MILLENNIUM STAR ATLAS
VOLUME I

MILLENNIUM STAR ATLAS

An All-Sky Atlas Comprising
One Million Stars to Visual Magnitude Eleven
from the Hipparcos and Tycho Catalogues
and Ten Thousand Nonstellar Objects

VOLUME I: 0 TO 8 HOURS

Roger W. Sinnott

Sky & Telescope

Michael A. C. Perryman

EUROPEAN SPACE AGENCY
FOR THE HIPPARCOS PROJECT

1997

SKY PUBLISHING CORPORATION

Cambridge, Massachusetts

EUROPEAN SPACE AGENCY

ESTEC, Noordwijk, The Netherlands

Principal Collaborators

TYCHO CATALOGUE

Erik Høg

Ulrich Bastian	Valeri V. Makarov
Claus Fabricius	Jean-Louis Halbwachs
Volkmar Großmann	Andreas Wicenec

HIPPARCOS CATALOGUE

Hans Schrijver

Michel Grenon	Lennart Lindegren
Jean Kovalevsky	François Mignard
Floor van Leeuwen	Catherine Turon

SKY PUBLISHING CORPORATION

Sally M. MacGillivray

E. Talmadge Mentall	Imelda B. Joson
Richard Tresch Fienberg	Samantha Parker
Gregg Dinderman	Leif J. Robinson

Copyright © 1997 by Sky Publishing Corporation

LIBRARY OF CONGRESS CATALOGUING-IN-PUBLICATION DATA

Sinnott, Roger W.
    Millennium Star Atlas: an all-sky atlas comprising one million stars to visual magnitude eleven from the Hipparcos and Tycho Catalogues and ten thousand nonstellar objects / Roger W. Sinnott, Michael A. C. Perryman.
        p.   cm.
    Includes bibliographical references and index.
    Contents: v.1. 0 to 8 hours — v.2. 8 to 16 hours — v.3. 16 to 24 hours.
    ISBN 0–933346–84–0 (3-vol. set: alk. paper). — ISBN 0–933346–81–6 (Vol. I: alk. paper). — ISBN 0–933346–82–4 (Vol. II: alk. paper). — ISBN 0–933346–83–2 (Vol. III: alk. paper).
    1. Stars—Atlases. 2. Astronomy—Charts, diagrams, etc.
I. Perryman, Michael A. C. II. Title.
      QB65.S62   1997   97–2552
                                                      CIP

CONTENTS

The region south and east of Rho Ophiuchi is so rich in bright nebulae and dark lanes that E. E. Barnard called it "one of the most extraordinary in the sky." The 1st-magnitude star Antares, seen here just below center, illuminates a large dust cloud to its north. Within the 9° field are three globular clusters as well, easily identified with the help of charts 1397 and 1398 of this atlas. The small ovals just above center are not nebulosities but ghost images of Antares, produced by the Schmidt optical system used to make this photograph.

INTRODUCTION

THROUGHOUT THE AGES star maps have served many needs. Celestial globes and seasonal charts of the night sky, depicting a few hundred stars at most, have helped initiate newcomers to astronomy and teach them the constellations. Early mariners and aviators used celestial charts to identify the navigational stars that were once so vital for a safe ocean passage. Special finder charts have helped astronomers point their telescopes. And when a new comet appears, the discoverer normally reaches for the most detailed map available to plot its location among the stars and claim credit for the find.

The *Millennium Star Atlas*, with its 1,548 charts, brings these orientational uses of star maps to a new plateau. At the same time, because it is based on the historic observations of the European Space Agency's Hipparcos satellite, this atlas contains more comprehensive data on the stars themselves than any previous work of its kind. The stars selected for plotting, their positions, and their brightnesses bear a one-to-one correspondence with those listed in that mission's Tycho Catalogue (with minor exceptions explained later). The stars' proper motions, distances, and variability information, when included, are from the smaller but more refined Hipparcos Catalogue (ESA, 1997). Further details of the spacecraft and its observations are found on page XXXI.

Plotted here are one million stars, three times as many as in any previous all-sky atlas. The sheer number can be a boon to "star-hoppers," people who center a telescope on a faint target by offsetting from brighter stars near it. An 8-inch (20-centimeter) telescope, operating at 50×, has a circular field of view about 1° across. In this atlas such a field typically contains 20 stars; in a less comprehensive one, the nearest plotted star is often wholly outside any 1° field.

Photographic charts, of course, plumb the sky to greater depths and reach fainter stars. But such charts lack the precise grid and labeling possible in a printed atlas. And photographs do not conspicuously differentiate between moderately bright and faint stars. Also, the emulsion's response to star colors usually differs from that of the human eye, making star patterns harder to reconcile with a telescopic view.

Our portrayal of nonstellar objects is also a step forward. This is the first large atlas to show the orientations of all galaxies plotted, an advance over the tradition of horizontal ovals for all but the largest examples. Outlines of many bright and dark nebulae have been painstakingly transferred from wide-field images, both photographic and electronic. Many open and globular clusters are—for the first time—precisely located by the brightest individual stars they contain.

No star atlas or catalogue has ever had a truly sharp magnitude cutoff, despite the best intentions of its makers, and this one is no exception. Stars a little brighter than the nominal magnitude limit may have been omitted, and variable stars complicate the definition of any selection threshold. The magnitudes of the faintest stars tend to be less accurately determined than the rest, and later observations may turn up stars that should cross the line in one direction or the other.

Yet this atlas probably comes closer to the ideal of completeness than any previous work. Tycho's one million stars form a nearly unbiased sampling of the entire sky. Earlier censuses have been inadequate in the far-southern sky simply because more astronomers and observatories have operated from the Northern Hemisphere. In addition, astronomers of the past who compiled astrometric catalogues had other concerns besides completeness on their minds. They sought fainter stars in the star-poor areas than elsewhere, because a prime goal was to avoid wide gaps in the network of reference stars around the sky.

Table I. Stars by Brightness

Magnitude Class	Range Included	Number by Magnitude	Cumulative Total
−1	−1.50 to −0.51	2	2
0	−0.50 to +0.49	6	8
+1	+0.50 to +1.49	14	22
+2	+1.50 to +2.49	71	93
+3	+2.50 to +3.49	190	283
+4	+3.50 to +4.49	610	893
+5	+4.50 to +5.49	1,929	2,822
+6	+5.50 to +6.49	5,946	8,768
+7	+6.50 to +7.49	17,765	26,533
+8	+7.50 to +8.49	51,094	77,627
+9	+8.50 to +9.49	140,062	217,689
+10	+9.50 to +10.49	368,275	585,964
+11	+10.50 to +11.49	452,516	1,038,480
+12	+11.50 and fainter	19,852	1,058,332

Paul Lind

A giant region of ionized hydrogen, the California Nebula lies in southern Perseus about 13° north of the Pleiades. What makes it glow is 4th-magnitude Xi Persei, the bright type-O star below and right of center in this photograph. Also known as NGC 1499, the nebula is shown as a 2½°-long outline on charts 117 and 118. Except as noted otherwise, all photographs have north up.

While Tycho is known to have missed stars at the hearts of some dense open clusters, its overall sampling is believed to be 99.9 percent complete to visual magnitude 10.0 and 90 percent complete to 10.5. The inclusion rate then falls off rapidly for fainter stars, as shown in Table I. To be accepted into the Tycho Catalogue, a star had to be detected reliably many times. Thus even this compilation has a frayed bottom edge, owing to the limited number of scans during the mission and the statistics of the sampling process.

For centuries celestial cartographers have debated how best to depict stars of different brightnesses. Stars were traditionally assigned to whole-magnitude bins, a choice dictated as much by drafting capability as by a desire to place each star in its proper magnitude class. But the computer plotting of the *Millennium Star Atlas* has made a continuous range of dot sizes possible. For example, a star of magnitude 4.51 has a slightly larger disk than one of magnitude 4.73, and this

difference should be discernible with a magnifier and measuring reticle on the charts themselves. At the same time, stars of magnitude 4.49 and 4.51 appear almost identical, as they should, even though they belong to separate magnitude classes (4th and 5th, respectively). In a binned atlas they would appear to differ by a whole magnitude.

The tapered magnitude scale includes another novel feature of this atlas. Some earlier cartographers have opted for an inverse linear relationship between stellar magnitudes and disk diameters. In that scheme, if an 8th-magnitude star is represented by a 1-millimeter disk and a 7th-magnitude star by a 2-mm disk, then a 6th-magnitude star would be 3 mm across, and so on. But this procedure tends to exaggerate the apparent brightnesses of stars in the middle of the plotted range. Other atlas makers have argued that the *areas* of the plotted disks should be proportional to brightnesses calculated from the magnitudes. Since a star of magnitude 3.0 is about 2.51 times brighter than one of magnitude 4.0, by this rule its disk should be 2.51 times larger in area (1.58 times larger in diameter).

However, neither strategy accurately reflects human sensory response. The modern magnitude scale, like the decibel scale used in acoustics, was suggested by Fechner's law of 1858, which states that a sensation is proportional to the logarithm of the stimulus. Psychologists have long known that this is not true (Stevens, 1961) and that a power law more accurately describes the human response to stimuli of various intensities. San Diego State University astronomer Andrew T. Young (1984, 1990) first pointed out the relevance of these findings to star charts. The *Millennium Star Atlas* is the first full-fledged work to adopt a power law for star magnitudes, though the charts appearing in *Sky & Telescope* magazine have done so since 1992. (The exact relationship between dot size and magnitude is stated mathematically on page XI.) As a result, the relative prominences of stars plotted here should rather faithfully match what you see in the sky.

REFERENCE SYSTEM

The grid lines in this atlas give the positions of objects in what are commonly called 2000.0 coordinates—those measured from the celestial equator and equinox at the start of the year 2000. Specifically, the atlas uses the International Celestial Reference System (ICRS) defined by a set of highly accurate measurements of extragalactic radio sources. The ICRS officially replaced the earlier FK5/J2000.0 system (Fricke et al., 1988) following a 1995 recommendation of the International Astronomical Union's Working Group on Reference Frames. Even so, the ICRS differs from the FK5 system by less than 0.1 arcsecond, an amount that is utterly inappreciable at the scale of the charts.

However, the epoch of the positions (as distinct from the chart equinox) is formally 1991.25. All stars in the atlas, and all configurations of double and multiple stars, are plotted as measured by Hipparcos during the $3\frac{1}{2}$-year period centered on this epoch in early April of 1991. The vast majority of stars have such slow motions across the sky that there is no detectable shift at the scale of this atlas in the $8\frac{3}{4}$ years between 1991.25 and 2000.0. The most extreme cases are Barnard's Star on chart 1273 and Kapteyn's Star on chart 437. To adjust the plotted positions of these stars to epoch 2000.0, they could be shifted by 0.9 and 0.8 mm, respectively, along their proper-motion arrows.

CHART PROJECTION AND SCALE

Each chart embraces an area of the sky measuring 5.4° by 7.4°. On a map of the world, France occupies a comparable portion of the globe. Many complex cartographic projections have been devised for situations where an even greater section of a sphere must be shown on a flat chart, but they always force some type of tradeoff, such as sacrificing a uniform scale to preserve angular relationships. No such compromise has been necessary in the *Millennium Star Atlas*.

We have chosen the simple conic projection (Raisz, 1938), which has several advantages over other types. All meridians of right ascension are strictly perpendicular to the parallels of declination, and the parallels are equally spaced. The scale is perfectly linear along all the meridian lines on each chart and along the central parallel. In the east-west direction, adjacent charts overlap perfectly. The maximum scale error occurs along the upper and lower edges, where it is about 0.2 percent for charts within 60° of the celestial equator and never more than 0.4 percent near the poles. Anywhere on a chart, a measured position angle differs by less than 0.2° from that on the sky itself. In both scale and position angle, these errors are virtually imperceptible—in any case, they are likely to be smaller than those that arise from age- and humidity-related distortions of the paper.

The atlas's scale, 100 arcseconds per millimeter, makes it easy to measure angular separations with a ruler. Coincidentally, photographs taken at the focal plane of an 8-inch (20-cm) f/10 Schmidt-Cassegrain telescope have very nearly the same scale as these charts.

THE STARS

The brightest stars are known today by their common names, mostly passed down from Arabic sources in antiquity. For these the atlas adopts the spellings recommended by Yale University astronomer Dorrit Hoffleit (1982). They and many other naked-eye stars also usually have a Flamsteed number, a Bayer (Greek-letter) label, or both. A few, especially among the southern constellations, are still known by a single Roman letter: an uppercase A through Q or a lowercase a through z. And sometimes the letter, Greek or Roman, is followed by a superscript digit to distinguish the bright components of a double star or a small group of stars in a given constellation.

In speech and writing, these letters and numbers would always be accompanied by the name of the constellation in which the star lies. The 88 constellations,

Table II. Constellation Names and Abbreviations

And	Andromeda, Andromedae	Lac	Lacerta, Lacertae
Ant	Antlia, Antliae	Leo	Leo, Leonis
Aps	Apus, Apodis	Lep	Lepus, Leporis
Aql	Aquila, Aquilae	Lib	Libra, Librae
Aqr	Aquarius, Aquarii	LMi	Leo Minor, Leonis Minoris
Ara	Ara, Arae	Lup	Lupus, Lupi
Ari	Aries, Arietis	Lyn	Lynx, Lyncis
Aur	Auriga, Aurigae	Lyr	Lyra, Lyrae
Boo	Bootes, Bootis	Men	Mensa, Mensae
Cae	Caelum, Caeli	Mic	Microscopium, Microscopii
Cam	Camelopardalis, Camelopardalis	Mon	Monoceros, Monocerotis
Cap	Capricornus, Capricorni	Mus	Musca, Muscae
Car	Carina, Carinae	Nor	Norma, Normae
Cas	Cassiopeia, Cassiopeiae	Oct	Octans, Octantis
Cen	Centaurus, Centauri	Oph	Ophiuchus, Ophiuchi
Cep	Cepheus, Cephei	Ori	Orion, Orionis
Cet	Cetus, Ceti	Pav	Pavo, Pavonis
Cha	Chamaeleon, Chamaeleontis	Peg	Pegasus, Pegasi
Cir	Circinus, Circini	Per	Perseus, Persei
CMa	Canis Major, Canis Majoris	Phe	Phoenix, Phoenicis
CMi	Canis Minor, Canis Minoris	Pic	Pictor, Pictoris
Cnc	Cancer, Cancri	PsA	Piscis Austrinus, Piscis Austrini
Col	Columba, Columbae	Psc	Pisces, Piscium
Com	Coma Berenices, Comae Berenices	Pup	Puppis, Puppis
CrA	Corona Australis, Coronae Australis	Pyx	Pyxis, Pyxidis
CrB	Corona Borealis, Coronae Borealis	Ret	Reticulum, Reticuli
Crt	Crater, Crateris	Scl	Sculptor, Sculptoris
Cru	Crux, Crucis	Sco	Scorpius, Scorpii
Crv	Corvus, Corvi	Sct	Scutum, Scuti
CVn	Canes Venatici, Canum Venaticorum	Ser	Serpens, Serpentis
Cyg	Cygnus, Cygni	Sex	Sextans, Sextantis
Del	Delphinus, Delphini	Sge	Sagitta, Sagittae
Dor	Dorado, Doradus	Sgr	Sagittarius, Sagittarii
Dra	Draco, Draconis	Tau	Taurus, Tauri
Equ	Equuleus, Equulei	Tel	Telescopium, Telescopii
Eri	Eridanus, Eridani	TrA	Triangulum Australe, Trianguli Australis
For	Fornax, Fornacis	Tri	Triangulum, Trianguli
Gem	Gemini, Geminorum	Tuc	Tucana, Tucanae
Gru	Grus, Gruis	UMa	Ursa Major, Ursae Majoris
Her	Hercules, Herculis	UMi	Ursa Minor, Ursae Minoris
Hor	Horologium, Horologii	Vel	Vela, Velorum
Hya	Hydra, Hydrae	Vir	Virgo, Virginis
Hyi	Hydrus, Hydri	Vol	Volans, Volantis
Ind	Indus, Indi	Vul	Vulpecula, Vulpeculae

After each abbreviation is the full constellation name, followed by the genitive, or possessive, form used with star designations.

along with the genitive forms used in such designations, are listed in Table II. The lowercase Greek letters can be found in Table III. Examples are α Centauri, 61 Cygni, 19 ϕ^2 Ceti, 78 β Geminorum, 111 Tauri, and d¹ Puppis. Since the constellation name can always be found elsewhere on a given chart, it is usually omitted from the star labels. The rare exceptions are when a star's traditional designation implies it lies in a *different* constellation from that set by the modern boundaries. For all such rogue stars the three-letter abbreviation of the original constellation is retained in the label, as in the case of 10 UMa in Lynx, 63 Oph in Sagittarius, and 67 ρ Aql in Delphinus.

Table III. Lowercase Greek Letters

α alpha	η eta	ν nu	τ tau
β beta	θ theta	ξ xi	υ upsilon
γ gamma	ι iota	o omicron	ϕ phi
δ delta	κ kappa	π pi	χ chi
ϵ epsilon	λ lambda	ρ rho	ψ psi
ζ zeta	μ mu	σ sigma	ω omega

Today's constellation boundaries are not the gracefully curving lines that adorn many early star maps and globes. Instead they are rigorously defined by line segments running along meridians of right ascension and parallels of declination, carving up the sky like a cosmic jigsaw puzzle. When Belgian astronomer Eugène Delporte set up these lines in 1930 under the auspices of the International Astronomical Union, he was actually extending to the northern sky a set of boundaries similarly defined many years earlier for the southern sky by Benjamin A. Gould. And because Gould had used equinox 1875.0 in his definitions, Delporte continued that practice. After 125 years of precession, these lines appear somewhat skewed with respect to those for equinox 2000.0, an effect most noticeable on charts of the polar regions.

The brightnesses of all plotted stars closely reflect their *V* values according to Johnson *UBV* photometry, a system widely used in modern astronomy. This choice makes the plotted star patterns reasonably similar to what the human eye sees, with or without a telescope. Some patterns may look quite different when recorded with a blue-sensitive photographic emulsion or a red-sensitive CCD imager. For example, a star of spectral type *O* or *B* would appear more prominent in blue light, and less so in red light, than it does in this atlas. The reverse is true for, say, spectral type *M*.

Specifically, the *V* magnitudes used for plotting are derived from the V_T and B_T values in the Tycho Catalogue through a transformation worked out by Hipparcos project astronomers. While the systematic error of this conversion is less than 0.05 magnitude for all but the reddest stars, the deviation from a ground-based photoelectric *V* can amount to 0.1 or 0.2 magnitude in individual cases. Such errors, however, are virtually unnoticeable in the plotted symbols.

For all stars of magnitude 2.0 and fainter, the dot diameter in millimeters, *d,* is related to the *V* magnitude as follows:

$$\log_{10}d = 0.135\,(8.7-V),$$
$$V = 8.7 - 7.41\log_{10}d.$$

If these relationships had been retained for the 48 stars in the sky brighter than magnitude 2.0, as listed in Table IV, their dot sizes would have become excessive. Therefore, these stars are plotted as if their magnitudes were 2.0 also. The table gives *V* magnitudes and *B−V* color indexes from the Hipparcos Catalogue, which are somewhat improved over those in Tycho. In the case of double stars, the listed color index is that of the brighter component.

Distances to stars within 200 light-years of the Sun are included in Table IV, as they are for more than 10,000 stars in the atlas itself. Error estimates for these Hipparcos distances vary somewhat according to the star's magnitude and position on the sky. Typically the satellite measured star positions with an accuracy of

Table IV. The Brightest Stars

Name	Designation		V Mag. (*)	B−V	Distance (ly)	Chart
Sirius	9	α CMa	−1.44	0.01	8.60	322
Canopus		α Car	−0.62	0.16	—	454
Rigil Kent		α Cen	−0.28c	0.71	4.40	985
Arcturus	16	α Boo	−0.05v	1.24	37	696
Vega	3	α Lyr	0.03v	0.00	25.3	1153
Capella	13	α Aur	0.08v	0.80	42	73
Rigel	19	β Ori	0.18v	−0.03	—	279
Procyon	10	α CMi	0.40	0.43	11.4	224
Achernar		α Eri	0.45v	−0.16	144	478
Betelgeuse	58	α Ori	0.45v	1.50	—	229
—		β Cen	0.61v	−0.23	—	986
Altair	53	α Aql	0.76v	0.22	16.8	1267
Acrux		α Cru	0.77c	−0.24	—	1002
Aldebaran	87	α Tau	0.87	1.54	65	185
Spica	67	α Vir	0.98v	−0.24	—	818
Antares	21	α Sco	1.06v	1.86	—	1397
Pollux	78	β Gem	1.16	0.99	34	129
Fomalhaut	24	α PsA	1.17	0.14	25.1	1401
—		β Cru	1.25v	−0.24	—	988
Deneb	50	α Cyg	1.25v	0.09	—	1107
Regulus	32	α Leo	1.36	−0.09	78	732
Adhara	21	ε CMa	1.50	−0.21	—	369
Castor	66	α Gem	1.58c	0.03	52	130
Gacrux		γ Cru	1.59v	1.60	88	989
Shaula	35	λ Sco	1.62v	−0.23	—	1438
Bellatrix	24	γ Ori	1.64	−0.22	—	230
Alnath	112	β Tau	1.65	−0.13	131	136
Miaplacidus		β Car	1.67	0.07	111	1017
Alnilam	46	ε Ori	1.69v	−0.18	—	254
Alnair		α Gru	1.73	−0.07	101	1467
Alnitak	50	ζ Ori	1.74c	−0.20	—	253
—		γ² Vel	1.75v	−0.14	—	966
Alioth	77	ε UMa	1.76v	−0.02	81	573
Mirphak	33	α Per	1.79	0.48	—	78
Kaus Australis	20	ε Sgr	1.79	−0.03	145	1436
Dubhe	50	α UMa	1.81c	1.06	124	561
—	25	δ CMa	1.83	0.67	—	345
Alkaid	85	η UMa	1.85	−0.10	101	588
Avior		ε Car	1.86v	1.20	—	996
—		θ Sco	1.86c	0.41	—	1458
Menkalinan	34	β Aur	1.90v	0.08	82	92
Atria		α TrA	1.91	1.45	—	1533
Alhena	24	γ Gem	1.93	0.00	105	179
—		δ Vel	1.93	0.04	80	981
Peacock		α Pav	1.94	−0.12	183	1490
Polaris	1	α UMi	1.97v	0.64	—	2
Mirzam	2	β CMa	1.98v	−0.24	—	323
Alphard	30	α Hya	1.99	1.44	177	806

*The letter *c* refers to the combined magnitude of a double star and *v* to the median magnitude of a variable star.

about 0.001 arcsecond, and the same applies to the parallax values obtained as Hipparcos and the Earth orbited the Sun. The quoted distances, obtained trigonometrically from these parallaxes, are generally reliable to 1.5 percent at 50 light-years, 3 percent at 100 light-years, and 6 percent at 200 light-years.

Accuracies like these are unprecedented in astronomy. The situation was rather different back in 1933, when the brilliant orange star Arcturus (α Bootis) played a symbolic role at that year's Century of Progress Exposition in Chicago. At nearby Yerkes

Observatory, astronomers trained their great refractor on Arcturus so its light, focused on a photocell, could send a telegraph signal that would turn on the fairground lights. Then believed to lie at a distance of 40 light-years, Arcturus would have emitted the light just at the time four decades earlier when Chicago was holding its famous Columbian Exposition of 1893. Hipparcos, however, has now pegged Arcturus's true distance at 36.7 ± 0.4 light-years.

The 20 stars in this atlas that are closest to the Sun, as given in the Hipparcos Catalogue, are listed in Table V. But this sample is by no means a complete inventory of the Sun's vicinity. The satellite could not detect low-luminosity dwarf stars with apparent magnitudes fainter than about 12.

Table V. Stars Near the Sun

Name	V Mag.	Absolute Mag.	Distance (ly)	Chart
Proxima Centauri	11.01	15.45	4.22	985
α Centauri A	−0.01	4.34	4.40	985
α Centauri B	1.35	5.70	4.40	985
Barnard's Star	9.54	13.24	5.94	1273
Lalande 21185	7.49	10.46	8.31	636
Sirius	−1.44	1.45	8.60	322
Ross 154	10.37	13.00	9.69	1390
18 ε Eridani	3.72	6.18	10.5	308
Lacaille 9352	7.35	9.76	10.7	1423
Ross 128	11.12	13.50	10.9	775
61 Cygni A	5.20	7.49	11.4	1146
61 Cygni B	6.05	8.33	11.4	1146
Procyon	0.40	2.68	11.4	224
BD +59° 1915 B	9.70	11.97	11.5	1078
BD +59° 1915 A	8.94	11.18	11.6	1078
Groombridge 34	8.09	10.33	11.6	106
ε Indi	4.69	6.89	11.8	1486
52 τ Ceti	3.49	5.68	11.9	337
HIP 5643	12.10	14.25	12.1	339
Luyten's Star	9.84	11.94	12.4	224

Variable stars. For any star whose brightness fluctuates over time, the magnitude range, or amplitude, is the best guide to the equipment needed to monitor its changes. The *Millennium Star Atlas* indicates this quantity, for stars in the Hipparcos Catalogue, by a concentric circle around the star's disk. While the size of this circle has no significance, its style does. A *solid circle* means the star varies by more than 1 magnitude, shining more than 2½ times brighter at its peak than at its low point. Such a change is easily noticed by anyone who ranks the star from night to night relative to those in its vicinity, and a careful observer can compile a revealing light curve from a series of visual estimates alone.

Similarly, a *dashed circle* means the variation lies in the range of 0.1 to 1.0 magnitude. In this case establishing a light curve demands a CCD imager or photoelectric photometer and a careful choice of comparison stars. A star with a *dotted circle* varies less than 0.1 magnitude, a change so subtle that detection requires high-precision photometry. The atlas contains some 820 large-amplitude variables (solid circles), 4,600 moderate variables (dashed circles), and 3,300 small-amplitude variables (dotted circles).

Most variables are further characterized by a code of one or two italic characters in parentheses, as explained on page XXXIV. The letter tells the broad category to which the star belongs, and the digit is a guide to the period range. Among the letters used, *e* denotes an eclipsing binary (type E, EA, EB, or EW) or a rotating binary with ellipsoidal components (Ell); *c* is a Cepheid (Cδ, CW, CWa, CWb) or a β Cephei star; *m* means a Mira variable; and *d* is either a δ Scuti or SX Phoenicis star. In addition, *r* is an RR Lyrae variable (RR, RRab, RRb, RRc); *s* is a semiregular variable (SR, SRa, SRb, SRc, SRd); and *i* is an irregular (I, Ia, Ib, In, InT, Is, Isa, Isb) or a slow irregular (L, Lb, Lc) variable. A UV Ceti flare star is marked *f*, while *x* refers to a nova (N, Na, Nr), novalike (Nl) variable, or a Z Andromedae cataclysmic variable. Finally, *v* is a catchall for the rarer variables whose prototypes are α² Canum Venaticorum, α Cygni, BY Draconis, FK Comae Berenices, γ Cassiopeiae, PV Telescopii, R Coronae Borealis, RS Canum Venaticorum, RV Tauri, S Doradus, and SX Arietis; it can also mean a Wolf-Rayet eruptive star (WR), a small-amplitude red variable, a small-amplitude multiperiod pulsating star, an X-ray novalike system, or an X-ray pulsar. The letter is omitted for a variable of unknown type.

In this atlas a variable star's dot size in most cases represents its median *V* magnitude from the Hipparcos Catalogue. For example, an eclipsing binary may spend most of the time at magnitude 3.0 and briefly fade to 5.0; its dot size might thus be that of a 3.1-magnitude star, surrounded by a somewhat larger (and in this case solid) amplitude circle. Similar to an average magnitude over time, the median value was obtained by arranging all the Hipparcos measurements for a given star in a sequence from faintest to brightest and adopting the middle, or 50th-percentile, value.

A different treatment applies to variables that belong to a close double system shown as a single dot with a tick. In this case the dot is enlarged to show the pair's combined brightness, but the outer circle (dotted, dashed, or solid) still indicates the amplitude of the variable star alone. Other sources must be consulted to identify which component varies.

To illustrate the coding process, Table VI lists the

brightest variable star in each of the 11 broad categories, along with its median *V* magnitude, amplitude, period, and specific variability type, followed by the simplified code used in the atlas. The periods cited for R Hydrae, β Centauri, and 3 α Lyrae have been inserted in the table from prior ground-based observations. For these three stars and many others in the atlas an accurate period is not given in the Hipparcos Catalogue, either because the variability was irregular, the coverage of the light curve was inadequate, or the period was not evident in the analyses conducted so far.

Table VI. Brightest Variable of Each Class

Designation	V Mag.	Ampl.	Period (days)	Type	Atlas Class	Chart
43 β And	2.07	0.04	—	SR	(s)	125
α Eri*	0.45	0.06	—	I	(i)	478
XX Cam	7.30	0.1	—	UV	(f)	58
19 β Ori	0.18	0.03	2.07	α Cyg	(v1)	279
SS Lep	4.92	0.05	—	Z And	(x)	324
R Hya	6.40	3	388.87	M	(m3)	866
β Cen	0.61	0.04	0.16	β Cep	(c)	986
16 α Boo	−0.05	0.05	—	—	—	696
3 α Lyr	0.03	0.06	0.19	δ Sct	(d)	1153
53 α Aql*	0.76	0.05	7.95	EA	(e1)	1267
V2121 Cyg*	5.73	0.09	0.80	RRab	(r0)	1107

*Variability discovered by Hipparcos.

All told, the Hipparcos Catalogue characteristics of some 8,200 variable stars are included in this atlas. Among them are 5,100 new discoveries subsequently checked in Moscow at the Sternberg Astronomical Institute and the Institute of Astronomy. Official designations for well over 3,000 of these new discoveries are included on the charts.

Hipparcos scientists also identified 500 previously known variables for which they were not able to derive a period and corresponding amplitude by the time the Hipparcos Catalogue was completed. They appear in the atlas as normal stars but with variable-star designations. During the preparation of the atlas, other previously known variable stars were matched to stars in Tycho by the staff at Sky Publishing Corp. Their labels and coding have been included from the prior literature:

And: T, SX, UX, GG. *Aps:* T. *Aql:* RW, HK, V337, V342, V346, V374. *Aqr:* S, RY, SS, SV. *Ara:* U, RW, V349, V616, V620. *Ari:* ST. *Aur:* TT, TW, CO. *Boo:* Z, XY, CN. *Cae:* Y. *Cam:* R, T, V, TW, UX. *Cap:* S. *Car:* RW, ZZ, BO, CK, EV, HP, IW, V340. *Cas:* Y, WX, V379. *Cen:* RS, RW, TW, VX, AD, AQ, BF, LZ, MN, V346, V377, V646, V785. *Cep:* RY, TZ, KZ. *Cet:* W, RS, WX, YY, AI, AN. *Cha:* CI. *Cir:* BF. *CMa:* S,

FX. *CMi:* YY. *Cnc:* TW, UV, ZZ, BQ, BS, BW, BX, CY. *Col:* RV. *Crt:* RR, RW. *Cru:* X, AE, AG. *CVn:* TX, AV. *Cyg:* SS, UU, CE, CF, V395, V449, V697. *Del:* KP. *Dra:* Y, TY. *Eri:* U, SU, VY, BT, BZ, DD, DI. *For:* ST, SU. *Gem:* SS, SW, TU, TW, LT. *Her:* W, UV, UY, CF, DH, GN. *Hor:* RR. *Hya:* RR, FF, FS, FZ, HW, HX, HZ. *Hyi:* VW. *Ind:* R, S, W, X. *Lac:* R, RX, RZ, CX. *Leo:* VV, AF, CZ. *Lep:* RS, RZ. *Lib:* RR, EI. *Lyr:* X. *Mic:* S, VY. *Mon:* AP, V536. *Mus:* CX. *Oct:* S, T, U. *Oph:* R, S, RV, SS, V447, V551, V679, V988. *Ori:* V, RR, BN, DH, FX, LP, NV, V352, V372, V430, V431, V451. *Pav:* U, Z. *Peg:* X, RW, GH. *Per:* R, AF. *Phe:* W, AF, AN. *Pic:* RX, SV. *PsA:* V, SV, TV. *Psc:* S, RX, UY. *Pup:* U, SW, AU, CF, MQ, MW. *Pyx:* TT. *Ret:* RX. *Scl:* V, XY, YY, YZ, ZZ, AB, AC, AF. *Sco:* RU, SV, TX, AI, V380, V499, V635, V727, V764, V883, V885. *Ser:* EG. *Sge:* R, V, W. *Sgr:* UX, AR, BQ, V771, V2349. *Tau:* R, W, WW, CH, ET, V624. *Tel:* RR, BR, NV. *TrA:* W. *Tuc:* S, U. *UMa:* RS, RT, AC. *UMi:* R Cep, T. *Vel:* U, RS, RW, SZ, WY, GG, GL, GM. *Vir:* X, V, RX, TZ, BG, CH, CO, CQ, ES. *Vul:* S, DR.

A few hundred more variables, known to spend at least some time at magnitude 9 or brighter, were found to be missing entirely from the Tycho Catalogue. A fair number of these are Mira stars that were probably too faint for detection during much of the Hipparcos mission. The following stars have been added to the atlas as small open circles. Their positions, as plotted, are uncertain by 1 arcminute or more:

And: U, V, X, Y, RR, RW, UZ. *Aps:* WW. *Aql:* W, X, Z, RS, RU, RV, XY. *Aqr:* Y, W, RR, RS, RV, RW. *Ari:* U. *Aur:* U, W, RR. *Cam:* SU. *Cap:* R, RU, TU. *Car:* RZ. *Cas:* S, RR, RV, VZ. *Cen:* TU, V418, V760. *Cep:* X, Y, RR, SZ. *Cet:* S, V, Z, UV, WW. *Cha:* R. *CMa:* GP. *CMi:* T, V. *Cnc:* U. *Col:* W. *CrB:* W, Z. *Crt:* U. *Cyg:* ST, TU, TW, UX, WY, AU, CU, DR, FF. *Del:* T, V, X, Z. *Dra:* U, W, X, RU, RV, SV, WZ. *Equ:* R. *Eri:* SS, SX. *Gem:* S, T, U. *Gru:* R. *Her:* R, RT, RV, RY, RZ, SV, TV. *Hya:* RS, RZ, ST, UZ, WX. *Leo:* S. *Lib:* U, V, RT. *Lup:* Y. *Lyn:* U, X. *Lyr:* V, RY, TW. *Mon:* Y, RR, BX. *Oph:* T, W, RR, RT, RU, SV. *Ori:* T, V345. *Pav:* W, SU. *Peg:* T, V, RR, RT, RU, RV, SU, SW, TV. *Per:* RR, RX. *Phe:* R, T, V, RR. *PsA:* R, S, RY, ST. *Psc:* R, T. *Pup:* CH. *Pyx:* S. *Scl:* U. *Sco:* RT, RW. *Ser:* T. *Sgr:* Z, RX, SW, TW, TY, FN, V1017, V1977. *Tau:* V, Z, VY. *Tel:* R. *Tuc:* R. *UMa:* X, RR, RU. *Vir:* T, Y, SU, SV.

Finally, an × marks the approximate locations of 170 historical novae and supernovae that attained magnitude 9 or brighter. One is the supernova that burst into view in the year 1006 in Lupus (chart 929) and may have reached magnitude –9, judging by observational records from China, Egypt, and Iraq. Another, near the heart of the Andromeda Galaxy (chart 105), brightened to magnitude 5.7 in 1885 and remained visible for five years. The most recent nova plotted in the atlas (chart 1415) is that discovered by William Liller in Scorpius in June 1997.

Double and multiple stars. In most other star atlases, double and multiple stars are simply flagged (if at all) by a horizontal bar through the star's symbol. Users have been left pretty much in the dark as to the components' angular separation and orientation on the sky. Even specialized double-star catalogues have been confusing to use. The most recent ground-based measurement of a double star may be decades old and, through orbital motion or proper motion, might not reflect the pair's current appearance.

However, because Hipparcos made all its measurements in a narrow time frame centered on early 1991, all the double-star information presented in this atlas *is* fairly current. Pairs separated by more than 30 arcseconds are plotted as two individual stars, while those closer than 30 arcseconds are shown as a single star with a tick attached. The length of the tick exaggerates the true separation, as explained below, and the tick's orientation is that from the primary star to its fainter companion on the sky.

Table VII lists the brightest stars marked as doubles in the atlas along with their separations and position angles for early 1991. Among these, the white-dwarf companions of Sirius and Procyon proved too difficult for the satellite, for each primary star outshines its companion by some 10,000 times. The configurations of these two pairs have been calculated from the orbital elements of W. H. van den Bos and K. Aa. Strand, respectively (Worley and Heintz, 1983).

Even so, as the accompanying diagram indicates, Hipparcos demonstrated a remarkable ability to measure very close pairs. A backyard observer cannot expect to resolve all these stars. A useful visibility guide is the famous criterion put forth in 1865 by English amateur William Rutter Dawes, one of the most experienced double-star observers of his day. Dawes stated that a high-quality refractor, under good conditions, should just resolve two 6th-magnitude stars separated by $4.56/A$ arcseconds, where A is the telescope's aperture in inches. A 3-inch (7.6-cm) telescope should be able to split pairs as close as 1.5 arcseconds, and a 12½-inch (30-cm) may reach 0.36 arcsecond, provided the

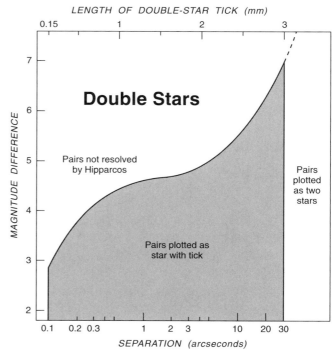

For double stars with separations greater than 30 arcseconds, the dot sizes in the atlas give a fair idea of how much the components differ in brightness. While the charts do not supply this information for closer pairs, the gray domain of the graph shows the range of differences encountered. Three magnitudes correspond to a 16-fold brightness change, and seven magnitudes to a factor of more than 600.

atmosphere is tranquil enough. Unequal pairs normally must be farther apart to be resolved at all.

Table VII. Brightest Double Stars

Name	Designation			V Mags. A	V Mags. B	Sep. (")	P.A. (°)	Chart
Sirius	9	α	CMa	–1.44	8.49	3.5	346	322
Rigil Kent		α	Cen	–0.01	1.35	19.1	215	985
Arcturus*	16	α	Boo	0.00	3.33	0.3	198	696
Procyon	10	α	CMi	0.40	10.3	5.2	28	224
—		β	Cen	0.66	4.03	0.9	234	986
Acrux		α	Cru	1.34	1.73	4.1	113	1002
Alnitak	50	ζ	Ori	1.88	4.01	2.4	164	253
—		θ	Sco	1.91	5.30	6.5	315	1458
Castor	66	α	Gem	1.93	2.97	3.1	76	130
—		δ	Vel	1.97	5.55	0.7	5	981
Dubhe	50	α	UMa	1.88	4.80	0.7	270	561
Avior*		ε	Car	2.03	3.99	0.5	132	996
Mizar	79	ζ	UMa	2.23	3.85	14.4	152	572
Almaak	57	γ	And	2.19	4.88	9.6	63	101
Algieba	41	γ	Leo	2.33	3.48	4.6	124	708
—	7	δ	Sco	2.42	4.64	0.1	344	1398
Mintaka*	34	δ	Ori	2.53	3.88	0.3	140	254

*Duplicity discovered by Hipparcos.

While the chart legend gives a rough idea of the correspondence between tick size and separation, a better estimate is often needed. If a loupe or optical comparator is used to measure the length, L, of a tick in millimeters, the separation in arcseconds, s, can be obtained from this formula:

$$\log_{10} s = (L - 1.30)/1.15.$$

Thus, a 2-mm tick implies a separation of 4.1 arcseconds, and a 1-mm tick 0.5 arcsecond. The very shortest ticks, barely visible in the printed atlas, signify a separation of only 0.1 arcsecond. Such pairs are so close that even the best ground-based telescopes may not be able to resolve them without a specialized technique such as speckle interferometry.

A tick does not imply that the components of a double star are physically connected. They might simply be close together along the line of sight ("optical pairs"), a frequent occurrence in open clusters and crowded areas of the Milky Way. But in many cases Hipparcos was able to measure the distances to the individual components, and these measurements (when less than 200 light-years) are listed together next to the star and tick. If the distances to both components differ by less than the measurement uncertainty, up to 6 percent at 200 light-years, then it is quite likely that the stars really do form a gravitationally bound pair.

Altogether about 22,200 ticks are plotted on stars in this atlas. Of these, 12,400 come from stars specifically targeted by Hipparcos; 9,800 are from Tycho for stars closer than 30 arcseconds and individually observed. We purposely suppressed Tycho-derived ticks for a double or multiple system that was also observed by Hipparcos, because not doing so would have introduced additional ticks 180° apart when the two instruments occasionally differed as to which was the brighter component. For plotting purposes the location of the brighter Tycho component has been adopted. But the tick information is from Hipparcos when available, and otherwise from Tycho.

Of course, many binaries are known in which one or both components are fainter than the atlas's magnitude limit. In such cases the primary star, when plotted, is not identified as part of a binary system.

Observing guides often refer to double stars by a special designation consisting of the discoverer's name and a serial number. For example, Σ 1728 refers to one of Wilhelm Struve's finds early in the 19th century. More than 100 distinct names of discoverers with numbers are found in the literature. Such designations could not be included in this atlas, especially because the separate pairings within a multiple system are frequently credited to different observers. The star Σ 1728 is better known as 42 α Comae Berenices, and it is simply marked "42 α" on chart 699.

Looking up detailed information on double stars

may become simpler in the future with a new nomenclature introduced by Belgian astronomers Jean Dommanget and Omer Nys in their *Catalogue of Components of Double and Multiple Stars* (1994). They have created a unique CCDM identifier from each system's equinox-2000.0 coordinates. For example, the well-known double-double ε Lyrae is CCDM 18443+3938. Even though the CCDM designation is not included in the atlas, a reasonable guess at its value can be made from the system's right ascension and declination, as read off chart 1132 or 1153 for ε Lyrae.

Fast-moving stars. Table VIII lists the 20 stars in this atlas whose locations, relative to the ICRS grid, change most rapidly over time. These stars, and all others found in the Hipparcos Catalogue to have a proper motion exceeding 0.2 arcsecond per year, are shown with a thin arrow extending in the direction of motion on the sky. The arrow's length, measured from the rim of the star's disk to the tip of the arrowhead, gives the angular distance traversed by the star in 1,000 years. Interestingly, the charts include many examples of stars moving on nearly parallel paths, clearly suggesting a common motion through space.

Table VIII. Stars of High Proper Motion

Name	V Mag.	Annual Motion (")	P.A. (°)	Chart
Barnard's Star	9.54	10.358	355.6	1273
Kapteyn's Star	8.86	8.671	131.4	437
Groombridge 1830	6.42	7.058	145.4	634
Lacaille 9352	7.35	6.896	78.9	1423
CD −37° 15492	8.56	6.100	112.5	410
HIP 67593	13.31	5.834	23.0	673
61 Cygni A	5.20	5.281	51.9	1146
61 Cygni B	6.05	5.172	52.6	1146
Lalande 21185	7.49	4.802	186.9	636
ε Indi	4.69	4.704	122.7	1486
Gliese 412	8.82	4.511	282.1	615
o² Eridani	4.43	4.088	213.2	282
Proxima Centauri	11.01	3.853	281.5	985
μ Cassiopeiae	5.17	3.777	115.1	64
Luyten's Star	9.84	3.738	171.2	224
α Centauri B	1.35	3.724	284.8	985
α Centauri A	−0.01	3.710	277.5	985
Washington 5583	9.44	3.681	195.8	837
Washington 5584	9.07	3.681	195.7	837
Lacaille 8760	6.69	3.455	250.6	1428

To a first approximation, then, a *Millennium Star Atlas* for A.D. 3000 would look much like the present one but with all arrowed stars transferred to the tips of their arrowheads. The maximum shift for slower-moving stars is about 2 mm, so their configurations would remain pretty much the same. However, the

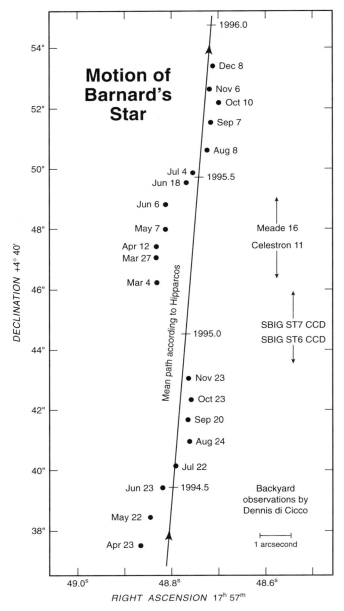

The northward migration of Barnard's Star can easily be followed month by month with a CCD camera and a modest telescope. Even the expected east-west oscillation, caused by parallax at the star's distance of 5.94 light-years, shows up in the plotted points. Because the star was measured against reference-star positions predating the Hipparcos Catalogue, it is not surprising that the points appear systematically shifted about a half arcsecond to the east relative to the mean path determined by the satellite.

absence of an arrow in this atlas does not *guarantee* that a star is a slow mover. Arrows are plotted only for stars specifically targeted by Hipparcos, and not for additional high-proper-motion candidates that may yet be found in the Tycho data.

Similarly, backtracking a star's position by twice the length of its arrow leads to its location at roughly the time of Ptolemy's *Almagest* (A.D. 137). For the bright star Arcturus (chart 696), it was the 1° discrepancy between Ptolemy's position and the contemporary one

that caught the attention of English astronomer Edmond Halley, leading to his discovery of stellar proper motions in 1718.

Barnard's Star, which has the highest known proper motion of all, appears with an exceedingly long arrow on chart 1273. It passed the small galaxy CGCG 56 – 3 in about 1971 and continues northward through Ophiuchus at a rate of 10.4 arcseconds per year. Using CCD-equipped 11- and 16-inch (28- and 40-cm) telescopes from suburban Boston, *Sky & Telescope* associate editor Dennis di Cicco was able to follow its motion month by month in 1994–95, as shown in the diagram at left. Along with the star's proper motion, his measurements reveal the yearly oscillation due to parallax. Such observations were long believed possible at only the best-equipped professional observatories.

The proper-motion arrows of a binary star's components sometimes diverge slightly, as in the case of 61 Cygni (chart 1146) and α Centauri (chart 985). The explanation of this oddity is that any orbital motion of the components was necessarily mixed with the stars' common proper motion when Hipparcos made its measurements in 1989–93. Gravitationally bound pairs of stars do not really diverge, but to plot them with parallel arrows would misrepresent the observations. If the components' 1,000-year motions were plotted literally, they would trace an elongated double helix on the sky.

Richness of star fields. Anyone paging through the atlas must be struck by variations in the number of stars across the sky. The fields of some open clusters are so thickly populated that the plotted star disks congeal like frogs' eggs. Other regions as large as 2 square degrees contain not a single star registered by the Tycho star-mapper, as on chart 1397. Free of the biases and shortcomings of previous surveys, these charts give the best-yet picture of the panoply of stars in all corners of the heavens.

In a broad sense the densest regions trace the shape of the Milky Way. For this reason the atlas omits the contour lines often used on other atlases; indeed, the very concept of a sharp edge is unrealistic. The changing star count from chart to chart is a much better clue as to where the Milky Way's richest star clouds lie.

Table IX summarizes the distribution of stars plotted in this atlas by constellation, taking into account the standard boundaries and the constellation areas in square degrees as originally calculated by A. E. Levin (1935). We see that Hydra is the largest constellation in size, and that it contains 238 stars to magnitude 6.5. But Hydra lies well away from the Milky Way, and

Table IX. Star Counts by Constellation

Const.	Area (sq. deg.)	Stars to V Mag. 6.5	Stars to V Mag. 10.0	Total Stars	Stars per sq. deg.	Const.	Area (sq. deg.)	Stars to V Mag. 6.5	Stars to V Mag. 10.0	Total Stars	Stars per sq. deg.
Cru	68.447	49	1,514	5,209	76	Dra	1,082.952	211	8,082	24,164	22
TrA	109.978	35	2,051	8,012	73	Hya	1,302.844	238	10,298	28,418	22
Nor	165.290	44	2,867	11,419	69	Oct	291.045	60	2,184	6,280	22
Cyg	803.983	262	14,376	49,948	62	Dor	179.173	29	1,264	3,794	21
Cir	93.353	39	1,678	5,757	62	Mic	209.513	43	1,474	4,413	21
Vel	499.649	214	9,154	30,304	61	Oph	948.340	174	6,703	19,694	21
Pup	673.434	237	11,040	37,683	56	Tri	131.847	25	1,043	2,719	21
Lac	200.688	68	3,070	10,874	54	Cae	124.865	20	816	2,504	20
Car	494.184	225	8,272	26,016	53	Ind	294.006	42	1,973	5,880	20
CMa	380.118	147	6,286	19,471	51	Men	153.484	22	1,129	3,069	20
Ara	237.057	71	3,883	12,063	51	Equ	71.641	16	567	1,429	20
Mus	138.355	62	2,044	6,839	49	Lyn	545.386	97	4,030	10,814	20
Cas	598.407	157	8,340	28,326	47	Peg	1,120.794	177	8,271	22,149	20
Sge	79.923	26	1,238	3,690	46	Cap	413.947	81	2,943	8,175	20
Lyr	286.476	73	3,889	13,093	46	Cnc	505.872	104	3,733	9,564	19
Vul	268.165	68	3,867	11,870	44	UMi	255.864	39	1,623	4,614	18
Pyx	220.833	41	2,781	9,605	43	Hyi	243.035	33	1,522	4,242	17
Mon	481.569	138	8,325	20,589	43	Tuc	294.557	45	1,858	5,070	17
Lup	333.683	127	4,248	14,063	42	Ret	113.936	23	703	1,905	17
Cen	1,060.422	281	13,779	43,862	41	Tau	797.249	223	5,382	12,630	16
Aps	206.327	39	2,429	8,405	41	Lib	538.052	83	3,184	8,505	16
CrA	127.696	46	1,822	4,879	38	Hor	248.885	30	1,406	3,930	16
Del	188.549	44	2,338	7,179	38	Gru	365.513	55	2,029	5,702	16
Per	614.997	158	6,542	21,279	35	CrB	178.710	37	926	2,757	15
Sco	496.783	167	6,072	16,856	34	Crt	282.398	33	1,540	4,269	15
CMi	183.367	47	2,438	6,127	33	Eri	1,137.919	194	6,468	17,084	15
Ant	238.901	42	2,452	7,976	33	PsA	245.375	47	1,341	3,665	15
Aur	657.438	152	7,471	21,470	33	Aqr	979.854	172	5,624	14,395	15
Aql	652.473	124	7,033	20,982	32	Ser	636.928	108	3,883	9,193	14
Cep	587.787	152	6,370	18,281	31	UMa	1,279.660	209	6,376	18,442	14
And	722.278	152	7,471	22,407	31	Crv	183.801	29	950	2,648	14
Vol	141.354	31	1,408	4,338	31	For	397.502	59	1,930	5,466	14
Tel	251.512	57	2,840	7,680	31	Phe	469.319	71	2,242	6,331	13
Gem	513.761	119	6,355	15,460	30	Sex	313.515	38	1,751	4,221	13
Sgr	867.432	194	10,138	26,101	30	Psc	889.417	150	4,691	11,812	13
Ori	594.120	204	6,987	16,765	28	LMi	231.956	37	1,070	2,966	13
Col	270.184	68	2,441	7,459	28	Ari	441.395	86	2,415	5,540	13
Pav	377.666	87	3,439	10,410	28	Boo	906.831	144	4,100	11,332	12
Lep	290.291	73	2,727	7,794	27	CVn	465.194	59	1,836	5,681	12
Cam	756.828	152	6,267	19,692	26	Scl	474.764	52	2,048	5,750	12
Sct	109.114	29	1,016	2,745	25	Vir	1,294.428	169	6,059	15,353	12
Her	1,225.148	245	10,043	30,623	25	Leo	946.964	123	4,389	10,852	11
Pic	246.739	49	2,003	6,046	25	Cet	1,231.411	189	5,567	13,991	11
Cha	131.592	31	1,072	3,219	24	Com	386.475	66	1,508	4,054	10

three others, led by Centaurus, actually top Hydra in naked-eye star count. On the other hand, Equuleus is the second-smallest constellation in terms of area and the very poorest in naked-eye stars. The picture changes subtly when fainter stars are included. Cygnus features more stars in binoculars and small telescopes than Centaurus, probably because the galactic equator runs more centrally through Cygnus. This atlas plots nearly 50,000 stars in Cygnus alone.

A better measure of richness is the star density, found by dividing a constellation's star count by its area. Because Table IX is arranged in order of decreasing star density (last column), we see that Coma Berenices, a constellation rich in galaxies, is actually the sparsest in stars. It averages only 10 plotted stars per square degree because it lies about as far from the Milky Way as it possibly could. In fact, the north galactic pole is plotted in Coma on chart 653.

Does Sagittarius, home of the galactic center (chart 1416), have the richest star fields? No—it is quite ordinary with a mere 30 stars per square degree. Scorpius to its west averages 34. The winners are those constellations situated in the fore and aft directions along our own spiral arm of the Milky Way galaxy. They include Cygnus on the one hand and the southern star clouds of Puppis, Vela, Circinus, Norma, and Triangulum Australe on the other. The richest fields of all are found in tiny Crux, with 76 stars per square degree. Under good conditions, a sweep across Crux with 7 × 50 binoculars might catch well over 3,000 stars in a single view.

NONSTELLAR OBJECTS

The earliest sky observers called almost anything that did not appear to be a star a *nebula,* which is Latin for "cloud." By the late 18th century, however, as Charles Messier in France, William Herschel in England, and others brought better and larger telescopes into use, many of these objects proved to be composed of individual stars. A stellar grouping that appeared loose and irregular came to be called an *open cluster,* while one that was round and especially rich was dubbed a *globular cluster.* Not until the early 20th century did astronomers establish that a large percentage of the remaining nebulae were, in fact, vast aggregations of stars far beyond the confines of our own Milky Way *galaxy.* By analogy, these objects became known as galaxies too. The symbols used in this atlas to distinguish true nebulae from star clusters and galaxies are based on the modern understanding of their nature.

In selecting objects to plot, our criteria differed greatly from one category to another so that a generous sampling of each could be included. Modern surveys of the southern sky, especially those conducted at the European Southern Observatory (Lauberts, 1982), have done much to overcome the Northern Hemisphere bias present in earlier compilations of nonstellar objects. At the same time, we resisted the temptation to plot every entry in J. L. E. Dreyer's *New General Catalogue* (1888) and *Index Catalogue* (1895, 1908), partly to avoid the misidentifications, duplicate entries, and uneven sky penetration of those works. Nevertheless, Dreyer's are still the most convenient designations in wide use today. For nonstellar objects of all types, the atlas gives NGC or IC numbers wherever possible.

Our starting point was the database compiled for *Sky Catalogue 2000.0, Volume 2* (Hirshfeld and Sinnott, 1985), which gives the positions and detailed characteristics of several thousand galaxies, nebulae, and star clusters, along with citations for their popular names. However, while that work can serve as a valuable companion to the *Millennium Star Atlas,* many more objects have been brought in from other tabulations. Three times as many galaxies are plotted here, for example, along with many hundreds of galaxy clusters.

The methods needed to observe nonstellar objects vary greatly. Some of the largest nebulae and open clusters are best viewed with binoculars or a low-power telescope. Dimmer, more compact ones, including the majority of galaxies, are seen much better with an 8-inch (20-cm) or larger telescope at a dark observing site. Others will tax even the largest amateur telescopes and beg to be imaged photographically or with a CCD. Nevertheless, everything plotted in this atlas should be within reach, one way or another, of equipment in the hands of today's amateur astronomer.

Nebulae. Bright nebulae are often highly irregular or wispy in shape. In a telescope they tend to appear white or colorless, for there's not enough light to excite our color vision. When photographed or imaged electronically, however, a nebula frequently appears strongly colored in a manner that provides clues to its composition and origins. Ionized hydrogen (H II) regions have a red color, while reflection nebulae are typically blue because they glow from starlight scattered by interstellar dust.

For this atlas the outlines of bright nebulae larger than about 10 arcminutes across have been traced from photographs of the National Geographic Society-Palomar Observatory Sky Survey and other sources. Small open squares locate the more compact examples. Apart from popular names, Messier numbers, and NGC or IC numbers, the atlas gives designations that

The Cocoon in Cygnus, also designated IC 5146, is an emission nebula energized by the 10th-magnitude B star at its center. Around this glowing cloud, a ring of cooler, dark matter seems to obscure the background stars. When matching this ½°-wide field to the same region on chart 1104, note that north lies toward upper right.

Chuck Vaughn

acknowledge astronomers who have studied particular objects: Cederblad (Ced); Gum; Minkowski (M1-92); Rodgers, Campbell, and Whiteoak (RCW); Sharpless (Sh2); van den Bergh (vdB); van den Bergh and Herbst (vdBH).

Dark nebulae—clumps of interstellar matter that hide stars from view—are indicated by dashed irregular outlines or small dashed squares. They also reveal their presence where the star density drops abruptly in an otherwise thickly populated section of the Milky Way. The first extensive photographic survey of dark nebulae was that done by American astronomer E. E. Barnard (1927), and his numerical designations are preceded by the letter B. Objects not observed by Barnard are labeled with their Lynds (LDN), Bernes (Be), Sandqvist (Sa), or Sandqvist and Lindroos (SL) designations.

Planetary nebulae are shells of ionized gas surrounding extremely hot stars. Having nothing to do with planets, they get their name from a telescopic resemblance to the planet Uranus. On closer inspection many appear ringlike and have a greenish hue, while others are decorated with faint outer halos and festoons. Because their appearance is highly dependent on the equipment used to observe them, this atlas gives only a rough idea of their overall angular diameters. In a few cases the central star, as observed by Tycho, appears superimposed on the identifying symbol. Planetaries lacking an NGC or IC number are identified by their PK designation from the *Catalogue of Galactic Planetary Nebulae* (Perek and Kohoutek, 1967). For eighty-eight of the more than 500 planetaries plotted here, Brian A. Skiff (1995) furnished improved positions.

A few members of our Local Group of galaxies harbor nebulous regions that are bright enough to be observed visually or imaged with small telescopes. By far the richest in such targets is the Large Magellanic Cloud (LMC), for which nearly 100 compact nebulosities have been culled from the extensive catalogue of Eduardo Bica et al. (1996). These objects, all of which have total *V* magnitudes brighter than 12.5, appear to be H II regions in which a stellar association or young cluster is embedded. Many have NGC or IC numbers; others bear designations from the work of Henize (N), Heydari-Malayeri et al. (HNT), or the other astronomers who have studied the LMC and are listed near the end of the next section. Nine small nebulosities, all having NGC or IC numbers, are plotted in the Small Magellanic Cloud as well.

Especially adventuresome observers may want to seek out the nebulous knots in two of our giant spiral

Martin Germano

Floating like a soap bubble among the stars of Lynx, this planetary nebula is known as PK 164+31.1. While it is plotted on chart 51, the 16.8-magnitude central star is much too faint to appear in the atlas.

neighbors. Five are plotted within the Andromeda Galaxy, M31 (chart 105). NGC 206 is the most conspicuous of these; the rest carry BA numbers from the listing of Walter Baade and Halton Arp (1964). In the Triangulum Galaxy, M33 (chart 146), are found NGC 604 and three other fairly bright nebulosities identified by the prefix A (Humphreys and Sandage, 1980). Guided tours of many more sights in M31 and M33 can be found in the *Observing Handbook and Catalogue of Deep-Sky Objects* (Luginbuhl and Skiff, 1989).

Open and globular star clusters. Containing at most a few hundred stars, open clusters are relatively nearby congregations along the spiral arms of our galaxy. The best-known examples are the Pleiades in Taurus (chart 163) and the Praesepe or Beehive in Cancer (chart 712). Those that formed fairly recently on the cosmic time scale—within the last few million years—often retain traces of their original gas and dust. The atlas uses dashed circles to indicate the locations and approximate diameters of open clusters.

Because open clusters rank among the sky's best-known sights, it would be natural to assume that their locations are well-documented in the astronomical literature. Surprisingly, however, just the opposite appears to be true. While plotting the charts for this atlas we encountered many cases in which the catalogue position was off, occasionally by $\frac{1}{4}°$ or more. The telltale sign was a cluster symbol noticeably off-center with respect to the clump of the brightest member stars observed by Tycho. In dozens of such cases the cluster's symbol has been recentered.

For the very largest open clusters, the scale of the charts made it impractical to plot a dashed circle. One

Preston Scott Justis

Preston Scott Justis

Among the best-known summer sights for small telescopes, the great globular cluster M13 in Hercules is pictured here with north to the upper left. Note that the cluster's outermost fringes, barely detectable on this photograph, are included in its overall diameter indicated on chart 1159; telescope users generally see a somewhat smaller core. In the top-left corner of this view lies a 12th-magnitude galaxy, NGC 6207.

A fine open cluster in Camelopardalis, NGC 1502 appears to contain about 50 member stars in this photograph. Nearly a third as many can also be counted on chart 43.

example is the Alpha Persei Cluster; another is the sprinkling of faint naked-eye stars in Coma Berenices. Both the Hyades (chart 185) and the Ursa Major Moving Cluster (charts 556–578) lie within 200 light-years of the Sun, so their members can be singled out from background stars by individual light-year labels. In fact, the three-dimensional structure of these two clusters has been revealed for the first time by Hipparcos's distance measurements.

When not identified by NGC or IC numbers, open clusters are labeled with the designations of astronomers or observatories that have specialized in their study. Many names are spelled out in full; those that are abbreviated in the atlas are Barkhatova (Bark), Berkeley (Berk), Biurakan (Biur), Collinder (Cr), Dolidze (Do), Dolidze-Dzimselejsvili (DoDz), Feinstein (Fein), Iskudarian (Isk), Lindsay (L), Markarian (Mrk), Melotte (Mel), Ruprecht (Ru), Stephenson (Steph), Trumpler (Tr), van den Bergh (vdB), van den Bergh-Hagen (vdB-Ha), and Westerlund (Westr).

Globular clusters are a different breed from their open cousins, for they contain tens or hundreds of thousands of stars each and are found far-flung throughout the disk and halo of our galaxy. For these our primary source is Skiff (1996), and the plotted symbols represent his angular sizes in an isophotal system similar to that in wide use for galaxies. Many globulars are known by their Messier, NGC, or IC numbers. Other designations include those of Arp-

Madore (abbreviated AM), Palomar (Pal), Ruprecht (Ru), Tonantzintla (Ton), and the United Kingdom Schmidt telescope (UKS). The two brightest, 47 Tucanae and ω Centauri, still carry the star names assigned to them by early astronomers. At the other end of the visibility scale, the very dim Eridanus and Pyxis globulars are known simply by the constellations in which they lie.

This atlas shows nearly 700 open clusters and 144 globular clusters belonging to our own galaxy. Additionally, in and around the Large Magellanic Cloud are plotted more than 200 clusters with an integrated V magnitude brighter than 12.5 (Bica et al., 1996). Of these only 15 seem to resemble the globulars of the Milky Way, according to a study by W. E. Harris and R. Racine (1979). The rest appear bluer, younger, and less round than our home-grown variety, suggesting a rather different evolution, and they are simply plotted with open-cluster symbols. The SL clusters come from the Shapley-Lindsay catalogue of 1963; other designations include Hodge (H), Lucke-Hodge (LH), Hodge-Sexton (HS), Bica et al. (BCDSP), European Southern Observatory (ESO), Robertson (Rob), Lortet-Testor (LT), Kontizas et al. (KMHK), and Bhatia et al. (BRHT).

Similarly, the charts of the Small Magellanic Cloud show a total of 45 clusters, 10 of which are marked as true globulars in the Milky Way sense. For nearly all of these, astrometric positions are from Douglas L. Welch (1991). The L prefix refers to numbers from the 1958 catalogue of E. M. Lindsay.

National Optical Astronomy Observatories

Because it appears nearly face on to our view, the spiral galaxy NGC 4622 in Centaurus is shown nearly round on chart 935. Recently this unusual object raised eyebrows among galactic dynamicists, for it appears to have two sets of spiral arms winding in opposite directions.

Martin Germano

Located in eastern Cetus less than 1° north of M77, the edge-on spiral NGC 1055 is nearly bisected by a prominent dust lane. Together with the bright foreground stars, this 11th-magnitude galaxy can be found on chart 262.

M31, M33, and the Fornax Dwarf (chart 403) are the only other galaxies whose brightest star clusters have been included in this atlas. M31's eight globulars and one open cluster are all brighter than magnitude 15 visually (Crampton et al., 1985), and they appear almost starlike in a telescope. The two brightest globulars in M33, designated C39 and U49, have magnitudes of 15.9 and 16.2, respectively (Christian and Schommer, 1982). The Fornax Dwarf's five globulars, which range in magnitude from 12.6 to 15.6 (Skiff, 1996), may well be easier targets telescopically than the sprawling, ultradim galaxy itself.

Galaxies. More than 8,000 small ovals of various shapes, sizes, and orientations are sprinkled throughout the *Millennium Star Atlas* charts. Each is a galaxy, and each contains anywhere from a few hundred thousand stars to a million million or more. In the relatively nearby spiral M31, the most luminous individual stars are scarcely brighter than magnitude 16.

Our selection began with all galaxies in the *Lyon-Meudon Extragalactic Database* (LEDA) having a total *B* (blue-light) magnitude of 13.7 or brighter (Paturel, 1997). To these were added a number of fainter galaxies between 13.7 and 14.5, including most in this range with NGC numbers or well-measured angular sizes and orientations. Since a typical galaxy appears about 0.7 magnitude brighter in yellow light, for visual observers the atlas can be considered fairly complete in galaxies to about *V* magnitude 13.5.

Unfortunately, position angles were found missing from the astronomical literature for nearly one-third of our entire sample. In a major effort especially for this

Kim Zussman

This trio of bright galaxies in Draco fits easily in a 100-power view or a small telescope's CCD frame, for NGC 5985 (left) lies just 13 arcminutes from NGC 5981 (right). Midway between the two spirals is an 11th-magnitude elliptical galaxy, NGC 5982. In comparing the photograph to the same region on chart 553, note that north is toward the upper right.

atlas, we have tried to "fill in the blanks" with the help of the online Digitized Sky Survey maintained by the Space Telescope Science Institute. Numerous photographs have also been consulted, such as those in the *Carnegie Atlas of Galaxies* (Sandage and Bedke, 1994).

Even so, the galaxy orientations found here must be treated with caution. While the goal has been to orient each galaxy according to its outermost features, this determination depends on many factors intrinsic to the galaxy and the way it was imaged. Barred spirals can be especially troublesome in this regard. In addi-

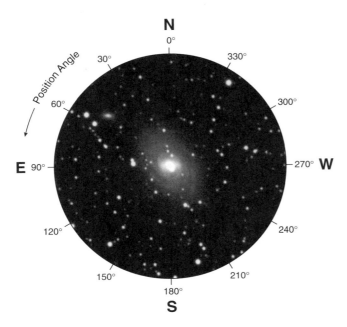

Position angles in a telescope field are measured from north through east, south, and west. The greatest extent of the galaxy NGC 1169 lies toward position angle 30° (and 210°), and that is the way it appears on chart 79 of the atlas. However, it is easy to see from the bright central region of this barred spiral why someone working with a photograph of much shorter exposure could assign an orientation of 90° by mistake.

tion, spot checks revealed a surprising number of erroneous position angles that have found their way into existing databases and catalogues. Especially alarming were many cases of east-west or mirror-image reversals, apparently caused by someone measuring angles clockwise rather than counterclockwise from north, or by viewing a plate from the wrong side. At the suggestion of Georges Paturel (Observatoire de Lyon), we concentrated our checking on the declination zone between 0° and –20° and corrected many errors of this type. Nevertheless, the mirror-image problem may still affect a few percent of the plotted galaxies all over the sky.

Misidentifications are another source of frustration for anyone engaged in deep-sky observing, and this problem is especially chronic among the NGC and IC galaxies. As to labels and positions, when LEDA differed from the *Revised New General Catalogue of Nonstellar Astronomical Objects* (Sulentic and Tifft, 1973), *Uranometria 2000.0* (Tirion et al., 1987), *NGC 2000.0* (Sinnott, 1988), or the online SIMBAD database (Centre de Données astronomiques de Strasbourg, 1997) we have tried to resolve the problem with the help of Dreyer's original compilation as reprinted by the Royal Astronomical Society, London (1962). Often Dreyer's descriptions provide better clues than his tabulated sky positions. For example, if he mentions "★ 2′ sp" (a star lying 2 arcminutes south-preced-

ing), a glance at several possible candidates in the Digitized Sky Survey may quickly locate the galaxy originally observed.

Despite the similarity of symbols, a small face-on galaxy can always be told from a variable star by the type of label it has. The majority of galaxies carry a simple NGC number up to 7840 (and no prefix) or a series of digits preceded by the letters IC, UGC, MCG, CGCG, or ESO. Interestingly enough, the atlas occasionally shows a Tycho star very nearly centered on a galaxy's symbol. Some of these are true foreground stars, as we have confirmed, but others are almost surely Tycho's measurement of the nucleus of the galaxy itself. (Such an artifact seems to have occurred, for example, for NGC 5260 on chart 865.) Deciding the issue one way or the other is complicated by the fact that the central region of a galaxy is often overexposed on all available photographs. Perhaps some user of this atlas will systematically check out such galaxies, taking advantage of the greater dynamic range of a CCD camera or the observer's own eye.

Finally, our selection includes 26 members of the Local Group, the loose collection of galaxies bunched together with our own Milky Way in a volume of space about three million light-years across. They comprise such familiar targets as M31, M33, and the Magellanic Clouds, along with an assortment of small elliptical and dwarf-irregular galaxies. The relative nearness of Local Group members gives them a large angular size, but that is no guarantee they are easy to observe. In a

Martin Germano

The Pegasus Dwarf, a small irregular galaxy belonging to the Local Group, is only about one-fifteenth as large as our Milky Way. While its overall light matches that of a 12th-magnitude star, the glow is spread across nearly 0.1° of sky and presents quite a challenge to visual observers. This object is plotted on chart 1232.

few the light is so dispersed that they have exceedingly low surface brightnesses; they are included for the sake of interest rather than observability.

In fact, the sizes of nearly all the galaxies plotted in this atlas are those within which the surface brightness exceeds one star of B magnitude 25 per square arcsecond—a criterion recommended by Gérard de Vaucouleurs et al. (1991). For the very dimmest members of the Local Group, however, York University astronomer Marshall McCall (1997) points out that such a definition leads to a diameter of zero! He has supplied, as an alternative, "dynamical boundaries" along with position angles and aspect ratios. Because the extreme edges of these objects are far too subtle to detect by ordinary means, the atlas shows ellipses that are 30 percent as large as McCall's dynamical values for the following Local Group galaxies: Sculptor Dwarf, Fornax, Carina, Leo I through III, Ursa Minor, Draco, Andromeda I through III, and Sextans I. Their chart numbers can be found in the index.

The most recent addition to the Local Group, called the Antlia Dwarf (Whiting et al., 1997), appears on chart 899. Further such discoveries are almost sure to come.

Galaxy clusters. Barely accessible to amateur astronomers before the CCD era, rich clusters of galaxies were the subject of much pioneering work by University of California astronomer George O. Abell, who examined photographic plates of the original Palomar Sky Survey in the 1950s. He was attracted to these "galaxian archipelagos," as he called them, by the promise they offered to provide a three-dimensional picture of the distribution of matter in the universe.

Abell's 1958 catalogue included only those galaxy clusters that could be photographed from Palomar Mountain. Then in 1980 he began work on a southern extension, examining additional Schmidt plates taken at the Anglo-Australian Observatory. Following Abell's death in 1984, his colleagues Harold Corwin and Ronald Olowin compiled a list of additional southern clusters in a supplement and reobserved some of the northern ones. Their final compilation (Abell et al., 1989) includes 4,073 clusters having at least 30 members that are not more than 2 magnitudes fainter than the third-brightest member galaxy.

At Corwin's suggestion, only the very nearest galaxy clusters (those assigned to Abell distance classes 1 through 4) are retained in our sample. This selection

Kim Zussman

Spanning some $1\frac{1}{2}°$ of sky, this great cluster of galaxies in Hercules contains at least 50 members visible in this photograph of its central region. A dozen of the brightest ones also appear individually on chart 1230 of the atlas.

reduces their number to 675 and helps to ensure that each plotted cluster has at least 10 members of magnitude 16.4 or brighter in blue light. They should have appeal as observing targets because, to our knowledge, they have never before been included in a star atlas. To avoid excessive clutter, the pentagon symbol and cluster label have been suppressed whenever more than a few of the individual member galaxies were bright enough to be plotted on their own.

Quasars and other special objects. Also known as quasi-stellar objects or QSOs, quasars remain of intense interest to cosmologists today. Because they lie at immense distances but are fairly bright, they are among the most luminous objects in the universe. Our sample includes all known quasars brighter than visual magnitude 16.0, along with their close cousins, the BL Lacertae objects. Some 250 in all, they have been selected from the catalogue of M. P. Véron-Cetty and P. Véron (1996).

A few of the brightest quasars, such as 12.9-magnitude 3C 273 in Virgo, can be spotted visually in a 6-inch (15-cm) telescope. All the rest can be imaged with modest equipment. But because most of these objects lie well below the atlas's magnitude cutoff for stars, proper identification normally requires a detailed finder chart showing equally faint foreground stars in the same field. Their locations are simply marked by the open-cross symbol shown in the legend.

The open-cross symbol also marks a few exceptional objects in this atlas that are *not* quasars, even though each member of this menagerie rightfully deserves a unique symbol all its own. For example, plotted on chart 179 is the high-energy gamma-ray source Geminga, showing both its location and proper motion as recently determined by John R. Mattox and colleagues (1997). Cassiopeia A, on chart 1070, is the strongest radio source in the sky. Chart 1269 shows the location of the celebrated 14th-magnitude object known as SS 433. And on chart 1416, a few arcminutes from the adopted origin of the galactic coordinate system, lies Sagittarius A* (Rogers et al., 1994), the radio source and probable black hole that mark the exact center of the Milky Way.

Additional information about the *Millennium Star Atlas* is available on Sky Publishing Corporation's Web site, SKY Online, at

http://www.skypub.com/msa/msa.html

Further details of the Hipparcos satellite and the *Hipparcos and Tycho Catalogues* can be found on the European Space Agency's Hipparcos page at

http://astro.estec.esa.nl/Hipparcos/hipparcos.html

ABOUT THE PHOTOGRAPHS

To record PK 164+31.1 (page XIX), NGC 1055 (page XXI), NGC 1169, and the Pegasus Dwarf (page XXII), California astrophotographer MARTIN GERMANO used a 14½-inch (37-cm) f/5 Newtonian with coma corrector; his exposure times were 105, 125, 120, and 165 minutes, respectively. PRESTON SCOTT JUSTIS of Virginia Beach, Virginia, used a 10-inch (25-cm) f/6 Newtonian and coma corrector for NGC 1502 and M13 (page XX); his exposures were 60 and 90 minutes. PAUL LIND designed and built his own 8-inch (20-cm) f/3.6 hyperbolic astrograph to capture the California Nebula (page VIII); he made this 120-minute exposure through a red filter at a site in central Arizona. SHIGEMI NUMAZAWA took his 8-inch f/1.5 Schmidt camera to Coonabarabran, Australia, to photograph the Antares region (page VI). Later, at his darkroom in Niigata City, Japan, he printed the 8-minute exposure and used the technique of unsharp masking to bring out details in the nebulosity. CHUCK VAUGHN captured the Cocoon (page XVIII) in a 90-minute exposure with his 12½-inch (30-cm) f/9 Ritchey-Chrétien reflector in Fremont, California. KIM ZUSSMAN, with a 14½-inch f/8 Cassegrain reflector in Thousand Oaks, California, exposed the NGC 5985 group (page XXI) for 120 minutes and the Hercules Cluster (page XXIII) for 204 minutes. All these images were made on gas-hypersensitized Kodak Technical Pan film, except the NOAO view of NGC 4622 (page XXI), which was taken on a blue-sensitive spectroscopic emulsion with the Cerro Tololo 4-meter reflector in Chile.

REFERENCES AND BIBLIOGRAPHY

LISTED HERE ARE works cited in the Introduction or found most useful during preparation of the atlas. Commonly used acronyms and designation prefixes are given in brackets after some of the source catalogues.

GENERAL

Burnham, R., Jr., *Burnham's Celestial Handbook,* New York, 1978: Dover Publications.

Delporte, E., *Délimitation Scientifique des Constellations,* Cambridge, 1930: Cambridge University Press.

Dreyer, J. L. E., *New General Catalogue of Nebulae and Clusters of Stars (1888), Index Catalogue (1895), Second Index Catalogue (1908),* London, 1962: Royal Astronomical Society. [NGC, IC]

ESA, *The Hipparcos and Tycho Catalogues,* ESA SP-1200, Noordwijk, 1997: European Space Agency.

Fricke, W., H. Schwan, and T. Lederle, *Fifth Fundamental Catalogue (FK5), Part I: The Basic Fundamental Stars,* Veröffentlichungen Astronomisches Rechen–Institut Heidelberg, 32, Karlsruhe, 1988: G. Braun. [FK5]

Hearnshaw, J. B., "Origins of the Stellar Magnitude Scale," *Sky & Telescope,* 84, 494–99, November 1992.

Hirshfeld, A., and R. W. Sinnott, eds., *Sky Catalogue 2000.0, Volume 2: Double Stars, Variable Stars and Nonstellar Objects,* Cambridge, MA, 1985: Sky Publishing Corp. and Cambridge University Press. [SC2]

Hirshfeld, A., R. W. Sinnott, and F. Ochsenbein, *Sky Catalogue 2000.0, Volume 1: Stars to Magnitude 8.0,* 2nd edition, Cambridge, MA, 1991: Sky Publishing Corp. and Cambridge University Press. [SC1]

Levin, A. E., "Areas of Constellations," *British Astronomical Association Handbook for 1935,* 34.

Luginbuhl, C. B., and B. A. Skiff, *Observing Handbook and Catalogue of Deep-Sky Objects,* Cambridge, 1989: Cambridge University Press.

Mallas, J. H., and E. Kreimer, *The Messier Album,* Cambridge, MA, 1978: Sky Publishing Corp. [M]

Minkowski, R. L., and G. O. Abell, "The National Geographic Society–Palomar Observatory Sky Survey," Appendix II in *Basic Astronomical Data,* K. Aa. Strand, ed., Chicago, 1963: University of Chicago Press.

Osterbrock, D. E., *Yerkes Observatory, 1892–1950,* Chicago, 1997: University of Chicago Press.

Ptolemy, C., *Almagest,* years 127–141. A machine-readable version, described by C. Jaschek in *Bulletin d'Information du Centre de Données Stellaires,* 33, 145, 1987, is distributed by the Astronomical Data Center, NASA GSFC, on the CD-ROM *Selected Astronomical Catalogs,* 3, 1996.

Raisz, E., *General Cartography,* New York, 1938: McGraw-Hill.

Sinnott, R. W., ed., *NGC 2000.0: The Complete New General Catalogue and Index Catalogues of Nebulae and Star Clusters by J. L. E. Dreyer,* Cambridge, MA, 1988: Sky Publishing Corp. and Cambridge University Press.

Smithsonian Astrophysical Observatory *Star Catalog,* Washington, DC, 1966, 1971: Smithsonian Institution. [SAO]

Stevens, S. S., "To Honor Fechner and Repeal His Law," *Science,* 133, 80, January 13, 1961.

Sulentic, J. W., and W. G. Tifft, *The Revised New General Catalogue of Nonstellar Astronomical Objects,* Tuscon, AZ, 1980: University of Arizona Press. [RNGC]

Tirion, W., *Sky Atlas 2000.0,* Cambridge, MA, 1981: Sky Publishing Corp. and Cambridge University Press.

Tirion, W., B. Rappaport, and G. Lovi, *Uranometria 2000.0,* Richmond, VA, 1987: Willmann-Bell.

Van Biesbroeck, G., "Star Catalogues and Charts," Appendix I in *Basic Astronomical Data,* K. Aa. Strand, ed., Chicago, 1963: University of Chicago Press.

Vehrenberg, H., *Atlas of Deep-Sky Splendors,* 4th edition, Cambridge, MA, 1983: Sky Publishing Corp.

Young, A. T., *NASA Conference Publication* 2350, 8, 1984.

Young, A. T., "How We Perceive Star Brightnesses," *Sky & Telescope,* 79, 311–12, March 1990.

NAMED ASTRONOMICAL OBJECTS

Allen, R. H., *Star Names: Their Lore and Meaning,* New York, 1963: Dover Publications.

Fernandez, A., M.–C. Lortet, and F. Spite, "The First Dictionary of the Nomenclature of Celestial Objects," *Astronomy and Astrophysics Supplement Series,* 52, 1983.

Hoffleit, D., "Discordances in Star Designations," *Bulletin d'Information du Centre de Données Stellaires,* 17, 38, 1979.

Hoffleit, D., *The Bright Star Catalogue,* 4th revised edition, New Haven, CT, 1982: Yale University Observatory.

Spite, F., and R. Lahmek, "Stars Named After Astronomers' Names," *Bulletin d'Information du Centre de Données Stellaires,* 22, 105, 1982.

Wagman, M., "Flamsteed's Missing Stars," *Journal for the History of Astronomy,* 18, 209, 1987.

VARIABLE STARS

Central Bureau for Astronomical Telegrams (CBAT), Smithsonian Astrophysical Observatory, Cambridge, MA, 1997: International Astronomical Union. The CBAT Computer Service provided positions and designations of recent novae. http://cfa-www.harvard.edu/cfa/ps/cbat.html

Clark, D. H., and F. R. Stephenson, *The Historical Supernovae*, New York, 1977: Pergamon Press.

Kholopov, P. N., "On the Classification of Variable Stars," *Variable Stars*, 21, 465, 1981.

Kholopov, P. N., et al., *General Catalogue of Variable Stars*, 4th edition, Moscow, 1985: Nauka. [GCVS]

Scovil, C. E., *The AAVSO Variable Star Atlas*, 2nd edition, Cambridge, MA, 1990: American Association of Variable Star Observers.

DOUBLE AND MULTIPLE STARS

Ashbrook, J., "The Eagle Eye of William Rutter Dawes," in *The Astronomical Scrapbook*, Cambridge, MA, 1984: Sky Publishing Corp. and Cambridge University Press.

Couteau, P., *Observing Visual Double Stars*, Cambridge, MA, 1981: MIT Press.

Dommanget, J. and O. Nys, "Catalogue of Components of Double and Multiple Stars," *Communications*, Observatoire Royale de Belgique, Series A, No. 115, 1994.

Jones, K. G., ed., *Webb Society Deep-Sky Observer's Handbook*, Vol. 1, Double Stars, Short Hills, NJ, 1979: Enslow Publishers.

Worley, C. E., and G. G. Douglass, *Washington Catalog of Visual Double Stars 1984.0*, Washington, DC, 1984: U. S. Naval Observatory. [WDS]

Worley, C. E., and W. D. Heintz, "Fourth Catalog of Orbits of Visual Binary Stars," *Publications* of the U. S. Naval Observatory, 2nd Series, 24, Part 7, Washington, DC, 1983.

BRIGHT NEBULAE

Baade, W., and H. Arp, "Positions of Emission Nebulae in M31," *Astrophysical Journal*, 139, 1027, 1964. [BA]

Bica, E., J. J. Clariá, H. Dottori, J. F. C. Santos, Jr., and A. E. Piatti, "Integrated *UBV* Photometry of 624 Star Clusters and Associations in the Large Magellanic Cloud," *Astrophysical Journal Supplement Series*, 102, 57, 1996.

Cederblad, S., "Catalogue of Bright Diffuse Galactic Nebulae," *Meddelanden fran Lunds astronomiska observatorium*, Ser. 2, 12, No. 119, 1946. [Ced]

Dufour, R. J., "The Chemical Composition of Selected HII Regions in the Magellanic Clouds," *Astrophysical Journal*, 195, 315, 1975.

Gum, C. S., "A Survey of Southern HII Regions," *Memoirs of the Royal Astronomical Society*, 67, 21, 1955. [Gum]

Humphreys, R., and A. Sandage, "On the Stellar Content and Structure of the Spiral Galaxy M33," *Astrophysical Journal Supplement Series*, 44, 319, 1980.

Jones, K. G., ed., *Webb Society Deep-Sky Observer's Handbook*, Vol. 2, Planetary and Gaseous Nebulae, Hillside, NJ, 1979: Enslow Publishers.

Lynds, B. T., "Catalogue of Bright Nebulae," *Astrophysical Journal Supplement Series*, 12, 163, 1965. [LBN]

Neckel, T., and H. Vehrenberg, *Atlas of Galactic Nebulae*, Dusseldorf, 1985, 1987, and 1990: Treugesell-Verlag.

Numazawa, S., *The Deep Sky*, Tokyo, 1992: Seibundo Shinkosha.

Sharpless, S., "A Catalogue of HII Regions," *Astrophysical Journal Supplement Series*, 4, 257, 1959. [Sh2]

van den Bergh, S., "A Study of Reflection Nebulae," *Astronomical Journal*, 71, 990, 1966. [vdB]

DARK NEBULAE

Barnard, E. E., "Catalogue of 349 Dark Objects in the Sky," in *A Photographic Atlas of Selected Regions of the Milky Way*, Washington, DC, 1927: Carnegie Institution. [B]

Bernes, C., "A Catalogue of Bright Nebulosities in Opaque Dust Clouds," *Astronomy and Astrophysics Supplement Series*, 29, 65, 1977. [Be]

Bok, B. J., and C. S. Cordwell, *A Study of Dark Nebulae*, Tucson, 1971: Steward Observatory, University of Arizona.

Lynds, B. T., "Catalogue of Dark Nebulae," *Astrophysical Journal Supplement Series*, 7, 1, 1962. [LDN]

Malin, D. F., "Dust Clouds of Sagittarius," *Sky & Telescope*, 63, 254, March 1982.

Sandqvist, Aa., "More Southern Dark Dust Clouds," *Astronomy and Astrophysics*, 57, 467, 1977. [Sa]

Sandqvist, Aa., and K. P. Lindroos, "Interstellar Formaldehyde in Southern Dark Dust Clouds," *Astronomy and Astrophysics*, 53, 179, 1976. [SL]

PLANETARY NEBULAE

Acker, A., et al., *The Strasbourg–ESO Catalogue of Galactic Planetary Nebulae*, Garching bei München, 1992: European Southern Observatory.

Jones, K. G., ed., *Webb Society Deep-Sky Observer's Handbook*, Vol. 2, Planetary and Gaseous Nebulae, Hillside, NJ, 1979: Enslow Publishers.

Perek, L., and L. Kohoutek, *Catalogue of Galactic Planetary Nebulae*, Prague, 1967: Academia Publishing House of the Czechoslovak Academy of Sciences. [PK]

Skiff, B. A., private communication, August 5, 1995.

OPEN AND GLOBULAR CLUSTERS

Alter, G., B. Balasz, and J. Ruprecht, *Catalogue of Star Clusters and Associations,* 2nd edition, Budapest, 1970: Akademiai Kiado.

Bica, E., J. J. Clariá, H. Dottori, J. F. C. Santos, Jr., and A. E. Piatti, "Integrated *UBV* Photometry of 624 Star Clusters and Associations in the Large Magellanic Cloud," *Astrophysical Journal Supplement Series,* 102, 57, 1996.

Christian, C. A., and R. A. Schommer, "The Cluster System of M33," *Astrophysical Journal Supplement Series,* 49, 405, 1982.

Crampton, D., A. P. Cowley, D. Schade, and P. Chayer, "The M31 Globular Cluster System," *Astrophysical Journal,* 288, 494, 1985.

di Cicco, D., "The Curious Case of IC 1257," *Sky & Telescope,* 93, 113, May 1997.

Hanes, D., and B. Madore, eds., *Globular Clusters,* Cambridge, 1980: Cambridge University Press.

Harris, W. E., R. L. Phelps, B. F. Madore, O. Pevunova, B. A. Skiff, C. Crute, B. Wilson, and B. A. Archinal, "IC 1257: A New Globular Cluster in the Galactic Halo," *Astronomical Journal,* 113, 688, 1997.

Harris, W. E., and R. Racine, "Globular Clusters in Galaxies," *Annual Review of Astronomy and Astrophysics,* 17, 241, 1979.

Hodge, P. W., *The Andromeda Galaxy,* Dordrecht, The Netherlands, 1992: Kluwer Academic Publishers.

Jones, K. G., ed., *Webb Society Deep-Sky Observer's Handbook,* Vol. 3, Open and Globular Clusters, Hillside, NJ, 1980: Enslow Publishers.

Lindsay, E. M., "The Cluster System of the Small Magellanic Cloud," *Monthly Notices* of the Royal Astronomical Society, 118, 172, 1958. [L]

Lynga, G., *Catalogue of Open Cluster Data,* Lund, 1981, revised 1983: Lund Observatory.

Lynga, G., "Open Clusters in Our Galaxy," *Astronomy and Astrophysics,* 109, 213, 1982.

Ruprecht, J., B. Balazs, and R. E. White, *Catalogue of Star Clusters and Associations,* Supplement I, Budapest, 1981: Akademiai Kiado.

Shapley, H., and E. M. Lindsay, "A Catalogue of Clusters in the Large Magellanic Cloud," *Irish Astronomical Journal,* 6, 74, 1963. [SL]

Skiff, B. A., private communication, May 12, 1996.

Terzan, A., "Quatre nouveaux amas stellaires dans la direction de le région centrale de la Galaxie," *Astronomy and Astrophysics,* 12, 477, 1971.

Welch, D. L., "Accurate Positions for SMC Clusters," *Astronomical Journal,* 101, 538, 1991.

GALAXIES

Centre de Données astronomiques de Strasbourg, *Set of Identifications, Measurements, and Bibliography for Astro-nomical Data,* machine-readable database as of 1997: Université de Strasbourg. [SIMBAD]

de Vaucouleurs, G., A. de Vaucouleurs, H. G. Corwin, Jr., R. J. Buta, G. Paturel, and P. Fouqué, *Third Reference Catalogue of Bright Galaxies,* New York, 1991: Springer-Verlag. [RC3]

Jones, K. G., ed., *Webb Society Deep-Sky Observer's Handbook,* Vol. 4, Galaxies, Hillside, NJ, 1981: Enslow Publishers.

Lauberts, A., *The ESO/Uppsala Survey of the ESO(B) Atlas,* 1982: European Southern Observatory. [ESO]

McCall, M. L., private communication, March 19, 1997.

Nilson, P. N., *Uppsala General Catalogue of Galaxies,* Uppsala, 1973: Uppsala Astronomical Observatory. [UGC]

Paturel, G., *Lyon-Meudon Extragalactic Database,* Lyon, 1997: CRAL-Observatoire de Lyon. [LEDA] http://www-obs.univ-lyon1.fr

Sandage, A., *The Hubble Atlas of Galaxies,* Washington, DC, 1961: Carnegie Institution.

Sandage, A., and J. Bedke, *The Carnegie Atlas of Galaxies,* Washington, DC, 1994: Carnegie Institution.

Sandage, A., and G. A. Tammann, *A Revised Shapley-Ames Catalog of Bright Galaxies,* Washington, DC, 1981: Carnegie Institution.

Space Telescope Science Institute, *The STScI Digitized Sky Survey,* Baltimore, MD, 1995: Association of Universities for Research in Astronomy. http://stdatu.stsci.edu/dss/

Vorontsov-Velyaminov, B. A., et al., *Morphological Catalog of Galaxies,* Parts I–V, Moscow, 1962–74: Moscow State University. [MCG]

Whiting, A. B., M. J. Irwin, and G. T. K. Hau, "A New Galaxy in the Local Group: The Antlia Dwarf Galaxy," *Astronomical Journal,* in press, 1997.

Zwicky, F., E. Herzog, P. Wild, M. Karpowicz, and C. T. Kowal, *Catalogue of Galaxies and Clusters of Galaxies,* Pasadena, CA, 1968: California Institute of Technology. [CGCG]

CLUSTERS OF GALAXIES

Abell, G. O., "The Distribution of Rich Clusters of Galaxies," *Astrophysical Journal Supplement Series,* 3, 211, 1958. [A]

Abell, G. O., H. G. Corwin, Jr., and R. P. Olowin, "A Catalogue of Rich Clusters of Galaxies," *Astrophysical Journal Supplement Series,* 70, 1, 1989. A machine-readable version is distributed by the Astronomical Data Center, NASA GSFC, on the CD-ROM *Selected Astronomical Catalogs,* 1, 1992. [A, AS]

Jones, K. G., ed., *Webb Society Deep-Sky Observer's Handbook,* Vol. 5, Clusters of Galaxies, Hillside, NJ, 1982: Enslow Publishers.

QUASARS AND OTHER
HIGH-ENERGY SOURCES

Bennett, A. S., "The Preparation of the Revised 3C Catalogue of Radio Sources," *Monthly Notices* of the Royal Astronomical Society, 125, 75, 1962. [3C]

Burbidge, G., and A. Hewitt, "A Catalog of Quasars Near and Far," *Sky & Telescope,* 88, 32, December 1994.

Ekers, J. A., "The Parkes Catalogue of Radio Sources," *Australian Journal of Physics,* Astrophysical Supplement, No. 7, 1, 1969. [PKS]

Mattox, J. R., J. P. Halpern, and P. A. Caraveo, "Timing the Geminga Pulsar with Gamma-Ray Observations," *Astrophysical Journal,* in press, 1997.

Rogers, A. E. E., et al., "Small-Scale Structure and Position of Sagittarius A* from VLBI at 3 Millimeter Wavelength," *Astrophysical Journal,* 434, L59–L62, October 20, 1994.

Véron-Cetty, M.-P., and P. Véron, "Quasars and Active Nuclei," 7th edition, ESO *Scientific Report* 17, Munich, 1996: European Southern Observatory. A machine-readable version is distributed by the Astronomical Data Center, NASA GSFC, on the CD-ROM *Selected Astronomical Catalogs,* 3, 1996.

ACKNOWLEDGMENTS

THIS ENDEAVOR grew in grandeur and complexity with the dreams of its creators. In 1992, while developing software to produce star charts for *Sky & Telescope* magazine, associate editor Roger W. Sinnott realized that a new star atlas could be produced largely by computer-generated graphics—a far cry from the years of toil by teams of drafting experts that such projects required in the past. But what niche would such an atlas occupy among the excellent atlases already in print? How could it stand apart?

ESA's Hipparcos satellite was then finishing its monumental survey of the heavens, and Sinnott wondered if its bounty might somehow be incorporated. At first the main attraction was the Tycho Catalogue, whose uniform sampling of stars around the sky would overcome the common failing of celestial atlases in the past. In May 1995, an auspicious meeting between Sky Publishing Corporation president Richard Tresch Fienberg and Hipparcos astronomer Daniel Egret (Observatoire de Strasbourg, France) quickly led to formal discussions with Michael Perryman (ESA–ESTEC, The Netherlands), ESA's project scientist for the Hipparcos mission since 1980 and chair of its science team. The *Millennium Star Atlas* was under way.

At first Sinnott envisioned using only a subset of the Tycho data to create an atlas with a few hundred charts. But Perryman pointed out many ways in which the more accurate Hipparcos findings could enhance the work, putting the atlas truly in a class by itself. And, viewed in that light, why shouldn't it include all of Tycho as well? In this manner the project ballooned to become the largest star atlas ever produced.

Joining the atlas effort on the European side was Hans Schrijver (SRON–Utrecht, The Netherlands), who had been responsible for monitoring and calibrating the satellite's performance during the mission and who later coordinated the final results as they were readied for publication. For this atlas Schrijver extracted the subsets of the Hipparcos Catalogue used to present stellar distances, proper motions, variability, and duplicity.

Erik Høg (Copenhagen University Observatory, Denmark), who had proposed the instrumental concepts underlying the Tycho experiment back in 1982, went on to lead the Tycho consortium and prepare its catalogue for publication. Valeri Makarov, also at Copenhagen, was closely involved with the Tycho calibrations and reductions. These two astronomers provided the concise version of Tycho that was used to plot all the atlas's stars.

Many other ESA astronomers played key roles through their long-time involvement and dedication to the Hipparcos mission. Lennart Lindegren (Lund Observatory, Sweden) and Jean Kovalevsky (Observatoire de la Côte d'Azur, Grasse, France) led the two consortia responsible for analyzing the Hipparcos data. Catherine Turon (Observatoire de Paris-Meudon, France) headed the consortium that prepared the *Hipparcos Input Catalogue*. Volkmar Großmann (Tübingen, Germany) and Jean-Louis Halbwachs (Strasbourg, France) had primary roles in the Tycho photometry, while Floor van Leeuwen and Dafydd Wynn Evans (Royal Greenwich Observatory, Cambridge, U. K.), François Mignard (Observatoire de la Côte d'Azur, Grasse, France) and Michel Grenon (Observatoire de Genève, Switzerland) oversaw the Hipparcos photometry and classification of variable stars. Lindegren and Mignard, along with Staffan Söderhjelm (Lund Observatory) and Pier Luigi Bernacca (Asiago Observatory, Italy), had overall responsibility for the parameters of double and multiple stars.

Across the Atlantic, back at Sky Publishing, Fienberg began to assemble the mounting resources that would bring the project to fruition. E. Talmadge Mentall, Sinnott's colleague almost from the start, measured images of 2,000 galaxies to obtain orientations and sizes missing from the literature. He also meticulously researched and drafted all the outlines of large bright and dark nebulae.

As overall project manager, Sally MacGillivray masterfully handled the publishing and printing arrangements and coordinated the massive effort needed to finalize the raw charts as they came from the computer. At this stage Imelda B. Joson joined the project; she and Mentall painstakingly annotated the charts, ever watchful for programming bugs and labeling ambiguities. As a further check, *Sky & Telescope* associate editor Samantha Parker carefully inspected hundreds of charts and thereby discovered the mirror-image problem with existing galaxy databases that is discussed in the Introduction. Many other members of the magazine's staff took time from their duties (and their weekends) to examine the charts from the perspective of observers: Edwin L. Aguirre, J. Kelly Beatty, Dennis di Cicco, Stuart J. Goldman, Timothy Lyster, Alan M. MacRobert, Carolyn C. Petersen, Joshua Roth, and Steven Simpson. Nina R. Barron proofread the front and back matter. Many a glitch was caught in time, thanks to their shrewdness and attention to detail.

Throughout, *Sky & Telescope* editor in chief Leif J. Robinson was the principal astronomical consultant, drawing on his familiarity with the sky as viewed by professionals and amateurs, other atlas projects, and printing technology. Janet A. Mattei (American Association of Variable Star Observers, Cambridge, Massachusetts) offered valuable suggestions on the coding and labeling of variables. Brian A. Skiff (Lowell Observatory, Flagstaff, Arizona) furnished his extensive personal lists of corrections to previously published data on globular clusters and planetary nebulae. Georges Paturel (Observatoire de Lyon, France) and Harold Corwin (California Institute of Technology, Pasadena, California) made helpful suggestions on galaxies and galaxy clusters.

Finally, Sky Publishing's Gregg Dinderman brought to bear his years of expertise as a technical illustrator, advising on aesthetic issues, preparing the chart keys, and placing outlines of nebulae with the dedicated help of Maureen A. Kehoe and Jim Zaccaria. Cartographer Martin von Wyss of Hybrid Designs, Cambridge, Massachusetts, put the finishing touches on many hundreds of charts. Their judgment is evident throughout the atlas, particularly in the more congested regions. Many other adjustments and file manipulations were contracted to Jeff Mead, Victor Curran, and the staff at Dartmouth Publishing, Inc., in Watertown, Massachusetts. The slipcase, binding design, and typography owe their elegance to the artistry of Christopher Kuntze.

THE HIPPARCOS MISSION: AN OVERVIEW

THE EUROPEAN SPACE AGENCY's Hipparcos satellite, launched by an Ariane rocket in August 1989 and operated until mid-1993, was the first spacecraft dedicated to the wholesale measurement of star positions, distances, and proper motions with extreme accuracy. The satellite's name pays tribute to the Greek astronomer Hipparchus, who in the 2nd century B.C. produced the first useful star catalogue and is widely acclaimed to be the founder of positional astronomy, or astrometry. Without continual improvements in the reference frame provided by such measurements, astronomers would learn very little about the motions of the planets, the sizes of stars, and the scale of the universe.

More than 200 scientists participated in the planning and development of the Hipparcos mission since its acceptance by ESA in 1980. Within hours of the launch, however, their hopes and those of astronomers around the world were nearly dashed by the failure of the satellite's apogee-boost motor. The mishap left the satellite in a highly elongated orbit instead of the planned geostationary one. Four times a day Hipparcos dipped in and out of the Van Allen radiation belts, which increased background noise in the detectors and threatened to harm the power-producing solar-cell panels. The mission's architects worked feverishly to adjust their observing strategy. They also enlisted the help of additional ground stations to receive the satellite's transmissions, which would soon stream data back to Earth at the rate of about 200 megabytes per day.

With the mission heroically saved from disaster, groups of the same scientists began a large-scale, coordinated analysis of the satellite data. In the end the results surpassed, in both quantity and quality, even the most optimistic expectations before launch. Two major new stellar databases emerged: Hipparcos, containing high-accuracy astrometric and photometric data for 118,218 stars; and Tycho, having somewhat lower accuracy but for 1,058,332 stars (including the majority of those in Hipparcos). The two were published as the *Hipparcos and Tycho Catalogues*, ESA SP-1200, in June 1997.

The *Millennium Star Atlas* uses, as its core star list, the entire contents of the Tycho database. The Tycho star positions are accurate to about 0.03 arcsecond,

and comparisons with earlier, ground-based catalogues confirm the overall reliability of the survey. In addition, the atlas incorporates the cream of the findings from the Hipparcos side of the mission in its star-distance labels, proper-motion arrows, double-star ticks, and variable-star codes. The Tycho Catalogue also contains lower-accuracy data on each star's proper motion, parallax, and photometric variability. Because they are less reliably determined, these "Tycho only" data have not been retained in the atlas. They hold great promise for astrophysical and statistical studies but would be of limited value to the amateur observer.

Spacecraft operation. Completing a single slow revolution once every two hours, the Hipparcos satellite scanned the sky in a complex series of precessing great circles. On board was a split mirror that simultaneously fed starlight from two fields of view, 58° apart on the sky, to a 12-inch (30-cm) Schmidt telescope. At this instrument's focal surface, stars from the two overlapping fields crossed a grating with 2,688 parallel slits, producing a continuous pattern of light fluctuations that served as grist for the huge computational mill that would follow. All the while the satellite's attitude had to be monitored continuously, the task of a separate star mapper. As a side benefit, the star mapper provided the independent data stream that became the basis of the million-star Tycho Catalogue.

The data analysis for the main Hipparcos mission involved sorting out, in a grand mathematical solution, which stars were crossing the two fields of view at specific times and what their positions and proper motions must be to account for the light fluctuations observed through the lifetime of the mission. An added complexity was the bending of starlight by the Sun's gravity predicted by Einstein's general theory of relativity. While a carefully designed ground-based telescope can detect such bending very near the Sun during a total solar eclipse, Hipparcos was sensitive enough to detect the effect on stars more than 90° away, over more than half the sky! In an interesting byproduct of the mission, Hipparcos confirmed to within one part in a thousand the amount of bending actually forecast by Einstein.

For the mission to work properly the list of Hipparcos stars had to be selected carefully and fixed in advance of the satellite launch. These targets formed the *Hipparcos Input Catalogue* (HIC). During the satellite's 3½-year period of operation, each entry was observed at some 100 to 150 distinct epochs (crossings of the telescope's fields of view), corresponding to some 25 to 60 distinct scanning configurations. For each star there were basically five unknowns: the right ascension and declination, the two proper-motion components, and the trigonometric parallax associated with the star's distance. And since there were more than 100,000 stars in the HIC, the reduction effort was tantamount to solving a vast array of mathematical equations that contained more than 500,000 unknowns.

Many HIC entries were known a priori to be, or subsequently found to be, double or multiple. The interplay of separation, multiplicity, component variability, and orbital motion sometimes made it difficult to interpret these observations uniquely, especially when there was a large magnitude difference between components. Handling such uncertainties was a major challenge in the four-year period between the end of the mission and the publication of the data.

Proceeding from nearly 1,000 gigabits of raw data, the global analysis of the satellite's observations was a lengthy and complex process. Two scientific teams, or consortia, developed software to analyze the Hipparcos data independently as a check on each other's work. A third consortium was responsible for the Tycho reductions, and a fourth for compiling the *Hipparcos Input Catalogue* before launch from the best available ground-based data. The publication of the catalogues in 1997 marked the formal end of ESA's involvement in the Hipparcos mission and brought supreme satisfaction to the hundreds of astronomers involved, many of whom had devoted two decades to the undertaking.

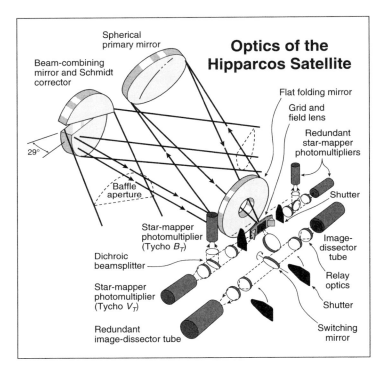

Inside the slowly turning Hipparcos satellite, a fixed composite mirror reflected two fields of view 58° apart into a common direction. A Schmidt telescope focused the overlapping fields onto a single grating that modulated the light as individual stars drifted by, allowing highly accurate comparisons of transit times. Processing the voluminous data required a very accurate knowledge of the satellite's orientation at all times. This orientation, along with data for the million-star Tycho Catalogue, was derived from separate detectors and a star-mapper grid on one side of the main grating.

HOW TO USE THIS ATLAS

THE *MILLENNIUM STAR ATLAS* contains about 1,058,000 stars, all those observed by the European Space Agency's Hipparcos spacecraft. More than 10,000 nonstellar objects have been included from other sources. The chart arrangement and scale have been chosen to make the atlas practical and efficient to use, considering the wealth of information it contains.

The atlas divides the celestial sphere into three lunes, or gores, each spanning a particular range of right ascension from pole to pole. Volume I covers from 0^h to 8^h, Volume II from 8^h to 16^h, and Volume III from 16^h to 24^h. Often just one of the three, encompassing the sky overhead and along the meridian from north to south, is all that will be needed for an observing session at the telescope. The following table tells which volume is most useful during specific seasons and observing times:

MONTH OF YEAR	TIME OF NIGHT				
	8 pm	*10 pm*	*Midnight*	*2 am*	*4 am*
January	I	I		II	II
February	I		II	II	II
March		II	II	II	
April	II	II	II		III
May	II	II		III	III
June	II		III	III	III
July		III	III	III	
August	III	III	III		I
September	III	III		I	I
October	III		I	I	I
November		I	I	I	
December	I	I	I		II

CHART SCALE AND GRID LINES

Each chart embraces a very small sky area, roughly that seen with a pair of 7 × 50 binoculars. North is up. Right ascensions are labeled along the top and bottom of each page, and declinations are printed at 1° intervals along the side of the chart. The grid lines, based on the International Celestial Reference System (ICRS), are consistent with coordinates measured from the 2000.0 equator and equinox.

The chart scale is 100 arcseconds per millimeter throughout. The 1° spacing of the declination grid lines may also be used to estimate angular separations on the sky.

Constellation boundaries are shown as gray lines. The ecliptic, the Sun's apparent path in the course of the year, is a dashed line marked at 1° intervals with ecliptic longitude. Another dashed line traces the galactic equator, the adopted plane of the Milky Way; it is labeled at 1° intervals with galactic longitude.

FINDING A CELESTIAL OBJECT

At the end of each volume, four chart keys show at a glance the region of sky covered. Chart numbers are the large numerals at the lower outside corner of each atlas page. Charts 1 through 516 are found in Volume I, 517 through 1032 in Volume II, and 1033 through 1548 in Volume III. An index lists the charts containing bright or unusual stars and deep-sky objects bearing popular names.

Within each volume, the charts start at the north celestial pole and work southward through consecutive declination bands in 6° steps. The central declination of the band is printed in large numerals at the upper outside corner of each chart.

If you know only the ICRS or 2000.0 coordinates of an object you are seeking, three steps will quickly locate the chart on which it lies: (1) Select the volume covering the general range of right ascension. (2) Flip through the pages to the desired declination band. (3) Turn consecutive pages left or right to locate the right ascension being sought.

Each pair of facing charts forms a continuous stretch of sky with a narrow overlap down the middle. Turning pages from front to back through the volume moves west, toward decreasing right ascension. Turning the pages from back to front moves east, toward increasing right ascension. (These rules apply until a volume boundary is reached at right ascension 0^h, 8^h, or 16^h. While the chart immediately west of chart 763 is 764 in Volume II, that to its east is 1302 in Volume III, as the chart keys in both volumes make clear.)

Centered near the top of each chart is a small up

arrow labeled with the chart number(s) immediately to the north. At the bottom of each chart, a down arrow identifies adjacent chart(s) to the south.

THE STARS

In the legend at the bottom of each left-hand page, a tapered scale of black disks shows the range of symbols used for individual stars. The smaller the disk the fainter the star, particular sizes being shown for visual (V) magnitude 2.0 (brightest), 3.0, 4.0, and so on up to 11.0 (faintest). The stars on the charts themselves can have these or any intermediate sizes, so that relative brightnesses are faithfully portrayed. An exception has been made for the four dozen brightest stars of all, listed in Table IV on page XI. To avoid excessively large disks, these well-known stars are plotted as if they, too, were of magnitude 2.0.

Only stars brighter than about magnitude 6 are visible to the naked eye. Some of these have popular names, such as Sirius or Polaris, while many more carry a Flamsteed number, a Bayer (Greek-letter) designation, or both.

Finally, every star that was found by Hipparcos to lie within 200 light-years of the Sun is labeled with its measured distance in light-years (ly). The light-year value, divided by 3.26, gives the distance in parsecs.

Variable stars. A black disk surrounded by some type of open circle identifies a variable star listed in the Hipparcos Catalogue. A variable is also identified by its standard designation, either an uppercase Roman letter from R to Z, a two-letter pair such as AX or CQ, or the letter V followed by 334 or a higher number. The constellation is omitted, even though it would always be included when mentioning the star in speech or writing, because a constellation label appears elsewhere on the same chart.

The size of a variable star's central disk corresponds to its median magnitude, as measured by Hipparcos, rather than to its maximum or minimum value. A surrounding dotted circle means that the amplitude of the light fluctuations is less than 0.1 magnitude. A dashed circle means the variation falls in the range of 0.1 to 1.0 magnitude. A solid circle implies the range is 1.0 or greater, and in this case the changes are obvious in a telescope even to the casual observer.

Next to the star or its designation, in parentheses, a lowercase italic letter identifies the broad class to which the variable belongs and a single digit its approximate period (expressed logarithmically), according to the following schemes:

VARIABILITY CLASS		PERIOD IN DAYS
(*e*) Eclipsing	(*s*) Semiregular	(*0*) Less than 1
(*c*) Cepheid	(*i*) Irregular	(*1*) 1 to 9
(*m*) Mira	(*f*) UV Ceti	(*2*) 10 to 99
(*d*) δ Scuti	(*x*) Novalike	(*3*) 100 to 999
(*r*) RR Lyrae	(*v*) Other	(*4*) 1,000 or more

Mnemonically, it may help to note that the period code equals the number of digits used to express the whole number of days in the period.

For example, a star marked "RV (*e1*)" appears on chart 1274 of a region in Ophiuchus. The label tells us the star is RV Ophiuchi, an eclipsing binary with a period between 1 and 9 days. For more about the plotting of variable stars, including the complete correspondence between these variability classes and the standard variable-star types, see page XII.

Some well-known variable stars were not observed by Hipparcos, generally because of their faint magnitude at the time of the mission, and they have been added from other sources. For example, locations of historical novae and supernovae are marked with a simple × and the letters N or SN followed by the year of appearance. Mira variables that spend much of the time near or fainter than the cutoff magnitude appear as small open circles. They can be distinguished from face-on galaxies by their designations.

Stars of high proper motion. All stars found in the Hipparcos Catalogue to have a proper motion greater than 0.2 arcsecond per year are plotted with an attached arrow showing the direction of this motion. The arrow's length represents the angular distance the star will move on the sky during one millennium. For example, at the chart scale of 100 arcseconds per millimeter, a 5-mm arrow means the star will move 500 arcseconds in 1,000 years. The length of an arrow should always be measured from just outside the rim of the star's disk (where the shaft begins) to the tip of the arrowhead.

Double and multiple stars. When the components of a double or multiple star are separated by more than 30 arcseconds, they are plotted individually with overlapping disks. But if the separation is less than 30 arcseconds, a single, enlarged disk representing the combined light is plotted at the brightest member's location with a protruding "tick" for each companion. The orientation and length of this tick, derived from Hipparcos measurements, show the state of the system at the catalogue epoch (1991.25). Most double and multiple stars with separations larger than a few tenths of an arcsecond retain nearly the same configuration for many decades.

To express angular separations meaningfully, the lengths of double-star ticks are greatly exaggerated. They are plotted on a logarithmic scale so that the closer, more interesting pairs are better distinguished. Three examples are shown in the legend, but ticks with lengths corresponding to any separation from 0.1 to 30 arcseconds are found throughout the atlas. Each tick begins just outside the rim of the primary star's enlarged disk and extends radially outward in the companion star's direction on the sky. When using the atlas at the telescope, it is important to remember that many optical systems present an inverted or mirror-reversed view.

NONSTELLAR OBJECTS

The legend on the right-hand chart pages explains the symbols used for nebulae, star clusters, galaxies, galaxy clusters, and quasars. Many of the brightest and most striking nonstellar objects are still best known from Charles Messier's observations with small comet-seeking telescopes in the late 18th century; they carry the letter M followed by a number from 1 to 110. Thousands of other objects were enumerated by J. L. E. Dreyer in his famous *New General Catalogue* (1888), or in its two supplements together known as the *Index Catalogue* (1895 and 1908). In this atlas NGC numbers (from 1 to 7840) are printed without any prefix; IC numbers (1 to 5386) are preceded by the letters IC.

Nebulae. Large, bright nebulae are plotted with a continuous and irregular outline that indicates their approximate extent on long-exposure photographs. Those measuring about 10 arcminutes across or smaller are marked with an open square. Similarly, dark nebulae are shown by a dashed outline when large, or by a small dashed square when they span 10 arcminutes or less. Planetary nebulae are usually too small to plot to scale; the symbols in the legend give an idea of their diameter, including any extremely faint outer halo that may be present. When not identified by an NGC or IC number, nebulae carry the designations assigned by the astronomers who discovered or studied them, as explained in the Introduction.

Open and globular star clusters. For many clusters the brighter stars are plotted individually. Open clusters are marked by a dashed open circle and globular clusters by a solid open circle and cross. The circle's diameter represents the approximate visual extent of the cluster. A minimal symbol, given in the legend, marks clusters smaller than 5 arcminutes across. When lacking an NGC or IC number, a cluster is designated by the name of an astronomer or observatory and a serial number.

Galaxies. The completeness limit for galaxies is a total visual magnitude brighter than about 13.5, though a number of fainter ones are included as well. All large galaxies are shown by an ellipse whose aspect ratio and orientation correspond to those on time-exposure photographs with large telescopes or CCD images. If a galaxy's major axis is smaller than 2 arcminutes it is plotted as 2 arcminutes, and if the minor axis is smaller than 1 arcminute it is plotted as 1 arcminute. This procedure preserves some idea of the orientation, even for very tiny objects.

Quasars. An open-centered cross is used for objects that are nearly stellar in appearance but well below the atlas's magnitude cutoff for stars. They are included for their astrophysical aura. Extragalactic quasars and their cousins, the BL Lacertae objects, make up the great majority of these, selected to be 16th magnitude or brighter visually. They are identified by such prefixes as PKS for a number in the Parkes radio survey and 3C for a number in the revised third Cambridge radio survey. The same open-cross symbol has been used for a handful of high-energy sources within our own galaxy, even though they are not quasars. These include several pulsars, the Geminga gamma-ray source, and the galactic center itself.

Galaxy clusters. A pentagon symbol marks a rich cluster of galaxies that has at least 10 members of 16th magnitude or brighter. In many cases, along with the pentagon, several of the brightest member galaxies are plotted individually. The prefix A refers to a number from the original northern and southern Abell catalogues; AS denotes a cluster in the southern supplement. The pentagon simply marks the cluster's location without indicating its angular extent. Most galaxy clusters in the atlas are smaller than $\frac{1}{4}°$ across.

CHARTS 1–516

Right Ascension 0 to 8 Hours

+90°

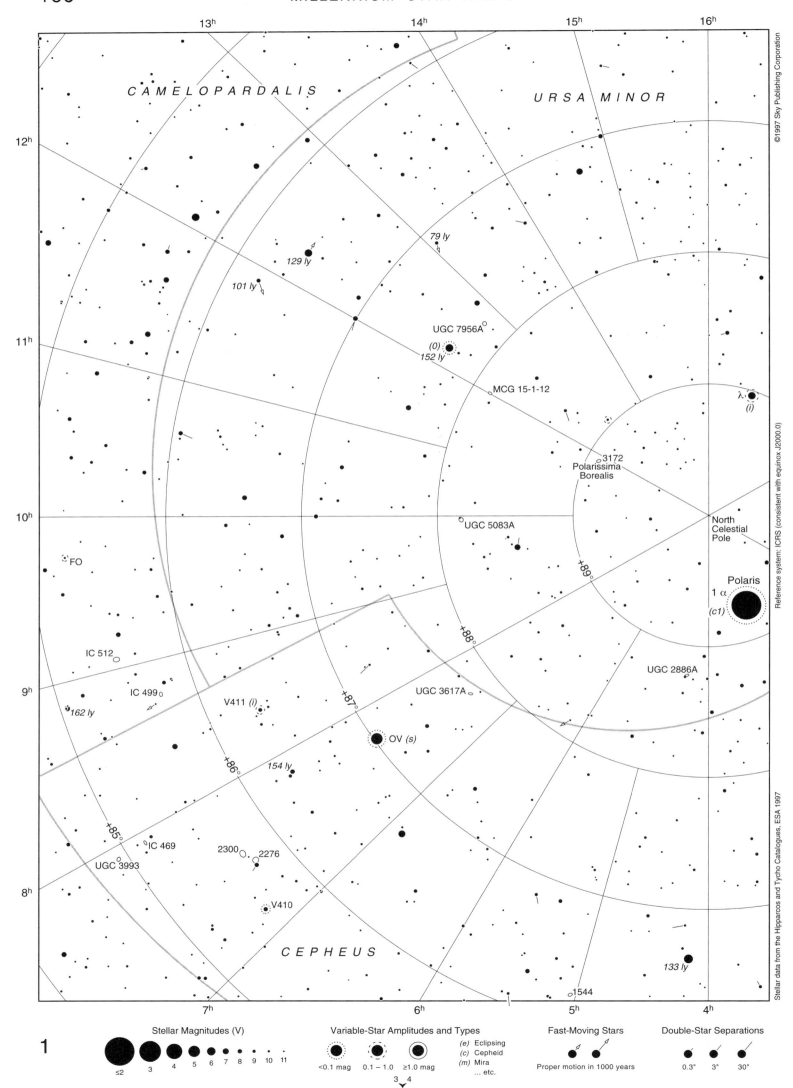

CAMELOPARDALIS

URSA MINOR

13ʰ   14ʰ   15ʰ   16ʰ

12ʰ

129 ly

79 ly

101 ly

11ʰ

UGC 7956A

(0)
152 ly

MCG 15-1-12

λ
(i)

3172
Polarissima
Borealis

10ʰ

UGC 5083A

North
Celestial
Pole

+89°

FO

Polaris

1 α

(c1)

IC 512

UGC 2886A

IC 499

9ʰ

UGC 3617A

162 ly

V411 (i)

+87°

+88°

OV (s)

+86°

154 ly

+85°

IC 469

UGC 3993

2300   2276

8ʰ

V410

CEPHEUS

133 ly

1544

7ʰ   6ʰ   5ʰ   4ʰ

©1997 Sky Publishing Corporation

Reference system: ICRS (consistent with equinox J2000.0)

Stellar data from the Hipparcos and Tycho Catalogues, ESA 1997

1

Stellar Magnitudes (V)

≤2   3   4   5   6   7   8   9   10   11

Variable-Star Amplitudes and Types

<0.1 mag   0.1 – 1.0   ≥1.0 mag

(e) Eclipsing
(c) Cepheid
(m) Mira
... etc.

Fast-Moving Stars

Proper motion in 1000 years

Double-Star Separations

0.3"   3"   30"

3   4

MILLENNIUM STAR ATLAS

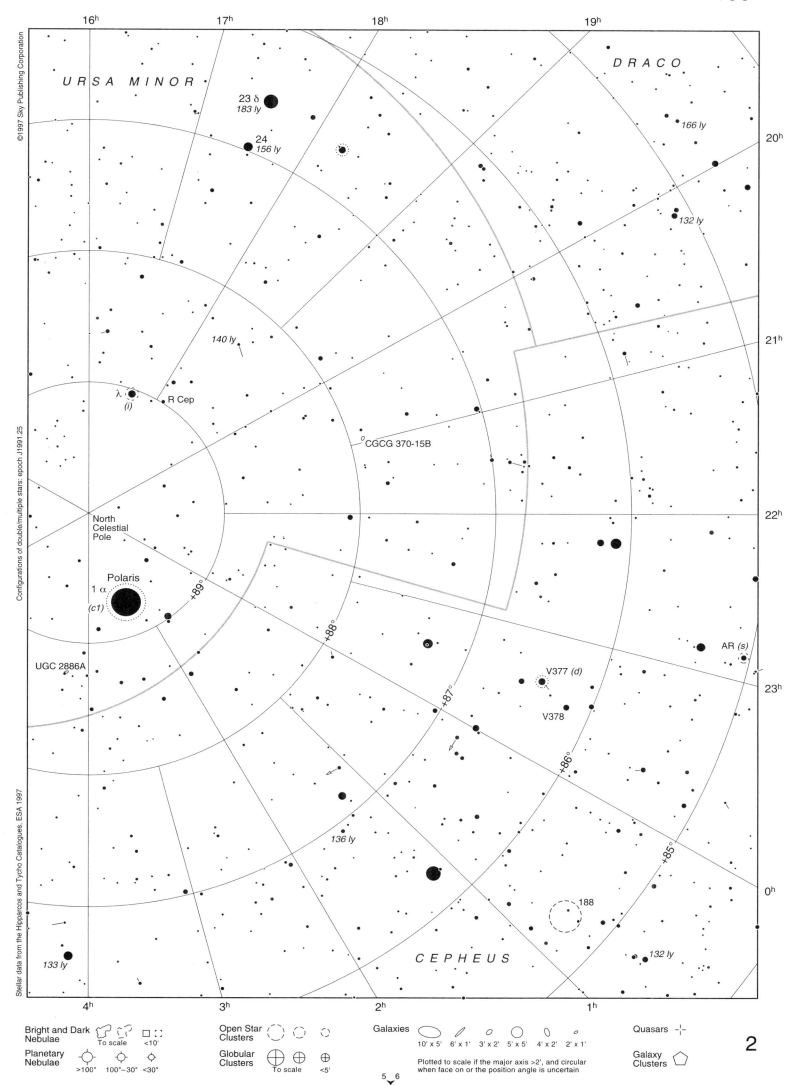

Configurations of double/multiple stars: epoch J1991.25

Stellar data from the Hipparcos and Tycho Catalogues, ESA 1997

URSA MINOR

DRACO

23 δ
183 ly

24
156 ly

166 ly

132 ly

140 ly

λ
(i)   R Cep

ᵒ CGCG 370-15B

North
Celestial
Pole

+89°

+88°

+87°

+86°

+85°

Polaris
1 α
(c1)

AR *(s)*

V377 *(d)*

V378

UGC 2886A

136 ly

188

CEPHEUS

133 ly

132 ly

Bright and Dark Nebulae	Open Star Clusters	Galaxies	Quasars

To scale   <10'

Planetary
Nebulae
>100"   100"–30"   <30"

Globular
Clusters
To scale   <5'

Galaxies
10' x 5'   6' x 1'   3' x 2'   5' x 5'   4' x 2'   2' x 1'

Plotted to scale if the major axis >2', and circular
when face on or the position angle is uncertain

Galaxy
Clusters

2

5 6

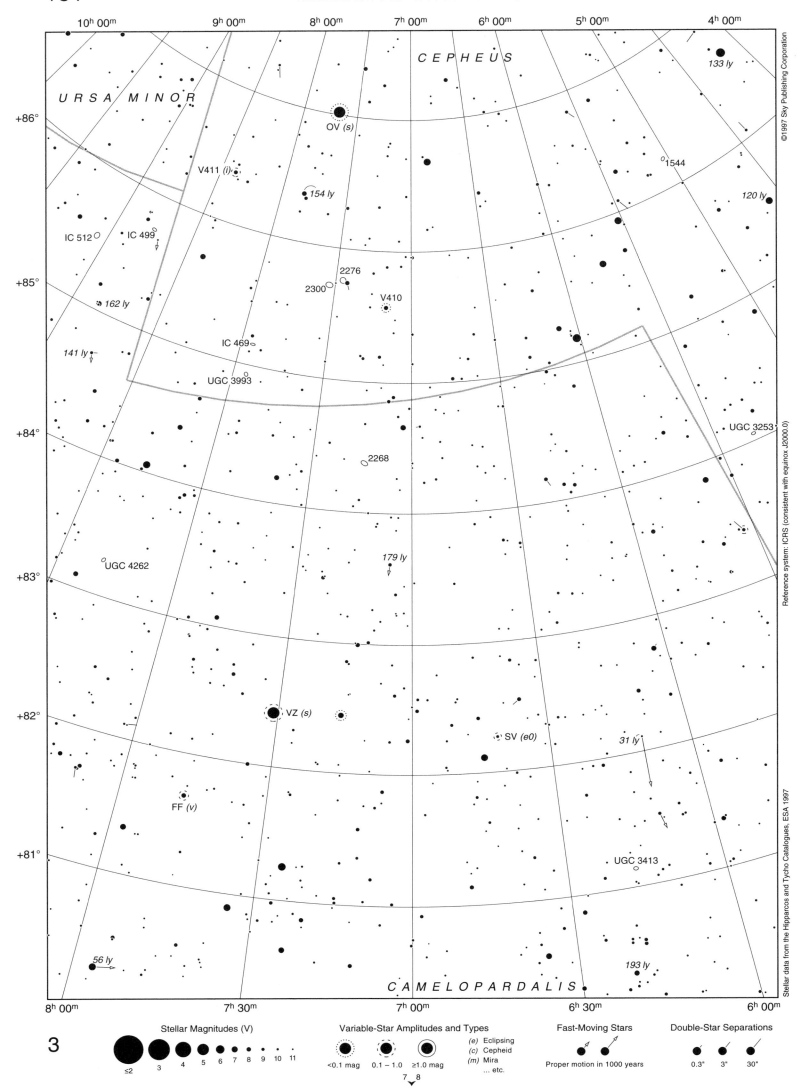

©1997 Sky Publishing Corporation

Reference system: ICRS (consistent with equinox J2000.0)

Stellar data from the Hipparcos and Tycho Catalogues, ESA 1997

CEPHEUS

URSA MINOR

133 ly

OV (s)

V411 (i)

154 ly

1544

120 ly

IC 512 ○   IC 499

2276
2300
V410

162 ly

IC 469

141 ly

UGC 3993

UGC 3253

2268

179 ly

UGC 4262

VZ (s)

SV (e0)

31 ly

FF (v)

UGC 3413

56 ly

193 ly

CAMELOPARDALIS

Stellar Magnitudes (V)

≤2　3　4　5　6　7　8　9　10　11

Variable-Star Amplitudes and Types

<0.1 mag　0.1 – 1.0　≥1.0 mag

(e) Eclipsing
(c) Cepheid
(m) Mira
... etc.

Fast-Moving Stars

Proper motion in 1000 years

Double-Star Separations

0.3"　3"　30"

3

7　8

©1997 Sky Publishing Corporation

Configurations of double/multiple stars: epoch J1991.25

Stellar data from the Hipparcos and Tycho Catalogues, ESA 1997

8ʰ 00ᵐ   7ʰ 00ᵐ   6ʰ 00ᵐ   5ʰ 00ᵐ   4ʰ 00ᵐ   3ʰ 00ᵐ   2ʰ 00ᵐ

154 ly

C E P H E U S

+86°

2300
2276

V410

133 ly

1544

+85°

120 ly

C A M E L O P A R D A L I S

V406

+84°

UGC 3253

V408 *(i)*

+83°

113 ly

V409

(e)

31 ly

+82°

164 ly

V407 *(d0)*

⊙ EZ *(r0)*

+81°

C E P H E U S

C A M

6ʰ 00ᵐ   5ʰ 30ᵐ   5ʰ 00ᵐ   4ʰ 30ᵐ   4ʰ 00ᵐ

Bright and Dark Nebulae	Open Star Clusters	Galaxies	Quasars

To scale   <10'

Planetary Nebulae
>100" 100"–30" <30"

Globular Clusters
To scale   <5'

Galaxies
10' x 5'   6' x 1'   3' x 2'   5' x 5'   4' x 2'   2' x 1'

Plotted to scale if the major axis >2', and circular
when face on or the position angle is uncertain

Galaxy Clusters

4

9 10

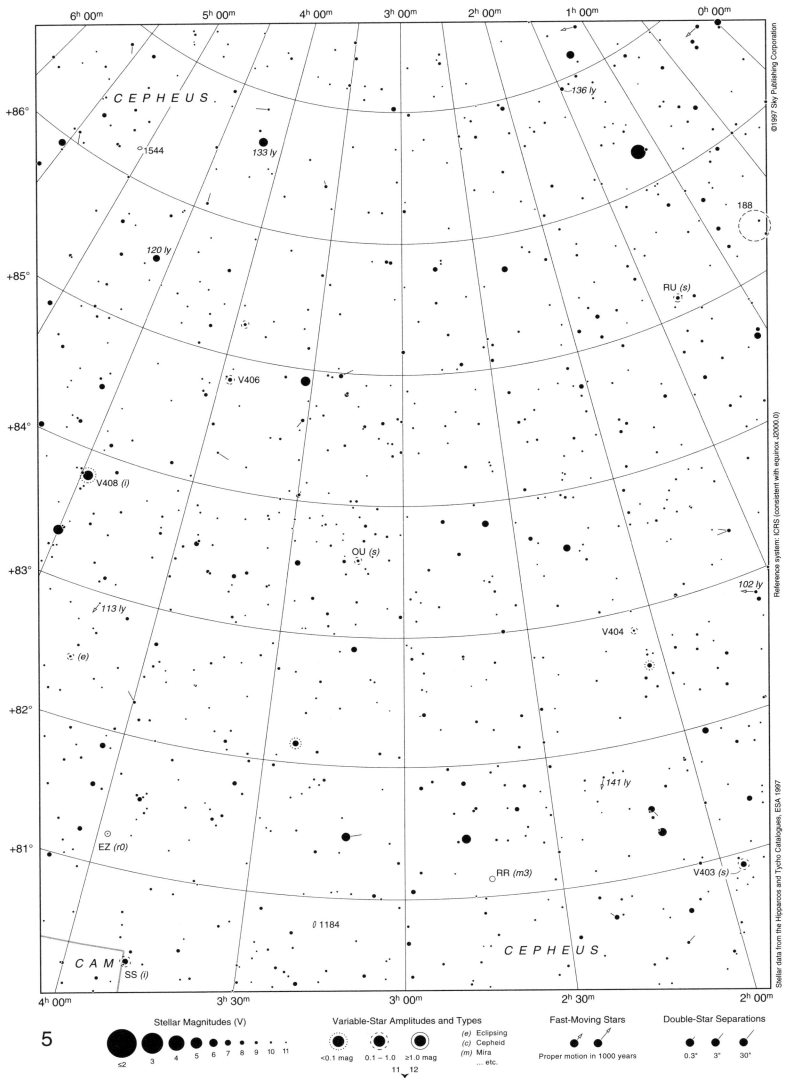

CEPHEUS

○ 1544

133 ly

120 ly

V406

V408 (i)

113 ly

◌ (e)

OU (s)

EZ (r0)

RR (m3)

θ 1184

CAM

SS (i)

CEPHEUS

136 ly

188

RU (s)

102 ly

V404

141 ly

V403 (s)

6h 00m   5h 00m   4h 00m   3h 00m   2h 00m   1h 00m   0h 00m

+86°

+85°

+84°

+83°

+82°

+81°

4h 00m   3h 30m   3h 00m   2h 30m   2h 00m

© 1997 Sky Publishing Corporation

Reference system: ICRS (consistent with equinox J2000.0)

Stellar data from the Hipparcos and Tycho Catalogues, ESA 1997

5

Stellar Magnitudes (V)

≤2   3   4   5   6   7   8   9   10   11

Variable-Star Amplitudes and Types

<0.1 mag   0.1 – 1.0   ≥1.0 mag

(e) Eclipsing
(c) Cepheid
(m) Mira
... etc.

11   12

Fast-Moving Stars

Proper motion in 1000 years

Double-Star Separations

0.3"   3"   30"

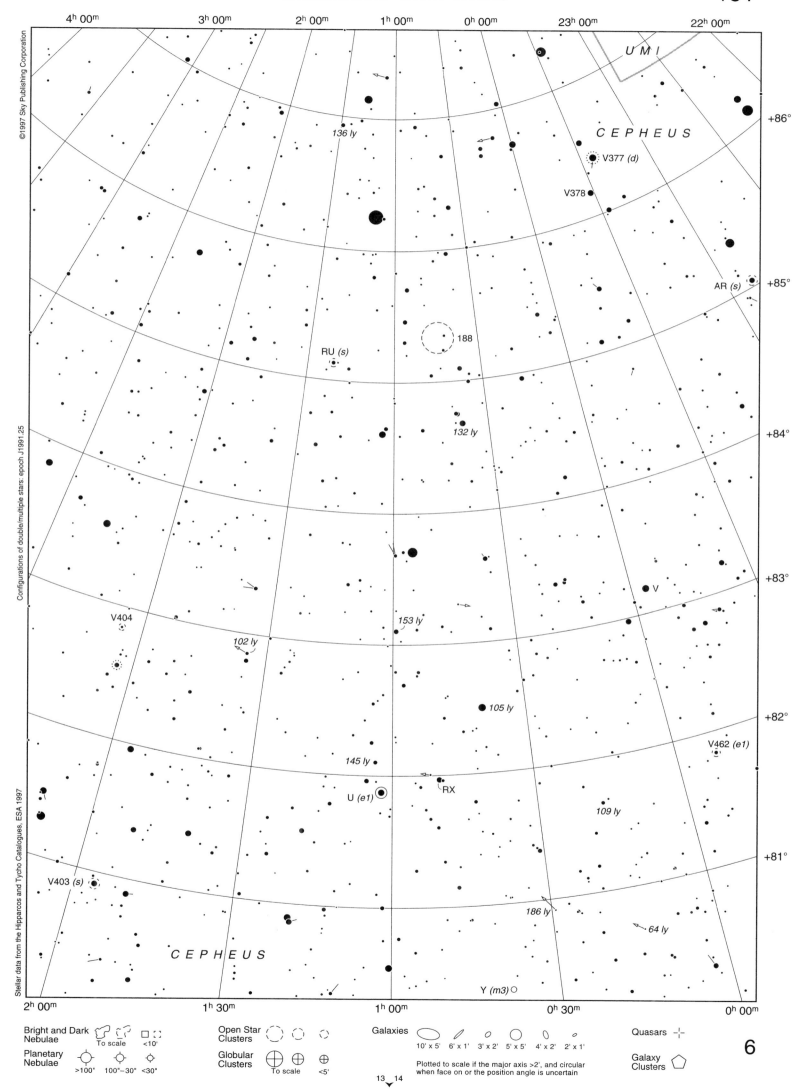

U M I

C E P H E U S

136 ly

V377 (d)

V378

AR (s)

+86°

+85°

188

RU (s)

132 ly

+84°

V

+83°

V404

153 ly

102 ly

105 ly

+82°

V462 (e1)

145 ly

U (e1)

RX

109 ly

+81°

V403 (s)

186 ly

64 ly

C E P H E U S

Y (m3)

Bright and Dark
Nebulae
To scale   <10'

Open Star
Clusters

Galaxies

10' x 5' 6' x 1' 3' x 2' 5' x 5' 4' x 2' 2' x 1'

Quasars

Planetary
Nebulae
>100" 100"-30" <30"

Globular
Clusters
To scale   <5'

Plotted to scale if the major axis >2', and circular
when face on or the position angle is uncertain

Galaxy
Clusters

6

13   14

4h 00m   3h 00m   2h 00m   1h 00m   0h 00m   23h 00m   22h 00m

2h 00m   1h 30m   1h 00m   0h 30m   0h 00m

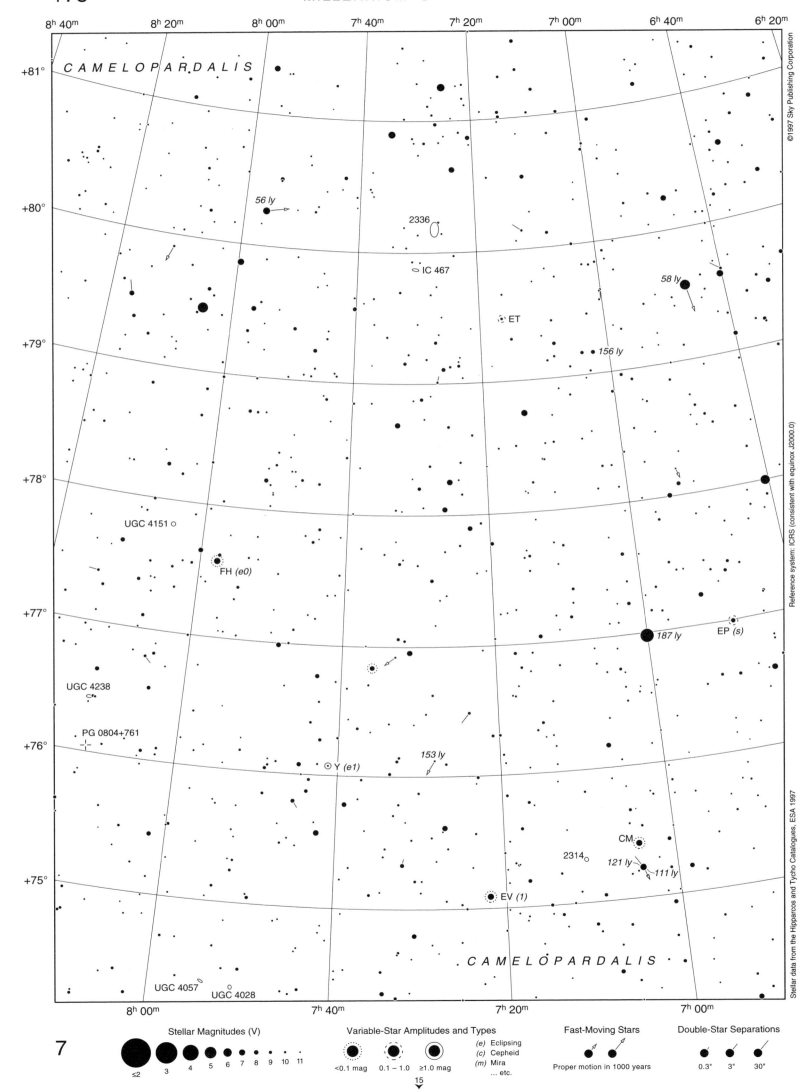

©1997 Sky Publishing Corporation

Reference system: ICRS (consistent with equinox J2000.0)

Stellar data from the Hipparcos and Tycho Catalogues, ESA 1997

CAMELOPARDALIS

56 ly

2336

IC 467

58 ly

ET

156 ly

UGC 4151

FH (e0)

UGC 4238

PG 0804+761

Y (e1)

153 ly

187 ly

EP (s)

CM

2314

121 ly

111 ly

EV (1)

CAMELOPARDALIS

UGC 4057

UGC 4028

7

Stellar Magnitudes (V)

≤2   3   4   5   6   7   8   9   10   11

Variable-Star Amplitudes and Types

<0.1 mag   0.1 – 1.0   ≥1.0 mag

(e) Eclipsing
(c) Cepheid
(m) Mira
... etc.

Fast-Moving Stars

Proper motion in 1000 years

Double-Star Separations

0.3"   3"   30"

15

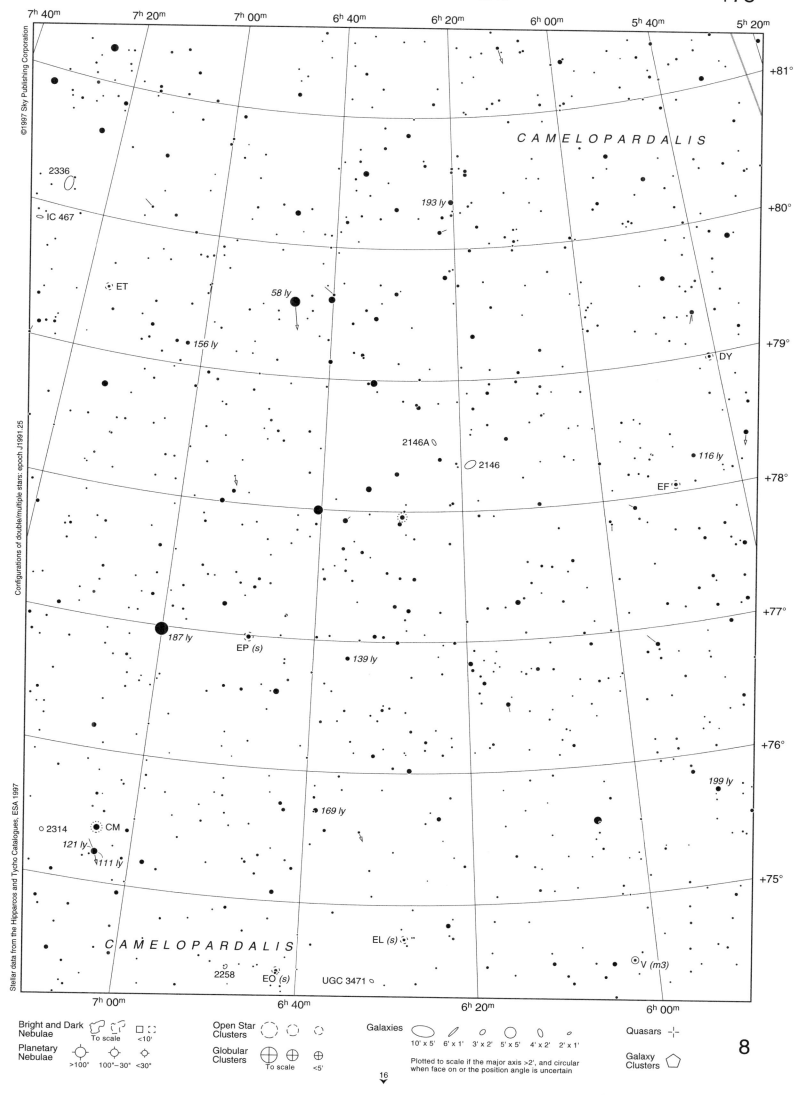

CAMELOPARDALIS

2336

IC 467

ET

193 ly

58 ly

156 ly

DY

2146A

2146

116 ly

EF

187 ly

EP (s)

139 ly

199 ly

169 ly

CM

2314

121 ly

111 ly

CAMELOPARDALIS

EL (s)

V (m3)

2258

EO (s)

UGC 3471

Bright and Dark Nebulae	Open Star Clusters	Galaxies	Quasars
To scale <10'	To scale	10' x 5' 6' x 1' 3' x 2' 5' x 5' 4' x 2' 2' x 1'	
Planetary Nebulae	Globular Clusters		Galaxy Clusters
>100" 100"–30" <30"	To scale <5'	Plotted to scale if the major axis >2', and circular when face on or the position angle is uncertain	

8

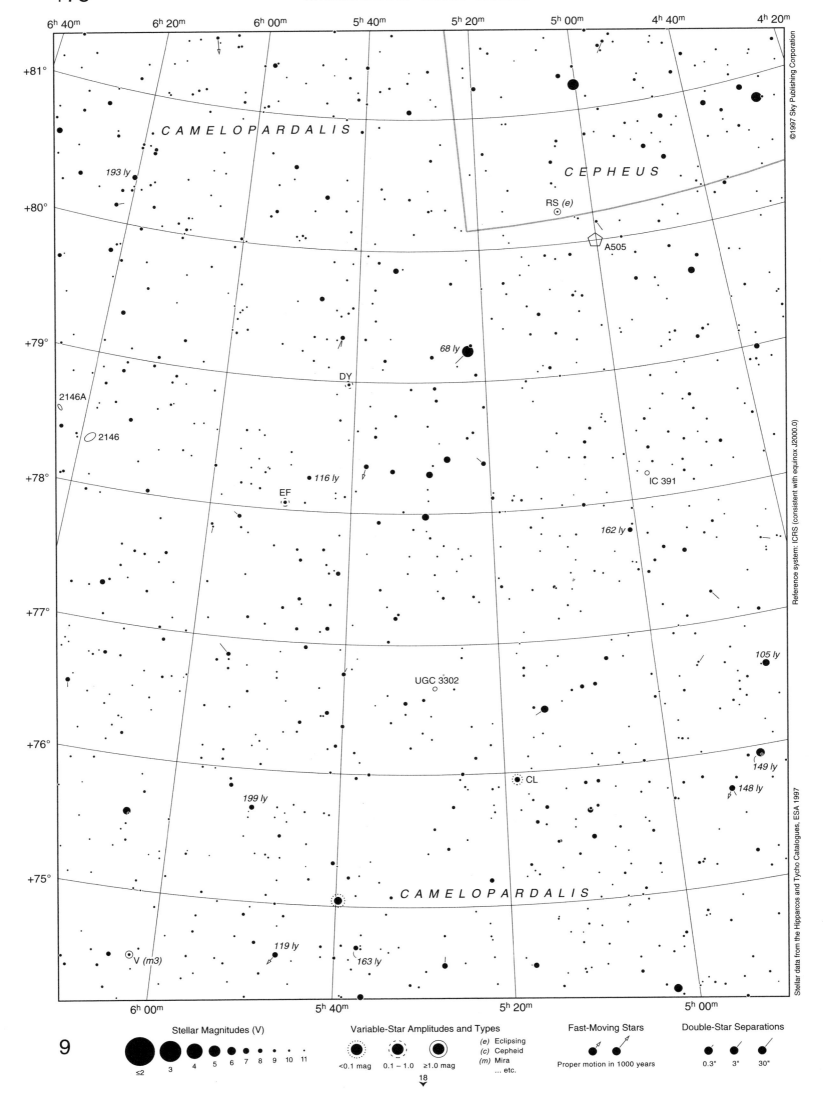

©1997 Sky Publishing Corporation

Reference system: ICRS (consistent with equinox J2000.0)

Stellar data from the Hipparcos and Tycho Catalogues, ESA 1997

Stellar Magnitudes (V)

≤2　3　4　5　6　7　8　9　10　11

Variable-Star Amplitudes and Types

<0.1 mag　　0.1 – 1.0　　≥1.0 mag

(e) Eclipsing
(c) Cepheid
(m) Mira
... etc.

Fast-Moving Stars

Proper motion in 1000 years

Double-Star Separations

0.3"　3"　30"

9

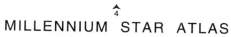

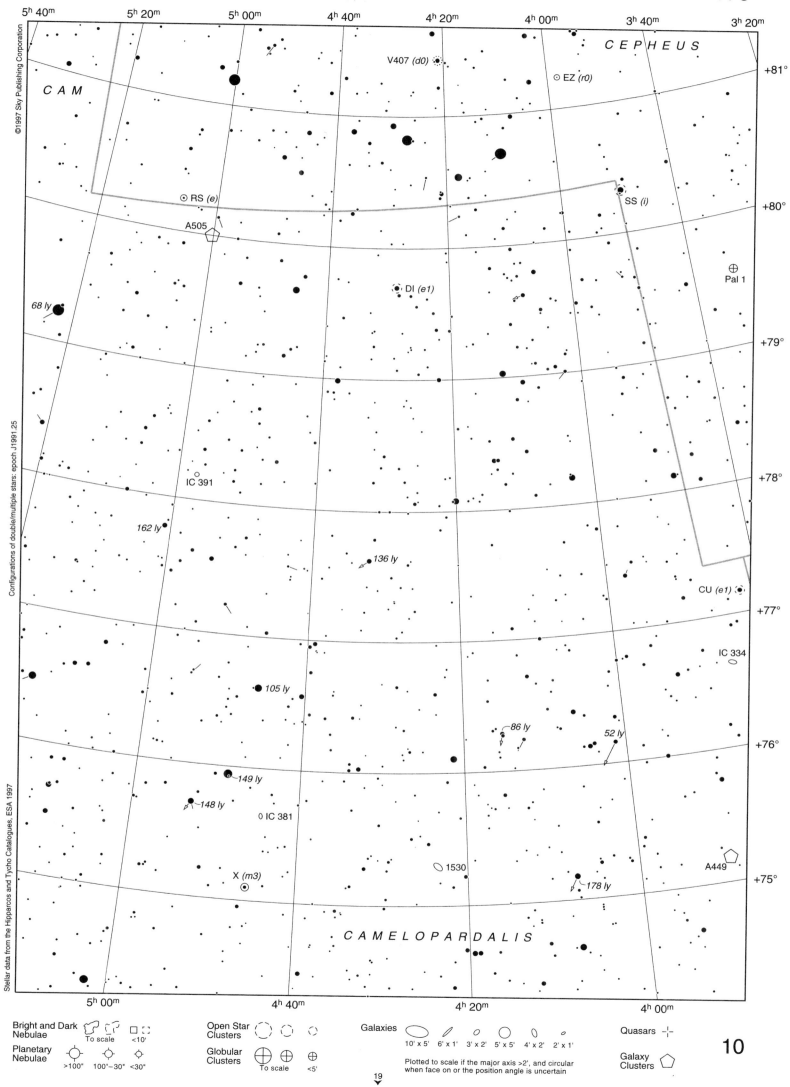

©1997 Sky Publishing Corporation

C E P H E U S

C A M

V407 (d0)

EZ (r0)

RS (e)

SS (i)

A505

Pal 1

DI (e1)

68 ly

IC 391

CU (e1)

162 ly

136 ly

IC 334

105 ly

86 ly

52 ly

149 ly

148 ly

0 IC 381

1530

A449

X (m3)

178 ly

C A M E L O P A R D A L I S

Configurations of double/multiple stars: epoch J1991.25

Stellar data from the Hipparcos and Tycho Catalogues, ESA 1997

Bright and Dark Nebulae

To scale   <10'

Planetary Nebulae

>100"   100"–30"   <30"

Open Star Clusters

Globular Clusters

To scale   <5'

Galaxies

10' x 5'   6' x 1'   3' x 2'   5' x 5'   4' x 2'   2' x 1'

Plotted to scale if the major axis >2', and circular when face on or the position angle is uncertain

Quasars

Galaxy Clusters

10

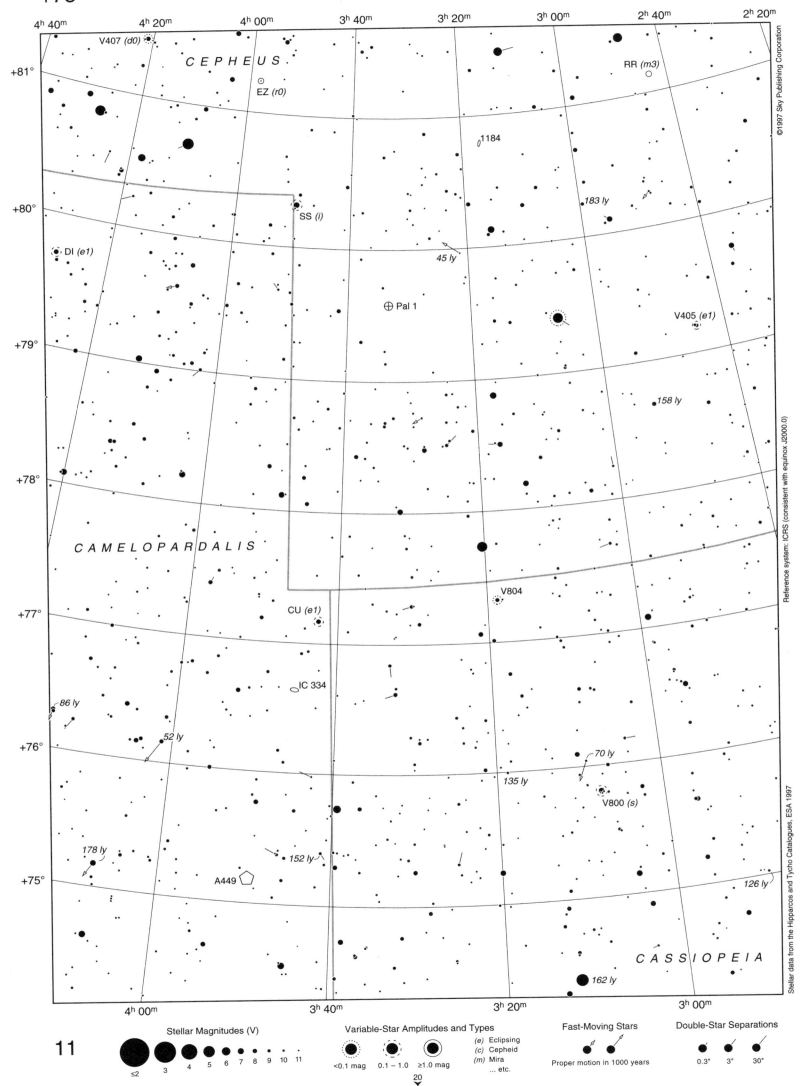

CEPHEUS

CAMELOPARDALIS

CASSIOPEIA

V407 (d0)
EZ (r0)
RR (m3)
1184
183 ly
SS (i)
45 ly
DI (e1)
Pal 1
V405 (e1)
158 ly
V804
CU (e1)
IC 334
86 ly
52 ly
70 ly
135 ly
V800 (s)
178 ly
152 ly
A449
126 ly
162 ly

Stellar Magnitudes (V)

≤2 3 4 5 6 7 8 9 10 11

Variable-Star Amplitudes and Types

<0.1 mag   0.1 – 1.0   ≥1.0 mag

(e) Eclipsing
(c) Cepheid
(m) Mira
... etc.

Fast-Moving Stars

Proper motion in 1000 years

Double-Star Separations

0.3" 3" 30"

11

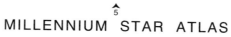

+78°

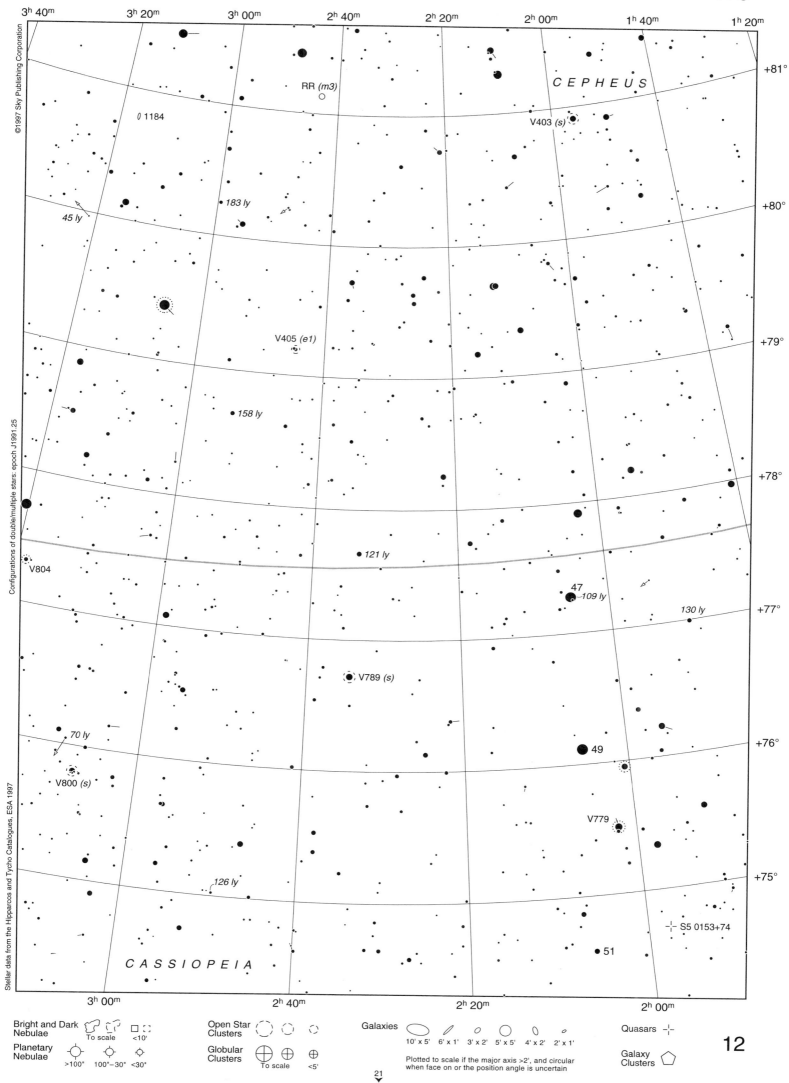

Configurations of double/multiple stars: epoch J1991.25

Stellar data from the Hipparcos and Tycho Catalogues, ESA 1997

CEPHEUS

RR (m3)

θ 1184

V403 (s)

45 ly

183 ly

V405 (e1)

158 ly

121 ly

V804

47
—109 ly

130 ly

V789 (s)

70 ly

49

V800 (s)

V779

126 ly

S5 0153+74

51

CASSIOPEIA

+81°
+80°
+79°
+78°
+77°
+76°
+75°

3ʰ 40ᵐ   3ʰ 20ᵐ   3ʰ 00ᵐ   2ʰ 40ᵐ   2ʰ 20ᵐ   2ʰ 00ᵐ   1ʰ 40ᵐ   1ʰ 20ᵐ

3ʰ 00ᵐ   2ʰ 40ᵐ   2ʰ 20ᵐ   2ʰ 00ᵐ

Bright and Dark Nebulae			
To scale	<10'		

Planetary Nebulae
>100" 100"–30" <30"

Open Star Clusters

Globular Clusters
To scale <5'

Galaxies
10' x 5'   6' x 1'   3' x 2'   5' x 5'   4' x 2'   2' x 1'

Plotted to scale if the major axis >2', and circular when face on or the position angle is uncertain

Quasars

Galaxy Clusters

12

21

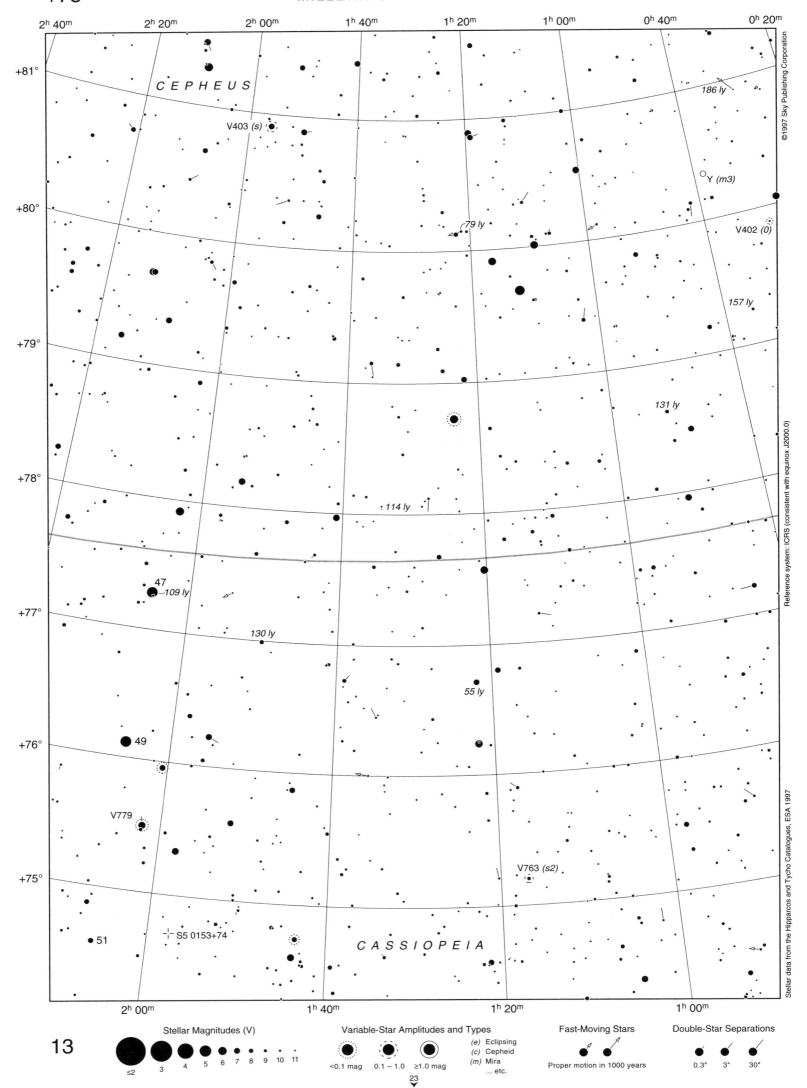

CEPHEUS

V403 (s)

Y (m3)

186 ly

V402 (0)

79 ly

157 ly

131 ly

47
109 ly

114 ly

130 ly

55 ly

49

V779

V763 (s2)

51

S5 0153+74

CASSIOPEIA

13

Stellar Magnitudes (V)

≤2   3   4   5   6   7   8   9   10   11

Variable-Star Amplitudes and Types

<0.1 mag   0.1 – 1.0   ≥1.0 mag

(e) Eclipsing
(c) Cepheid
(m) Mira
... etc.

Fast-Moving Stars

Proper motion in 1000 years

Double-Star Separations

0.3"   3"   30"

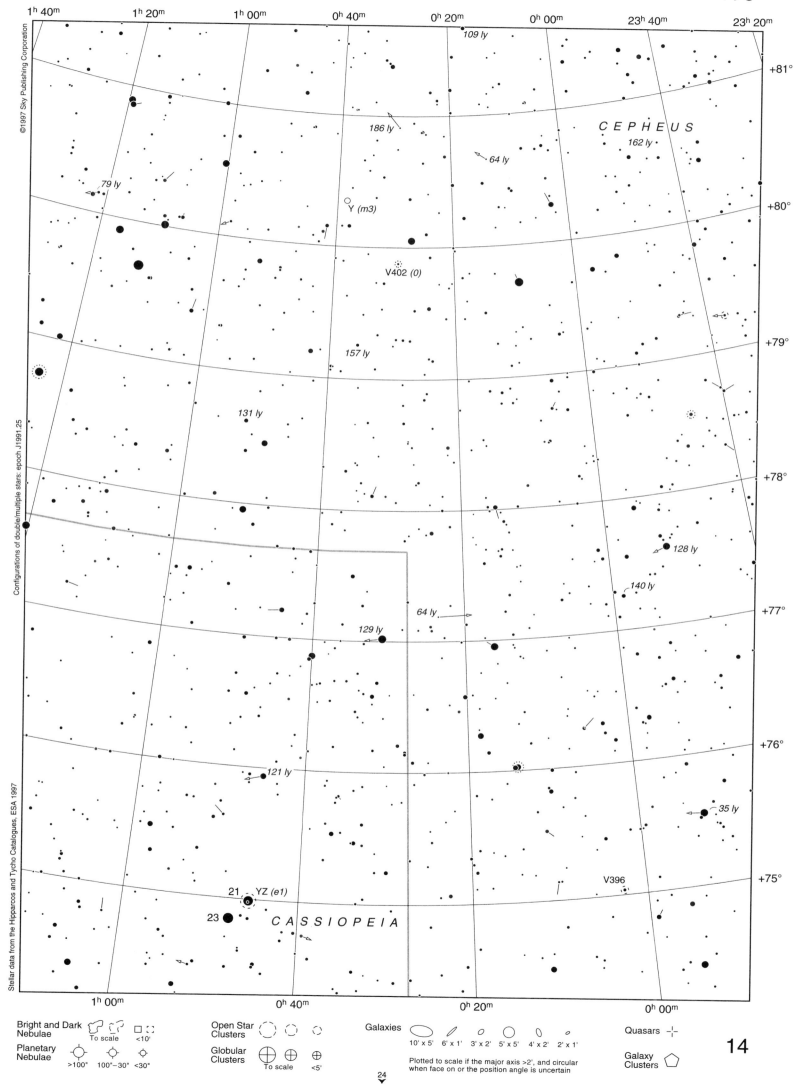

Configurations of double/multiple stars: epoch J1991.25

Stellar data from the Hipparcos and Tycho Catalogues, ESA 1997

C E P H E U S

C A S S I O P E I A

| Bright and Dark Nebulae | Open Star Clusters | Galaxies | Quasars |

Bright and Dark Nebulae — To scale — <10'

Planetary Nebulae — >100" — 100"–30" — <30"

Open Star Clusters

Globular Clusters — To scale — <5'

Galaxies — 10' x 5' — 6' x 1' — 3' x 2' — 5' x 5' — 4' x 2' — 2' x 1'

Plotted to scale if the major axis >2', and circular when face on or the position angle is uncertain

Quasars

Galaxy Clusters

14

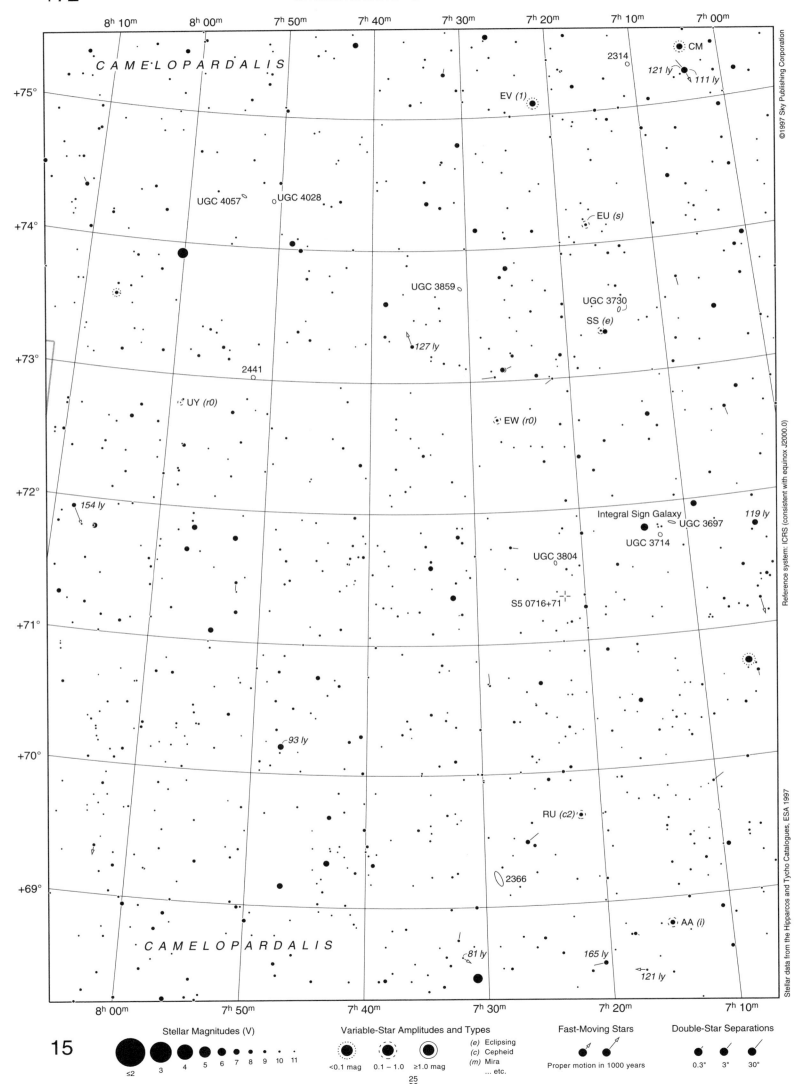

15

Stellar Magnitudes (V)

≤2 3 4 5 6 7 8 9 10 11

Variable-Star Amplitudes and Types

<0.1 mag   0.1 – 1.0   ≥1.0 mag

(e) Eclipsing
(c) Cepheid
(m) Mira
... etc.

Fast-Moving Stars

Proper motion in 1000 years

Double-Star Separations

0.3" 3" 30"

25

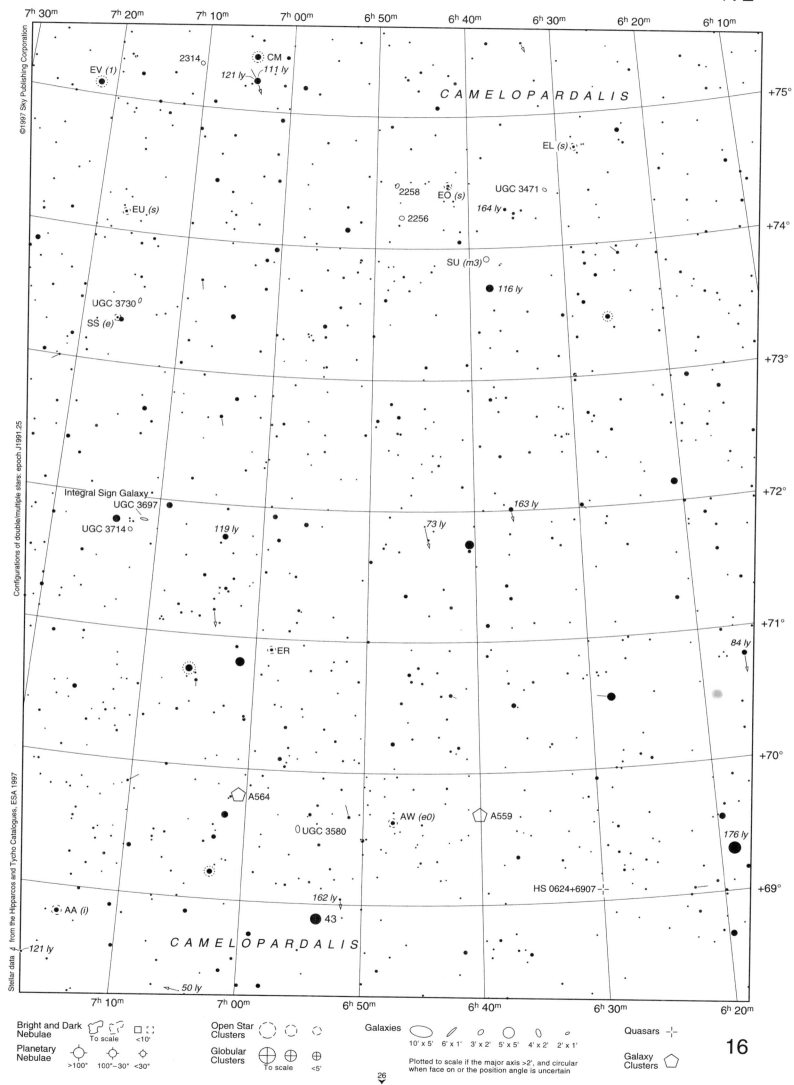
7ʰ 30ᵐ 7ʰ 20ᵐ 7ʰ 10ᵐ 7ʰ 00ᵐ 6ʰ 50ᵐ 6ʰ 40ᵐ 6ʰ 30ᵐ 6ʰ 20ᵐ 6ʰ 10ᵐ

©1997 Sky Publishing Corporation

Configurations of double/multiple stars: epoch J1991.25

Stellar data from the Hipparcos and Tycho Catalogues, ESA 1997

EV *(1)*

2314

CM

121 ly 111 ly

C A M E L O P A R D A L I S

EL *(s)*

2258 EO *(s)* UGC 3471

2256 164 ly

EU *(s)*

SU *(m3)*

116 ly

UGC 3730

SS *(e)*

+75°

+74°

+73°

+72°

+71°

+70°

+69°

Integral Sign Galaxy
UGC 3697

UGC 3714

119 ly

163 ly

73 ly

ER

84 ly

A564

AW *(e0)* A559

UGC 3580

176 ly

HS 0624+6907

162 ly

AA *(i)*

43

121 ly

C A M E L O P A R D A L I S

50 ly

7ʰ 10ᵐ 7ʰ 00ᵐ 6ʰ 50ᵐ 6ʰ 40ᵐ 6ʰ 30ᵐ 6ʰ 20ᵐ

Bright and Dark Nebulae
To scale   <10'

Planetary Nebulae
>100"   100"–30"   <30"

Open Star Clusters

Globular Clusters
To scale   <5'

Galaxies
10' x 5'   6' x 1'   3' x 2'   5' x 5'   4' x 2'   2' x 1'

Plotted to scale if the major axis >2', and circular
when face on or the position angle is uncertain

Quasars

Galaxy Clusters

16

26

+72°

MILLENNIUM STAR ATLAS

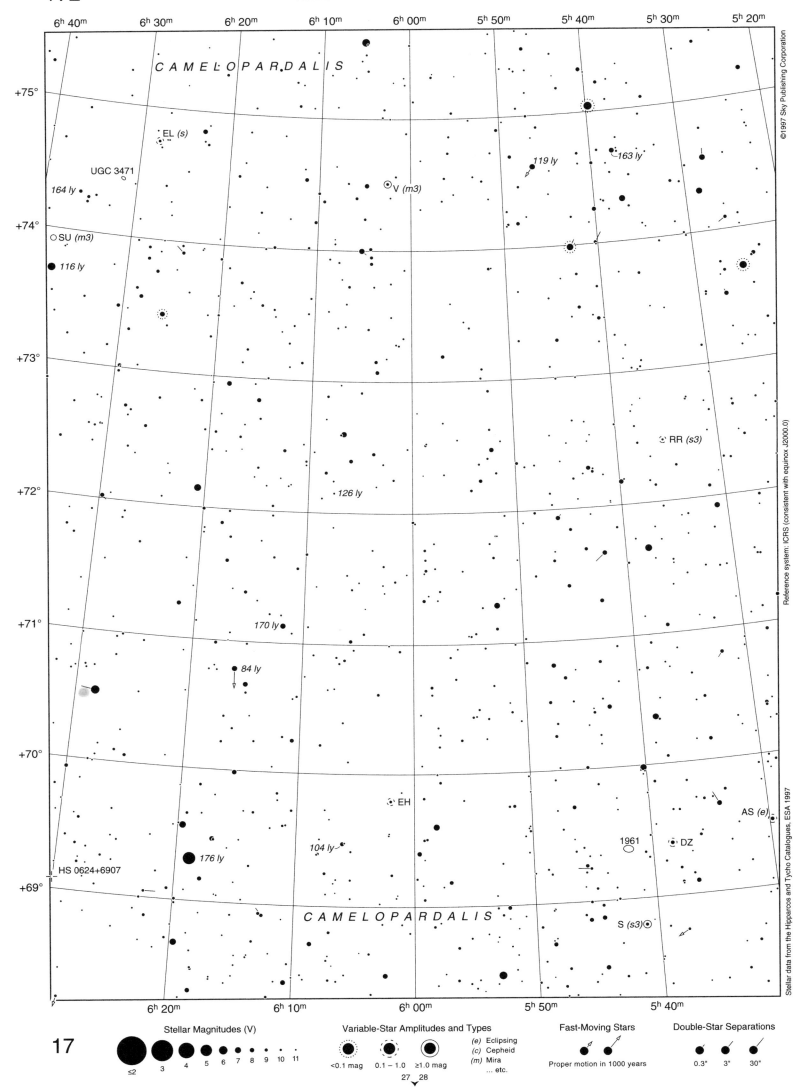

CAMELOPARDALIS

EL (s)

UGC 3471

164 ly

SU (m3)

116 ly

119 ly

163 ly

V (m3)

RR (s3)

126 ly

170 ly

84 ly

EH

104 ly

176 ly

HS 0624+6907

1961

DZ

AS (e)

S (s3)

CAMELOPARDALIS

©1997 Sky Publishing Corporation

Reference system: ICRS (consistent with equinox J2000.0)

Stellar data from the Hipparcos and Tycho Catalogues, ESA 1997

17

Stellar Magnitudes (V)

≤2   3   4   5   6   7   8   9   10   11

Variable-Star Amplitudes and Types

<0.1 mag   0.1 – 1.0   ≥1.0 mag

(e) Eclipsing
(c) Cepheid
(m) Mira
... etc.

Fast-Moving Stars

Proper motion in 1000 years

Double-Star Separations

0.3"   3"   30"

©1997 Sky Publishing Corporation

Configurations of double/multiple stars: epoch J1991.25

Stellar data from the Hipparcos and Tycho Catalogues, ESA 1997

5ʰ 50ᵐ 5ʰ 40ᵐ 5ʰ 30ᵐ 5ʰ 20ᵐ 5ʰ 10ᵐ 5ʰ 00ᵐ 4ʰ 50ᵐ 4ʰ 40ᵐ 4ʰ 30ᵐ

CAMELOPARDALIS

X (m3)

+75°

119 ly

163 ly

158 ly

+74°

BN (v1)

A527

130 ly

+73°

1573

DN (e0)

RR (s3)

+72°

+71°

+70°

1961

DZ

AS (e)

BS

139 ly

CAMELOPARDALIS

+69°

S (s3)

DW   105 ly

UX (i)

IC 396

5ʰ 40ᵐ 5ʰ 30ᵐ 5ʰ 20ᵐ 5ʰ 10ᵐ 5ʰ 00ᵐ 4ʰ 50ᵐ

Bright and Dark Nebulae	Open Star Clusters	Galaxies	Quasars

Bright and Dark Nebulae To scale <10'

Planetary Nebulae >100" 100"–30" <30"

Open Star Clusters

Globular Clusters To scale <5'

Galaxies 10' x 5' 6' x 1' 3' x 2' 5' x 5' 4' x 2' 2' x 1'

Plotted to scale if the major axis >2', and circular when face on or the position angle is uncertain

Quasars

Galaxy Clusters

18

29

MILLENNIUM STAR ATLAS

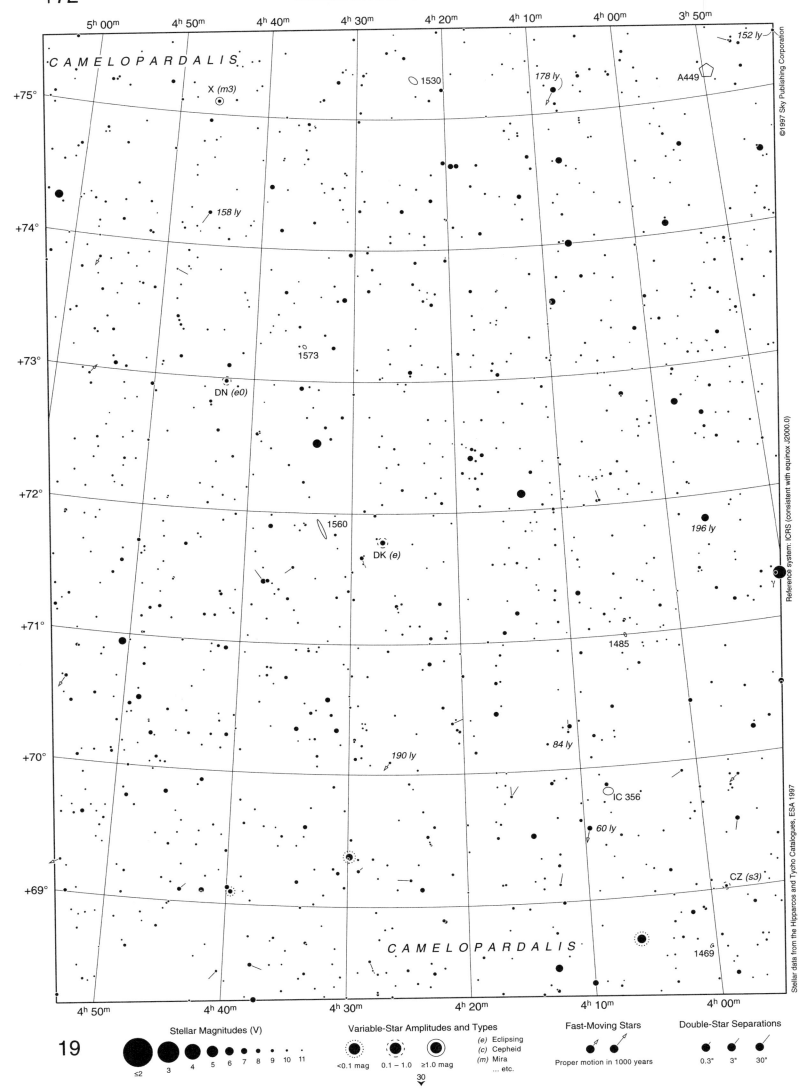

©1997 Sky Publishing Corporation

Reference system: ICRS (consistent with equinox J2000.0)

Stellar data from the Hipparcos and Tycho Catalogues, ESA 1997

CAMELOPARDALIS

X (m3)

1530

178 ly

152 ly

A449

158 ly

1573

DN (e0)

1560

DK (e)

196 ly

γ

1485

84 ly

190 ly

IC 356

60 ly

CZ (s3)

CAMELOPARDALIS

1469

19

Stellar Magnitudes (V)

≤2   3   4   5   6   7   8   9   10   11

Variable-Star Amplitudes and Types

<0.1 mag   0.1 – 1.0   ≥1.0 mag

(e) Eclipsing
(c) Cepheid
(m) Mira
... etc.

30

Fast-Moving Stars

Proper motion in 1000 years

Double-Star Separations

0.3"   3"   30"

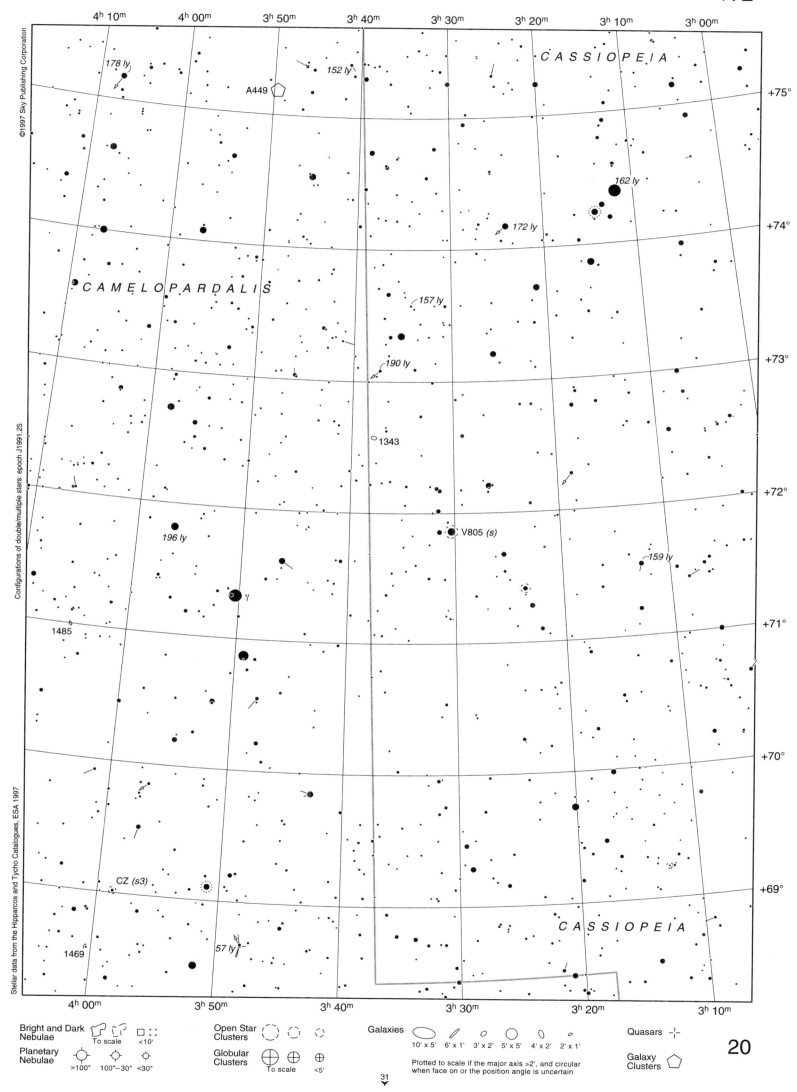

Configurations of double/multiple stars: epoch J1991.25

Stellar data from the Hipparcos and Tycho Catalogues, ESA 1997

CASSIOPEIA

178 ly

152 ly

A449

162 ly

172 ly

CAMELOPARDALIS

157 ly

190 ly

1343

V805 (s)

196 ly

159 ly

γ

1485

CASSIOPEIA

CZ (s3)

1469

57 ly

Bright and Dark
Nebulae
To scale   <10'

Planetary
Nebulae
>100"   100"−30"   <30"

Open Star
Clusters

Globular
Clusters
To scale   <5'

Galaxies
10' x 5'   6' x 1'   3' x 2'   5' x 5'   4' x 2'   2' x 1'

Plotted to scale if the major axis >2', and circular
when face on or the position angle is uncertain

Quasars

Galaxy
Clusters

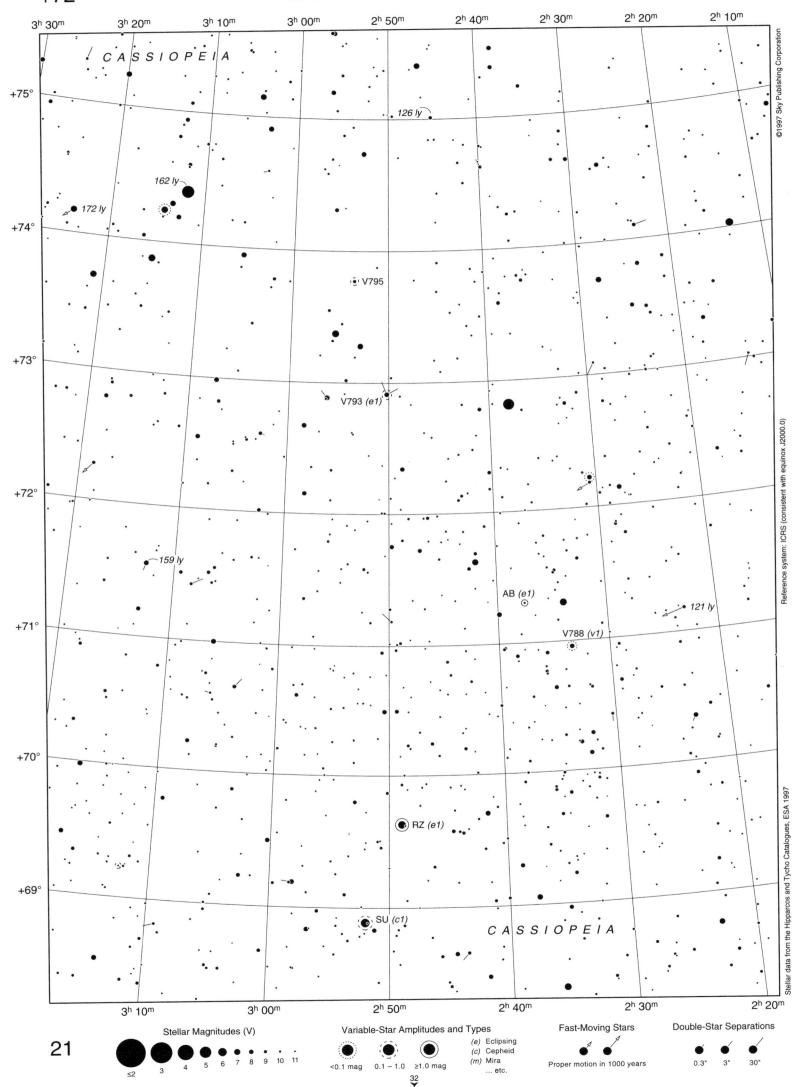

CASSIOPEIA

126 ly

162 ly

172 ly

V795

V793 (e1)

159 ly

AB (e1)

121 ly

V788 (v1)

RZ (e1)

SU (c1)

CASSIOPEIA

©1997 Sky Publishing Corporation

Reference system: ICRS (consistent with equinox J2000.0)

Stellar data from the Hipparcos and Tycho Catalogues, ESA 1997

21

Stellar Magnitudes (V)

≤2 3 4 5 6 7 8 9 10 11

Variable-Star Amplitudes and Types

<0.1 mag   0.1 – 1.0   ≥1.0 mag

(e) Eclipsing
(c) Cepheid
(m) Mira
... etc.

Fast-Moving Stars

Proper motion in 1000 years

Double-Star Separations

0.3"   3"   30"

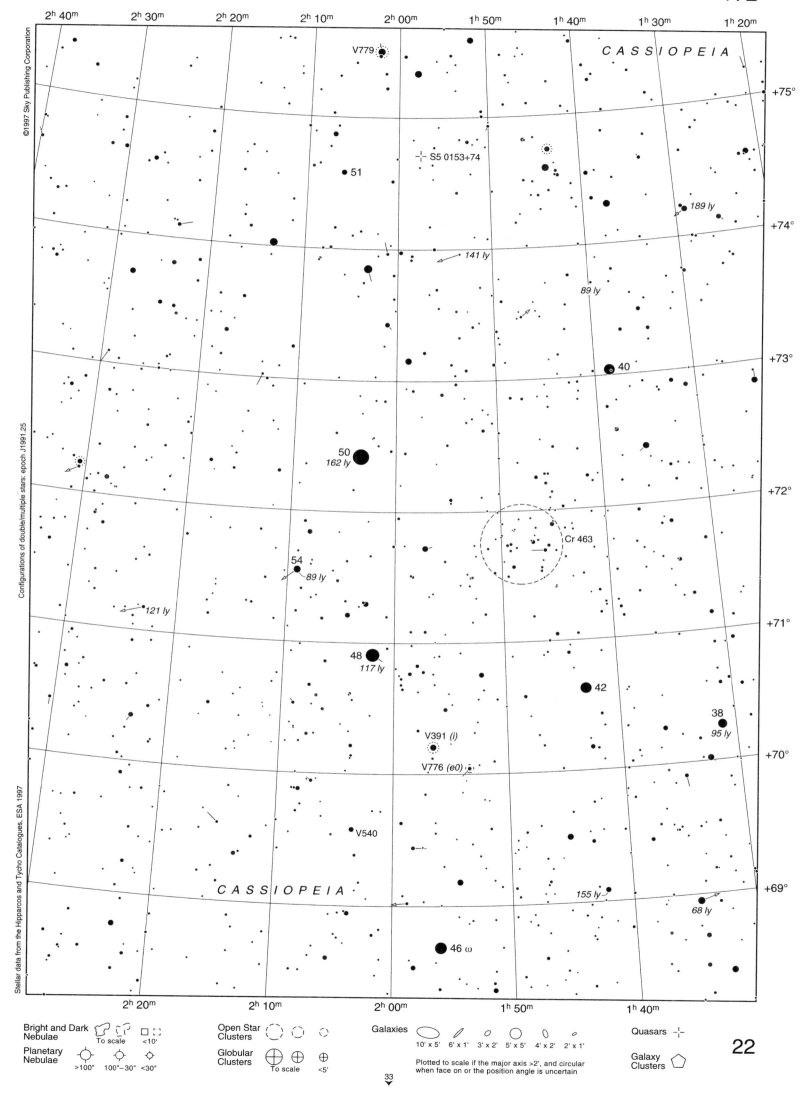

CASSIOPEIA

V779

S5 0153+74

51

189 ly

141 ly

89 ly

40

50
162 ly

Cr 463

54
89 ly

121 ly

48
117 ly

42

38
95 ly

V391 (i)

V776 (e0)

V540

155 ly

68 ly

CASSIOPEIA

46 ω

| Bright and Dark Nebulae | To scale | <10' |
| Planetary Nebulae | >100" | 100"–30" | <30" |

| Open Star Clusters | | |
| Globular Clusters | To scale | <5' |

Galaxies
10' x 5' 6' x 1' 3' x 2' 5' x 5' 4' x 2' 2' x 1'

Plotted to scale if the major axis >2', and circular when face on or the position angle is uncertain

Quasars

Galaxy Clusters

22

33

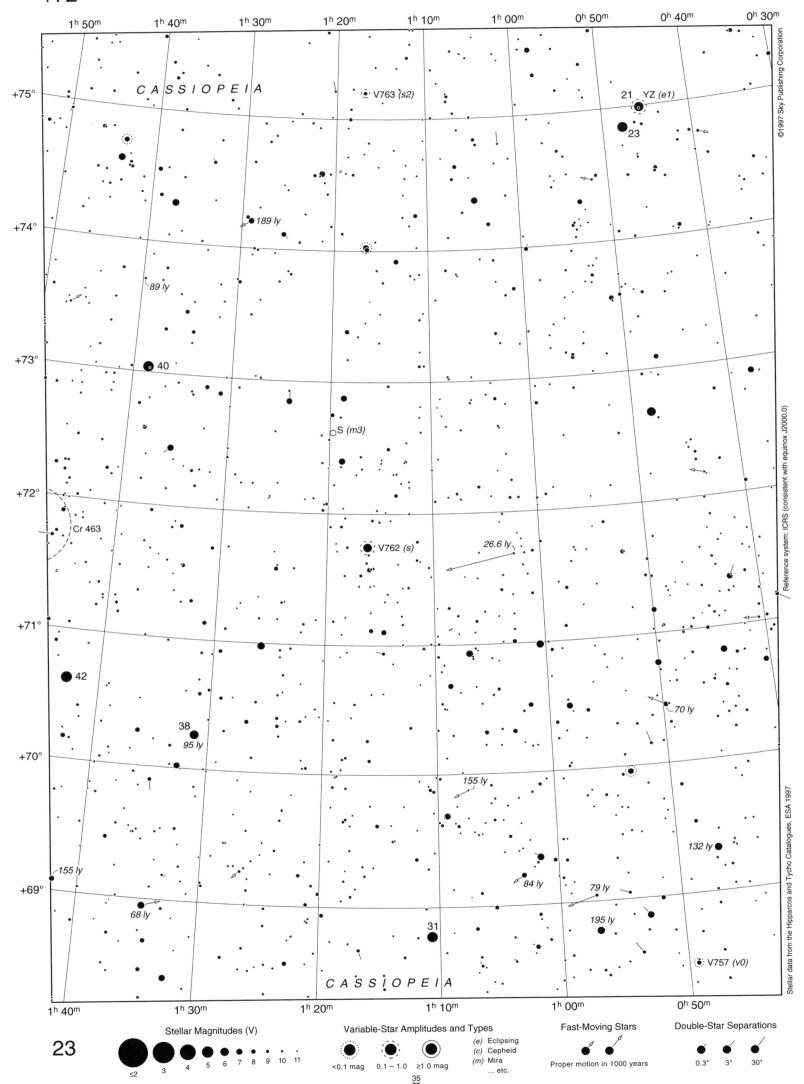

©1997 Sky Publishing Corporation

Reference system: ICRS (consistent with equinox J2000.0)

Stellar data from the Hipparcos and Tycho Catalogues, ESA 1997

23

Stellar Magnitudes (V)

≤2 3 4 5 6 7 8 9 10 11

Variable-Star Amplitudes and Types

<0.1 mag   0.1 – 1.0   ≥1.0 mag

(e) Eclipsing
(c) Cepheid
(m) Mira
... etc.

Fast-Moving Stars

Proper motion in 1000 years

Double-Star Separations

0.3" 3" 30"

35

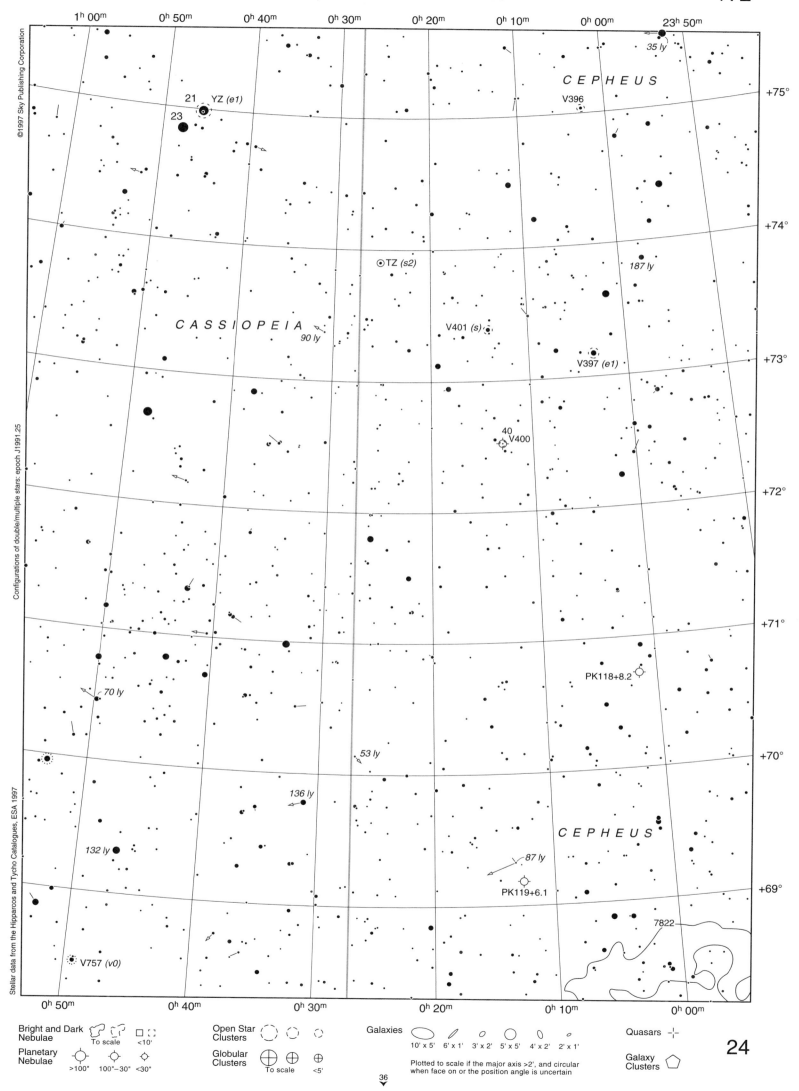

C E P H E U S

V396

21   YZ (e1)

23

CASSIOPEIA

TZ (s2)

187 ly

90 ly

V401 (s)

V397 (e1)

40
V400

PK118+8.2

70 ly

53 ly

136 ly

C E P H E U S

132 ly

87 ly

PK119+6.1

7822

V757 (v0)

35 ly

+75°

+74°

+73°

+72°

+71°

+70°

+69°

1ʰ 00ᵐ   0ʰ 50ᵐ   0ʰ 40ᵐ   0ʰ 30ᵐ   0ʰ 20ᵐ   0ʰ 10ᵐ   0ʰ 00ᵐ   23ʰ 50ᵐ

0ʰ 50ᵐ   0ʰ 40ᵐ   0ʰ 30ᵐ   0ʰ 20ᵐ   0ʰ 10ᵐ   0ʰ 00ᵐ

Bright and Dark Nebulae	Open Star Clusters	Galaxies	Quasars

Bright and Dark Nebulae   To scale   <10'
Planetary Nebulae   >100"   100"–30"   <30"
Open Star Clusters
Globular Clusters   To scale   <5'
Galaxies   10' x 5'   6' x 1'   3' x 2'   5' x 5'   4' x 2'   2' x 1'
Plotted to scale if the major axis >2', and circular when face on or the position angle is uncertain
Quasars
Galaxy Clusters

24

14

36

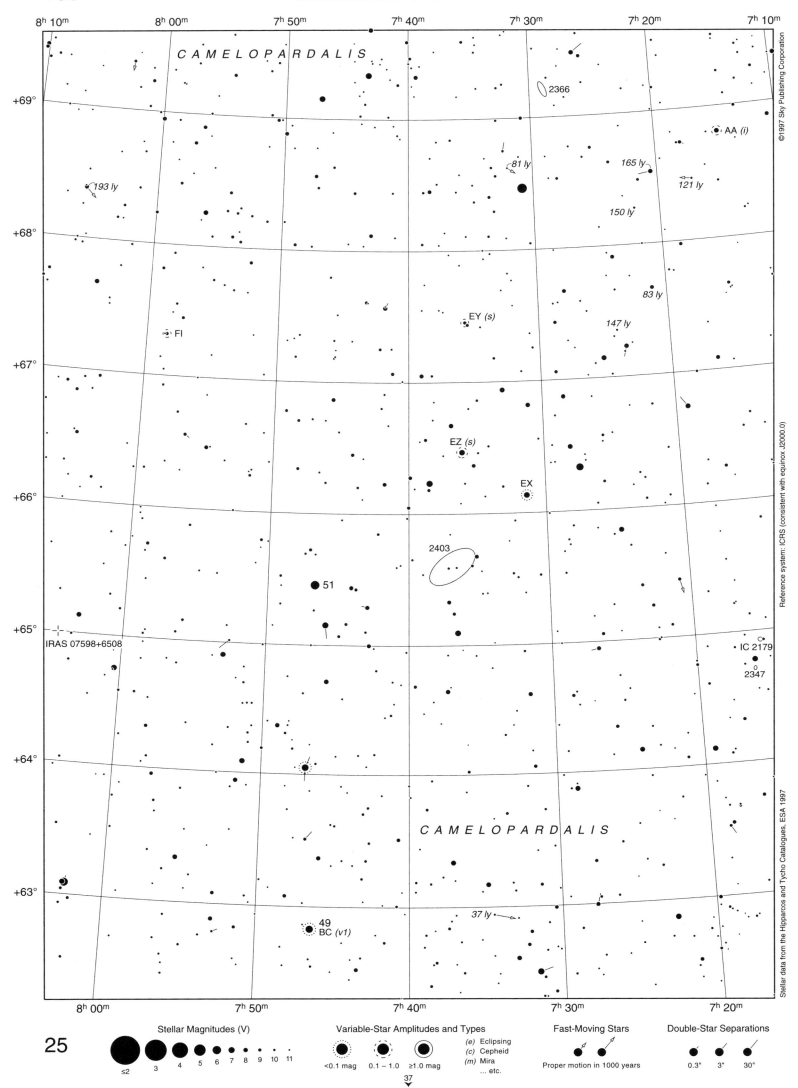

Reference system: ICRS (consistent with equinox J2000.0)

Stellar data from the Hipparcos and Tycho Catalogues, ESA 1997

CAMELOPARDALIS

2366

AA (i)

81 ly

165 ly

121 ly

150 ly

193 ly

83 ly

EY (s)

147 ly

FI

EZ (s)

EX

2403

51

IC 2179

IRAS 07598+6508

2347

CAMELOPARDALIS

37 ly

49
BC (v1)

25

Stellar Magnitudes (V)
≤2 3 4 5 6 7 8 9 10 11

Variable-Star Amplitudes and Types
<0.1 mag   0.1 – 1.0   ≥1.0 mag

(e) Eclipsing
(c) Cepheid
(m) Mira
... etc.

Fast-Moving Stars
Proper motion in 1000 years

Double-Star Separations
0.3"   3"   30"

37

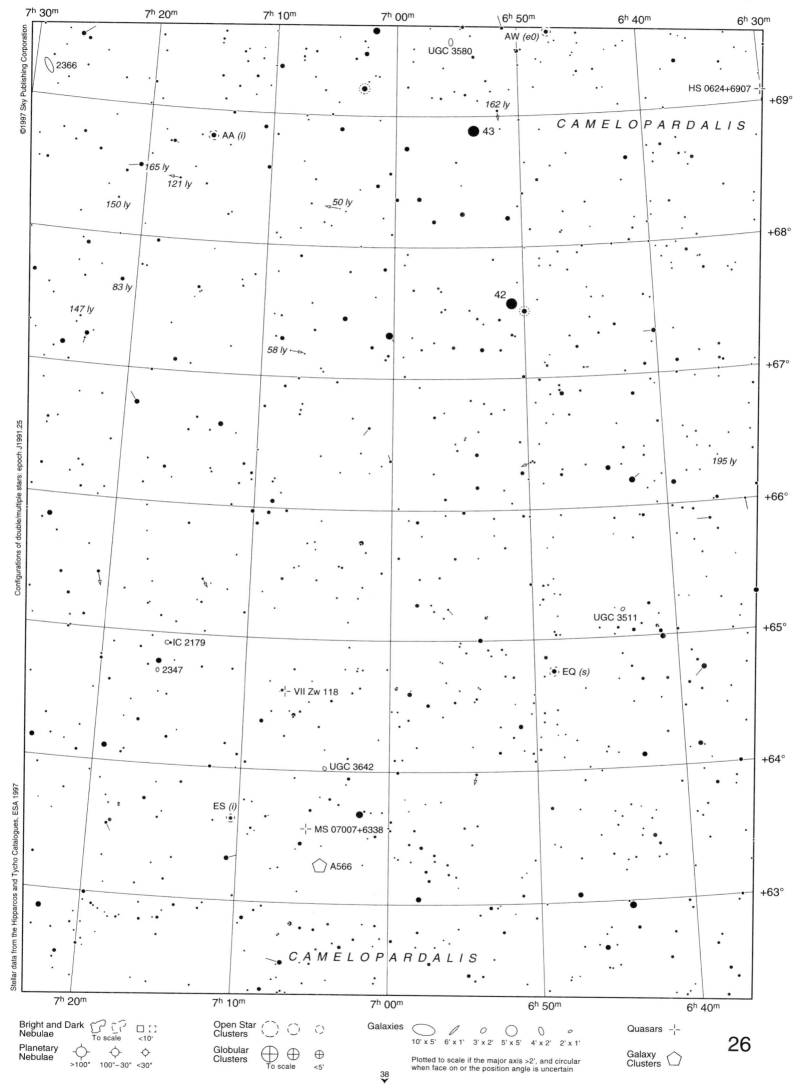

©1997 Sky Publishing Corporation

Configurations of double/multiple stars: epoch J1991.25

Stellar data from the Hipparcos and Tycho Catalogues, ESA 1997

2366

HS 0624+6907

UGC 3580

AW (e0)

C A M E L O P A R D A L I S

162 ly

43

AA (i)

165 ly

121 ly

150 ly

50 ly

83 ly

42

147 ly

58 ly

195 ly

UGC 3511

IC 2179

EQ (s)

2347

VII Zw 118

UGC 3642

ES (i)

MS 07007+6338

A566

C A M E L O P A R D A L I S

+69°

+68°

+67°

+66°

+65°

+64°

+63°

7h 30m   7h 20m   7h 10m   7h 00m   6h 50m   6h 40m   6h 30m

7h 20m   7h 10m   7h 00m   6h 50m   6h 40m

| Bright and Dark Nebulae | To scale | <10' | Open Star Clusters | Galaxies | Quasars |
| Planetary Nebulae | >100" 100"–30" <30" | Globular Clusters | To scale <5' | 10' x 5' 6' x 1' 3' x 2' 5' x 5' 4' x 2' 2' x 1' | Galaxy Clusters |

Plotted to scale if the major axis >2', and circular when face on or the position angle is uncertain

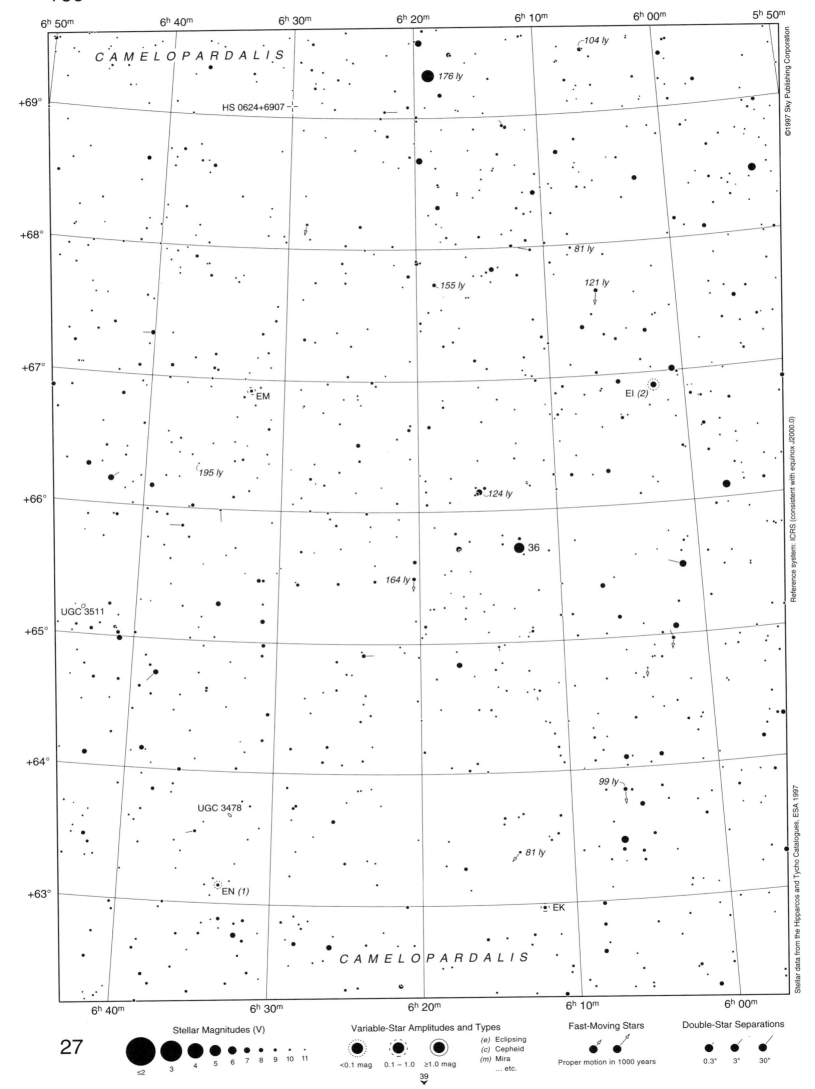

©1997 Sky Publishing Corporation

Reference system: ICRS (consistent with equinox J2000.0)

Stellar data from the Hipparcos and Tycho Catalogues, ESA 1997

Stellar Magnitudes (V)

≤2   3   4   5   6   7   8   9   10   11

Variable-Star Amplitudes and Types

<0.1 mag   0.1 – 1.0   ≥1.0 mag

(e) Eclipsing
(c) Cepheid
(m) Mira
... etc.

Fast-Moving Stars

Proper motion in 1000 years

Double-Star Separations

0.3"   3"   30"

27

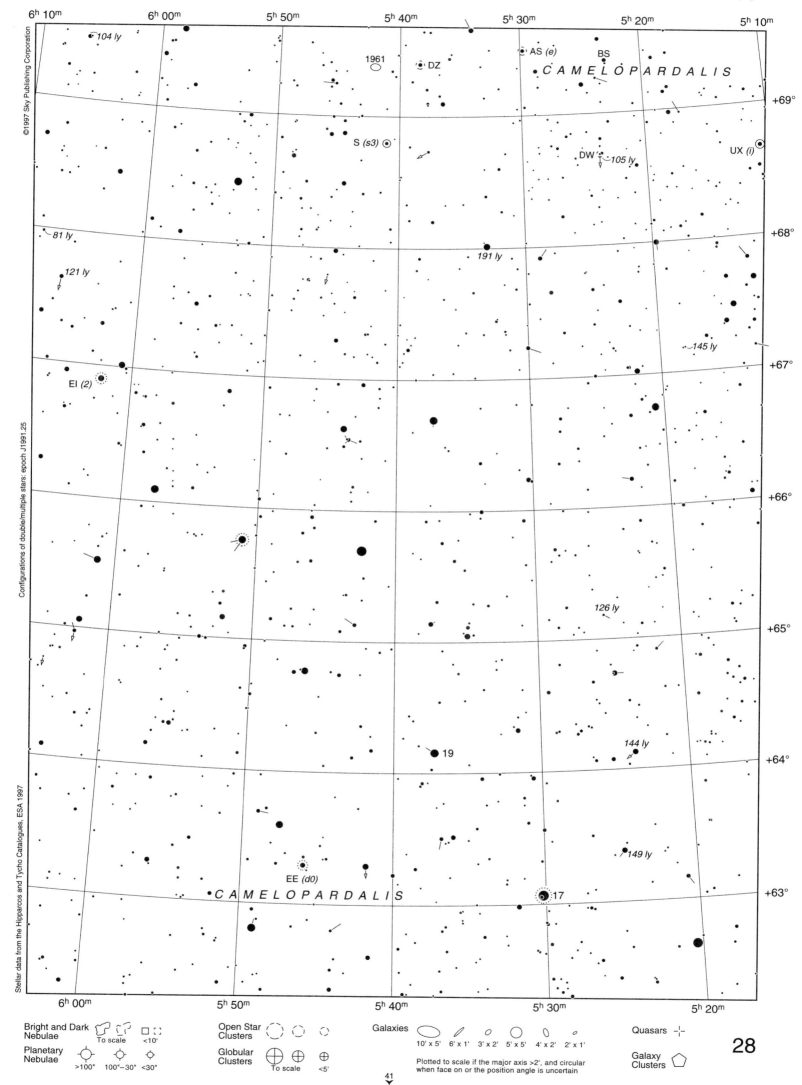

6h 10m · 6h 00m · 5h 50m · 5h 40m · 5h 30m · 5h 20m · 5h 10m

©1997 Sky Publishing Corporation

104 ly

1961

DZ

AS (e) BS

CAMELOPARDALIS

+69°

S (s3)

DW 105 ly

UX (i)

81 ly

191 ly

+68°

121 ly

145 ly

+67°

EI (2)

+66°

126 ly

+65°

19

144 ly

+64°

149 ly

EE (d0)

CAMELOPARDALIS

17

+63°

Configurations of double/multiple stars: epoch J1991.25

Stellar data from the Hipparcos and Tycho Catalogues, ESA 1997

6h 00m · 5h 50m · 5h 40m · 5h 30m · 5h 20m

Bright and Dark Nebulae
To scale   <10'

Open Star Clusters

Galaxies
10' x 5'   6' x 1'   3' x 2'   5' x 5'   4' x 2'   2' x 1'

Quasars

Planetary Nebulae
>100"   100"–30"   <30"

Globular Clusters
To scale   <5'

Plotted to scale if the major axis >2', and circular when face on or the position angle is uncertain

Galaxy Clusters

28

41

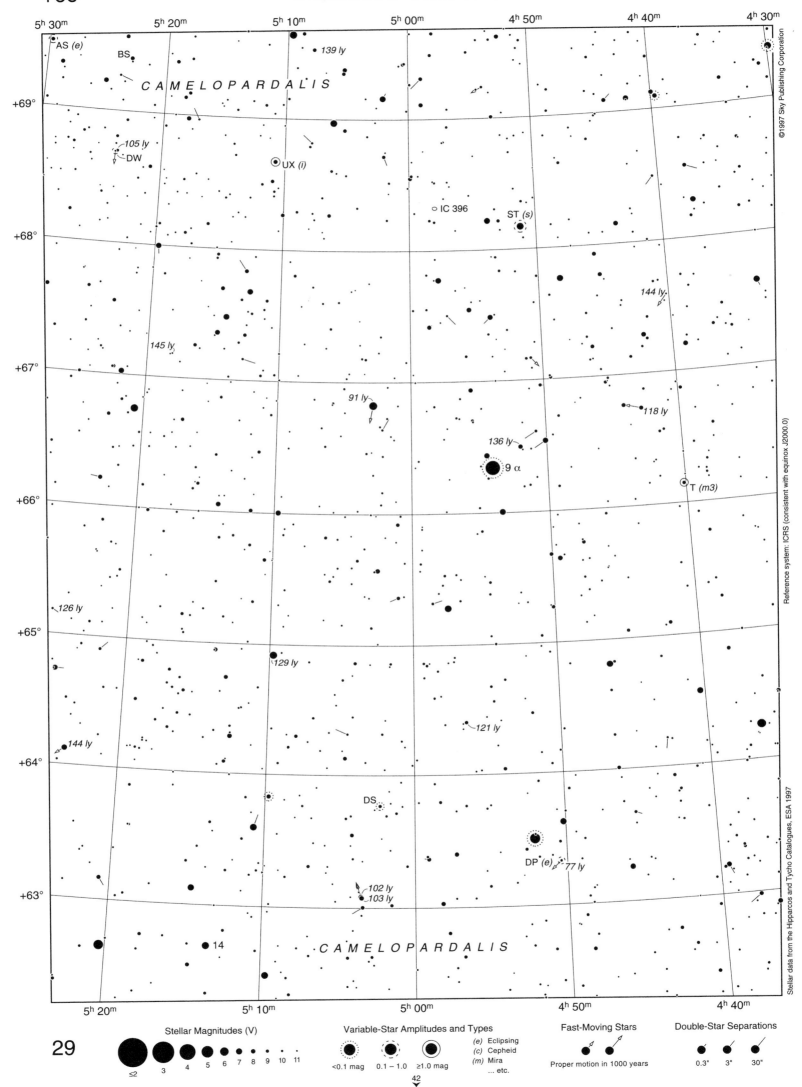

©1997 Sky Publishing Corporation

Reference system: ICRS (consistent with equinox J2000.0)

Stellar data from the Hipparcos and Tycho Catalogues, ESA 1997

AS (e)
BS
CAMELOPARDALIS
139 ly
105 ly
DW
UX (i)
IC 396
ST (s)
144 ly
145 ly
91 ly
118 ly
136 ly
9 α
T (m3)
126 ly
129 ly
121 ly
144 ly
DS
DP (e) 77 ly
102 ly
103 ly
CAMELOPARDALIS
14

Stellar Magnitudes (V)

29

≤2   3   4   5   6   7   8   9   10 11

Variable-Star Amplitudes and Types

<0.1 mag   0.1 – 1.0   ≥1.0 mag

(e) Eclipsing
(c) Cepheid
(m) Mira
... etc.

Fast-Moving Stars

Proper motion in 1000 years

Double-Star Separations

0.3"   3"   30"

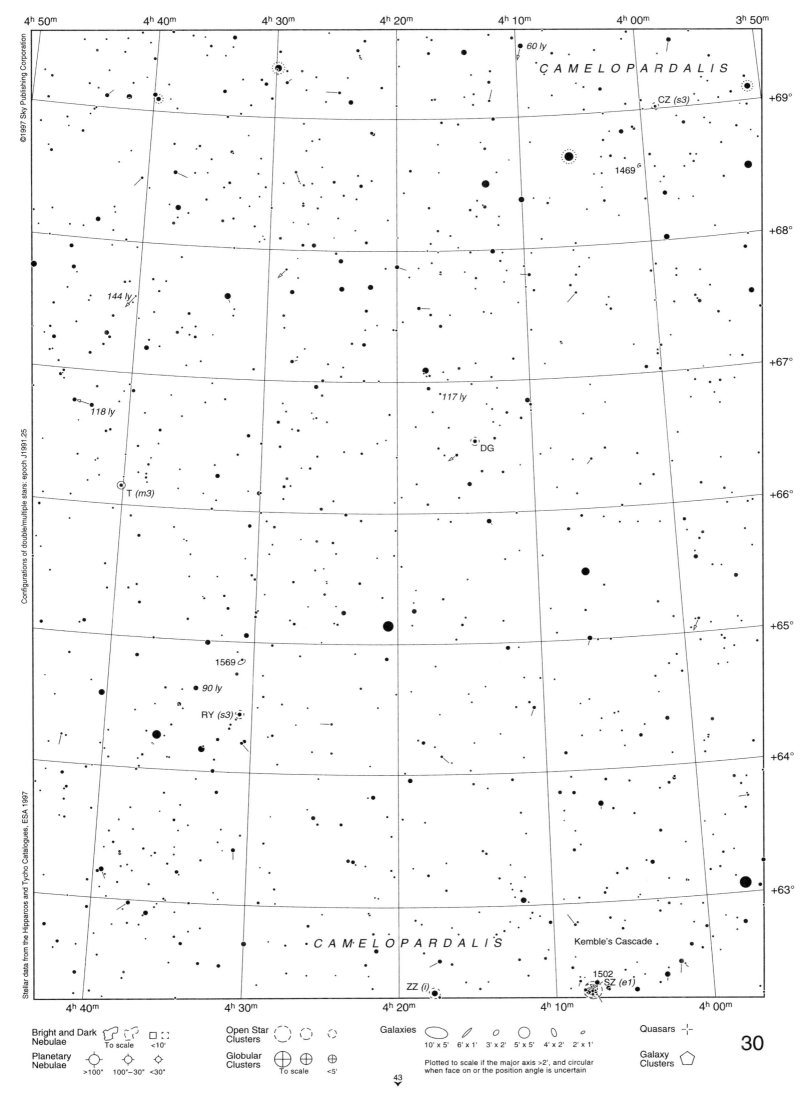

CAMELOPARDALIS

CZ (s3)

1469

60 ly

144 ly

118 ly

117 ly

DG

T (m3)

1569

90 ly

RY (s3)

CAMELOPARDALIS

Kemble's Cascade

1502
SZ (e1)

ZZ (i)

Bright and Dark
Nebulae
To scale   <10'

Planetary
Nebulae
>100" 100"–30" <30"

Open Star
Clusters
To scale   <10'

Globular
Clusters
To scale   <5'

Galaxies
10' x 5' 6' x 1' 3' x 2' 5' x 5' 4' x 2' 2' x 1'

Plotted to scale if the major axis >2', and circular
when face on or the position angle is uncertain

Quasars

Galaxy
Clusters

30

43

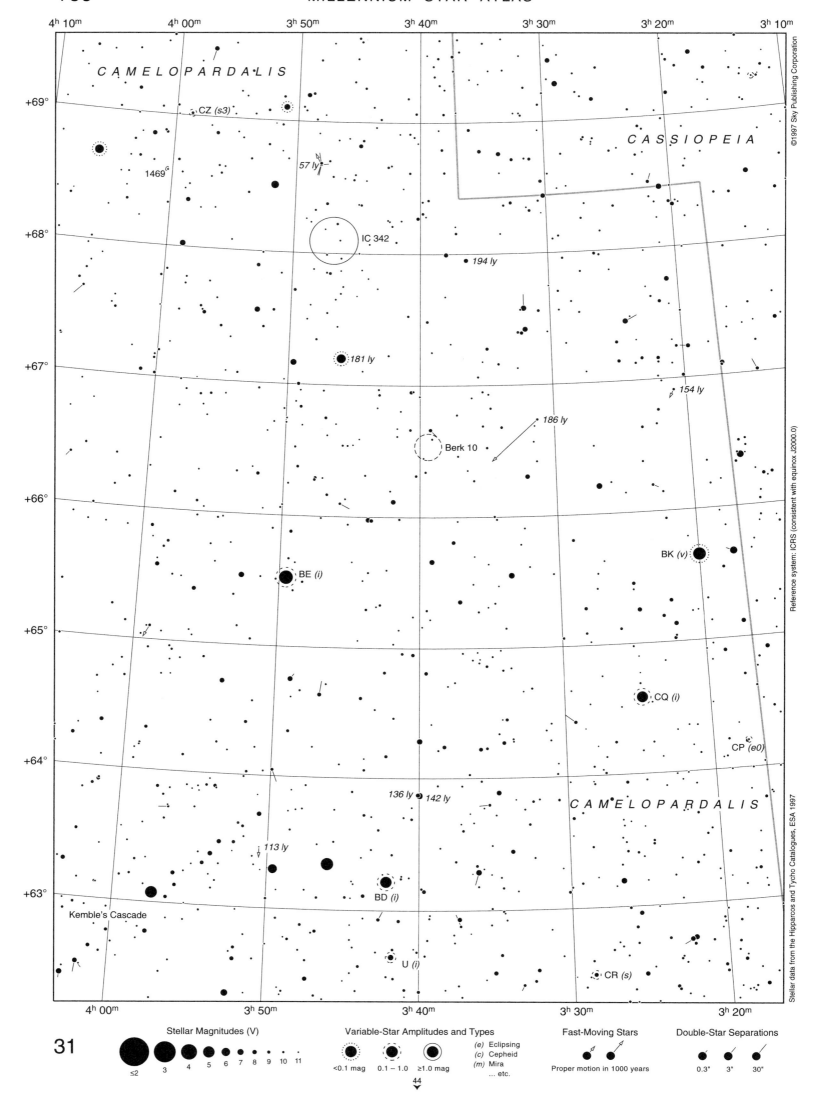

©1997 Sky Publishing Corporation

Reference system: ICRS (consistent with equinox J2000.0)

Stellar data from the Hipparcos and Tycho Catalogues, ESA 1997

CAMELOPARDALIS

CZ (s3)

1469

57 ly

CASSIOPEIA

IC 342

194 ly

181 ly

154 ly

186 ly

Berk 10

BK (v)

BE (i)

CQ (i)

CP (e0)

CAMELOPARDALIS

136 ly   142 ly

113 ly

BD (i)

Kemble's Cascade

U (i)

CR (s)

31

Stellar Magnitudes (V)

≤2   3   4   5   6   7   8   9   10 11

Variable-Star Amplitudes and Types

<0.1 mag   0.1 – 1.0   ≥1.0 mag

(e) Eclipsing
(c) Cepheid
(m) Mira
... etc.

Fast-Moving Stars

Proper motion in 1000 years

Double-Star Separations

0.3"   3"   30"

44

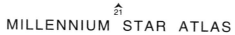
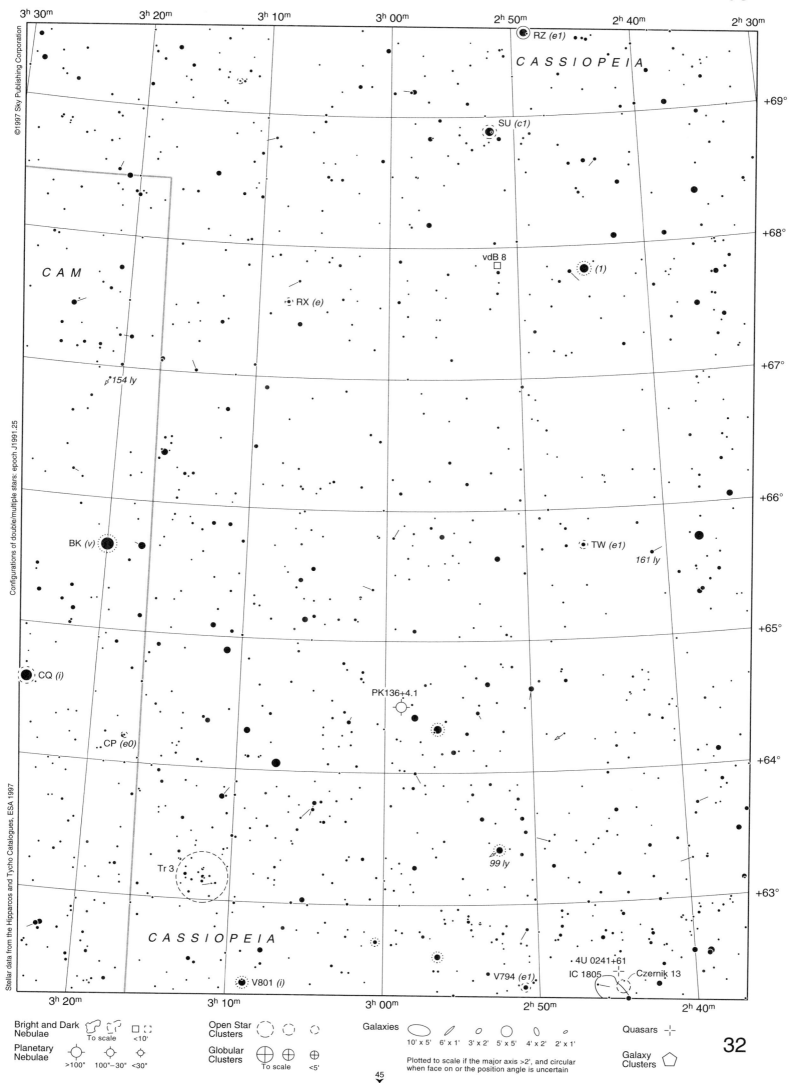

CASSIOPEIA

RZ *(e1)*

SU *(c1)*

CAM

vdB 8

(1)

RX *(e)*

β *154 ly*

BK *(v)*

TW *(e1)*

161 ly

CQ *(i)*

PK136+4.1

CP *(e0)*

Tr 3

99 ly

CASSIOPEIA

4U 0241+61

IC 1805

Czernik 13

V794 *(e1)*

V801 *(i)*

Bright and Dark Nebulae
To scale   <10'

Planetary Nebulae
>100"   100"-30"   <30"

Open Star Clusters

Globular Clusters
To scale   <5'

Galaxies
10' x 5'   6' x 1'   3' x 2'   5' x 5'   4' x 2'   2' x 1'

Plotted to scale if the major axis >2', and circular when face on or the position angle is uncertain

Quasars

Galaxy Clusters

32

45

MILLENNIUM STAR ATLAS

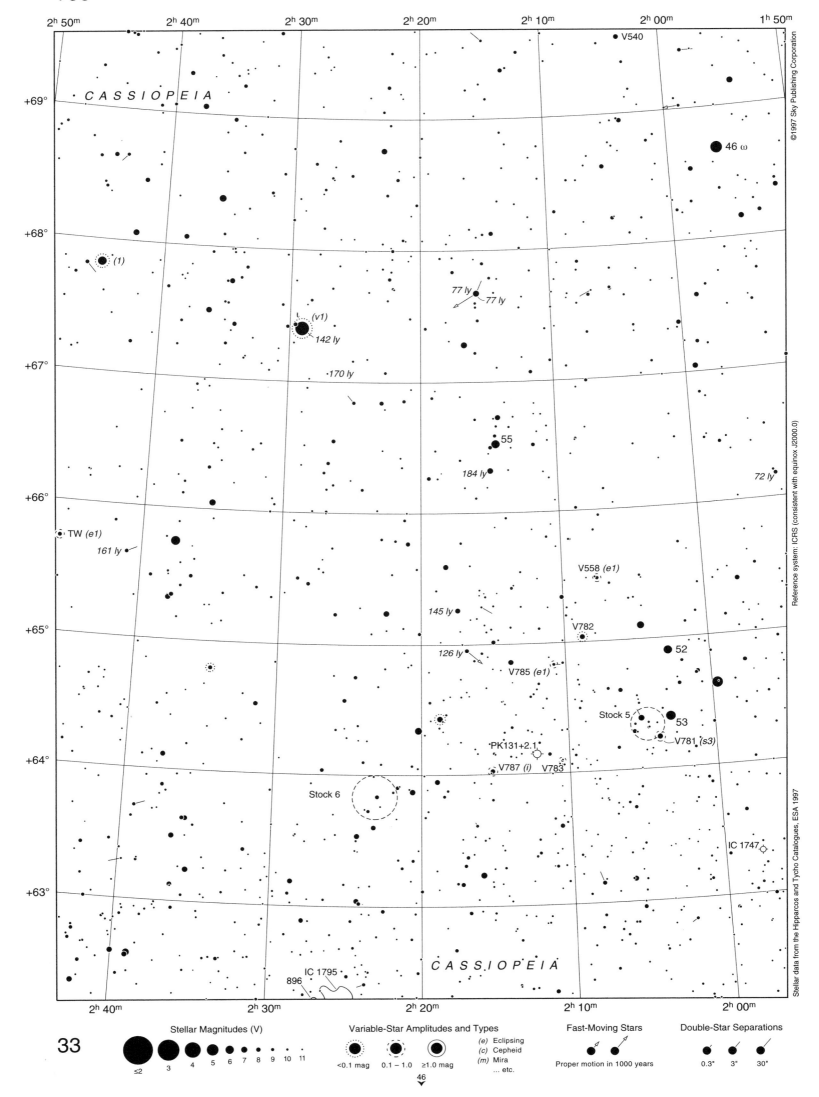

©1997 Sky Publishing Corporation

Reference system: ICRS (consistent with equinox J2000.0)

Stellar data from the Hipparcos and Tycho Catalogues, ESA 1997

33

Stellar Magnitudes (V)

≤2 3 4 5 6 7 8 9 10 11

Variable-Star Amplitudes and Types

<0.1 mag   0.1 – 1.0   ≥1.0 mag

(e) Eclipsing
(c) Cepheid
(m) Mira
... etc.

Fast-Moving Stars

Proper motion in 1000 years

Double-Star Separations

0.3"   3"   30"

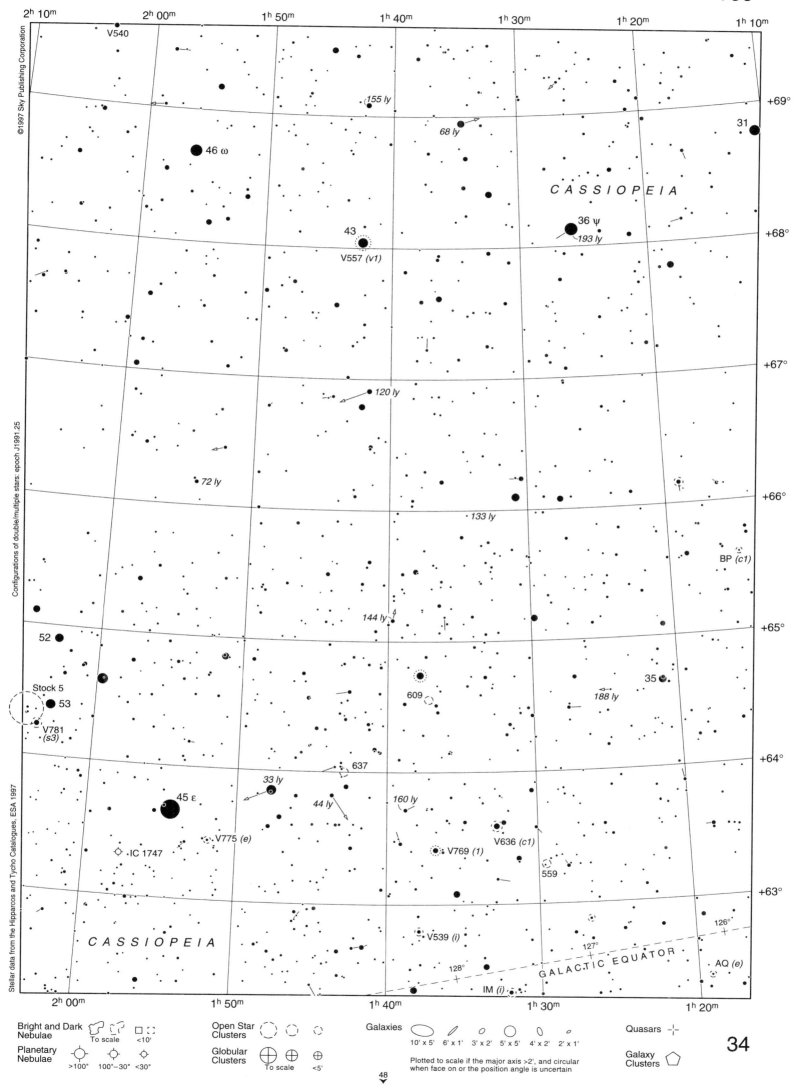

22

2h 10m   2h 00m   1h 50m   1h 40m   1h 30m   1h 20m   1h 10m

V540

155 ly

68 ly

31

+69°

46 ω

CASSIOPEIA

36 ψ

43

193 ly

+68°

V557 (v1)

120 ly

+67°

72 ly

133 ly

+66°

BP (c1)

144 ly

+65°

52

609

35

188 ly

Stock 5

53

V781 (s3)

637

+64°

33 ly

45 ε

44 ly

160 ly

V775 (e)

V636 (c1)

IC 1747

V769 (1)

559

+63°

CASSIOPEIA

V539 (i)

126°

127°

128°

GALACTIC EQUATOR

AQ (e)

IM (i)

2h 00m   1h 50m   1h 40m   1h 30m   1h 20m

Bright and Dark Nebulae — To scale   <10'

Planetary Nebulae — >100"   100"–30"   <30'

Open Star Clusters — To scale   <10'

Globular Clusters — To scale   <5'

Galaxies — 10' x 5'   6' x 1'   3' x 2'   5' x 5'   4' x 2'   2' x 1'

Plotted to scale if the major axis >2', and circular when face on or the position angle is uncertain

Quasars

Galaxy Clusters

34

48

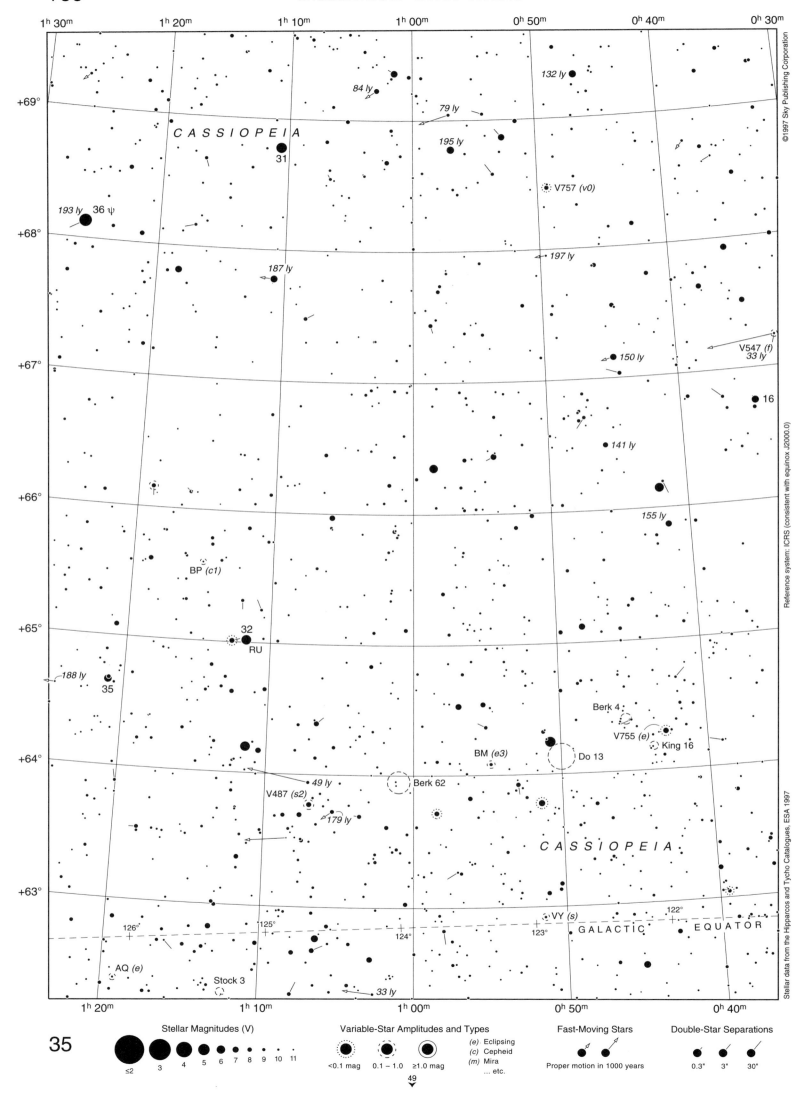

©1997 Sky Publishing Corporation

Reference system: ICRS (consistent with equinox J2000.0)

Stellar data from the Hipparcos and Tycho Catalogues, ESA 1997

CASSIOPEIA

84 ly
79 ly
132 ly
195 ly
31
V757 (v0)
193 ly   36 ψ
197 ly
187 ly
V547 (f)
33 ly
150 ly
16
141 ly
155 ly
BP (c1)
32
RU
188 ly
35
Berk 4
V755 (e)
BM (e3)   Do 13   King 16
49 ly
Berk 62
V487 (s2)
179 ly
CASSIOPEIA
VY (s)
126°   125°   124°   123°   122°   GALACTIC   EQUATOR
AQ (e)
Stock 3
33 ly

35

Stellar Magnitudes (V)

≤2   3   4   5   6   7   8   9   10   11

Variable-Star Amplitudes and Types

<0.1 mag   0.1 – 1.0   ≥1.0 mag

(e) Eclipsing
(c) Cepheid
(m) Mira
... etc.

Fast-Moving Stars

Proper motion in 1000 years

Double-Star Separations

0.3"   3"   30"

49

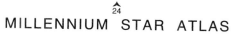
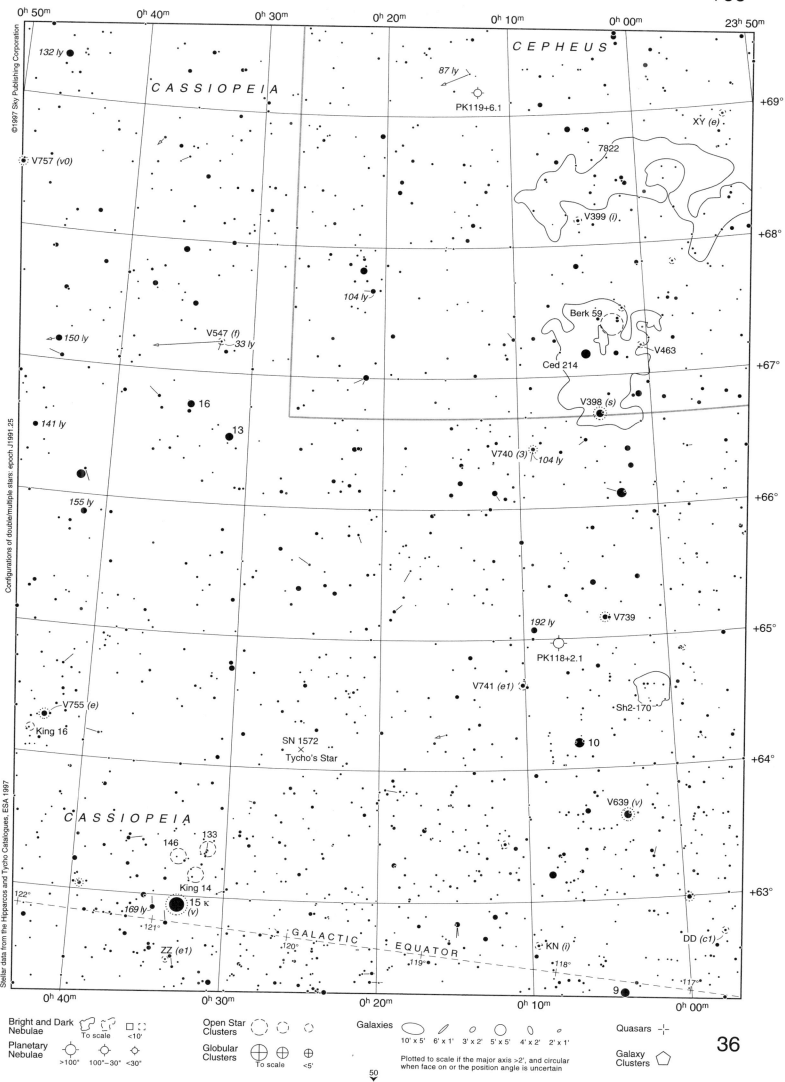

Configurations of double/multiple stars: epoch J1991.25

Stellar data from the Hipparcos and Tycho Catalogues, ESA 1997

0ʰ 50ᵐ   0ʰ 40ᵐ   0ʰ 30ᵐ   0ʰ 20ᵐ   0ʰ 10ᵐ   0ʰ 00ᵐ   23ʰ 50ᵐ

C E P H E U S

C A S S I O P E I A

132 ly

PK119+6.1

87 ly

XY *(e)*

7822

V757 *(v0)*

V399 *(i)*

+69°

+68°

104 ly

Berk 59

V463

V547 *(f)*
33 ly

Ced 214

150 ly

+67°

16

141 ly

13

V398 *(s)*

V740 *(3)*   *104 ly*

155 ly

+66°

192 ly

V739

PK118+2.1

V755 *(e)*

V741 *(e1)*

Sh2-170

King 16

10

+65°

SN 1572
×
Tycho's Star

+64°

C A S S I O P E I A

V639 *(v)*

146   133

King 14

122°

DD *(c1)*

15 κ
(v)
169 ly

121°

ZZ *(e1)*

KN *(i)*

120°

GALACTIC   EQUATOR

119°

118°

9

117°

+63°

0ʰ 40ᵐ   0ʰ 30ᵐ   0ʰ 20ᵐ   0ʰ 10ᵐ   0ʰ 00ᵐ

Bright and Dark
Nebulae

To scale   <10'

Planetary
Nebulae
   >100"   100"–30"   <30"

Open Star
Clusters

Globular
Clusters
   To scale   <5'

Galaxies

10' x 5'   6' x 1'   3' x 2'   5' x 5'   4' x 2'   2' x 1'

Plotted to scale if the major axis >2', and circular
when face on or the position angle is uncertain

Quasars

Galaxy
Clusters

36

50

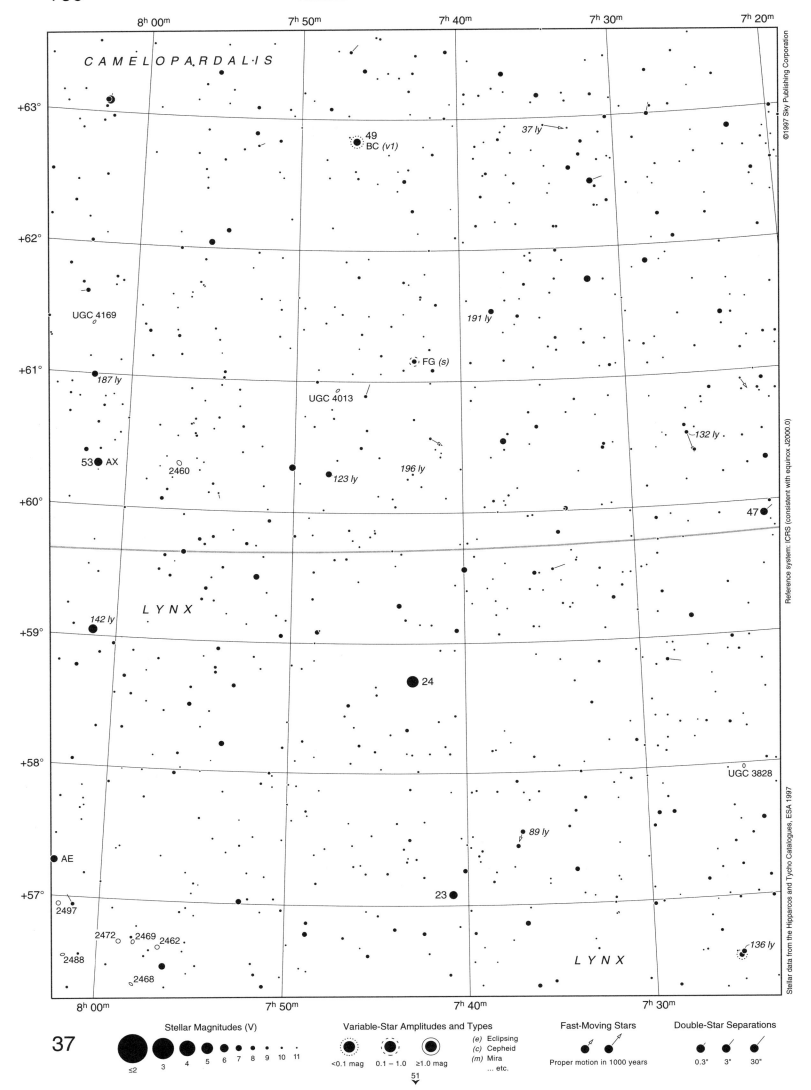

Reference system: ICRS (consistent with equinox J2000.0)

Stellar data from the Hipparcos and Tycho Catalogues, ESA 1997

Stellar Magnitudes (V)

≤2 3 4 5 6 7 8 9 10 11

Variable-Star Amplitudes and Types

<0.1 mag   0.1 – 1.0   ≥1.0 mag

(e) Eclipsing
(c) Cepheid
(m) Mira
... etc.

Fast-Moving Stars

Proper motion in 1000 years

Double-Star Separations

0.3"   3"   30"

37

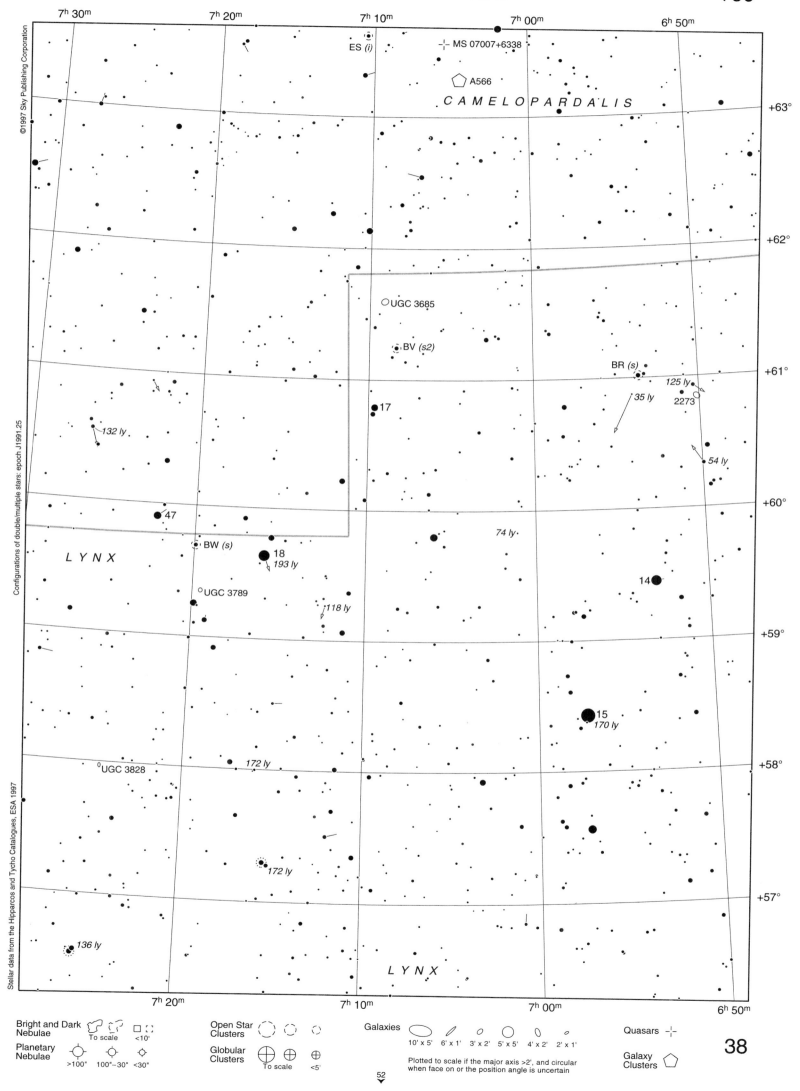

7h 30m 7h 20m 7h 10m 7h 00m 6h 50m

ES (i)

-|- MS 07007+6338

A566

C A M E L O P A R D A L I S +63°

+62°

UGC 3685

BV (s2)

BR (s) +61°

125 ly
2273

17

35 ly

132 ly

54 ly

+60°

47

74 ly

BW (s)

L Y N X

18
193 ly

14

UGC 3789

118 ly

+59°

15
170 ly

UGC 3828

172 ly

+58°

172 ly

+57°

136 ly

L Y N X

7h 20m 7h 10m 7h 00m 6h 50m

©1997 Sky Publishing Corporation

Configurations of double/multiple stars: epoch J1991.25

Stellar data from the Hipparcos and Tycho Catalogues, ESA 1997

Bright and Dark Nebulae
To scale <10'

Planetary Nebulae
>100" 100"–30" <30"

Open Star Clusters
To scale <10'

Globular Clusters
To scale <5'

Galaxies
10' x 5' 6' x 1' 3' x 2' 5' x 5' 4' x 2' 2' x 1'
Plotted to scale if the major axis >2', and circular when face on or the position angle is uncertain

Quasars -|-

Galaxy Clusters

38

52

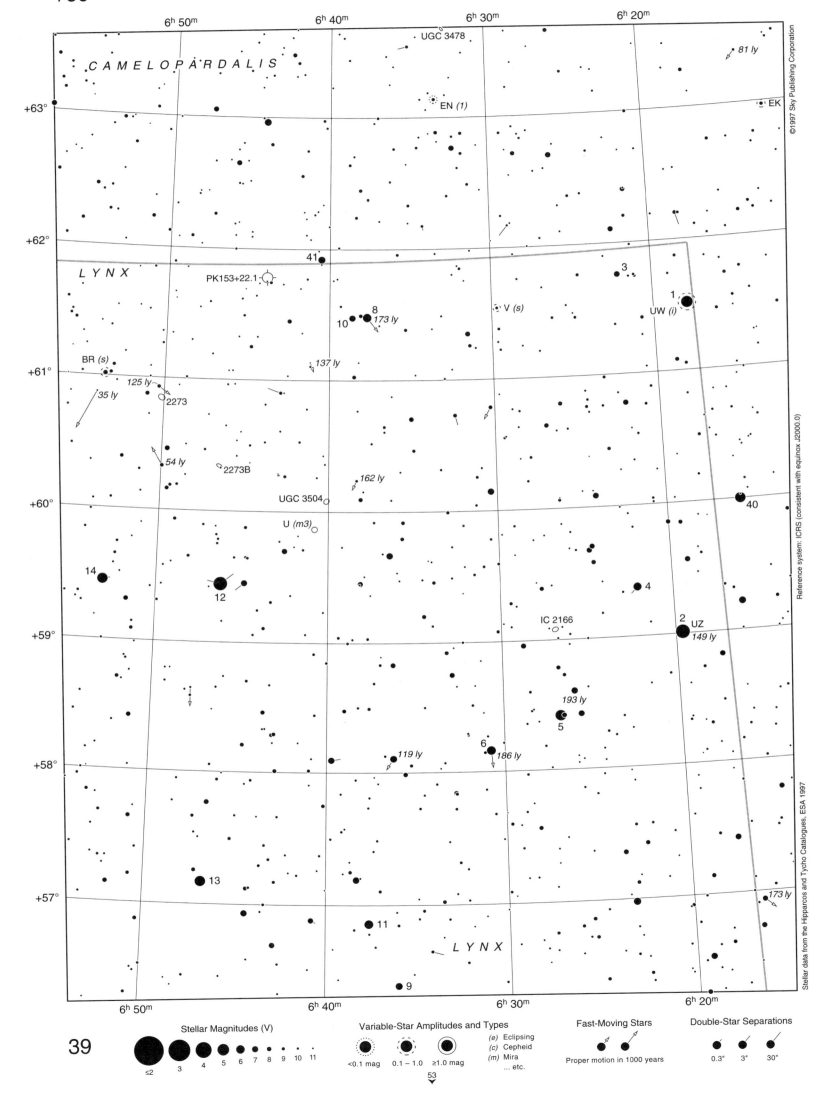

©1997 Sky Publishing Corporation

Reference system: ICRS (consistent with equinox J2000.0)

Stellar data from the Hipparcos and Tycho Catalogues, ESA 1997

39

Stellar Magnitudes (V)

≤2   3   4   5   6   7   8   9   10   11

Variable-Star Amplitudes and Types

<0.1 mag   0.1 – 1.0 mag   ≥1.0 mag

(e) Eclipsing
(c) Cepheid
(m) Mira
... etc.

Fast-Moving Stars

Proper motion in 1000 years

Double-Star Separations

0.3"   3"   30"

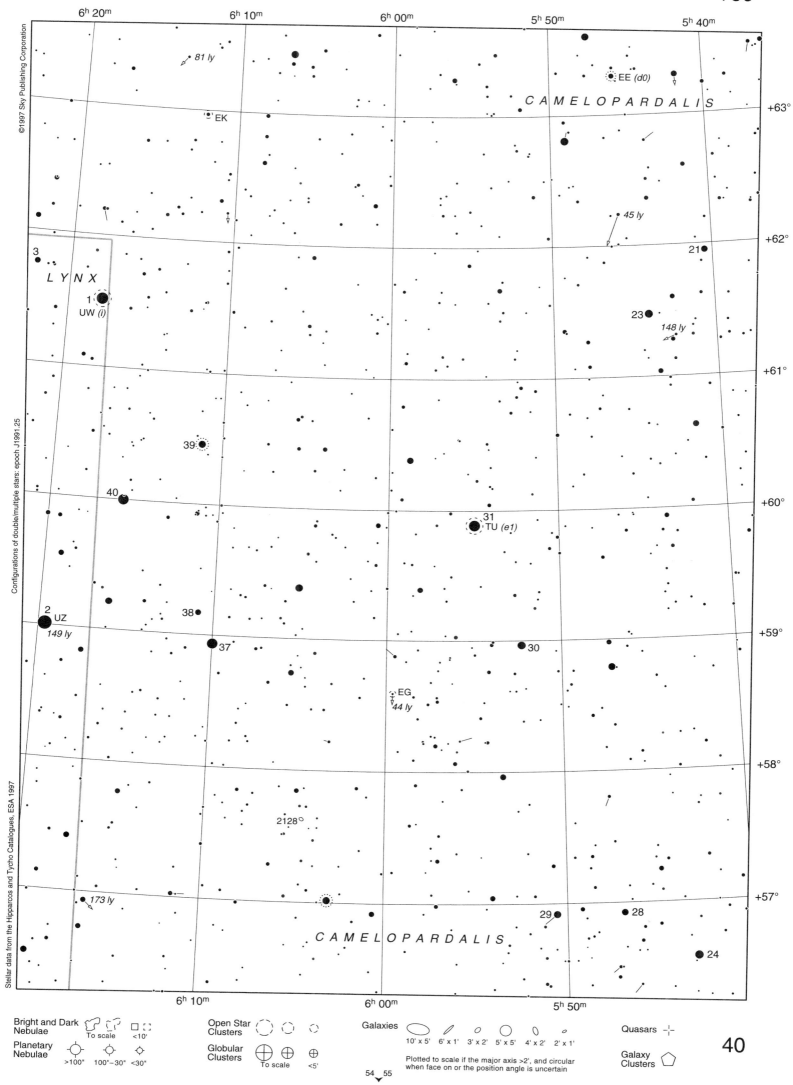

Configurations of double/multiple stars: epoch J1991.25

Stellar data from the Hipparcos and Tycho Catalogues, ESA 1997

CAMELOPARDALIS

EE *(d0)*

81 ly

EK

45 ly

21

23

148 ly

L Y N X

3

1
UW *(i)*

39

40

31
TU *(e1)*

30

2 UZ
149 ly

38

37

EG
44 ly

2128°

173 ly

29

28

24

CAMELOPARDALIS

Bright and Dark Nebulae			Open Star Clusters			Galaxies							Quasars
To scale		<10'	To scale		<10'	10' x 5'	6' x 1'	3' x 2'	5' x 5'	4' x 2'	2' x 1'		

Planetary Nebulae
>100" 100"–30" <30"

Globular Clusters
To scale <5'

Plotted to scale if the major axis >2', and circular when face on or the position angle is uncertain

Quasars

Galaxy Clusters

40

54 55

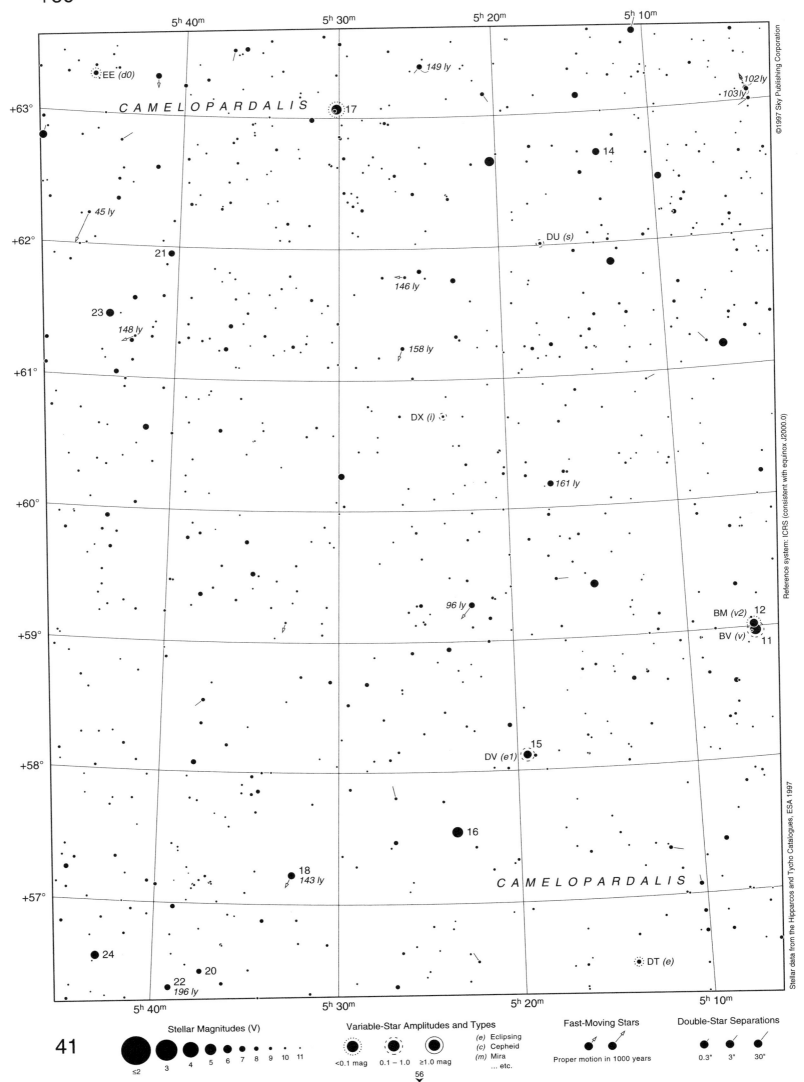

©1997 Sky Publishing Corporation

Reference system: ICRS (consistent with equinox J2000.0)

Stellar data from the Hipparcos and Tycho Catalogues, ESA 1997

Stellar Magnitudes (V)

≤2 3 4 5 6 7 8 9 10 11

Variable-Star Amplitudes and Types

<0.1 mag   0.1 – 1.0   ≥1.0 mag

(e) Eclipsing
(c) Cepheid
(m) Mira
... etc.

Fast-Moving Stars

Proper motion in 1000 years

Double-Star Separations

0.3"   3"   30"

56

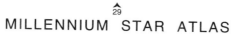
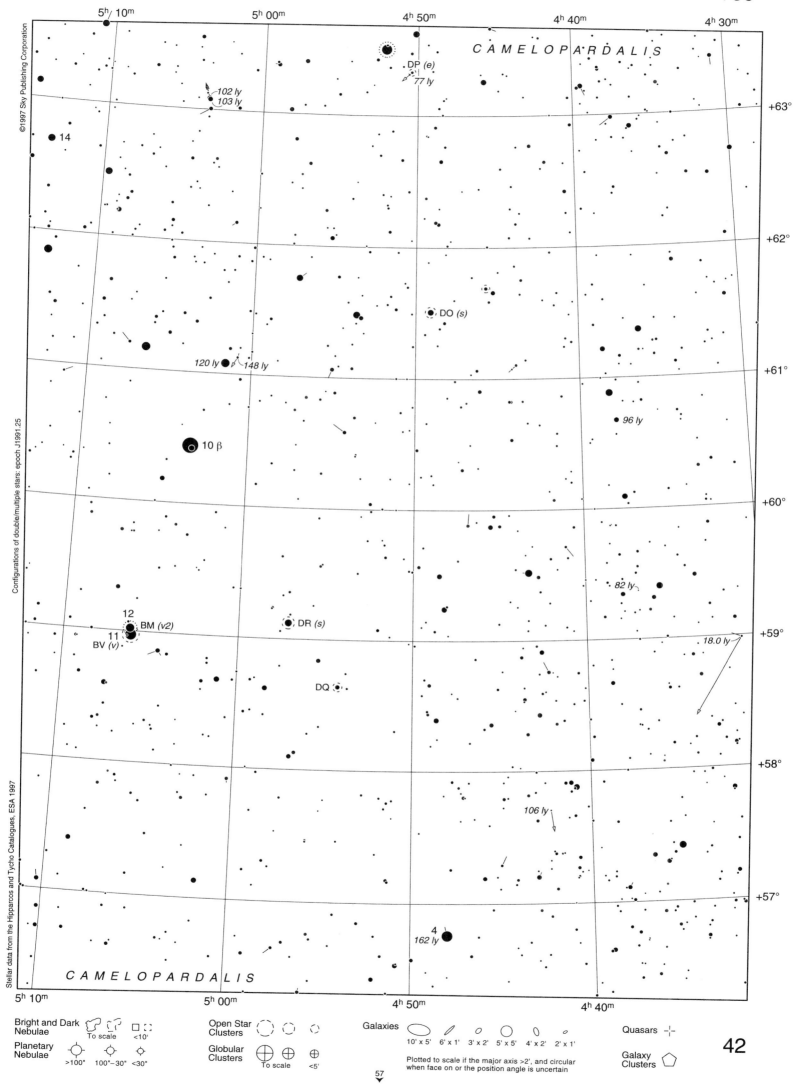

Configurations of double/multiple stars: epoch J1991.25

Stellar data from the Hipparcos and Tycho Catalogues, ESA 1997

5ʰ 10ᵐ   5ʰ 00ᵐ   4ʰ 50ᵐ   4ʰ 40ᵐ   4ʰ 30ᵐ

C A M E L O P A R D A L I S

+63°

14

DP (e)
77 ly

102 ly
103 ly

DO (s)

+62°

120 ly   148 ly

+61°

96 ly

10 β

82 ly

+60°

12
BM (v2)
11
BV (v)

DR (s)

18.0 ly

+59°

DQ

106 ly

+58°

+57°

4
162 ly

5ʰ 10ᵐ   5ʰ 00ᵐ   4ʰ 50ᵐ   4ʰ 40ᵐ

C A M E L O P A R D A L I S

Bright and Dark Nebulae
To scale   <10'

Open Star Clusters

Galaxies
10' x 5'   6' x 1'   3' x 2'   5' x 5'   4' x 2'   2' x 1'

Quasars

Planetary Nebulae
>100"   100"–30"   <30"

Globular Clusters
To scale   <5'

Plotted to scale if the major axis >2', and circular when face on or the position angle is uncertain

Galaxy Clusters

42

57

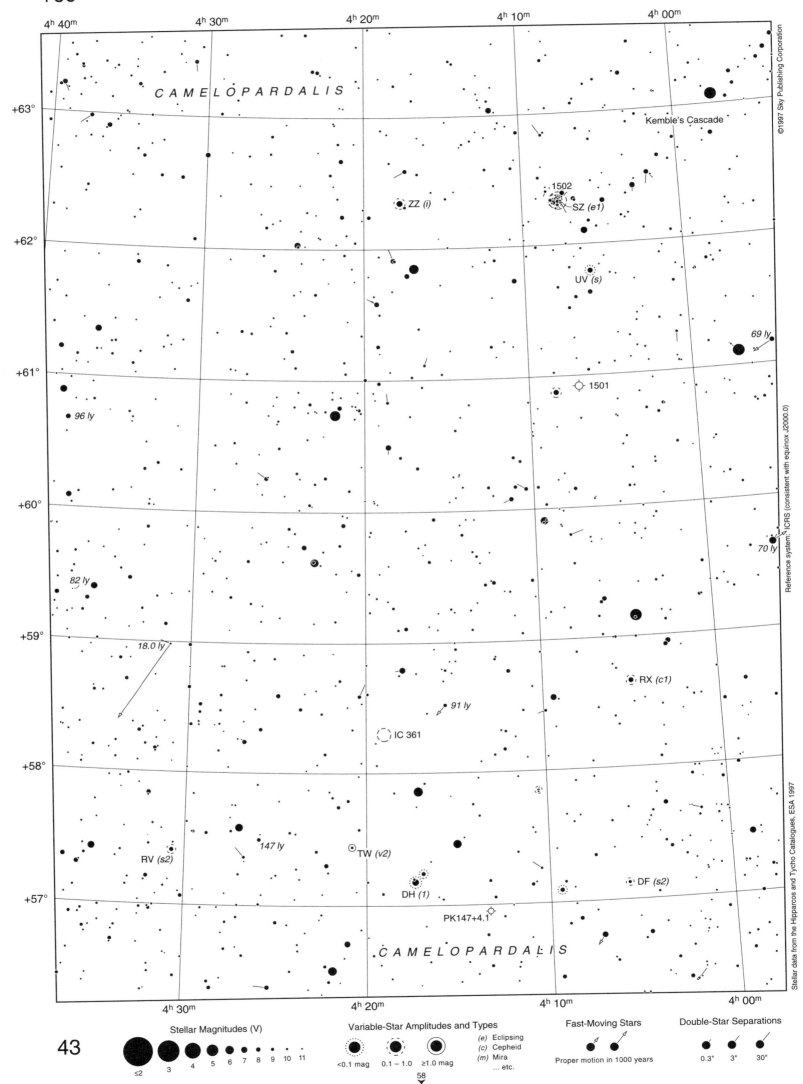

CAMELOPARDALIS

Kemble's Cascade

1502

ZZ (i)

SZ (e1)

UV (s)

69 ly

1501

96 ly

70 ly

82 ly

18.0 ly

RX (c1)

91 ly

IC 361

147 ly

RV (s2)

TW (v2)

DF (s2)

DH (1)

PK147+4.1

CAMELOPARDALIS

43

Stellar Magnitudes (V)

≤2   3   4   5   6   7   8   9   10   11

Variable-Star Amplitudes and Types

<0.1 mag   0.1 – 1.0   ≥1.0 mag

(e) Eclipsing
(c) Cepheid
(m) Mira
... etc.

Fast-Moving Stars

Proper motion in 1000 years

Double-Star Separations

0.3"   3"   30"

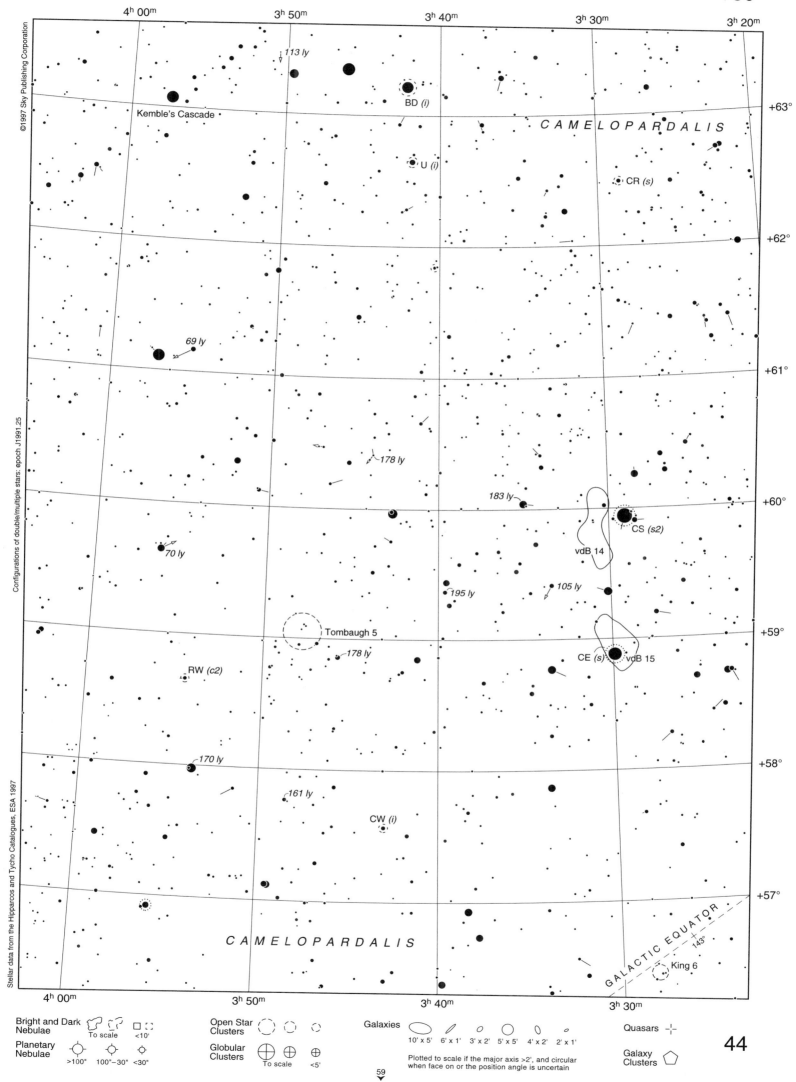

Kemble's Cascade

CAMELOPARDALIS

BD (i)

U (i)

CR (s)

113 ly

69 ly

178 ly

183 ly

105 ly

CS (s2)

vdB 14

70 ly

195 ly

Tombaugh 5

178 ly

RW (c2)

CE (s)   vdB 15

170 ly

161 ly

CW (i)

CAMELOPARDALIS

GALACTIC EQUATOR

143°

King 6

Bright and Dark Nebulae			Open Star Clusters			Galaxies						Quasars
To scale		<10'				10' x 5'	6' x 1'	3' x 2'	5' x 5'	4' x 2'	2' x 1'	
Planetary Nebulae			Globular Clusters									Galaxy Clusters
>100"	100"–30"	<30"	To scale		<5'	Plotted to scale if the major axis >2', and circular when face on or the position angle is uncertain						

59

44

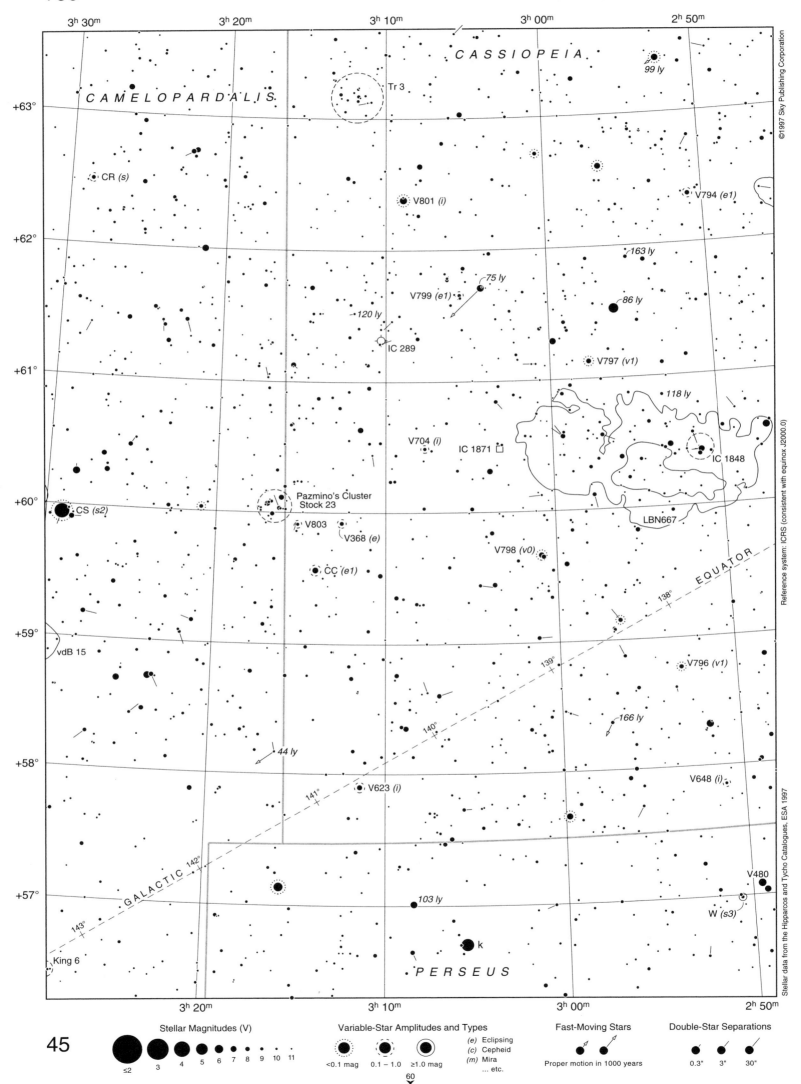

©1997 Sky Publishing Corporation

Reference system: ICRS (consistent with equinox J2000.0)

Stellar data from the Hipparcos and Tycho Catalogues, ESA 1997

45

Stellar Magnitudes (V)

≤2   3   4   5   6   7   8 9 10 11

Variable-Star Amplitudes and Types

<0.1 mag   0.1 – 1.0   ≥1.0 mag

(e) Eclipsing
(c) Cepheid
(m) Mira
... etc.

Fast-Moving Stars

Proper motion in 1000 years

Double-Star Separations

0.3"   3"   30"

60

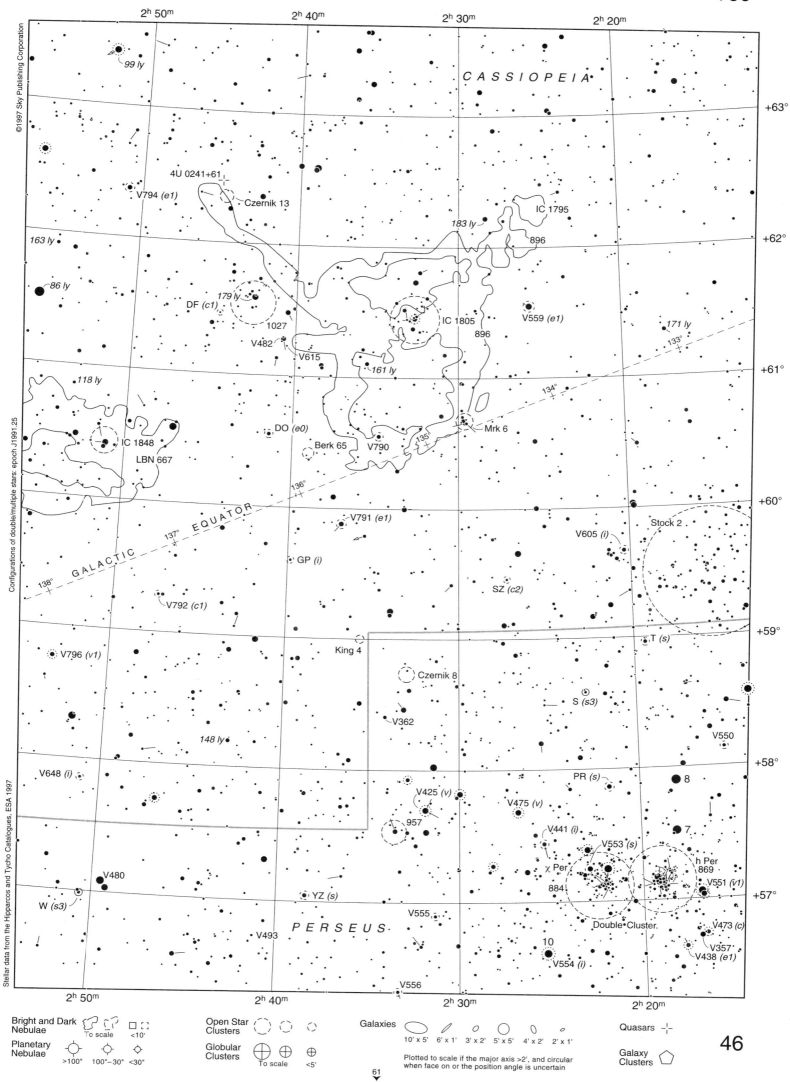

CASSIOPEIA

+63°

+62°

+61°

+60°

+59°

+58°

+57°

©1997 Sky Publishing Corporation

Configurations of double/multiple stars: epoch J1991.25

Stellar data from the Hipparcos and Tycho Catalogues, ESA 1997

2ʰ 50ᵐ
2ʰ 40ᵐ
2ʰ 30ᵐ
2ʰ 20ᵐ

99 ly

4U 0241+61
V794 (e1)
Czernik 13

IC 1795
896

183 ly

163 ly

86 ly

179 ly
DF (c1)
1027
V482
V615

IC 1805
896

V559 (e1)

171 ly
133°

118 ly

161 ly

134°

IC 1848
LBN 667

DO (e0)
Berk 65
V790

135°
Mrk 6

136°

V791 (e1)

GALACTIC   EQUATOR
137°

GP (i)

Stock 2

V605 (i)

138°

V792 (c1)

SZ (c2)

King 4

T (s)

V796 (v1)

Czernik 8

S (s3)

148 ly

V362

V550

V648 (i)

PR (s)

8

V425 (v)

V475 (v)

957

V441 (i)

7

V553 (s)

h Per
869

V480

χ Per

884

V551 (v1)

W (s3)

YZ (s)

V555

Double Cluster.

V473 (c)

V493

PERSEUS

10

V357
V438 (e1)

V554 (i)

V556

Bright and Dark Nebulae ⌇ ⌇ ◻ To scale <10'
Planetary Nebulae ✳ ✛ ◇ >100" 100"–30" <30"
Open Star Clusters ◌ ◌ ◌
Globular Clusters ⊕ ⊕ ⊕ To scale <5'
Galaxies ⬭ ⬩ ◦ ◯ ⬭ ◦ 10' x 5' 6' x 1' 3' x 2' 5' x 5' 4' x 2' 2' x 1'
Plotted to scale if the major axis >2', and circular when face on or the position angle is uncertain
Quasars ┼
Galaxy Clusters ⬠

46

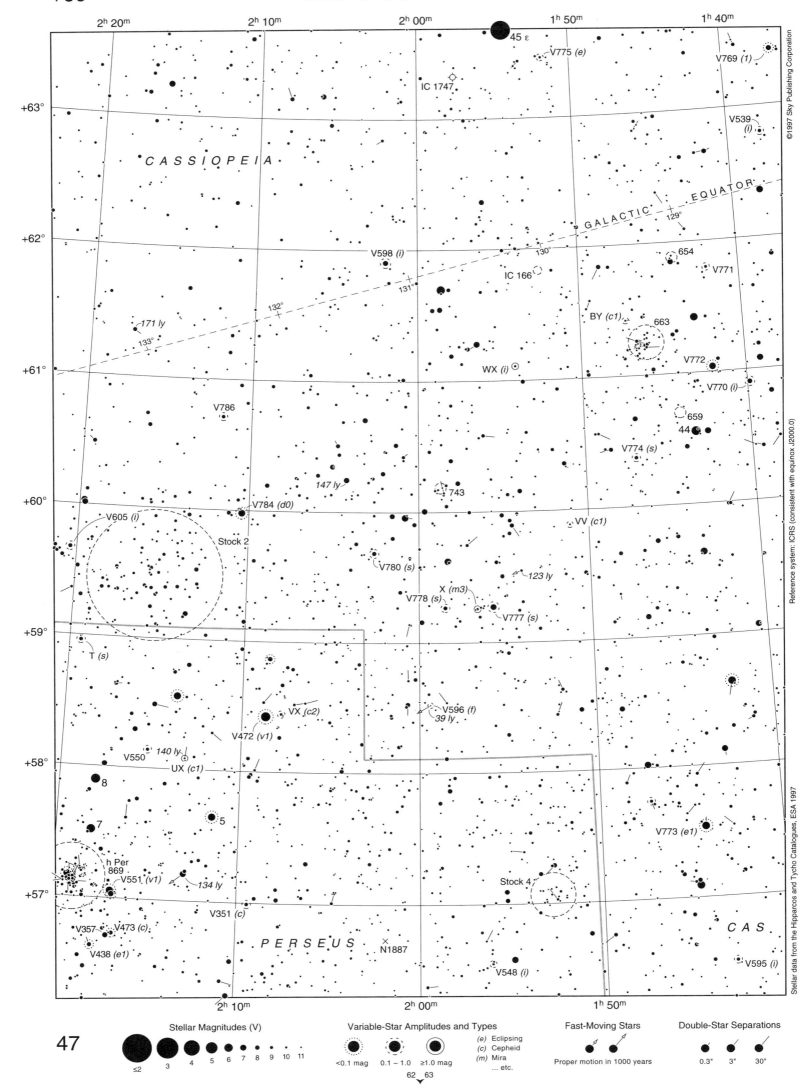

+63°

+62°

+61°

+60°

+59°

+58°

+57°

2ʰ 20ᵐ   2ʰ 10ᵐ   2ʰ 00ᵐ   1ʰ 50ᵐ   1ʰ 40ᵐ

45 ε

V775 (e)

V769 (1)

IC 1747

V539 (i)

CASSIOPEIA

GALACTIC EQUATOR

129°

V598 (i)

130°

654

V771

131°

BY (c1)   663

132°

V772

171 ly

133°

WX (i)

V770 (i)

IC 166

V786

659

44

V774 (s)

147 ly

743

V784 (d0)

VV (c1)

V605 (i)

Stock 2

123 ly

V780 (s)

X (m3)

V778 (s)

V777 (s)

T (s)

V596 (f)
39 ly

VX (c2)

V472 (v1)

V550   140 ly

UX (c1)

8

5

7

V773 (e1)

h Per
869

Stock 4

V551 (v1)

134 ly

V351 (c)

CAS

V357   V473 (c)

PERSEUS

V438 (e1)

N1887

V595 (i)

V548 (i)

Stellar Magnitudes (V)

≤2   3   4   5   6   7   8   9 10 11

Variable-Star Amplitudes and Types

<0.1 mag   0.1 – 1.0   ≥1.0 mag

(e) Eclipsing
(c) Cepheid
(m) Mira
... etc.

Fast-Moving Stars

Proper motion in 1000 years

Double-Star Separations

0.3"   3"   30"

Reference system: ICRS (consistent with equinox J2000.0)

Stellar data from the Hipparcos and Tycho Catalogues, ESA 1997

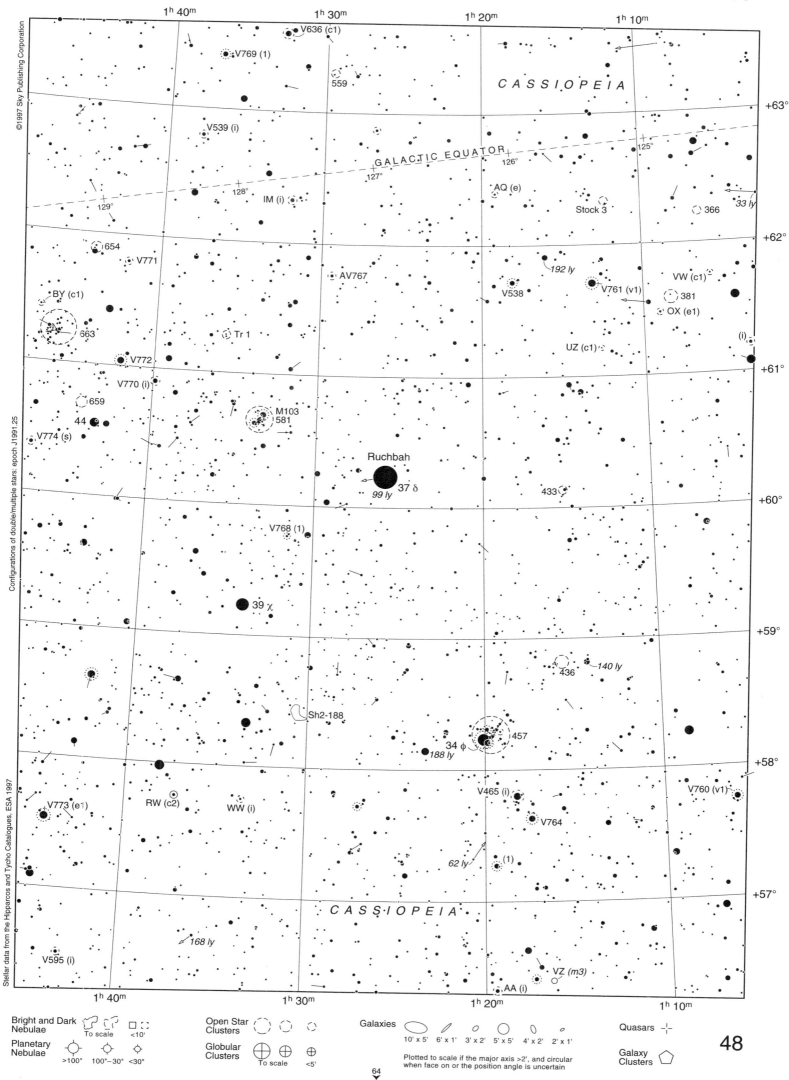

CASSIOPEIA

+63°

GALACTIC EQUATOR

126°
125°
127°
128°
129°

AQ (e)
Stock 3
366
33 ly

+62°

654
V771
AV767
192 ly
VW (c1)
V538
V761 (v1)
381
OX (e1)
BY (c1)
Tr 1
663
UZ (c1)
(i)
V772
V770 (i)
+61°
659
M103
44
581
V774 (s)
Ruchbah
37 δ
433
99 ly
+60°
V768 (1)

39 χ
+59°

436
140 ly
Sh2-188
34 φ
457
188 ly
+58°
V465 (i)
V760 (v1)
V773 (e1)
RW (c2)
WW (i)
V764
62 ly
(1)
+57°
168 ly
CASSIOPEIA
V595 (i)
VZ (m3)
AA (i)

V636 (c1)
V769 (1)
559
V539 (i)
IM (i)

1h 40m
1h 30m
1h 20m
1h 10m

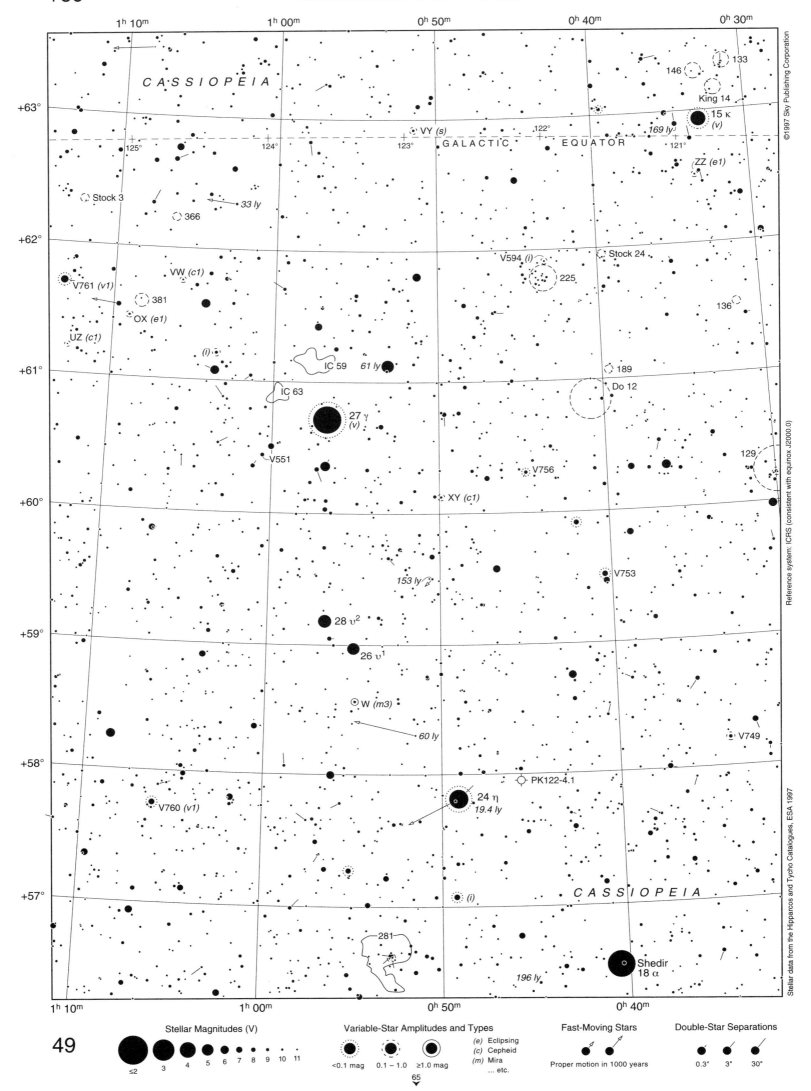

CASSIOPEIA

+63°

VY (s)   GALACTIC   EQUATOR

125°   124°   123°   122°   121°

Stock 3

33 ly

366

+62°

V761 (v1)   VW (c1)   V594 (i)   Stock 24

381   225   136

OX (e1)

UZ (c1)

(i)   IC 59   61 ly   189

+61°   IC 63   Do 12

27 γ   129
(v)

V551   V756

XY (c1)

+60°

V753

153 ly

28 υ²

26 υ¹

W (m3)

60 ly   V749

+58°   PK122-4.1

24 η   V760 (v1)   19.4 ly

+57°   (i)   CASSIOPEIA

281

196 ly   Shedir
18 α

1ʰ 10ᵐ   1ʰ 00ᵐ   0ʰ 50ᵐ   0ʰ 40ᵐ

49

Stellar Magnitudes (V)
≤2   3   4   5   6   7 8 9 10 11

Variable-Star Amplitudes and Types
<0.1 mag   0.1 – 1.0   ≥1.0 mag

(e) Eclipsing
(c) Cepheid
(m) Mira
... etc.

Fast-Moving Stars
Proper motion in 1000 years

Double-Star Separations
0.3"   3"   30"

+60°

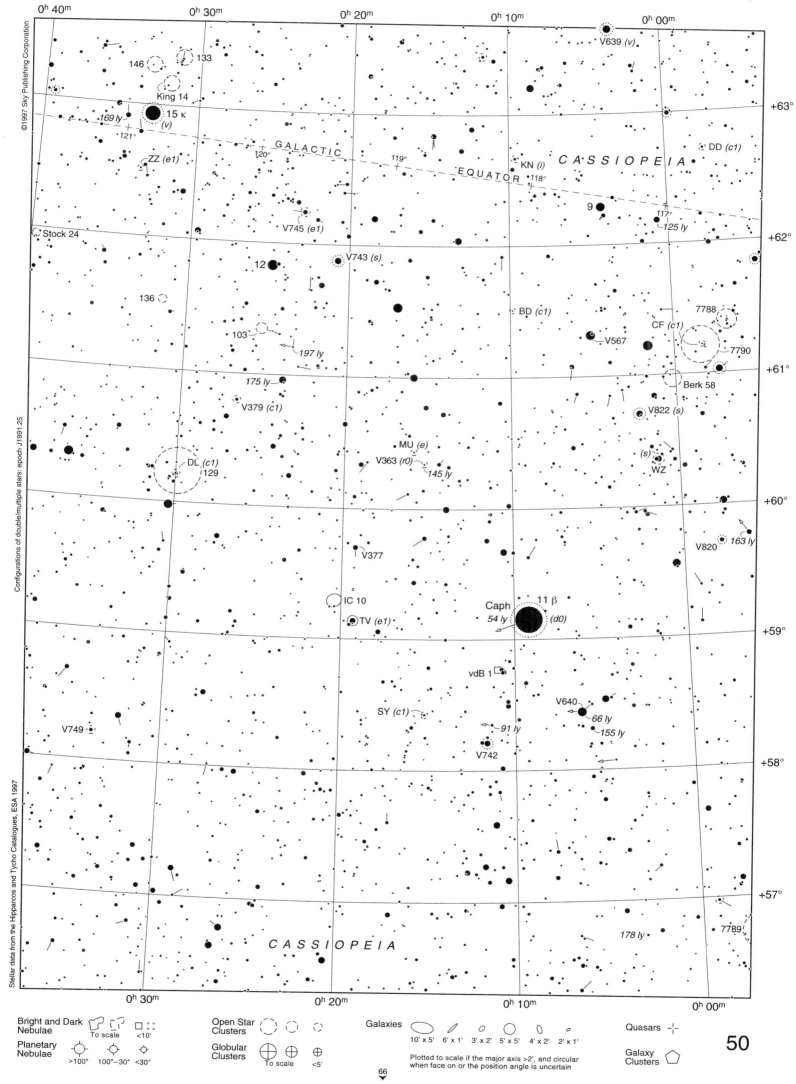

Configurations of double/multiple stars: epoch J1991.25

Stellar data from the Hipparcos and Tycho Catalogues, ESA 1997

0ʰ 40ᵐ   0ʰ 30ᵐ   0ʰ 20ᵐ   0ʰ 10ᵐ   0ʰ 00ᵐ

V639 (v)

146   133

King 14

15 κ
(v)

169 ly

121°

ZZ (e1)

DD (c1)

GALACTIC   120°   119°   KN (i)   CASSIOPEIA

EQUATOR   118°

V745 (e1)   9   117°
125 ly

Stock 24   +62°

V743 (s)

12   BD (c1)   7788

136   CF (c1)   7790

103   V567
197 ly   +61°

175 ly   Berk 58

V379 (c1)   V822 (s)

MU (e)   (s)
V363 (r0)   WZ
145 ly

DL (c1)
129   +60°

V377   V820   163 ly

IC 10   11 β
Caph   (d0)
TV (e1)   54 ly

+59°

vdB 1

V640
SY (c1)   66 ly
91 ly   155 ly

V749   V742   +58°

178 ly   7789   +57°

CASSIOPEIA

0ʰ 30ᵐ   0ʰ 20ᵐ   0ʰ 10ᵐ   0ʰ 00ᵐ

+63°

Bright and Dark Nebulae   Open Star Clusters   Galaxies   Quasars

To scale   <10'   10'×5' 6'×1' 3'×2' 5'×5' 4'×2' 2'×1'

Planetary Nebulae   Globular Clusters   Galaxy Clusters

>100" 100"−30" <30'   To scale <5'   Plotted to scale if the major axis >2', and circular when face on or the position angle is uncertain

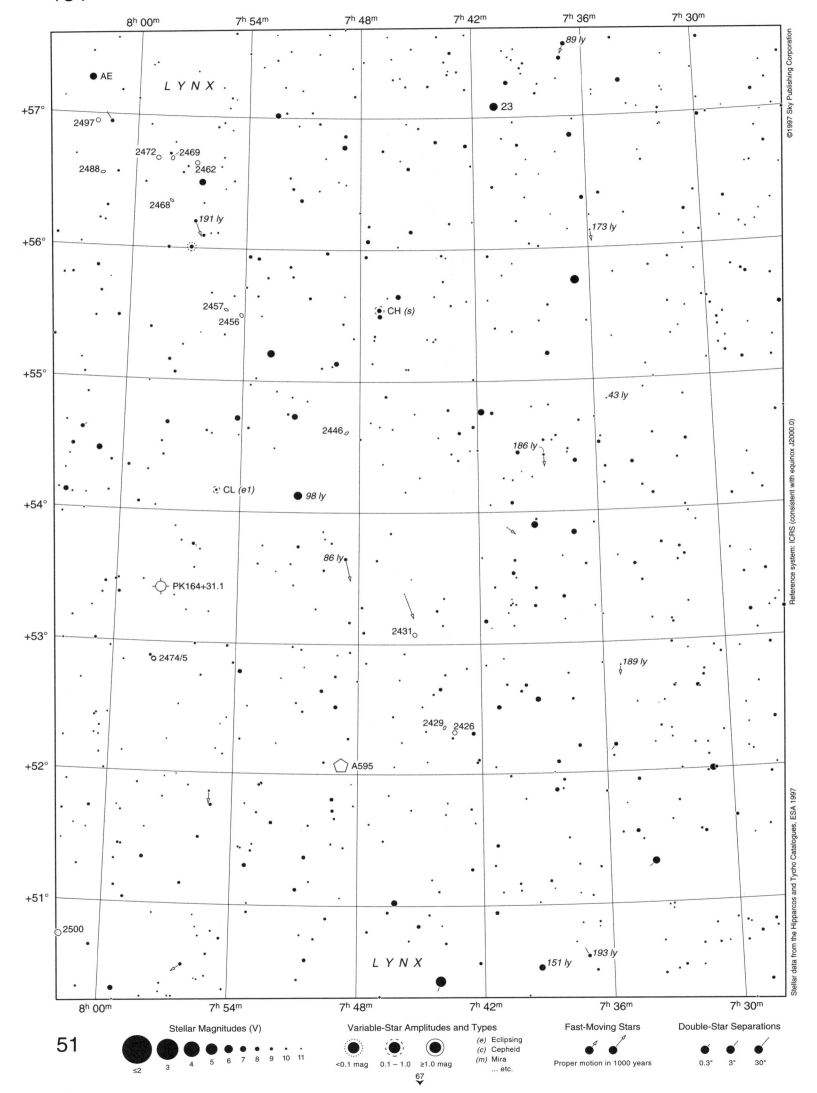

51

Stellar Magnitudes (V)

≤2   3   4   5   6   7   8   9   10   11

Variable-Star Amplitudes and Types

<0.1 mag   0.1 – 1.0   ≥1.0 mag

(e) Eclipsing
(c) Cepheid
(m) Mira
... etc.

Fast-Moving Stars

Proper motion in 1000 years

Double-Star Separations

0.3"   3"   30"

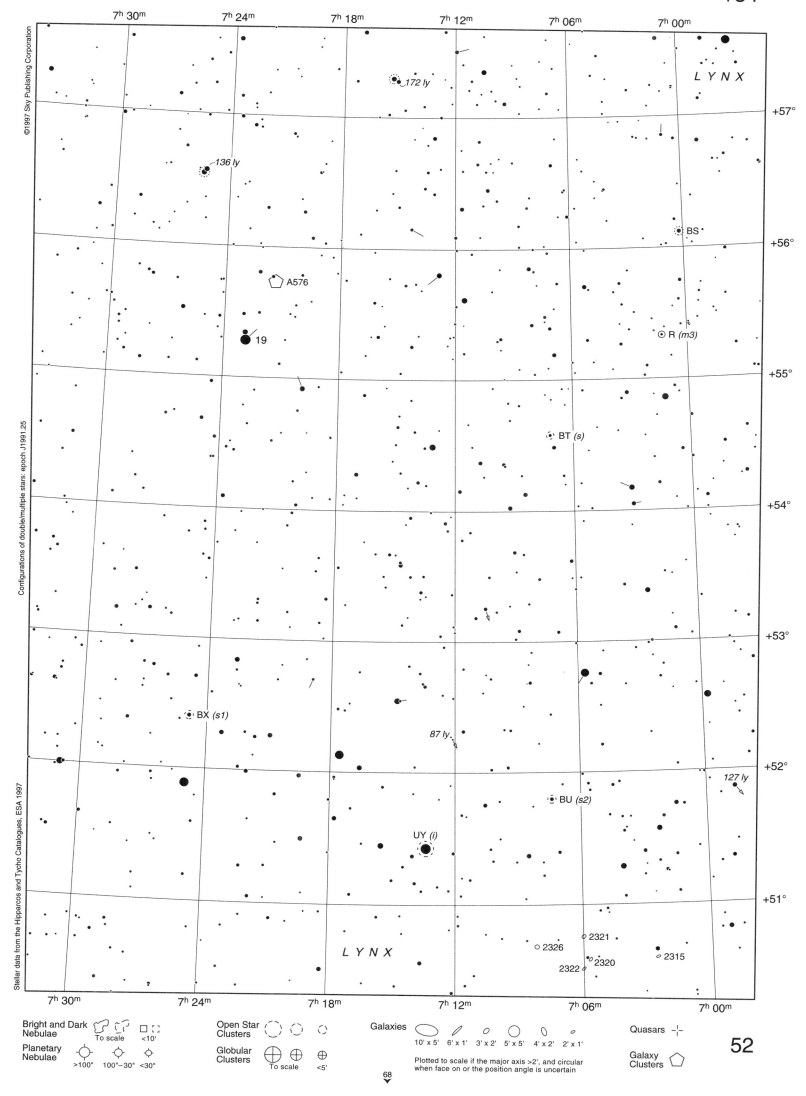

©1997 Sky Publishing Corporation

Configurations of double/multiple stars: epoch J1991.25

Stellar data from the Hipparcos and Tycho Catalogues, ESA 1997

7ʰ 30ᵐ   7ʰ 24ᵐ   7ʰ 18ᵐ   7ʰ 12ᵐ   7ʰ 06ᵐ   7ʰ 00ᵐ

L Y N X

172 ly

+57°

136 ly

BS

+56°

A576

R (m3)

19

+55°

BT (s)

+54°

+53°

BX (s1)

87 ly

+52°

127 ly

BU (s2)

UY (i)

+51°

2321
2326
2320
2322   2315

L Y N X

7ʰ 30ᵐ   7ʰ 24ᵐ   7ʰ 18ᵐ   7ʰ 12ᵐ   7ʰ 06ᵐ   7ʰ 00ᵐ

Bright and Dark Nebulae	Open Star Clusters	Galaxies	Quasars
To scale <10'		10' x 5' 6' x 1' 3' x 2' 5' x 5' 4' x 2' 2' x 1'	
Planetary Nebulae	Globular Clusters		Galaxy Clusters
>100" 100"−30" <30"	To scale <5'	Plotted to scale if the major axis >2', and circular when face on or the position angle is uncertain	

52

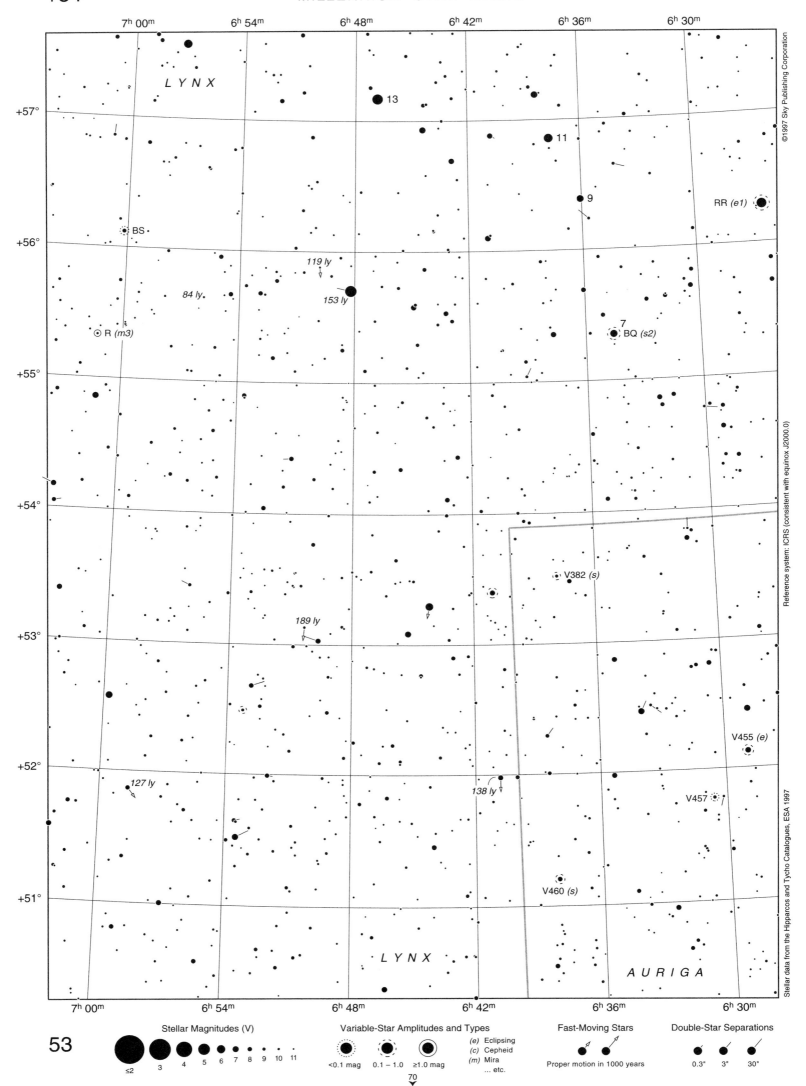

©1997 Sky Publishing Corporation

Reference system: ICRS (consistent with equinox J2000.0)

Stellar data from the Hipparcos and Tycho Catalogues, ESA 1997

LYNX

13

11

9

RR (e1)

BS

119 ly

84 ly

153 ly

R (m3)

7
BQ (s2)

189 ly

V382 (s)

127 ly

V455 (e)

138 ly

V457

V460 (s)

LYNX

AURIGA

Stellar Magnitudes (V)

≤2 3 4 5 6 7 8 9 10 11

Variable-Star Amplitudes and Types

<0.1 mag   0.1 – 1.0   ≥1.0 mag

(e) Eclipsing
(c) Cepheid
(m) Mira
... etc.

Fast-Moving Stars

Proper motion in 1000 years

Double-Star Separations

0.3"   3"   30"

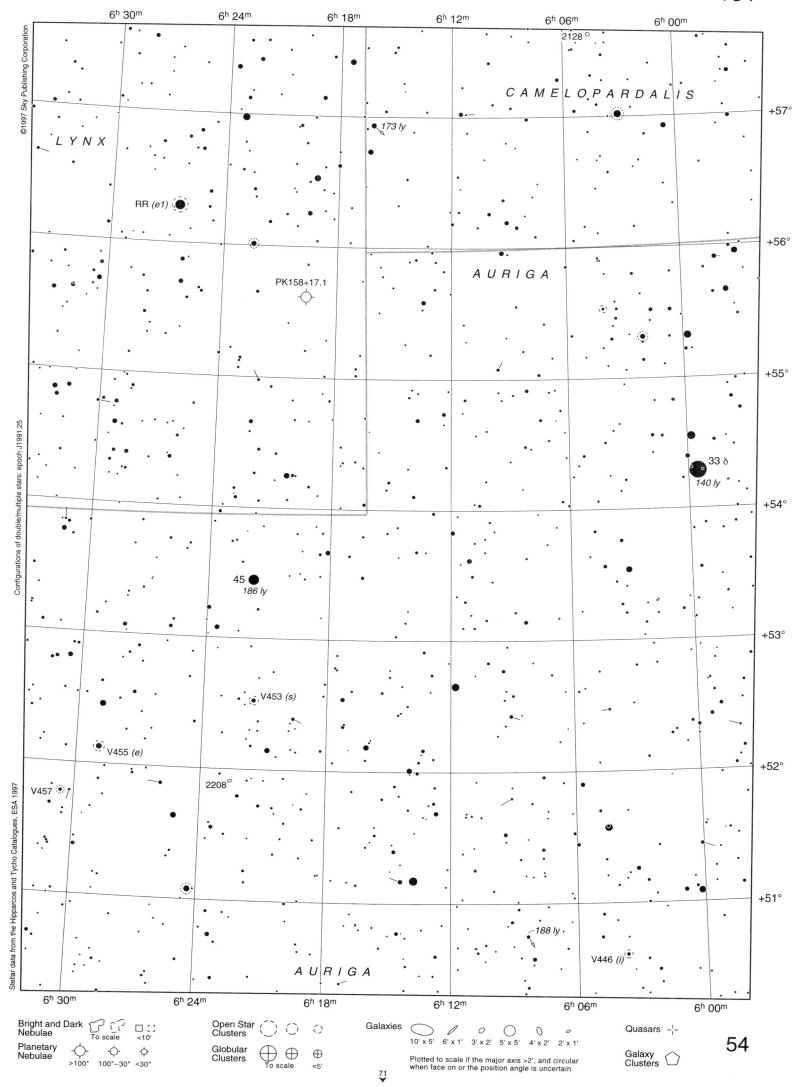

6h 30m 6h 24m 6h 18m 6h 12m 6h 06m 6h 00m

2128 °

C A M E L O P A R D A L I S

+57°

L Y N X

173 ly

RR (e1)

+56°

A U R I G A

PK158+17.1

+55°

33 δ
140 ly

+54°

45
186 ly

+53°

V453 (s)

+52°

V455 (e)

V457

2208 °

+51°

188 ly

V446 (i)

A U R I G A

6h 30m 6h 24m 6h 18m 6h 12m 6h 06m

Bright and Dark Nebulae
To scale   <10'

Planetary Nebulae
>100" 100"–30" <30"

Open Star Clusters

Globular Clusters
To scale   <5'

Galaxies
10' x 5' 6' x 1' 3' x 2' 5' x 5' 4' x 2' 2' x 1'

Plotted to scale if the major axis >2', and circular when face on or the position angle is uncertain

Quasars

Galaxy Clusters

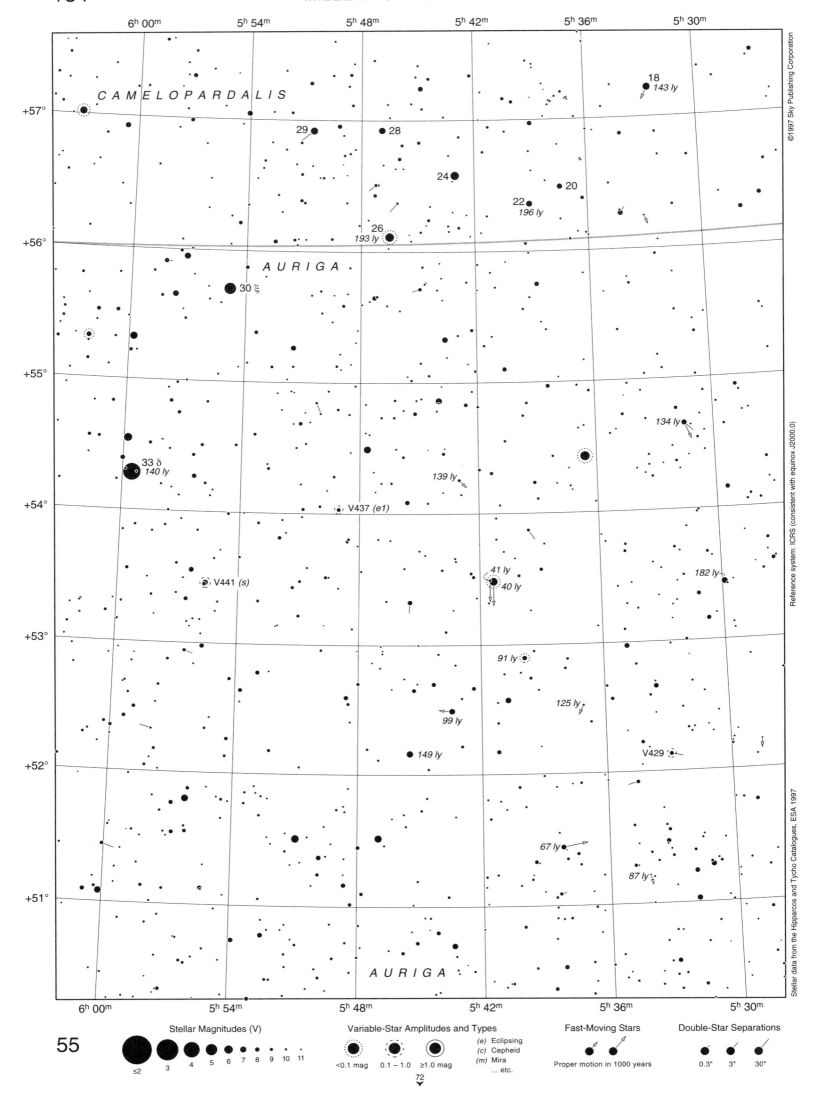

MILLENNIUM STAR ATLAS

CAMELOPARDALIS

AURIGA

18
143 ly

29   28

24

22
196 ly

20

26
193 ly

30 ξ

33 δ
140 ly

134 ly

139 ly

182 ly

V437 (e1)

V441 (s)

41 ly
40 ly

91 ly

125 ly

99 ly

149 ly

V429

67 ly

87 ly

AURIGA

Reference system: ICRS (consistent with equinox J2000.0)

Stellar data from the Hipparcos and Tycho Catalogues, ESA 1997

Stellar Magnitudes (V)

≤2   3   4   5   6   7   8 9 10 11

Variable-Star Amplitudes and Types

<0.1 mag   0.1 – 1.0   ≥1.0 mag

(e) Eclipsing
(c) Cepheid
(m) Mira
... etc.

Fast-Moving Stars

Proper motion in 1000 years

Double-Star Separations

0.3"   3"   30"

72

MILLENNIUM STAR ATLAS

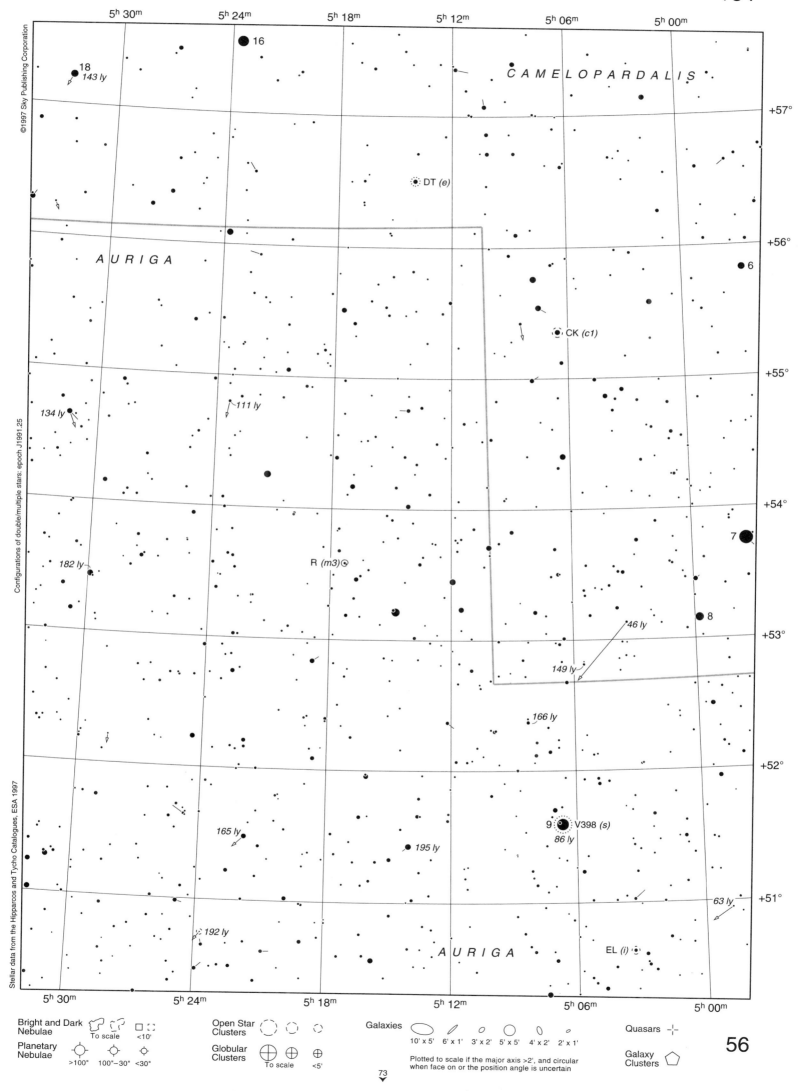

©1997 Sky Publishing Corporation

Configurations of double/multiple stars: epoch J1991.25

Stellar data from the Hipparcos and Tycho Catalogues, ESA 1997

CAMELOPARDALIS

AURIGA

DT (e)

CK (c1)

R (m3)

V398 (s)

EL (i)

AURIGA

18
143 ly

16

6

7

8

46 ly

149 ly

166 ly

9

86 ly

63 ly

134 ly

111 ly

182 ly

165 ly

195 ly

192 ly

5h 30m   5h 24m   5h 18m   5h 12m   5h 06m   5h 00m

+57°

+56°

+55°

+54°

+53°

+52°

+51°

Bright and Dark Nebulae
To scale   <10'

Planetary Nebulae
>100"   100"–30"   <30"

Open Star Clusters

Globular Clusters
To scale   <5'

Galaxies
10' x 5'   6' x 1'   3' x 2'   5' x 5'   4' x 2'   2' x 1'

Plotted to scale if the major axis >2', and circular when face on or the position angle is uncertain

Quasars

Galaxy Clusters

56

73

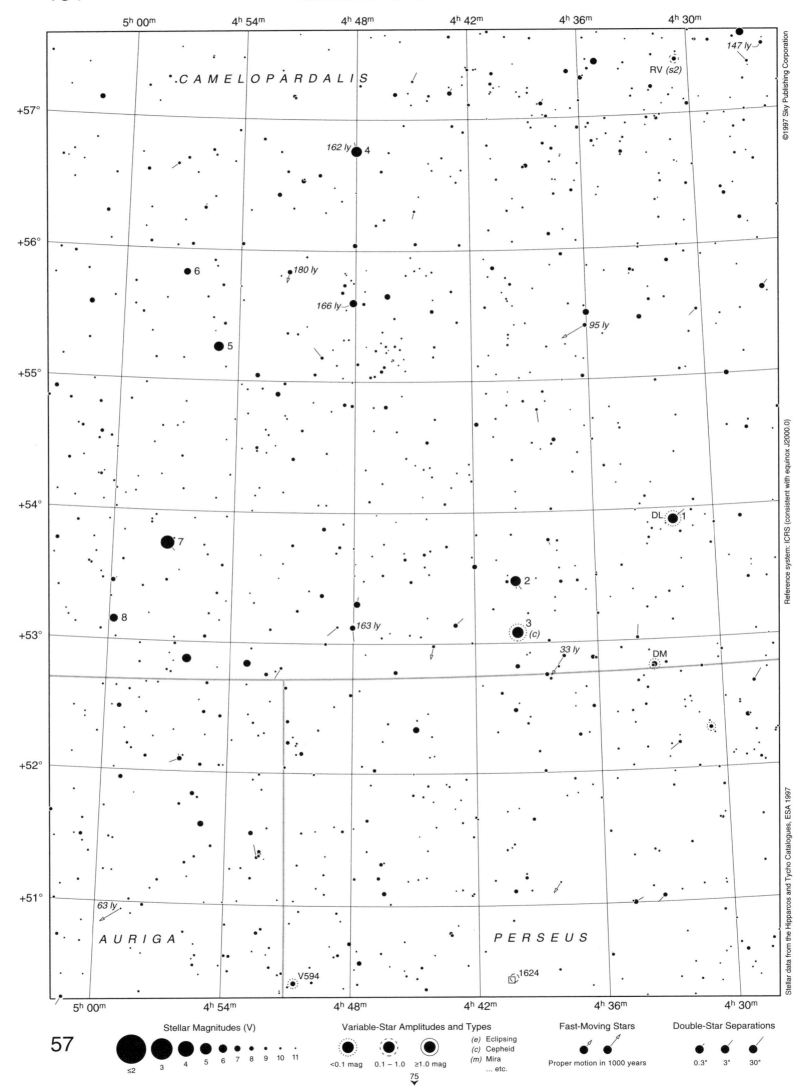

©1997 Sky Publishing Corporation

Reference system: ICRS (consistent with equinox J2000.0)

Stellar data from the Hipparcos and Tycho Catalogues, ESA 1997

CAMELOPARDALIS

AURIGA

PERSEUS

Stellar Magnitudes (V)

≤2 3 4 5 6 7 8 9 10 11

Variable-Star Amplitudes and Types

<0.1 mag   0.1 – 1.0   ≥1.0 mag

(e) Eclipsing
(c) Cepheid
(m) Mira
... etc.

Fast-Moving Stars

Proper motion in 1000 years

Double-Star Separations

0.3"   3"   30"

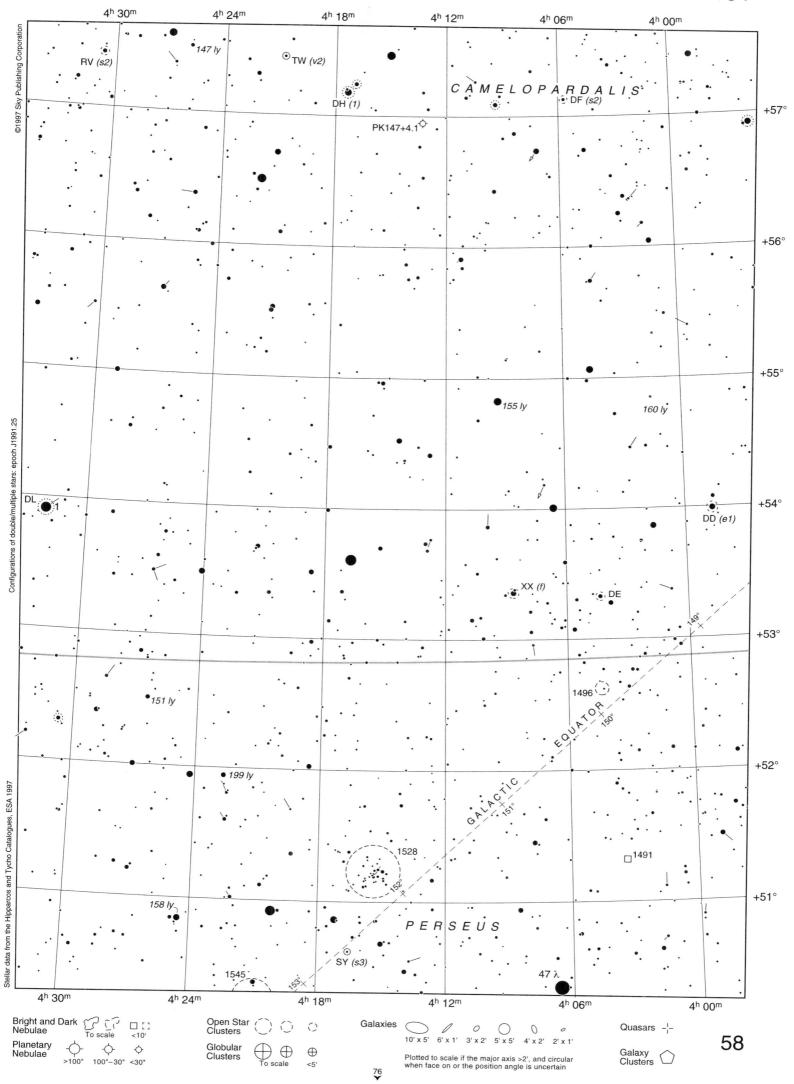

Configurations of double/multiple stars: epoch J1991.25

Stellar data from the Hipparcos and Tycho Catalogues, ESA 1997

RV (s2)
147 ly
TW (v2)
DH (1)
CAMELOPARDALIS
DF (s2)
PK147+4.1
+57°
+56°
155 ly
160 ly
+55°
DL 1
+54°
DD (e1)
XX (f)
DE
149°
+53°
1496
150°
EQUATOR
151 ly
GALACTIC
151°
199 ly
1491
+52°
1528
152°
158 ly
+51°
PERSEUS
1545
153°
SY (s3)
47 λ

4h 30m   4h 24m   4h 18m   4h 12m   4h 06m   4h 00m

Bright and Dark Nebulae
To scale   <10'

Planetary Nebulae
>100"   100"–30"   <30"

Open Star Clusters

Globular Clusters
To scale   <5'

Galaxies
10' x 5'   6' x 1'   3' x 2'   5' x 5'   4' x 2'   2' x 1'
Plotted to scale if the major axis >2', and circular when face on or the position angle is uncertain

Quasars

Galaxy Clusters

58

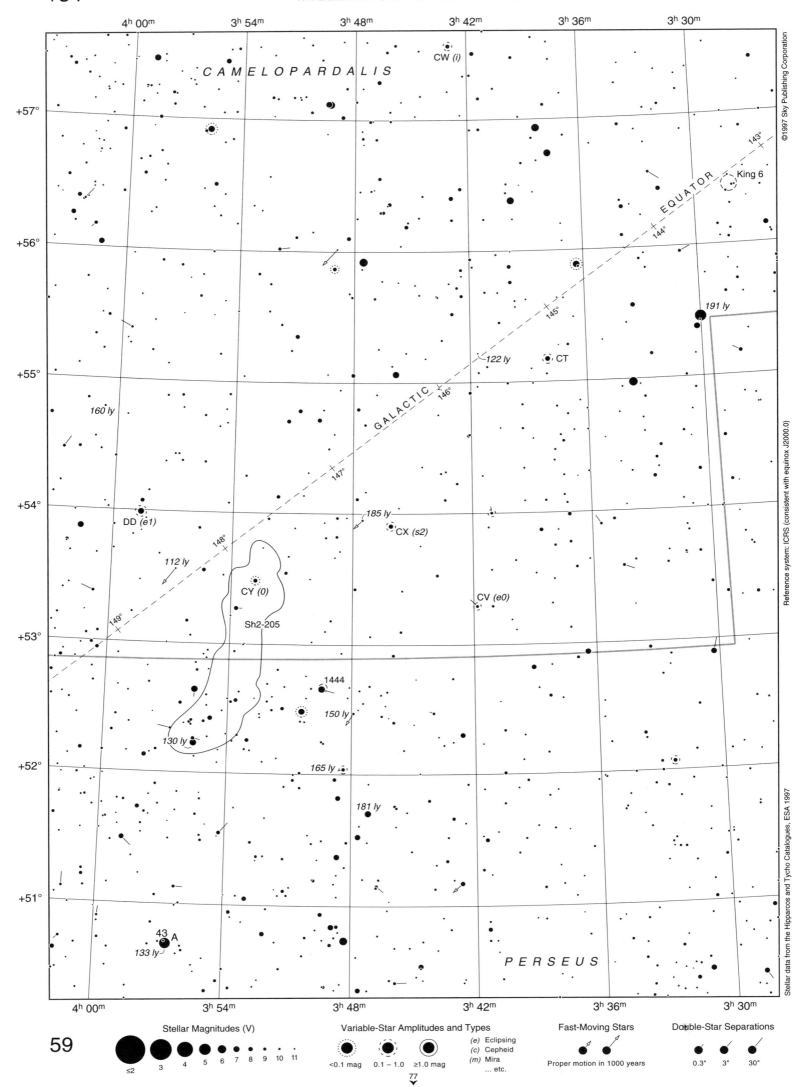

44

CAMELOPARDALIS

CW (i)

King 6

EQUATOR

191 ly

143°

144°

145°

122 ly

CT

146°

GALACTIC

160 ly

147°

185 ly

DD (e1)

148°

CX (s2)

112 ly

CY (0)

CV (e0)

149°

Sh2-205

1444

150 ly

130 ly

165 ly

181 ly

43 A

133 ly

PERSEUS

©1997 Sky Publishing Corporation

Reference system: ICRS (consistent with equinox J2000.0)

Stellar data from the Hipparcos and Tycho Catalogues, ESA 1997

59

Stellar Magnitudes (V)	Variable-Star Amplitudes and Types	Fast-Moving Stars	Double-Star Separations

≤2 3 4 5 6 7 8 9 10 11

<0.1 mag   0.1 – 1.0   ≥1.0 mag

(e) Eclipsing
(c) Cepheid
(m) Mira
... etc.

Proper motion in 1000 years

0.3"   3"   30"

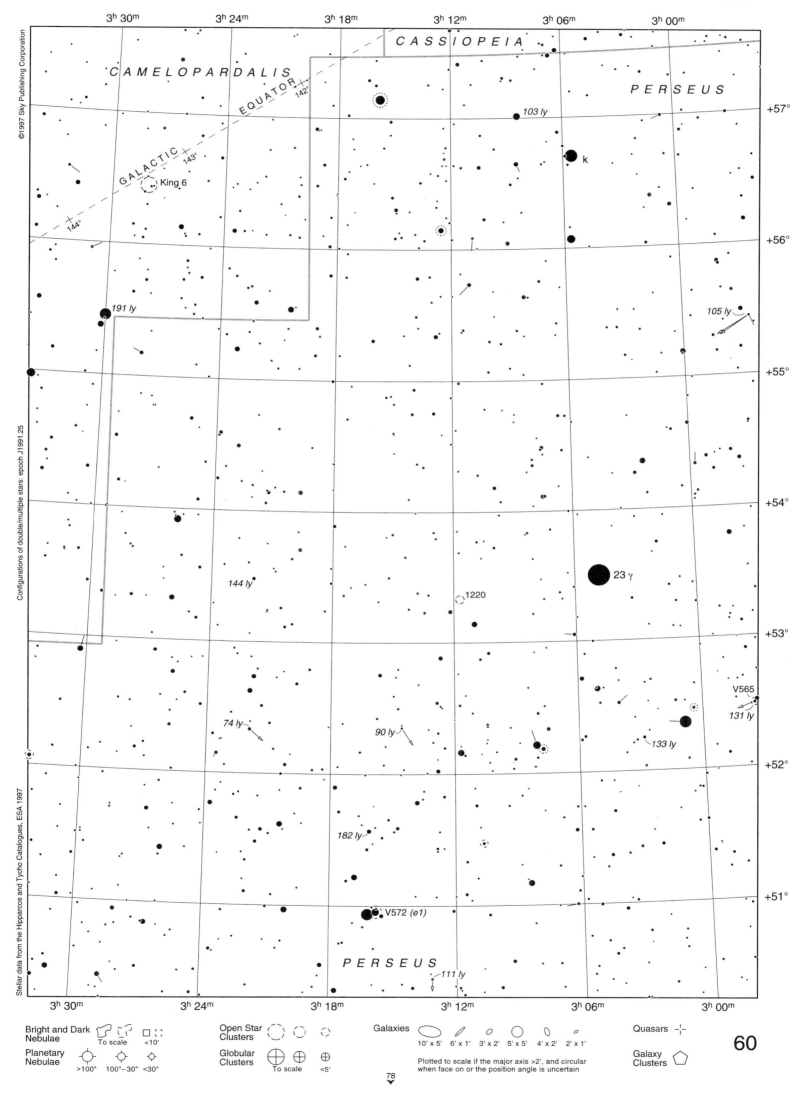

CASSIOPEIA

CAMELOPARDALIS

PERSEUS

GALACTIC EQUATOR

142°

143°

King 6

144°

103 ly

k

191 ly

105 ly

144 ly

1220

23 γ

74 ly

90 ly

V565

131 ly

133 ly

182 ly

V572 (e1)

PERSEUS

111 ly

3h 30m   3h 24m   3h 18m   3h 12m   3h 06m   3h 00m

+57°
+56°
+55°
+54°
+53°
+52°
+51°

Bright and Dark Nebulae   Open Star Clusters   Galaxies   Quasars
To scale   <10'   Galaxy Clusters
Planetary Nebulae   Globular Clusters   10' x 5' 6' x 1' 3' x 2' 5' x 5' 4' x 2' 2' x 1'
>100" 100"–30" <30"   To scale   <5'   Plotted to scale if the major axis >2', and circular
                                                             when face on or the position angle is uncertain

60

78

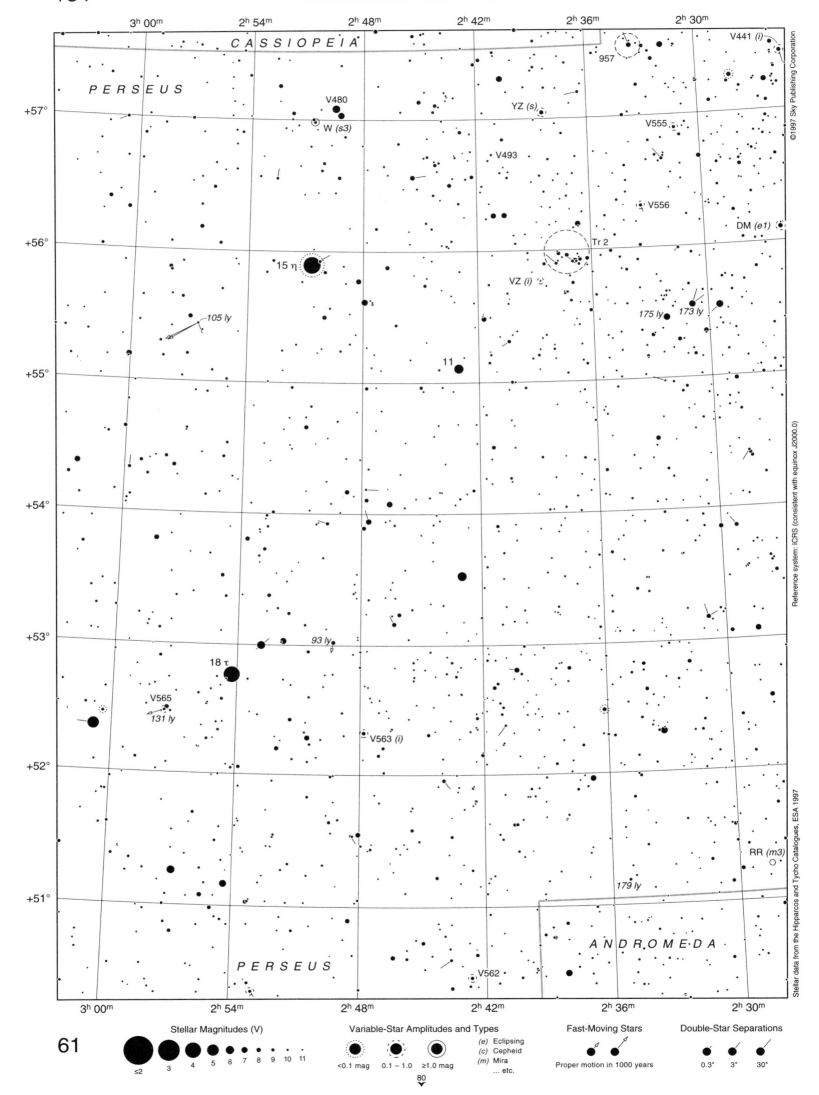

©1997 Sky Publishing Corporation

Reference system: ICRS (consistent with equinox J2000.0)

Stellar data from the Hipparcos and Tycho Catalogues, ESA 1997

CASSIOPEIA

PERSEUS

V480

W (s3)

YZ (s)

V493

957

V441 (i)

V555

V556

DM (e1)

Tr 2

VZ (i)

15 η

105 ly

175 ly   173 ly

11

18 τ

93 ly

V565

131 ly

V563 (i)

RR (m3)

179 ly

ANDROMEDA

PERSEUS

V562

61

Stellar Magnitudes (V)

≤2   3   4   5   6   7   8   9   10   11

Variable-Star Amplitudes and Types

<0.1 mag   0.1 – 1.0   ≥1.0 mag

(e) Eclipsing
(c) Cepheid
(m) Mira
... etc.

80

Fast-Moving Stars

Proper motion in 1000 years

Double-Star Separations

0.3"   3"   30"

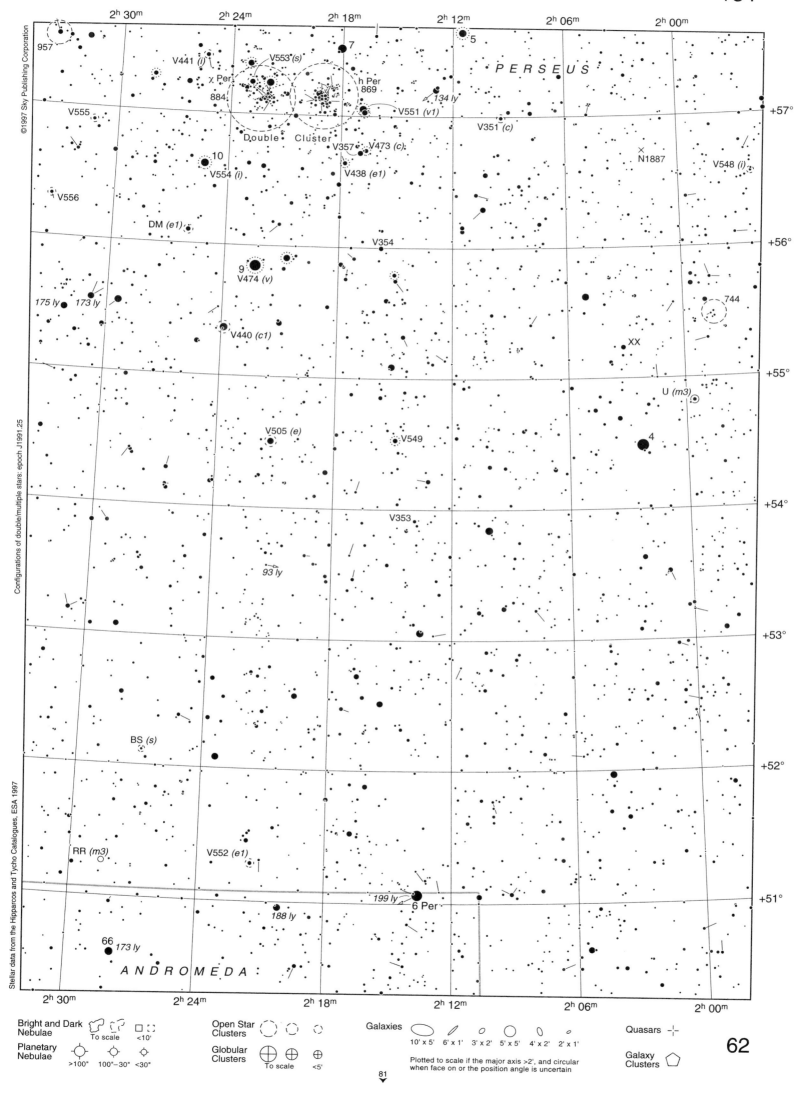

PERSEUS

957

V441 (i)
V553 (s)
χ Per
884
Double Cluster
h Per
869
V555
V551 (v1)
134 ly
V351 (c)
10
N1887
V548 (i)
V554 (i)
V357 V473 (c)
V556
V438 (e1)
DM (e1)
V354
9
V474 (v)
744
175 ly 173 ly
XX
V440 (c1)
U (m3)
4
V505 (e)
V549
V353
93 ly
BS (s)
RR (m3)
V552 (e1)
199 ly
6 Per
188 ly
66 173 ly
ANDROMEDA

2h 30m · 2h 24m · 2h 18m · 2h 12m · 2h 06m · 2h 00m

+57°
+56°
+55°
+54°
+53°
+52°
+51°

7
5

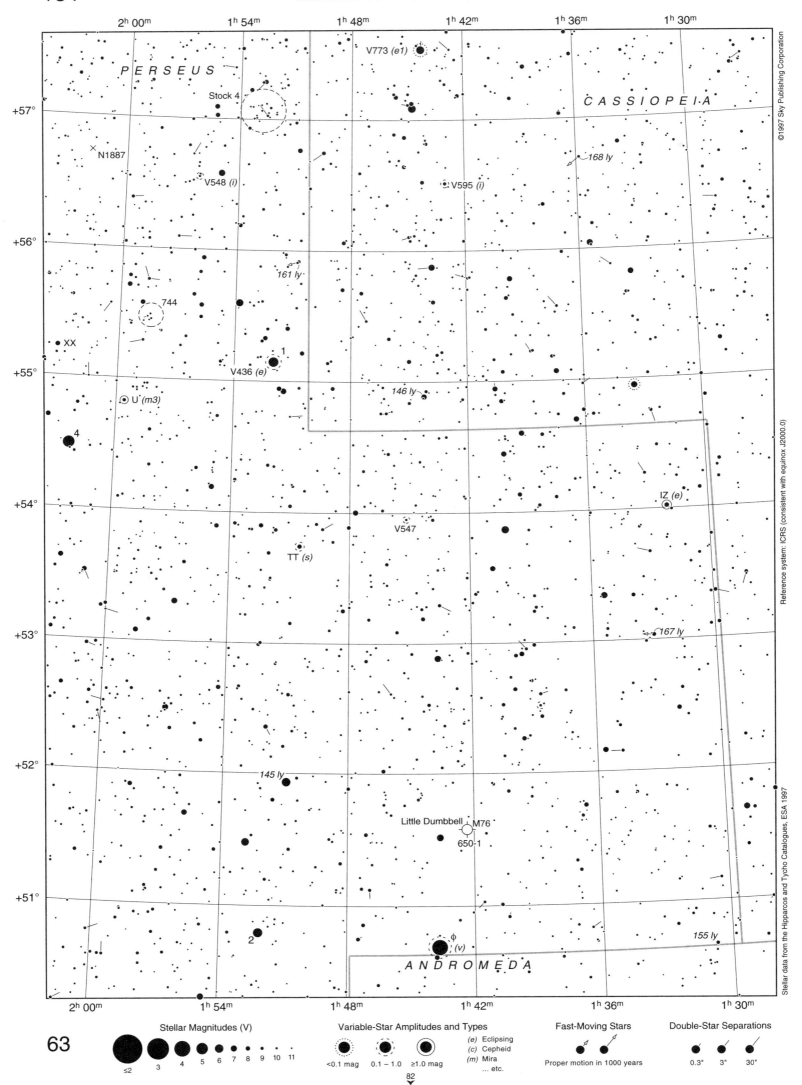

PERSEUS

CASSIOPEIA

ANDROMEDA

Stock 4

× N1887

V548 (i)

V773 (e1)

V595 (i)

168 ly

161 ly

744

XX

1

V436 (e)

146 ly

U (m3)

4

IZ (e)

V547

TT (s)

167 ly

145 ly

Little Dumbbell   M76

650-1

φ
(v)

155 ly

Stellar Magnitudes (V)

≤2   3   4   5   6   7   8   9   10   11

Variable-Star Amplitudes and Types

<0.1 mag   0.1 – 1.0   ≥1.0 mag

(e) Eclipsing
(c) Cepheid
(m) Mira
... etc.

Fast-Moving Stars

Proper motion in 1000 years

Double-Star Separations

0.3"   3"   30"

82

48

+54°

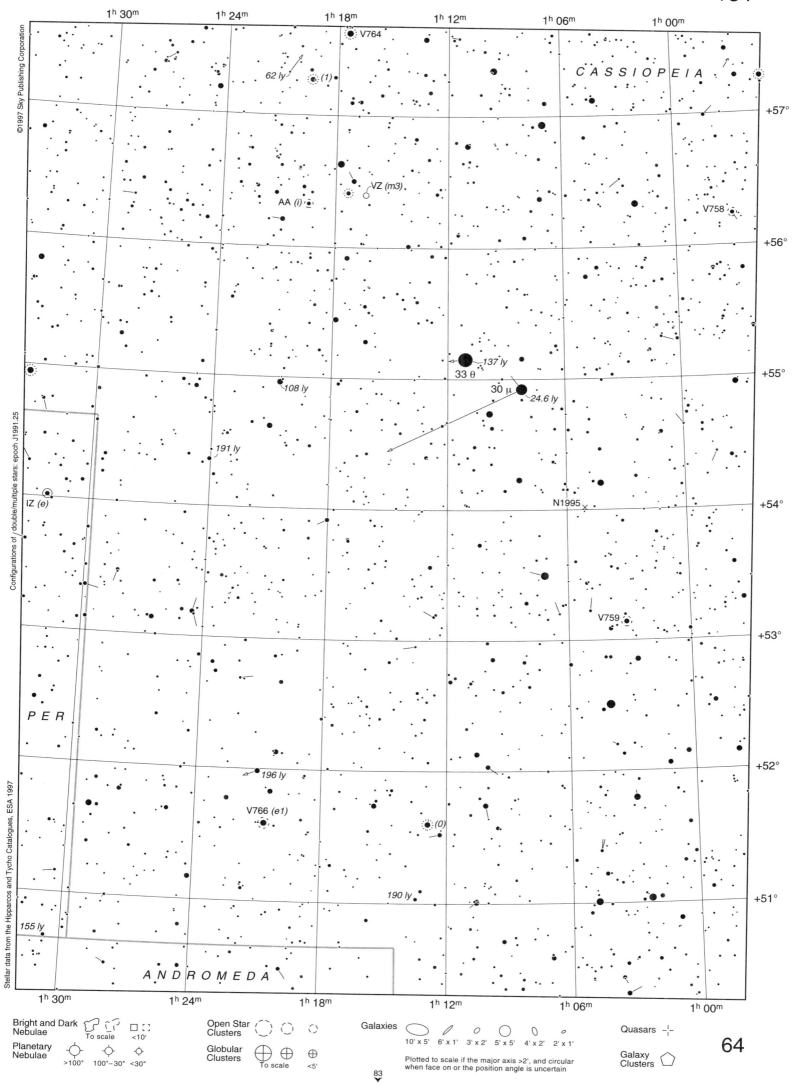

CASSIOPEIA

1ʰ 30ᵐ   1ʰ 24ᵐ   1ʰ 18ᵐ   1ʰ 12ᵐ   1ʰ 06ᵐ   1ʰ 00ᵐ

V764

62 ly   (1)

+57°

VZ (m3)

AA (i)   V758

+56°

33 θ   137 ly

108 ly   30 μ   +55°
24.6 ly

191 ly

N1995   ×   +54°

IZ (e)

V759   +53°

P E R

196 ly   +52°

V766 (e1)

(0)

190 ly   +51°

155 ly

A N D R O M E D A

1ʰ 30ᵐ   1ʰ 24ᵐ   1ʰ 18ᵐ   1ʰ 12ᵐ   1ʰ 06ᵐ   1ʰ 00ᵐ

Configurations of / double/multiple stars: epoch J1991.25

Stellar data from the Hipparcos and Tycho Catalogues, ESA 1997

Bright and Dark Nebulae
To scale   <10'

Planetary Nebulae
>100"   100"–30"   <30"

Open Star Clusters

Globular Clusters
To scale   <5'

Galaxies
10' x 5'   6' x 1'   3' x 2'   5' x 5'   4' x 2'   2' x 1'

Plotted to scale if the major axis >2', and circular when face on or the position angle is uncertain

Quasars

Galaxy Clusters

64

83

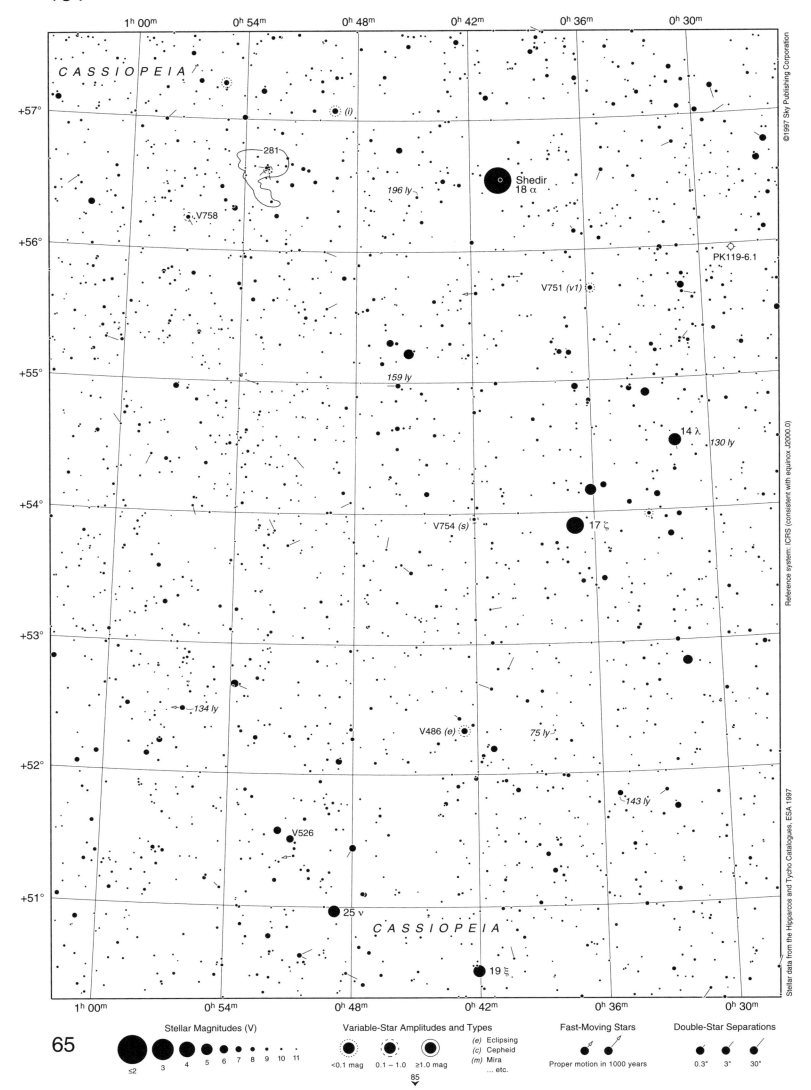

©1997 Sky Publishing Corporation

Reference system: ICRS (consistent with equinox J2000.0)

Stellar data from the Hipparcos and Tycho Catalogues, ESA 1997

CASSIOPEIA

(i)

281

V758

196 ly

Shedir
18 α

PK119-6.1

V751 (v1)

159 ly

14 λ   130 ly

17 ζ

V754 (s)

134 ly

V486 (e)   75 ly

143 ly

V526

25 ν

CASSIOPEIA

19 ξ

Stellar Magnitudes (V)

≤2   3   4   5   6   7 8 9 10 11

Variable-Star Amplitudes and Types

<0.1 mag   0.1 – 1.0   ≥1.0 mag

(e) Eclipsing
(c) Cepheid
(m) Mira
... etc.

Fast-Moving Stars

Proper motion in 1000 years

Double-Star Separations

0.3"   3"   30"

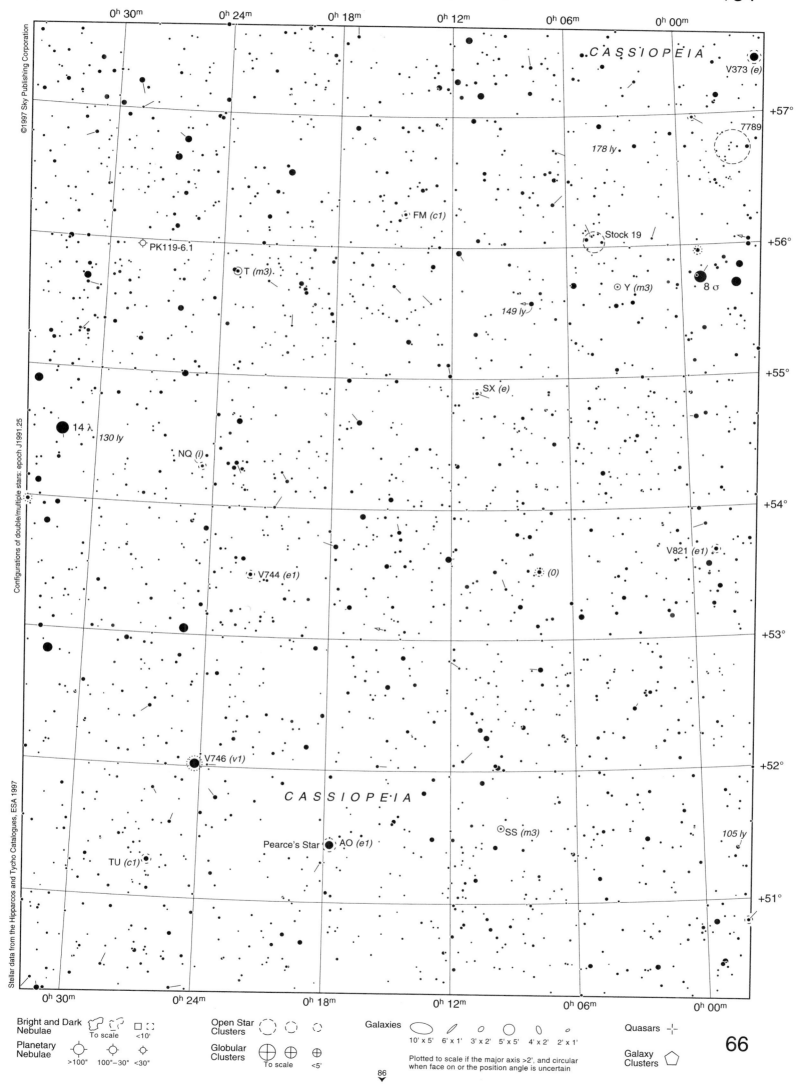

Configurations of double/multiple stars: epoch J1991.25

Stellar data from the Hipparcos and Tycho Catalogues, ESA 1997

CASSIOPEIA

V373 (e)

7789

178 ly

FM (c1)

Stock 19

PK119-6.1

T (m3)

Y (m3)

8 σ

149 ly

SX (e)

14 λ   130 ly

NQ (i)

V821 (e1)

V744 (e1)

(0)

V746 (v1)

CASSIOPEIA

SS (m3)

105 ly

Pearce's Star   AO (e1)

TU (c1)

+57°
+56°
+55°
+54°
+53°
+52°
+51°

0ʰ 30ᵐ   0ʰ 24ᵐ   0ʰ 18ᵐ   0ʰ 12ᵐ   0ʰ 06ᵐ   0ʰ 00ᵐ

86
▾

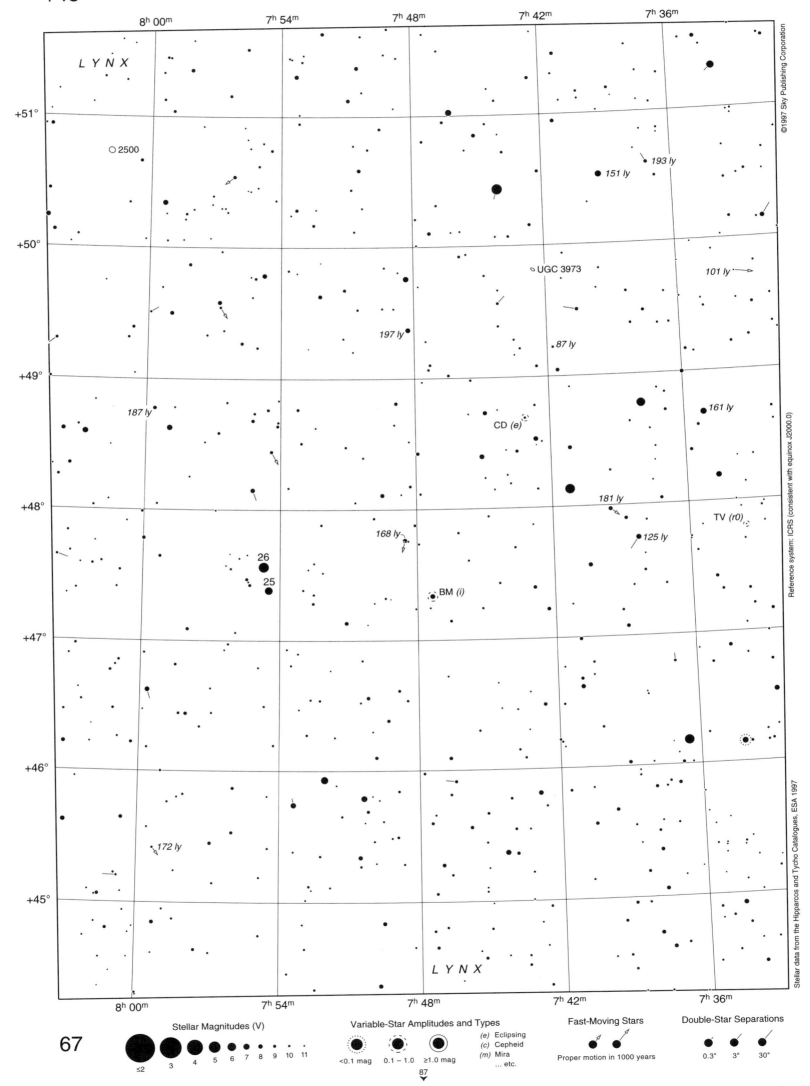

+48°

LYNX

+51°

○ 2500

193 ly
151 ly

+50°

UGC 3973
101 ly

197 ly
87 ly

+49°

187 ly

161 ly

CD (e)

181 ly
TV (r0)

125 ly

168 ly

+48°

26
25

BM (i)

+47°

+46°

172 ly

+45°

LYNX

8h 00m   7h 54m   7h 48m   7h 42m   7h 36m

67

Stellar Magnitudes (V)
≤2 3 4 5 6 7 8 9 10 11

Variable-Star Amplitudes and Types
<0.1 mag   0.1 – 1.0   ≥1.0 mag
(e) Eclipsing
(c) Cepheid
(m) Mira
... etc.

Fast-Moving Stars
Proper motion in 1000 years

Double-Star Separations
0.3"   3"   30"

87

Reference system: ICRS (consistent with equinox J2000.0)

Stellar data from the Hipparcos and Tycho Catalogues, ESA 1997

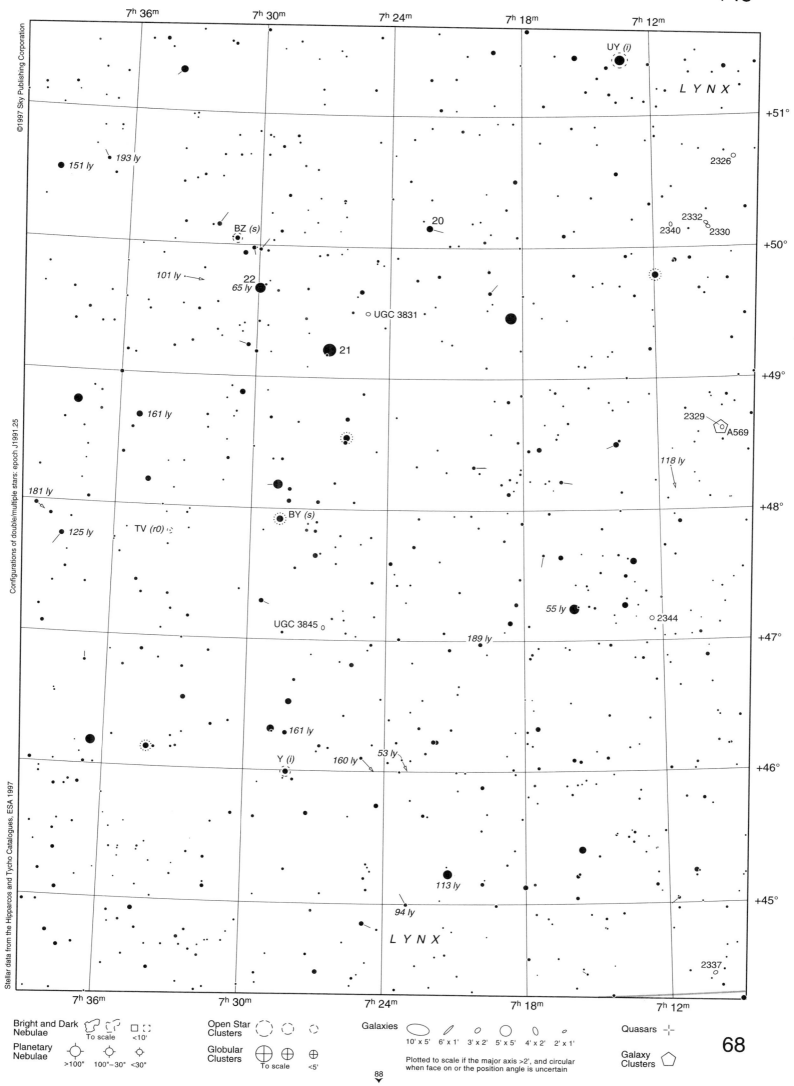

L Y N X

UY (i)

2326

2332
2340 2330

20

BZ (s)

101 ly
22
65 ly

UGC 3831

21

2329
A569

118 ly

161 ly

181 ly

BY (s)

125 ly

TV (r0)

55 ly
2344

UGC 3845

189 ly

161 ly

Y (i)
160 ly   53 ly

113 ly

94 ly

L Y N X

2337

193 ly
151 ly

Bright and Dark
Nebulae
To scale   <10'
Planetary
Nebulae
>100" 100"–30" <30"

Open Star
Clusters
Globular
Clusters
To scale   <5'

Galaxies

10' x 5'   6' x 1'   3' x 2'   5' x 5'   4' x 2'   2' x 1'

Plotted to scale if the major axis >2', and circular
when face on or the position angle is uncertain

Quasars

Galaxy
Clusters

68

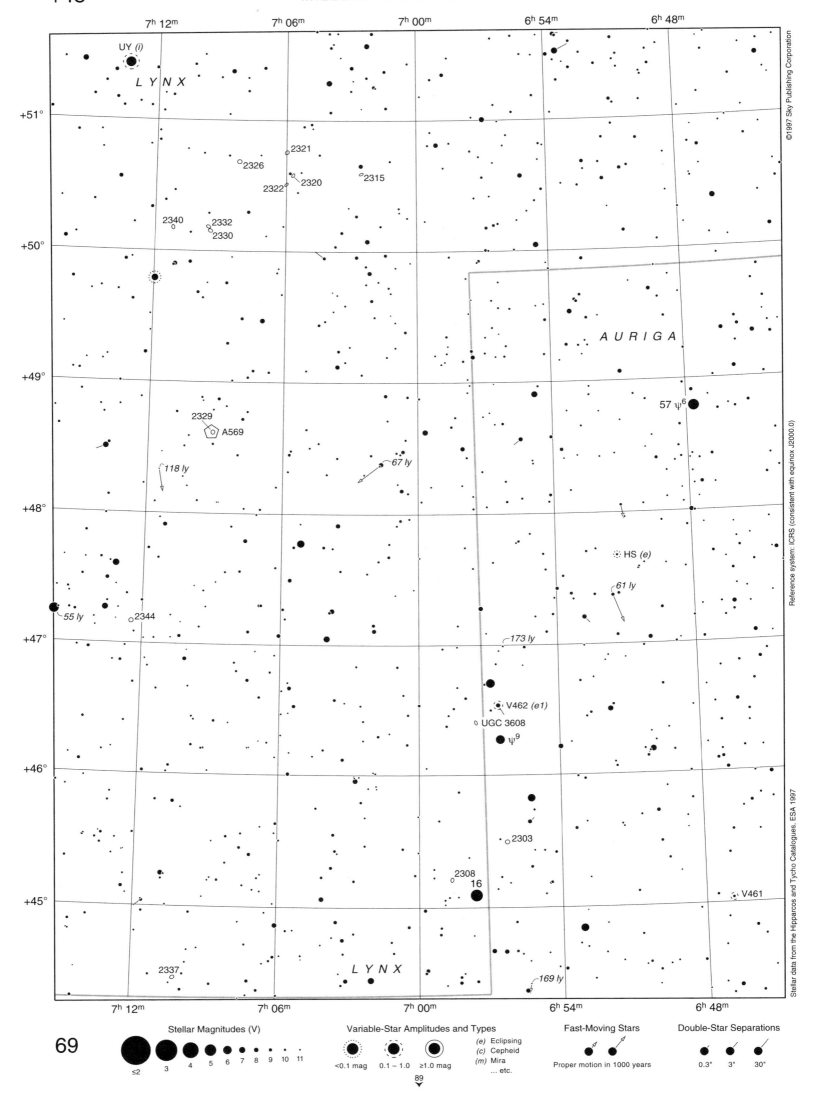

©1997 Sky Publishing Corporation

Reference system: ICRS (consistent with equinox J2000.0)

Stellar data from the Hipparcos and Tycho Catalogues, ESA 1997

69

Stellar Magnitudes (V)

≤2 3 4 5 6 7 8 9 10 11

Variable-Star Amplitudes and Types

<0.1 mag   0.1 – 1.0   ≥1.0 mag

(e) Eclipsing
(c) Cepheid
(m) Mira
... etc.

Fast-Moving Stars

Proper motion in 1000 years

Double-Star Separations

0.3"   3"   30"

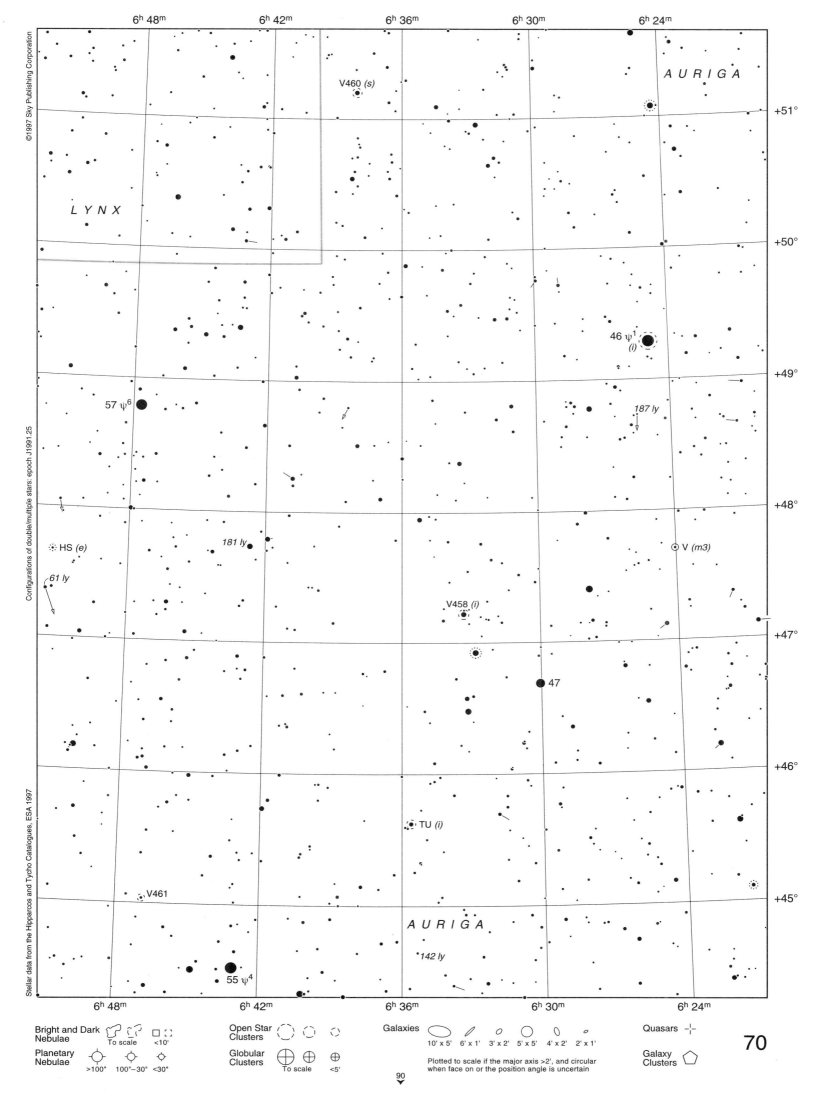

AURIGA

LYNX

V460 (s)

46 ψ¹ (i)

57 ψ⁶

187 ly

HS (e)

181 ly

V (m3)

61 ly

V458 (i)

47

TU (i)

V461

AURIGA

142 ly

55 ψ⁴

Bright and Dark Nebulae — To scale — <10'

Planetary Nebulae — >100" — 100"–30" — <30"

Open Star Clusters

Globular Clusters — To scale — <5'

Galaxies — 10' x 5' — 6' x 1' — 3' x 2' — 5' x 5' — 4' x 2' — 2' x 1'

Plotted to scale if the major axis >2', and circular when face on or the position angle is uncertain

Quasars

Galaxy Clusters

70

MILLENNIUM STAR ATLAS

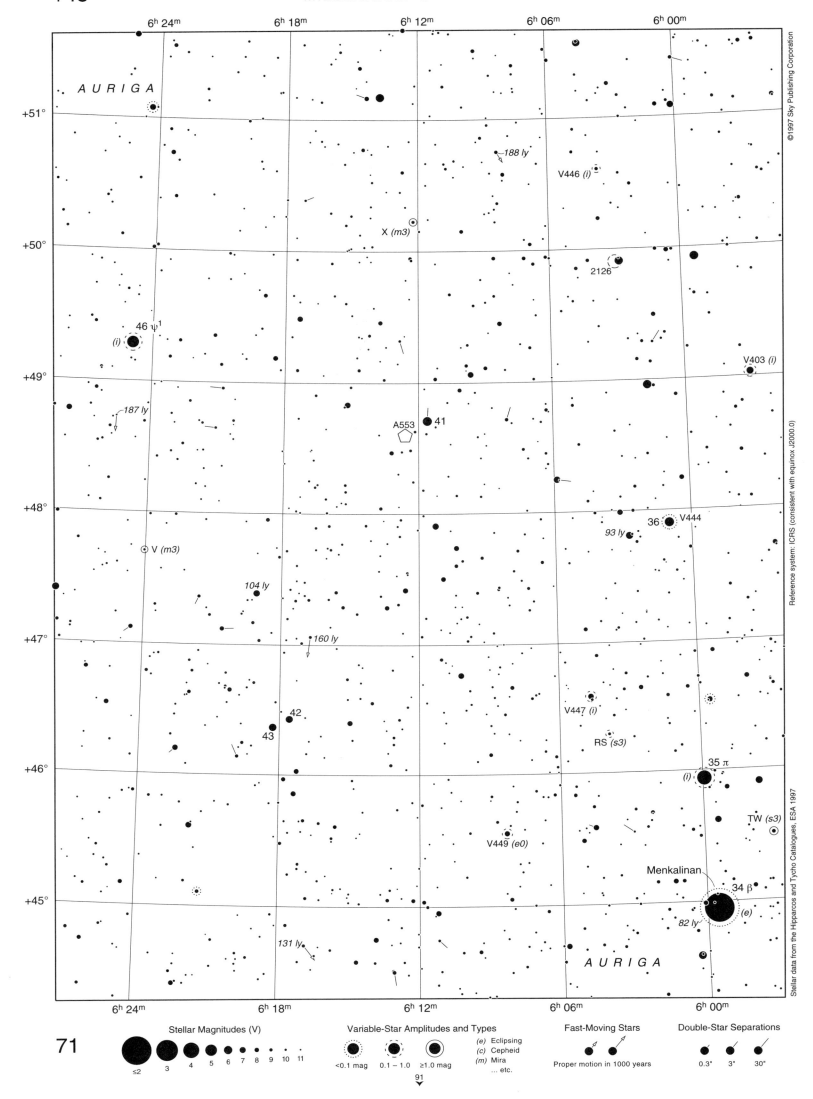

AURIGA

188 ly

V446 (i)

X (m3)

2126

46 ψ¹

(i)

V403 (i)

187 ly

A553 · 41

36 V444

93 ly

V (m3)

104 ly

160 ly

V447 (i)

42

RS (s3)

43

35 π

(i)

TW (s3)

V449 (e0)

Menkalinan

34 β

(e)

82 ly

AURIGA

131 ly

Stellar Magnitudes (V)

≤2 3 4 5 6 7 8 9 10 11

Variable-Star Amplitudes and Types

<0.1 mag   0.1 – 1.0   ≥1.0 mag

(e) Eclipsing
(c) Cepheid
(m) Mira
... etc.

Fast-Moving Stars

Proper motion in 1000 years

Double-Star Separations

0.3"   3"   30"

©1997 Sky Publishing Corporation

Reference system: ICRS (consistent with equinox J2000.0)

Stellar data from the Hipparcos and Tycho Catalogues, ESA 1997

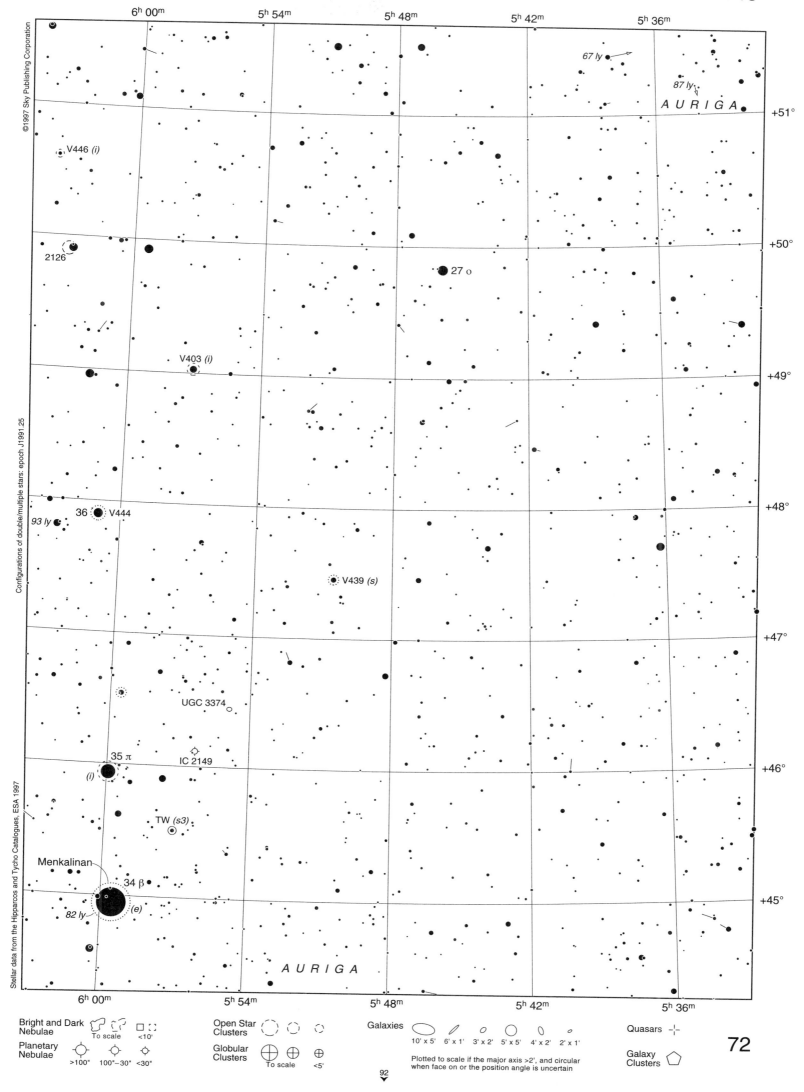

©1997 Sky Publishing Corporation

Configurations of double/multiple stars: epoch J1991.25

Stellar data from the Hipparcos and Tycho Catalogues, ESA 1997

6ʰ 00ᵐ   5ʰ 54ᵐ   5ʰ 48ᵐ   5ʰ 42ᵐ   5ʰ 36ᵐ

67 ly

87 ly

A U R I G A

+51°

V446 (i)

2126

27 o

+50°

V403 (i)

+49°

36   V444

93 ly

+48°

V439 (s)

+47°

UGC 3374

35 π

IC 2149

+46°

(i)

TW (s3)

Menkalinan

34 β

82 ly   (e)

A U R I G A

+45°

6ʰ 00ᵐ   5ʰ 54ᵐ   5ʰ 48ᵐ   5ʰ 42ᵐ   5ʰ 36ᵐ

Bright and Dark Nebulae
To scale   <10'

Planetary Nebulae
>100"   100"–30"   <30"

Open Star Clusters

Globular Clusters
To scale   <5'

Galaxies

10' x 5'   6' x 1'   3' x 2'   5' x 5'   4' x 2'   2' x 1'

Plotted to scale if the major axis >2', and circular
when face on or the position angle is uncertain

Quasars

Galaxy Clusters

72

92

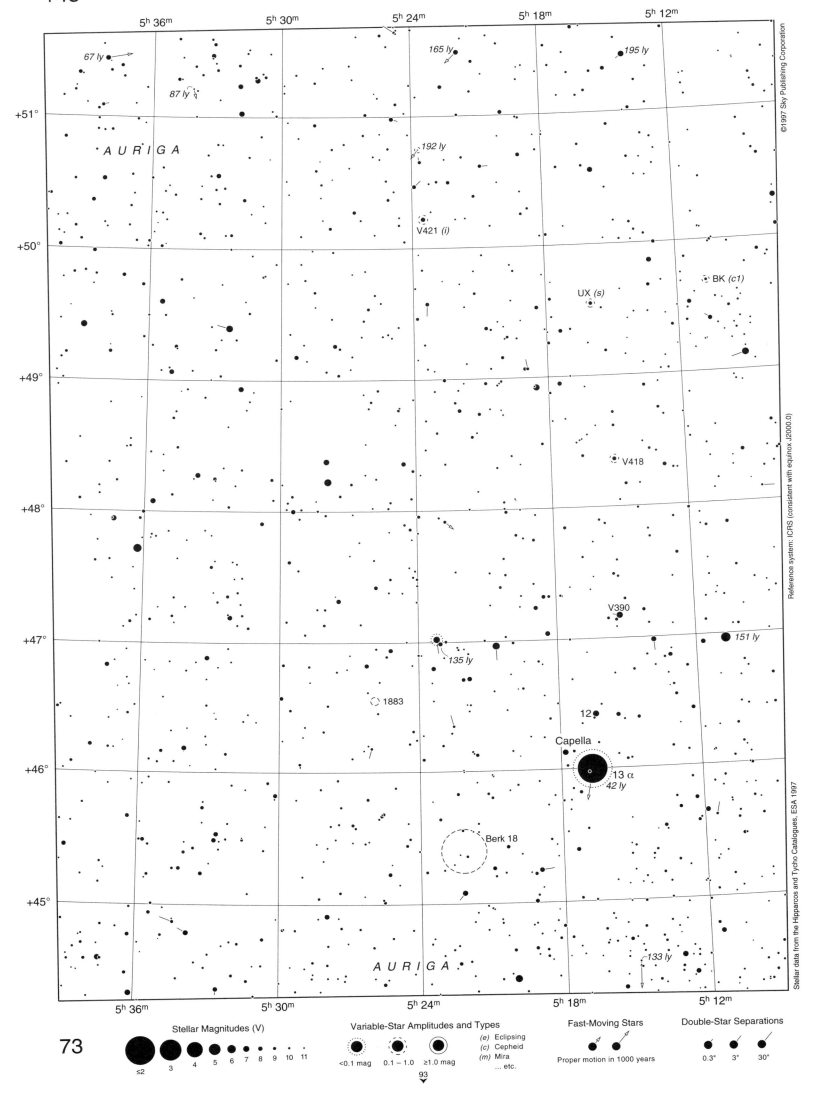

67 ly

87 ly

165 ly

195 ly

A U R I G A

192 ly

V421 (i)

UX (s)

BK (c1)

V418

V390

151 ly

135 ly

1883

12

Capella

13 α
42 ly

Berk 18

A U R I G A

133 ly

73

Stellar Magnitudes (V)

≤2   3   4   5   6   7   8   9   10   11

Variable-Star Amplitudes and Types

<0.1 mag   0.1 – 1.0   ≥1.0 mag

(e) Eclipsing
(c) Cepheid
(m) Mira
... etc.

Fast-Moving Stars

Proper motion in 1000 years

Double-Star Separations

0.3"   3"   30"

93

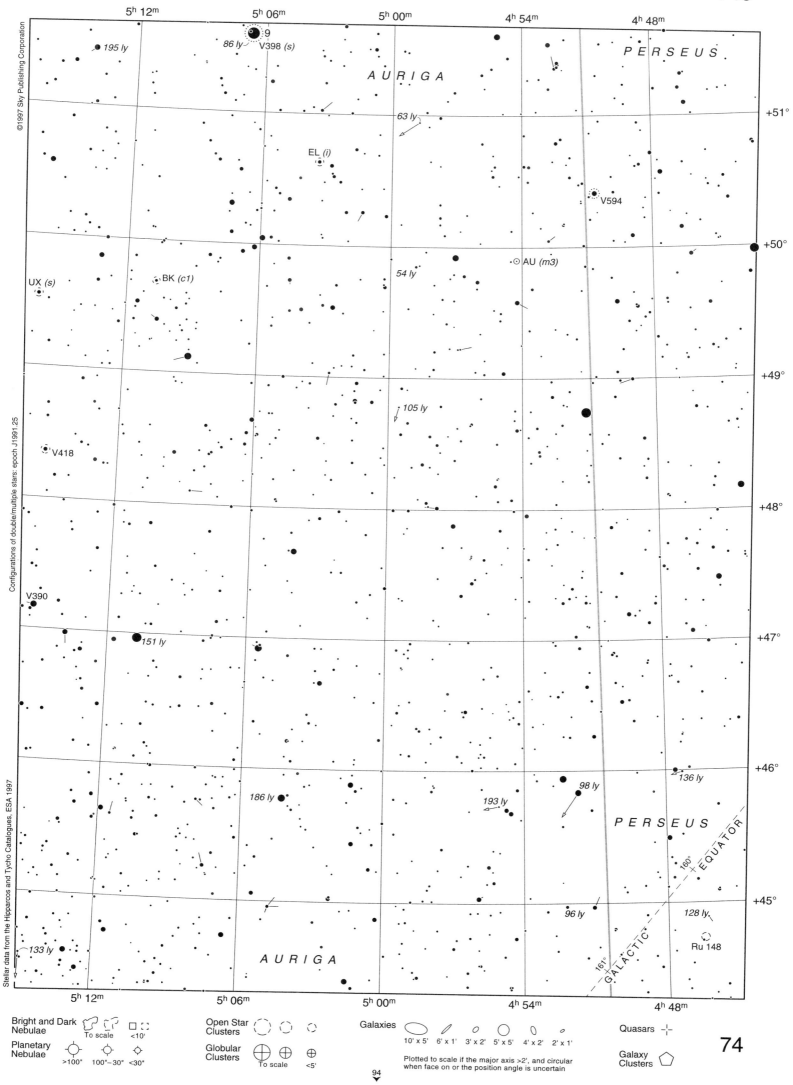

Bright and Dark Nebulae			Open Star Clusters			Galaxies						Quasars
To scale	<10'				<10'	10' x 5'	6' x 1'	3' x 2'	5' x 5'	4' x 2'	2' x 1'	
Planetary Nebulae			Globular Clusters									Galaxy Clusters
>100"	100"–30"	<30"	To scale	<5'		Plotted to scale if the major axis >2', and circular when face on or the position angle is uncertain						

74

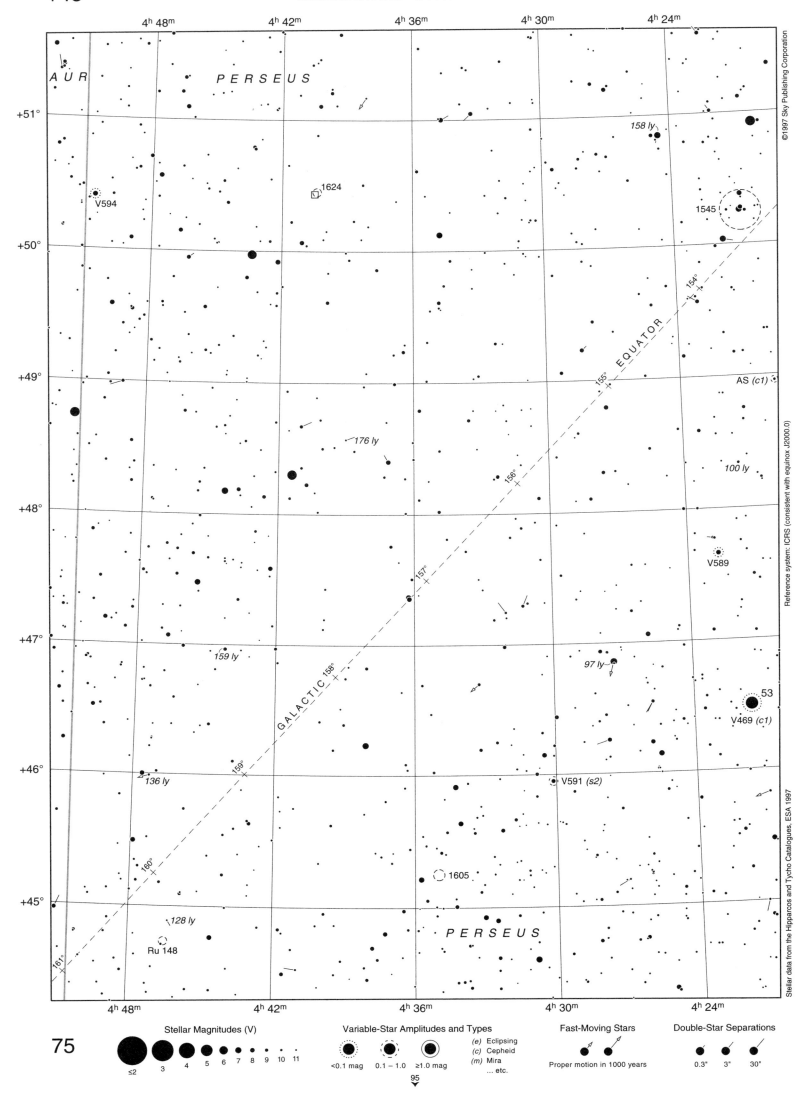

©1997 Sky Publishing Corporation

Reference system: ICRS (consistent with equinox J2000.0)

Stellar data from the Hipparcos and Tycho Catalogues, ESA 1997

Stellar Magnitudes (V)
≤2 3 4 5 6 7 8 9 10 11

Variable-Star Amplitudes and Types
<0.1 mag   0.1 – 1.0   ≥1.0 mag

(e) Eclipsing
(c) Cepheid
(m) Mira
... etc.

Fast-Moving Stars
Proper motion in 1000 years

Double-Star Separations
0.3"   3"   30"

75

MILLENNIUM STAR ATLAS

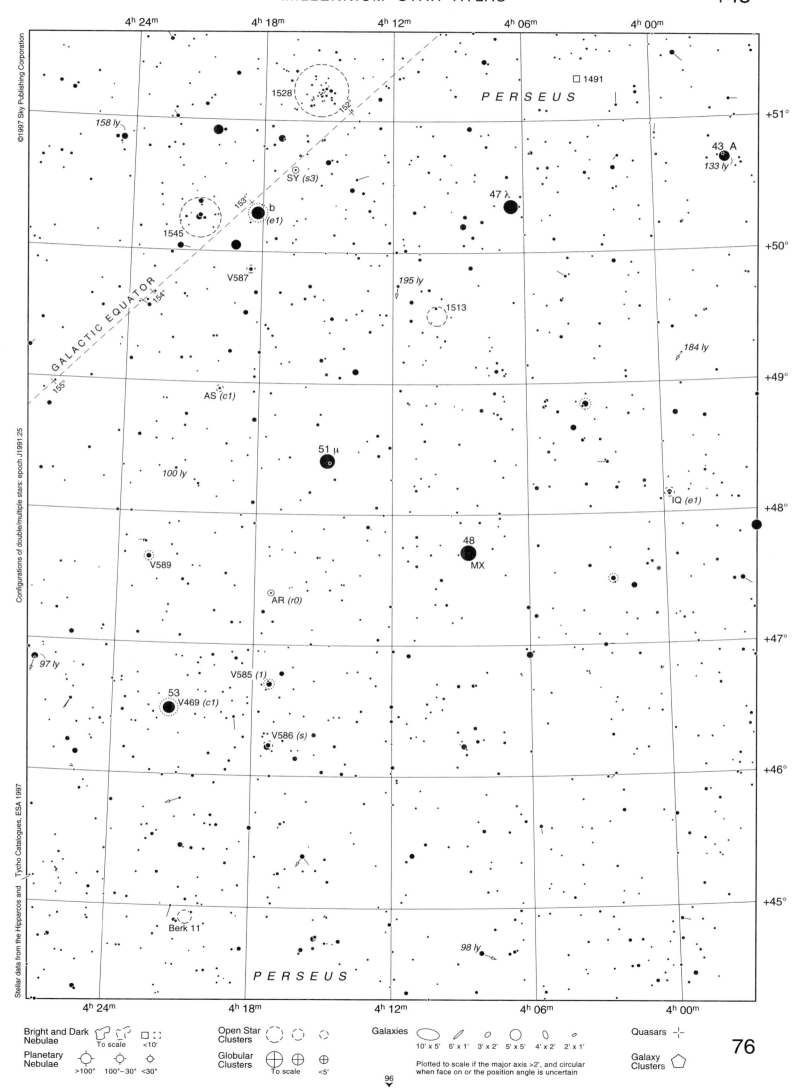

Configurations of double/multiple stars: epoch J1991.25

Stellar data from the Hipparcos and Tycho Catalogues, ESA 1997

PERSEUS

1491

1528

152

SY (s3)

158 ly

153°

1545

b (e1)

V587

154°

155°

43 A

133 ly

47 λ

195 ly

1513

184 ly

AS (c1)

51 μ

100 ly

IQ (e1)

48
MX

V589

AR (r0)

97 ly

V585 (1)

53
V469 (c1)

V586 (s)

Berk 11

98 ly

PERSEUS

Bright and Dark Nebulae	To scale	<10'	Open Star Clusters	Galaxies	10' x 5'	6' x 1'	3' x 2'	5' x 5'	4' x 2'	2' x 1'	Quasars

Planetary Nebulae >100" 100"–30" <30"

Globular Clusters To scale <5'

Galaxy Clusters

Plotted to scale if the major axis >2', and circular when face on or the position angle is uncertain

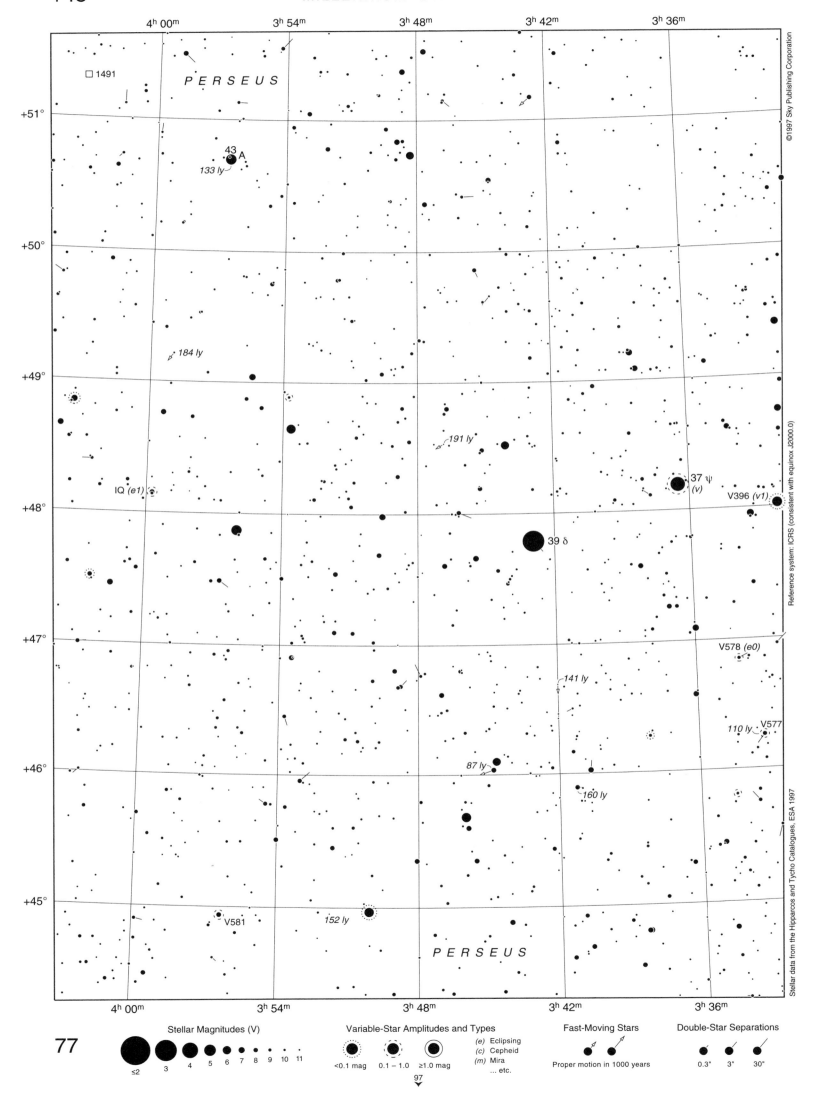

PERSEUS

□ 1491

43 A
133 ly

184 ly

191 ly

IQ *(e1)*

37 ψ
(v)

V396 *(v1)*

39 δ

V578 *(e0)*

141 ly

110 ly V577

87 ly

160 ly

V581   *152 ly*

PERSEUS

77

Stellar Magnitudes (V)

≤2 3 4 5 6 7 8 9 10 11

Variable-Star Amplitudes and Types

<0.1 mag   0.1 – 1.0   ≥1.0 mag

(e) Eclipsing
(c) Cepheid
(m) Mira
... etc.

Fast-Moving Stars

Proper motion in 1000 years

Double-Star Separations

0.3"   3"   30"

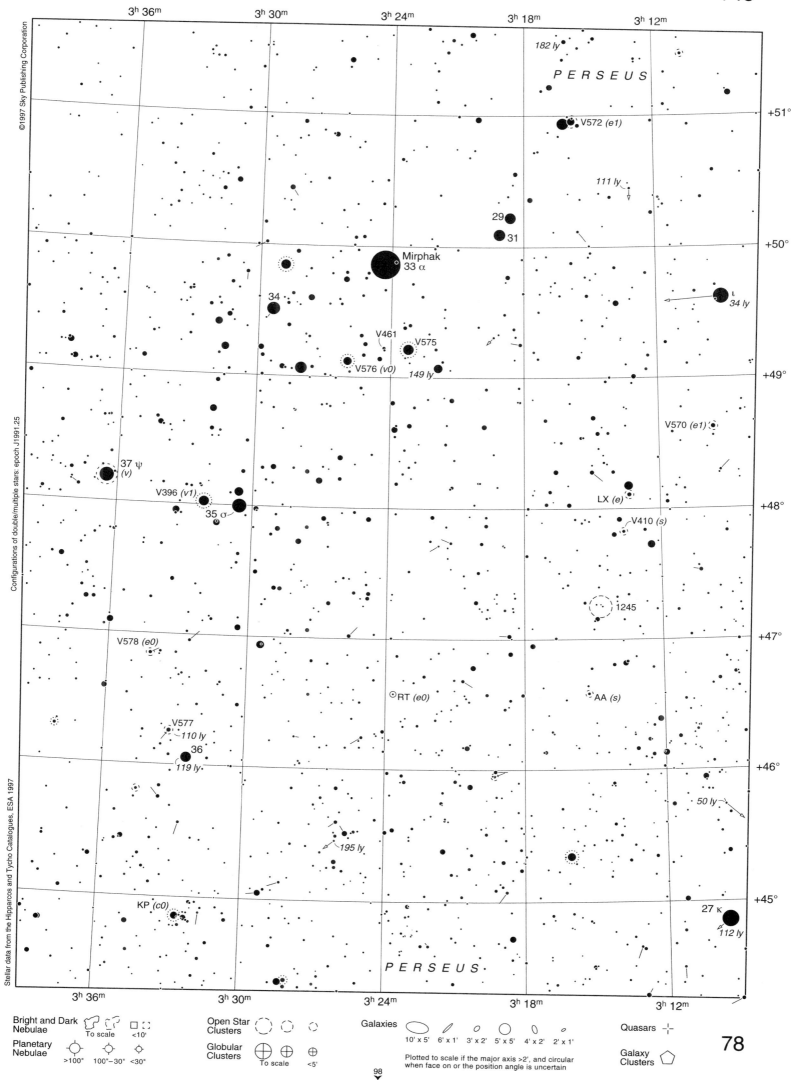

Configurations of double/multiple stars: epoch J1991.25

Stellar data from the Hipparcos and Tycho Catalogues, ESA 1997

P E R S E U S

182 ly

3h 36m   3h 30m   3h 24m   3h 18m   3h 12m

+51°

V572 (e1)

111 ly

29
31

Mirphak
33 α

+50°

34

ι
34 ly

V461   V575
V576 (v0)
149 ly

+49°

V570 (e1)

37 ψ
(v)

V396 (v1)
35 σ

LX (e)

V410 (s)

+48°

1245

V578 (e0)

RT (e0)

AA (s)

+47°

V577
110 ly
36
119 ly

50 ly

195 ly

+46°

KP (c0)

27 κ
112 ly

+45°

P E R S E U S

3h 36m   3h 30m   3h 24m   3h 18m   3h 12m

Bright and Dark
Nebulae   To scale   <10'
Planetary
Nebulae   >100" 100"-30" <30"

Open Star
Clusters   To scale   <5'
Globular
Clusters   To scale   <5'

Galaxies
10' x 5' 6' x 1' 3' x 2' 5' x 5' 4' x 2' 2' x 1'

Plotted to scale if the major axis >2', and circular
when face on or the position angle is uncertain

Quasars

Galaxy
Clusters

78

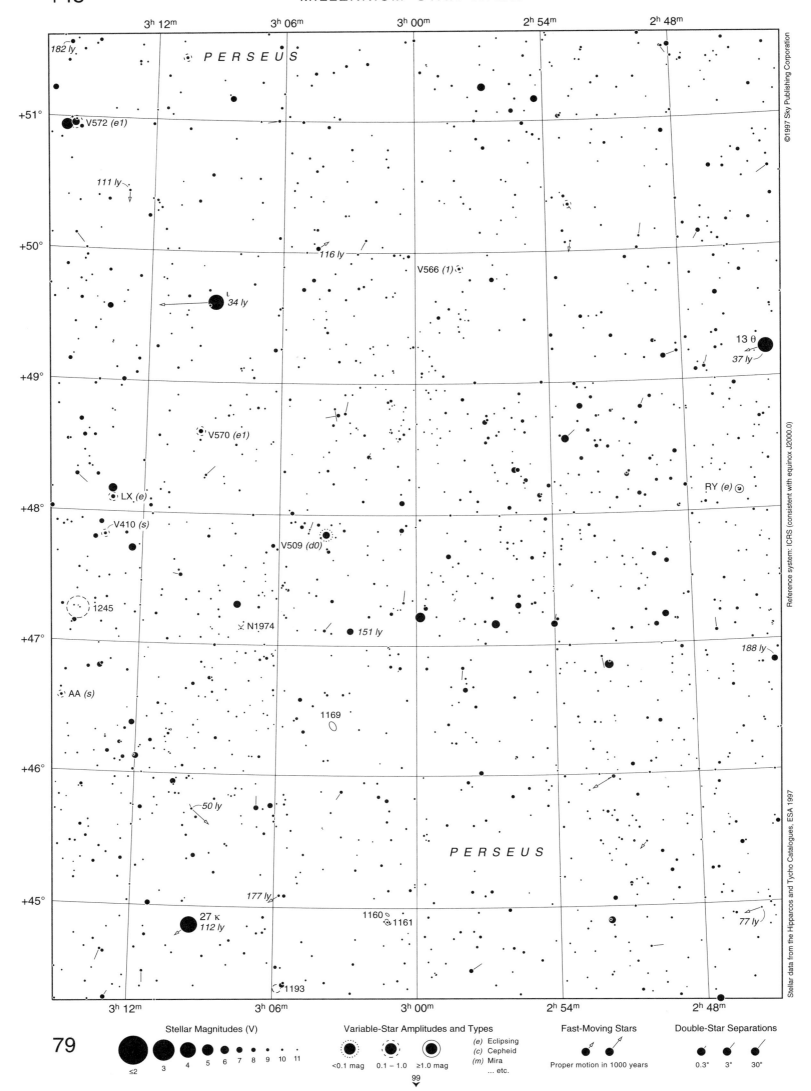

©1997 Sky Publishing Corporation

Reference system: ICRS (consistent with equinox J2000.0)

Stellar data from the Hipparcos and Tycho Catalogues, ESA 1997

PERSEUS

182 ly

V572 (e1)

111 ly

116 ly

V566 (1)

34 ly

13 θ
37 ly

V570 (e1)

RY (e)

LX (e)

V410 (s)

V509 (d0)

1245

N1974

151 ly

188 ly

AA (s)

1169

50 ly

PERSEUS

177 ly

27 κ
112 ly

1160
1161

77 ly

1193

Stellar Magnitudes (V)

≤2 3 4 5 6 7 8 9 10 11

Variable-Star Amplitudes and Types

<0.1 mag   0.1 – 1.0   ≥1.0 mag

(e) Eclipsing
(c) Cepheid
(m) Mira
... etc.

Fast-Moving Stars

Proper motion in 1000 years

Double-Star Separations

0.3"   3"   30"

99

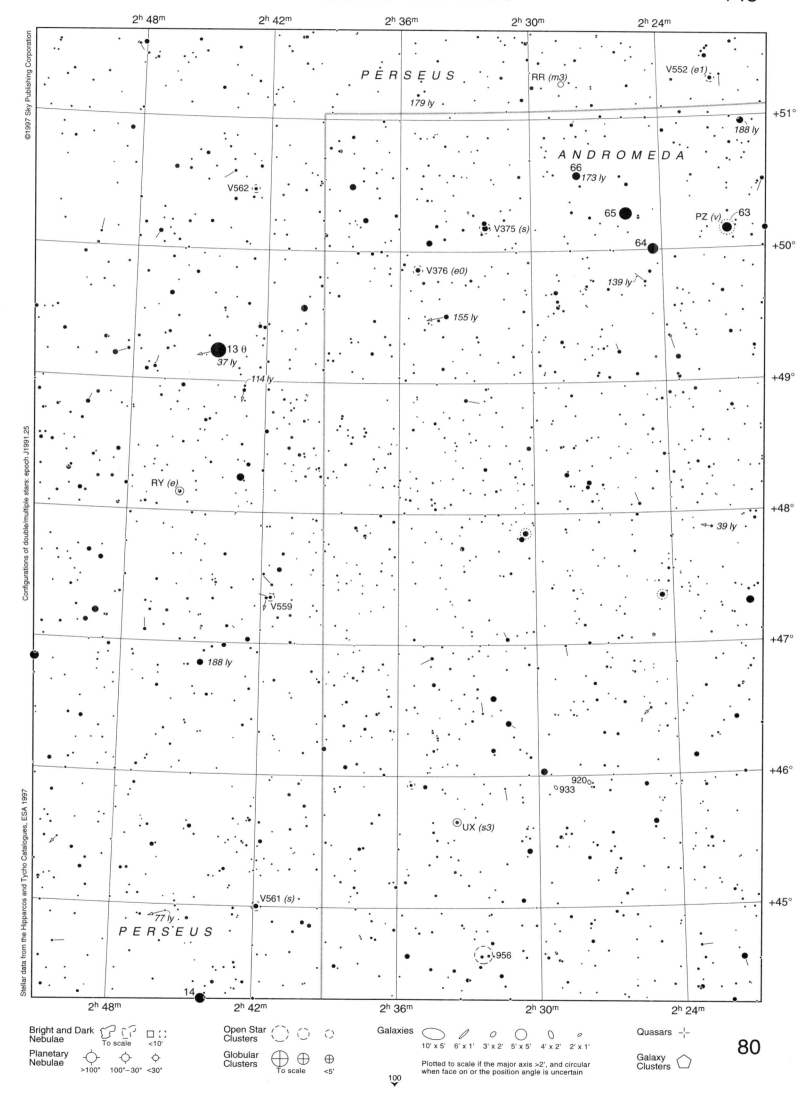

©1997 Sky Publishing Corporation

Configurations of double/multiple stars: epoch J1991.25

Stellar data from the Hipparcos and Tycho Catalogues, ESA 1997

PERSEUS

RR (m3)

179 ly

V552 (e1)

188 ly

ANDROMEDA

66
173 ly

V562

65

V375 (s)

PZ (v)   63

64

V376 (e0)

139 ly

155 ly

13 θ
37 ly

114 ly

RY (e)

39 ly

V559

188 ly

920
933

UX (s3)

V561 (s)

77 ly

956

PERSEUS

14

Bright and Dark Nebulae	To scale <10'
Planetary Nebulae	>100" 100"–30" <30"
Open Star Clusters	
Globular Clusters	To scale <5'
Galaxies	10' x 5' 6' x 1' 3' x 2' 5' x 5' 4' x 2' 2' x 1'
	Plotted to scale if the major axis >2', and circular when face on or the position angle is uncertain
Quasars	
Galaxy Clusters	

100

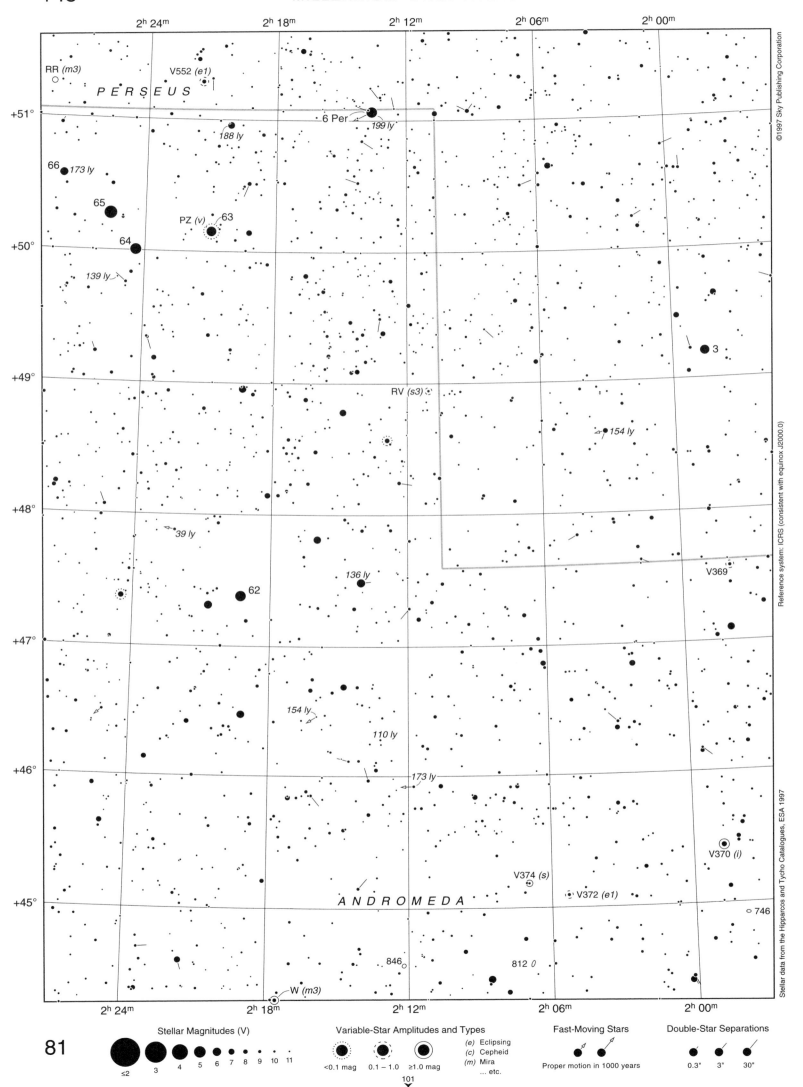

Reference system: ICRS (consistent with equinox J2000.0)

Stellar data from the Hipparcos and Tycho Catalogues, ESA 1997

81

Stellar Magnitudes (V)

≤2 3 4 5 6 7 8 9 10 11

Variable-Star Amplitudes and Types

<0.1 mag   0.1 – 1.0   ≥1.0 mag

(e) Eclipsing
(c) Cepheid
(m) Mira
... etc.

Fast-Moving Stars

Proper motion in 1000 years

Double-Star Separations

0.3"   3"   30"

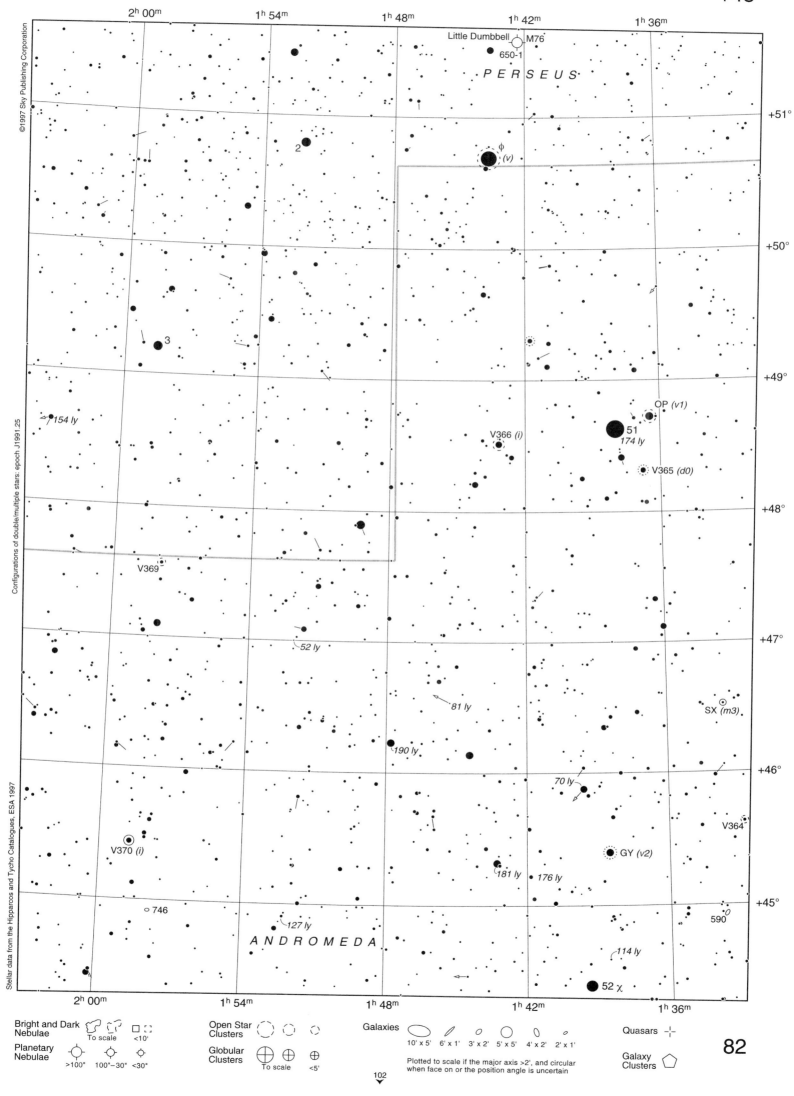

Configurations of double/multiple stars: epoch J1991.25

Stellar data from the Hipparcos and Tycho Catalogues, ESA 1997

2ʰ 00ᵐ 1ʰ 54ᵐ 1ʰ 48ᵐ 1ʰ 42ᵐ 1ʰ 36ᵐ

+51°
+50°
+49°
+48°
+47°
+46°
+45°

Little Dumbbell M76
650-1
P E R S E U S
φ (v)
2
3
154 ly
V366 (i)
OP (v1)
51
174 ly
V365 (d0)
V369
52 ly
81 ly
SX (m3)
190 ly
70 ly
V364
V370 (i)
GY (v2)
181 ly 176 ly
746
590
127 ly
114 ly
A N D R O M E D A
52 χ

Bright and Dark Nebulae
To scale   <10'
Planetary Nebulae
>100" 100"–30" <30"

Open Star Clusters
Globular Clusters
To scale   <5'

Galaxies
10' x 5' 6' x 1' 3' x 2' 5' x 5' 4' x 2' 2' x 1'
Plotted to scale if the major axis >2', and circular when face on or the position angle is uncertain

Quasars

Galaxy Clusters

82

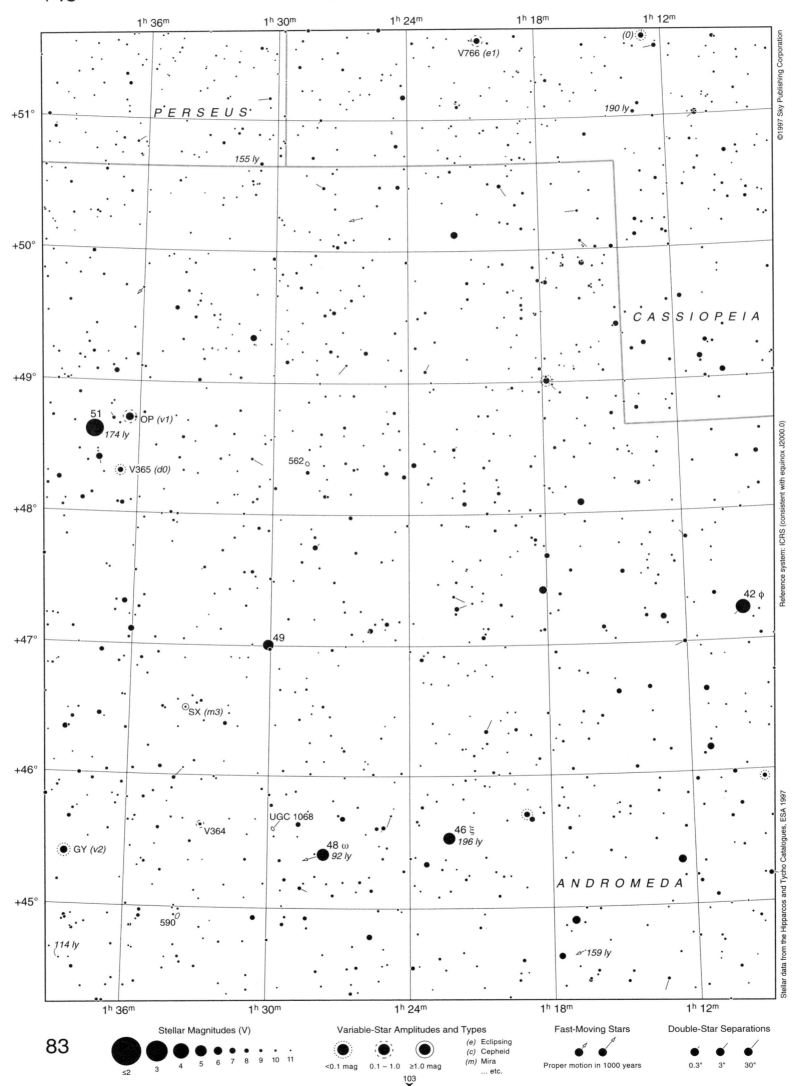

©1997 Sky Publishing Corporation

Reference system: ICRS (consistent with equinox J2000.0)

Stellar data from the Hipparcos and Tycho Catalogues, ESA 1997

1h 36m 1h 30m 1h 24m 1h 18m 1h 12m

V766 (e1)

(0)

190 ly

P E R S E U S

155 ly

+51°

+50°

+49°

C A S S I O P E I A

51
OP (v1)
174 ly
V365 (d0)

562

42 φ

+48°

49

SX (m3)

42 φ

+47°

UGC 1068
V364
48 ω
92 ly
46 ξ
196 ly

+46°

GY (v2)

A N D R O M E D A

590

114 ly

159 ly

+45°

1h 36m 1h 30m 1h 24m 1h 18m 1h 12m

Stellar Magnitudes (V)

≤2   3   4   5   6   7 8 9 10 11

Variable-Star Amplitudes and Types

<0.1 mag   0.1 – 1.0   ≥1.0 mag

(e) Eclipsing
(c) Cepheid
(m) Mira
... etc.

Fast-Moving Stars

Proper motion in 1000 years

Double-Star Separations

0.3"   3"   30"

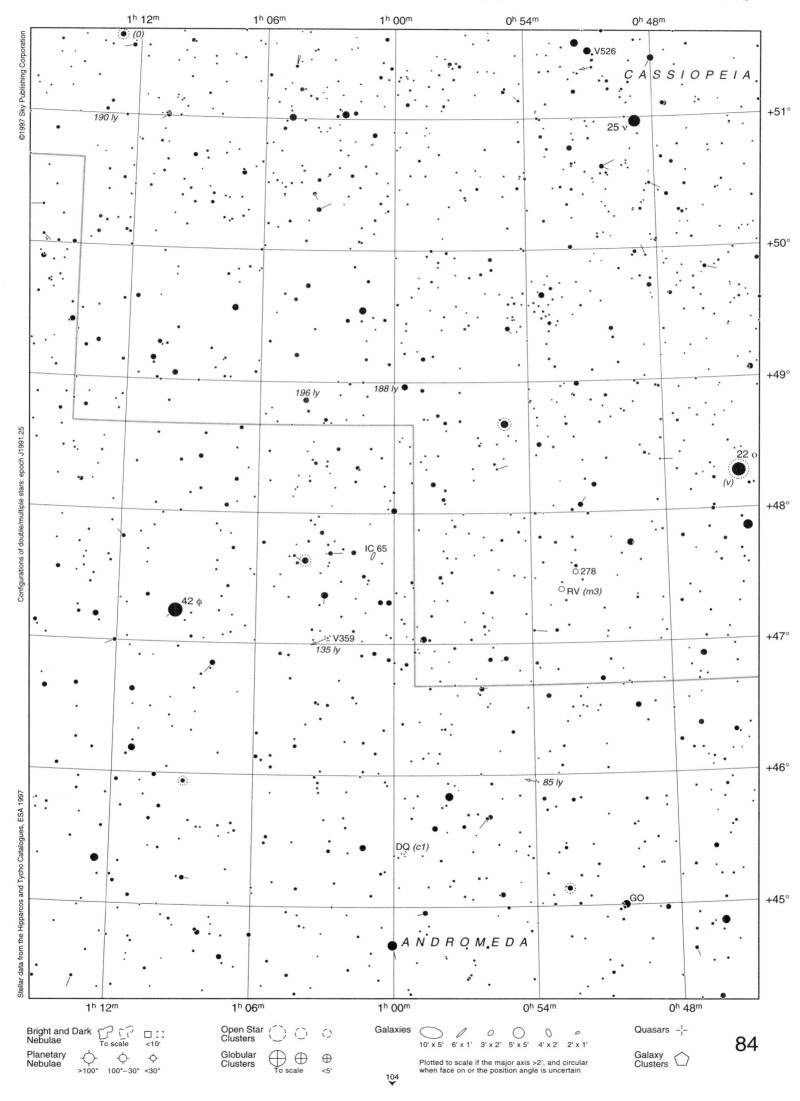

Configurations of double/multiple stars: epoch J1991.25

Stellar data from the Hipparcos and Tycho Catalogues, ESA 1997

1ʰ 12ᵐ   1ʰ 06ᵐ   1ʰ 00ᵐ   0ʰ 54ᵐ   0ʰ 48ᵐ

+51°   +50°   +49°   +48°   +47°   +46°   +45°

C A S S I O P E I A

V526

25 ν

22 ο
(v)

190 ly

196 ly   188 ly

IC 65

42 φ

278
RV (m3)

V359
135 ly

85 ly

DQ (c1)

GO

A N D R O M E D A

(0)

Bright and Dark Nebulae	Open Star Clusters	Galaxies	Quasars
To scale <10'		10' x 5' 6' x 1' 3' x 2' 5' x 5' 4' x 2' 2' x 1'	
Planetary Nebulae	Globular Clusters		Galaxy Clusters
>100" 100"–30" <30"	To scale <5'	Plotted to scale if the major axis >2', and circular when face on or the position angle is uncertain	

84

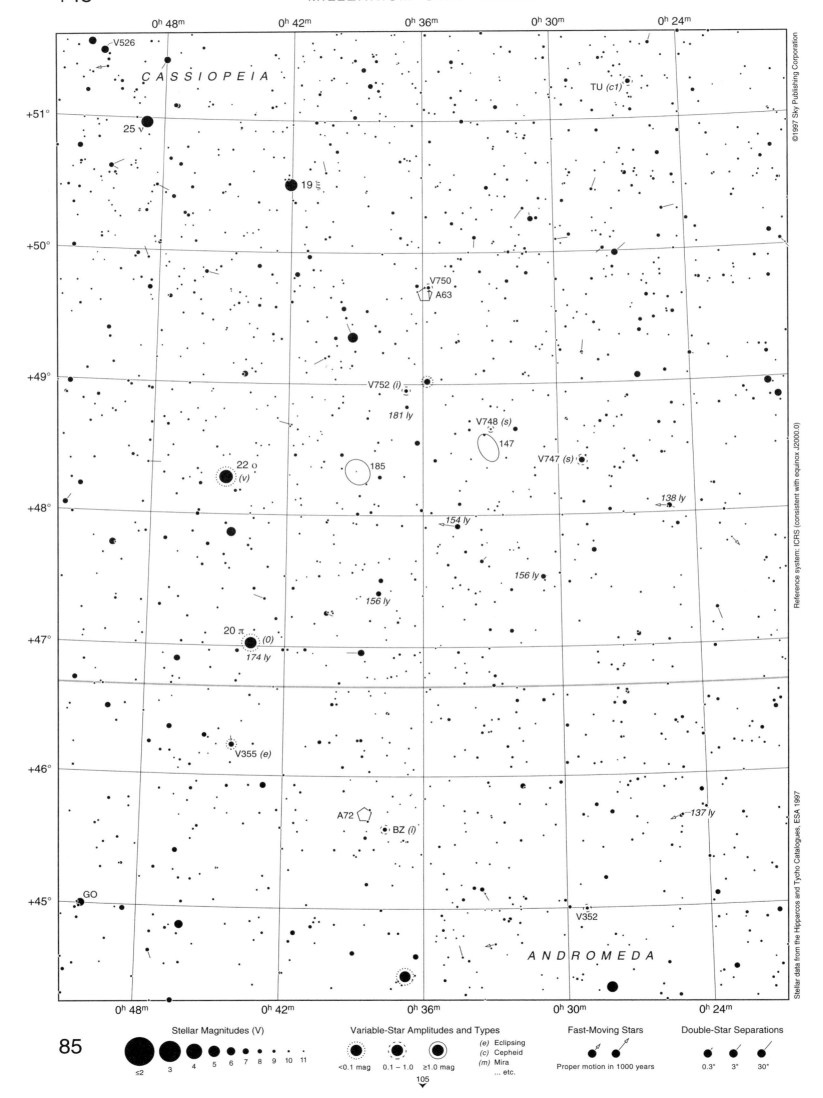

CASSIOPEIA

V526

25 ν

19 ξ

V750
A63

V752 (i)

181 ly

V748 (s)
147

V747 (s)

22 o
(v)

185

138 ly

154 ly

156 ly

156 ly

20 π
(0)
174 ly

V355 (e)

A72

BZ (i)

137 ly

GO

V352

ANDROMEDA

TU (c1)

©1997 Sky Publishing Corporation

Reference system: ICRS (consistent with equinox J2000.0)

Stellar data from the Hipparcos and Tycho Catalogues, ESA 1997

Stellar Magnitudes (V)

≤2   3   4   5   6   7   8   9   10   11

Variable-Star Amplitudes and Types

<0.1 mag   0.1 – 1.0   ≥1.0 mag

(e) Eclipsing
(c) Cepheid
(m) Mira
... etc.

Fast-Moving Stars

Proper motion in 1000 years

Double-Star Separations

0.3"   3"   30"

105

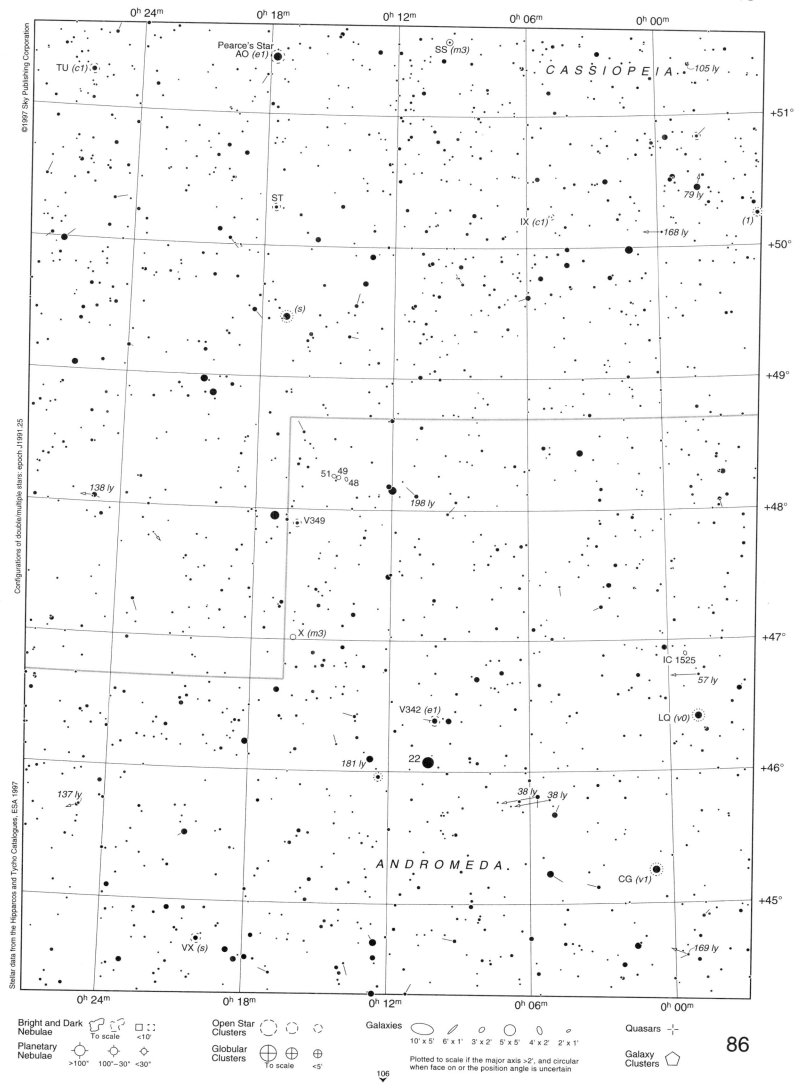

Configurations of double/multiple stars: epoch J1991.25

Stellar data from the Hipparcos and Tycho Catalogues, ESA 1997

CASSIOPEIA

Pearce's Star
AO (e1)

TU (c1)

SS (m3)

105 ly

ST

79 ly

IX (c1)

168 ly

(1)

(s)

138 ly

51 49
48

198 ly

V349

X (m3)

IC 1525

57 ly

V342 (e1)

LQ (v0)

181 ly

22

38 ly 38 ly

137 ly

ANDROMEDA

CG (v1)

VX (s)

169 ly

0h 24m   0h 18m   0h 12m   0h 06m   0h 00m

+51°
+50°
+49°
+48°
+47°
+46°
+45°

Bright and Dark Nebulae
To scale   <10'

Planetary Nebulae
>100"   100"-30"   <30"

Open Star Clusters

Globular Clusters
To scale   <5'

Galaxies
10' x 5'   6' x 1'   3' x 2'   5' x 5'   4' x 2'   2' x 1'

Plotted to scale if the major axis >2', and circular when face on or the position angle is uncertain

Quasars

Galaxy Clusters

86

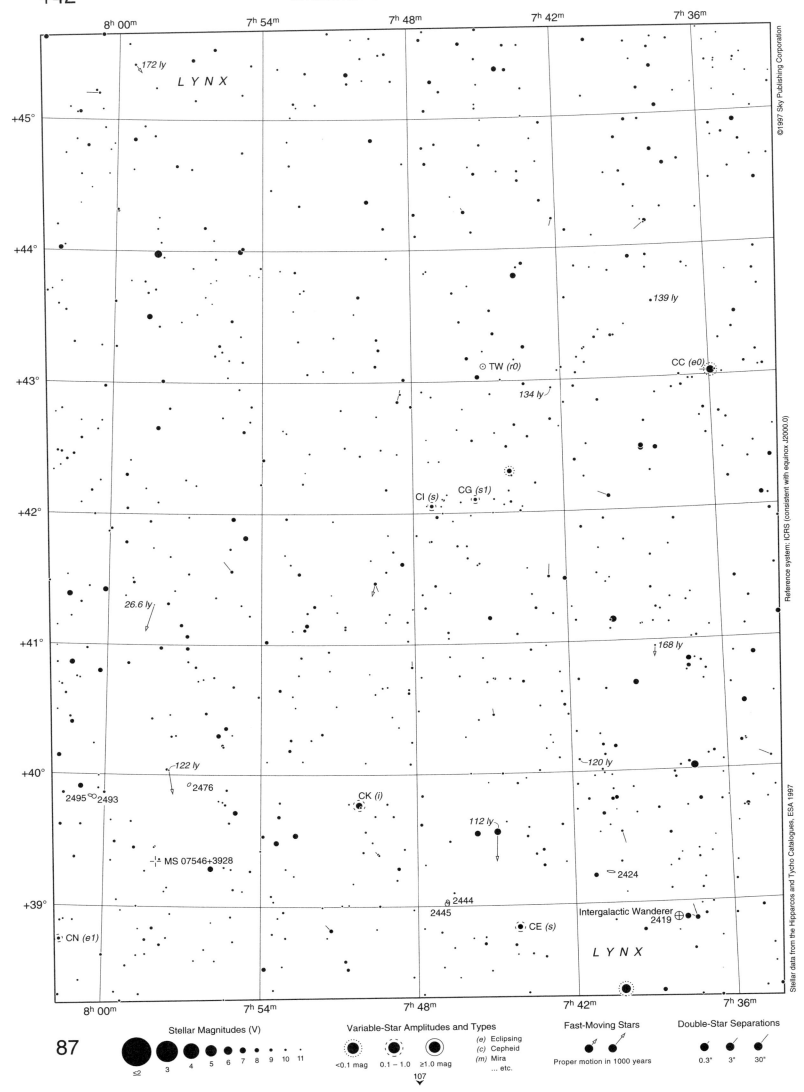

LYNX

172 ly

139 ly

TW (r0)

CC (e0)

134 ly

CG (s1)

CI (s)

26.6 ly

168 ly

122 ly

120 ly

2476

2495 2493

CK (i)

112 ly

MS 07546+3928

2424

2444

2445

Intergalactic Wanderer
2419

CE (s)

CN (e1)

LYNX

©1997 Sky Publishing Corporation

Reference system: ICRS (consistent with equinox J2000.0)

Stellar data from the Hipparcos and Tycho Catalogues, ESA 1997

87

Stellar Magnitudes (V)

≤2   3   4   5   6   7   8   9   10   11

Variable-Star Amplitudes and Types

<0.1 mag   0.1 – 1.0   ≥1.0 mag

(e) Eclipsing
(c) Cepheid
(m) Mira
... etc.

Fast-Moving Stars

Proper motion in 1000 years

Double-Star Separations

0.3"   3"   30"

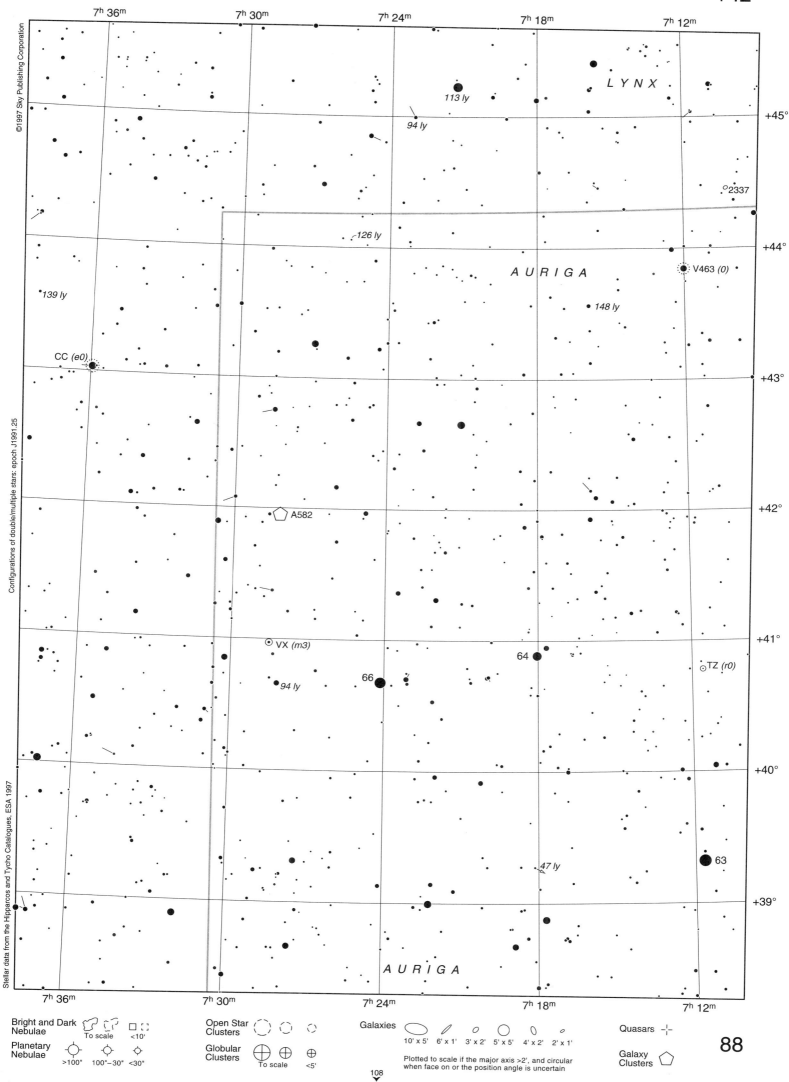

Configurations of double/multiple stars: epoch J1991.25

Stellar data from the Hipparcos and Tycho Catalogues, ESA 1997

L Y N X

113 ly

94 ly

2337

126 ly

A U R I G A

V463 (0)

139 ly

148 ly

CC (e0)

A582

+45°

+44°

+43°

+42°

+41°

+40°

+39°

VX (m3)

64

TZ (r0)

66

94 ly

63

47 ly

A U R I G A

7ʰ 36ᵐ   7ʰ 30ᵐ   7ʰ 24ᵐ   7ʰ 18ᵐ   7ʰ 12ᵐ

Bright and Dark Nebulae
To scale   <10'

Planetary Nebulae
>100"   100"–30"   <30"

Open Star Clusters

Globular Clusters
To scale   <5'

Galaxies
10' x 5'   6' x 1'   3' x 2'   5' x 5'   4' x 2'   2' x 1'

Plotted to scale if the major axis >2', and circular when face on or the position angle is uncertain

Quasars

Galaxy Clusters

88

108

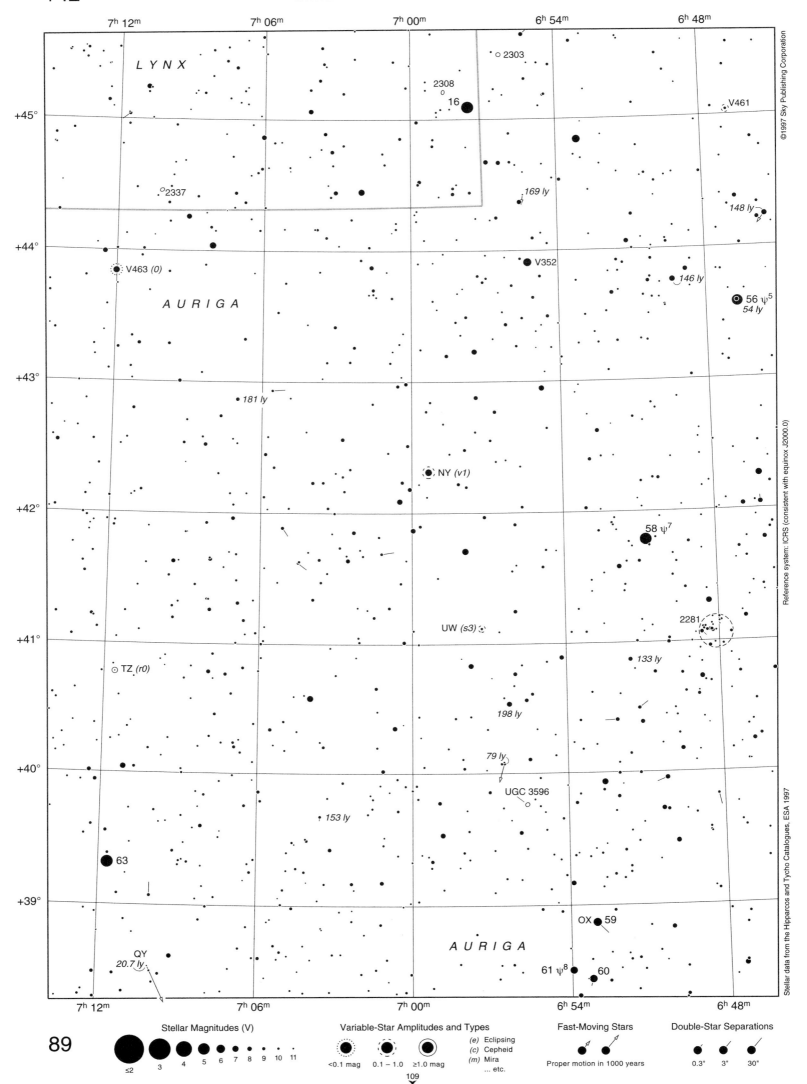

©1997 Sky Publishing Corporation

Reference system: ICRS (consistent with equinox J2000.0)

Stellar data from the Hipparcos and Tycho Catalogues, ESA 1997

Stellar Magnitudes (V)

≤2 3 4 5 6 7 8 9 10 11

Variable-Star Amplitudes and Types

<0.1 mag   0.1 – 1.0 mag   ≥1.0 mag

(e) Eclipsing
(c) Cepheid
(m) Mira
... etc.

Fast-Moving Stars

Proper motion in 1000 years

Double-Star Separations

0.3"   3"   30"

$\overset{\uparrow}{70}$

+42°

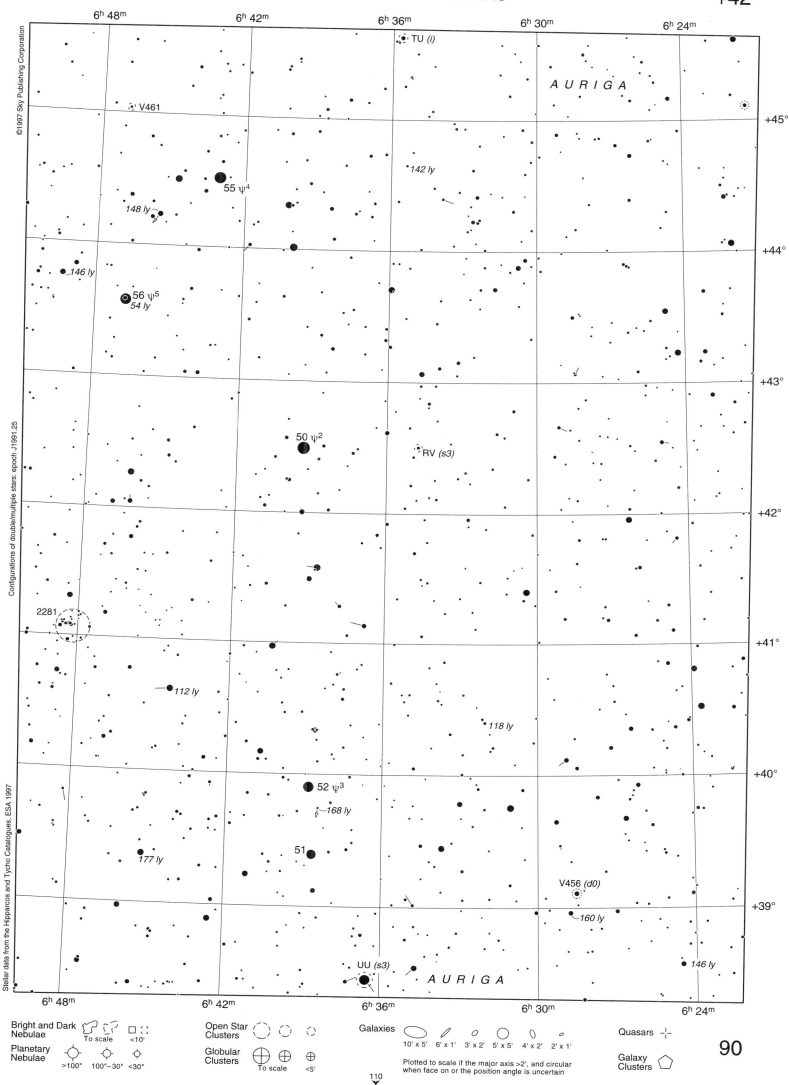

6h 48m 6h 42m 6h 36m 6h 30m 6h 24m

©1997 Sky Publishing Corporation

Configurations of double/multiple stars: epoch J1991.25

Stellar data from the Hipparcos and Tycho Catalogues, ESA 1997

TU (i)

A U R I G A

V461

142 ly

55 ψ⁴

148 ly

146 ly

56 ψ⁵
54 ly

+45°

+44°

+43°

50 ψ²

RV (s3)

+42°

2281

112 ly

118 ly

+41°

+40°

52 ψ³

168 ly

51

177 ly

V456 (d0)

+39°

160 ly

146 ly

UU (s3)

A U R I G A

6h 48m 6h 42m 6h 36m 6h 30m 6h 24m

Bright and Dark
Nebulae
To scale   <10'

Planetary
Nebulae
>100" 100"–30" <30"

Open Star
Clusters

Globular
Clusters
To scale   <5'

Galaxies
10' x 5' 6' x 1' 3' x 2' 5' x 5' 4' x 2' 2' x 1'

Plotted to scale if the major axis >2', and circular
when face on or the position angle is uncertain

Quasars

Galaxy
Clusters

90

110

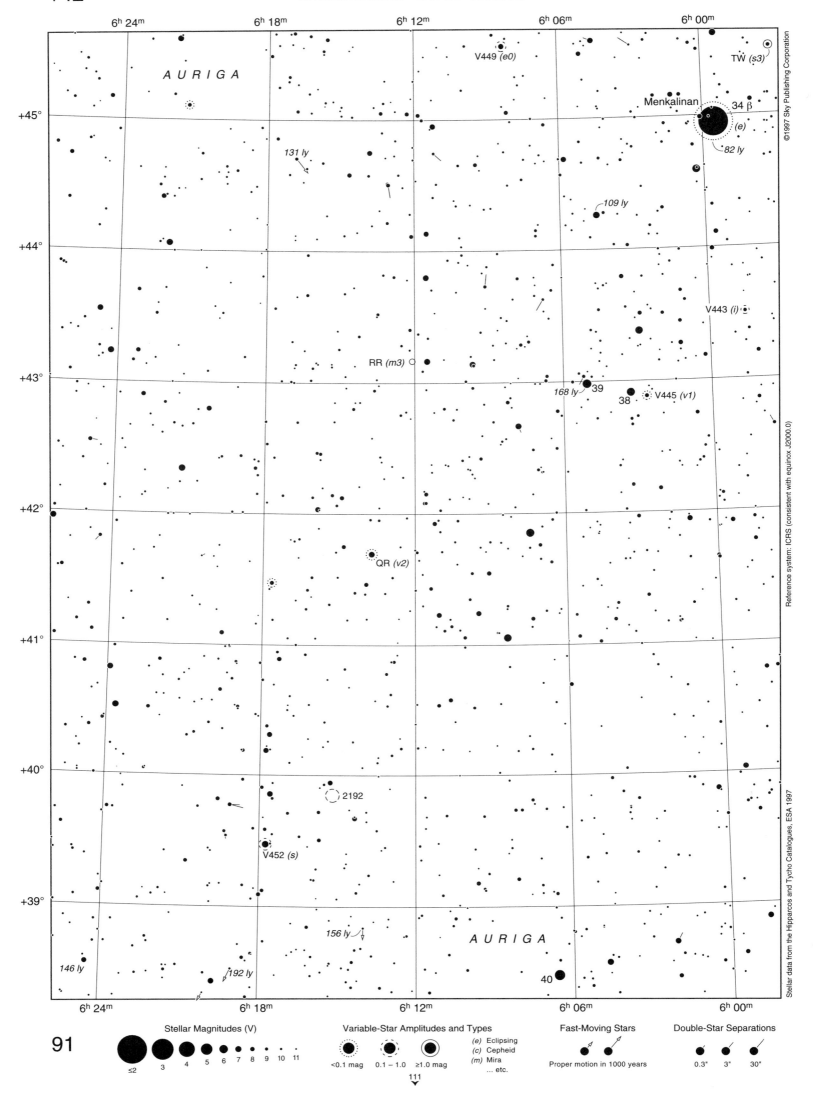

©1997 Sky Publishing Corporation

Reference system: ICRS (consistent with equinox J2000.0)

Stellar data from the Hipparcos and Tycho Catalogues, ESA 1997

AURIGA

Menkalinan

TW *(s3)*

34 β

(e)

82 ly

V449 *(e0)*

131 ly

109 ly

V443 *(i)*

RR *(m3)*

168 ly 39

38 V445 *(v1)*

QR *(v2)*

2192

V452 *(s)*

156 ly

AURIGA

146 ly

192 ly

40

Stellar Magnitudes (V)

≤2 3 4 5 6 7 8 9 10 11

Variable-Star Amplitudes and Types

<0.1 mag   0.1 − 1.0   ≥1.0 mag

(e) Eclipsing
(c) Cepheid
(m) Mira
... etc.

Fast-Moving Stars

Proper motion in 1000 years

Double-Star Separations

0.3" 3" 30"

111

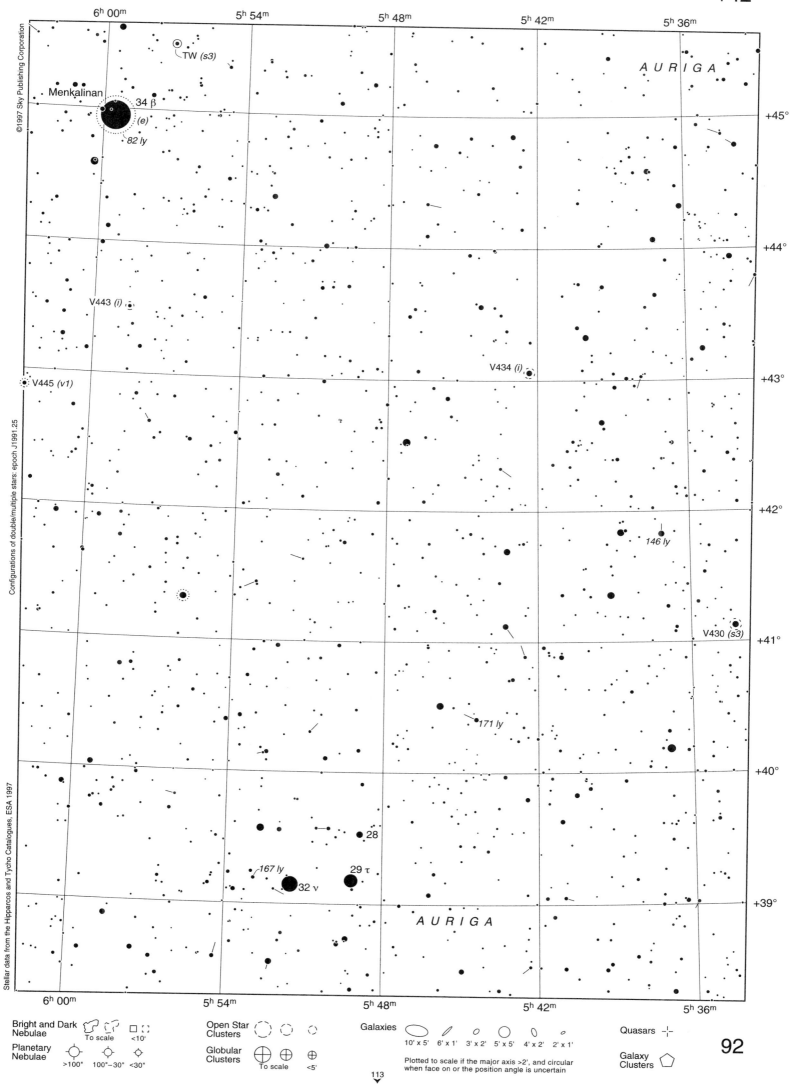

AURIGA

TW *(s3)*

Menkalinan

34 β

(e)

82 *ly*

V443 *(i)*

V434 *(i)*

V445 *(v1)*

146 *ly*

V430 *(s3)*

171 *ly*

28

167 *ly*

29 τ

32 ν

AURIGA

+45°

+44°

+43°

+42°

+41°

+40°

+39°

6ʰ 00ᵐ   5ʰ 54ᵐ   5ʰ 48ᵐ   5ʰ 42ᵐ   5ʰ 36ᵐ

Bright and Dark Nebulae	To scale <10'	
Planetary Nebulae	>100" 100"–30" <30"	
Open Star Clusters		
Globular Clusters	To scale <5'	

Galaxies

10' x 5'   6' x 1'   3' x 2'   5' x 5'   4' x 2'   2' x 1'

Plotted to scale if the major axis >2', and circular when face on or the position angle is uncertain

Quasars

Galaxy Clusters

92

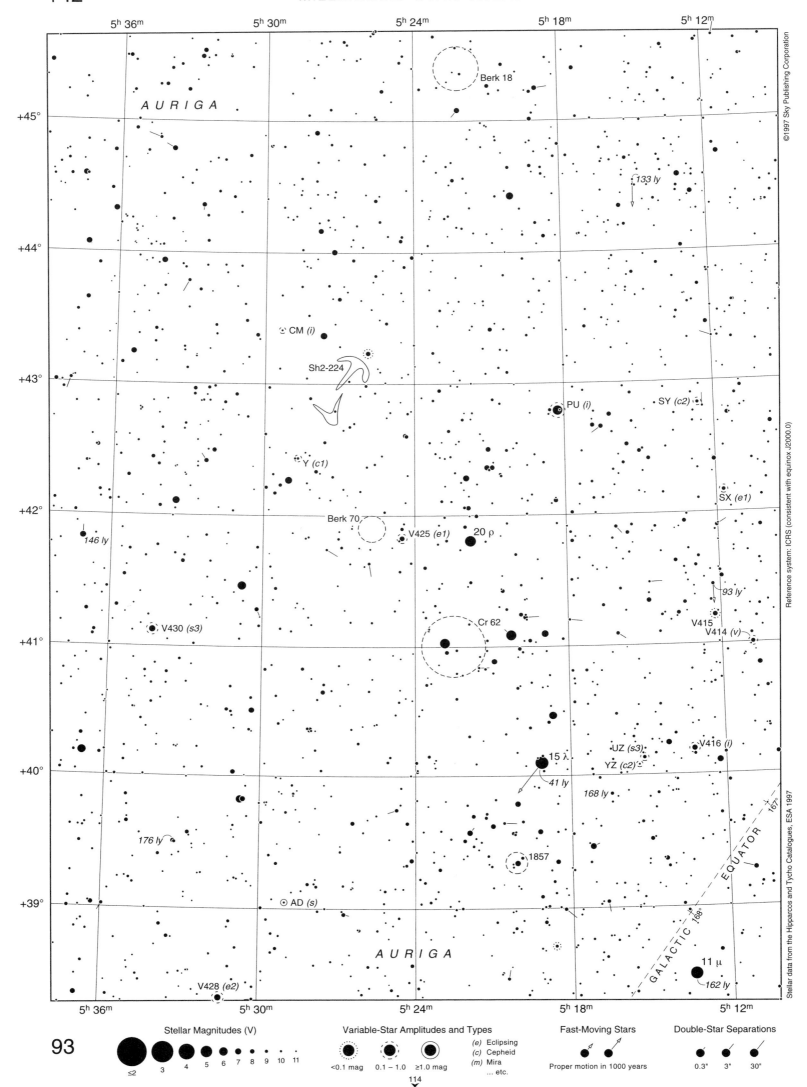

©1997 Sky Publishing Corporation

Reference system: ICRS (consistent with equinox J2000.0)

Stellar data from the Hipparcos and Tycho Catalogues, ESA 1997

AURIGA

Berk 18

133 ly

CM (i)

Sh2-224

PU (i)

SY (c2)

Y (c1)

SX (e1)

Berk 70

V425 (e1)

20 ρ

146 ly

93 ly

V430 (s3)

Cr 62

V415

V414 (v)

15 λ

UZ (s3)

V416 (i)

YZ (c2)

41 ly

168 ly

176 ly

1857

GALACTIC 168°

EQUATOR

167°

AD (s)

AURIGA

11 μ

162 ly

V428 (e2)

Stellar Magnitudes (V)

≤2 3 4 5 6 7 8 9 10 11

Variable-Star Amplitudes and Types

<0.1 mag   0.1 – 1.0   ≥1.0 mag

(e) Eclipsing
(c) Cepheid
(m) Mira
... etc.

Fast-Moving Stars

Proper motion in 1000 years

Double-Star Separations

0.3"   3"   30"

114

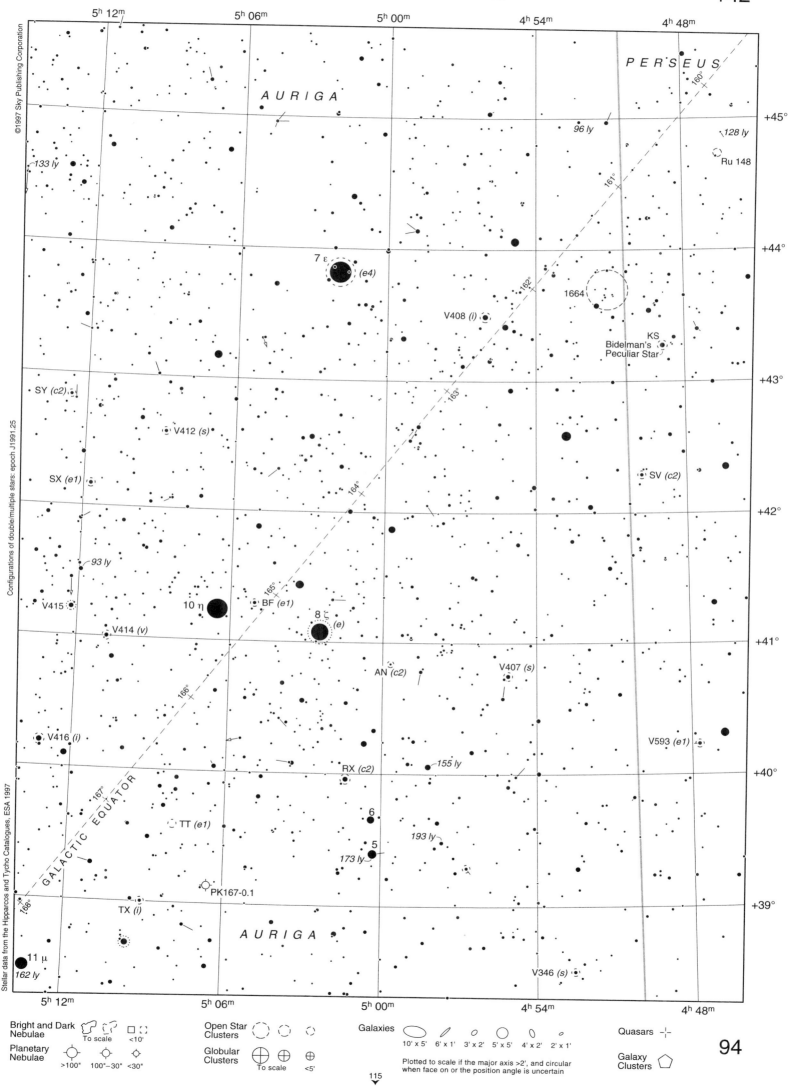

PERSEUS

AURIGA

96 ly

128 ly

133 ly

Ru 148

7 ε   (e4)

1664

V408 (i)

KS
Bidelman's
Peculiar Star

SY (c2)

163°

V412 (s)

SV (c2)

SX (e1)

164°

93 ly

165°

10 η   BF (e1)

V415

8 ζ   (e)

V414 (v)

AN (c2)

V407 (s)

166°

V416 (i)

V593 (e1)

155 ly

167°

RX (c2)

6

TT (e1)

5

193 ly

173 ly

PK167-0.1

168°

TX (i)

AURIGA

11 μ
162 ly

V346 (s)

GALACTIC EQUATOR

5h 12m   5h 06m   5h 00m   4h 54m   4h 48m

+45°
+44°
+43°
+42°
+41°
+40°
+39°

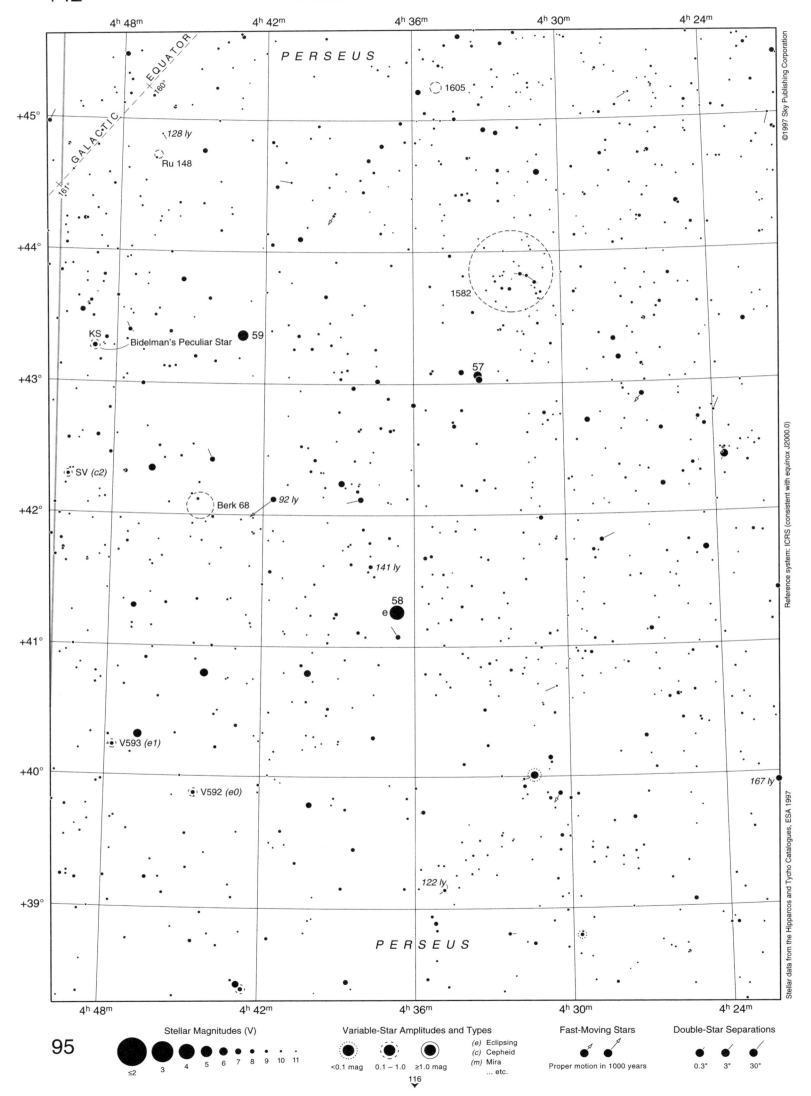

©1997 Sky Publishing Corporation

Reference system: ICRS (consistent with equinox J2000.0)

Stellar data from the Hipparcos and Tycho Catalogues, ESA 1997

PERSEUS

Ru 148

128 ly

1605

1582

KS
Bidelman's Peculiar Star
59

57

SV *(c2)*

Berk 68
92 ly

141 ly

58
e

V593 *(e1)*

V592 *(e0)*

122 ly

167 ly

PERSEUS

Stellar Magnitudes (V)

≤2 3 4 5 6 7 8 9 10 11

Variable-Star Amplitudes and Types

<0.1 mag   0.1 – 1.0   ≥1.0 mag

(e) Eclipsing
(c) Cepheid
(m) Mira
... etc.

Fast-Moving Stars

Proper motion in 1000 years

Double-Star Separations

0.3"   3"   30"

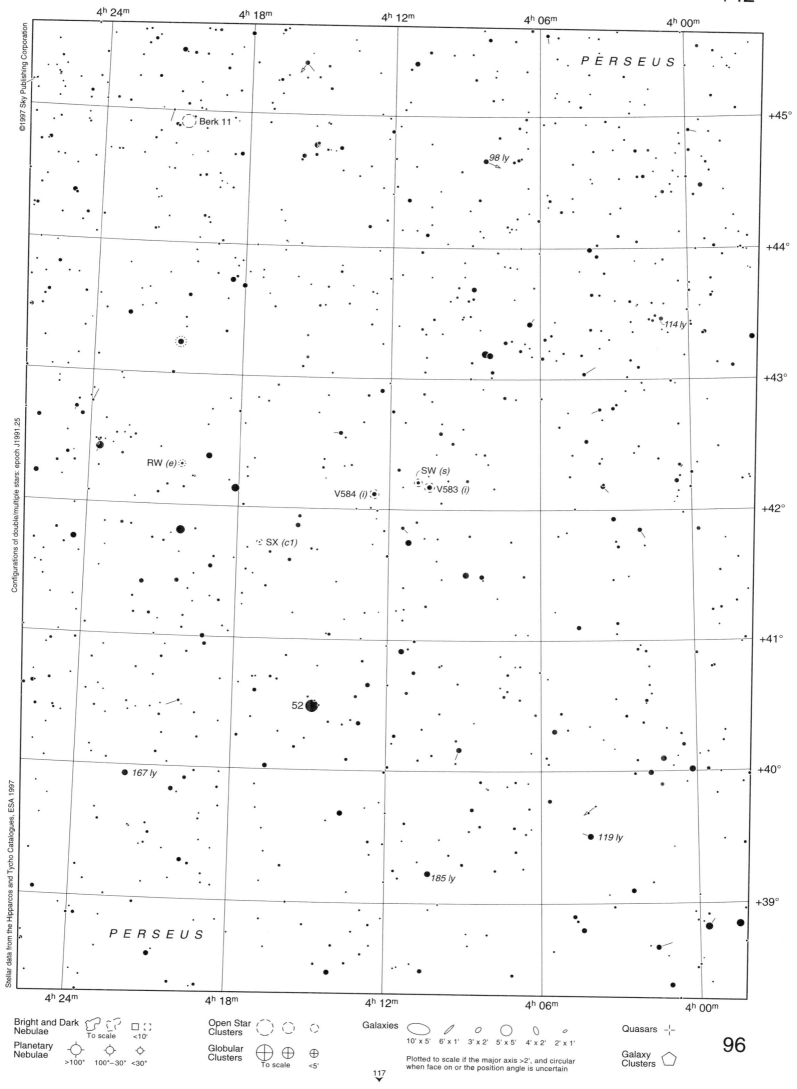

Configurations of double/multiple stars: epoch J1991.25

Stellar data from the Hipparcos and Tycho Catalogues, ESA 1997

P E R S E U S

4ʰ 24ᵐ   4ʰ 18ᵐ   4ʰ 12ᵐ   4ʰ 06ᵐ   4ʰ 00ᵐ

+45°
+44°
+43°
+42°
+41°
+40°
+39°

Berk 11

98 ly

114 ly

RW (e)

SW (s)

V584 (i)   V583 (i)

SX (c1)

52

167 ly

119 ly

185 ly

P E R S E U S

Bright and Dark Nebulae
To scale   <10'

Planetary Nebulae
>100"   100"–30"   <30"

Open Star Clusters

Globular Clusters
To scale   <5'

Galaxies
10' x 5'   6' x 1'   3' x 2'   5' x 5'   4' x 2'   2' x 1'

Plotted to scale if the major axis >2', and circular when face on or the position angle is uncertain

Quasars

Galaxy Clusters

96

117

76

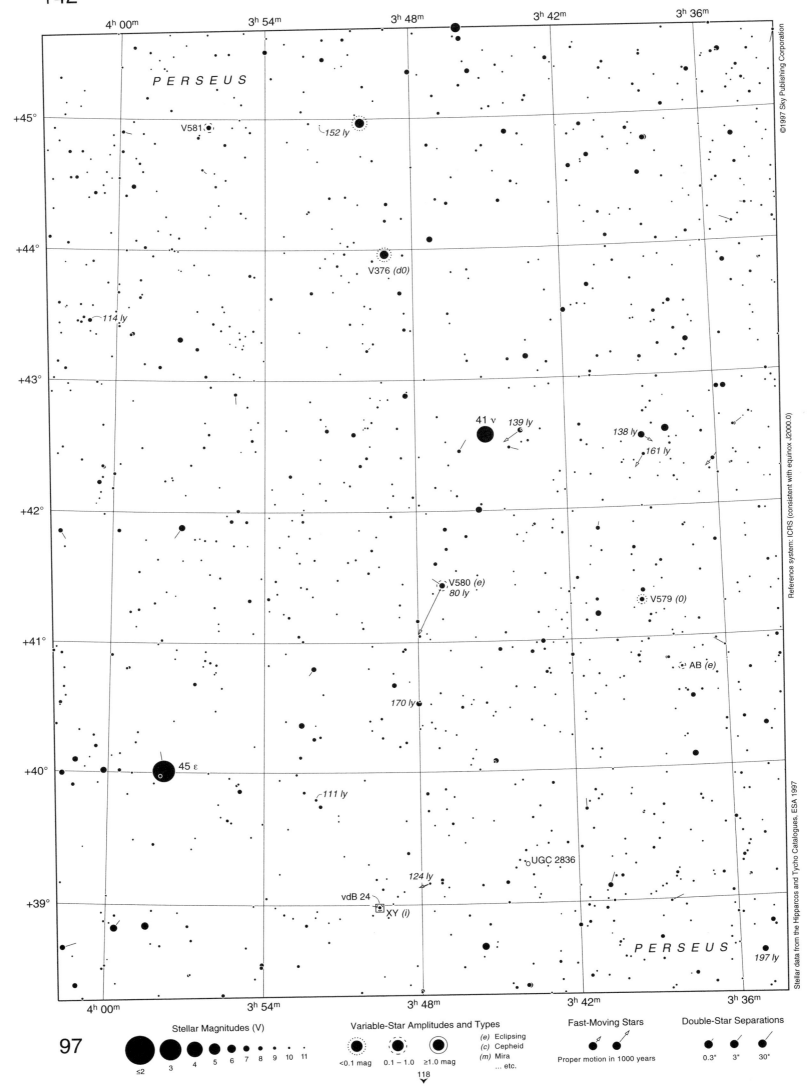

© 1997 Sky Publishing Corporation

Reference system: ICRS (consistent with equinox J2000.0)

Stellar data from the Hipparcos and Tycho Catalogues, ESA 1997

P E R S E U S

V581
152 ly
V376 (d0)
114 ly
41 ν   139 ly
138 ly
161 ly
V580 (e)
80 ly
V579 (0)
AB (e)
170 ly
45 ε
111 ly
UGC 2836
124 ly
vdB 24
XY (i)
P E R S E U S
197 ly

97

Stellar Magnitudes (V)	Variable-Star Amplitudes and Types	Fast-Moving Stars	Double-Star Separations

≤2   3   4   5   6   7   8   9   10   11

<0.1 mag   0.1 – 1.0   ≥1.0 mag

(e) Eclipsing
(c) Cepheid
(m) Mira
... etc.

Proper motion in 1000 years

0.3"   3"   30"

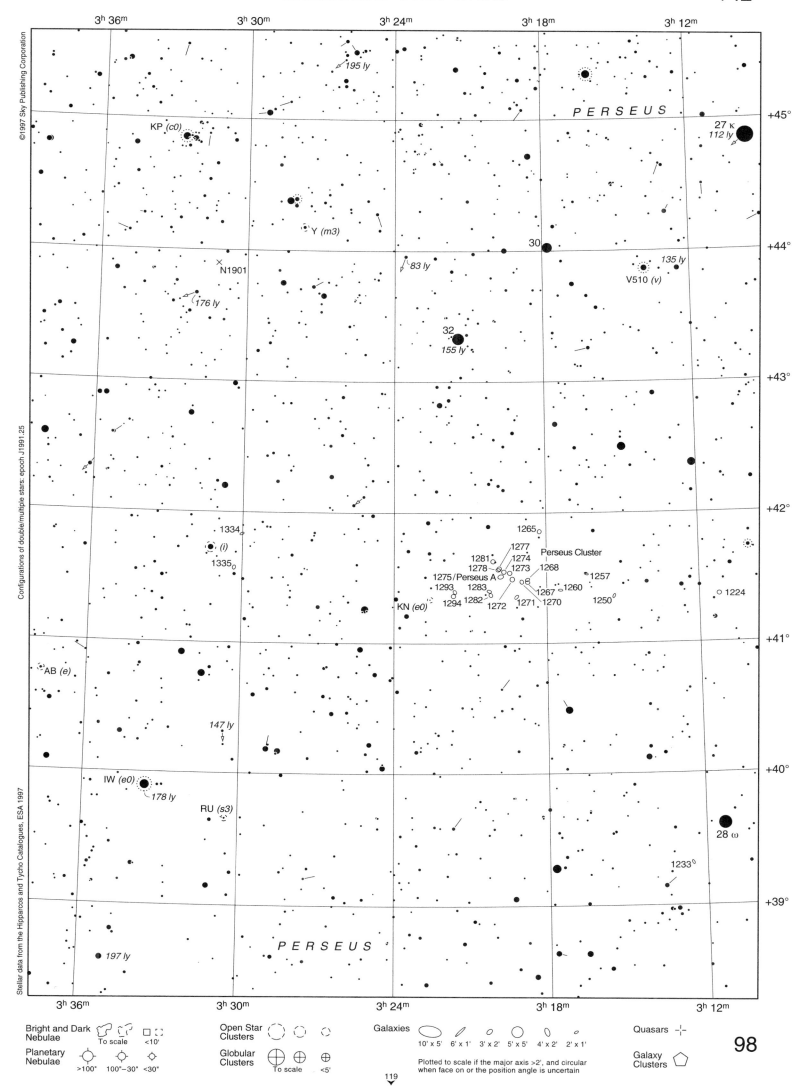

Configurations of double/multiple stars: epoch J1991.25

Stellar data from the Hipparcos and Tycho Catalogues, ESA 1997

P E R S E U S

3ʰ 36ᵐ   3ʰ 30ᵐ   3ʰ 24ᵐ   3ʰ 18ᵐ   3ʰ 12ᵐ

+45°
+44°
+43°
+42°
+41°
+40°
+39°

195 ly

KP (c0)

27 κ
112 ly

30

Y (m3)

N1901

176 ly

83 ly

135 ly
V510 (v)

32
155 ly

1334

(i)

1335

1265

Perseus Cluster
1277
1281 1274
1278 1273   1268
1275 / Perseus A   1257
1293   1283   1260
          1267
KN (e0)   1294 1282 1272 1271 1270 1250   1224

AB (e)

147 ly

IW (e0)

178 ly

RU (s3)

28 ω

1233

197 ly

P E R S E U S

3ʰ 36ᵐ   3ʰ 30ᵐ   3ʰ 24ᵐ   3ʰ 18ᵐ   3ʰ 12ᵐ

Bright and Dark
Nebulae   To scale   <10'

Planetary
Nebulae   >100" 100"–30" <30"

Open Star
Clusters

Globular
Clusters   To scale   <5'

Galaxies
10' x 5' 6' x 1' 3' x 2' 5' x 5' 4' x 2' 2' x 1'

Plotted to scale if the major axis >2', and circular
when face on or the position angle is uncertain

Quasars

Galaxy
Clusters

98

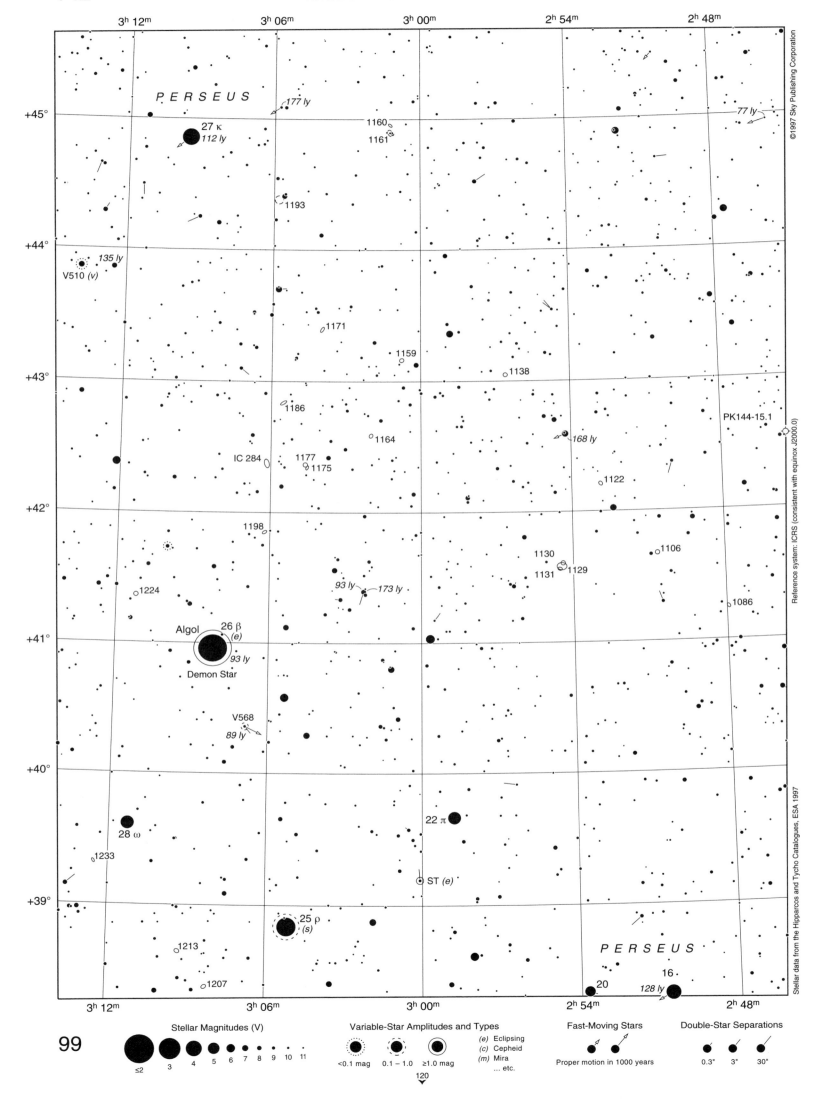

PERSEUS

27 κ
112 ly

177 ly

1160
1161

77 ly

1193

135 ly
V510 (v)

1171

1159

1138

1186

1164

PK144-15.1

IC 284

1177
1175

168 ly

1122

1198

1130
1131 1129

1106

1224

93 ly   173 ly

1086

Algol   26 β
(e)

93 ly

Demon Star

V568

89 ly

28 ω

22 π

1233

ST (e)

25 ρ
(s)

PERSEUS

1213

16

1207

20

128 ly

©1997 Sky Publishing Corporation

Reference system: ICRS (consistent with equinox J2000.0)

Stellar data from the Hipparcos and Tycho Catalogues, ESA 1997

99

Stellar Magnitudes (V)

≤2   3   4   5   6   7   8   9   10   11

Variable-Star Amplitudes and Types

<0.1 mag   0.1 – 1.0   ≥1.0 mag

(e) Eclipsing
(c) Cepheid
(m) Mira
... etc.

Fast-Moving Stars

Proper motion in 1000 years

Double-Star Separations

0.3"   3"   30"

120

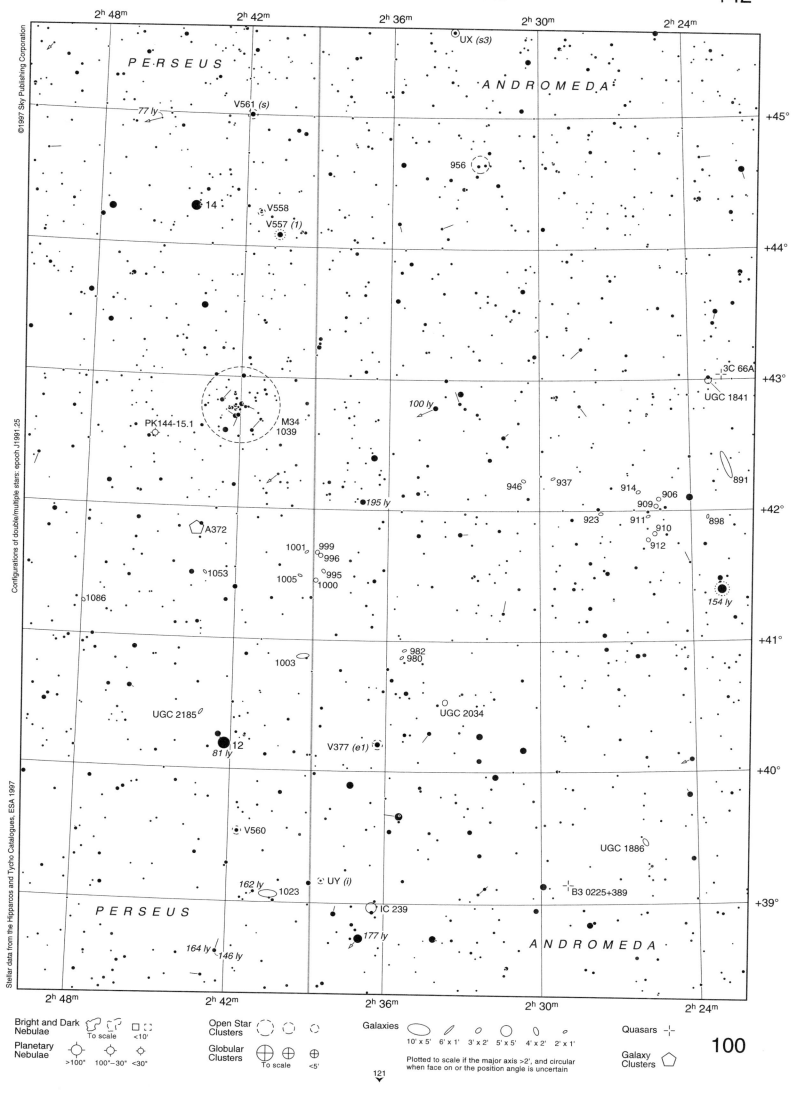

Configurations of double/multiple stars: epoch J1991.25

Stellar data from the Hipparcos and Tycho Catalogues, ESA 1997

P E R S E U S

A N D R O M E D A

UX (s3)

956

77 ly

V561 (s)

14

V558

V557 (1)

3C 66A

UGC 1841

100 ly

PK144-15.1

M34
1039

946   937

914   906

909

891

923   911   910

912   898

A372

1001   999

996

1053   1005   995

1000

1086

154 ly

195 ly

982
980

1003

UGC 2185

UGC 2034

12

81 ly

V377 (e1)

UGC 1886

V560

B3 0225+389

162 ly   1023

UY (i)

P E R S E U S

IC 239

A N D R O M E D A

164 ly   146 ly

177 ly

+45°

+44°

+43°

+42°

+41°

+40°

+39°

2ʰ 48ᵐ   2ʰ 42ᵐ   2ʰ 36ᵐ   2ʰ 30ᵐ   2ʰ 24ᵐ

100

121

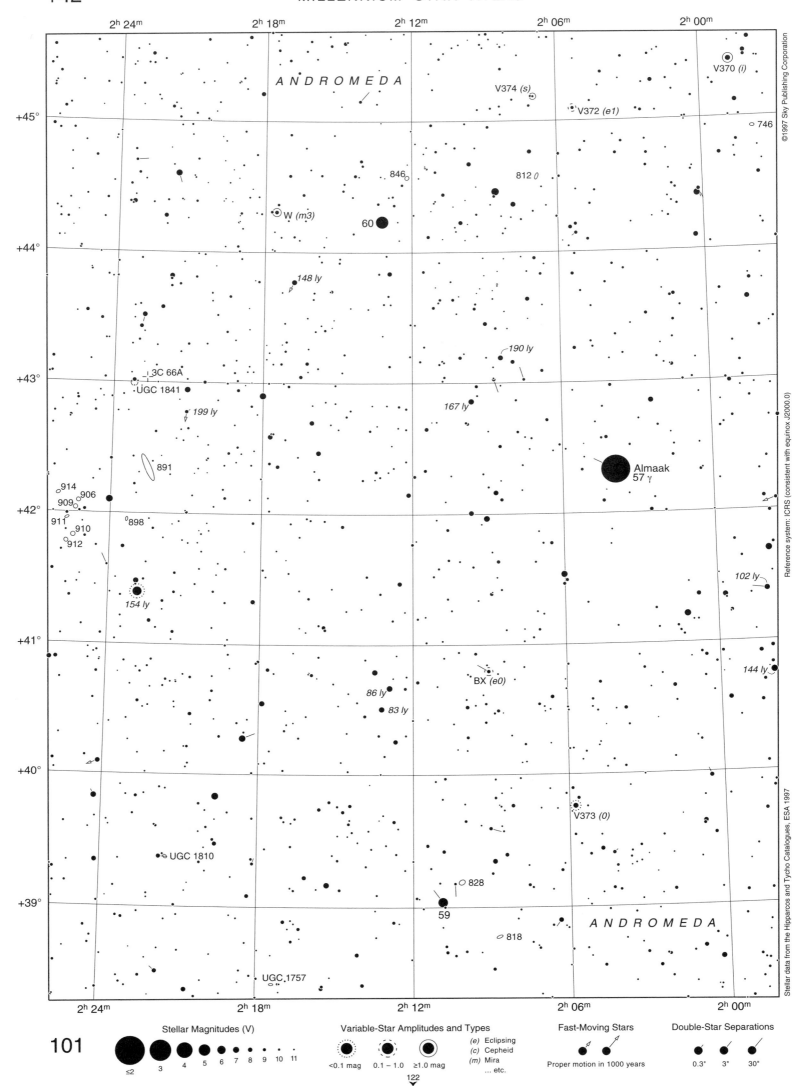

©1997 Sky Publishing Corporation

Reference system: ICRS (consistent with equinox J2000.0)

Stellar data from the Hipparcos and Tycho Catalogues, ESA 1997

ANDROMEDA

V374 (s)
V372 (e1)
V370 (i)
746
846
812 0
60
W (m3)
148 ly
190 ly
3C 66A
UGC 1841
167 ly
199 ly
Almaak
57 γ
891
914
906
909
911
910
912
898
102 ly
154 ly
144 ly
86 ly
BX (e0)
83 ly
V373 (0)
UGC 1810
828
59
UGC 1757
818
ANDROMEDA

101

Stellar Magnitudes (V)

≤2   3   4   5   6   7   8   9   10   11

Variable-Star Amplitudes and Types

<0.1 mag   0.1 – 1.0   ≥1.0 mag

(e) Eclipsing
(c) Cepheid
(m) Mira
... etc.

Fast-Moving Stars

Proper motion in 1000 years

Double-Star Separations

0.3"   3"   30"

122

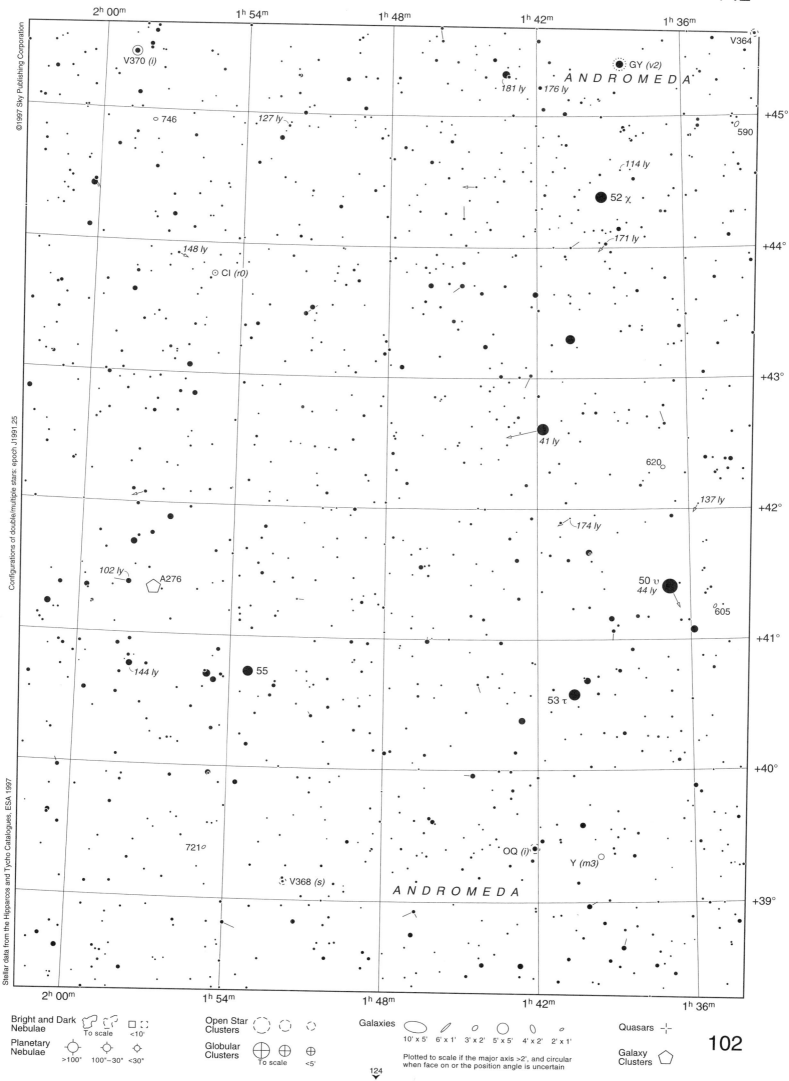

©1997 Sky Publishing Corporation

Configurations of double/multiple stars: epoch J1991.25

Stellar data from the Hipparcos and Tycho Catalogues, ESA 1997

A N D R O M E D A

GY (v2)

V364

V370 (i)

181 ly   176 ly

746   127 ly

590

114 ly

52 χ

148 ly   171 ly

Cl (r0)

41 ly

620

137 ly

174 ly

102 ly   A276

50 υ
44 ly

605

144 ly   55

53 τ

7211

OQ (i)   Y (m3)

V368 (s)

A N D R O M E D A

+45°

+44°

+43°

+42°

+41°

+40°

+39°

2h 00m   1h 54m   1h 48m   1h 42m   1h 36m

Bright and Dark Nebulae
To scale   <10'
Planetary Nebulae
>100"   100"–30"   <30"

Open Star Clusters

Globular Clusters
To scale   <5'

Galaxies
10' x 5'   6' x 1'   3' x 2'   5' x 5'   4' x 2'   2' x 1'

Plotted to scale if the major axis >2', and circular when face on or the position angle is uncertain

Quasars

Galaxy Clusters

102

124

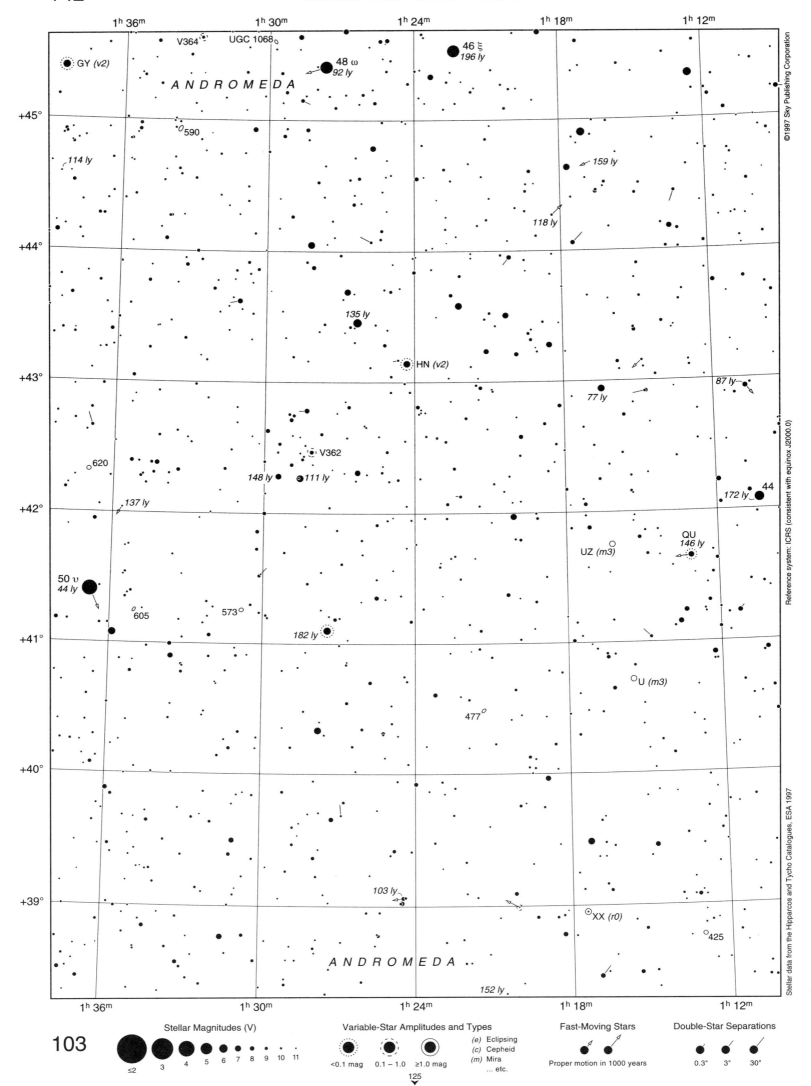

©1997 Sky Publishing Corporation

Reference system: ICRS (consistent with equinox J2000.0)

Stellar data from the Hipparcos and Tycho Catalogues, ESA 1997

ANDROMEDA

GY *(v2)*

V364   UGC 1068

48 ω
92 ly

46 ξ
196 ly

590

114 ly

159 ly

118 ly

135 ly

HN *(v2)*

87 ly

77 ly

V362

620

148 ly   111 ly

137 ly

44
172 ly

QU
146 ly

UZ *(m3)*

50 υ
44 ly

605   573

182 ly

U *(m3)*

477

103 ly

XX *(r0)*

425

152 ly

ANDROMEDA

Stellar Magnitudes (V)

≤2   3   4   5   6   7   8   9   10   11

Variable-Star Amplitudes and Types

<0.1 mag   0.1 – 1.0   ≥1.0 mag

(e) Eclipsing
(c) Cepheid
(m) Mira
... etc.

Fast-Moving Stars

Proper motion in 1000 years

Double-Star Separations

0.3"   3"   30"

125

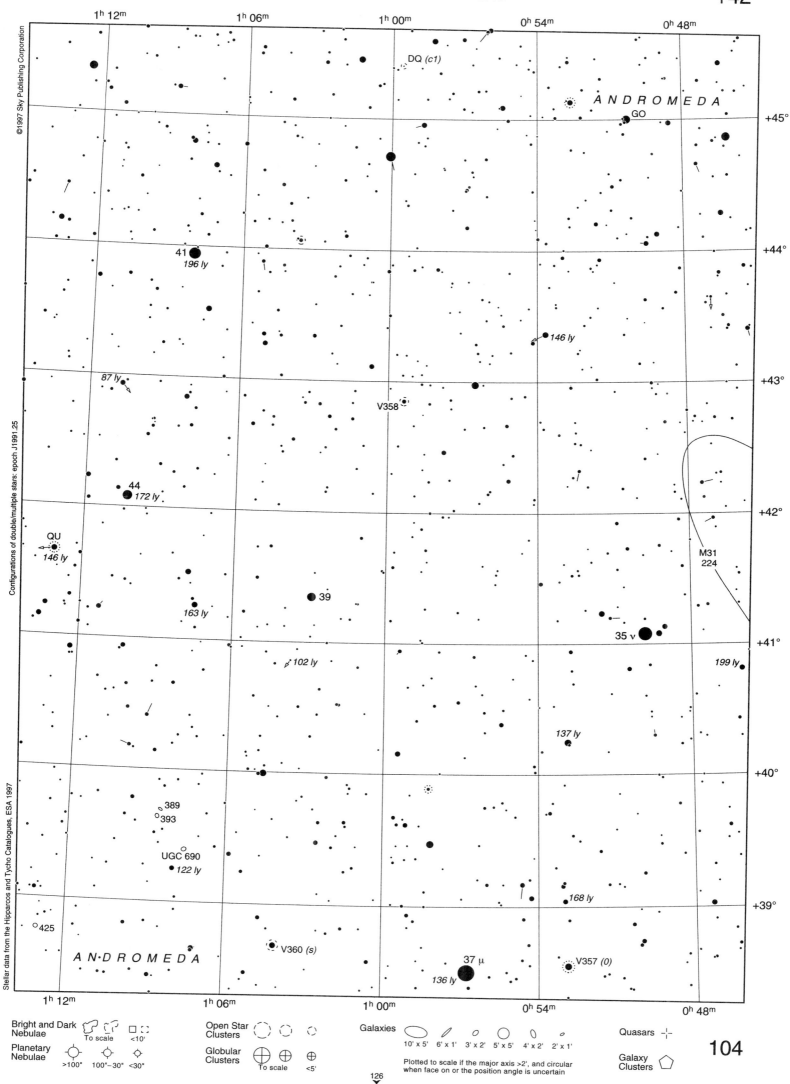

©1997 Sky Publishing Corporation

Configurations of double/multiple stars: epoch J1991.25

Stellar data from the Hipparcos and Tycho Catalogues, ESA 1997

1h 12m   1h 06m   1h 00m   0h 54m   0h 48m

DQ (c1)

A N D R O M E D A

GO

+45°

41
196 ly

+44°

146 ly

87 ly

+43°

V358

44
172 ly

+42°

QU
146 ly

M31
224

39

163 ly

35 ν
199 ly

+41°

102 ly

137 ly

+40°

389
393

UGC 690
122 ly

168 ly

+39°

425

A N · D R O M E D A

V360 (s)

37 μ
136 ly

V357 (0)

1h 12m   1h 06m   1h 00m   0h 54m   0h 48m

Bright and Dark
Nebulae
To scale   <10'

Planetary
Nebulae
>100" 100"–30" <30"

Open Star
Clusters

Globular
Clusters
To scale   <5'

Galaxies
10' x 5' 6' x 1' 3' x 2' 5' x 5' 4' x 2' 2' x 1'

Plotted to scale if the major axis >2', and circular
when face on or the position angle is uncertain

Quasars

Galaxy
Clusters

104

126

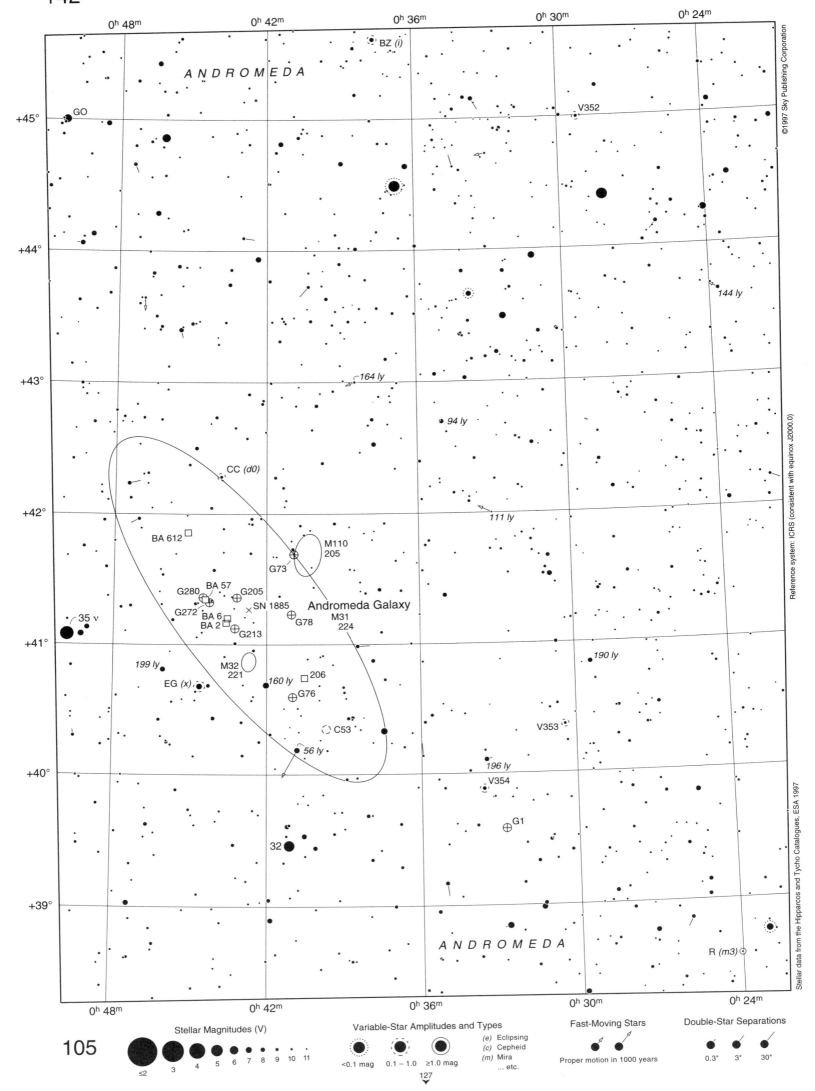

105

Stellar Magnitudes (V)	Variable-Star Amplitudes and Types	Fast-Moving Stars	Double-Star Separations

≤2   3   4   5   6   7   8   9   10   11

<0.1 mag   0.1 – 1.0   ≥1.0 mag

(e) Eclipsing
(c) Cepheid
(m) Mira
... etc.

Proper motion in 1000 years

0.3"   3"   30"

127

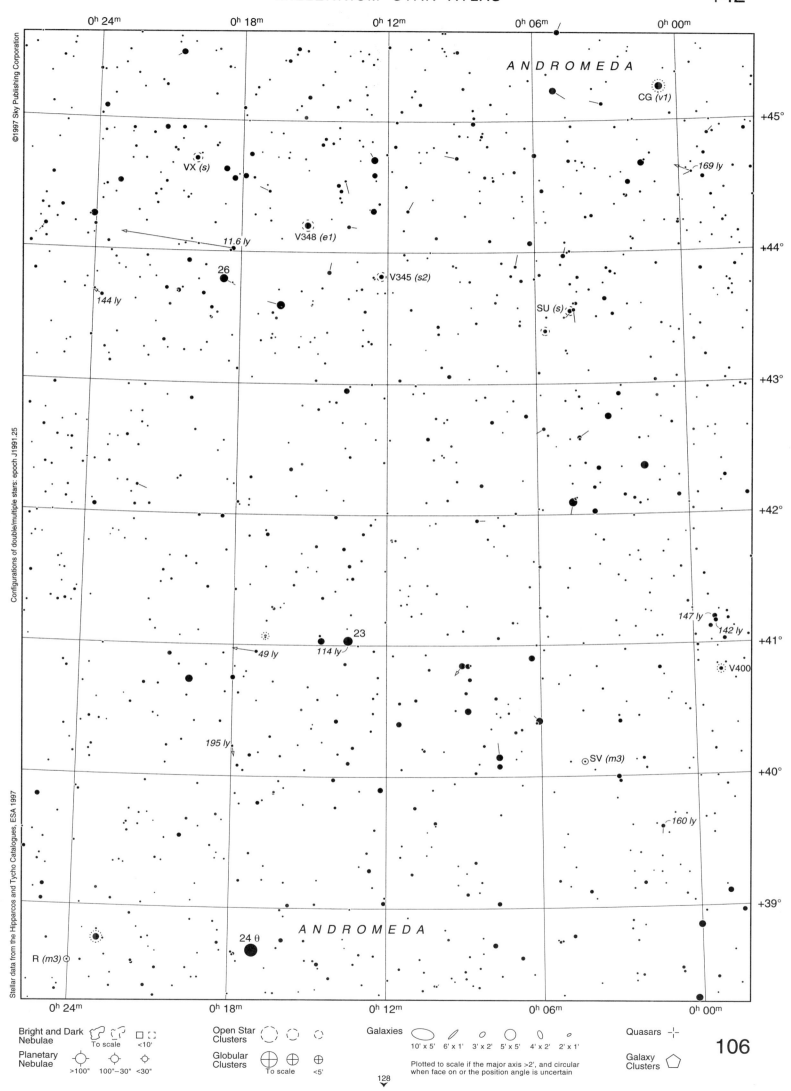

ANDROMEDA

CG (v1)

169 ly

VX (s)

V348 (e1)

11.6 ly

26

144 ly

V345 (s2)

SU (s)

147 ly

142 ly

V400

23

49 ly

114 ly

SV (m3)

195 ly

160 ly

ANDROMEDA

24 θ

R (m3)

Bright and Dark Nebulae			Open Star Clusters			Galaxies						Quasars
	To scale	<10'				10' x 5'	6' x 1'	3' x 2'	5' x 5'	4' x 2'	2' x 1'	

Planetary Nebulae
>100"   100"–30"   <30"

Globular Clusters
To scale   <5'

Galaxy Clusters

Plotted to scale if the major axis >2', and circular when face on or the position angle is uncertain

87

MILLENNIUM STAR ATLAS

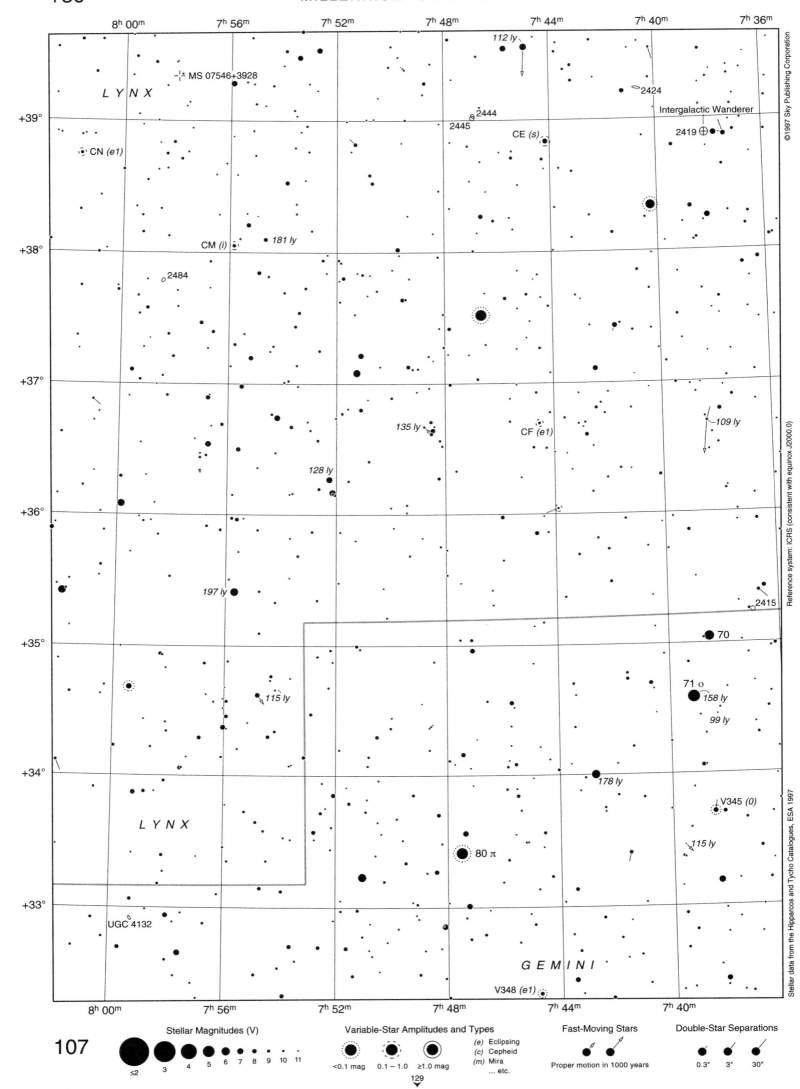

©1997 Sky Publishing Corporation

Reference system: ICRS (consistent with equinox J2000.0)

Stellar data from the Hipparcos and Tycho Catalogues, ESA 1997

LYNX

MS 07546+3928

CN (e1)

CM (i)   181 ly

2484

112 ly

2444
2445

CE (s)

2424

Intergalactic Wanderer

2419

135 ly

CF (e1)

128 ly

109 ly

197 ly

2415

70

115 ly

71 o
158 ly

99 ly

178 ly

V345 (0)

115 ly

LYNX

80 π

UGC 4132

GEMINI

V348 (e1)

107

Stellar Magnitudes (V)

≤2   3   4   5   6   7   8   9   10   11

Variable-Star Amplitudes and Types

<0.1 mag   0.1 – 1.0   ≥1.0 mag

(e) Eclipsing
(c) Cepheid
(m) Mira
... etc.

Fast-Moving Stars

Proper motion in 1000 years

Double-Star Separations

0.3"   3"   30"

129

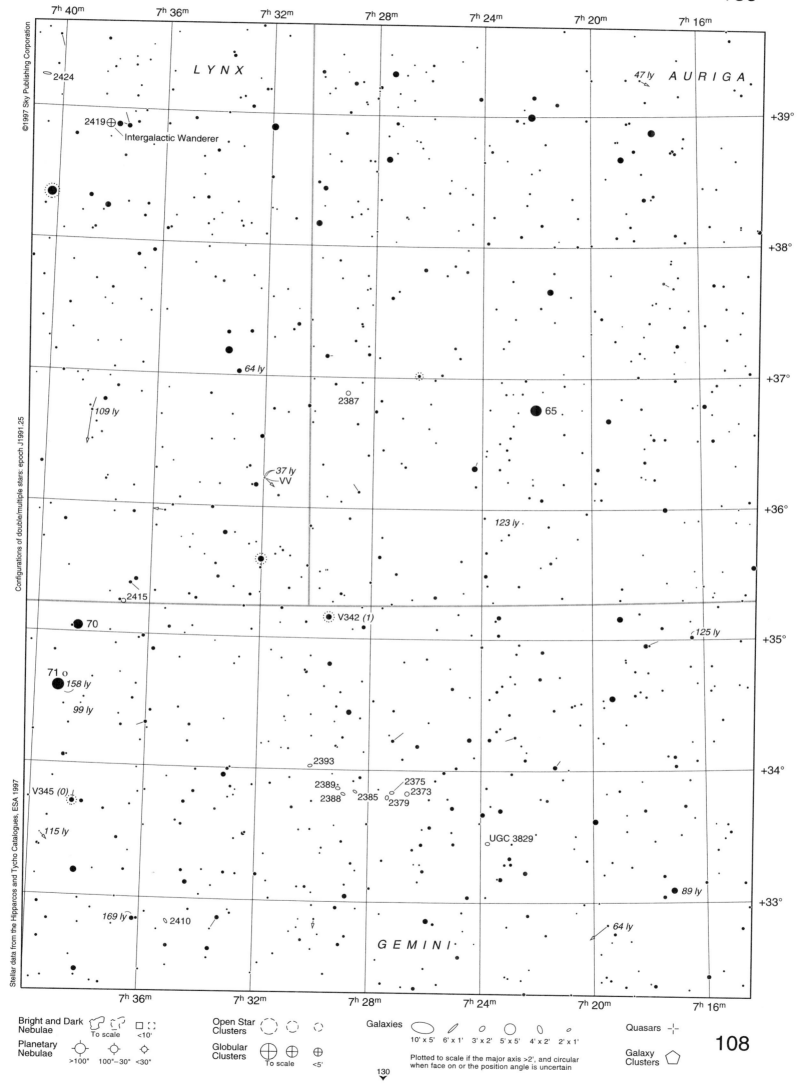

L Y N X

A U R I G A

2424

2419 ⊕
Intergalactic Wanderer

47 ly

+39°

+38°

64 ly

+37°

109 ly

2387

65

37 ly
VV

+36°

123 ly

2415

125 ly

70

V342 (1)

+35°

71 o
158 ly

99 ly

2393

+34°

2389   2375
2388   2385   2373
             2379

V345 (0)

115 ly

UGC 3829

89 ly

+33°

169 ly   2410

64 ly

G E M I N I

Bright and Dark
Nebulae
                    To scale   <10'

Planetary
Nebulae
            >100" 100"–30" <30"

Open Star
Clusters

Globular
Clusters
            To scale   <5'

Galaxies
        10' x 5' 6' x 1' 3' x 2' 5' x 5' 4' x 2' 2' x 1'

Plotted to scale if the major axis >2', and circular
when face on or the position angle is uncertain

Quasars

Galaxy
Clusters

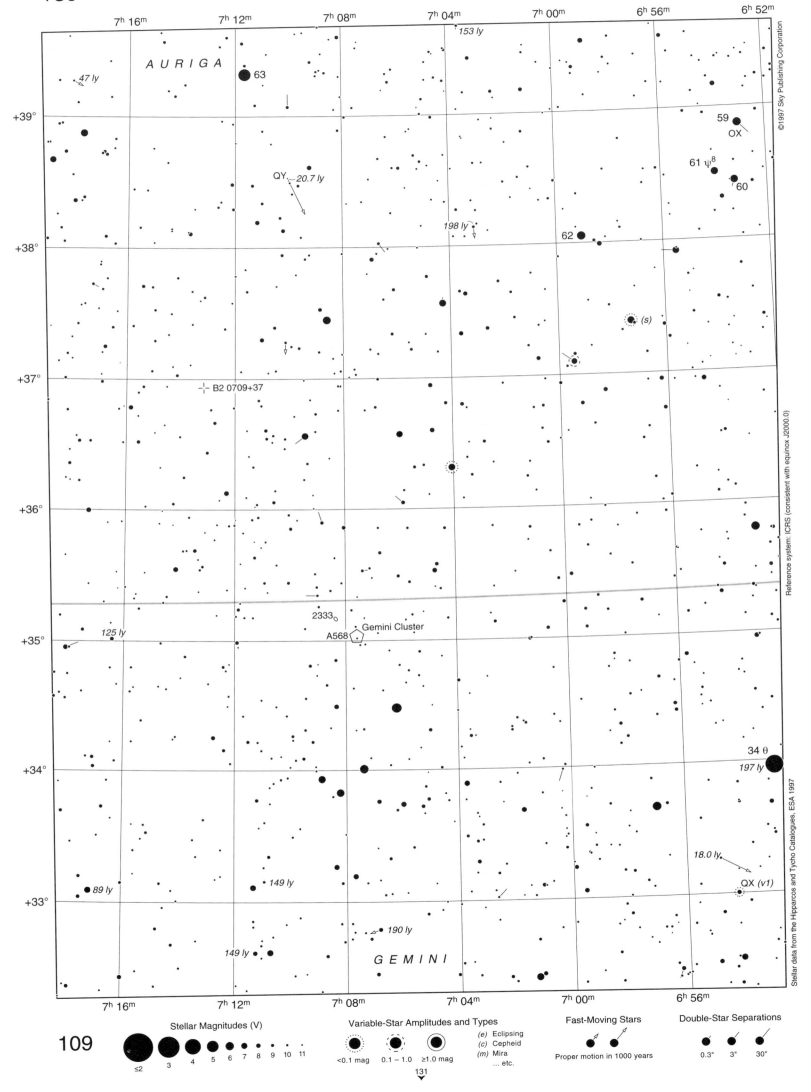

AURIGA

GEMINI

©1997 Sky Publishing Corporation

Reference system: ICRS (consistent with equinox J2000.0)

Stellar data from the Hipparcos and Tycho Catalogues, ESA 1997

47 ly

63

QY 20.7 ly

153 ly

59
OX

61 ψ⁸
60

62

(s)

198 ly

B2 0709+37

2333

Gemini Cluster
A568

125 ly

34 θ
197 ly

18.0 ly

QX (v1)

89 ly

149 ly

190 ly

149 ly

109

Stellar Magnitudes (V)

≤2   3   4   5   6   7   8   9   10   11

Variable-Star Amplitudes and Types

<0.1 mag   0.1 – 1.0   ≥1.0 mag

(e) Eclipsing
(c) Cepheid
(m) Mira
... etc.

Fast-Moving Stars

Proper motion in 1000 years

Double-Star Separations

0.3"   3"   30"

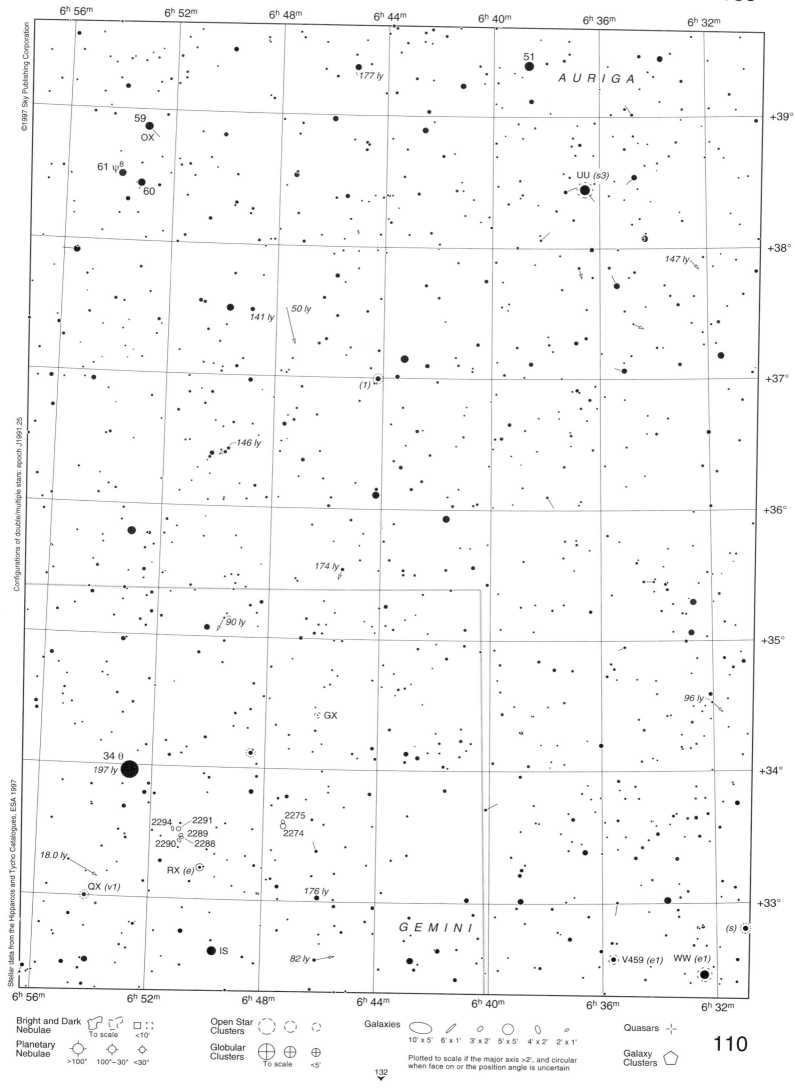

Configurations of double/multiple stars: epoch J1991.25

Stellar data from the Hipparcos and Tycho Catalogues, ESA 1997

AURIGA

51

59
OX

61 ψ8
60

UU (s3)

147 ly

177 ly

141 ly   50 ly

146 ly

(1)

174 ly

90 ly

96 ly

GX

34 θ
197 ly

2294   2291
2289
2290   2288

2275
2274

18.0 ly

RX (e)

QX (v1)

176 ly

GEMINI

IS   82 ly

V459 (e1)   WW (e1)

(s)

+39°

+38°

+37°

+36°

+35°

+34°

+33°

6ʰ 56ᵐ   6ʰ 52ᵐ   6ʰ 48ᵐ   6ʰ 44ᵐ   6ʰ 40ᵐ   6ʰ 36ᵐ   6ʰ 32ᵐ

Bright and Dark
Nebulae   To scale   <10'

Planetary
Nebulae   >100" 100"–30" <30"

Open Star
Clusters

Globular
Clusters   To scale   <5'

Galaxies

10' x 5'   6' x 1'   3' x 2'   5' x 5'   4' x 2'   2' x 1'

Plotted to scale if the major axis >2', and circular
when face on or the position angle is uncertain

Quasars –|–

Galaxy
Clusters

110

132

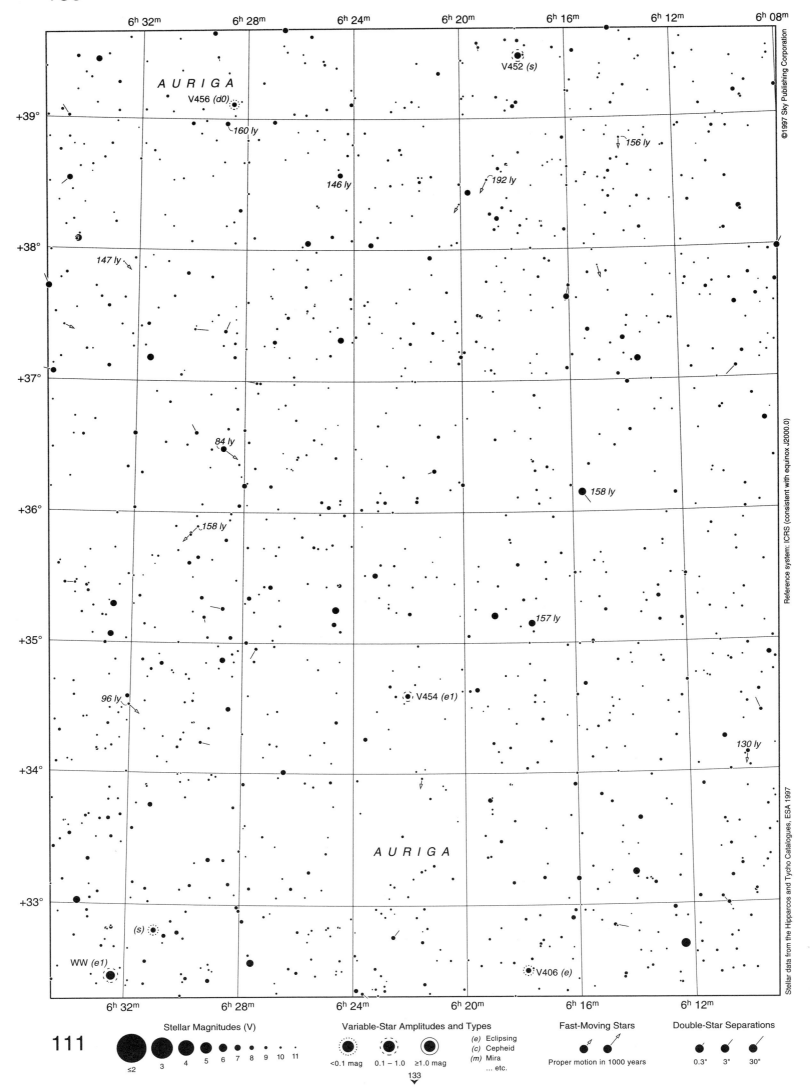

AURIGA

V452 (s)

V456 (d0)

160 ly

156 ly

146 ly

192 ly

147 ly

84 ly

158 ly

158 ly

96 ly

157 ly

V454 (e1)

130 ly

AURIGA

(s)

WW (e1)

V406 (e)

©1997 Sky Publishing Corporation

Reference system: ICRS (consistent with equinox J2000.0)

Stellar data from the Hipparcos and Tycho Catalogues, ESA 1997

111

Stellar Magnitudes (V)	Variable-Star Amplitudes and Types	Fast-Moving Stars	Double-Star Separations

Stellar Magnitudes (V)

≤2   3   4   5   6   7   8   9   10   11

Variable-Star Amplitudes and Types

<0.1 mag   0.1 – 1.0   ≥1.0 mag

(e) Eclipsing
(c) Cepheid
(m) Mira
... etc.

Fast-Moving Stars

Proper motion in 1000 years

Double-Star Separations

0.3"   3"   30"

MILLENNIUM STAR ATLAS

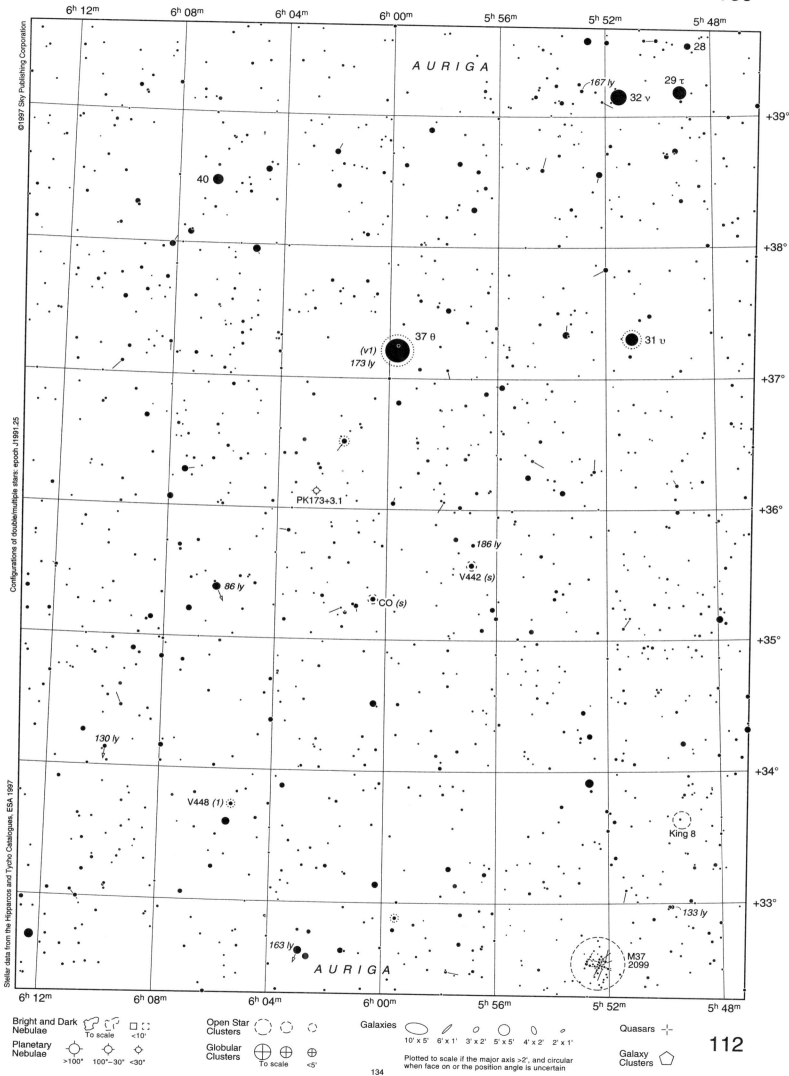

©1997 Sky Publishing Corporation

Configurations of double/multiple stars: epoch J1991.25

Stellar data from the Hipparcos and Tycho Catalogues, ESA 1997

A U R I G A

28

167 ly
29 τ
32 ν

40

+39°

+38°

37 θ
(v1)
173 ly

31 υ

+37°

PK173+3.1

186 ly
V442 (s)

86 ly

CO (s)

+36°

+35°

130 ly

V448 (1)

King 8

+34°

133 ly

163 ly
A U R I G A

M37
2099

+33°

Bright and Dark Nebulae	Open Star Clusters	Galaxies

Bright and Dark
Nebulae
To scale   <10'

Planetary
Nebulae
>100"   100"–30"   <30"

Open Star
Clusters

Globular
Clusters
To scale   <5'

Galaxies
10' x 5' 6' x 1' 3' x 2' 5' x 5' 4' x 2' 2' x 1'

Plotted to scale if the major axis >2', and circular
when face on or the position angle is uncertain

Quasars

Galaxy
Clusters

112

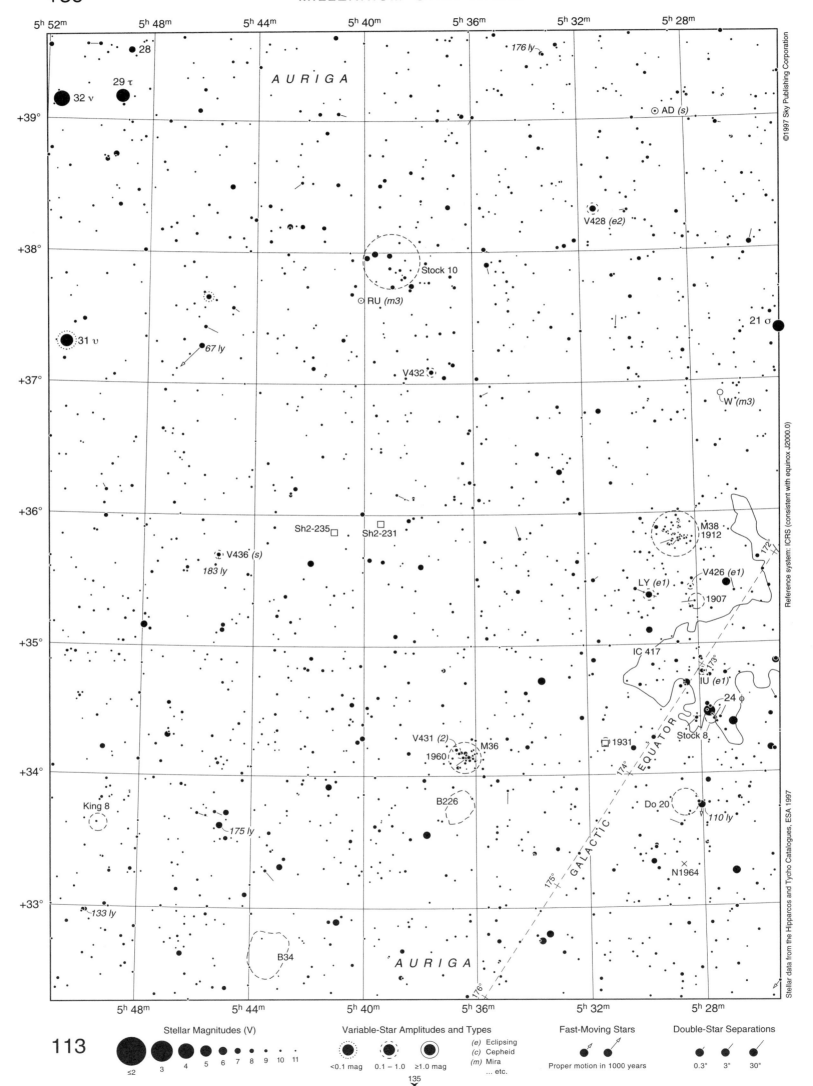

©1997 Sky Publishing Corporation

Reference system: ICRS (consistent with equinox J2000.0)

Stellar data from the Hipparcos and Tycho Catalogues, ESA 1997

A U R I G A

5h 52m   5h 48m   5h 44m   5h 40m   5h 36m   5h 32m   5h 28m

+39°

28

29 τ

32 ν

⊙ AD (s)

176 ly

V428 (e2)

+38°

Stock 10

⊙ RU (m3)

21 σ

31 υ

67 ly

V432

W (m3)

+37°

+36°

Sh2-235   Sh2-231

M38
1912

V436 (s)

183 ly

V426 (e1)

LY (e1)

1907

IC 417

+35°

IU (e1)

24 φ

Stock 8

V431 (2)   M36

1960

1931

B226

Do 20

110 ly

+34°

King 8

B34

175 ly

N1964

133 ly

GALACTIC EQUATOR

172°

173°

174°

175°

176°

+33°

A U R I G A

5h 48m   5h 44m   5h 40m   5h 36m   5h 32m   5h 28m

Stellar Magnitudes (V)

≤2   3   4   5   6   7   8   9   10   11

Variable-Star Amplitudes and Types

<0.1 mag   0.1 – 1.0 mag   ≥1.0 mag

(e) Eclipsing
(c) Cepheid
(m) Mira
... etc.

Fast-Moving Stars

Proper motion in 1000 years

Double-Star Separations

0.3"   3"   30"

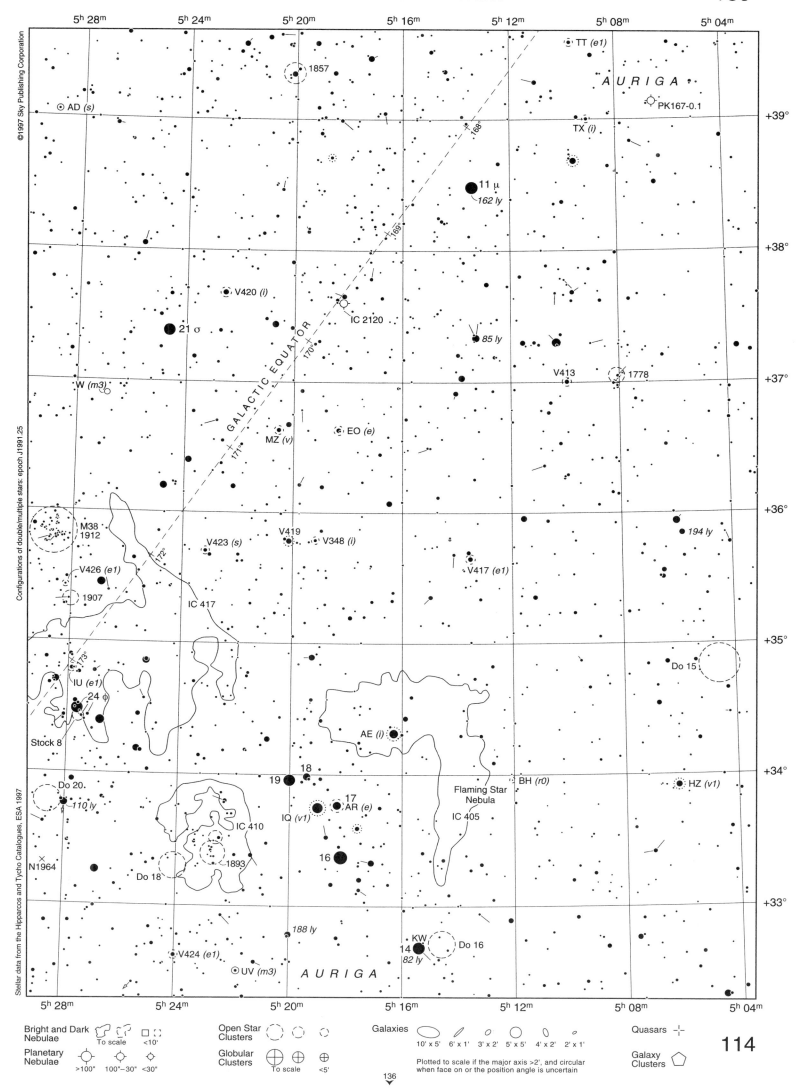

AURIGA

TT (e1)

PK167-0.1

1857

AD (s)

TX (i)

168°

11 μ
162 ly

V420 (i)

IC 2120

21 σ

85 ly

169°

V413   1778

170°

W (m3)

EO (e)

MZ (v)

171°

GALACTIC EQUATOR

M38
1912

V423 (s)   V419   V348 (i)

194 ly

V426 (e1)

V417 (e1)

1907

IC 417

172°

Do 15

173°

IU (e1)

24 φ

AE (i)

Stock 8

Flaming Star
Nebula

BH (r0)

HZ (v1)

18

19

Do 20.

17
AR (e)

110 ly

IQ (v1)

IC 410

IC 405

N1964

1893

16

Do 18

188 ly

KW
Do 16
14
82 ly

V424 (e1)

UV (m3)   A U R I G A

Bright and Dark
Nebulae
To scale   <10'

Open Star
Clusters

Galaxies

10' x 5'   6' x 1'   3' x 2'   5' x 5'   4' x 2'   2' x 1'

Quasars

Planetary
Nebulae
>100"   100"–30"   <30"

Globular
Clusters
To scale   <5'

Galaxy
Clusters

Plotted to scale if the major axis >2', and circular
when face on or the position angle is uncertain

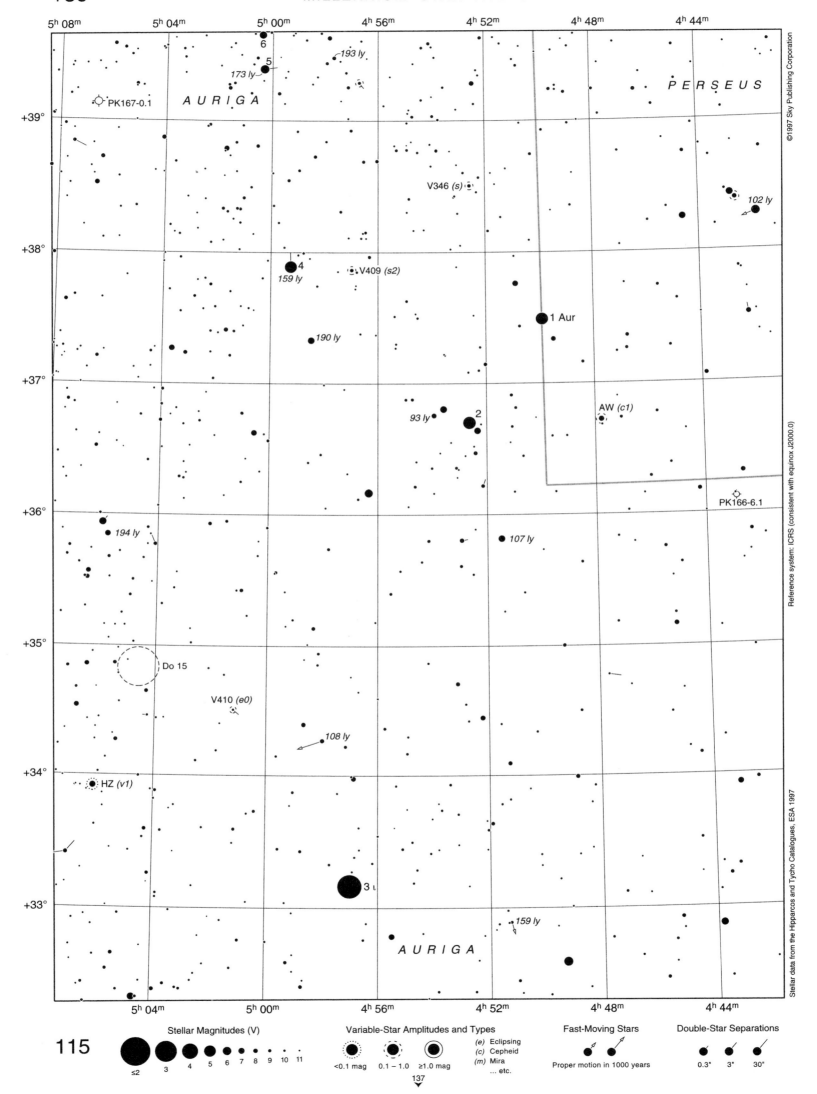

©1997 Sky Publishing Corporation

Reference system: ICRS (consistent with equinox J2000.0)

Stellar data from the Hipparcos and Tycho Catalogues, ESA 1997

PERSEUS

AURIGA

PK167-0.1

193 ly

173 ly

6

5

V346 (s)

102 ly

4

159 ly

V409 (s2)

1 Aur

190 ly

93 ly

2

AW (c1)

194 ly

107 ly

PK166-6.1

Do 15

V410 (e0)

108 ly

HZ (v1)

3 ι

AURIGA

159 ly

Stellar Magnitudes (V)

≤2 3 4 5 6 7 8 9 10 11

Variable-Star Amplitudes and Types

<0.1 mag   0.1 – 1.0   ≥1.0 mag

(e) Eclipsing
(c) Cepheid
(m) Mira
... etc.

Fast-Moving Stars

Proper motion in 1000 years

Double-Star Separations

0.3"   3"   30"

137

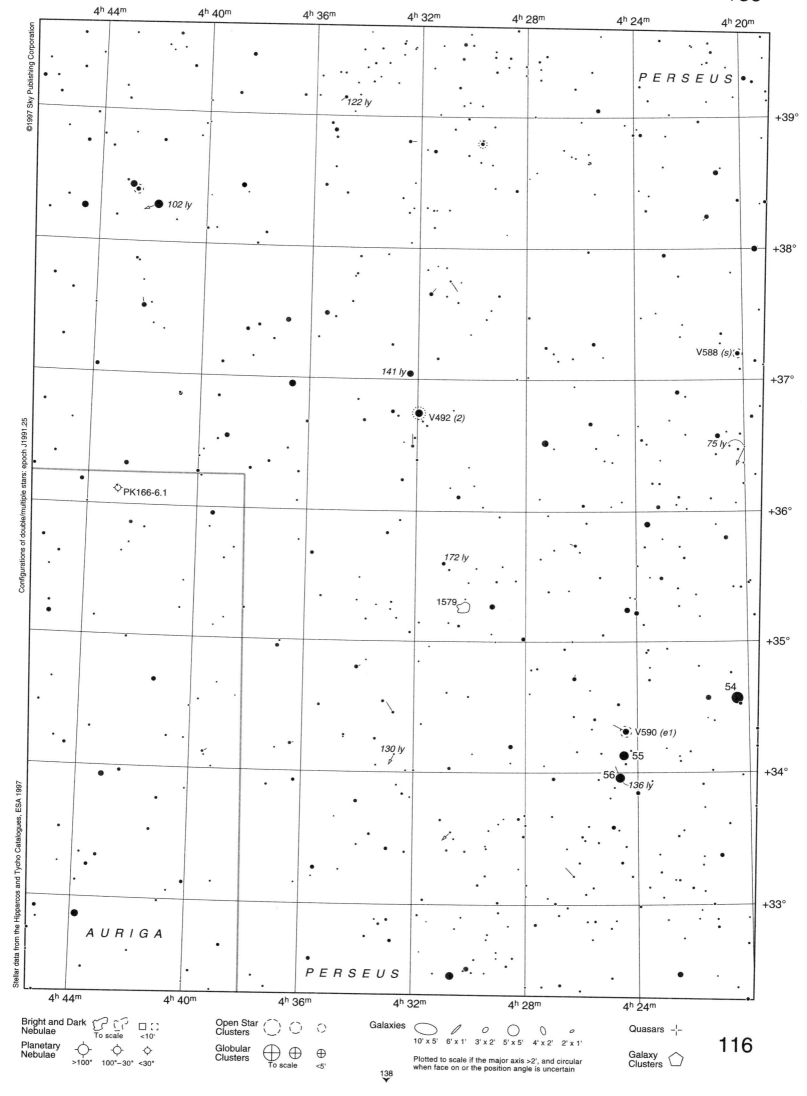

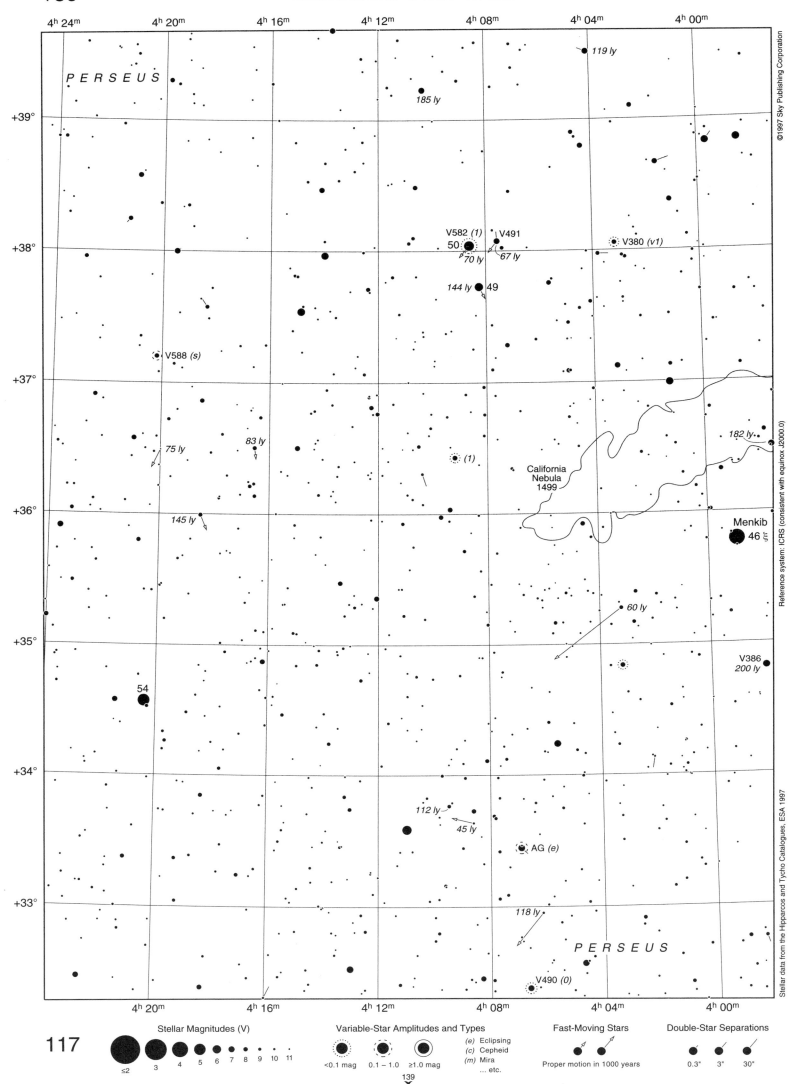

P E R S E U S

119 ly

185 ly

V582 (1) V491
50   V380 (v1)
70 ly 67 ly

144 ly 49

V588 (s)

(1)

California
Nebula
1499

182 ly

75 ly

83 ly

Menkib
46 ξ

145 ly

60 ly

V386
200 ly

54

112 ly
45 ly

AG (e)

118 ly

P E R S E U S

V490 (0)

©1997 Sky Publishing Corporation

Reference system: ICRS (consistent with equinox J2000.0)

Stellar data from the Hipparcos and Tycho Catalogues, ESA 1997

Stellar Magnitudes (V)

≤2   3   4   5   6   7 8 9 10 11

Variable-Star Amplitudes and Types

<0.1 mag   0.1 – 1.0   ≥1.0 mag

(e) Eclipsing
(c) Cepheid
(m) Mira
... etc.

Fast-Moving Stars

Proper motion in 1000 years

Double-Star Separations

0.3"   3"   30"

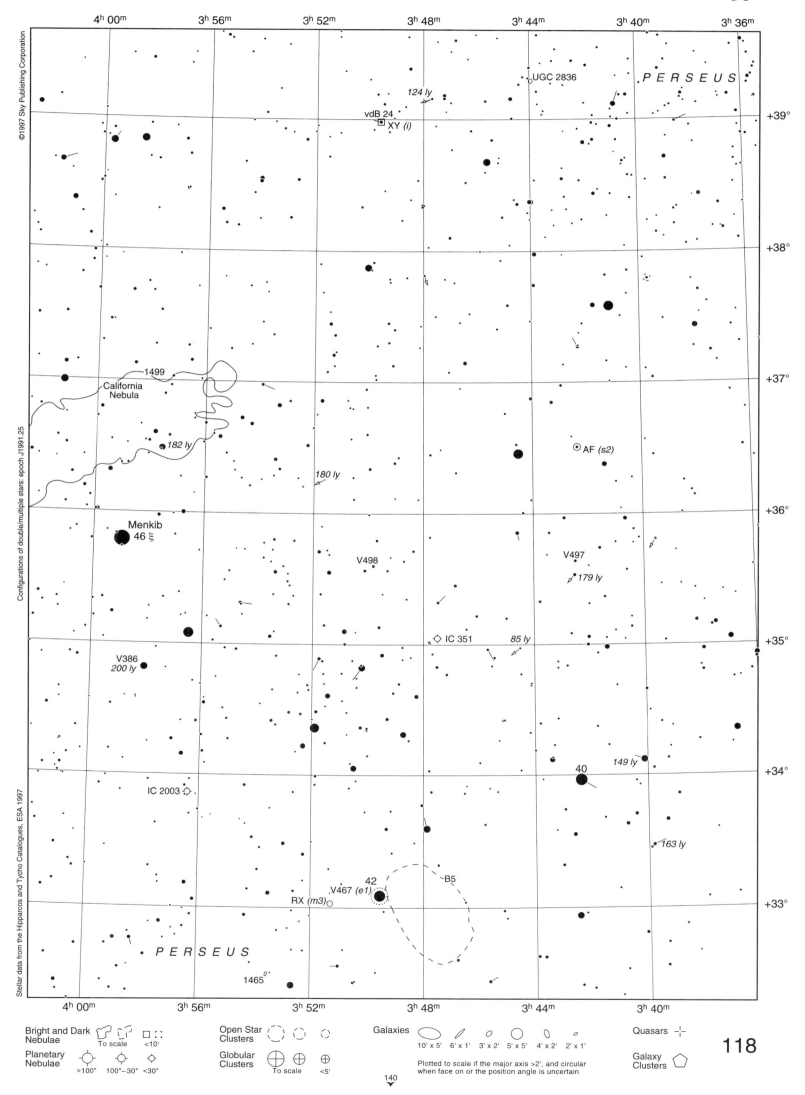

PERSEUS

UGC 2836

124 ly

vdB 24
☐• XY (i)

+39°

+38°

1499

California
Nebula

182 ly

180 ly

⊙ AF (s2)

+37°

Menkib
46 ξ

+36°

V498

V497

179 ly

V386
200 ly

◇ IC 351

85 ly

+35°

IC 2003 ◇

40

149 ly

163 ly

+34°

42

B5

.V467 (e1)
RX (m3) ○

+33°

PERSEUS

1465

©1997 Sky Publishing Corporation

Configurations of double/multiple stars: epoch J1991.25

Stellar data from the Hipparcos and Tycho Catalogues, ESA 1997

Bright and Dark Nebulae	Open Star Clusters	Galaxies	Quasars

Bright and Dark
Nebulae
To scale   <10'

Planetary
Nebulae
>100" 100"–30" <30'

Open Star
Clusters

Globular
Clusters
To scale <5'

Galaxies
10' x 5' 6' x 1' 3' x 2' 5' x 5' 4' x 2' 2' x 1'

Plotted to scale if the major axis >2', and circular
when face on or the position angle is uncertain

Quasars

Galaxy
Clusters

MILLENNIUM STAR ATLAS

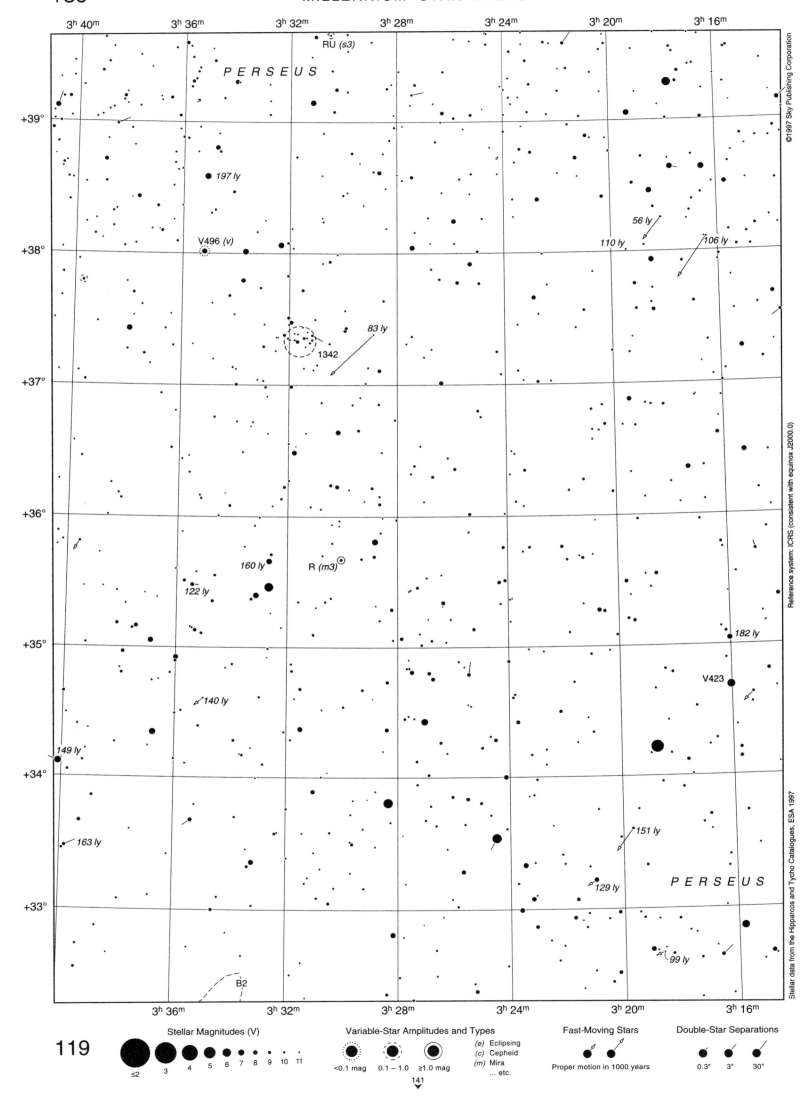

Reference system: ICRS (consistent with equinox J2000.0)

Stellar data from the Hipparcos and Tycho Catalogues, ESA 1997

P E R S E U S

RU *(s3)*

197 ly

V496 *(v)*

56 ly

110 ly

106 ly

83 ly

1342

160 ly

R *(m3)*

122 ly

182 ly

V423

140 ly

149 ly

151 ly

163 ly

129 ly

P E R S E U S

99 ly

B2

119

Stellar Magnitudes (V)

≤2   3   4   5   6   7   8   9   10   11

Variable-Star Amplitudes and Types

<0.1 mag   0.1 – 1.0   ≥1.0 mag

(e) Eclipsing
(c) Cepheid
(m) Mira
... etc.

Fast-Moving Stars

Proper motion in 1000 years

Double-Star Separations

0.3"   3"   30"

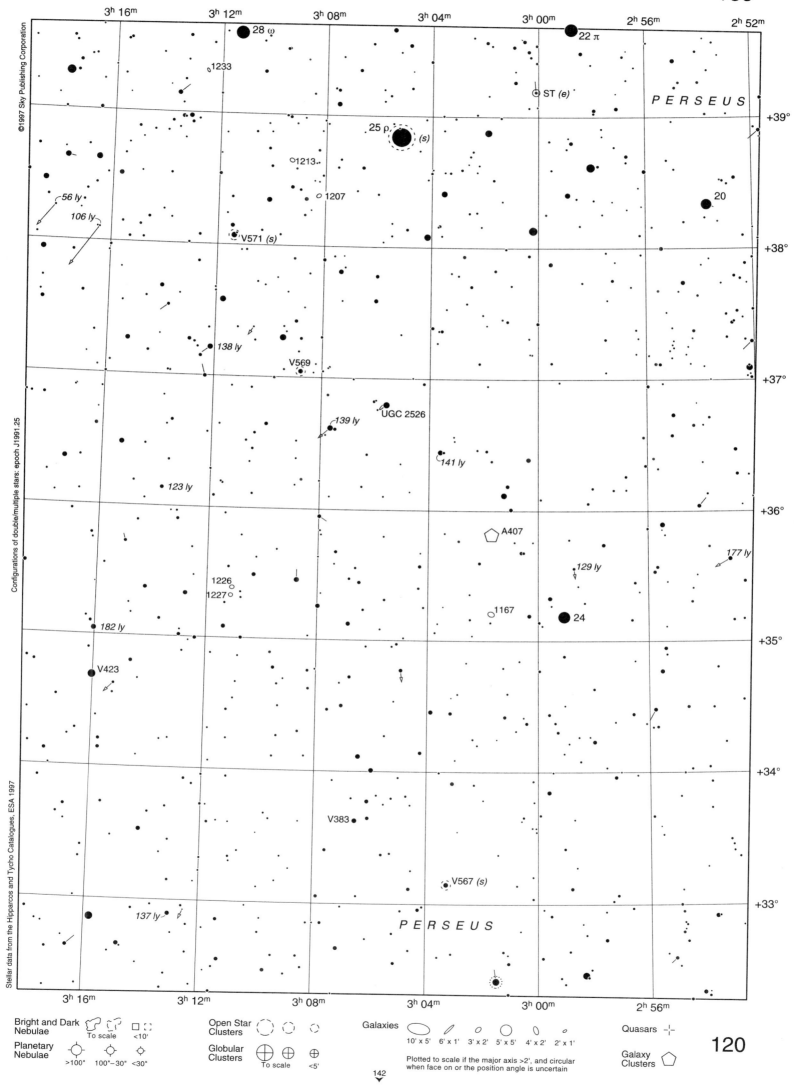

PERSEUS

PERSEUS

Bright and Dark Nebulae
To scale   <10'

Planetary Nebulae
>100"   100"–30"   <30"

Open Star Clusters

Globular Clusters
To scale   <5'

Galaxies
10' x 5'   6' x 1'   3' x 2'   5' x 5'   4' x 2'   2' x 1'

Plotted to scale if the major axis >2', and circular when face on or the position angle is uncertain

Quasars

Galaxy Clusters

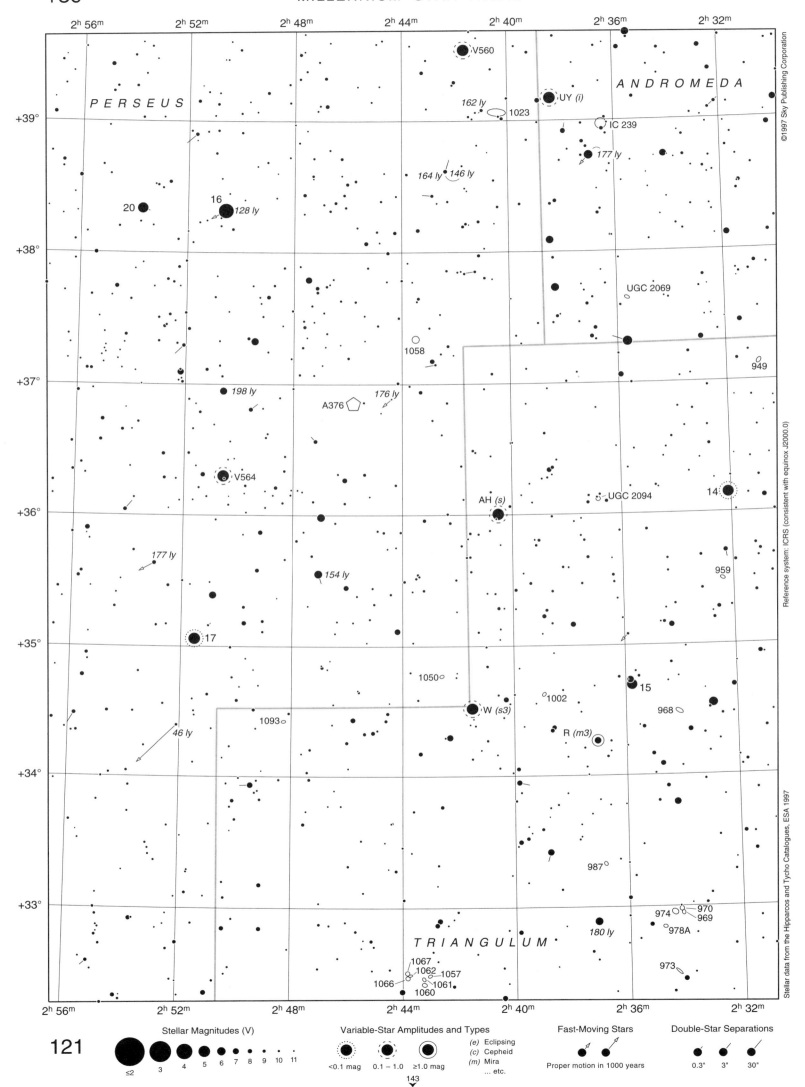

©1997 Sky Publishing Corporation

Reference system: ICRS (consistent with equinox J2000.0)

Stellar data from the Hipparcos and Tycho Catalogues, ESA 1997

PERSEUS

ANDROMEDA

TRIANGULUM

121

Stellar Magnitudes (V)

≤2   3   4   5   6   7   8   9   10   11

Variable-Star Amplitudes and Types

<0.1 mag   0.1 – 1.0   ≥1.0 mag

(e) Eclipsing
(c) Cepheid
(m) Mira
... etc.

Fast-Moving Stars

Proper motion in 1000 years

Double-Star Separations

0.3"   3"   30"

143

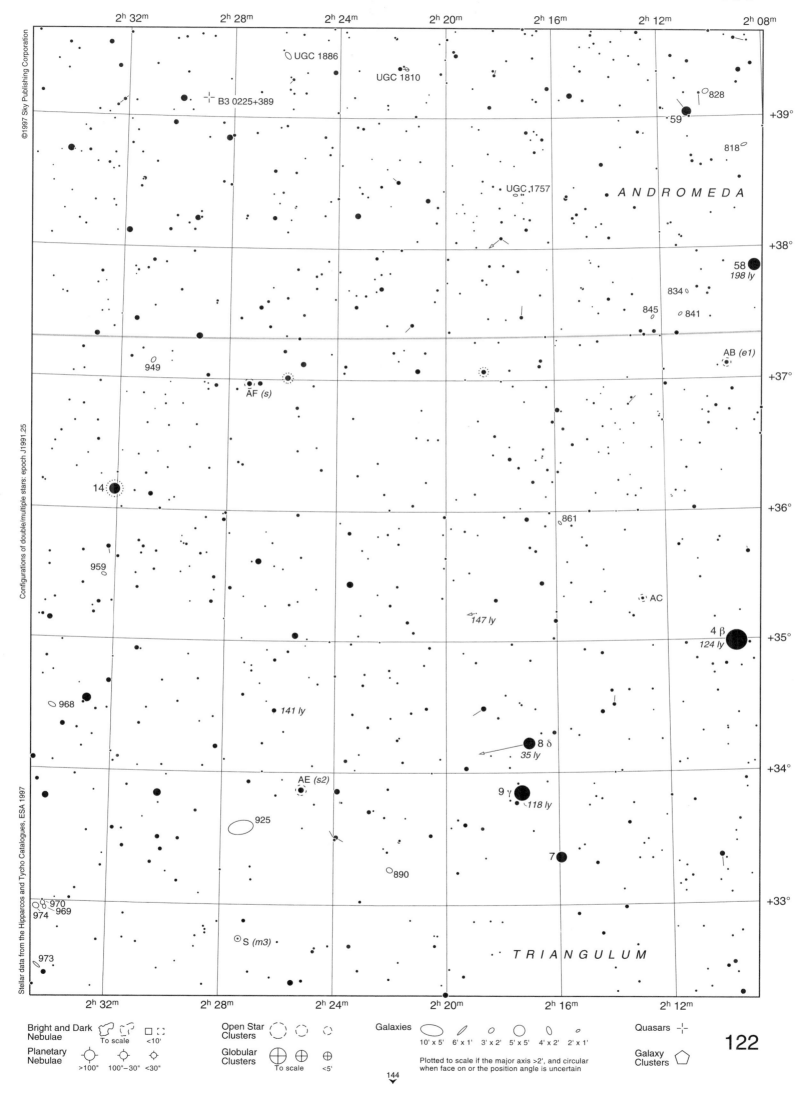

UGC 1886

UGC 1810

B3 0225+389

828

59

818

UGC 1757

A N D R O M E D A

58
198 ly

834

845   841

AB (e1)

949

ĀF (s)

14

861

959

AC

147 ly

4 β
124 ly

968

141 ly

8 δ
35 ly

AE (s2)

9 γ
118 ly

925

7

890

970
974   969

S (m3)

T R I A N G U L U M

973

Bright and Dark
Nebulae
To scale   <10'

Planetary
Nebulae
>100"   100"–30"   <30"

Open Star
Clusters

Globular
Clusters
To scale   <5'

Galaxies
10' x 5'   6' x 1'   3' x 2'   5' x 5'   4' x 2'   2' x 1'

Plotted to scale if the major axis >2', and circular
when face on or the position angle is uncertain

Quasars

Galaxy
Clusters

122

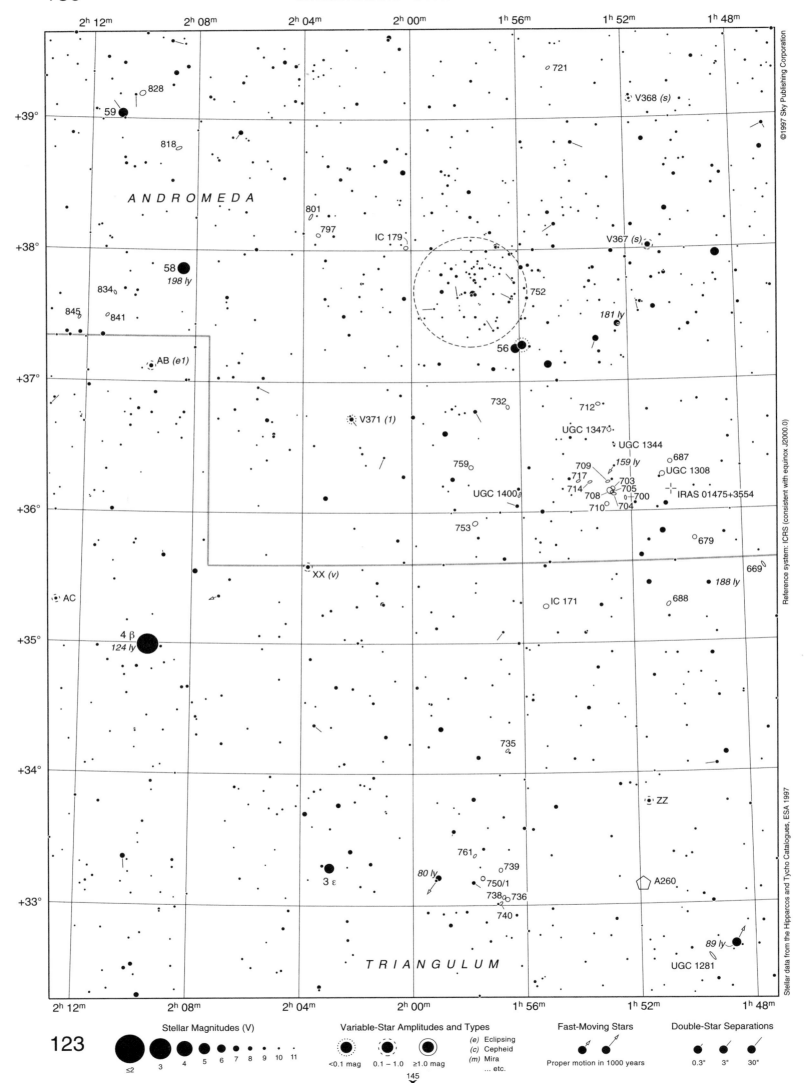

©1997 Sky Publishing Corporation

Reference system: ICRS (consistent with equinox J2000.0)

Stellar data from the Hipparcos and Tycho Catalogues, ESA 1997

ANDROMEDA

TRIANGULUM

59
828
818
58
198 ly
834
845
841
AB *(e1)*
AC
4 β
124 ly
3 ε

801
797
IC 179
752
56
V371 *(1)*
732
759
UGC 1400
753
XX *(v)*
735
80 ly
761
739
750/1
738 736
740

721
V368 *(s)*
V367 *(s)*
181 ly
712
UGC 1347
UGC 1344
709   *159 ly*
717   703
714   705
708   700
710   704
UGC 1281
688
IC 171
ZZ
A260
89 ly
687
UGC 1308
IRAS 01475+3554
679
669
188 ly

123

Stellar Magnitudes (V)
≤2 3 4 5 6 7 8 9 10 11

Variable-Star Amplitudes and Types
<0.1 mag   0.1 – 1.0   ≥1.0 mag

(e) Eclipsing
(c) Cepheid
(m) Mira
... etc.

Fast-Moving Stars
Proper motion in 1000 years

Double-Star Separations
0.3"   3"   30"

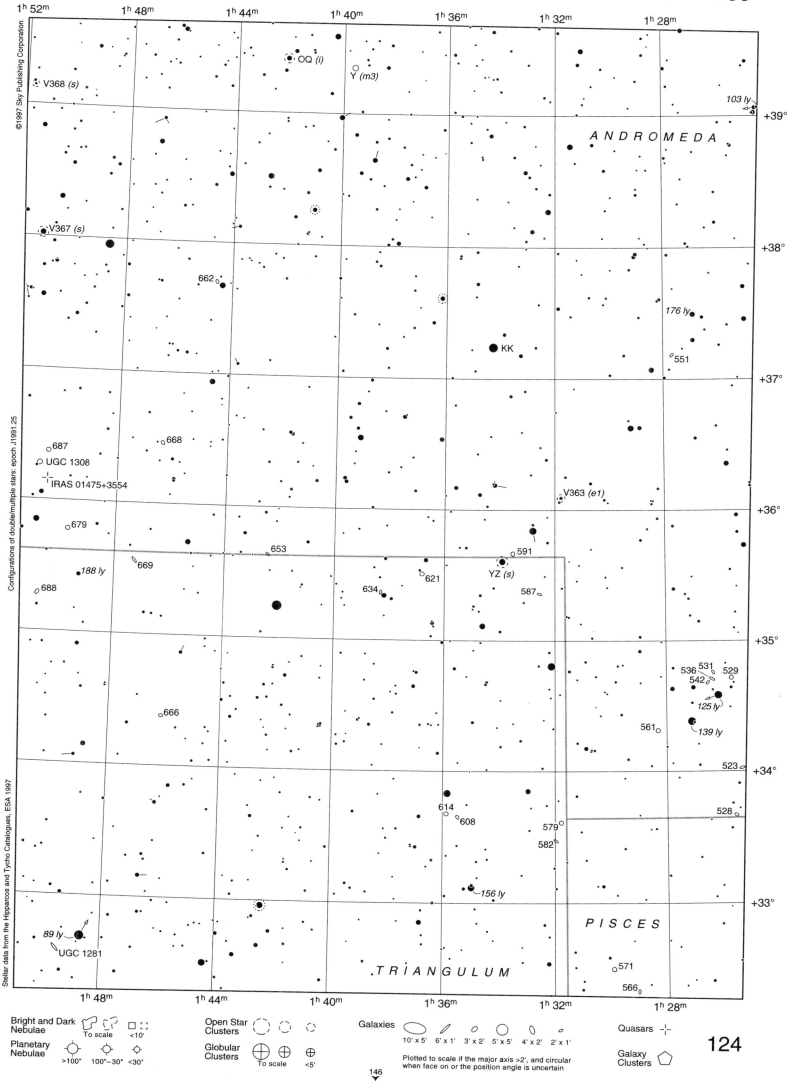

ANDROMEDA

PISCES

TRIANGULUM

OQ *(i)*

Y *(m3)*

V368 *(s)*

103 ly

V367 *(s)*

662

176 ly

KK

551

687

668

UGC 1308

IRAS 01475+3554

V363 *(e1)*

679

653

591

188 ly

669

YZ *(s)*

688

621

587

634

536 531
542 529

666

125 ly

561

139 ly

523

528

614

608

579

582

156 ly

89 ly

UGC 1281

571

566

Bright and Dark Nebulae	To scale	<10"
Planetary Nebulae	>100" 100"–30" <30"	
Open Star Clusters		
Globular Clusters	To scale <5'	
Galaxies	10' x 5' 6' x 1' 3' x 2' 5' x 5' 4' x 2' 2' x 1'	
Quasars		
Galaxy Clusters		

Plotted to scale if the major axis >2', and circular when face on or the position angle is uncertain

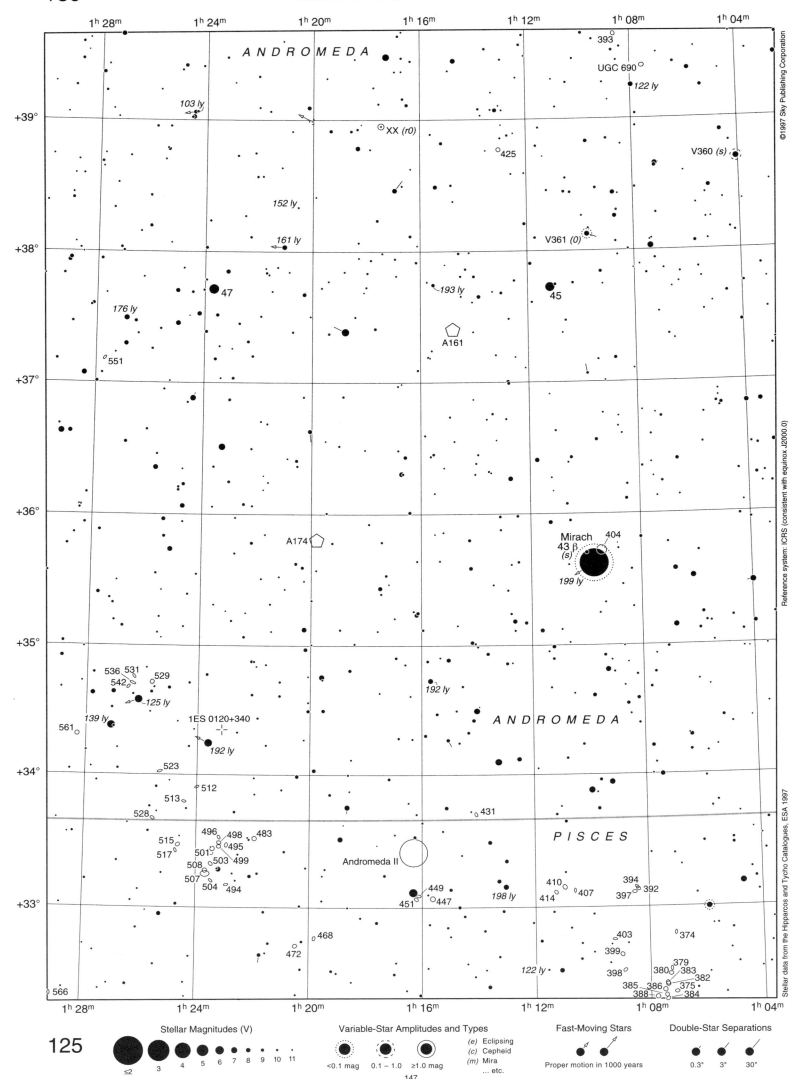

©1997 Sky Publishing Corporation

Reference system: ICRS (consistent with equinox J2000.0)

Stellar data from the Hipparcos and Tycho Catalogues, ESA 1997

ANDROMEDA

103 ly
152 ly
161 ly
176 ly
47
551
193 ly
45
A161
XX (r0)
425
393
UGC 690
122 ly
V360 (s)
V361 (0)

A174

Mirach
43 β
(s)
404
199 ly

536 531
542   529
125 ly
139 ly
561
1ES 0120+340
192 ly
523
512
513
528

515
517
496 498 483
495
501
508 503 499
507
504 494

ANDROMEDA

192 ly
431

Andromeda II

449
451   447

PISCES

198 ly
410
414   407
394
397   392

468
472

403
399
122 ly
398
380 379
385 386
388
383
382
375
384
374

566

125

ANDROMEDA

Stellar Magnitudes (V)

≤2 3 4 5 6 7 8 9 10 11

Variable-Star Amplitudes and Types

<0.1 mag   0.1 – 1.0   ≥1.0 mag

(e) Eclipsing
(c) Cepheid
(m) Mira
... etc.

Fast-Moving Stars

Proper motion in 1000 years

Double-Star Separations

0.3"   3"   30"

147

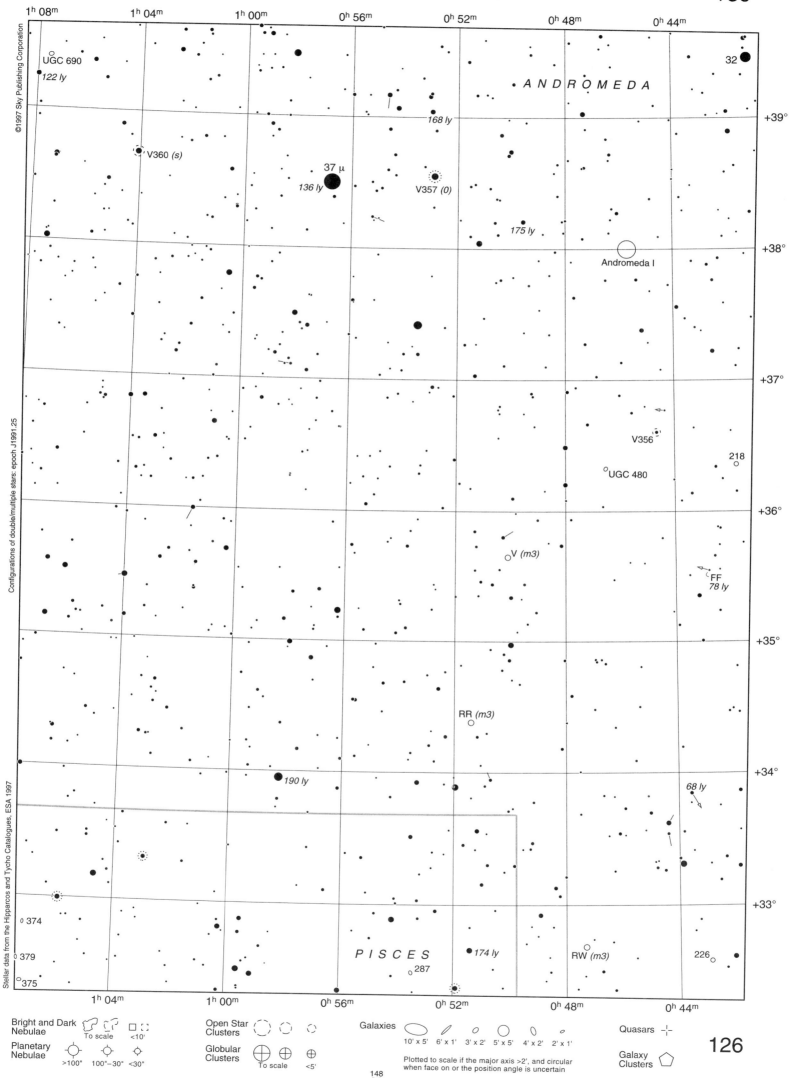

Configurations of double/multiple stars: epoch J1991.25

Stellar data from the Hipparcos and Tycho Catalogues, ESA 1997

UGC 690
122 ly

V360 *(s)*

37 μ
136 ly

V357 *(0)*

168 ly

175 ly

A N D R O M E D A

32

Andromeda I

V356

218

UGC 480

V *(m3)*

FF
78 ly

RR *(m3)*

190 ly

68 ly

RW *(m3)*

226

P I S C E S
174 ly

287

374

379

375

Bright and Dark
Nebulae
To scale   <10'

Planetary
Nebulae
>100"   100"–30"   <30"

Open Star
Clusters

Globular
Clusters
To scale   <5'

Galaxies
10' x 5'   6' x 1'   3' x 2'   5' x 5'   4' x 2'   2' x 1'

Plotted to scale if the major axis >2', and circular
when face on or the position angle is uncertain

Quasars

Galaxy
Clusters

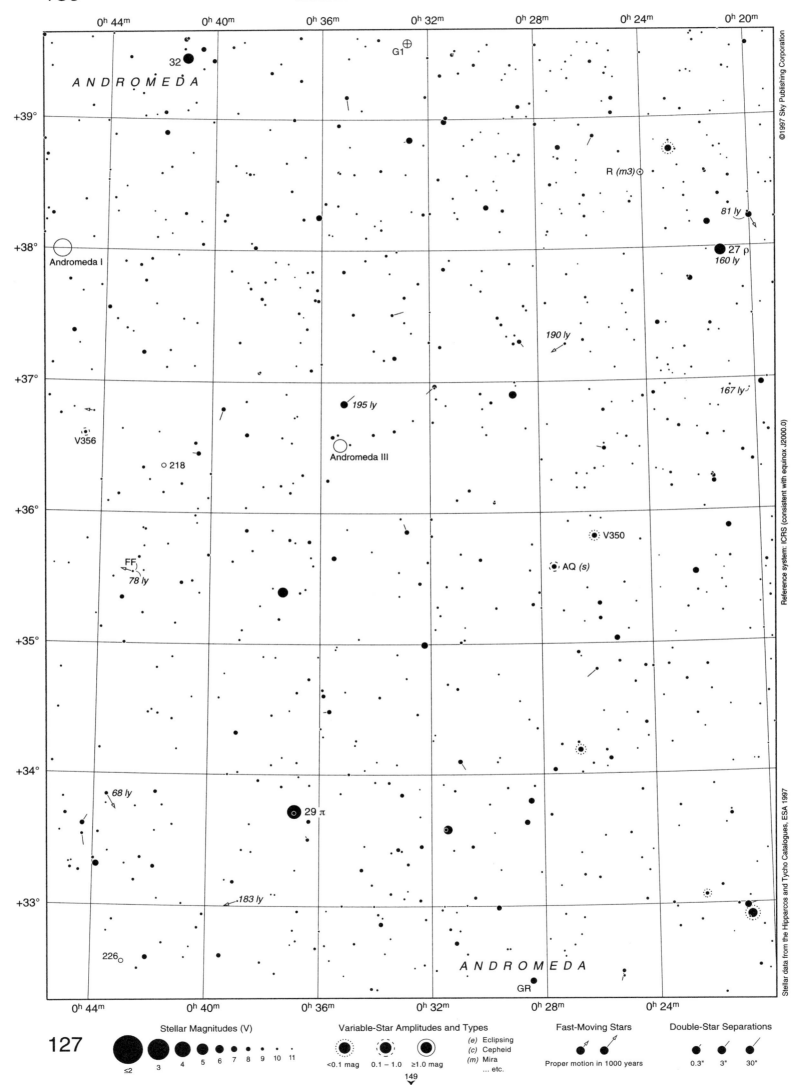

©1997 Sky Publishing Corporation

Reference system: ICRS (consistent with equinox J2000.0)

Stellar data from the Hipparcos and Tycho Catalogues, ESA 1997

ANDROMEDA

32

G1

R (m3)⊙

81 ly

27 ρ
160 ly

190 ly

167 ly

195 ly

Andromeda I

V356

○ 218

Andromeda III

V350

AQ (s)

FF
78 ly

29 π

68 ly

183 ly

226○

ANDROMEDA

GR

127

Stellar Magnitudes (V)

≤2   3   4   5   6 7 8 9 10 11

Variable-Star Amplitudes and Types

<0.1 mag   0.1 – 1.0   ≥1.0 mag

(e) Eclipsing
(c) Cepheid
(m) Mira
... etc.

Fast-Moving Stars

Proper motion in 1000 years

Double-Star Separations

0.3"   3"   30"

149

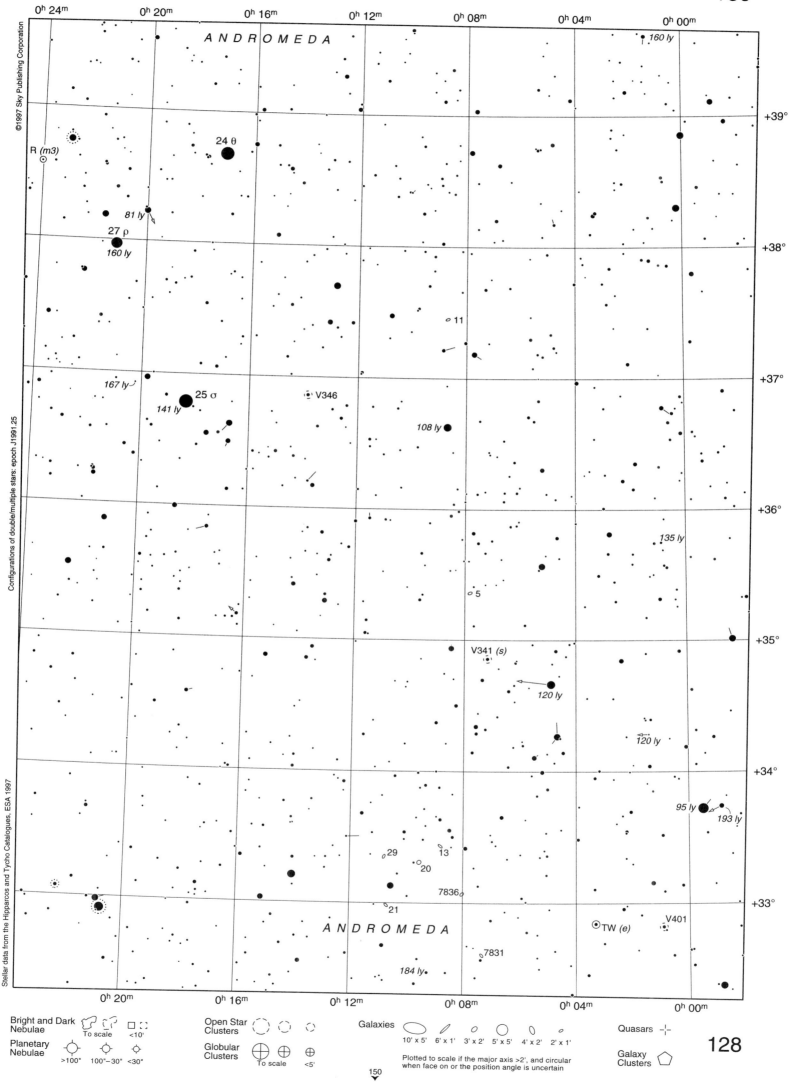

ANDROMEDA

©1997 Sky Publishing Corporation

Configurations of double/multiple stars: epoch J1991.25

Stellar data from the Hipparcos and Tycho Catalogues, ESA 1997

R (m3)

24 θ

81 ly

27 ρ

160 ly

160 ly

167 ly

25 σ

141 ly

V346

108 ly

11

135 ly

5

V341 (s)

120 ly

120 ly

95 ly

193 ly

29

13

20

7836

21

184 ly

ANDROMEDA

TW (e)

V401

7831

0h 24m 0h 20m 0h 16m 0h 12m 0h 08m 0h 04m 0h 00m

+39°

+38°

+37°

+36°

+35°

+34°

+33°

0h 20m 0h 16m 0h 12m 0h 08m 0h 04m 0h 00m

Bright and Dark Nebulae

To scale   <10'

Planetary Nebulae

>100"   100"–30"   <30"

Open Star Clusters

Globular Clusters

To scale   <5'

Galaxies

10' x 5'   6' x 1'   3' x 2'   5' x 5'   4' x 2'   2' x 1'

Plotted to scale if the major axis >2', and circular when face on or the position angle is uncertain

Quasars

Galaxy Clusters

128

150

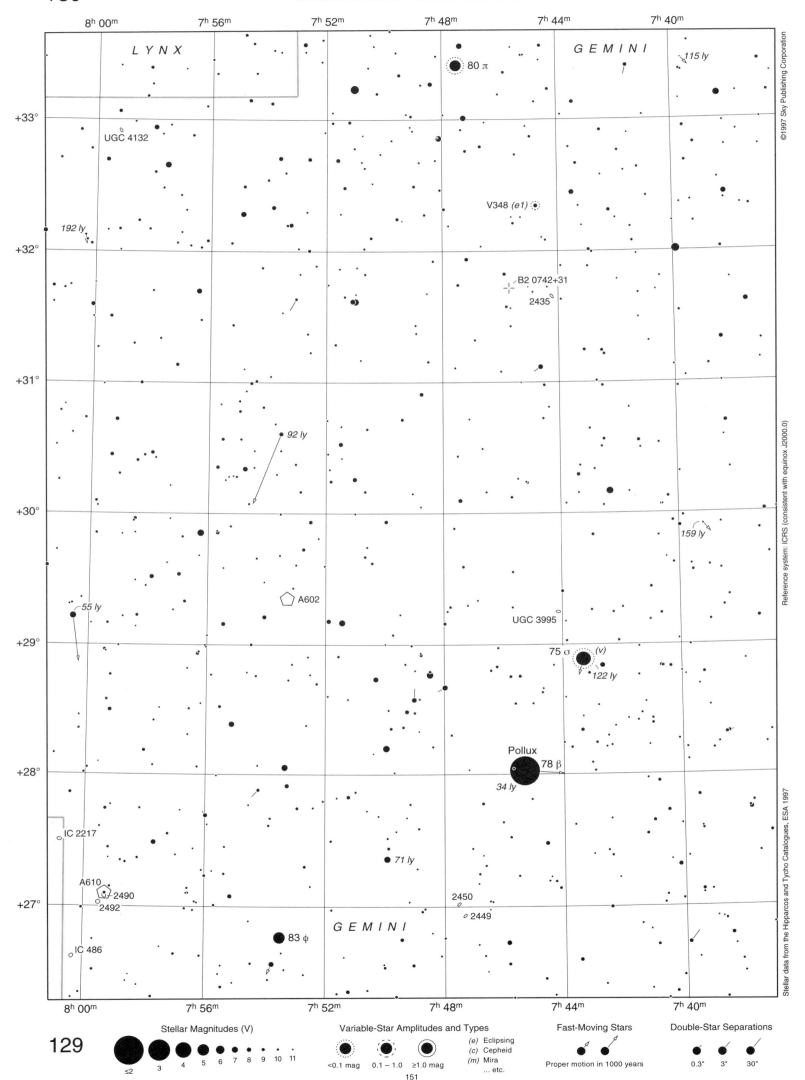

©1997 Sky Publishing Corporation

Reference system: ICRS (consistent with equinox J2000.0)

Stellar data from the Hipparcos and Tycho Catalogues, ESA 1997

LYNX

GEMINI

80 π

115 ly

UGC 4132

V348 (e1)

192 ly

B2 0742+31

2435

92 ly

159 ly

A602

UGC 3995

55 ly

75 σ   (v)

122 ly

Pollux

78 β

34 ly

IC 2217

71 ly

A610

2450

2490

2449

2492

GEMINI

IC 486

83 φ

129

Stellar Magnitudes (V)

≤2   3   4   5   6   7   8   9 10 11

Variable-Star Amplitudes and Types

<0.1 mag   0.1 – 1.0   ≥1.0 mag

(e) Eclipsing
(c) Cepheid
(m) Mira
... etc.

Fast-Moving Stars

Proper motion in 1000 years

Double-Star Separations

0.3"   3"   30"

151

MILLENNIUM STAR ATLAS

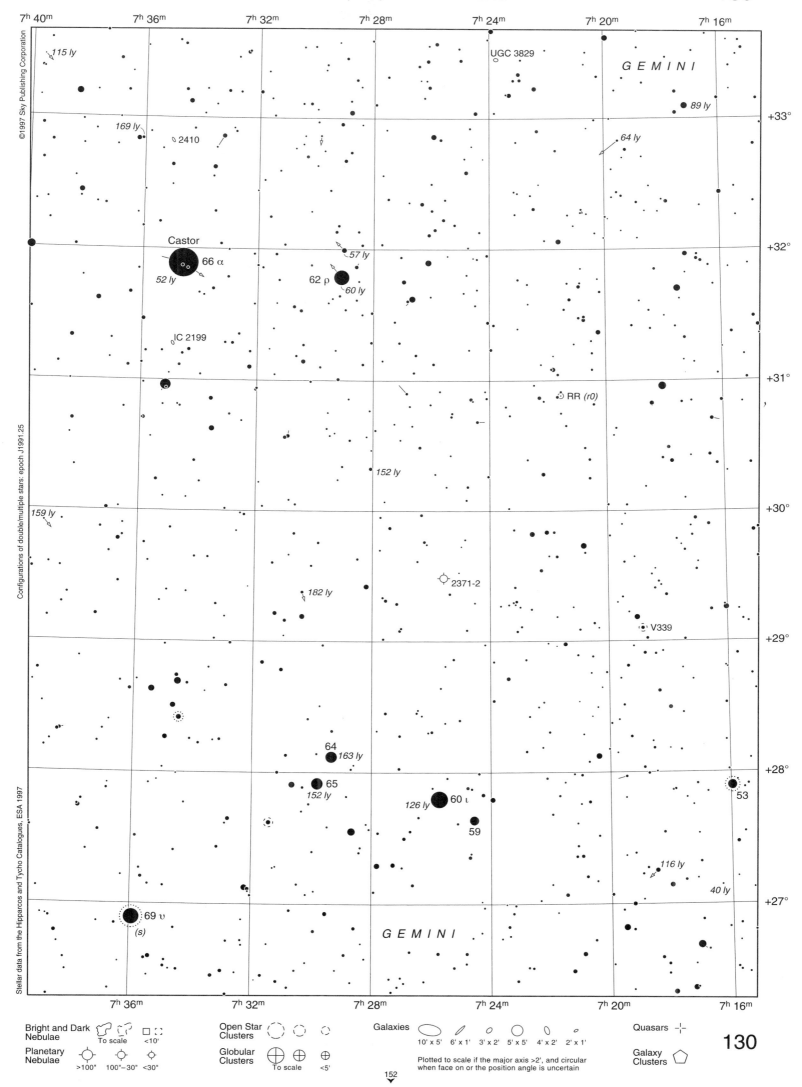

Configurations of double/multiple stars: epoch J1991.25

Stellar data from the Hipparcos and Tycho Catalogues, ESA 1997

115 ly

UGC 3829

GEMINI

89 ly

169 ly

○ 2410

64 ly

57 ly

Castor

66 α

52 ly

62 ρ

60 ly

○ IC 2199

RR *(r0)*

+33°

+32°

+31°

152 ly

159 ly

2371-2

182 ly

V339

+30°

+29°

64   163 ly

65

152 ly

60 ι

126 ly

53

59

116 ly

40 ly

69 υ

(s)

GEMINI

+28°

+27°

7ʰ 40ᵐ   7ʰ 36ᵐ   7ʰ 32ᵐ   7ʰ 28ᵐ   7ʰ 24ᵐ   7ʰ 20ᵐ   7ʰ 16ᵐ

7ʰ 36ᵐ   7ʰ 32ᵐ   7ʰ 28ᵐ   7ʰ 24ᵐ   7ʰ 20ᵐ   7ʰ 16ᵐ

Bright and Dark Nebulae
To scale   <10'

Planetary Nebulae
>100"   100"–30"   <30"

Open Star Clusters

Globular Clusters
To scale   <5'

Galaxies
10' x 5'   6' x 1'   3' x 2'   5' x 5'   4' x 2'   2' x 1'

Plotted to scale if the major axis >2', and circular when face on or the position angle is uncertain

Quasars

Galaxy Clusters

152

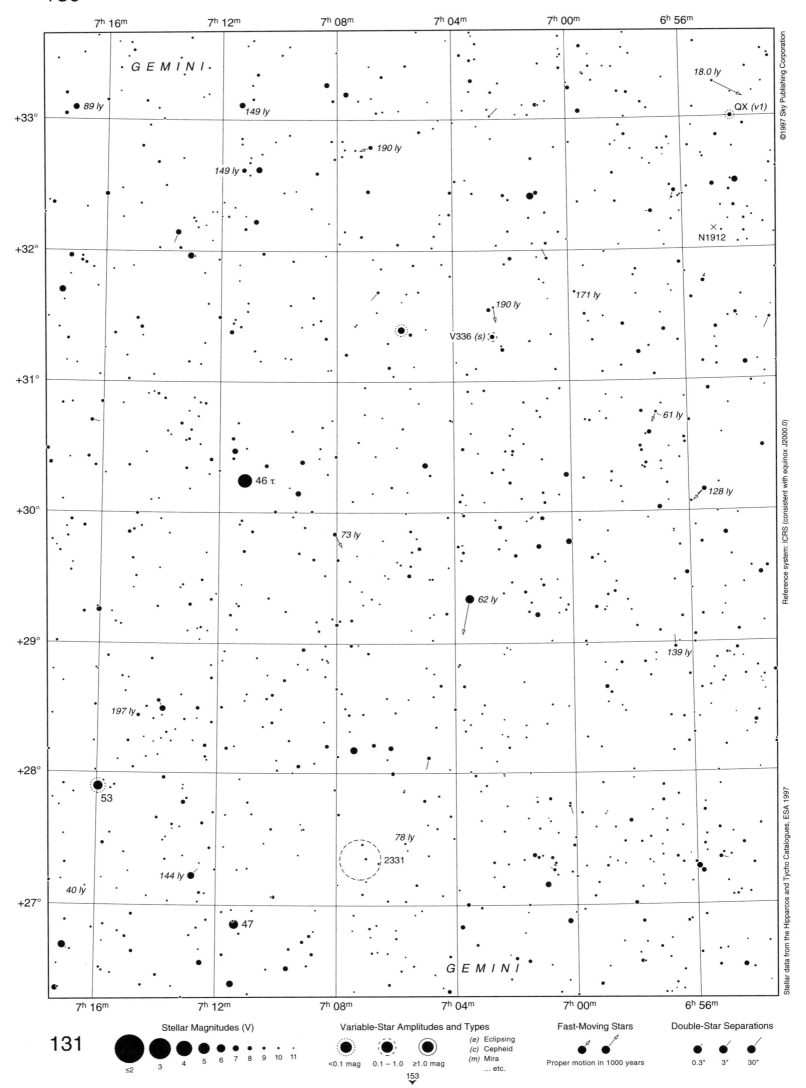

Stellar Magnitudes (V)

≤2 3 4 5 6 7 8 9 10 11

Variable-Star Amplitudes and Types

<0.1 mag   0.1 – 1.0   ≥1.0 mag

(e) Eclipsing
(c) Cepheid
(m) Mira
... etc.

Fast-Moving Stars

Proper motion in 1000 years

Double-Star Separations

0.3"   3"   30"

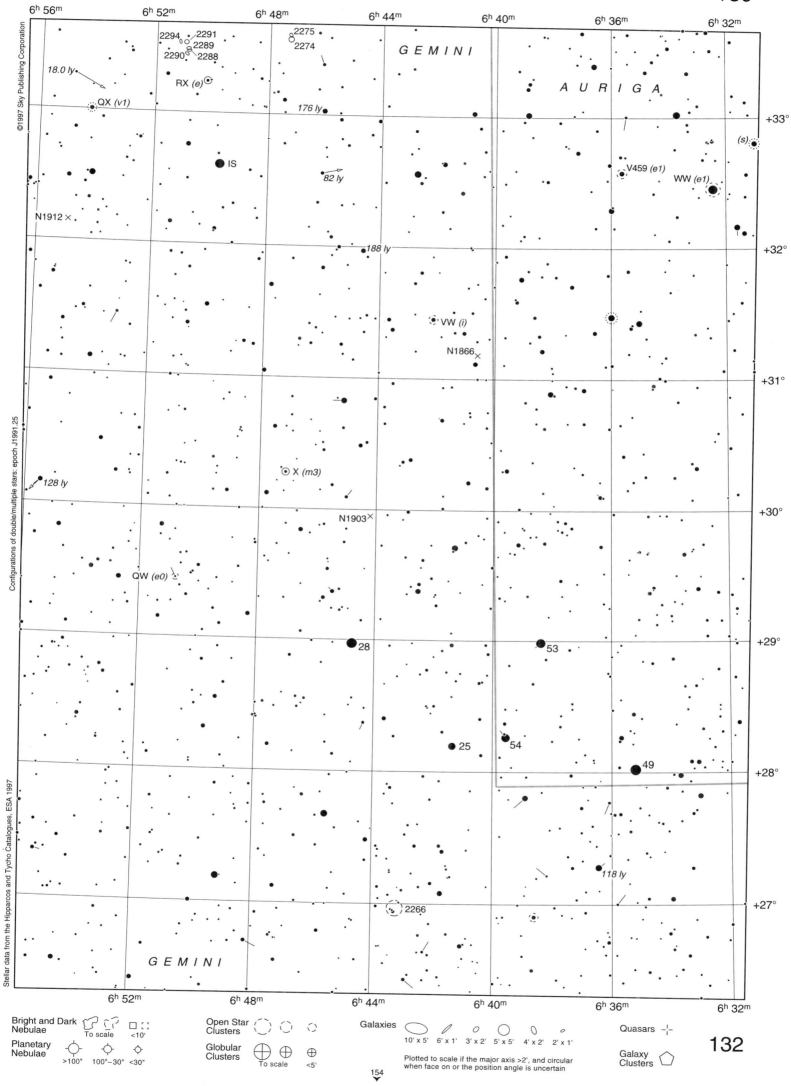

Configurations of double/multiple stars: epoch J1991.25

Stellar data from the Hipparcos and Tycho Catalogues, ESA 1997

6h 56m   6h 52m   6h 48m   6h 44m   6h 40m   6h 36m   6h 32m

2294   2291
2289
2290   2288

2275
2274

GEMINI

AURIGA

RX (e)

+33°

18.0 ly

QX (v1)

176 ly

IS

82 ly

(s)

V459 (e1)

WW (e1)

N1912

+32°

188 ly

VW (i)

N1866

+31°

X (m3)

128 ly

N1903

+30°

QW (e0)

28

53

+29°

25   54

49   +28°

118 ly

GEMINI

2266   +27°

6h 52m   6h 48m   6h 44m   6h 40m   6h 36m   6h 32m

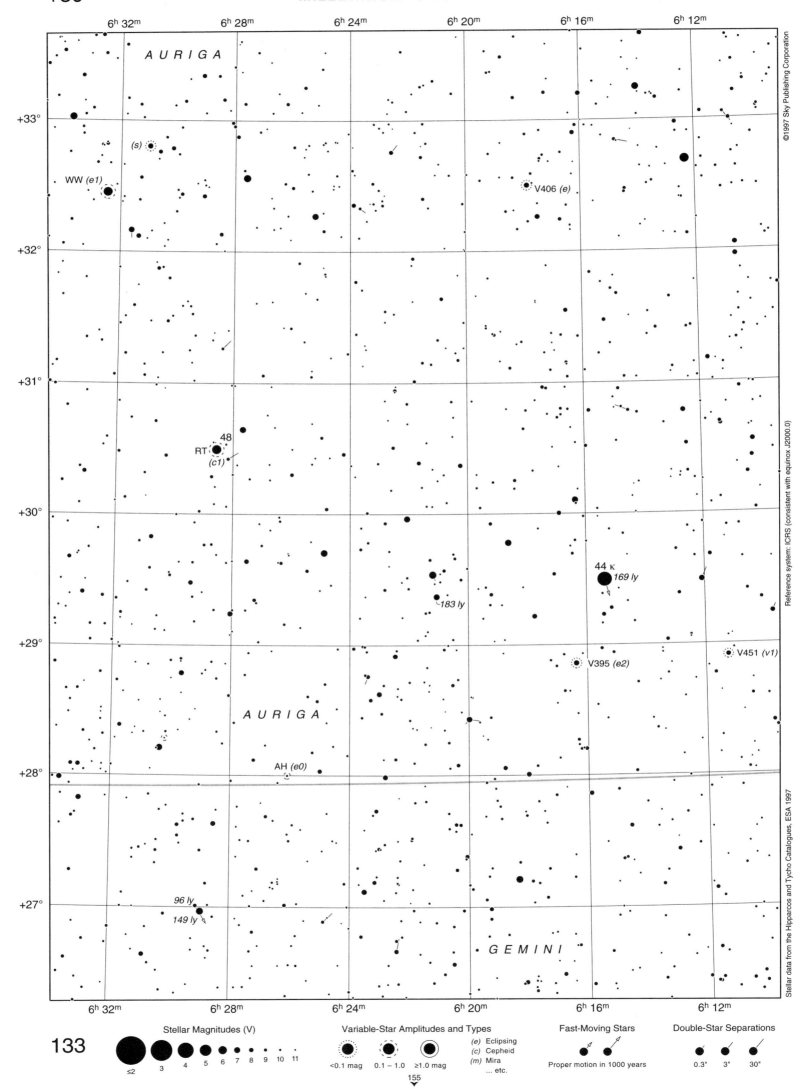

©1997 Sky Publishing Corporation

Reference system: ICRS (consistent with equinox J2000.0)

Stellar data from the Hipparcos and Tycho Catalogues, ESA 1997

133

Stellar Magnitudes (V)

≤2 3 4 5 6 7 8 9 10 11

Variable-Star Amplitudes and Types

<0.1 mag   0.1 – 1.0   ≥1.0 mag

(e) Eclipsing
(c) Cepheid
(m) Mira
... etc.

Fast-Moving Stars

Proper motion in 1000 years

Double-Star Separations

0.3"   3"   30"

©1997 Sky Publishing Corporation

Configurations of double/multiple stars: epoch J1991.25

Stellar data from the Hipparcos and Tycho Catalogues, ESA 1997

King 8

A U R I G A

133 ly

163 ly

M37
2099

160 ly

V440

CQ *(e)*

150 ly

FU *(i)*

□ Sh2-241

Basel 4

V394 *(s)*

V438

V451 *(v1)*

V450 *(s)*

Simeis
147

136

145 ly

G E M I N I

116 ly

V781 *(e0)*

136 ly

V593 *(v)*

AA *(c2)*

T A U R U S

GALACTIC EQUATOR

18°

183°

6h 12m 6h 08m 6h 04m 6h 00m 5h 56m 5h 52m 5h 48m

+33°

+32°

+31°

+30°

+29°

+28°

+27°

6h 08m 6h 04m 6h 00m 5h 56m 5h 52m

Bright and Dark Nebulae	⌒ ⌒ □ ⌐
To scale	<10'
Planetary Nebulae	⊕ ⬙ ◇
>100"	100"–30" <30"

Open Star Clusters	⊙ ◌ ○
Globular Clusters	⊕ ⊕ ⊕
To scale	<5'

Galaxies ⬯ ╱ ○ ○ ○ ○
10' x 5' 6' x 1' 3' x 2' 5' x 5' 4' x 2' 2' x 1'

Plotted to scale if the major axis >2', and circular
when face on or the position angle is uncertain

Quasars -|-

Galaxy Clusters ⬠

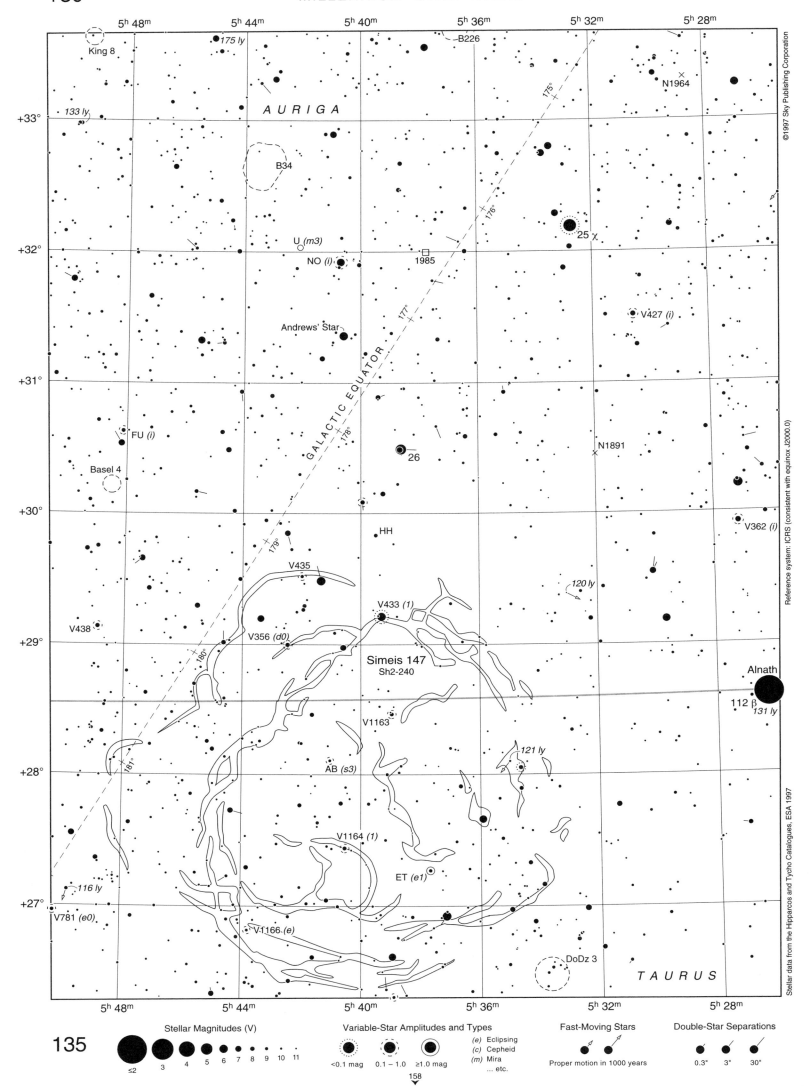

King 8

175 ly

B226

N1964

×

A U R I G A

133 ly

B34

©1997 Sky Publishing Corporation

25 χ

U (m3)

NO (i)

1985

176°

V427 (i)

175°

Andrews' Star

177°

GALACTIC EQUATOR

FU (i)

178°

26

N1891

Basel 4

Reference system: ICRS (consistent with equinox J2000.0)

HH

V362 (i)

179°

120 ly

V435

V433 (1)

V438

V356 (d0)

180°

Simeis 147
Sh2-240

Alnath

V1163

112 β
131 ly

121 ly

181°

AB (s3)

Stellar data from the Hipparcos and Tycho Catalogues, ESA 1997

V1164 (1)

ET (e1)

116 ly

V781 (e0)

V1166 (e)

DoDz 3

T A U R U S

5ʰ 48ᵐ   5ʰ 44ᵐ   5ʰ 40ᵐ   5ʰ 36ᵐ   5ʰ 32ᵐ   5ʰ 28ᵐ

135

Stellar Magnitudes (V)

≤2 3 4 5 6 7 8 9 10 11

Variable-Star Amplitudes and Types

<0.1 mag   0.1 – 1.0   ≥1.0 mag

(e) Eclipsing
(c) Cepheid
(m) Mira
... etc.

Fast-Moving Stars

Proper motion in 1000 years

Double-Star Separations

0.3"   3"   30"

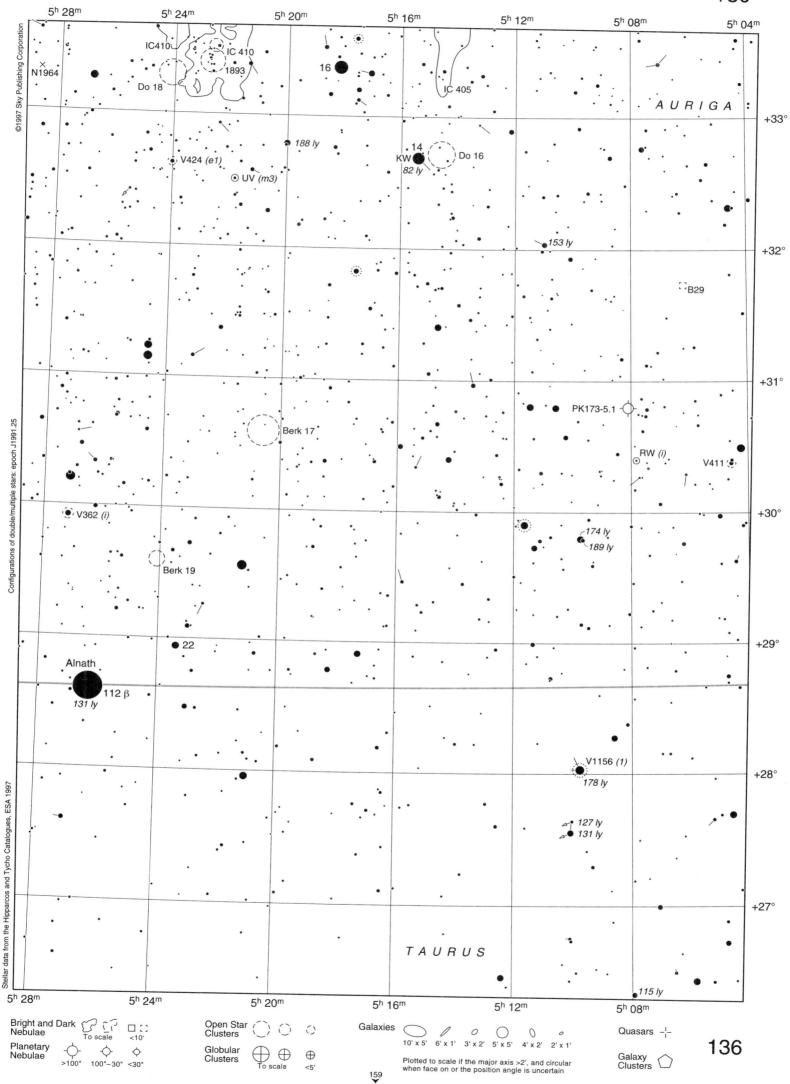

Configurations of double/multiple stars: epoch J1991.25

Stellar data from the Hipparcos and Tycho Catalogues, ESA 1997

IC410
IC 410
1893
Do 18
N1964
16
AURIGA
188 ly
V424 (e1)
14
KW
Do 16
82 ly
UV (m3)
IC 405
153 ly
B29
Berk 17
PK173-5.1
RW (i)
V411
V362 (i)
174 ly
189 ly
Berk 19
22
Alnath
112 β
131 ly
V1156 (1)
178 ly
127 ly
131 ly
TAURUS
115 ly

Bright and Dark Nebulae		Open Star Clusters		Galaxies		Quasars

Bright and Dark Nebulae
To scale   <10'
Planetary Nebulae
>100" 100"–30" <30"
Open Star Clusters
Globular Clusters
To scale   <5'
Galaxies
10' x 5' 6' x 1' 3' x 2' 5' x 5' 4' x 2' 2' x 1'
Plotted to scale if the major axis >2', and circular when face on or the position angle is uncertain
Quasars
Galaxy Clusters

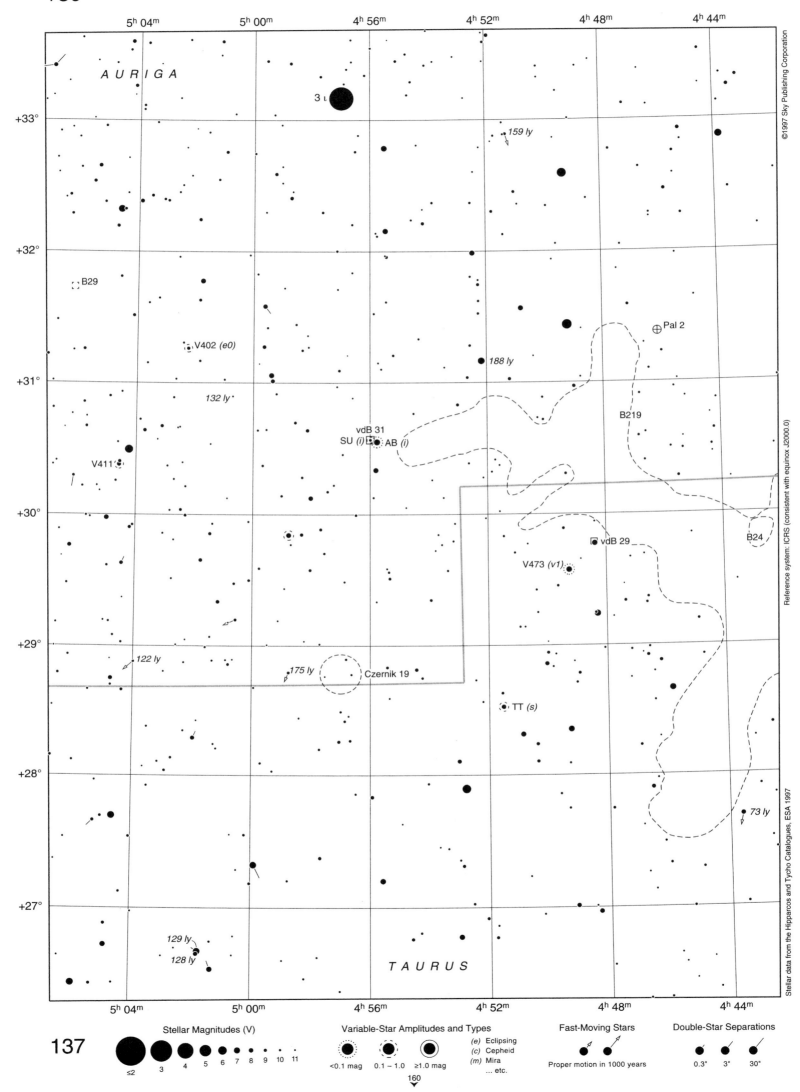

©1997 Sky Publishing Corporation

Reference system: ICRS (consistent with equinox J2000.0)

Stellar data from the Hipparcos and Tycho Catalogues, ESA 1997

A U R I G A

3 ι

159 ly

B29

V402 (e0)

188 ly

132 ly

Pal 2

B219

vdB 31

SU (i)   AB (i)

V411

B24

vdB 29

V473 (v1)

122 ly

175 ly   Czernik 19

TT (s)

73 ly

129 ly

128 ly

T A U R U S

Stellar Magnitudes (V)

≤2   3   4   5   6   7 8 9 10 11

Variable-Star Amplitudes and Types

<0.1 mag   0.1 – 1.0   ≥1.0 mag

(e) Eclipsing
(c) Cepheid
(m) Mira
... etc.

Fast-Moving Stars

Proper motion in 1000 years

Double-Star Separations

0.3"   3"   30"

160

MILLENNIUM STAR ATLAS

+30°

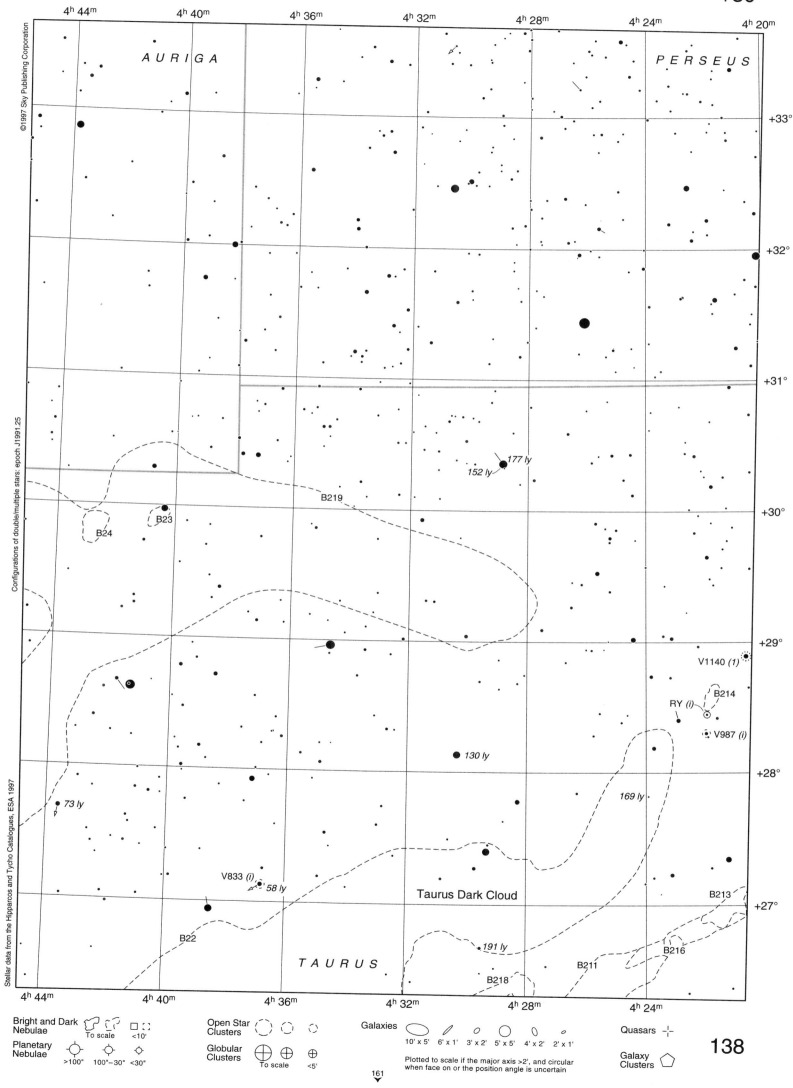

Configurations of double/multiple stars: epoch J1991.25

Stellar data from the Hipparcos and Tycho Catalogues, ESA 1997

4ʰ 44ᵐ   4ʰ 40ᵐ   4ʰ 36ᵐ   4ʰ 32ᵐ   4ʰ 28ᵐ   4ʰ 24ᵐ   4ʰ 20ᵐ

A U R I G A

P E R S E U S

+33°

+32°

+31°

177 ly
152 ly

B219

+30°

B23

B24

V1140 (1)

+29°

B214

RY (i)

V987 (i)

130 ly

+28°

169 ly

73 ly

V833 (i)
58 ly

Taurus Dark Cloud

B213

+27°

B22

191 ly

B216

T A U R U S

B211

B218

4ʰ 44ᵐ   4ʰ 40ᵐ   4ʰ 36ᵐ   4ʰ 32ᵐ   4ʰ 28ᵐ   4ʰ 24ᵐ

Bright and Dark Nebulae			Open Star Clusters			Galaxies						Quasars
To scale		<10'				10' x 5'	6' x 1'	3' x 2'	5' x 5'	4' x 2'	2' x 1'	
Planetary Nebulae			Globular Clusters									Galaxy Clusters
>100"	100"–30"	<30"	To scale		<5'	Plotted to scale if the major axis >2', and circular when face on or the position angle is uncertain						

138

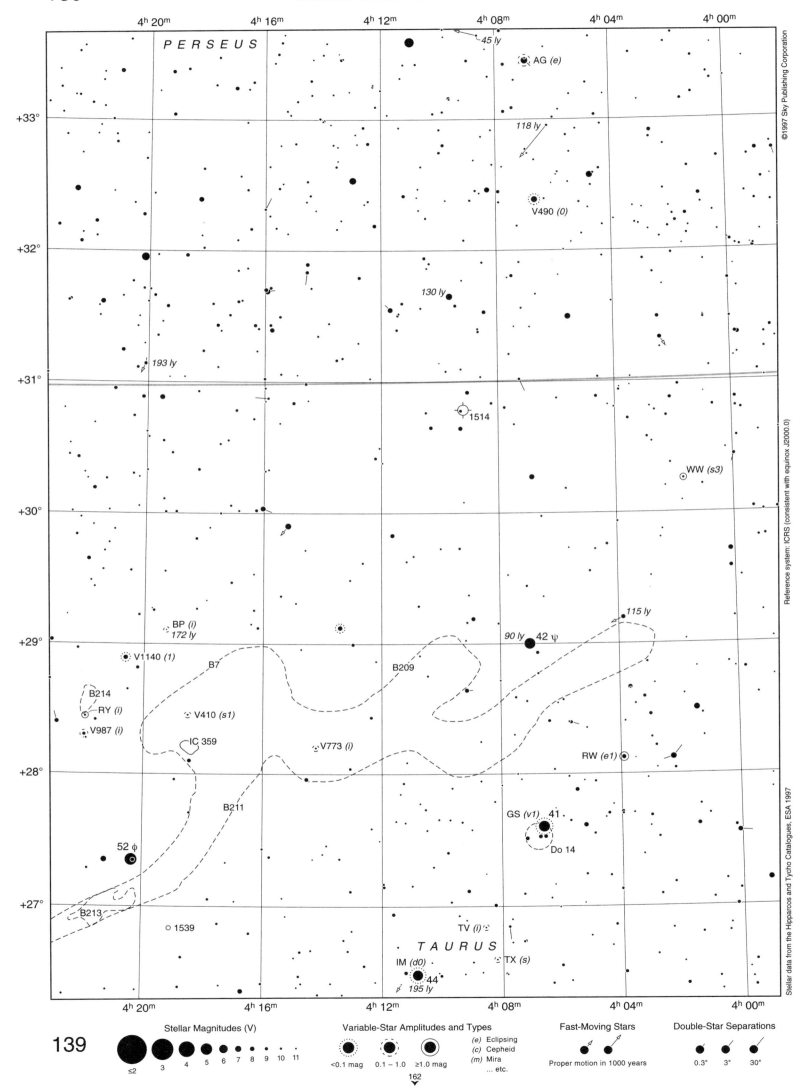

©1997 Sky Publishing Corporation

Reference system: ICRS (consistent with equinox J2000.0)

Stellar data from the Hipparcos and Tycho Catalogues, ESA 1997

PERSEUS

45 ly

AG (e)

118 ly

V490 (0)

130 ly

193 ly

1514

WW (s3)

115 ly

BP (i)
172 ly

90 ly 42 ψ

V1140 (1)

B7

B209

B214

RY (i)

V410 (s1)

V987 (i)

IC 359

V773 (i)

RW (e1)

B211

GS (v1) 41

52 φ

Do 14

B213

1539

TV (i)

TAURUS

IM (d0)

TX (s)

44

195 ly

Stellar Magnitudes (V)

≤2 3 4 5 6 7 8 9 10 11

Variable-Star Amplitudes and Types

<0.1 mag   0.1 – 1.0   ≥1.0 mag

(e) Eclipsing
(c) Cepheid
(m) Mira
... etc.

Fast-Moving Stars

Proper motion in 1000 years

Double-Star Separations

0.3"   3"   30"

162

MILLENNIUM STAR ATLAS

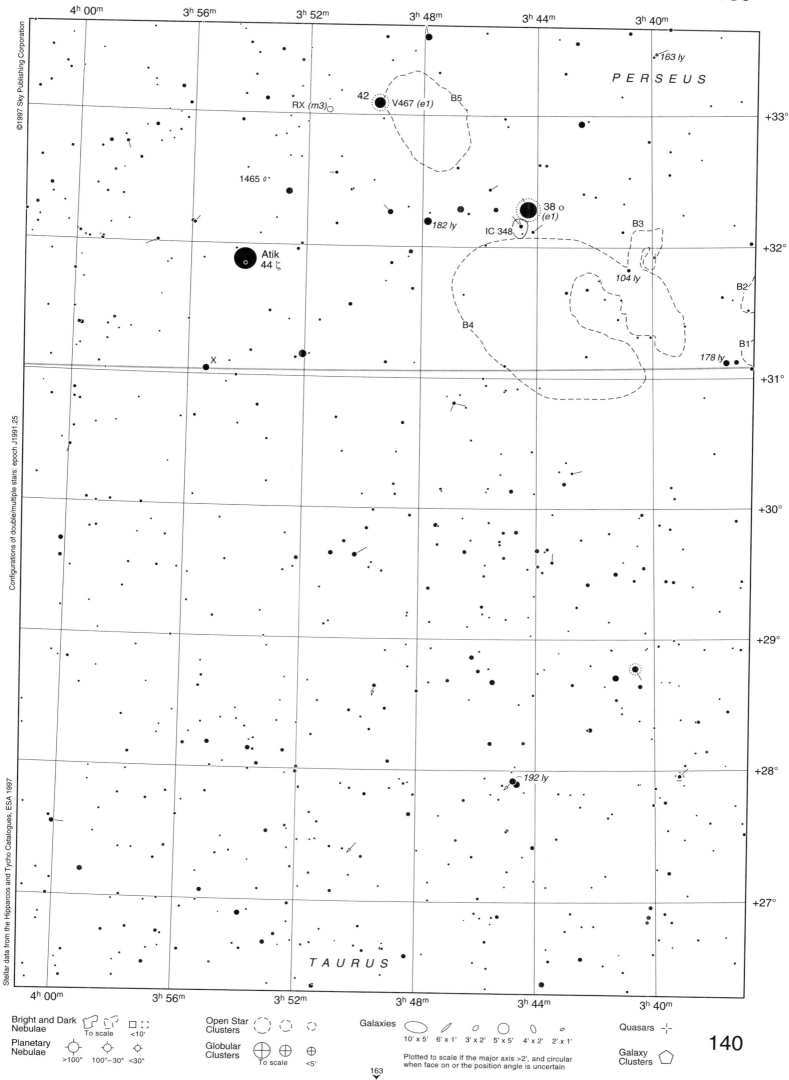

PERSEUS

163 ly

42   V467 (e1)   B5

RX (m3)

1465 o

38 o
(e1)

182 ly   IC 348   B3

Atik
44 ζ   104 ly   B2

B4   B1

X   178 ly

+33°
+32°
+31°
+30°
+29°
+28°
+27°

192 ly

TAURUS

Configurations of double/multiple stars: epoch J1991.25

Stellar data from the Hipparcos and Tycho Catalogues, ESA 1997

Bright and Dark Nebulae	Open Star Clusters	Galaxies	Quasars

Bright and Dark Nebulae
To scale   <10'

Planetary Nebulae
>100"   100"–30"   <30"

Open Star Clusters

Globular Clusters
To scale   <5'

Galaxies
10' x 5'   6' x 1'   3' x 2'   5' x 5'   4' x 2'   2' x 1'

Plotted to scale if the major axis >2', and circular when face on or the position angle is uncertain

Quasars

Galaxy Clusters

163

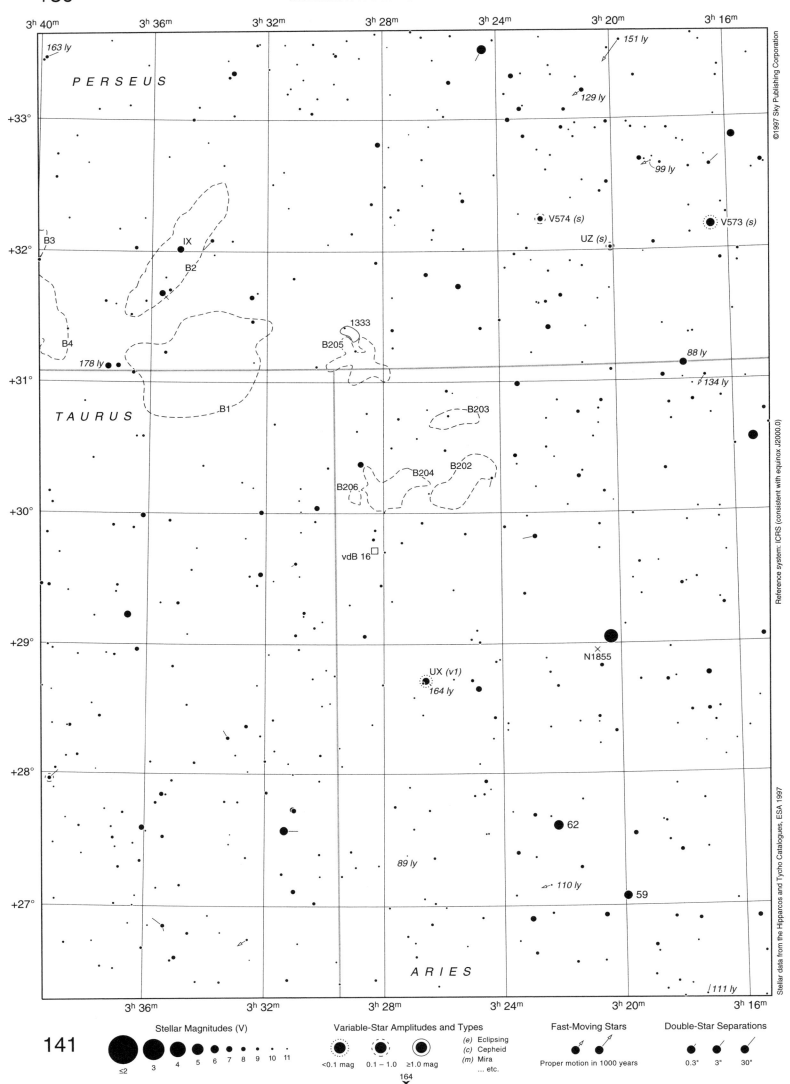

©1997 Sky Publishing Corporation

Reference system: ICRS (consistent with equinox J2000.0)

Stellar data from the Hipparcos and Tycho Catalogues, ESA 1997

PERSEUS

TAURUS

ARIES

163 ly

B3

B4

178 ly

IX

B2

1333

B205

B1

B203

B204   B202

B206

vdB 16

151 ly

129 ly

99 ly

V574 (s)

UZ (s)

V573 (s)

88 ly

134 ly

N1855

UX (v1)

164 ly

62

89 ly

110 ly

59

111 ly

141

Stellar Magnitudes (V)

≤2   3   4   5   6   7   8   9   10   11

Variable-Star Amplitudes and Types

<0.1 mag   0.1 – 1.0   ≥1.0 mag

(e) Eclipsing
(c) Cepheid
(m) Mira
... etc.

Fast-Moving Stars

Proper motion in 1000 years

Double-Star Separations

0.3"   3"   30"

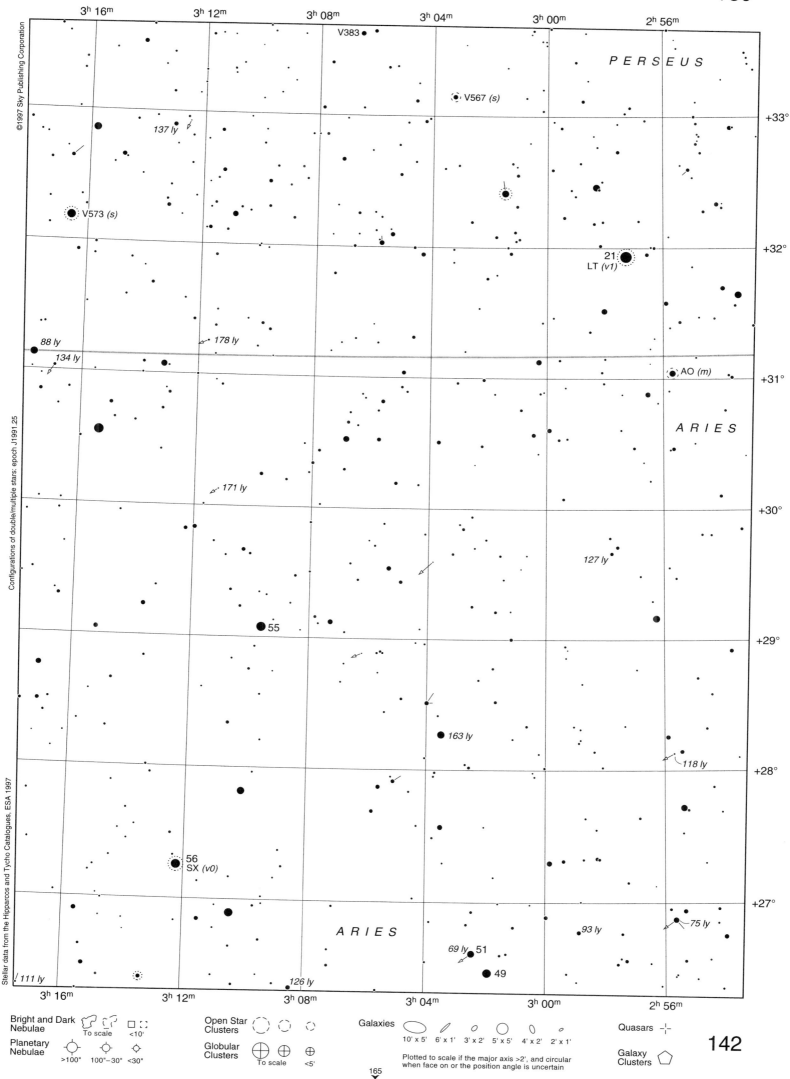

Configurations of double/multiple stars: epoch J1991.25

Stellar data from the Hipparcos and Tycho Catalogues, ESA 1997

P E R S E U S

V383 •

V567 (s)

137 ly

V573 (s)

21
LT (v1)

88 ly
134 ly

178 ly

AO (m)

A R I E S

171 ly

127 ly

55

163 ly

118 ly

56
SX (v0)

A R I E S

93 ly

75 ly

69 ly 51

49

111 ly

126 ly

3h 16m   3h 12m   3h 08m   3h 04m   3h 00m   2h 56m

+33°
+32°
+31°
+30°
+29°
+28°
+27°

| Bright and Dark Nebulae | Open Star Clusters | Galaxies | Quasars |

Bright and Dark Nebulae
To scale   <10'

Planetary Nebulae
>100" 100"–30" <30"

Open Star Clusters

Globular Clusters
To scale   <5'

Galaxies
10' x 5' 6' x 1' 3' x 2' 5' x 5' 4' x 2' 2' x 1'

Plotted to scale if the major axis >2', and circular when face on or the position angle is uncertain

Quasars

Galaxy Clusters

142

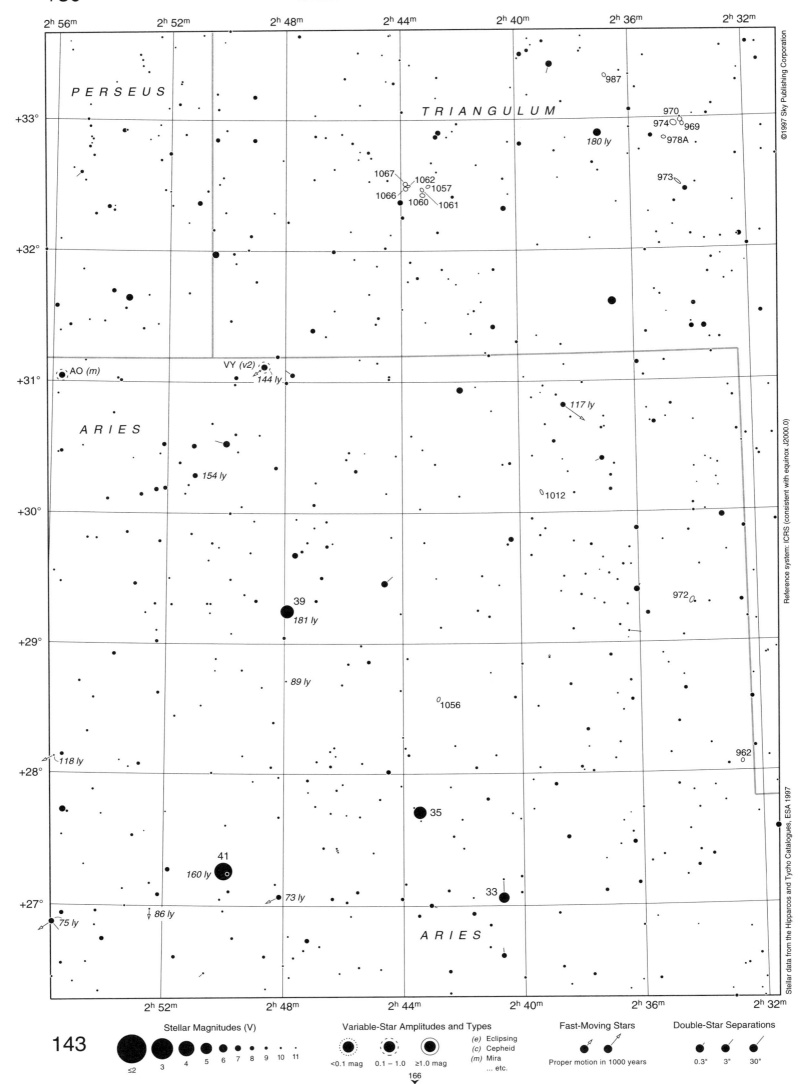

P E R S E U S

T R I A N G U L U M

+33°

987

970
974 969
180 ly
978A

1067
1066 1062
1060 1057
1061

973

+32°

AO (m)

VY (v2)
144 ly

+31°

A R I E S

117 ly

154 ly

1012

+30°

39
181 ly

972

89 ly

+29°

1056

118 ly

962

+28°

35

41
160 ly

33

73 ly

+27°

86 ly

75 ly

A R I E S

©1997 Sky Publishing Corporation

Reference system: ICRS (consistent with equinox J2000.0)

Stellar data from the Hipparcos and Tycho Catalogues, ESA 1997

143

Stellar Magnitudes (V)

≤2 3 4 5 6 7 8 9 10 11

Variable-Star Amplitudes and Types

<0.1 mag 0.1 – 1.0 ≥1.0 mag

(e) Eclipsing
(c) Cepheid
(m) Mira
... etc.

Fast-Moving Stars

Proper motion in 1000 years

Double-Star Separations

0.3" 3" 30"

166

MILLENNIUM STAR ATLAS

+30°

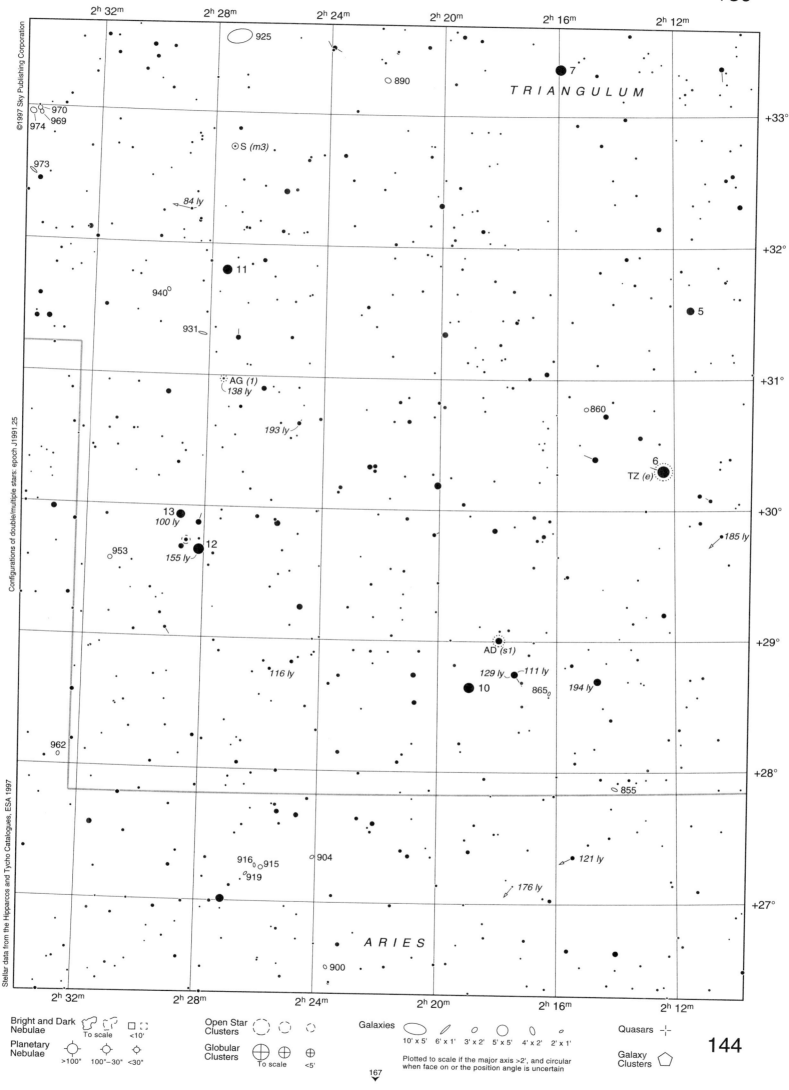

Configurations of double/multiple stars: epoch J1991.25

Stellar data from the Hipparcos and Tycho Catalogues, ESA 1997

2ʰ 32ᵐ   2ʰ 28ᵐ   2ʰ 24ᵐ   2ʰ 20ᵐ   2ʰ 16ᵐ   2ʰ 12ᵐ

925

890

7

TRIANGULUM

+33°

970
969
974

973

84 ly

11

940

5

931

AG *(1)*
138 ly

193 ly

860

6
TZ *(e)*

+31°

13
100 ly

12
155 ly

953

185 ly

+30°

116 ly

AD *(s1)*

129 ly   111 ly

10   865

194 ly

+29°

962

855

+28°

916   915
919

904

121 ly

176 ly

+27°

ARIES

900

2ʰ 32ᵐ   2ʰ 28ᵐ   2ʰ 24ᵐ   2ʰ 20ᵐ   2ʰ 16ᵐ   2ʰ 12ᵐ

Bright and Dark Nebulae   To scale   <10'

Planetary Nebulae   >100"   100"–30"   <30"

Open Star Clusters

Globular Clusters   To scale   <5'

Galaxies   10' x 5'   6' x 1'   3' x 2'   5' x 5'   4' x 2'   2' x 1'

Plotted to scale if the major axis >2', and circular when face on or the position angle is uncertain

Quasars

Galaxy Clusters

144

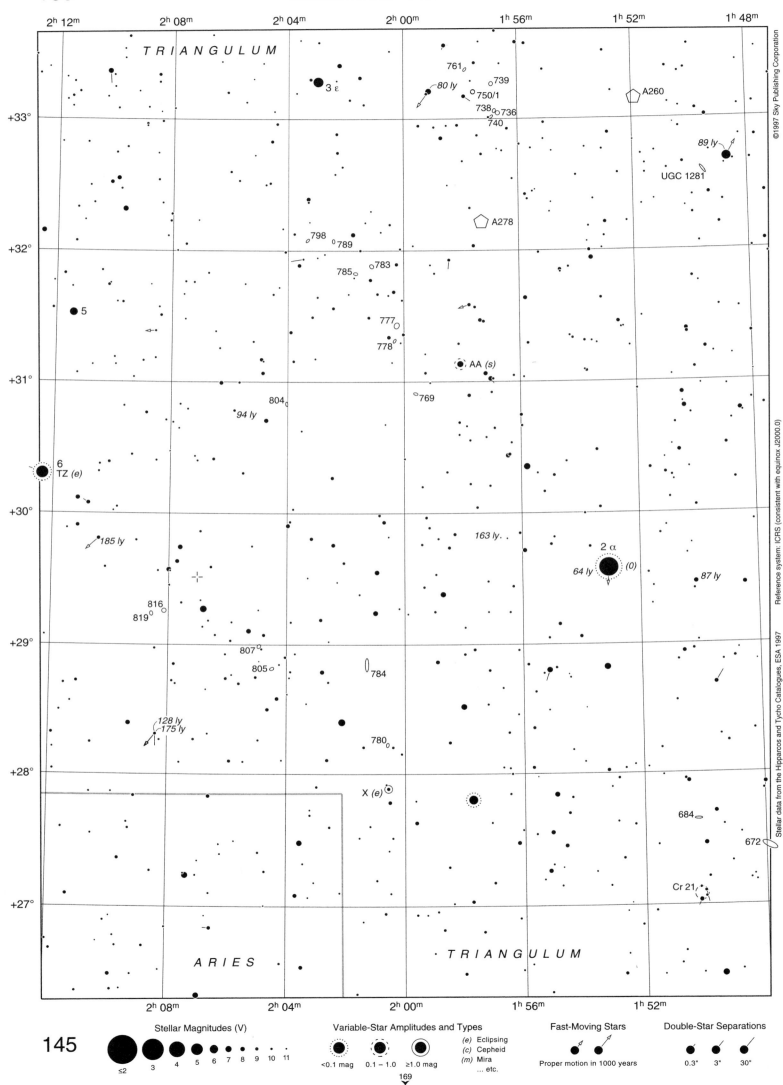

T R I A N G U L U M

761
739
80 ly
750/1
738
736
740

A260

89 ly

UGC 1281

A278

798
789
785 783

5

777
778

AA (s)

804
94 ly

769

6
TZ (e)

185 ly

163 ly

2 α
64 ly (0)

87 ly

816
819

807
805

784

128 ly
175 ly

780

X (e)

684

672

Cr 21

A R I E S

T R I A N G U L U M

Stellar Magnitudes (V)

≤2 3 4 5 6 7 8 9 10 11

Variable-Star Amplitudes and Types

<0.1 mag   0.1 – 1.0   ≥1.0 mag

(e) Eclipsing
(c) Cepheid
(m) Mira
... etc.

169

Fast-Moving Stars

Proper motion in 1000 years

Double-Star Separations

0.3"   3"   30"

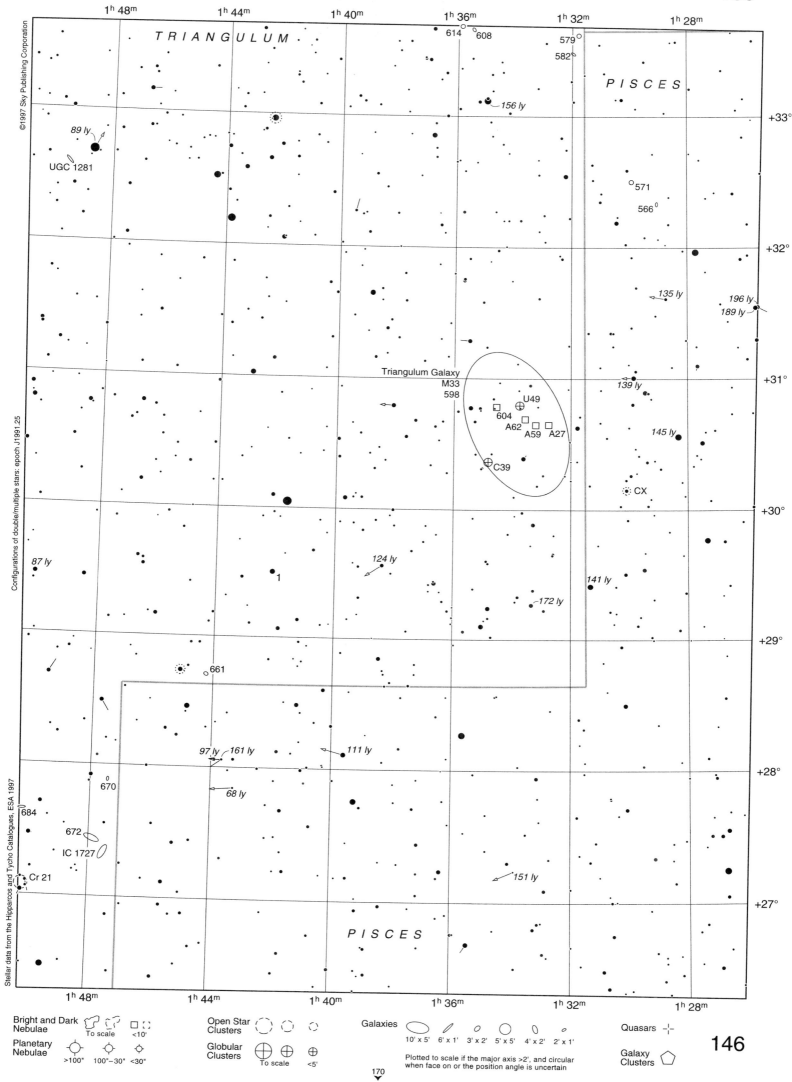

TRIANGULUM

PISCES

614 608
579
582

156 ly

571
566

89 ly
UGC 1281

135 ly

196 ly
189 ly

Triangulum Galaxy
M33
598

139 ly

U49
604
A62
A59 A27

C39

145 ly

CX

+33°
+32°
+31°
+30°
+29°
+28°
+27°

87 ly

1

124 ly

172 ly

141 ly

661

97 ly 161 ly

111 ly

670

68 ly

684

672
IC 1727

151 ly

Cr 21

PISCES

1ʰ 48ᵐ 1ʰ 44ᵐ 1ʰ 40ᵐ 1ʰ 36ᵐ 1ʰ 32ᵐ 1ʰ 28ᵐ

Bright and Dark Nebulae	To scale <10'
Planetary Nebulae	>100" 100"–30" <30"
Open Star Clusters	
Globular Clusters	To scale <5'
Galaxies	10' x 5' 6' x 1' 3' x 2' 5' x 5' 4' x 2' 2' x 1'
Quasars	
Galaxy Clusters	

Plotted to scale if the major axis >2', and circular when face on or the position angle is uncertain

146

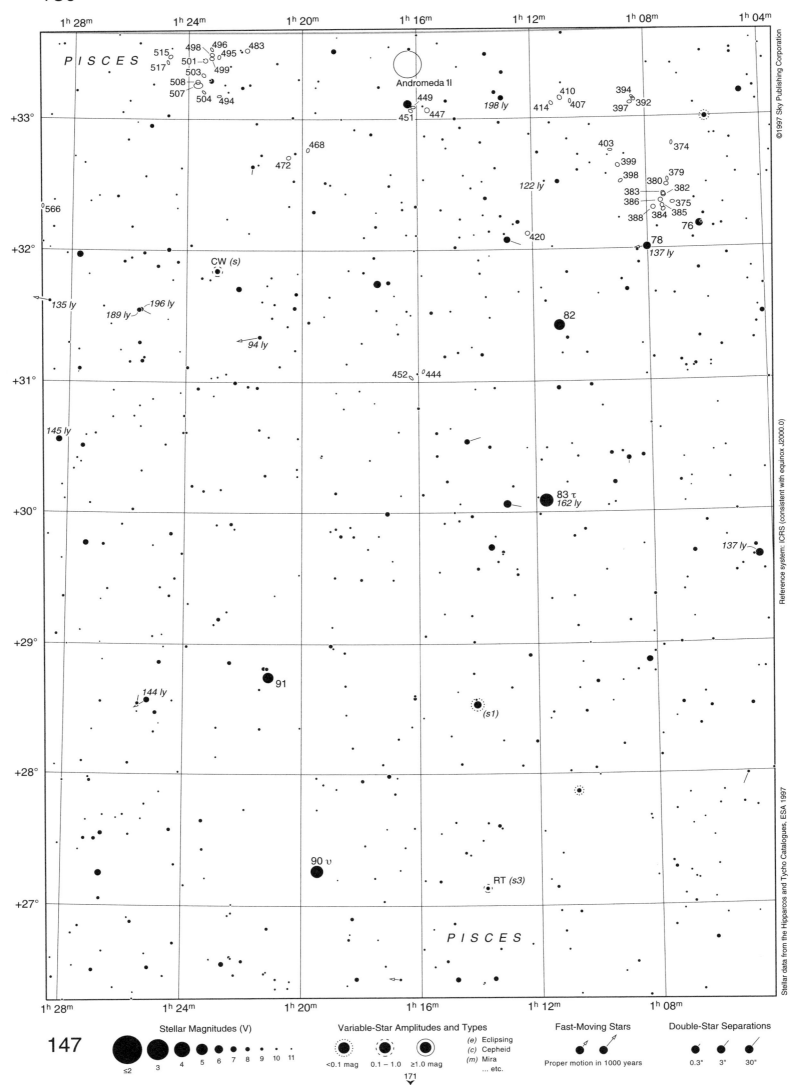
PISCES

515
517
498 496
495 483
501
499
503
508
507 504 494

Andromeda II

449
451 447

468
472

198 ly

410
414 407
394
397 392

403
399
398 374
383 382 379
386 384 380 375
388 385 78 76
137 ly

566

420
CW (s)

135 ly 196 ly
189 ly

82

94 ly

452 444

145 ly

83 τ
162 ly

137 ly

91

144 ly

(s1)

90 υ

RT (s3)

PISCES

147

©1997 Sky Publishing Corporation

Reference system: ICRS (consistent with equinox J2000.0)

Stellar data from the Hipparcos and Tycho Catalogues, ESA 1997

Stellar Magnitudes (V)

≤2   3   4   5 6 7 8 9 10 11

Variable-Star Amplitudes and Types

<0.1 mag   0.1 – 1.0   ≥1.0 mag

(e) Eclipsing
(c) Cepheid
(m) Mira
... etc.

Fast-Moving Stars

Proper motion in 1000 years

Double-Star Separations

0.3"   3"   30"

171

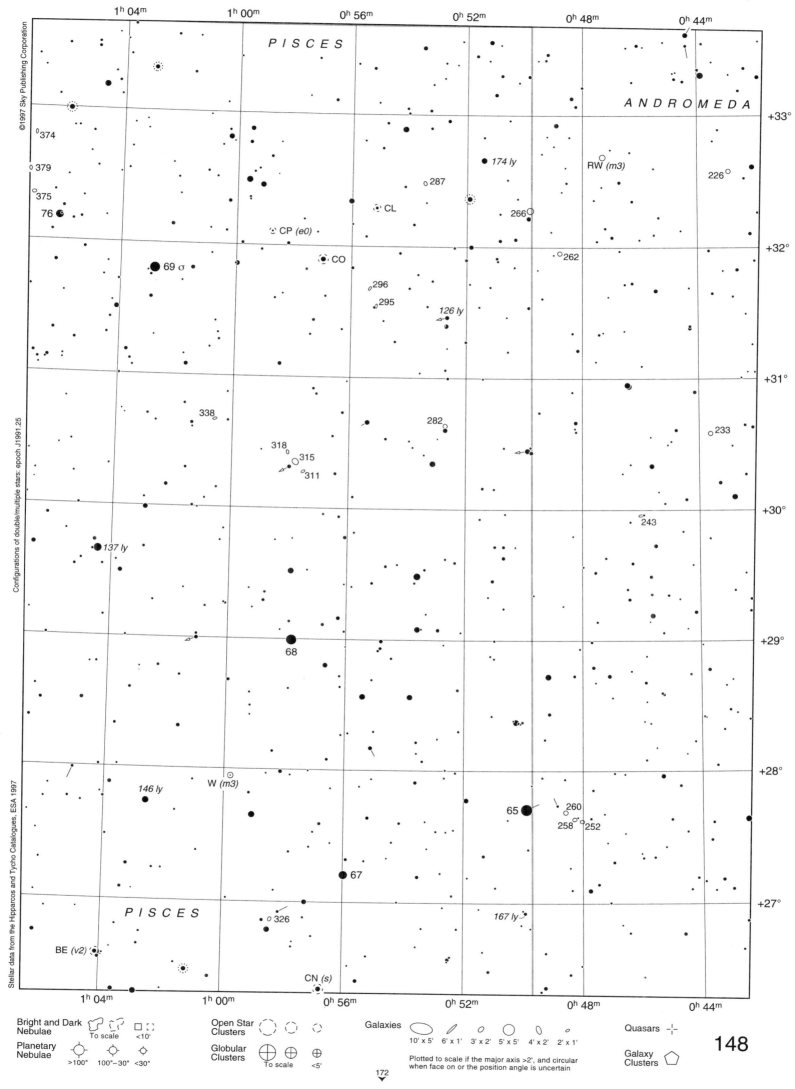

©1997 Sky Publishing Corporation

Configurations of double/multiple stars: epoch J1991.25

Stellar data from the Hipparcos and Tycho Catalogues, ESA 1997

P I S C E S

A N D R O M E D A

1ʰ 04ᵐ   1ʰ 00ᵐ   0ʰ 56ᵐ   0ʰ 52ᵐ   0ʰ 48ᵐ   0ʰ 44ᵐ

+33°

ᵒ374
ᵒ 379
ᵒ 375
76
69 σ

174 ly
RW (m3)
ᵒ 287
CL
266
226ᵒ
+32°
ᵒ262
CP (e0)
CO
ᵒ296
ᵒ295
126 ly
338
282ᵒ
233ᵒ
+31°
318ᵒ
ᵒ315
ᵒ311
243
+30°
137 ly
68
+29°
146 ly
W (m3)
65
260
258   252
+28°
67
+27°
P I S C E S
ᵒ326
167 ly
BE (v2)
CN (s)

1ʰ 04ᵐ   1ʰ 00ᵐ   0ʰ 56ᵐ   0ʰ 52ᵐ   0ʰ 48ᵐ   0ʰ 44ᵐ

Bright and Dark Nebulae   To scale   <10'

Open Star Clusters

Galaxies   10' x 5'   6' x 1'   3' x 2'   5' x 5'   4' x 2'   2' x 1'

Quasars

Planetary Nebulae   >100"   100"–30"   <30"

Globular Clusters   To scale   <5'

Plotted to scale if the major axis >2', and circular when face on or the position angle is uncertain

Galaxy Clusters

148

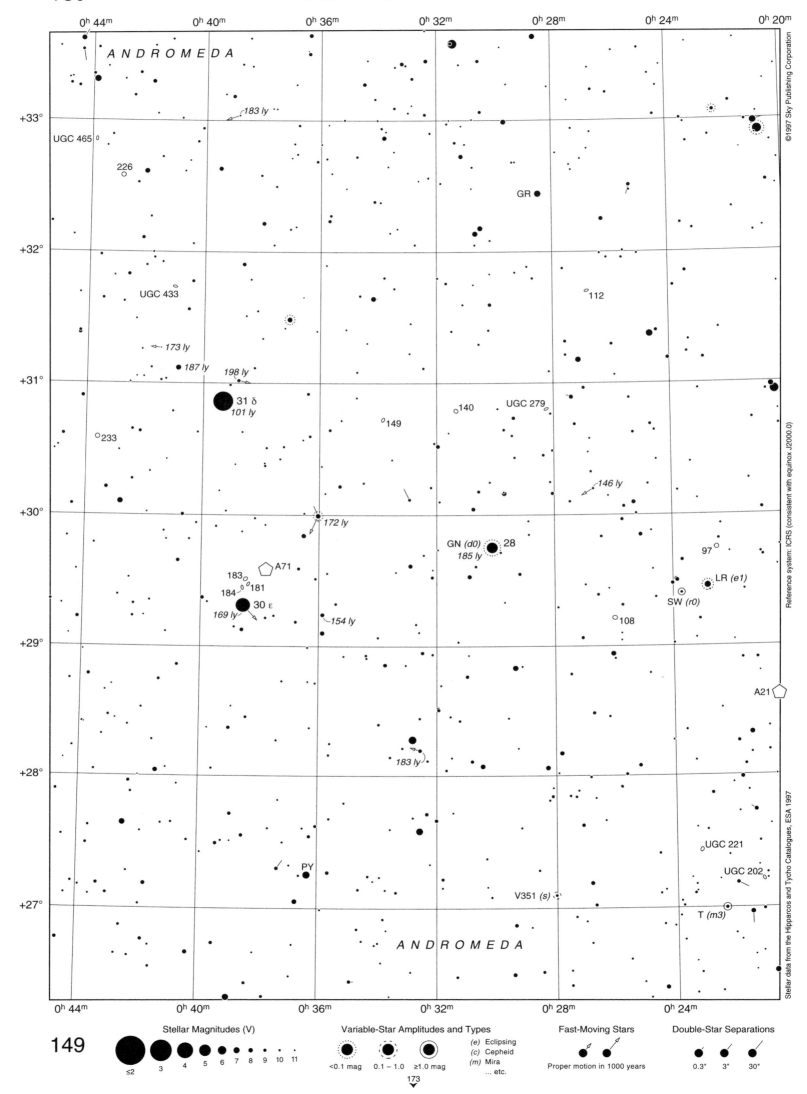

©1997 Sky Publishing Corporation

Reference system: ICRS (consistent with equinox J2000.0)

Stellar data from the Hipparcos and Tycho Catalogues, ESA 1997

A N D R O M E D A

UGC 465

226

GR

UGC 433

112

173 ly

187 ly   198 ly

31 δ
101 ly

233

149

140   UGC 279

146 ly

172 ly

GN (d0)   28
185 ly

A71

183   181
184

30 ε
169 ly

97

LR (e1)

SW (r0)

154 ly

108

A21

183 ly

UGC 221

PY

UGC 202

V351 (s)

T (m3)

A N D R O M E D A

149

Stellar Magnitudes (V)
≤2   3   4   5   6   7   8   9   10   11

Variable-Star Amplitudes and Types
<0.1 mag   0.1 – 1.0   ≥1.0 mag

(e) Eclipsing
(c) Cepheid
(m) Mira
... etc.

Fast-Moving Stars
Proper motion in 1000 years

Double-Star Separations
0.3"   3"   30"

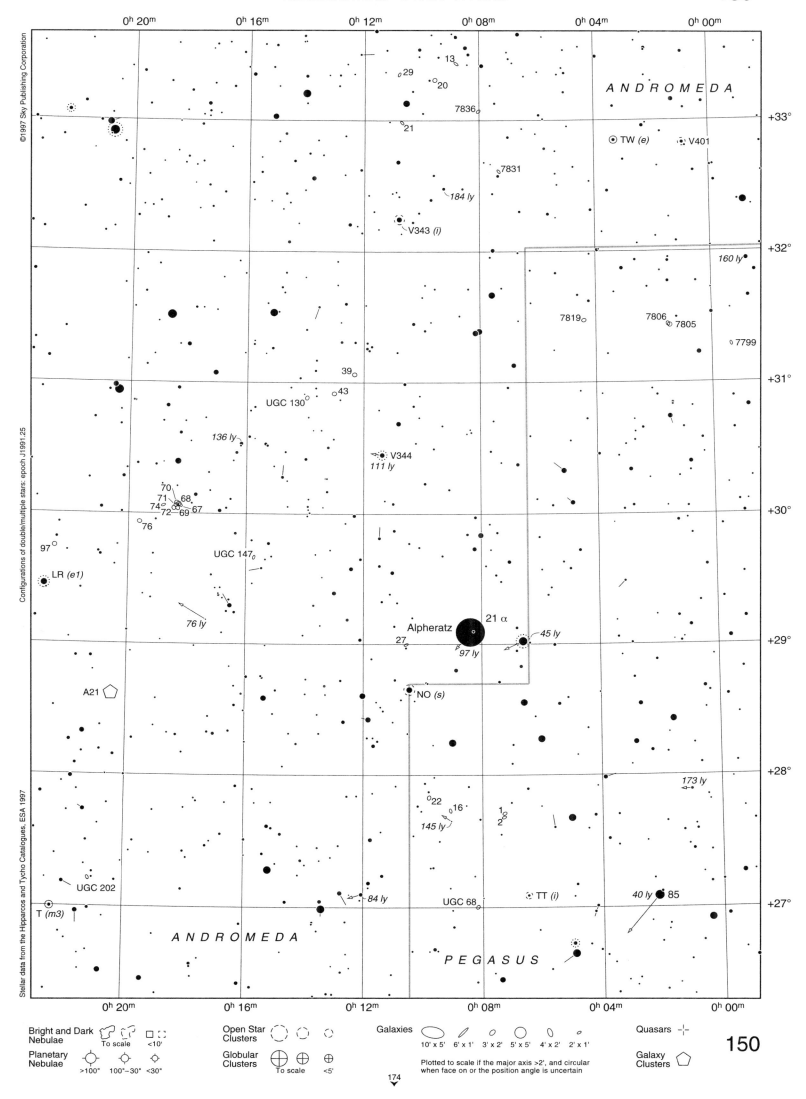

ANDROMEDA

13
29
20
7836
21
TW (e)   V401
7831
184 ly
160 ly
V343 (i)
7819   7806   7805
7799
39
43
UGC 130
136 ly
V344
111 ly
70
71   68
74   67
72   69
76
97
UGC 147
LR (e1)
76 ly
21 α
Alpheratz   45 ly
27   97 ly
A21   NO (s)
173 ly
22
16   1
2
145 ly
84 ly   UGC 68   TT (i)   40 ly   85
UGC 202
T (m3)
ANDROMEDA
PEGASUS

Bright and Dark
Nebulae   Open Star
Clusters   Galaxies   Quasars
To scale   <10'   To scale   10' x 5' 6' x 1' 3' x 2' 5' x 5' 4' x 2' 2' x 1'
Planetary   Globular   Galaxy
Nebulae   Clusters   Clusters
>100" 100"–30" <30'   To scale   <5'   Plotted to scale if the major axis >2', and circular
when face on or the position angle is uncertain

150

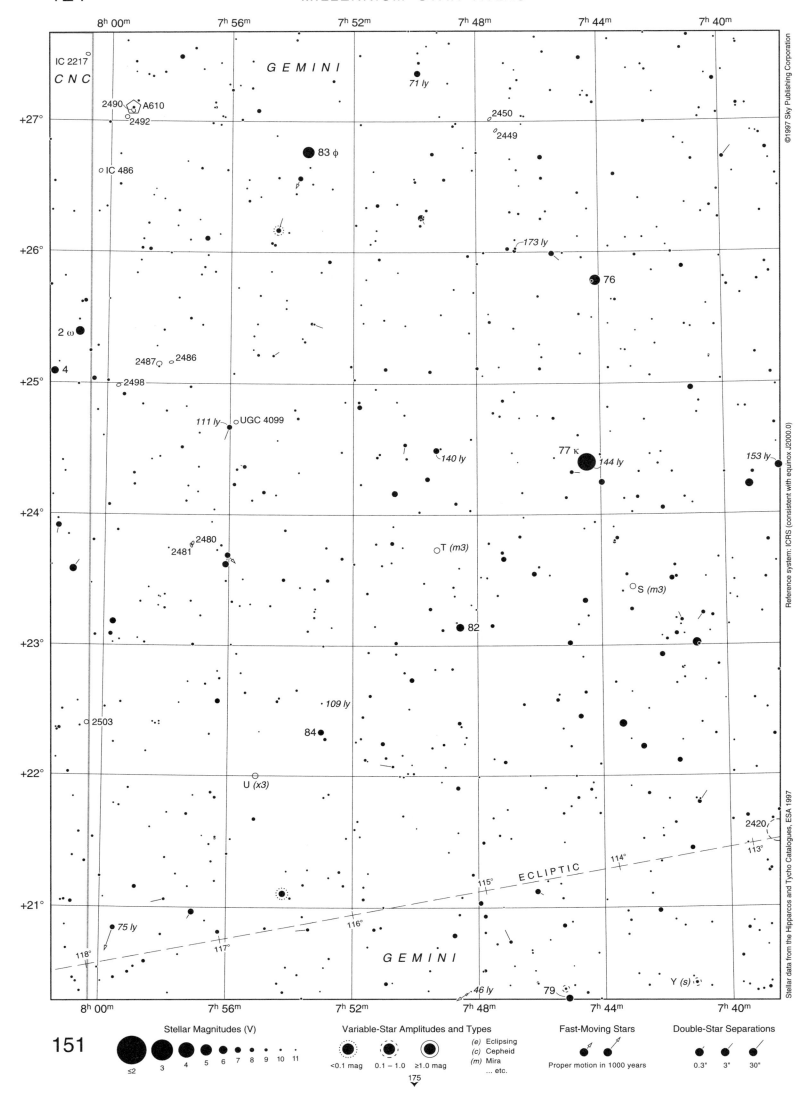

©1997 Sky Publishing Corporation

Reference system: ICRS (consistent with equinox J2000.0)

Stellar data from the Hipparcos and Tycho Catalogues, ESA 1997

151

Stellar Magnitudes (V)

≤2   3   4   5   6   7 8 9 10 11

Variable-Star Amplitudes and Types

<0.1 mag   0.1 – 1.0   ≥1.0 mag

(e) Eclipsing
(c) Cepheid
(m) Mira
... etc.

175

Fast-Moving Stars

Proper motion in 1000 years

Double-Star Separations

0.3"   3"   30"

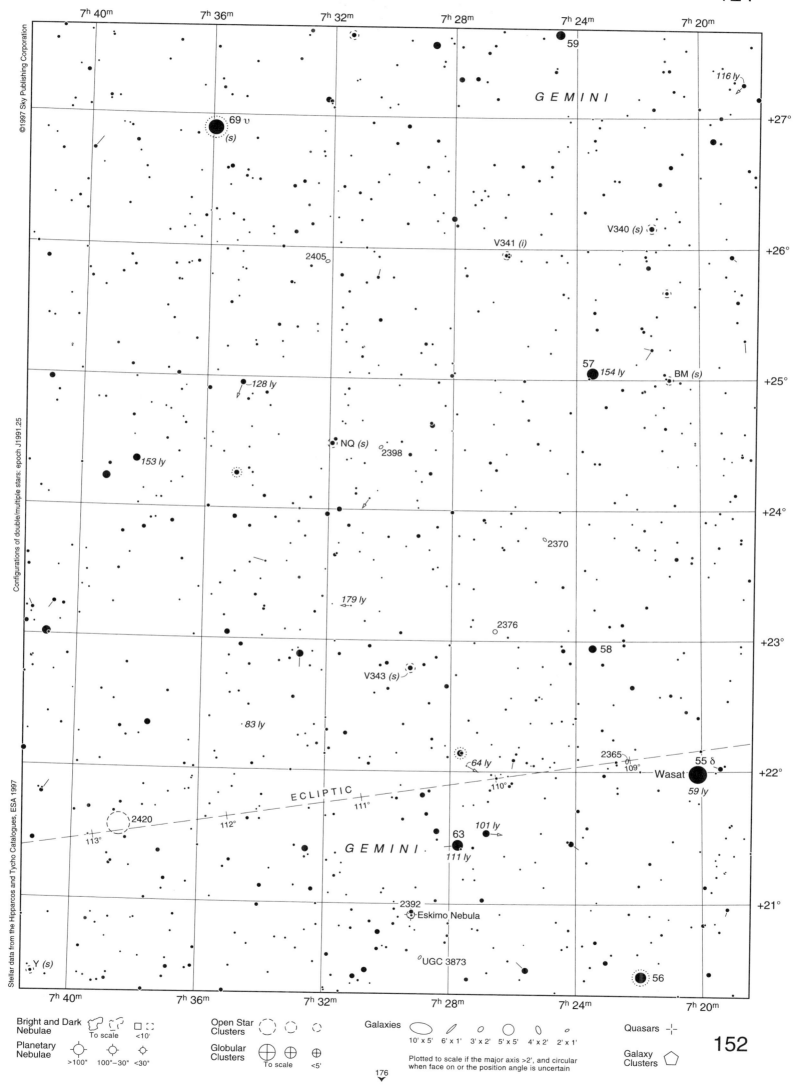

Configurations of double/multiple stars: epoch J1991.25

Stellar data from the Hipparcos and Tycho Catalogues, ESA 1997

Bright and Dark Nebulae — To scale — <10'

Planetary Nebulae — >100" — 100"–30" — <30'

Open Star Clusters

Globular Clusters — To scale — <5'

Galaxies — 10' x 5' — 6' x 1' — 3' x 2' — 5' x 5' — 4' x 2' — 2' x 1'

Plotted to scale if the major axis >2', and circular when face on or the position angle is uncertain

Quasars

Galaxy Clusters

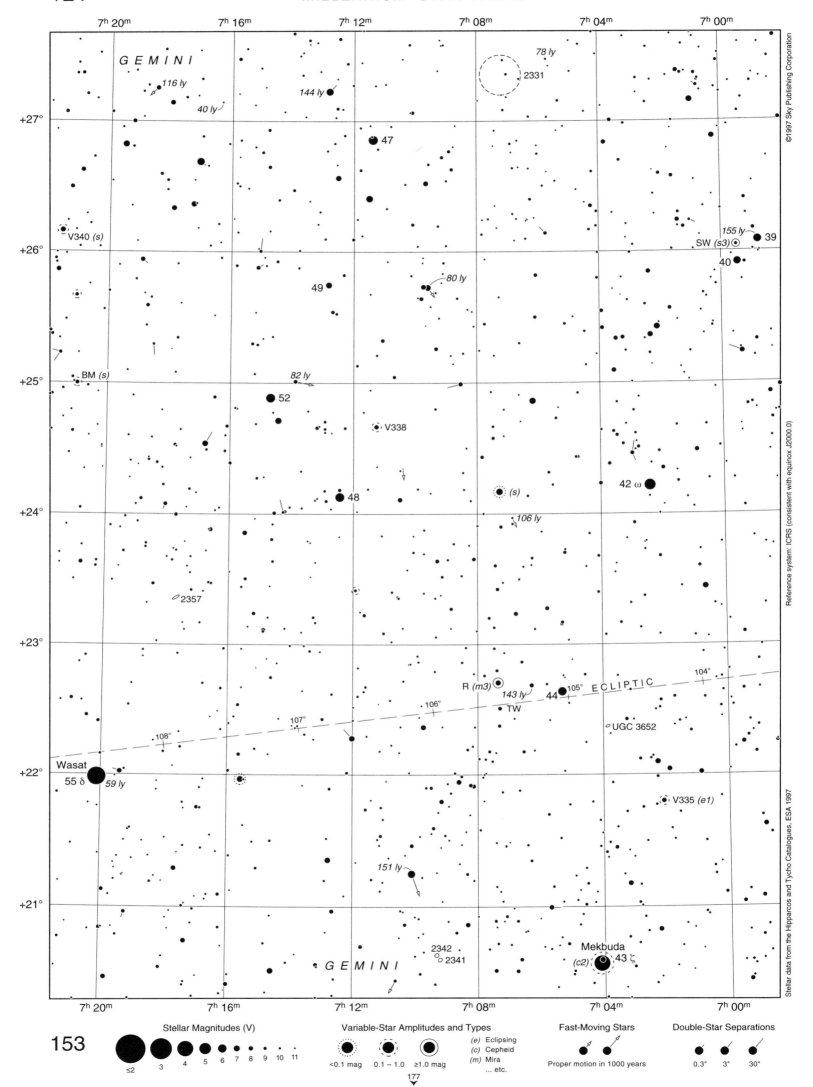

©1997 Sky Publishing Corporation

Reference system: ICRS (consistent with equinox J2000.0)

Stellar data from the Hipparcos and Tycho Catalogues, ESA 1997

153

Stellar Magnitudes (V)

≤2 3 4 5 6 7 8 9 10 11

Variable-Star Amplitudes and Types

<0.1 mag   0.1 − 1.0   ≥1.0 mag

(e) Eclipsing
(c) Cepheid
(m) Mira
... etc.

Fast-Moving Stars

Proper motion in 1000 years

Double-Star Separations

0.3"   3"   30"

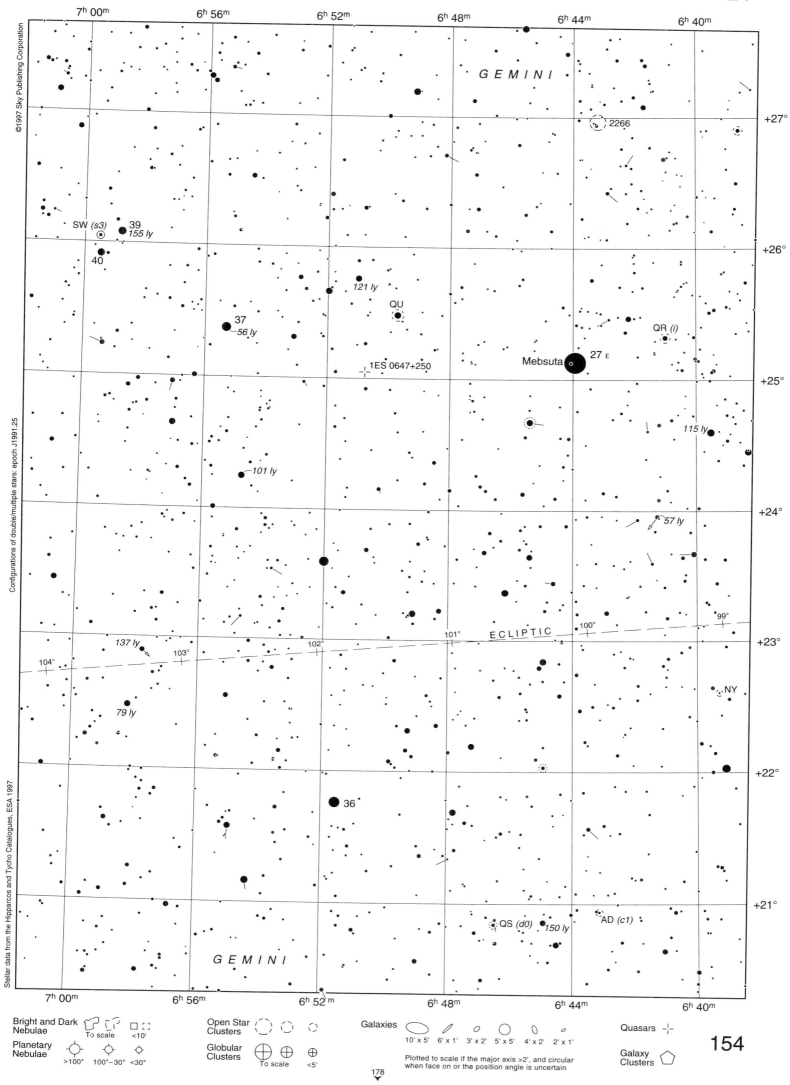

©1997 Sky Publishing Corporation

Configurations of double/multiple stars: epoch J1991.25

Stellar data from the Hipparcos and Tycho Catalogues, ESA 1997

G E M I N I

2266

SW (s3)
39
155 ly

40

121 ly

QU

37
56 ly

QR (i)

Mebsuta   27 ε

1ES 0647+250

115 ly

101 ly

57 ly

ECLIPTIC

137 ly

104°   103°   102°   101°   100°   99°

NY

79 ly

36

QS (d0)   150 ly   AD (c1)

G E M I N I

+27°

+26°

+25°

+24°

+23°

+22°

+21°

7ʰ 00ᵐ   6ʰ 56ᵐ   6ʰ 52ᵐ   6ʰ 48ᵐ   6ʰ 44ᵐ   6ʰ 40ᵐ

| Bright and Dark Nebulae | Open Star Clusters | Galaxies | Quasars |
| Planetary Nebulae | Globular Clusters | | Galaxy Clusters |

To scale   <10'

>100" 100"–30" <30'

To scale   <5'

10' x 5' 6' x 1' 3' x 2' 5' x 5' 4' x 2' 2' x 1'

Plotted to scale if the major axis >2', and circular when face on or the position angle is uncertain

154

178

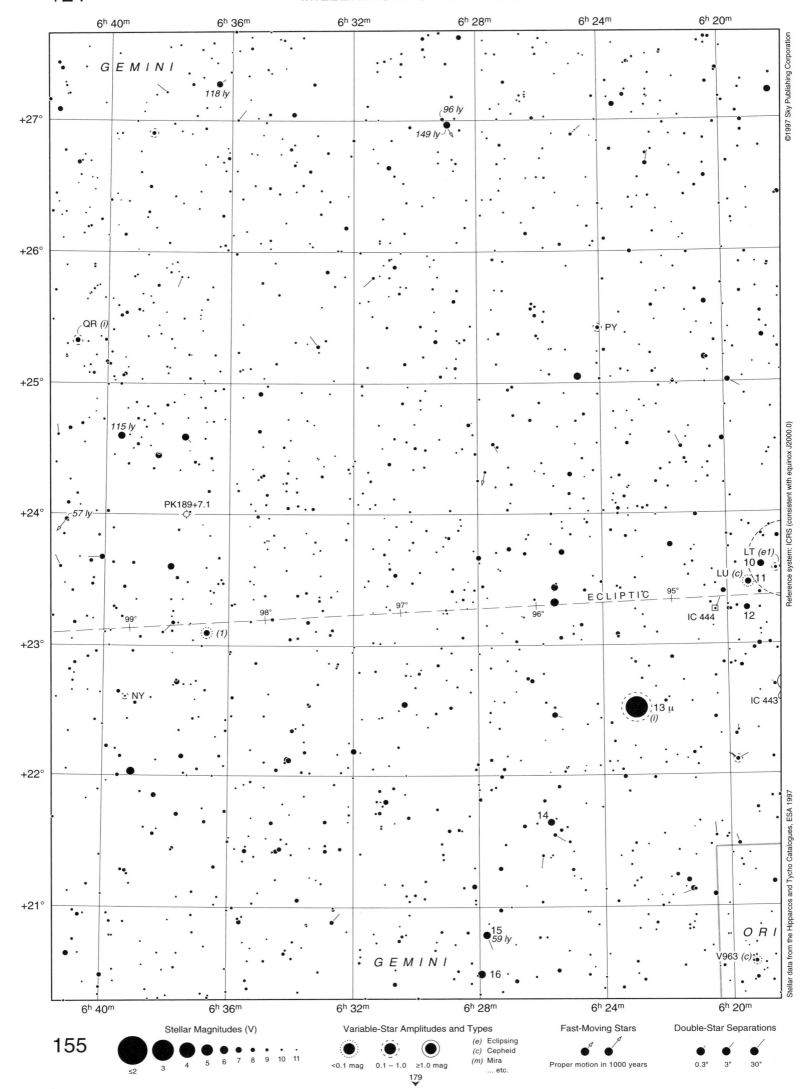

©1997 Sky Publishing Corporation

Reference system: ICRS (consistent with equinox J2000.0)

Stellar data from the Hipparcos and Tycho Catalogues, ESA 1997

GEMINI

118 ly

96 ly

149 ly

QR (i)

PY

115 ly

57 ly

PK189+7.1

LT (e1)
10
LU (c)
11
IC 444
12

ECLIPTIC
95°
96°
97°
98°
99°

(1)

NY

13 μ
(i)

IC 443

14

ORI

15
59 ly

GEMINI

16

V963 (c)

Stellar Magnitudes (V)

≤2   3   4   5   6   7   8   9   10   11

Variable-Star Amplitudes and Types

<0.1 mag   0.1 – 1.0   ≥1.0 mag

(e) Eclipsing
(c) Cepheid
(m) Mira
... etc.

Fast-Moving Stars

Proper motion in 1000 years

Double-Star Separations

0.3"   3"   30"

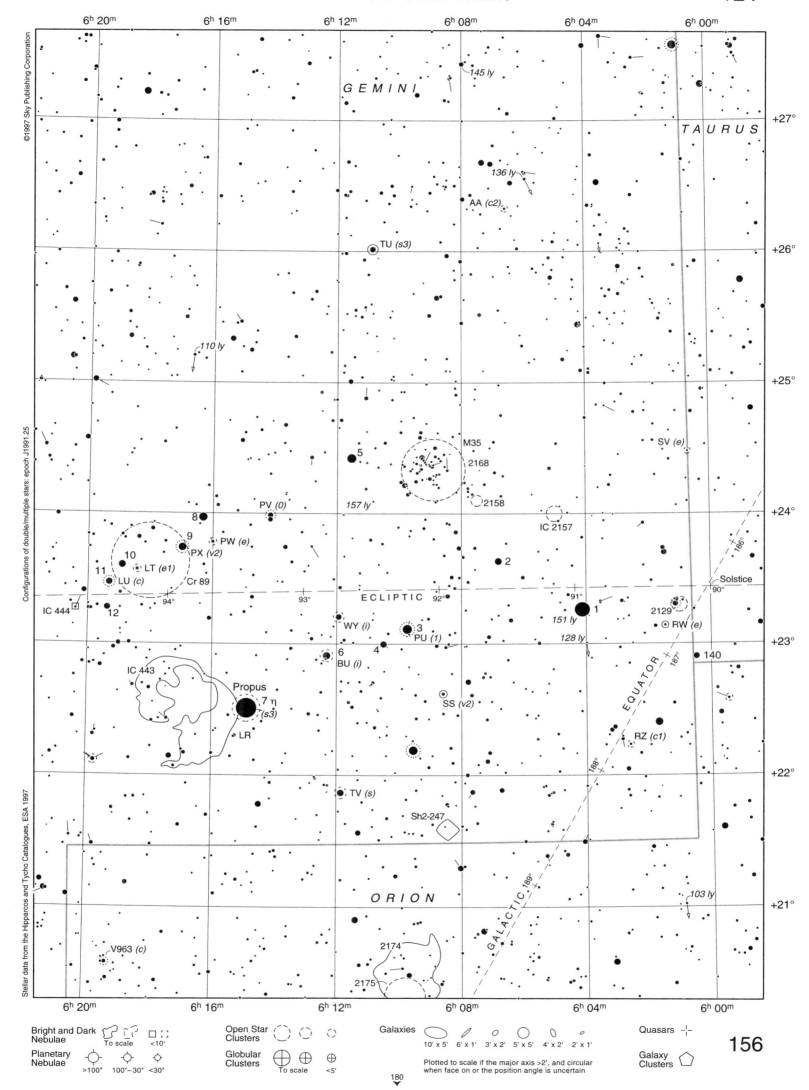

GEMINI

TAURUS

ORION

+27°
+26°
+25°
+24°
+23°
+22°
+21°

6h 20m   6h 16m   6h 12m   6h 08m   6h 04m   6h 00m

145 ly
136 ly
AA (c2)
TU (s3)
110 ly
M35
2168
5
2158
157 ly
IC 2157
SV (e)
PV (0)
8
9
PW (e)
PX (v2)
10
LT (e1)
Cr 89
11
LU (c)
12
IC 444
94°   93°   ECLIPTIC   92°   91°   90° Solstice
186°
2
151 ly   128 ly   187°   140
2129
RW (e)
WY (i)
PU (1)   3
6   4
BU (i)
IC 443
SS (v2)
Propus
7 η
(s3)
LR
RZ (c1)
EQUATOR
188°
TV (s)
Sh2-247
V963 (c)
GALACTIC 189°
103 ly
2174
2175

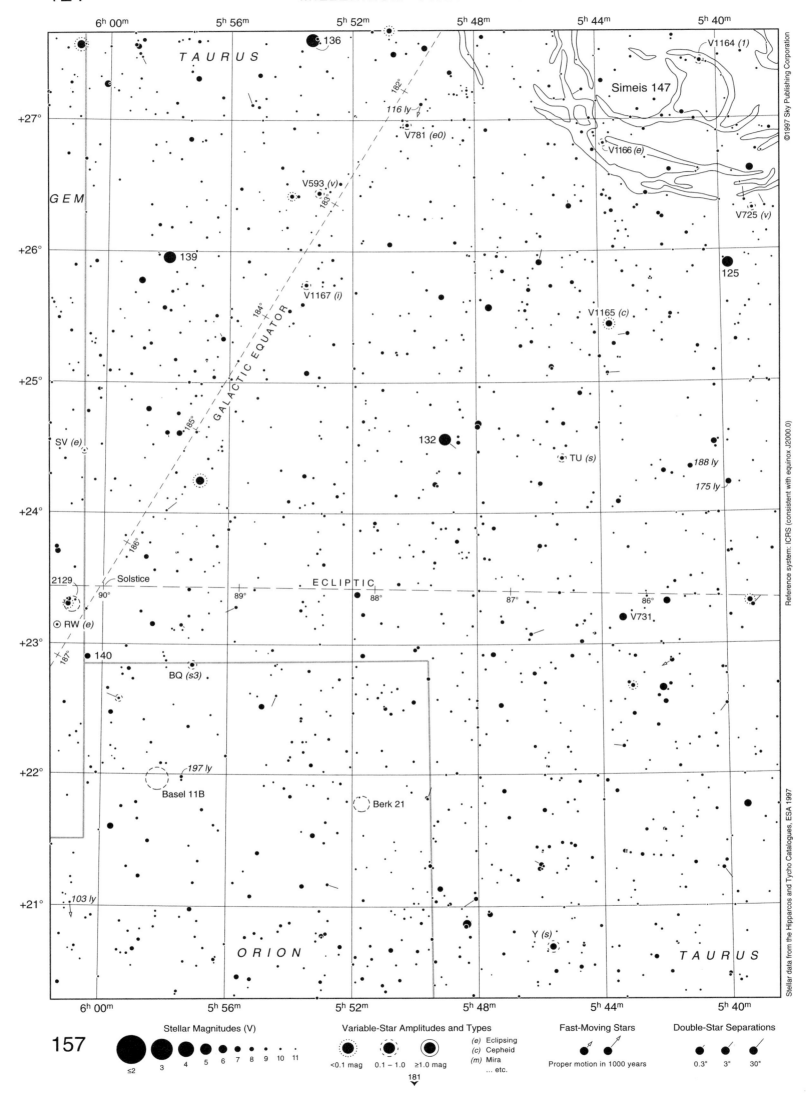

©1997 Sky Publishing Corporation

Reference system: ICRS (consistent with equinox J2000.0)

Stellar data from the Hipparcos and Tycho Catalogues, ESA 1997

157

Stellar Magnitudes (V)
≤2 3 4 5 6 7 8 9 10 11

Variable-Star Amplitudes and Types
<0.1 mag   0.1 – 1.0   ≥1.0 mag
(e) Eclipsing
(c) Cepheid
(m) Mira
... etc.

Fast-Moving Stars
Proper motion in 1000 years

Double-Star Separations
0.3"   3"   30"

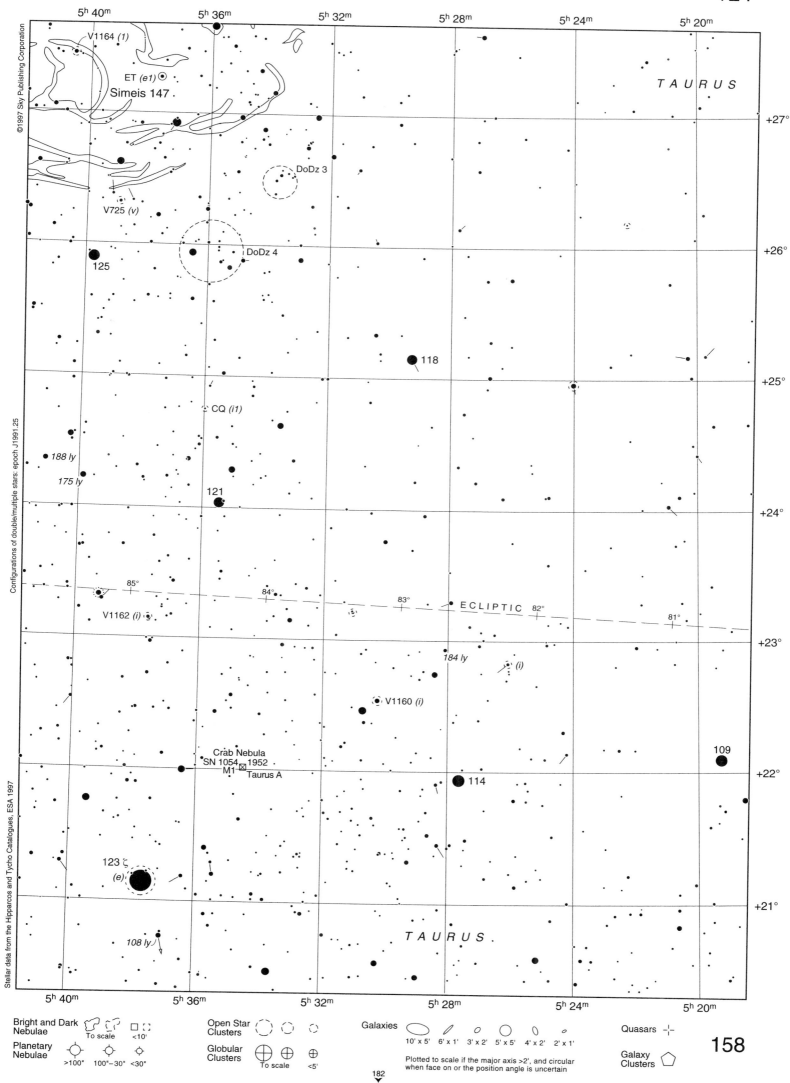

Configurations of double/multiple stars: epoch J1991.25

Stellar data from the Hipparcos and Tycho Catalogues, ESA 1997

V1164 (1)

ET (e1)

Simeis 147

V725 (v)

DoDz 3

DoDz 4

125

118

CQ (i1)

188 ly

175 ly

121

85°   84°   83°   ECLIPTIC   82°   81°
ECLIPTIC

V1162 (i)

+27°
+26°
+25°
+24°
+23°

184 ly
(i)

V1160 (i)

Crab Nebula
SN 1054 ⊠ 1952
M1   Taurus A

109

114

+22°

123 ζ
(e)

+21°

T A U R U S

108 ly

5h 40m   5h 36m   5h 32m   5h 28m   5h 24m   5h 20m

T A U R U S

Bright and Dark
Nebulae
To scale <10'

Planetary
Nebulae
>100" 100"–30" <30"

Open Star
Clusters

Globular
Clusters
To scale <5'

Galaxies
10' x 5' 6' x 1' 3' x 2' 5' x 5' 4' x 2' 2' x 1'

Plotted to scale if the major axis >2', and circular
when face on or the position angle is uncertain

Quasars

Galaxy
Clusters

182

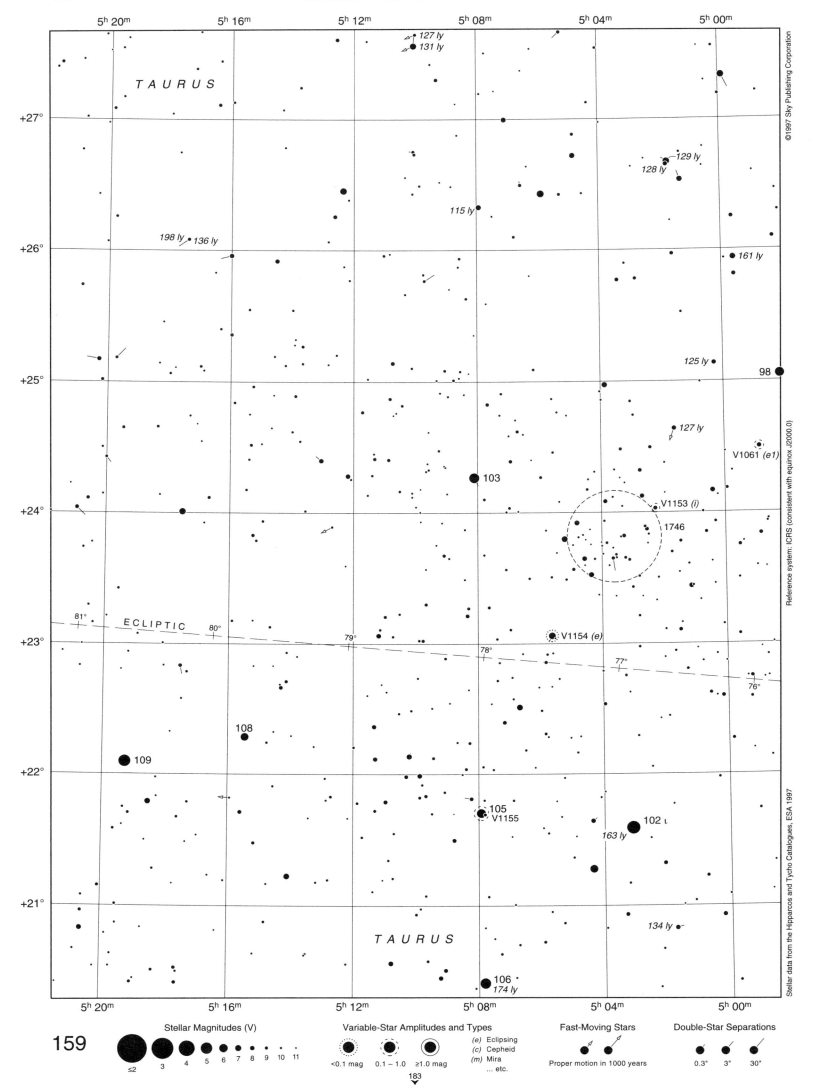

©1997 Sky Publishing Corporation

Reference system: ICRS (consistent with equinox J2000.0)

Stellar data from the Hipparcos and Tycho Catalogues, ESA 1997

TAURUS

127 ly
131 ly

129 ly
128 ly

115 ly

198 ly · 136 ly

161 ly

125 ly

98

127 ly

V1061 (e1)

103

V1153 (i)

1746

ECLIPTIC

V1154 (e)

108

109

105
V1155

102 ι

163 ly

134 ly

TAURUS

106
174 ly

159

Stellar Magnitudes (V)
≤2 3 4 5 6 7 8 9 10 11

Variable-Star Amplitudes and Types
<0.1 mag   0.1 – 1.0   ≥1.0 mag

(e) Eclipsing
(c) Cepheid
(m) Mira
... etc.

Fast-Moving Stars
Proper motion in 1000 years

Double-Star Separations
0.3"   3"   30"

136

183

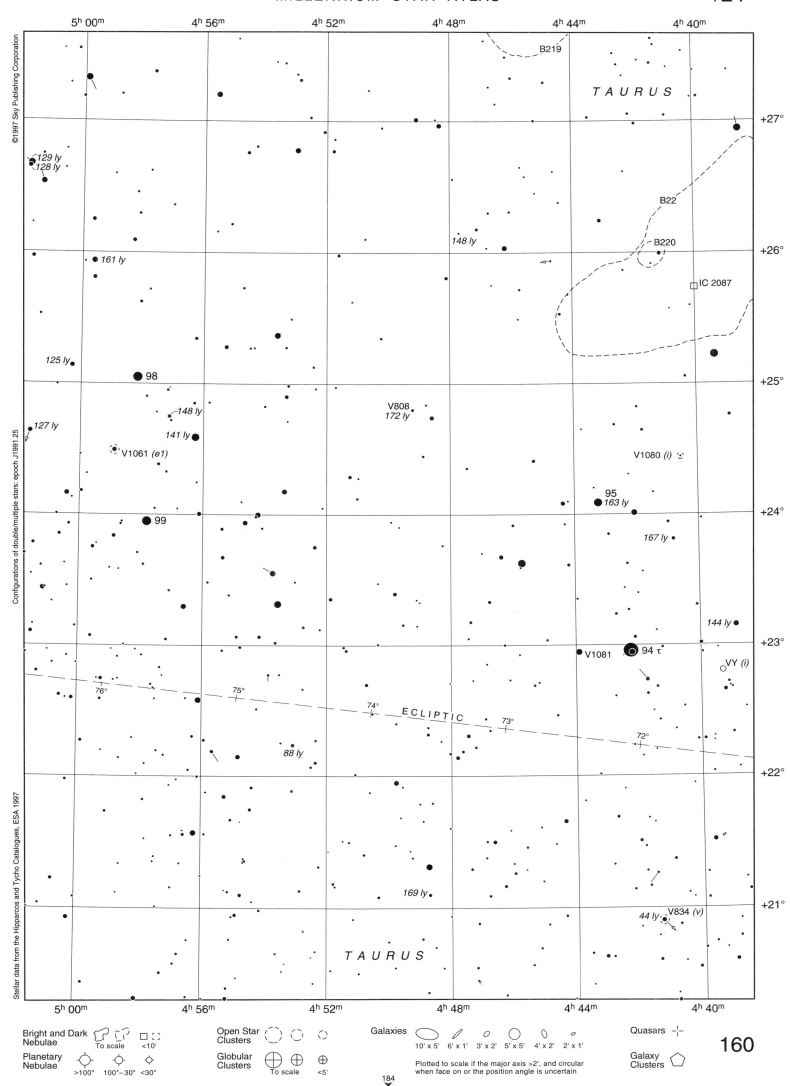

B219

T A U R U S

129 ly
128 ly

B22

B220

IC 2087

161 ly

148 ly

125 ly

98

127 ly

148 ly

V808
172 ly

141 ly

V1061 *(e1)*

V1080 *(i)*

95
163 ly

99

167 ly

144 ly

94 τ

V1081

VY *(i)*

76°

75°

74° *E C L I P T I C* 73°

72°

88 ly

169 ly

V834 *(v)*

44 ly

T A U R U S

Bright and Dark Nebulae	To scale	<10'	
Planetary Nebulae	>100" 100"−30" <30"		
Open Star Clusters			
Globular Clusters	To scale <5'		
Galaxies	10' x 5' 6' x 1' 3' x 2' 5' x 5' 4' x 2' 2' x 1'		
	Plotted to scale if the major axis >2', and circular when face on or the position angle is uncertain		
Quasars			
Galaxy Clusters			

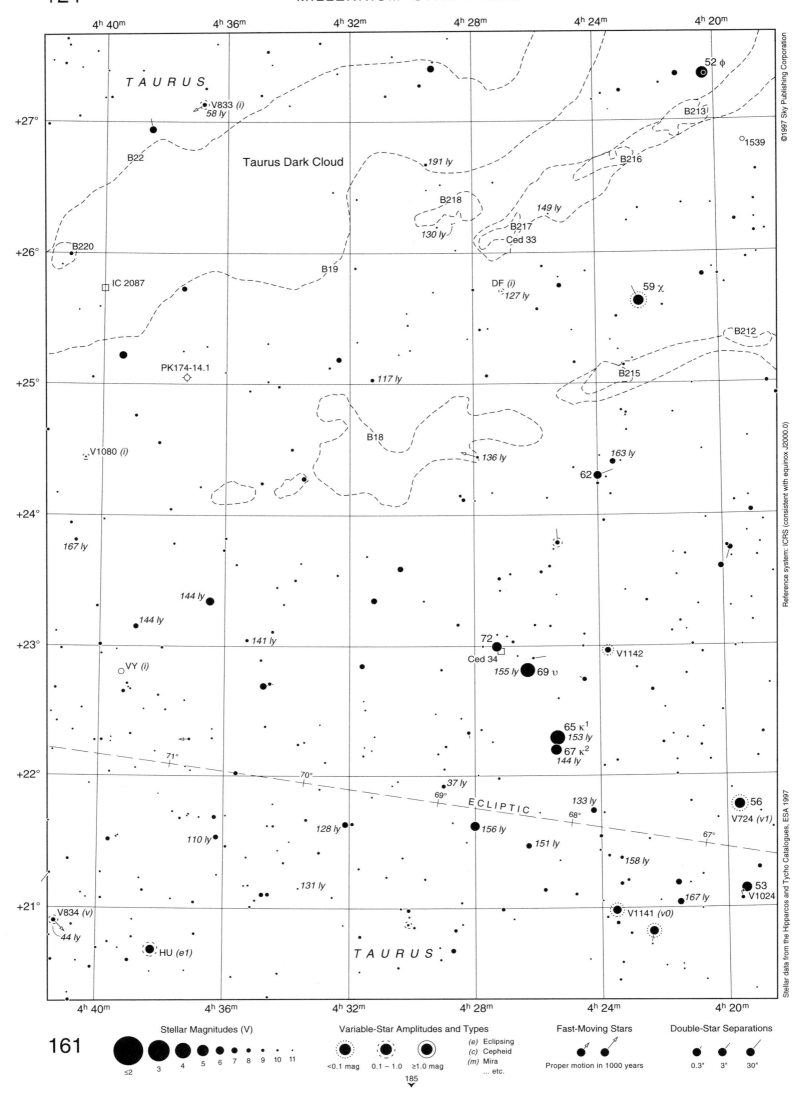

©1997 Sky Publishing Corporation

Reference system: ICRS (consistent with equinox J2000.0)

Stellar data from the Hipparcos and Tycho Catalogues, ESA 1997

TAURUS

Taurus Dark Cloud

V833 (i)
58 ly

B22

191 ly

B218

B220

IC 2087

B19

130 ly

B217
Ced 33

149 ly

52 φ

B213

B216

1539

59 χ

DF (i)
127 ly

B212

PK174-14.1

117 ly

B215

V1080 (i)

B18

136 ly

163 ly

62

167 ly

144 ly

144 ly

141 ly

72
Ced 34

V1142

155 ly 69 υ

65 κ¹
153 ly
67 κ²
144 ly

VY (i)

71°

70°

37 ly

69°

ECLIPTIC

133 ly

68°

156 ly

151 ly

56

V724 (v1)

128 ly

110 ly

158 ly

67°

131 ly

167 ly

53
V1024

V834 (v)

V1141 (v0)

44 ly

HU (e1)

TAURUS

Stellar Magnitudes (V)

≤2   3   4   5   6   7   8   9 10 11

Variable-Star Amplitudes and Types

<0.1 mag   0.1 – 1.0   ≥1.0 mag

(e) Eclipsing
(c) Cepheid
(m) Mira
... etc.

185

Fast-Moving Stars

Proper motion in 1000 years

Double-Star Separations

0.3"   3"   30"

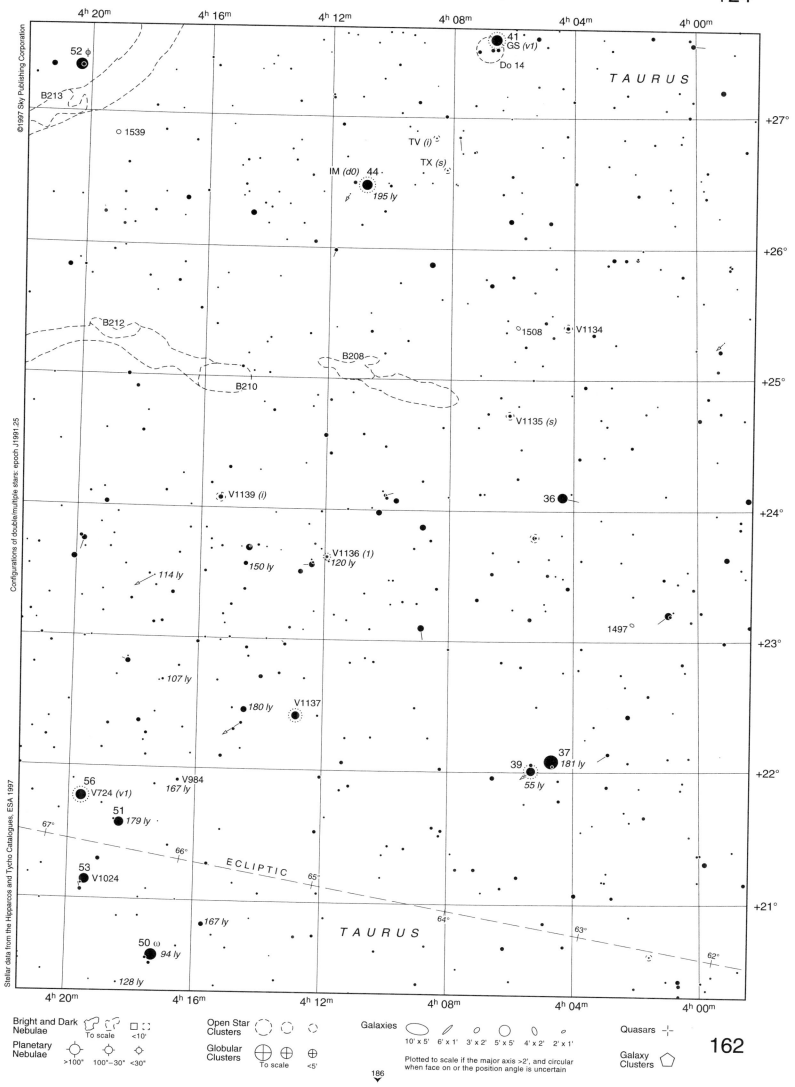

Configurations of double/multiple stars: epoch J1991.25

Stellar data from the Hipparcos and Tycho Catalogues, ESA 1997

T A U R U S

B213

52 φ

1539

TV (i)
TX (s)

41
GS (v1)
Do 14

IM (d0) 44
195 ly

B212

B208
B210

1508
V1134

V1135 (s)

V1139 (i)

36

114 ly

150 ly

V1136 (1)
120 ly

1497

107 ly

180 ly
V1137

37
181 ly

39
55 ly

56
V724 (v1)

V984
167 ly

51
179 ly

67°
66°
ECLIPTIC
65°

53
V1024

64°
63°
62°

T A U R U S

50 ω
94 ly

128 ly

Bright and Dark
Nebulae
To scale   <10'

Planetary
Nebulae
>100" 100"–30" <30"

Open Star
Clusters

Globular
Clusters
To scale   <5'

Galaxies
10' x 5' 6' x 1' 3' x 2' 5' x 5' 4' x 2' 2' x 1'

Plotted to scale if the major axis >2', and circular
when face on or the position angle is uncertain

Quasars

Galaxy
Clusters

162

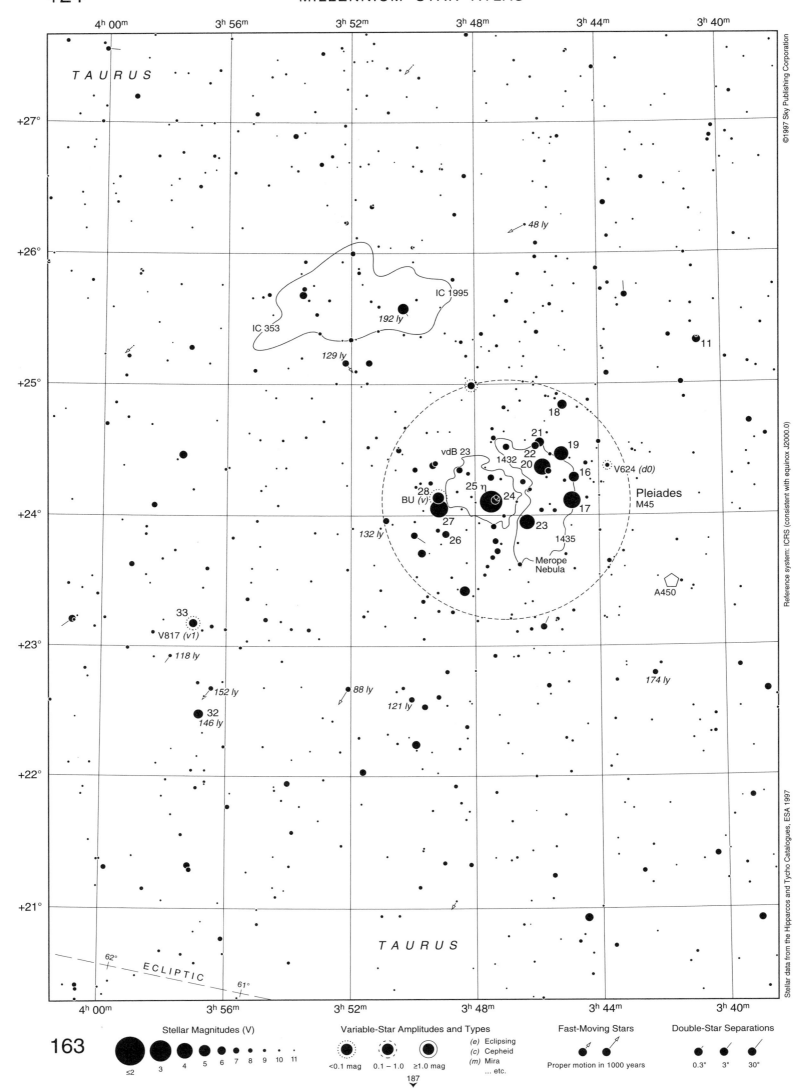

©1997 Sky Publishing Corporation

Reference system: ICRS (consistent with equinox J2000.0)

Stellar data from the Hipparcos and Tycho Catalogues, ESA 1997

TAURUS

IC 1995
IC 353
192 ly
129 ly

48 ly

11

18
21
vdB 23
1432
22
20
19
16
V624 (d0)
25 η
28
BU (v)
24
17
Pleiades
M45
27
23
26
132 ly
1435
Merope
Nebula
A450

33
V817 (v1)
118 ly
152 ly
88 ly
121 ly
174 ly
32
146 ly

TAURUS

62°
ECLIPTIC
61°

163

Stellar Magnitudes (V)
≤2   3   4   5   6   7   8   9   10   11

Variable-Star Amplitudes and Types
<0.1 mag   0.1 – 1.0   ≥1.0 mag

(e) Eclipsing
(c) Cepheid
(m) Mira
... etc.

Fast-Moving Stars
Proper motion in 1000 years

Double-Star Separations
0.3"   3"   30"

187

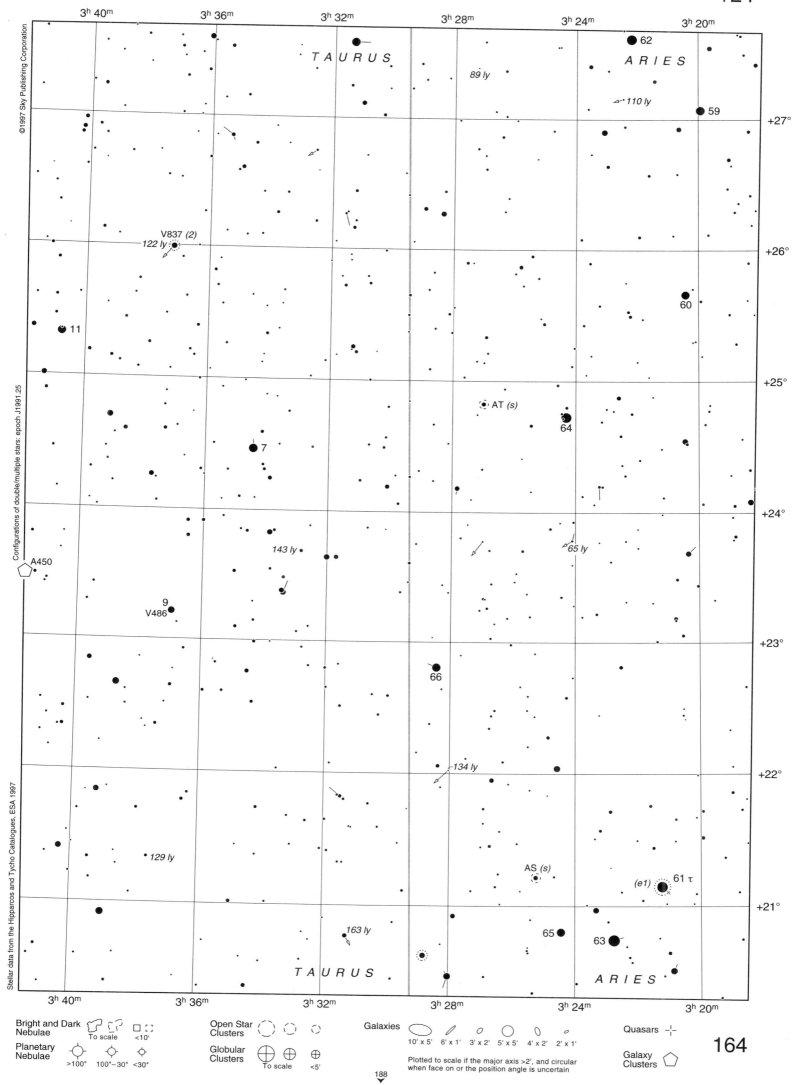

Configurations of double/multiple stars: epoch J1991.25

Stellar data from the Hipparcos and Tycho Catalogues, ESA 1997

TAURUS

ARIES

89 ly

110 ly

62

59

V837 (2)
122 ly

60

11

AT (s)

64

7

143 ly

65 ly

A450

9
V486

66

134 ly

129 ly

AS (s)

(e1)   61 τ

163 ly

65

63

TAURUS

ARIES

Bright and Dark Nebulae
To scale   <10'

Planetary Nebulae
>100" 100"–30" <30"

Open Star Clusters

Globular Clusters
To scale   <5'

Galaxies
10' x 5' 6' x 1' 3' x 2' 5' x 5' 4' x 2' 2' x 1'

Plotted to scale if the major axis >2', and circular when face on or the position angle is uncertain

Quasars

Galaxy Clusters

188

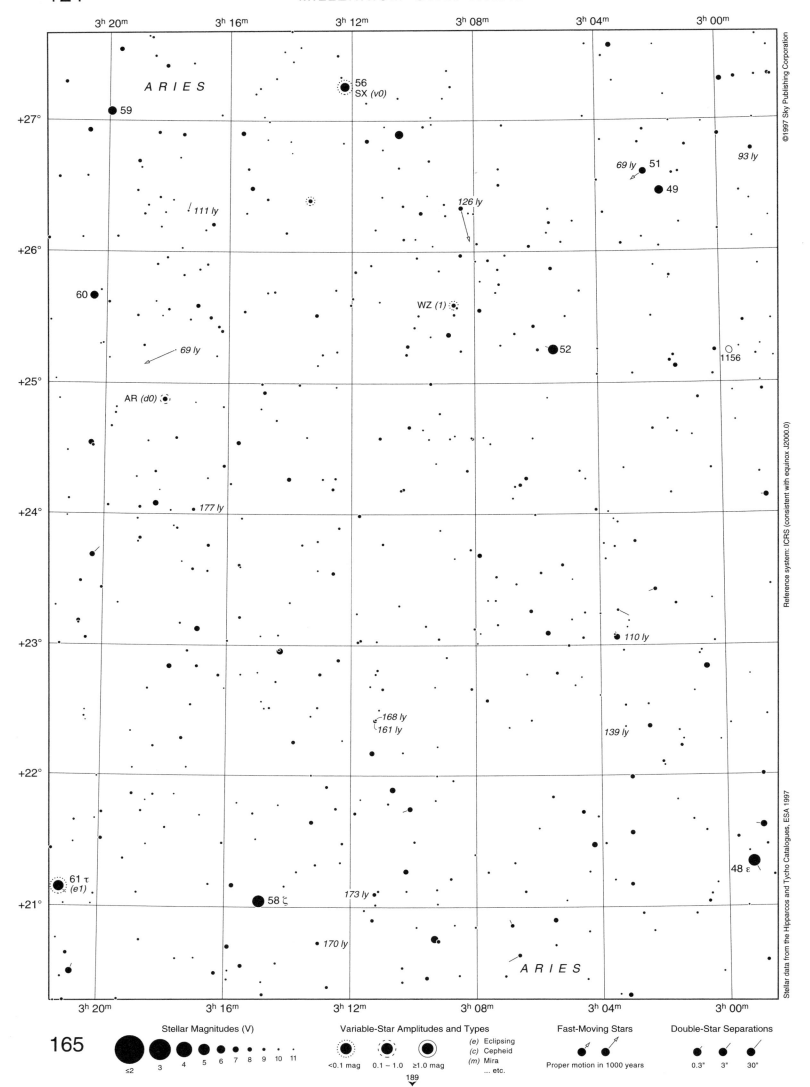

ARIES

56
SX (v0)

59

69 ly 51
49

93 ly

111 ly

126 ly

60

69 ly

WZ (1)

52

1156

AR (d0)

177 ly

110 ly

168 ly
161 ly

139 ly

61 τ
(e1)

58 ζ

173 ly

48 ε

170 ly

ARIES

Stellar Magnitudes (V)

≤2   3   4   5   6   7   8   9   10   11

Variable-Star Amplitudes and Types

<0.1 mag   0.1 – 1.0   ≥1.0 mag

(e) Eclipsing
(c) Cepheid
(m) Mira
... etc.

Fast-Moving Stars

Proper motion in 1000 years

Double-Star Separations

0.3"   3"   30"

189

©1997 Sky Publishing Corporation

Reference system: ICRS (consistent with equinox J2000.0)

Stellar data from the Hipparcos and Tycho Catalogues, ESA 1997

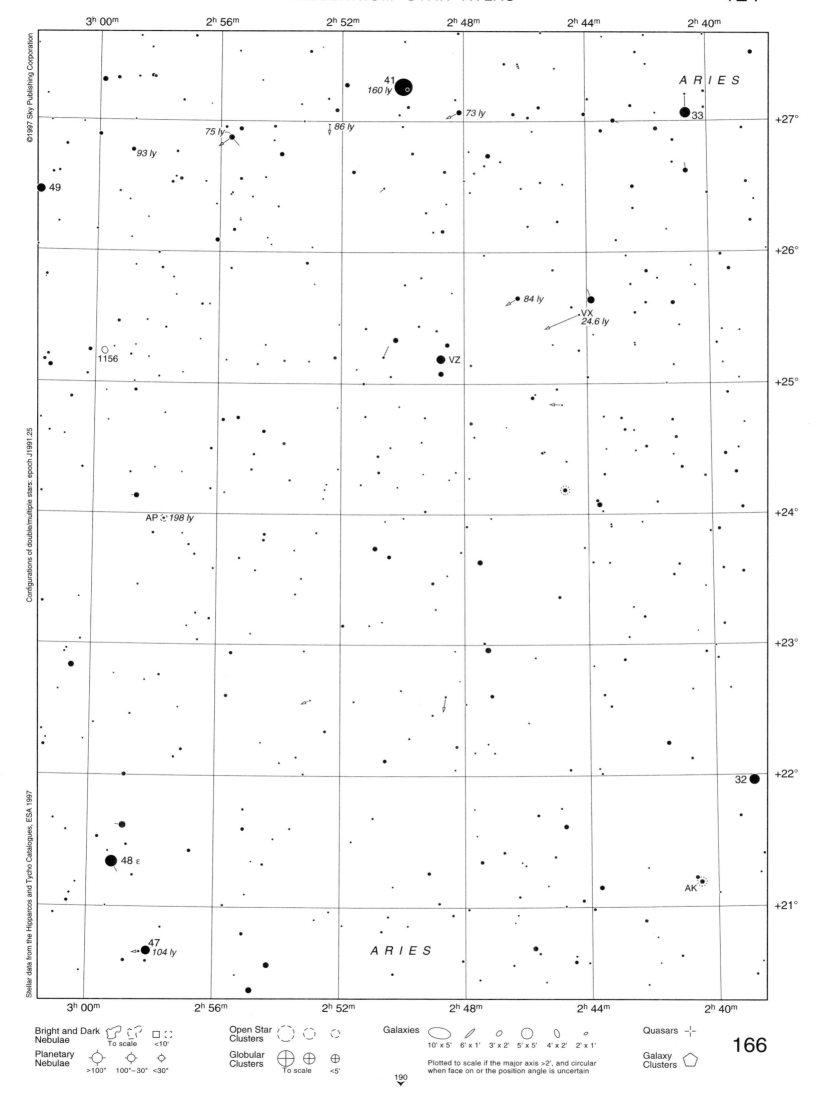

Bright and Dark
Nebulae
To scale   <10'

Planetary
Nebulae
>100" 100"–30" <30"

Open Star
Clusters

Globular
Clusters
To scale   <5'

Galaxies
10' x 5' 6' x 1' 3' x 2' 5' x 5' 4' x 2' 2' x 1'

Plotted to scale if the major axis >2', and circular
when face on or the position angle is uncertain

Quasars

Galaxy
Clusters

166

190

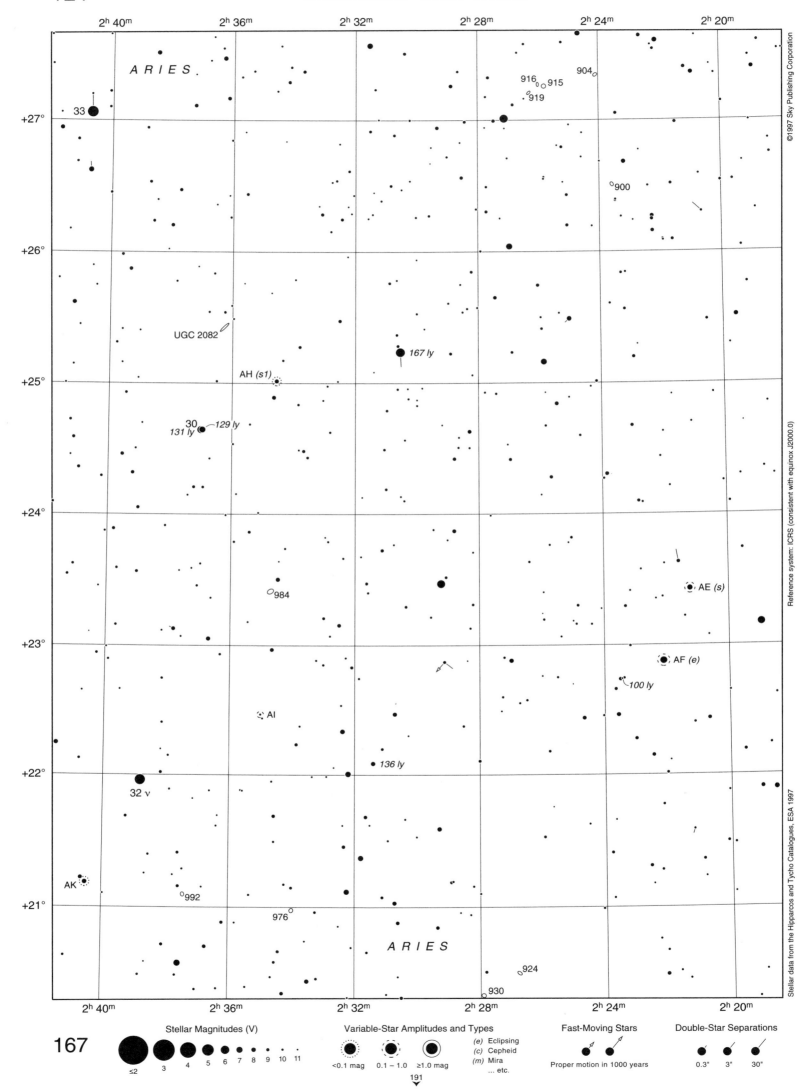

©1997 Sky Publishing Corporation

Reference system: ICRS (consistent with equinox J2000.0)

Stellar data from the Hipparcos and Tycho Catalogues, ESA 1997

ARIES

33

916 915
919
904
900

UGC 2082

AH (s1)

167 ly

30
131 ly 129 ly

984

AE (s)

AF (e)
100 ly

AI

136 ly

32 ν

AK
992

976

ARIES

924

930

Stellar Magnitudes (V)

167

≤2   3   4   5   6   7   8   9   10   11

Variable-Star Amplitudes and Types

<0.1 mag   0.1 – 1.0   ≥1.0 mag

(e) Eclipsing
(c) Cepheid
(m) Mira
... etc.

Fast-Moving Stars

Proper motion in 1000 years

Double-Star Separations

0.3"   3"   30"

191

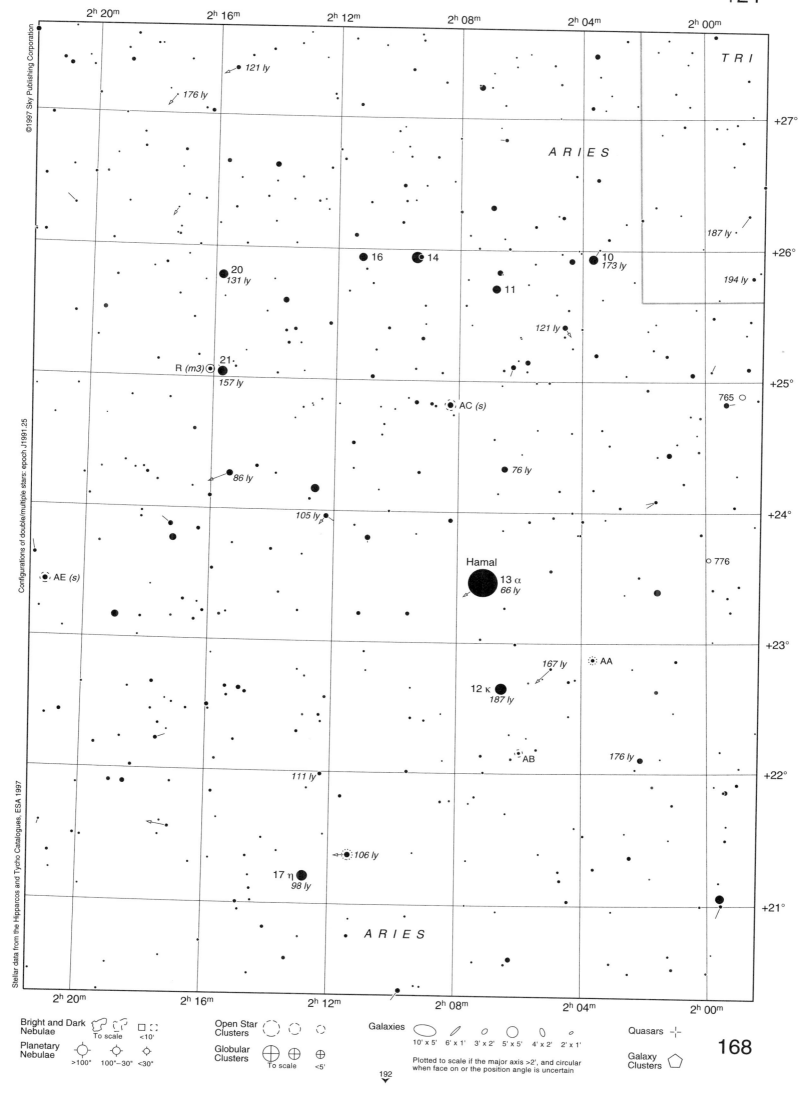

Configurations of double/multiple stars: epoch J1991.25

Stellar data from the Hipparcos and Tycho Catalogues, ESA 1997

T R I

A R I E S

121 ly
176 ly

20
131 ly

16   14

10
173 ly

11

187 ly

194 ly

121 ly

R (m3)   21
157 ly

765

AC (s)

86 ly

76 ly

105 ly

Hamal
13 α
66 ly

776

AE (s)

AA

167 ly

12 κ
187 ly

AB

176 ly

111 ly

106 ly

17 η
98 ly

A R I E S

+27°
+26°
+25°
+24°
+23°
+22°
+21°

2ʰ 20ᵐ   2ʰ 16ᵐ   2ʰ 12ᵐ   2ʰ 08ᵐ   2ʰ 04ᵐ   2ʰ 00ᵐ

| Bright and Dark Nebulae | To scale | <10' |
| Planetary Nebulae | >100" 100"–30" <30" | |

| Open Star Clusters | | <10' |
| Globular Clusters | To scale | <5' |

Galaxies
10' x 5'   6' x 1'   3' x 2'   5' x 5'   4' x 2'   2' x 1'

Plotted to scale if the major axis >2', and circular when face on or the position angle is uncertain

Quasars

Galaxy Clusters

192

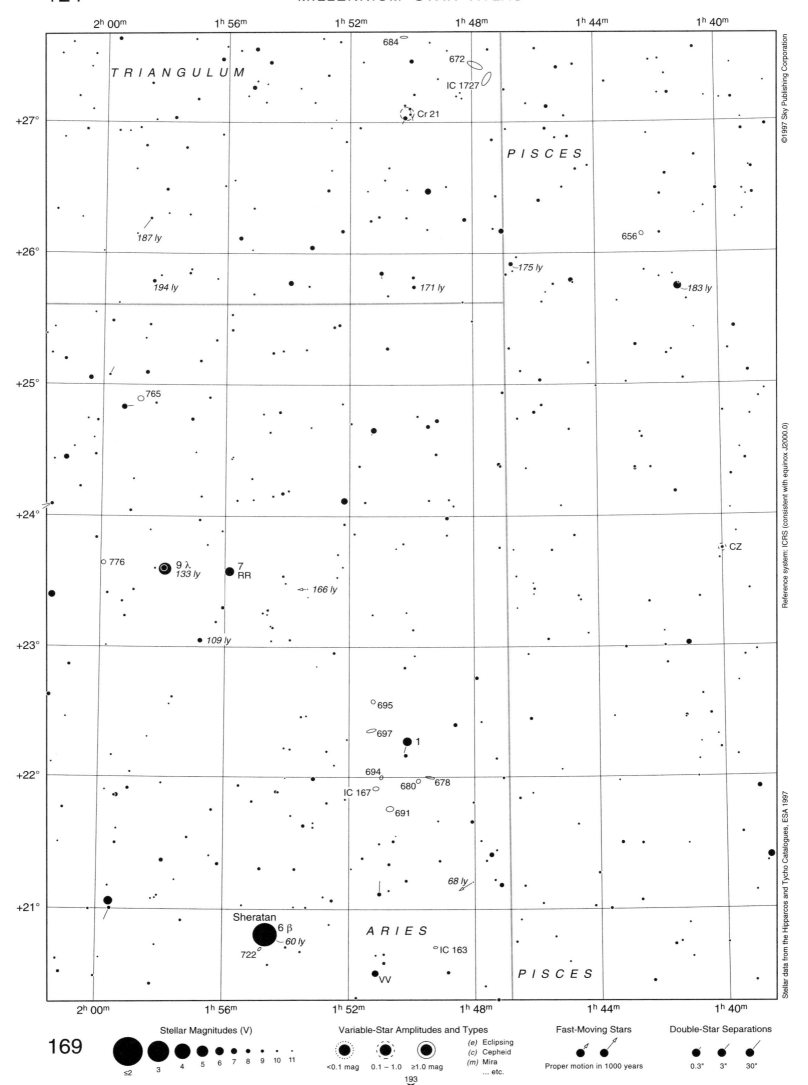

©1997 Sky Publishing Corporation

Reference system: ICRS (consistent with equinox J2000.0)

Stellar data from the Hipparcos and Tycho Catalogues, ESA 1997

TRIANGULUM

PISCES

684

672

IC 1727

Cr 21

656

187 ly

194 ly

171 ly

175 ly

183 ly

765

776

9 λ
133 ly

7
RR

166 ly

109 ly

CZ

695

697

1

694

680   678

IC 167

691

68 ly

Sheratan
6 β
60 ly

722

A R I E S

IC 163

VV

P I S C E S

Stellar Magnitudes (V)

≤2   3   4   5   6   7   8   9   10   11

Variable-Star Amplitudes and Types

<0.1 mag   0.1 – 1.0   ≥1.0 mag

(e) Eclipsing
(c) Cepheid
(m) Mira
... etc.

Fast-Moving Stars

Proper motion in 1000 years

Double-Star Separations

0.3"   3"   30"

193

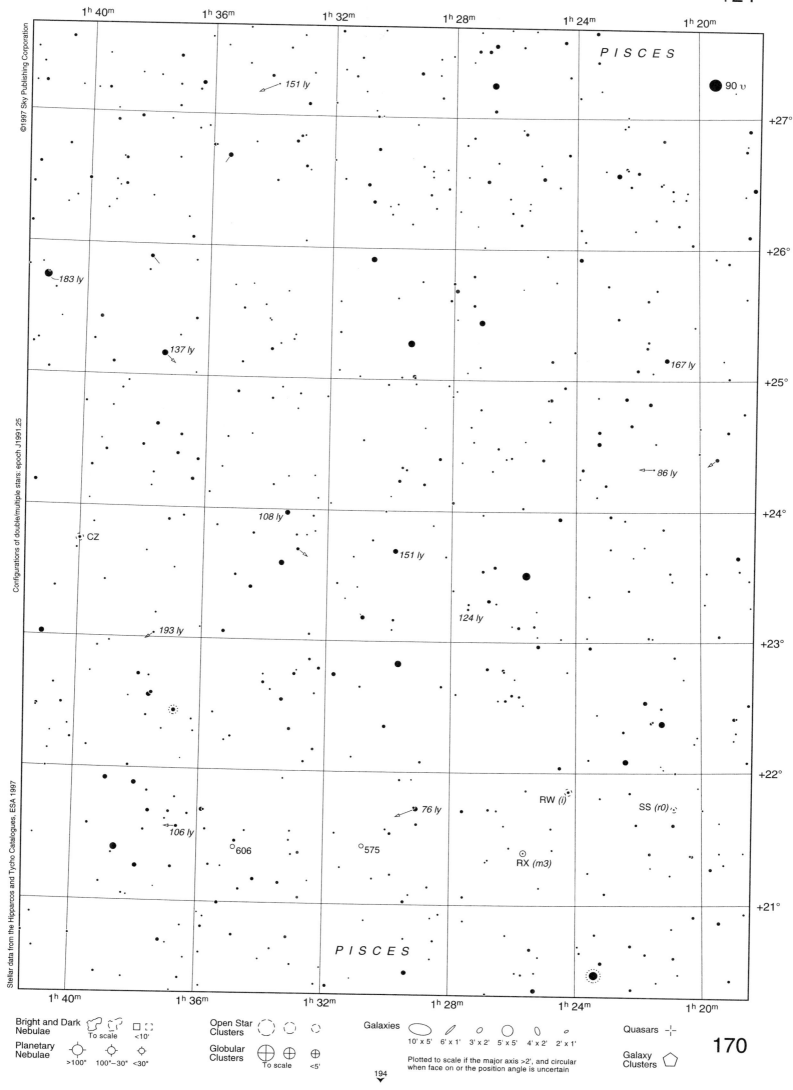

Configurations of double/multiple stars: epoch J1991.25

Stellar data from the Hipparcos and Tycho Catalogues, ESA 1997

P I S C E S

90 υ

151 ly

183 ly

137 ly

167 ly

86 ly

108 ly

CZ

151 ly

193 ly

124 ly

RW *(i)*

SS *(r0)*

76 ly

106 ly

○ 606

○ 575

RX *(m3)*

P I S C E S

+27°

+26°

+25°

+24°

+23°

+22°

+21°

1ʰ 40ᵐ 1ʰ 36ᵐ 1ʰ 32ᵐ 1ʰ 28ᵐ 1ʰ 24ᵐ 1ʰ 20ᵐ

Bright and Dark Nebulae			Open Star Clusters			Galaxies						Quasars
To scale		<10'				10' x 5'	6' x 1'	3' x 2'	5' x 5'	4' x 2'	2' x 1'	
Planetary Nebulae			Globular Clusters									Galaxy Clusters
>100"	100"–30"	<30"	To scale	<5'			Plotted to scale if the major axis >2', and circular when face on or the position angle is uncertain					

170

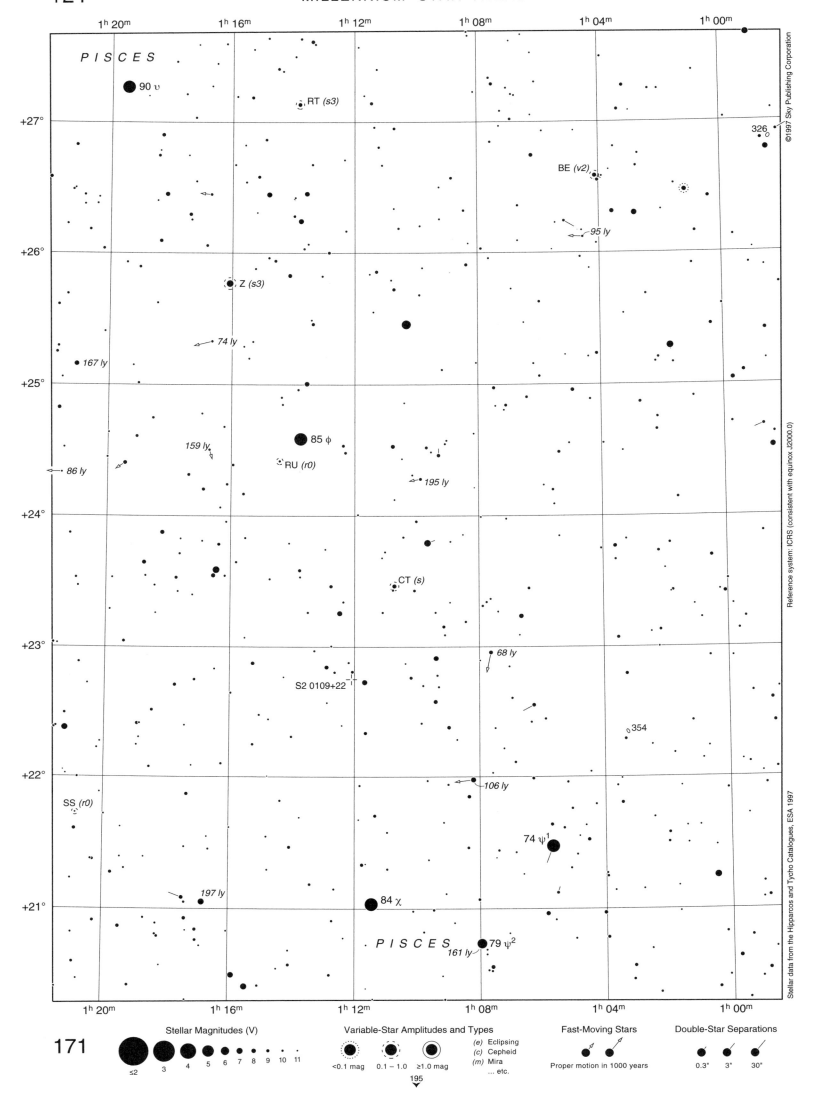

©1997 Sky Publishing Corporation

Reference system: ICRS (consistent with equinox J2000.0)

Stellar data from the Hipparcos and Tycho Catalogues, ESA 1997

PISCES

90 υ

RT (s3)

326

BE (v2)

95 ly

Z (s3)

74 ly

167 ly

85 φ

RU (r0)

159 ly

86 ly

195 ly

CT (s)

68 ly

S2 0109+22

354

106 ly

SS (r0)

74 ψ¹

197 ly

84 χ

PISCES

79 ψ²

161 ly

171

Stellar Magnitudes (V)

≤2 3 4 5 6 7 8 9 10 11

Variable-Star Amplitudes and Types

<0.1 mag   0.1 – 1.0   ≥1.0 mag

(e) Eclipsing
(c) Cepheid
(m) Mira
... etc.

Fast-Moving Stars

Proper motion in 1000 years

Double-Star Separations

0.3"   3"   30"

195

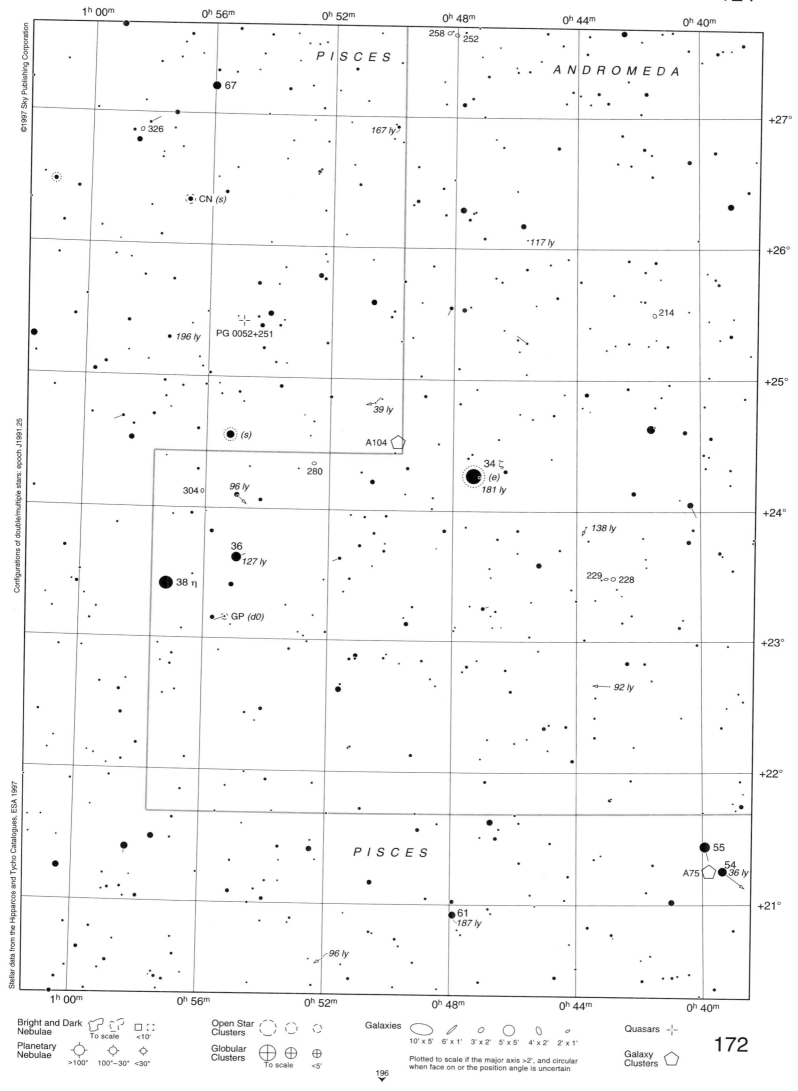
1ʰ 00ᵐ   0ʰ 56ᵐ   0ʰ 52ᵐ   0ʰ 48ᵐ   0ʰ 44ᵐ   0ʰ 40ᵐ

258 ☐ ○ 252

P I S C E S   A N D R O M E D A

67

○ 326

167 ly

+27°

CN (s)

117 ly

+26°

196 ly   ○ 214

PG 0052+251

+25°

39 ly

A104

34 ζ
(e)
181 ly

280 ○

304 ○   96 ly

138 ly

+24°

36
127 ly

229 ○ ○ 228

38 η

GP (d0)

92 ly

+23°

+22°

P I S C E S

55

A75   54
36 ly

61
187 ly   +21°

96 ly

1ʰ 00ᵐ   0ʰ 56ᵐ   0ʰ 52ᵐ   0ʰ 48ᵐ   0ʰ 44ᵐ   0ʰ 40ᵐ

Bright and Dark
Nebulae
To scale   <10'

Open Star
Clusters

Galaxies

Quasars —|—

Planetary
Nebulae
>100" 100"–30" <30'

Globular
Clusters
To scale   <5'

10' x 5' 6' x 1' 3' x 2' 5' x 5' 4' x 2' 2' x 1'

Galaxy
Clusters

Plotted to scale if the major axis >2', and circular
when face on or the position angle is uncertain

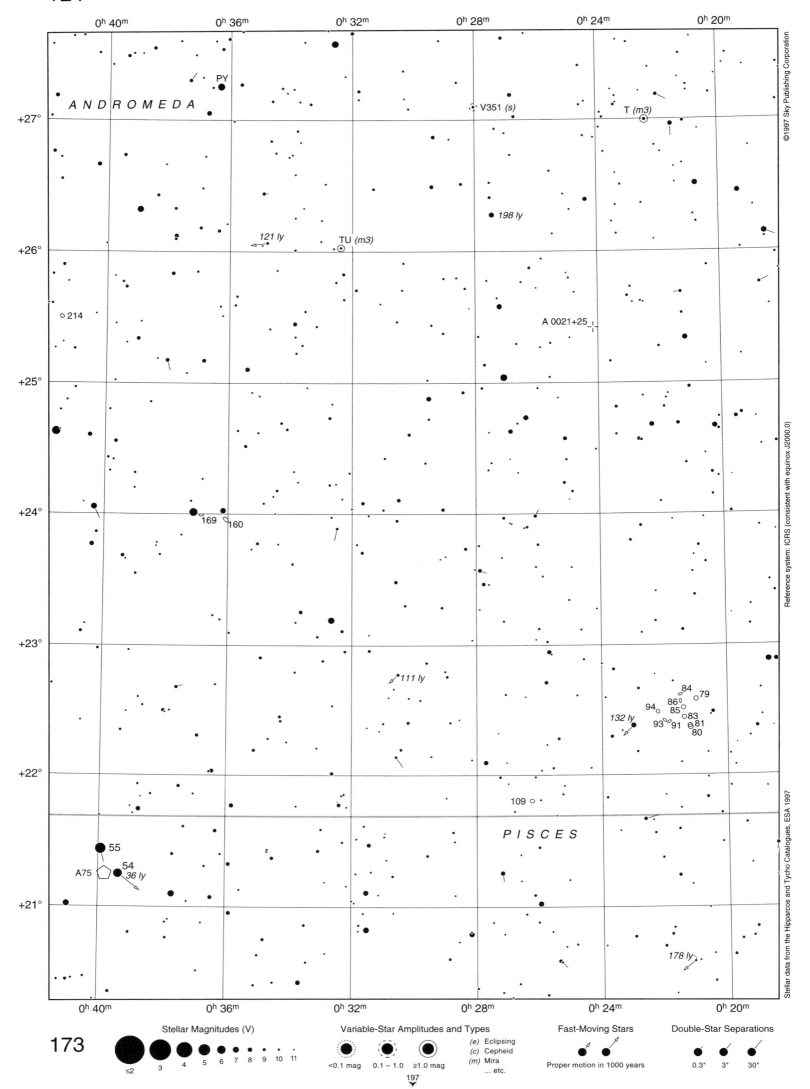

ANDROMEDA

PY

V351 (s)

T (m3)

+27°

198 ly

121 ly

TU (m3)

+26°

○ 214

A 0021+25

+25°

169 ○ 160

+24°

111 ly

84
86 ○ 79
94 ○ 85
132 ly ○ 83
93 91 ○ 81
80

+23°

+22°

109 ○

PISCES

55

54
A75
36 ly

+21°

©1997 Sky Publishing Corporation

Reference system: ICRS (consistent with equinox J2000.0)

Stellar data from the Hipparcos and Tycho Catalogues, ESA 1997

173

| Stellar Magnitudes (V) | Variable-Star Amplitudes and Types | Fast-Moving Stars | Double-Star Separations |

≤2 3 4 5 6 7 8 9 10 11

<0.1 mag   0.1 – 1.0   ≥1.0 mag

(e) Eclipsing
(c) Cepheid
(m) Mira
... etc.

Proper motion in 1000 years

0.3"   3"   30"

197

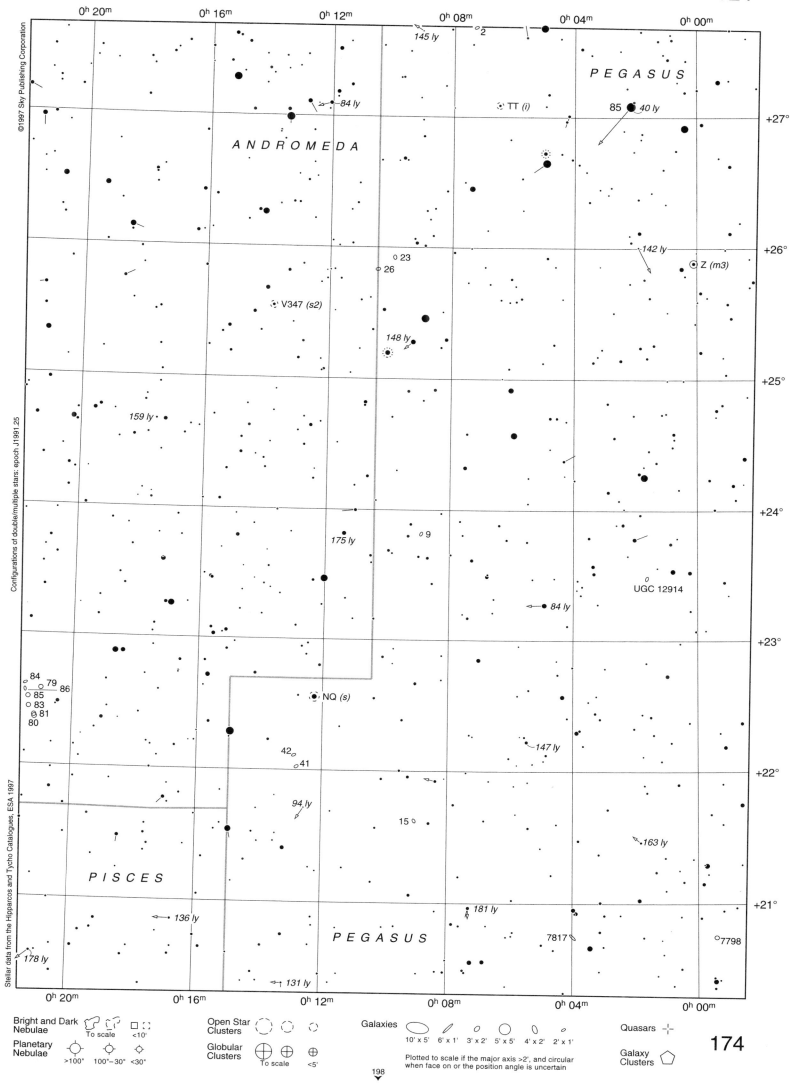

P E G A S U S

A N D R O M E D A

P I S C E S

P E G A S U S

145 ly

TT (i)

85   40 ly

84 ly

142 ly

Z (m3)

23
26

V347 (s2)

148 ly

159 ly

175 ly

9

UGC 12914

84 ly

84   79
86
85
83
81
80

NQ (s)

147 ly

42
41

94 ly

15

163 ly

136 ly

181 ly

7817   7798

178 ly

131 ly

0ʰ 20ᵐ   0ʰ 16ᵐ   0ʰ 12ᵐ   0ʰ 08ᵐ   0ʰ 04ᵐ   0ʰ 00ᵐ

+27°
+26°
+25°
+24°
+23°
+22°
+21°

Bright and Dark
Nebulae
To scale   <10'
Planetary
Nebulae
>100"   100"–30"   <30'

Open Star
Clusters
Globular
Clusters
To scale   <5'

Galaxies
10' x 5'   6' x 1'   3' x 2'   5' x 5'   4' x 2'   2' x 1'

Plotted to scale if the major axis >2', and circular
when face on or the position angle is uncertain

Quasars

Galaxy
Clusters

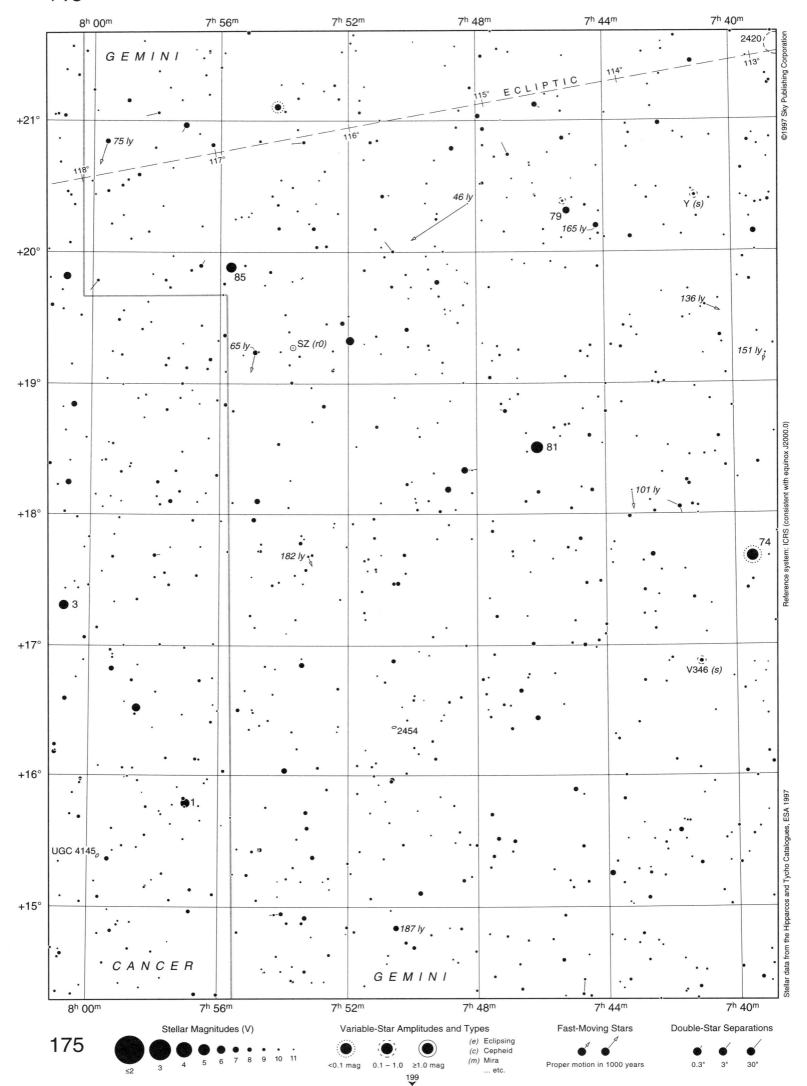

GEMINI

ECLIPTIC

75 ly

46 ly

Y (s)

79

165 ly

85

136 ly

65 ly

SZ (r0)

151 ly

81

101 ly

74

3

182 ly

V346 (s)

2454

1

UGC 4145

2420

113°

114°

115°

116°

117°

118°

187 ly

CANCER

GEMINI

Stellar Magnitudes (V)

≤2   3   4   5   6   7   8   9   10   11

Variable-Star Amplitudes and Types

<0.1 mag   0.1 – 1.0   ≥1.0 mag

(e) Eclipsing
(c) Cepheid
(m) Mira
... etc.

Fast-Moving Stars

Proper motion in 1000 years

Double-Star Separations

0.3"   3"   30"

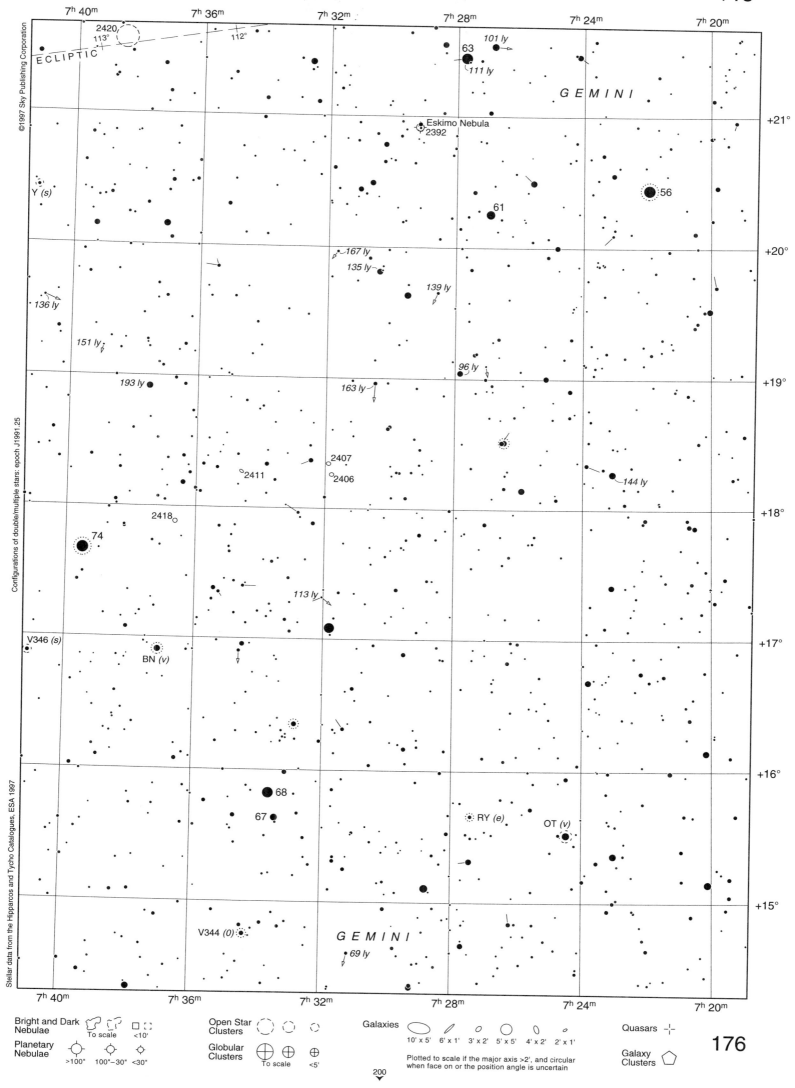

©1997 Sky Publishing Corporation

Configurations of double/multiple stars: epoch J1991.25

Stellar data from the Hipparcos and Tycho Catalogues, ESA 1997

ECLIPTIC

2420
113°

112°

GEMINI

Eskimo Nebula
2392

Y (s)

61

56

167 ly
135 ly

136 ly

139 ly

151 ly

96 ly

193 ly

163 ly

144 ly

2407
2411   2406

2418

74

113 ly

V346 (s)

BN (v)

68
67

RY (e)

OT (v)

V344 (0)

GEMINI

69 ly

63
101 ly
111 ly

7ʰ 40ᵐ   7ʰ 36ᵐ   7ʰ 32ᵐ   7ʰ 28ᵐ   7ʰ 24ᵐ   7ʰ 20ᵐ

+21°
+20°
+19°
+18°
+17°
+16°
+15°

Bright and Dark
Nebulae
To scale   <10'

Planetary
Nebulae
>100"   100"−30"   <30"

Open Star
Clusters

Globular
Clusters
To scale   <5'

Galaxies
10' x 5'   6' x 1'   3' x 2'   5' x 5'   4' x 2'   2' x 1'

Plotted to scale if the major axis >2', and circular
when face on or the position angle is uncertain

Quasars

Galaxy
Clusters

200

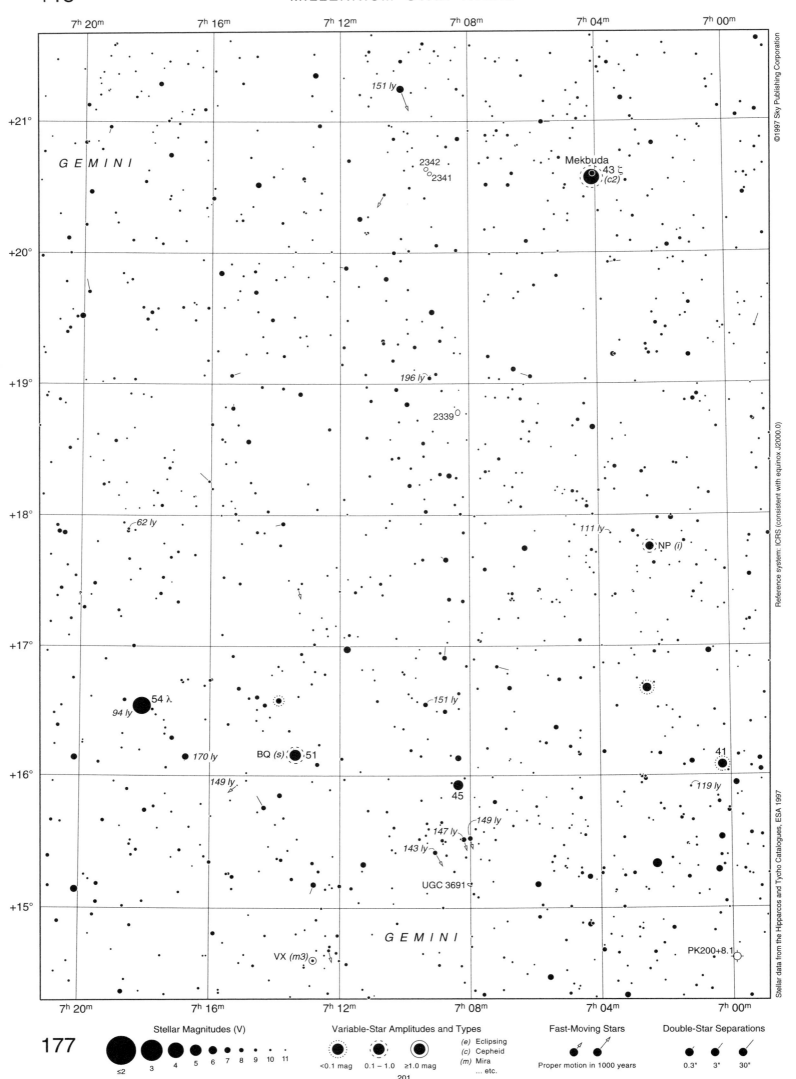

©1997 Sky Publishing Corporation

Reference system: ICRS (consistent with equinox J2000.0)

Stellar data from the Hipparcos and Tycho Catalogues, ESA 1997

G E M I N I

151 ly

2342
2341

Mekbuda
43 ζ
(c2)

196 ly

2339

62 ly

111 ly

NP (i)

54 λ
94 ly

151 ly

170 ly

BQ (s) 51

41

149 ly

45

119 ly

149 ly
147 ly
143 ly

UGC 3691

G E M I N I

VX (m3)

PK200+8.1

Stellar Magnitudes (V)

≤2 3 4 5 6 7 8 9 10 11

Variable-Star Amplitudes and Types

<0.1 mag   0.1 – 1.0   ≥1.0 mag

(e) Eclipsing
(c) Cepheid
(m) Mira
... etc.

Fast-Moving Stars

Proper motion in 1000 years

Double-Star Separations

0.3"   3"   30"

201

MILLENNIUM STAR ATLAS

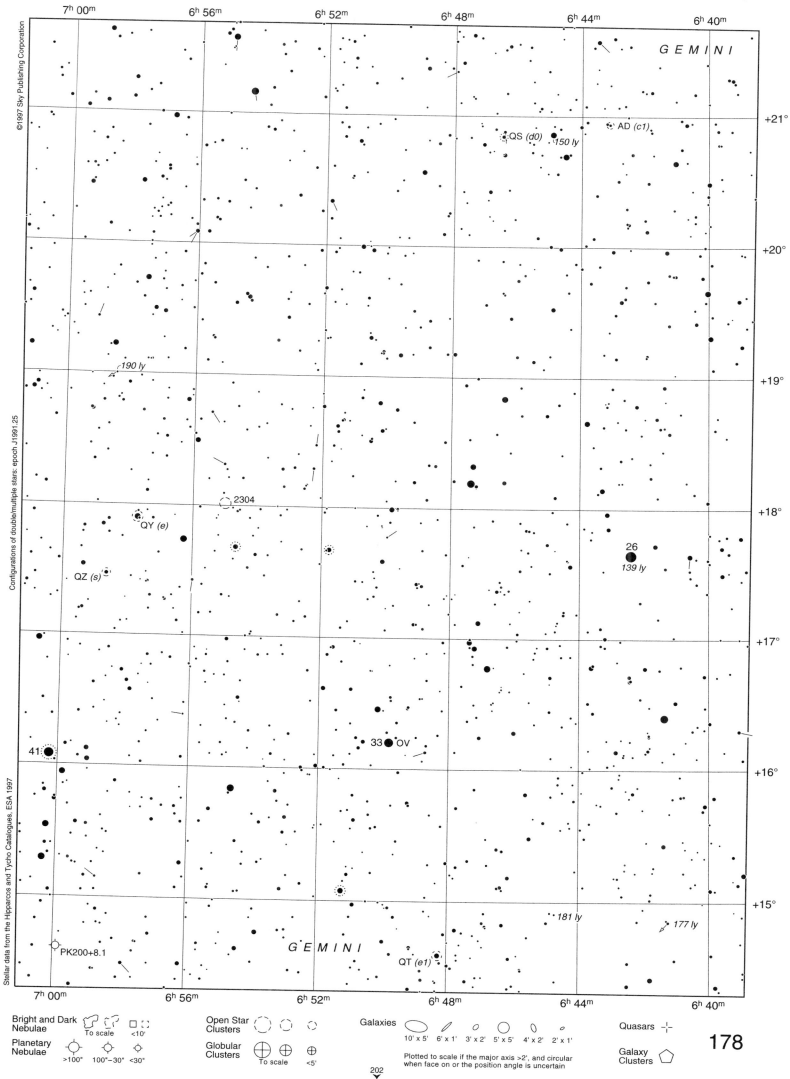

G E M I N I

QS *(d0)*

150 ly

AD *(c1)*

190 ly

2304

QY *(e)*

QZ *(s)*

26

139 ly

41

33 OV

PK200+8.1

G E M I N I

181 ly

177 ly

QT *(e1)*

Configurations of double/multiple stars: epoch J1991.25

Stellar data from the Hipparcos and Tycho Catalogues, ESA 1997

Bright and Dark Nebulae	Open Star Clusters	Galaxies	Quasars

Bright and Dark Nebulae — To scale — <10'

Planetary Nebulae — >100" — 100"–30" — <30"

Open Star Clusters

Globular Clusters — To scale — <5'

Galaxies — 10' x 5' — 6' x 1' — 3' x 2' — 5' x 5' — 4' x 2' — 2' x 1'

Plotted to scale if the major axis >2', and circular when face on or the position angle is uncertain

Quasars

Galaxy Clusters

178

202

MILLENNIUM STAR ATLAS

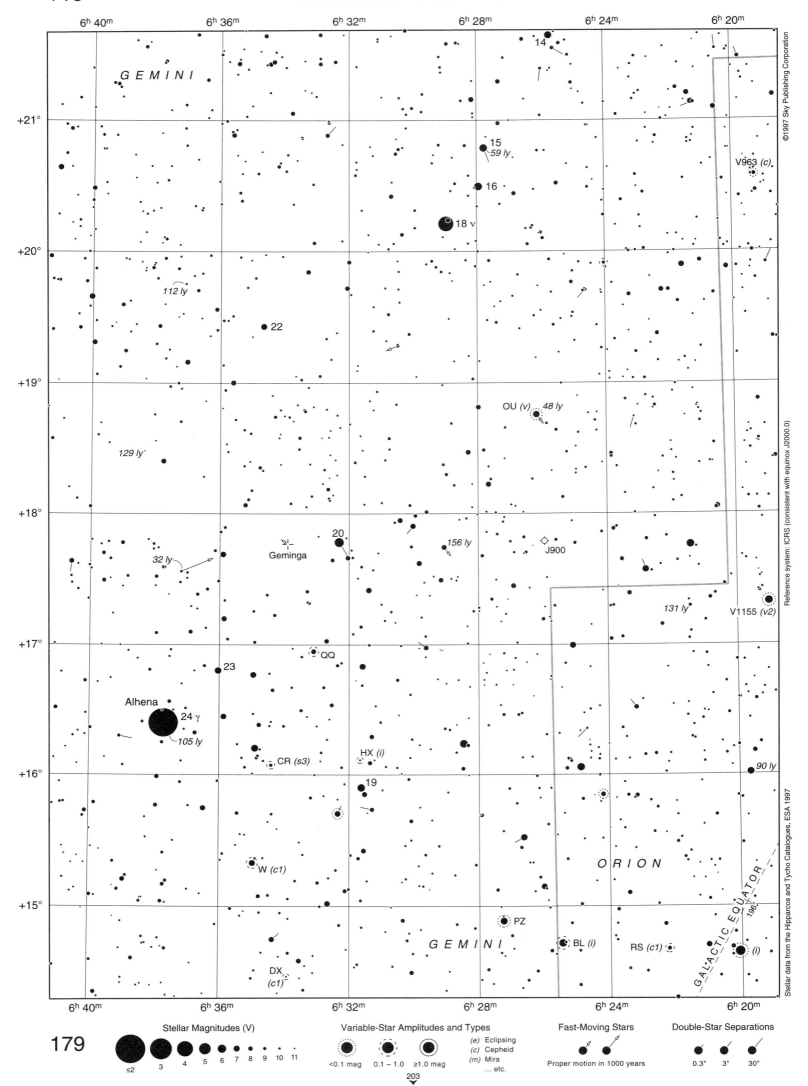

Reference system: ICRS (consistent with equinox J2000.0)

Stellar data from the Hipparcos and Tycho Catalogues, ESA 1997

GEMINI

ORION

GEMINI

GALACTIC EQUATOR

14

15
59 ly

16

18 ν

V963 (c)

112 ly

22

129 ly

OU (v) 48 ly

32 ly

Geminga

20

156 ly

J900

131 ly

V1155 (v2)

QQ

23

Alhena

24 γ

105 ly

CR (s3)

HX (i)

19

90 ly

W (c1)

PZ

BL (i)

RS (c1)

(i)

DX
(c1)

179

Stellar Magnitudes (V)

≤2   3   4   5   6   7   8   9   10   11

Variable-Star Amplitudes and Types

<0.1 mag   0.1 – 1.0   ≥1.0 mag

(e) Eclipsing
(c) Cepheid
(m) Mira
... etc.

Fast-Moving Stars

Proper motion in 1000 years

Double-Star Separations

0.3"   3"   30"

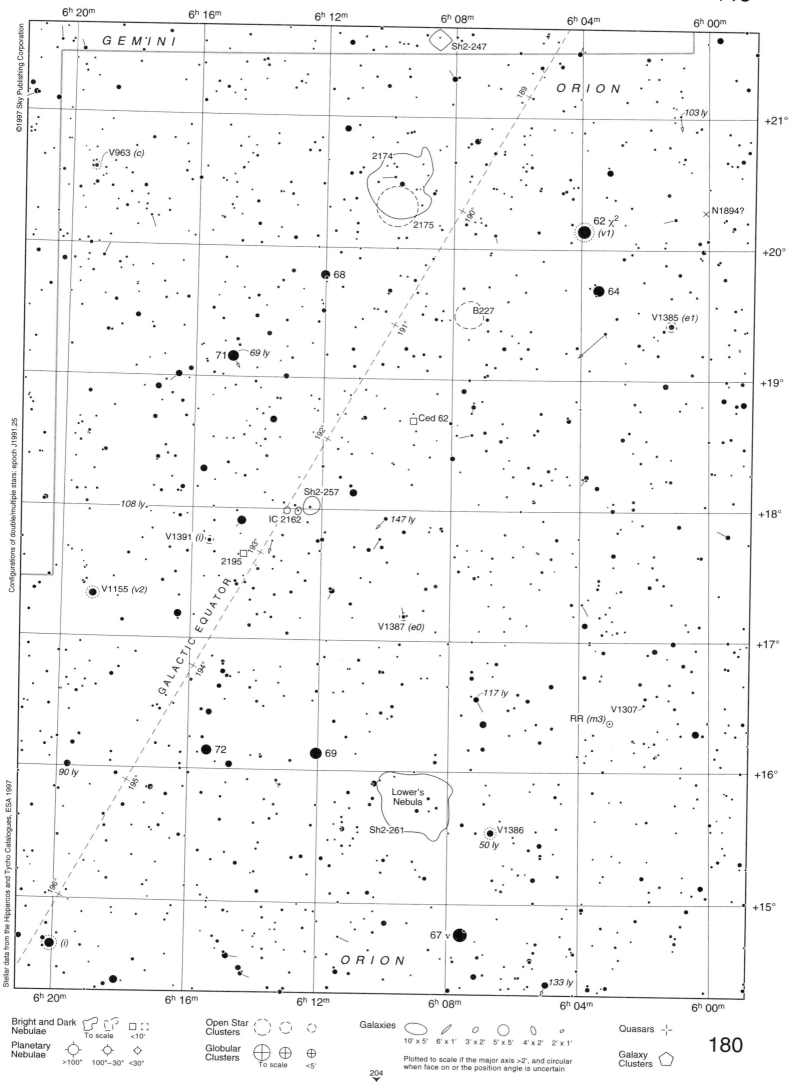

G E M I N I

Sh2-247

O R I O N

189

103 ly

2174

190°

2175

62 χ²
(v1)

N1894?

68

191°

64

B227

V1385 (e1)

V963 (c)

71   69 ly

192°

Ced 62

108 ly

Sh2-257

IC 2162

147 ly

V1391 (i)

193°

2195

V1155 (v2)

V1387 (e0)

117 ly

194°

V1307

RR (m3)

72   69

195°

90 ly

Lower's
Nebula

Sh2-261   V1386

50 ly

196°

(i)

67 v

O R I O N

133 ly

GALACTIC EQUATOR

Bright and Dark
Nebulae   To scale   <10'

Open Star
Clusters

Galaxies

Quasars

Planetary
Nebulae   >100" 100"–30" <30"

Globular
Clusters   To scale   <5'

10' x 5'   6' x 1'   3' x 2'   5' x 5'   4' x 2'   2' x 1'

Galaxy
Clusters

Plotted to scale if the major axis >2', and circular
when face on or the position angle is uncertain

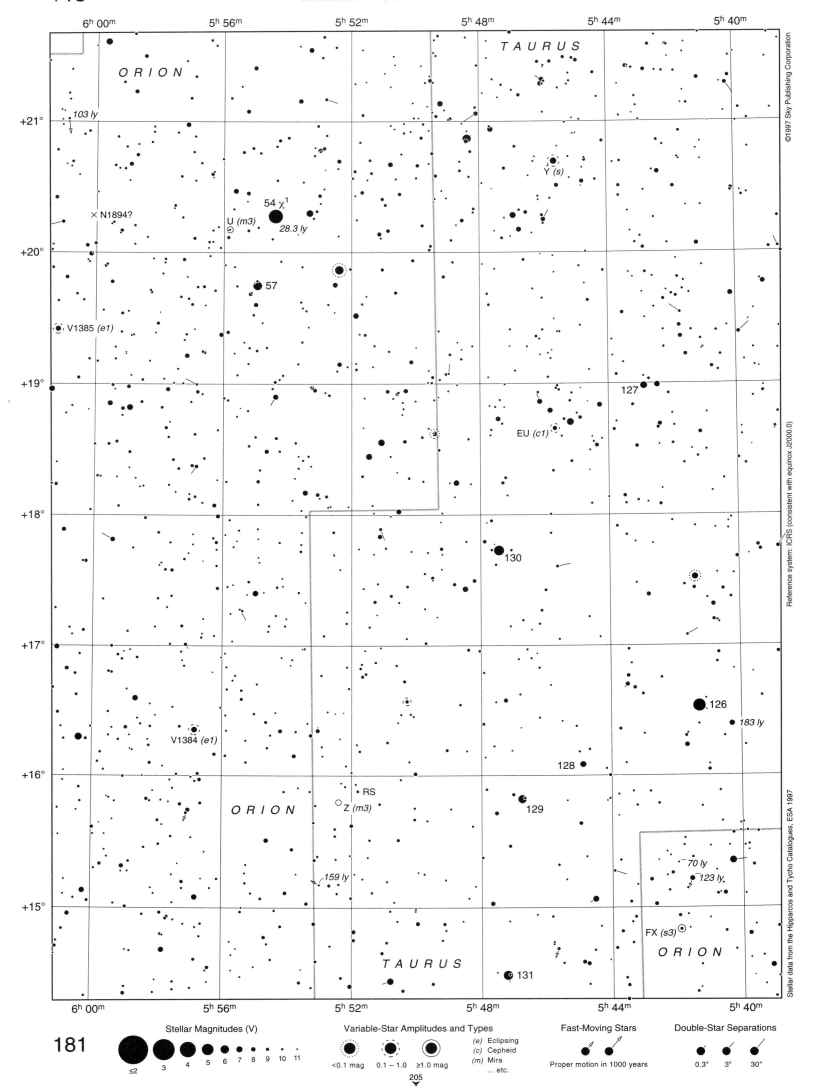

©1997 Sky Publishing Corporation

Reference system: ICRS (consistent with equinox J2000.0)

Stellar data from the Hipparcos and Tycho Catalogues, ESA 1997

181

Stellar Magnitudes (V)

≤2 3 4 5 6 7 8 9 10 11

Variable-Star Amplitudes and Types

<0.1 mag   0.1 – 1.0   ≥1.0 mag

(e) Eclipsing
(c) Cepheid
(m) Mira
... etc.

Fast-Moving Stars

Proper motion in 1000 years

Double-Star Separations

0.3"   3"   30"

MILLENNIUM STAR ATLAS

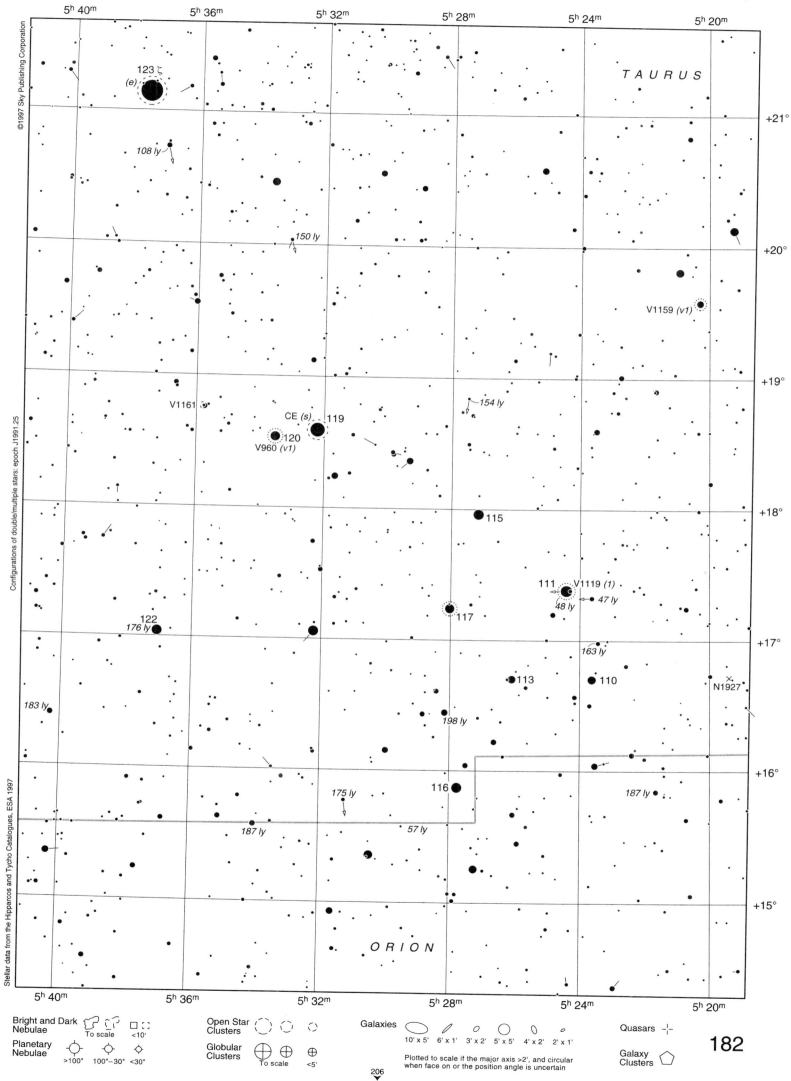

© 1997 Sky Publishing Corporation

Configurations of double/multiple stars: epoch J1991.25

Stellar data from the Hipparcos and Tycho Catalogues, ESA 1997

T A U R U S

123 ζ
(e)

108 ly

150 ly

V1159 *(v1)*

V1161

CE *(s)* 119

120
V960 *(v1)*

154 ly

115

111 V1119 *(1)*
48 ly   47 ly

122
176 ly

117

163 ly

113   110

N1927

183 ly

198 ly

116

175 ly   187 ly

187 ly   57 ly

O R I O N

5ʰ 40ᵐ   5ʰ 36ᵐ   5ʰ 32ᵐ   5ʰ 28ᵐ   5ʰ 24ᵐ   5ʰ 20ᵐ

+21°

+20°

+19°

+18°

+17°

+16°

+15°

Bright and Dark Nebulae				Open Star Clusters			Galaxies							Quasars
	To scale	<10'					10' x 5'	6' x 1'	3' x 2'	5' x 5'	4' x 2'	2' x 1'		

Planetary Nebulae
>100"   100"–30"   <30"

Globular Clusters
To scale   <5'

Plotted to scale if the major axis >2', and circular when face on or the position angle is uncertain

Galaxy Clusters

206

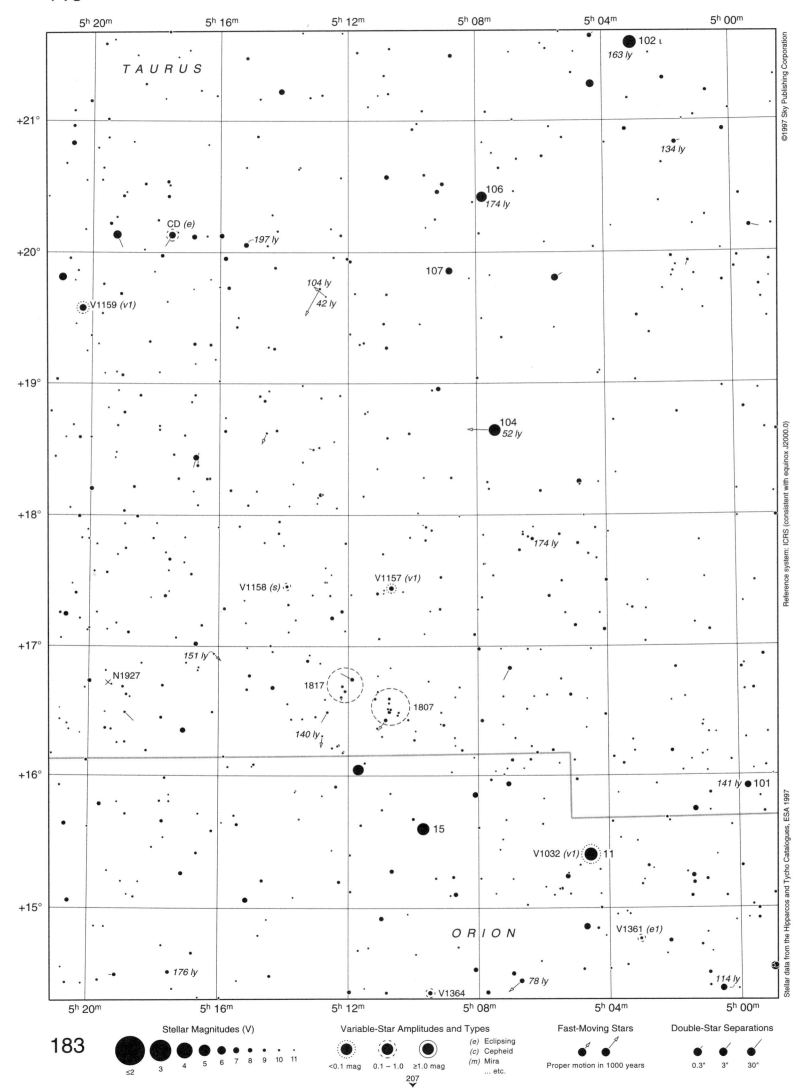

©1997 Sky Publishing Corporation

Reference system: ICRS (consistent with equinox J2000.0)

Stellar data from the Hipparcos and Tycho Catalogues, ESA 1997

183

Stellar Magnitudes (V)

≤2   3   4   5   6   7 8 9 10 11

Variable-Star Amplitudes and Types

<0.1 mag   0.1 − 1.0   ≥1.0 mag

(e) Eclipsing
(c) Cepheid
(m) Mira
... etc.

Fast-Moving Stars

Proper motion in 1000 years

Double-Star Separations

0.3"   3"   30"

207

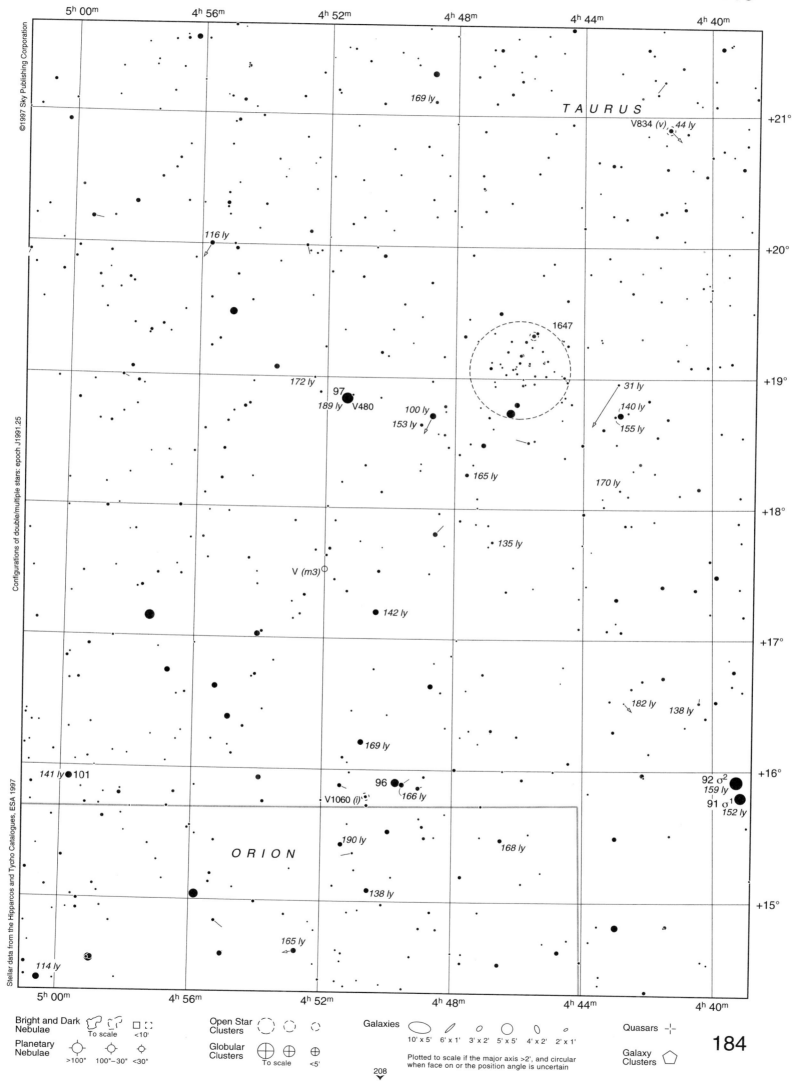

Configurations of double/multiple stars: epoch J1991.25

Stellar data from the Hipparcos and Tycho Catalogues, ESA 1997

5h 00m   4h 56m   4h 52m   4h 48m   4h 44m   4h 40m

+21°
+20°
+19°
+18°
+17°
+16°
+15°

T A U R U S

V834 (v)   44 ly

169 ly

116 ly

1647

172 ly

97

189 ly   V480

100 ly

153 ly

31 ly

140 ly

155 ly

165 ly

170 ly

135 ly

V (m3)

142 ly

182 ly   138 ly

169 ly

141 ly   101

92 σ²

159 ly

91 σ¹

152 ly

96

166 ly

V1060 (i)

190 ly

168 ly

O R I O N

138 ly

165 ly

114 ly

5h 00m   4h 56m   4h 52m   4h 48m   4h 44m   4h 40m

Bright and Dark
Nebulae   To scale   <10'

Planetary
Nebulae   >100" 100"–30" <30"

Open Star
Clusters

Globular
Clusters   To scale   <5'

Galaxies   10' x 5' 6' x 1' 3' x 2' 5' x 5' 4' x 2' 2' x 1'

Plotted to scale if the major axis >2', and circular
when face on or the position angle is uncertain

Quasars

Galaxy
Clusters

184

208

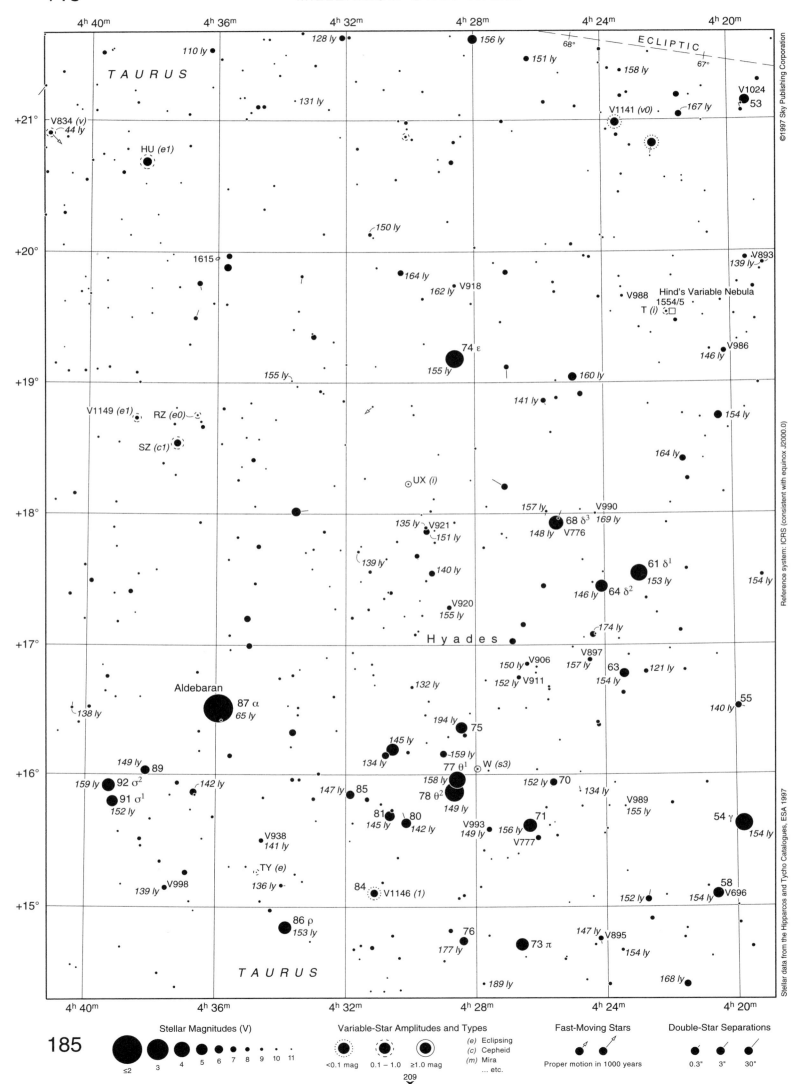

©1997 Sky Publishing Corporation

Reference system: ICRS (consistent with equinox J2000.0)

Stellar data from the Hipparcos and Tycho Catalogues, ESA 1997

Stellar Magnitudes (V)

≤2 3 4 5 6 7 8 9 10 11

Variable-Star Amplitudes and Types

<0.1 mag   0.1 – 1.0   ≥1.0 mag

(e) Eclipsing
(c) Cepheid
(m) Mira
... etc.

Fast-Moving Stars

Proper motion in 1000 years

Double-Star Separations

0.3"   3"   30"

MILLENNIUM STAR ATLAS

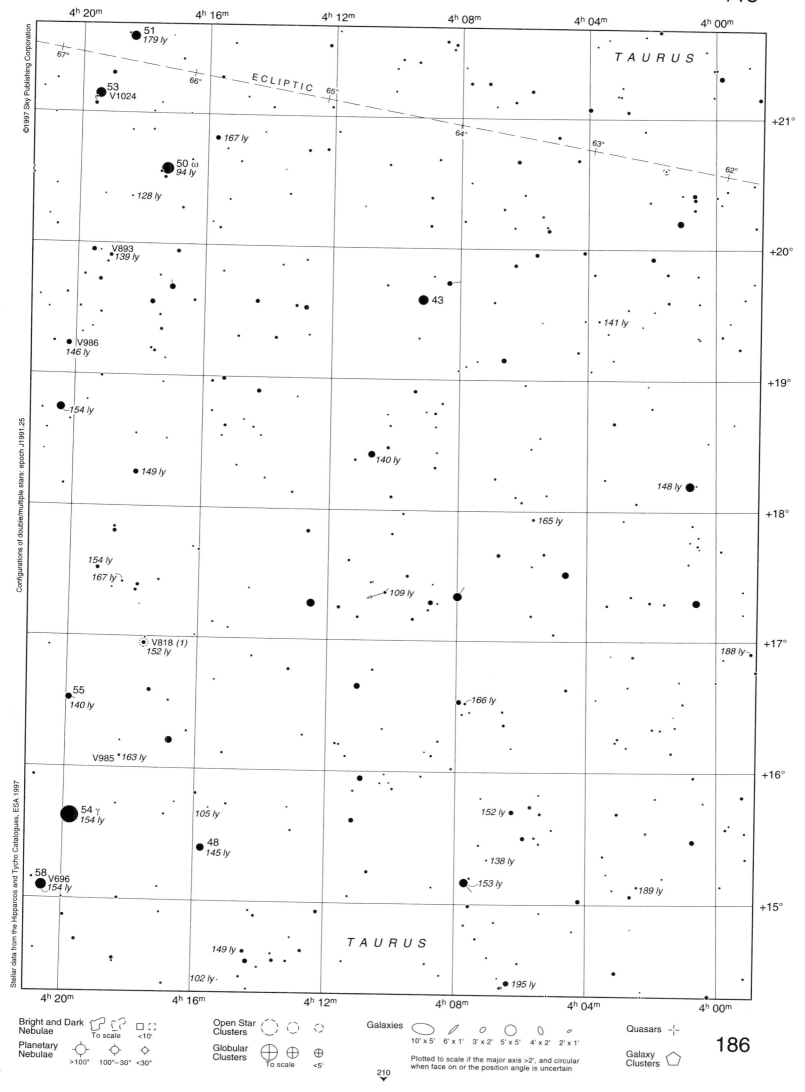

T A U R U S

E C L I P T I C

51
179 ly

53
V1024

167 ly

50 ω
94 ly

128 ly

V893
139 ly

43

141 ly

V986
146 ly

154 ly

149 ly

140 ly

148 ly

165 ly

154 ly
167 ly

109 ly

188 ly

V818 (1)
152 ly

55
140 ly

166 ly

V985 · 163 ly

152 ly

54 γ
154 ly

105 ly

48
145 ly

138 ly

58
V696
154 ly

153 ly

189 ly

T A U R U S

149 ly

102 ly ·

195 ly

Bright and Dark
Nebulae
To scale   <10'

Planetary
Nebulae
>100" 100"–30" <30"

Open Star
Clusters
To scale   <10'

Globular
Clusters
To scale   <5'

Galaxies
10' x 5' 6' x 1' 3' x 2' 5' x 5' 4' x 2' 2' x 1'

Plotted to scale if the major axis >2', and circular
when face on or the position angle is uncertain

Quasars

Galaxy
Clusters

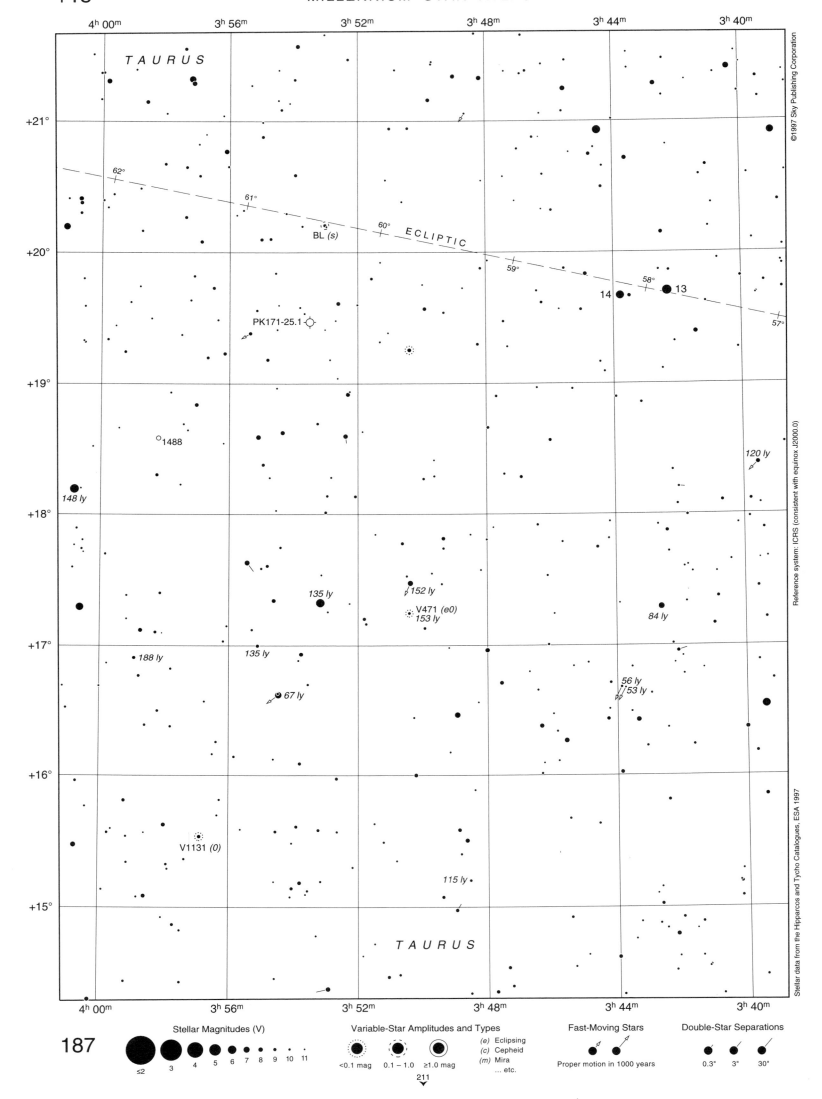

TAURUS

ECLIPTIC

62°
61°
60°
59°
58°
57°

BL (s)

14   13

PK171-25.1

1488

120 ly

148 ly

135 ly

152 ly

V471 (e0)
153 ly

84 ly

188 ly

135 ly

56 ly
53 ly

67 ly

V1131 (0)

115 ly

TAURUS

Stellar Magnitudes (V)

≤2   3   4   5   6   7   8   9   10   11

Variable-Star Amplitudes and Types

<0.1 mag   0.1 – 1.0   ≥1.0 mag

(e) Eclipsing
(c) Cepheid
(m) Mira
... etc.

Fast-Moving Stars

Proper motion in 1000 years

Double-Star Separations

0.3"   3"   30"

MILLENNIUM STAR ATLAS

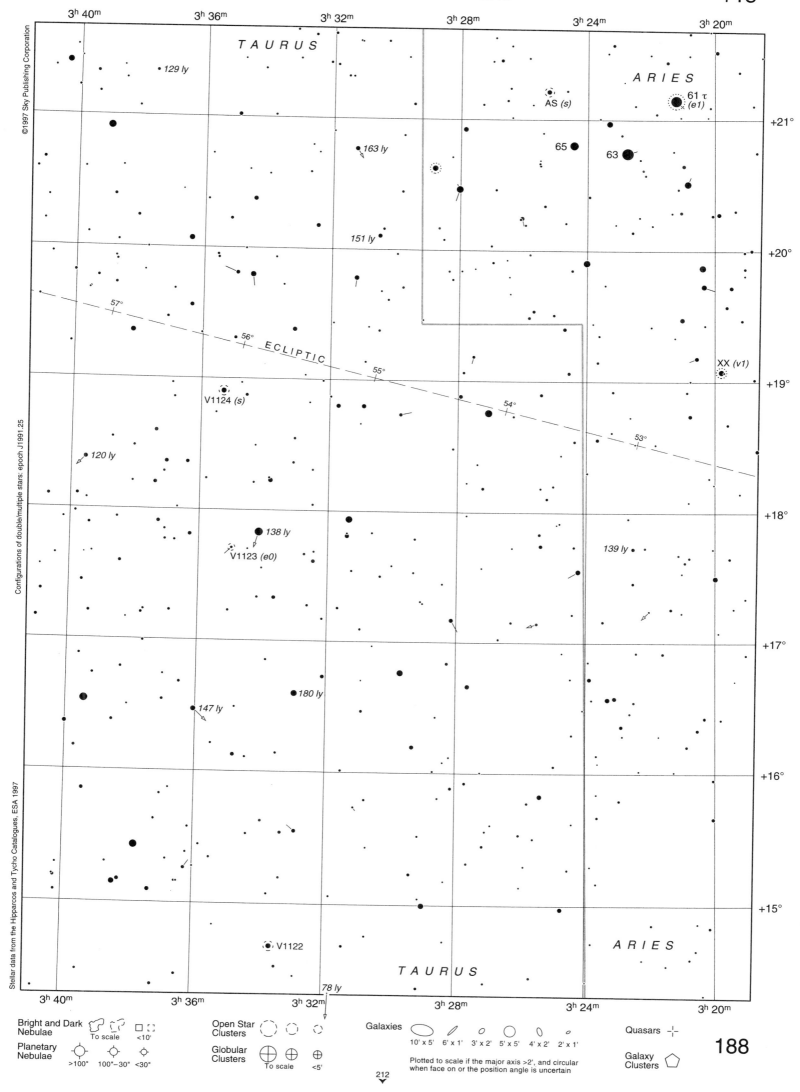

Configurations of double/multiple stars: epoch J1991.25

Stellar data from the Hipparcos and Tycho Catalogues, ESA 1997

T A U R U S

A R I E S

129 ly

AS (s)

61 τ
(e1)

65

63

163 ly

151 ly

57°

ECLIPTIC

56°

55°

54°

53°

XX (v1)

V1124 (s)

120 ly

138 ly

V1123 (e0)

139 ly

180 ly

147 ly

A R I E S

V1122

T A U R U S

78 ly

+21°

+20°

+19°

+18°

+17°

+16°

+15°

3ʰ 40ᵐ 3ʰ 36ᵐ 3ʰ 32ᵐ 3ʰ 28ᵐ 3ʰ 24ᵐ 3ʰ 20ᵐ

Bright and Dark Nebulae — To scale — <10'

Planetary Nebulae — >100" — 100"–30" — <30"

Open Star Clusters

Globular Clusters — To scale — <5'

Galaxies — 10' x 5' — 6' x 1' — 3' x 2' — 5' x 5' — 4' x 2' — 2' x 1'

Plotted to scale if the major axis >2', and circular when face on or the position angle is uncertain

Quasars

Galaxy Clusters

188

212

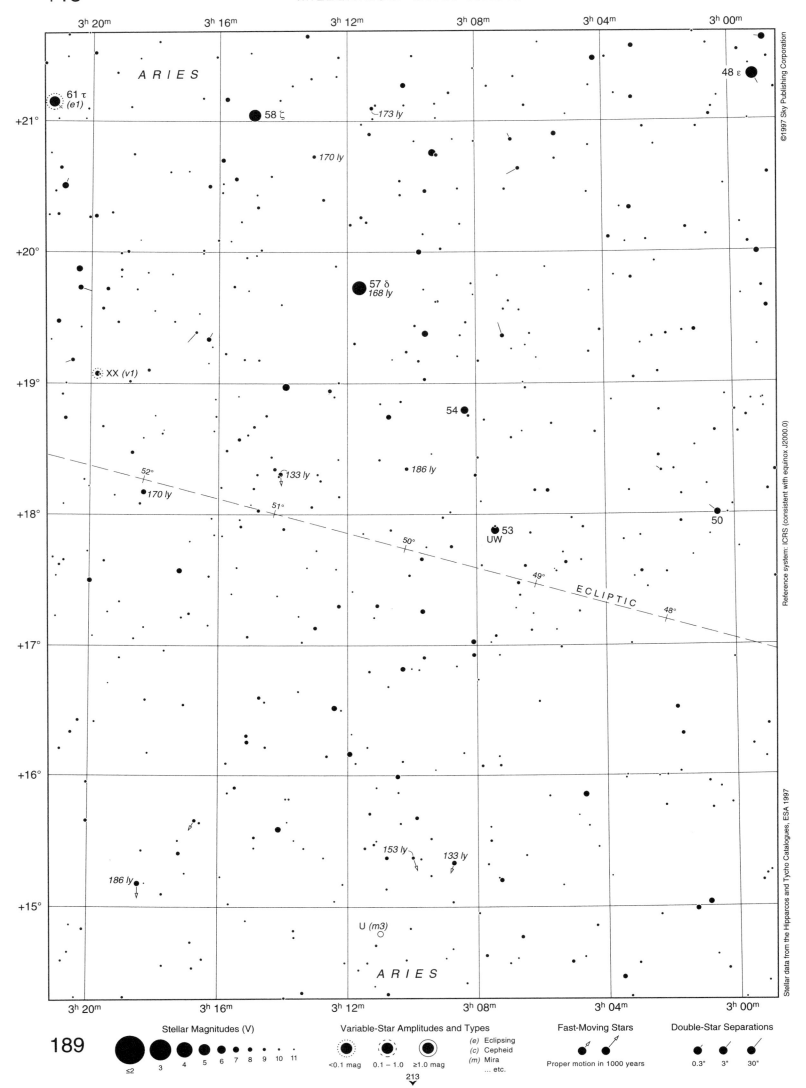

©1997 Sky Publishing Corporation

Reference system: ICRS (consistent with equinox J2000.0)

Stellar data from the Hipparcos and Tycho Catalogues, ESA 1997

189

Stellar Magnitudes (V)

≤2 3 4 5 6 7 8 9 10 11

Variable-Star Amplitudes and Types

<0.1 mag   0.1 – 1.0   ≥1.0 mag

(e) Eclipsing
(c) Cepheid
(m) Mira
... etc.

Fast-Moving Stars

Proper motion in 1000 years

Double-Star Separations

0.3"   3"   30"

MILLENNIUM STAR ATLAS

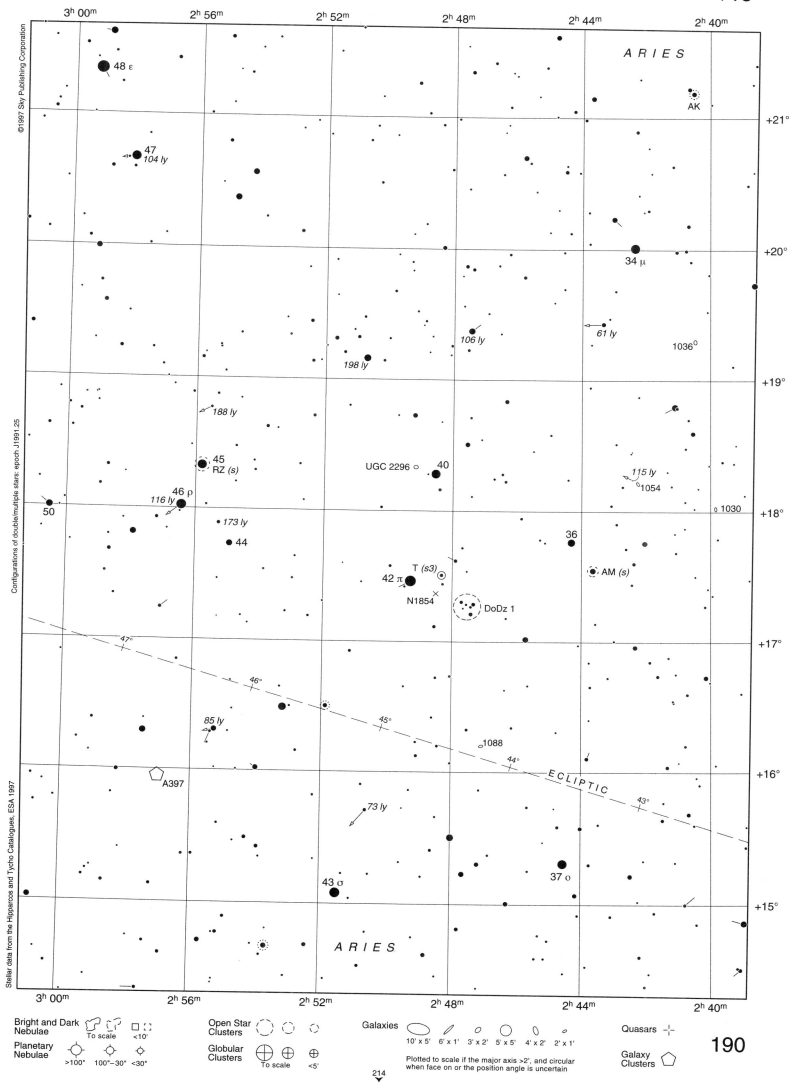

ARIES

AK

48 ε

47
104 ly

34 μ

61 ly

1036°

106 ly

198 ly

188 ly

45
RZ (s)

UGC 2296

40

115 ly
1054

50

46 ρ

116 ly

1030

173 ly

44

36

T (s3)

AM (s)

42 π

N1854

DoDz 1

47°

46°

85 ly

45°

1088

44°

A397

ECLIPTIC

73 ly

43°

37 ο

43 σ

ARIES

©1997 Sky Publishing Corporation

Configurations of double/multiple stars: epoch J1991.25

Stellar data from the Hipparcos and Tycho Catalogues, ESA 1997

Bright and Dark Nebulae		To scale		<10'

Planetary Nebulae
>100" 100"–30" <30"

Open Star Clusters

Globular Clusters
To scale <5'

Galaxies
10' x 5'   6' x 1'   3' x 2'   5' x 5'   4' x 2'   2' x 1'

Plotted to scale if the major axis >2', and circular when face on or the position angle is uncertain

Quasars

Galaxy Clusters

190

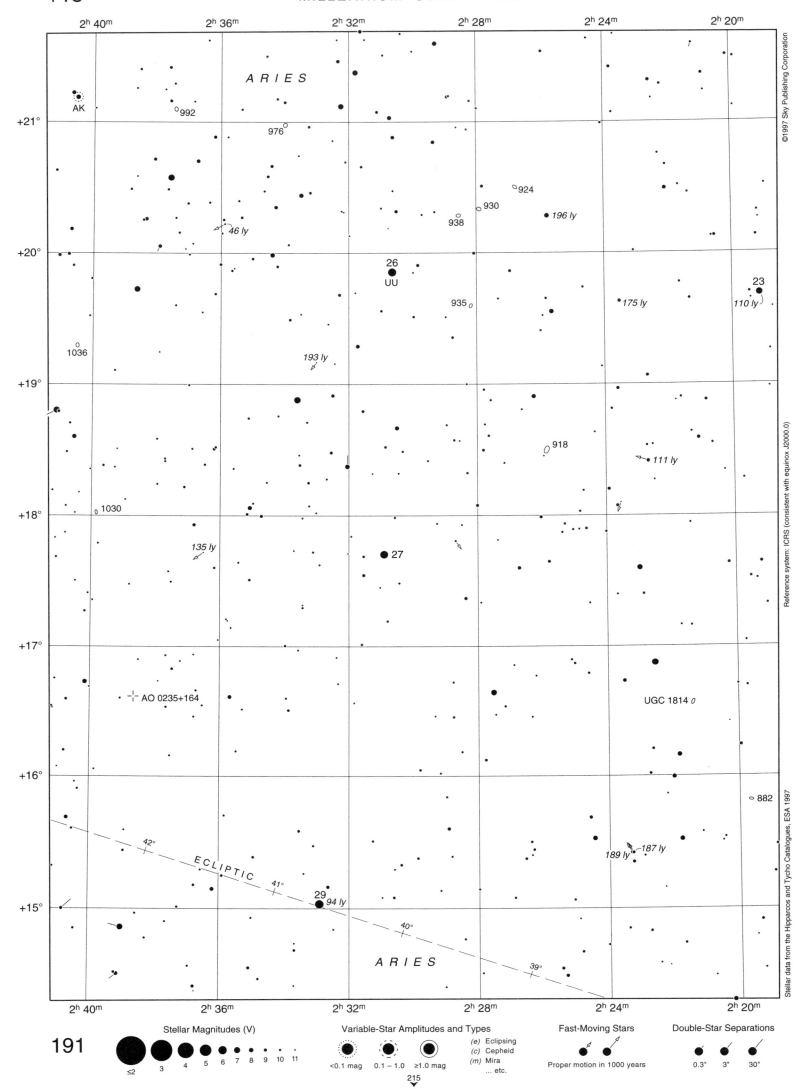

©1997 Sky Publishing Corporation

Reference system: ICRS (consistent with equinox J2000.0)

Stellar data from the Hipparcos and Tycho Catalogues, ESA 1997

Stellar Magnitudes (V)

≤2 3 4 5 6 7 8 9 10 11

Variable-Star Amplitudes and Types

<0.1 mag   0.1 – 1.0   ≥1.0 mag

(e) Eclipsing
(c) Cepheid
(m) Mira
... etc.

Fast-Moving Stars

Proper motion in 1000 years

Double-Star Separations

0.3"   3"   30"

191

215

MILLENNIUM STAR ATLAS

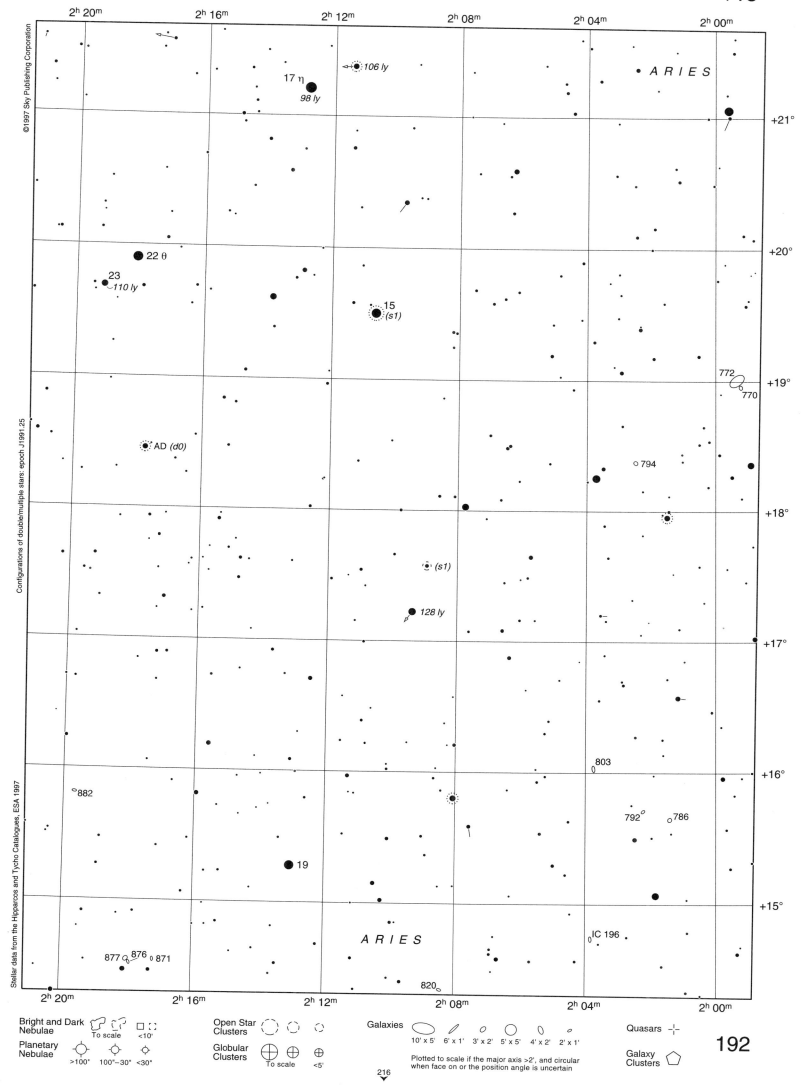

©1997 Sky Publishing Corporation

Configurations of double/multiple stars: epoch J1991.25

Stellar data from the Hipparcos and Tycho Catalogues, ESA 1997

A R I E S

17 η
98 ly

106 ly

22 θ

23
110 ly

15
(s1)

772
770

AD (d0)

794

(s1)

128 ly

803

882

19

792 786

IC 196

877 876 871

820

2ʰ 20ᵐ   2ʰ 16ᵐ   2ʰ 12ᵐ   2ʰ 08ᵐ   2ʰ 04ᵐ   2ʰ 00ᵐ

+21°
+20°
+19°
+18°
+17°
+16°
+15°

A R I E S

Bright and Dark Nebulae	Open Star Clusters	Galaxies	Quasars

To scale   <10'

Planetary Nebulae

>100"   100"–30"   <30"

Globular Clusters

To scale   <5'

10' x 5'   6' x 1'   3' x 2'   5' x 5'   4' x 2'   2' x 1'

Plotted to scale if the major axis >2', and circular when face on or the position angle is uncertain

Galaxy Clusters

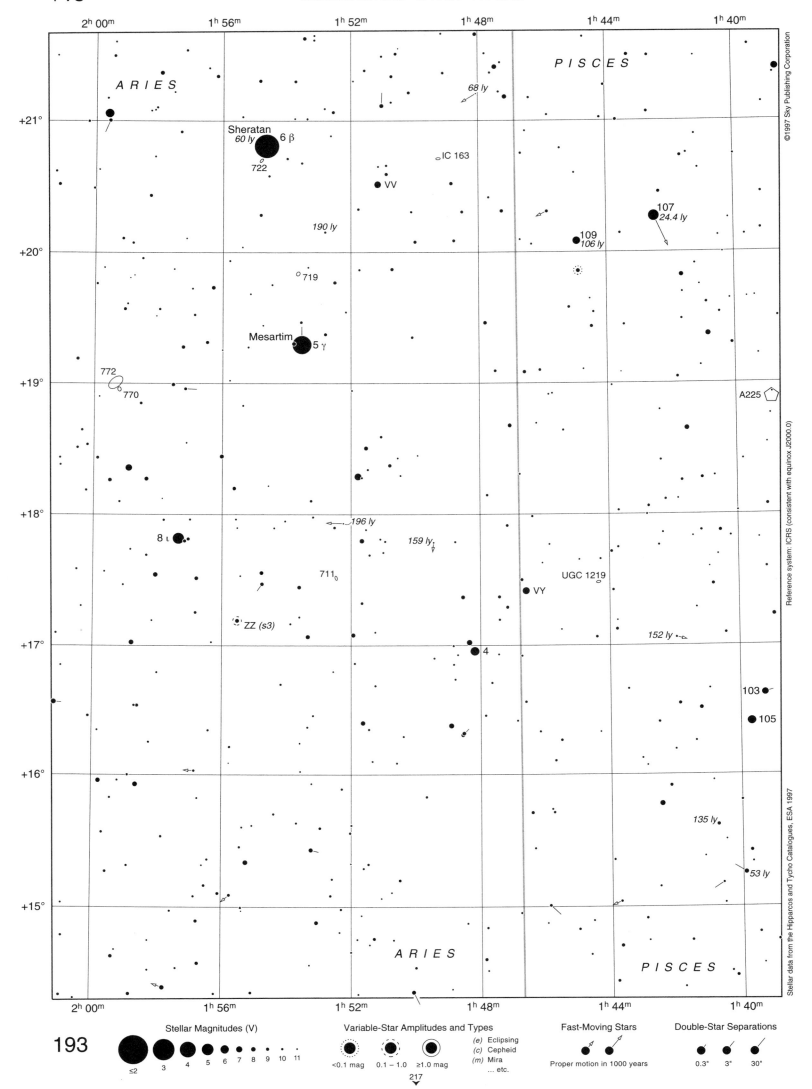

169

2h 00m   1h 56m   1h 52m   1h 48m   1h 44m   1h 40m

PISCES

ARIES

+21°

Sheratan
60 ly   6 β
722

68 ly

IC 163

VV

190 ly

107
24.4 ly

109
106 ly

+20°

719

Mesartim   5 γ

772
770

+19°

A225

196 ly

8 ι

159 ly

711

UGC 1219

VY

ZZ (s3)

152 ly

+17°

4

103

105

+16°

135 ly

53 ly

+15°

ARIES

PISCES

2h 00m   1h 56m   1h 52m   1h 48m   1h 44m   1h 40m

193

Stellar Magnitudes (V)
≤2   3   4   5   6   7   8   9   10   11

Variable-Star Amplitudes and Types
<0.1 mag   0.1 – 1.0   ≥1.0 mag
(e) Eclipsing
(c) Cepheid
(m) Mira
... etc.

Fast-Moving Stars
Proper motion in 1000 years

Double-Star Separations
0.3"   3"   30"

217

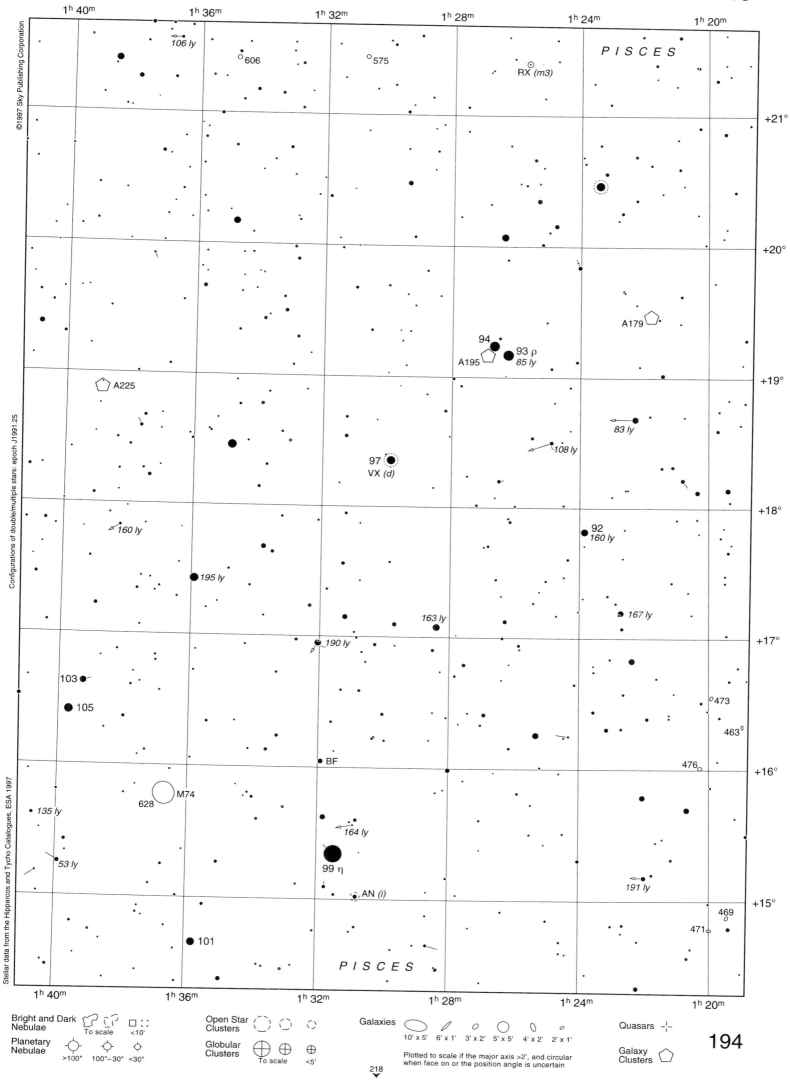

PISCES

606

575

RX (m3)

A179

94

A195

93 ρ
85 ly

A225

83 ly

108 ly

97
VX (d)

92
160 ly

160 ly

195 ly

167 ly

163 ly

103

190 ly

473

105

463

476

BF

628   M74

135 ly

164 ly

53 ly

99 η

191 ly

AN (i)

101

469

471

PISCES

Configurations of double/multiple stars: epoch J1991.25

Stellar data from the Hipparcos and Tycho Catalogues, ESA 1997

Bright and Dark
Nebulae   To scale   <10'

Planetary
Nebulae   >100" 100"–30" <30'

Open Star
Clusters

Globular
Clusters   To scale   <5'

Galaxies

10' x 5'   6' x 1'   3' x 2'   5' x 5'   4' x 2'   2' x 1'

Plotted to scale if the major axis >2', and circular
when face on or the position angle is uncertain

Quasars

Galaxy
Clusters

194

218

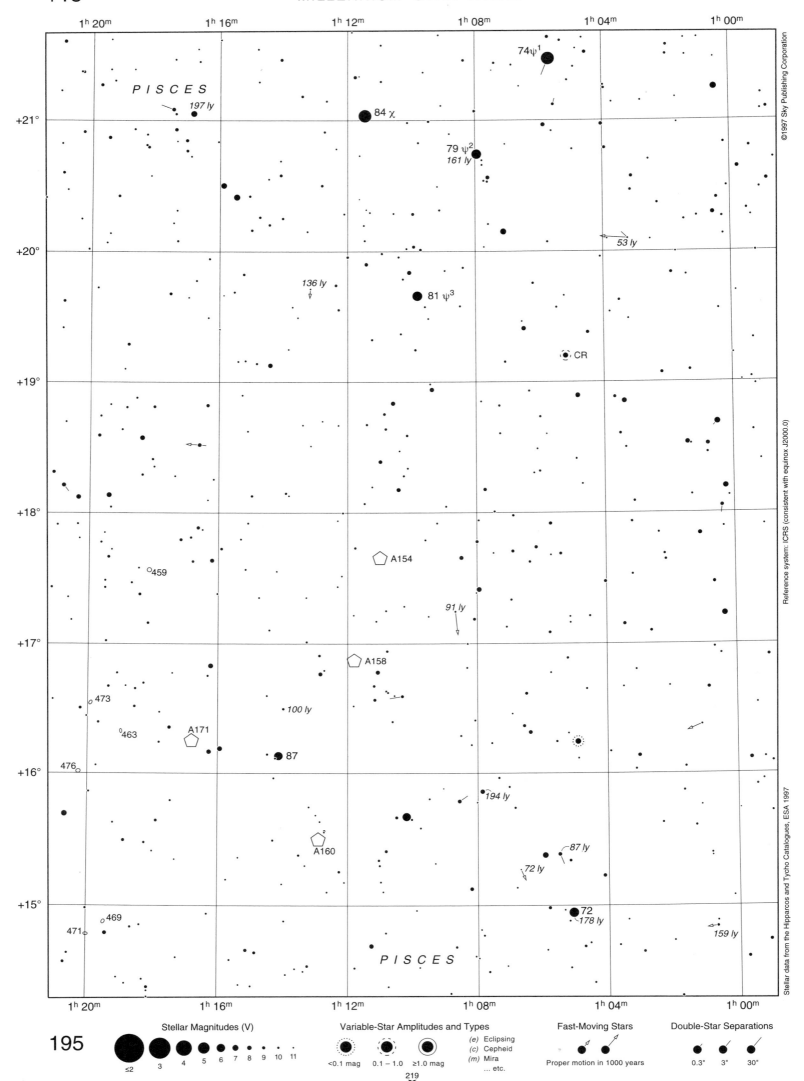

©1997 Sky Publishing Corporation

Reference system: ICRS (consistent with equinox J2000.0)

Stellar data from the Hipparcos and Tycho Catalogues, ESA 1997

PISCES

74 ψ¹

84 χ

79 ψ²
161 ly

197 ly

53 ly

136 ly

81 ψ³

CR

A154

91 ly

A158

ᵒ459

100 ly

ᵒ473

A171

ᵒ463

87

476 ᵒ

194 ly

A160

87 ly

72 ly

72
178 ly

ᵒ469

471 ᵒ

159 ly

PISCES

195

Stellar Magnitudes (V)

●●●●●●• · · · ·
≤2 3 4 5 6 7 8 9 10 11

Variable-Star Amplitudes and Types

<0.1 mag   0.1 – 1.0   ≥1.0 mag

(e) Eclipsing
(c) Cepheid
(m) Mira
... etc.

Fast-Moving Stars

Proper motion in 1000 years

Double-Star Separations

0.3"   3"   30"

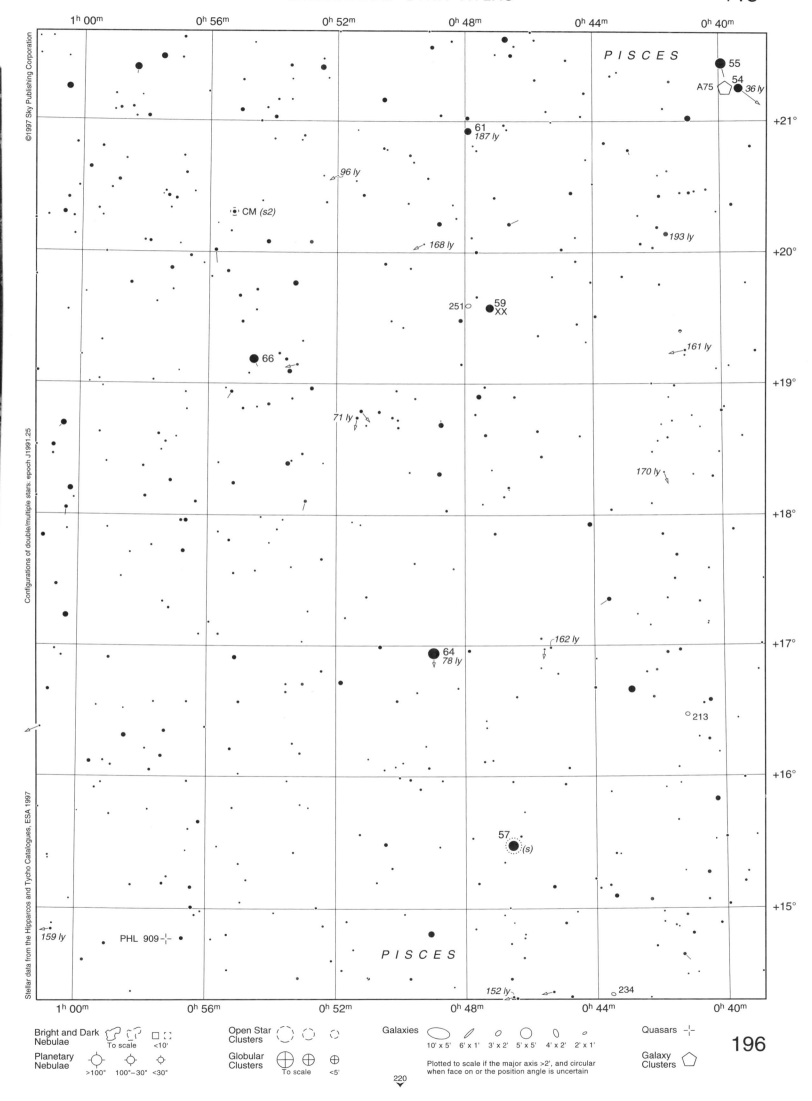

PISCES

55
A75
54
36 ly

61
187 ly

96 ly

CM (s2)

168 ly

193 ly

251
59
XX

161 ly

66

71 ly

170 ly

64
78 ly

162 ly

213

57
(s)

159 ly
PHL 909

PISCES

152 ly
234

| Bright and Dark Nebulae | To scale | <10' | Open Star Clusters | | To scale | Galaxies | 10' x 5' | 6' x 1' | 3' x 2' | 5' x 5' | 4' x 2' | 2' x 1' | Quasars |
| Planetary Nebulae | >100" | 100"–30" | <30" | Globular Clusters | To scale | <5' | Plotted to scale if the major axis >2', and circular when face on or the position angle is uncertain | | | | | | Galaxy Clusters |

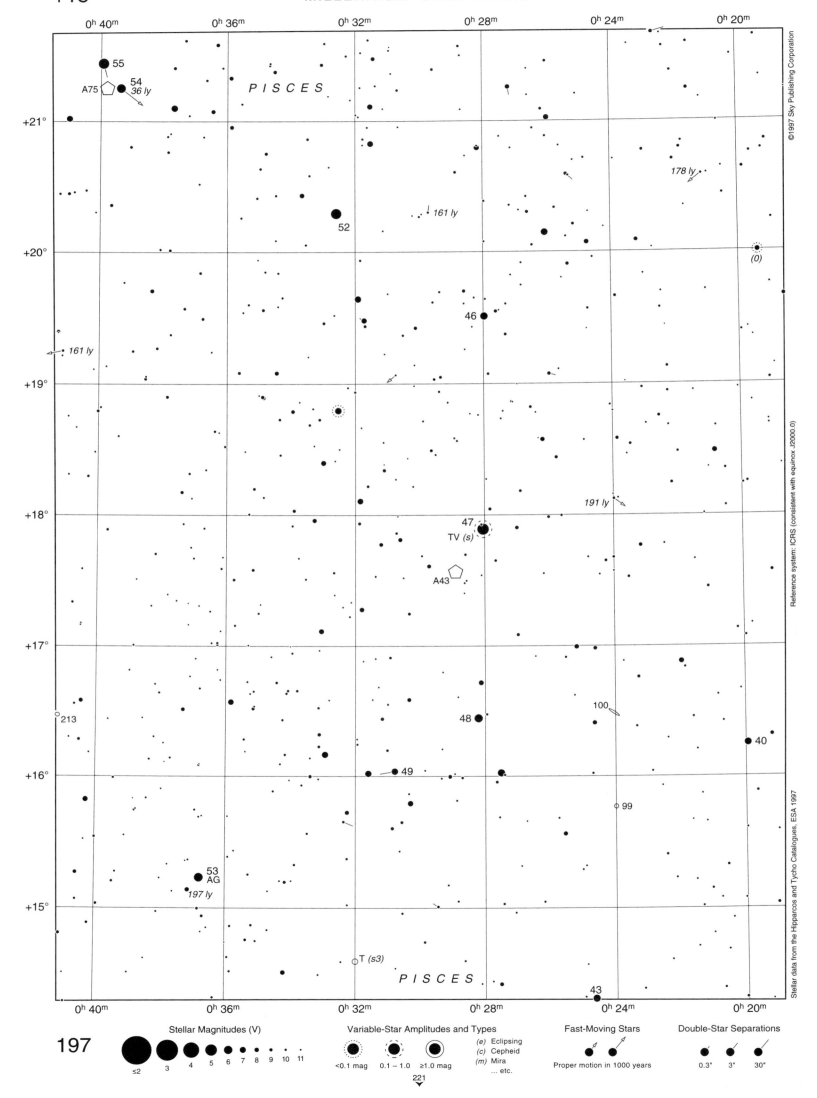

©1997 Sky Publishing Corporation

Reference system: ICRS (consistent with equinox J2000.0)

Stellar data from the Hipparcos and Tycho Catalogues, ESA 1997

P I S C E S

P I S C E S

55
A75
54
36 ly

52

161 ly

178 ly

(0)

46

161 ly

47
TV (s)

191 ly

A43

213

100

48

40

49

99

53
AG
197 ly

T (s3)

43

197

Stellar Magnitudes (V)

≤2   3   4   5   6   7 8 9 10 11

Variable-Star Amplitudes and Types

<0.1 mag   0.1 − 1.0   ≥1.0 mag

(e) Eclipsing
(c) Cepheid
(m) Mira
... etc.

Fast-Moving Stars

Proper motion in 1000 years

Double-Star Separations

0.3"   3"   30"

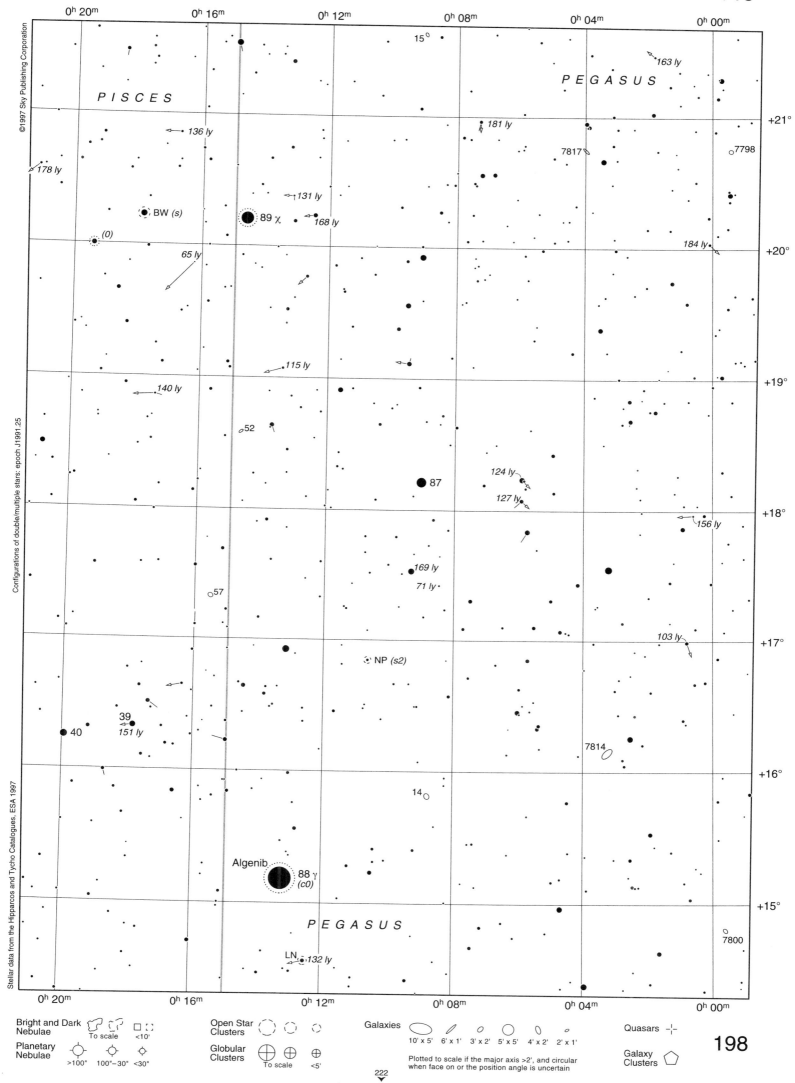

PISCES

PEGASUS

136 ly

178 ly

163 ly

181 ly

7817   7798

BW (s)

131 ly

89 χ   168 ly

(0)

184 ly

65 ly

115 ly

140 ly

52

124 ly

87   127 ly

156 ly

169 ly
71 ly

57

103 ly

NP (s2)

39
40   151 ly

7814

14

Algenib

88 γ
(c0)

PEGASUS

LN 132 ly

15⁰

7800

Bright and Dark
Nebulae
To scale   <10'
Planetary
Nebulae
>100" 100"–30" <30'

Open Star
Clusters

Globular
Clusters
To scale   <5'

Galaxies
10' x 5'   6' x 1'   3' x 2'   5' x 5'   4' x 2'   2' x 1'

Plotted to scale if the major axis >2', and circular
when face on or the position angle is uncertain

Quasars

Galaxy
Clusters

198

222

+12°

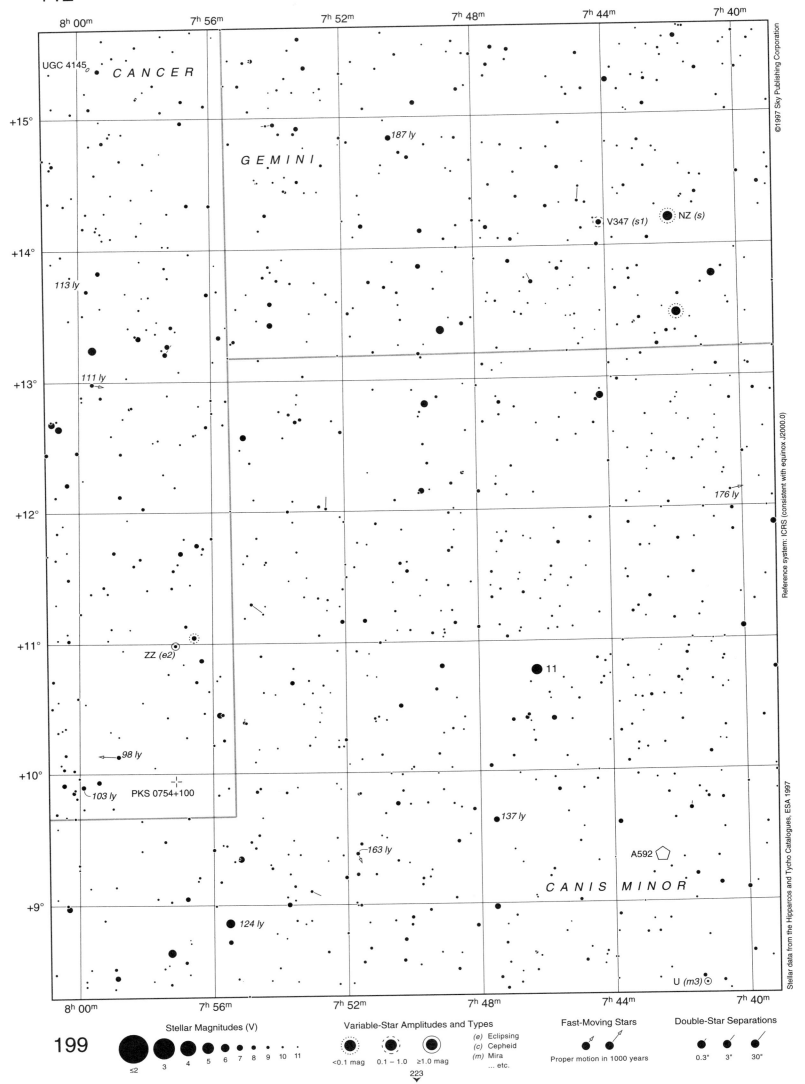

©1997 Sky Publishing Corporation

Reference system: ICRS (consistent with equinox J2000.0)

Stellar data from the Hipparcos and Tycho Catalogues, ESA 1997

UGC 4145

CANCER

GEMINI

187 ly

V347 (s1)   NZ (s)

113 ly

111 ly

176 ly

ZZ (e2)

11

98 ly

PKS 0754+100

103 ly

137 ly

163 ly

A592

CANIS   MINOR

124 ly

U (m3)

199

Stellar Magnitudes (V)

≤2   3   4   5   6   7   8   9   10   11

Variable-Star Amplitudes and Types

<0.1 mag   0.1 – 1.0   ≥1.0 mag

(e) Eclipsing
(c) Cepheid
(m) Mira
... etc.

Fast-Moving Stars

Proper motion in 1000 years

Double-Star Separations

0.3"   3"   30"

223

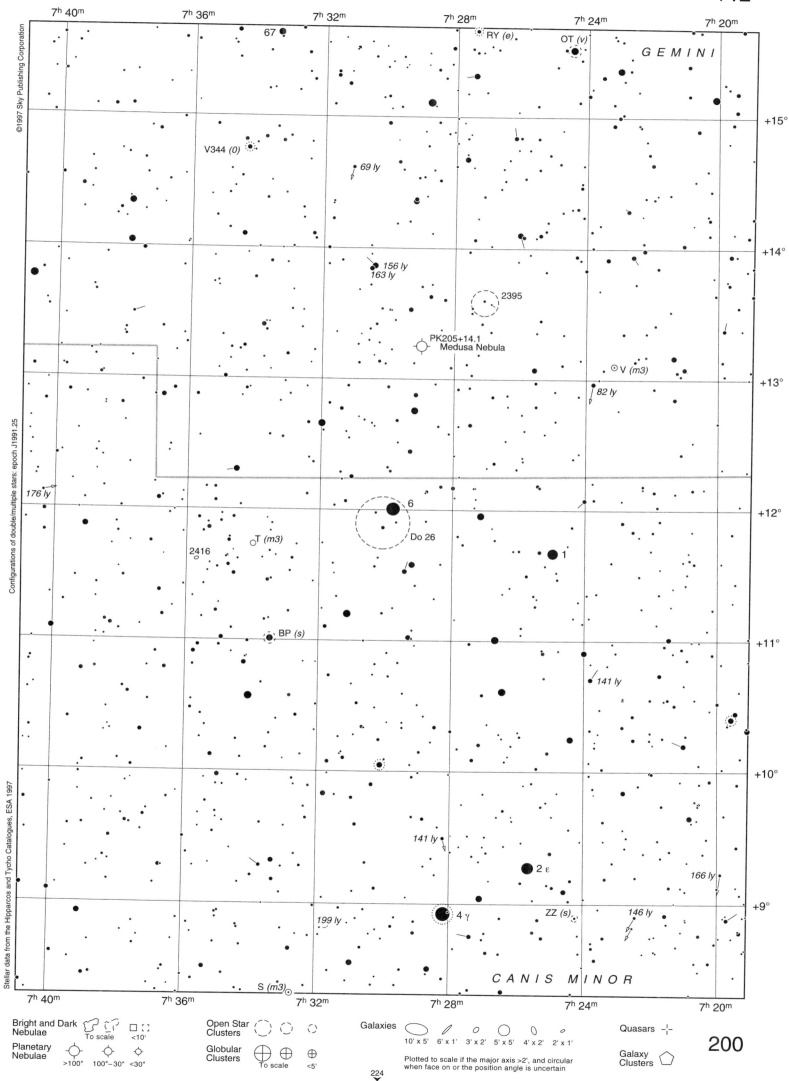

GEMINI

CANIS MINOR

Bright and Dark Nebulae
To scale   <10'

Planetary Nebulae
>100"   100"−30"   <30"

Open Star Clusters

Globular Clusters
To scale   <5'

Galaxies
10' x 5'   6' x 1'   3' x 2'   5' x 5'   4' x 2'   2' x 1'

Plotted to scale if the major axis >2', and circular when face on or the position angle is uncertain

Quasars

Galaxy Clusters

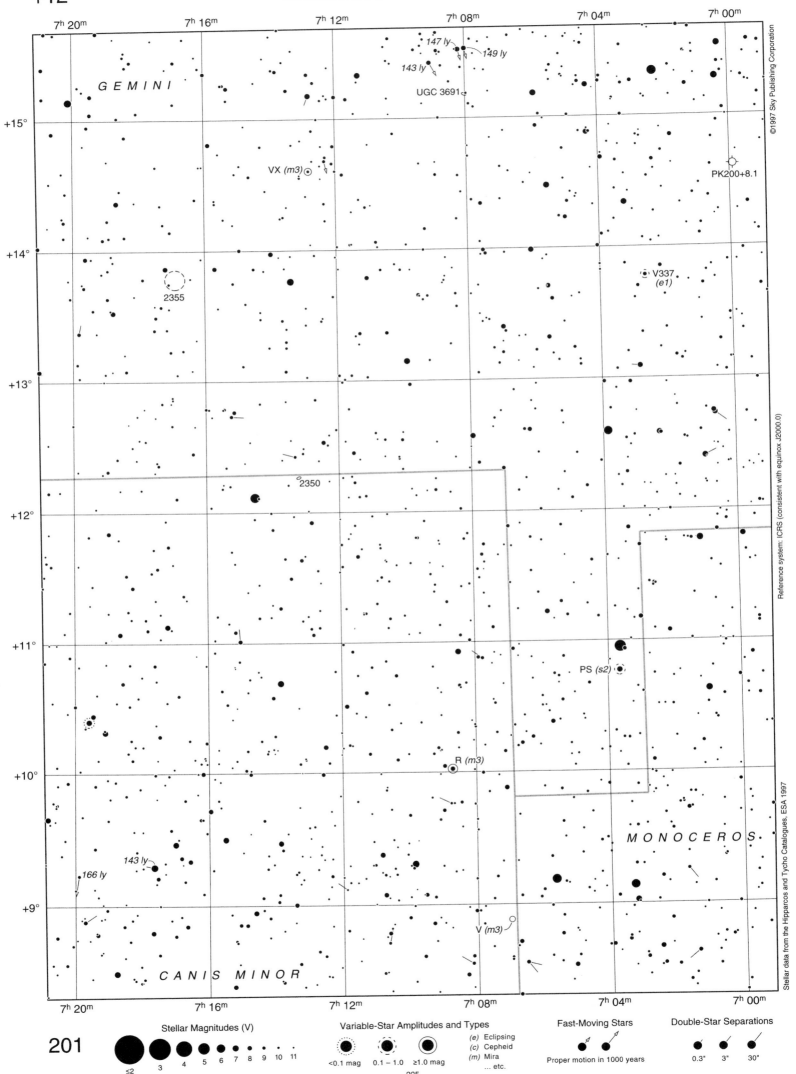

©1997 Sky Publishing Corporation

Reference system: ICRS (consistent with equinox J2000.0)

Stellar data from the Hipparcos and Tycho Catalogues, ESA 1997

GEMINI

VX *(m3)*

2355

2350

UGC 3691

147 ly

149 ly

143 ly

PK200+8.1

V337 *(e1)*

PS *(s2)*

R *(m3)*

MONOCEROS

143 ly

166 ly

V *(m3)*

CANIS MINOR

201

Stellar Magnitudes (V)

≤2   3   4   5   6   7   8   9   10   11

Variable-Star Amplitudes and Types

<0.1 mag   0.1 – 1.0   ≥1.0 mag

(e) Eclipsing
(c) Cepheid
(m) Mira
... etc.

Fast-Moving Stars

Proper motion in 1000 years

Double-Star Separations

0.3"   3"   30"

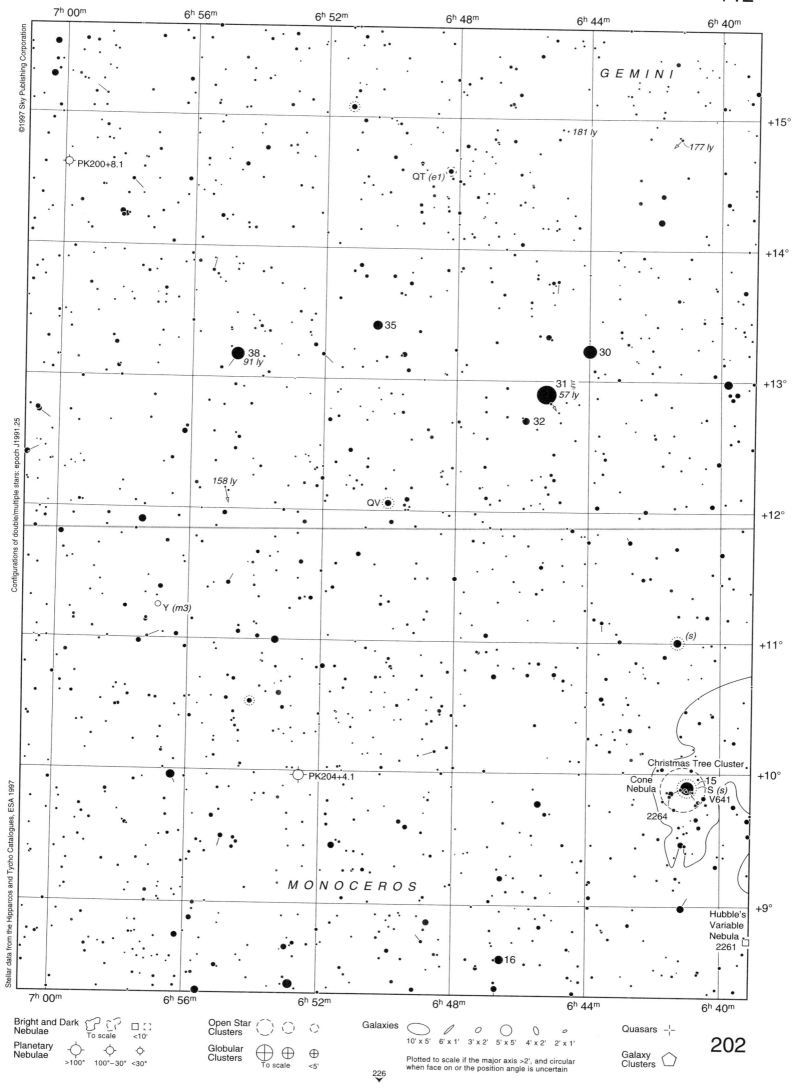

©1997 Sky Publishing Corporation

Configurations of double/multiple stars: epoch J1991.25

Stellar data from the Hipparcos and Tycho Catalogues, ESA 1997

GEMINI

181 ly
177 ly

PK200+8.1

QT (e1)

35

38
91 ly

30

31 ξ
57 ly

32

158 ly

QV

Y (m3)

(s)

Christmas Tree Cluster

Cone
Nebula   15
S (s)
V641

2264

PK204+4.1

MONOCEROS

Hubble's
Variable
Nebula
2261

16

Legend:

Bright and Dark Nebulae — To scale / <10'

Planetary Nebulae — >100" / 100"–30" / <30"

Open Star Clusters — To scale

Globular Clusters — To scale / <5'

Galaxies — 10' x 5' / 6' x 1' / 3' x 2' / 5' x 5' / 4' x 2' / 2' x 1'

Plotted to scale if the major axis >2', and circular when face on or the position angle is uncertain

Quasars — ┼

Galaxy Clusters

202

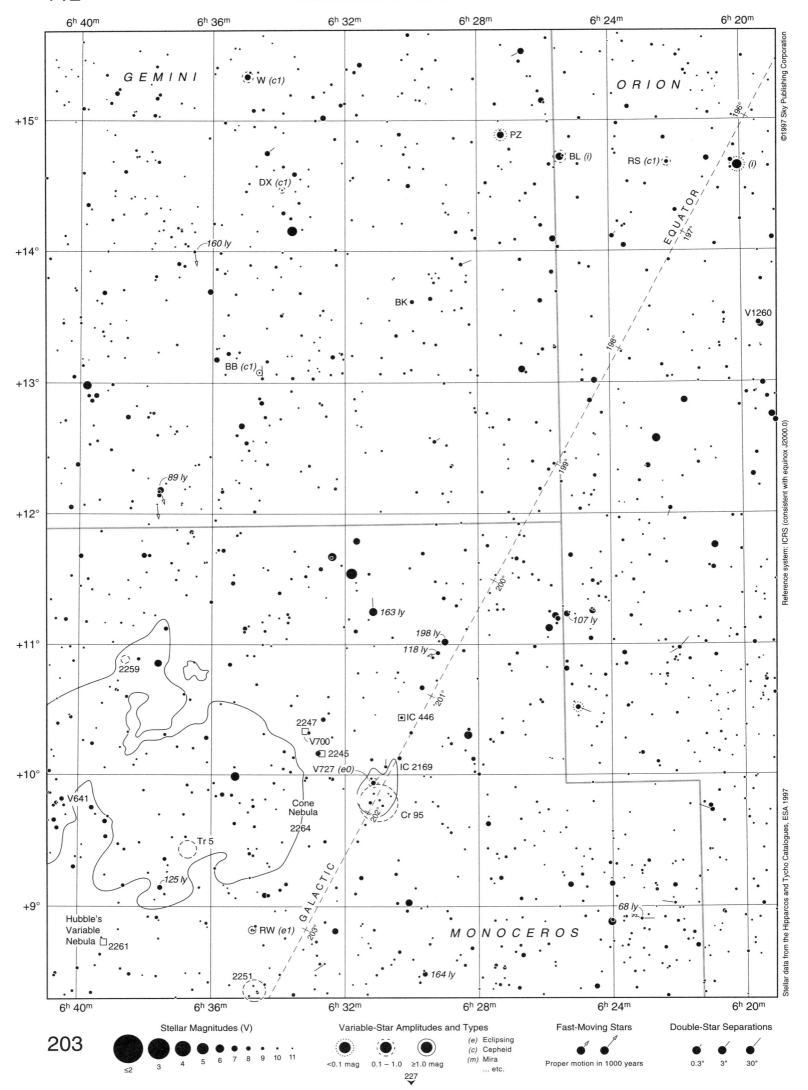

©1997 Sky Publishing Corporation

Reference system: ICRS (consistent with equinox J2000.0)

Stellar data from the Hipparcos and Tycho Catalogues, ESA 1997

GEMINI

ORION

W *(c1)*

PZ

DX *(c1)*

BL *(i)*

RS *(c1)*

(i)

160 ly

BK

V1260

BB *(c1)*

89 ly

163 ly

107 ly

198 ly

118 ly

2259

IC 446

2247
V700
2245
V727 *(e0)*
IC 2169

Cone
Nebula
2264

Cr 95

V641

Tr 5

125 ly

68 ly

Hubble's
Variable
Nebula 2261

RW *(e1)*

MONOCEROS

2251

164 ly

EQUATOR

196°
197°
198°
199°
200°
201°
202°
203°

GALACTIC

203

Stellar Magnitudes (V)

≤2   3   4   5   6   7   8   9   10   11

Variable-Star Amplitudes and Types

<0.1 mag   0.1 – 1.0   ≥1.0 mag

(e) Eclipsing
(c) Cepheid
(m) Mira
... etc.

Fast-Moving Stars

Proper motion in 1000 years

Double-Star Separations

0.3"   3"   30"

227

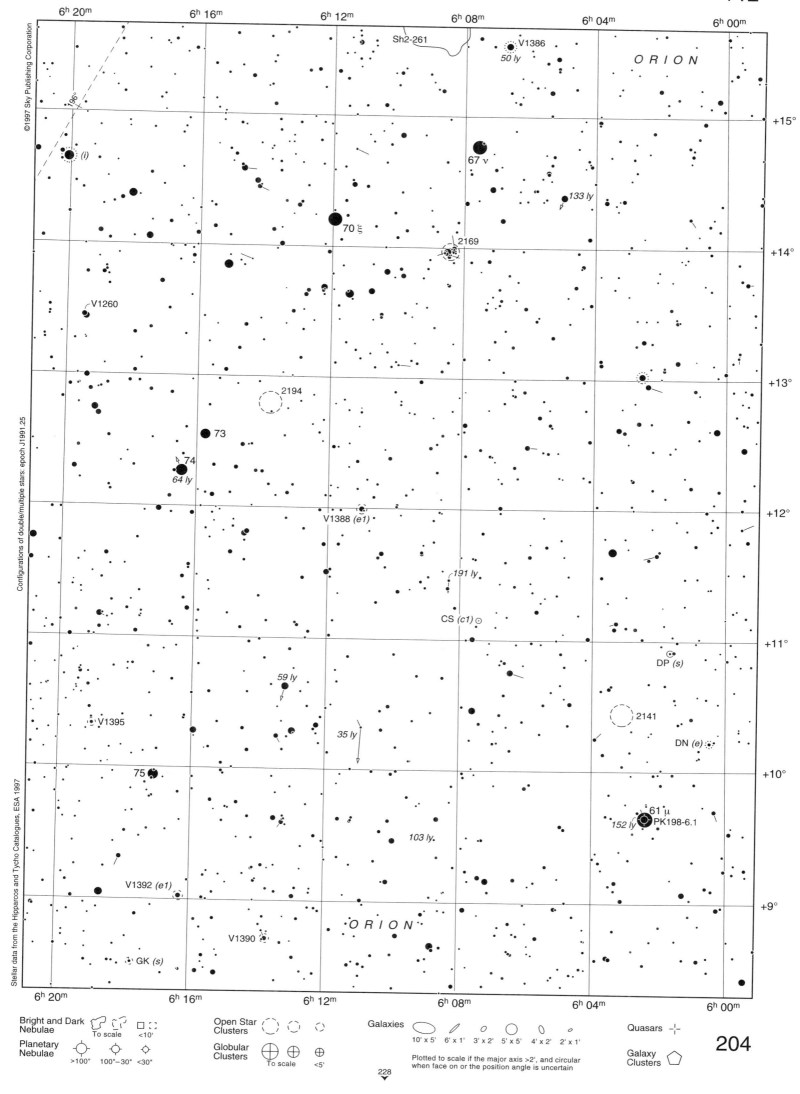

ORION

Sh2-261

V1386
50 ly

67 ν

133 ly

70 ξ

2169

V1260

2194

73

74
64 ly

V1388 (e1)

191 ly

CS (c1)

DP (s)

59 ly

V1395

2141

35 ly

DN (e)

75

61 μ
152 ly PK198-6.1

103 ly

V1392 (e1)

V1390

ORION

GK (s)

©1997 Sky Publishing Corporation

Configurations of double/multiple stars: epoch J1991.25

Stellar data from the Hipparcos and Tycho Catalogues, ESA 1997

Bright and Dark
Nebulae
To scale   <10'

Planetary
Nebulae
>100" 100"–30" <30"

Open Star
Clusters
To scale

Globular
Clusters
To scale   <5'

Galaxies
10' x 5' 6' x 1' 3' x 2' 5' x 5' 4' x 2' 2' x 1'

Plotted to scale if the major axis >2', and circular
when face on or the position angle is uncertain

Quasars

Galaxy
Clusters

204

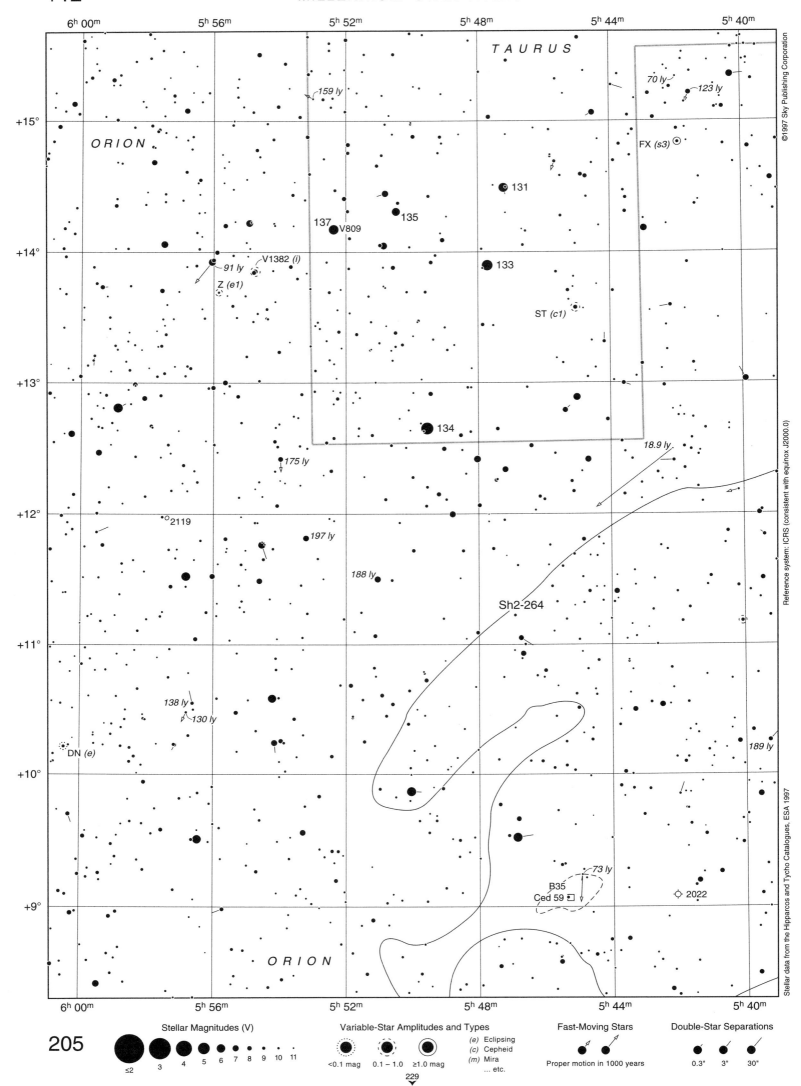

©1997 Sky Publishing Corporation

Reference system: ICRS (consistent with equinox J2000.0)

Stellar data from the Hipparcos and Tycho Catalogues, ESA 1997

205

Stellar Magnitudes (V)
≤2 3 4 5 6 7 8 9 10 11

Variable-Star Amplitudes and Types
<0.1 mag   0.1 – 1.0   ≥1.0 mag

(e) Eclipsing
(c) Cepheid
(m) Mira
... etc.

Fast-Moving Stars
Proper motion in 1000 years

Double-Star Separations
0.3"   3"   30"

MILLENNIUM STAR ATLAS

+12°

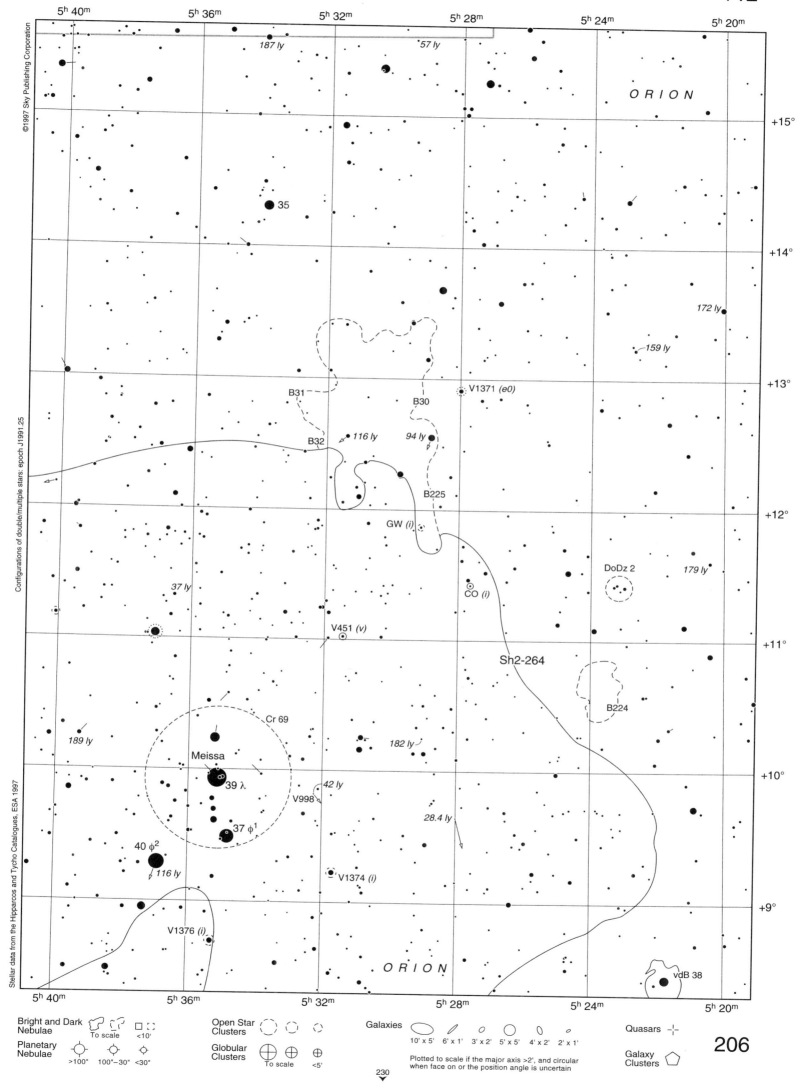

O R I O N

5ʰ 40ᵐ   5ʰ 36ᵐ   5ʰ 32ᵐ   5ʰ 28ᵐ   5ʰ 24ᵐ   5ʰ 20ᵐ

+15°

+14°

+13°

+12°

+11°

+10°

+9°

187 ly

57 ly

172 ly

159 ly

B31

B30

V1371 (e0)

B32

116 ly

94 ly

B225

GW (i)

DoDz 2

179 ly

CO (i)

37 ly

V451 (v)

Sh2-264

B224

Cr 69

189 ly

182 ly

Meissa

39 λ

42 ly

V998

28.4 ly

40 φ²

37 φ¹

116 ly

V1374 (i)

V1376 (i)

O R I O N

vdB 38

35

5ʰ 40ᵐ   5ʰ 36ᵐ   5ʰ 32ᵐ   5ʰ 28ᵐ   5ʰ 24ᵐ   5ʰ 20ᵐ

Bright and Dark Nebulae   To scale   <10'

Planetary Nebulae   >100"   100"–30"   <30"

Open Star Clusters

Globular Clusters   To scale   <5'

Galaxies   10' x 5'   6' x 1'   3' x 2'   5' x 5'   4' x 2'   2' x 1'

Plotted to scale if the major axis >2', and circular when face on or the position angle is uncertain

Quasars

Galaxy Clusters

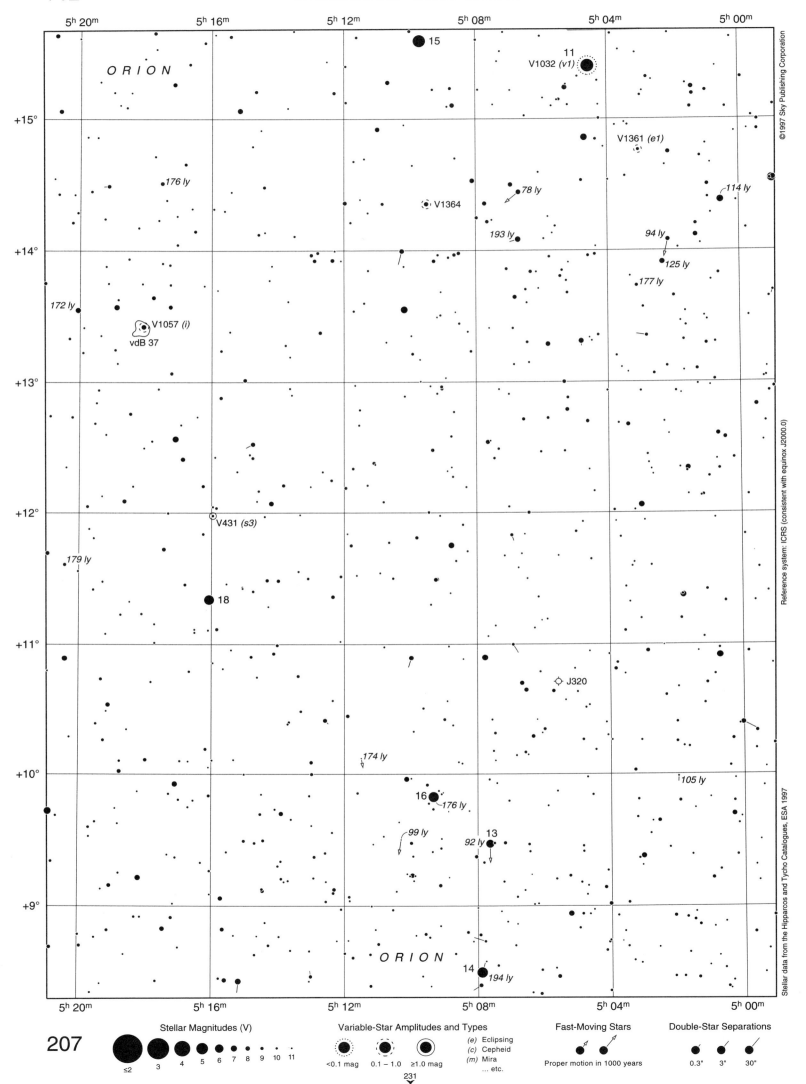

ORION

V1032 (v1)
11

V1361 (e1)

78 ly

V1364

114 ly

193 ly

94 ly

176 ly

125 ly

177 ly

172 ly

V1057 (i)
vdB 37

179 ly

V431 (s3)

18

J320

174 ly

105 ly

16
176 ly

99 ly

13
92 ly

ORION

14
194 ly

©1997 Sky Publishing Corporation

Reference system: ICRS (consistent with equinox J2000.0)

Stellar data from the Hipparcos and Tycho Catalogues, ESA 1997

207

Stellar Magnitudes (V)
≤2   3   4   5   6   7   8   9   10   11

Variable-Star Amplitudes and Types
<0.1 mag   0.1 – 1.0   ≥1.0 mag

(e) Eclipsing
(c) Cepheid
(m) Mira
... etc.

Fast-Moving Stars
Proper motion in 1000 years

Double-Star Separations
0.3"   3"   30"

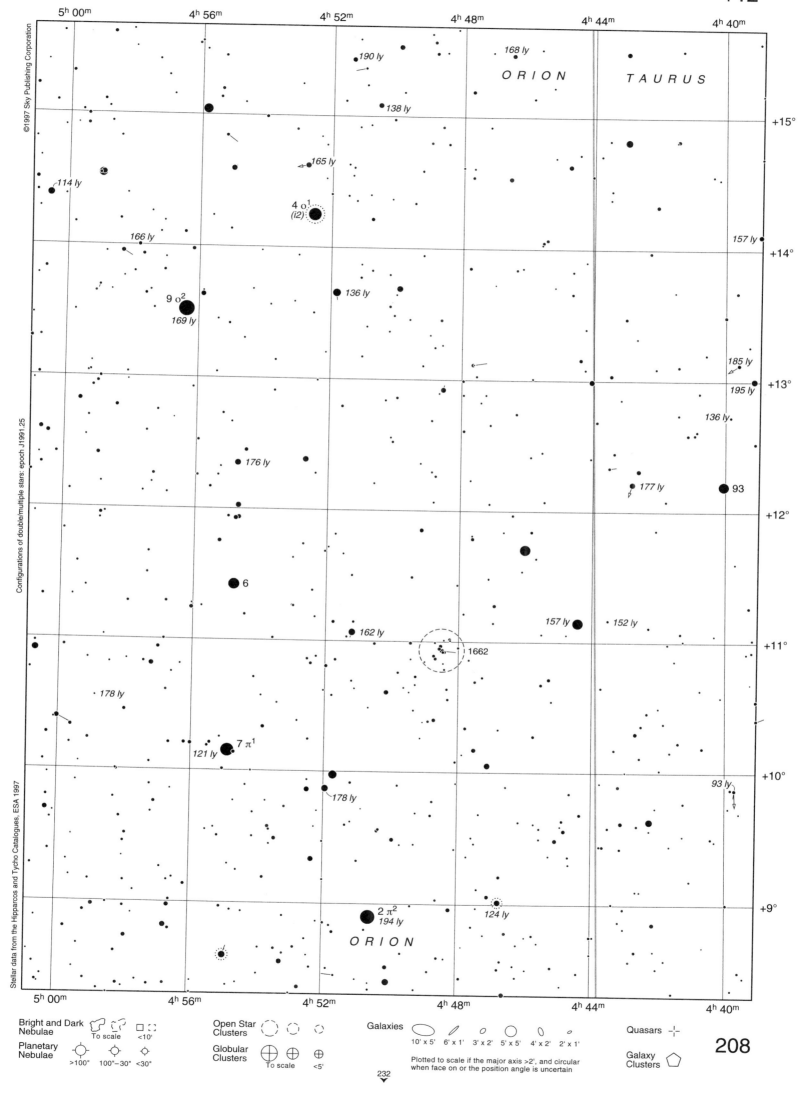

190 ly

168 ly

ORION　　*TAURUS*

138 ly

+15°

165 ly

157 ly

4 o¹
(i2)

166 ly

+14°

9 o²
169 ly

136 ly

185 ly

+13°

195 ly

136 ly

176 ly

177 ly

93

+12°

6

157 ly　152 ly

162 ly

+11°

1662

178 ly

7 π¹
121 ly

+10°

178 ly

93 ly

2 π²
194 ly

124 ly

+9°

ORION

©1997 Sky Publishing Corporation

Configurations of double/multiple stars: epoch J1991.25

Stellar data from the Hipparcos and Tycho Catalogues, ESA 1997

Bright and Dark Nebulae	To scale	<10'	Open Star Clusters	Galaxies		Quasars

Planetary Nebulae
>100" 100"–30" <30"

Globular Clusters
To scale <5'

10' x 5' 6' x 1' 3' x 2' 5' x 5' 4' x 2' 2' x 1'

Plotted to scale if the major axis >2', and circular when face on or the position angle is uncertain

Galaxy Clusters

208

MILLENNIUM STAR ATLAS

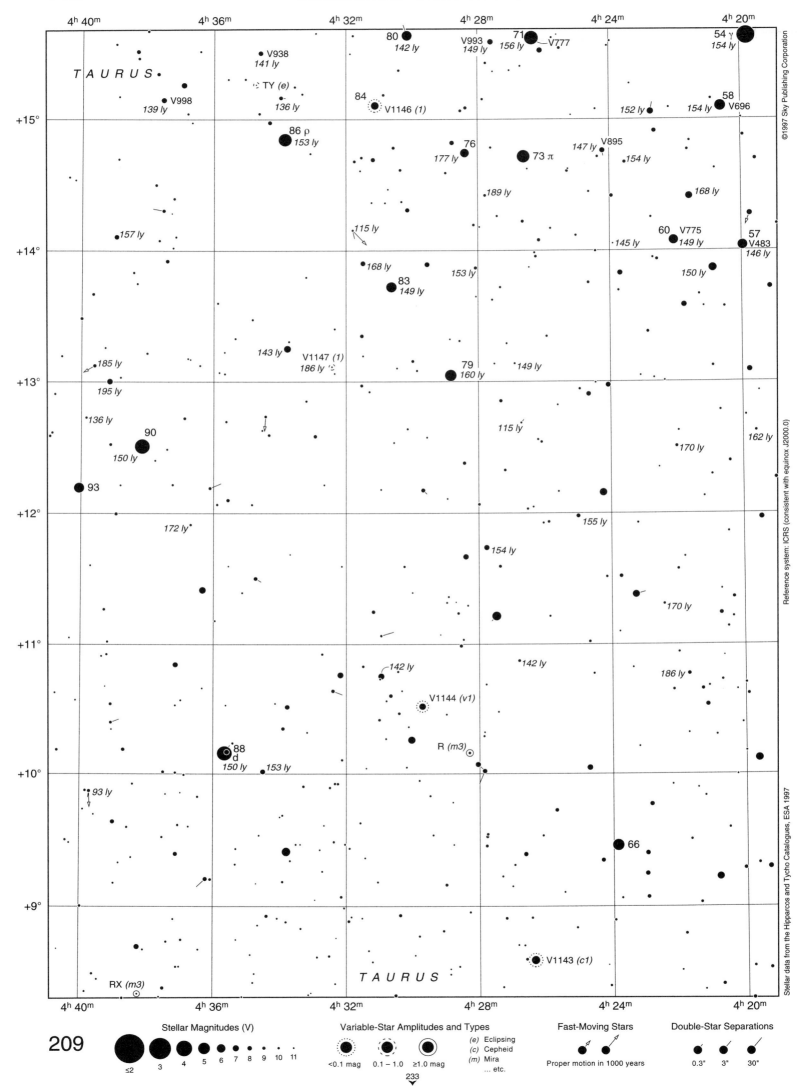

Reference system: ICRS (consistent with equinox J2000.0)

Stellar data from the Hipparcos and Tycho Catalogues, ESA 1997

209

Stellar Magnitudes (V)

≤2 3 4 5 6 7 8 9 10 11

Variable-Star Amplitudes and Types

<0.1 mag   0.1 – 1.0   ≥1.0 mag

(e) Eclipsing
(c) Cepheid
(m) Mira
... etc.

Fast-Moving Stars

Proper motion in 1000 years

Double-Star Separations

0.3" 3" 30"

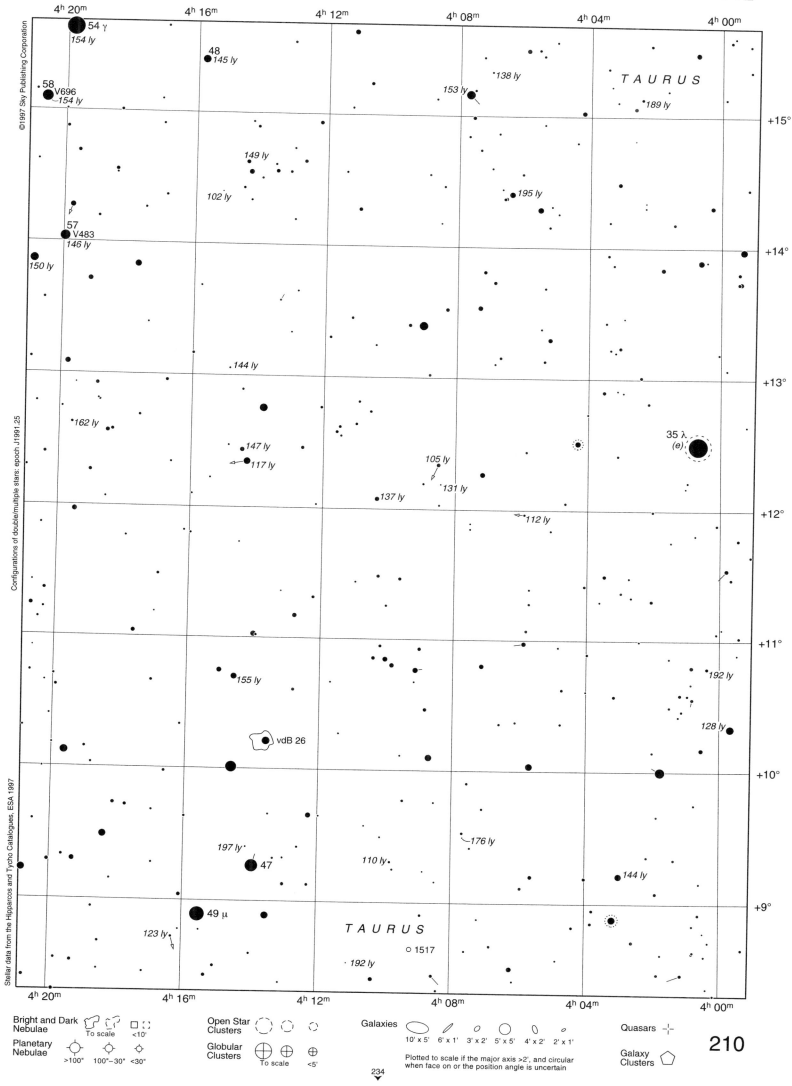

4ʰ 20ᵐ   4ʰ 16ᵐ   4ʰ 12ᵐ   4ʰ 08ᵐ   4ʰ 04ᵐ   4ʰ 00ᵐ

54 γ
154 ly

48
145 ly

58
V696
154 ly

138 ly

T A U R U S

153 ly

189 ly

+15°

149 ly

195 ly

102 ly

57
V483
146 ly

150 ly

+14°

144 ly

+13°

162 ly

35 λ
(e)

147 ly

105 ly

117 ly

131 ly

137 ly

112 ly

+12°

155 ly

192 ly

128 ly

vdB 26

+11°

+10°

176 ly

197 ly

110 ly

47

144 ly

+9°

49 μ

T A U R U S

123 ly

○ 1517

192 ly

4ʰ 20ᵐ   4ʰ 16ᵐ   4ʰ 12ᵐ   4ʰ 08ᵐ   4ʰ 04ᵐ   4ʰ 00ᵐ

Bright and Dark
Nebulae   To scale   <10'

Open Star
Clusters

Galaxies

Quasars

Planetary
Nebulae   >100" 100"–30" <30'

Globular
Clusters   To scale   <5'

10' x 5'   6' x 1'   3' x 2'   5' x 5'   4' x 2'   2' x 1'

Galaxy
Clusters

Plotted to scale if the major axis >2', and circular
when face on or the position angle is uncertain

210

234

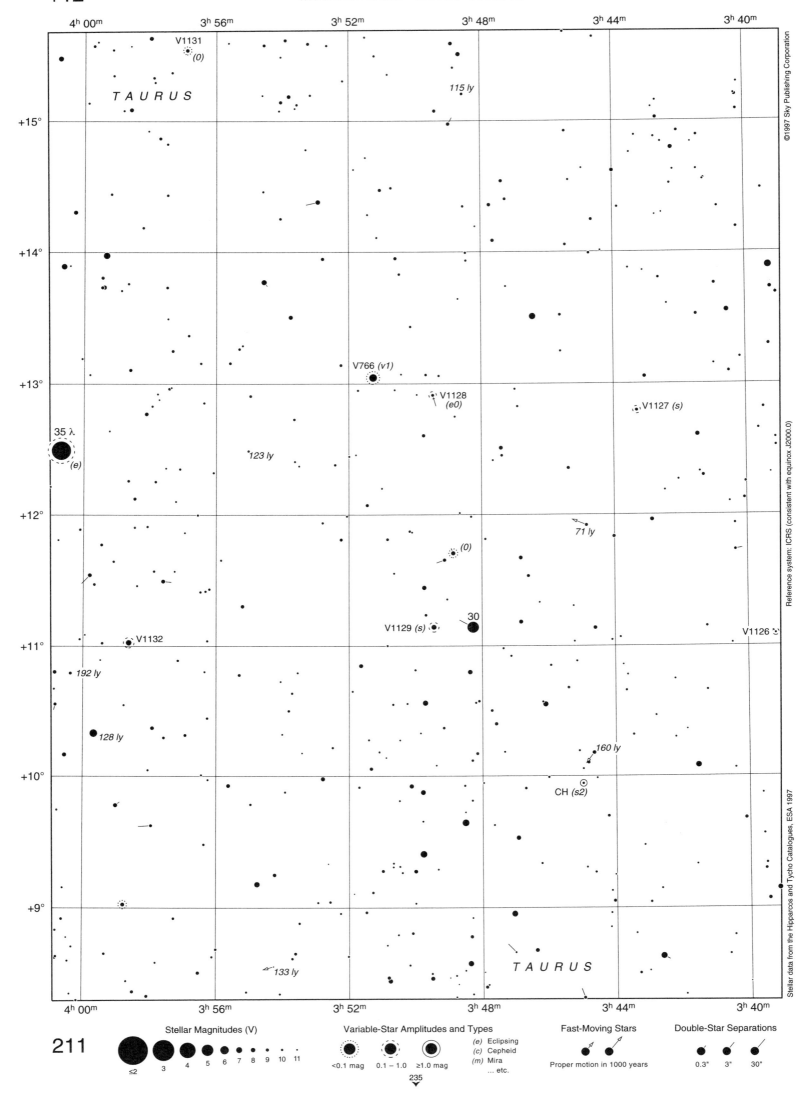

©1997 Sky Publishing Corporation

Reference system: ICRS (consistent with equinox J2000.0)

Stellar data from the Hipparcos and Tycho Catalogues, ESA 1997

TAURUS

V1131

(0)

115 ly

V766 (v1)

V1128
(e0)

V1127 (s)

35 λ

123 ly

(e)

71 ly

(0)

30

V1129 (s)

V1126

V1132

192 ly

128 ly

160 ly

CH (s2)

133 ly

TAURUS

211

Stellar Magnitudes (V)

≤2   3   4   5   6   7   8   9   10   11

Variable-Star Amplitudes and Types

<0.1 mag   0.1 – 1.0   ≥1.0 mag

(e) Eclipsing
(c) Cepheid
(m) Mira
... etc.

Fast-Moving Stars

Proper motion in 1000 years

Double-Star Separations

0.3"   3"   30"

235

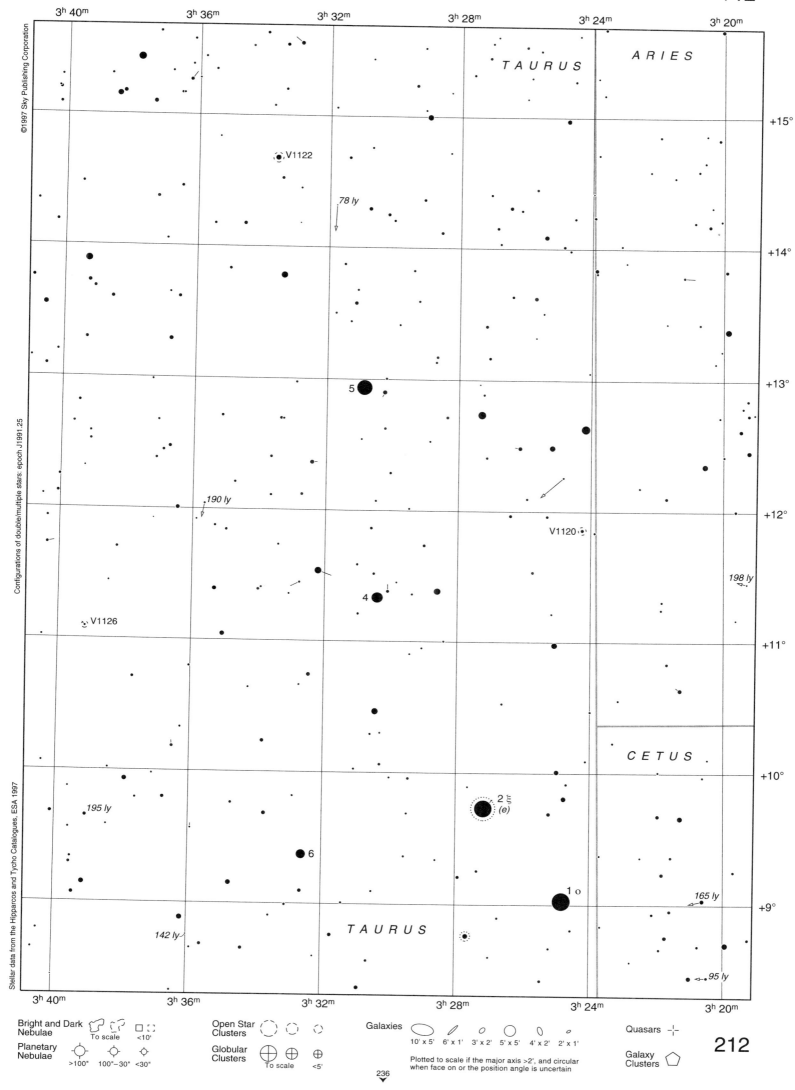

3ʰ 40ᵐ   3ʰ 36ᵐ   3ʰ 32ᵐ   3ʰ 28ᵐ   3ʰ 24ᵐ   3ʰ 20ᵐ

T A U R U S

A R I E S

+15°

V1122

78 ly

+14°

5

+13°

190 ly

V1120

+12°

198 ly

V1126

4

+11°

C E T U S

+10°

2 ξ
(e)

195 ly

6

1 o

165 ly

142 ly

T A U R U S

95 ly

+9°

3ʰ 40ᵐ   3ʰ 36ᵐ   3ʰ 32ᵐ   3ʰ 28ᵐ   3ʰ 24ᵐ   3ʰ 20ᵐ

Bright and Dark Nebulae			Open Star Clusters			Galaxies						Quasars
To scale		<10'				10' x 5'	6' x 1'	3' x 2'	5' x 5'	4' x 2'	2' x 1'	

Planetary Nebulae			Globular Clusters				Galaxy Clusters
>100"	100"–30"	<30"	To scale	<5'		Plotted to scale if the major axis >2', and circular when face on or the position angle is uncertain	

212

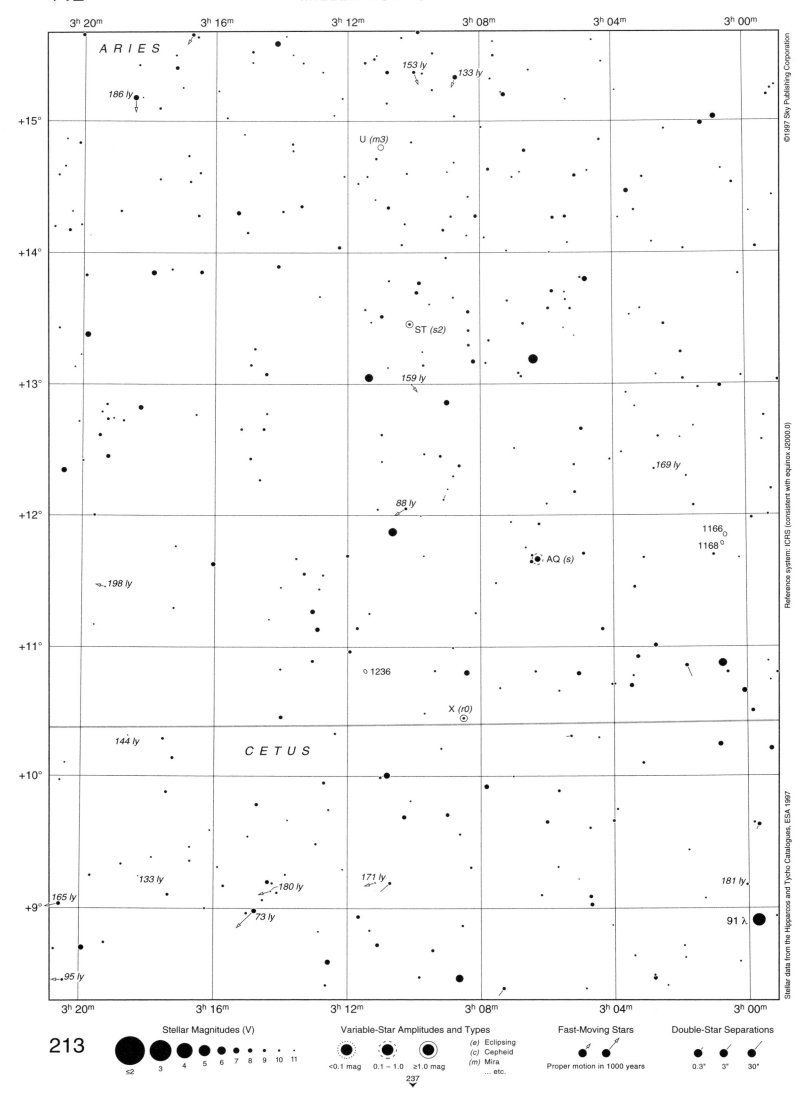

©1997 Sky Publishing Corporation

Reference system: ICRS (consistent with equinox J2000.0)

Stellar data from the Hipparcos and Tycho Catalogues, ESA 1997

ARIES

153 ly

133 ly

186 ly

U (m3)

ST (s2)

159 ly

169 ly

88 ly

1166
1168

.198 ly

AQ (s)

1236

X (r0)

144 ly

CETUS

133 ly

180 ly

171 ly

181 ly

165 ly

73 ly

95 ly

91 λ

213

Stellar Magnitudes (V)

≤2 3 4 5 6 7 8 9 10 11

Variable-Star Amplitudes and Types

<0.1 mag   0.1 – 1.0   ≥1.0 mag

(e) Eclipsing
(c) Cepheid
(m) Mira
... etc.

Fast-Moving Stars

Proper motion in 1000 years

Double-Star Separations

0.3"   3"   30"

MILLENNIUM STAR ATLAS

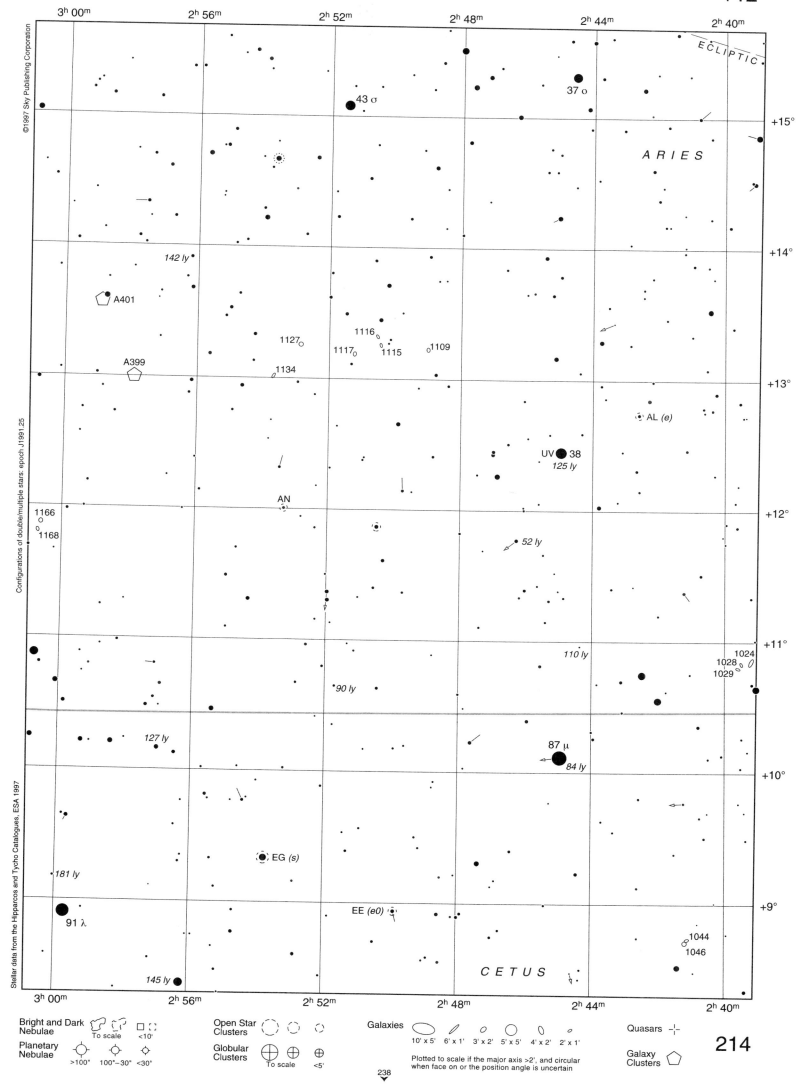

Configurations of double/multiple stars: epoch J1991.25

Stellar data from the Hipparcos and Tycho Catalogues, ESA 1997

E C L I P T I C

A R I E S

C E T U S

43 σ

37 o

142 ly

A401

A399

1127

1116

1117   1115   1109

1134

AL (e)

UV ● 38

125 ly

AN

1166
1168

52 ly

110 ly

1024
1028
1029

90 ly

127 ly

87 μ

84 ly

181 ly

EG (s)

91 λ

EE (e0)

1044
1046

145 ly

3ʰ 00ᵐ	2ʰ 56ᵐ	2ʰ 52ᵐ	2ʰ 48ᵐ

+15°
+14°
+13°
+12°
+11°
+10°
+9°

Legend

Bright and Dark Nebulae — To scale / <10'

Planetary Nebulae — >100" / 100"–30" / <30"

Open Star Clusters

Globular Clusters — To scale / <5'

Galaxies — 10' x 5' / 6' x 1' / 3' x 2' / 5' x 5' / 4' x 2' / 2' x 1'

Plotted to scale if the major axis >2', and circular when face on or the position angle is uncertain

Quasars

Galaxy Clusters

238

214

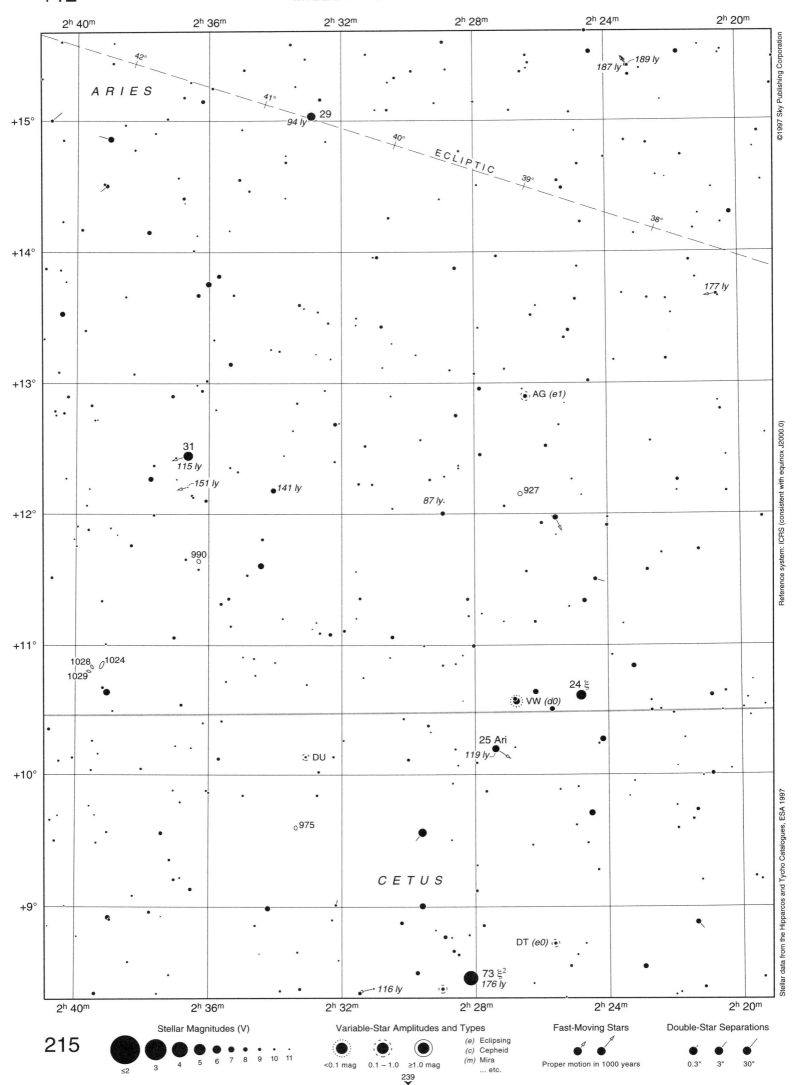

©1997 Sky Publishing Corporation

Reference system: ICRS (consistent with equinox J2000.0)

Stellar data from the Hipparcos and Tycho Catalogues, ESA 1997

ARIES

42°

41°

29
94 ly

40°

ECLIPTIC

39°

38°

187 ly   189 ly

177 ly

AG (e1)

31
115 ly

151 ly

141 ly

87 ly.

927

990

1028   1024
1029

24 ξ

VW (d0)

25 Ari
119 ly

DU

975

CETUS

DT (e0)

73 ξ²
176 ly

116 ly

215

Stellar Magnitudes (V)

≤2   3   4   5   6   7   8   9   10   11

Variable-Star Amplitudes and Types

<0.1 mag   0.1 – 1.0   ≥1.0 mag

(e) Eclipsing
(c) Cepheid
(m) Mira
... etc.

Fast-Moving Stars

Proper motion in 1000 years

Double-Star Separations

0.3"   3"   30"

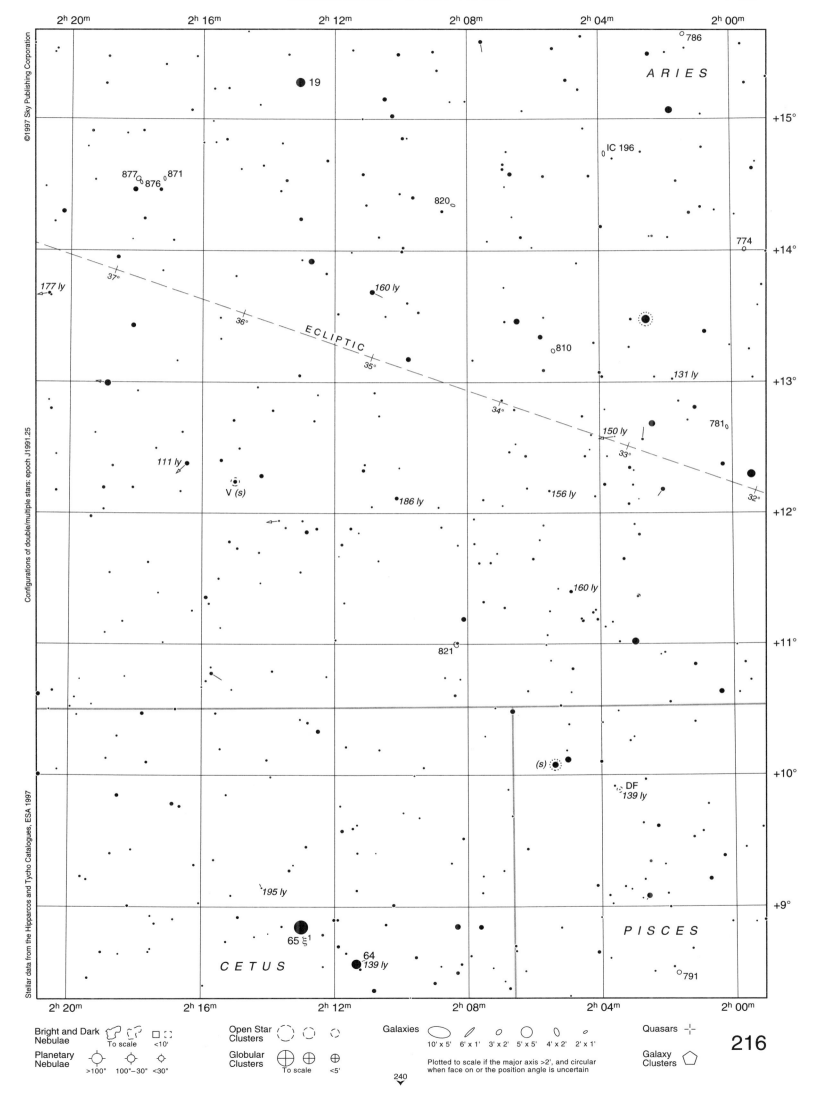

2ʰ 20ᵐ 2ʰ 16ᵐ 2ʰ 12ᵐ 2ʰ 08ᵐ 2ʰ 04ᵐ 2ʰ 00ᵐ

ARIES

786

19

877 876 871

IC 196

820

+15°

774

+14°

37°

177 ly

160 ly

36°

ECLIPTIC

35°

810

131 ly

+13°

34°

781

150 ly

33°

111 ly

156 ly

+12°

V (s)

186 ly

32°

160 ly

821

+11°

(s)

DF
139 ly

+10°

195 ly

+9°

65 ξ¹

PISCES

64
139 ly

791

C E T U S

2ʰ 20ᵐ 2ʰ 16ᵐ 2ʰ 12ᵐ 2ʰ 08ᵐ 2ʰ 04ᵐ 2ʰ 00ᵐ

Bright and Dark Nebulae				Open Star Clusters			Galaxies							Quasars	

Bright and Dark Nebulae — To scale — <10'

Planetary Nebulae — >100" 100"–30" <30"

Open Star Clusters

Globular Clusters — To scale — <5'

Galaxies — 10' x 5' 6' x 1' 3' x 2' 5' x 5' 4' x 2' 2' x 1'

Plotted to scale if the major axis >2', and circular when face on or the position angle is uncertain

Quasars

Galaxy Clusters

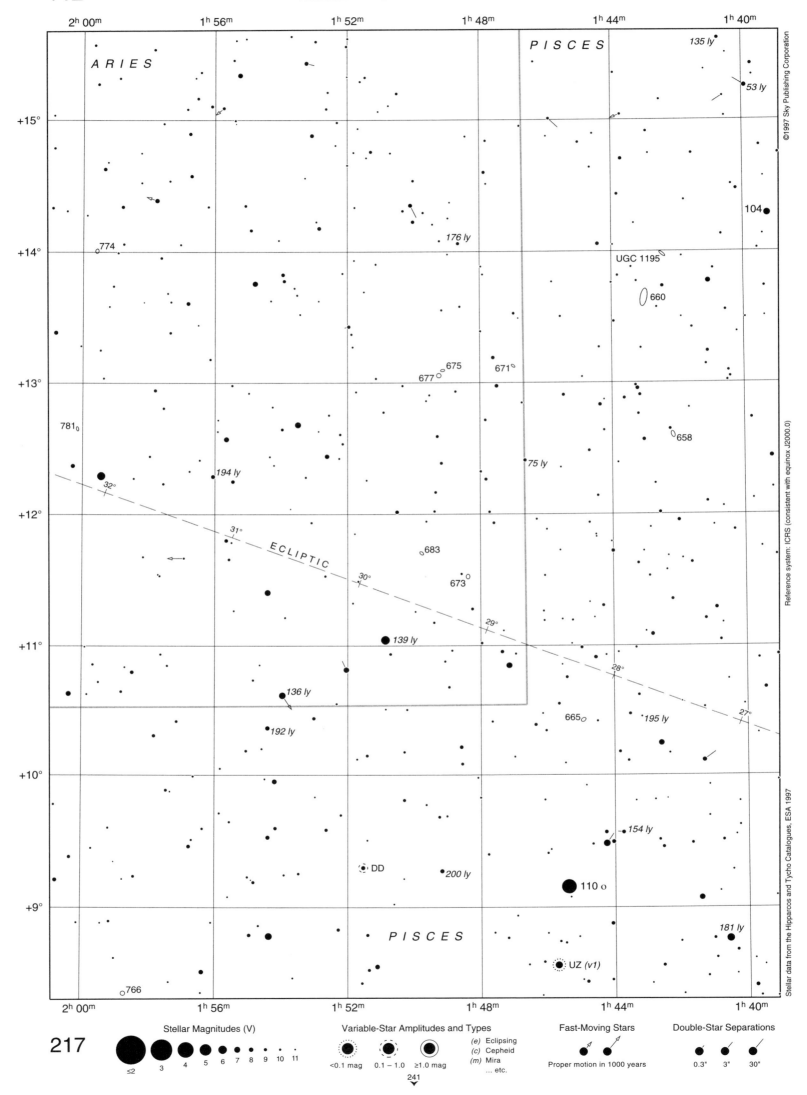

©1997 Sky Publishing Corporation

Reference system: ICRS (consistent with equinox J2000.0)

Stellar data from the Hipparcos and Tycho Catalogues, ESA 1997

ARIES

PISCES

135 ly
53 ly

104

774

176 ly

UGC 1195

660

781₀

677 675 671

32°

194 ly

658

75 ly

31°

ECLIPTIC

683

30°

673

139 ly

29°

28°

136 ly

192 ly

665

195 ly

27°

154 ly

DD

200 ly

110 ○

PISCES

181 ly

UZ (v1)

766

217

Stellar Magnitudes (V)

≤2   3   4   5   6 7 8 9 10 11

Variable-Star Amplitudes and Types

<0.1 mag   0.1 – 1.0   ≥1.0 mag

(e) Eclipsing
(c) Cepheid
(m) Mira
... etc.

Fast-Moving Stars

Proper motion in 1000 years

Double-Star Separations

0.3"   3"   30"

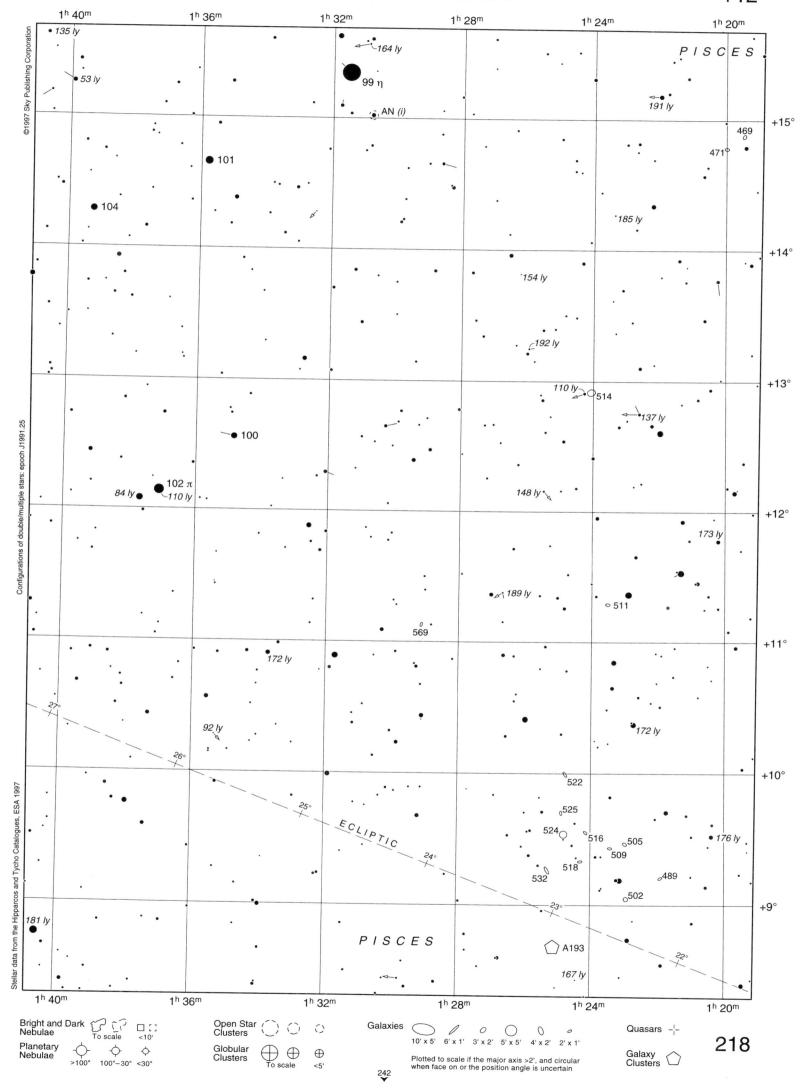

PISCES

99 η

164 ly

135 ly

53 ly

101

104

100

102 π

84 ly

110 ly

191 ly

469

471

185 ly

154 ly

192 ly

110 ly · 514

137 ly

148 ly

173 ly

189 ly

511

569

172 ly

92 ly

172 ly

522

525

524

516

505

509

518

532

502

489

176 ly

181 ly

PISCES

A193

167 ly

ECLIPTIC

27°

26°

25°

24°

23°

22°

AN (i)

+15°

+14°

+13°

+12°

+11°

+10°

+9°

©1997 Sky Publishing Corporation

Configurations of double/multiple stars: epoch J1991.25

Stellar data from the Hipparcos and Tycho Catalogues, ESA 1997

1ʰ 40ᵐ   1ʰ 36ᵐ   1ʰ 32ᵐ   1ʰ 28ᵐ   1ʰ 24ᵐ   1ʰ 20ᵐ

Bright and Dark Nebulae	Open Star Clusters	Galaxies						Quasars
To scale <10'	To scale <10'	10' x 5' 6' x 1' 3' x 2' 5' x 5' 4' x 2' 2' x 1'						
Planetary Nebulae >100" 100"–30" <30"	Globular Clusters To scale <5'	Plotted to scale if the major axis >2', and circular when face on or the position angle is uncertain						Galaxy Clusters

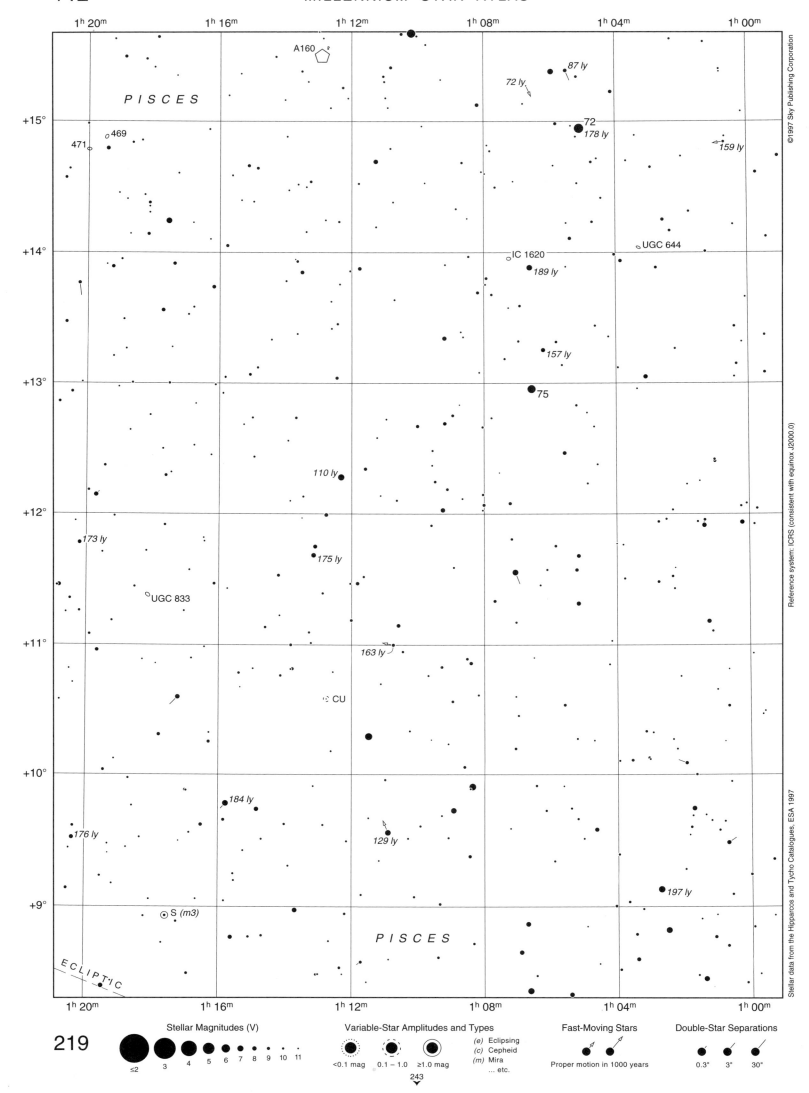

PISCES

1ʰ 20ᵐ   1ʰ 16ᵐ   1ʰ 12ᵐ   1ʰ 08ᵐ   1ʰ 04ᵐ   1ʰ 00ᵐ

+15°
+14°
+13°
+12°
+11°
+10°
+9°

A160

87 ly
72 ly
72
178 ly
159 ly

UGC 644
IC 1620
189 ly

157 ly

75

469
471

110 ly

173 ly
175 ly

UGC 833

163 ly

CU

184 ly

176 ly
129 ly

197 ly

S (m3)

PISCES

ECLIPTIC

©1997 Sky Publishing Corporation

Reference system: ICRS (consistent with equinox J2000.0)

Stellar data from the Hipparcos and Tycho Catalogues, ESA 1997

219

Stellar Magnitudes (V)
≤2   3   4   5   6   7   8   9   10   11

Variable-Star Amplitudes and Types
<0.1 mag   0.1 – 1.0   ≥1.0 mag

(e) Eclipsing
(c) Cepheid
(m) Mira
... etc.

Fast-Moving Stars
Proper motion in 1000 years

Double-Star Separations
0.3"   3"   30"

MILLENNIUM STAR ATLAS

+12°

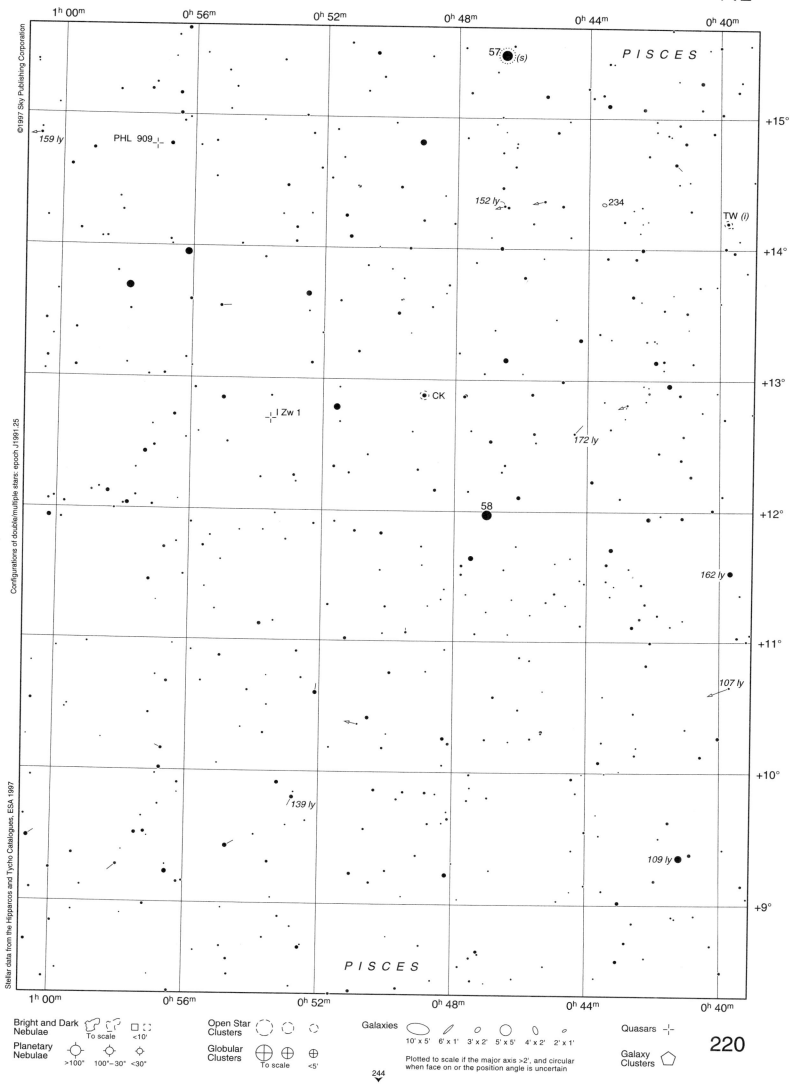

Configurations of double/multiple stars: epoch J1991.25

Stellar data from the Hipparcos and Tycho Catalogues, ESA 1997

PISCES

PISCES

159 ly

PHL 909

152 ly

234

TW (i)

57 (s)

I Zw 1

CK

172 ly

58

162 ly

107 ly

139 ly

109 ly

+15°

+14°

+13°

+12°

+11°

+10°

+9°

1ʰ 00ᵐ 0ʰ 56ᵐ 0ʰ 52ᵐ 0ʰ 48ᵐ 0ʰ 44ᵐ 0ʰ 40ᵐ

Bright and Dark Nebulae	Open Star Clusters	Galaxies						Quasars
To scale <10'	To scale	10' x 5'	6' x 1'	3' x 2'	5' x 5'	4' x 2'	2' x 1'	
Planetary Nebulae	Globular Clusters							Galaxy Clusters
>100" 100"–30" <30"	To scale <5'	Plotted to scale if the major axis >2', and circular when face on or the position angle is uncertain						

220

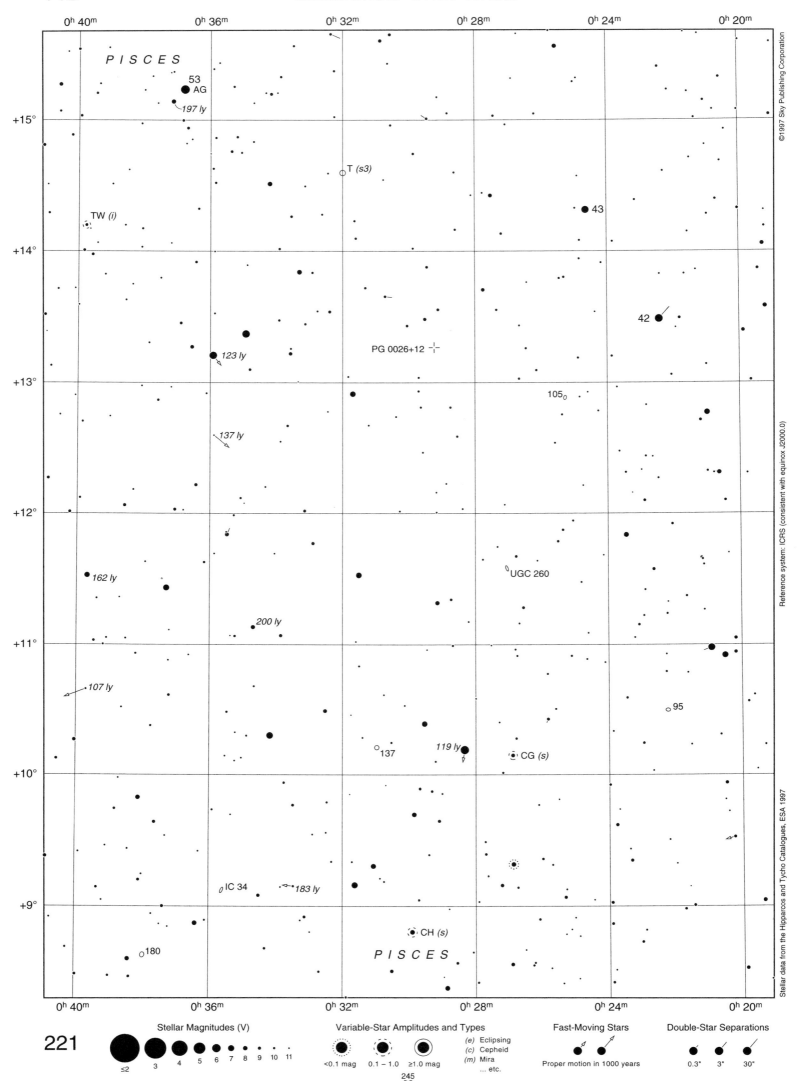

©1997 Sky Publishing Corporation

Reference system: ICRS (consistent with equinox J2000.0)

Stellar data from the Hipparcos and Tycho Catalogues, ESA 1997

PISCES

53
AG
197 ly

T (s3)

43

TW (i)

42

123 ly

PG 0026+12

105₀

137 ly

UGC 260

162 ly

200 ly

95

107 ly

137

119 ly

CG (s)

IC 34

183 ly

CH (s)

PISCES

180

Stellar Magnitudes (V)

≤2 3 4 5 6 7 8 9 10 11

Variable-Star Amplitudes and Types

<0.1 mag   0.1 – 1.0   ≥1.0 mag

(e) Eclipsing
(c) Cepheid
(m) Mira
... etc.

245

Fast-Moving Stars

Proper motion in 1000 years

Double-Star Separations

0.3"   3"   30"

MILLENNIUM STAR ATLAS

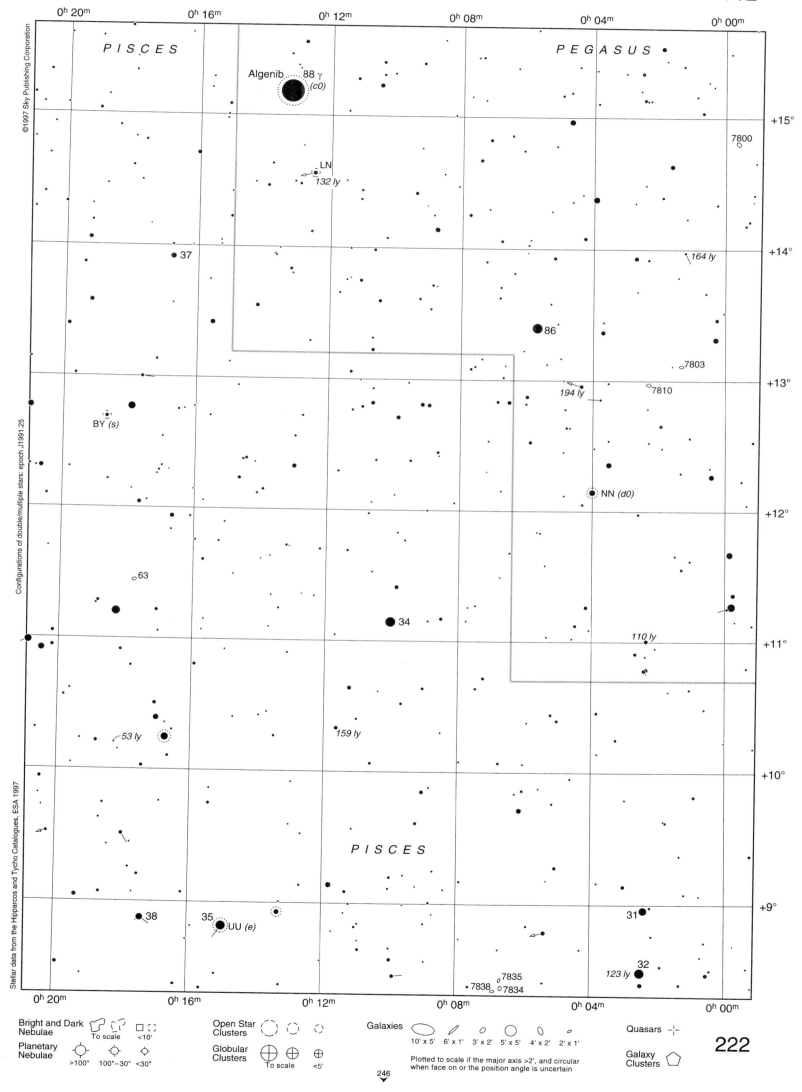

PISCES

PEGASUS

Algenib 88 γ (c0)

LN 132 ly

37

164 ly

86

7800

7803

194 ly 7810

BY (s)

NN (d0)

63

34

159 ly

110 ly

53 ly

PISCES

38

35 UU (e)

31

32 123 ly

7835
7838 7834

Bright and Dark Nebulae — To scale <10'

Planetary Nebulae — >100" 100"–30" <30"

Open Star Clusters — To scale <5'

Globular Clusters — To scale <5'

Galaxies — 10' x 5' 6' x 1' 3' x 2' 5' x 5' 4' x 2' 2' x 1'

Plotted to scale if the major axis >2', and circular when face on or the position angle is uncertain

Quasars

Galaxy Clusters

246

222

+6°

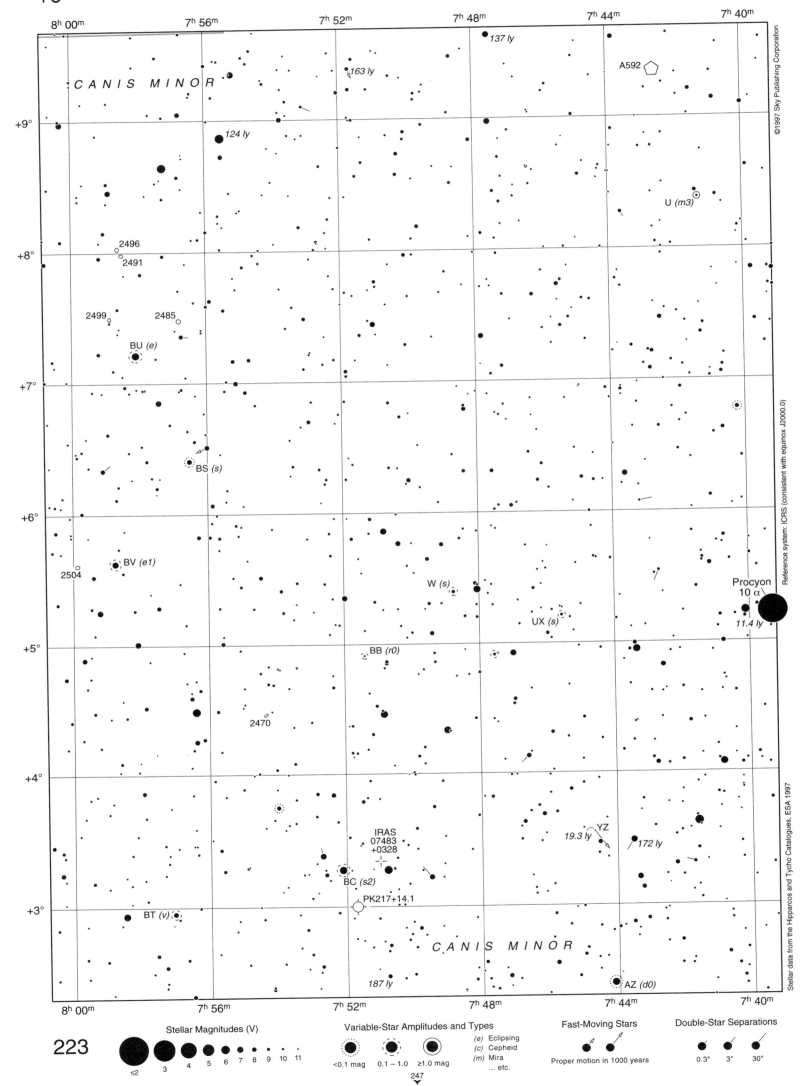

©1997 Sky Publishing Corporation

Reference system: ICRS (consistent with equinox J2000.0)

Stellar data from the Hipparcos and Tycho Catalogues, ESA 1997

CANIS MINOR

137 ly

163 ly

A592

U (m3)

124 ly

2496
2491

2499   2485

BU (e)

BS (s)

BV (e1)
2504

W (s)
Procyon
10 α
UX (s)
11.4 ly

BB (r0)

2470

IRAS
07483
+0328
YZ
19.3 ly   172 ly
BC (s2)

PK217+14.1

BT (v)

CANIS MINOR

187 ly
AZ (d0)

223

Stellar Magnitudes (V)

≤2   3   4   5   6   7   8   9   10   11

Variable-Star Amplitudes and Types

<0.1 mag   0.1 – 1.0   ≥1.0 mag

(e) Eclipsing
(c) Cepheid
(m) Mira
... etc.

Fast-Moving Stars

Proper motion in 1000 years

Double-Star Separations

0.3"   3"   30"

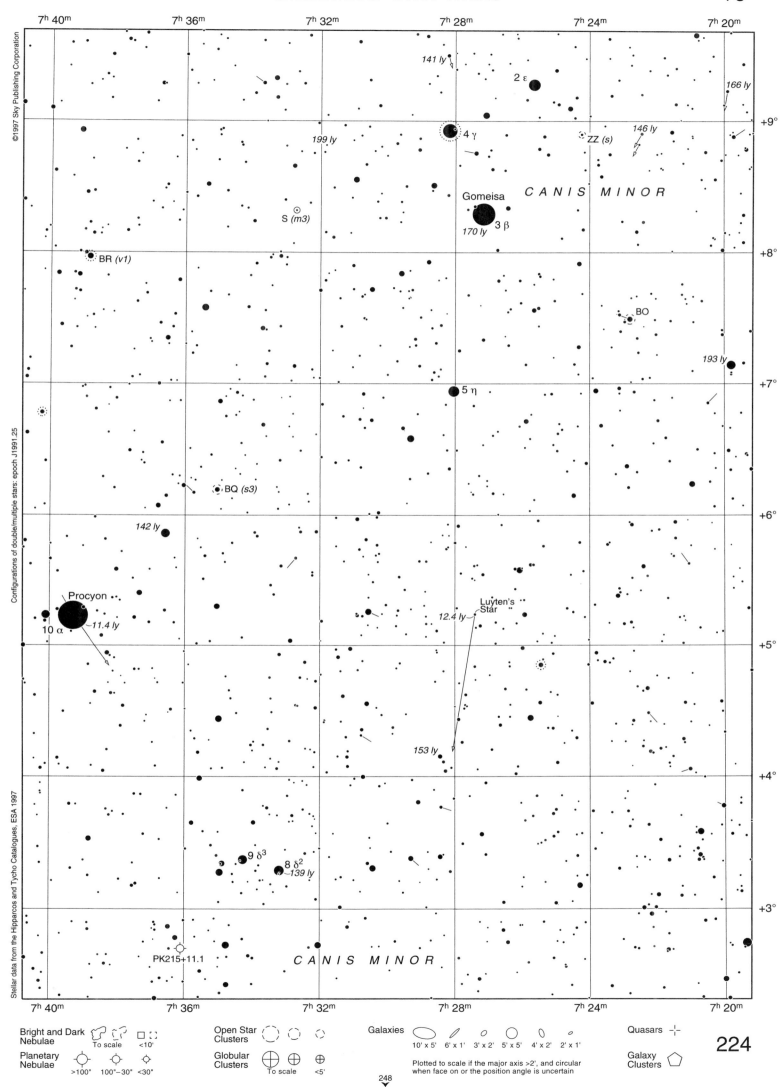

Configurations of double/multiple stars: epoch J1991.25

Stellar data from the Hipparcos and Tycho Catalogues, ESA 1997

7ʰ 40ᵐ   7ʰ 36ᵐ   7ʰ 32ᵐ   7ʰ 28ᵐ   7ʰ 24ᵐ   7ʰ 20ᵐ

+9°
+8°
+7°
+6°
+5°
+4°
+3°

141 ly

2 ε

4 γ

199 ly

ZZ (s)

146 ly

166 ly

Gomeisa

CANIS MINOR

S (m3)

3 β

170 ly

BR (v1)

BO

193 ly

5 η

BQ (s3)

142 ly

Procyon

Luyten's Star

12.4 ly

10 α

−11.4 ly

153 ly

9 δ³

8 δ²

−139 ly

PK215+11.1

CANIS MINOR

Bright and Dark
Nebulae
To scale   <10'

Planetary
Nebulae
>100" 100"–30" <30"

Open Star
Clusters

Globular
Clusters
To scale   <5'

Galaxies
10' x 5' 6' x 1' 3' x 2' 5' x 5' 4' x 2' 2' x 1'

Plotted to scale if the major axis >2', and circular
when face on or the position angle is uncertain

Quasars

Galaxy
Clusters

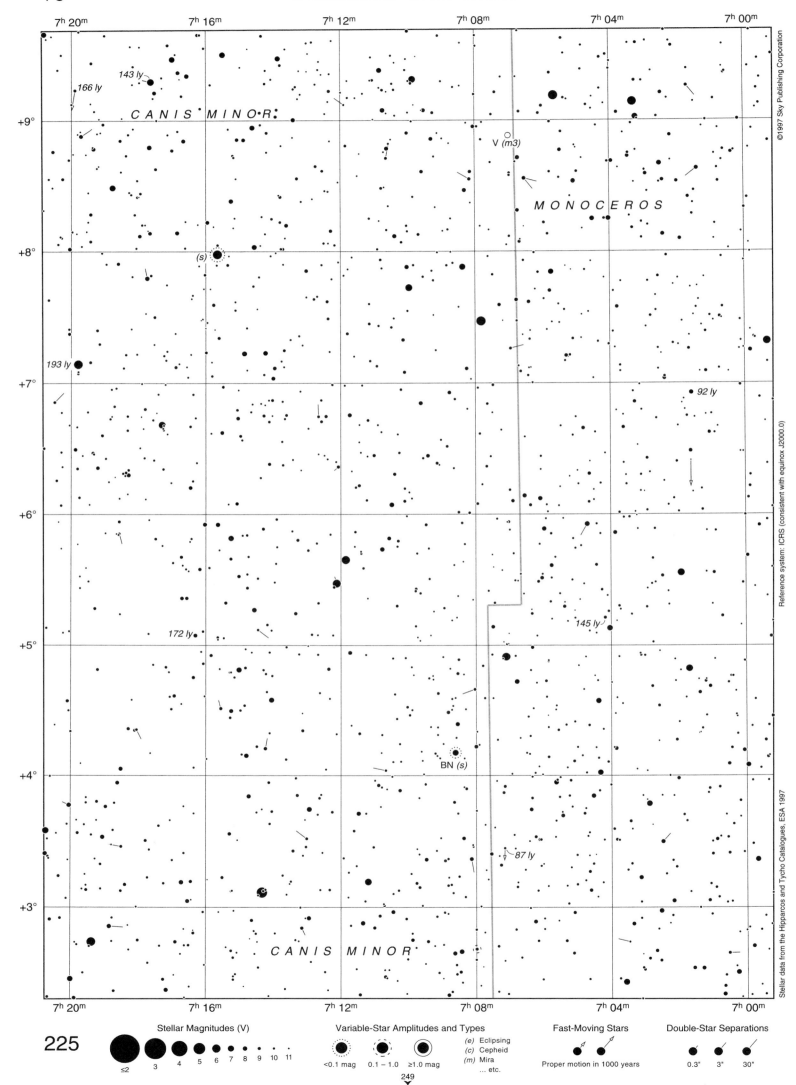

©1997 Sky Publishing Corporation

Reference system: ICRS (consistent with equinox J2000.0)

Stellar data from the Hipparcos and Tycho Catalogues, ESA 1997

CANIS MINOR

MONOCEROS

CANIS MINOR

V (m3)

BN (s)

143 ly
166 ly
193 ly
172 ly
92 ly
145 ly
87 ly

Stellar Magnitudes (V)

≤2 3 4 5 6 7 8 9 10 11

Variable-Star Amplitudes and Types

<0.1 mag   0.1 – 1.0   ≥1.0 mag

(e) Eclipsing
(c) Cepheid
(m) Mira
... etc.

Fast-Moving Stars

Proper motion in 1000 years

Double-Star Separations

0.3"   3"   30"

225

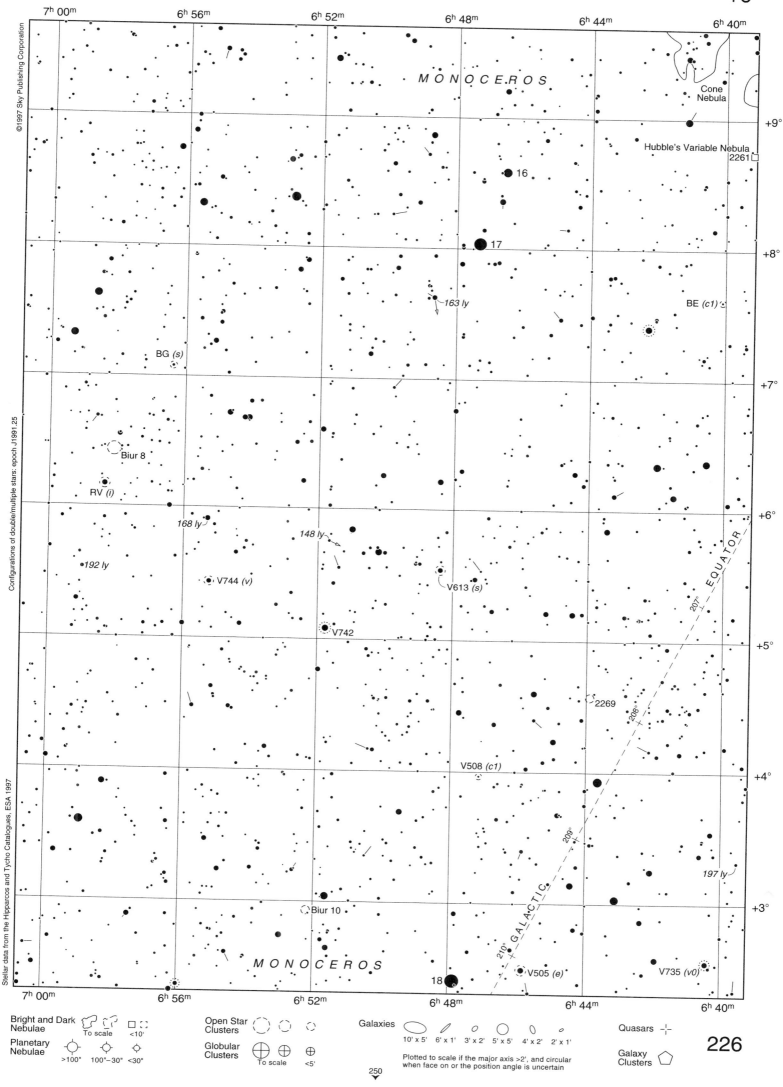

MONOCEROS

Cone Nebula

Hubble's Variable Nebula
2261

16

17

163 ly

BE (c1)

BG (s)

Biur 8

RV (i)

168 ly

148 ly

192 ly

V744 (v)

V613 (s)

V742

EQUATOR

207°

2269

208°

V508 (c1)

209°

197 ly

Biur 10

GALACTIC

MONOCEROS

210°

V505 (e)

V735 (v0)

18

Configurations of double/multiple stars: epoch J1991.25

Stellar data from the Hipparcos and Tycho Catalogues, ESA 1997

Bright and Dark Nebulae		

To scale   <10'

Open Star Clusters

Galaxies

Quasars

Planetary Nebulae

>100" 100"–30" <30"

Globular Clusters

To scale   <5'

10' x 5' 6' x 1' 3' x 2' 5' x 5' 4' x 2' 2' x 1'

Plotted to scale if the major axis >2', and circular
when face on or the position angle is uncertain

Galaxy Clusters

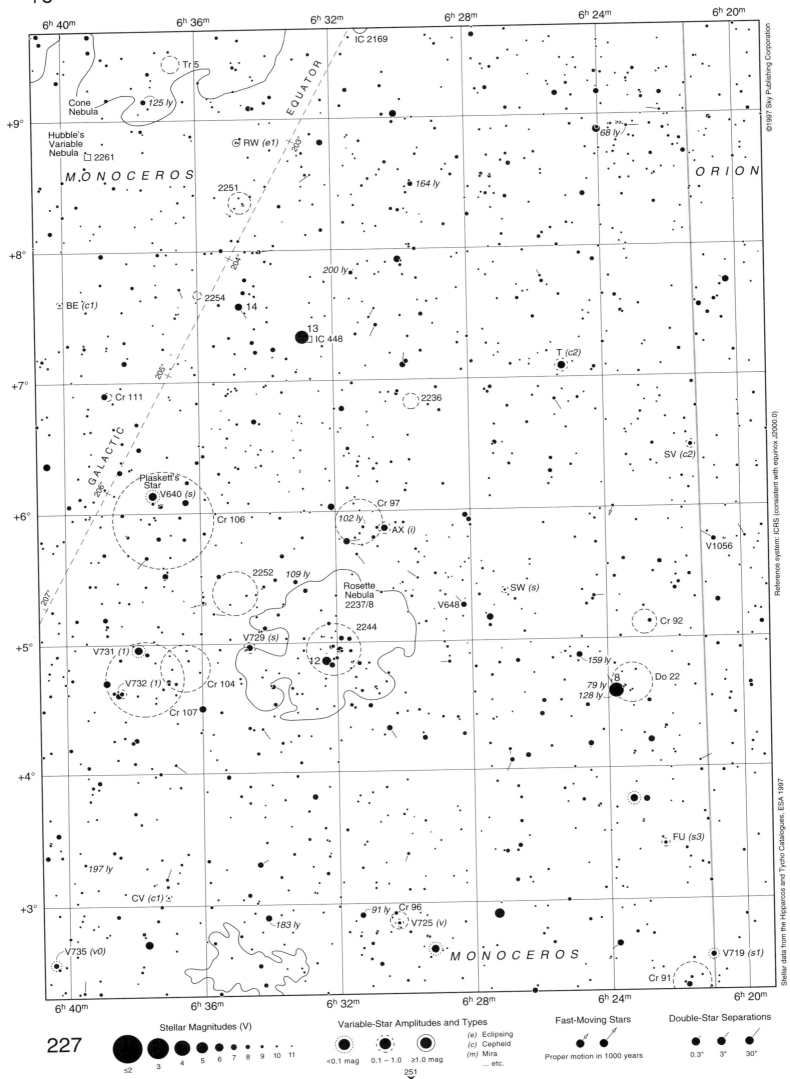

227

Stellar Magnitudes (V)

≤2 3 4 5 6 7 8 9 10 11

Variable-Star Amplitudes and Types

<0.1 mag   0.1 – 1.0   ≥1.0 mag

(e) Eclipsing
(c) Cepheid
(m) Mira
... etc.

Fast-Moving Stars

Proper motion in 1000 years

Double-Star Separations

0.3" 3" 30"

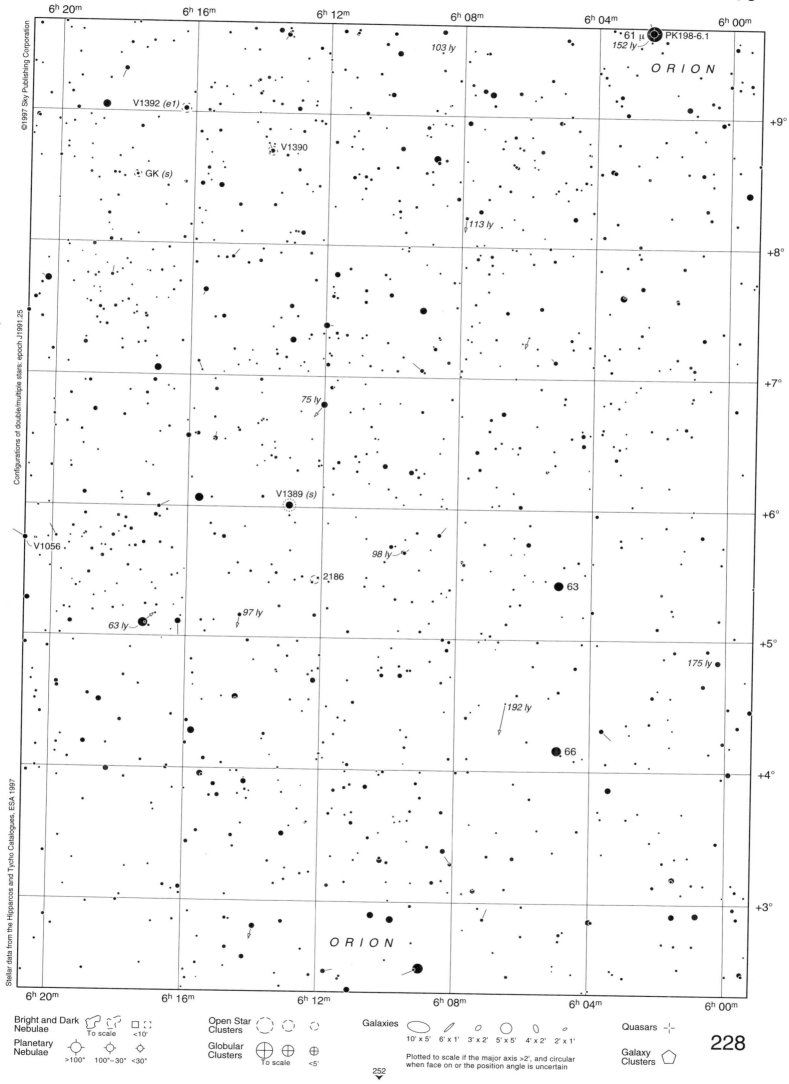

ORION

61 μ   PK198-6.1
152 ly

103 ly

V1392 (e1)

V1390

GK (s)

113 ly

75 ly

V1389 (s)

V1056

98 ly

2186

63

97 ly

63 ly

175 ly

192 ly

66

ORION

Bright and Dark Nebulae
To scale   <10'

Planetary Nebulae
>100"   100"–30"   <30"

Open Star Clusters

Globular Clusters
To scale   <5'

Galaxies
10' x 5'   6' x 1'   3' x 2'   5' x 5'   4' x 2'   2' x 1'

Plotted to scale if the major axis >2', and circular
when face on or the position angle is uncertain

Quasars

Galaxy Clusters

228

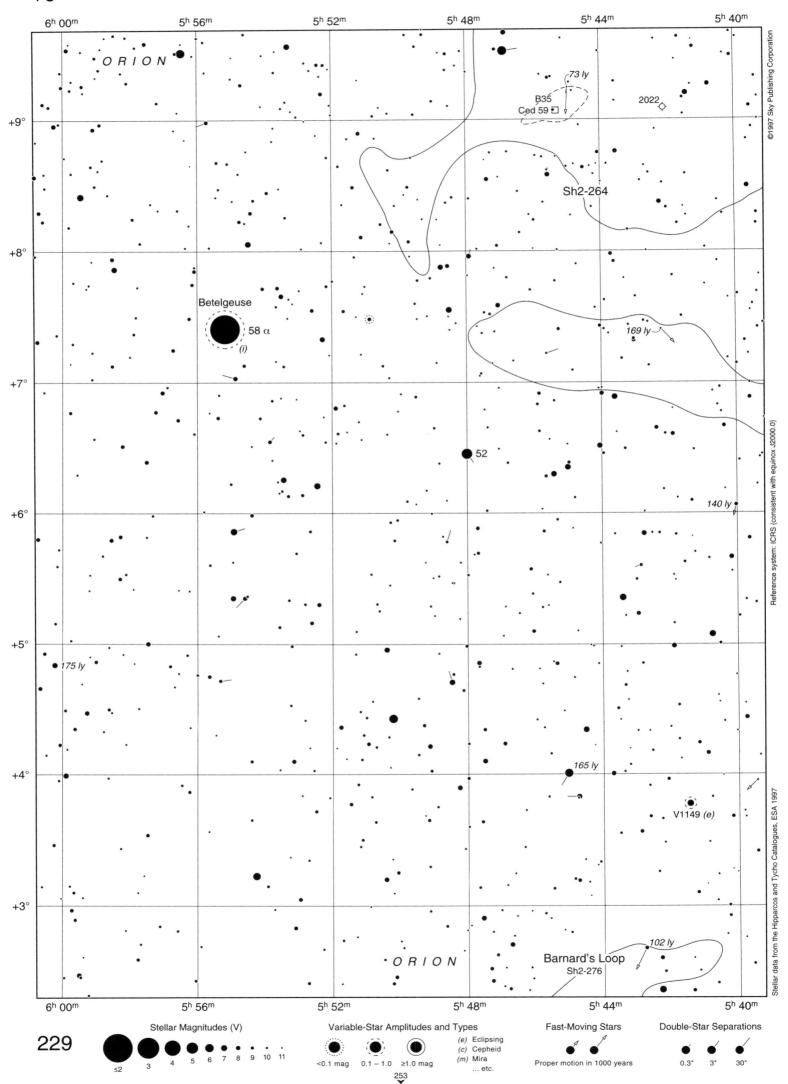

©1997 Sky Publishing Corporation

Reference system: ICRS (consistent with equinox J2000.0)

Stellar data from the Hipparcos and Tycho Catalogues, ESA 1997

ORION

Sh2-264

B35
Ced 59

2022

73 ly

Betelgeuse

58 α

(i)

52

169 ly

140 ly

175 ly

165 ly

V1149 (e)

ORION

Barnard's Loop
Sh2-276

102 ly

229

Stellar Magnitudes (V)

≤2   3   4   5   6   7   8   9   10   11

Variable-Star Amplitudes and Types

<0.1 mag   0.1 – 1.0   ≥1.0 mag

(e) Eclipsing
(c) Cepheid
(m) Mira
... etc.

Fast-Moving Stars

Proper motion in 1000 years

Double-Star Separations

0.3"   3"   30"

253

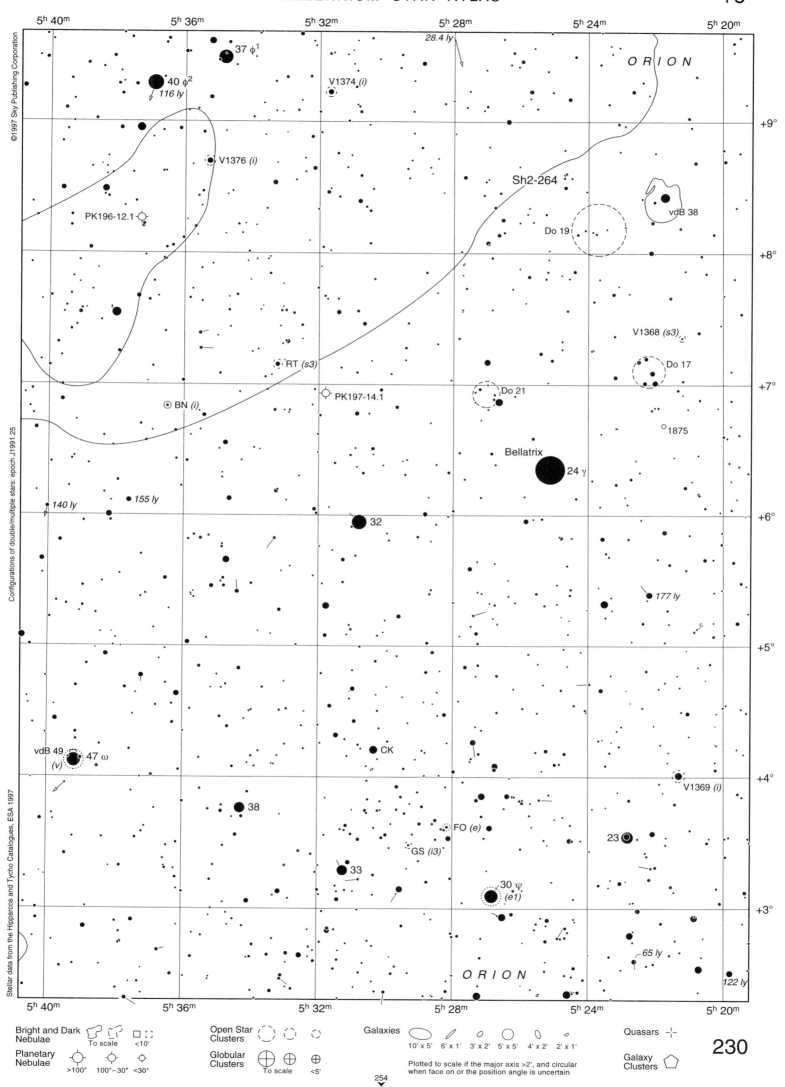

ORION

28.4 ly

Sh2-264

vdB 38

Do 19

37 φ¹

40 φ²
116 ly

V1374 (i)

V1376 (i)

PK196-12.1

V1368 (s3)

Do 17

RT (s3)

Do 21

BN (i)

PK197-14.1

1875

Bellatrix

24 γ

140 ly

155 ly

32

177 ly

vdB 49

47 ω
(v)

CK

V1369 (i)

38

23

FO (e)

GS (i3)

33

30 ψ
(e1)

65 ly

ORION

122 ly

Bright and Dark Nebulae — To scale — <10'

Planetary Nebulae — >100" — 100"–30" — <30"

Open Star Clusters

Globular Clusters — To scale — <5'

Galaxies — 10' x 5' — 6' x 1' — 3' x 2' — 5' x 5' — 4' x 2' — 2' x 1'

Plotted to scale if the major axis >2', and circular when face on or the position angle is uncertain

Quasars

Galaxy Clusters

230

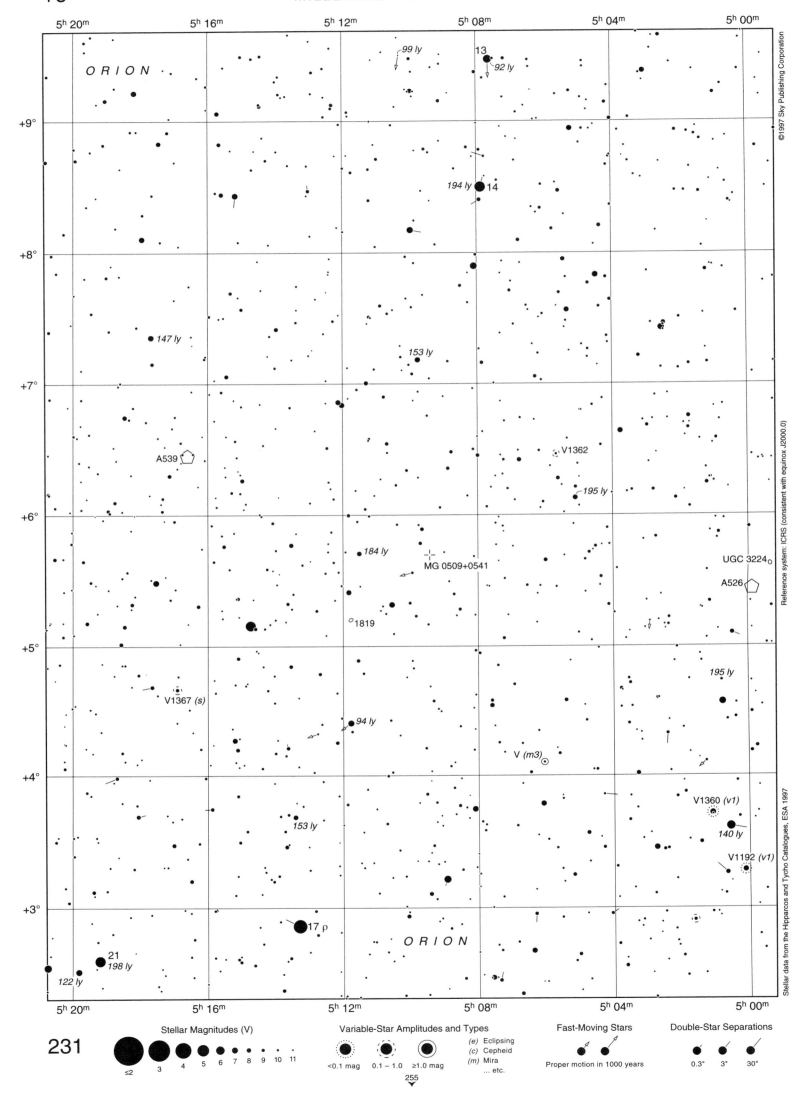

ORION

99 ly

13
92 ly

194 ly 14

147 ly

153 ly

A539

V1362

195 ly

UGC 3224

A526

184 ly

MG 0509+0541

1819

195 ly

V1367 (s)

94 ly

V (m3)

V1360 (v1)

153 ly

140 ly

V1192 (v1)

17 ρ

ORION

21
198 ly

122 ly

231

Stellar Magnitudes (V)

≤2   3   4   5   6   7   8   9 10 11

Variable-Star Amplitudes and Types

<0.1 mag   0.1 – 1.0   ≥1.0 mag

(e) Eclipsing
(c) Cepheid
(m) Mira
... etc.

Fast-Moving Stars

Proper motion in 1000 years

Double-Star Separations

0.3"   3"   30"

255

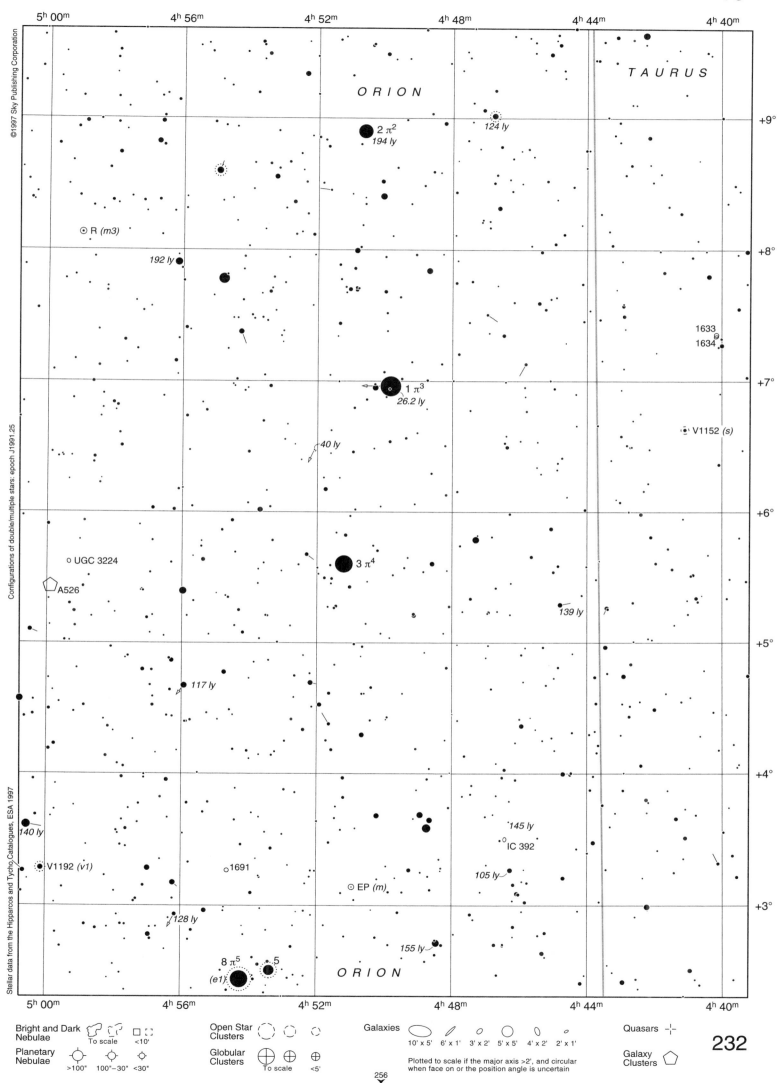

TAURUS

ORION

2 π^2
194 ly

124 ly

R (m3)

192 ly

1633
1634

1 π^3
26.2 ly

V1152 (s)

40 ly

UGC 3224

A526

3 π^4

139 ly

117 ly

140 ly

145 ly
IC 392

V1192 (v1)

1691

105 ly

EP (m)

128 ly

155 ly

8 π^5 5

(e1)

ORION

Bright and Dark Nebulae			

To scale   <10'

Planetary Nebulae

>100"   100"–30"   <30"

Open Star Clusters

Globular Clusters

To scale   <5'

Galaxies

10' x 5'   6' x 1'   3' x 2'   5' x 5'   4' x 2'   2' x 1'

Plotted to scale if the major axis >2', and circular when face on or the position angle is uncertain

Quasars

Galaxy Clusters

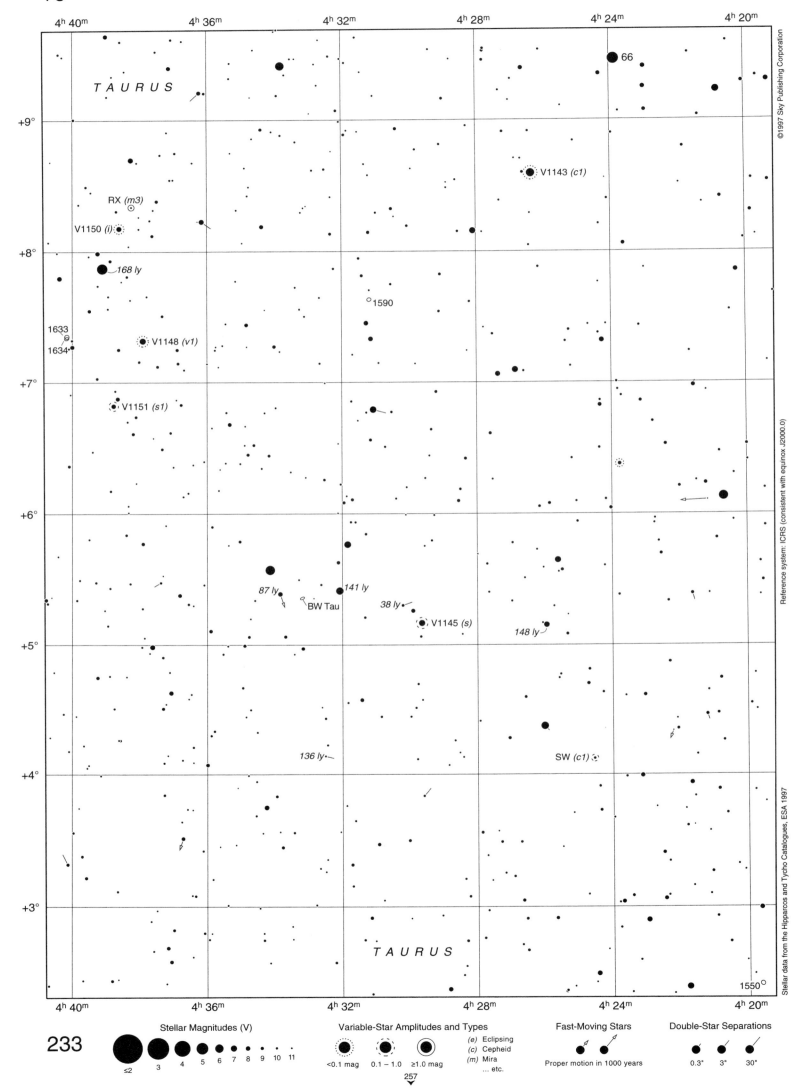

©1997 Sky Publishing Corporation

Reference system: ICRS (consistent with equinox J2000.0)

Stellar data from the Hipparcos and Tycho Catalogues, ESA 1997

TAURUS

66

V1143 (c1)

RX (m3)

V1150 (i)

168 ly

○ 1590

1633
1634

V1148 (v1)

V1151 (s1)

87 ly

141 ly

BW Tau

38 ly

V1145 (s)

148 ly

136 ly

SW (c1)

TAURUS

1550 ○

Stellar Magnitudes (V)

≤2   3   4   5   6 7 8 9 10 11

Variable-Star Amplitudes and Types

<0.1 mag   0.1 – 1.0   ≥1.0 mag

(e) Eclipsing
(c) Cepheid
(m) Mira
... etc.

Fast-Moving Stars

Proper motion in 1000 years

Double-Star Separations

0.3"   3"   30"

210

+6°

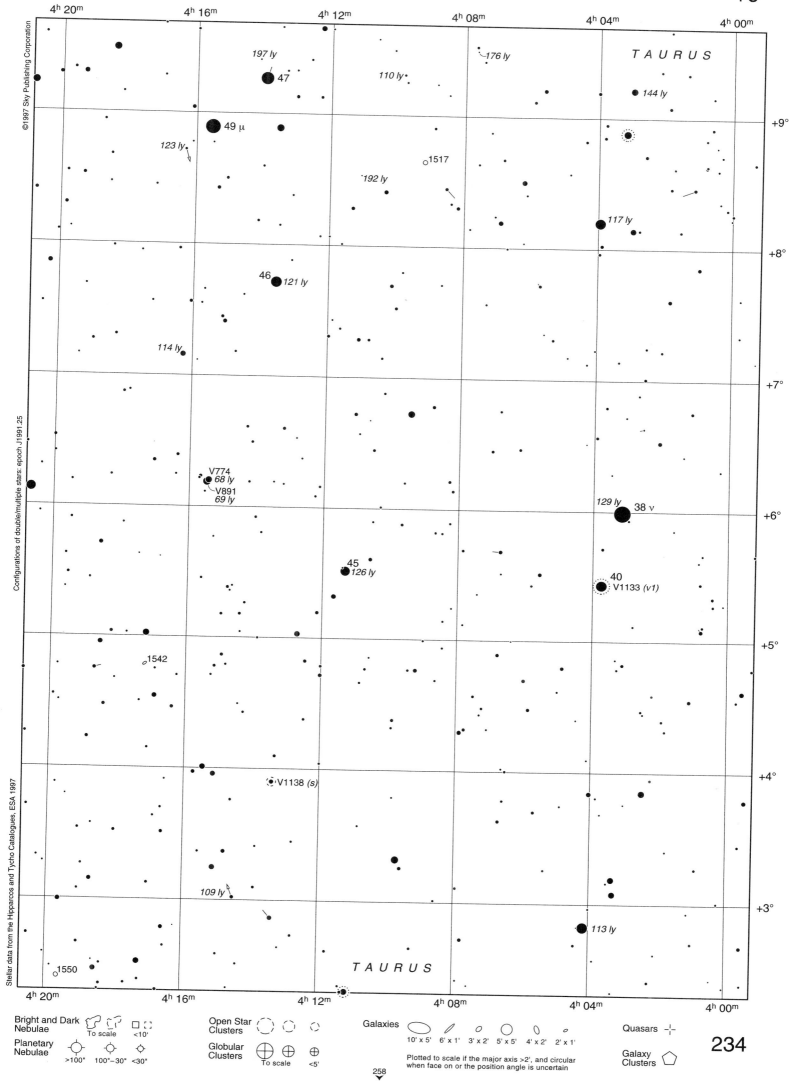

Configurations of double/multiple stars: epoch J1991.25

Stellar data from the Hipparcos and Tycho Catalogues, ESA 1997

4ʰ 20ᵐ   4ʰ 16ᵐ   4ʰ 12ᵐ   4ʰ 08ᵐ   4ʰ 04ᵐ   4ʰ 00ᵐ

T A U R U S

197 ly
47
49 μ
123 ly
46 121 ly
114 ly
V774
68 ly
V891
69 ly
45
126 ly
1542
V1138 (s)
109 ly
1550

176 ly
110 ly
1517
192 ly

144 ly
117 ly
129 ly   38 ν
40
V1133 (v1)
113 ly

+9°
+8°
+7°
+6°
+5°
+4°
+3°

T A U R U S

Bright and Dark Nebulae
To scale   <10'

Planetary Nebulae
>100"   100"–30"   <30"

Open Star Clusters

Globular Clusters
To scale   <5'

Galaxies
10' x 5'   6' x 1'   3' x 2'   5' x 5'   4' x 2'   2' x 1'

Plotted to scale if the major axis >2', and circular when face on or the position angle is uncertain

Quasars

Galaxy Clusters

258

234

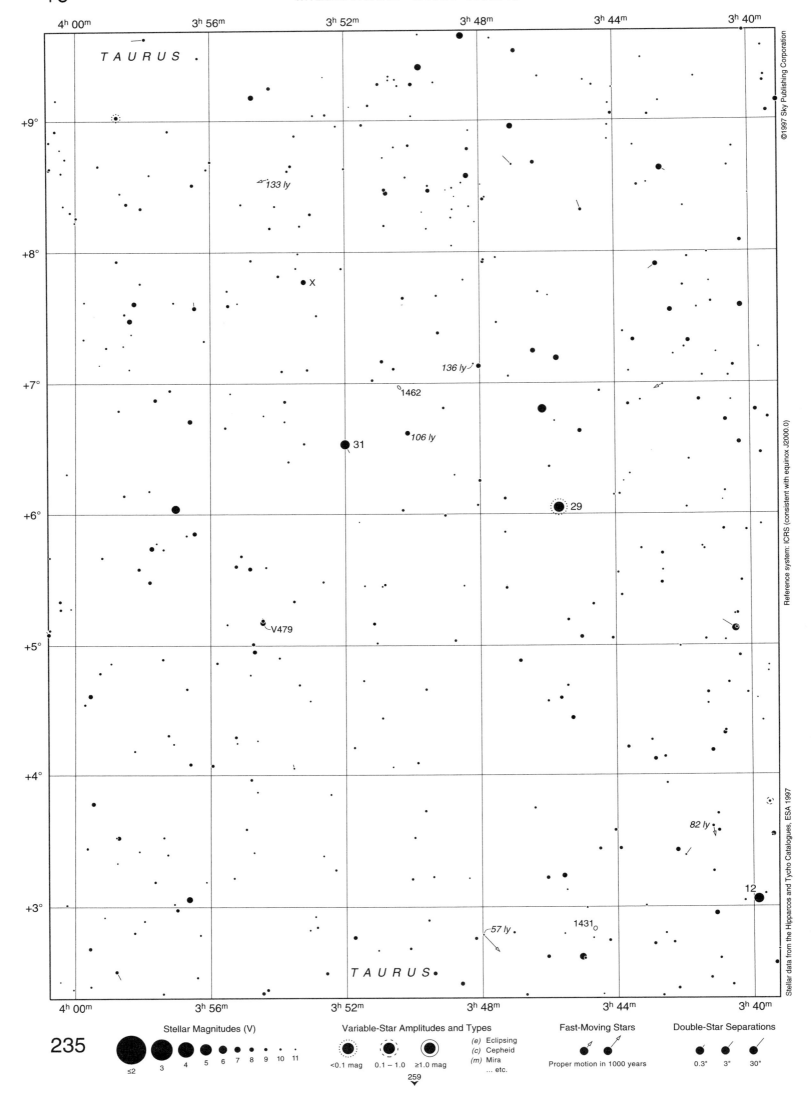

TAURUS

+9°

133 ly

+8°

X

136 ly

+7°

1462

106 ly

31

29

+6°

V479

+5°

82 ly

12

+4°

1431

57 ly

+3°

TAURUS

©1997 Sky Publishing Corporation

Reference system: ICRS (consistent with equinox J2000.0)

Stellar data from the Hipparcos and Tycho Catalogues, ESA 1997

Stellar Magnitudes (V)

≤2 3 4 5 6 7 8 9 10 11

Variable-Star Amplitudes and Types

<0.1 mag   0.1 – 1.0   ≥1.0 mag

(e) Eclipsing
(c) Cepheid
(m) Mira
... etc.

Fast-Moving Stars

Proper motion in 1000 years

Double-Star Separations

0.3"   3"   30"

259

MILLENNIUM STAR ATLAS

+6°

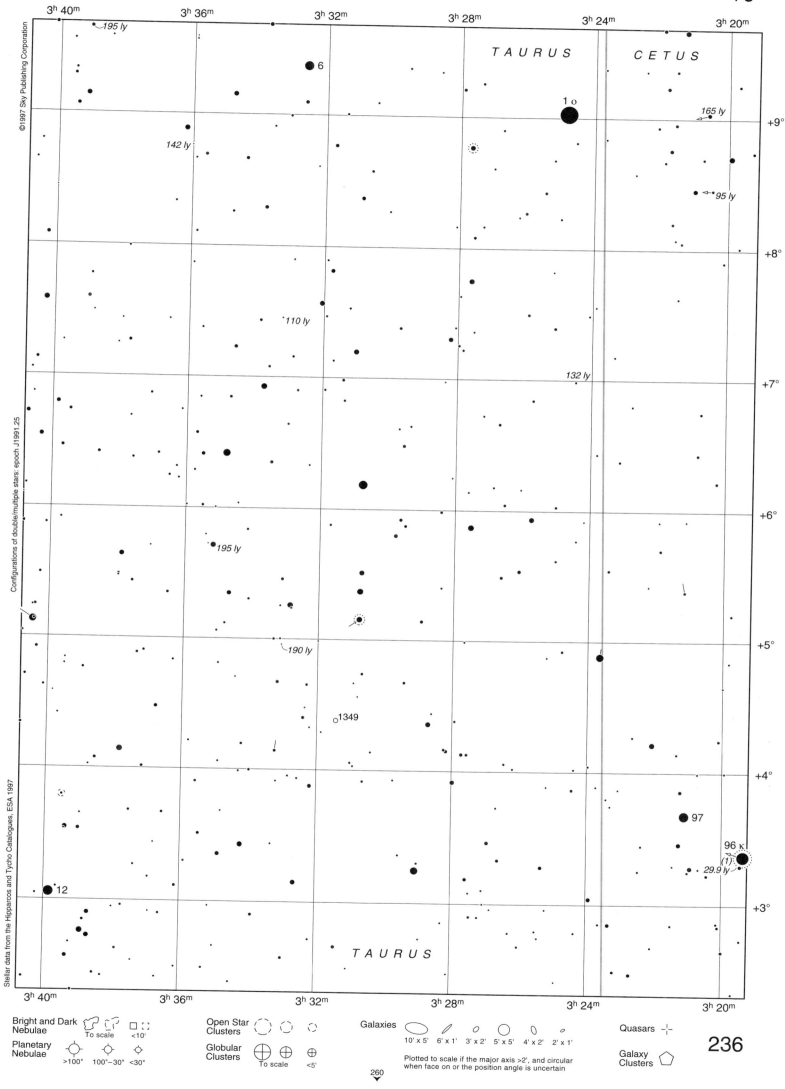

Configurations of double/multiple stars: epoch J1991.25

Stellar data from the Hipparcos and Tycho Catalogues, ESA 1997

T A U R U S *C E T U S*

T A U R U S

3ʰ 40ᵐ	3ʰ 36ᵐ	3ʰ 32ᵐ	3ʰ 28ᵐ	3ʰ 24ᵐ	3ʰ 20ᵐ

195 ly
6
1 ο
142 ly
165 ly
95 ly
110 ly
132 ly
195 ly
190 ly
1349
97
96 κ
(1)
29.9 ly
12

+9°
+8°
+7°
+6°
+5°
+4°
+3°

Bright and Dark Nebulae   To scale   <10'

Planetary Nebulae   >100"   100"–30"   <30"

Open Star Clusters

Globular Clusters   To scale   <5'

Galaxies   10' x 5'   6' x 1'   3' x 2'   5' x 5'   4' x 2'   2' x 1'

Plotted to scale if the major axis >2', and circular when face on or the position angle is uncertain

Quasars –|–

Galaxy Clusters

236

260

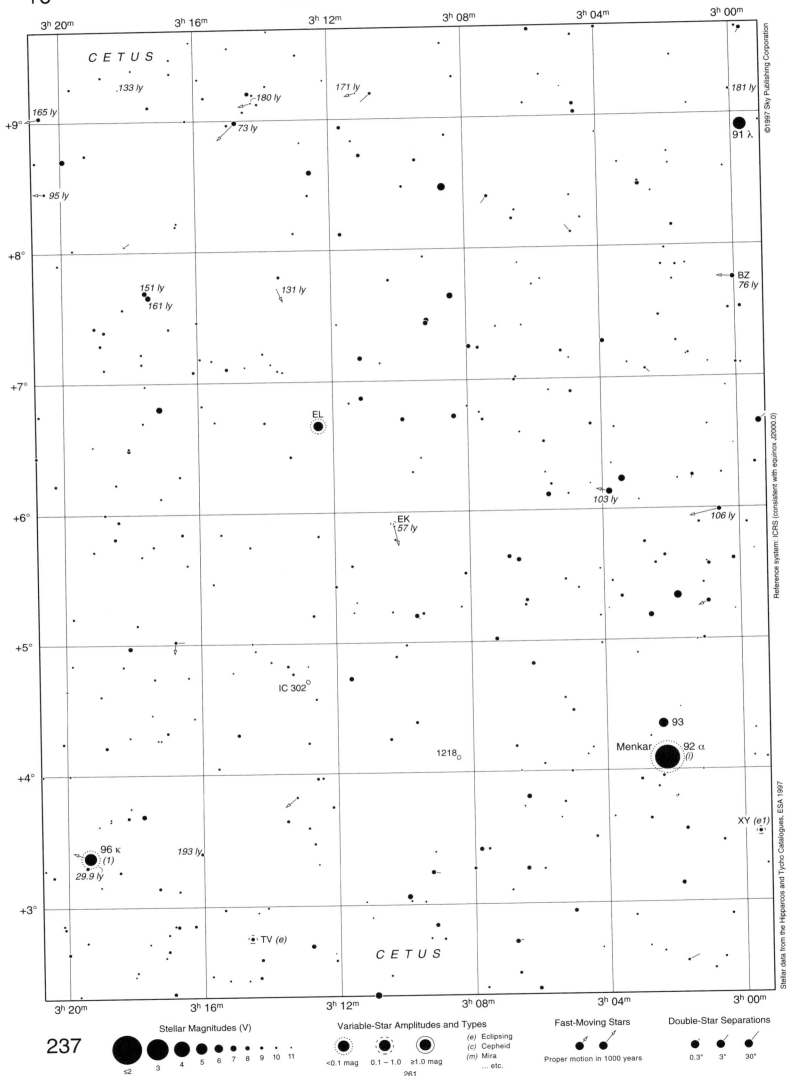

CETUS

3h 20m   3h 16m   3h 12m   3h 08m   3h 04m   3h 00m

.133 ly

165 ly   180 ly
+9°   171 ly   181 ly
              73 ly   91 λ

95 ly

+8°   BZ
                    151 ly   131 ly   76 ly
                    161 ly

+7°
                              EL

+6°   103 ly
                    EK   106 ly
                    57 ly

+5°

                    IC 302

                                                           93
+4°   1218   Menkar   92 α
                                                       (i)

                                                                        XY (e1)
         96 κ
            (1)   193 ly
+3°   29.9 ly

                              TV (e)

CETUS

3h 20m   3h 16m   3h 12m   3h 08m   3h 04m   3h 00m

©1997 Sky Publishing Corporation

Reference system: ICRS (consistent with equinox J2000.0)

Stellar data from the Hipparcos and Tycho Catalogues, ESA 1997

Stellar Magnitudes (V)

5   6   7   8   9   10 11

≤2   3   4

Variable-Star Amplitudes and Types

<0.1 mag   0.1 – 1.0   ≥1.0 mag

(e) Eclipsing
(c) Cepheid
(m) Mira
... etc.

Fast-Moving Stars

Proper motion in 1000 years

Double-Star Separations

0.3"   3"   30"

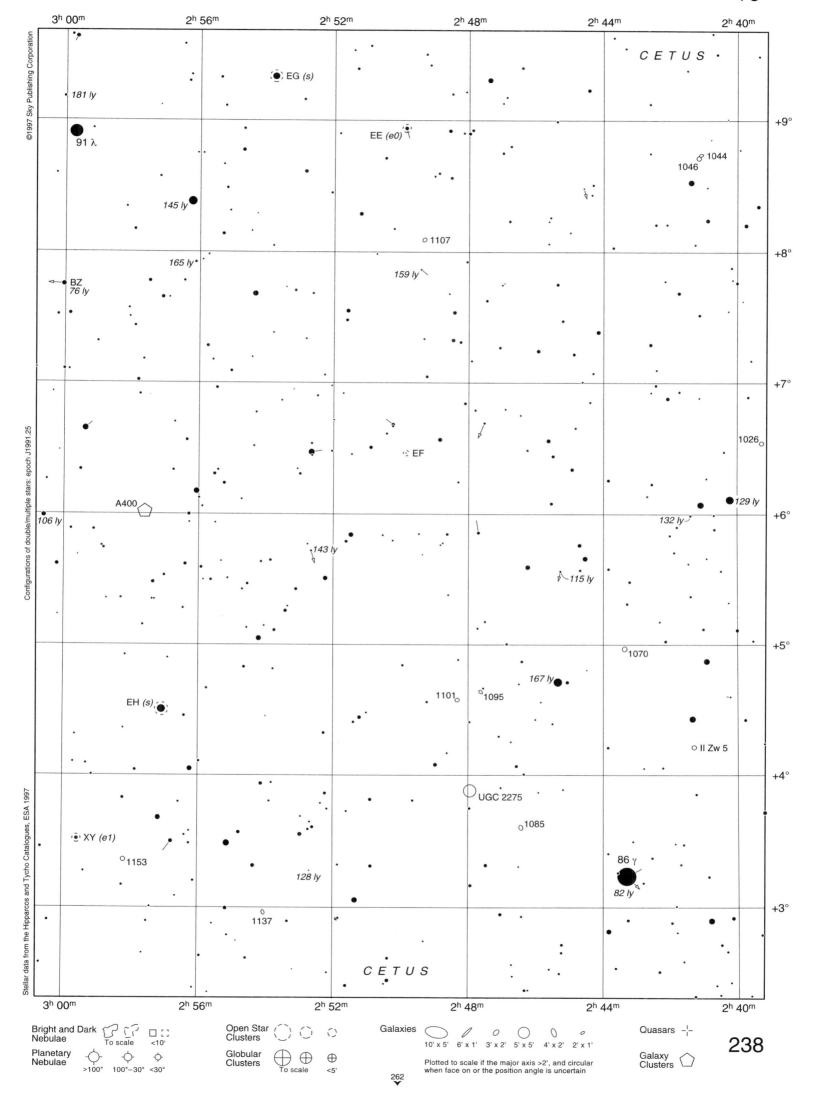

CETUS

EG (s)

181 ly

+9°

91 λ

EE (e0)

145 ly

1046 ♂ 1044

○ 1107

+8°

165 ly

159 ly

BZ
76 ly

1026 ○

EF

+6°

A400

129 ly

106 ly

132 ly

143 ly

115 ly

+5°

○ 1070

EH (s)

167 ly

1101 ○ ○ 1095

○ II Zw 5

+4°

UGC 2275

○ 1085

XY (e1)

○ 1153

86 γ

128 ly

82 ly

+3°

○ 1137

CETUS

3h 00m   2h 56m   2h 52m   2h 48m   2h 44m   2h 40m

Bright and Dark
Nebulae   To scale   <10'

Planetary
Nebulae   >100" 100"–30" <30"

Open Star
Clusters

Globular
Clusters   To scale   <5'

Galaxies

10' x 5' 6' x 1' 3' x 2' 5' x 5' 4' x 2' 2' x 1'

Plotted to scale if the major axis >2', and circular
when face on or the position angle is uncertain

Quasars

Galaxy
Clusters

238

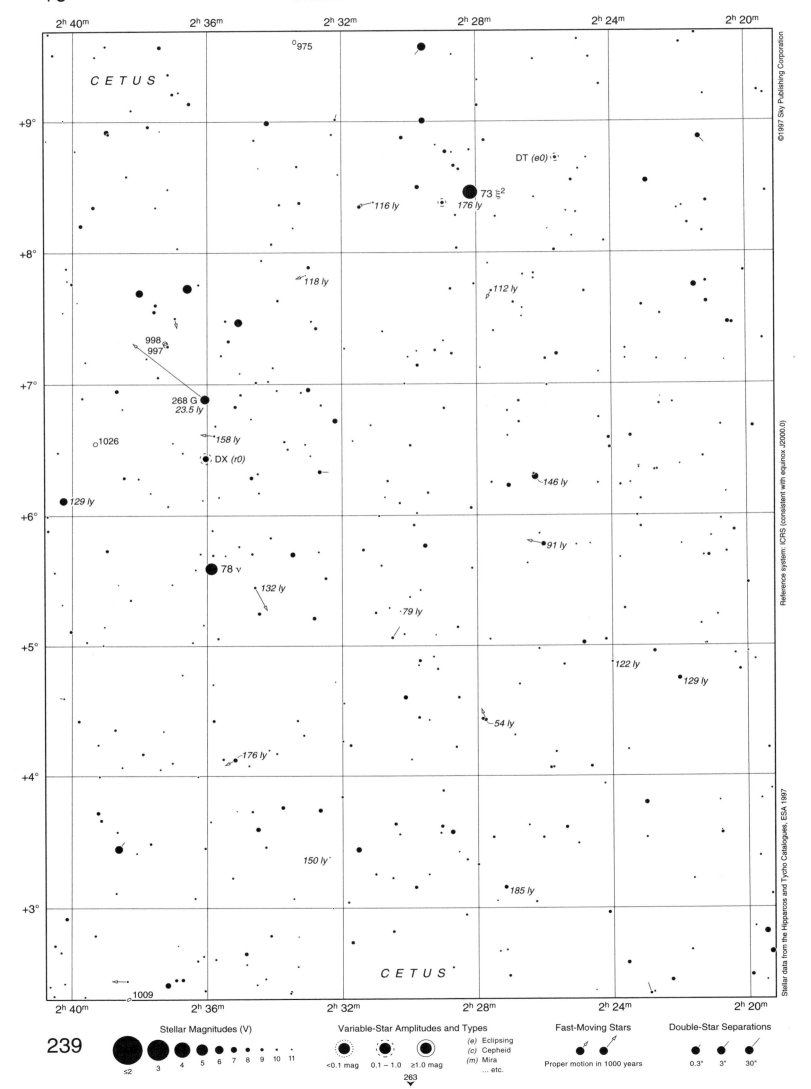

C E T U S

DT (e0)

116 ly

176 ly

73 ξ²

118 ly

112 ly

998
997

268 G
23.5 ly

1026

158 ly

DX (r0)

146 ly

129 ly

91 ly

78 ν

132 ly

79 ly

122 ly

129 ly

54 ly

176 ly

150 ly

185 ly

C E T U S

1009

©1997 Sky Publishing Corporation

Reference system: ICRS (consistent with equinox J2000.0)

Stellar data from the Hipparcos and Tycho Catalogues, ESA 1997

239

Stellar Magnitudes (V)

≤2   3   4   5   6   7   8   9   10   11

Variable-Star Amplitudes and Types

<0.1 mag   0.1 – 1.0   ≥1.0 mag

(e) Eclipsing
(c) Cepheid
(m) Mira
... etc.

Fast-Moving Stars

Proper motion in 1000 years

Double-Star Separations

0.3"   3"   30"

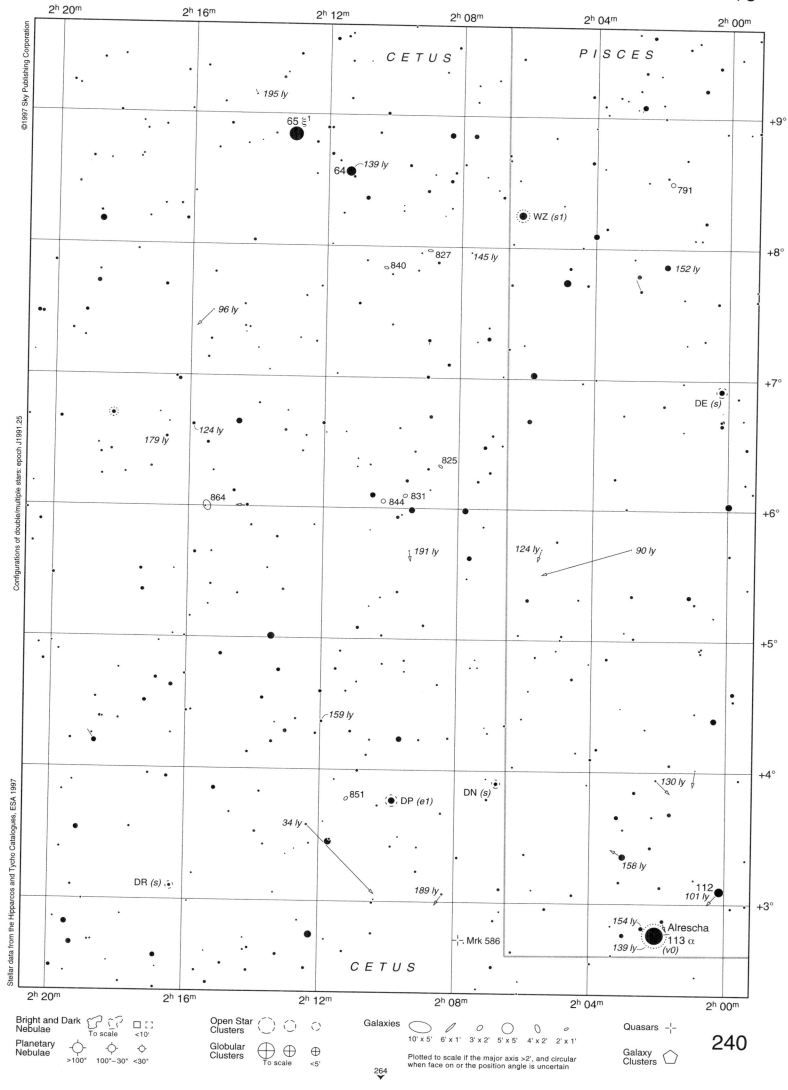

2ʰ20ᵐ   2ʰ16ᵐ   2ʰ12ᵐ   2ʰ08ᵐ   2ʰ04ᵐ   2ʰ00ᵐ

©1997 Sky Publishing Corporation

CETUS   *PISCES*

195 ly

65 ξ¹

64   *139 ly*

○ 791

WZ *(s1)*

○ 827   *145 ly*
○ 840

● *152 ly*

96 ly

+9°

+8°

Configurations of double/multiple stars: epoch J1991.25

DE *(s)*

179 ly   *124 ly*

○ 825

864   ○ 844 ○ 831

+7°

+6°

191 ly   *124 ly*   *90 ly*

Stellar data from the Hipparcos and Tycho Catalogues, ESA 1997

159 ly

+5°

+4°

130 ly

○ 851   DP *(e1)*   DN *(s)*

34 ly

158 ly

DR *(s)*

112
101 ly

189 ly

154 ly   Alrescha
┼ Mrk 586   113 α
139 ly   *(v0)*

+3°

CETUS

2ʰ20ᵐ   2ʰ16ᵐ   2ʰ12ᵐ   2ʰ08ᵐ   2ʰ04ᵐ   2ʰ00ᵐ

Bright and Dark Nebulae
To scale   <10'

Planetary Nebulae
>100"   100"–30"   <30"

Open Star Clusters

Globular Clusters
To scale   <5'

Galaxies
10' x 5'   6' x 1'   3' x 2'   5' x 5'   4' x 2'   2' x 1'
Plotted to scale if the major axis >2', and circular when face on or the position angle is uncertain

Quasars

Galaxy Clusters

240

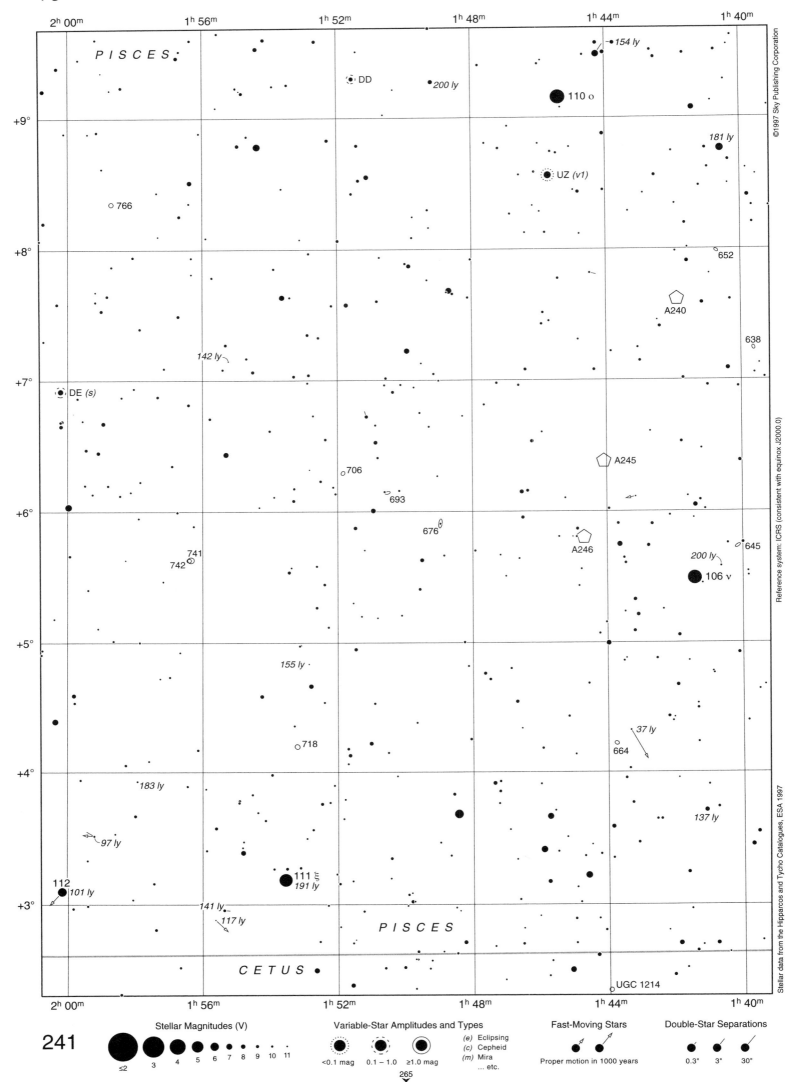

PISCES

DD

200 ly

154 ly

110 o

181 ly

UZ (v1)

766

652

A240

638

142 ly

DE (s)

A245

706

693

676

A246

741
742

200 ly

645

106 ν

155 ly

718

37 ly

664

183 ly

137 ly

97 ly

112
101 ly

111 ξ
191 ly

141 ly

117 ly

PISCES

CETUS

UGC 1214

2ʰ 00ᵐ   1ʰ 56ᵐ   1ʰ 52ᵐ   1ʰ 48ᵐ   1ʰ 44ᵐ   1ʰ 40ᵐ

241

Stellar Magnitudes (V)

≤2   3   4   5   6   7   8   9   10   11

Variable-Star Amplitudes and Types

<0.1 mag   0.1 – 1.0   ≥1.0 mag

(e) Eclipsing
(c) Cepheid
(m) Mira
... etc.

Fast-Moving Stars

Proper motion in 1000 years

Double-Star Separations

0.3"   3"   30"

265

MILLENNIUM STAR ATLAS

+6°

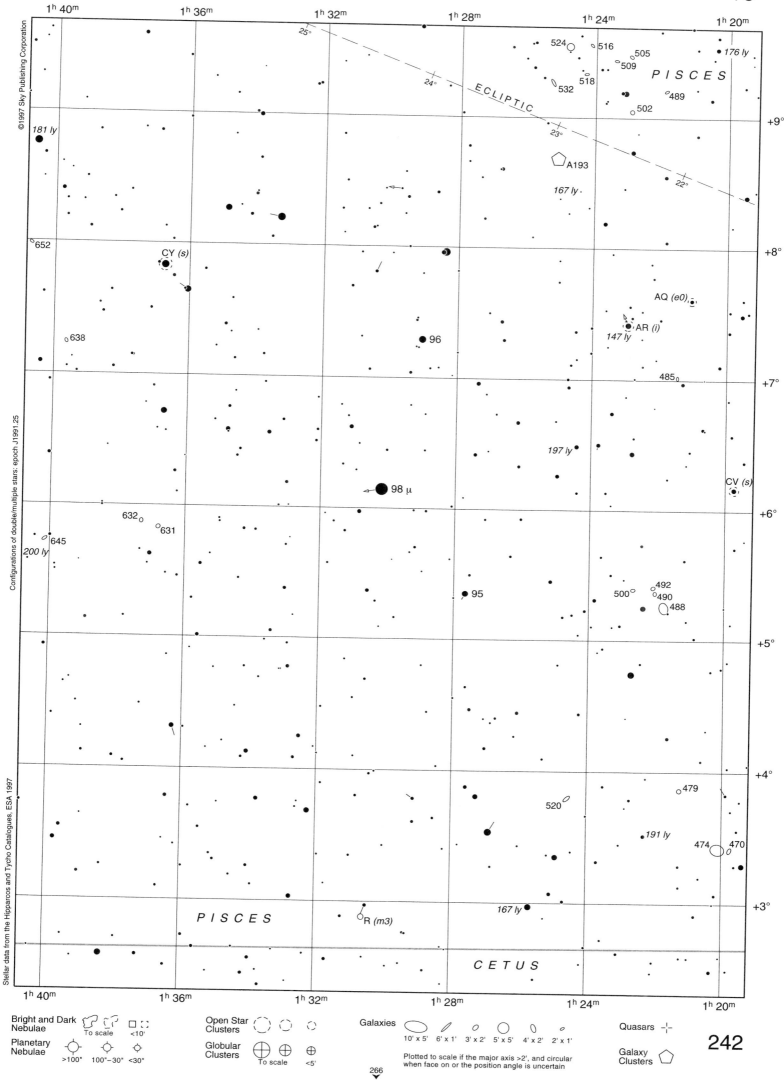

Configurations of double/multiple stars: epoch J1991.25

Stellar data from the Hipparcos and Tycho Catalogues, ESA 1997

1ʰ 40ᵐ   1ʰ 36ᵐ   1ʰ 32ᵐ   1ʰ 28ᵐ   1ʰ 24ᵐ   1ʰ 20ᵐ

PISCES

ECLIPTIC

CETUS

+9°   +8°   +7°   +6°   +5°   +4°   +3°

Bright and Dark Nebulae — To scale   <10'

Planetary Nebulae — >100"   100"–30"   <30"

Open Star Clusters — To scale   <10'

Globular Clusters — To scale   <5'

Galaxies — 10' x 5'   6' x 1'   3' x 2'   5' x 5'   4' x 2'   2' x 1'

Plotted to scale if the major axis >2', and circular when face on or the position angle is uncertain

Quasars

Galaxy Clusters

242

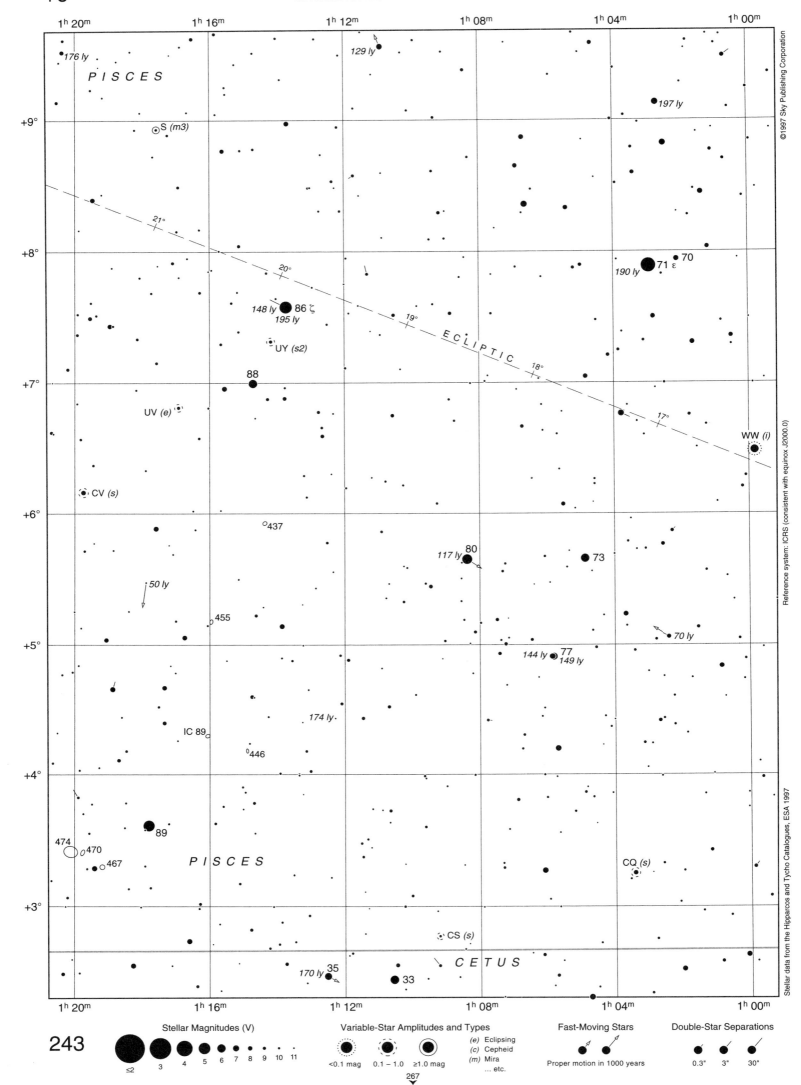

243

Stellar Magnitudes (V)

≤2 3 4 5 6 7 8 9 10 11

Variable-Star Amplitudes and Types

<0.1 mag   0.1 – 1.0   ≥1.0 mag

(e) Eclipsing
(c) Cepheid
(m) Mira
... etc.

Fast-Moving Stars

Proper motion in 1000 years

Double-Star Separations

0.3"   3"   30"

267

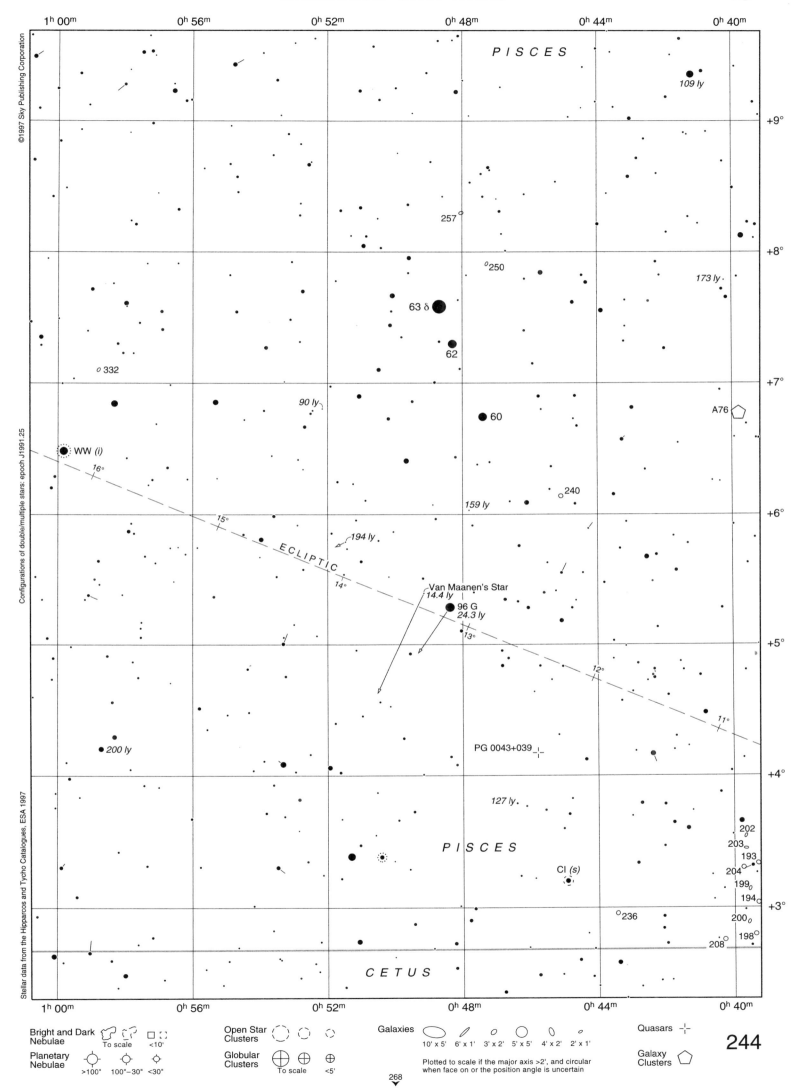

PISCES

257
250
63 δ
62
o 332
90 ly
60
A76
WW (i)
16°
240
15°
159 ly
ECLIPTIC
194 ly
14°
Van Maanen's Star
14.4 ly
96 G
24.3 ly
13°
12°
11°
200 ly
PG 0043+039
127 ly
PISCES
202
203
193
Cl (s)
204
199
194
236
200
208
198
+9°
+8°
+7°
+6°
+5°
+4°
+3°

CETUS

173 ly
109 ly

Bright and Dark Nebulae	To scale <10'	
Planetary Nebulae	>100" 100"–30" <30"	
Open Star Clusters	To scale	
Globular Clusters	To scale <5'	
Galaxies	10' x 5' 6' x 1' 3' x 2' 5' x 5' 4' x 2' 2' x 1'	
Quasars		
Galaxy Clusters		

Plotted to scale if the major axis >2', and circular when face on or the position angle is uncertain

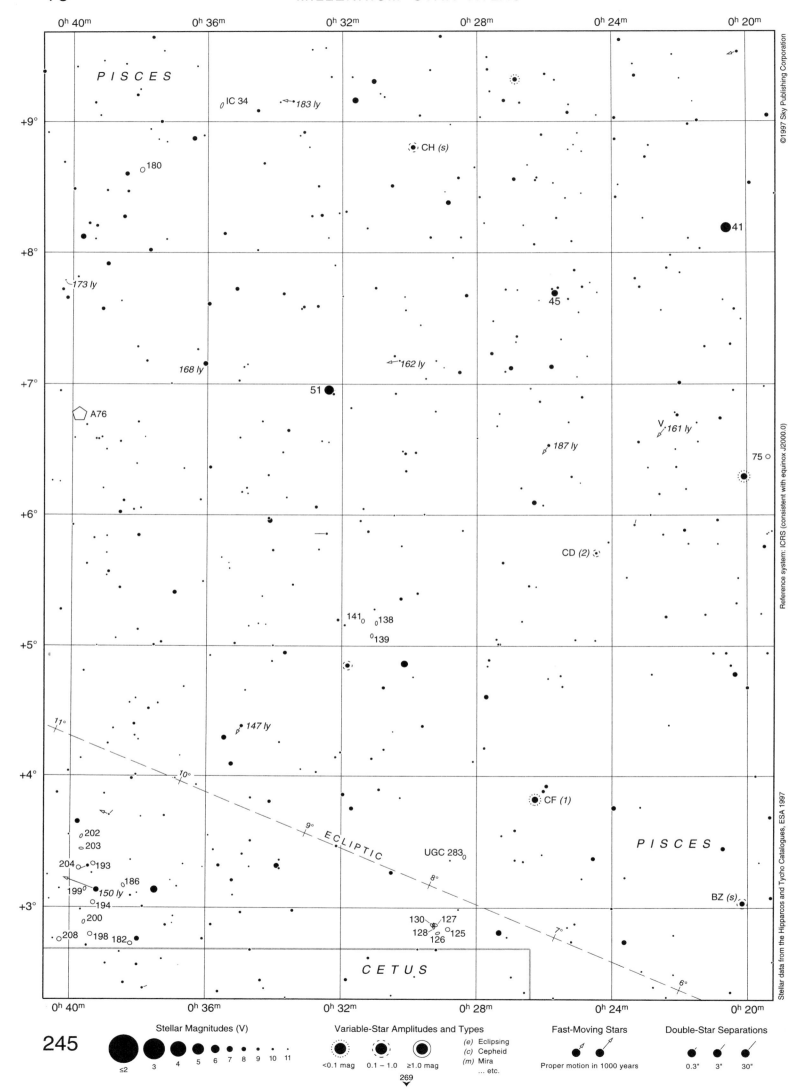

©1997 Sky Publishing Corporation

Reference system: ICRS (consistent with equinox J2000.0)

Stellar data from the Hipparcos and Tycho Catalogues, ESA 1997

245

Stellar Magnitudes (V)

≤2   3   4   5   6 7 8 9 10 11

Variable-Star Amplitudes and Types

<0.1 mag   0.1 – 1.0   ≥1.0 mag

(e) Eclipsing
(c) Cepheid
(m) Mira
... etc.

Fast-Moving Stars

Proper motion in 1000 years

Double-Star Separations

0.3"   3"   30"

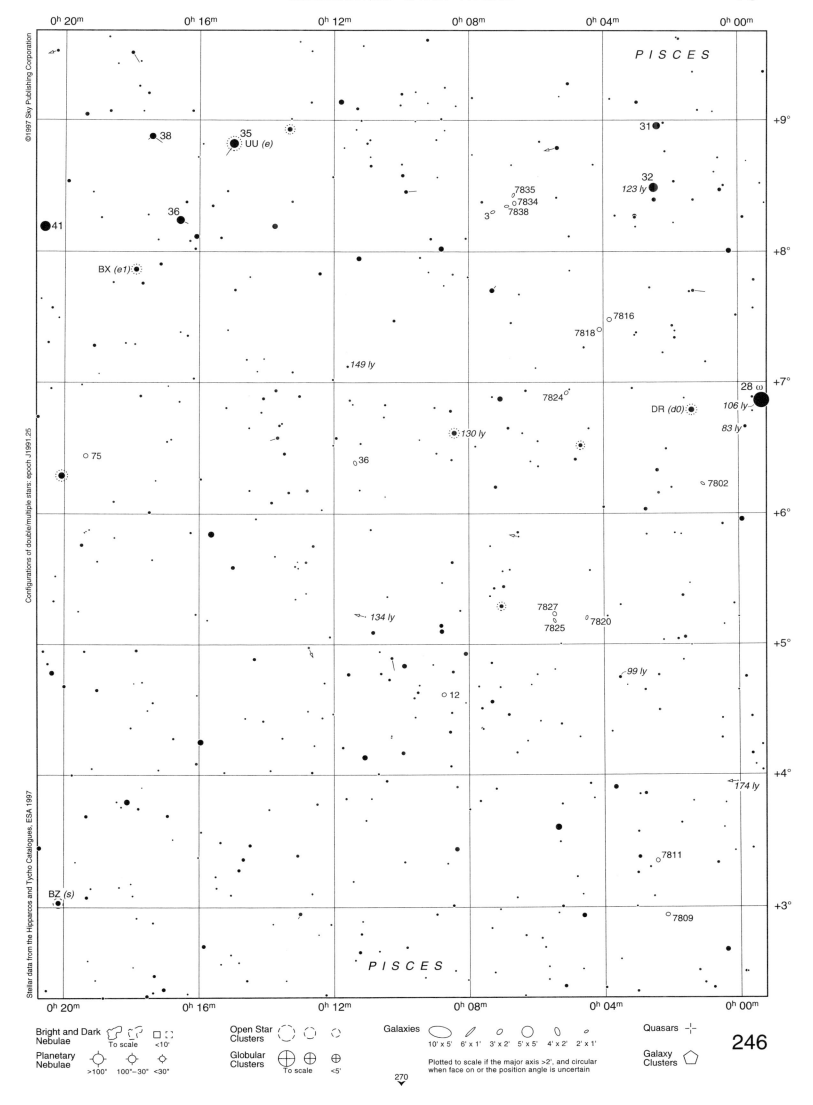

P I S C E S

31

32
123 ly

7835
7834
3
7838

BX *(e1)*

7816

7818

149 ly

28 ω
106 ly

DR *(d0)*

83 ly

7824

130 ly

75

36

7802

134 ly

7827
7825

7820

99 ly

12

174 ly

7811

BZ *(s)*

7809

P I S C E S

38

35
UU *(e)*

36

41

Bright and Dark Nebulae
To scale   <10'

Planetary Nebulae
>100"   100"–30"   <30"

Open Star Clusters

Globular Clusters
To scale   <5'

Galaxies
10' x 5'   6' x 1'   3' x 2'   5' x 5'   4' x 2'   2' x 1'

Plotted to scale if the major axis >2', and circular when face on or the position angle is uncertain

Quasars

Galaxy Clusters

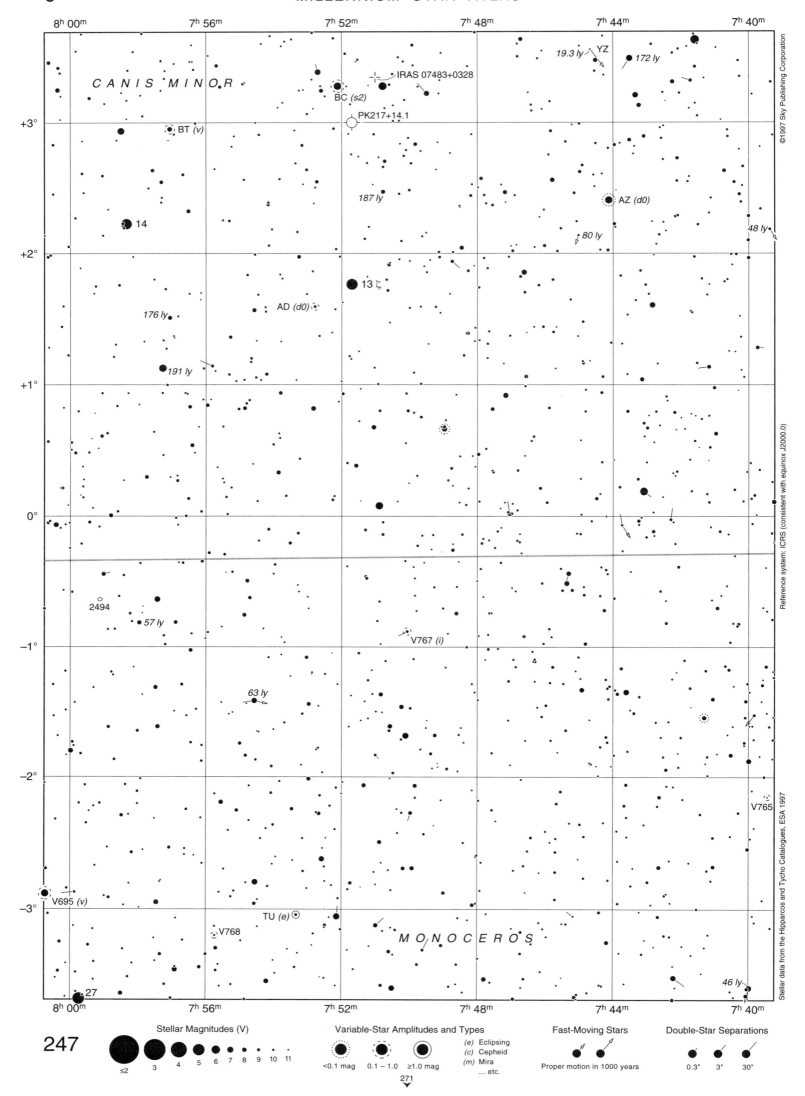

©1997 Sky Publishing Corporation

Reference system: ICRS (consistent with equinox J2000.0)

Stellar data from the Hipparcos and Tycho Catalogues, ESA 1997

247

Stellar Magnitudes (V)

≤2 3 4 5 6 7 8 9 10 11

Variable-Star Amplitudes and Types

<0.1 mag   0.1 – 1.0   ≥1.0 mag

(e) Eclipsing
(c) Cepheid
(m) Mira
... etc.

Fast-Moving Stars

Proper motion in 1000 years

Double-Star Separations

0.3"   3"   30"

271

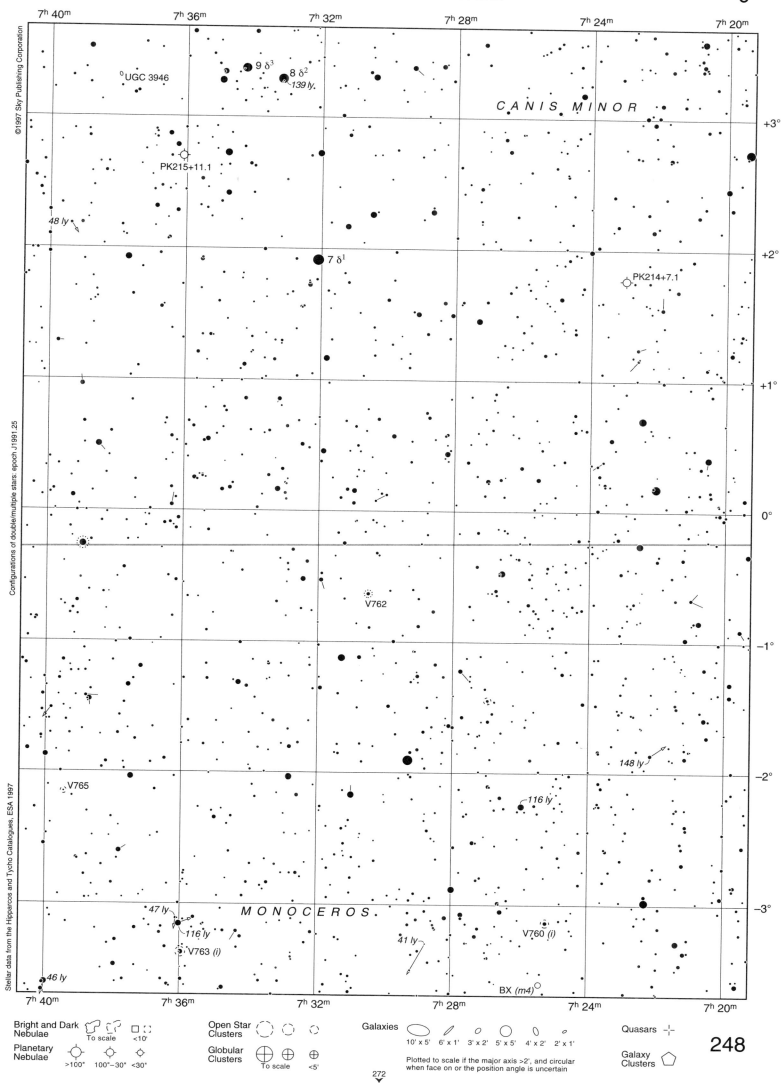

Configurations of double/multiple stars: epoch J1991.25

Stellar data from the Hipparcos and Tycho Catalogues, ESA 1997

7ʰ 40ᵐ   7ʰ 36ᵐ   7ʰ 32ᵐ   7ʰ 28ᵐ   7ʰ 24ᵐ   7ʰ 20ᵐ

UGC 3946

9 δ³

8 δ²
139 ly.

CANIS MINOR

+3°

PK215+11.1

48 ly

+2°

7 δ¹

PK214+7.1

+1°

0°

V762

-1°

148 ly

V765

116 ly

-2°

MONOCEROS

47 ly

116 ly

V760 (i)

41 ly

-3°

V763 (i)

46 ly

BX (m4)

7ʰ 40ᵐ   7ʰ 36ᵐ   7ʰ 32ᵐ   7ʰ 28ᵐ   7ʰ 24ᵐ   7ʰ 20ᵐ

Bright and Dark Nebulae
To scale   <10'

Planetary Nebulae
>100"   100"–30"   <30"

Open Star Clusters

Globular Clusters
To scale   <5'

Galaxies
10' x 5'   6' x 1'   3' x 2'   5' x 5'   4' x 2'   2' x 1'

Plotted to scale if the major axis >2', and circular when face on or the position angle is uncertain

Quasars

Galaxy Clusters

248

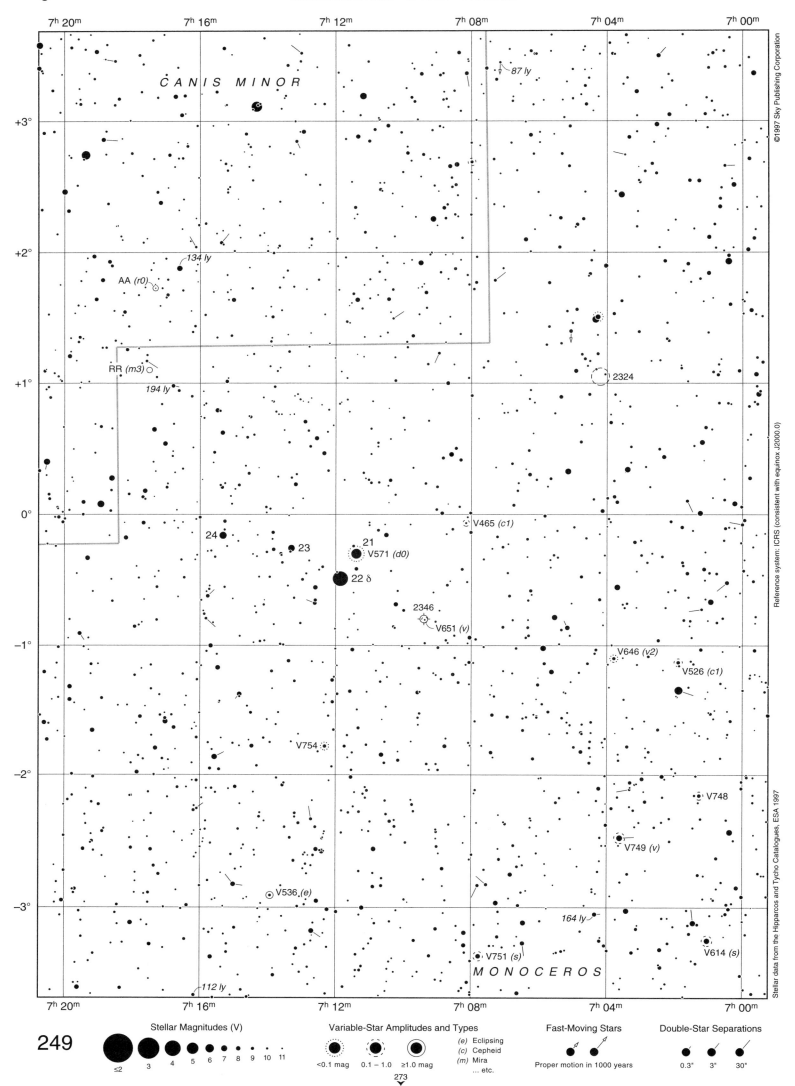

©1997 Sky Publishing Corporation

Reference system: ICRS (consistent with equinox J2000.0)

Stellar data from the Hipparcos and Tycho Catalogues, ESA 1997

CANIS MINOR

87 ly

134 ly

AA (r0)

RR (m3)

194 ly

2324

V465 (c1)

24

23

21

V571 (d0)

22 δ

2346

V651 (v)

V646 (v2)

V526 (c1)

V754

V748

V749 (v)

V536 (e)

164 ly

V751 (s)

V614 (s)

MONOCEROS

112 ly

Stellar Magnitudes (V)

≤2   3   4   5   6   7   8   9 10 11

Variable-Star Amplitudes and Types

<0.1 mag   0.1 − 1.0   ≥1.0 mag

(e) Eclipsing
(c) Cepheid
(m) Mira
... etc.

Fast-Moving Stars

Proper motion in 1000 years

Double-Star Separations

0.3"   3"   30"

273

0°

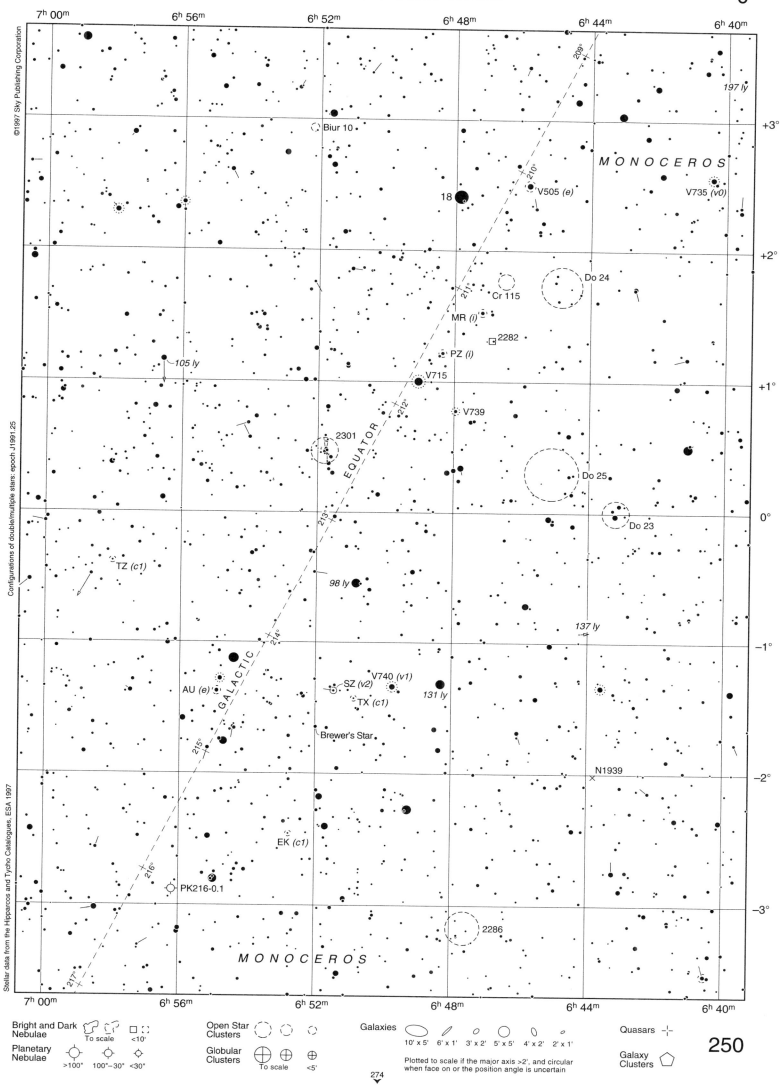

Configurations of double/multiple stars: epoch J1991.25

Stellar data from the Hipparcos and Tycho Catalogues, ESA 1997

7ʰ 00ᵐ   6ʰ 56ᵐ   6ʰ 52ᵐ   6ʰ 48ᵐ   6ʰ 44ᵐ   6ʰ 40ᵐ

209°

197 ly

+3°

Biur 10

MONOCEROS

210°

V505 (e)   V735 (v0)

18

+2°

Do 24

211°   Cr 115

MR (i)

2282

PZ (i)

+1°

105 ly   V715

212°   V739

2301

Do 25

213°   EQUATOR   0°

Do 23

TZ (c1)

98 ly

137 ly

214°   GALACTIC   −1°

V740 (v1)

AU (e)   SZ (v2)

TX (c1)   131 ly

Brewer's Star

215°   N1939   −2°

EK (c1)

216°

PK216-0.1

2286

−3°

MONOCEROS

217°

7ʰ 00ᵐ   6ʰ 56ᵐ   6ʰ 52ᵐ   6ʰ 48ᵐ   6ʰ 44ᵐ   6ʰ 40ᵐ

Bright and Dark Nebulae — To scale — <10'   Open Star Clusters   Galaxies — 10' x 5' 6' x 1' 3' x 2' 5' x 5' 4' x 2' 2' x 1'   Quasars

Planetary Nebulae — >100" 100"–30" <30"   Globular Clusters — To scale — <5'   Galaxy Clusters

Plotted to scale if the major axis >2', and circular when face on or the position angle is uncertain

250

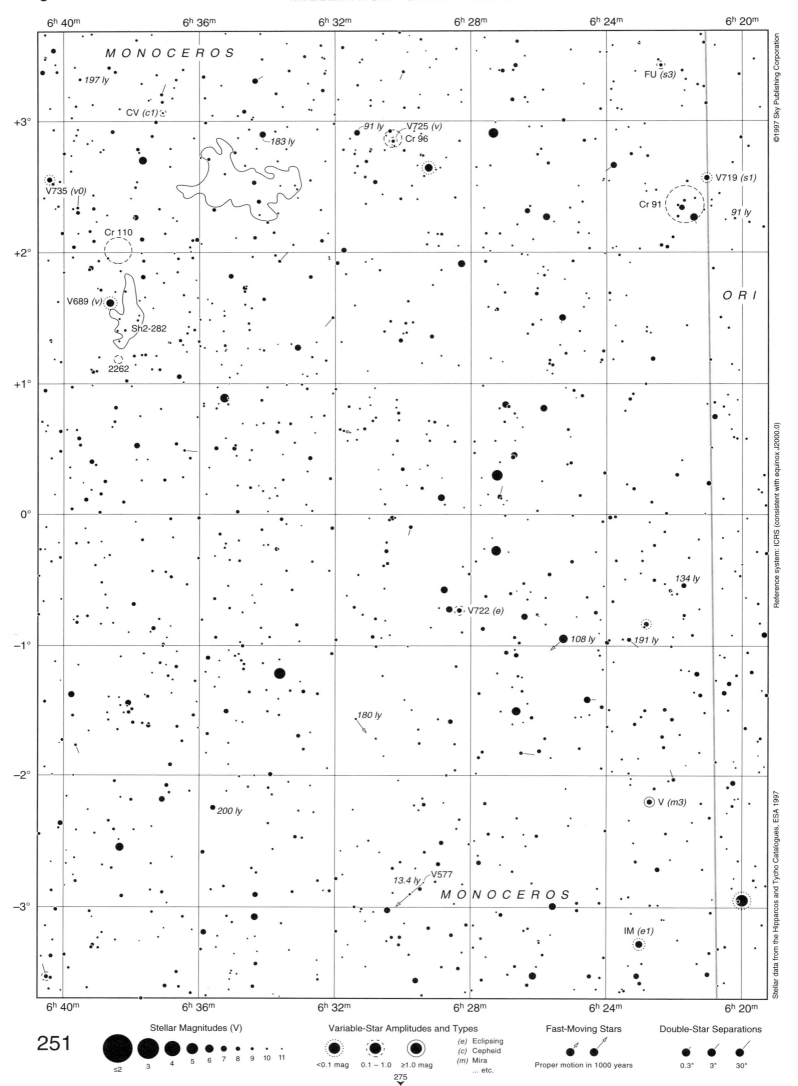

©1997 Sky Publishing Corporation

Reference system: ICRS (consistent with equinox J2000.0)

Stellar data from the Hipparcos and Tycho Catalogues, ESA 1997

MONOCEROS

ORI

197 ly

CV (c1)

FU (s3)

183 ly

91 ly   V725 (v)
             Cr 96

V735 (v0)

V719 (s1)

Cr 91

91 ly

Cr 110

V689 (v)

Sh2-282

2262

134 ly

V722 (e)

108 ly   191 ly

180 ly

200 ly

V (m3)

13.4 ly   V577

MONOCEROS

IM (e1)

251

Stellar Magnitudes (V)

≤2   3   4   5   6   7   8   9   10   11

Variable-Star Amplitudes and Types

<0.1 mag   0.1 – 1.0   ≥1.0 mag

(e) Eclipsing
(c) Cepheid
(m) Mira
... etc.

Fast-Moving Stars

Proper motion in 1000 years

Double-Star Separations

0.3"   3"   30"

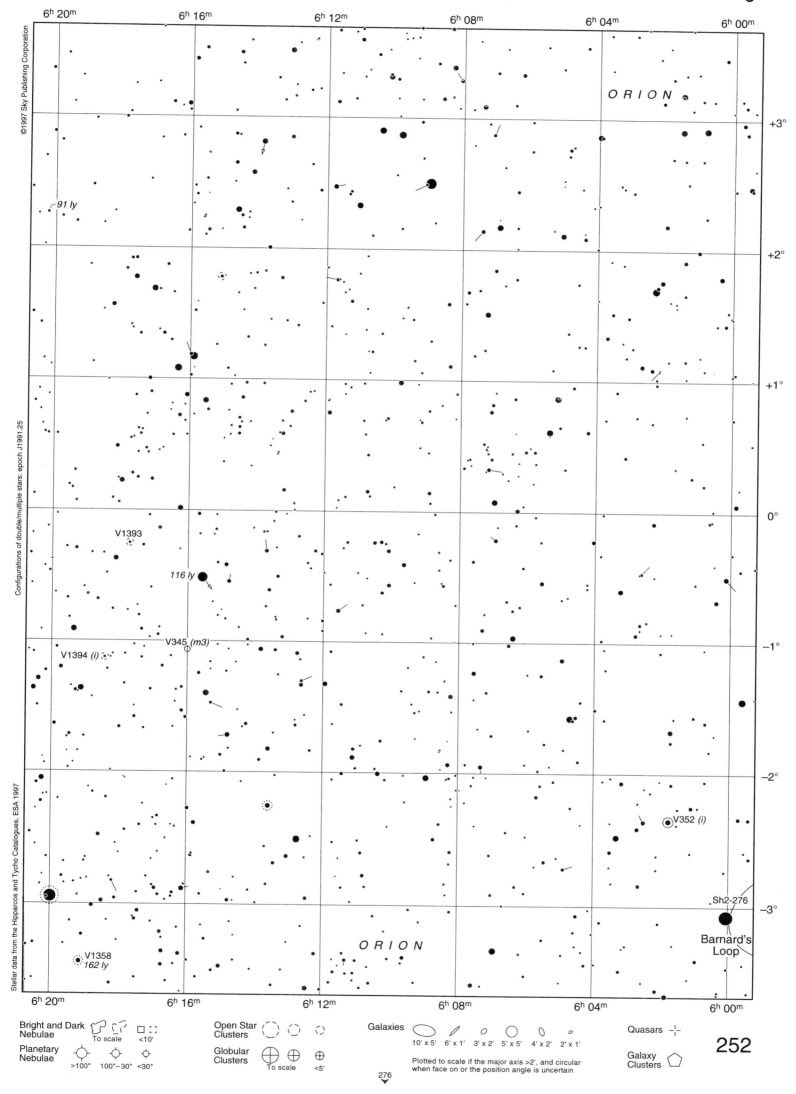

ORION

6h 20m 6h 16m 6h 12m 6h 08m 6h 04m 6h 00m

+3°

+2°

91 ly

+1°

V1393

116 ly

0°

V345 (m3)

−1°

V1394 (i)

V352 (i)

−2°

Sh2-276

−3°

Barnard's
Loop

V1358
162 ly

6h 20m 6h 16m 6h 12m 6h 08m 6h 04m 6h 00m

ORION

©1997 Sky Publishing Corporation

Configurations of double/multiple stars: epoch J1991.25

Stellar data from the Hipparcos and Tycho Catalogues, ESA 1997

Bright and Dark
Nebulae
To scale   <10'

Planetary
Nebulae
>100" 100"–30" <30"

Open Star
Clusters

Globular
Clusters
To scale   <5'

Galaxies

10' x 5' 6' x 1' 3' x 2' 5' x 5' 4' x 2' 2' x 1'

Plotted to scale if the major axis >2', and circular
when face on or the position angle is uncertain

Quasars

Galaxy
Clusters

252

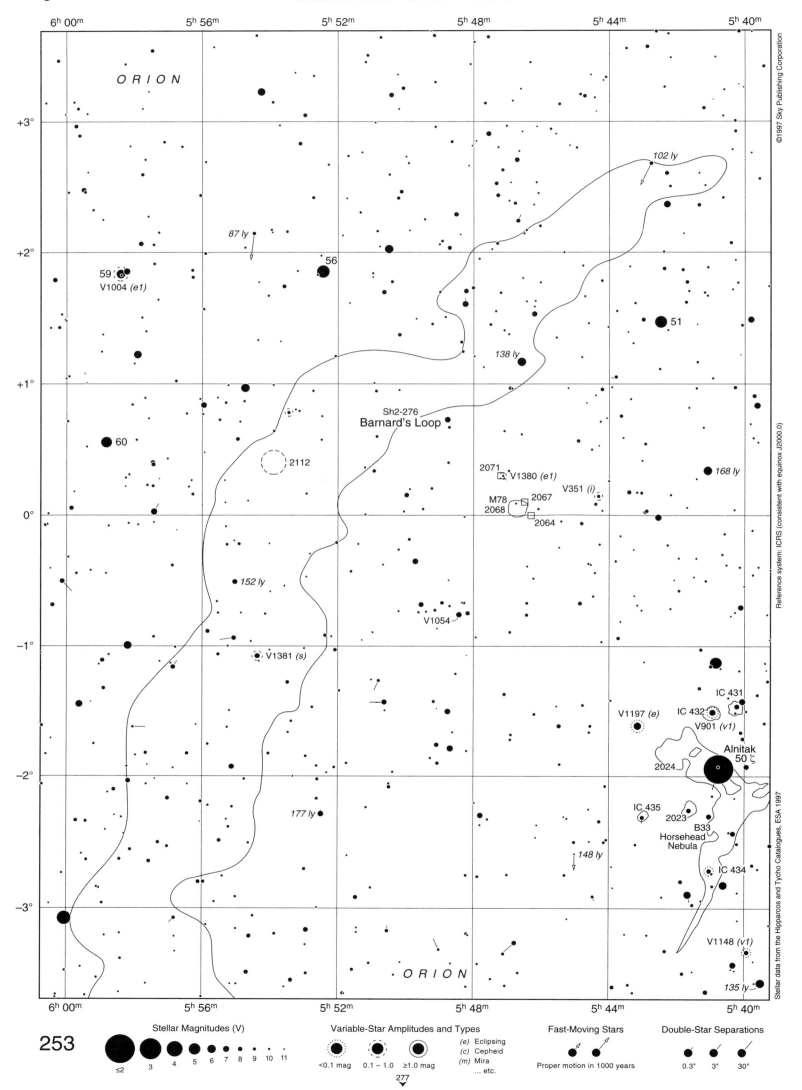

ORION

87 ly

59 60
V1004 (e1)

56

102 ly

51

138 ly

60

Sh2-276
Barnard's Loop

2112

2071
V1380 (e1)

V351 (i)

168 ly

M78
2068

2067

2064

152 ly

V1054

V1381 (s)

IC 431

V1197 (e)

IC 432

V901 (v1)

Alnitak
50 ζ

2024

177 ly

IC 435

2023

B33
Horsehead
Nebula

148 ly

IC 434

V1148 (v1)

ORION

135 ly

Stellar Magnitudes (V)

≤2 3 4 5 6 7 8 9 10 11

Variable-Star Amplitudes and Types

<0.1 mag   0.1 – 1.0   ≥1.0 mag

(e) Eclipsing
(c) Cepheid
(m) Mira
... etc.

Fast-Moving Stars

Proper motion in 1000 years

Double-Star Separations

0.3"   3"   30"

©1997 Sky Publishing Corporation

Reference system: ICRS (consistent with equinox J2000.0)

Stellar data from the Hipparcos and Tycho Catalogues, ESA 1997

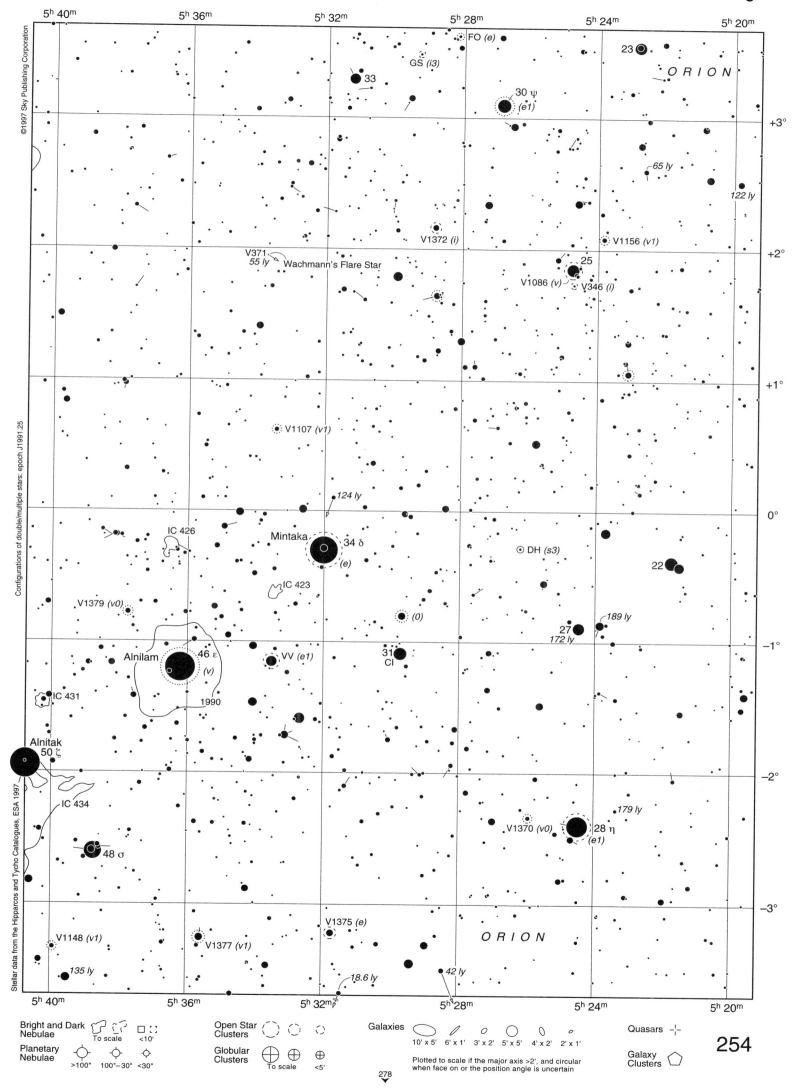

0°

©1997 Sky Publishing Corporation

Configurations of double/multiple stars: epoch J1991.25

Stellar data from the Hipparcos and Tycho Catalogues, ESA 1997

5ʰ 40ᵐ   5ʰ 36ᵐ   5ʰ 32ᵐ   5ʰ 28ᵐ   5ʰ 24ᵐ   5ʰ 20ᵐ

FO (e)

GS (i3)

33

30 ψ (e1)

23

O R I O N

+3°

65 ly

122 ly

V1372 (i)

V1156 (v1)

+2°

V371
55 ly   Wachmann's Flare Star

25

V1086 (v)   V346 (i)

+1°

V1107 (v1)

124 ly

IC 426

Mintaka   34 δ
(e)

DH (s3)

22

IC 423

0°

V1379 (v0)

(0)

189 ly

27
172 ly

−1°

Alnilam   46 ε
(v)

VV (e1)

31
CI

IC 431

1990

Alnitak
50 ζ

−2°

IC 434

179 ly

V1370 (v0)   28 η
(e1)

48 σ

−3°

V1375 (e)

O R I O N

V1148 (v1)

V1377 (v1)

135 ly

18.6 ly

42 ly

5ʰ 40ᵐ   5ʰ 36ᵐ   5ʰ 32ᵐ   5ʰ 28ᵐ   5ʰ 24ᵐ   5ʰ 20ᵐ

Bright and Dark
Nebulae
To scale   <10'

Planetary
Nebulae
>100"   100"−30"   <30"

Open Star
Clusters

Globular
Clusters
To scale   <5'

Galaxies
10' x 5'   6' x 1'   3' x 2'   5' x 5'   4' x 2'   2' x 1'

Plotted to scale if the major axis >2', and circular
when face on or the position angle is uncertain

Quasars

Galaxy
Clusters

254

278

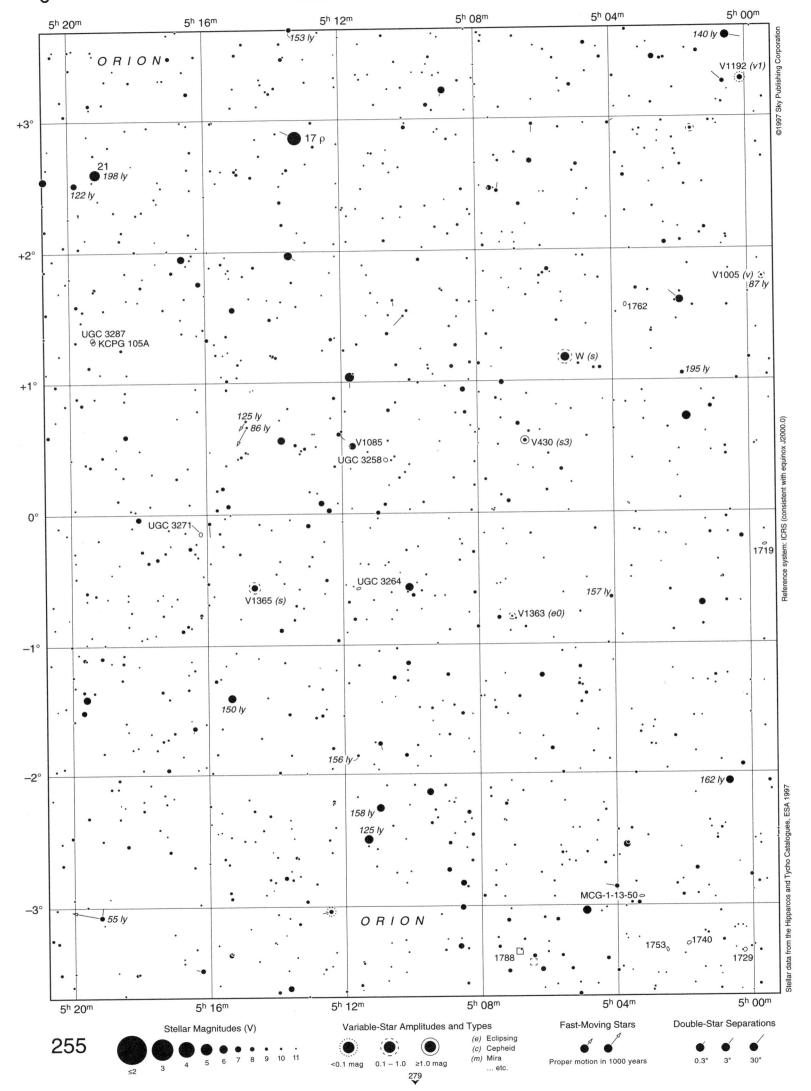

ORION

5ʰ 20ᵐ   5ʰ 16ᵐ   5ʰ 12ᵐ   5ʰ 08ᵐ   5ʰ 04ᵐ   5ʰ 00ᵐ

+3°
+2°
+1°
0°
−1°
−2°
−3°

153 ly
140 ly
V1192 (v1)
17 ρ
21
198 ly
122 ly
V1005 (v)
87 ly
1762
UGC 3287
KCPG 105A
W (s)
195 ly
125 ly
86 ly
V1085
V430 (s3)
UGC 3258
UGC 3271
1719
UGC 3264
V1365 (s)
157 ly
V1363 (e0)
150 ly
156 ly
162 ly
158 ly
125 ly
MCG-1-13-50
ORION
55 ly
1753
1740
1729
1788

255

Stellar Magnitudes (V)

≤2   3   4   5   6   7   8   9   10   11

Variable-Star Amplitudes and Types

<0.1 mag   0.1 − 1.0   ≥1.0 mag

(e) Eclipsing
(c) Cepheid
(m) Mira
... etc.

Fast-Moving Stars

Proper motion in 1000 years

Double-Star Separations

0.3"   3"   30"

279

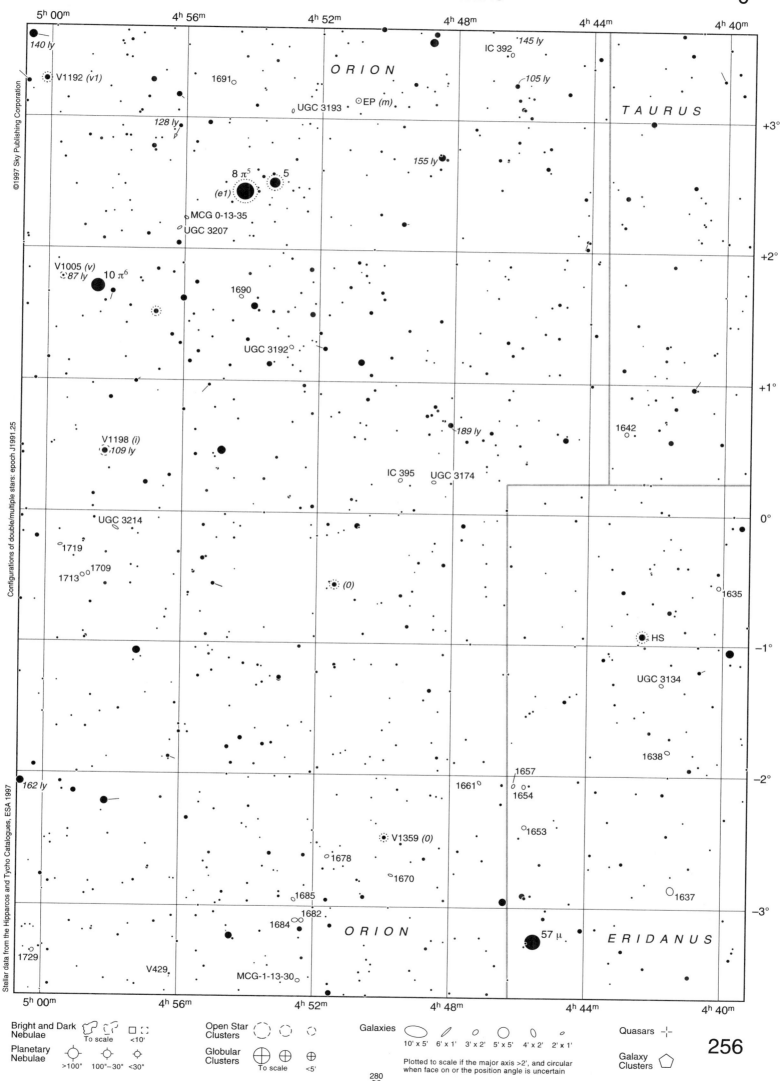

5h 00m · 4h 56m · 4h 52m · 4h 48m · 4h 44m · 4h 40m

140 ly

V1192 *(v1)*

1691

ORION

IC 392 *145 ly*

UGC 3193

EP *(m)*

105 ly

TAURUS

128 ly

+3°

8 π⁵ 5

(e1)

155 ly

MCG 0-13-35

UGC 3207

+2°

V1005 *(v)*

87 ly 10 π⁶

1690

UGC 3192

V1198 *(i)*

109 ly

189 ly

1642

+1°

IC 395 UGC 3174

UGC 3214

0°

1719

1713 1709

(0)

1635

HS

UGC 3134

-1°

1657

1661 1654

1638

162 ly

-2°

V1359 *(0)*

1653

1678

1670

1685

1637

1682

-3°

1684

1729

ORION

57 μ

ERIDANUS

V429

MCG-1-13-30

5h 00m · 4h 56m · 4h 52m · 4h 48m · 4h 44m · 4h 40m

Bright and Dark Nebulae	Open Star Clusters	Galaxies	Quasars

Bright and Dark Nebulae — To scale — <10'

Planetary Nebulae — >100" 100"–30" <30'

Open Star Clusters

Globular Clusters — To scale — <5'

Galaxies — 10' x 5' 6' x 1' 3' x 2' 5' x 5' 4' x 2' 2' x 1'

Plotted to scale if the major axis >2', and circular when face on or the position angle is uncertain

Quasars

Galaxy Clusters

256

280

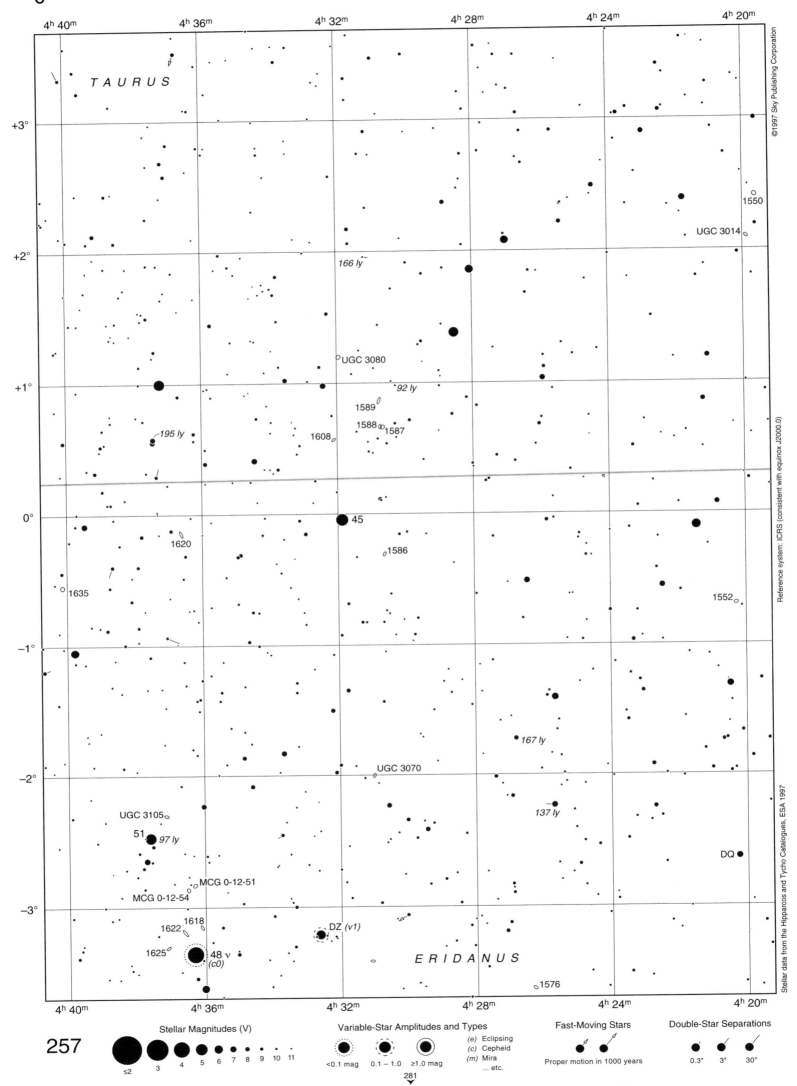

©1997 Sky Publishing Corporation

Reference system: ICRS (consistent with equinox J2000.0)

Stellar data from the Hipparcos and Tycho Catalogues, ESA 1997

TAURUS

1550
UGC 3014

166 ly

UGC 3080

92 ly

1589
1588 1587
1608

195 ly

45

1586

1620

1635

1552

167 ly

UGC 3070

137 ly

UGC 3105
51 97 ly

DQ

MCG 0-12-51
MCG 0-12-54

1618
1622
DZ (v1)
1625
48 ν
(c0)

ERIDANUS

1576

257

Stellar Magnitudes (V)

≤2   3   4   5 6 7 8 9 10 11

Variable-Star Amplitudes and Types

<0.1 mag   0.1 – 1.0   ≥1.0 mag

(e) Eclipsing
(c) Cepheid
(m) Mira
... etc.

Fast-Moving Stars

Proper motion in 1000 years

Double-Star Separations

0.3"   3"   30"

281

0°

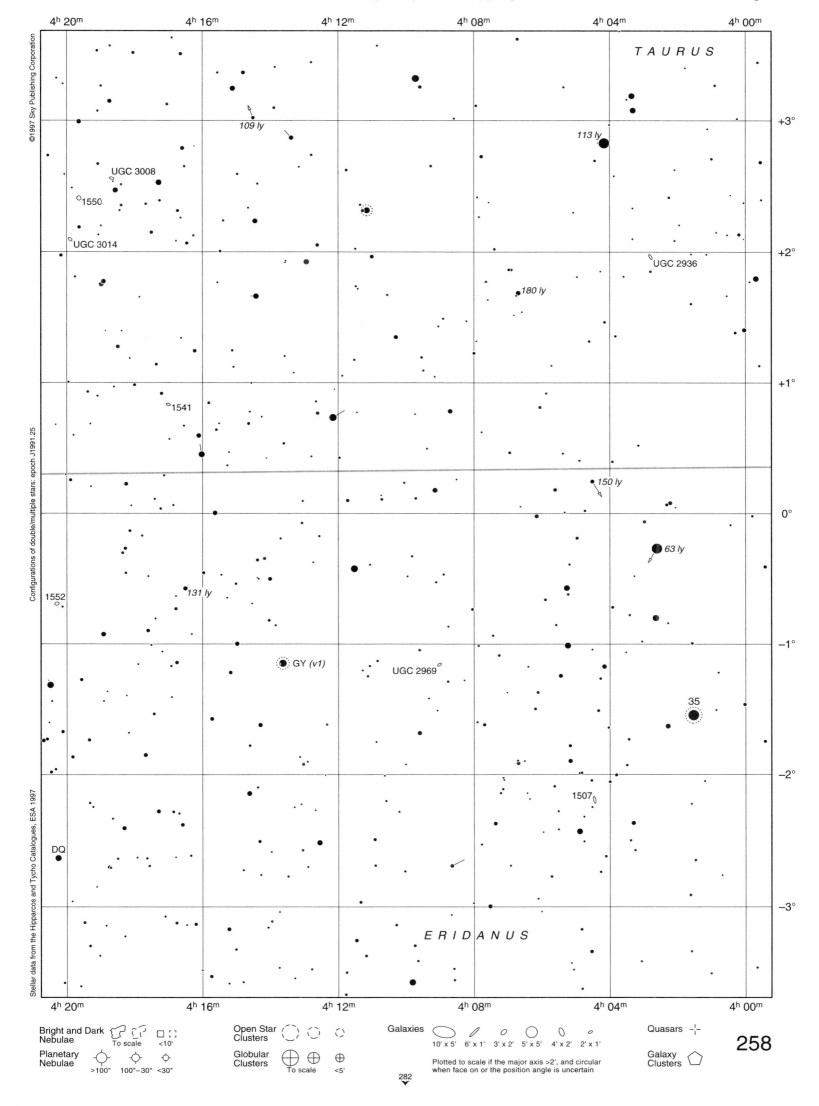

T A U R U S

109 ly

113 ly

UGC 3008

1550

UGC 3014

UGC 2936

180 ly

+3°

+2°

1541

+1°

150 ly

63 ly

1552

131 ly

0°

−1°

GY (v1)

UGC 2969

35

−2°

1507

DQ

−3°

E R I D A N U S

4h 20m   4h 16m   4h 12m   4h 08m   4h 04m   4h 00m

Bright and Dark Nebulae	Planetary Nebulae	Open Star Clusters	Globular Clusters	Galaxies	Quasars	Galaxy Clusters

Bright and Dark Nebulae To scale <10'

Planetary Nebulae >100" 100"−30" <30"

Open Star Clusters

Globular Clusters To scale <5'

Galaxies 10' x 5' 6' x 1' 3' x 2' 5' x 5' 4' x 2' 2' x 1'

Plotted to scale if the major axis >2', and circular when face on or the position angle is uncertain

Quasars

Galaxy Clusters

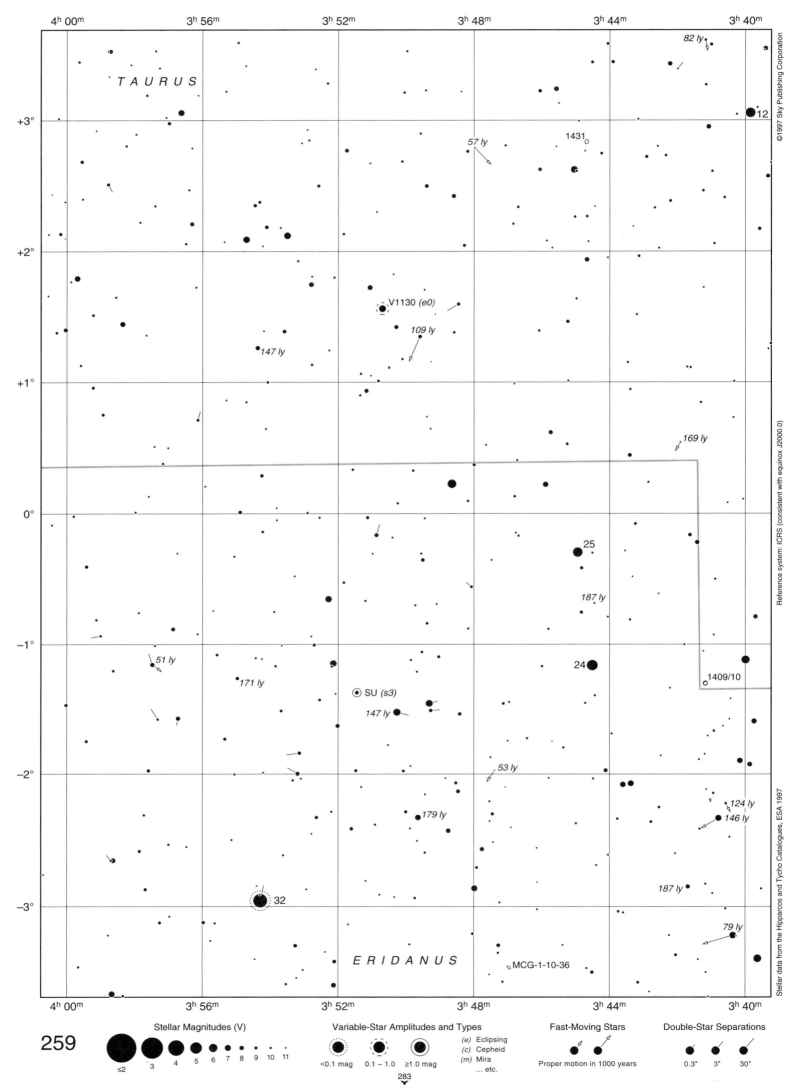

©1997 Sky Publishing Corporation

Reference system: ICRS (consistent with equinox J2000.0)

Stellar data from the Hipparcos and Tycho Catalogues, ESA 1997

T A U R U S

V1130 (e0)

57 ly

1431

82 ly

12

147 ly

109 ly

169 ly

25

187 ly

51 ly

171 ly

24

1409/10

SU (s3)

147 ly

124 ly

146 ly

53 ly

179 ly

187 ly

32

79 ly

E R I D A N U S

MCG-1-10-36

Stellar Magnitudes (V)

≤2 3 4 5 6 7 8 9 10 11

Variable-Star Amplitudes and Types

<0.1 mag   0.1 – 1.0   ≥1.0 mag

(e) Eclipsing
(c) Cepheid
(m) Mira
... etc.

Fast-Moving Stars

Proper motion in 1000 years

Double-Star Separations

0.3"   3"   30"

0°

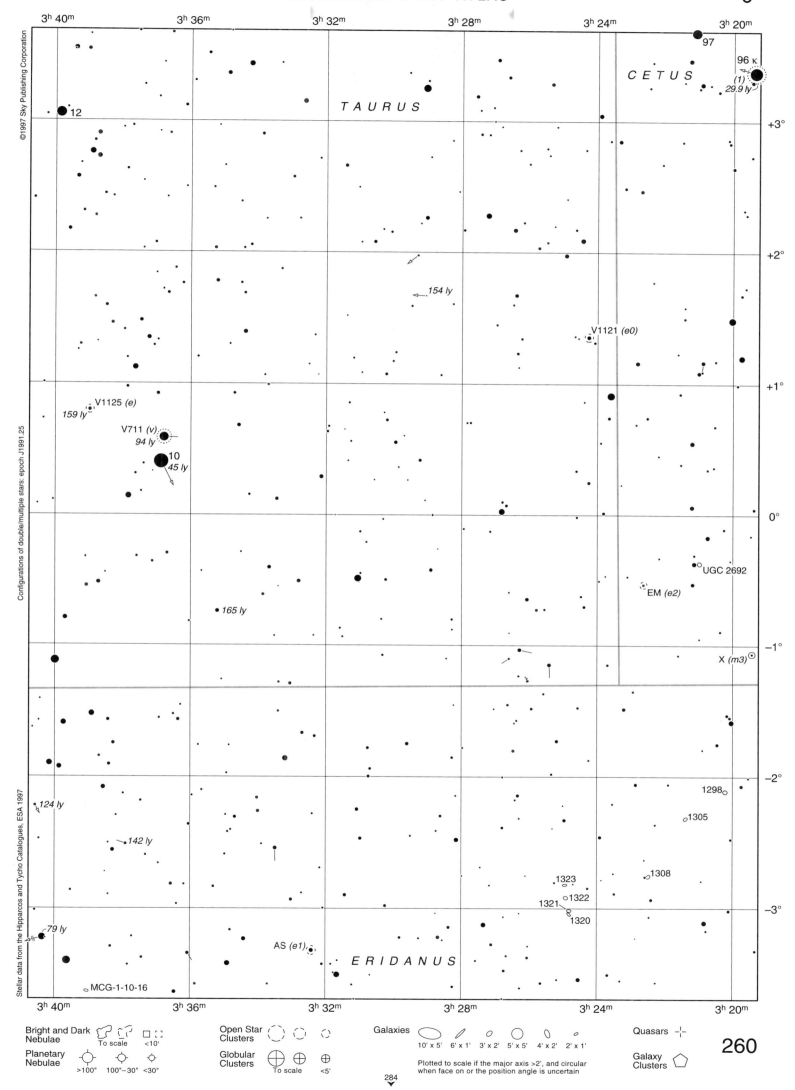

Configurations of double/multiple stars: epoch J1991.25

Stellar data from the Hipparcos and Tycho Catalogues, ESA 1997

3ʰ 40ᵐ   3ʰ 36ᵐ   3ʰ 32ᵐ   3ʰ 28ᵐ   3ʰ 24ᵐ   3ʰ 20ᵐ

C E T U S

96 κ

(1)

29.9 ly

97

12

T A U R U S

+3°

+2°

154 ly

V1121 (e0)

+1°

V1125 (e)

159 ly

V711 (v)

94 ly

10

45 ly

0°

UGC 2692

EM (e2)

165 ly

−1°

X (m3)

−2°

1298

1305

124 ly

1308

142 ly

1323

1321   1322

1320

−3°

79 ly

AS (e1)

E R I D A N U S

MCG-1-10-16

3ʰ 40ᵐ   3ʰ 36ᵐ   3ʰ 32ᵐ   3ʰ 28ᵐ   3ʰ 24ᵐ   3ʰ 20ᵐ

| Bright and Dark Nebulae | Open Star Clusters | Galaxies | Quasars |
| Planetary Nebulae | Globular Clusters | | Galaxy Clusters |

To scale   <10'

>100"   100"–30"   <30'

To scale   <5'

10' x 5'   6' x 1'   3' x 2'   5' x 5'   4' x 2'   2' x 1'

Plotted to scale if the major axis >2', and circular when face on or the position angle is uncertain

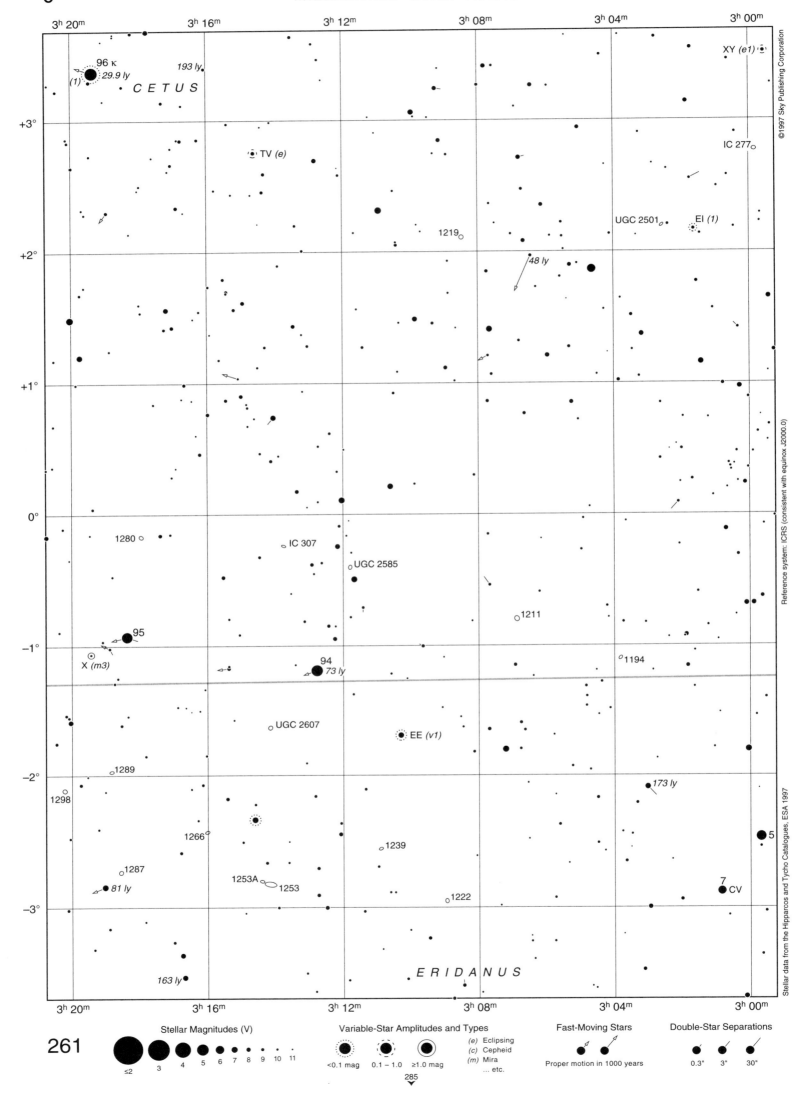

©1997 Sky Publishing Corporation

Reference system: ICRS (consistent with equinox J2000.0)

Stellar data from the Hipparcos and Tycho Catalogues, ESA 1997

Stellar Magnitudes (V)

≤2 3 4 5 6 7 8 9 10 11

Variable-Star Amplitudes and Types

<0.1 mag   0.1 – 1.0   ≥1.0 mag

(e) Eclipsing
(c) Cepheid
(m) Mira
... etc.

Fast-Moving Stars

Proper motion in 1000 years

Double-Star Separations

0.3"   3"   30"

285

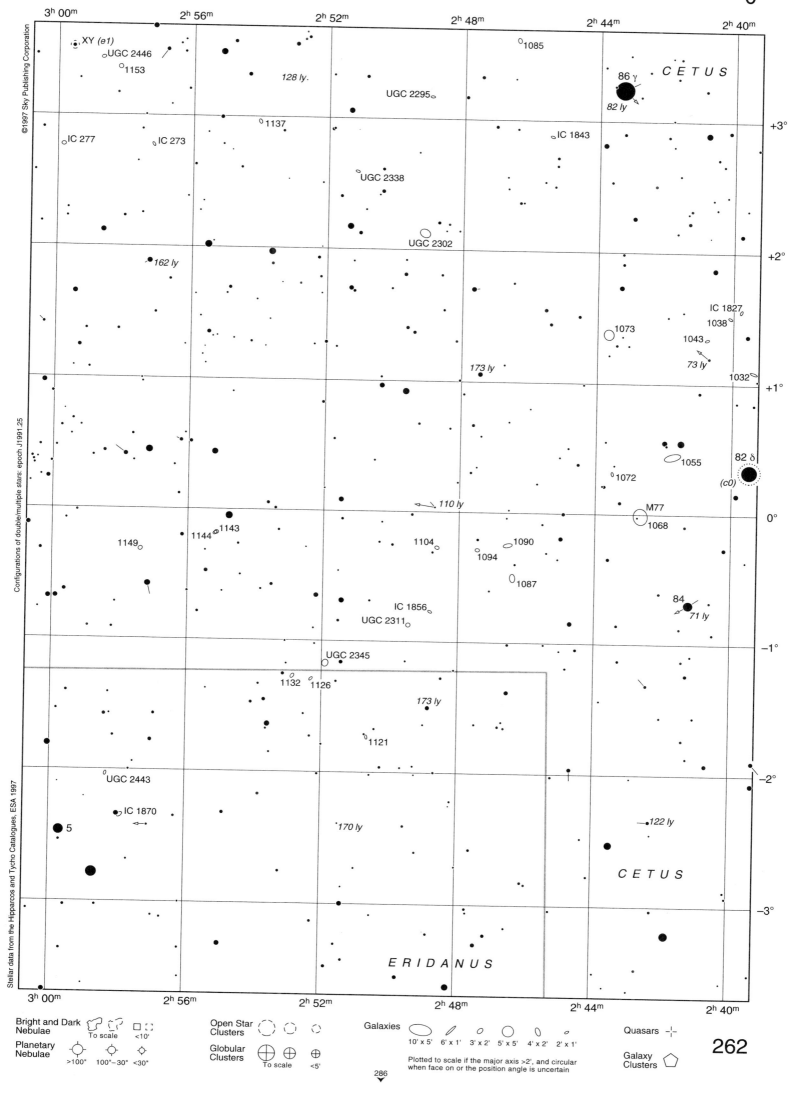

XY *(e1)*
UGC 2446
1153
1085
CETUS
86 γ
82 ly
128 ly.
UGC 2295
IC 277
IC 273
1137
IC 1843
UGC 2338
IC 1827
1038
UGC 2302
+3°
162 ly
1073
1043
73 ly
1032
+2°
173 ly
+1°
82 δ
1055
(c0)
1072
M77
110 ly
1068
1149
1144 1143
1104
1090
1094
1087
IC 1856
84
71 ly
UGC 2311
0°
UGC 2345
-1°
1132 1126
173 ly
1121
UGC 2443
-2°
IC 1870
122 ly
5
170 ly
CETUS
-3°
ERIDANUS

3ʰ 00ᵐ   2ʰ 56ᵐ   2ʰ 52ᵐ   2ʰ 48ᵐ   2ʰ 44ᵐ   2ʰ 40ᵐ

Bright and Dark Nebulae

To scale   <10'

Planetary Nebulae

>100" 100"–30" <30"

Open Star Clusters

Globular Clusters

To scale   <5'

Galaxies

10' x 5'   6' x 1'   3' x 2'   5' x 5'   4' x 2'   2' x 1'

Plotted to scale if the major axis >2', and circular when face on or the position angle is uncertain

Quasars

Galaxy Clusters

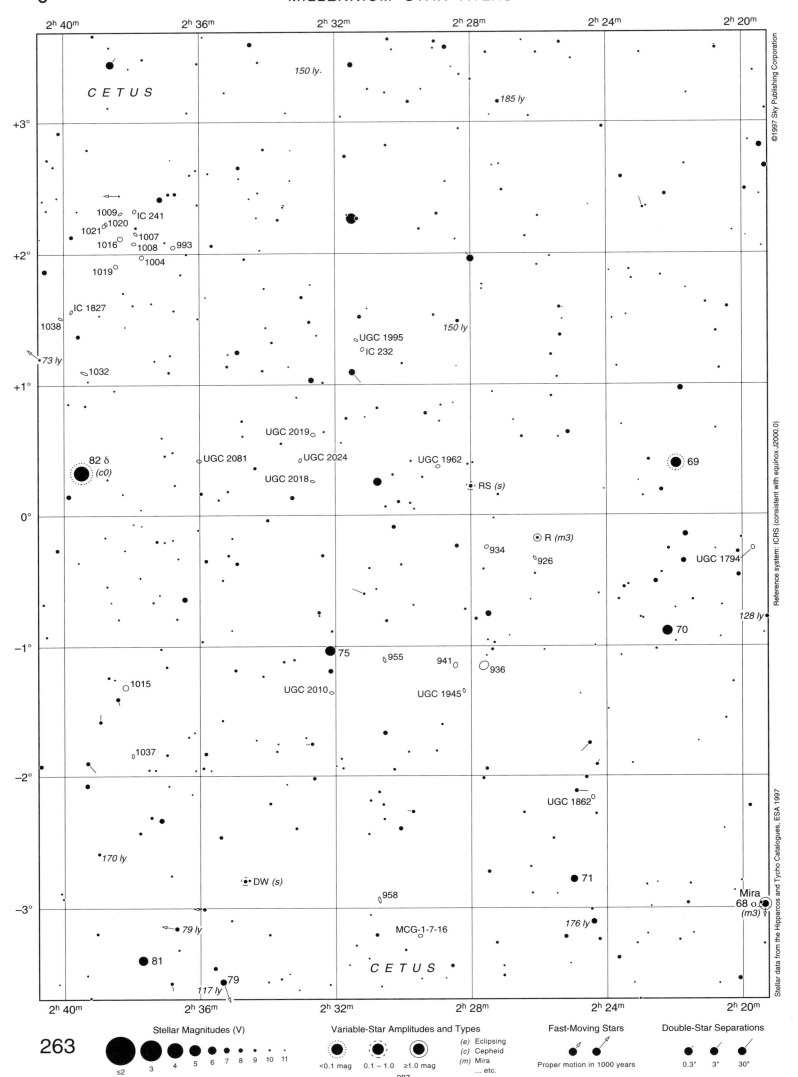

©1997 Sky Publishing Corporation

Reference system: ICRS (consistent with equinox J2000.0)

Stellar data from the Hipparcos and Tycho Catalogues, ESA 1997

2ʰ 40ᵐ   2ʰ 36ᵐ   2ʰ 32ᵐ   2ʰ 28ᵐ   2ʰ 24ᵐ   2ʰ 20ᵐ

C E T U S

150 ly.

185 ly

+3°

1009 IC 241
1021 1020
1016 1007
1008 993
1004
+2°
1019

IC 1827
1038
UGC 1995
150 ly
IC 232
73 ly
1032
+1°

UGC 2019
82 δ UGC 2081 UGC 2024 UGC 1962 69
(c0) UGC 2018 RS (s)

0°
R (m3)
934 926
UGC 1794
128 ly
70
75 955 941 936
-1°
1015 UGC 2010 UGC 1945

1037
-2°
UGC 1862

170 ly
71
DW (s)
958
Mira
68 (m3)
-3°
MCG-1-7-16 176 ly
79 ly
81
C E T U S
79
117 ly

2ʰ 40ᵐ   2ʰ 36ᵐ   2ʰ 32ᵐ   2ʰ 28ᵐ   2ʰ 24ᵐ   2ʰ 20ᵐ

Stellar Magnitudes (V)
≤2   3   4   5   6   7   8   9   10 11

Variable-Star Amplitudes and Types
<0.1 mag   0.1 – 1.0   ≥1.0 mag

(e) Eclipsing
(c) Cepheid
(m) Mira
... etc.

Fast-Moving Stars
Proper motion in 1000 years

Double-Star Separations
0.3"   3"   30"

0°

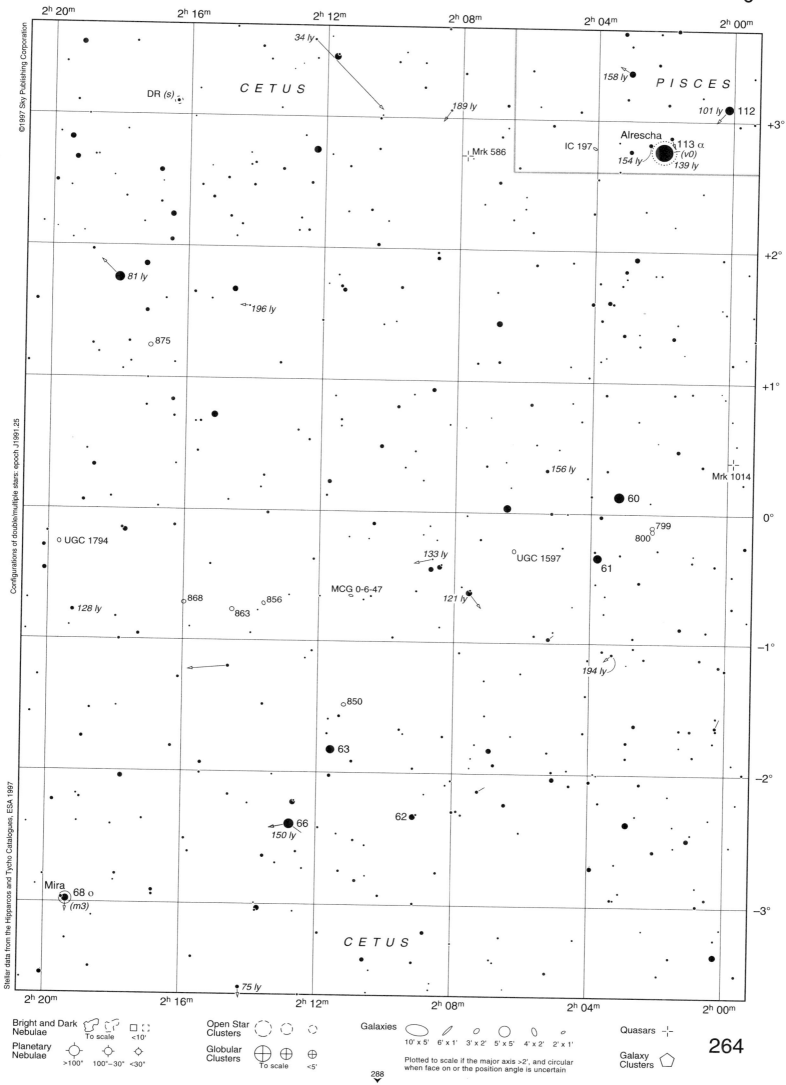

2h 20m   2h 16m   2h 12m   2h 08m   2h 04m   2h 00m

34 ly

C E T U S

P I S C E S

158 ly

189 ly

+3°

DR (s)

101 ly   112

Mrk 586

Alrescha

IC 197   113 α
(v0)
154 ly   139 ly

81 ly

+2°

196 ly

875

+1°

156 ly

Mrk 1014

60

0°

799

UGC 1794

800

UGC 1597

61

133 ly

128 ly

868   856

MCG 0-6-47   121 ly

863

-1°

194 ly

850

63

-2°

66

62

150 ly

Mira   68 o

(m3)

-3°

C E T U S

75 ly

Bright and Dark Nebulae   To scale   <10'

Planetary Nebulae   >100"   100"-30"   <30"

Open Star Clusters

Globular Clusters   To scale   <5'

Galaxies   10' x 5'   6' x 1'   3' x 2'   5' x 5'   4' x 2'   2' x 1'

Plotted to scale if the major axis >2', and circular when face on or the position angle is uncertain

Quasars

Galaxy Clusters

264

288

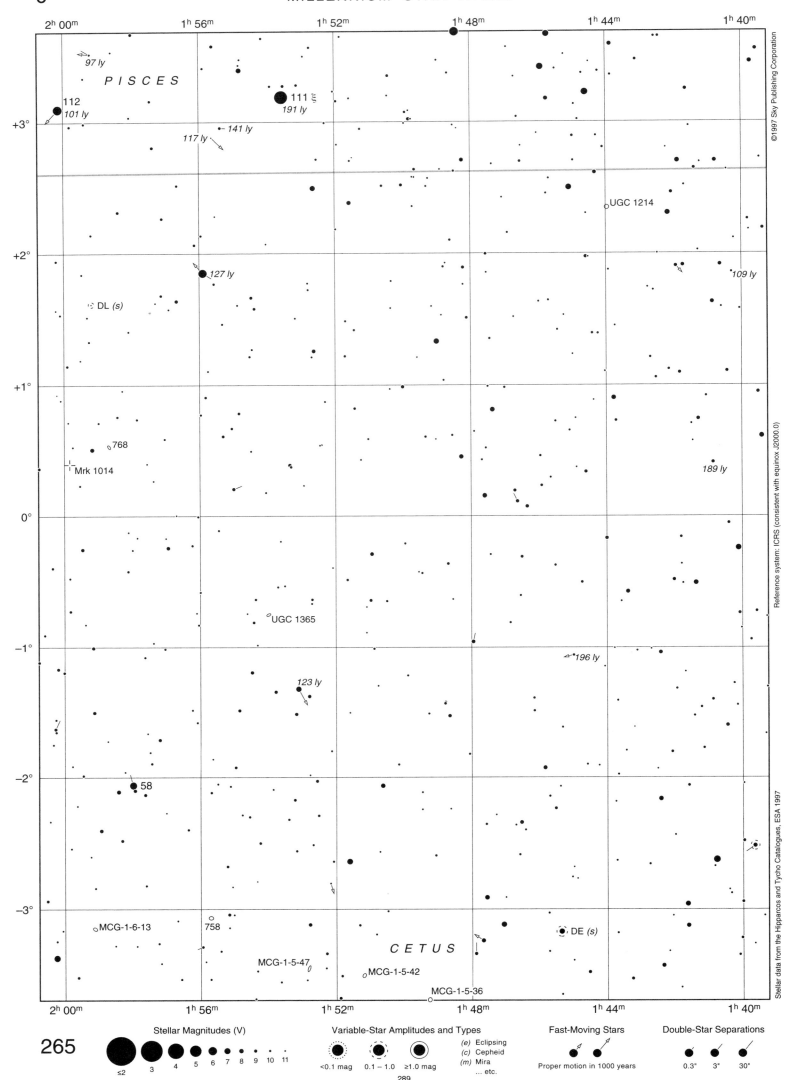

©1997 Sky Publishing Corporation

Reference system: ICRS (consistent with equinox J2000.0)

Stellar data from the Hipparcos and Tycho Catalogues, ESA 1997

PISCES

112
101 ly

97 ly

111 ξ
191 ly

141 ly

117 ly

UGC 1214

127 ly

109 ly

DL (s)

768

189 ly

Mrk 1014

UGC 1365

196 ly

123 ly

58

MCG-1-6-13

758

DE (s)

CETUS

MCG-1-5-47

MCG-1-5-42

MCG-1-5-36

Stellar Magnitudes (V)

≤2   3   4   5   6   7   8   9 10 11

Variable-Star Amplitudes and Types

<0.1 mag   0.1 – 1.0   ≥1.0 mag

(e) Eclipsing
(c) Cepheid
(m) Mira
... etc.

Fast-Moving Stars

Proper motion in 1000 years

Double-Star Separations

0.3"   3"   30"

289

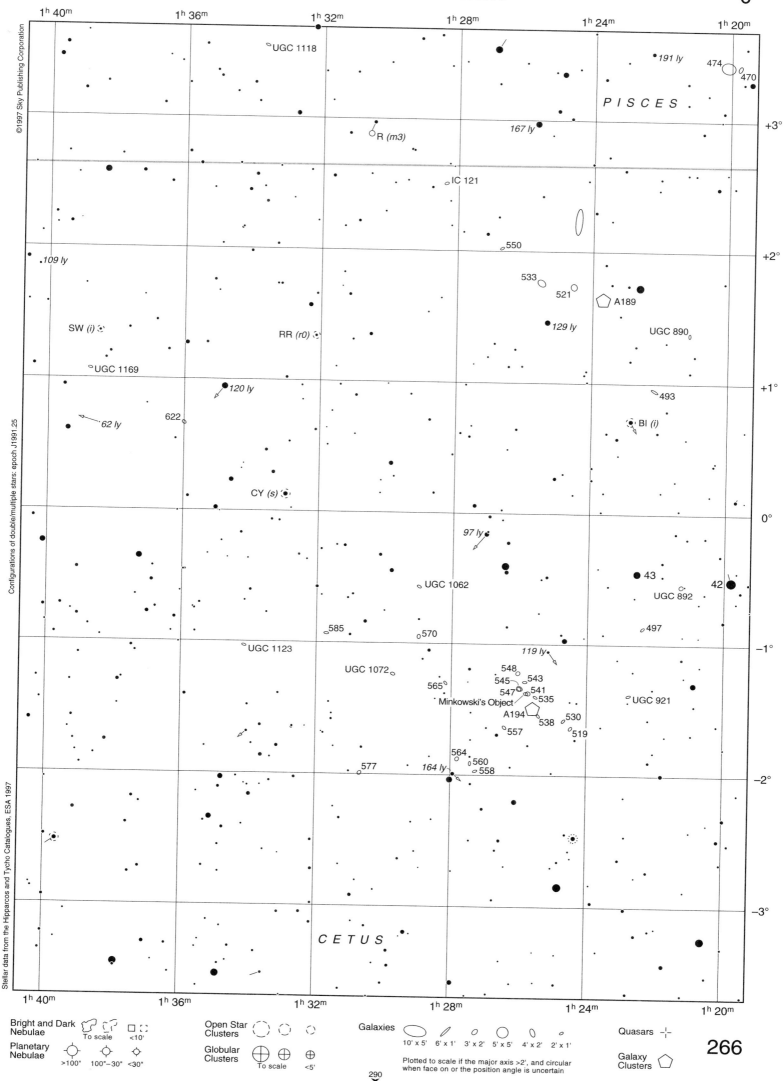

Bright and Dark Nebulae
To scale   <10'

Planetary Nebulae
>100"   100"–30"   <30"

Open Star Clusters

Globular Clusters
To scale   <5'

Galaxies
10' x 5'   6' x 1'   3' x 2'   5' x 5'   4' x 2'   2' x 1'

Plotted to scale if the major axis >2', and circular when face on or the position angle is uncertain

Quasars

Galaxy Clusters

266

290

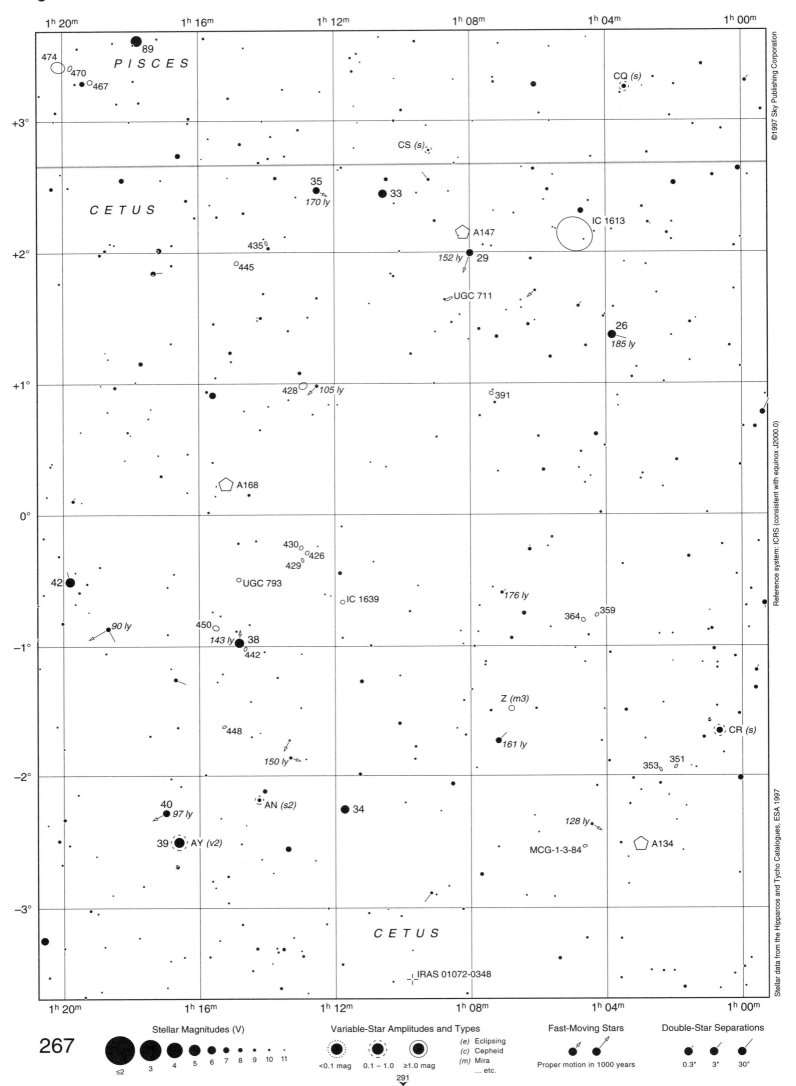

Reference system: ICRS (consistent with equinox J2000.0)

Stellar data from the Hipparcos and Tycho Catalogues, ESA 1997

267

Stellar Magnitudes (V)

≤2 3 4 5 6 7 8 9 10 11

Variable-Star Amplitudes and Types

<0.1 mag   0.1 – 1.0   ≥1.0 mag

(e) Eclipsing
(c) Cepheid
(m) Mira
... etc.

Fast-Moving Stars

Proper motion in 1000 years

Double-Star Separations

0.3"   3"   30"

291

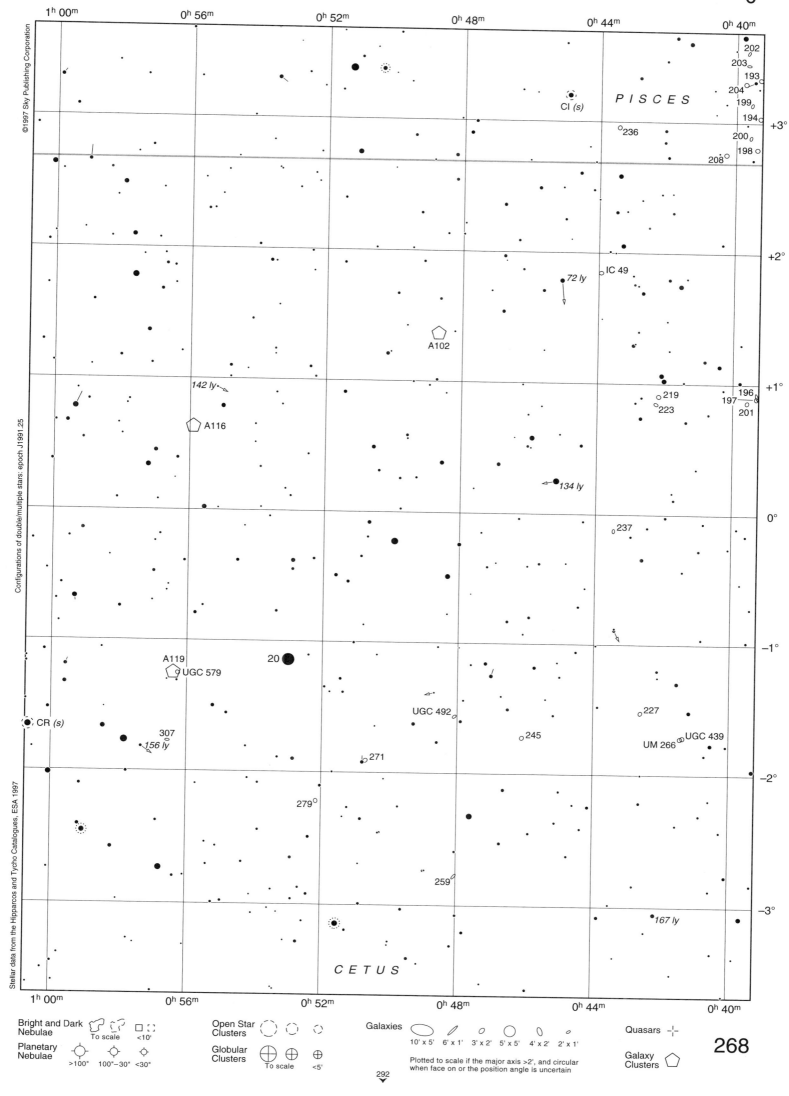

P I S C E S

CI (s)

+3°

236

IC 49

72 ly

+2°

A102

142 ly

+1°

A116

219
223

197 196
201

134 ly

0°

237

A119
UGC 579

20

0°

UGC 492

227

CR (s)

307
156 ly

245

UM 266 UGC 439

271

−2°

279

259

−3°

167 ly

C E T U S

1ʰ 00ᵐ   0ʰ 56ᵐ   0ʰ 52ᵐ   0ʰ 48ᵐ   0ʰ 44ᵐ   0ʰ 40ᵐ

Bright and Dark Nebulae	To scale	□ ⬚ <10'
Planetary Nebulae	>100" 100"–30"	<30"
Open Star Clusters	○ ○	○
Globular Clusters	⊕ ⊕	⊕ <5'
	To scale	

Galaxies   10' x 5'   6' x 1'   3' x 2'   5' x 5'   4' x 2'   2' x 1'

Plotted to scale if the major axis >2', and circular when face on or the position angle is uncertain

Quasars -|-

Galaxy Clusters

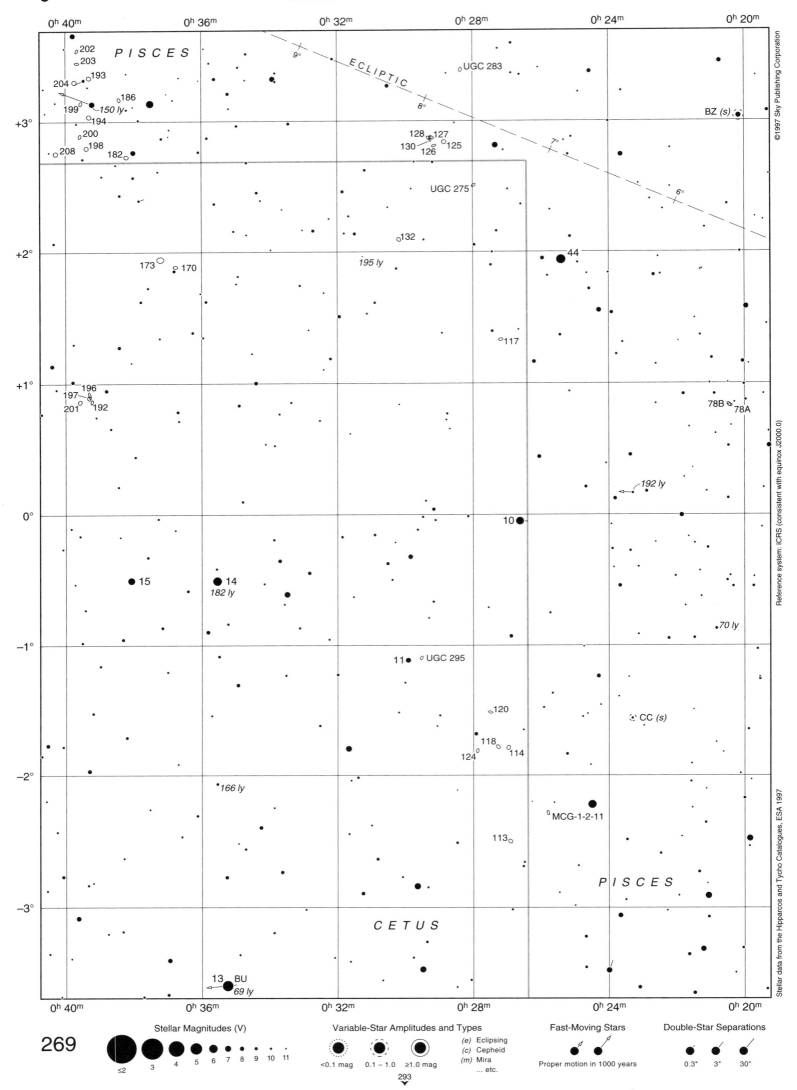

©1997 Sky Publishing Corporation

Reference system: ICRS (consistent with equinox J2000.0)

Stellar data from the Hipparcos and Tycho Catalogues, ESA 1997

269

Stellar Magnitudes (V)	Variable-Star Amplitudes and Types	Fast-Moving Stars	Double-Star Separations

Stellar Magnitudes (V) ≤2 3 4 5 6 7 8 9 10 11

Variable-Star Amplitudes and Types
<0.1 mag   0.1 – 1.0   ≥1.0 mag

(e) Eclipsing
(c) Cepheid
(m) Mira
... etc.

Fast-Moving Stars
Proper motion in 1000 years

Double-Star Separations
0.3"   3"   30"

293

MILLENNIUM STAR ATLAS

0°

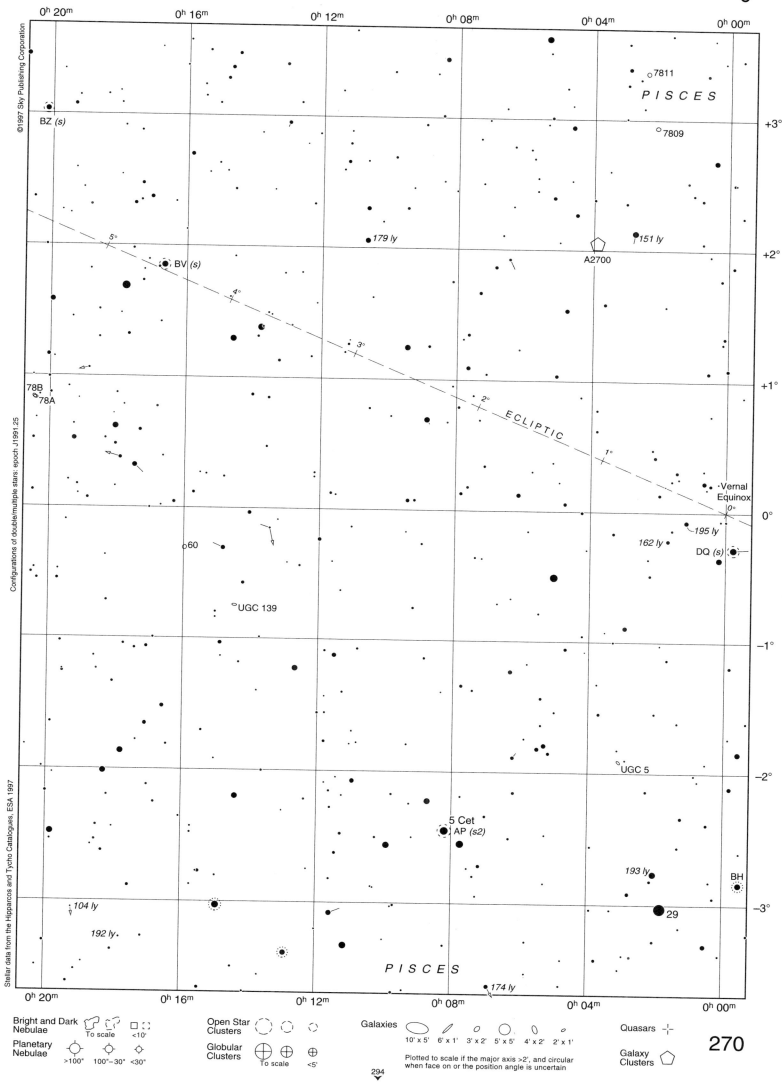

Configurations of double/multiple stars: epoch J1991.25

Stellar data from the Hipparcos and Tycho Catalogues, ESA 1997

BZ (s)

PISCES

7811

7809

+3°

179 ly

151 ly

+2°

BV (s)

A2700

5°

4°

3°

ECLIPTIC

2°

1°

78B
78A

+1°

60

Vernal
Equinox
0°

0°

195 ly

162 ly

DQ (s)

UGC 139

−1°

UGC 5

−2°

5 Cet
AP (s2)

193 ly

BH

104 ly

29

−3°

192 ly

PISCES

174 ly

0h 20m   0h 16m   0h 12m   0h 08m   0h 04m   0h 00m

Bright and Dark Nebulae		Open Star Clusters			Galaxies						Quasars
Planetary Nebulae		Globular Clusters			10' x 5' 6' x 1' 3' x 2' 5' x 5' 4' x 2' 2' x 1'						Galaxy Clusters
>100" 100"–30" <30"		To scale <5'									

To scale   <10'

Plotted to scale if the major axis >2', and circular
when face on or the position angle is uncertain

270

−6°

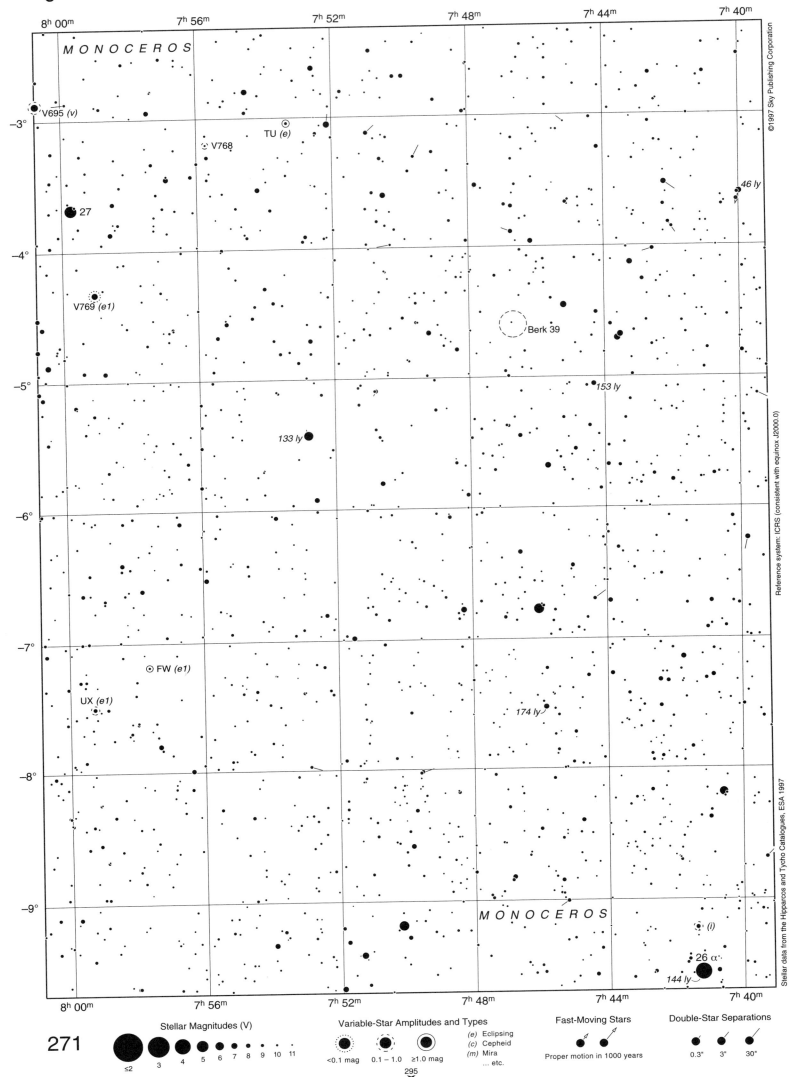

©1997 Sky Publishing Corporation

Reference system: ICRS (consistent with equinox J2000.0)

Stellar data from the Hipparcos and Tycho Catalogues, ESA 1997

271

Stellar Magnitudes (V)

≤2   3   4   5   6   7   8   9   10   11

Variable-Star Amplitudes and Types

<0.1 mag   0.1 − 1.0   ≥1.0 mag

(e) Eclipsing
(c) Cepheid
(m) Mira
... etc.

Fast-Moving Stars

Proper motion in 1000 years

Double-Star Separations

0.3"   3"   30"

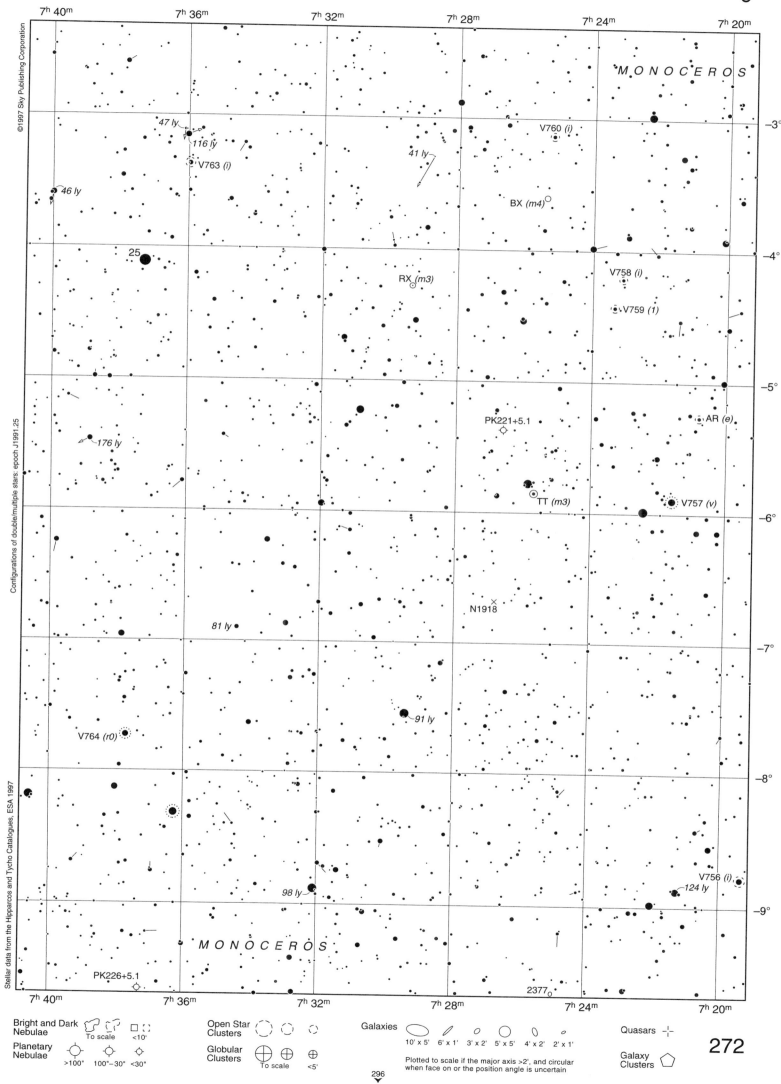

MONOCEROS

7h 40m 7h 36m 7h 32m 7h 28m 7h 24m 7h 20m

©1997 Sky Publishing Corporation

Configurations of double/multiple stars: epoch J1991.25

Stellar data from the Hipparcos and Tycho Catalogues, ESA 1997

V760 (i)

47 ly
116 ly
V763 (i)

41 ly

BX (m4)

46 ly

25

RX (m3)

V758 (i)

V759 (1)

−3°

−4°

PK221+5.1

AR (e)

176 ly

TT (m3)

V757 (v)

−5°

−6°

N1918

81 ly

−7°

91 ly

V764 (r0)

−8°

98 ly

V756 (i)
124 ly

−9°

MONOCEROS

PK226+5.1

2377

7h 40m 7h 36m 7h 32m 7h 28m 7h 24m 7h 20m

Bright and Dark Nebulae
To scale   <10'

Planetary Nebulae
>100"   100"–30"   <30"

Open Star Clusters

Globular Clusters
To scale   <5'

Galaxies
10' x 5' 6' x 1' 3' x 2' 5' x 5' 4' x 2' 2' x 1'

Plotted to scale if the major axis >2', and circular when face on or the position angle is uncertain

Quasars

Galaxy Clusters

272

-6°

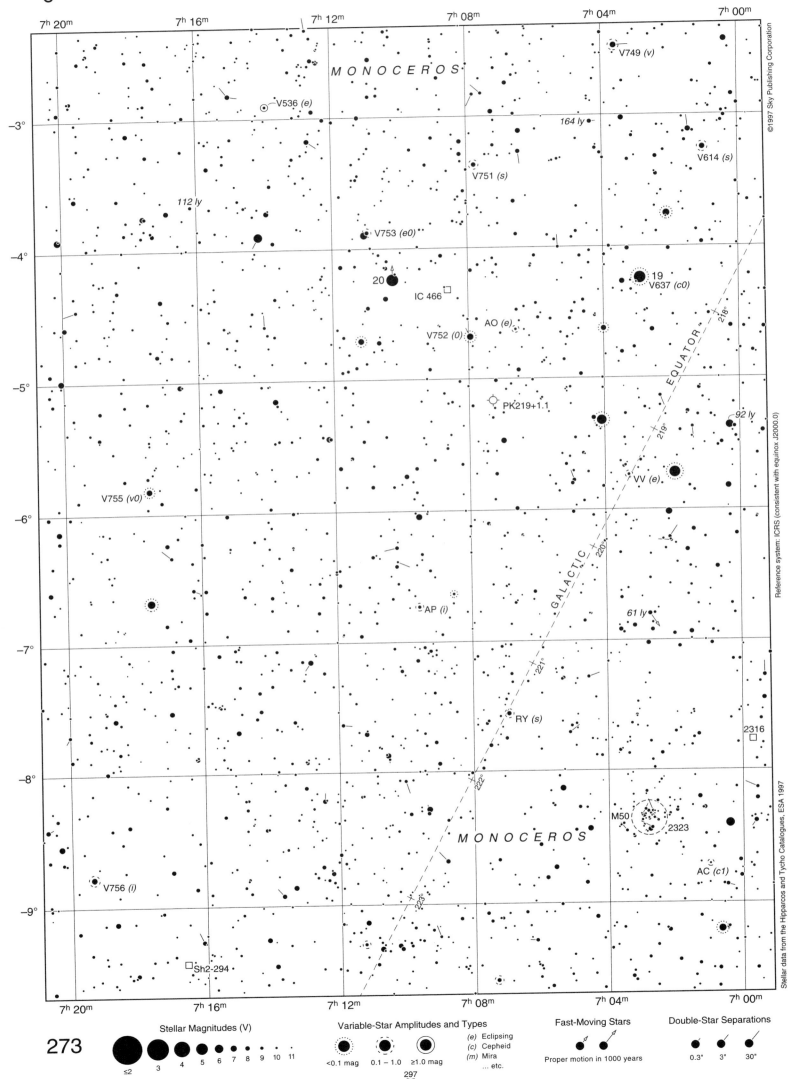

©1997 Sky Publishing Corporation

Reference system: ICRS (consistent with equinox J2000.0)

Stellar data from the Hipparcos and Tycho Catalogues, ESA 1997

MONOCEROS

V749 (v)
164 ly
V614 (s)
V536 (e)
V751 (s)
112 ly
V753 (e0)
20
19
IC 466
V637 (c0)
AO (e)
V752 (0)
218°
PK219+1.1
92 ly
219°
VV (e)
V755 (v0)
220°
AP (i)
61 ly
221°
RY (s)
2316
222°
M50
2323
MONOCEROS
AC (c1)
V756 (i)
223°
Sh2-294

EQUATOR

GALACTIC

273

Stellar Magnitudes (V)

≤2 3 4 5 6 7 8 9 10 11

Variable-Star Amplitudes and Types

<0.1 mag   0.1 – 1.0   ≥1.0 mag

(e) Eclipsing
(c) Cepheid
(m) Mira
... etc.

Fast-Moving Stars

Proper motion in 1000 years

Double-Star Separations

0.3"   3"   30"

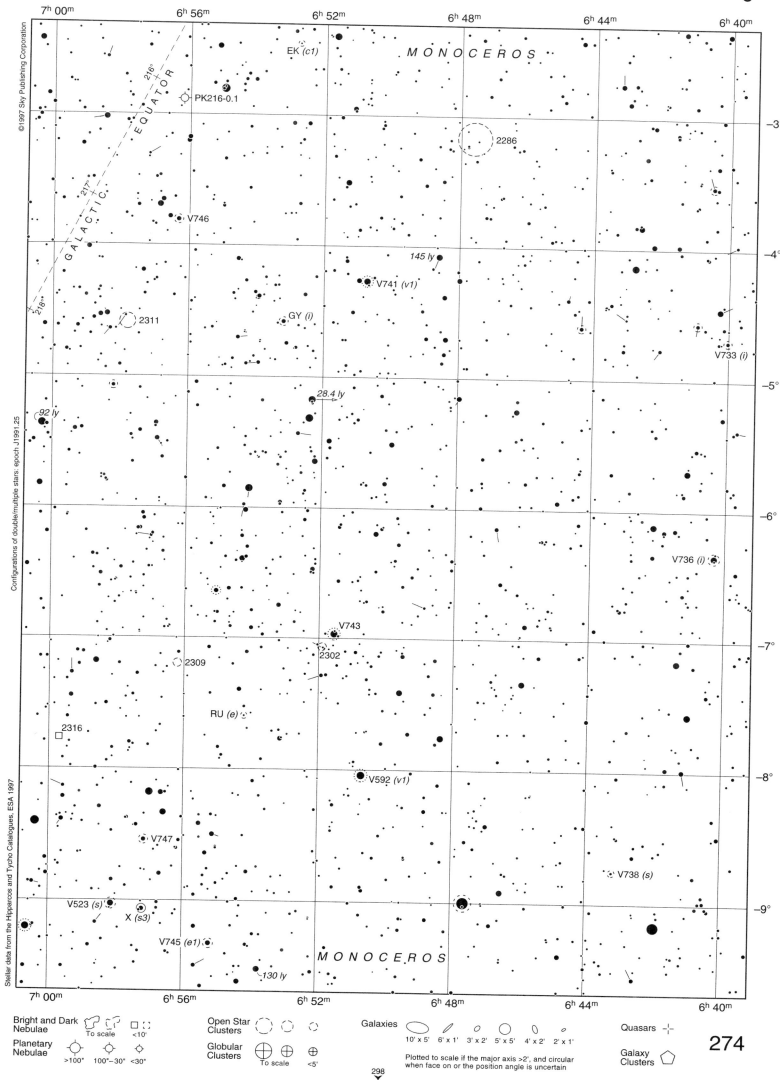

Configurations of double/multiple stars: epoch J1991.25

Stellar data from the Hipparcos and Tycho Catalogues, ESA 1997

7ʰ 00ᵐ   6ʰ 56ᵐ   6ʰ 52ᵐ   6ʰ 48ᵐ   6ʰ 44ᵐ   6ʰ 40ᵐ

EK (c1)

M O N O C E R O S

PK216-0.1

216°

EQUATOR

217°

GALACTIC

218°

V746

−3°

2286

145 ly

V741 (v1)

−4°

2311

GY (i)

V733 (i)

28.4 ly

−5°

92 ly

−6°

V736 (i)

V743

−7°

2309

2302

RU (e)

2316

V592 (v1)

−8°

V747

V738 (s)

V523 (s)

−9°

X (s3)

V745 (e1)

130 ly

M O N O C E R O S

7ʰ 00ᵐ   6ʰ 56ᵐ   6ʰ 52ᵐ   6ʰ 48ᵐ   6ʰ 44ᵐ   6ʰ 40ᵐ

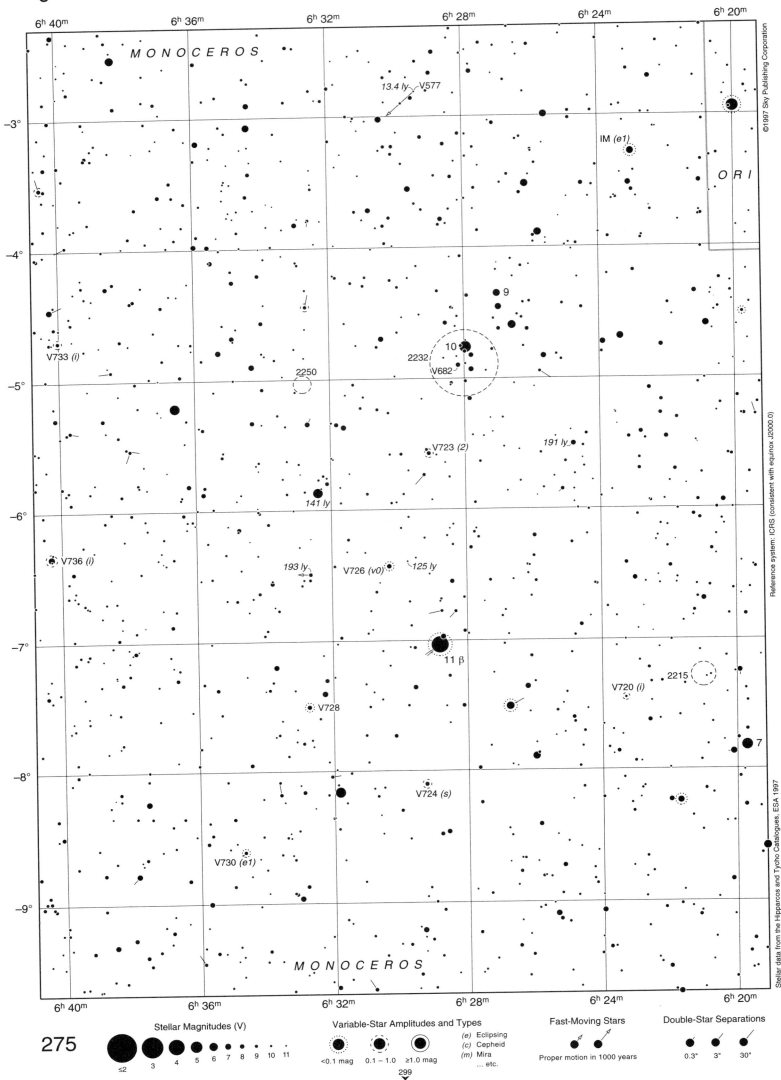

MONOCEROS

ORI

13.4 ly — V577

IM (e1)

9

10

2232

V682

2250

V733 (i)

V723 (2)

191 ly

141 ly

V736 (i)

193 ly   V726 (v0)   125 ly

11 β

2215

V720 (i)

V728

7

V724 (s)

V730 (e1)

MONOCEROS

275

Stellar Magnitudes (V)

≤2   3   4   5   6   7   8   9   10   11

Variable-Star Amplitudes and Types

<0.1 mag   0.1 – 1.0   ≥1.0 mag

(e) Eclipsing
(c) Cepheid
(m) Mira
... etc.

Fast-Moving Stars

Proper motion in 1000 years

Double-Star Separations

0.3"   3"   30"

MILLENNIUM STAR ATLAS

−6°

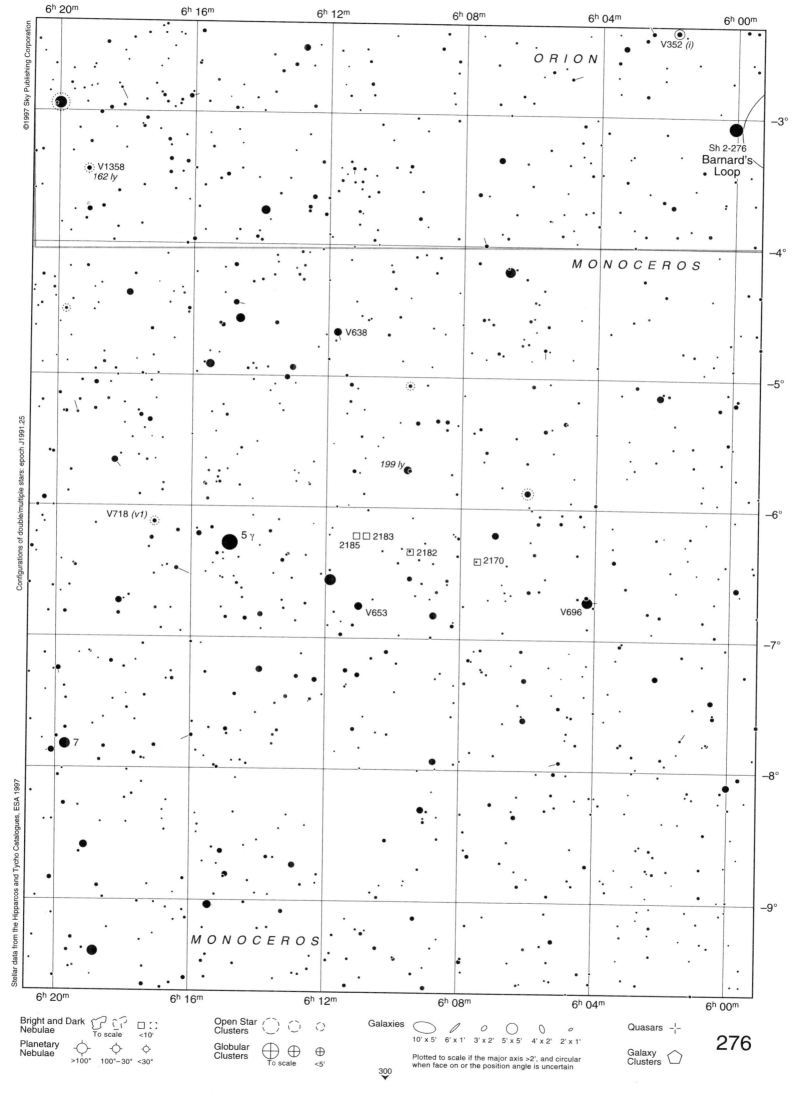

Configurations of double/multiple stars: epoch J1991.25

Stellar data from the Hipparcos and Tycho Catalogues, ESA 1997

O R I O N

V352 *(i)*

Sh 2-276
Barnard's
Loop

M O N O C E R O S

V1358
162 ly

V638

199 ly

V718 *(v1)*

5 γ

2185 ☐ ☐ 2183
2182
2170

V653

V696

7

M O N O C E R O S

Bright and Dark Nebulae	Open Star Clusters	Galaxies	Quasars

Bright and Dark Nebulae — To scale — <10'

Open Star Clusters

Planetary Nebulae — >100" 100"–30" <30'

Globular Clusters — To scale — <5'

Galaxies — 10' x 5' 6' x 1' 3' x 2' 5' x 5' 4' x 2' 2' x 1'

Plotted to scale if the major axis >2', and circular when face on or the position angle is uncertain

Quasars

Galaxy Clusters

276

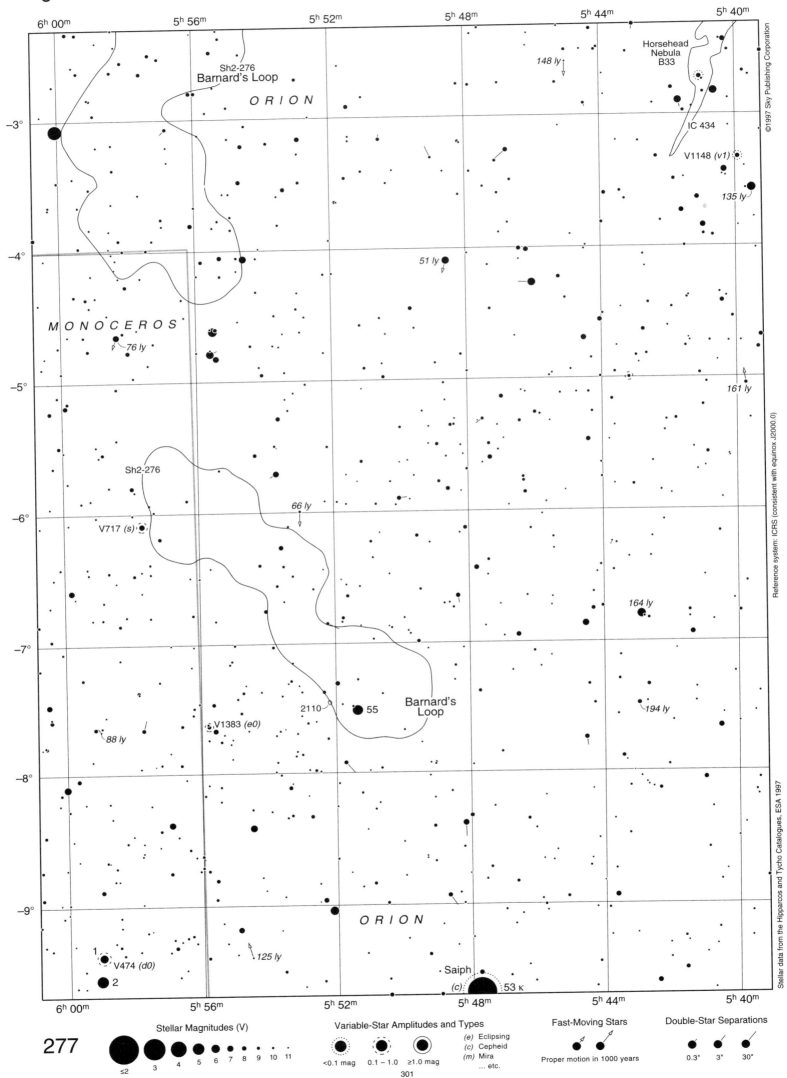

−6°

6h 00m   5h 56m   5h 52m   5h 48m   5h 44m   5h 40m

Sh2-276
Barnard's Loop

O R I O N

Horsehead
Nebula
B33

148 ly

IC 434

−3°

V1148 (v1)

135 ly

−4°

51 ly

M O N O C E R O S

76 ly

161 ly

−5°

Sh2-276

66 ly

164 ly

−6°

V717 (s)

Barnard's
Loop

2110   55

194 ly

−7°

V1383 (e0)

88 ly

−8°

O R I O N

−9°

1

125 ly

V474 (d0)

Saiph

2

(c)   53 κ

6h 00m   5h 56m   5h 52m   5h 48m   5h 44m   5h 40m

©1997 Sky Publishing Corporation

Reference system: ICRS (consistent with equinox J2000.0)

Stellar data from the Hipparcos and Tycho Catalogues, ESA 1997

Stellar Magnitudes (V)   Variable-Star Amplitudes and Types   Fast-Moving Stars   Double-Star Separations

277

≤2   3   4   5   6   7   8   9   10   11

<0.1 mag   0.1 – 1.0   ≥1.0 mag

(e) Eclipsing
(c) Cepheid
(m) Mira
... etc.

Proper motion in 1000 years

0.3"   3"   30"

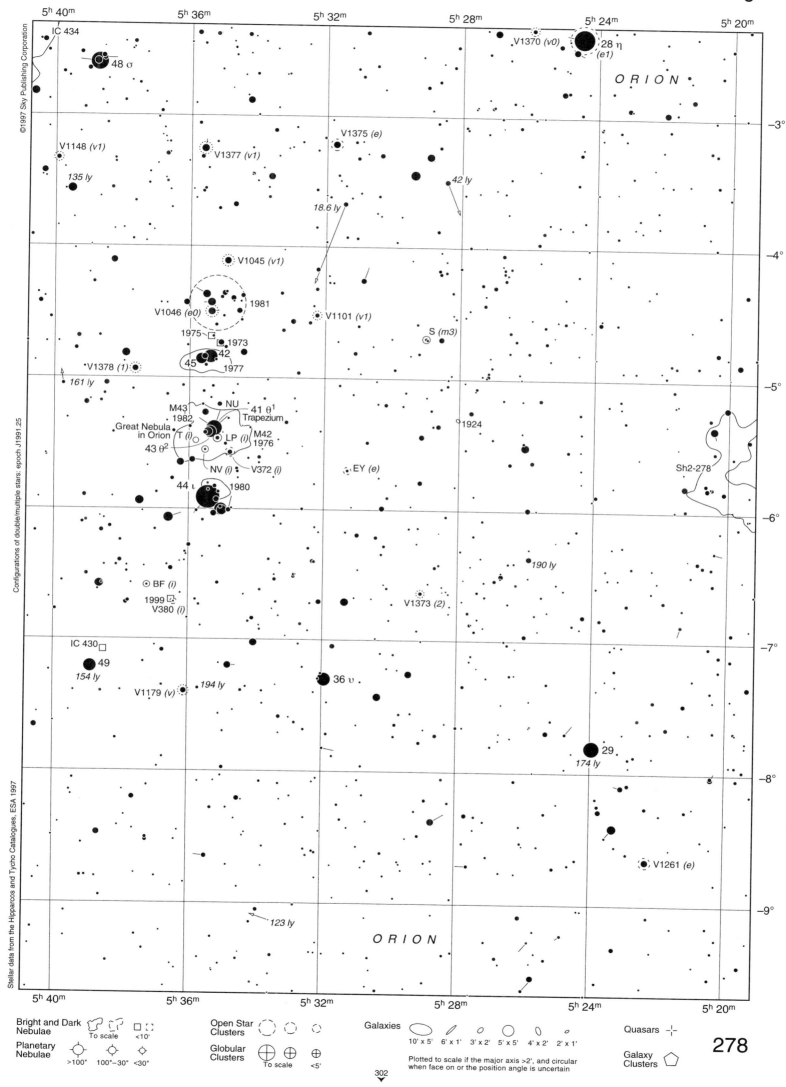

ORION

IC 434

48 σ

V1148 (v1)

135 ly

V1375 (e)

V1377 (v1)

V1370 (v0)

28 η
(e1)

42 ly

18.6 ly

V1045 (v1)

V1046 (e0)   1981

1975

1973

42

45   1977

V1378 (1)

161 ly

V1101 (v1)

S (m3)

1924

M43   NU   41 θ¹
1982   Trapezium

Great Nebula
in Orion   T (i)   LP (i)   M42
43 θ²   1976

NV (i)   V372 (i)

EY (e)

44 ι   1980

Sh2-278

BF (i)

1999
V380 (i)

V1373 (2)

190 ly

IC 430

49

154 ly

V1179 (v)   194 ly

36 υ

29

174 ly

V1261 (e)

123 ly

ORION

5ʰ 40ᵐ   5ʰ 36ᵐ   5ʰ 32ᵐ   5ʰ 28ᵐ   5ʰ 24ᵐ   5ʰ 20ᵐ

−3°

−4°

−5°

−6°

−7°

−8°

−9°

Bright and Dark
Nebulae
To scale   <10'

Planetary
Nebulae
>100"   100"–30"   <30"

Open Star
Clusters

Globular
Clusters
To scale   <5'

Galaxies

10' x 5'   6' x 1'   3' x 2'   5' x 5'   4' x 2'   2' x 1'

Plotted to scale if the major axis >2', and circular
when face on or the position angle is uncertain

Quasars

Galaxy
Clusters

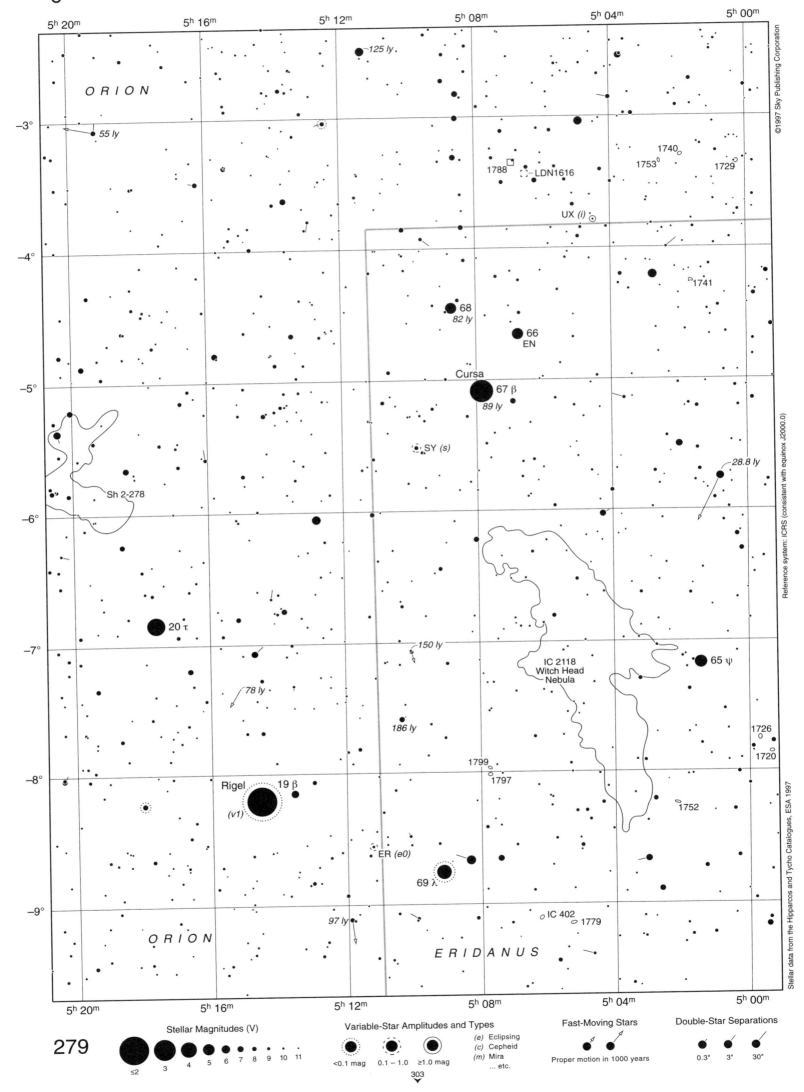

ORION

−3°

~125 ly

55 ly

1740
1788   LDN1616   1753°   1729

UX (i)

−4°

1741

68
82 ly

66
EN

Cursa

−5°

67 β
89 ly

SY (s)

28.8 ly

Sh 2-278

−6°

IC 2118
Witch Head
Nebula

65 ψ

20 τ

−7°

150 ly

78 ly

1726
186 ly

1720

1799
1797

−8°

Rigel   19 β

1752

(v1)

ER (e0)

69 λ

−9°

IC 402   1779

97 ly

ORION   ERIDANUS

©1997 Sky Publishing Corporation

Reference system: ICRS (consistent with equinox J2000.0)

Stellar data from the Hipparcos and Tycho Catalogues, ESA 1997

Stellar Magnitudes (V)

279

≤2   3   4   5   6   7   8   9   10   11

Variable-Star Amplitudes and Types

<0.1 mag   0.1 – 1.0   ≥1.0 mag

(e) Eclipsing
(c) Cepheid
(m) Mira
... etc.

Fast-Moving Stars

Proper motion in 1000 years

Double-Star Separations

0.3"   3"   30"

MILLENNIUM STAR ATLAS

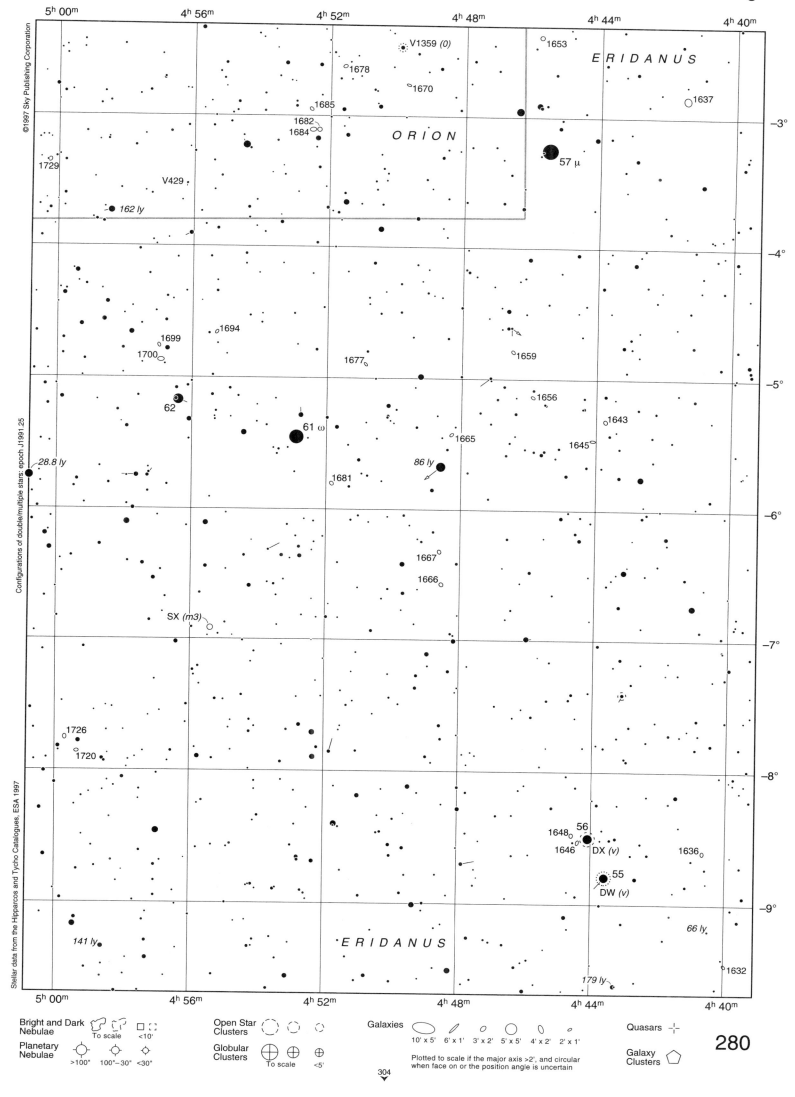

ERIDANUS

V1359 (0)
1653
1678
1670
1637
1685
ORION
1682
1684
57 μ
1729
V429
162 ly

1694
1699
1700
1677
1659
62
1656
61 ω
1643
1665
1645
28.8 ly
86 ly
1681

1667
1666

SX (m3)

1726
1720

56
1648
1646
DX (v)
1636
55
DW (v)
141 ly
ERIDANUS
66 ly
179 ly
1632

Legend

Bright and Dark Nebulae — To scale — <10'

Planetary Nebulae — >100" — 100"–30" — <30"

Open Star Clusters

Globular Clusters — To scale — <5'

Galaxies — 10' x 5' — 6' x 1' — 3' x 2' — 5' x 5' — 4' x 2' — 2' x 1'

Plotted to scale if the major axis >2', and circular when face on or the position angle is uncertain

Quasars

Galaxy Clusters

280

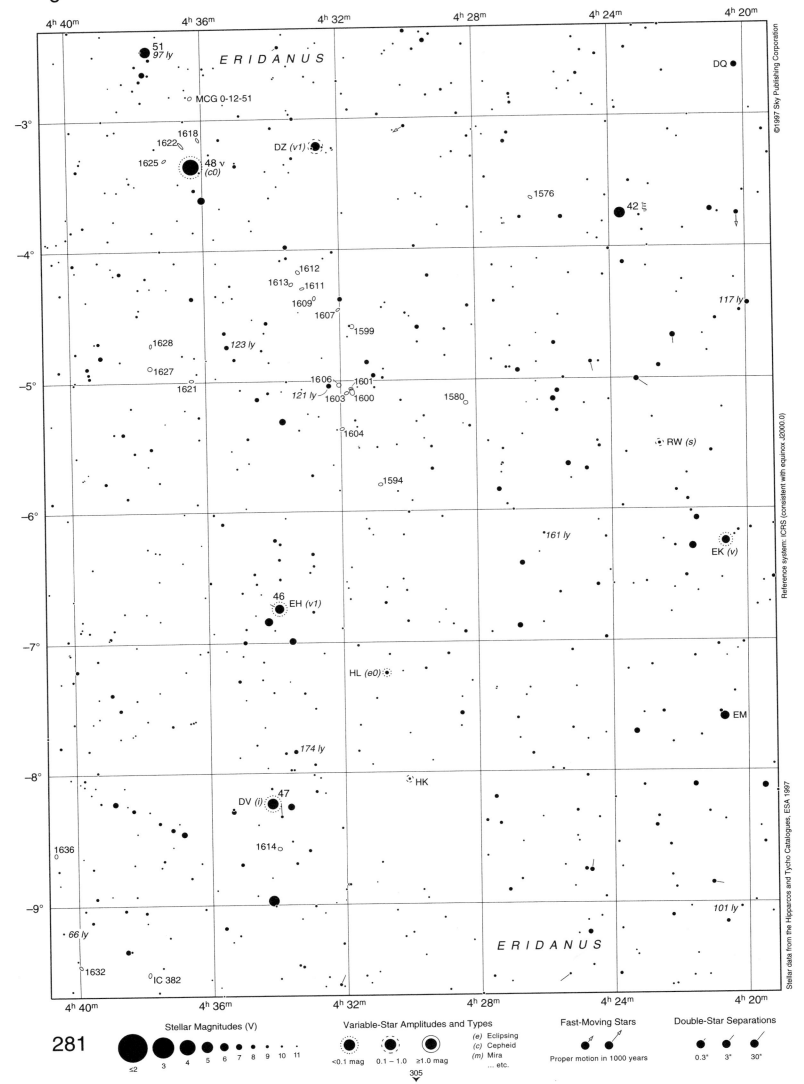

ERIDANUS

ERIDANUS

51
97 ly

DQ

MCG 0-12-51

1618
1622
1625
48 ν
(c0)

DZ (v1)

1576

42 ξ

117 ly

1612
1613
1609
1607
1611

1599

1628

123 ly

1627
1621

1606
1603 1600
121 ly

1601

1580

1604

RW (s)

1594

161 ly

EK (v)

46
EH (v1)

HL (e0)

EM

174 ly

HK

DV (i)
47

1636

1614

66 ly

1632

IC 382

101 ly

©1997 Sky Publishing Corporation

Reference system: ICRS (consistent with equinox J2000.0)

Stellar data from the Hipparcos and Tycho Catalogues, ESA 1997

281

Stellar Magnitudes (V)

≤2
3
4
5
6
7
8
9
10
11

Variable-Star Amplitudes and Types

<0.1 mag   0.1 – 1.0   ≥1.0 mag

(e) Eclipsing
(c) Cepheid
(m) Mira
... etc.

Fast-Moving Stars

Proper motion in 1000 years

Double-Star Separations

0.3"   3"   30"

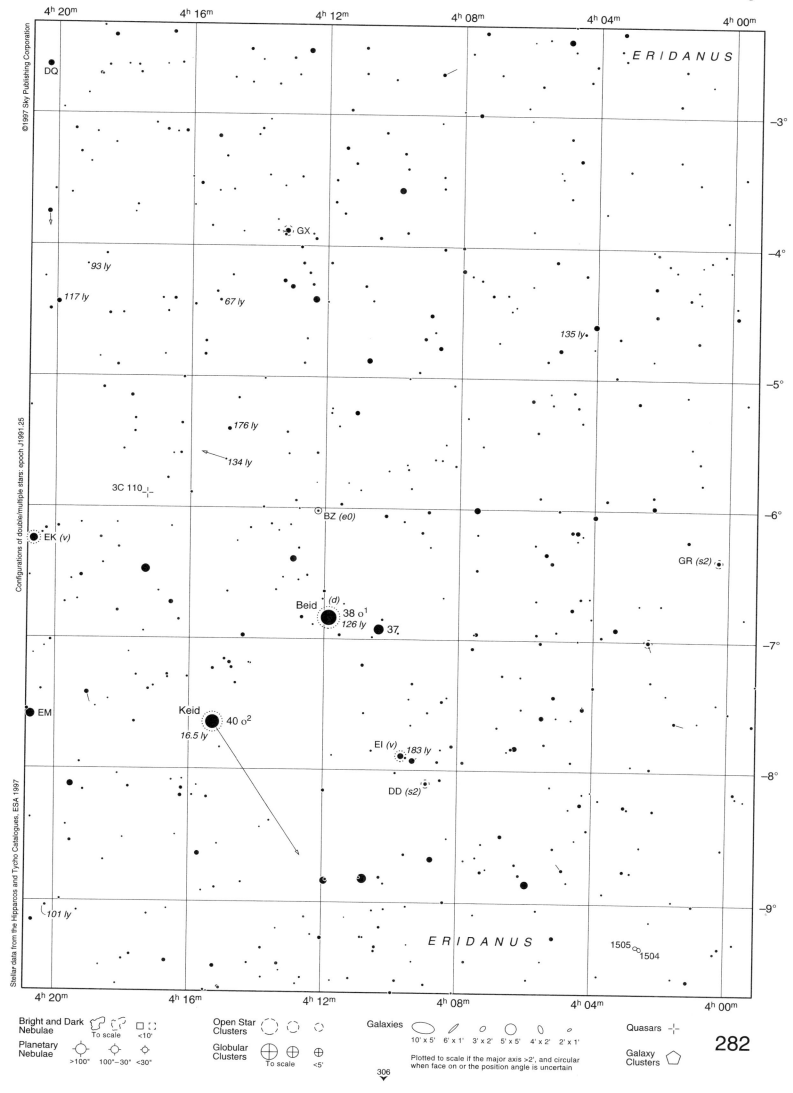

ERIDANUS

DQ

GX

93 ly

117 ly

67 ly

135 ly

176 ly

134 ly

3C 110

BZ (e0)

EK (v)

GR (s2)

Beid   (d)
38 o¹
126 ly   37

Keid   40 o²
16.5 ly

El (v)   183 ly

EM

DD (s2)

101 ly

ERIDANUS

1505 ⊙⊙ 1504

Bright and Dark Nebulae	Open Star Clusters	Galaxies	Quasars

To scale   <10'

Planetary Nebulae   >100"   100"–30"   <30"

Globular Clusters   To scale   <5'

Galaxies   10' x 5'   6' x 1'   3' x 2'   5' x 5'   4' x 2'   2' x 1'

Galaxy Clusters

Plotted to scale if the major axis >2', and circular when face on or the position angle is uncertain

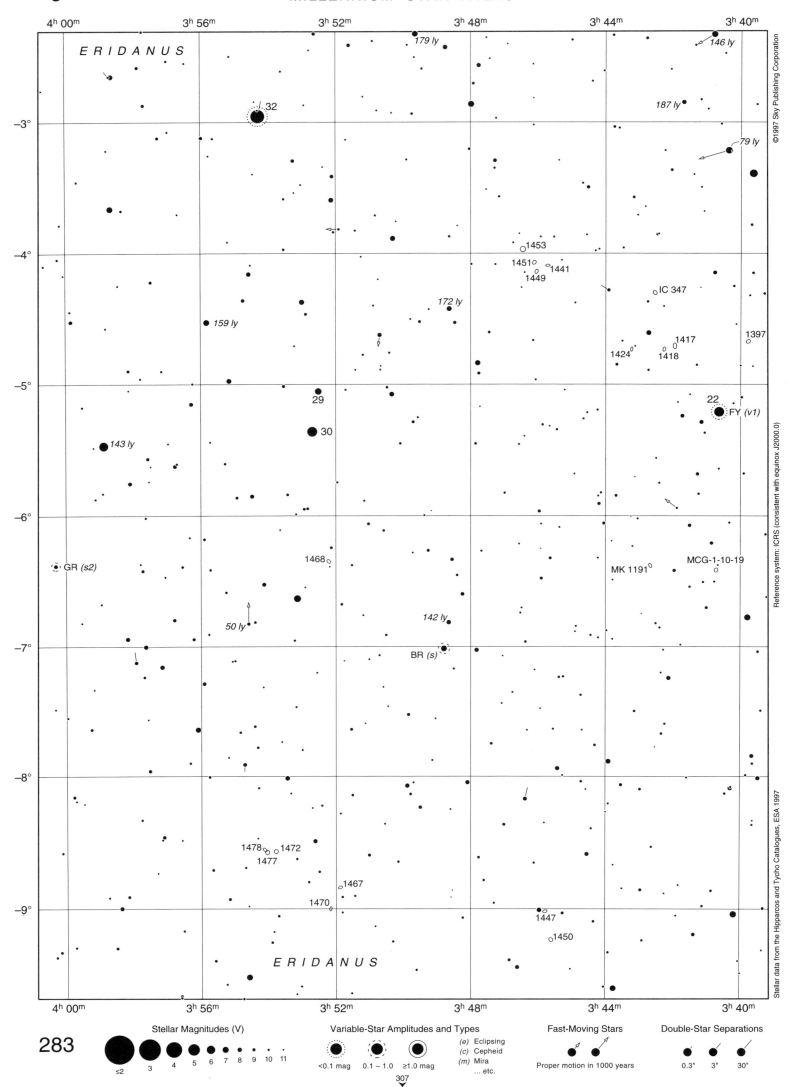

©1997 Sky Publishing Corporation

Reference system: ICRS (consistent with equinox J2000.0)

Stellar data from the Hipparcos and Tycho Catalogues, ESA 1997

ERIDANUS

179 ly

146 ly

187 ly

79 ly

32

1453

1451 1441
1449

IC 347

172 ly

1424 1417
1418

1397

159 ly

29

22
FY (v1)

30

143 ly

GR (s2)

1468

MK 1191

MCG-1-10-19

50 ly

142 ly

BR (s)

1478 1472
1477

1467

1470

1447

1450

ERIDANUS

Stellar Magnitudes (V)

≤2   3   4   5   6   7   8   9   10   11

Variable-Star Amplitudes and Types

<0.1 mag   0.1 − 1.0   ≥1.0 mag

(e) Eclipsing
(c) Cepheid
(m) Mira
... etc.

Fast-Moving Stars

Proper motion in 1000 years

Double-Star Separations

0.3"   3"   30"

MILLENNIUM STAR ATLAS

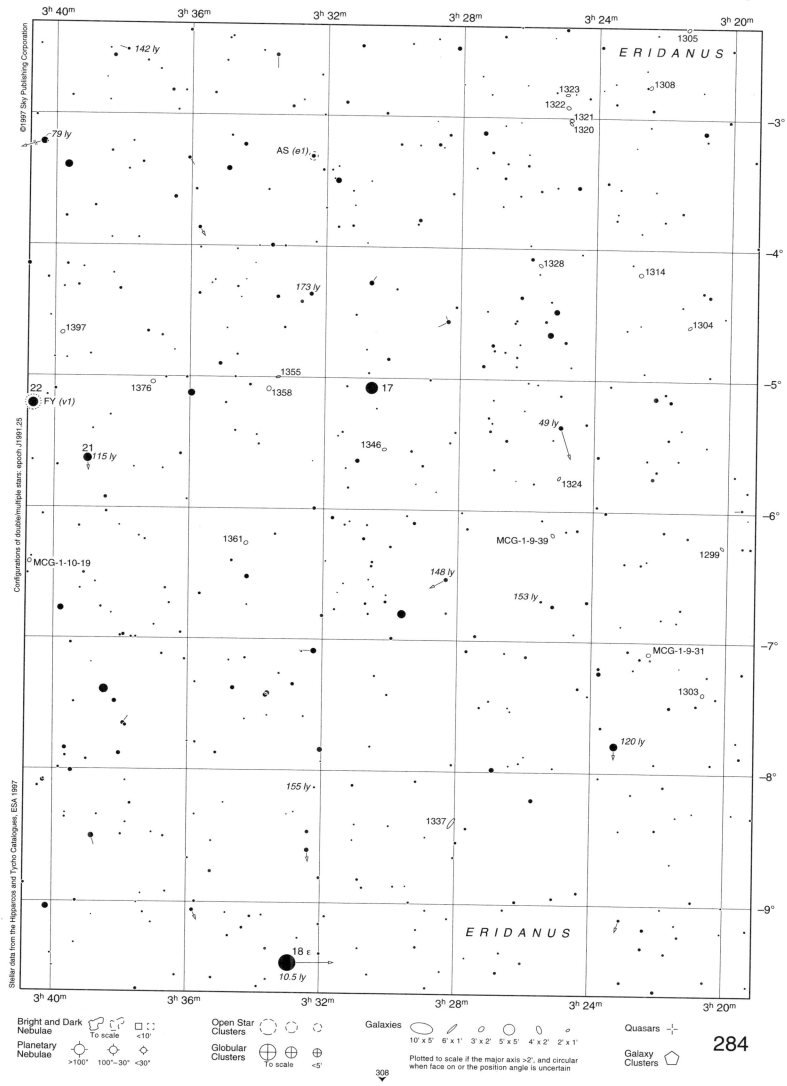

Configurations of double/multiple stars: epoch J1991.25

Stellar data from the Hipparcos and Tycho Catalogues, ESA 1997

3h 40m   3h 36m   3h 32m   3h 28m   3h 24m   3h 20m

ERIDANUS

1305

142 ly

1323
1322
1321
1320

1308

AS (e1)

79 ly

173 ly

1328

1314

1397

1304

1355

22
FY (v1)

1376

1358

17

21
115 ly

1346

49 ly

1324

1361

MCG-1-10-19

MCG-1-9-39

1299

148 ly

153 ly

MCG-1-9-31

1303

120 ly

155 ly

1337

ERIDANUS

18 ε

10.5 ly

3h 40m   3h 36m   3h 32m   3h 28m   3h 24m   3h 20m

−3°

−4°

−5°

−6°

−7°

−8°

−9°

Bright and Dark
Nebulae
To scale   <10'

Planetary
Nebulae
>100"   100"–30"   <30"

Open Star
Clusters

Globular
Clusters
To scale   <5'

Galaxies
10' x 5'   6' x 1'   3' x 2'   5' x 5'   4' x 2'   2' x 1'

Plotted to scale if the major axis >2', and circular
when face on or the position angle is uncertain

Quasars

Galaxy
Clusters

284

308

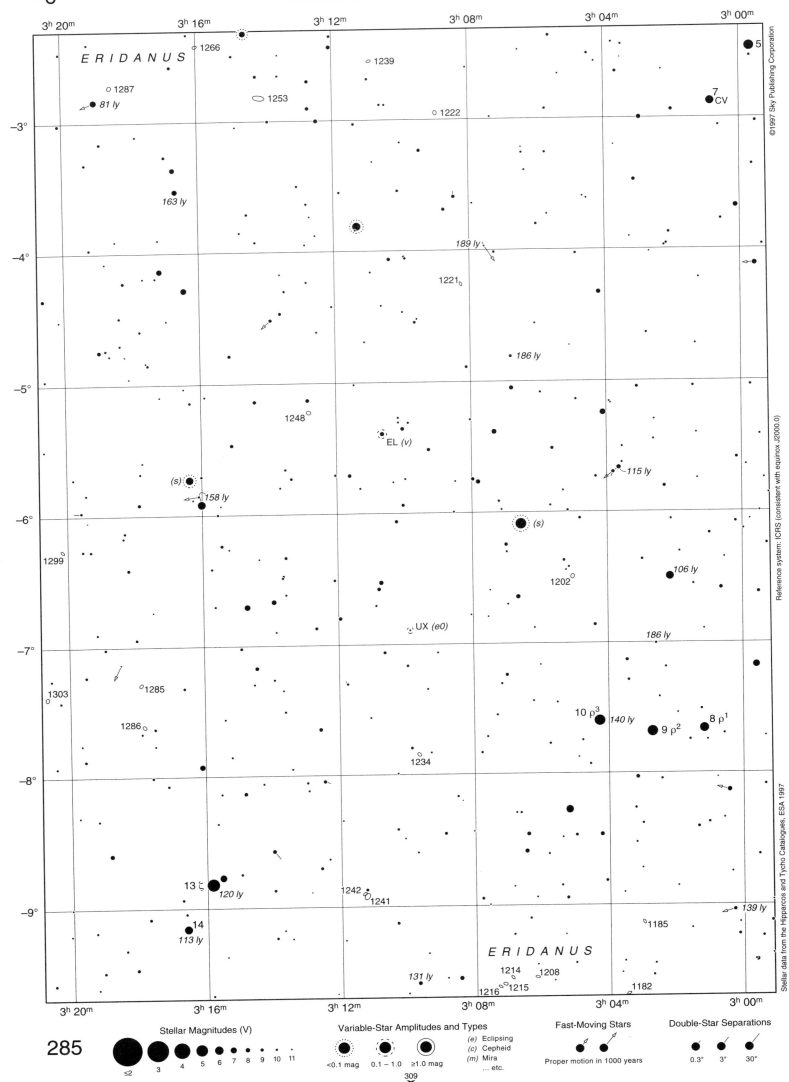

ERIDANUS

∘ 1266
∘ 1287
81 ly
1253
∘ 1239
∘ 1222

7 CV

163 ly

189 ly

1221 ∘

186 ly

1248 ∘

EL (v)

115 ly

(s)

158 ly

(s)

106 ly

1299 ∘

1202 ∘

186 ly

UX (e0)

1303 ∘
∘ 1285
1286 ∘

10 ρ³   140 ly
9 ρ²   8 ρ¹

1234

13 ζ
120 ly

1242 ∘
∘ 1241

139 ly

14
113 ly

∘ 1185

ERIDANUS

131 ly

1214
∘ 1208
1216 ∘ ∘ 1215

1182

Reference system: ICRS (consistent with equinox J2000.0)

Stellar data from the Hipparcos and Tycho Catalogues, ESA 1997

285

Stellar Magnitudes (V)

≤2   3   4   5   6   7   8   9   10   11

Variable-Star Amplitudes and Types

<0.1 mag   0.1 − 1.0   ≥1.0 mag

(e) Eclipsing
(c) Cepheid
(m) Mira
... etc.

Fast-Moving Stars

Proper motion in 1000 years

Double-Star Separations

0.3"   3"   30"

309

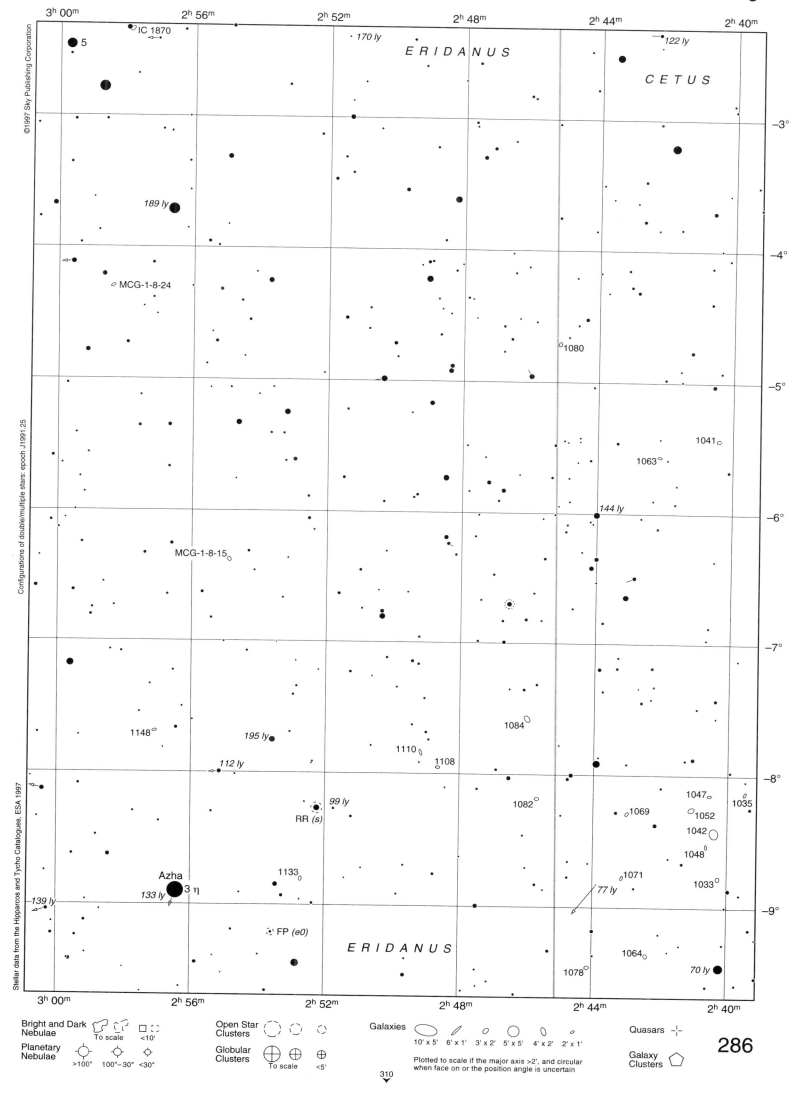

Configurations of double/multiple stars: epoch J1991.25

Stellar data from the Hipparcos and Tycho Catalogues, ESA 1997

3h 00m 2h 56m 2h 52m 2h 48m 2h 44m 2h 40m

5

IC 1870

· 170 ly

ERIDANUS

— 122 ly

CETUS

-3°

189 ly

-4°

MCG-1-8-24

1080

-5°

1041

1063

144 ly

-6°

MCG-1-8-15

-7°

1148

195 ly

1110

1084

112 ly

1108

-8°

99 ly

1082

1047

1035

RR (s)

1069

1052

1042

1048

Azha

1133

1071

1033

139 ly

133 ly

3 η

77 ly

-9°

FP (e0)

ERIDANUS

1064

1078

70 ly

3h 00m 2h 56m 2h 52m 2h 48m 2h 44m 2h 40m

Bright and Dark Nebulae
To scale   <10'

Planetary Nebulae
>100"   100"-30"   <30"

Open Star Clusters

Globular Clusters
To scale   <5'

Galaxies
10' x 5'   6' x 1'   3' x 2'   5' x 5'   4' x 2'   2' x 1'

Plotted to scale if the major axis >2', and circular when face on or the position angle is uncertain

Quasars

Galaxy Clusters

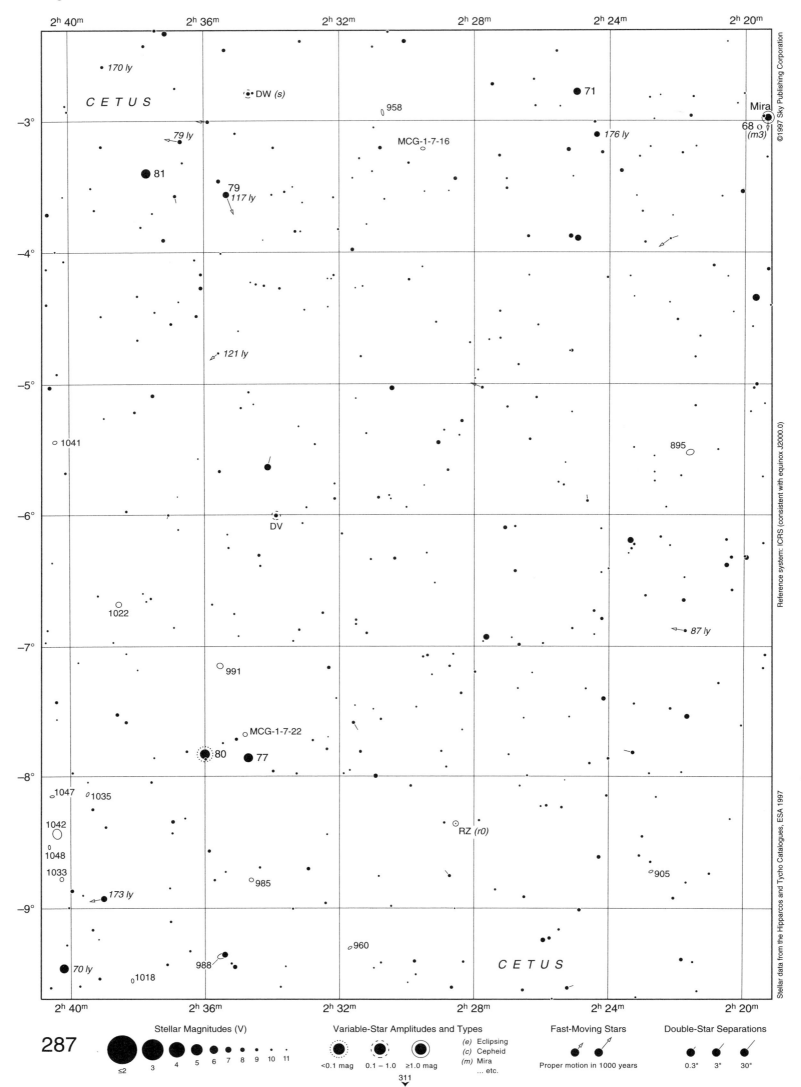

©1997 Sky Publishing Corporation

Reference system: ICRS (consistent with equinox J2000.0)

Stellar data from the Hipparcos and Tycho Catalogues, ESA 1997

CETUS

170 ly

DW (s)

958

MCG-1-7-16

71

Mira

68 o
(m3)

79 ly

176 ly

81

79
117 ly

121 ly

1041

895

DV

1022

87 ly

991

MCG-1-7-22

80   77

1047   1035

1042

RZ (r0)

1048

905

1033

985

173 ly

960

CETUS

70 ly

988

1018

Stellar Magnitudes (V)

≤2   3   4   5   6   7   8   9   10   11

Variable-Star Amplitudes and Types

<0.1 mag   0.1 − 1.0   ≥1.0 mag

(e) Eclipsing
(c) Cepheid
(m) Mira
... etc.

Fast-Moving Stars

Proper motion in 1000 years

Double-Star Separations

0.3"   3"   30"

311

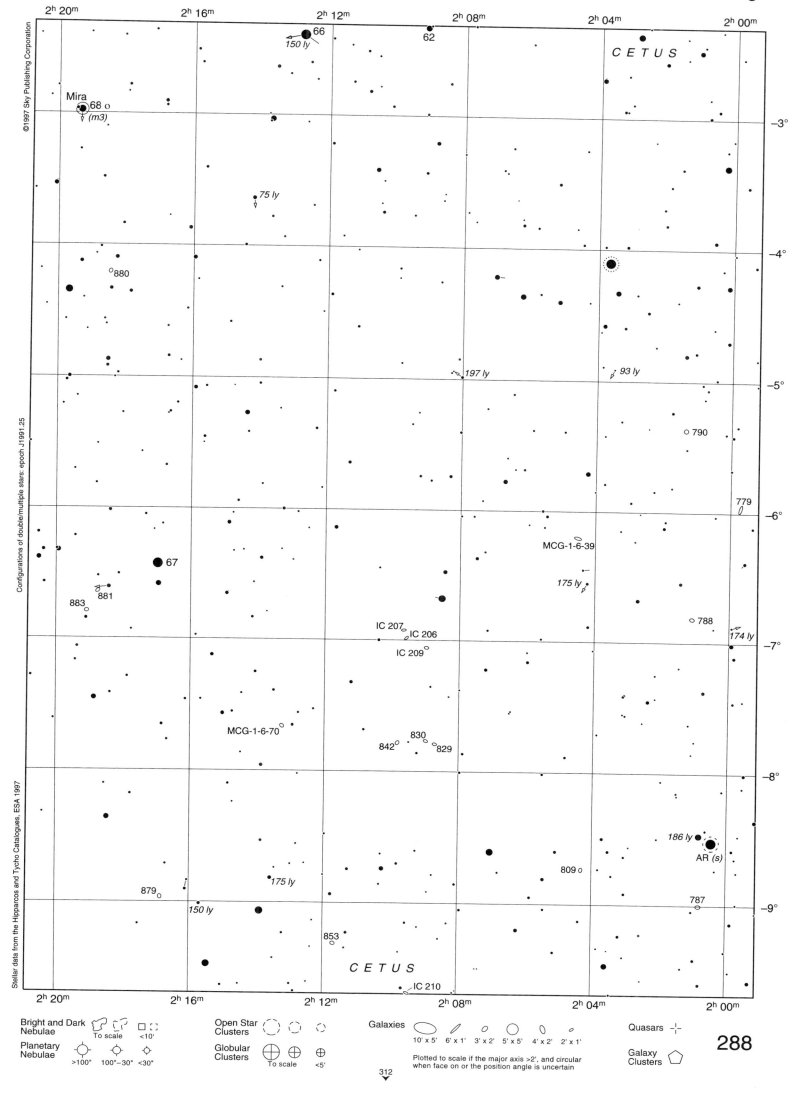

66
150 ly
62
CETUS

Mira
68 o
(m3)

−3°

75 ly

880
−4°

197 ly
93 ly

−5°

790

779

MCG-1-6-39
−6°

67
175 ly

881
883
788
174 ly

IC 207
IC 206
−7°

IC 209

MCG-1-6-70

830
842
829

−8°

186 ly
AR (s)

809 o

175 ly
879

787

150 ly
−9°

853

CETUS

IC 210

@1997 Sky Publishing Corporation

Configurations of double/multiple stars: epoch J1991.25

Stellar data from the Hipparcos and Tycho Catalogues, ESA 1997

Bright and Dark Nebulae
To scale   <10'

Planetary Nebulae
>100"   100"−30"   <30"

Open Star Clusters

Globular Clusters
To scale   <5'

Galaxies
10' x 5'   6' x 1'   3' x 2'   5' x 5'   4' x 2'   2' x 1'

Plotted to scale if the major axis >2', and circular when face on or the position angle is uncertain

Quasars

Galaxy Clusters

288

312

MILLENNIUM STAR ATLAS

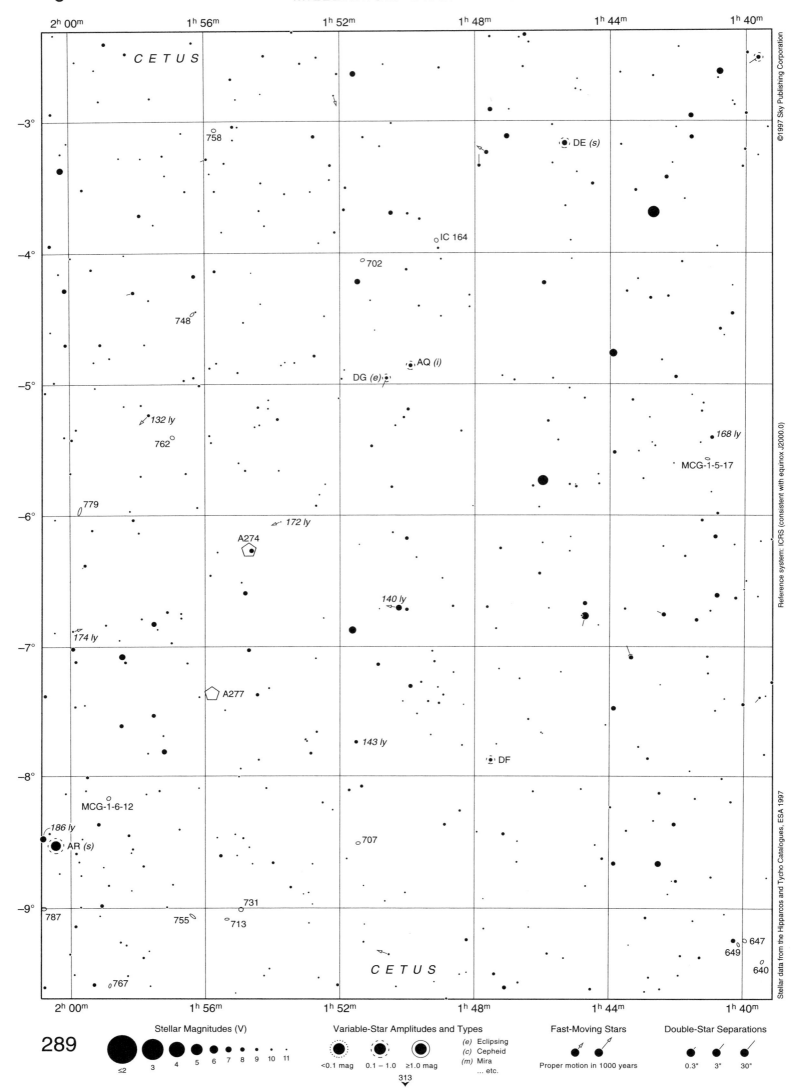

−6°

CETUS

758

IC 164

702

748

DE (s)

AQ (i)

DG (e)

132 ly

762

168 ly

MCG-1-5-17

779

172 ly

A274

140 ly

174 ly

A277

143 ly

DF

MCG-1-6-12

186 ly

AR (s)

707

731

787

755

713

649 647

640

CETUS

767

©1997 Sky Publishing Corporation

Reference system: ICRS (consistent with equinox J2000.0)

Stellar data from the Hipparcos and Tycho Catalogues, ESA 1997

289

| Stellar Magnitudes (V) | Variable-Star Amplitudes and Types | Fast-Moving Stars | Double-Star Separations |

≤2   3   4   5   6 7 8 9 10 11

<0.1 mag   0.1 – 1.0 mag   ≥1.0 mag

(e) Eclipsing
(c) Cepheid
(m) Mira
... etc.

Proper motion in 1000 years

0.3"   3"   30"

313

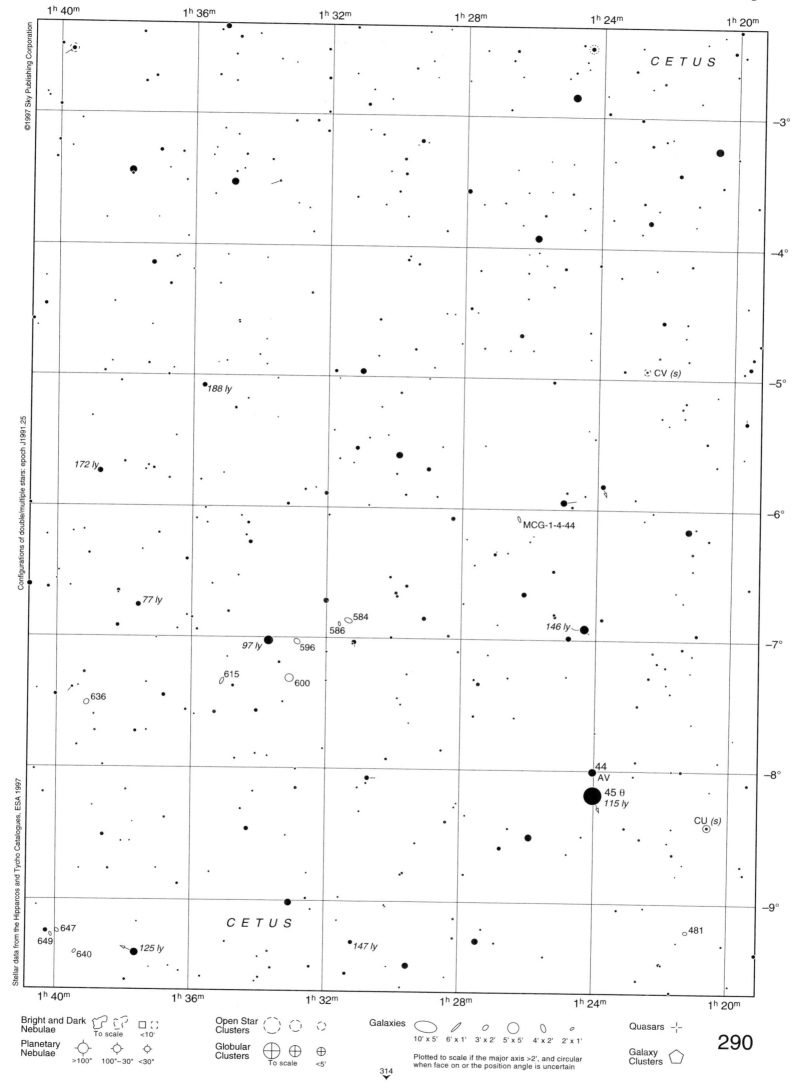

Configurations of double/multiple stars: epoch J1991.25

Stellar data from the Hipparcos and Tycho Catalogues, ESA 1997

C E T U S

CV *(s)*

MCG-1-4-44

188 ly

172 ly

77 ly

146 ly

97 ly

596

615

600

636

584
586

44
AV

45 θ
115 ly

CU *(s)*

C E T U S

647
649
640

125 ly

147 ly

481

Bright and Dark Nebulae			Open Star Clusters			Galaxies						Quasars
	To scale	<10'				10' x 5'	6' x 1'	3' x 2'	5' x 5'	4' x 2'	2' x 1'	
Planetary Nebulae			Globular Clusters									Galaxy Clusters
>100"	100"−30"	<30"	To scale		<5'	Plotted to scale if the major axis >2', and circular when face on or the position angle is uncertain						

290

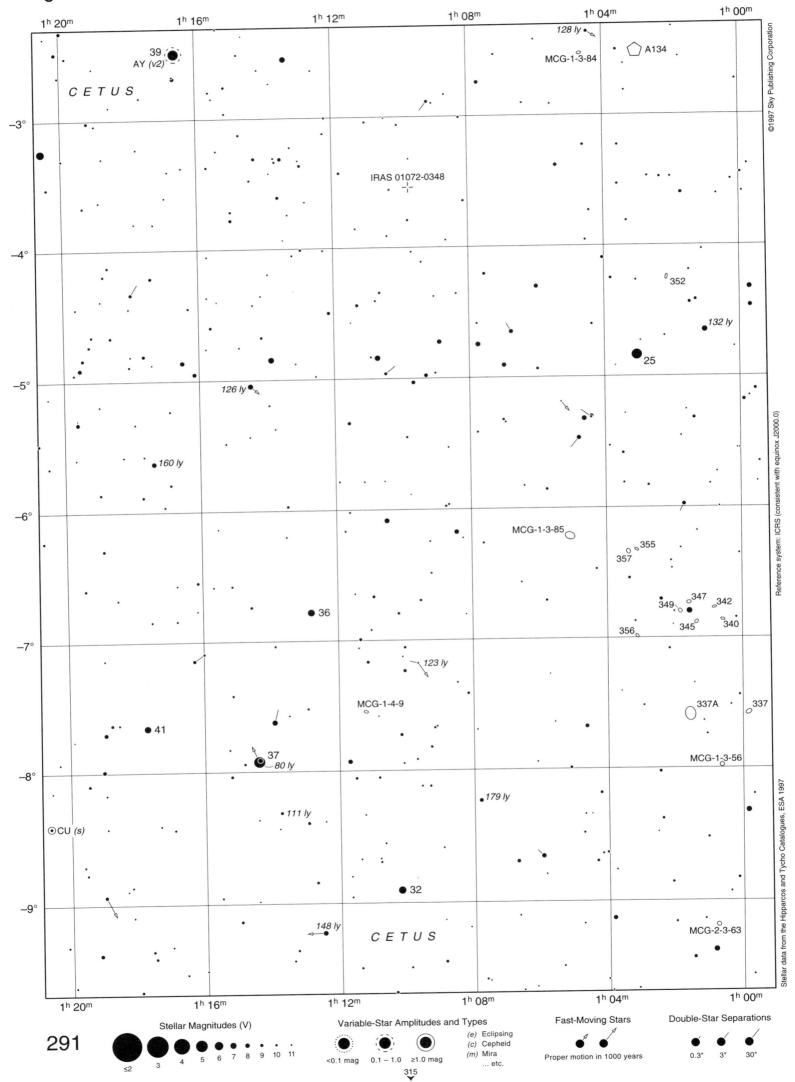

−6°

1ʰ 20ᵐ   1ʰ 16ᵐ   1ʰ 12ᵐ   1ʰ 08ᵐ   1ʰ 04ᵐ   1ʰ 00ᵐ

−3°

−4°

−5°

−6°

−7°

−8°

−9°

CETUS

39
AY *(v2)*

128 ly
MCG-1-3-84   A134

IRAS 01072-0348

⁰ 352

132 ly

25

126 ly

160 ly

MCG-1-3-85

355
357

349 ⁰ 347   342
345   340
356

36

123 ly

MCG-1-4-9

337A   337

41

37
80 ly

MCG-1-3-56

179 ly

⊙CU *(s)*

111 ly

32

148 ly   *CETUS*

MCG-2-3-63

©1997 Sky Publishing Corporation

Reference system: ICRS (consistent with equinox J2000.0)

Stellar data from the Hipparcos and Tycho Catalogues, ESA 1997

291

Stellar Magnitudes (V)
≤2 3 4 5 6 7 8 9 10 11

Variable-Star Amplitudes and Types
<0.1 mag   0.1 − 1.0   ≥1.0 mag

(e) Eclipsing
(c) Cepheid
(m) Mira
... etc.

Fast-Moving Stars
Proper motion in 1000 years

Double-Star Separations
0.3"   3"   30"

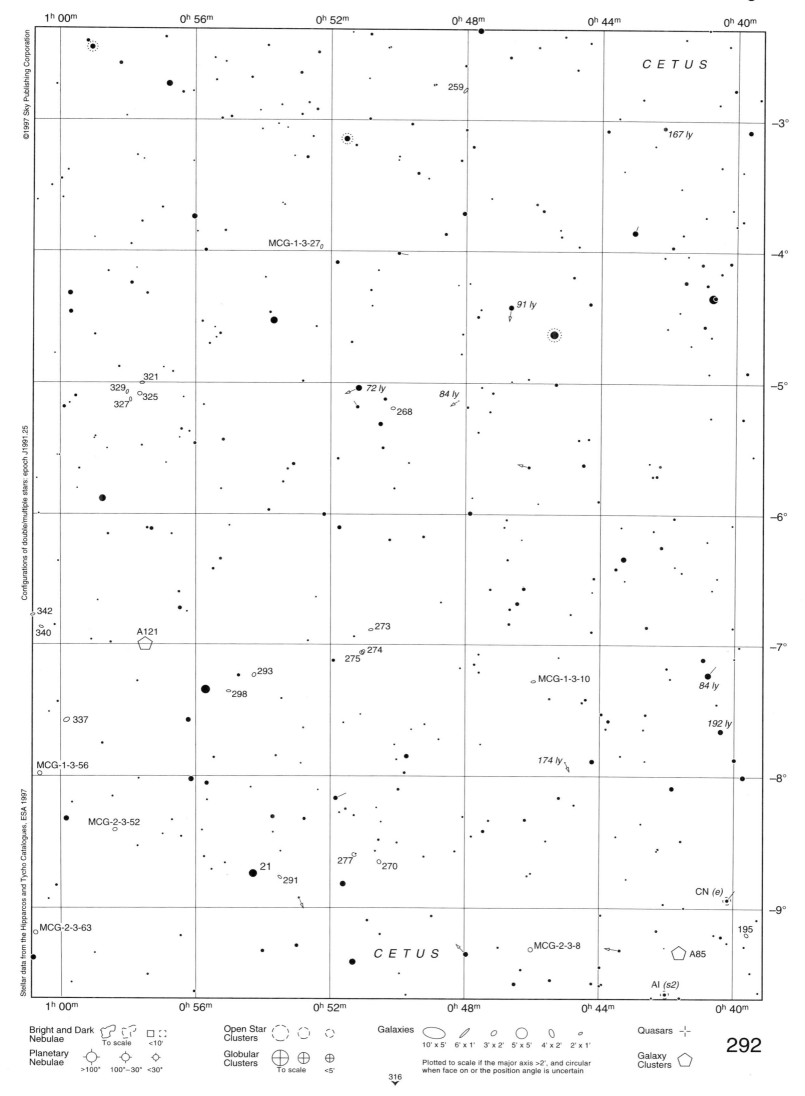

C E T U S

MCG-1-3-27₀

259

167 ly

91 ly

321
329₀   ○ 325
327₀

72 ly
○ 268

84 ly

342
340

A121

○ 273

○ 293   275 ○ 274

○ 298

○ 337

MCG-1-3-56

MCG-2-3-52

21
○ 291

277   ○ 270

MCG-2-3-63

MCG-1-3-10

84 ly

192 ly

174 ly

CN (e)

195

MCG-2-3-8

A85

AI (s2)

C E T U S

©1997 Sky Publishing Corporation

Configurations of double/multiple stars: epoch J1991.25

Stellar data from the Hipparcos and Tycho Catalogues, ESA 1997

Bright and Dark Nebulae	To scale	<10'		
Planetary Nebulae	>100" 100"−30" <30"			
Open Star Clusters				
Globular Clusters	To scale	<5'		

Galaxies

10' x 5'   6' x 1'   3' x 2'   5' x 5'   4' x 2'   2' x 1'

Plotted to scale if the major axis >2', and circular when face on or the position angle is uncertain

Quasars

Galaxy Clusters

292

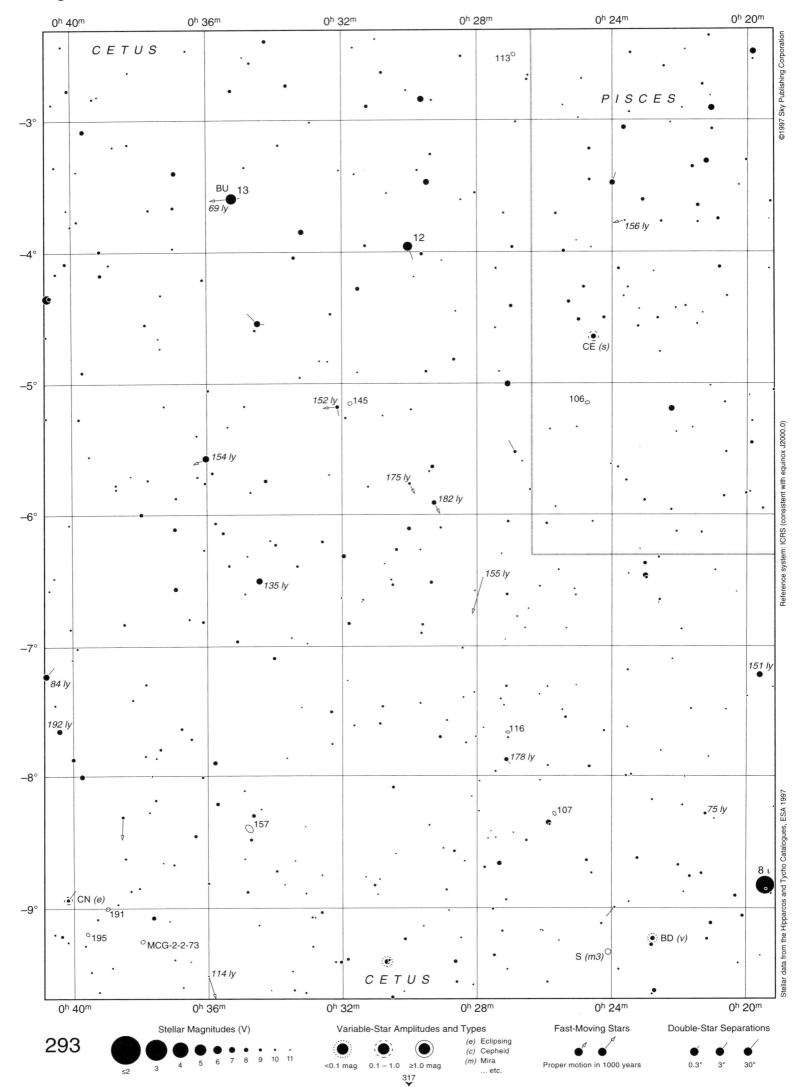

©1997 Sky Publishing Corporation

Reference system: ICRS (consistent with equinox J2000.0)

Stellar data from the Hipparcos and Tycho Catalogues, ESA 1997

Stellar Magnitudes (V)

≤2   3   4   5   6   7   8   9   10   11

Variable-Star Amplitudes and Types

<0.1 mag   0.1 – 1.0   ≥1.0 mag

(e) Eclipsing
(c) Cepheid
(m) Mira
... etc.

Fast-Moving Stars

Proper motion in 1000 years

Double-Star Separations

0.3"   3"   30"

317

0h 20m 0h 16m 0h 12m 0h 08m 0h 04m 0h 00m

5 Cet

AP (s2)

P I S C E S

193 ly

BH

104 ly

29

−3°

192 ly

174 ly

7832

164 ly

−4°

139 ly

−5°

179 ly

38

33
BC

30
YY (i)

83 ly

129 ly

−6°

64

54 47

151 ly

151 ly

50

AD (i)

151 ly

−7°

76 ly

MCG-1-1-30

−8°

115 ly

8 ι

−9°

C E T U S

165 ly

0h 20m 0h 16m 0h 12m 0h 08m 0h 04m 0h 00m

Bright and Dark Nebulae	Open Star Clusters	Galaxies	Quasars
To scale <10'		10' x 5' 6' x 1' 3' x 2' 5' x 5' 4' x 2' 2' x 1'	
Planetary Nebulae	Globular Clusters		Galaxy Clusters
>100" 100"–30" <30"	To scale <5'	Plotted to scale if the major axis >2', and circular when face on or the position angle is uncertain	

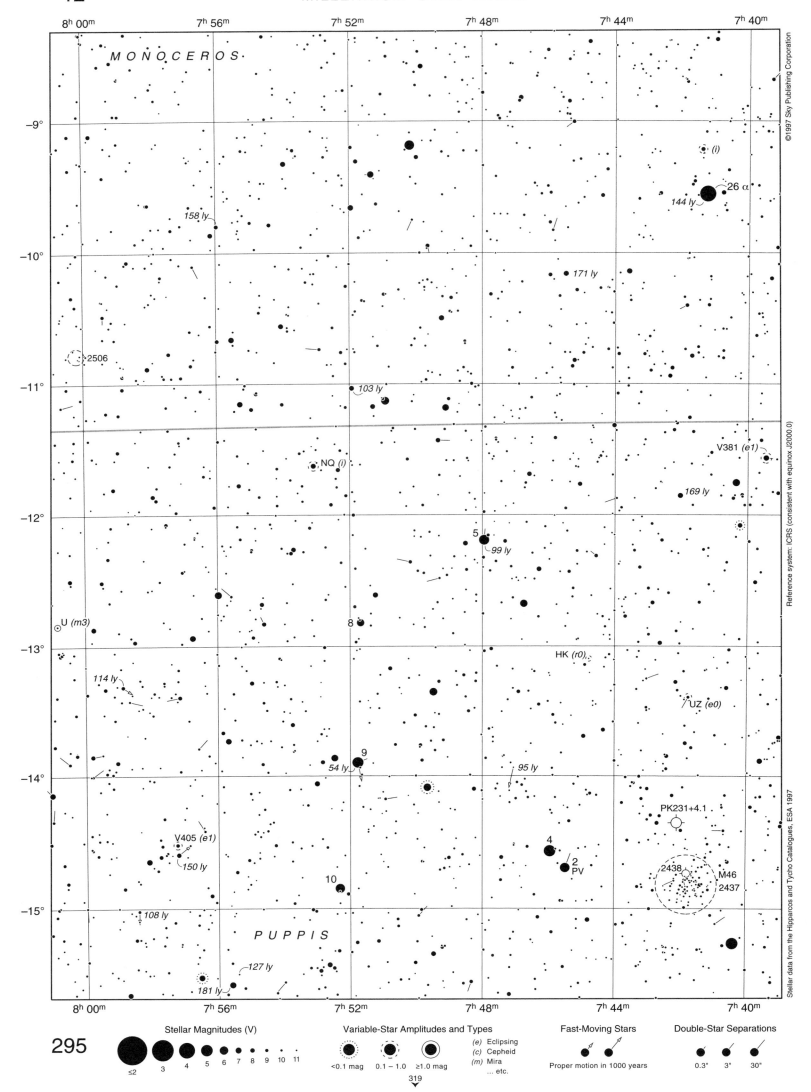

©1997 Sky Publishing Corporation

Reference system: ICRS (consistent with equinox J2000.0)

Stellar data from the Hipparcos and Tycho Catalogues, ESA 1997

MONOCEROS

PUPPIS

158 ly

2506

103 ly

NQ *(i)*

V381 *(e1)*

169 ly

5

99 ly

8

U *(m3)*

HK *(r0)*

UZ *(e0)*

114 ly

9

54 ly

95 ly

PK231+4.1

V405 *(e1)*

4

2
PV

150 ly

10

2438

M46
2437

108 ly

127 ly

181 ly

26 α

144 ly

171 ly

(i)

Stellar Magnitudes (V)

≤2   3   4   5   6   7   8   9 10 11

Variable-Star Amplitudes and Types

<0.1 mag   0.1 − 1.0   ≥1.0 mag

(e) Eclipsing
(c) Cepheid
(m) Mira
... etc.

Fast-Moving Stars

Proper motion in 1000 years

Double-Star Separations

0.3"   3"   30"

▼
319

272

−12°

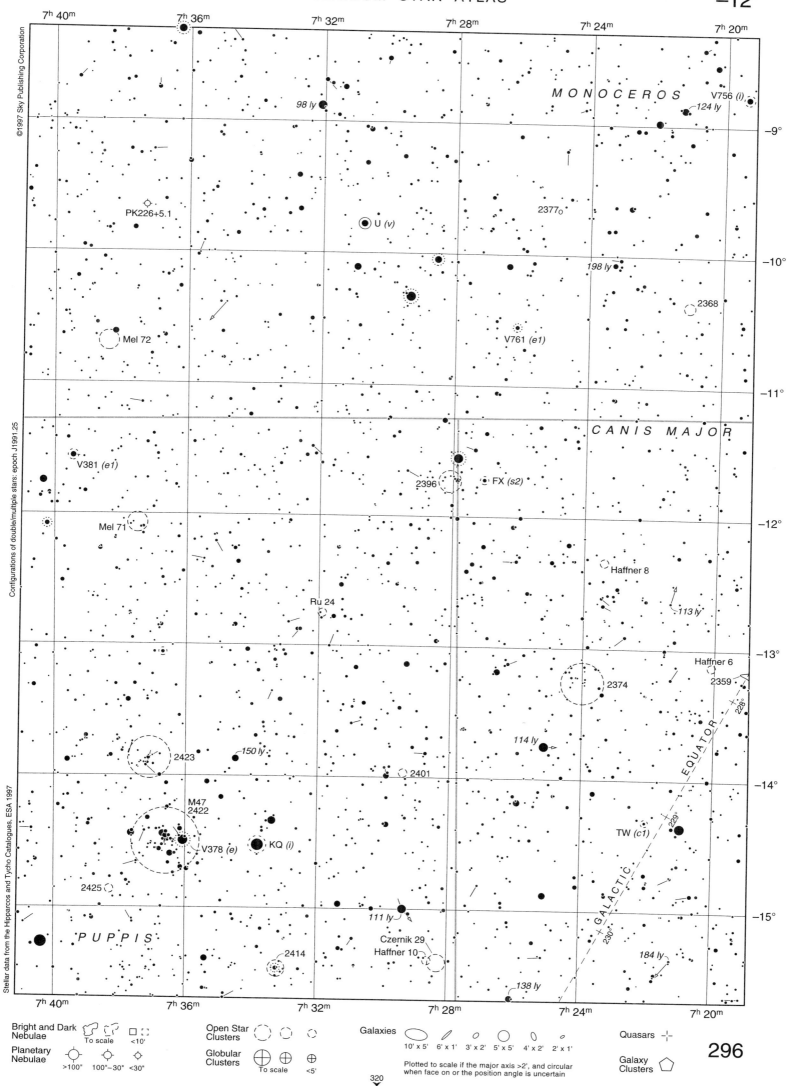

Configurations of double/multiple stars: epoch J1991.25

Stellar data from the Hipparcos and Tycho Catalogues, ESA 1997

7h 40m 7h 36m 7h 32m 7h 28m 7h 24m 7h 20m

MONOCEROS

V756 *(i)*

124 ly

−9°

98 ly

PK226+5.1

2377

U *(v)*

198 ly

−10°

2368

Mel 72

V761 *(e1)*

−11°

CANIS MAJOR

V381 *(e1)*

2396   FX *(s2)*

Mel 71

−12°

Haffner 8

113 ly

Ru 24

−13°

2374

Haffner 6

2359

2423   *150 ly*

228°

114 ly

2401

EQUATOR

−14°

M47
2422

V378 *(e)*   KQ *(i)*

TW *(c1)*

229°

2425

GALACTIC

PUPPIS

−15°

111 ly

2414

Czernik 29
Haffner 10

230°

184 ly

138 ly

7h 40m 7h 36m 7h 32m 7h 28m 7h 24m 7h 20m

Bright and Dark Nebulae   Open Star Clusters   Galaxies   Quasars

To scale   <10'   To scale   <10'   10' x 5'   6' x 1'   3' x 2'   5' x 5'   4' x 2'   2' x 1'

Planetary Nebulae   Globular Clusters

>100"   100"–30"   <30"   To scale   <5'   Plotted to scale if the major axis >2', and circular when face on or the position angle is uncertain   Galaxy Clusters

296

320

MILLENNIUM STAR ATLAS

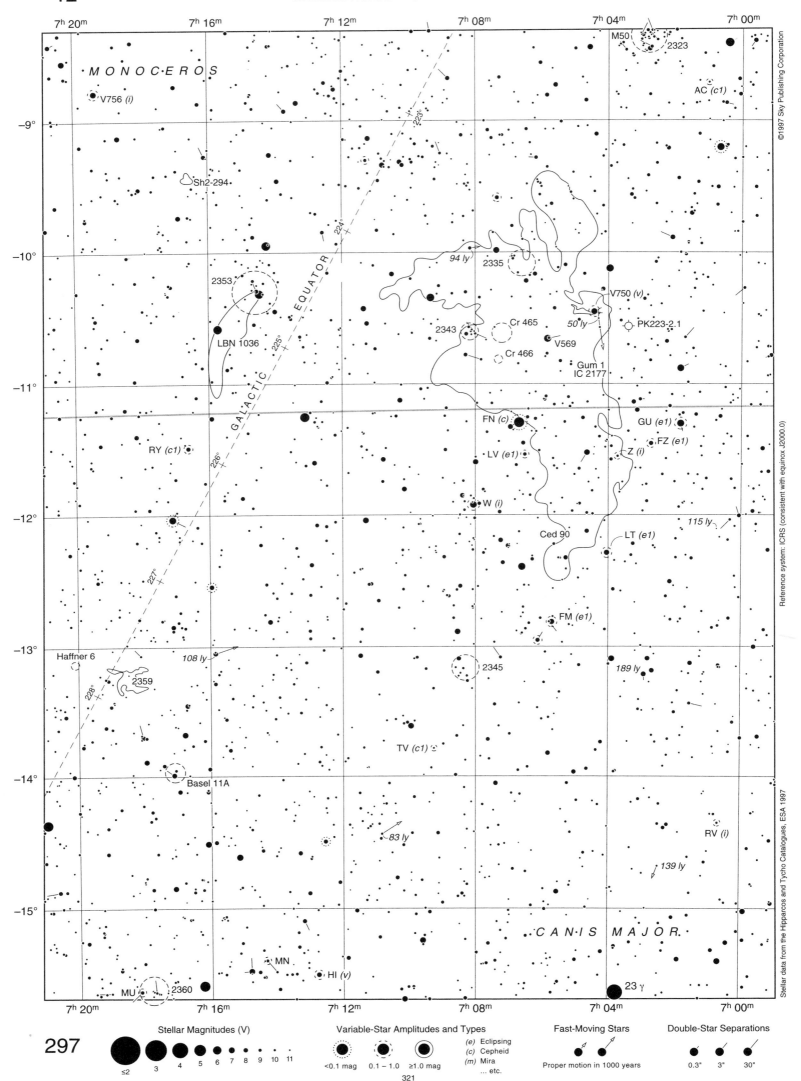

©1997 Sky Publishing Corporation

Reference system: ICRS (consistent with equinox J2000.0)

Stellar data from the Hipparcos and Tycho Catalogues, ESA 1997

MONOCEROS

V756 (i)

Sh2-294

2353

LBN 1036

94 ly   2335

V750 (v)

Cr 465   50 ly   PK223-2.1

2343   V569

Cr 466   Gum 1
IC 2177

FN (c)   GU (e1)

RY (c1)   FZ (e1)

LV (e1)   Z (i)

W (i)

Ced 90   LT (e1)   115 ly

FM (e1)

Haffner 6   108 ly   2345   189 ly

2359

TV (c1)

Basel 11A

83 ly   RV (i)

139 ly

CANIS MAJOR

MN

HI (v)

MU   2360   23 γ

M50   2323

AC (c1)

Stellar Magnitudes (V)

297   ≤2   3   4   5   6   7   8   9   10   11

Variable-Star Amplitudes and Types

<0.1 mag   0.1 – 1.0   ≥1.0 mag

(e) Eclipsing
(c) Cepheid
(m) Mira
... etc.

Fast-Moving Stars

Proper motion in 1000 years

Double-Star Separations

0.3"   3"   30"

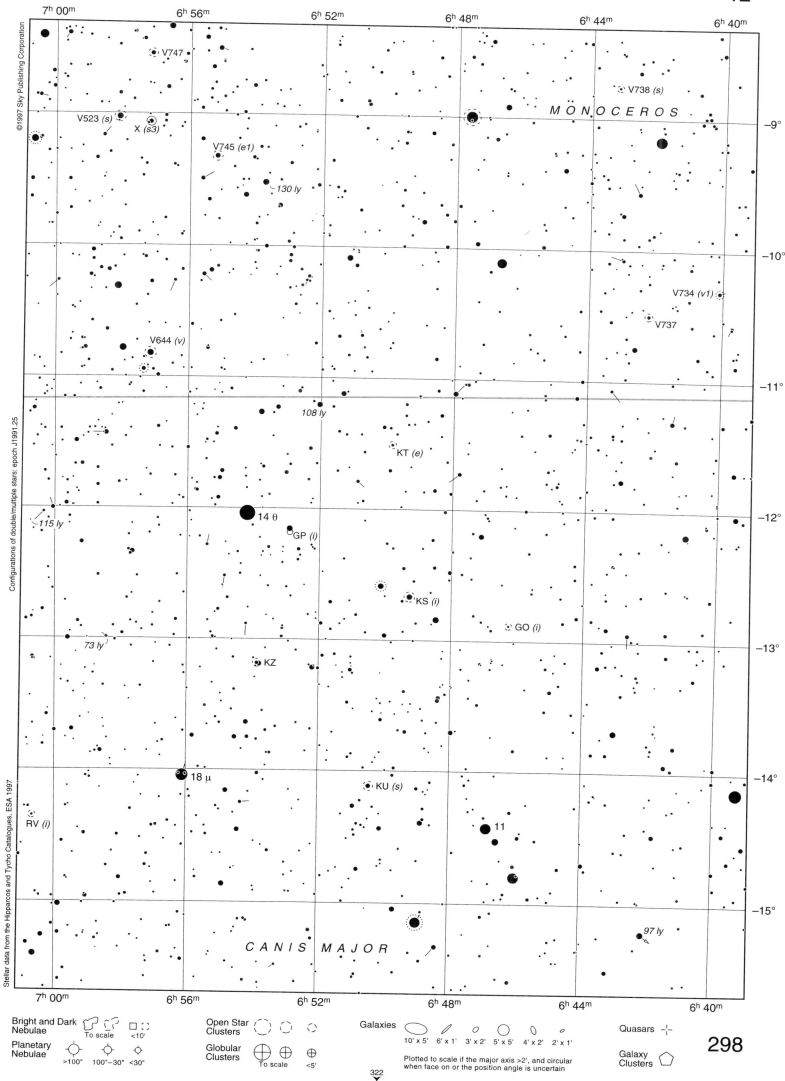

MONOCEROS

V747

V738 (s)

V523 (s)

X (s3)

V745 (e1)

130 ly

−9°

V734 (v1)

V737

−10°

V644 (v)

108 ly

KT (e)

−11°

115 ly

14 θ

GP (i)

KS (i)

GO (i)

−12°

73 ly

KZ

−13°

18 μ

KU (s)

RV (i)

11

−14°

97 ly

CANIS MAJOR

−15°

Bright and Dark Nebulae	Open Star Clusters	Galaxies	Quasars

To scale   <10'

Planetary Nebulae
>100"   100"–30"   <30"

Globular Clusters
To scale   <5'

Galaxies
10' x 5'   6' x 1'   3' x 2'   5' x 5'   4' x 2'   2' x 1'

Plotted to scale if the major axis >2', and circular when face on or the position angle is uncertain

Galaxy Clusters

298

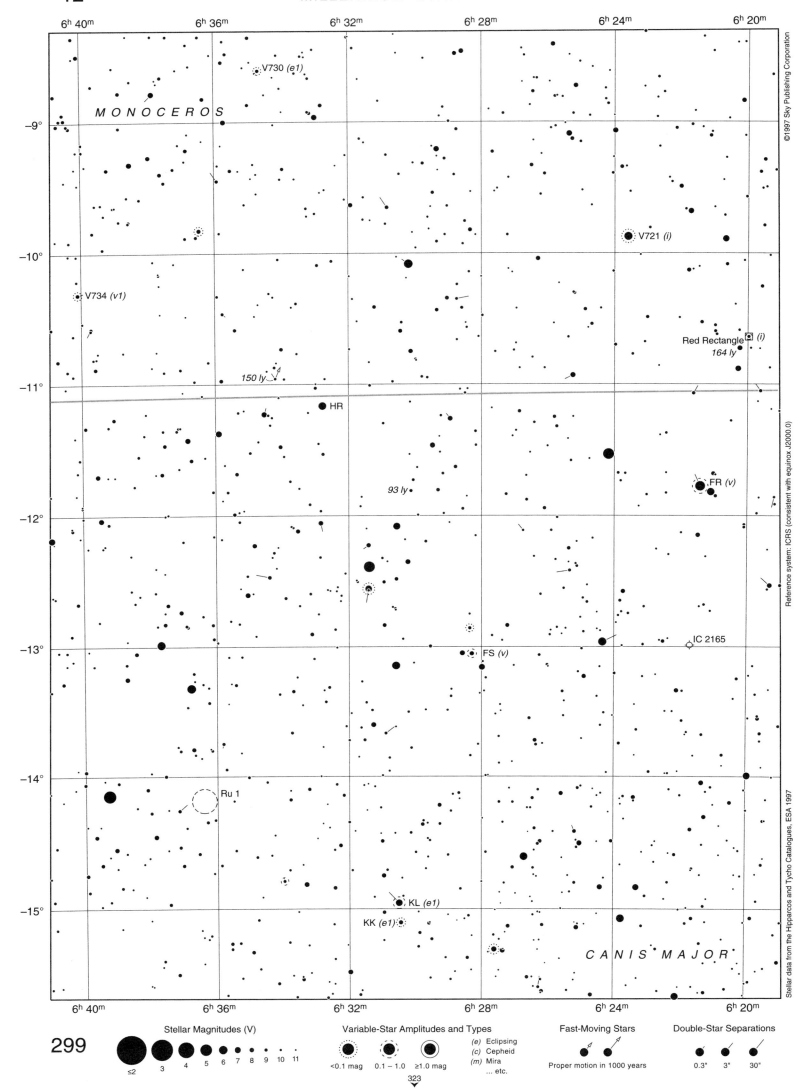

©1997 Sky Publishing Corporation

Reference system: ICRS (consistent with equinox J2000.0)

Stellar data from the Hipparcos and Tycho Catalogues, ESA 1997

MONOCEROS

V730 (e1)

V721 (i)

V734 (v1)

Red Rectangle (i)
164 ly

150 ly

HR

FR (v)

93 ly

IC 2165

FS (v)

Ru 1

KL (e1)

KK (e1)

CANIS MAJOR

Stellar Magnitudes (V)

≤2 3 4 5 6 7 8 9 10 11

Variable-Star Amplitudes and Types

<0.1 mag   0.1 – 1.0   ≥1.0 mag

(e) Eclipsing
(c) Cepheid
(m) Mira
... etc.

Fast-Moving Stars

Proper motion in 1000 years

Double-Star Separations

0.3"   3"   30"

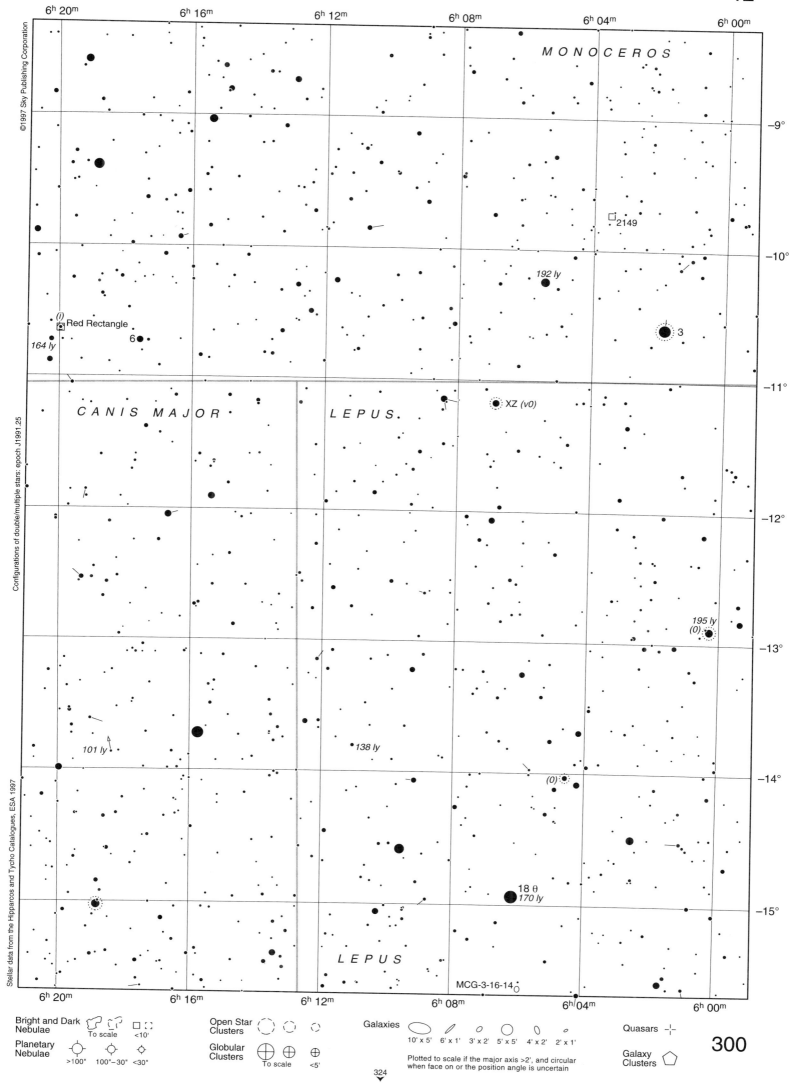

©1997 Sky Publishing Corporation

Configurations of double/multiple stars: epoch J1991.25

Stellar data from the Hipparcos and Tycho Catalogues, ESA 1997

MONOCEROS

2149

192 ly

(i)
Red Rectangle

164 ly

6

3

CANIS MAJOR

LEPUS

XZ (v0)

195 ly
(0)

101 ly

138 ly

(0)

18 θ
170 ly

LEPUS

MCG-3-16-14

6h 20m   6h 16m   6h 12m   6h 08m   6h 04m   6h 00m

−9°
−10°
−11°
−12°
−13°
−14°
−15°

Bright and Dark Nebulae			Open Star Clusters			Galaxies						Quasars
To scale		<10'				10' x 5'	6' x 1'	3' x 2'	5' x 5'	4' x 2'	2' x 1'	
Planetary Nebulae			Globular Clusters									Galaxy Clusters
>100"	100"-30"	<30"	To scale		<5'							

Plotted to scale if the major axis >2', and circular when face on or the position angle is uncertain

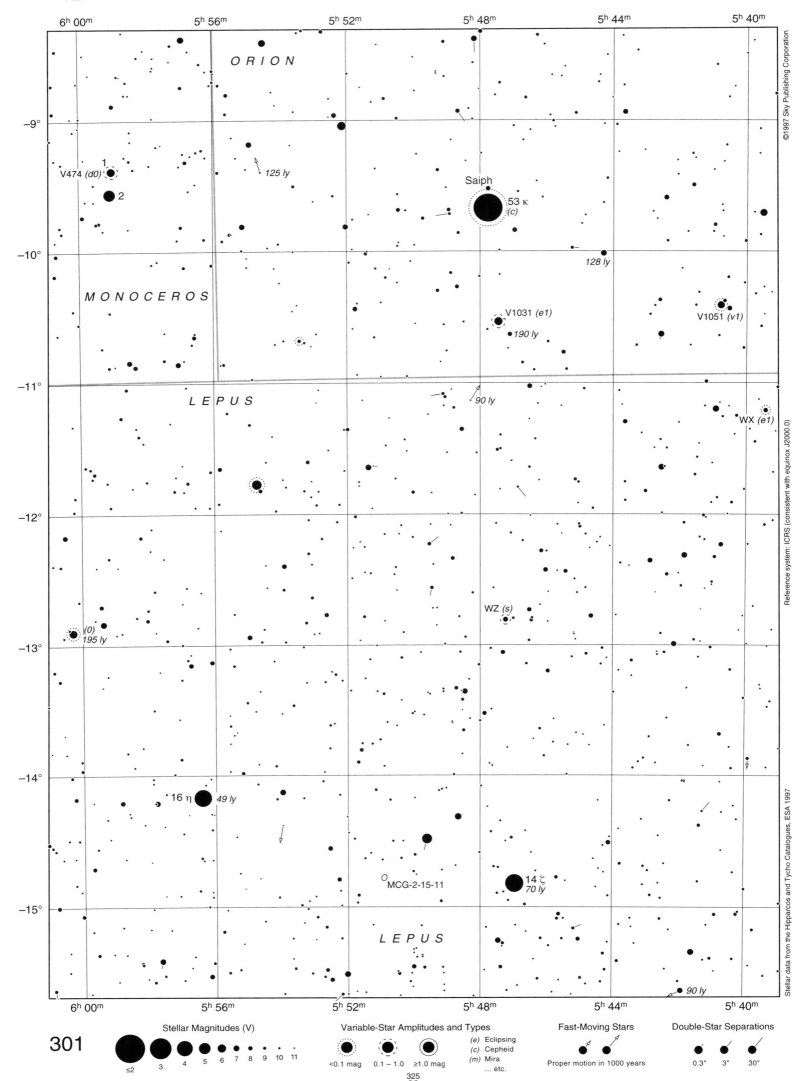

©1997 Sky Publishing Corporation

Reference system: ICRS (consistent with equinox J2000.0)

Stellar data from the Hipparcos and Tycho Catalogues, ESA 1997

ORION

V474 (d0)
1
2

MONOCEROS

Saiph
53 κ
(c)

125 ly

128 ly

V1031 (e1)
190 ly

V1051 (v1)

LEPUS

90 ly

WX (e1)

WZ (s)

(0)
195 ly

16 η   49 ly

MCG-2-15-11

14 ζ
70 ly

LEPUS

90 ly

301

Stellar Magnitudes (V)
≤2   3   4   5   6   7 8 9 10 11

Variable-Star Amplitudes and Types
<0.1 mag   0.1 − 1.0   ≥1.0 mag

(e) Eclipsing
(c) Cepheid
(m) Mira
... etc.

Fast-Moving Stars
Proper motion in 1000 years

Double-Star Separations
0.3"   3"   30"

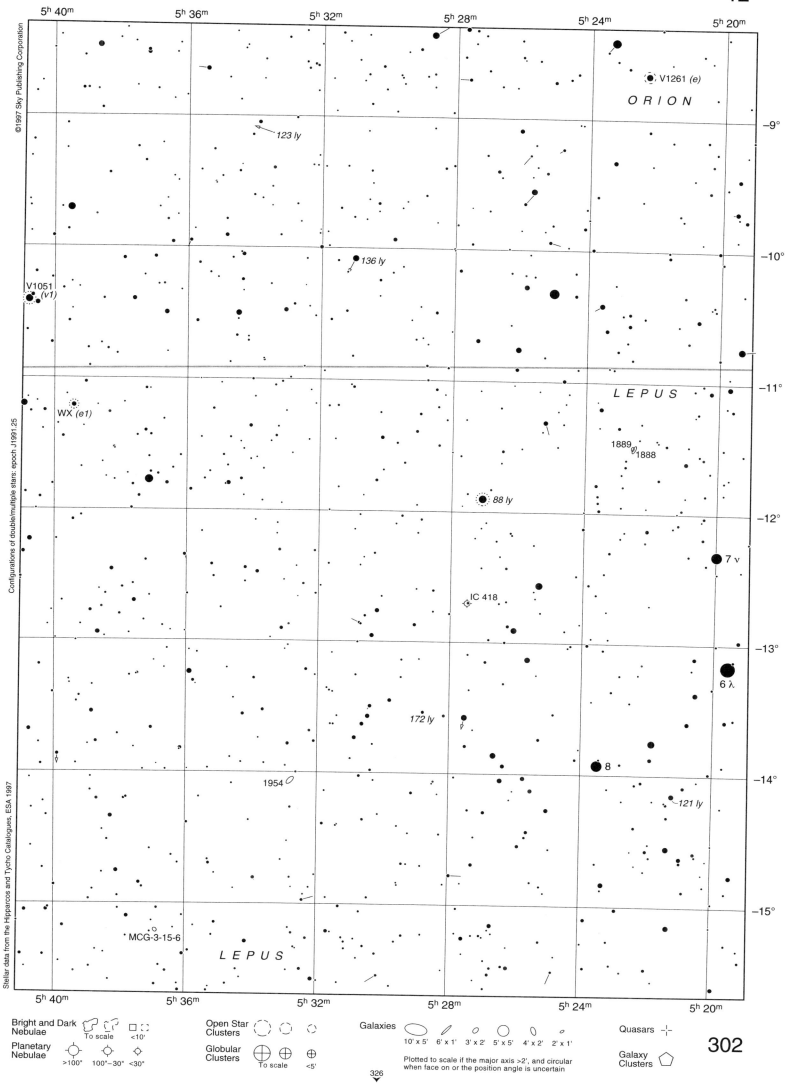

5ʰ 40ᵐ   5ʰ 36ᵐ   5ʰ 32ᵐ   5ʰ 28ᵐ   5ʰ 24ᵐ   5ʰ 20ᵐ

V1261 (e)

O R I O N

−9°

123 ly

136 ly

V1051
(v1)

−10°

L E P U S

−11°

WX (e1)

1889
1888

88 ly

−12°

7 ν

IC 418

6 λ

−13°

172 ly

8

1954

−14°

121 ly

MCG-3-15-6

−15°

L E P U S

5ʰ 40ᵐ   5ʰ 36ᵐ   5ʰ 32ᵐ   5ʰ 28ᵐ   5ʰ 24ᵐ   5ʰ 20ᵐ

Bright and Dark Nebulae
To scale   <10'

Planetary Nebulae
>100"   100"–30"   <30"

Open Star Clusters

Globular Clusters
To scale   <5'

Galaxies
10' x 5'   6' x 1'   3' x 2'   5' x 5'   4' x 2'   2' x 1'

Plotted to scale if the major axis >2', and circular when face on or the position angle is uncertain

Quasars

Galaxy Clusters

302

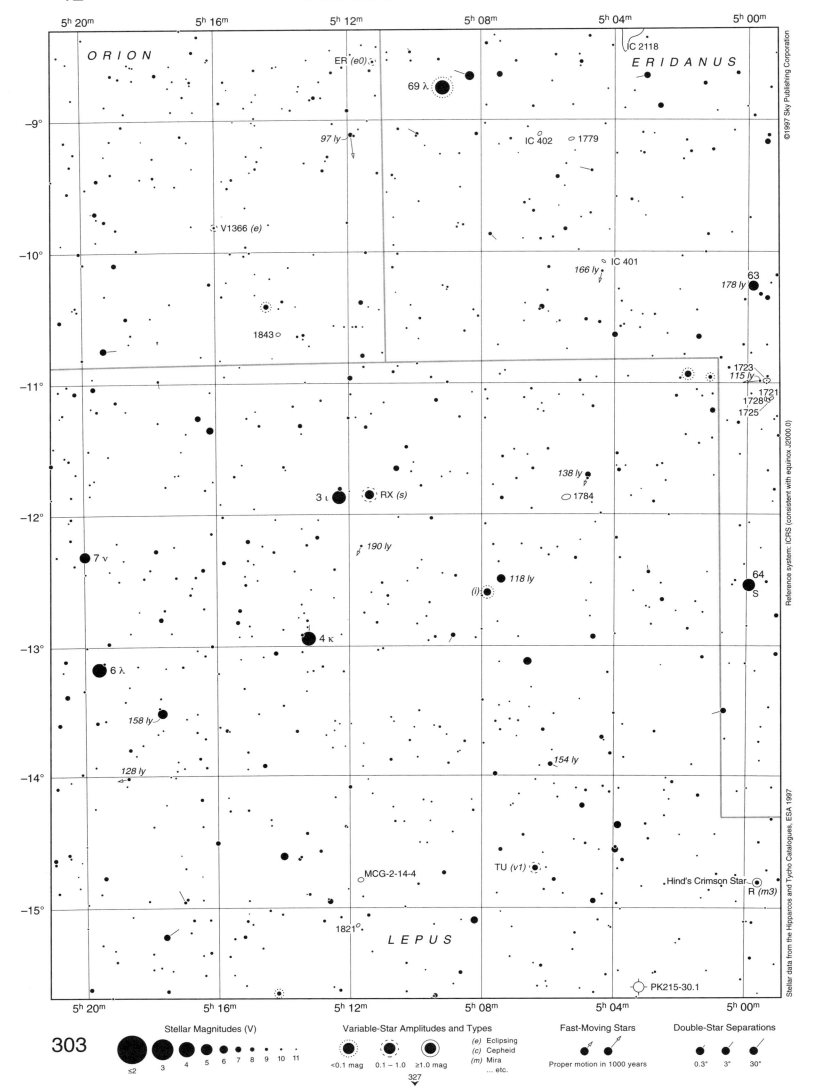

©1997 Sky Publishing Corporation

Reference system: ICRS (consistent with equinox J2000.0)

Stellar data from the Hipparcos and Tycho Catalogues, ESA 1997

303

Stellar Magnitudes (V)

≤2   3   4   5   6   7   8   9   10   11

Variable-Star Amplitudes and Types

<0.1 mag   0.1 − 1.0   ≥1.0 mag

(e) Eclipsing
(c) Cepheid
(m) Mira
... etc.

Fast-Moving Stars

Proper motion in 1000 years

Double-Star Separations

0.3"   3"   30"

327

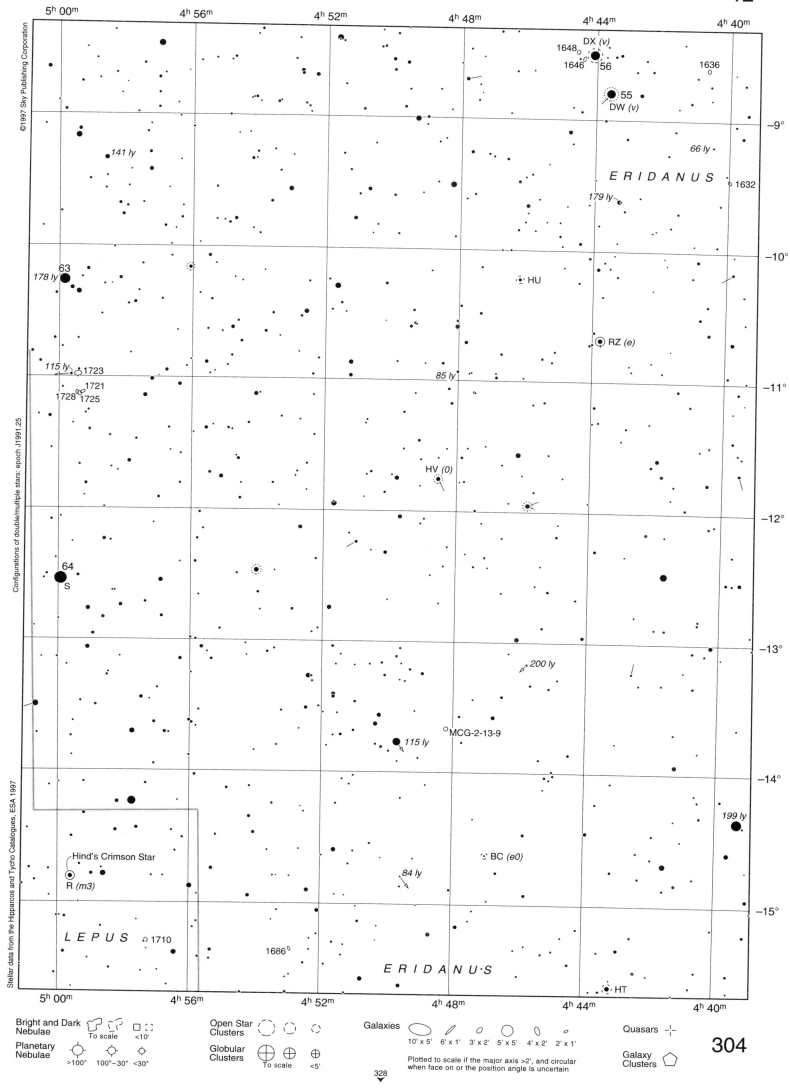

Configurations of double/multiple stars: epoch J1991.25

Stellar data from the Hipparcos and Tycho Catalogues, ESA 1997

E R I D A N U S

1648
1646
DX *(v)*
56
1636
55
DW *(v)*
1632
66 ly
179 ly

63
178 ly
HU
RZ *(e)*
115 ly   1723
1721
1728   1725
85 ly

HV *(0)*

64
S

200 ly

MCG-2-13-9
115 ly

199 ly

Hind's Crimson Star
BC *(e0)*
R *(m3)*
84 ly

L E P U S   1710
1686
E R I D A N U S

HT

Bright and Dark Nebulae	Open Star Clusters	Galaxies	Quasars

To scale   <10'

Planetary Nebulae   >100"   100"–30"   <30'

Globular Clusters   To scale   <5'

10' x 5'   6' x 1'   3' x 2'   5' x 5'   4' x 2'   2' x 1'

Galaxy Clusters

Plotted to scale if the major axis >2', and circular when face on or the position angle is uncertain

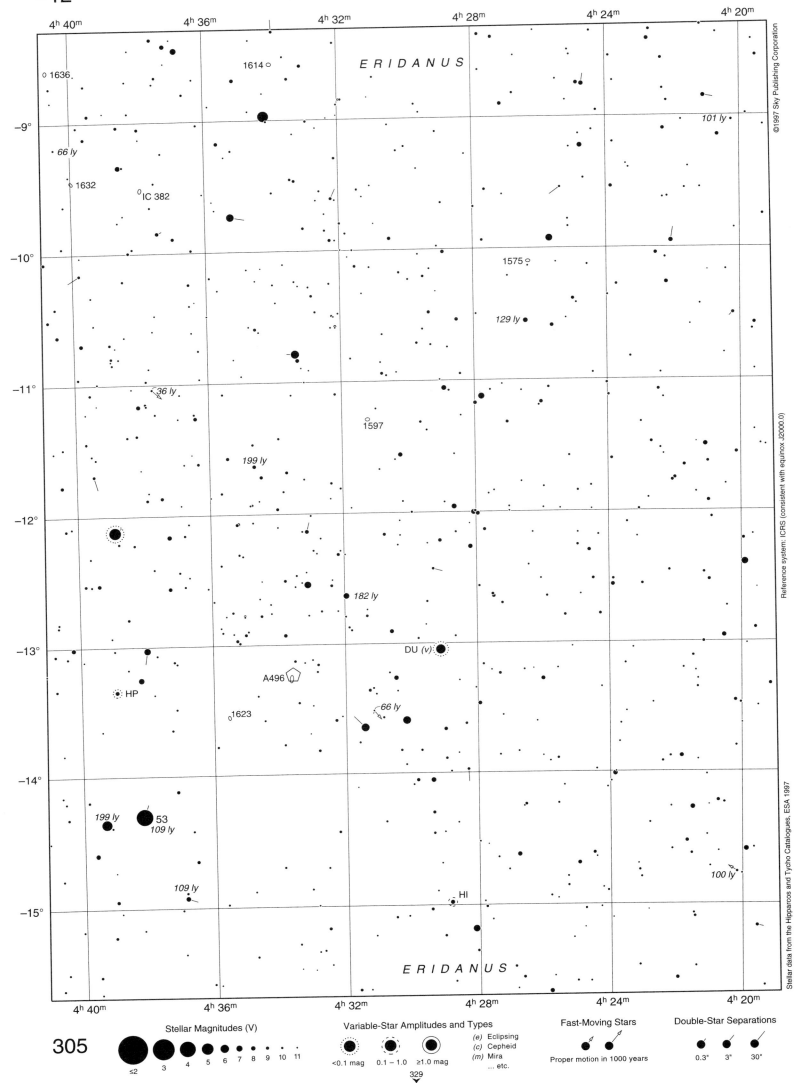

©1997 Sky Publishing Corporation

Reference system: ICRS (consistent with equinox J2000.0)

Stellar data from the Hipparcos and Tycho Catalogues, ESA 1997

305

Stellar Magnitudes (V)

≤2   3   4   5   6   7   8   9   10   11

Variable-Star Amplitudes and Types

<0.1 mag   0.1 – 1.0   ≥1.0 mag

(e) Eclipsing
(c) Cepheid
(m) Mira
... etc.

Fast-Moving Stars

Proper motion in 1000 years

Double-Star Separations

0.3"   3"   30"

−12°

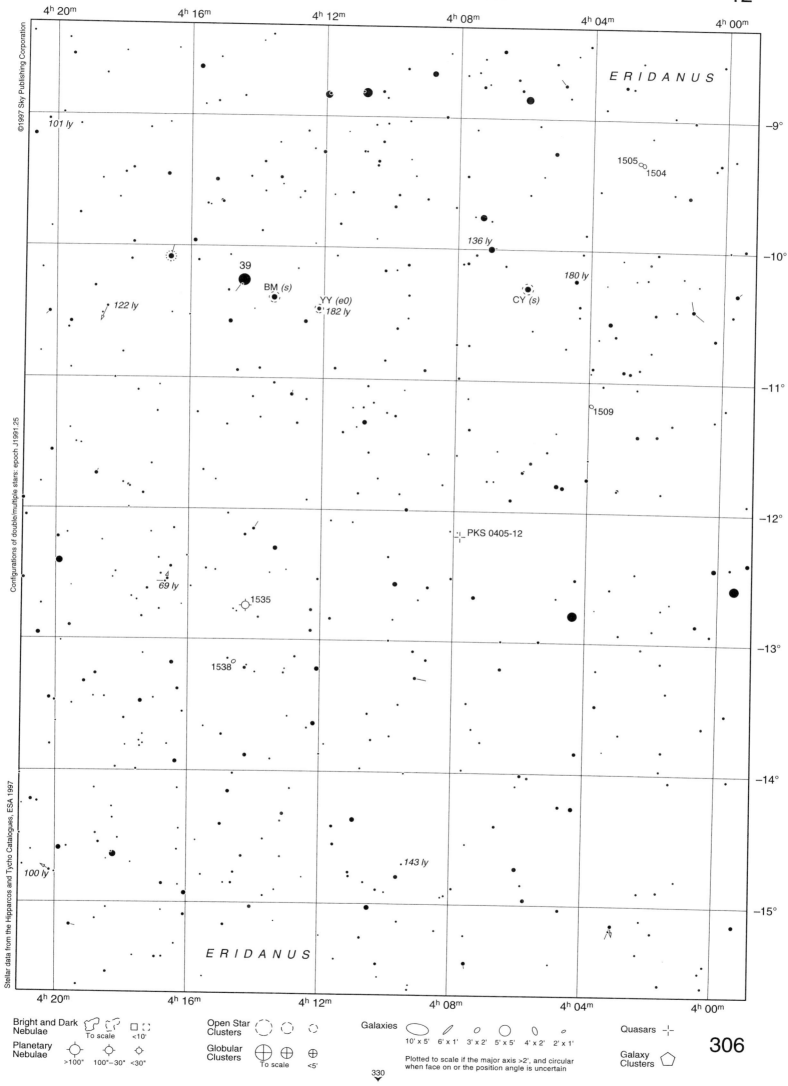

4ʰ 20ᵐ   4ʰ 16ᵐ   4ʰ 12ᵐ   4ʰ 08ᵐ   4ʰ 04ᵐ   4ʰ 00ᵐ

−9°
−10°
−11°
−12°
−13°
−14°
−15°

E R I D A N U S

101 ly
122 ly
39
BM (s)
YY (e0)
182 ly
136 ly
CY (s)
180 ly
1505
1504
1509
PKS 0405-12
4
69 ly
1535
1538
100 ly
143 ly

E R I D A N U S

Bright and Dark Nebulae	Open Star Clusters	Galaxies	Quasars

Bright and Dark Nebulae — To scale, <10'

Planetary Nebulae — >100", 100"–30", <30"

Open Star Clusters

Globular Clusters — To scale, <5'

Galaxies — 10' x 5', 6' x 1', 3' x 2', 5' x 5', 4' x 2', 2' x 1'

Plotted to scale if the major axis >2', and circular when face on or the position angle is uncertain

Quasars

Galaxy Clusters

306

330

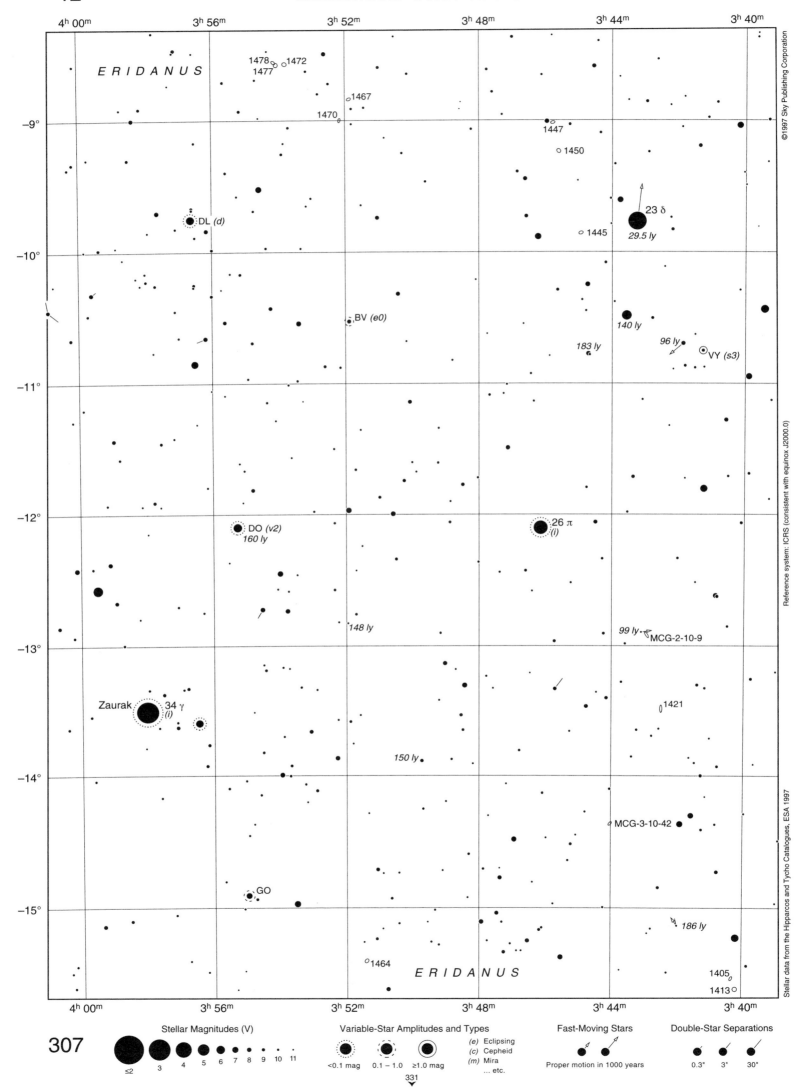

©1997 Sky Publishing Corporation

Reference system: ICRS (consistent with equinox J2000.0)

Stellar data from the Hipparcos and Tycho Catalogues, ESA 1997

ERIDANUS

1478 °1472
1477

°1467

1470 ₀

1447
°

1450

23 δ
29.5 ly

DL (d)

° 1445

140 ly

183 ly

96 ly

VY (s3)

BV (e0)

DO (v2)
160 ly

26 π
(i)

148 ly

99 ly MCG-2-10-9

Zaurak   34 γ
(i)

1421

150 ly

MCG-3-10-42

GO

186 ly

1464

ERIDANUS

1405
1413 °

Stellar Magnitudes (V)

≤2   3   4   5   6   7   8   9   10   11

Variable-Star Amplitudes and Types

<0.1 mag   0.1 − 1.0   ≥1.0 mag

(e) Eclipsing
(c) Cepheid
(m) Mira
... etc.

Fast-Moving Stars

Proper motion in 1000 years

Double-Star Separations

0.3"   3"   30"

MILLENNIUM STAR ATLAS

-12°

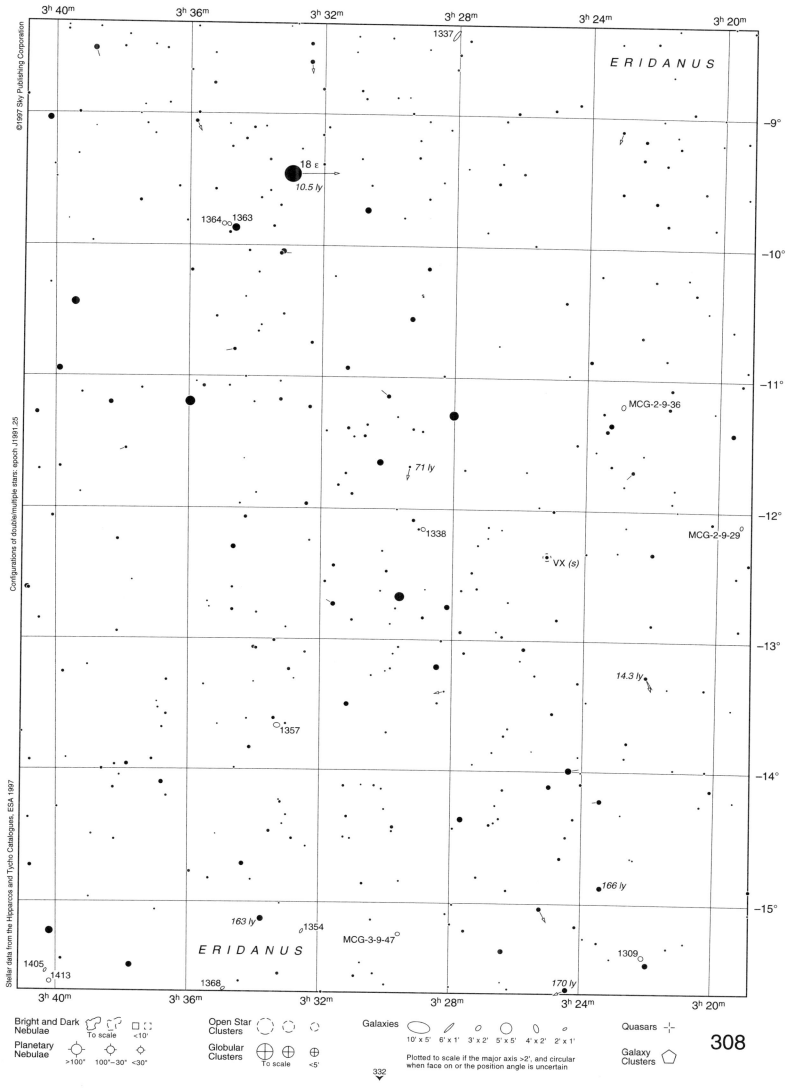

Configurations of double/multiple stars: epoch J1991.25

Stellar data from the Hipparcos and Tycho Catalogues, ESA 1997

E R I D A N U S

3ʰ 40ᵐ 3ʰ 36ᵐ 3ʰ 32ᵐ 3ʰ 28ᵐ 3ʰ 24ᵐ 3ʰ 20ᵐ

-9°

18 ε
10.5 ly

1364 1363

-10°

MCG-2-9-36

71 ly

-11°

MCG-2-9-29

1338

VX (s)

-12°

14.3 ly

-13°

1357

-14°

166 ly

163 ly 1354

E R I D A N U S

MCG-3-9-47

1309

1405
1413

1368

170 ly

-15°

3ʰ 40ᵐ 3ʰ 36ᵐ 3ʰ 32ᵐ 3ʰ 28ᵐ 3ʰ 24ᵐ 3ʰ 20ᵐ

Bright and Dark Nebulae				Open Star Clusters			Galaxies							Quasars
To scale		<10'					10' x 5'	6' x 1'	3' x 2'	5' x 5'	4' x 2'	2' x 1'		

Planetary Nebulae				Globular Clusters		
>100"	100"−30"	<30"		To scale		<5'

Galaxy Clusters

Plotted to scale if the major axis >2', and circular when face on or the position angle is uncertain

308

−12°

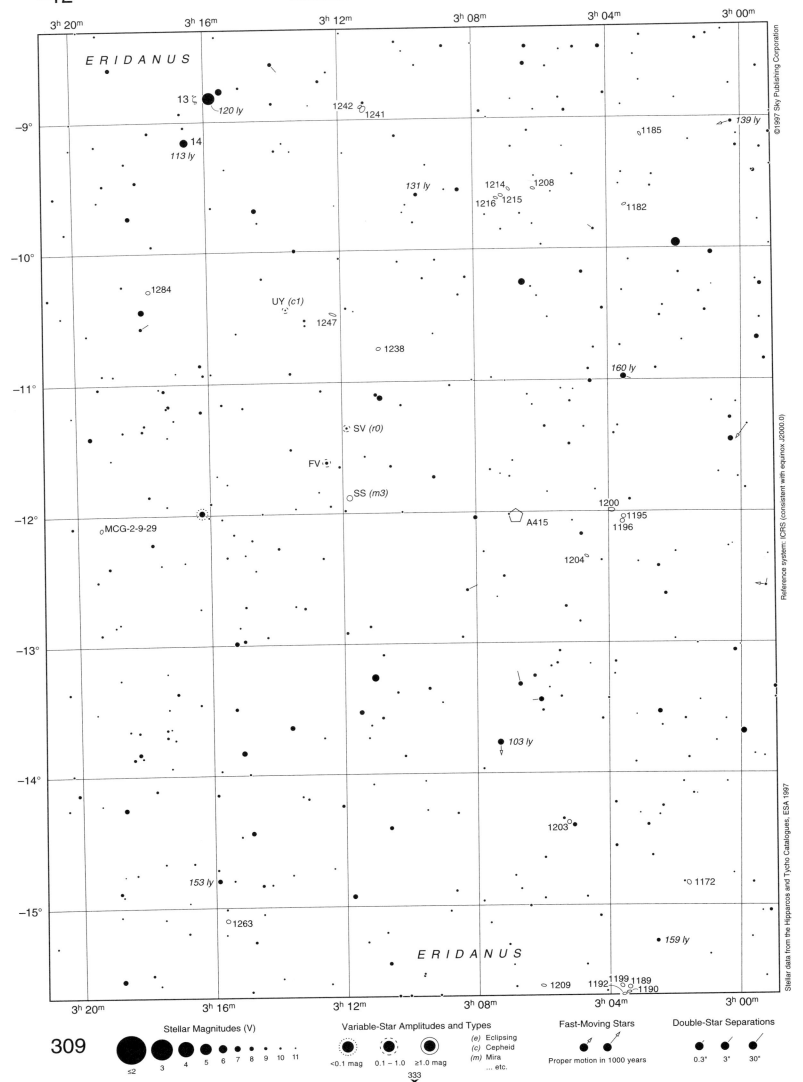

©1997 Sky Publishing Corporation

Reference system: ICRS (consistent with equinox J2000.0)

Stellar data from the Hipparcos and Tycho Catalogues, ESA 1997

E R I D A N U S

3ʰ 20ᵐ   3ʰ 16ᵐ   3ʰ 12ᵐ   3ʰ 08ᵐ   3ʰ 04ᵐ   3ʰ 00ᵐ

−9°

13 ζ
120 ly

14
113 ly

1242 1241

1185

139 ly

131 ly   1214 1208
1216 1215

1182

−10°

1284

UY (c1)

1247

1238

160 ly

−11°

SV (r0)

FV

SS (m3)

1200
A415   1195
1196

1204

−12°

MCG-2-9-29

103 ly

−13°

1203

−14°

153 ly

1172

1263

159 ly

−15°

E R I D A N U S

1209   1192 1199 1189
1190

3ʰ 20ᵐ   3ʰ 16ᵐ   3ʰ 12ᵐ   3ʰ 08ᵐ   3ʰ 04ᵐ   3ʰ 00ᵐ

309

Stellar Magnitudes (V)

≤2   3   4   5   6   7   8   9   10   11

Variable-Star Amplitudes and Types

<0.1 mag   0.1 – 1.0   ≥1.0 mag

(e) Eclipsing
(c) Cepheid
(m) Mira
... etc.

Fast-Moving Stars

Proper motion in 1000 years

Double-Star Separations

0.3"   3"   30"

333

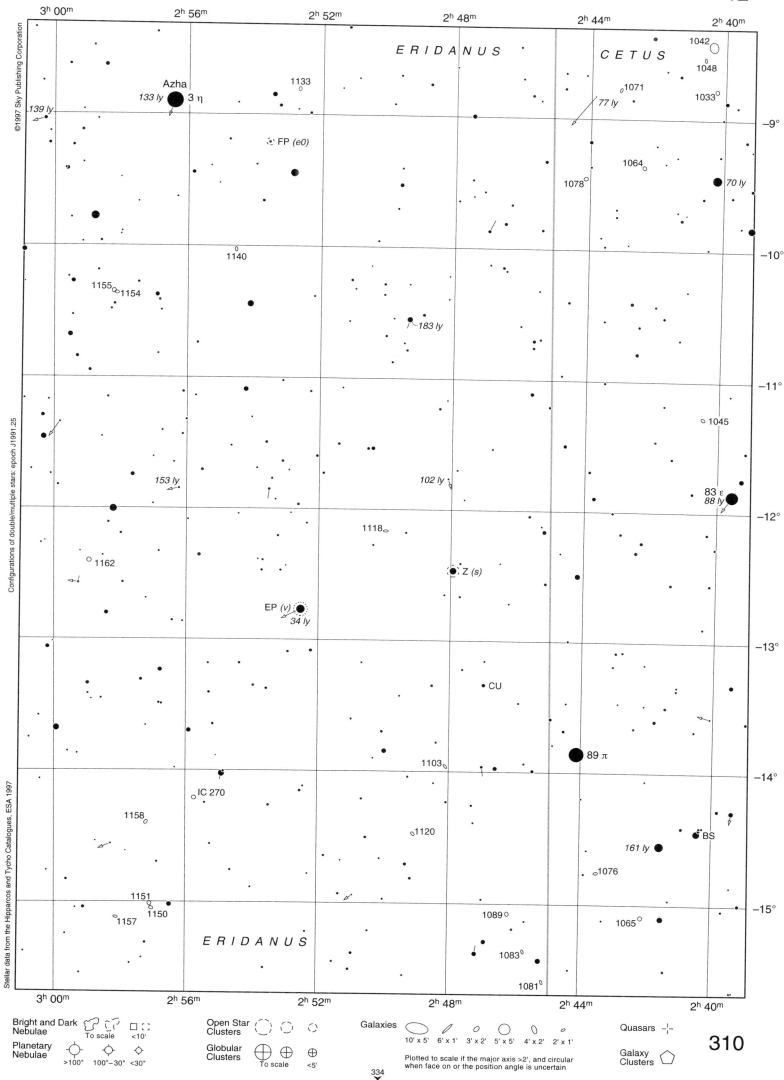

ERIDANUS

CETUS

Azha
133 ly 3 η

1133

FP (e0)

139 ly

1042
1048

1071

1033

77 ly

1064

1078

70 ly

−9°

1140

1155 1154

183 ly

−10°

153 ly

1045

102 ly

83 ε
88 ly

−11°

1118

1162

Z (s)

EP (v)
34 ly

−12°

CU

89 π

−13°

1103

IC 270

1158

1120

BS

161 ly

1076

−14°

1151

1150

1157

1089

1065

ERIDANUS

1083

1081

−15°

3ʰ 00ᵐ   2ʰ 56ᵐ   2ʰ 52ᵐ   2ʰ 48ᵐ   2ʰ 44ᵐ   2ʰ 40ᵐ

Bright and Dark Nebulae
To scale   <10'

Planetary Nebulae
>100"   100"–30"   <30"

Open Star Clusters

Globular Clusters
To scale   <5'

Galaxies
10' x 5'   6' x 1'   3' x 2'   5' x 5'   4' x 2'   2' x 1'

Plotted to scale if the major axis >2', and circular when face on or the position angle is uncertain

Quasars

Galaxy Clusters

310

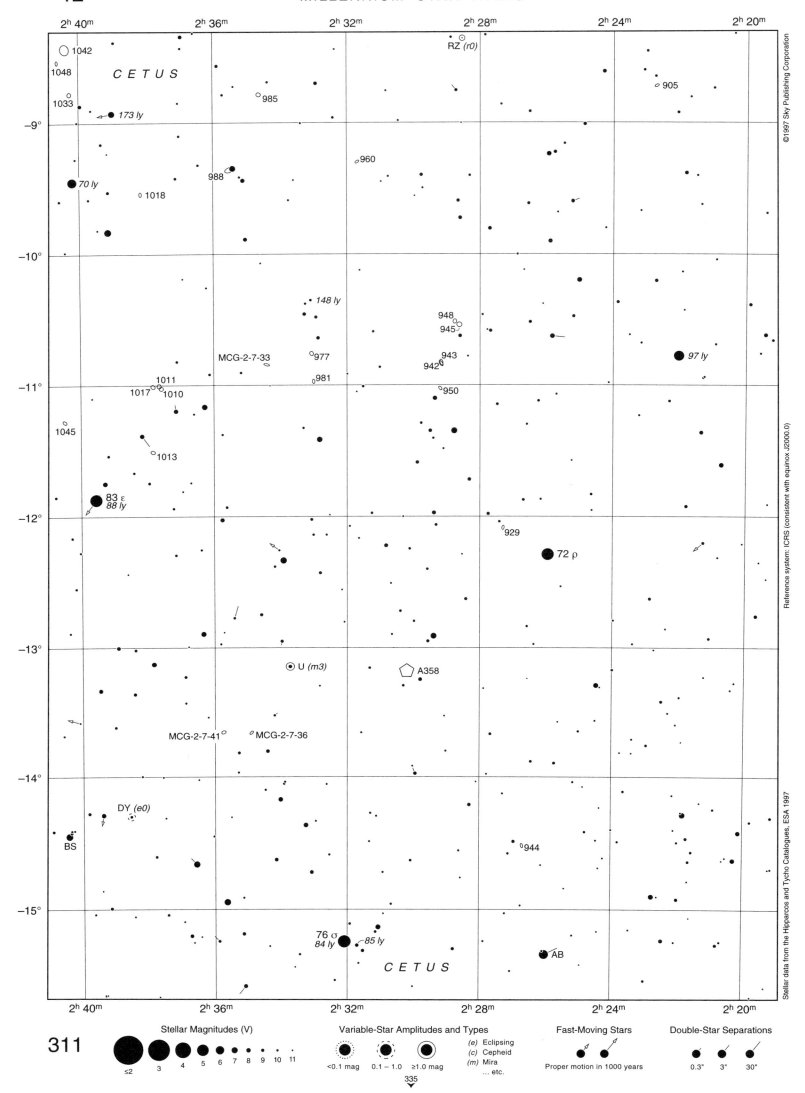

©1997 Sky Publishing Corporation

Reference system: ICRS (consistent with equinox J2000.0)

Stellar data from the Hipparcos and Tycho Catalogues, ESA 1997

311

Stellar Magnitudes (V)
≤2 3 4 5 6 7 8 9 10 11

Variable-Star Amplitudes and Types
<0.1 mag   0.1 – 1.0   ≥1.0 mag

(e) Eclipsing
(c) Cepheid
(m) Mira
... etc.

Fast-Moving Stars
Proper motion in 1000 years

Double-Star Separations
0.3"   3"   30"

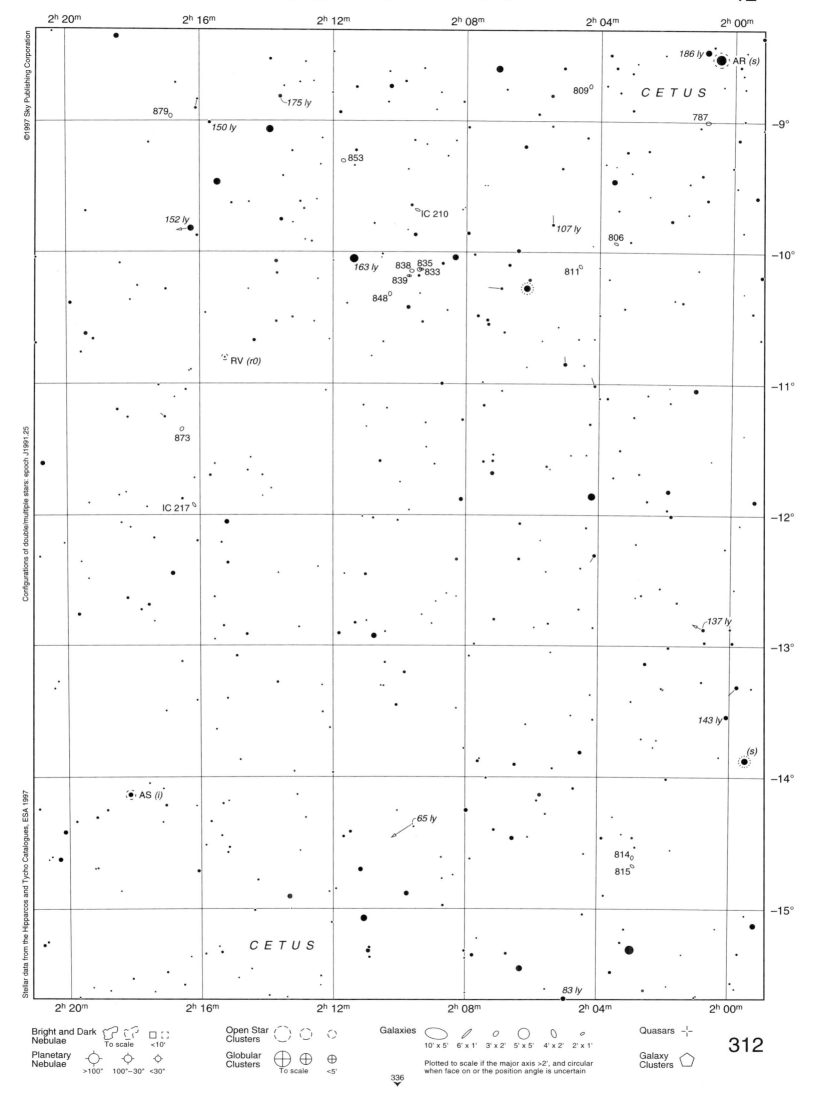

186 ly — AR (s)

809°

C E T U S

787

879°

175 ly

150 ly

853

152 ly

IC 210

107 ly

806

163 ly — 838 — 835
839 — 833
848°

811°

RV (r0)

873

IC 217°

137 ly

143 ly

(s)

AS (i)

65 ly

814°
815°

C E T U S

83 ly

Bright and Dark Nebulae			Open Star Clusters			Galaxies						Quasars
To scale		<10'				10' x 5'	6' x 1'	3' x 2'	5' x 5'	4' x 2'	2' x 1'	
Planetary Nebulae			Globular Clusters			Plotted to scale if the major axis >2', and circular when face on or the position angle is uncertain						Galaxy Clusters
>100"	100"−30"	<30"	To scale		<5'							

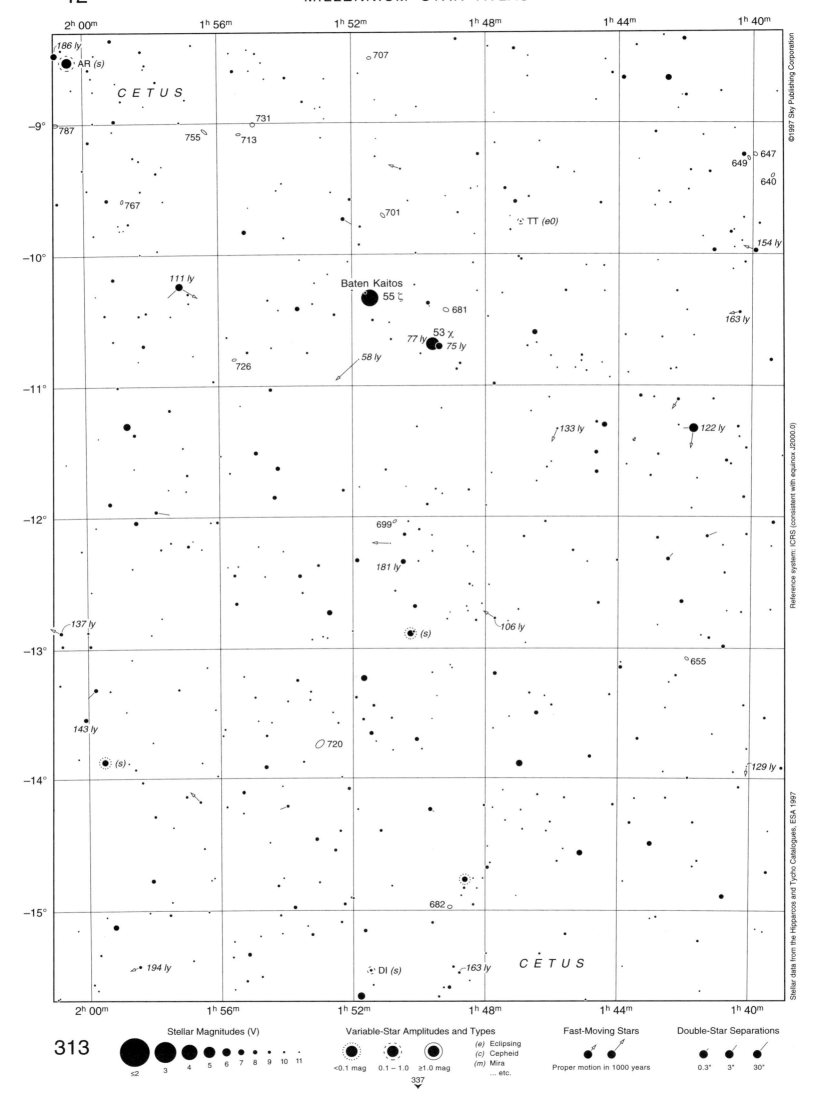

©1997 Sky Publishing Corporation

Reference system: ICRS (consistent with equinox J2000.0)

Stellar data from the Hipparcos and Tycho Catalogues, ESA 1997

186 ly

AR *(s)*

C E T U S

787   731

755   ⁰713

707

⁰767   ⁰701

649 ⁰647

640

TT *(e0)*

154 ly

111 ly

Baten Kaitos

55 ζ   ⁰ 681

163 ly

77 ly   53 χ

75 ly

⁰726   *58 ly*

133 ly   *122 ly*

699⁰

181 ly

137 ly   *106 ly*

(s)

⁰ 655

143 ly

⁰ 720

(s)   *129 ly*

682 ⁰

194 ly   DI *(s)*   *163 ly*   *C E T U S*

313

Stellar Magnitudes (V)

≤2   3   4   5   6   7   8   9   10   11

Variable-Star Amplitudes and Types

<0.1 mag   0.1 – 1.0   ≥1.0 mag

(e) Eclipsing
(c) Cepheid
(m) Mira
... etc.

Fast-Moving Stars

Proper motion in 1000 years

Double-Star Separations

0.3"   3"   30"

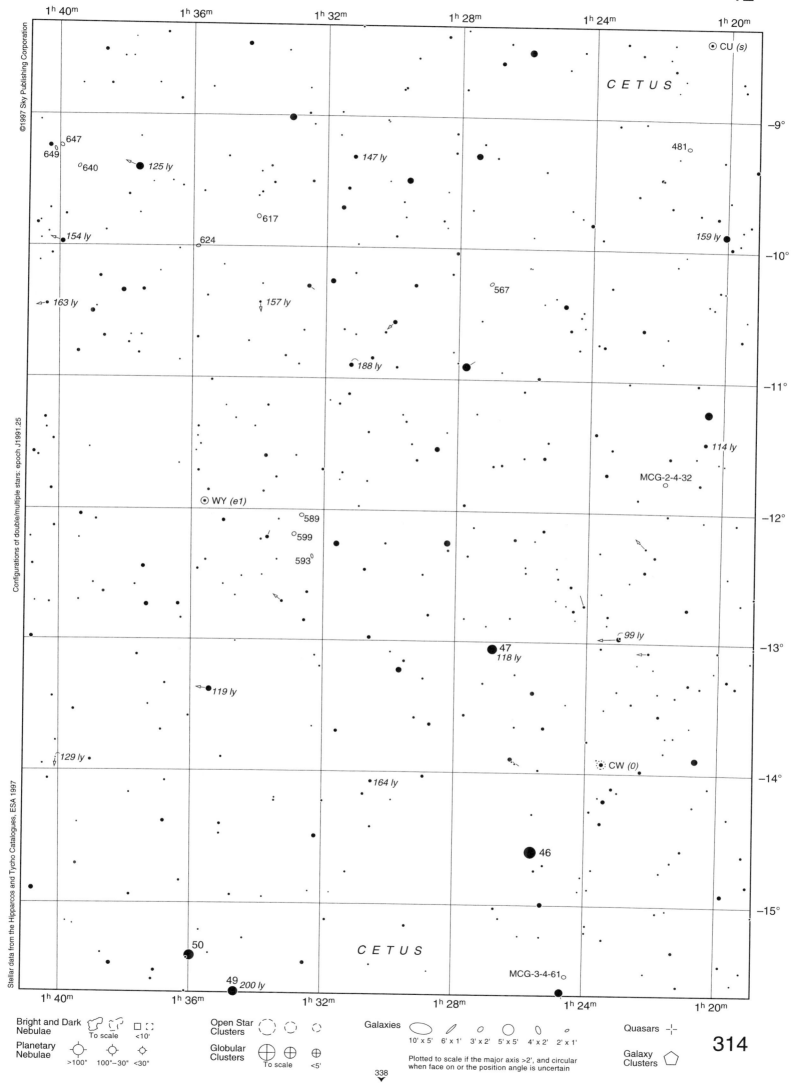

CETUS

647
649
640 125 ly
154 ly
617
624
147 ly
481
159 ly
163 ly
157 ly
567
188 ly
WY (e1)
589
599
593
MCG-2-4-32
114 ly
CU (s)
99 ly
47
118 ly
119 ly
129 ly
CW (0)
164 ly
46
50
49 200 ly
CETUS
MCG-3-4-61

Bright and Dark
Nebulae   To scale   <10'
Planetary
Nebulae   >100" 100"−30" <30'

Open Star
Clusters
Globular
Clusters   To scale   <5'

Galaxies
10' x 5' 6' x 1' 3' x 2' 5' x 5' 4' x 2' 2' x 1'
Plotted to scale if the major axis >2', and circular
when face on or the position angle is uncertain

Quasars

Galaxy
Clusters

314

338

MILLENNIUM STAR ATLAS

©1997 Sky Publishing Corporation

Reference system: ICRS (consistent with equinox J2000.0)

Stellar data from the Hipparcos and Tycho Catalogues, ESA 1997

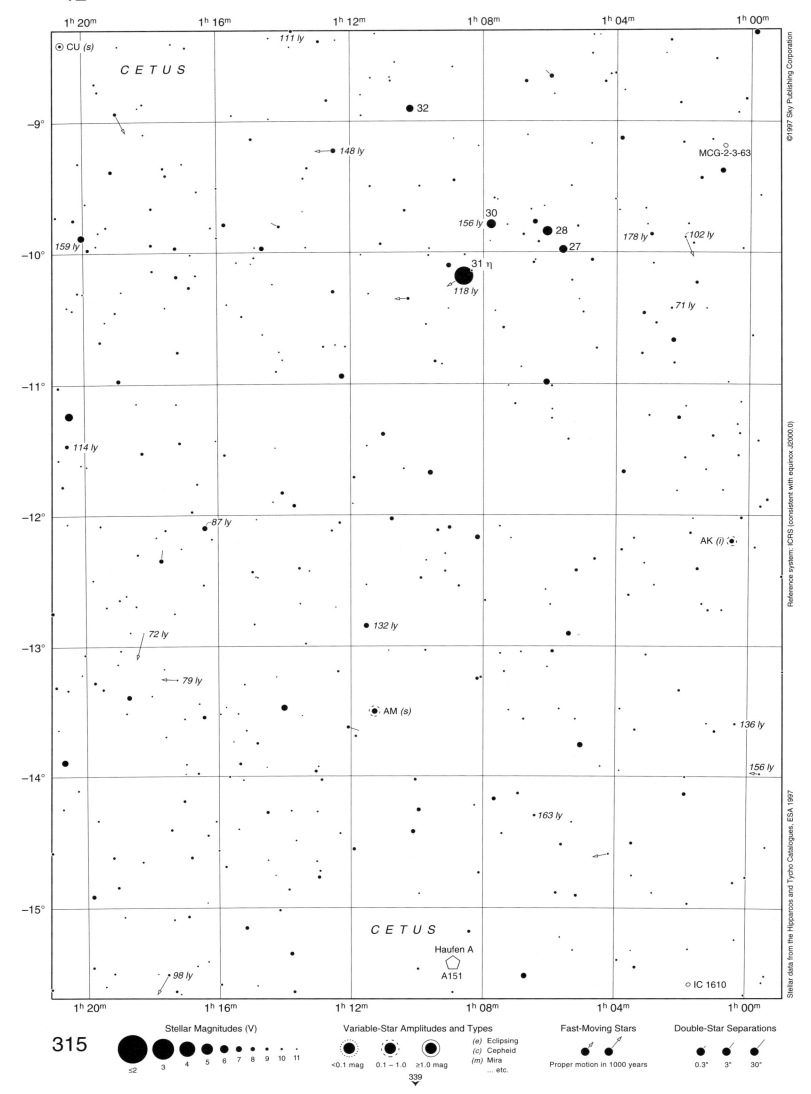

CU (s)

CETUS

111 ly

32

148 ly

MCG-2-3-63

30
156 ly
28
27
178 ly
102 ly

159 ly

31 η
118 ly

71 ly

114 ly

AK (i)

87 ly

72 ly

132 ly

79 ly

136 ly

AM (s)

156 ly

163 ly

CETUS

98 ly

Haufen A
A151

IC 1610

Stellar Magnitudes (V)

≤2 3 4 5 6 7 8 9 10 11

Variable-Star Amplitudes and Types

<0.1 mag   0.1 – 1.0   ≥1.0 mag

(e) Eclipsing
(c) Cepheid
(m) Mira
... etc.

Fast-Moving Stars

Proper motion in 1000 years

Double-Star Separations

0.3"   3"   30"

339

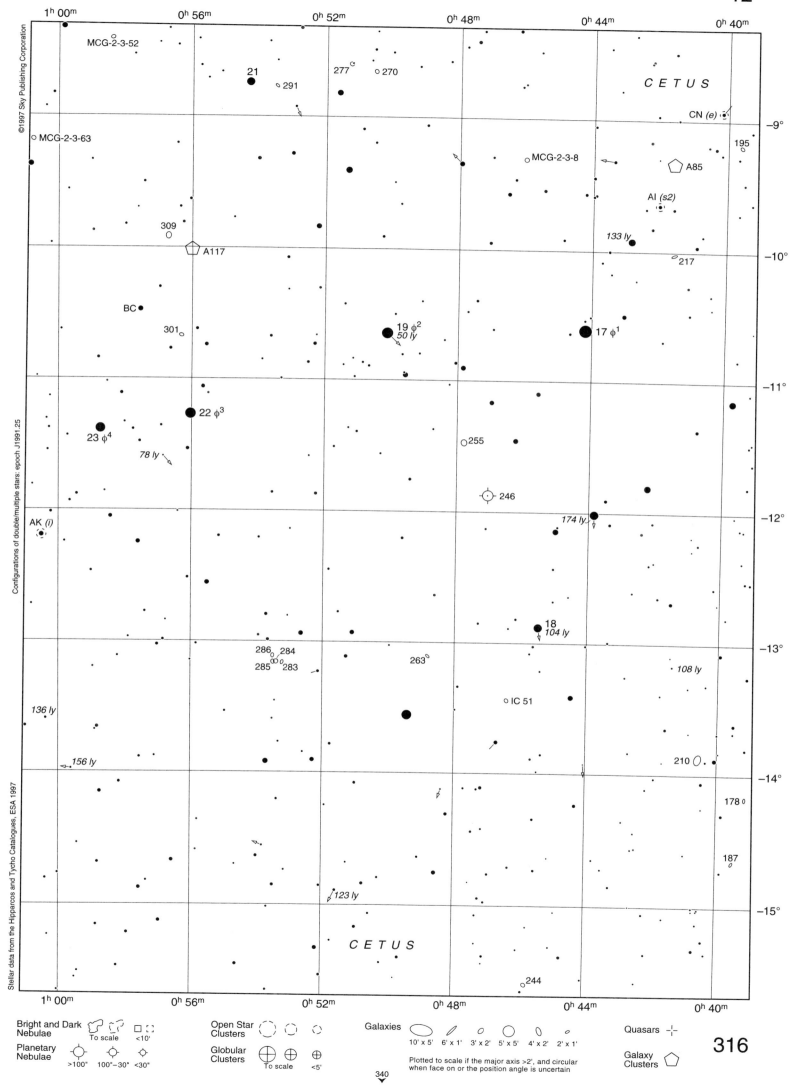

Configurations of double/multiple stars: epoch J1991.25

Stellar data from the Hipparcos and Tycho Catalogues, ESA 1997

MCG-2-3-52

MCG-2-3-63

21

291

277

270

CETUS

CN (e)

195

MCG-2-3-8

A85

AI (s2)

309

133 ly

A117

217

BC

301

19 φ²
50 ly

17 φ¹

22 φ³

23 φ⁴

78 ly

255

246

AK (i)

174 ly

18
104 ly

286   284
285   283

263

108 ly

136 ly

IC 51

156 ly

210

178 0

187

123 ly

CETUS

244

Bright and Dark Nebulae — To scale — <10'

Planetary Nebulae — >100" — 100"–30" — <30"

Open Star Clusters

Globular Clusters — To scale — <5'

Galaxies — 10' x 5' — 6' x 1' — 3' x 2' — 5' x 5' — 4' x 2' — 2' x 1'

Plotted to scale if the major axis >2', and circular when face on or the position angle is uncertain

Quasars

Galaxy Clusters

316

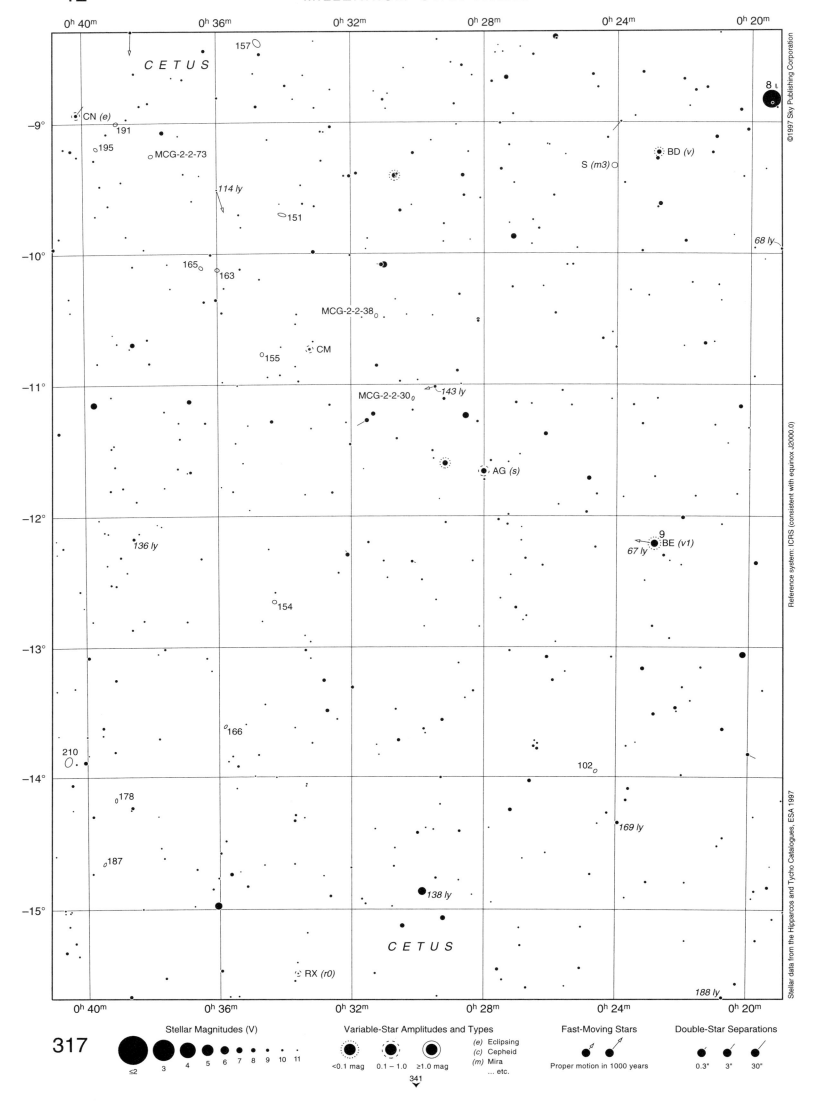

©1997 Sky Publishing Corporation

Reference system: ICRS (consistent with equinox J2000.0)

Stellar data from the Hipparcos and Tycho Catalogues, ESA 1997

317

Stellar Magnitudes (V)

≤2   3   4   5   6   7   8   9 10 11

Variable-Star Amplitudes and Types

<0.1 mag   0.1 – 1.0   ≥1.0 mag

(e) Eclipsing
(c) Cepheid
(m) Mira
... etc.

Fast-Moving Stars

Proper motion in 1000 years

Double-Star Separations

0.3"   3"   30"

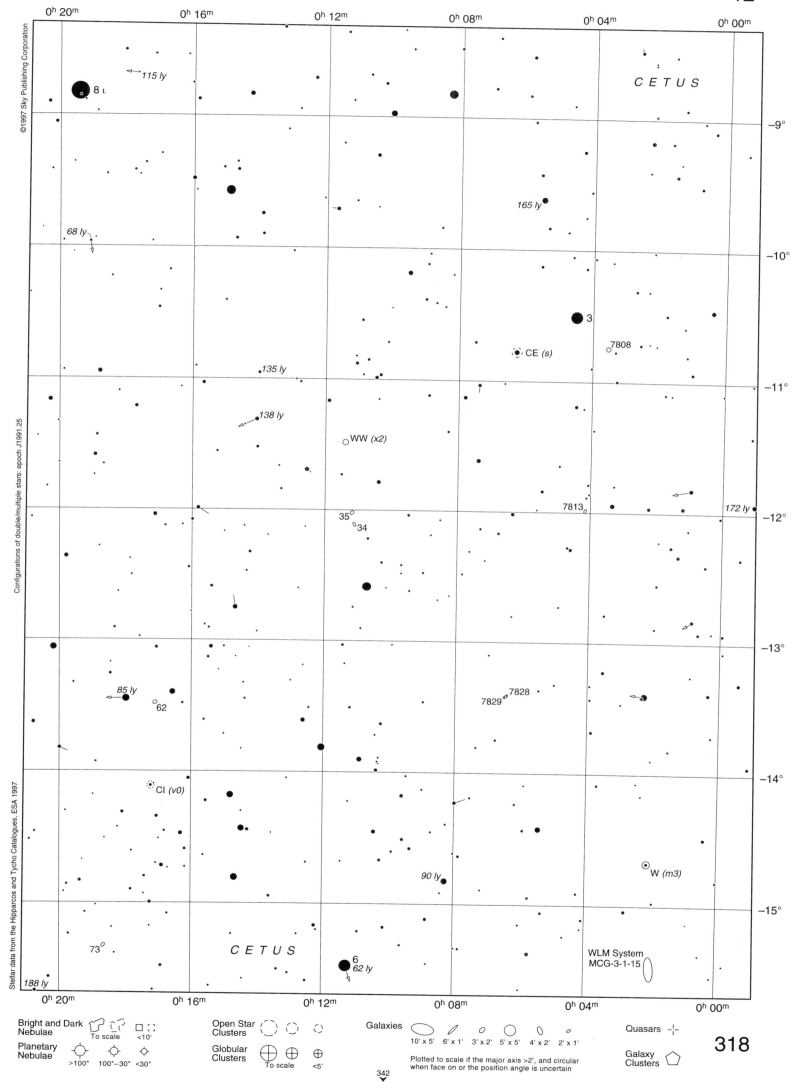

8 ι

115 ly

CETUS

68 ly

165 ly

3

7808

CE (s)

135 ly

138 ly

WW (x2)

7813

172 ly

35
34

85 ly

62

7829 7828

Cl (v0)

W (m3)

90 ly

73

CETUS

188 ly

6
62 ly

WLM System
MCG-3-1-15

Bright and Dark Nebulae	Open Star Clusters	Galaxies	Quasars
To scale <10'		10' x 5' 6' x 1' 3' x 2' 5' x 5' 4' x 2' 2' x 1'	
Planetary Nebulae	Globular Clusters		Galaxy Clusters
>100" 100"–30" <30"	To scale <5'	Plotted to scale if the major axis >2', and circular when face on or the position angle is uncertain	

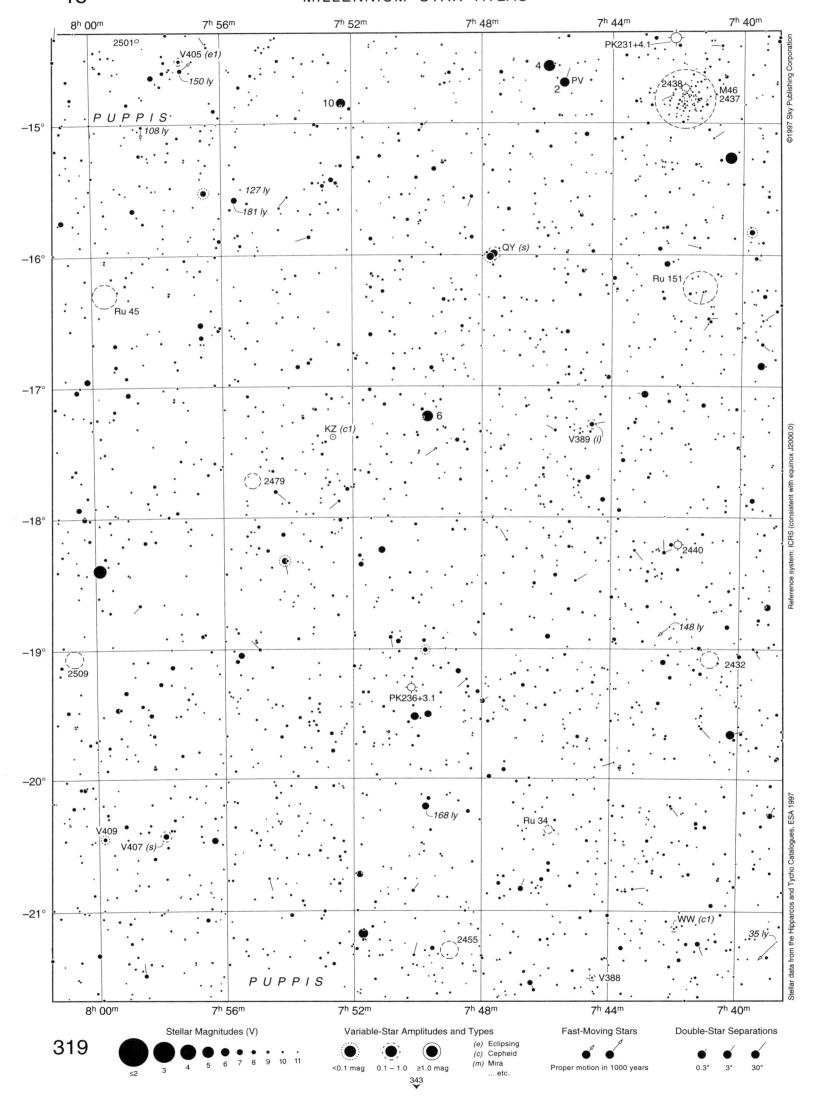

PUPPIS

PUPPIS

319

Stellar Magnitudes (V)

≤2   3   4   5   6   7   8   9   10   11

Variable-Star Amplitudes and Types

<0.1 mag   0.1 – 1.0   ≥1.0 mag

(e) Eclipsing
(c) Cepheid
(m) Mira
... etc.

Fast-Moving Stars

Proper motion in 1000 years

Double-Star Separations

0.3"   3"   30"

343

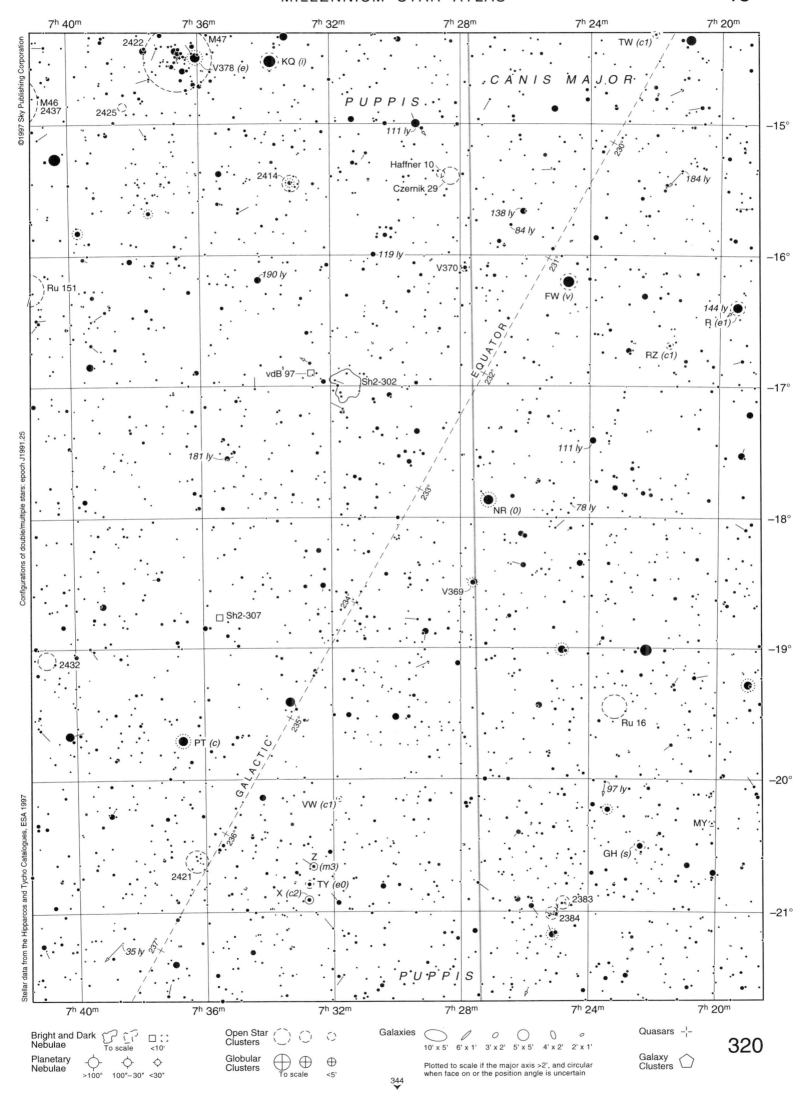

7h 40m   7h 36m   7h 32m   7h 28m   7h 24m   7h 20m

TW (c1)

CANIS MAJOR

2422   M47

V378 (e)   KQ (i)

PUPPIS

M46
2437

2425

−15°

2414

Haffner 10

111 ly

Czernik 29

184 ly

138 ly

84 ly

119 ly

−16°

190 ly

V370

23°

FW (v)

144 ly

R (e1)

Ru 151

23°

RZ (c1)

vdB 97

Sh2-302

EQUATOR

232°

−17°

181 ly

111 ly

233°

78 ly

NR (0)

−18°

234°

V369

Sh2-307

235°

−19°

2432

Ru 16

PT (c)

GALACTIC

235°

−20°

97 ly

VW (c1)

236°

MY

Z
(m3)

GH (s)

2421

TY (e0)

X (c2)

2383

2384

−21°

35 ly   237°

PUPPIS

7h 40m   7h 36m   7h 32m   7h 28m   7h 24m   7h 20m

Bright and Dark
Nebulae   To scale   <10'

Open Star
Clusters

Galaxies

10' x 5'   6' x 1'   3' x 2'   5' x 5'   4' x 2'   2' x 1'

Quasars

Planetary
Nebulae   >100"   100"–30"   <30"

Globular
Clusters   To scale   <5'

Plotted to scale if the major axis >2', and circular
when face on or the position angle is uncertain

Galaxy
Clusters

320

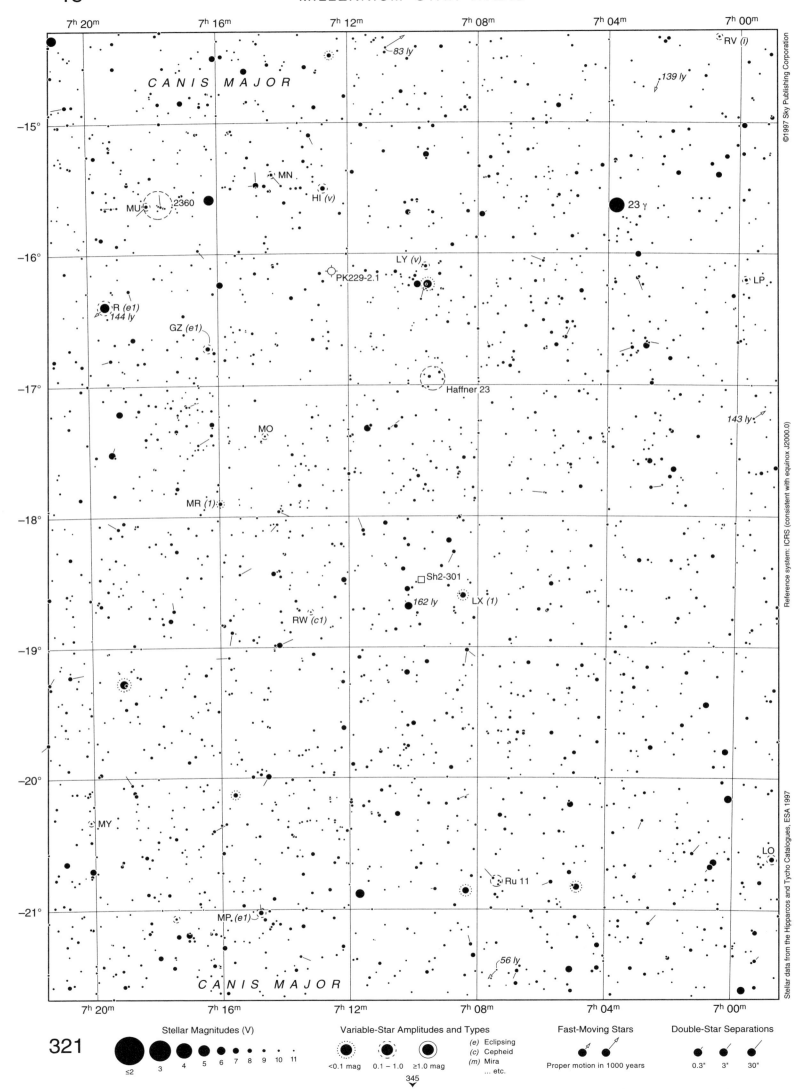

©1997 Sky Publishing Corporation

Reference system: ICRS (consistent with equinox J2000.0)

Stellar data from the Hipparcos and Tycho Catalogues, ESA 1997

CANIS MAJOR

CANIS MAJOR

23 γ

MU · 2360

MN

HI (v)

LY (v)

PK229-2.1

R (e1)
144 ly

GZ (e1)

Haffner 23

LP

MO

143 ly

MR (1)

Sh2-301

162 ly   LX (1)

RW (c1)

RV (i)

139 ly

MY

LO

Ru 11

MP (e1)

56 ly

321

Stellar Magnitudes (V)

≤2   3   4   5   6   7   8   9   10   11

Variable-Star Amplitudes and Types

<0.1 mag   0.1 – 1.0   ≥1.0 mag

(e) Eclipsing
(c) Cepheid
(m) Mira
... etc.

Fast-Moving Stars

Proper motion in 1000 years

Double-Star Separations

0.3"   3"   30"

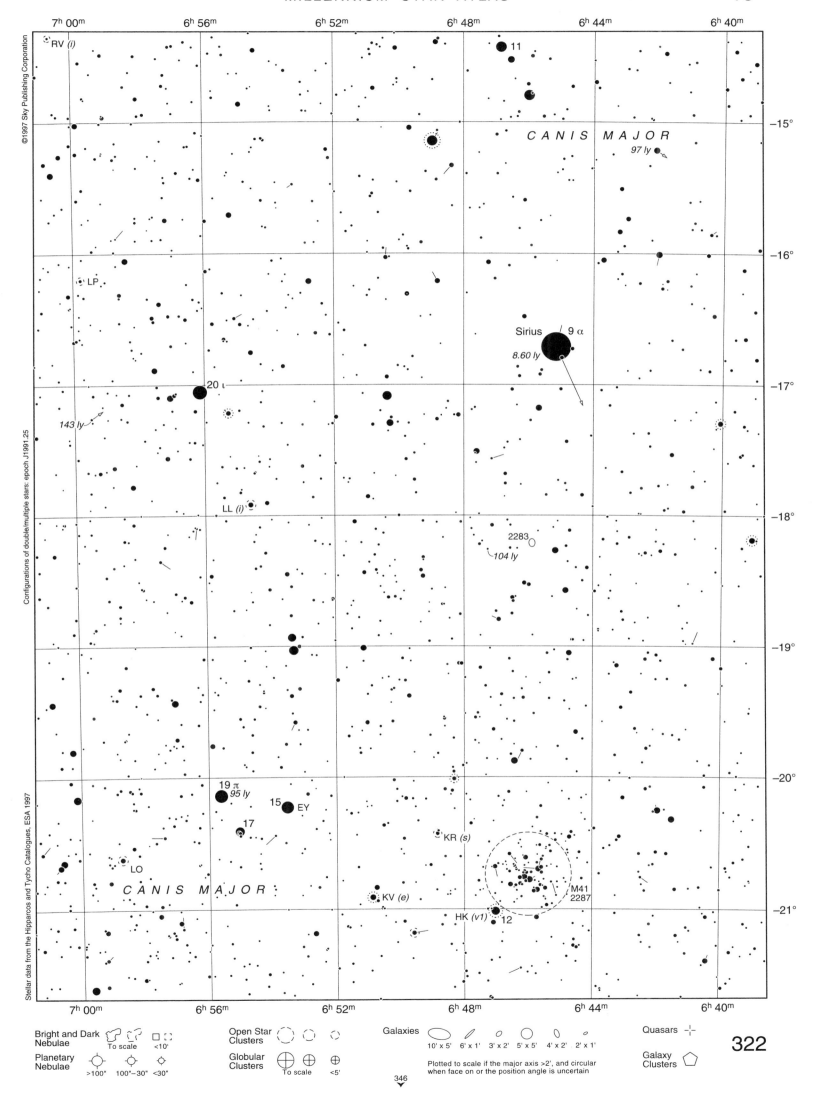

RV (i)

CANIS MAJOR

97 ly

LP

Sirius 9 α

20 ι

8.60 ly

143 ly

LL (i)

2283

104 ly

19 π
95 ly

15   EY

17

KR (s)

LO

CANIS MAJOR

KV (e)

M41
2287

HK (v1)   12

| Bright and Dark Nebulae | | | Open Star Clusters | | | Galaxies | | | | | | | Quasars |
| Planetary Nebulae | | | Globular Clusters | | | | | | | | | | Galaxy Clusters |

To scale   <10'

>100"   100"–30"   <30"

To scale   <5'

10' x 5' 6' x 1' 3' x 2' 5' x 5' 4' x 2' 2' x 1'

Plotted to scale if the major axis >2', and circular
when face on or the position angle is uncertain

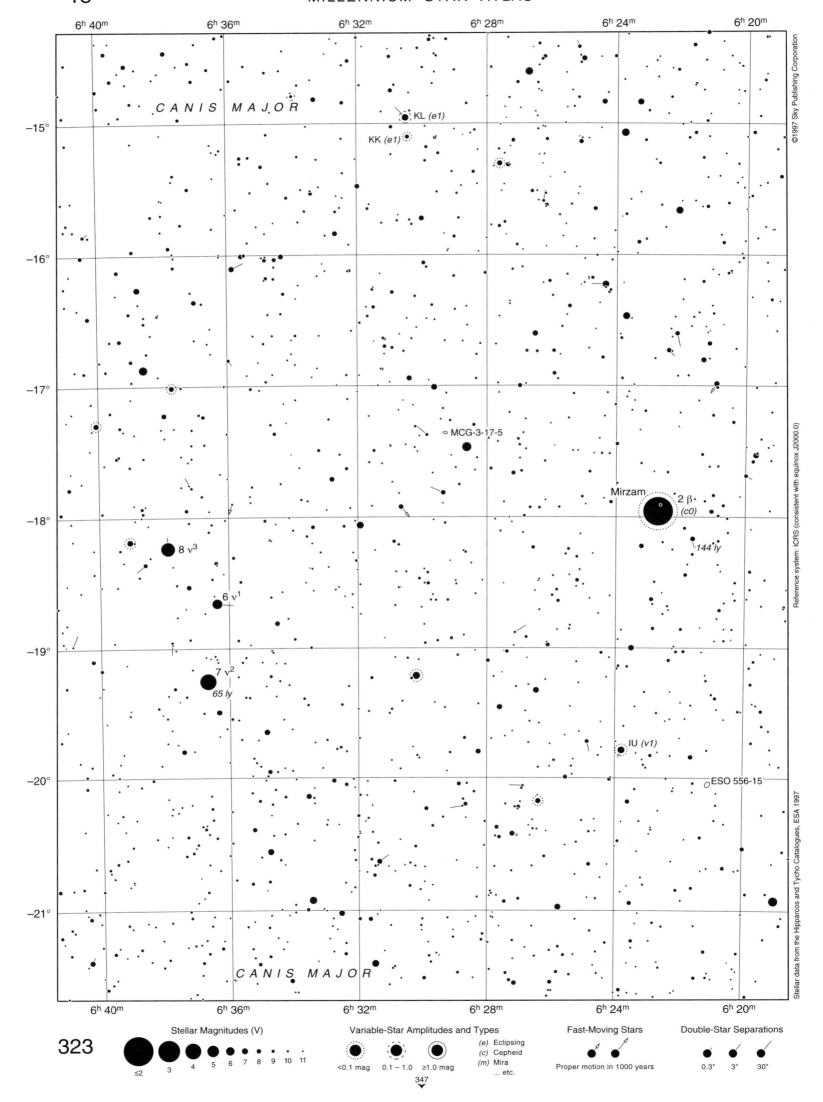

©1997 Sky Publishing Corporation

Reference system: ICRS (consistent with equinox J2000.0)

Stellar data from the Hipparcos and Tycho Catalogues, ESA 1997

Stellar Magnitudes (V)

≤2   3   4   5   6   7 8 9 10 11

Variable-Star Amplitudes and Types

<0.1 mag   0.1 – 1.0   ≥1.0 mag

(e) Eclipsing
(c) Cepheid
(m) Mira
... etc.

Fast-Moving Stars

Proper motion in 1000 years

Double-Star Separations

0.3"   3"   30"

323

347

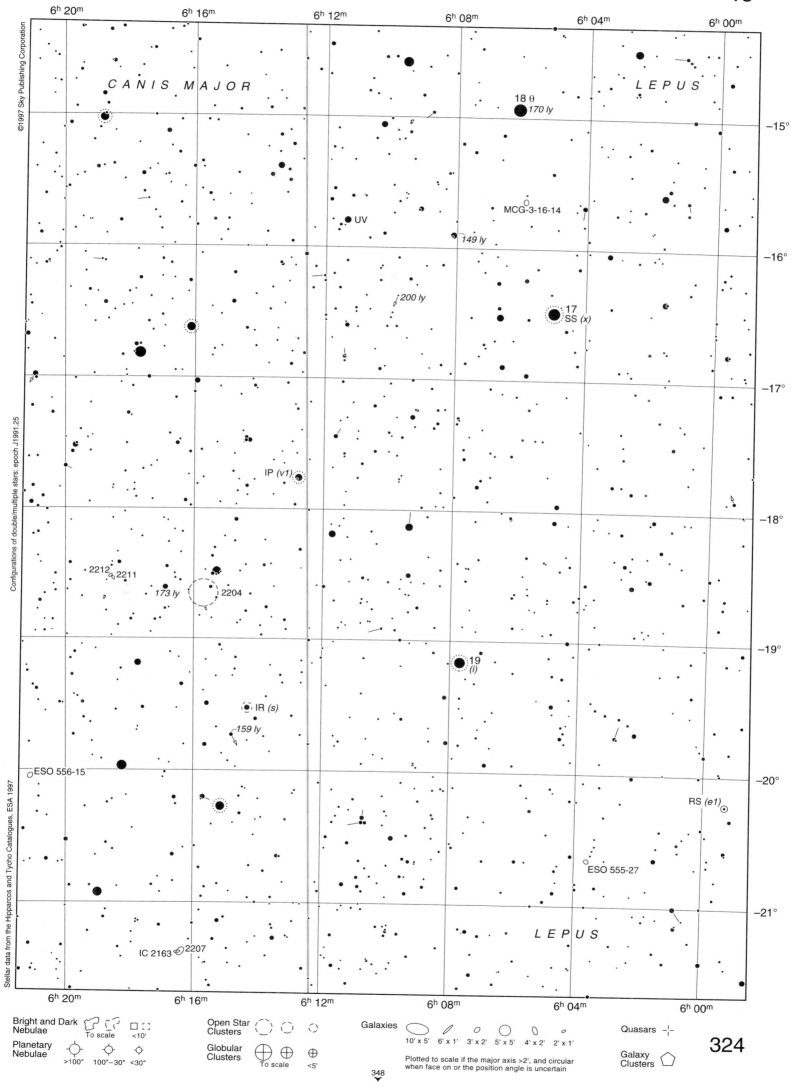

CANIS MAJOR

LEPUS

18 θ
170 ly

MCG-3-16-14

UV

149 ly

200 ly

17
SS (x)

−15°

−16°

−17°

−18°

IP (v1)

2212 2211

173 ly 2204

19
(i)

IR (s)

159 ly

ESO 556-15

RS (e1)

ESO 555-27

−19°

−20°

−21°

LEPUS

IC 2163 2207

Bright and Dark Nebulae				
To scale	<10'			

Planetary Nebulae >100" 100"−30" <30"

Open Star Clusters

Globular Clusters To scale <5'

Galaxies
10' x 5' 6' x 1' 3' x 2' 5' x 5' 4' x 2' 2' x 1'

Plotted to scale if the major axis >2', and circular
when face on or the position angle is uncertain

Quasars

Galaxy Clusters

324

348

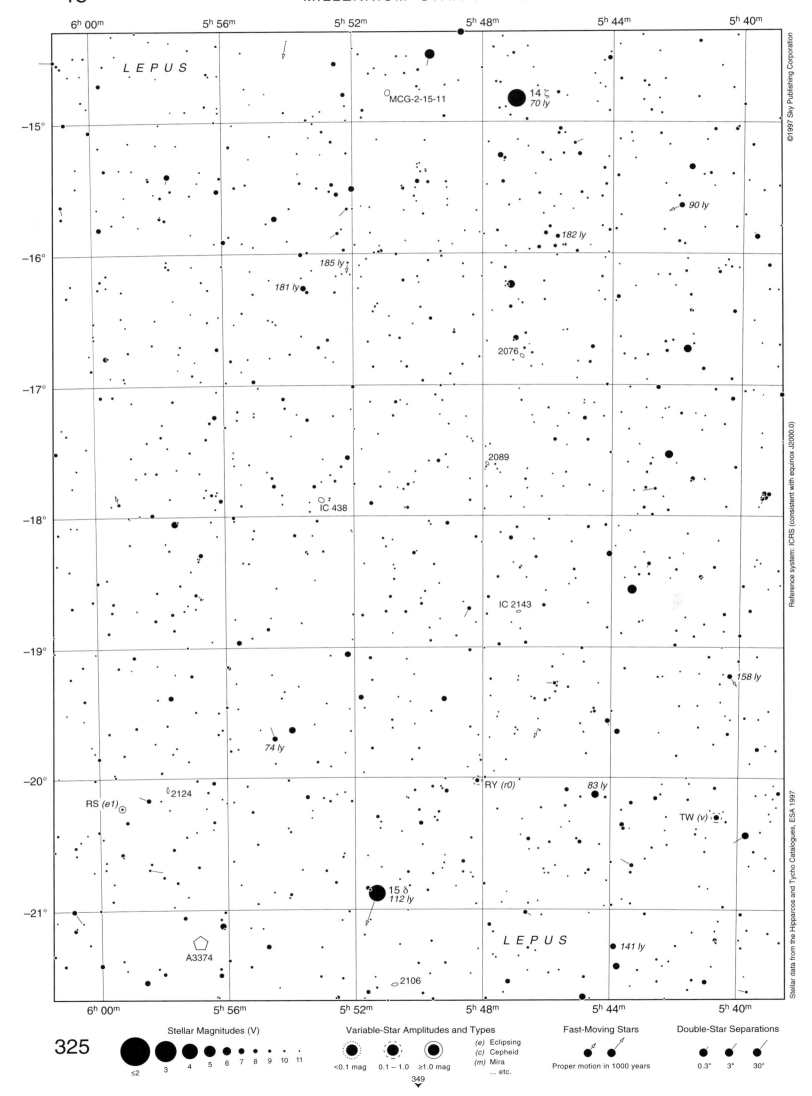

©1997 Sky Publishing Corporation

Reference system: ICRS (consistent with equinox J2000.0)

Stellar data from the Hipparcos and Tycho Catalogues, ESA 1997

LEPUS

MCG-2-15-11

14 ζ
70 ly

90 ly

182 ly

185 ly

181 ly

2076

2089

IC 438

IC 2143

158 ly

74 ly

RY (r0)

83 ly

RS (e1)

2124

TW (v)

15 δ
112 ly

LEPUS

141 ly

A3374

2106

325

Stellar Magnitudes (V)

≤2 3 4 5 6 7 8 9 10 11

Variable-Star Amplitudes and Types

<0.1 mag   0.1 – 1.0   ≥1.0 mag

(e) Eclipsing
(c) Cepheid
(m) Mira
... etc.

Fast-Moving Stars

Proper motion in 1000 years

Double-Star Separations

0.3"   3"   30"

349

MILLENNIUM STAR ATLAS

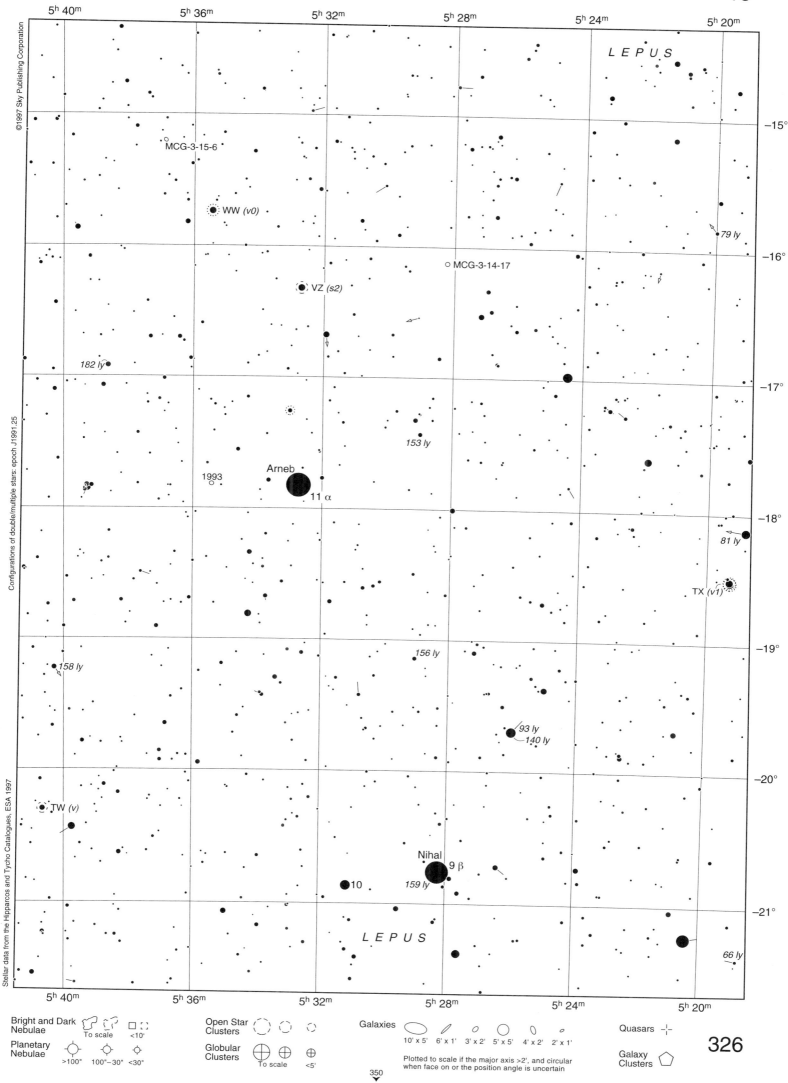

L E P U S

MCG-3-15-6

WW *(v0)*

−15°

79 ly

−16°

MCG-3-14-17

VZ *(s2)*

182 ly

−17°

153 ly

1993

Arneb

11 α

−18°

81 ly

TX *(v1)*

158 ly

156 ly

−19°

93 ly
140 ly

−20°

TW *(v)*

Nihal

9 β

10   159 ly

−21°

L E P U S

66 ly

Bright and Dark Nebulae			
To scale	<10'		

Planetary Nebulae
>100"   100"−30"   <30"

Open Star Clusters

Globular Clusters
To scale   <5'

Galaxies
10' x 5'   6' x 1'   3' x 2'   5' x 5'   4' x 2'   2' x 1'

Plotted to scale if the major axis >2', and circular when face on or the position angle is uncertain

Quasars

Galaxy Clusters

350

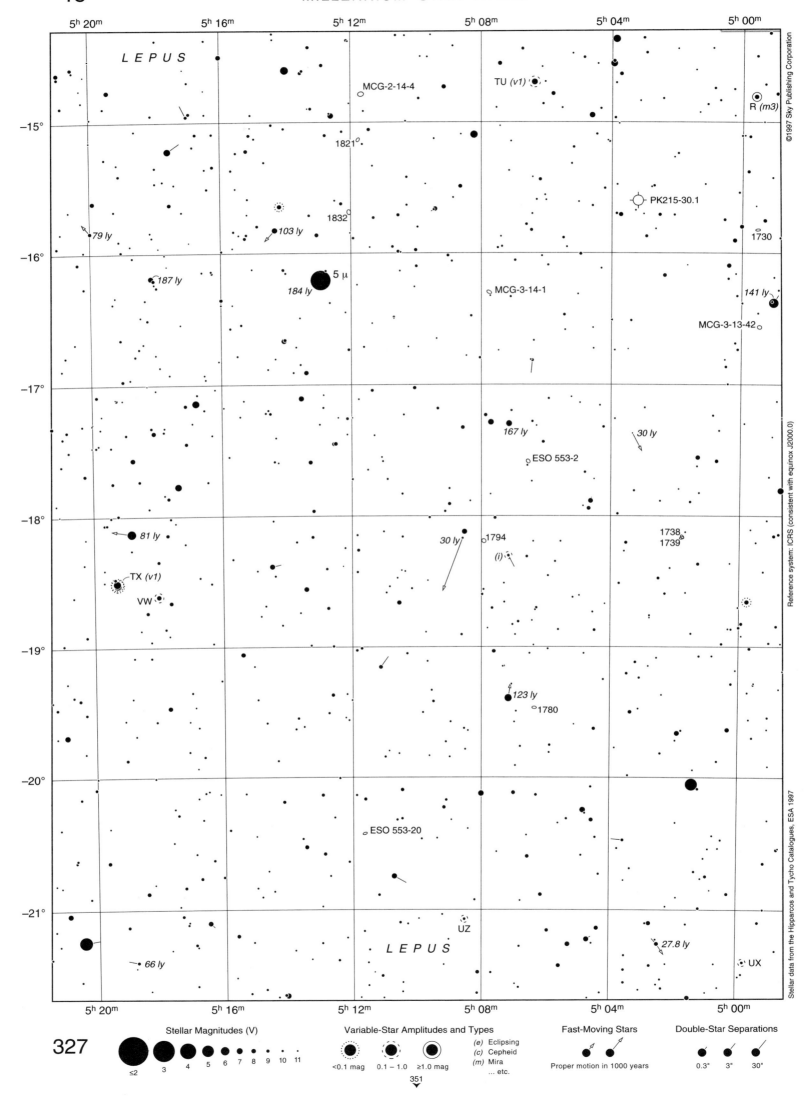

L E P U S

MCG-2-14-4

TU (v1)

R (m3)

1821

1832

PK215-30.1

1730

79 ly

103 ly

187 ly

5 μ

184 ly

MCG-3-14-1

141 ly

MCG-3-13-42

167 ly

30 ly

ESO 553-2

81 ly

1794

1738
1739

(i)

30 ly

TX (v1)

VW

123 ly

1780

ESO 553-20

UZ

L E P U S

27.8 ly

66 ly

UX

327

Stellar Magnitudes (V)

≤2   3   4   5   6   7 8 9 10 11

Variable-Star Amplitudes and Types

<0.1 mag   0.1 – 1.0   ≥1.0 mag

(e) Eclipsing
(c) Cepheid
(m) Mira
... etc.

Fast-Moving Stars

Proper motion in 1000 years

Double-Star Separations

0.3"   3"   30"

MILLENNIUM STAR ATLAS

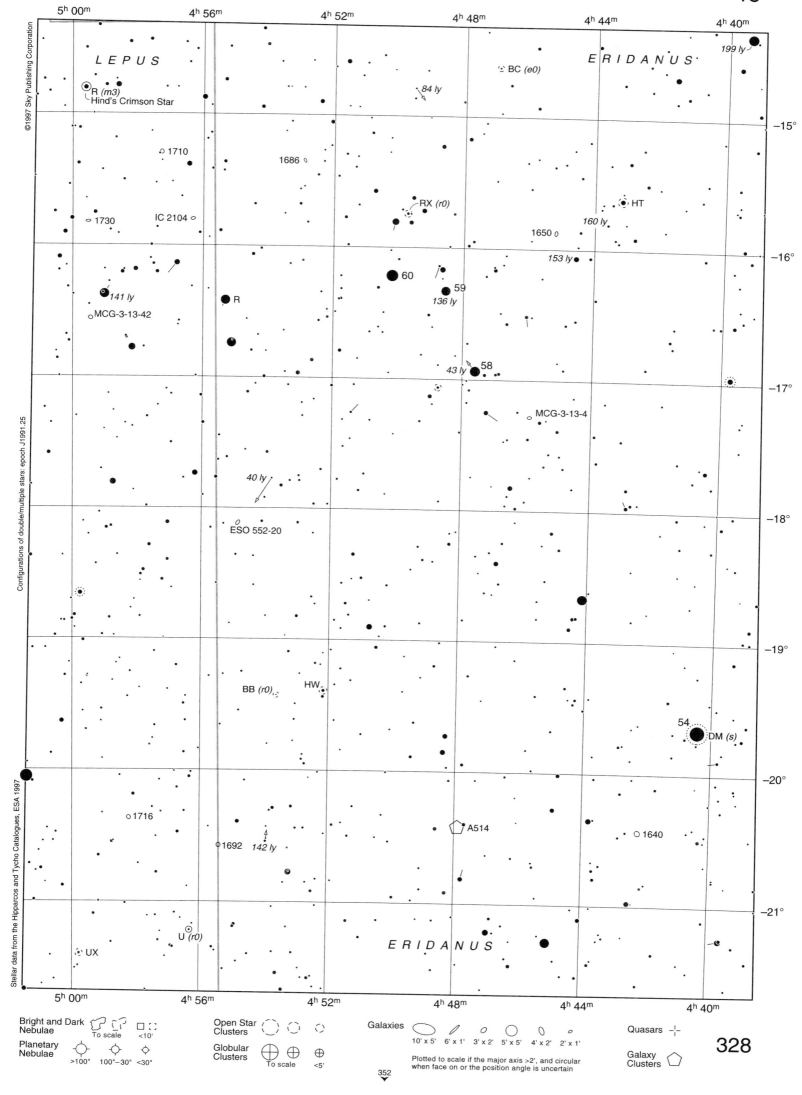

L E P U S

E R I D A N U S

199 ly

BC (e0)

84 ly

R (m3)
Hind's Crimson Star

1710

1686

IC 2104

RX (r0)

HT

1730

160 ly

1650

141 ly

153 ly

60

59

R

MCG-3-13-42

136 ly

58

43 ly

MCG-3-13-4

40 ly

ESO 552-20

BB (r0)

HW

54

DM (s)

1716

A514

1640

1692

142 ly

U (r0)

UX

E R I D A N U S

Bright and Dark
Nebulae
To scale   <10'

Open Star
Clusters

Galaxies

10' x 5'   6' x 1'   3' x 2'   5' x 5'   4' x 2'   2' x 1'

Quasars

Planetary
Nebulae
>100"   100"–30"   <30"

Globular
Clusters
To scale   <5'

Plotted to scale if the major axis >2', and circular
when face on or the position angle is uncertain

Galaxy
Clusters

328

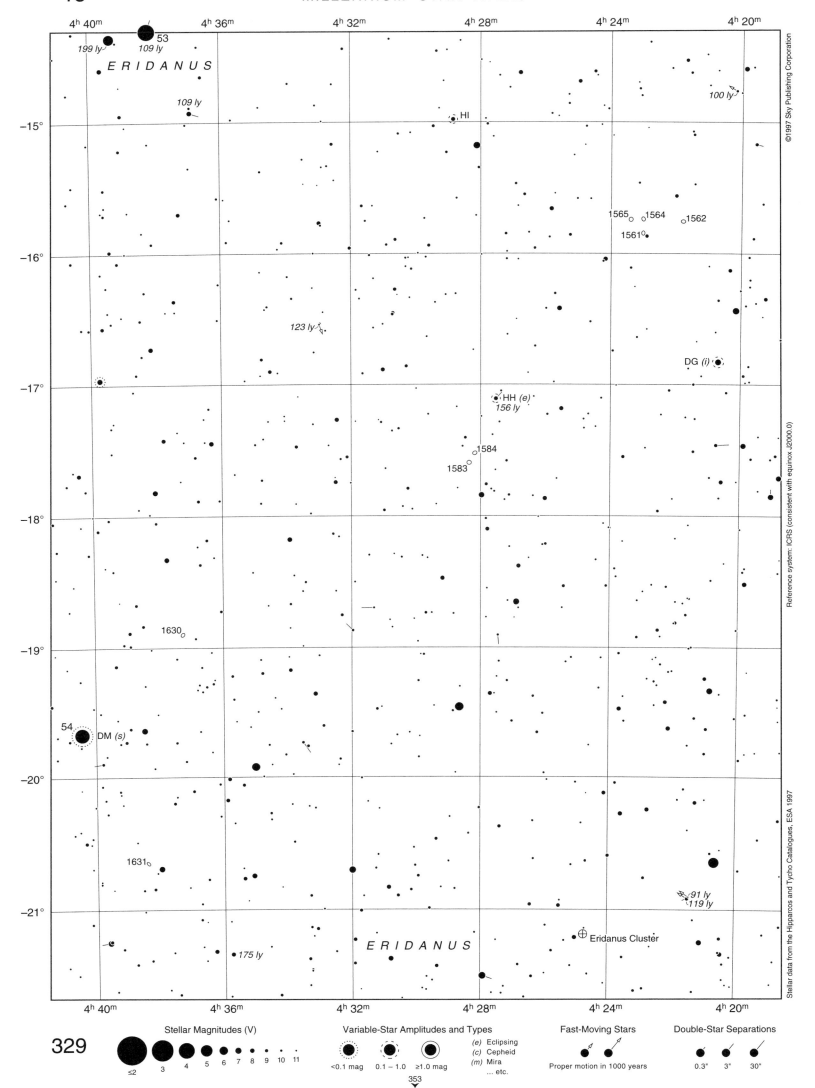

©1997 Sky Publishing Corporation

Reference system: ICRS (consistent with equinox J2000.0)

Stellar data from the Hipparcos and Tycho Catalogues, ESA 1997

Stellar Magnitudes (V)

≤2   3   4   5   6   7   8   9   10   11

Variable-Star Amplitudes and Types

<0.1 mag   0.1 – 1.0   ≥1.0 mag

(e) Eclipsing
(c) Cepheid
(m) Mira
... etc.

Fast-Moving Stars

Proper motion in 1000 years

Double-Star Separations

0.3"   3"   30"

MILLENNIUM STAR ATLAS

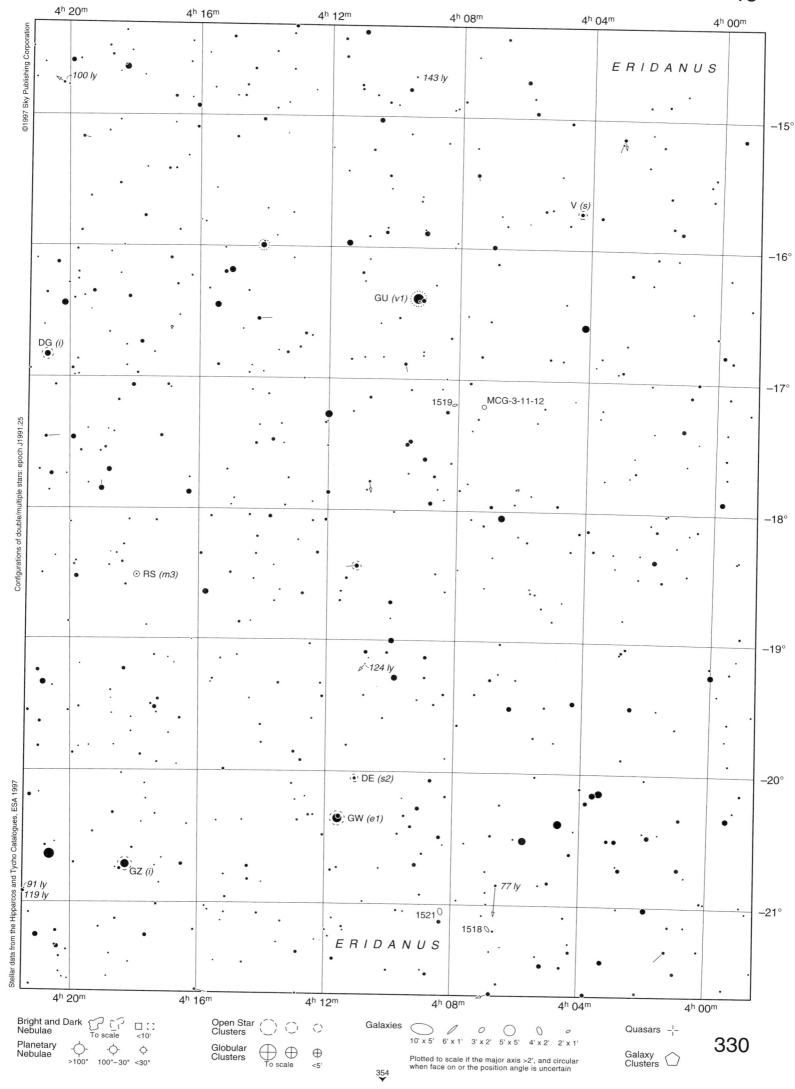

Configurations of double/multiple stars: epoch J1991.25

Stellar data from the Hipparcos and Tycho Catalogues, ESA 1997

ERIDANUS

100 ly

143 ly

−15°

V (s)

−16°

GU (v1)

DG (i)

−17°

1519   MCG-3-11-12

−18°

RS (m3)

−19°

124 ly

DE (s2)

−20°

GW (e1)

GZ (i)

91 ly
119 ly

77 ly

−21°

1521   1518

ERIDANUS

4ʰ 20ᵐ   4ʰ 16ᵐ   4ʰ 12ᵐ   4ʰ 08ᵐ   4ʰ 04ᵐ   4ʰ 00ᵐ

| Bright and Dark Nebulae | Open Star Clusters | Galaxies | Quasars |
| To scale   <10' | | 10' x 5'   6' x 1'   3' x 2'   5' x 5'   4' x 2'   2' x 1' | |

Planetary Nebulae
>100"   100"-30"   <30"

Globular Clusters
To scale   <5'

Plotted to scale if the major axis >2', and circular when face on or the position angle is uncertain

Galaxy Clusters

330

MILLENNIUM STAR ATLAS

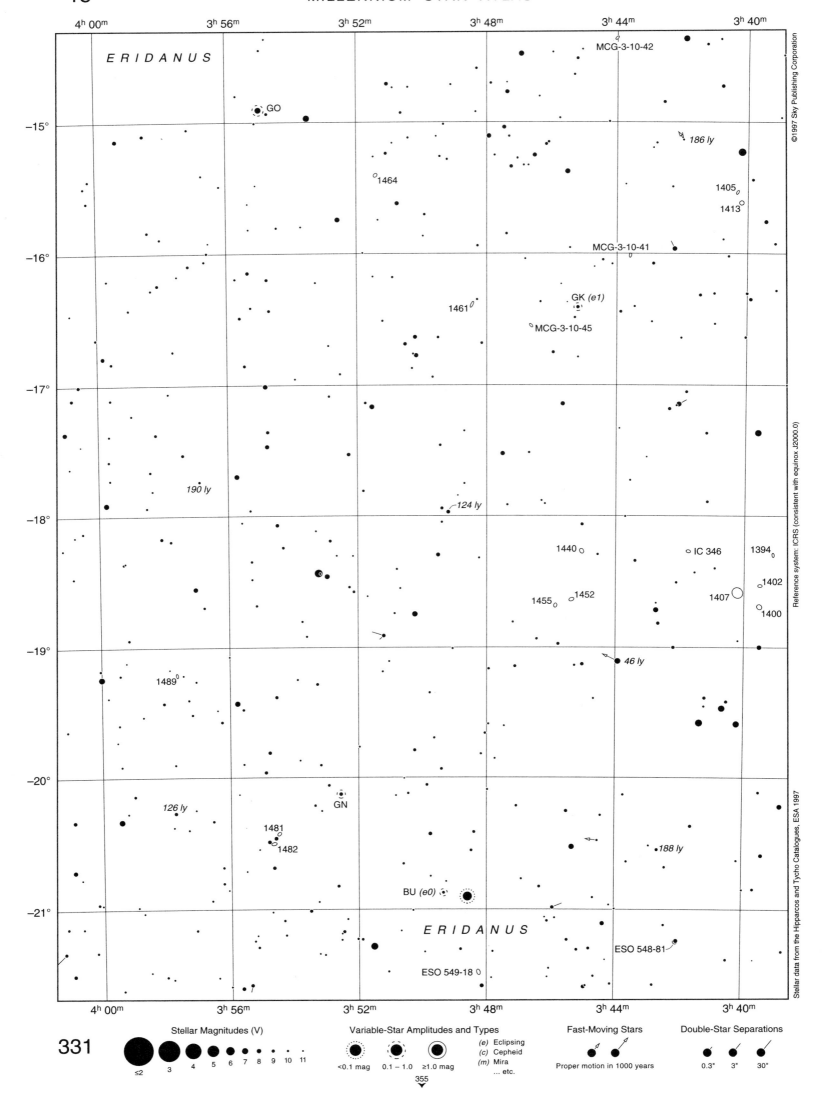

E R I D A N U S

MCG-3-10-42

GO

186 ly

1464

1405

1413

MCG-3-10-41

GK (e1)

1461

MCG-3-10-45

190 ly

124 ly

1440   IC 346   1394

1407   1402

1455   1452   1400

1489

46 ly

126 ly

GN

188 ly

1481

1482

BU (e0)

E R I D A N U S

ESO 548-81

ESO 549-18

©1997 Sky Publishing Corporation

Reference system: ICRS (consistent with equinox J2000.0)

Stellar data from the Hipparcos and Tycho Catalogues, ESA 1997

331

Stellar Magnitudes (V)	Variable-Star Amplitudes and Types	Fast-Moving Stars	Double-Star Separations

Stellar Magnitudes (V)

≤2   3   4   5   6   7   8   9   10   11

Variable-Star Amplitudes and Types

<0.1 mag   0.1 – 1.0   ≥1.0 mag

(e) Eclipsing
(c) Cepheid
(m) Mira
... etc.

Fast-Moving Stars

Proper motion in 1000 years

Double-Star Separations

0.3"   3"   30"

MILLENNIUM STAR ATLAS

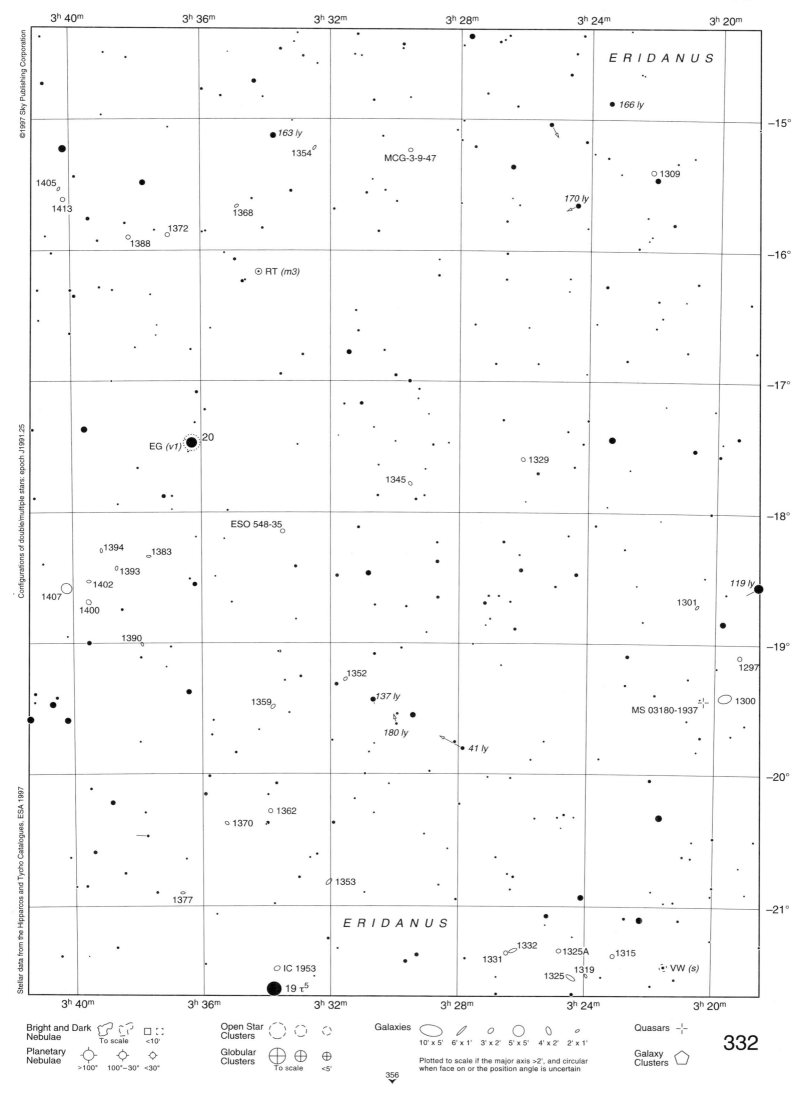

ERIDANUS

3h 40m   3h 36m   3h 32m   3h 28m   3h 24m   3h 20m

166 ly

−15°

163 ly
1354

MCG-3-9-47

○ 1309

170 ly

1405
1413

1368

1372
1388

−16°

⊙ RT *(m3)*

20

EG *(v1)*

○ 1329

1345 ○

−17°

ESO 548-35

○1394   ○1383

○1393

○1402

1407

○1400

1390

−18°

119 ly

1301

−19°

1352

1359 ○

137 ly

180 ly

41 ly

1297

MS 03180-1937   ○ 1300

−20°

○ 1362
1370   ○

1353

1377

−21°

ERIDANUS

○1332   ○1325A   ○1315

1331   1325   1319   ⊡ VW *(s)*

○ IC 1953

19 τ⁵

3h 40m   3h 36m   3h 32m   3h 28m   3h 24m   3h 20m

©1997 Sky Publishing Corporation

Configurations of double/multiple stars: epoch J1991.25

Stellar data from the Hipparcos and Tycho Catalogues, ESA 1997

Bright and Dark Nebulae   To scale   <10'

Open Star Clusters

Galaxies   10' x 5'   6' x 1'   3' x 2'   5' x 5'   4' x 2'   2' x 1'

Quasars

Planetary Nebulae   >100"   100"−30"   <30"

Globular Clusters   To scale   <5'

Plotted to scale if the major axis >2', and circular when face on or the position angle is uncertain

Galaxy Clusters

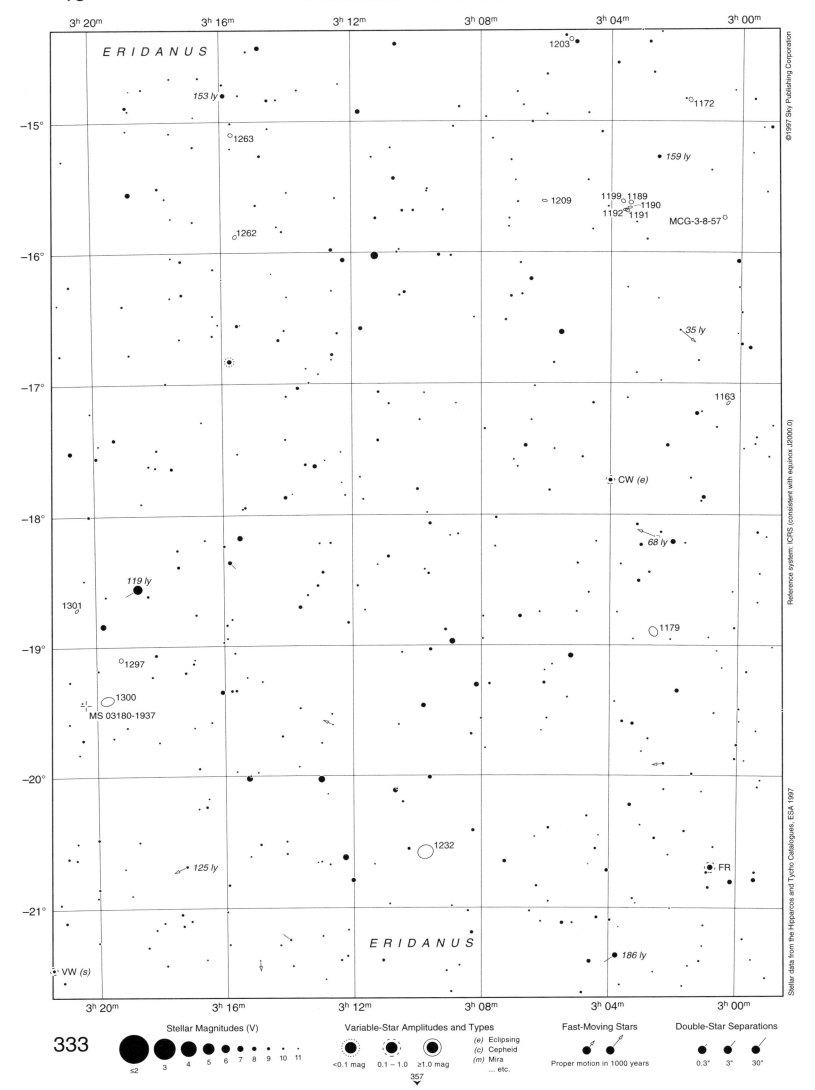

©1997 Sky Publishing Corporation

Reference system: ICRS (consistent with equinox J2000.0)

Stellar data from the Hipparcos and Tycho Catalogues, ESA 1997

ERIDANUS

153 ly

1263

1262

1203

1172

159 ly

1209   1199 1189
          1190
1192 1191
MCG-3-8-57

35 ly

1163

CW (e)

68 ly

119 ly

1301

1179

1297

1300
MS 03180-1937

1232

125 ly

FR

ERIDANUS

186 ly

VW (s)

Stellar Magnitudes (V)

≤2   3   4   5   6   7   8   9   10 11

Variable-Star Amplitudes and Types

<0.1 mag   0.1 – 1.0   ≥1.0 mag

(e) Eclipsing
(c) Cepheid
(m) Mira
... etc.

Fast-Moving Stars

Proper motion in 1000 years

Double-Star Separations

0.3"   3"   30"

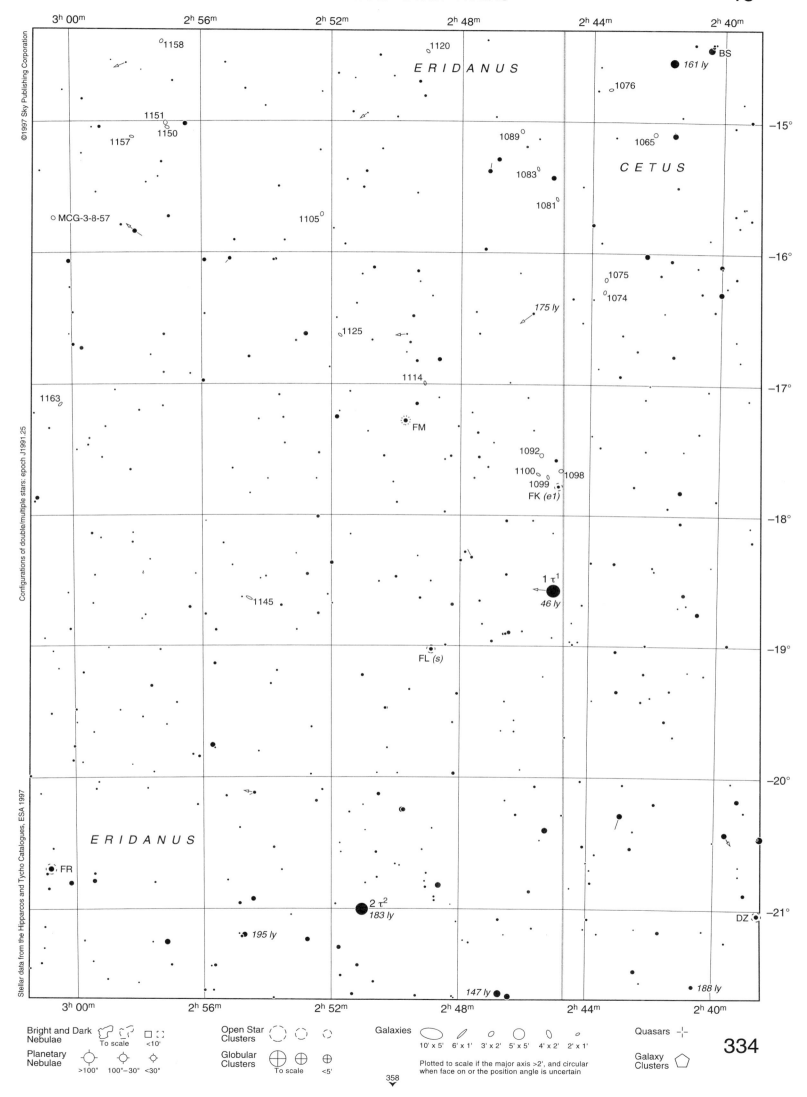

310

3ʰ 00ᵐ   2ʰ 56ᵐ   2ʰ 52ᵐ   2ʰ 48ᵐ   2ʰ 44ᵐ   2ʰ 40ᵐ

E R I D A N U S

C E T U S

−15°

−16°

−17°

−18°

−19°

−20°

−21°

1158
1120
BS
161 ly
1076
1151
1150
1157
1089
1065
1083
1081
MCG-3-8-57
1105
1075
1074
175 ly
1125
1114
1163
FM
1092
1100   1098
1099
FK (e1)
1 τ¹
46 ly
1145
FL (s)
E R I D A N U S
FR
2 τ²
183 ly
195 ly
147 ly
DZ
188 ly

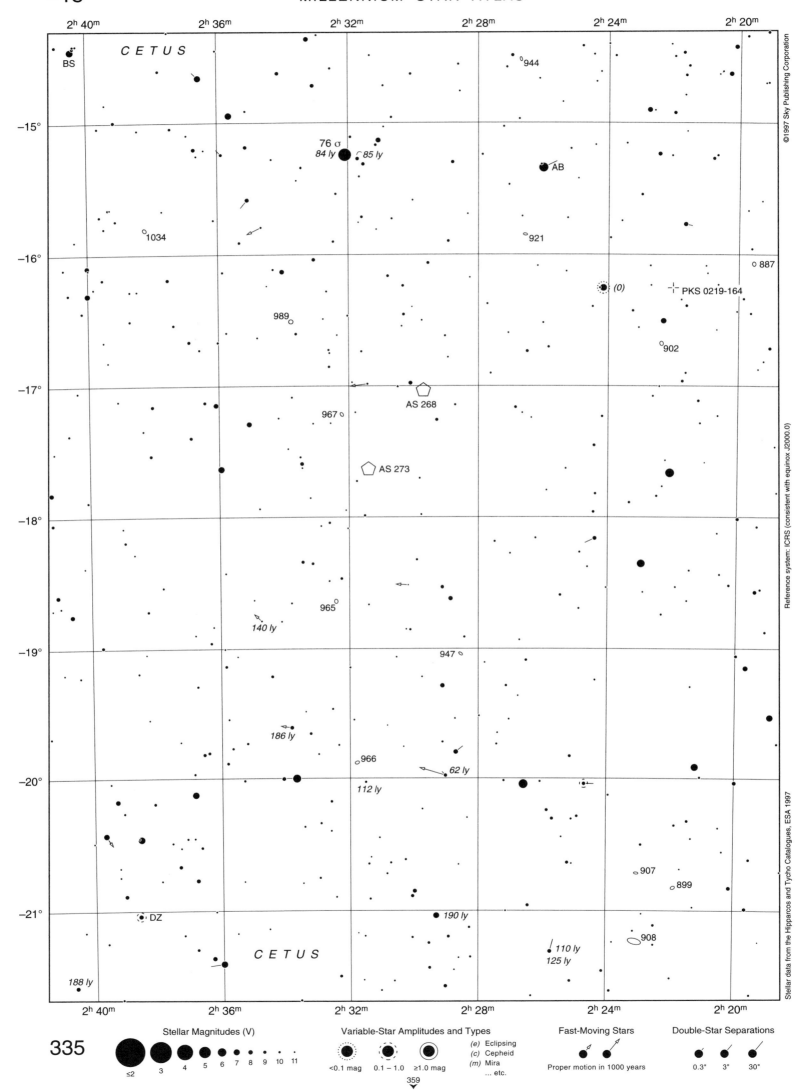

©1997 Sky Publishing Corporation

Reference system: ICRS (consistent with equinox J2000.0)

Stellar data from the Hipparcos and Tycho Catalogues, ESA 1997

CETUS

BS

76 σ
84 ly   85 ly

AB

944

921

1034

887

(0)

PKS 0219-164

989

902

AS 268

967

AS 273

965

140 ly

947

186 ly

966

62 ly

112 ly

DZ

907

899

190 ly

908

110 ly
125 ly

CETUS

188 ly

Stellar Magnitudes (V)

≤2   3   4   5   6 7 8 9 10 11

Variable-Star Amplitudes and Types

<0.1 mag   0.1 – 1.0   ≥1.0 mag

(e) Eclipsing
(c) Cepheid
(m) Mira
... etc.

Fast-Moving Stars

Proper motion in 1000 years

Double-Star Separations

0.3"   3"   30"

MILLENNIUM STAR ATLAS

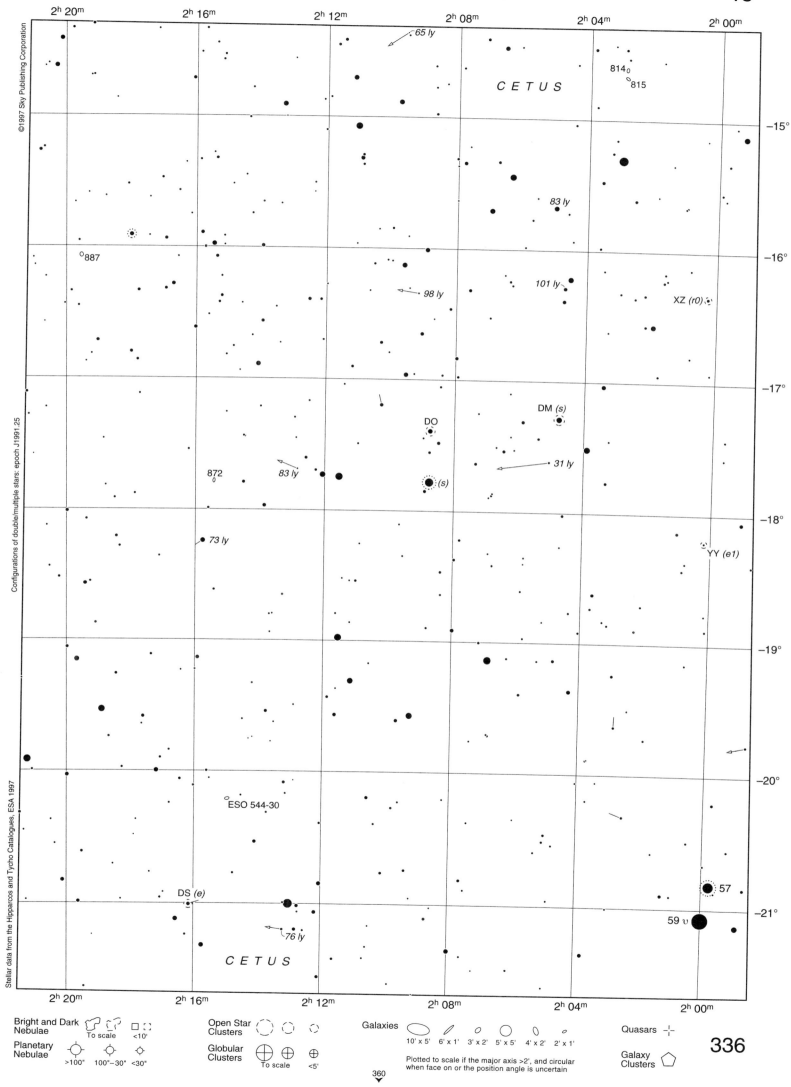

©1997 Sky Publishing Corporation

Configurations of double/multiple stars: epoch J1991.25

Stellar data from the Hipparcos and Tycho Catalogues, ESA 1997

2h 20m 2h 16m 2h 12m 2h 08m 2h 04m 2h 00m

65 ly

C E T U S

814₀
815

−15°

83 ly

−16°

887

98 ly

101 ly

XZ (r0)

DO

DM (s)

872₀

83 ly

31 ly

(s)

−17°

73 ly

−18°

YY (e1)

−19°

ESO 544-30

−20°

DS (e)

57

76 ly

59 υ

−21°

C E T U S

2h 20m 2h 16m 2h 12m 2h 08m 2h 04m 2h 00m

Bright and Dark Nebulae — To scale — <10'

Planetary Nebulae — >100" — 100"-30" — <30"

Open Star Clusters

Globular Clusters — To scale — <5'

Galaxies
10' x 5' — 6' x 1' — 3' x 2' — 5' x 5' — 4' x 2' — 2' x 1'

Plotted to scale if the major axis >2', and circular when face on or the position angle is uncertain

Quasars

Galaxy Clusters

336

360

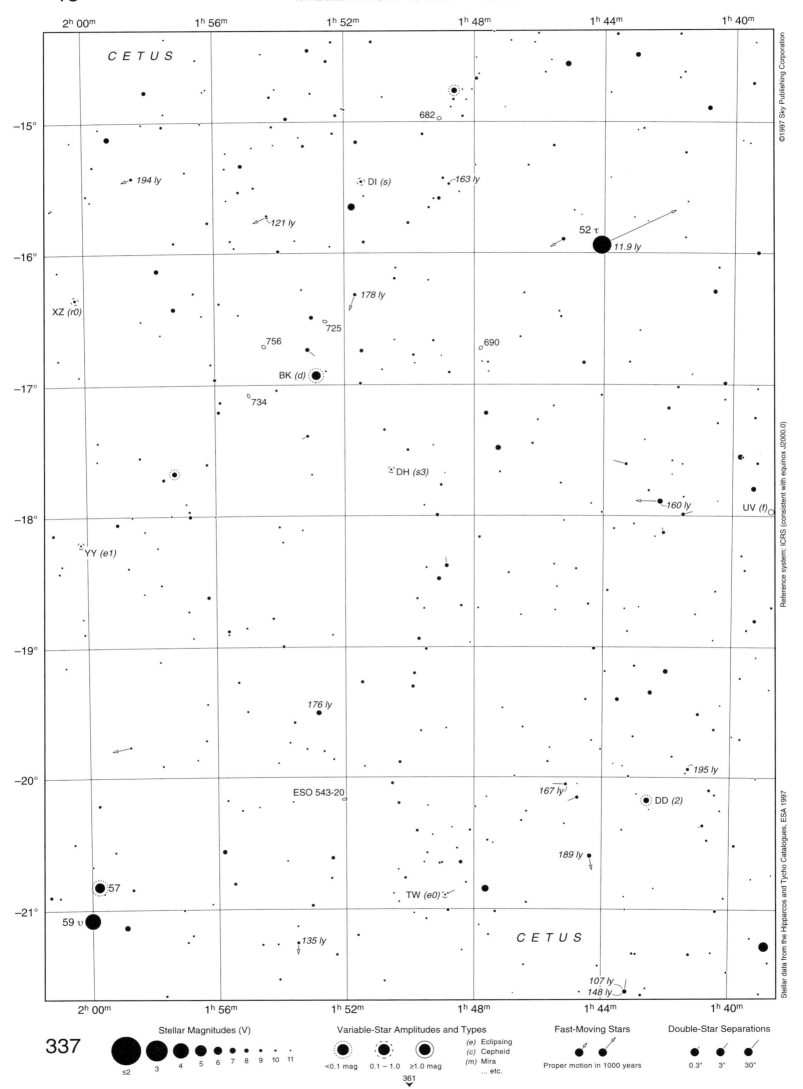

©1997 Sky Publishing Corporation

Reference system: ICRS (consistent with equinox J2000.0)

Stellar data from the Hipparcos and Tycho Catalogues, ESA 1997

CETUS

682 ○

194 ly

DI (s)   163 ly

121 ly

52 τ   11.9 ly

178 ly

XZ (r0)

725

756   690

BK (d)

734

DH (s3)

160 ly

UV (f) ○

YY (e1)

176 ly

195 ly

ESO 543-20

167 ly   DD (2)

189 ly

57

TW (e0)

CETUS

59 υ

135 ly

107 ly
148 ly

337

Stellar Magnitudes (V)

≤2   3   4   5   6   7   8   9   10   11

Variable-Star Amplitudes and Types

<0.1 mag   0.1 – 1.0   ≥1.0 mag

(e) Eclipsing
(c) Cepheid
(m) Mira
... etc.

Fast-Moving Stars

Proper motion in 1000 years

Double-Star Separations

0.3"   3"   30"

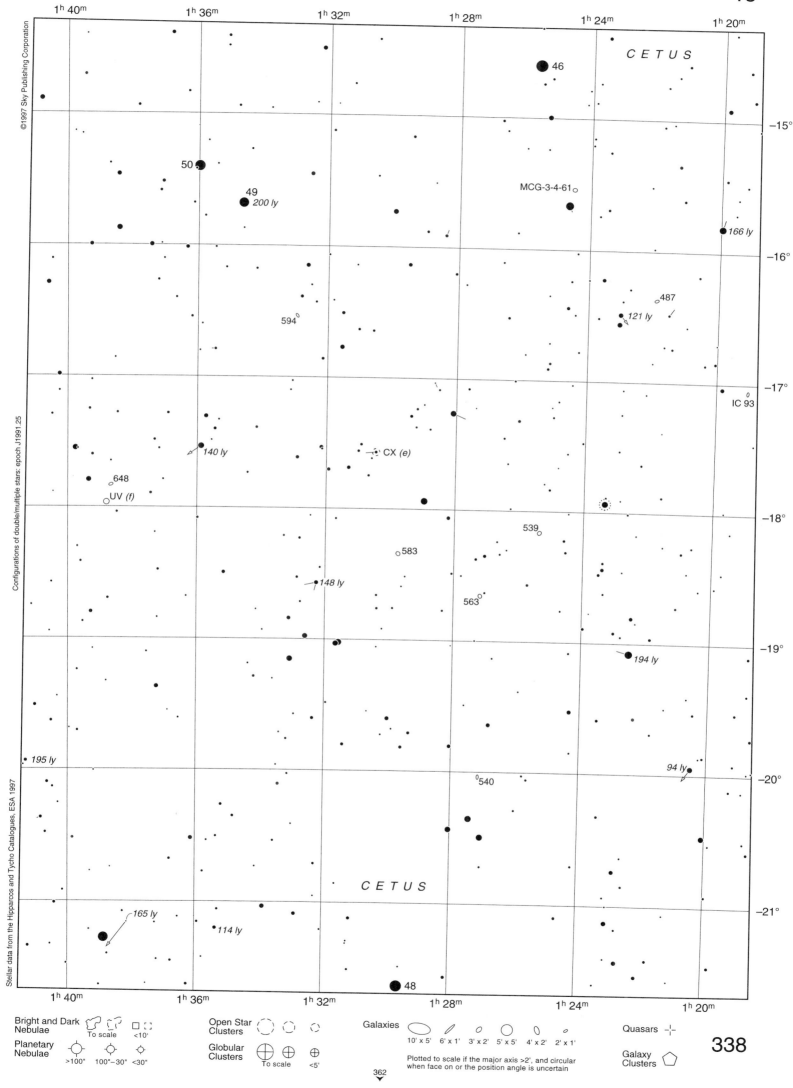

Configurations of double/multiple stars: epoch J1991.25

Stellar data from the Hipparcos and Tycho Catalogues. ESA 1997

CETUS

46

50

49
200 ly

MCG-3-4-61

166 ly

487
121 ly

594

IC 93

140 ly

CX (e)

648
UV (f)

539

583

148 ly

563

194 ly

195 ly

540

94 ly

CETUS

165 ly

114 ly

48

Bright and Dark Nebulae
To scale   <10'

Planetary Nebulae
>100"   100"−30"   <30'

Open Star Clusters

Globular Clusters
To scale   <5'

Galaxies
10' x 5'   6' x 1'   3' x 2'   5' x 5'   4' x 2'   2' x 1'

Plotted to scale if the major axis >2', and circular when face on or the position angle is uncertain

Quasars

Galaxy Clusters

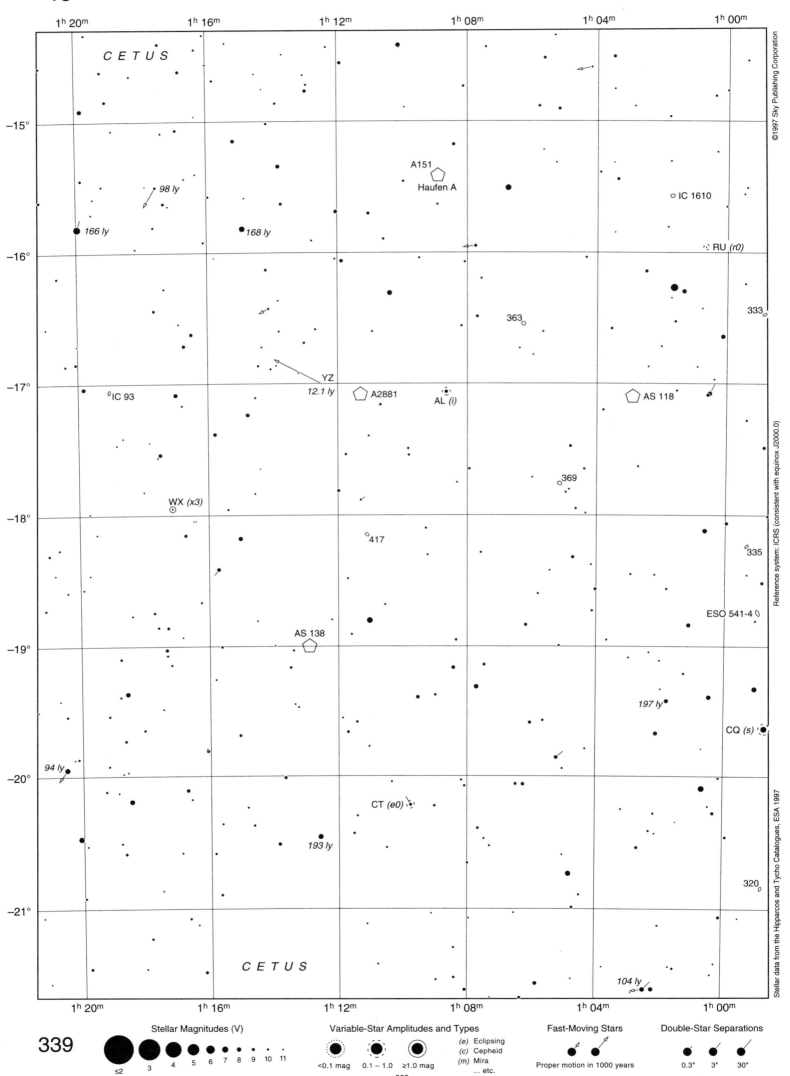

Reference system: ICRS (consistent with equinox J2000.0)

Stellar data from the Hipparcos and Tycho Catalogues, ESA 1997

CETUS

A151
Haufen A

○ IC 1610

98 ly

166 ly

168 ly

○ RU (r0)

333 ○

363 ○

YZ
12.1 ly

○ IC 93

A2881

AL (i)

AS 118

○ 369

WX (x3)

○ 417

○ 335

ESO 541-4 ○

AS 138

197 ly

CQ (s)

94 ly

CT (e0)

193 ly

320 ○

104 ly

CETUS

339

Stellar Magnitudes (V)

≤2   3   4   5   6   7   8   9   10   11

Variable-Star Amplitudes and Types

<0.1 mag   0.1 – 1.0   ≥1.0 mag

(e) Eclipsing
(c) Cepheid
(m) Mira
... etc.

Fast-Moving Stars

Proper motion in 1000 years

Double-Star Separations

0.3"   3"   30"

315

363

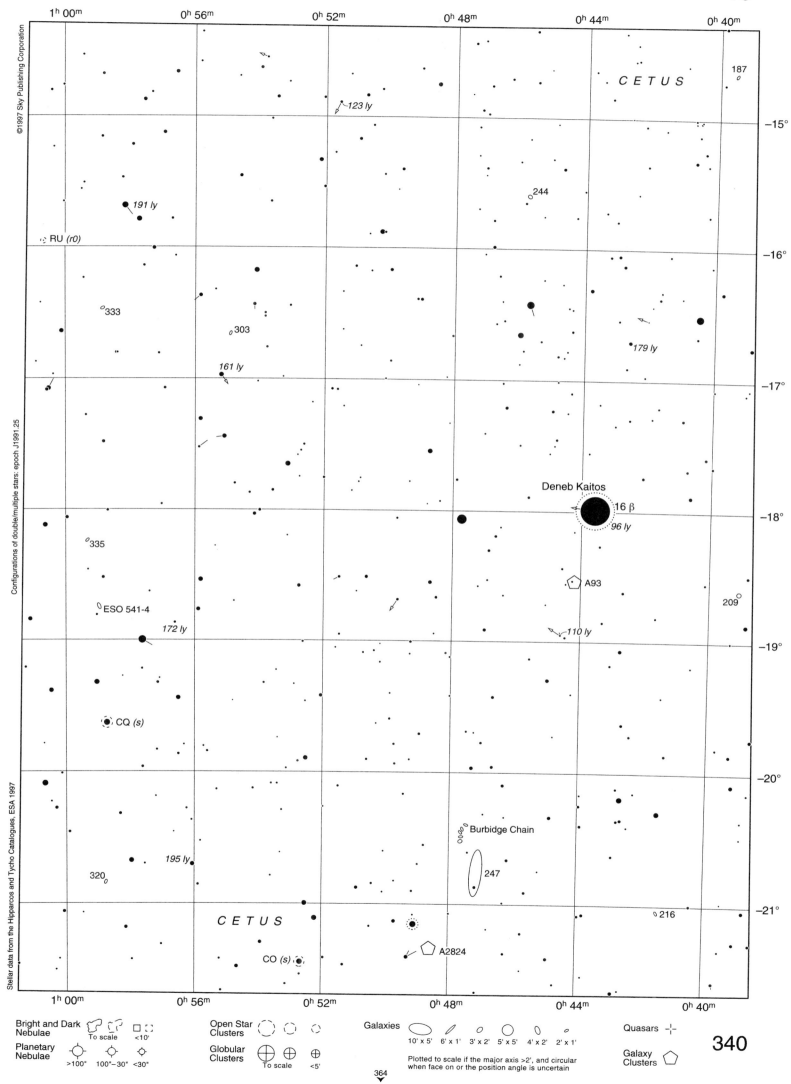

1h 00m
0h 56m
0h 52m
0h 48m
0h 44m
0h 40m

CETUS

187

123 ly

−15°

244

191 ly

RU (r0)

−16°

333

303

179 ly

161 ly

−17°

Deneb Kaitos

16 β

96 ly

−18°

335

A93

209

ESO 541-4

172 ly

110 ly

−19°

CQ (s)

−20°

Burbidge Chain

195 ly

247

320

216

−21°

CETUS

A2824

CO (s)

1h 00m
0h 56m
0h 52m
0h 48m
0h 44m
0h 40m

Bright and Dark Nebulae
To scale   <10'

Planetary Nebulae
>100"   100"−30"   <30"

Open Star Clusters

Globular Clusters
To scale   <5'

Galaxies
10' x 5'   6' x 1'   3' x 2'   5' x 5'   4' x 2'   2' x 1'

Plotted to scale if the major axis >2', and circular
when face on or the position angle is uncertain

Quasars

Galaxy Clusters

340

MILLENNIUM STAR ATLAS

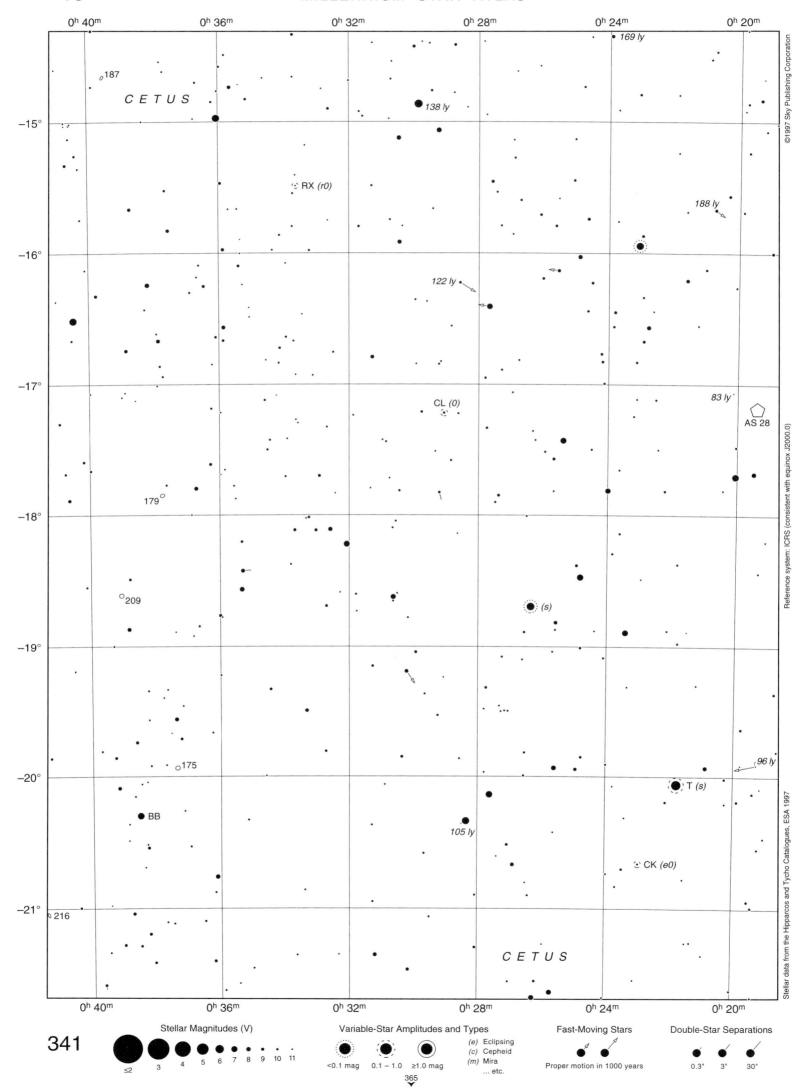

CETUS

187

138 ly

169 ly

RX (r0)

188 ly

122 ly

CL (0)

83 ly

AS 28

179

209

(s)

175

96 ly

T (s)

BB

105 ly

CK (e0)

216

CETUS

©1997 Sky Publishing Corporation

Reference system: ICRS (consistent with equinox J2000.0)

Stellar data from the Hipparcos and Tycho Catalogues, ESA 1997

341

Stellar Magnitudes (V)

≤2 3 4 5 6 7 8 9 10 11

Variable-Star Amplitudes and Types

<0.1 mag   0.1 – 1.0   ≥1.0 mag

(e) Eclipsing
(c) Cepheid
(m) Mira
... etc.

Fast-Moving Stars

Proper motion in 1000 years

Double-Star Separations

0.3"   3"   30"

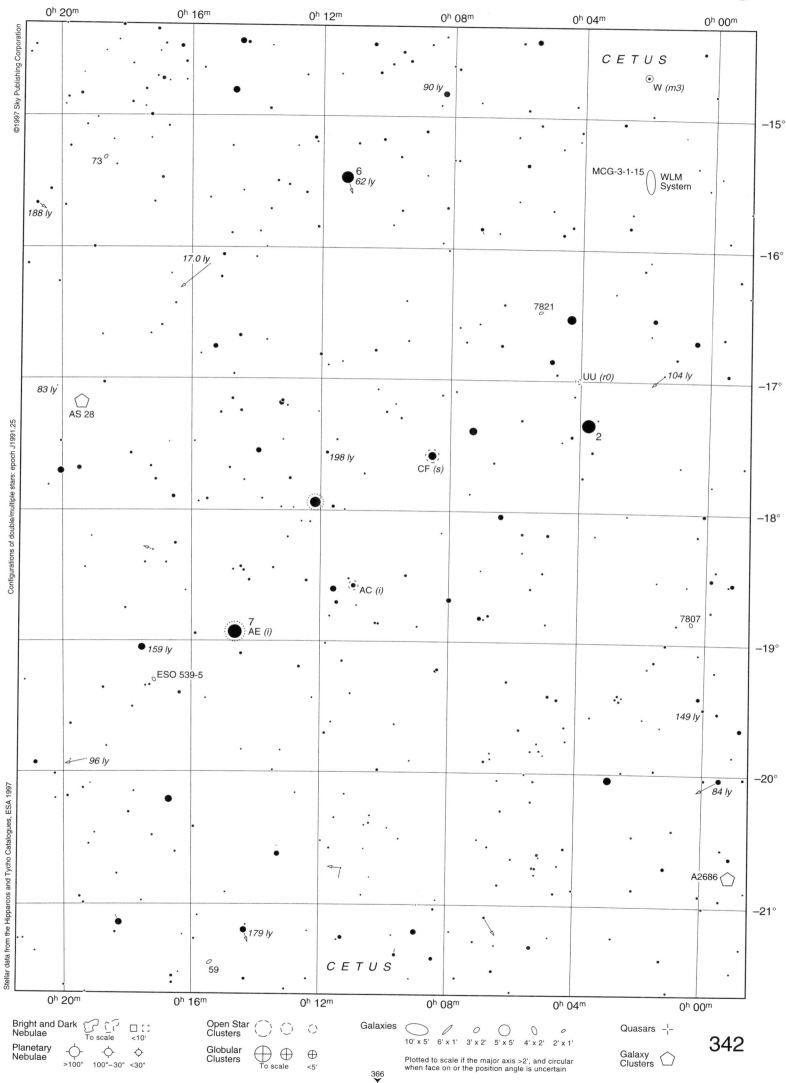

CETUS

W (m3)

MCG-3-1-15   WLM System

90 ly

73°

188 ly

6
62 ly

17.0 ly

7821

UU (r0)   104 ly

83 ly

AS 28

198 ly

CF (s)

2

AC (i)

7807

7
AE (i)

159 ly

ESO 539-5

149 ly

96 ly

84 ly

A2686

179 ly

59

CETUS

Bright and Dark Nebulae
To scale   <10'

Planetary Nebulae
>100"   100"–30"   <30"

Open Star Clusters

Globular Clusters
To scale   <5'

Galaxies
10' x 5'   6' x 1'   3' x 2'   5' x 5'   4' x 2'   2' x 1'

Plotted to scale if the major axis >2', and circular when face on or the position angle is uncertain

Quasars

Galaxy Clusters

366

−24°　　　　　　　　MILLENNIUM STAR ATLAS

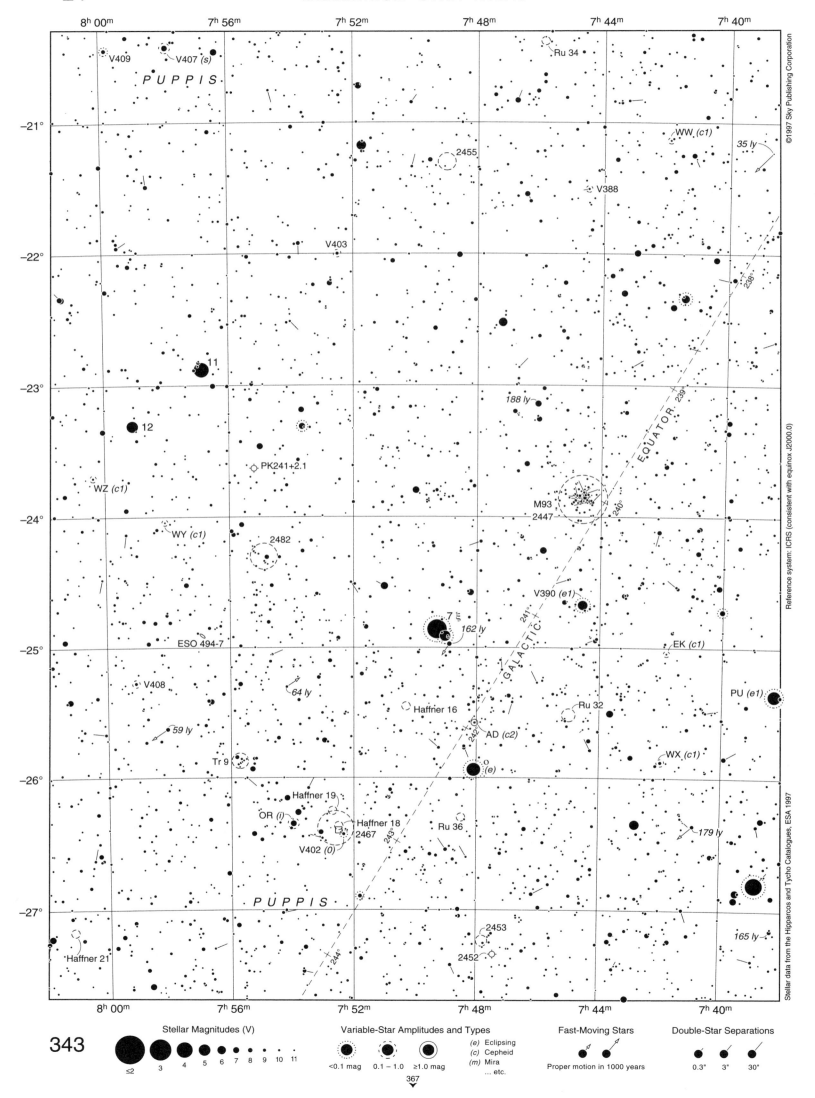

©1997 Sky Publishing Corporation

Reference system: ICRS (consistent with equinox J2000.0)

Stellar data from the Hipparcos and Tycho Catalogues, ESA 1997

343

Stellar Magnitudes (V)

≤2　3　4　5　6　7　8　9　10　11

Variable-Star Amplitudes and Types

<0.1 mag　　0.1 – 1.0　　≥1.0 mag

(e) Eclipsing
(c) Cepheid
(m) Mira
... etc.

Fast-Moving Stars

Proper motion in 1000 years

Double-Star Separations

0.3"　3"　30"

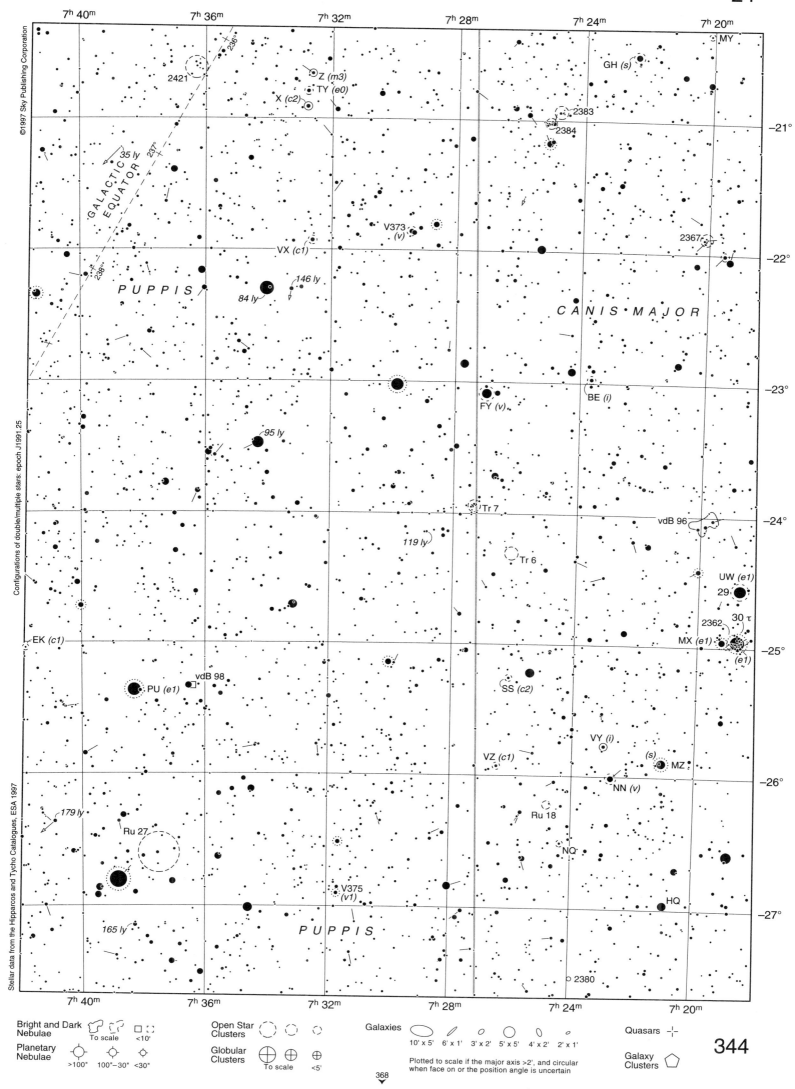

PUPPIS

CANIS MAJOR

PUPPIS

Bright and Dark Nebulae
To scale   <10'

Planetary Nebulae
>100"   100"−30"   <30"

Open Star Clusters

Globular Clusters
To scale   <5'

Galaxies
10' x 5'   6' x 1'   3' x 2'   5' x 5'   4' x 2'   2' x 1'

Plotted to scale if the major axis >2', and circular when face on or the position angle is uncertain

Quasars

Galaxy Clusters

344

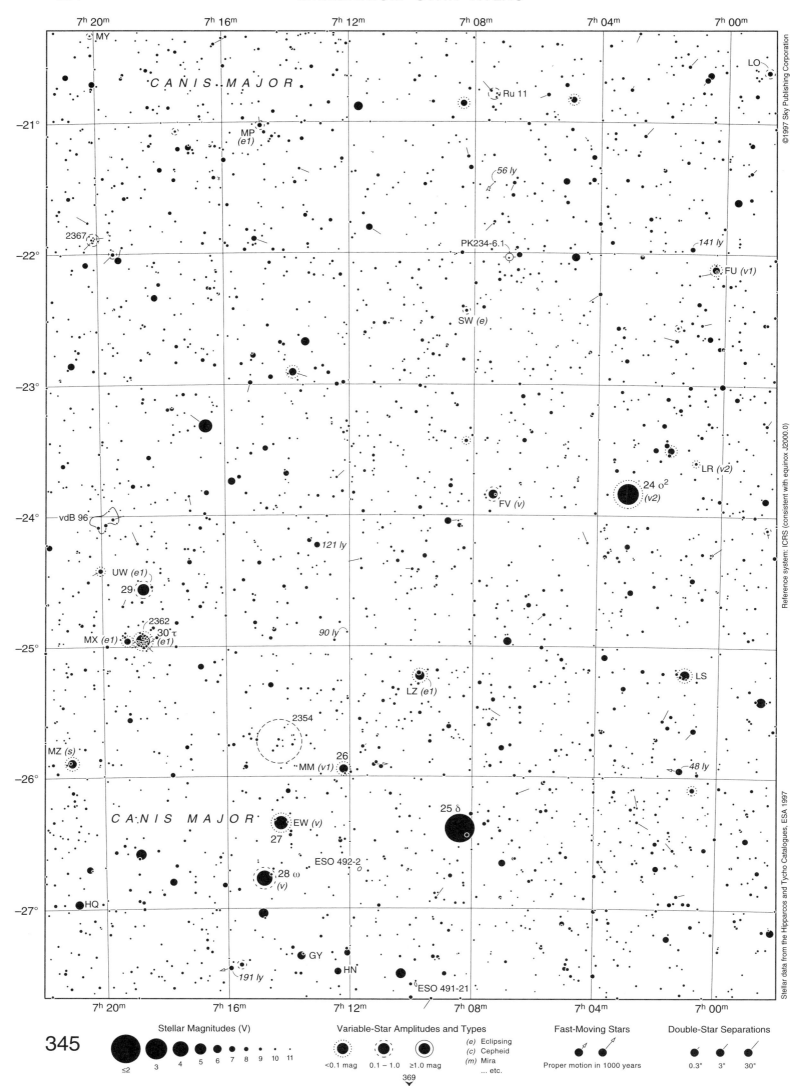

©1997 Sky Publishing Corporation

Reference system: ICRS (consistent with equinox J2000.0)

Stellar data from the Hipparcos and Tycho Catalogues, ESA 1997

345

Stellar Magnitudes (V)

≤2 3 4 5 6 7 8 9 10 11

Variable-Star Amplitudes and Types

<0.1 mag   0.1 – 1.0   ≥1.0 mag

(e) Eclipsing
(c) Cepheid
(m) Mira
... etc.

Fast-Moving Stars

Proper motion in 1000 years

Double-Star Separations

0.3" 3" 30"

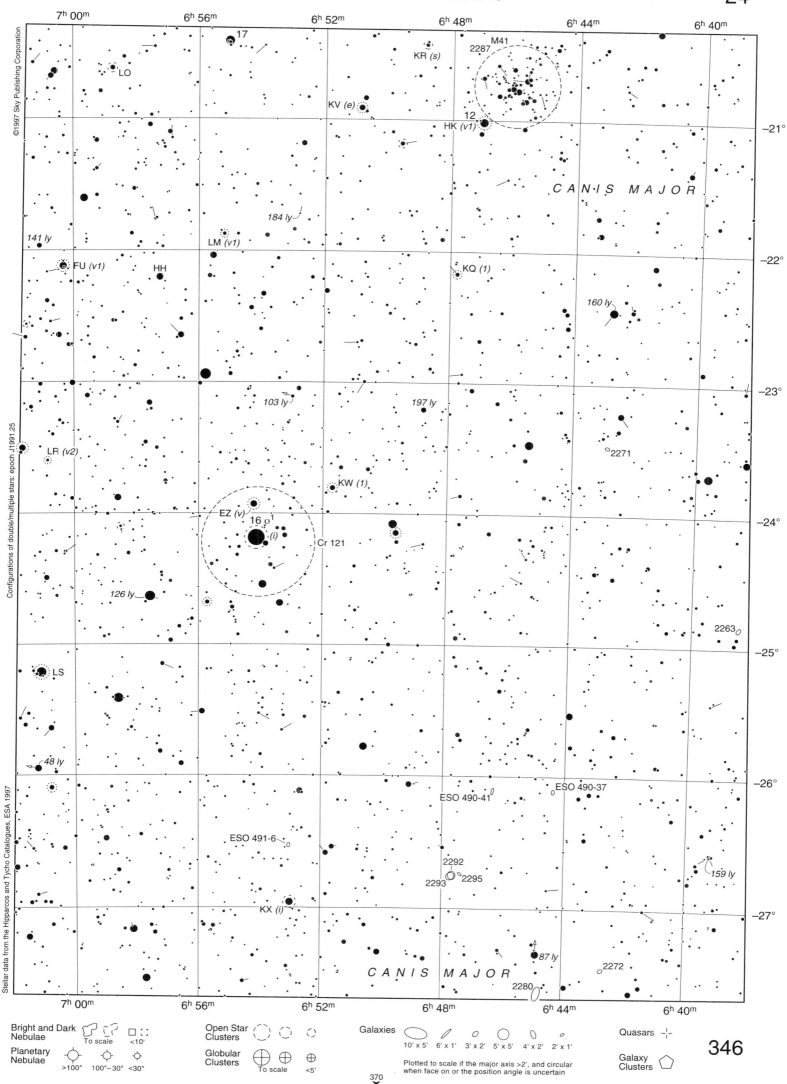

Configurations of double/multiple stars: epoch J1991.25

Stellar data from the Hipparcos and Tycho Catalogues, ESA 1997

CANIS MAJOR

CANIS MAJOR

17

LO

KR (s)
2287
M41

KV (e)
12
HK (v1)

184 ly

LM (v1)

141 ly

FU (v1)   HH

KQ (1)

160 ly

103 ly

197 ly

LR (v2)

2271

KW (1)

EZ (v)
16 ○¹
(i)
Cr 121

126 ly

2263

LS

48 ly

ESO 490-41
ESO 490-37

ESO 491-6

2292
2293 2295

159 ly

KX (i)

87 ly

2272

2280

Bright and Dark
Nebulae
To scale   <10'
Planetary
Nebulae
>100" 100"−30" <30"

Open Star
Clusters
Globular
Clusters
To scale   <5'

Galaxies
10' x 5' 6' x 1' 3' x 2' 5' x 5' 4' x 2' 2' x 1'

Plotted to scale if the major axis >2', and circular
when face on or the position angle is uncertain

Quasars

Galaxy
Clusters

346

370

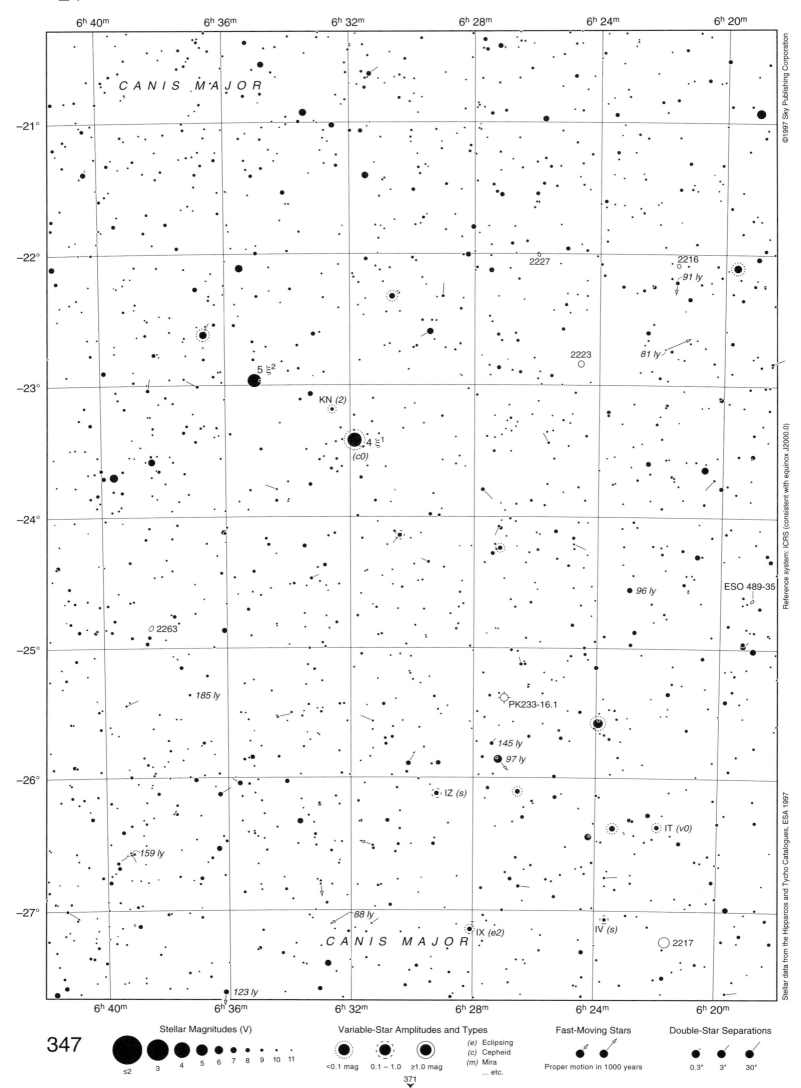

©1997 Sky Publishing Corporation

Reference system: ICRS (consistent with equinox J2000.0)

Stellar data from the Hipparcos and Tycho Catalogues, ESA 1997

CANIS MAJOR

2227

2216

91 ly

2223

81 ly

5 ξ²

KN (2)

4 ξ¹
(c0)

96 ly

ESO 489-35

O 2263

185 ly

PK233-16.1

145 ly

97 ly

IZ (s)

IT (v0)

159 ly

88 ly

IX (e2)

IV (s)

2217

CANIS MAJOR

Stellar Magnitudes (V)

≤2 3 4 5 6 7 8 9 10 11

Variable-Star Amplitudes and Types

<0.1 mag   0.1 − 1.0   ≥1.0 mag

(e) Eclipsing
(c) Cepheid
(m) Mira
... etc.

Fast-Moving Stars

Proper motion in 1000 years

Double-Star Separations

0.3"   3"   30"

MILLENNIUM STAR ATLAS

−24°

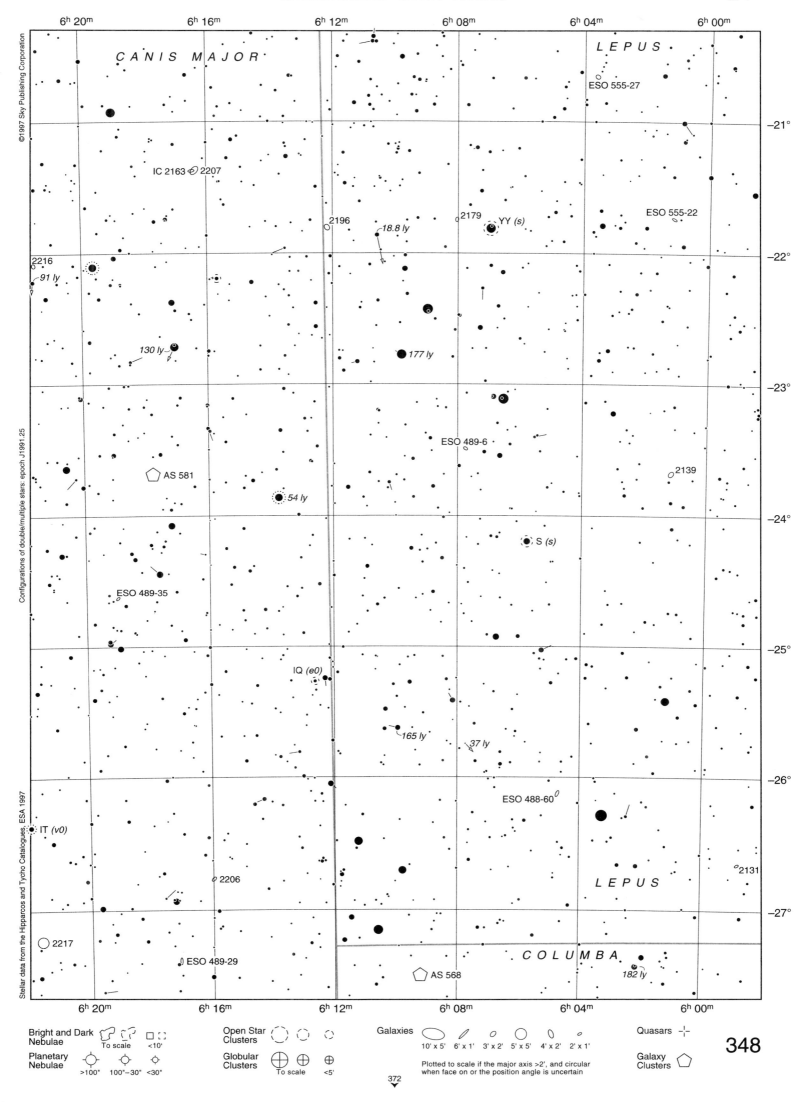

Configurations of double/multiple stars: epoch J1991.25

Stellar data from the Hipparcos and Tycho Catalogues, ESA 1997

CANIS MAJOR

LEPUS

ESO 555-27

IC 2163 ⌒ 2207

2196

18.8 ly

2179

YY (s)

ESO 555-22

2216

91 ly

130 ly

177 ly

ESO 489-6

2139

AS 581

54 ly

S (s)

ESO 489-35

IQ (e0)

165 ly

37 ly

ESO 488-60

IT (v0)

2206

2131

LEPUS

2217

ESO 489-29

COLUMBA

AS 568

182 ly

6h 20m   6h 16m   6h 12m   6h 08m   6h 04m   6h 00m

−21°
−22°
−23°
−24°
−25°
−26°
−27°

Bright and Dark Nebulae	To scale	<10'

Planetary Nebulae >100" 100"−30" <30'

Open Star Clusters

Globular Clusters To scale <5'

Galaxies 10' x 5' 6' x 1' 3' x 2' 5' x 5' 4' x 2' 2' x 1'

Plotted to scale if the major axis >2', and circular when face on or the position angle is uncertain

Quasars

Galaxy Clusters

348

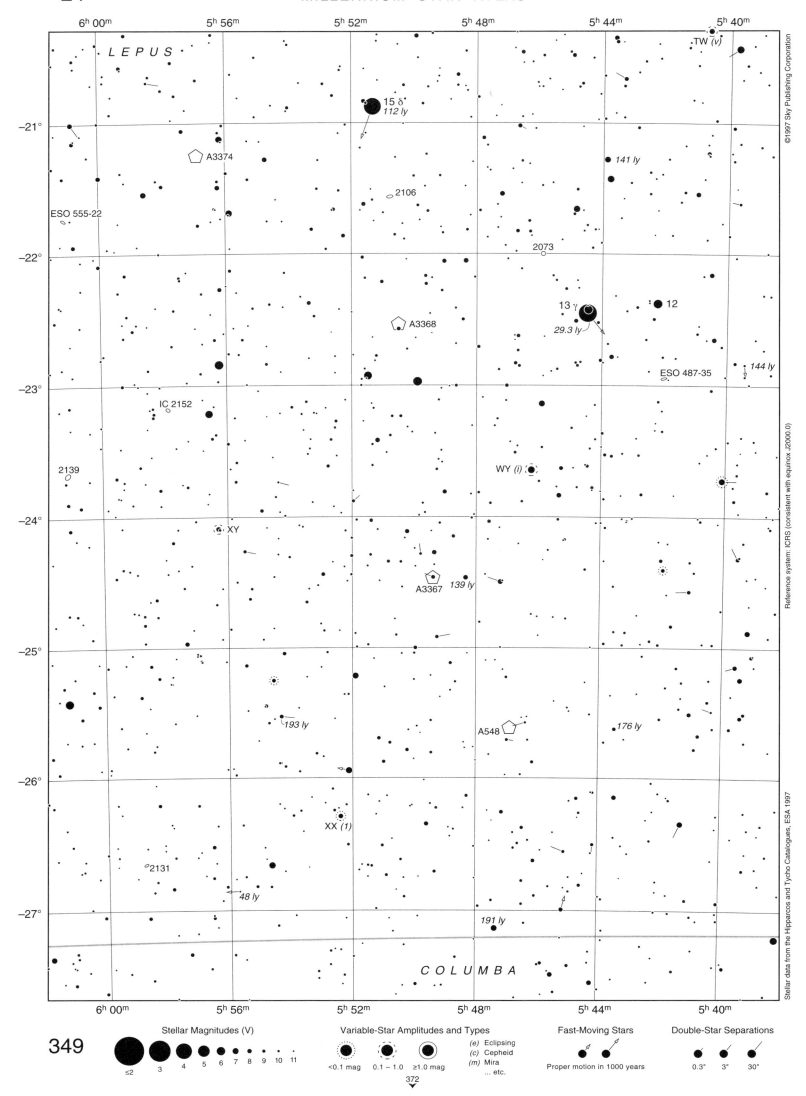

Reference system: ICRS (consistent with equinox J2000.0)

Stellar data from the Hipparcos and Tycho Catalogues, ESA 1997

LEPUS

TW *(v)*

15 δ
112 ly

A3374

ESO 555-22

141 ly

2106

2073

13 γ

12

29.3 ly

A3368

ESO 487-35

144 ly

IC 2152

2139

WY *(i)*

XY

A3367 *139 ly*

193 ly

A548 *176 ly*

XX *(1)*

2131

48 ly

191 ly

COLUMBA

Stellar Magnitudes (V)
≤2　3　4　5　6　7　8　9　10　11

Variable-Star Amplitudes and Types
<0.1 mag　0.1 − 1.0　≥1.0 mag

(e) Eclipsing
(c) Cepheid
(m) Mira
... etc.

Fast-Moving Stars
Proper motion in 1000 years

Double-Star Separations
0.3"　3"　30"

372

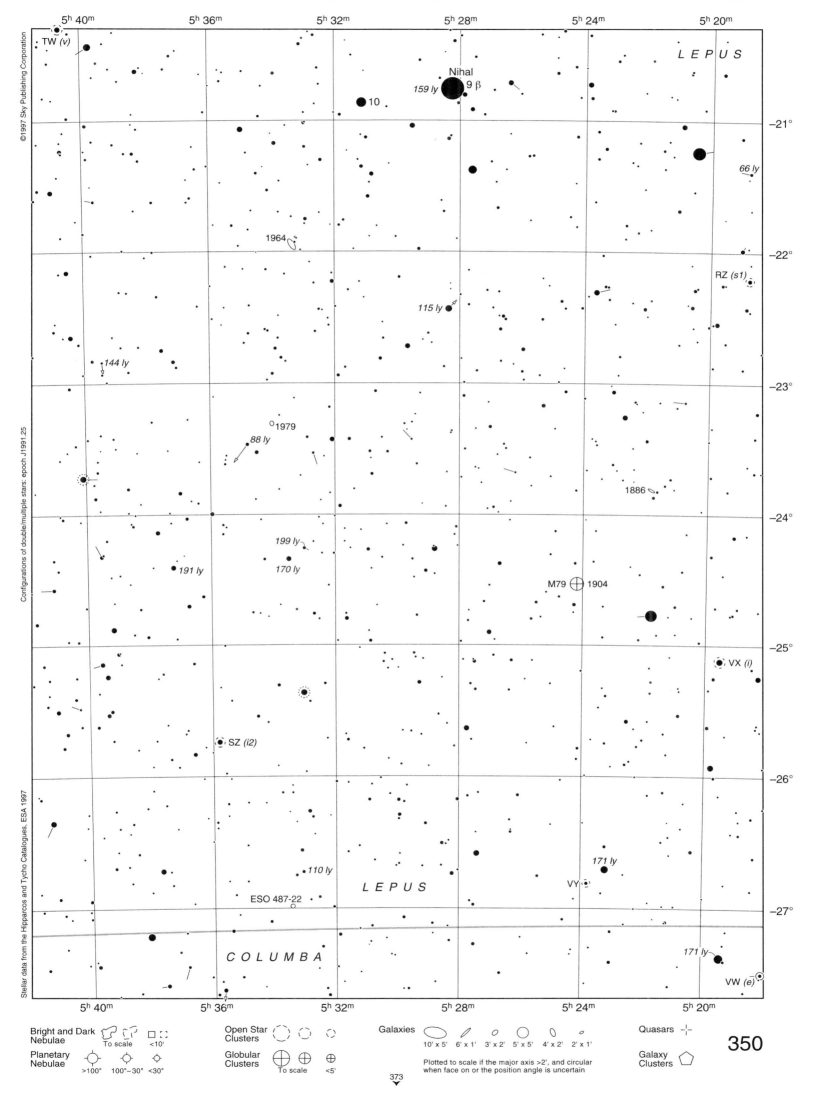

L E P U S

TW (v)

Nihal
9 β
159 ly

10

66 ly

1964

−21°

−22°

RZ (s1)

115 ly

144 ly

1979

88 ly

1886

−23°

−24°

199 ly

170 ly

191 ly

M79 ⊕ 1904

−25°

VX (i)

171 ly

VY

SZ (i2)

−26°

110 ly

L E P U S

ESO 487-22

−27°

C O L U M B A

171 ly

326

VW (e)

Bright and Dark Nebulae
To scale   <10'

Planetary Nebulae
>100" 100"–30" <30"

Open Star Clusters

Globular Clusters
To scale   <5'

Galaxies
10' x 5' 6' x 1' 3' x 2' 5' x 5' 4' x 2' 2' x 1'

Plotted to scale if the major axis >2', and circular when face on or the position angle is uncertain

Quasars

Galaxy Clusters

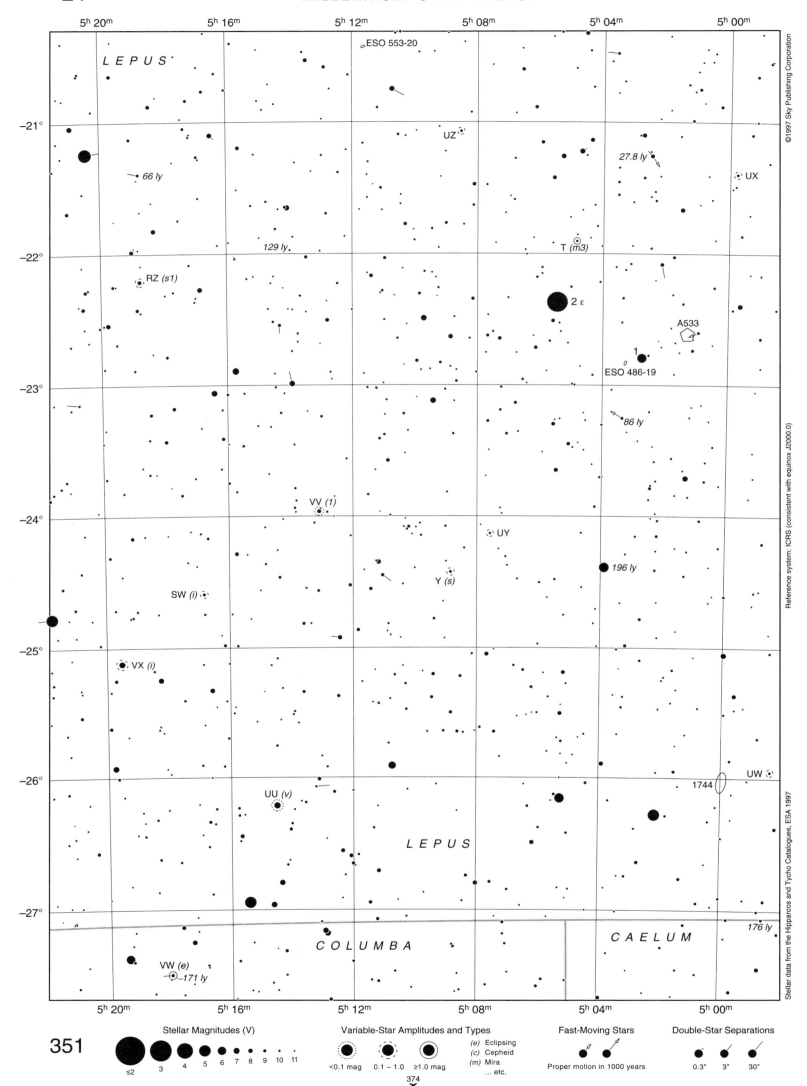

©1997 Sky Publishing Corporation

Reference system: ICRS (consistent with equinox J2000.0)

Stellar data from the Hipparcos and Tycho Catalogues, ESA 1997

351

Stellar Magnitudes (V)

≤2　3　4　5　6　7　8　9　10　11

Variable-Star Amplitudes and Types

<0.1 mag　0.1 − 1.0　≥1.0 mag

(e) Eclipsing
(c) Cepheid
(m) Mira
... etc.

Fast-Moving Stars

Proper motion in 1000 years

Double-Star Separations

0.3"　3"　30"

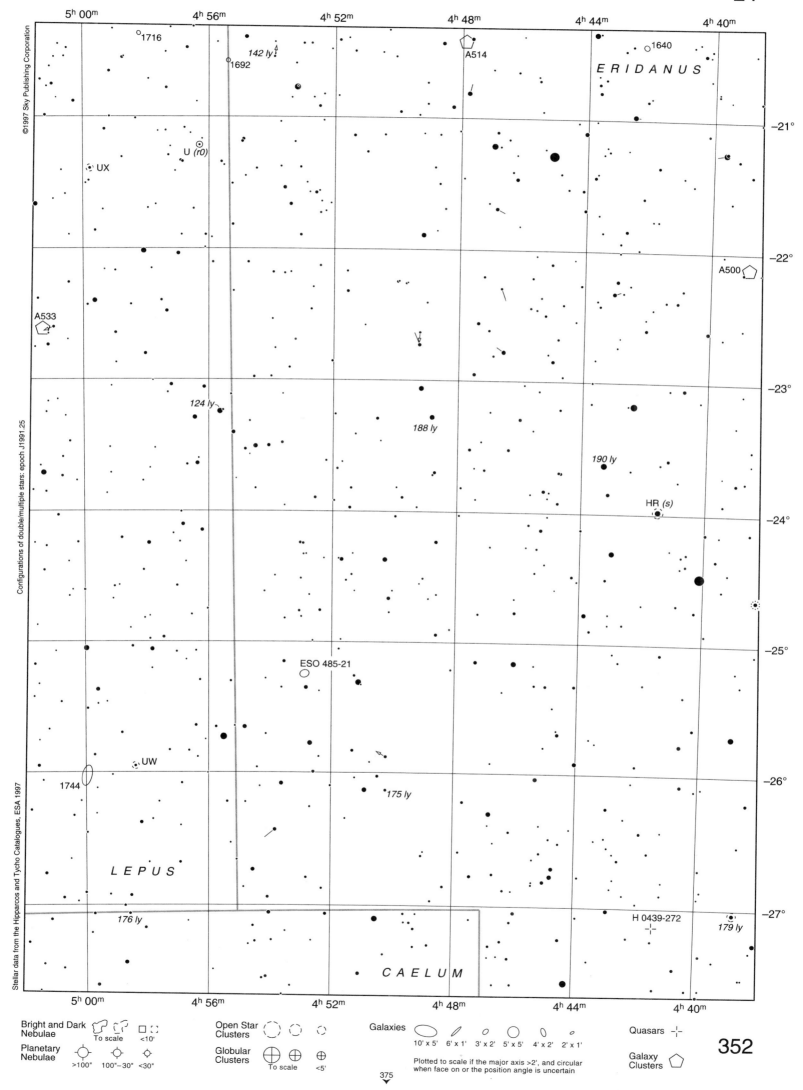

ERIDANUS

LEPUS

CAELUM

A514
A500
A533
1716
1692
1640
142 ly
U (r0)
UX
124 ly
188 ly
190 ly
HR (s)
ESO 485-21
UW
1744
175 ly
176 ly
179 ly
H 0439-272

Bright and Dark Nebulae
To scale   <10'

Planetary Nebulae
>100"   100"–30"   <30"

Open Star Clusters

Globular Clusters
To scale   <5'

Galaxies
10' x 5'   6' x 1'   3' x 2'   5' x 5'   4' x 2'   2' x 1'

Plotted to scale if the major axis >2', and circular when face on or the position angle is uncertain

Quasars

Galaxy Clusters

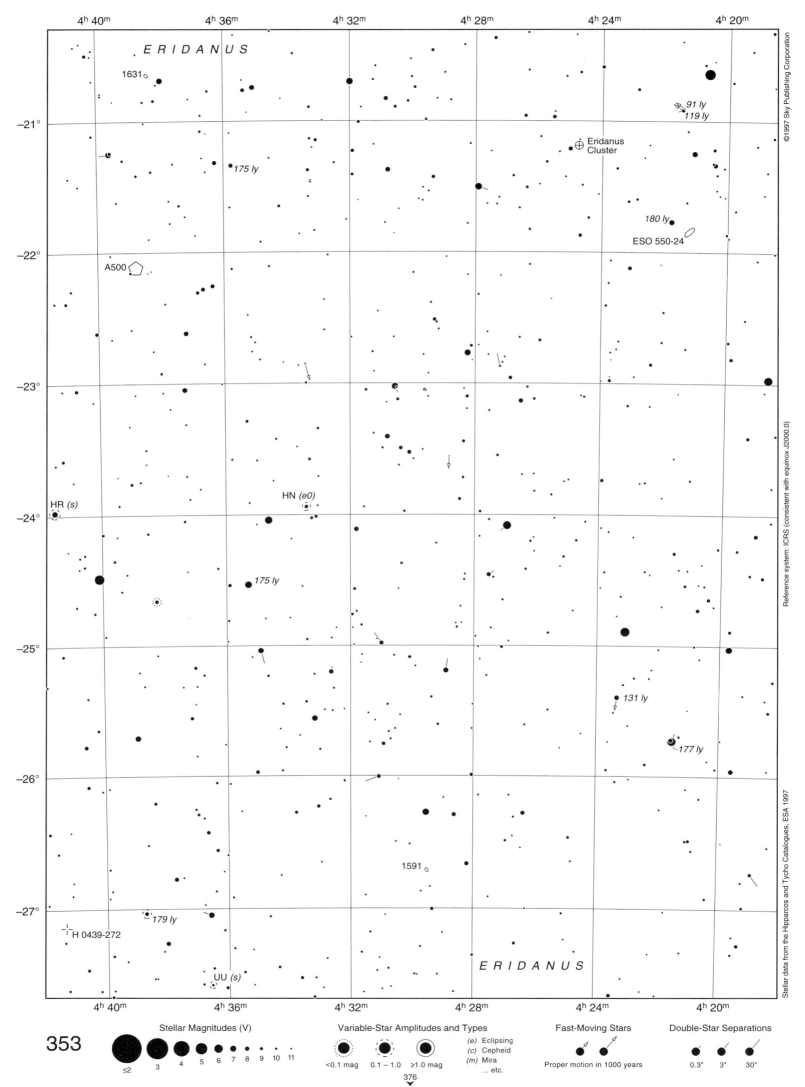

353

Stellar Magnitudes (V)

≤2 3 4 5 6 7 8 9 10 11

Variable-Star Amplitudes and Types

<0.1 mag   0.1 – 1.0   ≥1.0 mag

(e) Eclipsing
(c) Cepheid
(m) Mira
... etc.

Fast-Moving Stars

Proper motion in 1000 years

Double-Star Separations

0.3"   3"   30"

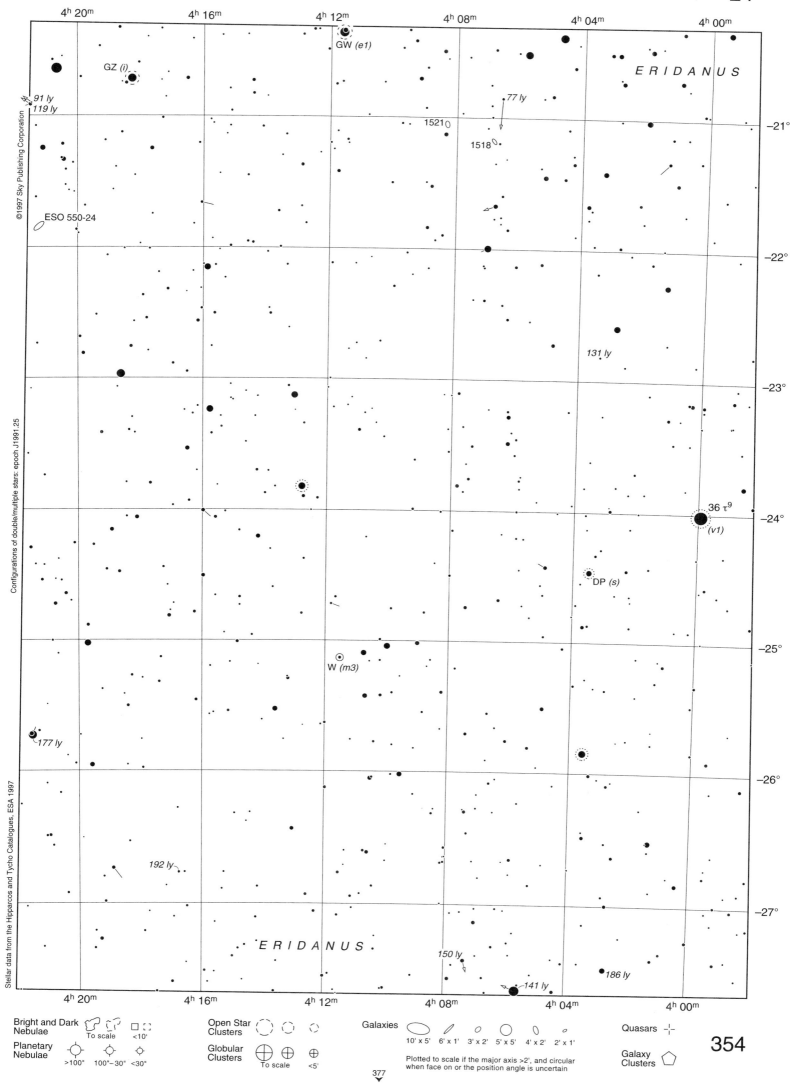

ERIDANUS

GZ *(i)*

GW *(e1)*

91 ly
119 ly

77 ly

1521

1518

ESO 550-24

131 ly

36 τ⁹
(v1)

DP *(s)*

177 ly

W *(m3)*

192 ly

ERIDANUS

150 ly

141 ly

186 ly

Bright and Dark Nebulae	To scale <10'	
Planetary Nebulae	>100" 100"−30" <30"	
Open Star Clusters		
Globular Clusters	To scale <5'	
Galaxies	10' x 5' 6' x 1' 3' x 2' 5' x 5' 4' x 2' 2' x 1'	
Quasars		
Galaxy Clusters		

Plotted to scale if the major axis >2', and circular when face on or the position angle is uncertain

354

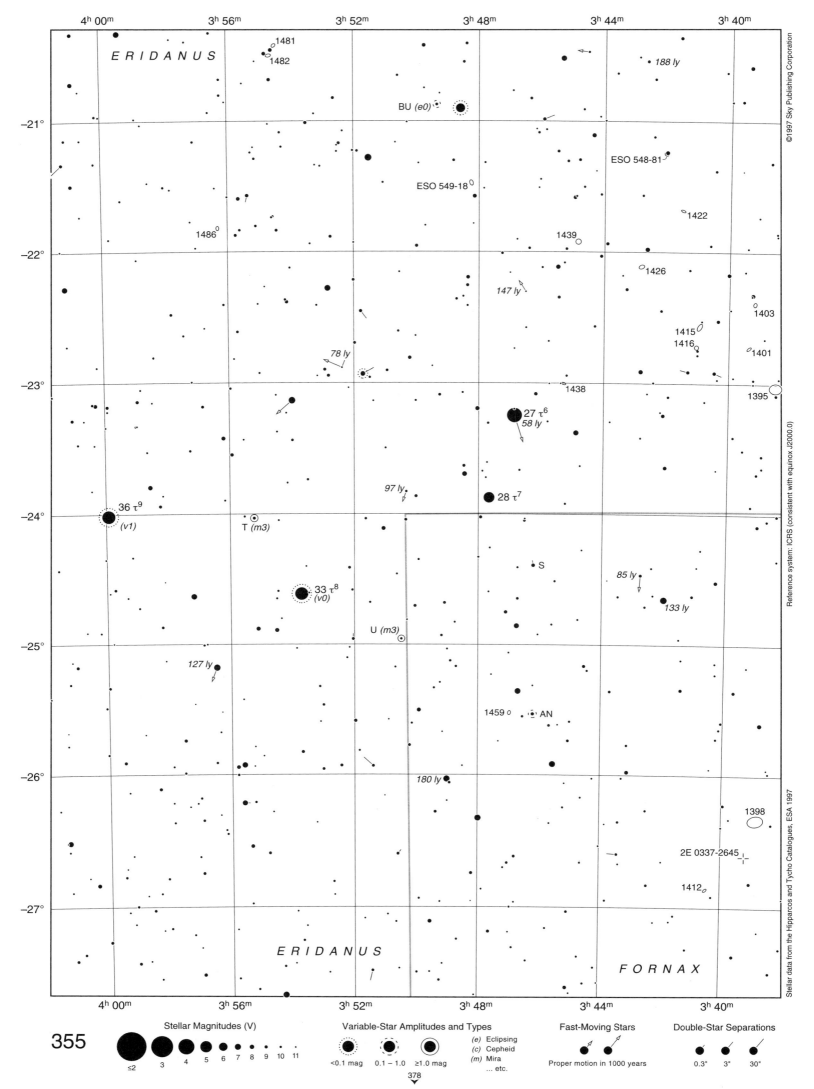

©1997 Sky Publishing Corporation

Reference system: ICRS (consistent with equinox J2000.0)

Stellar data from the Hipparcos and Tycho Catalogues, ESA 1997

ERIDANUS

BU (e0)

ESO 549-18 0

ESO 548-81

1486 0

188 ly

1422

1439

1426

147 ly

78 ly

1415
1416

1403

1401

1438

1395

27 τ⁶
58 ly

97 ly

28 τ⁷

36 τ⁹
(v1)

T (m3)

S

85 ly

133 ly

33 τ⁸
(v0)

U (m3)

127 ly

1459 o

AN

180 ly

1398

2E 0337-2645

1412 o

ERIDANUS

FORNAX

355

Stellar Magnitudes (V)

≤2 3 4 5 6 7 8 9 10 11

Variable-Star Amplitudes and Types

<0.1 mag   0.1 − 1.0   ≥1.0 mag

(e) Eclipsing
(c) Cepheid
(m) Mira
... etc.

Fast-Moving Stars

Proper motion in 1000 years

Double-Star Separations

0.3"   3"   30"

378

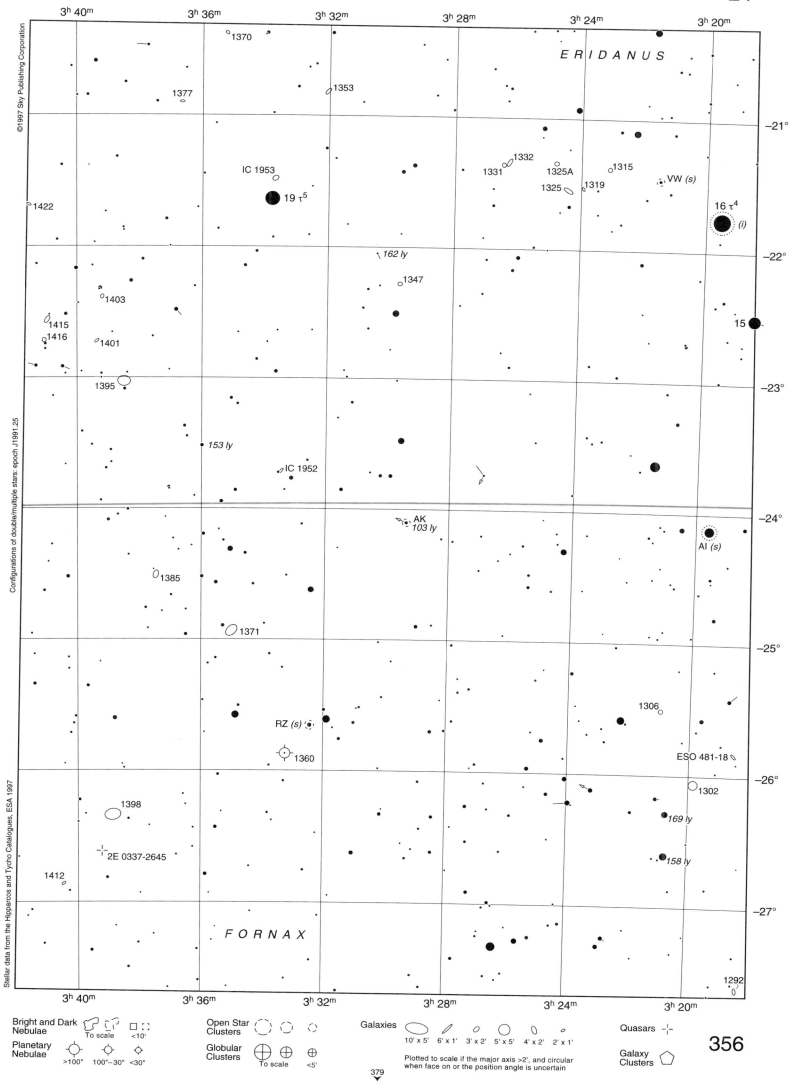

3ʰ 40ᵐ 3ʰ 36ᵐ 3ʰ 32ᵐ 3ʰ 28ᵐ 3ʰ 24ᵐ 3ʰ 20ᵐ

E R I D A N U S

1370
1353
1377

−21°

IC 1953
1331 1332 1325A 1315 VW *(s)*
19 τ⁵ 1325 1319

1422
16 τ⁴
(i)

−22°

162 ly
1347
15

1403
1415
1416 1401

1395
153 ly

−23°

IC 1952

AK
103 ly

−24°

Al *(s)*

1385

1371
−25°

1306

RZ *(s)*
1360 ESO 481-18

−26°
1302

1398
169 ly

2E 0337-2645
158 ly

1412

−27°

F O R N A X

1292

3ʰ 40ᵐ 3ʰ 36ᵐ 3ʰ 32ᵐ 3ʰ 28ᵐ 3ʰ 24ᵐ 3ʰ 20ᵐ

−24°

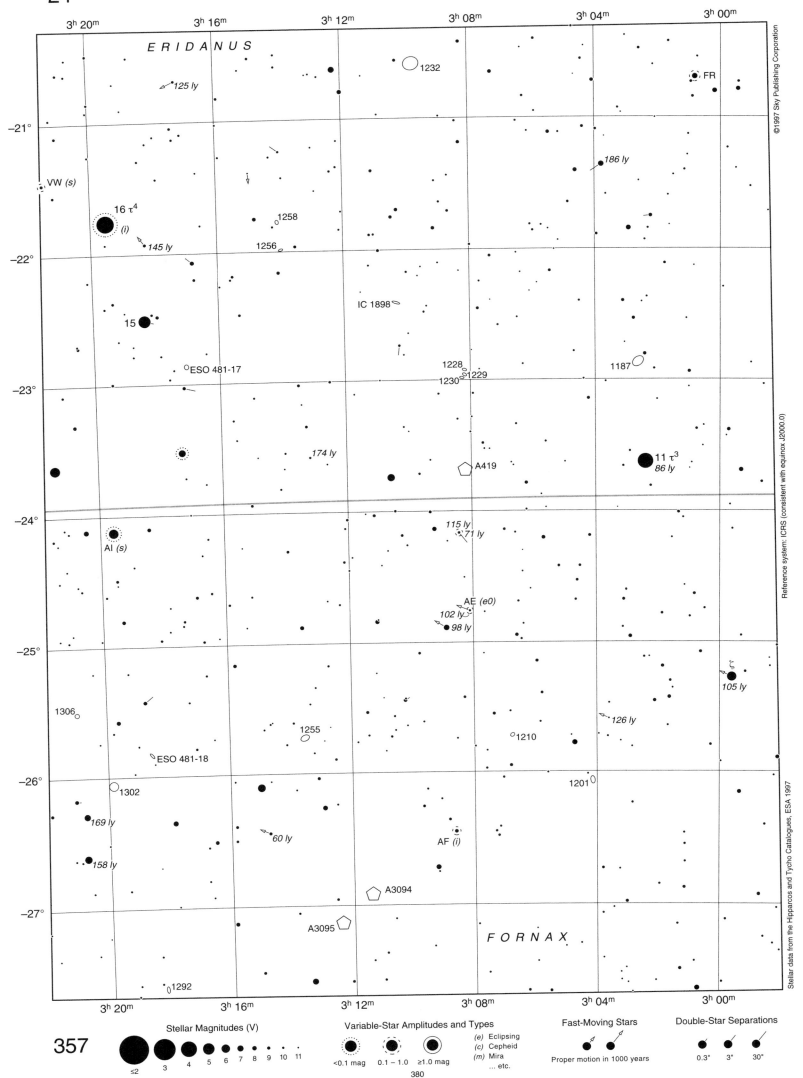

Reference system: ICRS (consistent with equinox J2000.0)

Stellar data from the Hipparcos and Tycho Catalogues, ESA 1997

357

Stellar Magnitudes (V)

≤2 3 4 5 6 7 8 9 10 11

Variable-Star Amplitudes and Types

<0.1 mag   0.1 – 1.0   ≥1.0 mag

(e) Eclipsing
(c) Cepheid
(m) Mira
... etc.

Fast-Moving Stars

Proper motion in 1000 years

Double-Star Separations

0.3"   3"   30"

▼
380

MILLENNIUM STAR ATLAS

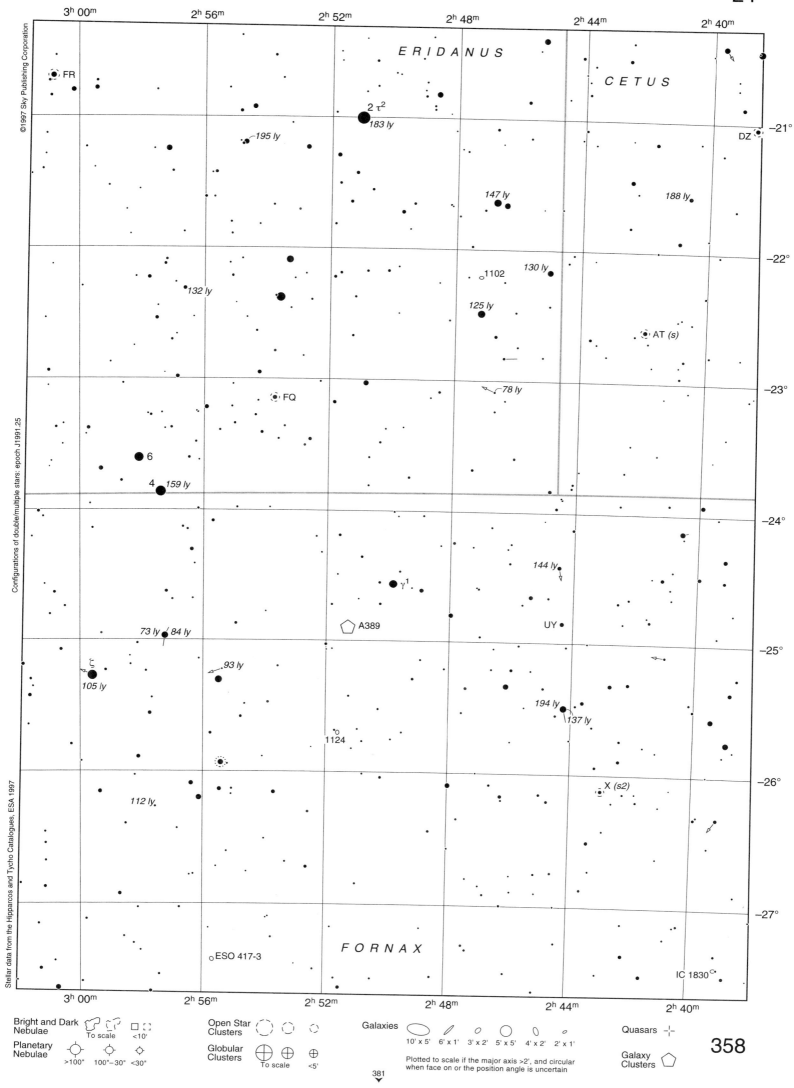

©1997 Sky Publishing Corporation

Configurations of double/multiple stars: epoch J1991.25

Stellar data from the Hipparcos and Tycho Catalogues, ESA 1997

ERIDANUS

CETUS

FR

2 τ²
183 ly

195 ly

DZ

147 ly

188 ly

1102
130 ly

132 ly

125 ly

AT (s)

FQ

78 ly

6

4 159 ly

γ¹

144 ly

A389

UY

73 ly 84 ly

ζ

93 ly

105 ly

194 ly
137 ly

1124

X (s2)

112 ly

FORNAX

ESO 417-3

IC 1830

Bright and Dark Nebulae		To scale	□ ⬚ <10'	Open Star Clusters			Galaxies							Quasars	╪

Bright and Dark Nebulae
To scale   □ <10'

Planetary Nebulae
>100"   100"−30"   <30"

Open Star Clusters

Globular Clusters
To scale   <5'

Galaxies
10' x 5'   6' x 1'   3' x 2'   5' x 5'   4' x 2'   2' x 1'

Plotted to scale if the major axis >2', and circular when face on or the position angle is uncertain

Quasars ╪

Galaxy Clusters ⬠

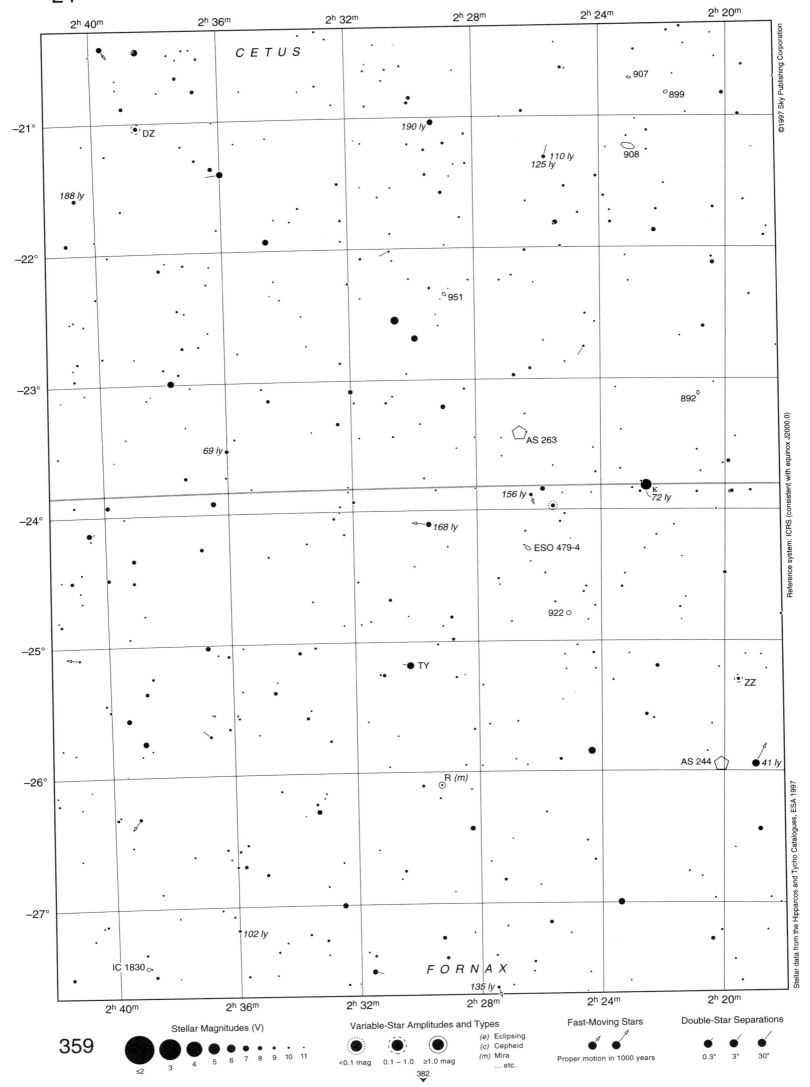

-24°

MILLENNIUM STAR ATLAS

©1997 Sky Publishing Corporation

Reference system: ICRS (consistent with equinox J2000.0)

Stellar data from the Hipparcos and Tycho Catalogues, ESA 1997

2ʰ 40ᵐ   2ʰ 36ᵐ   2ʰ 32ᵐ   2ʰ 28ᵐ   2ʰ 24ᵐ   2ʰ 20ᵐ

C E T U S

907

899

-21°   190 ly

908
110 ly
125 ly

188 ly

-22°   951

69 ly   892

AS 263

156 ly   κ
72 ly

-24°   168 ly

ESO 479-4

922

-25°   TY

ZZ

AS 244   41 ly

R (m)   -26°

-27°   102 ly

IC 1830

F O R N A X   135 ly

359

Stellar Magnitudes (V)

≤2   3   4   5   6   7   8   9 10 11

Variable-Star Amplitudes and Types

<0.1 mag   0.1 – 1.0   ≥1.0 mag

(e) Eclipsing
(c) Cepheid
(m) Mira
... etc.

Fast-Moving Stars

Proper motion in 1000 years

Double-Star Separations

0.3"   3"   30"

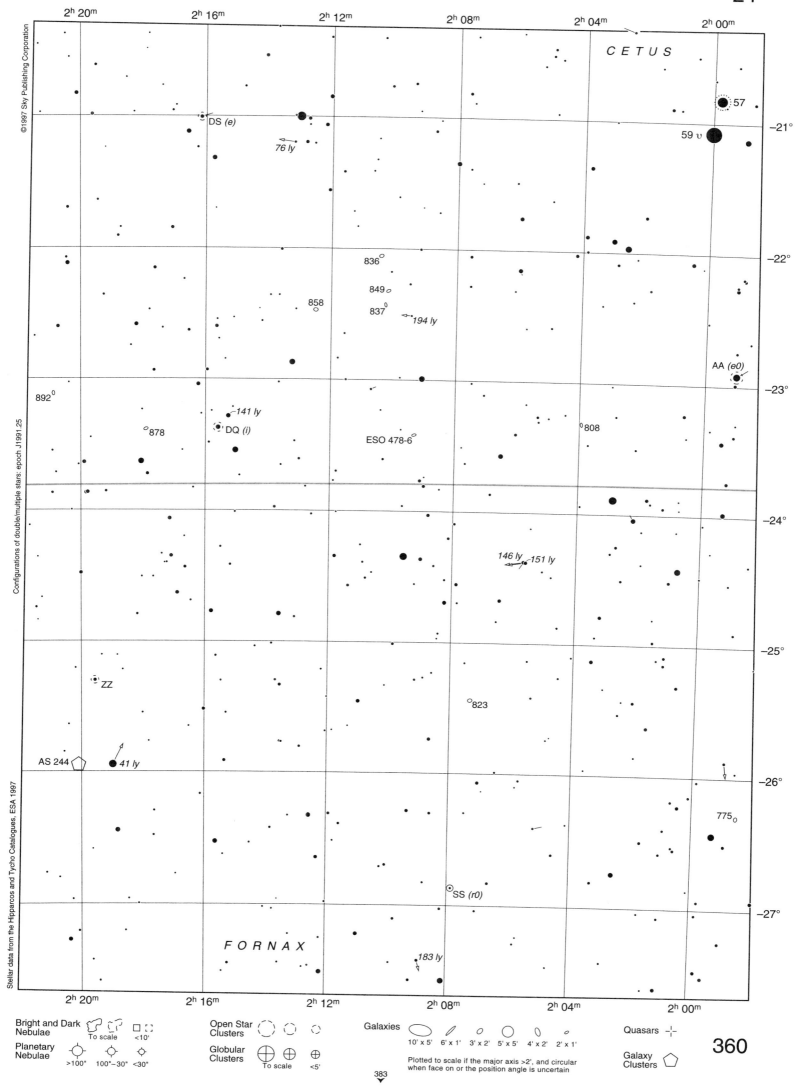

2h 20m 2h 16m 2h 12m 2h 08m 2h 04m 2h 00m

C E T U S

57

59 υ   −21°

DS (e)

76 ly

−22°

836

849

858   837   194 ly

AA (e0)

−23°

892

141 ly

878   DQ (i)

ESO 478-6   808

−24°

146 ly 151 ly

−25°

ZZ

823

AS 244   41 ly   −26°

775

F O R N A X

SS (r0)

−27°

183 ly

2h 20m 2h 16m 2h 12m 2h 08m 2h 04m 2h 00m

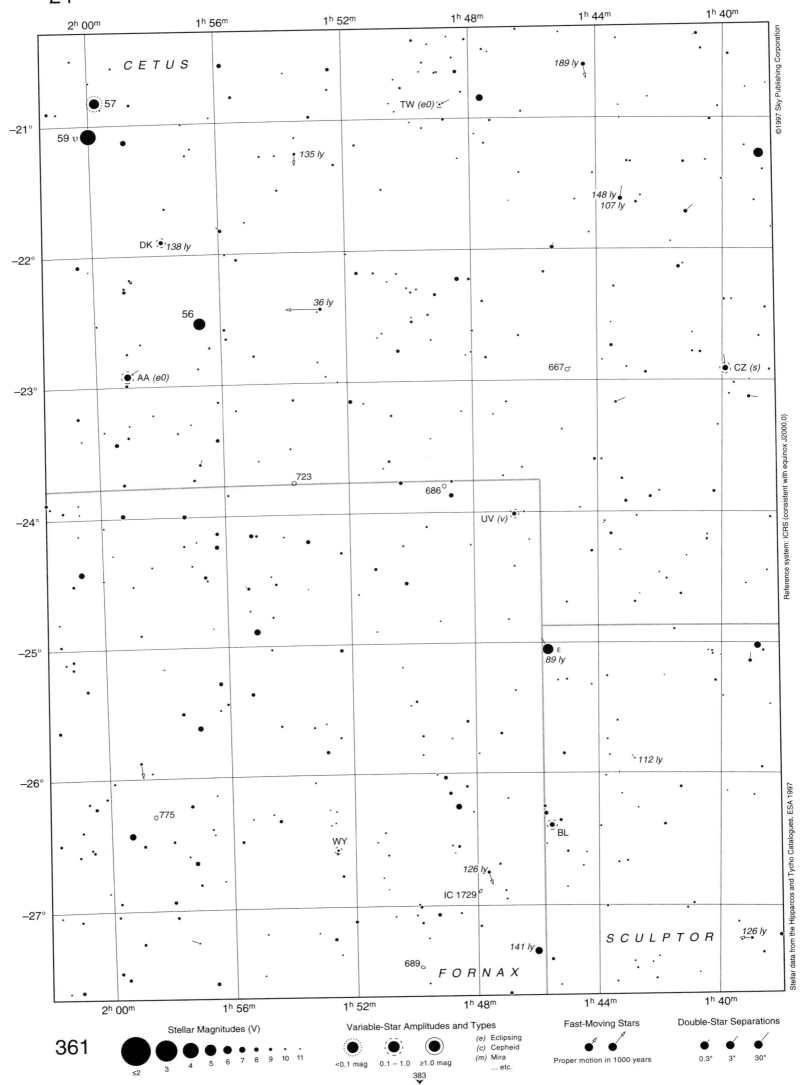

©1997 Sky Publishing Corporation

Reference system: ICRS (consistent with equinox J2000.0)

Stellar data from the Hipparcos and Tycho Catalogues, ESA 1997

CETUS

57

59 υ

135 ly

TW (e0)

189 ly

148 ly
107 ly

DK 138 ly

36 ly

56

AA (e0)

667

CZ (s)

723

686

UV (v)

ε
89 ly

112 ly

775

BL

WY

126 ly

IC 1729

SCULPTOR

126 ly

141 ly

689   FORNAX

361

Stellar Magnitudes (V)

≤2 3 4 5 6 7 8 9 10 11

Variable-Star Amplitudes and Types

<0.1 mag   0.1 – 1.0   ≥1.0 mag

(e) Eclipsing
(c) Cepheid
(m) Mira
... etc.

Fast-Moving Stars

Proper motion in 1000 years

Double-Star Separations

0.3"   3"   30"

383

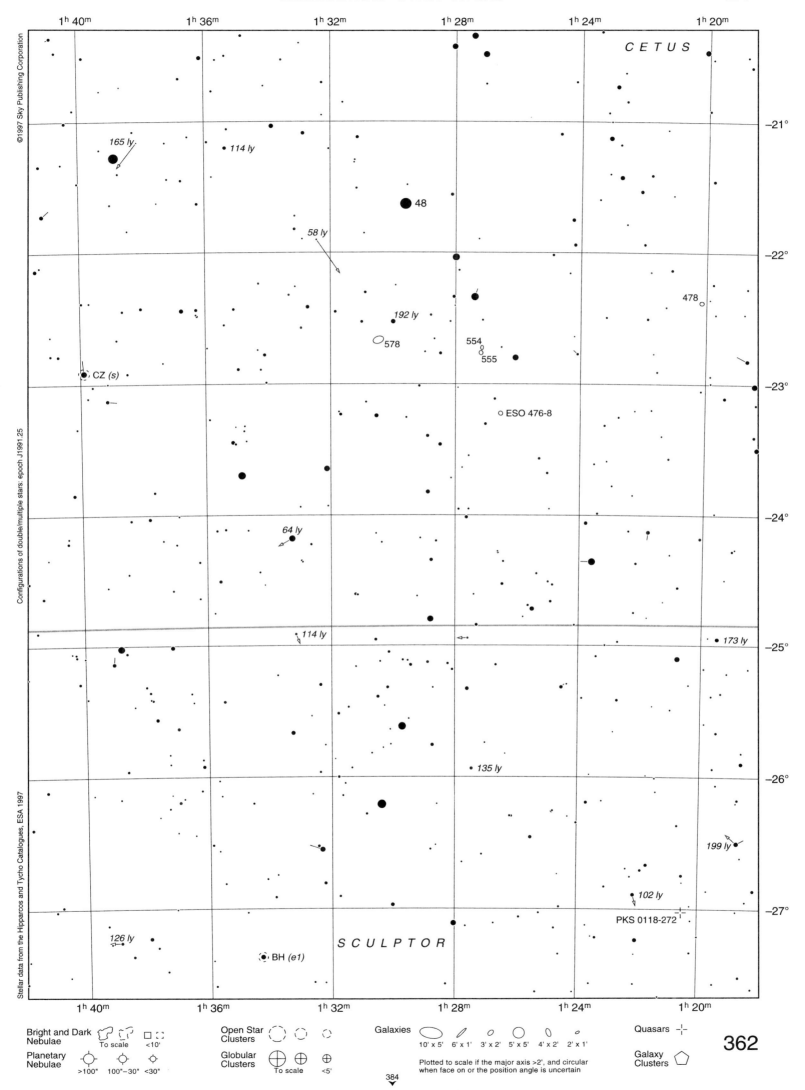

CETUS

165 ly

114 ly

48

58 ly

192 ly

578

554

555

478

CZ (s)

ESO 476-8

64 ly

114 ly

173 ly

135 ly

199 ly

102 ly

PKS 0118-272

126 ly

SCULPTOR

BH (e1)

1ʰ 40ᵐ   1ʰ 36ᵐ   1ʰ 32ᵐ   1ʰ 28ᵐ   1ʰ 24ᵐ   1ʰ 20ᵐ

−21°
−22°
−23°
−24°
−25°
−26°
−27°

Bright and Dark Nebulae	To scale	<10'	
Planetary Nebulae	>100" 100"–30" <30"		
Open Star Clusters			
Globular Clusters	To scale <5'		
Galaxies	10' x 5' 6' x 1' 3' x 2' 5' x 5' 4' x 2' 2' x 1'		
	Plotted to scale if the major axis >2', and circular when face on or the position angle is uncertain		
Quasars			
Galaxy Clusters			

362

384

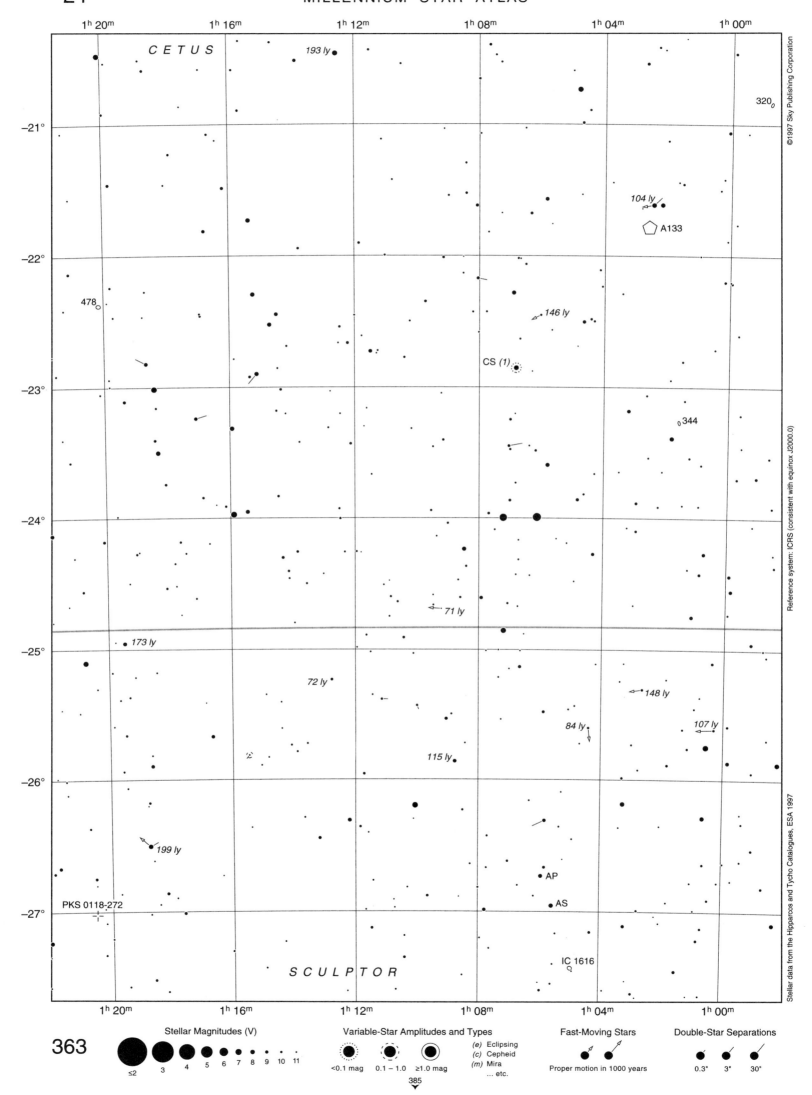

363

Stellar Magnitudes (V)

≤2 3 4 5 6 7 8 9 10 11

Variable-Star Amplitudes and Types

<0.1 mag   0.1 − 1.0   ≥1.0 mag

(e) Eclipsing
(c) Cepheid
(m) Mira
... etc.

Fast-Moving Stars

Proper motion in 1000 years

Double-Star Separations

0.3"   3"   30"

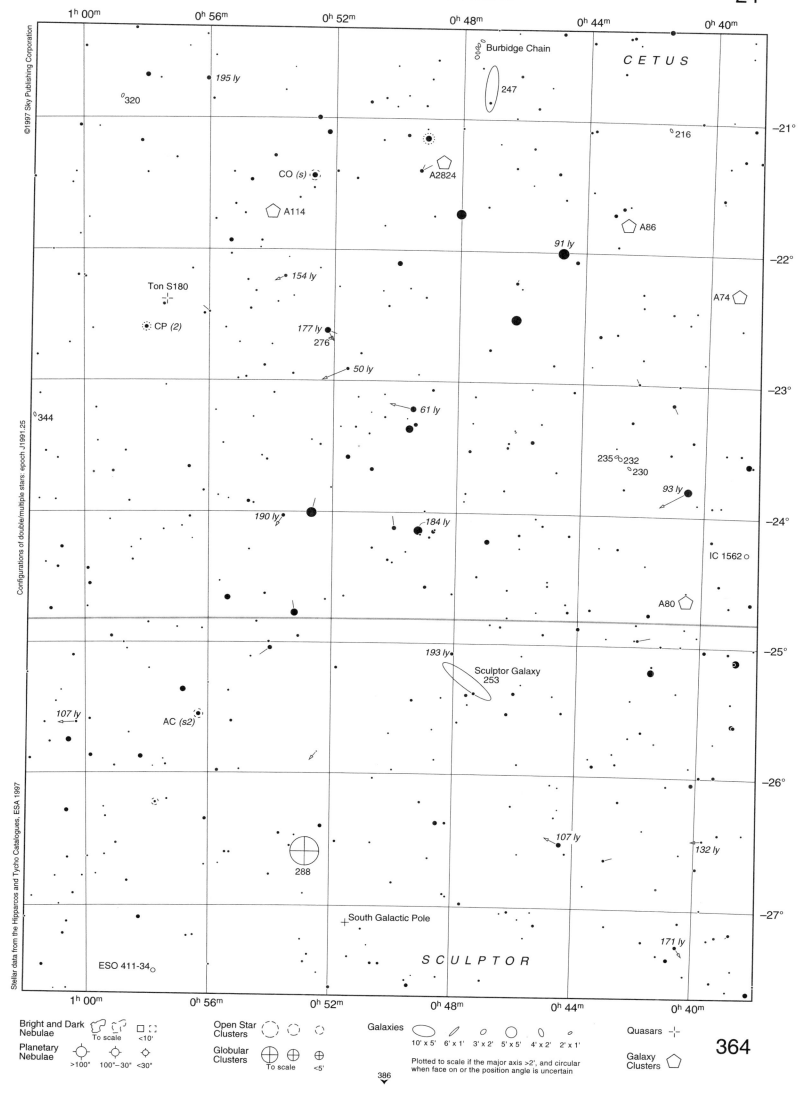

Configurations of double/multiple stars: epoch J1991.25

Stellar data from the Hipparcos and Tycho Catalogues, ESA 1997

Burbidge Chain

247

C E T U S

°216

CO (s)

A2824

A114

A86

91 ly

195 ly

°320

Ton S180

CP (2)

154 ly

A74

177 ly
276

50 ly

°344

61 ly

235 232
230

93 ly

190 ly

184 ly

IC 1562 °

A80

193 ly

Sculptor Galaxy
253

107 ly

AC (s2)

107 ly

132 ly

288

South Galactic Pole

171 ly

S C U L P T O R

ESO 411-34 °

Bright and Dark Nebulae					Open Star Clusters			Galaxies						Quasars

To scale <10'

Planetary Nebulae

>100" 100"−30" <30"

Globular Clusters

To scale <5'

Galaxies

10' x 5' 6' x 1' 3' x 2' 5' x 5' 4' x 2' 2' x 1'

Plotted to scale if the major axis >2', and circular
when face on or the position angle is uncertain

Quasars

Galaxy Clusters

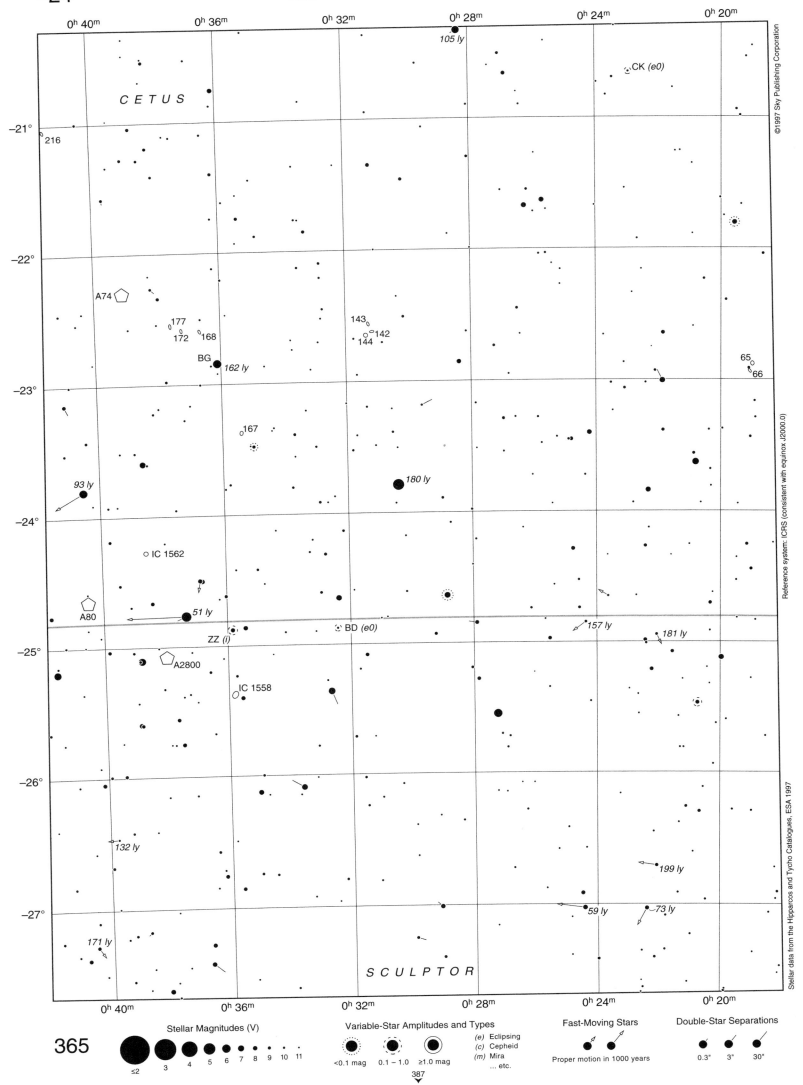

Stellar Magnitudes (V)

365

≤2 3 4 5 6 7 8 9 10 11

Variable-Star Amplitudes and Types

<0.1 mag   0.1 – 1.0   ≥1.0 mag

(e) Eclipsing
(c) Cepheid
(m) Mira
... etc.

387

Fast-Moving Stars

Proper motion in 1000 years

Double-Star Separations

0.3"   3"   30"

MILLENNIUM STAR ATLAS

−24°

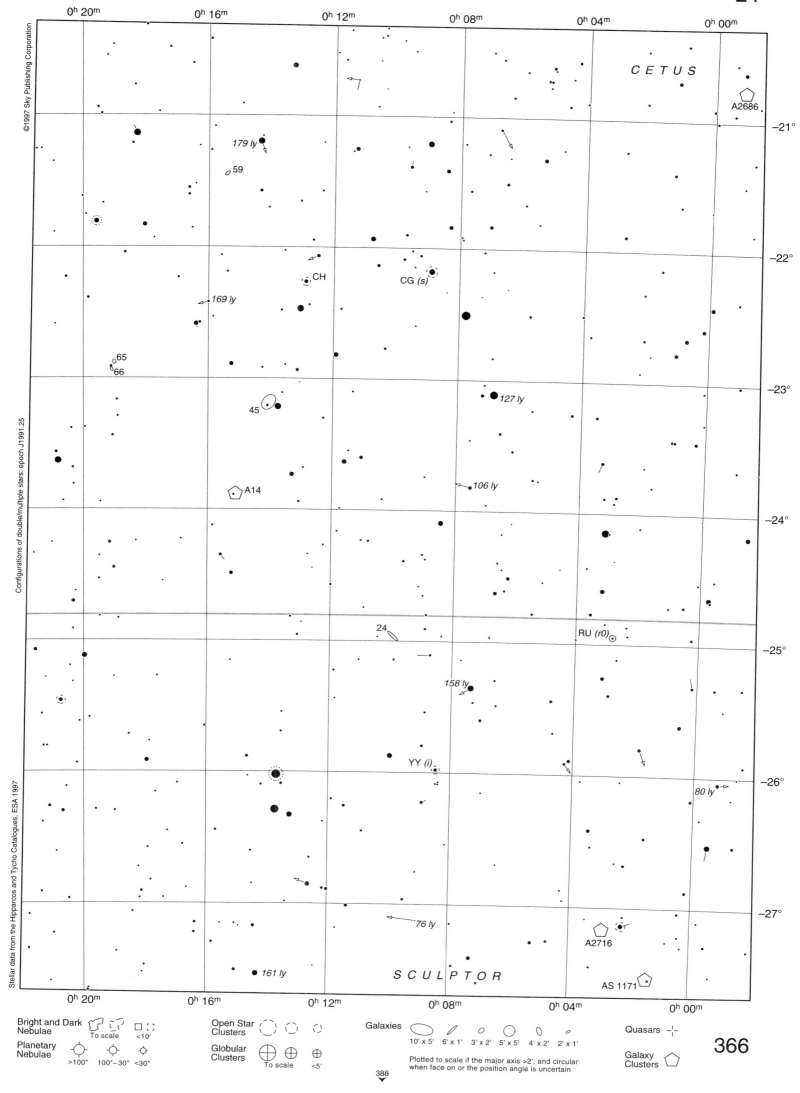

0ʰ 20ᵐ 0ʰ 16ᵐ 0ʰ 12ᵐ 0ʰ 08ᵐ 0ʰ 04ᵐ 0ʰ 00ᵐ

©1997 Sky Publishing Corporation

Configurations of double/multiple stars: epoch J1991.25

Stellar data from the Hipparcos and Tycho Catalogues, ESA 1997

CETUS

A2686

−21°

179 ly

59

CH

CG (s)

−22°

169 ly

65
66

45

127 ly

−23°

A14

106 ly

−24°

24

RU (r0)⊙

−25°

158 ly

YY (i)

80 ly

−26°

76 ly

A2716

161 ly

SCULPTOR

AS 1171

−27°

0ʰ 20ᵐ 0ʰ 16ᵐ 0ʰ 12ᵐ 0ʰ 08ᵐ 0ʰ 04ᵐ 0ʰ 00ᵐ

Bright and Dark Nebulae — To scale — <10'

Planetary Nebulae — >100" — 100"–30" — <30"

Open Star Clusters

Globular Clusters — To scale — <5'

Galaxies — 10' x 5' — 6' x 1' — 3' x 2' — 5' x 5' — 4' x 2' — 2' x 1'

Plotted to scale if the major axis >2', and circular when face on or the position angle is uncertain

Quasars

Galaxy Clusters

366

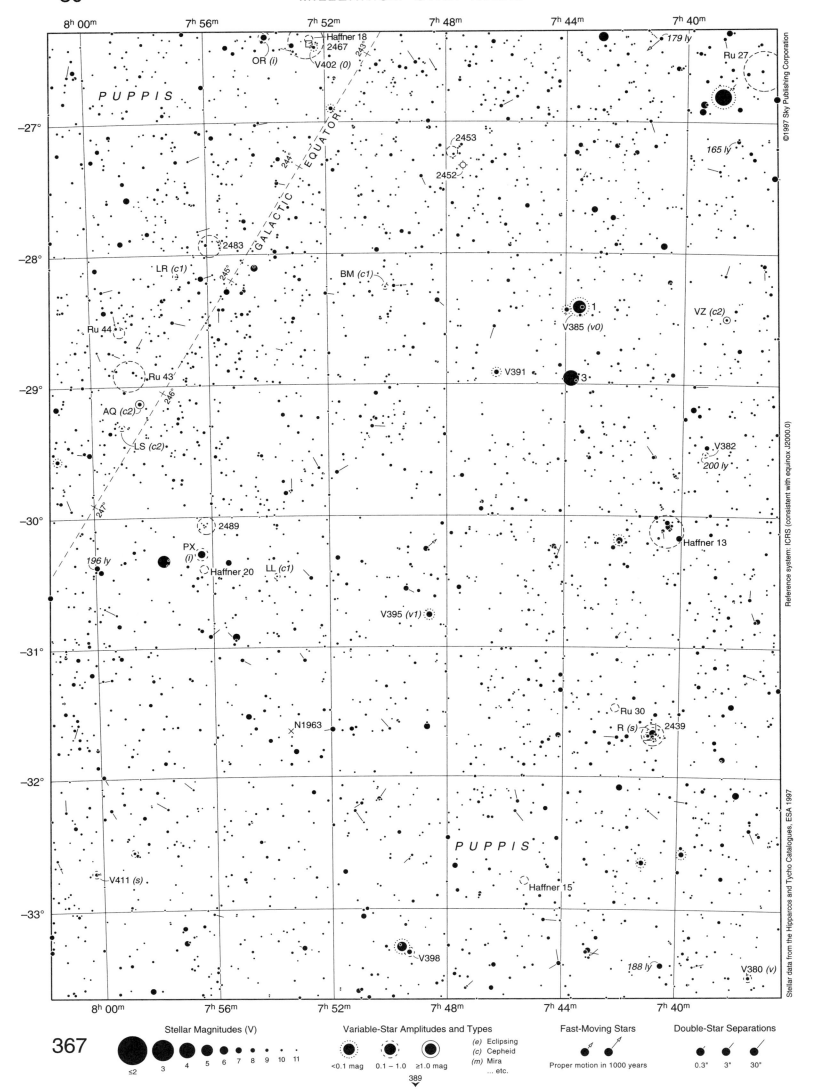

©1997 Sky Publishing Corporation

Reference system: ICRS (consistent with equinox J2000.0)

Stellar data from the Hipparcos and Tycho Catalogues, ESA 1997

367

Stellar Magnitudes (V)

≤2 3 4 5 6 7 8 9 10 11

Variable-Star Amplitudes and Types

<0.1 mag   0.1 – 1.0   ≥1.0 mag

(e) Eclipsing
(c) Cepheid
(m) Mira
... etc.

Fast-Moving Stars

Proper motion in 1000 years

Double-Star Separations

0.3"   3"   30"

-30°

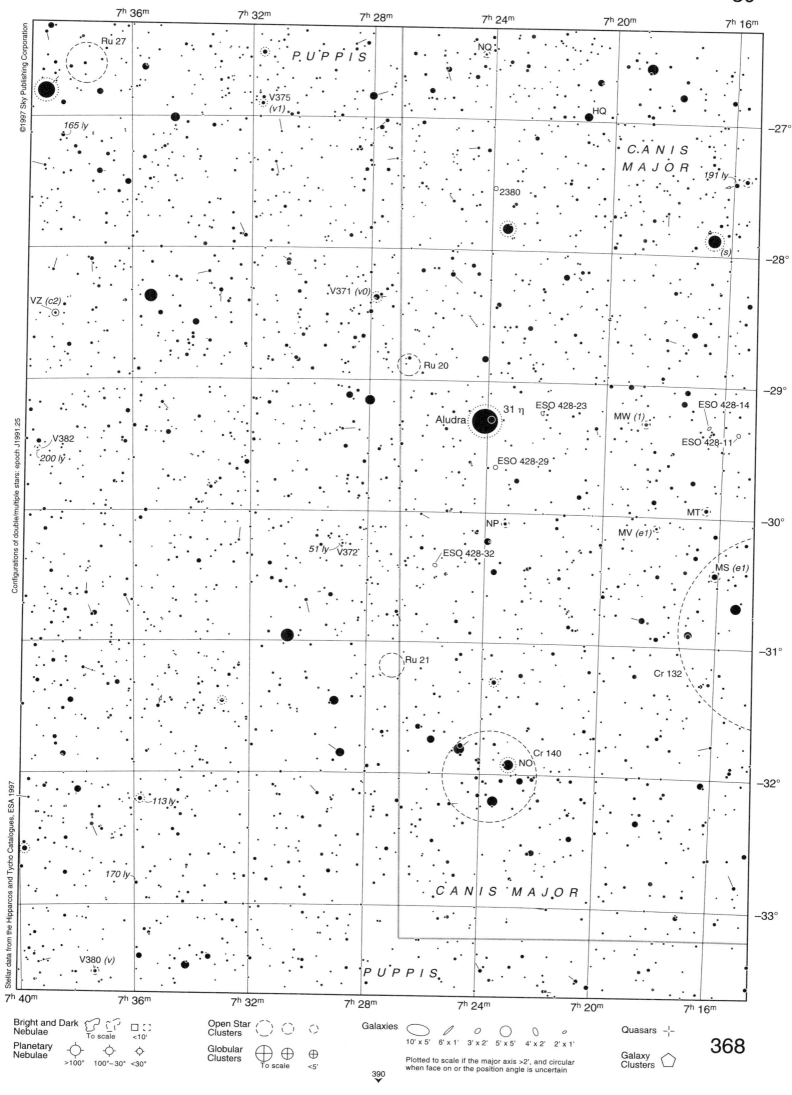

7h 36m   7h 32m   7h 28m   7h 24m   7h 20m   7h 16m

©1997 Sky Publishing Corporation

Ru 27

P U P P I S

NQ

165 ly

V375
(v1)

HQ

CANIS
MAJOR

-27°

191 ly

2380

(s)

-28°

VZ (c2)

V371 (v0)

Ru 20

-29°

31 η
Aludra

ESO 428-23

ESO 428-14

MW (1)

ESO 428-11

V382
200 ly

ESO 428-29

MT

Configurations of double/multiple stars: epoch J1991.25

NP

MV (e1)

-30°

51 ly
V372

ESO 428-32

MS (e1)

Ru 21

Cr 132

-31°

Cr 140

NO

113 ly

Stellar data from the Hipparcos and Tycho Catalogues, ESA 1997

170 ly

C A N I S   M A J O R

-32°

V380 (v)

P U P P I S

-33°

7h 40m   7h 36m   7h 32m   7h 28m   7h 24m   7h 20m   7h 16m

390

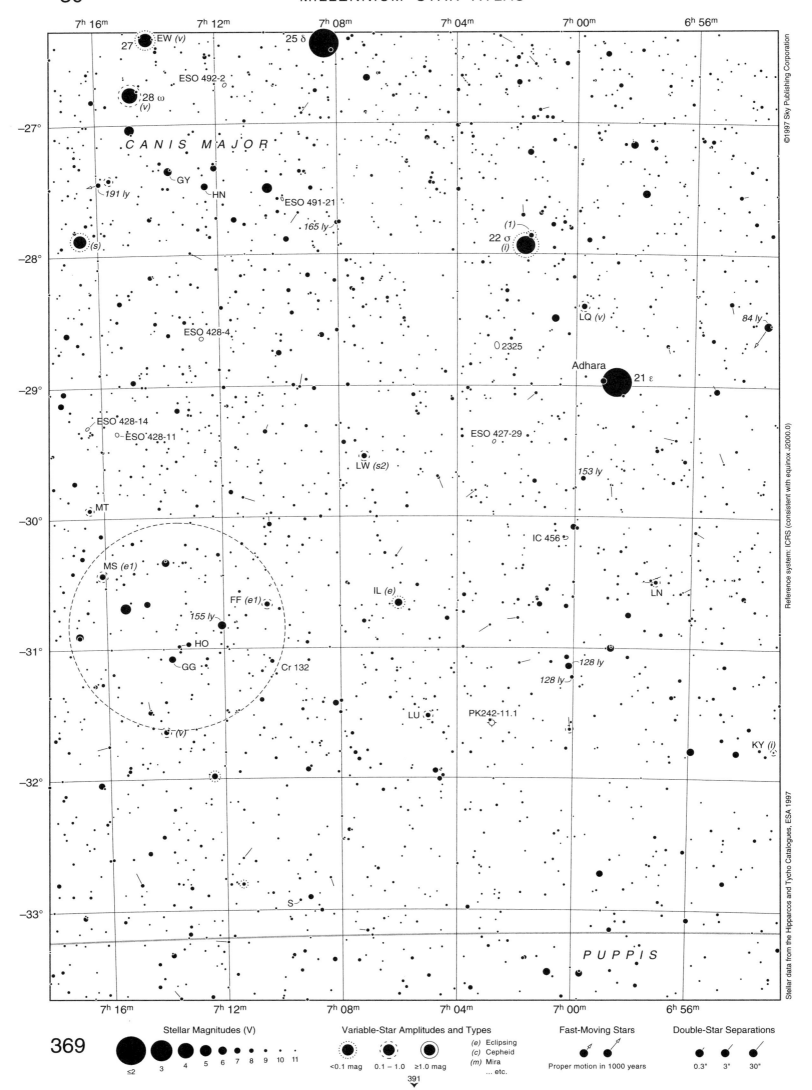

7h 16m   7h 12m   7h 08m   7h 04m   7h 00m   6h 56m

27   EW (v)

ESO 492-2

28 ω
(v)

−27°

C A N I S   M A J O R

GY

HN

ESO 491-21

191 ly

165 ly

(1)

22 σ
(i)

(s)

−28°

LQ (v)

84 ly

ESO 428-4

2325

Adhara

21 ε

−29°

ESO 428-14

ESO 428-11

ESO 427-29

LW (s2)

153 ly

MT

−30°

IC 456

MS (e1)

LN

FF (e1)

IL (e)

155 ly

HO

GG   Cr 132

128 ly

128 ly

(v)

LU   PK242-11.1

KY (i)

−31°

−32°

S

−33°

P U P P I S

7h 16m   7h 12m   7h 08m   7h 04m   7h 00m   6h 56m

©1997 Sky Publishing Corporation

Reference system: ICRS (consistent with equinox J2000.0)

Stellar data from the Hipparcos and Tycho Catalogues, ESA 1997

369

Stellar Magnitudes (V)

≤2   3   4   5   6   7   8   9   10   11

Variable-Star Amplitudes and Types

<0.1 mag   0.1 − 1.0   ≥1.0 mag

(e) Eclipsing
(c) Cepheid
(m) Mira
... etc.

Fast-Moving Stars

Proper motion in 1000 years

Double-Star Separations

0.3"   3"   30"

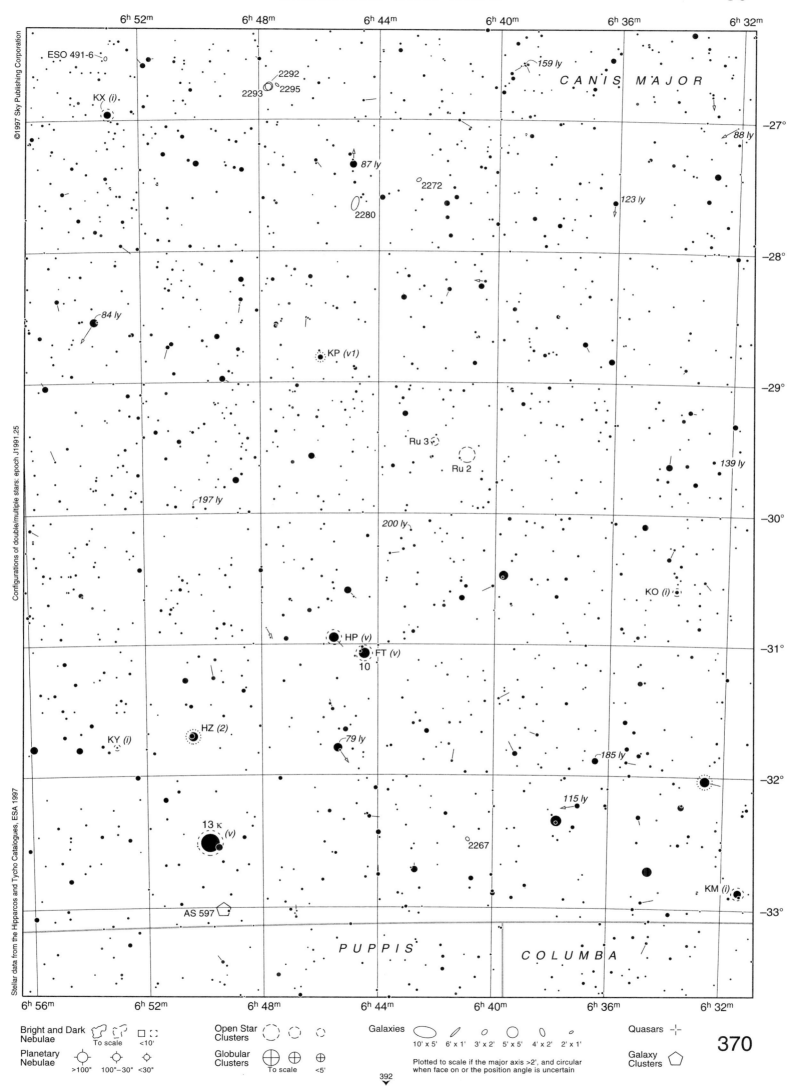

Configurations of double/multiple stars: epoch J1991.25

Stellar data from the Hipparcos and Tycho Catalogues, ESA 1997

ESO 491-6

KX (i)

2292
2293 2295

159 ly

C A N I S   M A J O R

87 ly

88 ly

2272

2280

123 ly

84 ly

KP (v1)

Ru 3

Ru 2

139 ly

197 ly

200 ly

KO (i)

HP (v)

FT (v)
10

KY (i)

HZ (2)

79 ly

185 ly

115 ly

13 κ (v)

2267

KM (i)

AS 597

P U P P I S

C O L U M B A

−27°

−28°

−29°

−30°

−31°

−32°

−33°

6ʰ 52ᵐ   6ʰ 48ᵐ   6ʰ 44ᵐ   6ʰ 40ᵐ   6ʰ 36ᵐ   6ʰ 32ᵐ

6ʰ 56ᵐ   6ʰ 52ᵐ   6ʰ 48ᵐ   6ʰ 44ᵐ   6ʰ 40ᵐ   6ʰ 36ᵐ   6ʰ 32ᵐ

Bright and Dark Nebulae		Open Star Clusters			Galaxies						Quasars
To scale	<10'				10' x 5'	6' x 1'	3' x 2'	5' x 5'	4' x 2'	2' x 1'	

Planetary Nebulae
>100" 100"−30" <30"

Globular Clusters
To scale <5'

Galaxies
Plotted to scale if the major axis >2', and circular when face on or the position angle is uncertain

Galaxy Clusters

Quasars

370

392

347

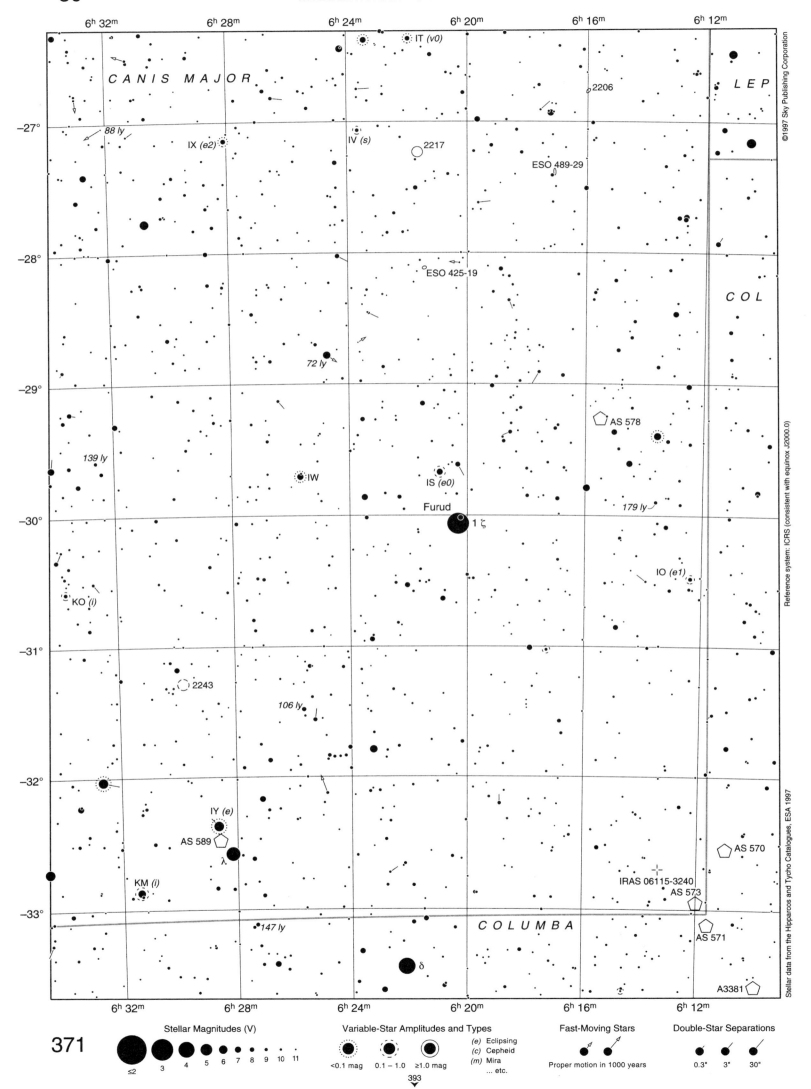

CANIS MAJOR

IT (v0)

IX (e2)

IV (s)

2206

LEP

2217

ESO 489-29

88 ly

−27°

ESO 425-19

COL

72 ly

AS 578

−28°

139 ly

IW

IS (e0)

179 ly

Furud

1 ζ

−29°

IO (e1)

−30°

KO (i)

2243

106 ly

−31°

IY (e)

AS 589

λ

AS 570

KM (i)

IRAS 06115-3240

AS 573

−32°

COLUMBA

AS 571

147 ly

δ

A3381

−33°

©1997 Sky Publishing Corporation

Reference system: ICRS (consistent with equinox J2000.0)

Stellar data from the Hipparcos and Tycho Catalogues, ESA 1997

6^h 32^m 6^h 28^m 6^h 24^m 6^h 20^m 6^h 16^m 6^h 12^m

371

Stellar Magnitudes (V)

≤2 3 4 5 6 7 8 9 10 11

Variable-Star Amplitudes and Types

<0.1 mag   0.1 – 1.0   ≥1.0 mag

(e) Eclipsing
(c) Cepheid
(m) Mira
... etc.

Fast-Moving Stars

Proper motion in 1000 years

Double-Star Separations

0.3" 3" 30"

393

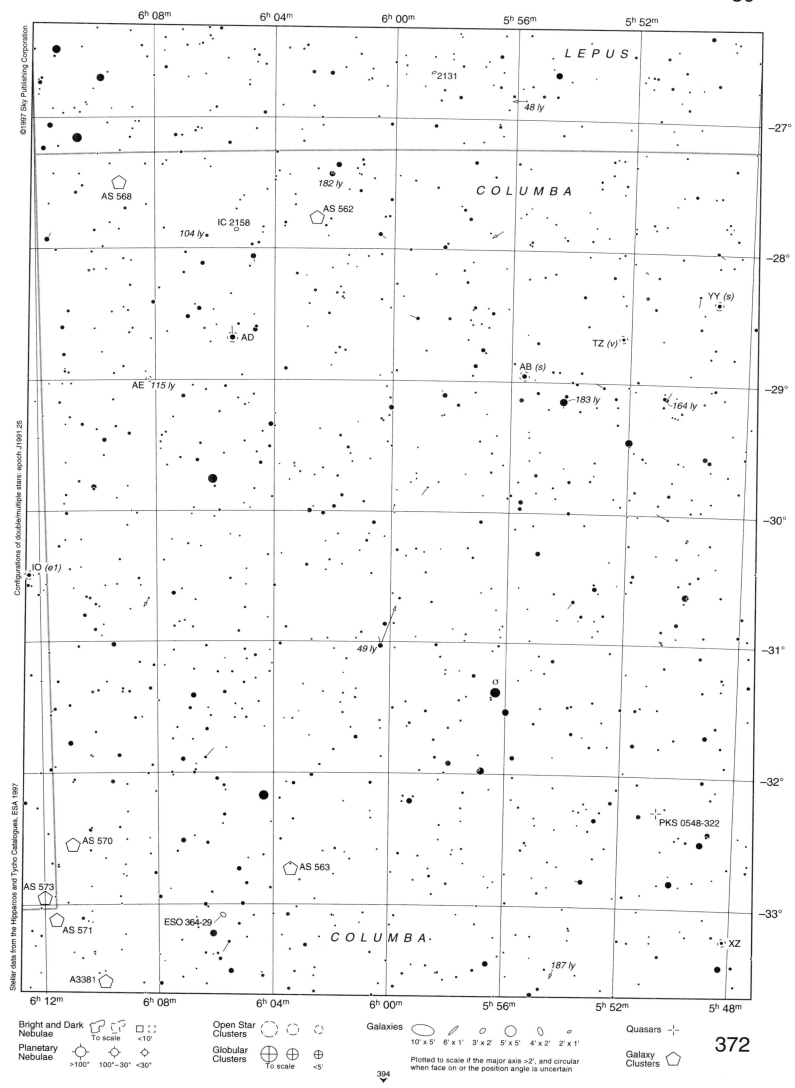

Configurations of double/multiple stars: epoch J1991.25

Stellar data from the Hipparcos and Tycho Catalogues, ESA 1997

L E P U S

2131

48 ly

C O L U M B A

AS 568

182 ly

AS 562

IC 2158

104 ly

YY (s)

TZ (v)

AD

AB (s)

AE 115 ly

183 ly

−164 ly

IO (e1)

49 ly

σ

PKS 0548-322

AS 570

AS 563

AS 573

ESO 364-29

XZ

AS 571

C O L U M B A

187 ly

A3381

−27°

−28°

−29°

−30°

−31°

−32°

−33°

6ʰ 08ᵐ 6ʰ 04ᵐ 6ʰ 00ᵐ 5ʰ 56ᵐ 5ʰ 52ᵐ

6ʰ 12ᵐ 6ʰ 08ᵐ 6ʰ 04ᵐ 6ʰ 00ᵐ 5ʰ 56ᵐ 5ʰ 52ᵐ 5ʰ 48ᵐ

Bright and Dark Nebulae	To scale <10'	**Galaxies** 10' x 5' 6' x 1' 3' x 2' 5' x 5' 4' x 2' 2' x 1'	**Quasars** —+—
Planetary Nebulae >100" 100"–30" <30"	**Open Star Clusters**		
	Globular Clusters To scale <5'	Plotted to scale if the major axis >2', and circular when face on or the position angle is uncertain	**Galaxy Clusters**

MILLENNIUM STAR ATLAS

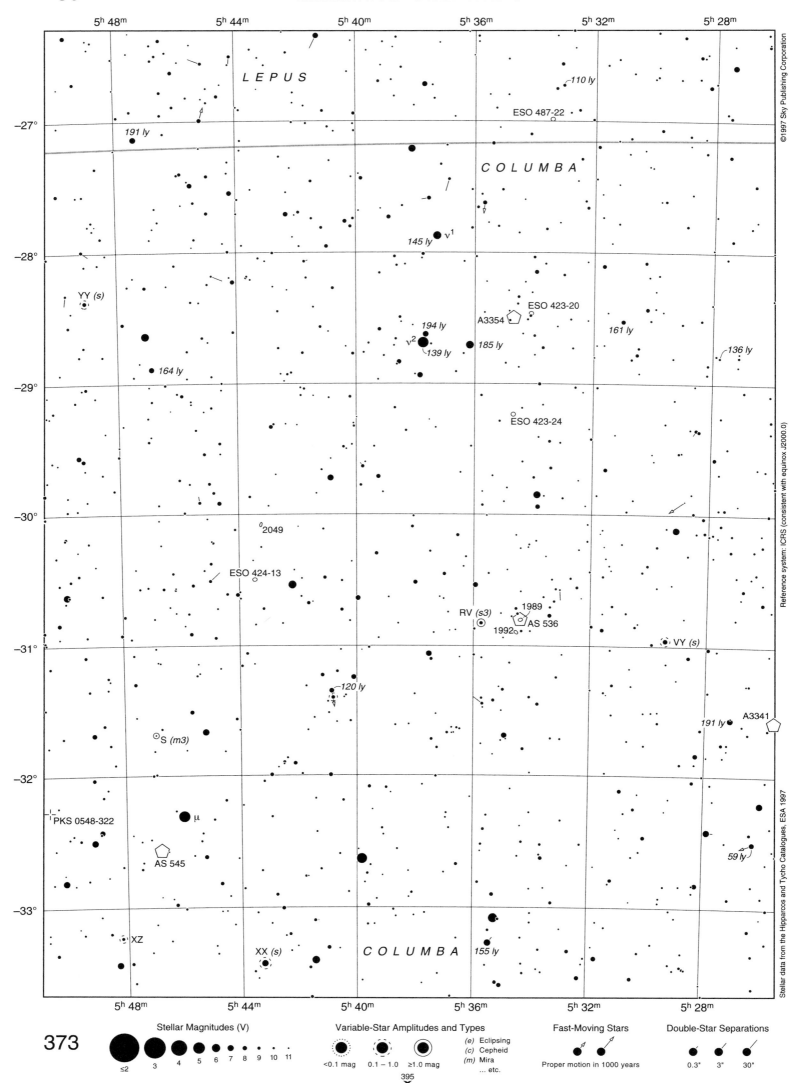

©1997 Sky Publishing Corporation

Reference system: ICRS (consistent with equinox J2000.0)

Stellar data from the Hipparcos and Tycho Catalogues, ESA 1997

L E P U S

110 ly

ESO 487-22

C O L U M B A

145 ly ν¹

YY (s)

194 ly
ν² 185 ly
139 ly

161 ly

136 ly

164 ly

ESO 423-20
A3354

ESO 423-24

2049

ESO 424-13

1989
RV (s3) AS 536
1992

VY (s)

120 ly

191 ly A3341

S (m3)

PKS 0548-322 μ

AS 545

59 ly

XZ

XX (s) C O L U M B A 155 ly

373

Stellar Magnitudes (V)

≤2 3 4 5 6 7 8 9 10 11

Variable-Star Amplitudes and Types

<0.1 mag 0.1 − 1.0 ≥1.0 mag

(e) Eclipsing
(c) Cepheid
(m) Mira
... etc.

Fast-Moving Stars

Proper motion in 1000 years

Double-Star Separations

0.3" 3" 30"

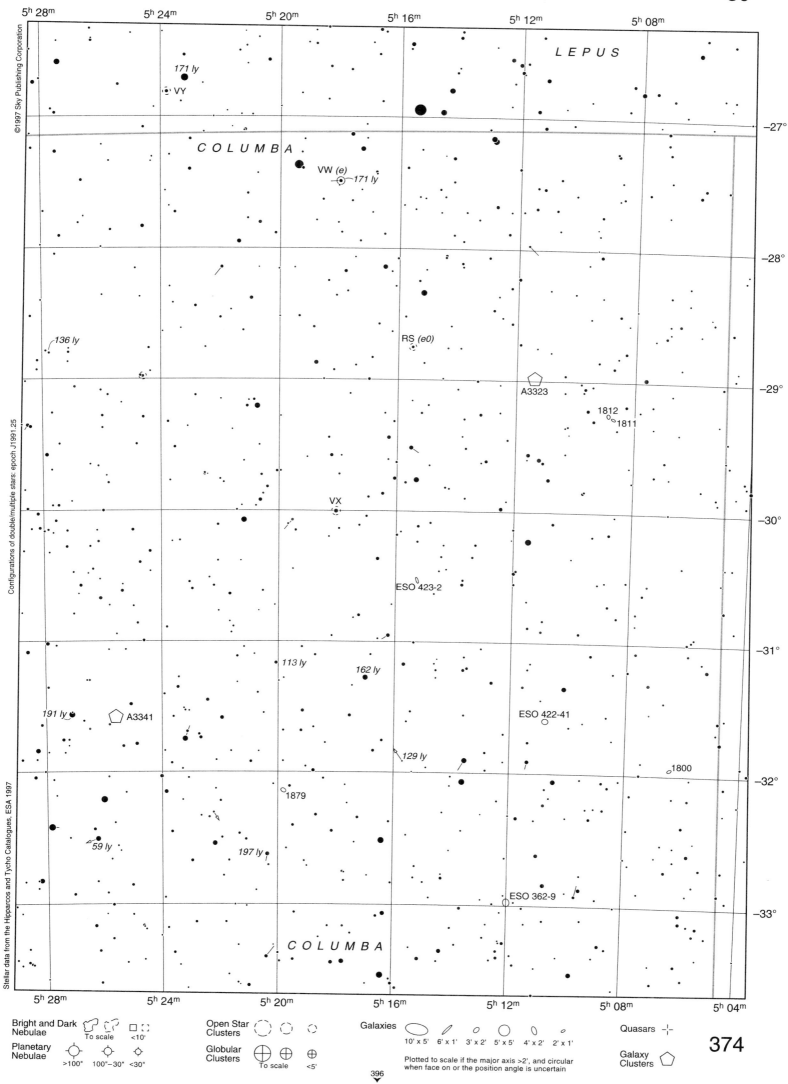

LEPUS

COLUMBA

171 ly
VY

VW (e) 171 ly

136 ly

RS (e0)

A3323

1812
1811

VX

ESO 423-2

113 ly

162 ly

191 ly

A3341

ESO 422-41

129 ly

1800

1879

59 ly

197 ly

ESO 362-9

COLUMBA

| Bright and Dark Nebulae | To scale | <10' | Open Star Clusters | To scale | <5' | Galaxies | 10' x 5' | 6' x 1' | 3' x 2' | 5' x 5' | 4' x 2' | 2' x 1' | Quasars |
| Planetary Nebulae | >100" 100"−30" <30" | Globular Clusters | | | | | | | | | | Galaxy Clusters |

Plotted to scale if the major axis >2', and circular when face on or the position angle is uncertain

374

-30°

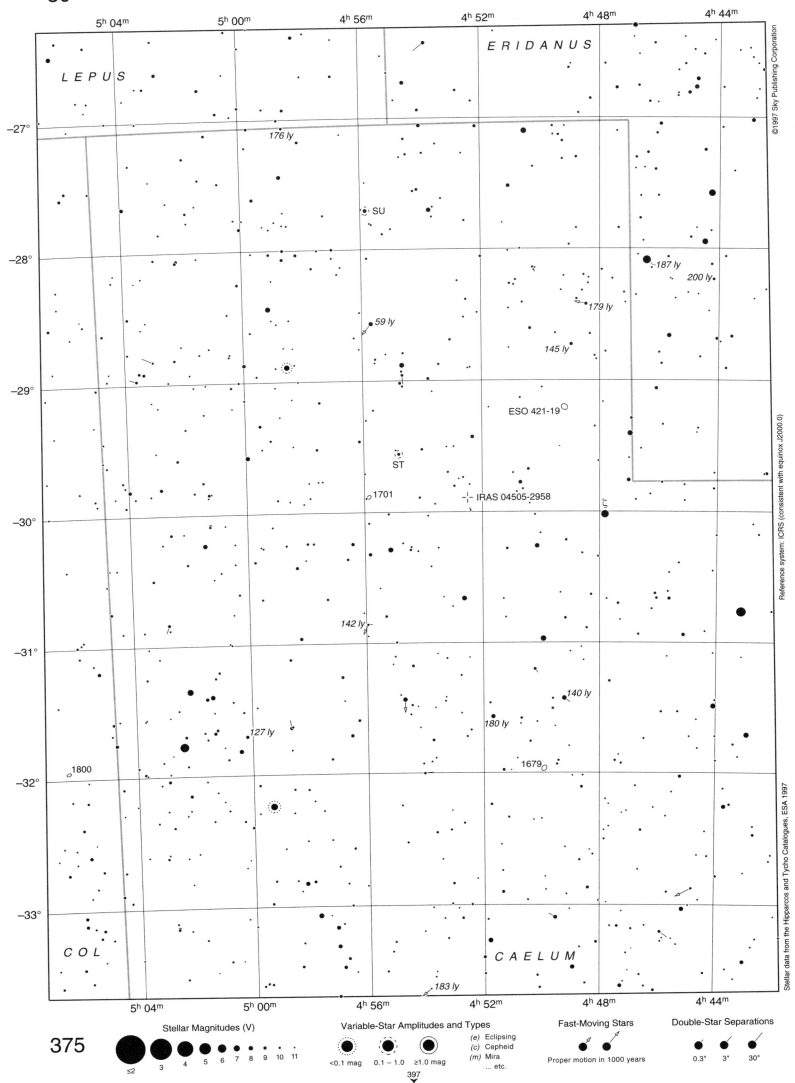

E R I D A N U S

L E P U S

-27°

176 ly

·○ SU

-28°

·○ *187 ly*

200 ly

179 ly

○ *59 ly*

145 ly

ESO 421-19 ○

·○ ST

○ 1701

─┼─ IRAS 04505-2958

ζ

-30°

142 ly

-31°

140 ly

127 ly

180 ly

○ 1800

1679 ○

-32°

C O L

C A E L U M

○ *183 ly*

©1997 Sky Publishing Corporation

Reference system: ICRS (consistent with equinox J2000.0)

Stellar data from the Hipparcos and Tycho Catalogues, ESA 1997

375

| Stellar Magnitudes (V) | Variable-Star Amplitudes and Types | Fast-Moving Stars | Double-Star Separations |

Stellar Magnitudes (V)
≤2 3 4 5 6 7 8 9 10 11

Variable-Star Amplitudes and Types
<0.1 mag   0.1 – 1.0   ≥1.0 mag

(e) Eclipsing
(c) Cepheid
(m) Mira
... etc.

Fast-Moving Stars
Proper motion in 1000 years

Double-Star Separations
0.3" 3" 30"

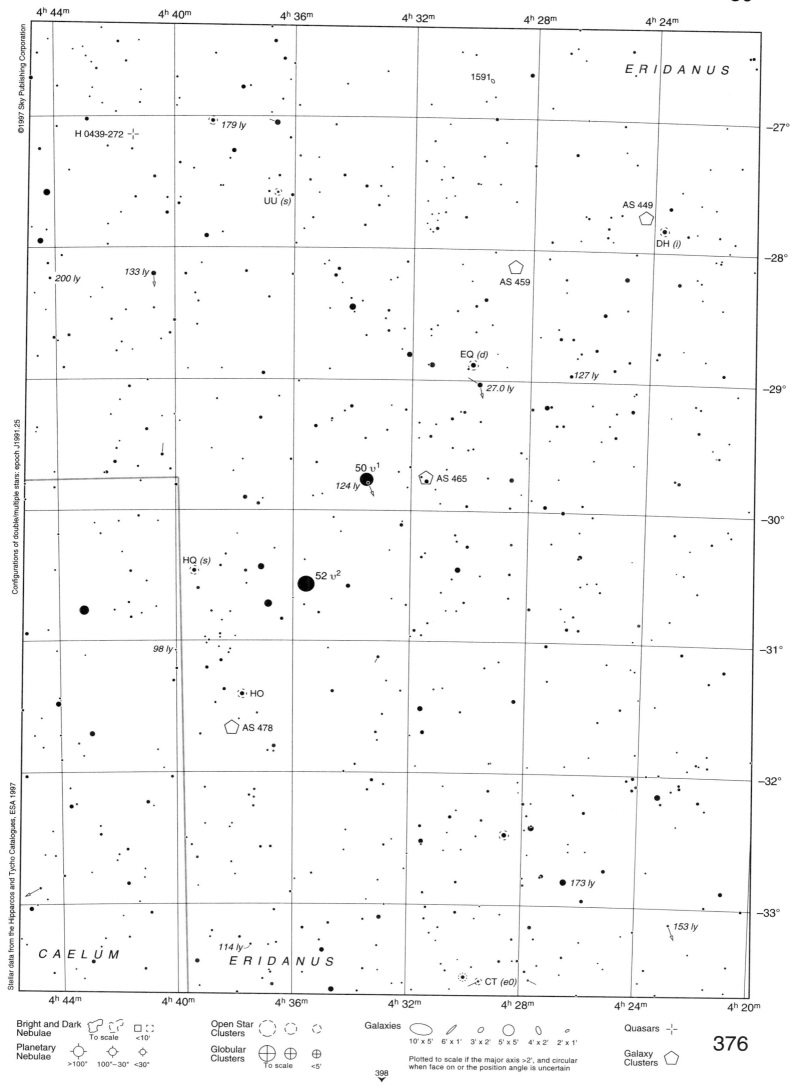

ERIDANUS

1591

H 0439-272

179 ly

UU (s)

AS 449

DH (i)

200 ly   133 ly

AS 459

EQ (d)

127 ly

27.0 ly

50 υ¹

124 ly   AS 465

HQ (s)

52 υ²

98 ly

HO

AS 478

173 ly

153 ly

114 ly

CAELUM   ERIDANUS

CT (e0)

©1997 Sky Publishing Corporation

Configurations of double/multiple stars: epoch J1991.25

Stellar data from the Hipparcos and Tycho Catalogues, ESA 1997

Bright and Dark Nebulae		Open Star Clusters			Galaxies						Quasars
To scale	<10'				10' x 5'	6' x 1'	3' x 2'	5' x 5'	4' x 2'	2' x 1'	
Planetary Nebulae		Globular Clusters									Galaxy Clusters
>100"	100"–30" <30"	To scale	<5'								

Plotted to scale if the major axis >2', and circular when face on or the position angle is uncertain

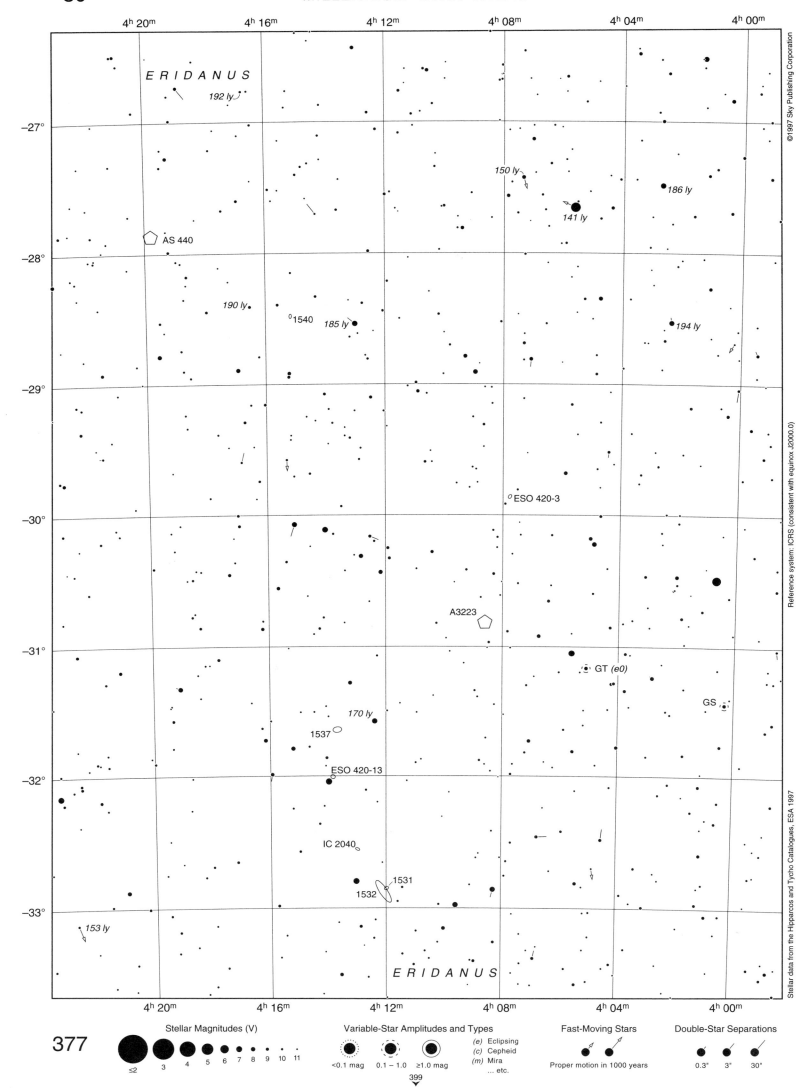

©1997 Sky Publishing Corporation

Reference system: ICRS (consistent with equinox J2000.0)

Stellar data from the Hipparcos and Tycho Catalogues, ESA 1997

ERIDANUS

192 ly

AS 440

150 ly

186 ly

141 ly

190 ly

1540

185 ly

194 ly

ESO 420-3

A3223

GT (e0)

GS

170 ly

1537

ESO 420-13

IC 2040

1531

1532

153 ly

ERIDANUS

Stellar Magnitudes (V)

≤2 3 4 5 6 7 8 9 10 11

Variable-Star Amplitudes and Types

<0.1 mag   0.1 – 1.0   ≥1.0 mag

(e) Eclipsing
(c) Cepheid
(m) Mira
... etc.

Fast-Moving Stars

Proper motion in 1000 years

Double-Star Separations

0.3"   3"   30"

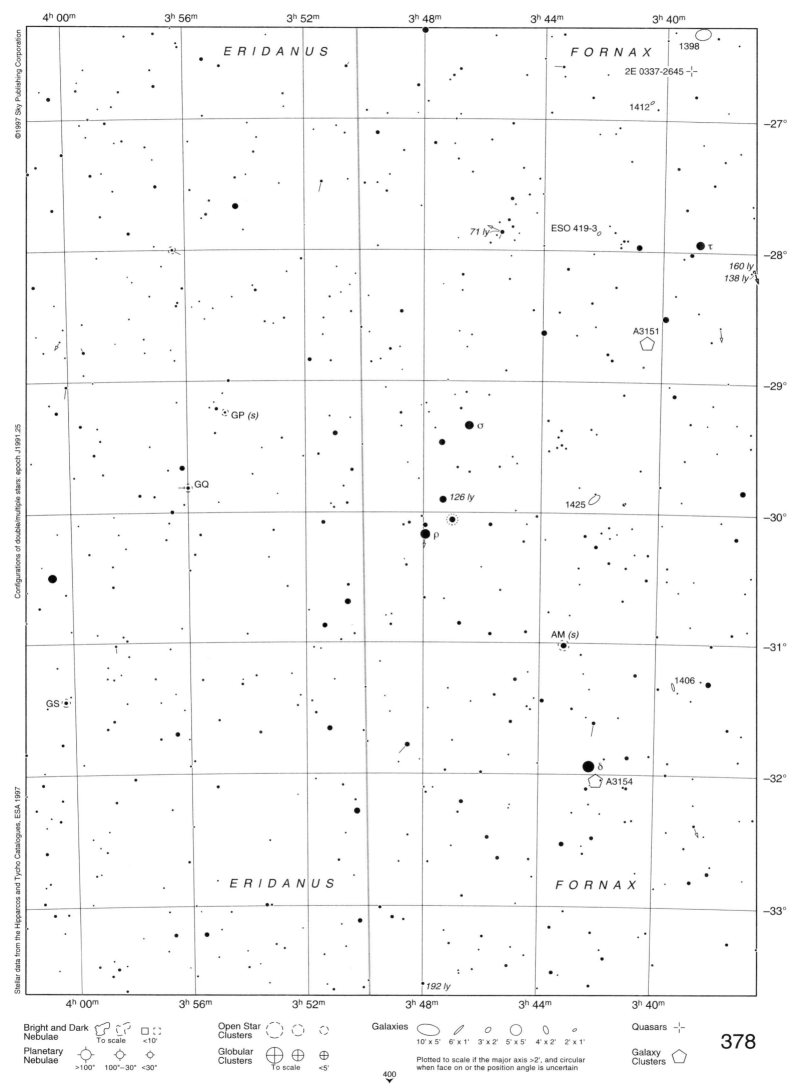

ERIDANUS

FORNAX

1398

2E 0337-2645

1412

71 ly

ESO 419-3

τ

160 ly
138 ly

A3151

GP (s)

σ

GQ

126 ly

1425

ρ

AM (s)

1406

GS

δ

A3154

ERIDANUS

FORNAX

192 ly

Bright and Dark
Nebulae
To scale   <10'

Planetary
Nebulae
>100" 100"−30" <30"

Open Star
Clusters

Globular
Clusters
To scale   <5'

Galaxies
10' x 5'   6' x 1'   3' x 2'   5' x 5'   4' x 2'   2' x 1'

Plotted to scale if the major axis >2', and circular
when face on or the position angle is uncertain

Quasars

Galaxy
Clusters

378

400

MILLENNIUM STAR ATLAS

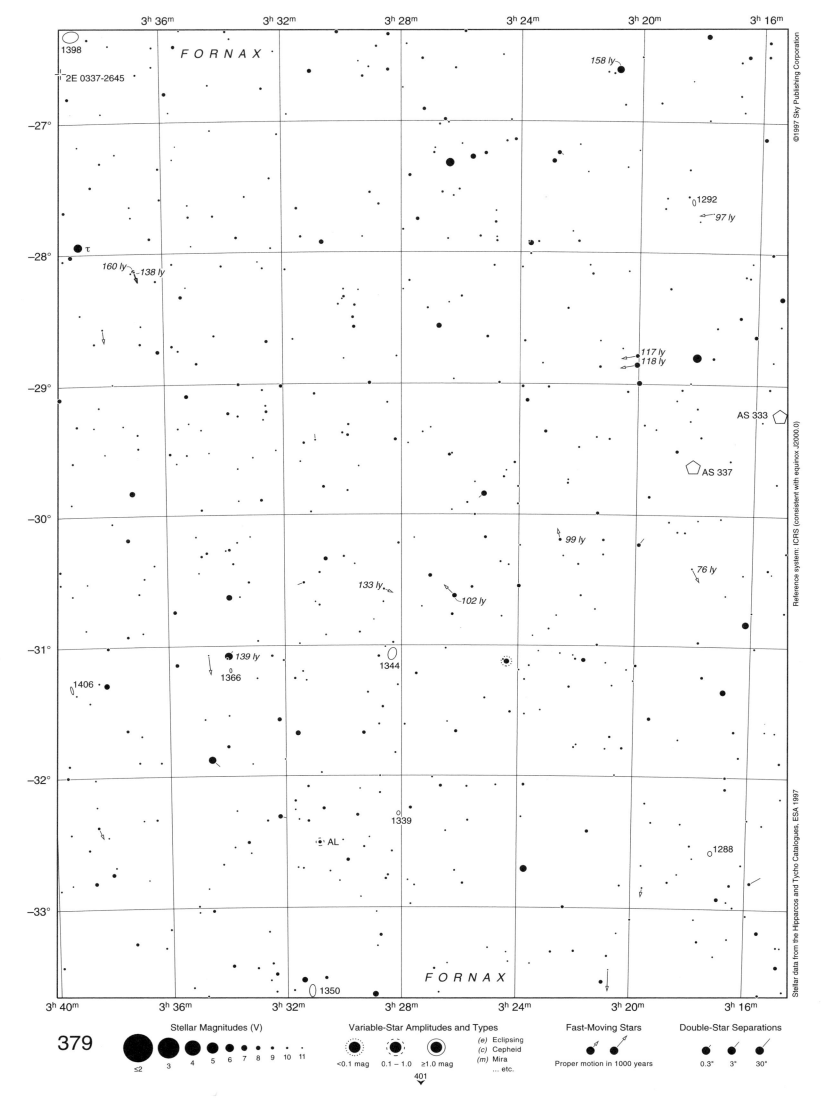

©1997 Sky Publishing Corporation

Reference system: ICRS (consistent with equinox J2000.0)

Stellar data from the Hipparcos and Tycho Catalogues, ESA 1997

F O R N A X

1398

2E 0337-2645

158 ly

1292

97 ly

τ

160 ly 138 ly

117 ly
118 ly

AS 333

AS 337

99 ly

76 ly

133 ly

102 ly

1344

139 ly

1366

1406

1350

1339

AL

1288

F O R N A X

Stellar Magnitudes (V)

≤2 3 4 5 6 7 8 9 10 11

379

Variable-Star Amplitudes and Types

<0.1 mag   0.1 – 1.0   ≥1.0 mag

(e) Eclipsing
(c) Cepheid
(m) Mira
... etc.

Fast-Moving Stars

Proper motion in 1000 years

Double-Star Separations

0.3"   3"   30"

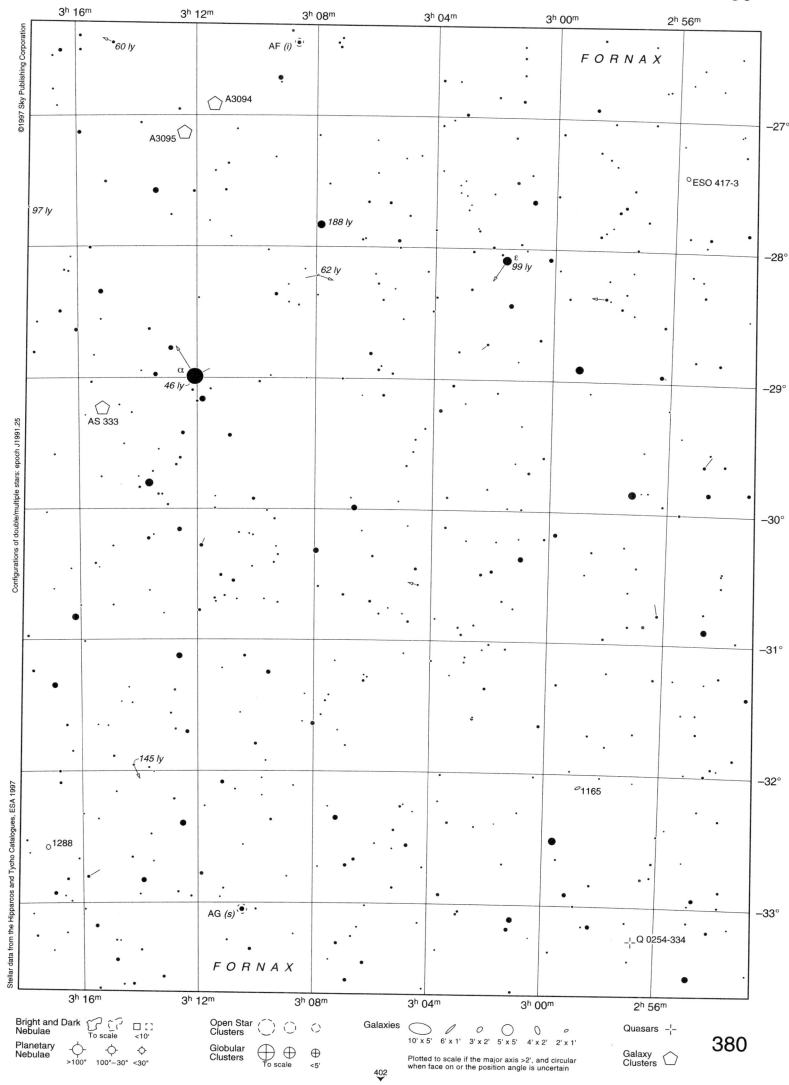

Configurations of double/multiple stars: epoch J1991.25

FORNAX

60 ly

AF (i)

A3094

A3095

97 ly

188 ly

ESO 417-3

ε
99 ly

62 ly

α

46 ly

AS 333

145 ly

1165

1288

AG (s)

Q 0254-334

FORNAX

3h 16m   3h 12m   3h 08m   3h 04m   3h 00m   2h 56m

−27°
−28°
−29°
−30°
−31°
−32°
−33°

| Bright and Dark Nebulae | Open Star Clusters | Galaxies | Quasars |
| Planetary Nebulae | Globular Clusters | | Galaxy Clusters |

To scale   <10'

>100"   100"–30"   <30"

To scale   <5'

10' x 5'   6' x 1'   3' x 2'   5' x 5'   4' x 2'   2' x 1'

Plotted to scale if the major axis >2', and circular
when face on or the position angle is uncertain

380

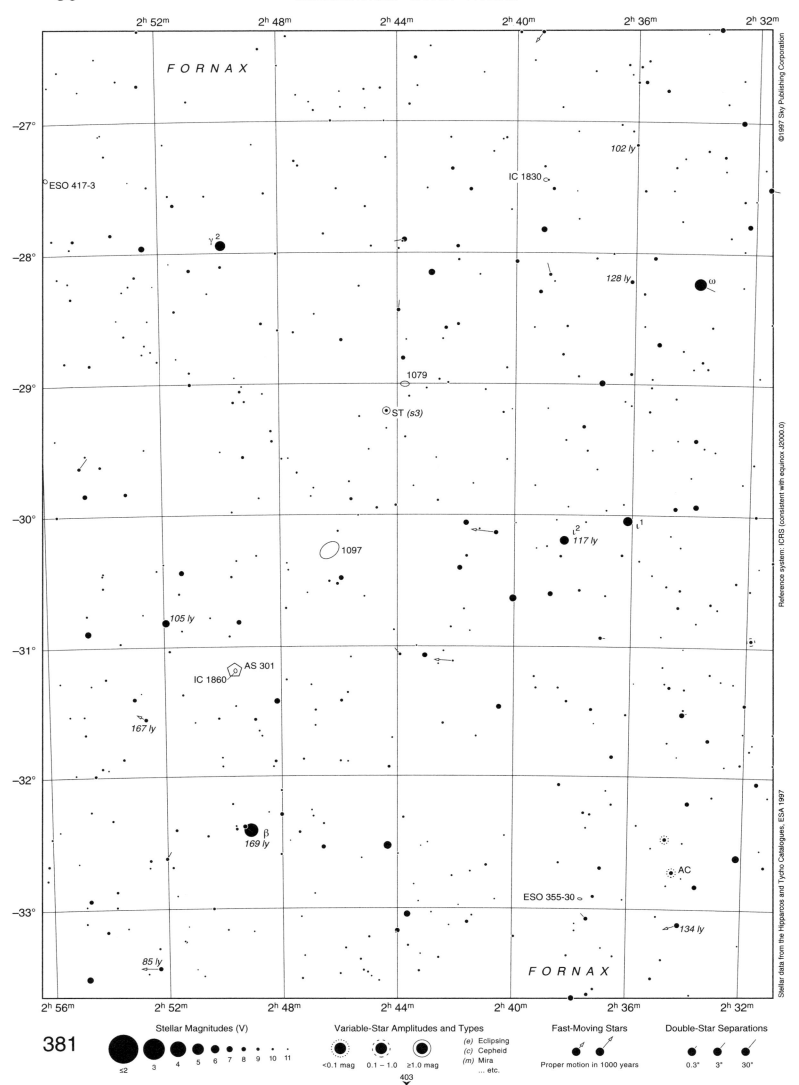

358

FORNAX

ESO 417-3

γ²

IC 1830 c

102 ly

128 ly

ω

1079

ST *(s3)*

1097

ι² 117 ly

ι¹

105 ly

IC 1860 ○ AS 301

167 ly

β
169 ly

AC

ESO 355-30 ○

134 ly

85 ly

FORNAX

381

Stellar Magnitudes (V)

≤2 3 4 5 6 7 8 9 10 11

Variable-Star Amplitudes and Types

<0.1 mag   0.1 − 1.0   ≥1.0 mag

(e) Eclipsing
(c) Cepheid
(m) Mira
... etc.

403

Fast-Moving Stars

Proper motion in 1000 years

Double-Star Separations

0.3"   3"   30"

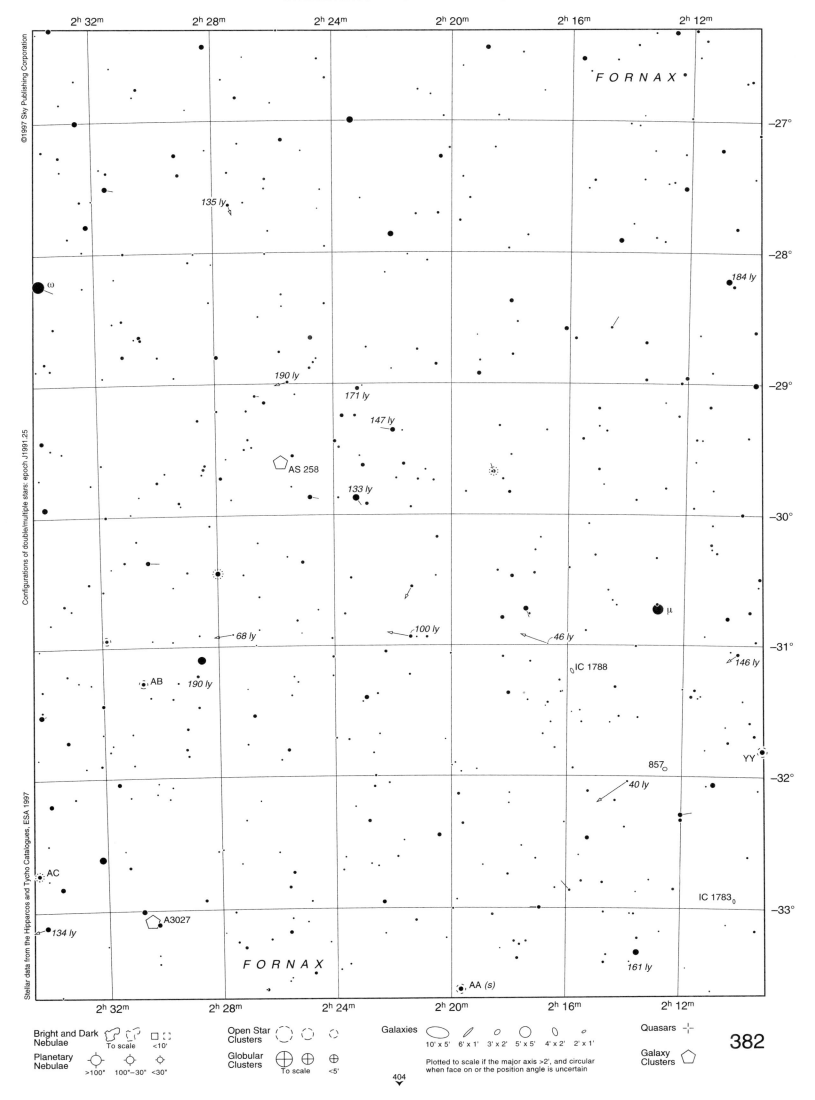

FORNAX

−27°

135 ly

−28°

184 ly

ω

190 ly

−29°

171 ly

147 ly

AS 258

133 ly

−30°

μ

68 ly

100 ly

46 ly

IC 1788

−31°

AB   190 ly

146 ly

857

YY

40 ly

AC

IC 1783

−32°

A3027

134 ly

161 ly

−33°

FORNAX

AA *(s)*

Bright and Dark Nebulae		

To scale   <10'

Planetary Nebulae

>100" 100"−30" <30"

Open Star Clusters

Globular Clusters

To scale   <5'

Galaxies

10' x 5'   6' x 1'   3' x 2'   5' x 5'   4' x 2'   2' x 1'

Plotted to scale if the major axis >2', and circular when face on or the position angle is uncertain

Quasars

Galaxy Clusters

MILLENNIUM STAR ATLAS

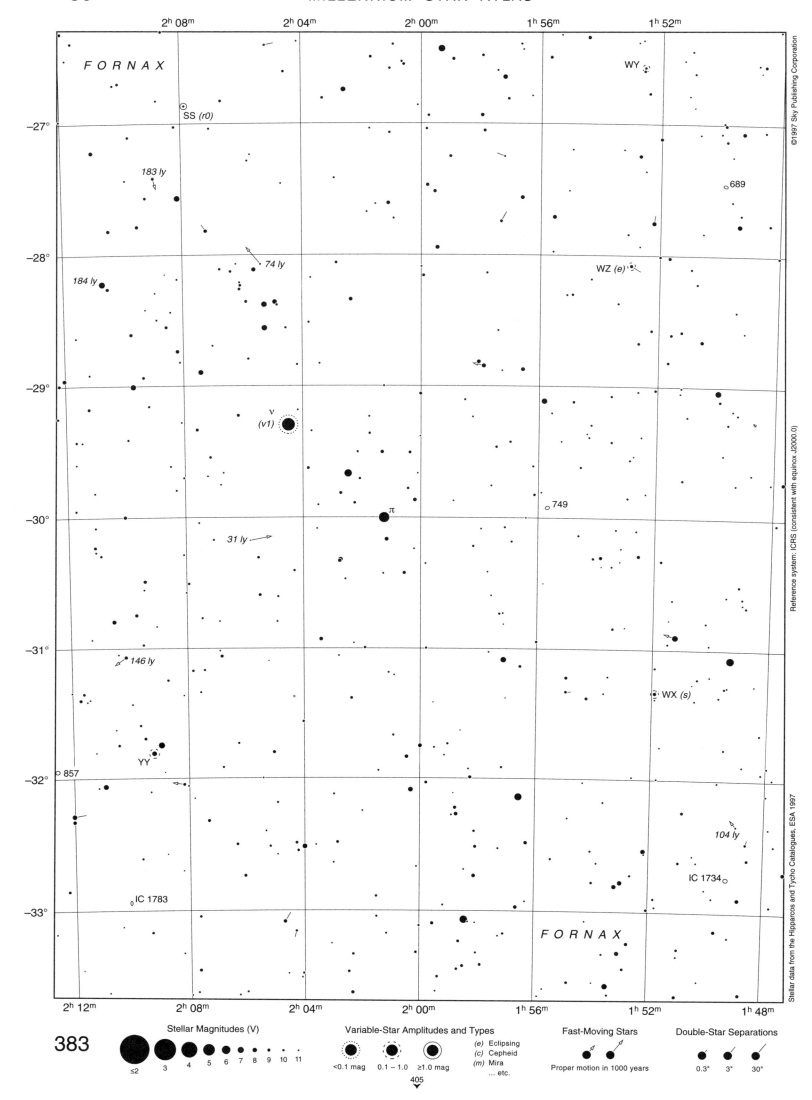

©1997 Sky Publishing Corporation

Reference system: ICRS (consistent with equinox J2000.0)

Stellar data from the Hipparcos and Tycho Catalogues, ESA 1997

F O R N A X

SS (r0)

183 ly

74 ly

184 ly

WY

689

WZ (e)

ν
(v1)

749

π

31 ly

146 ly

WX (s)

YY

857

104 ly

IC 1734

IC 1783

F O R N A X

383

Stellar Magnitudes (V)

≤2 3 4 5 6 7 8 9 10 11

Variable-Star Amplitudes and Types

<0.1 mag   0.1 – 1.0   ≥1.0 mag

(e) Eclipsing
(c) Cepheid
(m) Mira
... etc.

Fast-Moving Stars

Proper motion in 1000 years

Double-Star Separations

0.3"   3"   30"

MILLENNIUM STAR ATLAS

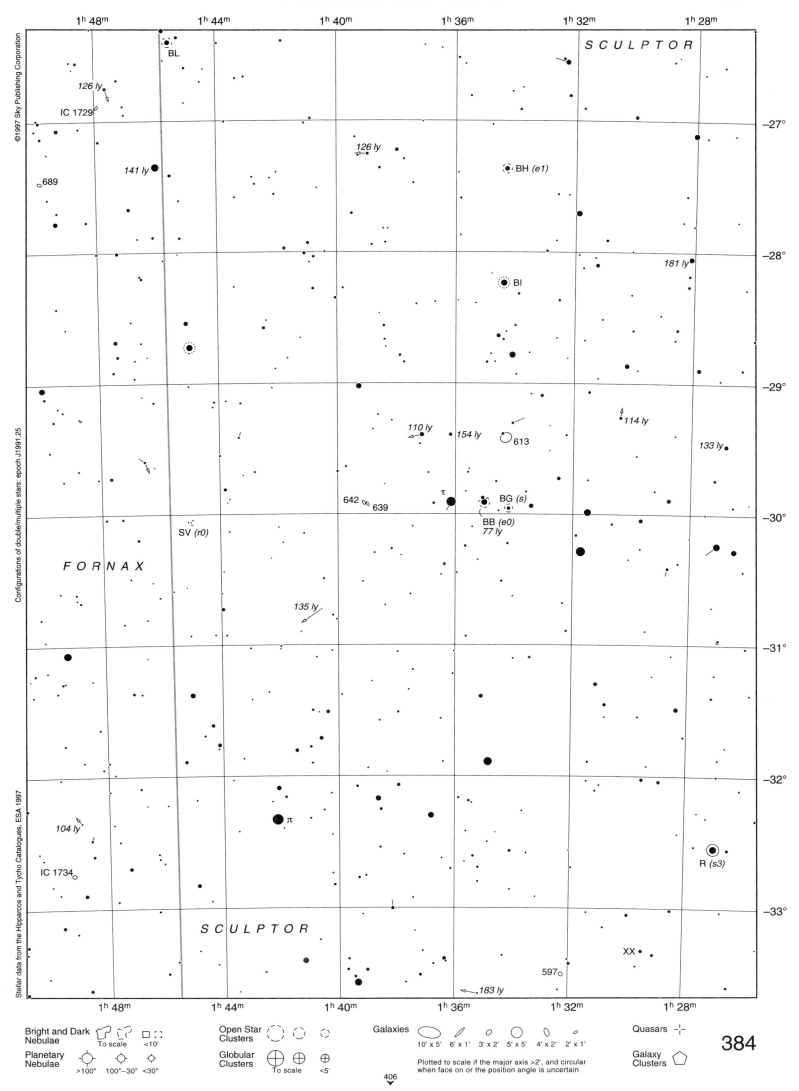

S C U L P T O R

BL

126 ly

IC 1729

141 ly

689

126 ly

BH *(e1)*

181 ly

BI

114 ly

110 ly   *154 ly*

613

133 ly

τ

642 ∞ 639

BG *(s)*

SV *(r0)*

BB *(e0)*
77 ly

F O R N A X

135 ly

104 ly

π

IC 1734

R *(s3)*

S C U L P T O R

XX

597

183 ly

Bright and Dark Nebulae		To scale		<10'		**Quasars**
Planetary Nebulae	>100"	100"–30"	<30"			**Galaxy Clusters**
Open Star Clusters						
Globular Clusters		To scale	<5'			
Galaxies	10' x 5'	6' x 1'	3' x 2'	5' x 5'	4' x 2'	2' x 1'

Plotted to scale if the major axis >2', and circular when face on or the position angle is uncertain

384

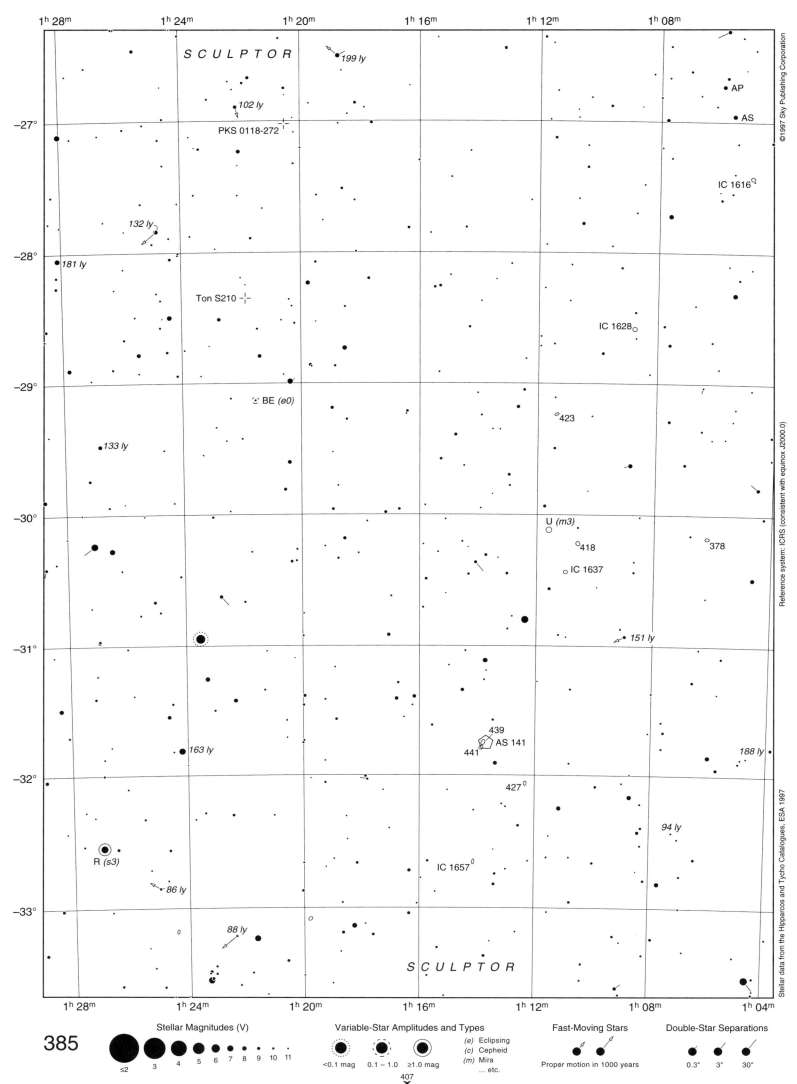

©1997 Sky Publishing Corporation

Reference system: ICRS (consistent with equinox J2000.0)

Stellar data from the Hipparcos and Tycho Catalogues, ESA 1997

S C U L P T O R

199 ly

102 ly

PKS 0118-272

AP

AS

IC 1616

132 ly

181 ly

Ton S210

IC 1628

133 ly

BE (e0)

423

U (m3)

418   378

IC 1637

151 ly

439
AS 141
441

188 ly

427

94 ly

R (s3)

IC 1657

86 ly

88 ly

S C U L P T O R

385

Stellar Magnitudes (V)

≤2   3   4   5   6   7   8   9   10   11

Variable-Star Amplitudes and Types

<0.1 mag   0.1 − 1.0   ≥1.0 mag

(e) Eclipsing
(c) Cepheid
(m) Mira
... etc.

Fast-Moving Stars

Proper motion in 1000 years

Double-Star Separations

0.3"   3"   30"

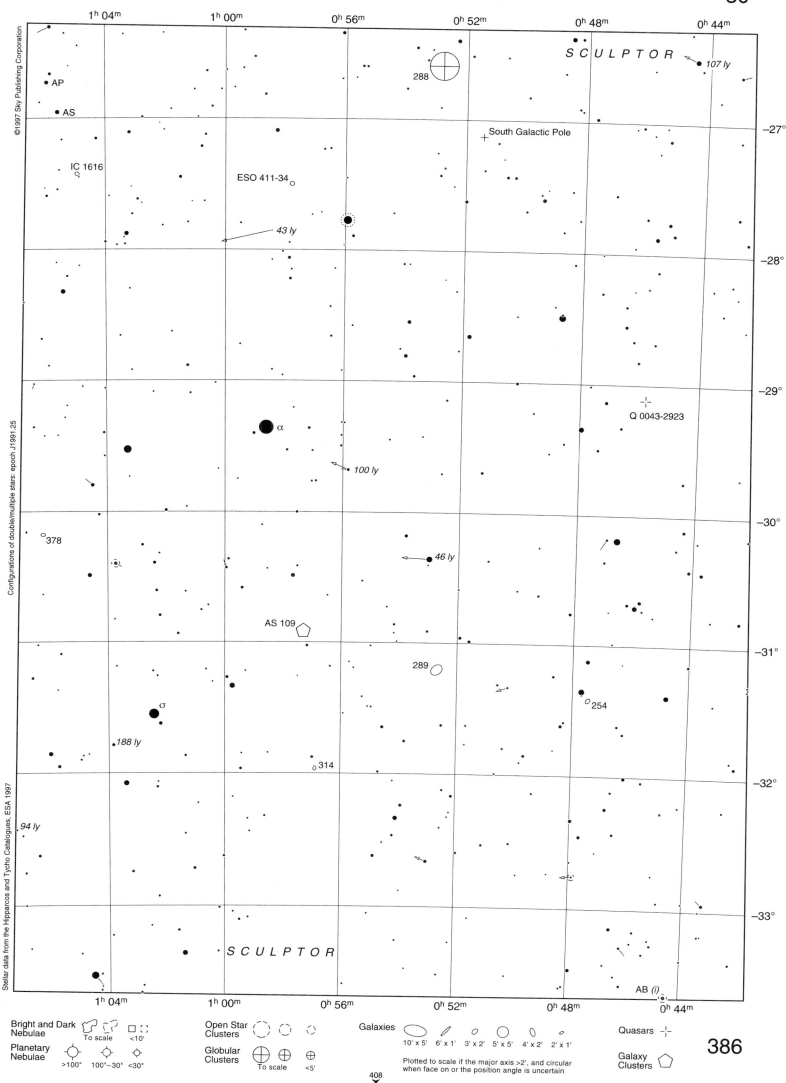

Configurations of double/multiple stars: epoch J1991.25

Stellar data from the Hipparcos and Tycho Catalogues, ESA 1997

S C U L P T O R

107 ly

South Galactic Pole

288

AP

AS

IC 1616

ESO 411-34

43 ly

−27°

−28°

α

100 ly

Q 0043-2923

−29°

378

46 ly

−30°

AS 109

289

254

−31°

σ

188 ly

314

−32°

94 ly

−33°

S C U L P T O R

AB (i)

Bright and Dark
Nebulae
To scale   <10'

Planetary
Nebulae
>100"   100"-30"   <30"

Open Star
Clusters

Globular
Clusters
To scale   <5'

Galaxies
10' x 5'   6' x 1'   3' x 2'   5' x 5'   4' x 2'   2' x 1'

Plotted to scale if the major axis >2', and circular
when face on or the position angle is uncertain

Quasars

Galaxy
Clusters

408

365

0h 44m 0h 40m 0h 36m 0h 32m 0h 28m 0h 24m

©1997 Sky Publishing Corporation

107 ly

132 ly

199 ly

S C U L P T O R

59 ly   73 ly

−27°

171 ly

150

−28°

182 ly

174

−29°

Reference system: ICRS (consistent with equinox J2000.0)

188 ly

−30°

AA (i)

160 ly

−31°

AV

59 ly

148

Stellar data from the Hipparcos and Tycho Catalogues, ESA 1997

−32°

IC 1554

150 ly

101

168 ly

η   (i)

AS 41

134   131

73 ly

S C U L P T O R

AB (i)   65 ly

115

0h 44m 0h 40m 0h 36m 0h 32m 0h 28m 0h 24m 0h 20m

387

Stellar Magnitudes (V)

≤2   3   4   5   6   7   8   9   10   11

Variable-Star Amplitudes and Types

<0.1 mag   0.1 – 1.0   ≥1.0 mag

(e) Eclipsing
(c) Cepheid
(m) Mira
... etc.

Fast-Moving Stars

Proper motion in 1000 years

Double-Star Separations

0.3"   3"   30"

409

MILLENNIUM STAR ATLAS

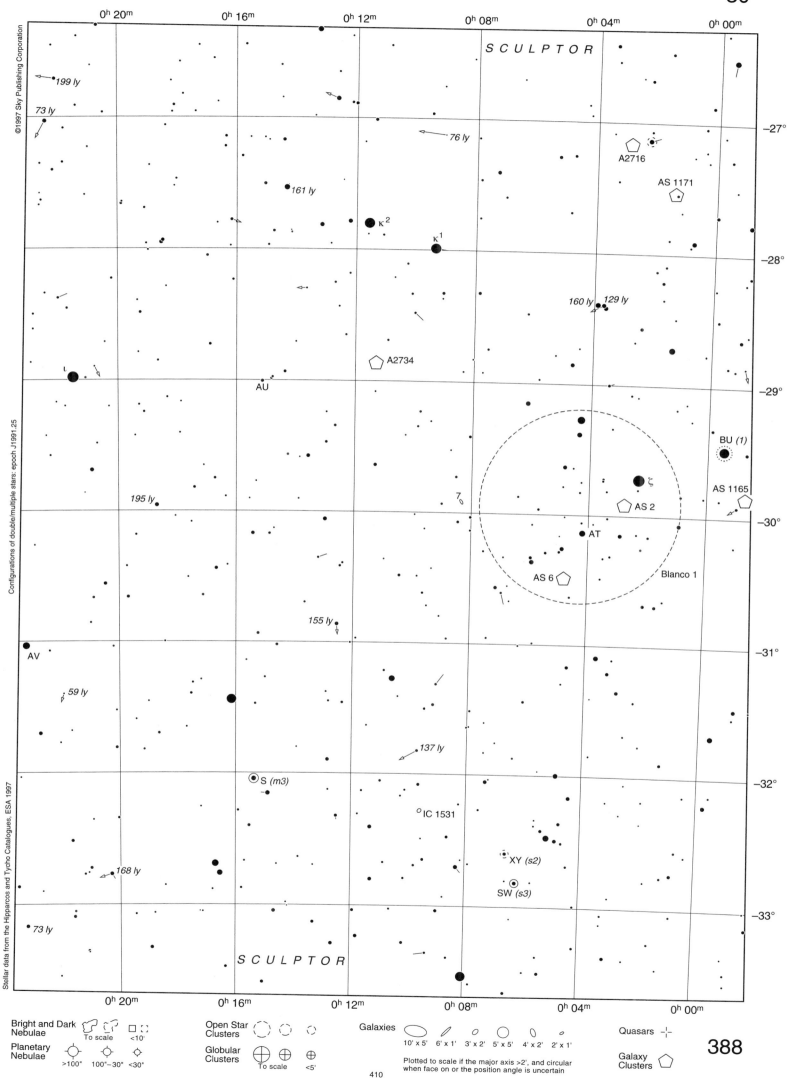

S C U L P T O R

0h 20m   0h 16m   0h 12m   0h 08m   0h 04m   0h 00m

199 ly

73 ly

-27°

76 ly

A2716

AS 1171

161 ly

κ^2

κ^1

-28°

160 ly   129 ly

A2734

AU

-29°

BU *(1)*

195 ly

ζ

AS 1165

7

AS 2

-30°

AT

AS 6   Blanco 1

155 ly

AV   -31°

59 ly

137 ly

S *(m3)*   -32°

IC 1531

XY *(s2)*

168 ly

SW *(s3)*

73 ly   -33°

S C U L P T O R

0h 20m   0h 16m   0h 12m   0h 08m   0h 04m   0h 00m

Bright and Dark Nebulae
To scale   <10'

Planetary Nebulae
>100"   100"–30"   <30"

Open Star Clusters

Globular Clusters
To scale   <5'

Galaxies
10' x 5'   6' x 1'   3' x 2'   5' x 5'   4' x 2'   2' x 1'

Plotted to scale if the major axis >2', and circular when face on or the position angle is uncertain

Quasars

Galaxy Clusters

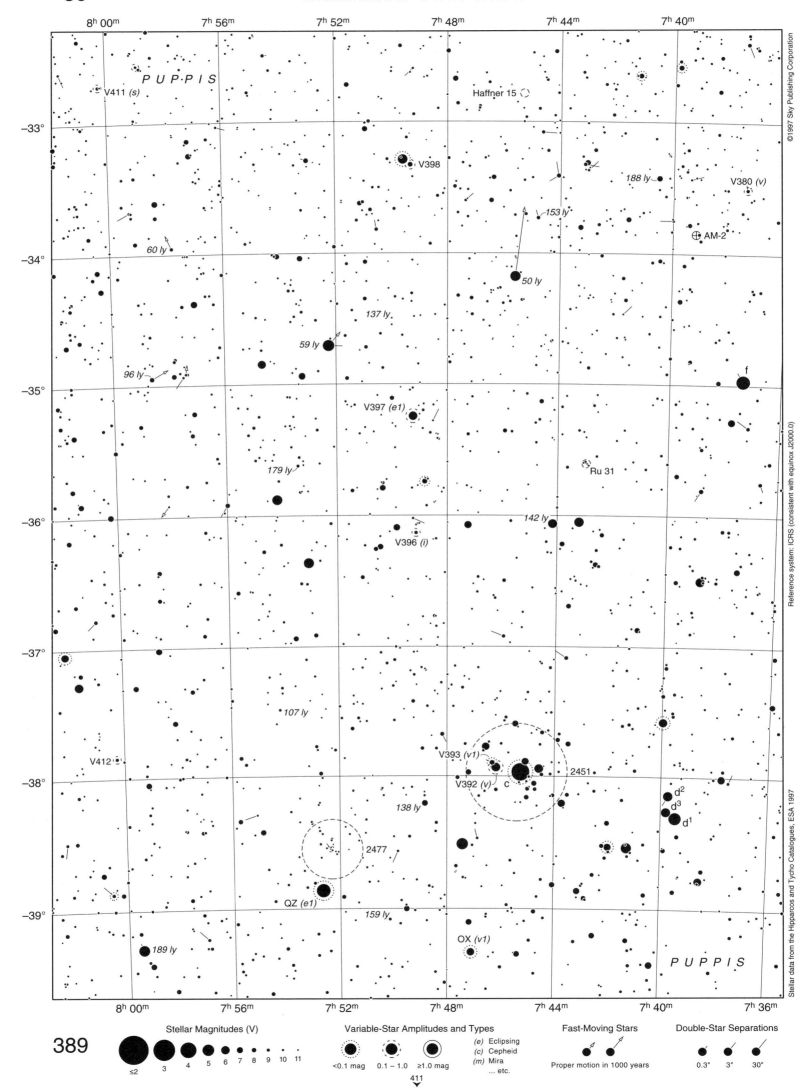

©1997 Sky Publishing Corporation

Reference system: ICRS (consistent with equinox J2000.0)

Stellar data from the Hipparcos and Tycho Catalogues, ESA 1997

Stellar Magnitudes (V)

≤2 3 4 5 6 7 8 9 10 11

Variable-Star Amplitudes and Types

<0.1 mag   0.1 − 1.0   ≥1.0 mag

(e) Eclipsing
(c) Cepheid
(m) Mira
... etc.

Fast-Moving Stars

Proper motion in 1000 years

Double-Star Separations

0.3"   3"   30"

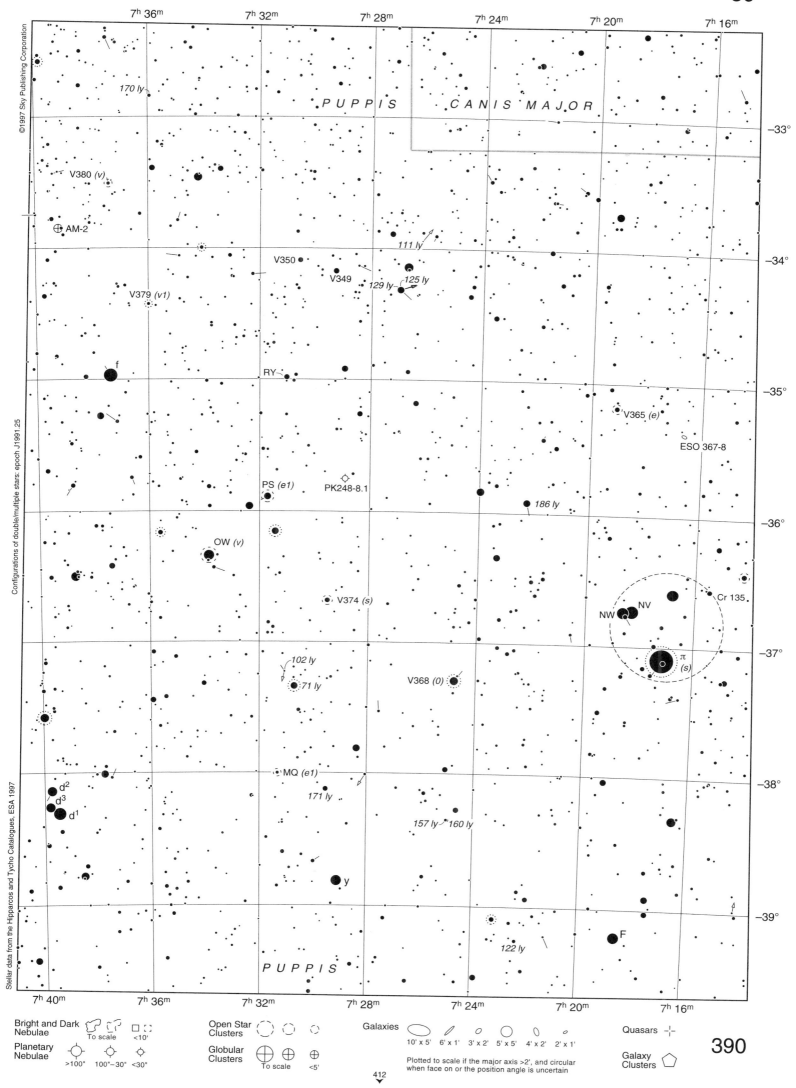

P U P P I S   C A N I S   M A J O R

170 ly

V380 (v)

AM-2

111 ly

V350

V349   129 ly   125 ly

V379 (v1)

f

RY

V365 (e)

ESO 367-8

PS (e1)   PK248-8.1

186 ly

OW (v)

V374 (s)

Cr 135

NW   NV

π (s)

102 ly

71 ly   V368 (0)

MQ (e1)

171 ly

d²
d³
d¹

157 ly 160 ly

y

F

122 ly

P U P P I S

Bright and Dark Nebulae   To scale   <10'

Planetary Nebulae   >100" 100"−30" <30"

Open Star Clusters

Globular Clusters   To scale   <5'

Galaxies   10' x 5' 6' x 1' 3' x 2' 5' x 5' 4' x 2' 2' x 1'

Plotted to scale if the major axis >2', and circular when face on or the position angle is uncertain

Quasars

Galaxy Clusters

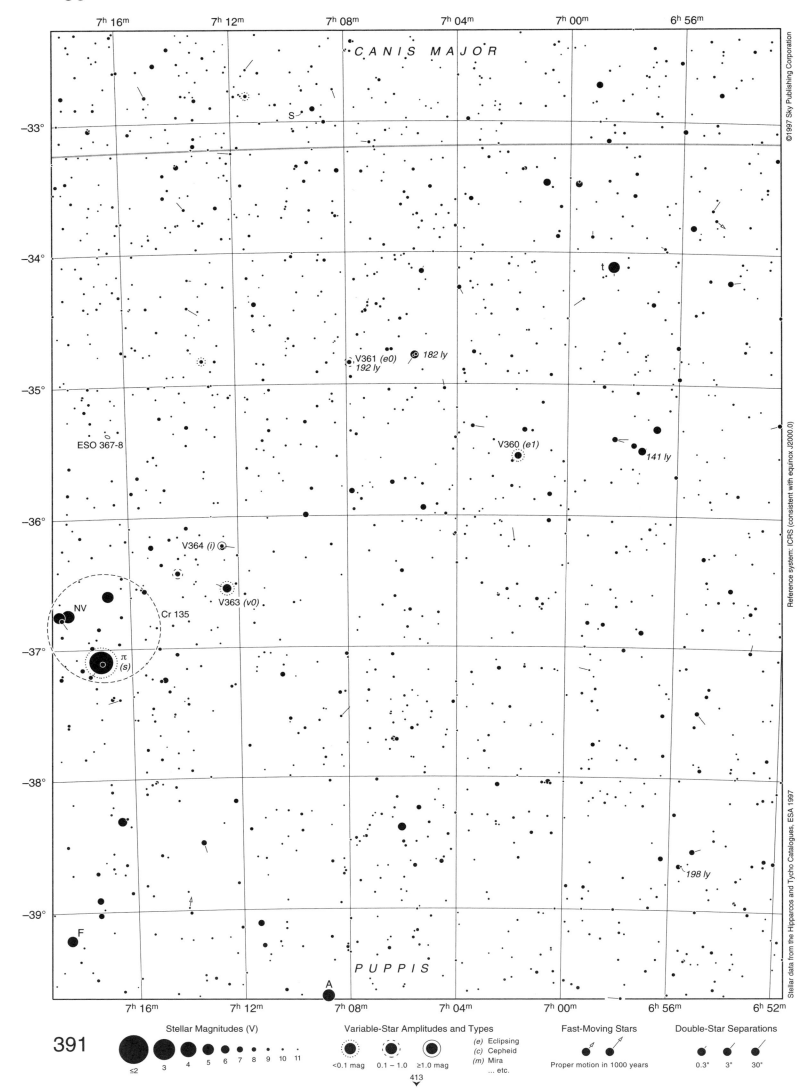

CANIS MAJOR

S

-33°

-34°

t

V361 (e0) 182 ly
192 ly

-35°

ESO 367-8

V360 (e1)

141 ly

-36°

V364 (i)

NV

V363 (v0)

Cr 135

π
(s)

-37°

198 ly

-38°

-39°

F

PUPPIS

A

© 1997 Sky Publishing Corporation

Reference system: ICRS (consistent with equinox J2000.0)

Stellar data from the Hipparcos and Tycho Catalogues, ESA 1997

391

Stellar Magnitudes (V)

≤2 3 4 5 6 7 8 9 10 11

Variable-Star Amplitudes and Types

<0.1 mag   0.1 – 1.0   ≥1.0 mag

(e) Eclipsing
(c) Cepheid
(m) Mira
... etc.

Fast-Moving Stars

Proper motion in 1000 years

Double-Star Separations

0.3"   3"   30"

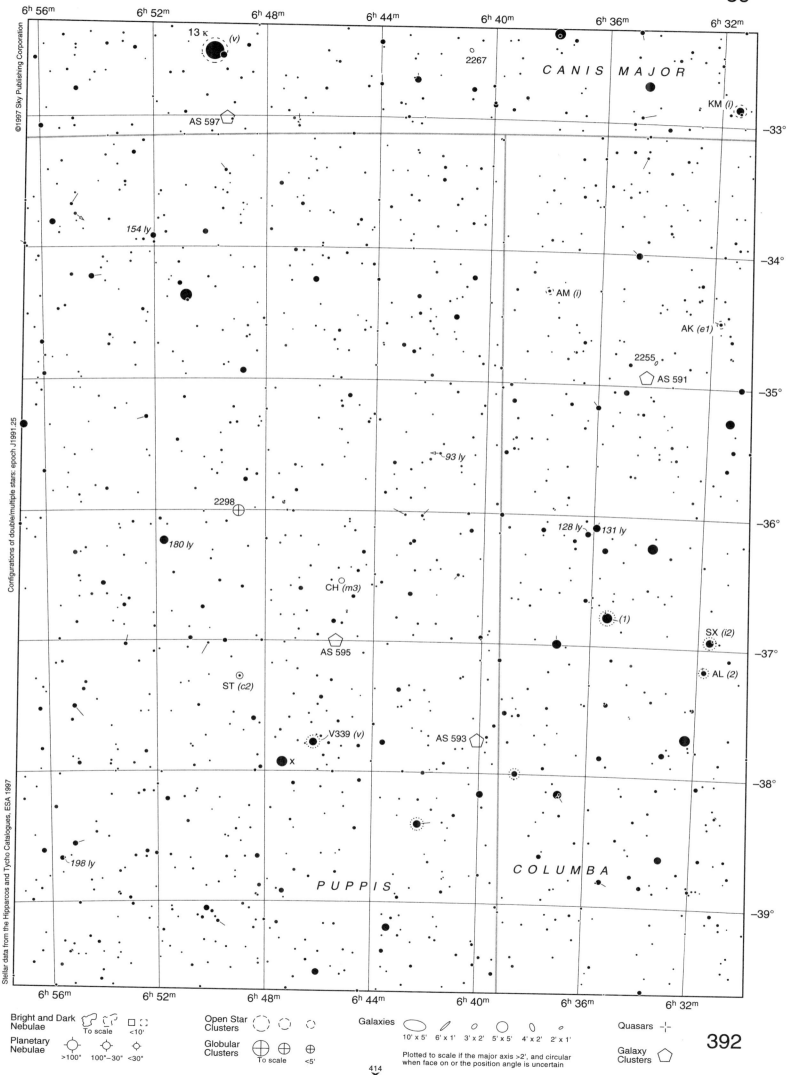

6ʰ 56ᵐ   6ʰ 52ᵐ   6ʰ 48ᵐ   6ʰ 44ᵐ   6ʰ 40ᵐ   6ʰ 36ᵐ   6ʰ 32ᵐ

13 κ (v)

CANIS MAJOR

AS 597

KM (i)

−33°

154 ly

AM (i)

AK (e1)

2255₀

AS 591

−34°

93 ly

2298

128 ly   131 ly

−35°

180 ly

CH (m3)

(1)

SX (i2)

−36°

AS 595

AL (2)

ST (c2)

V339 (v)

AS 593

x

−37°

−38°

198 ly

COLUMBA

PUPPIS

−39°

6ʰ 56ᵐ   6ʰ 52ᵐ   6ʰ 48ᵐ   6ʰ 44ᵐ   6ʰ 40ᵐ   6ʰ 36ᵐ   6ʰ 32ᵐ

2267

Bright and Dark Nebulae	To scale <10'	
Planetary Nebulae	>100" 100"–30" <30"	
Open Star Clusters		
Globular Clusters	To scale <5'	
Galaxies	10' x 5' 6' x 1' 3' x 2' 5' x 5' 4' x 2' 2' x 1'	
	Plotted to scale if the major axis >2', and circular when face on or the position angle is uncertain	
Quasars		
Galaxy Clusters		

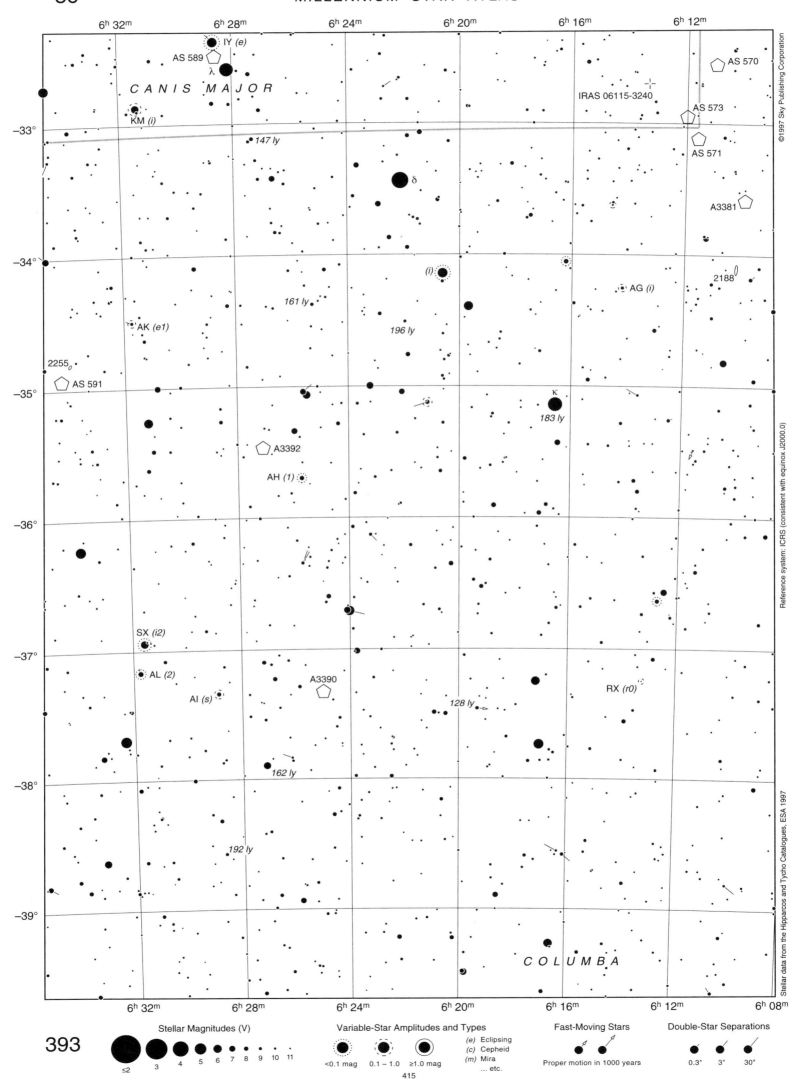

©1997 Sky Publishing Corporation

Reference system: ICRS (consistent with equinox J2000.0)

Stellar data from the Hipparcos and Tycho Catalogues, ESA 1997

CANIS MAJOR

COLUMBA

IY (e)
AS 589
λ
KM (i)
147 ly
δ
(i)
AK (e1)
161 ly
196 ly
2255₀
AS 591
κ
183 ly
A3392
AH (1)
AG (i)
2188
A3381
AS 570
AS 573
AS 571
IRAS 06115-3240
SX (i2)
AL (2)
AI (s)
A3390
128 ly
RX (r0)
162 ly
192 ly

Stellar Magnitudes (V)

≤2   3   4   5   6   7 8 9 10 11

Variable-Star Amplitudes and Types

<0.1 mag   0.1 – 1.0   ≥1.0 mag

(e) Eclipsing
(c) Cepheid
(m) Mira
... etc.

Fast-Moving Stars

Proper motion in 1000 years

Double-Star Separations

0.3"   3"   30"

415

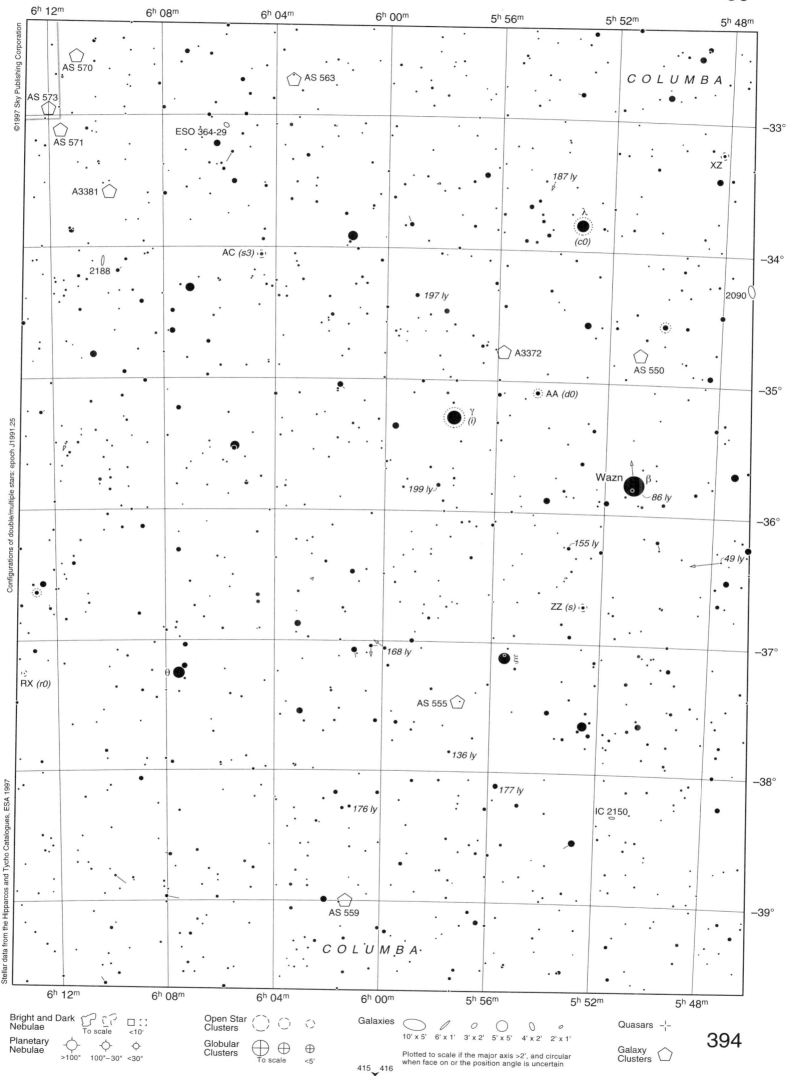

Configurations of double/multiple stars: epoch J1991.25

Stellar data from the Hipparcos and Tycho Catalogues, ESA 1997

COLUMBA

AS 570
AS 573
AS 563
AS 571
ESO 364-29
A3381
XZ
187 ly
λ
(c0)
AC (s3)
2188
−33°
197 ly
A3372
2090
AS 550
−34°
γ
(i)
AA (d0)
Wazn
β
86 ly
−35°
199 ly
155 ly
49 ly
ZZ (s)
−36°
168 ly
ξ
RX (r0)
θ
AS 555
−37°
136 ly
177 ly
176 ly
IC 2150
−38°
AS 559
COLUMBA
−39°

6h 12m 6h 08m 6h 04m 6h 00m 5h 56m 5h 52m 5h 48m

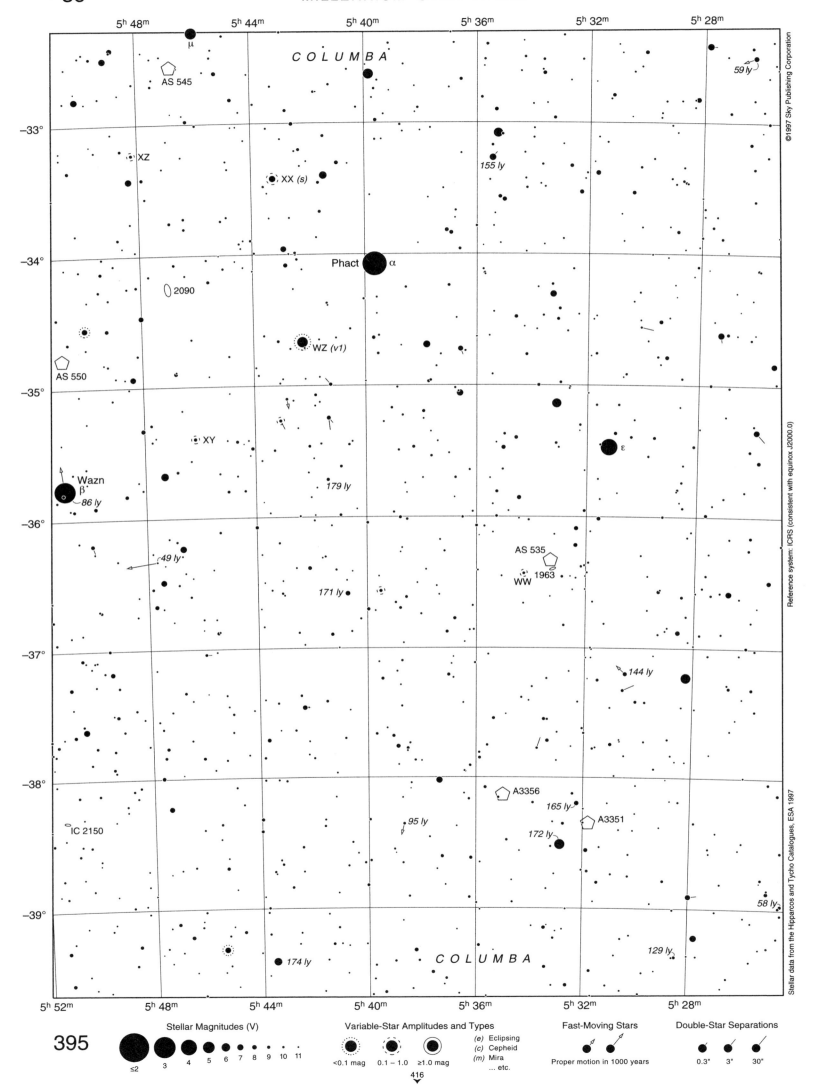

©1997 Sky Publishing Corporation

Reference system: ICRS (consistent with equinox J2000.0)

Stellar data from the Hipparcos and Tycho Catalogues, ESA 1997

COLUMBA

μ

AS 545

XZ

XX (s)

155 ly

Phact α

2090

WZ (v1)

AS 550

XY

Wazn
β
86 ly

ε

179 ly

AS 535
WW 1963

49 ly

171 ly

144 ly

A3356
165 ly
A3351

95 ly

172 ly

IC 2150

58 ly

129 ly

174 ly

COLUMBA

Stellar Magnitudes (V)

● ● ● ● ● ● • • · ·
≤2 3 4 5 6 7 8 9 10 11

Variable-Star Amplitudes and Types

⊙ ⊙ ◎
<0.1 mag   0.1 − 1.0   ≥1.0 mag

(e) Eclipsing
(c) Cepheid
(m) Mira
... etc.

Fast-Moving Stars

Proper motion in 1000 years

Double-Star Separations

0.3"   3"   30"

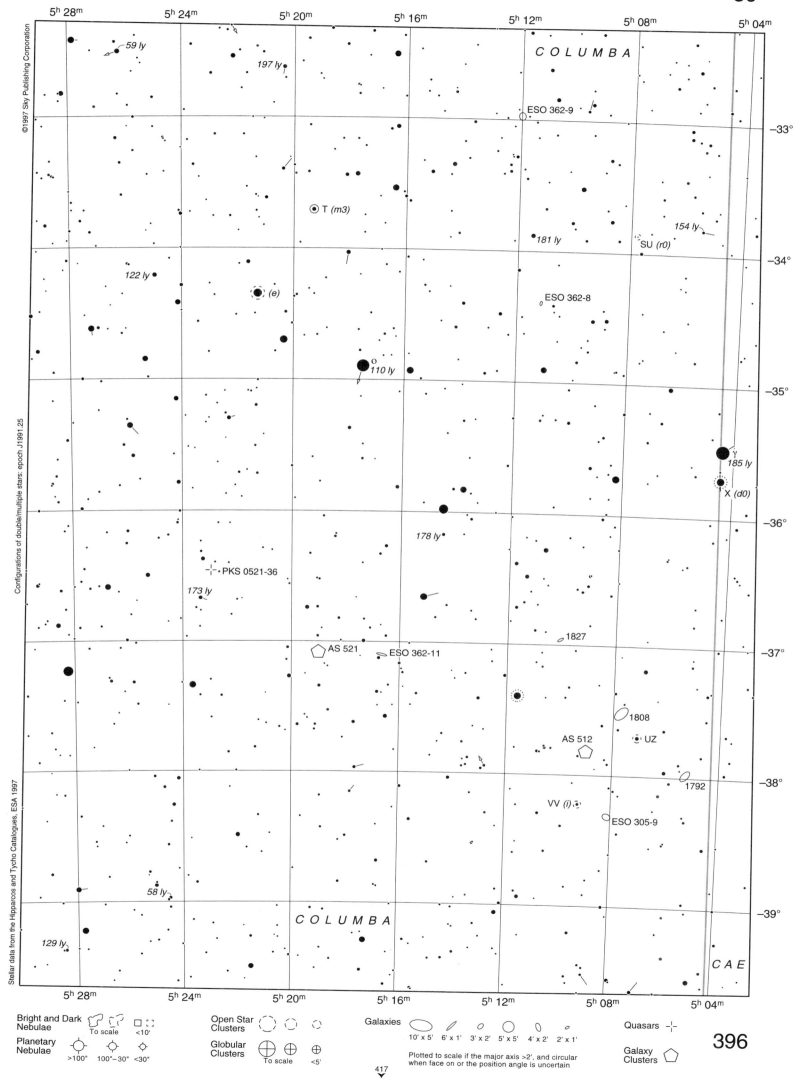

5ʰ 28ᵐ 5ʰ 24ᵐ 5ʰ 20ᵐ 5ʰ 16ᵐ 5ʰ 12ᵐ 5ʰ 08ᵐ 5ʰ 04ᵐ

C O L U M B A

59 ly

197 ly

ESO 362-9

−33°

T (m3)

181 ly

154 ly

SU (r0)

−34°

122 ly

(e)

ESO 362-8

O

110 ly

−35°

γ
185 ly

X (d0)

178 ly

−36°

PKS 0521-36

173 ly

1827

AS 521

ESO 362-11

−37°

1808

AS 512

UZ

1792

−38°

VV (i)

ESO 305-9

58 ly

−39°

C O L U M B A

129 ly

C A E

Legend

Bright and Dark Nebulae		Open Star Clusters		Galaxies		Quasars −⊢−
To scale	<10'			10' x 5' 6' x 1' 3' x 2' 5' x 5' 4' x 2' 2' x 1'		
Planetary Nebulae		Globular Clusters				Galaxy Clusters
>100" 100"−30" <30"		To scale <5'		Plotted to scale if the major axis >2', and circular when face on or the position angle is uncertain		

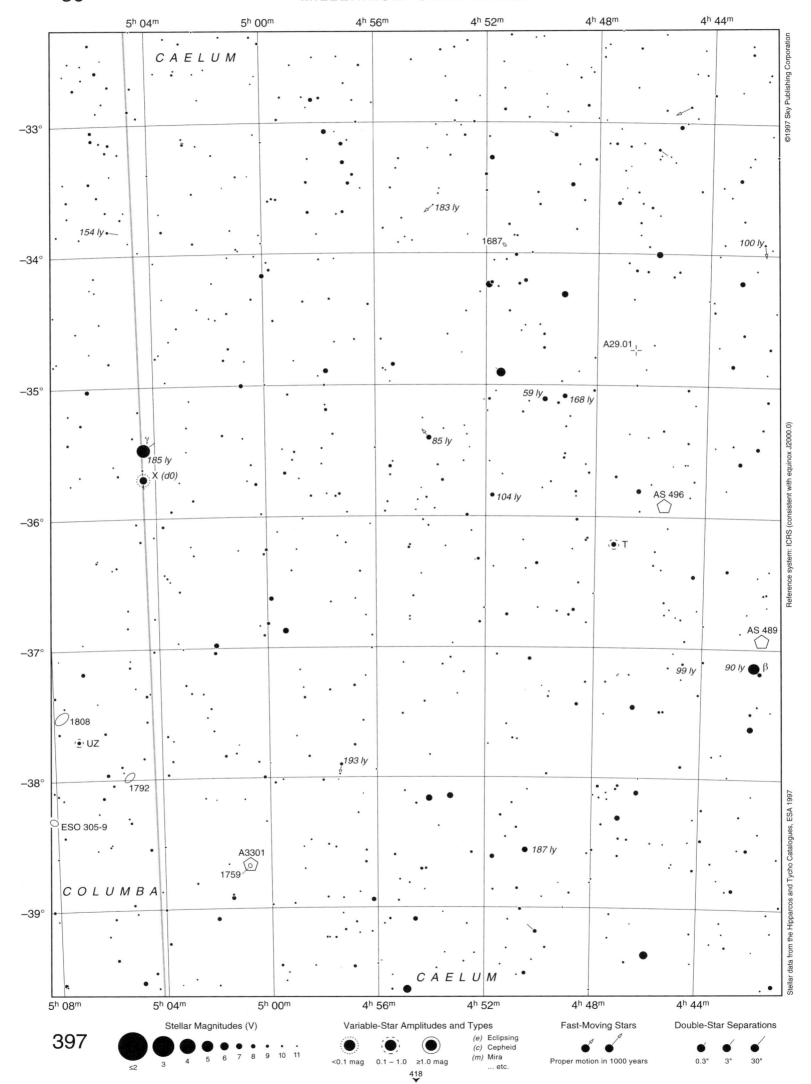

©1997 Sky Publishing Corporation

Reference system: ICRS (consistent with equinox J2000.0)

Stellar data from the Hipparcos and Tycho Catalogues, ESA 1997

CAELUM

154 ly

183 ly

1687

100 ly

A29.01

59 ly   168 ly

85 ly

γ
185 ly
X (d0)

104 ly

AS 496

T

AS 489

99 ly   90 ly β

1808

UZ

193 ly

1792

187 ly

ESO 305-9

A3301
1759

COLUMBA

CAELUM

Stellar Magnitudes (V)

≤2   3   4   5   6   7   8   9 10 11

Variable-Star Amplitudes and Types

<0.1 mag   0.1 – 1.0   ≥1.0 mag

(e) Eclipsing
(c) Cepheid
(m) Mira
... etc.

418

Fast-Moving Stars

Proper motion in 1000 years

Double-Star Separations

0.3"   3"   30"

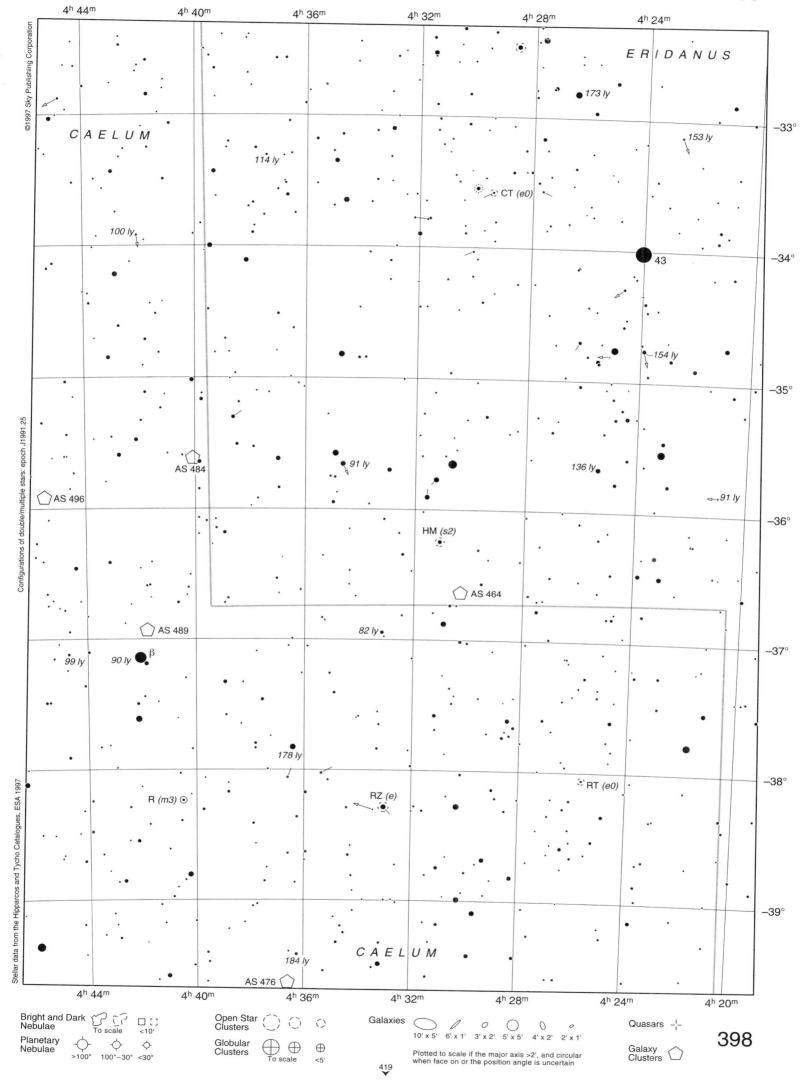

ERIDANUS

CAELUM

©1997 Sky Publishing Corporation

Configurations of double/multiple stars: epoch J1991.25

Stellar data from the Hipparcos and Tycho Catalogues, ESA 1997

173 ly

153 ly

−33°

114 ly

CT (e0)

100 ly

43

−34°

154 ly

−35°

AS 484

91 ly

136 ly

←·91 ly

AS 496

−36°

HM (s2)

AS 464

AS 489

82 ly

−37°

99 ly   90 ly   β

178 ly

RT (e0)

−38°

R (m3) ⊙

RZ (e)

−39°

CAELUM

184 ly

AS 476

Bright and Dark Nebulae
To scale   <10'

Planetary Nebulae
>100"   100"−30"   <30'

Open Star Clusters

Globular Clusters
To scale   <5'

Galaxies
10' x 5'   6' x 1'   3' x 2'   5' x 5'   4' x 2'   2' x 1'

Plotted to scale if the major axis >2', and circular when face on or the position angle is uncertain

Quasars

Galaxy Clusters

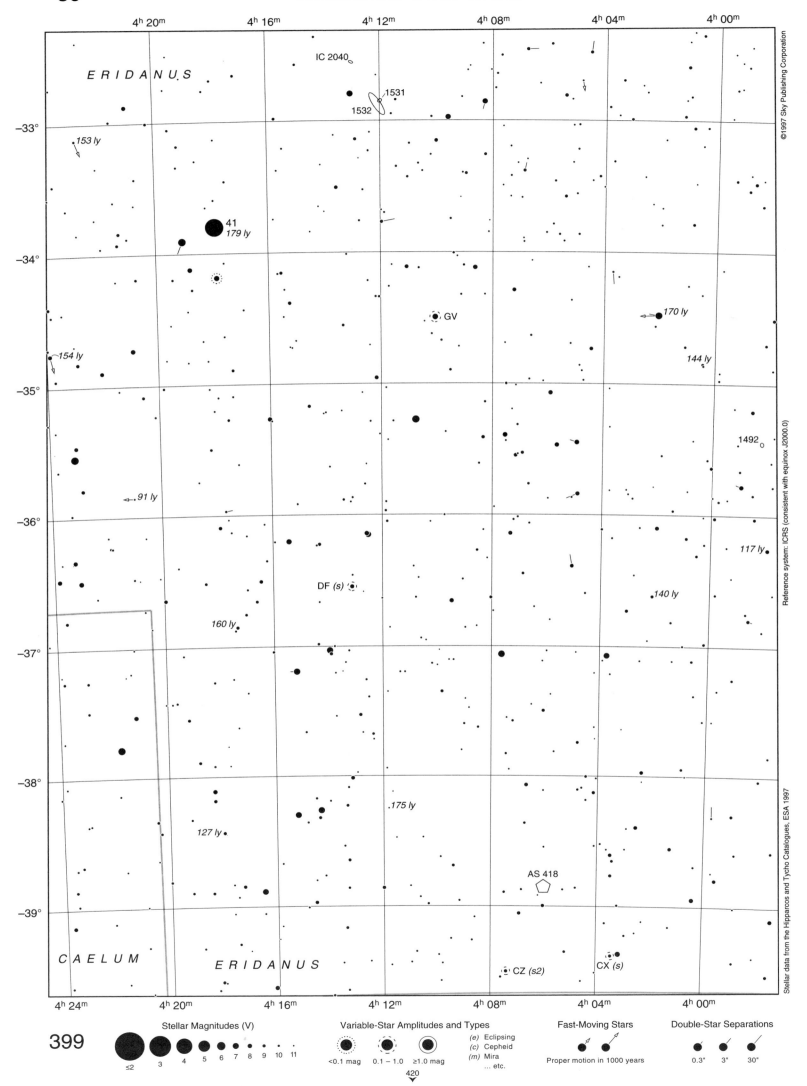

©1997 Sky Publishing Corporation

Reference system: ICRS (consistent with equinox J2000.0)

Stellar data from the Hipparcos and Tycho Catalogues, ESA 1997

E R I D A N U S

IC 2040

1531
1532

153 ly

41
179 ly

GV

170 ly

154 ly

144 ly

1492

91 ly

117 ly

DF (s)

140 ly

160 ly

175 ly

127 ly

AS 418

CAELUM

ERIDANUS

CZ (s2)

CX (s)

Stellar Magnitudes (V)

≤2 3 4 5 6 7 8 9 10 11

Variable-Star Amplitudes and Types

<0.1 mag   0.1 – 1.0   ≥1.0 mag

(e) Eclipsing
(c) Cepheid
(m) Mira
... etc.

Fast-Moving Stars

Proper motion in 1000 years

Double-Star Separations

0.3"   3"   30"

420

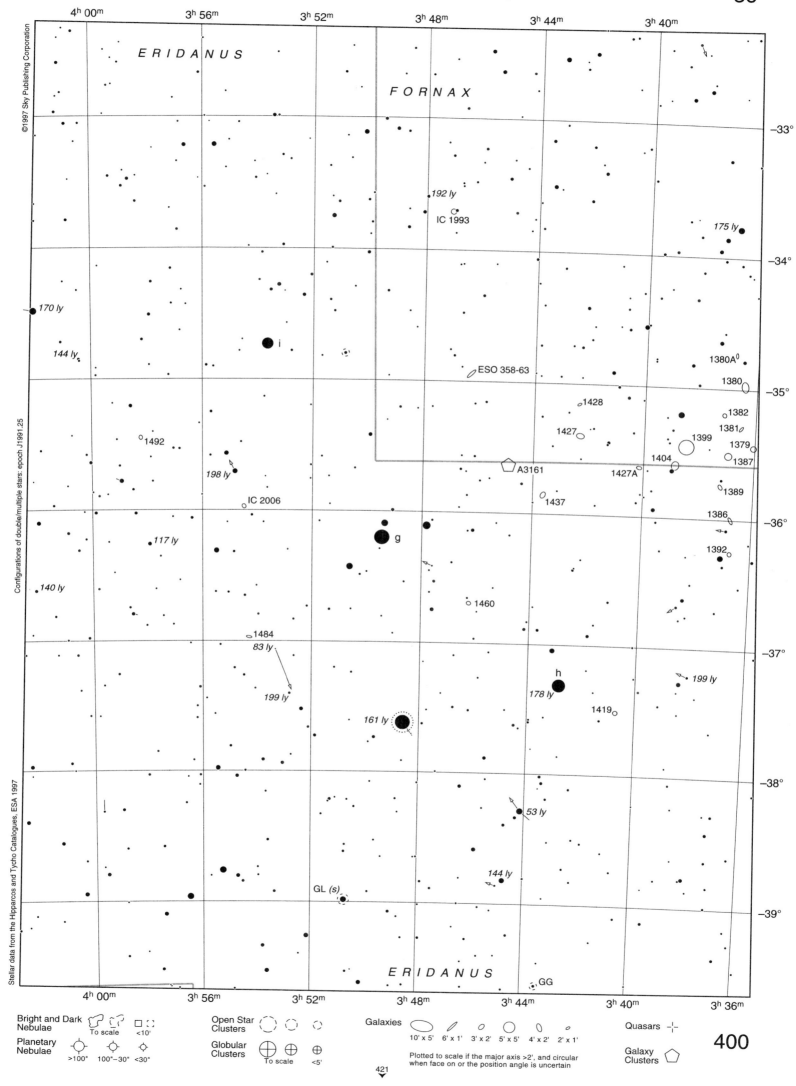

ERIDANUS

FORNAX

192 ly

IC 1993

175 ly

170 ly

144 ly

i

ESO 358-63

1380A⁰

1380

1428

1382

1492

1427

1381

1399

198 ly

1379

1404

1387

IC 2006

A3161

1427A

1389

1437

117 ly

1386

g

1392

140 ly

1460

1484

83 ly

h

199 ly

199 ly

178 ly

1419

161 ly

53 ly

144 ly

GL (s)

ERIDANUS

GG

Bright and Dark Nebulae			Open Star Clusters		Galaxies						Quasars
To scale		<10'	To scale	<10'	10' x 5'	6' x 1'	3' x 2'	5' x 5'	4' x 2'	2' x 1'	

Planetary Nebulae

>100"   100"−30"   <30"

Globular Clusters

To scale   <5'

Plotted to scale if the major axis >2', and circular when face on or the position angle is uncertain

Galaxy Clusters

400

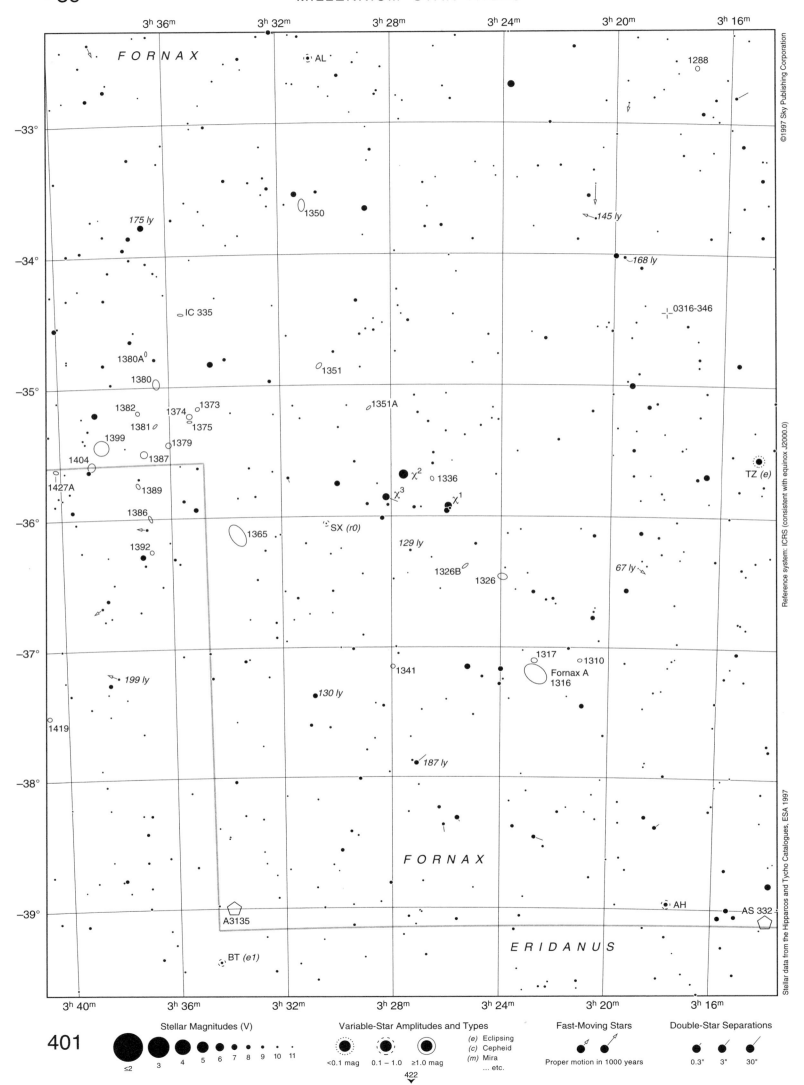

FORNAX

1288

AL

1350

175 ly

145 ly

168 ly

−33°

−34°

IC 335

0316-346

1380A

1380

1351

1382
1381
1374
1373
1375

1399

1351A

−35°

1404

1379
1387

TZ (e)

1427A

1389

χ² 1336

χ³

χ¹

1386

SX (r0)

129 ly

−36°

1365

1392

1326B 1326

67 ly

1317 1310

−37°

1341

Fornax A
1316

199 ly

130 ly

1419

187 ly

−38°

FORNAX

AH

AS 332

A3135

−39°

ERIDANUS

BT (e1)

3ʰ 40ᵐ   3ʰ 36ᵐ   3ʰ 32ᵐ   3ʰ 28ᵐ   3ʰ 24ᵐ   3ʰ 20ᵐ   3ʰ 16ᵐ

401

Stellar Magnitudes (V)

≤2   3   4   5   6   7   8   9   10 11

Variable-Star Amplitudes and Types

<0.1 mag   0.1 – 1.0   ≥1.0 mag

(e) Eclipsing
(c) Cepheid
(m) Mira
... etc.

422

Fast-Moving Stars

Proper motion in 1000 years

Double-Star Separations

0.3"   3"   30"

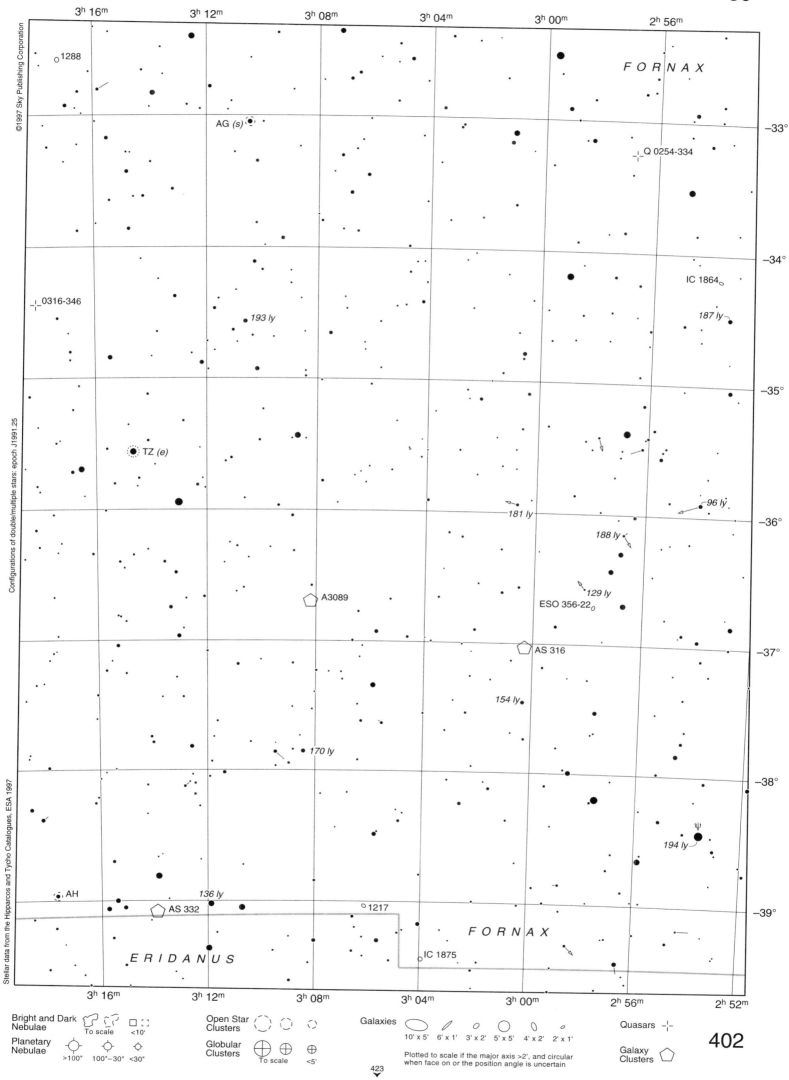

FORNAX

1288

AG (s)

Q 0254-334

0316-346

IC 1864

193 ly

187 ly

TZ (e)

96 ly

181 ly

188 ly

129 ly

A3089

ESO 356-22

AS 316

154 ly

170 ly

ψ

194 ly

AH

136 ly

AS 332

1217

FORNAX

ERIDANUS

IC 1875

Bright and Dark Nebulae

To scale <10'

Planetary Nebulae

>100" 100"−30" <30"

Open Star Clusters

Globular Clusters

To scale <5'

Galaxies

10' x 5' 6' x 1' 3' x 2' 5' x 5' 4' x 2' 2' x 1'

Plotted to scale if the major axis >2', and circular when face on or the position angle is uncertain

Quasars

Galaxy Clusters

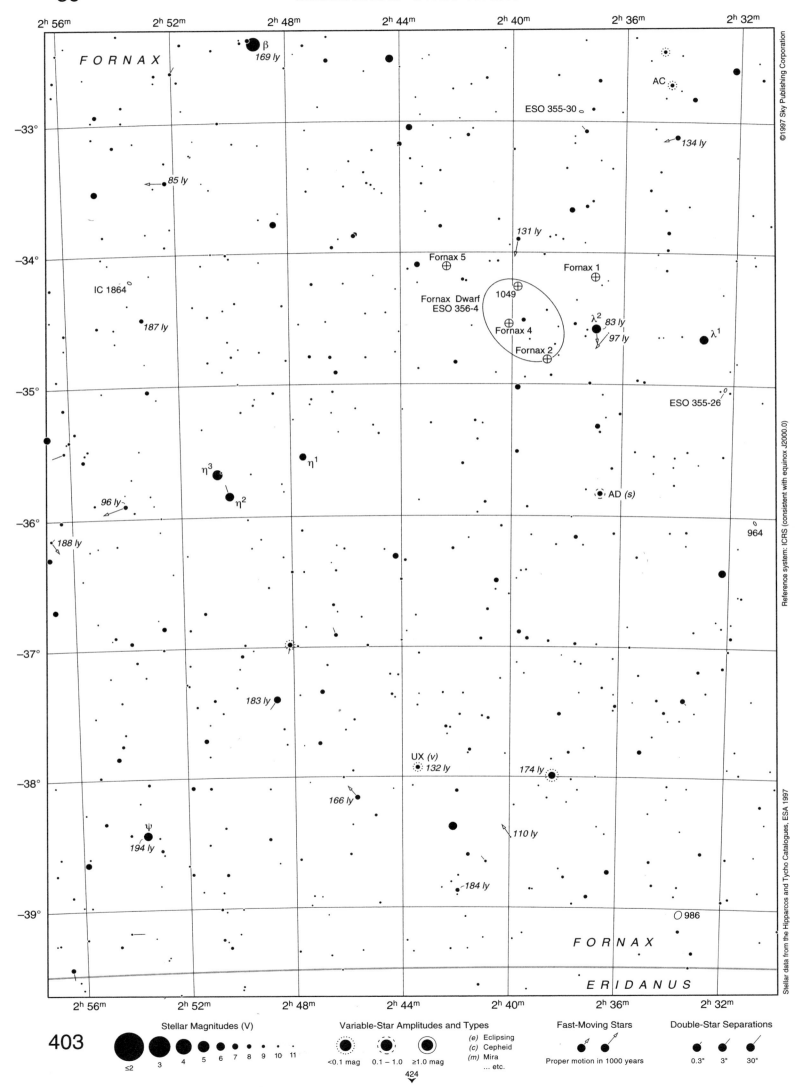

©1997 Sky Publishing Corporation

Reference system: ICRS (consistent with equinox J2000.0)

Stellar data from the Hipparcos and Tycho Catalogues, ESA 1997

FORNAX

β
169 ly

AC

ESO 355-30

134 ly

85 ly

131 ly

Fornax 5

Fornax 1

IC 1864

1049

187 ly

Fornax Dwarf
ESO 356-4

λ² 83 ly

Fornax 4

97 ly

λ¹

Fornax 2

ESO 355-26

η³

η¹

η²

AD (s)

96 ly

964

188 ly

183 ly

UX (v)
132 ly

174 ly

166 ly

110 ly

ψ

194 ly

184 ly

986

FORNAX

ERIDANUS

403

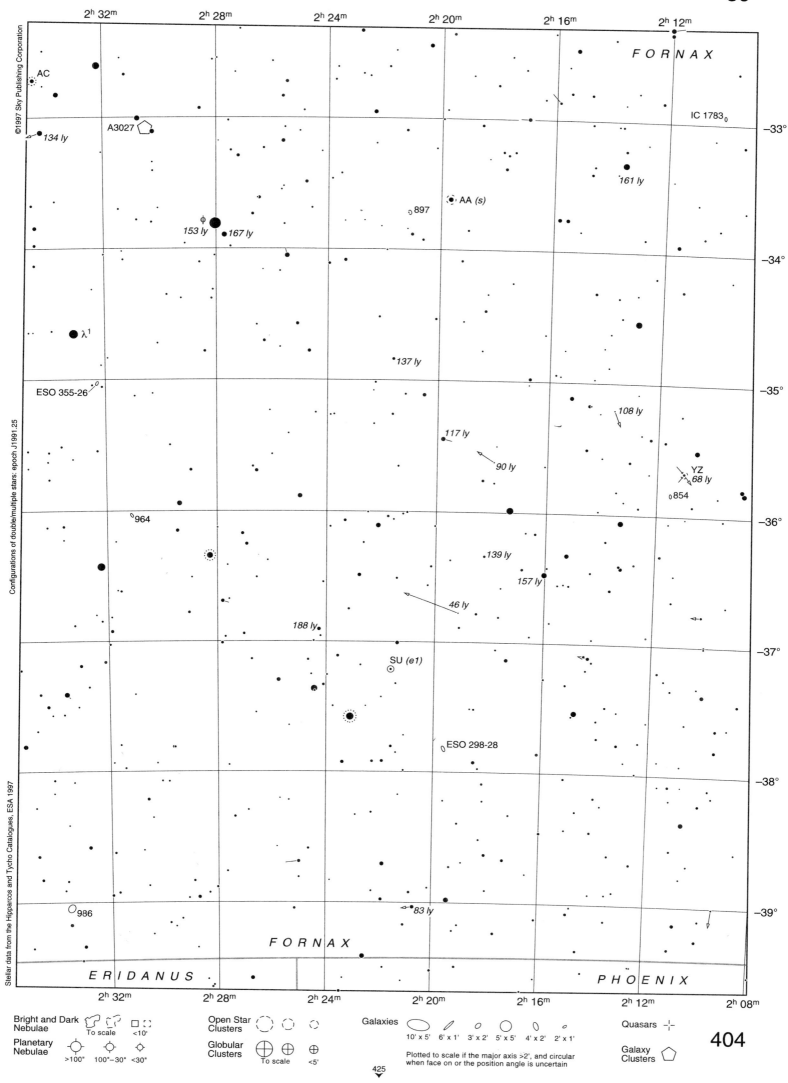

F O R N A X

IC 1783₀

AC

A3027

← 134 ly

φ
153 ly • 167 ly

161 ly

(•) AA (s)
₀ 897

λ¹

137 ly

−33°

−34°

ESO 355-26 ₀

108 ly

117 ly

90 ly

YZ
68 ly
₀ 854

−35°

₀ 964

139 ly

157 ly

46 ly

188 ly

46 ly

SU (e1)

ESO 298-28

−36°

−37°

−38°

₀ 986

← 83 ly

−39°

F O R N A X

E R I D A N U S

P H O E N I X

Bright and Dark Nebulae	To scale	<10'
Planetary Nebulae	>100" 100"−30"	<30"
Open Star Clusters		
Globular Clusters	To scale	<5'
Galaxies	10' x 5' 6' x 1' 3' x 2' 5' x 5' 4' x 2' 2' x 1'	

Plotted to scale if the major axis >2', and circular
when face on or the position angle is uncertain

Quasars

Galaxy Clusters

404

425

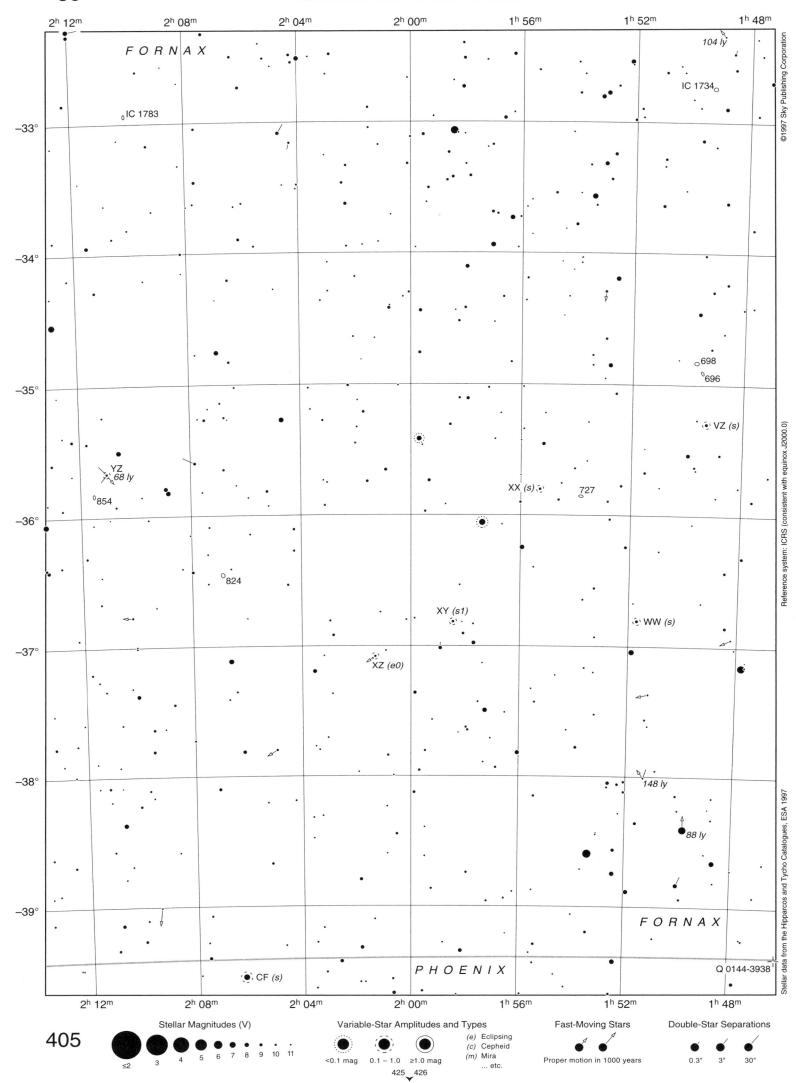

©1997 Sky Publishing Corporation

Reference system: ICRS (consistent with equinox J2000.0)

Stellar data from the Hipparcos and Tycho Catalogues, ESA 1997

FORNAX

IC 1783

104 ly

IC 1734

698
696

VZ (s)

YZ
68 ly

854

XX (s)   727

824

XY (s1)

WW (s)

XZ (e0)

148 ly

88 ly

FORNAX

PHOENIX

Q 0144-3938

CF (s)

405

Stellar Magnitudes (V)

≤2 3 4 5 6 7 8 9 10 11

Variable-Star Amplitudes and Types

<0.1 mag   0.1 − 1.0   ≥1.0 mag

425 426

(e) Eclipsing
(c) Cepheid
(m) Mira
... etc.

Fast-Moving Stars

Proper motion in 1000 years

Double-Star Separations

0.3"   3"   30"

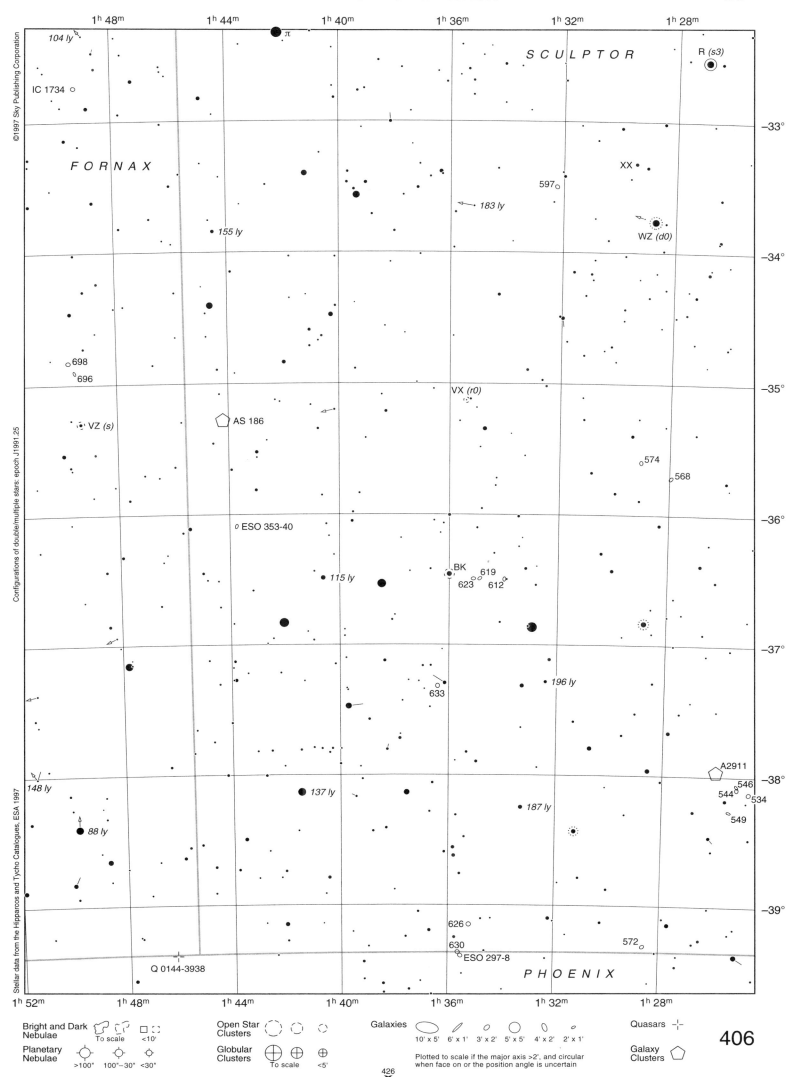

SCULPTOR

R (s3)

FORNAX

IC 1734

XX
597
183 ly
155 ly
WZ (d0)

698
696

VX (r0)
VZ (s)
AS 186
574
568

0 ESO 353-40

BK
619
115 ly
623
612

633
196 ly

A2911
546
148 ly
137 ly
544
534
88 ly
187 ly
549

626
630
572
ESO 297-8
Q 0144-3938
PHOENIX

Bright and Dark Nebulae
To scale
<10'

Planetary Nebulae
>100"
100"–30"
<30"

Open Star Clusters

Globular Clusters
To scale
<5'

Galaxies
10' x 5'
6' x 1'
3' x 2'
5' x 5'
4' x 2'
2' x 1'

Plotted to scale if the major axis >2', and circular when face on or the position angle is uncertain

Quasars

Galaxy Clusters

406

MILLENNIUM STAR ATLAS

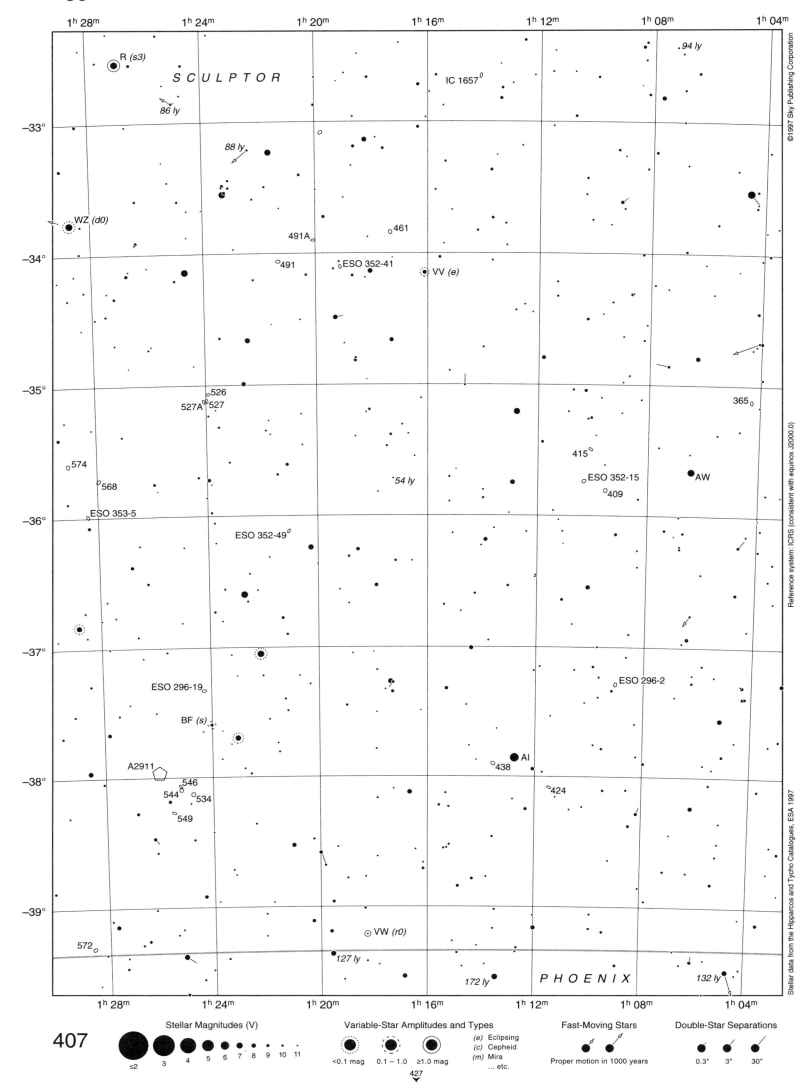

407

Stellar Magnitudes (V)
≤2 3 4 5 6 7 8 9 10 11

Variable-Star Amplitudes and Types
<0.1 mag   0.1 − 1.0   ≥1.0 mag

(e) Eclipsing
(c) Cepheid
(m) Mira
... etc.

Fast-Moving Stars
Proper motion in 1000 years

Double-Star Separations
0.3"   3"   30"

427

MILLENNIUM STAR ATLAS

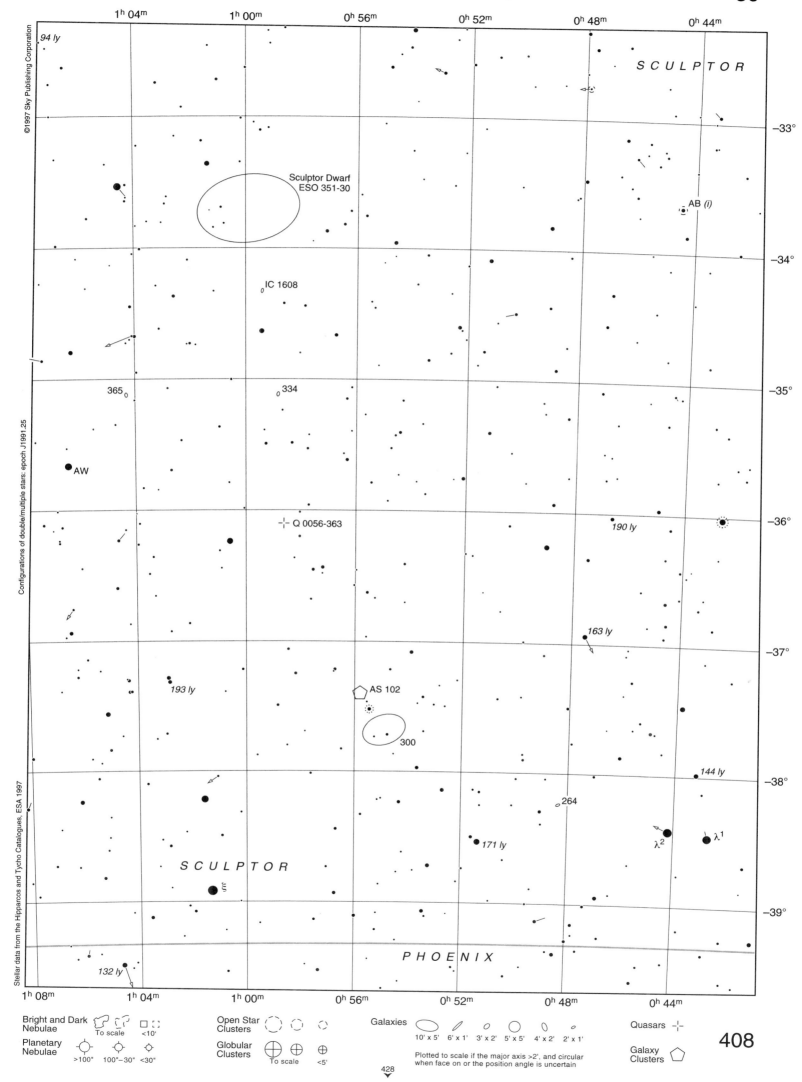

Configurations of double/multiple stars: epoch J1991.25

Stellar data from the Hipparcos and Tycho Catalogues, ESA 1997

S C U L P T O R

94 ly

Sculptor Dwarf
ESO 351-30

AB *(i)*

IC 1608

365₀

334

AW

Q 0056-363

190 ly

163 ly

193 ly

AS 102

300

144 ly

264

171 ly

λ²

λ¹

S C U L P T O R

ξ

P H O E N I X

132 ly

Bright and Dark Nebulae	To scale	□	<10'
Planetary Nebulae	>100" 100"−30" <30"		

Open Star Clusters		
Globular Clusters	To scale	<5'

Galaxies

10' x 5' 6' x 1' 3' x 2' 5' x 5' 4' x 2' 2' x 1'

Plotted to scale if the major axis >2', and circular
when face on or the position angle is uncertain

Quasars

Galaxy Clusters

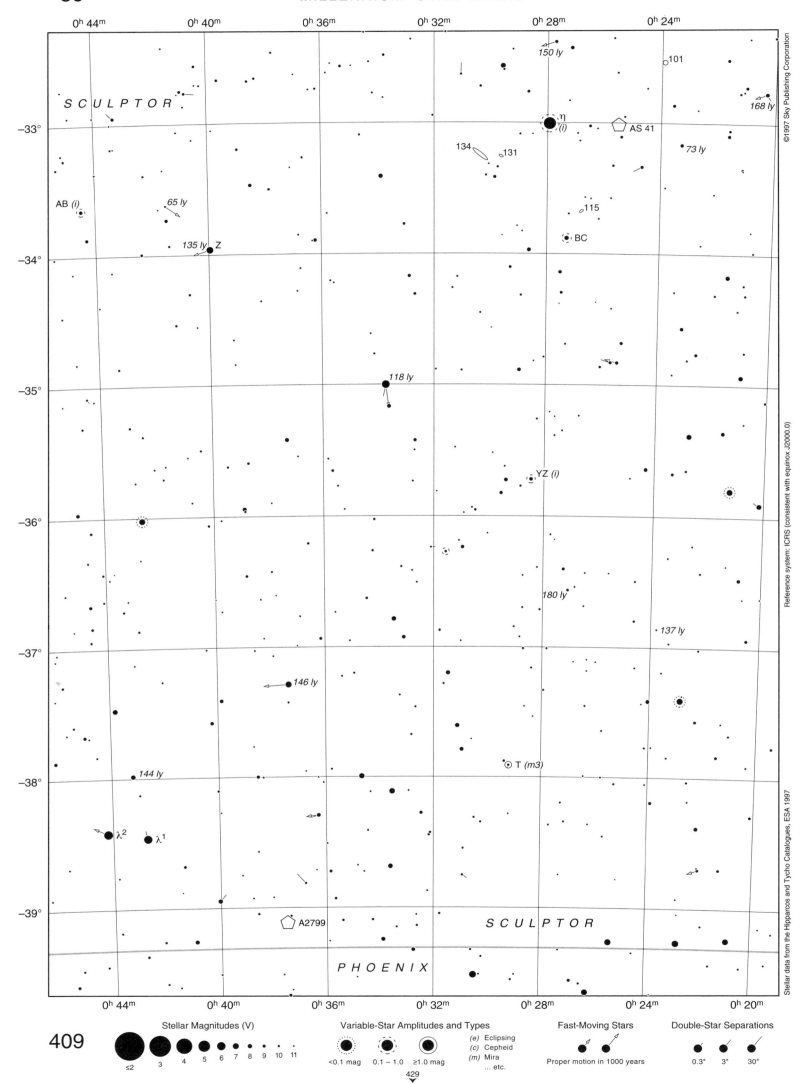

©1997 Sky Publishing Corporation

Reference system: ICRS (consistent with equinox J2000.0)

Stellar data from the Hipparcos and Tycho Catalogues, ESA 1997

Stellar Magnitudes (V)

≤2   3   4   5   6   7   8   9   10   11

Variable-Star Amplitudes and Types

<0.1 mag   0.1 − 1.0   ≥1.0 mag

(e) Eclipsing
(c) Cepheid
(m) Mira
... etc.

Fast-Moving Stars

Proper motion in 1000 years

Double-Star Separations

0.3"   3"   30"

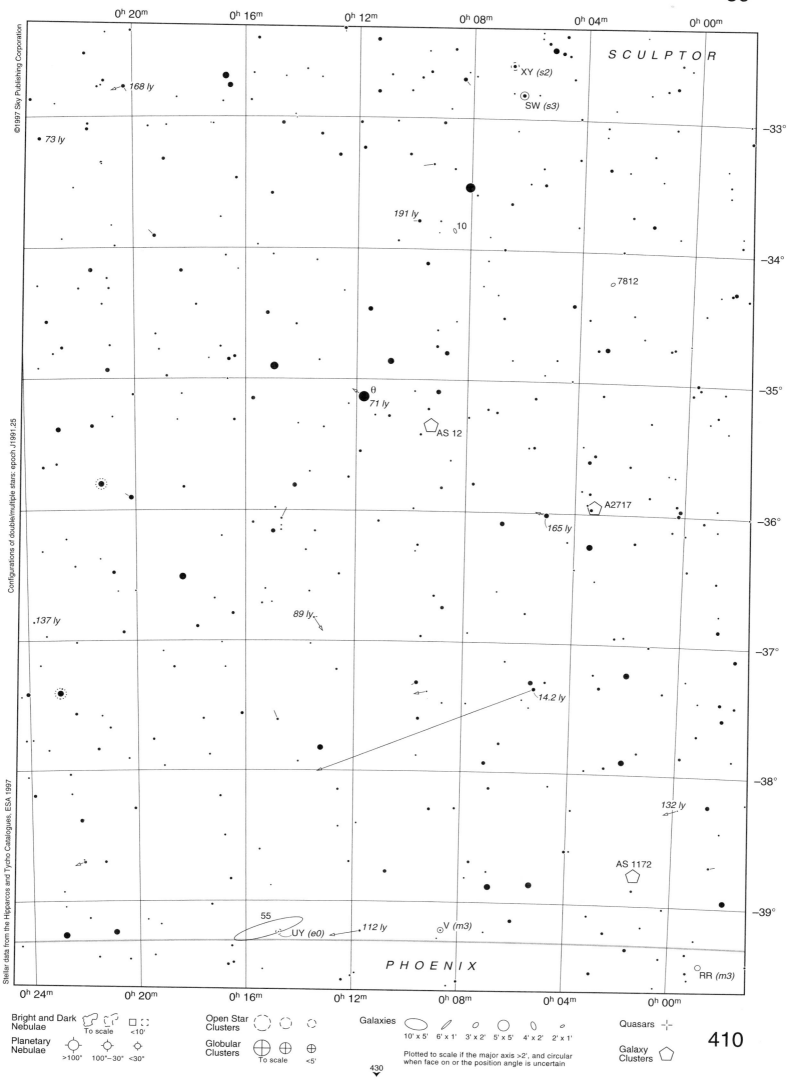
S C U L P T O R

XY (s2)

SW (s3)

168 ly

73 ly

−33°

191 ly

10

7812

−34°

θ

71 ly

AS 12

−35°

A2717

165 ly

−36°

137 ly

89 ly

14.2 ly

−37°

132 ly

AS 1172

−38°

55

UY (e0)   112 ly   V (m3)

−39°

P H O E N I X

RR (m3)

Bright and Dark Nebulae	Open Star Clusters	Galaxies	Quasars

To scale   <10'

To scale

Planetary Nebulae

>100" 100"−30" <30"

Globular Clusters

To scale   <5'

10' x 5'   6' x 1'   3' x 2'   5' x 5'   4' x 2'   2' x 1'

Plotted to scale if the major axis >2', and circular when face on or the position angle is uncertain

Galaxy Clusters

MILLENNIUM STAR ATLAS

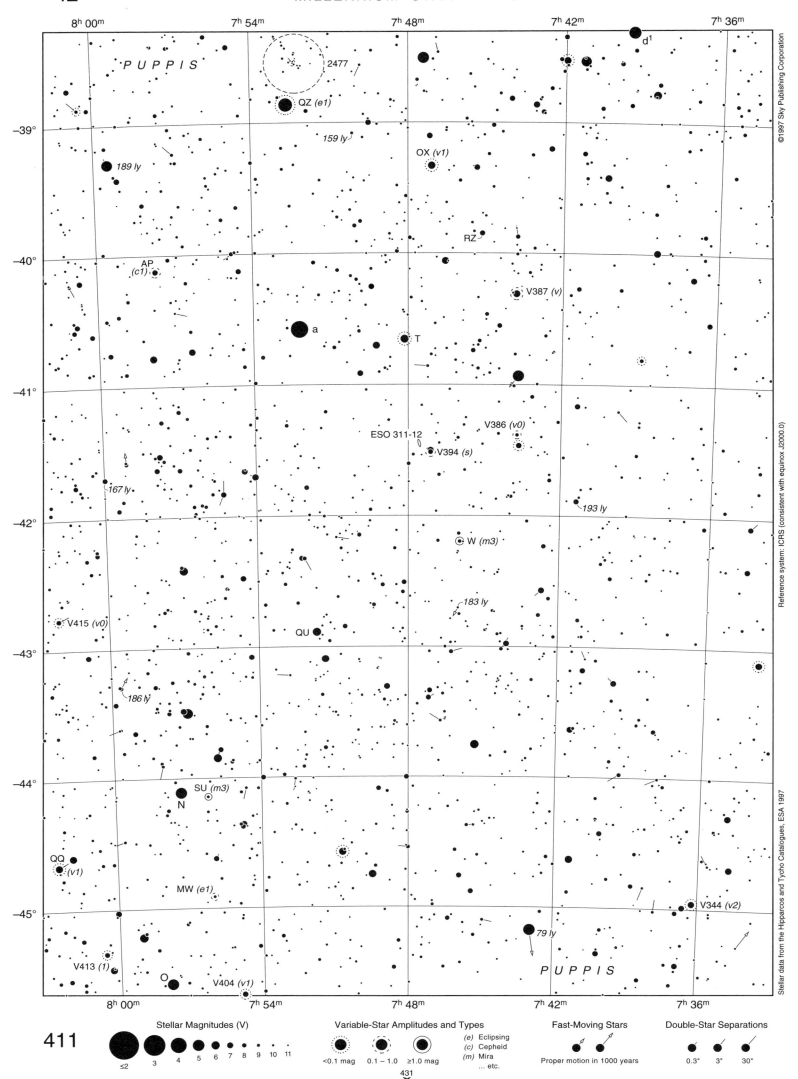

PUPPIS

2477

QZ (e1)

159 ly

189 ly

OX (v1)

RZ

−39°

AP
(c1)

−40°

V387 (v)

a

T

−41°

V386 (v0)

ESO 311-12

V394 (s)

167 ly

193 ly

−42°

W (m3)

183 ly

V415 (v0)

QU

−43°

186 ly

−44°

SU (m3)

N

79 ly

QQ

(v1)

MW (e1)

−45°

V344 (v2)

PUPPIS

V413 (1)

O

V404 (v1)

8ʰ 00ᵐ   7ʰ 54ᵐ   7ʰ 48ᵐ   7ʰ 42ᵐ   7ʰ 36ᵐ

d¹

©1997 Sky Publishing Corporation

Reference system: ICRS (consistent with equinox J2000.0)

Stellar data from the Hipparcos and Tycho Catalogues, ESA 1997

411

Stellar Magnitudes (V)

≤2   3   4   5   6   7   8   9   10   11

Variable-Star Amplitudes and Types

<0.1 mag   0.1 − 1.0   ≥1.0 mag

(e) Eclipsing
(c) Cepheid
(m) Mira
... etc.

Fast-Moving Stars

Proper motion in 1000 years

Double-Star Separations

0.3"   3"   30"

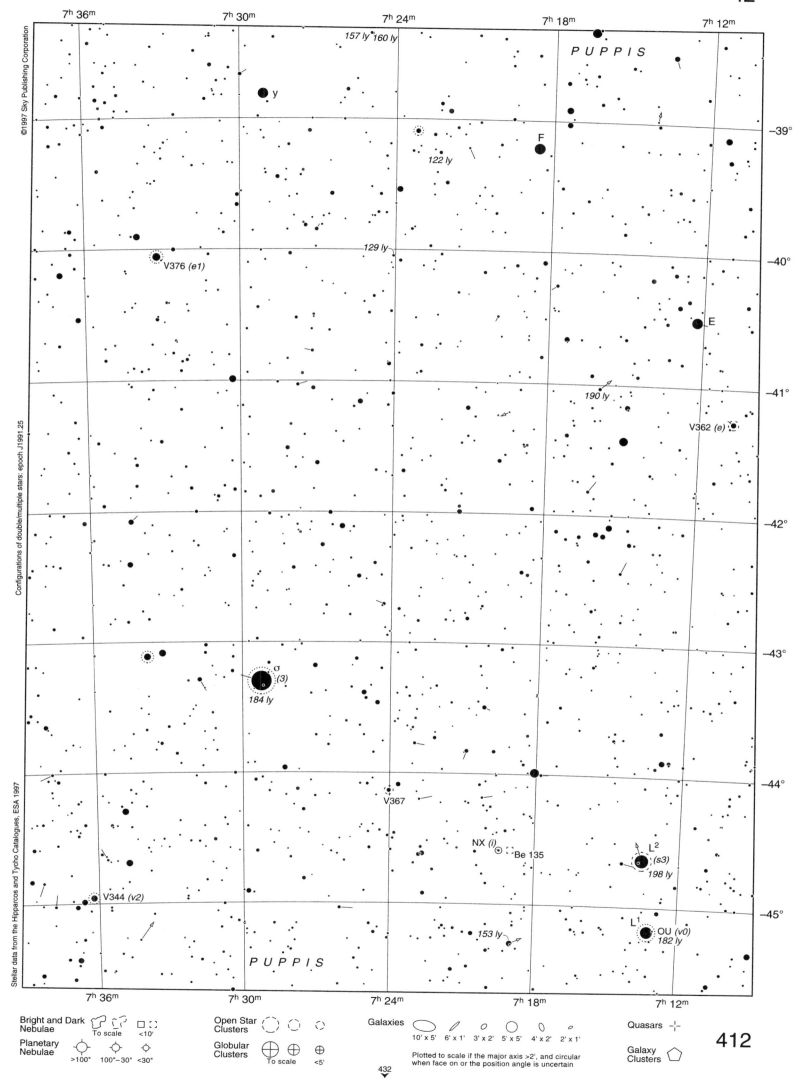

Configurations of double/multiple stars: epoch J1991.25

Stellar data from the Hipparcos and Tycho Catalogues, ESA 1997

PUPPIS

157 ly 160 ly

y

122 ly

F

129 ly

V376 (e1)

E

190 ly

V362 (e)

σ
(3)
184 ly

V367

NX (i)
Be 135

L²
(s3)
198 ly

V344 (v2)

153 ly

L¹
OU (v0)
182 ly

PUPPIS

Bright and Dark Nebulae	To scale	<10'	
Planetary Nebulae	>100" 100"–30" <30"		
Open Star Clusters			
Globular Clusters	To scale <5'		
Galaxies	10' x 5' 6' x 1' 3' x 2' 5' x 5' 4' x 2' 2' x 1'		
Quasars			
Galaxy Clusters			

Plotted to scale if the major axis >2', and circular
when face on or the position angle is uncertain

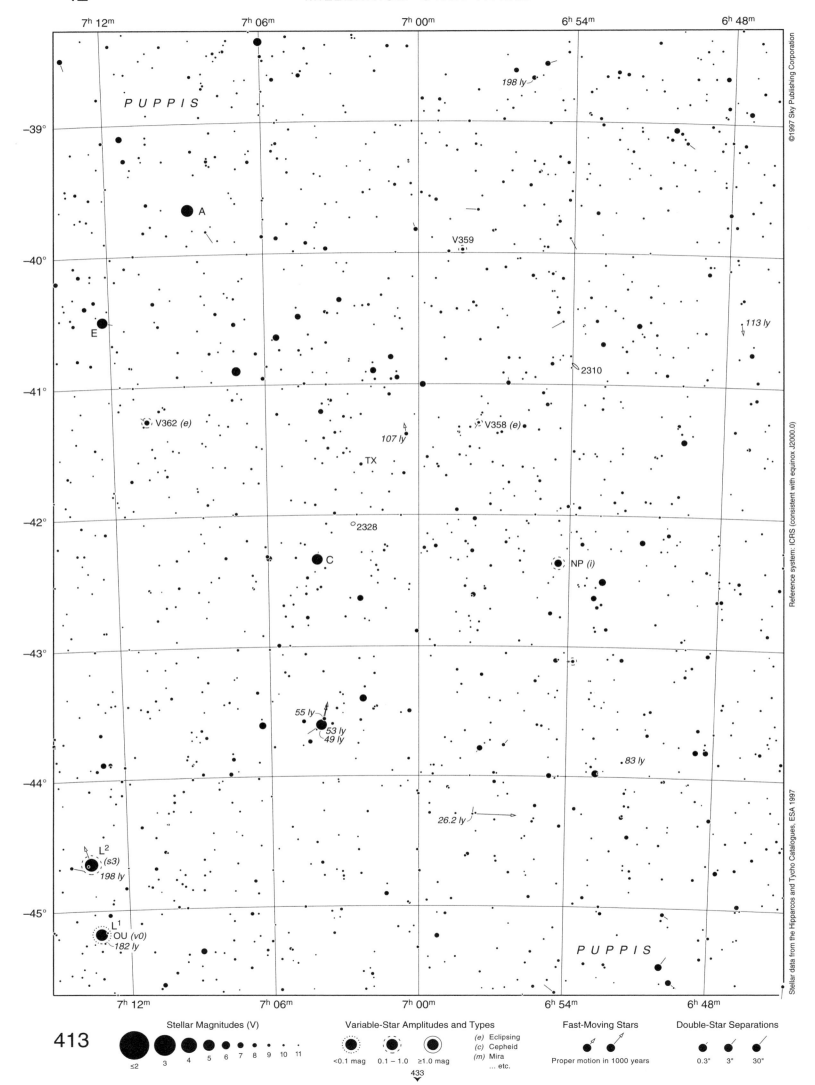

© 1997 Sky Publishing Corporation

Reference system: ICRS (consistent with equinox J2000.0)

Stellar data from the Hipparcos and Tycho Catalogues, ESA 1997

PUPPIS

A

E

V359

198 ly

113 ly

2310

V362 (e)

V358 (e)

107 ly

TX

2328

C

NP (i)

55 ly

53 ly
49 ly

83 ly

26.2 ly

L²
(s3)
198 ly

L¹
OU (v0)
182 ly

PUPPIS

413

Stellar Magnitudes (V)

≤2   3   4   5   6   7 8 9 10 11

Variable-Star Amplitudes and Types

<0.1 mag   0.1 – 1.0 mag   ≥1.0 mag

(e) Eclipsing
(c) Cepheid
(m) Mira
... etc.

Fast-Moving Stars

Proper motion in 1000 years

Double-Star Separations

0.3″   3″   30″

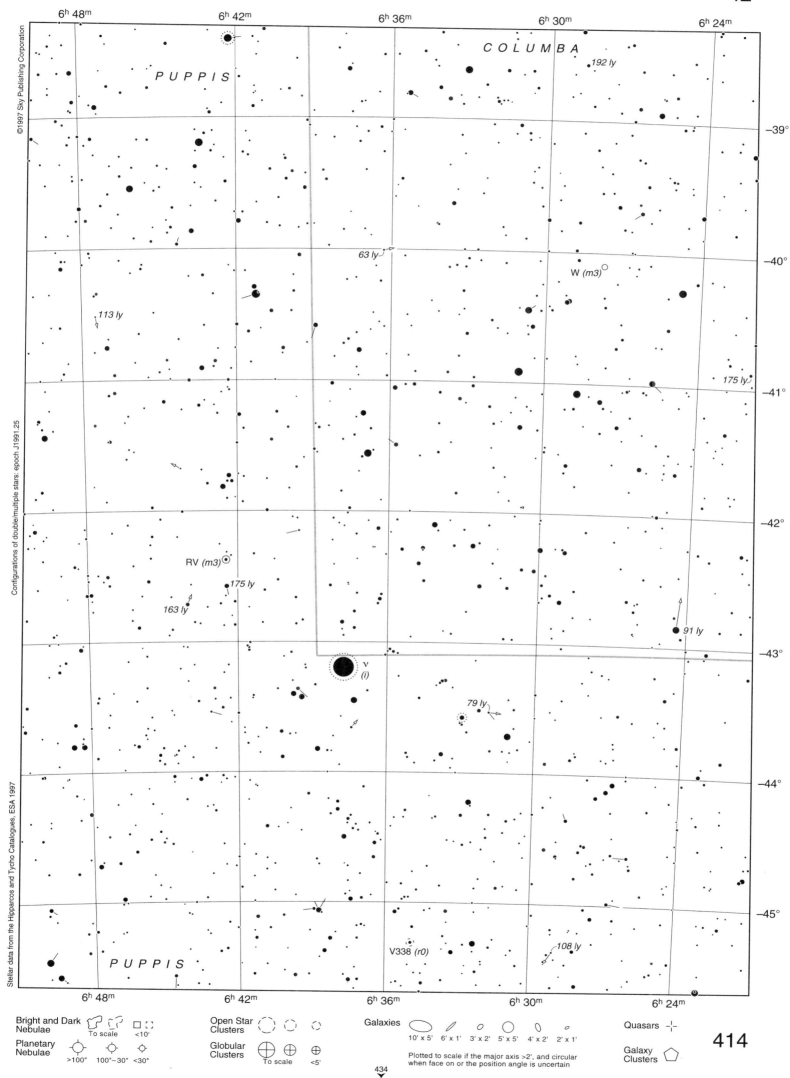

COLUMBA

PUPPIS

192 ly

63 ly

W (m3)

113 ly

175 ly

RV (m3)

175 ly

163 ly

91 ly

ν (i)

79 ly

PUPPIS

V338 (r0)

108 ly

Bright and Dark Nebulae	To scale	<10'		Open Star Clusters			Galaxies
Planetary Nebulae	>100" 100"−30" <30"			Globular Clusters	To scale <5'		10' x 5' 6' x 1' 3' x 2' 5' x 5' 4' x 2' 2' x 1'

Galaxies

10' x 5'   6' x 1'   3' x 2'   5' x 5'   4' x 2'   2' x 1'

Quasars

Galaxy Clusters

Plotted to scale if the major axis >2', and circular when face on or the position angle is uncertain

−42°

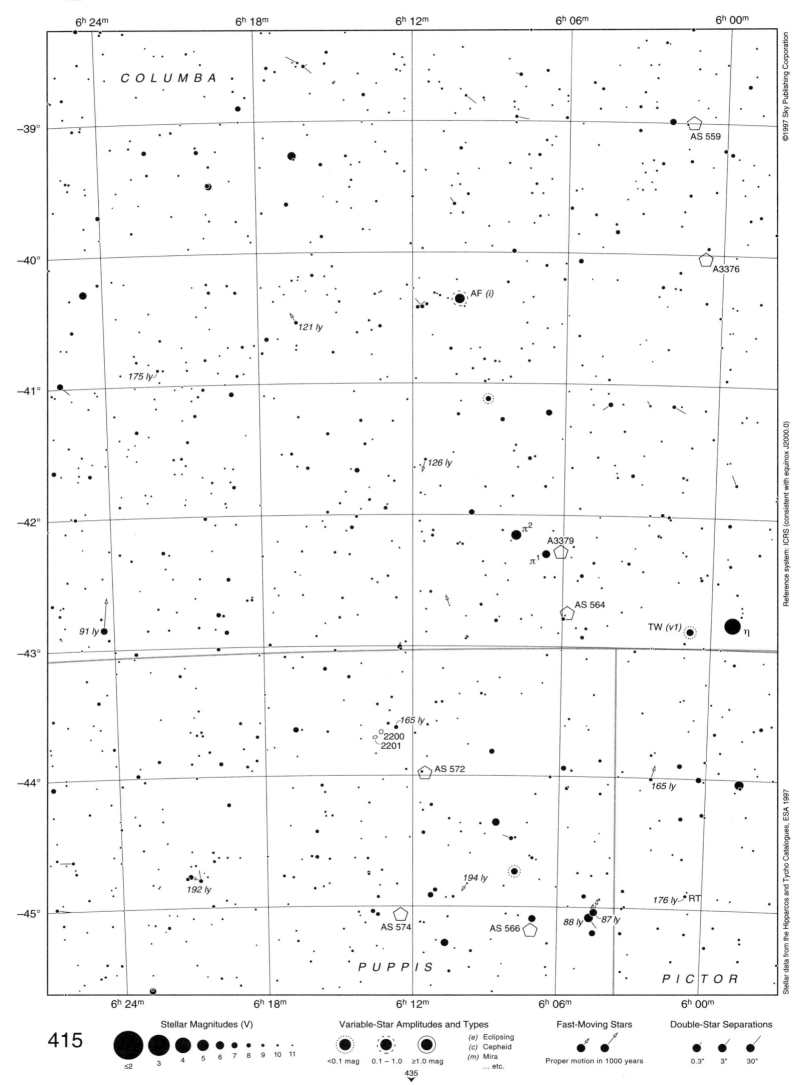

COLUMBA

AS 559

A3376

AF *(i)*

121 ly

175 ly

126 ly

π²

A3379

π¹

AS 564

TW *(v1)*

η

91 ly

165 ly

2200
2201

AS 572

165 ly

194 ly

192 ly

176 ly RT

AS 574

AS 566

88 ly *87 ly*

PUPPIS

PICTOR

Stellar Magnitudes (V)	Variable-Star Amplitudes and Types	Fast-Moving Stars	Double-Star Separations

≤2 3 4 5 6 7 8 9 10 11

<0.1 mag   0.1 − 1.0   ≥1.0 mag

(e) Eclipsing
(c) Cepheid
(m) Mira
    ... etc.

Proper motion in 1000 years

0.3"   3"   30"

©1997 Sky Publishing Corporation

Reference system: ICRS (consistent with equinox J2000.0)

Stellar data from the Hipparcos and Tycho Catalogues, ESA 1997

MILLENNIUM STAR ATLAS

−42°

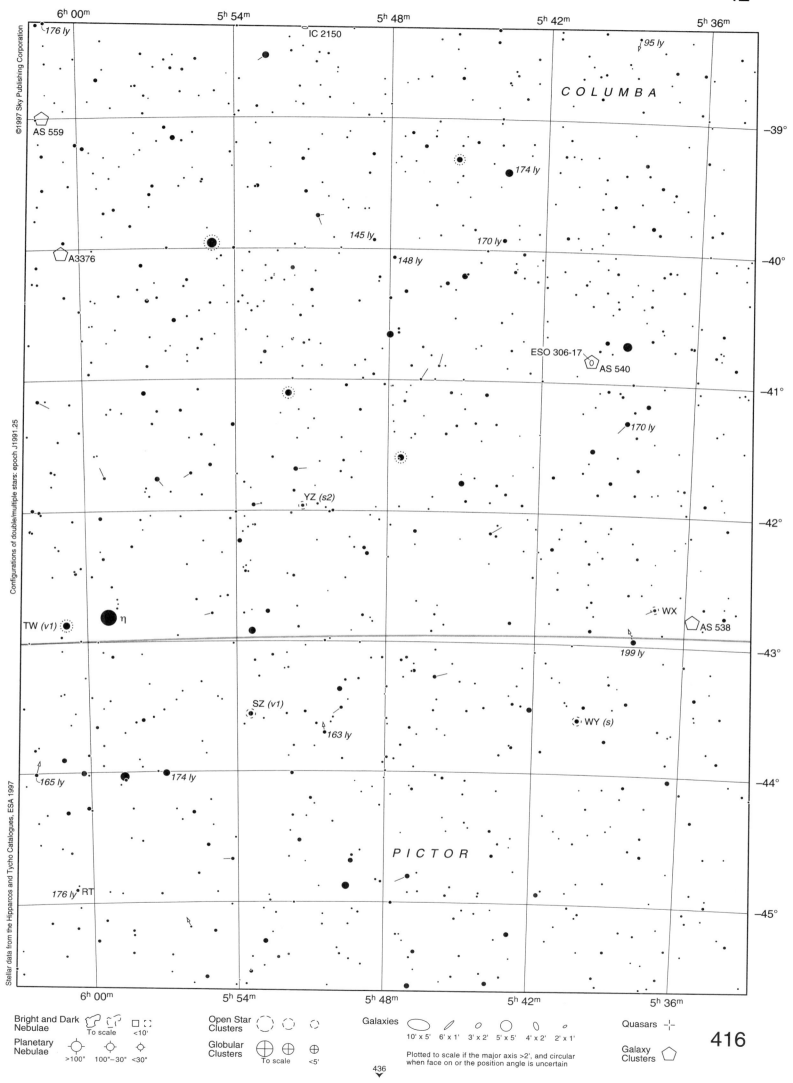

Configurations of double/multiple stars: epoch J1991.25

Stellar data from the Hipparcos and Tycho Catalogues, ESA 1997

6h 00m   5h 54m   5h 48m   5h 42m   5h 36m

176 ly

IC 2150

COLUMBA

95 ly

−39°

AS 559

174 ly

A3376

145 ly

148 ly

170 ly

−40°

ESO 306-17
AS 540

−41°

170 ly

YZ (s2)

−42°

η

WX

AS 538

TW (v1)

199 ly

−43°

SZ (v1)

WY (s)

163 ly

165 ly

174 ly

−44°

176 ly RT

PICTOR

−45°

6h 00m   5h 54m   5h 48m   5h 42m   5h 36m

Bright and Dark
Nebulae
To scale   <10'

Open Star
Clusters

Galaxies

10' x 5'   6' x 1'   3' x 2'   5' x 5'   4' x 2'   2' x 1'

Quasars

Planetary
Nebulae
>100" 100"–30" <30"

Globular
Clusters
To scale   <5'

Plotted to scale if the major axis >2', and circular
when face on or the position angle is uncertain

Galaxy
Clusters

416

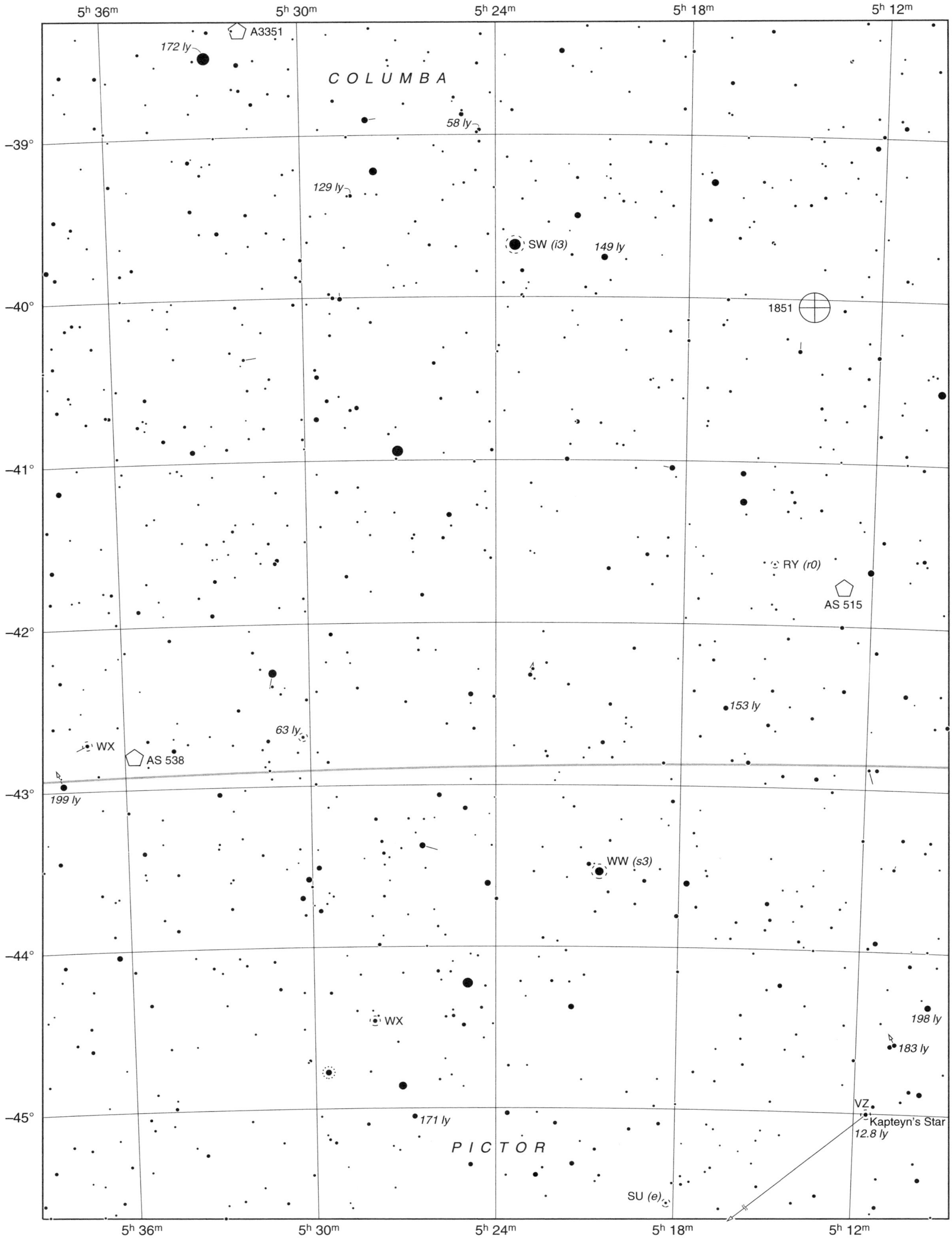
5h 36m
5h 30m
5h 24m
5h 18m
5h 12m
–39°
–40°
–41°
–42°
–43°
–44°
–45°
COLUMBA
PICTOR
A3351
172 ly
58 ly
129 ly
SW (i3)
149 ly
1851
RY (r0)
AS 515
153 ly
63 ly
WX
AS 538
199 ly
WW (s3)
WX
198 ly
183 ly
171 ly
VZ
Kapteyn's Star
12.8 ly
SU (e)

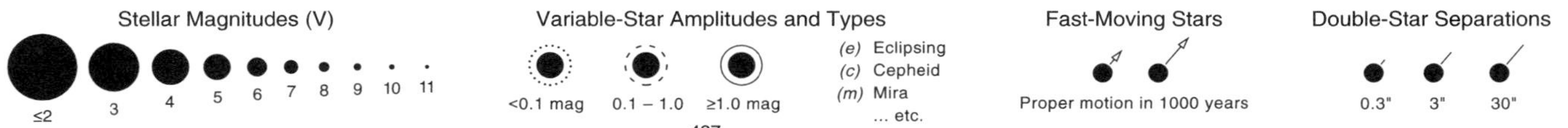
Stellar Magnitudes (V)
≤2
3
4
5
6
7
8
9
10
11
Variable-Star Amplitudes and Types
<0.1 mag
0.1 – 1.0
≥1.0 mag
(e) Eclipsing
(c) Cepheid
(m) Mira
... etc.
Fast-Moving Stars
Proper motion in 1000 years
Double-Star Separations
0.3"
3"
30"

©1997 Sky Publishing Corporation
Reference system: ICRS (consistent with equinox J2000.0)
Stellar data from the Hipparcos and Tycho Catalogues, ESA 1997

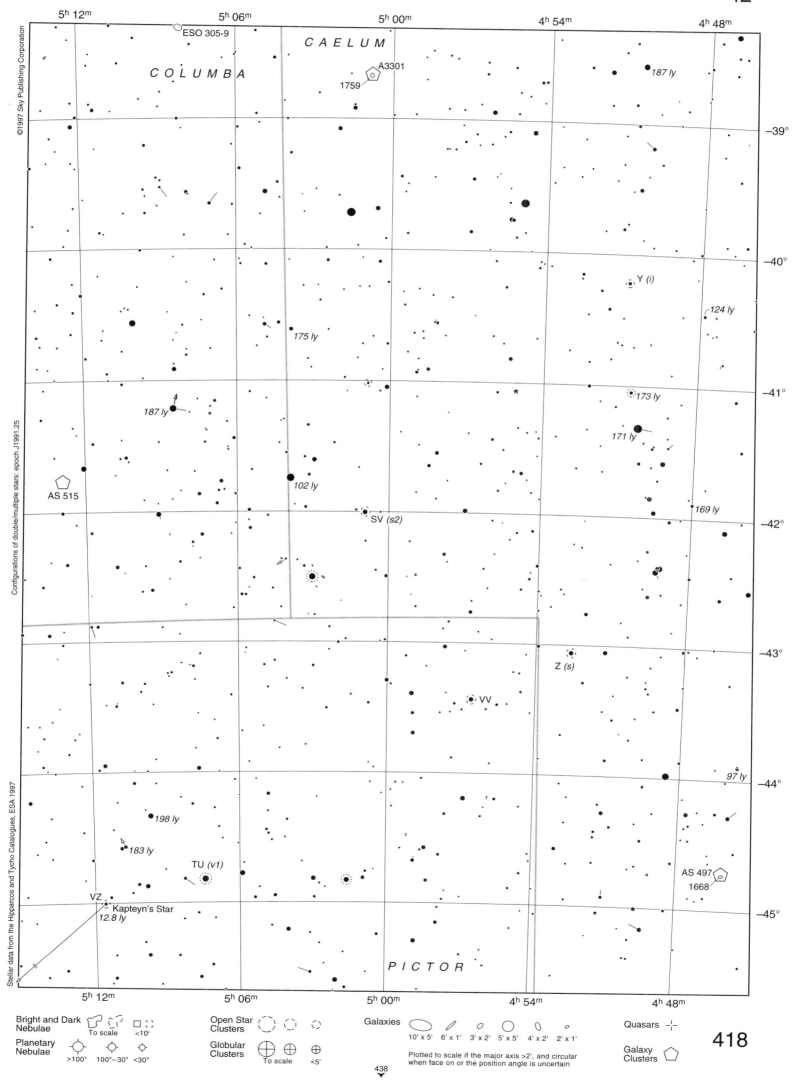

ESO 305-9

C A E L U M

A3301
1759

C O L U M B A

187 ly

−39°

Y (i)

−40°

124 ly

175 ly

173 ly

187 ly

171 ly

AS 515

102 ly

−41°

169 ly

SV (s2)

−42°

−43°

Z (s)

VV

97 ly

−44°

198 ly

183 ly

TU (v1)

AS 497
1668

VZ
Kapteyn's Star
12.8 ly

−45°

P I C T O R

Bright and Dark Nebulae				Open Star Clusters			Galaxies						Quasars	

Bright and Dark Nebulae — To scale — <10'

Planetary Nebulae — >100" — 100"–30" — <30'

Open Star Clusters

Globular Clusters — To scale — <5'

Galaxies — 10' x 5' — 6' x 1' — 3' x 2' — 5' x 5' — 4' x 2' — 2' x 1'

Plotted to scale if the major axis >2', and circular when face on or the position angle is uncertain

Quasars

Galaxy Clusters

438

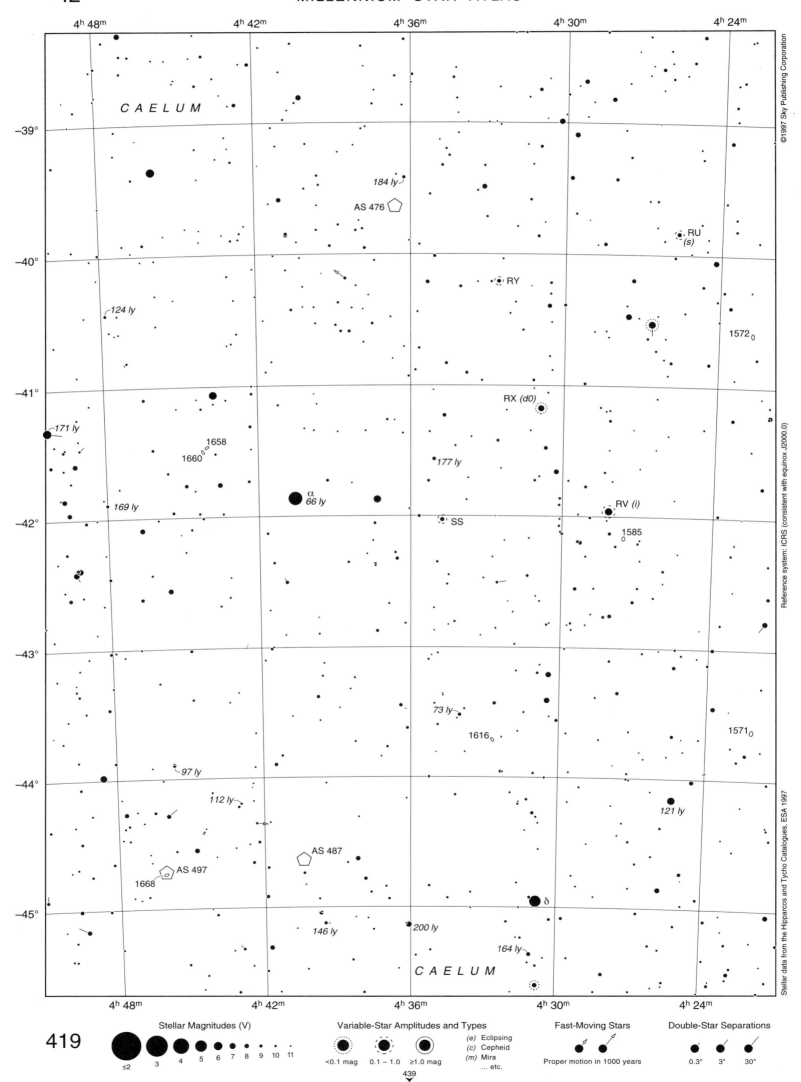

©1997 Sky Publishing Corporation

Reference system: ICRS (consistent with equinox J2000.0)

Stellar data from the Hipparcos and Tycho Catalogues, ESA 1997

CAELUM

184 ly
AS 476

RU
(s)

124 ly

RY

1572₀

−40°

RX (d0)

−41°

171 ly

1658
1660

177 ly

169 ly

α
66 ly

RV (i)

SS

1585₀

73 ly

1616₀

1571₀

97 ly

121 ly

112 ly

AS 487

AS 497

1668

δ

146 ly

200 ly

164 ly

CAELUM

Stellar Magnitudes (V)

≤2   3   4   5 6 7 8 9 10 11

Variable-Star Amplitudes and Types

<0.1 mag   0.1 – 1.0   ≥1.0 mag

(e) Eclipsing
(c) Cepheid
(m) Mira
... etc.

439

Fast-Moving Stars

Proper motion in 1000 years

Double-Star Separations

0.3"   3"   30"

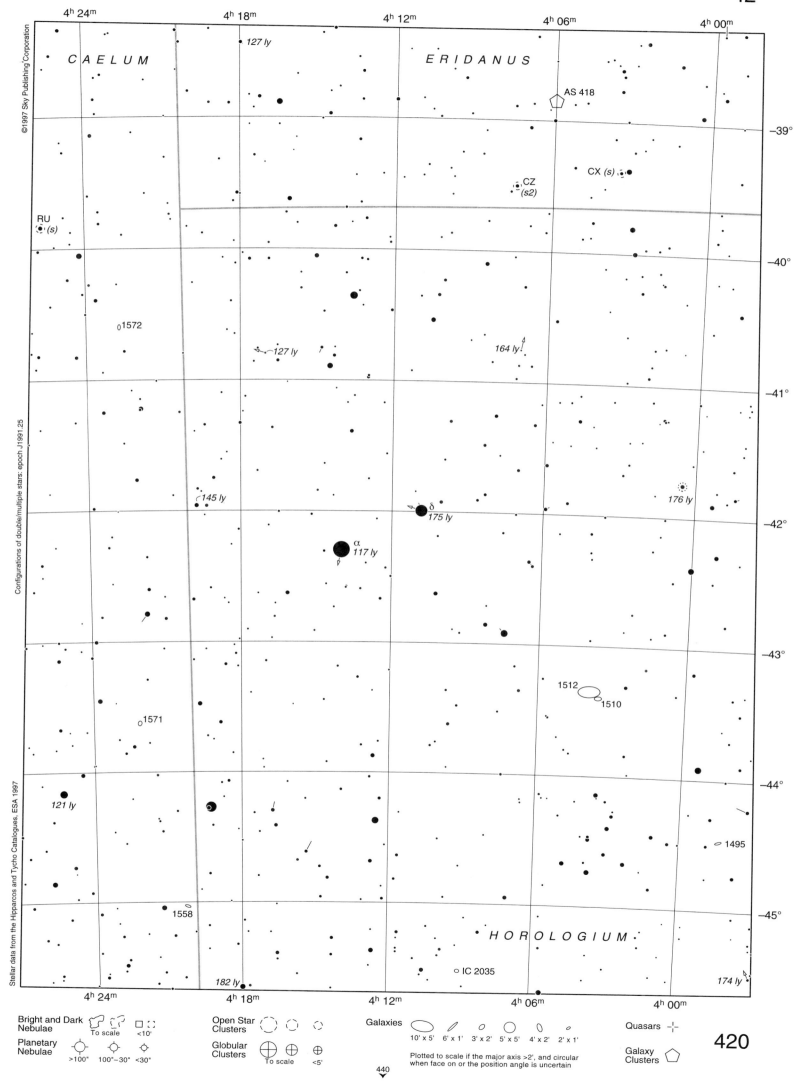

CAELUM

127 ly

ERIDANUS

AS 418

CX (s)

CZ
(s2)

RU
(s)

1572

127 ly

164 ly

145 ly

176 ly

δ
175 ly

α
117 ly

1512
1510

1571

121 ly

1495

1558

HOROLOGIUM

IC 2035

182 ly

174 ly

Bright and Dark Nebulae			
To scale		□	⬚ <10'

Planetary Nebulae
>100" 100"–30" <30"

Open Star Clusters

Globular Clusters
To scale <5'

Galaxies
10' x 5' 6' x 1' 3' x 2' 5' x 5' 4' x 2' 2' x 1'

Plotted to scale if the major axis >2', and circular when face on or the position angle is uncertain

Quasars

Galaxy Clusters

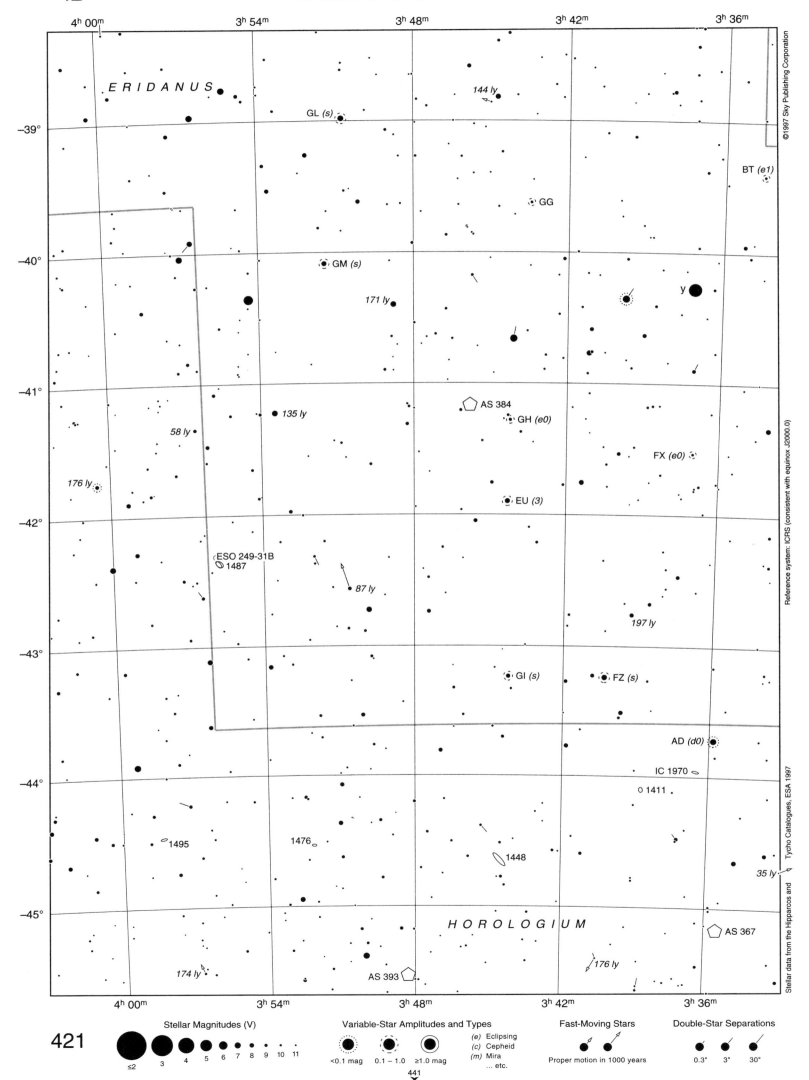

©1997 Sky Publishing Corporation

Reference system: ICRS (consistent with equinox J2000.0)

Stellar data from the Hipparcos and   Tycho Catalogues, ESA 1997

ERIDANUS

HOROLOGIUM

GL (s)

144 ly

GG

BT (e1)

GM (s)

171 ly

y

AS 384

GH (e0)

135 ly

58 ly

FX (e0)

176 ly

EU (3)

ESO 249-31B
1487

87 ly

197 ly

GI (s)

FZ (s)

AD (d0)

IC 1970

1411

1495

1476

1448

35 ly

AS 367

174 ly

176 ly

AS 393

421

Stellar Magnitudes (V)

≤2   3   4   5   6   7   8   9 10 11

Variable-Star Amplitudes and Types

<0.1 mag   0.1 − 1.0   ≥1.0 mag

(e) Eclipsing
(c) Cepheid
(m) Mira
... etc.

Fast-Moving Stars

Proper motion in 1000 years

Double-Star Separations

0.3"   3"   30"

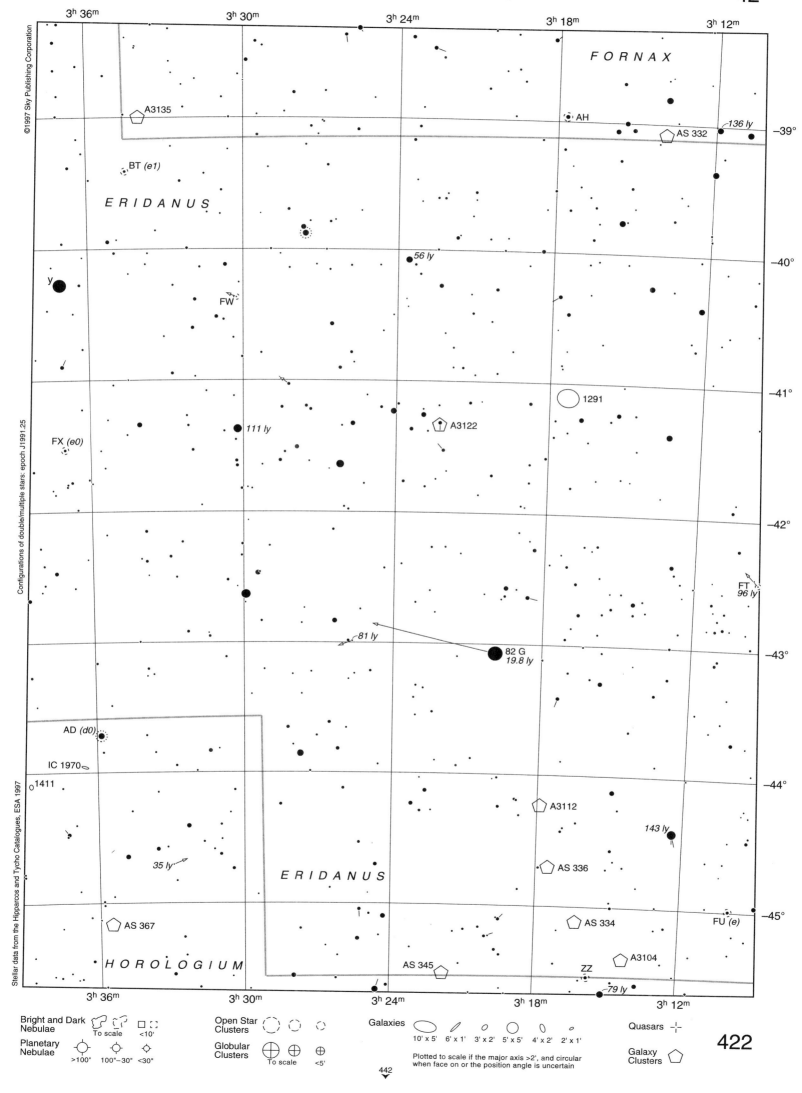

© 1997 Sky Publishing Corporation

Configurations of double/multiple stars: epoch J1991.25

Stellar data from the Hipparcos and Tycho Catalogues, ESA 1997

3ʰ 36ᵐ   3ʰ 30ᵐ   3ʰ 24ᵐ   3ʰ 18ᵐ   3ʰ 12ᵐ

F O R N A X

A3135

AH

AS 332

136 ly

−39°

BT *(e1)*

E R I D A N U S

y

56 ly

FW

−40°

1291

A3122

FX *(e0)*

111 ly

−41°

−42°

FT
96 ly

81 ly

82 G
19.8 ly

−43°

AD *(d0)*

IC 1970

1411

A3112

143 ly

35 ly

AS 336

E R I D A N U S

−44°

AS 367

AS 334

FU *(e)*

−45°

H O R O L O G I U M

AS 345

A3104

ZZ

79 ly

3ʰ 36ᵐ   3ʰ 30ᵐ   3ʰ 24ᵐ   3ʰ 18ᵐ   3ʰ 12ᵐ

Bright and Dark
Nebulae
To scale   <10'

Planetary
Nebulae
>100" 100"–30" <30"

Open Star
Clusters

Globular
Clusters
To scale   <5'

Galaxies
10' x 5' 6' x 1' 3' x 2' 5' x 5' 4' x 2' 2' x 1'

Plotted to scale if the major axis >2', and circular
when face on or the position angle is uncertain

Quasars

Galaxy
Clusters

442

422

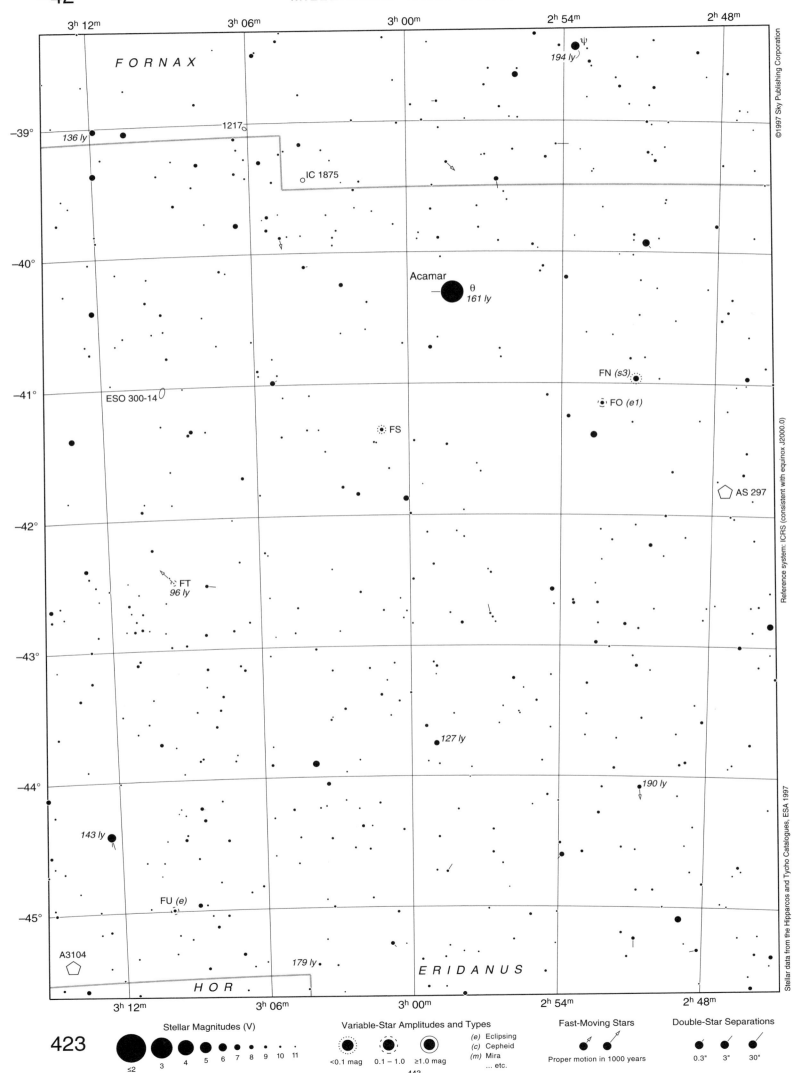

©1997 Sky Publishing Corporation

Reference system: ICRS (consistent with equinox J2000.0)

Stellar data from the Hipparcos and Tycho Catalogues, ESA 1997

FORNAX

194 ly
ψ

136 ly

1217

IC 1875

Acamar
θ
161 ly

FN (s3)

ESO 300-14

FO (e1)

FS

AS 297

FT
96 ly

127 ly

190 ly

143 ly

FU (e)

A3104

179 ly

HOR

ERIDANUS

Stellar Magnitudes (V)

≤2   3   4   5   6   7   8   9 10 11

Variable-Star Amplitudes and Types

<0.1 mag   0.1 – 1.0   ≥1.0 mag

(e) Eclipsing
(c) Cepheid
(m) Mira
... etc.

Fast-Moving Stars

Proper motion in 1000 years

Double-Star Separations

0.3"   3"   30"

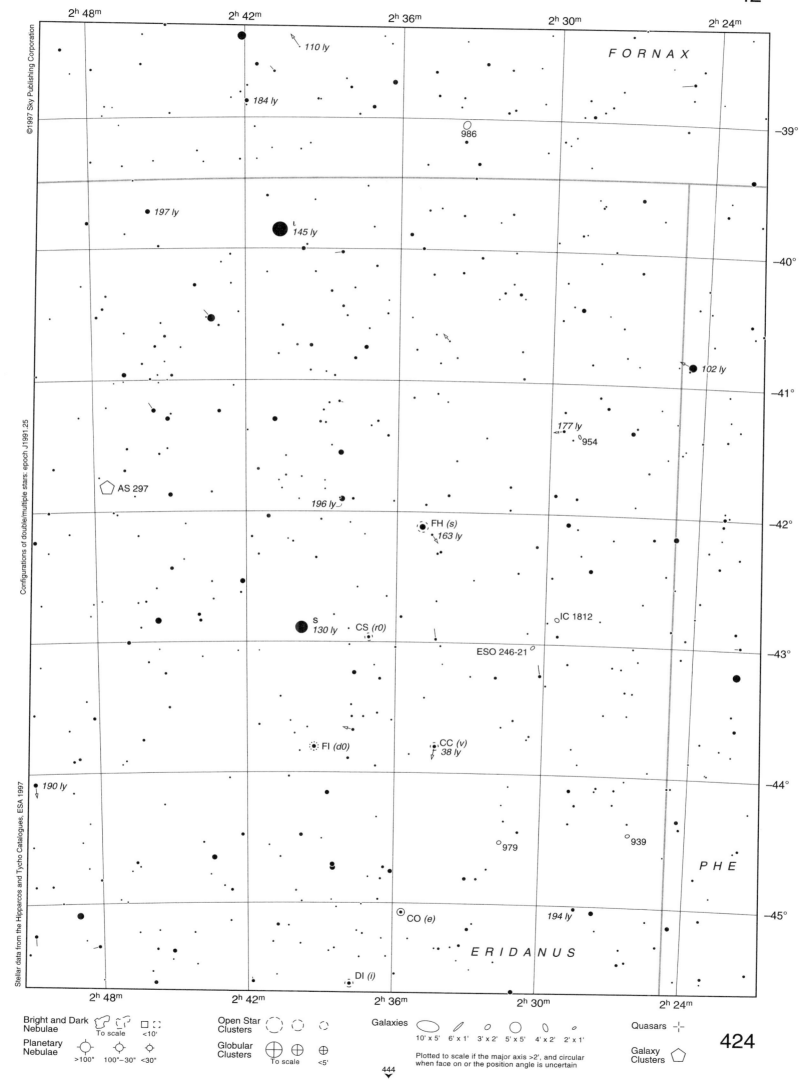

2ʰ 48ᵐ   2ʰ 42ᵐ   2ʰ 36ᵐ   2ʰ 30ᵐ   2ʰ 24ᵐ

F O R N A X

110 ly

184 ly

−39°

986

197 ly

ι
145 ly

−40°

102 ly

177 ly
954

−41°

AS 297

196 ly

FH (s)
163 ly

−42°

IC 1812

S
130 ly   CS (r0)

ESO 246-21

−43°

FI (d0)

CC (v)
38 ly

190 ly

−44°

979   939

P H E

CO (e)

194 ly

−45°

E R I D A N U S

DI (i)

2ʰ 48ᵐ   2ʰ 42ᵐ   2ʰ 36ᵐ   2ʰ 30ᵐ   2ʰ 24ᵐ

Bright and Dark
Nebulae
To scale   <10'

Planetary
Nebulae
>100" 100"−30" <30"

Open Star
Clusters

Globular
Clusters
To scale   <5'

Galaxies

10' x 5' 6' x 1' 3' x 2' 5' x 5' 4' x 2' 2' x 1'

Plotted to scale if the major axis >2', and circular
when face on or the position angle is uncertain

Quasars

Galaxy
Clusters

424

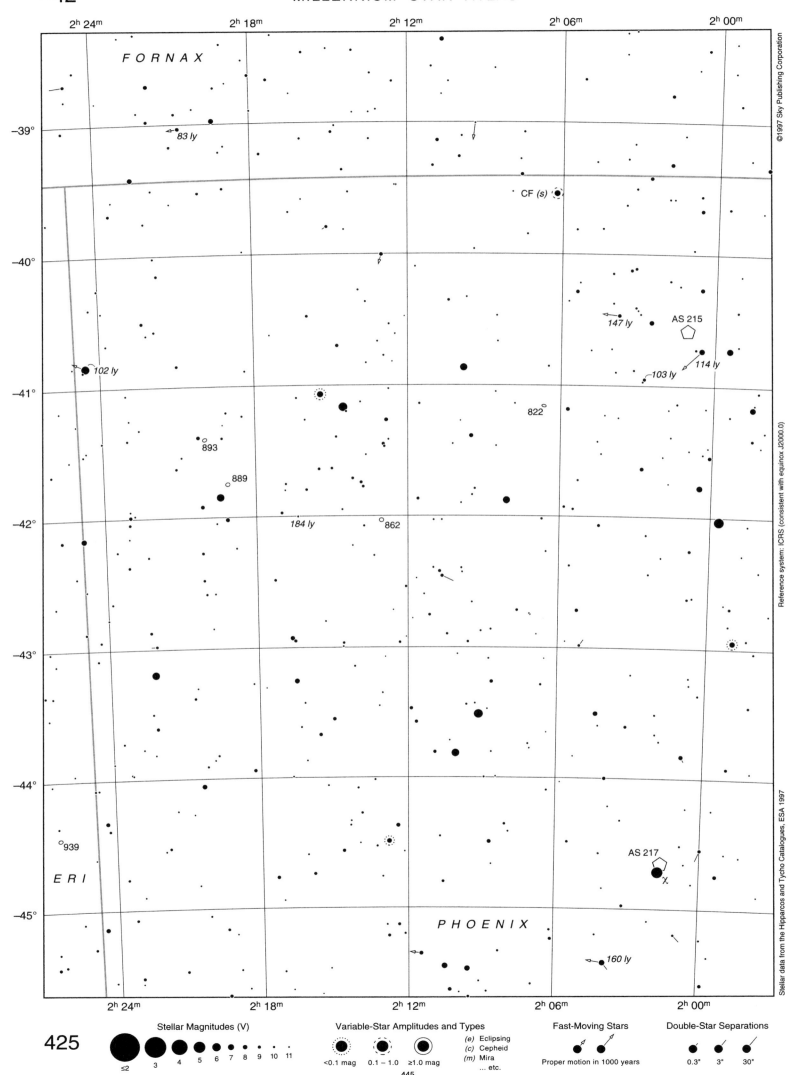

©1997 Sky Publishing Corporation

Reference system: ICRS (consistent with equinox J2000.0)

Stellar data from the Hipparcos and Tycho Catalogues, ESA 1997

425

Stellar Magnitudes (V)

≤2 3 4 5 6 7 8 9 10 11

Variable-Star Amplitudes and Types

<0.1 mag   0.1 – 1.0   ≥1.0 mag

(e) Eclipsing
(c) Cepheid
(m) Mira
... etc.

Fast-Moving Stars

Proper motion in 1000 years

Double-Star Separations

0.3"   3"   30"

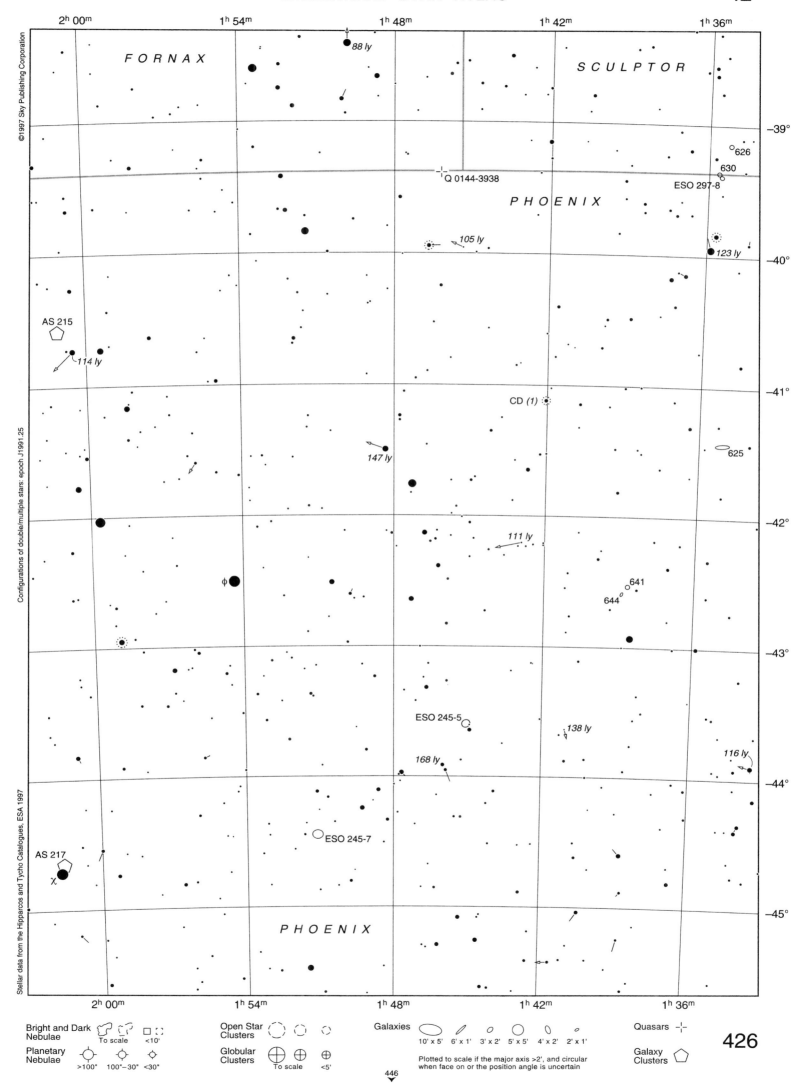

©1997 Sky Publishing Corporation

Configurations of double/multiple stars: epoch J1991.25

Stellar data from the Hipparcos and Tycho Catalogues, ESA 1997

FORNAX

SCULPTOR

PHOENIX

88 ly

Q 0144-3938

○626

630

ESO 297-8

105 ly

○123 ly

AS 215

114 ly

CD (1)

625

147 ly

111 ly

641

644

φ

ESO 245-5

138 ly

168 ly

116 ly

ESO 245-7

AS 217

χ

PHOENIX

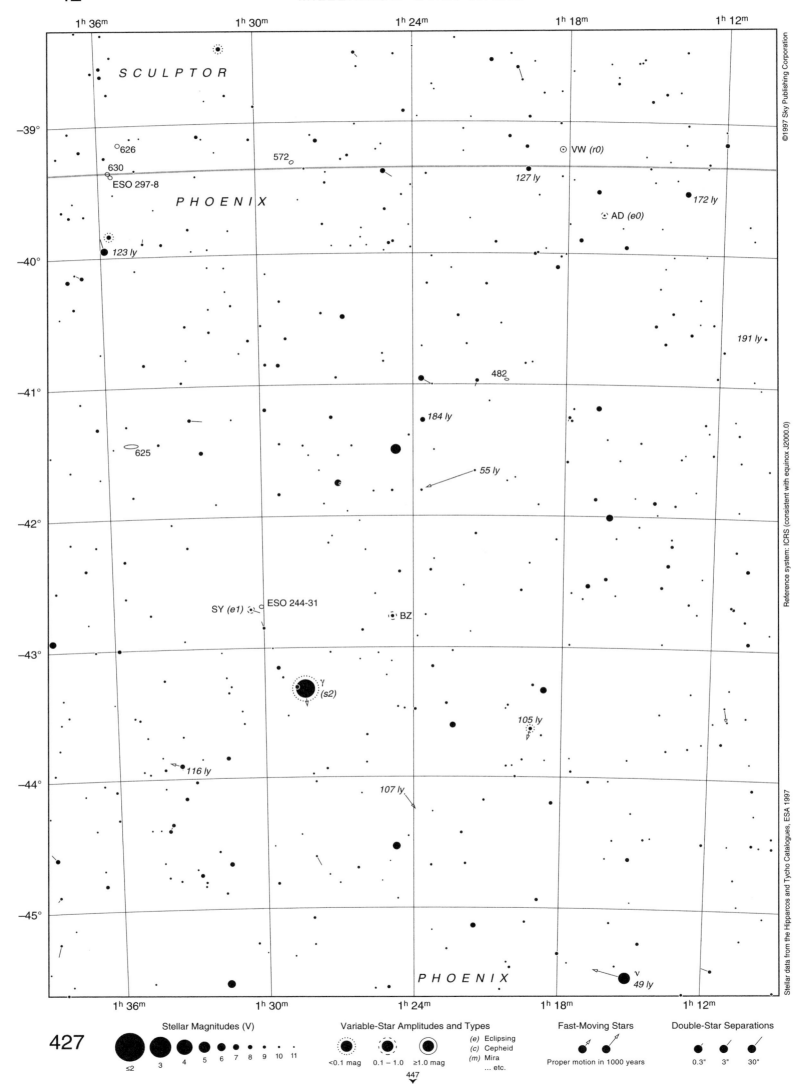

©1997 Sky Publishing Corporation

Reference system: ICRS (consistent with equinox J2000.0)

Stellar data from the Hipparcos and Tycho Catalogues, ESA 1997

427

Stellar Magnitudes (V)

≤2   3   4   5   6   7   8   9   10   11

Variable-Star Amplitudes and Types

<0.1 mag   0.1 – 1.0   ≥1.0 mag

(e) Eclipsing
(c) Cepheid
(m) Mira
... etc.

Fast-Moving Stars

Proper motion in 1000 years

Double-Star Separations

0.3"   3"   30"

MILLENNIUM STAR ATLAS

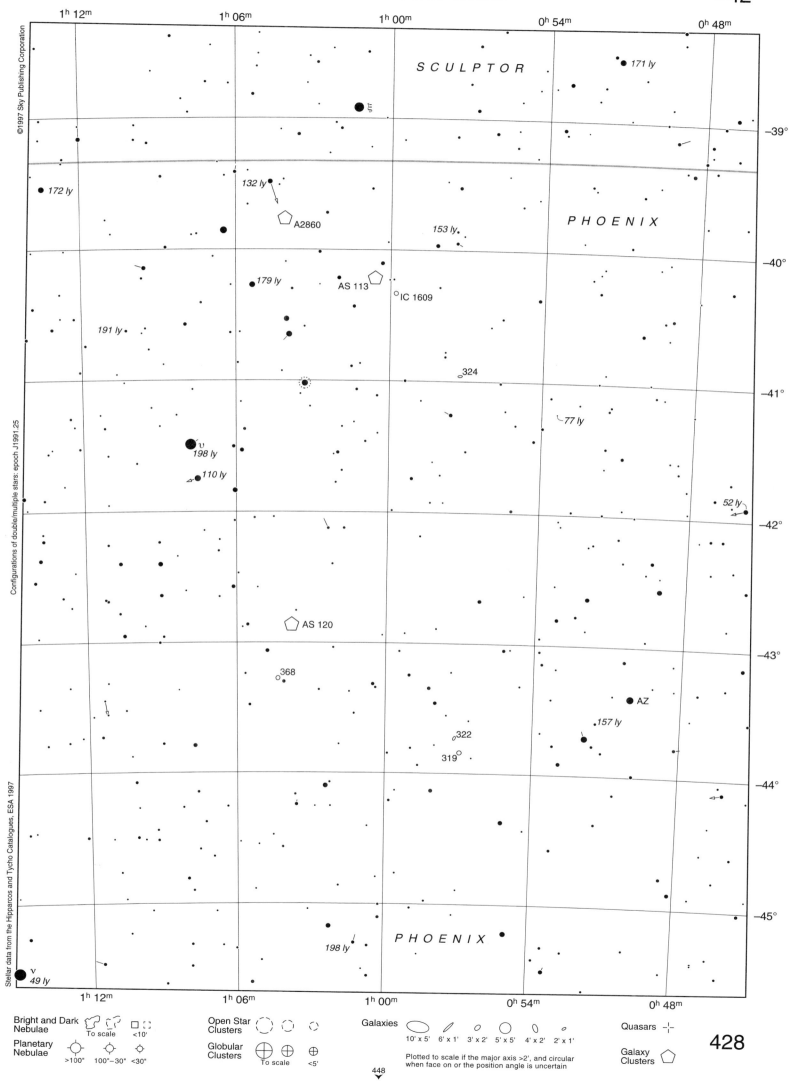

Configurations of double/multiple stars: epoch J1991.25

Stellar data from the Hipparcos and Tycho Catalogues, ESA 1997

S C U L P T O R

P H O E N I X

P H O E N I X

171 ly

ξ

172 ly

132 ly

A2860

153 ly

179 ly

AS 113

IC 1609

191 ly

324

77 ly

υ

198 ly

110 ly

52 ly

AS 120

368

AZ

322

157 ly

319

198 ly

ν
49 ly

1ʰ 12ᵐ   1ʰ 06ᵐ   1ʰ 00ᵐ   0ʰ 54ᵐ   0ʰ 48ᵐ

−39°
−40°
−41°
−42°
−43°
−44°
−45°

Bright and Dark Nebulae			

To scale   <10'

Planetary Nebulae
>100"   100"–30"   <30"

Open Star Clusters

Globular Clusters
To scale   <5'

Galaxies
10' x 5'   6' x 1'   3' x 2'   5' x 5'   4' x 2'   2' x 1'

Plotted to scale if the major axis >2', and circular when face on or the position angle is uncertain

Quasars

Galaxy Clusters

428

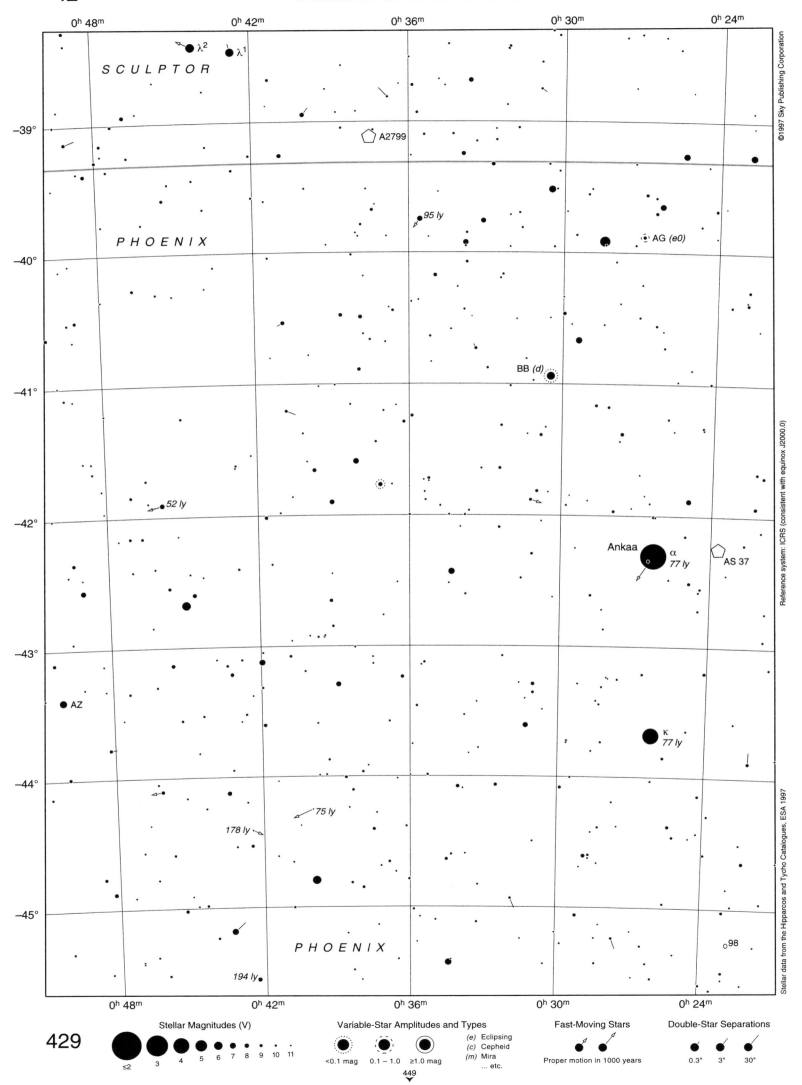

©1997 Sky Publishing Corporation

Reference system: ICRS (consistent with equinox J2000.0)

Stellar data from the Hipparcos and Tycho Catalogues, ESA 1997

429

Stellar Magnitudes (V)

≤2 3 4 5 6 7 8 9 10 11

Variable-Star Amplitudes and Types

<0.1 mag   0.1 – 1.0   ≥1.0 mag

(e) Eclipsing
(c) Cepheid
(m) Mira
... etc.

Fast-Moving Stars

Proper motion in 1000 years

Double-Star Separations

0.3"   3"   30"

449

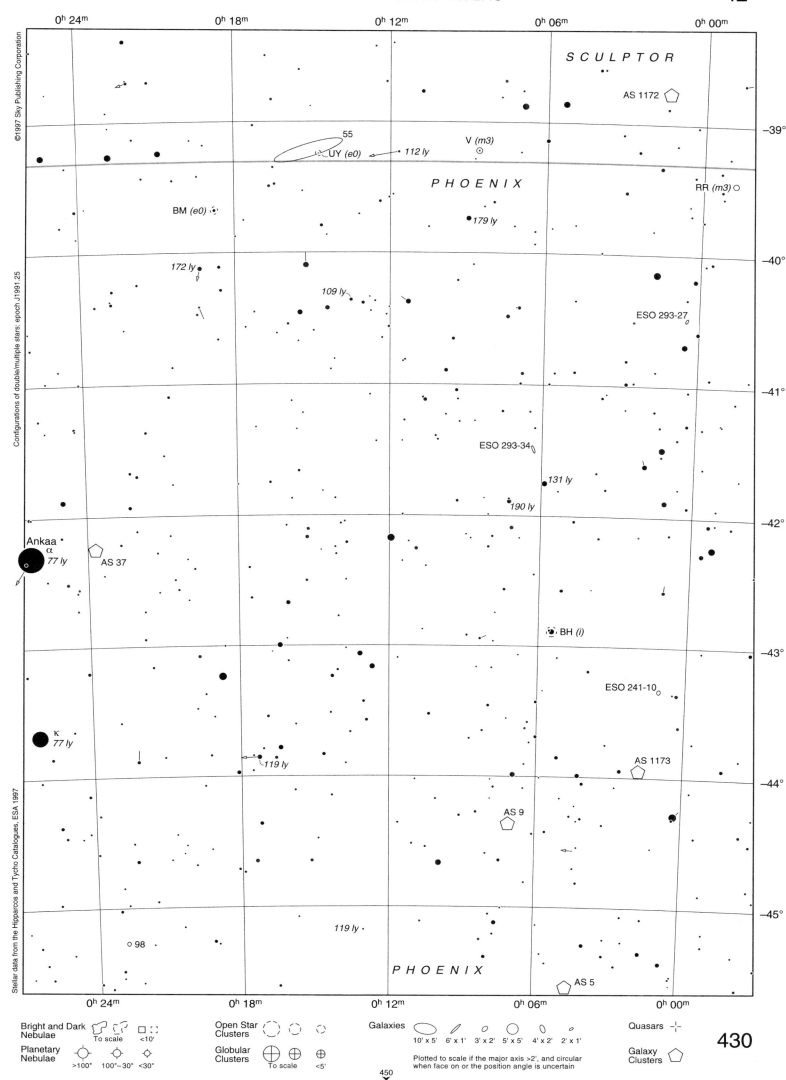

©1997 Sky Publishing Corporation

Configurations of double/multiple stars: epoch J1991.25

Stellar data from the Hipparcos and Tycho Catalogues, ESA 1997

SCULPTOR

AS 1172

−39°

55

UY (e0) → 112 ly

V (m3)

PHOENIX

RR (m3) ○

BM (e0)

179 ly

172 ly

−40°

109 ly

ESO 293-27

−41°

ESO 293-34

131 ly

190 ly

−42°

Ankaa
α
77 ly

AS 37

BH (i)

−43°

ESO 241-10

κ
77 ly

119 ly

AS 1173

−44°

AS 9

119 ly

−45°

○ 98

PHOENIX

AS 5

| Bright and Dark Nebulae | To scale | <10' | Open Star Clusters | Galaxies | 10' x 5' | 6' x 1' | 3' x 2' | 5' x 5' | 4' x 2' | 2' x 1' | Quasars |
| Planetary Nebulae | >100" | 100"−30" | <30" | Globular Clusters | To scale | <5' | Plotted to scale if the major axis >2', and circular when face on or the position angle is uncertain | | Galaxy Clusters |

MILLENNIUM STAR ATLAS

Reference system: ICRS (consistent with equinox J2000.0)

Stellar data from the Hipparcos and Tycho Catalogues, ESA 1997

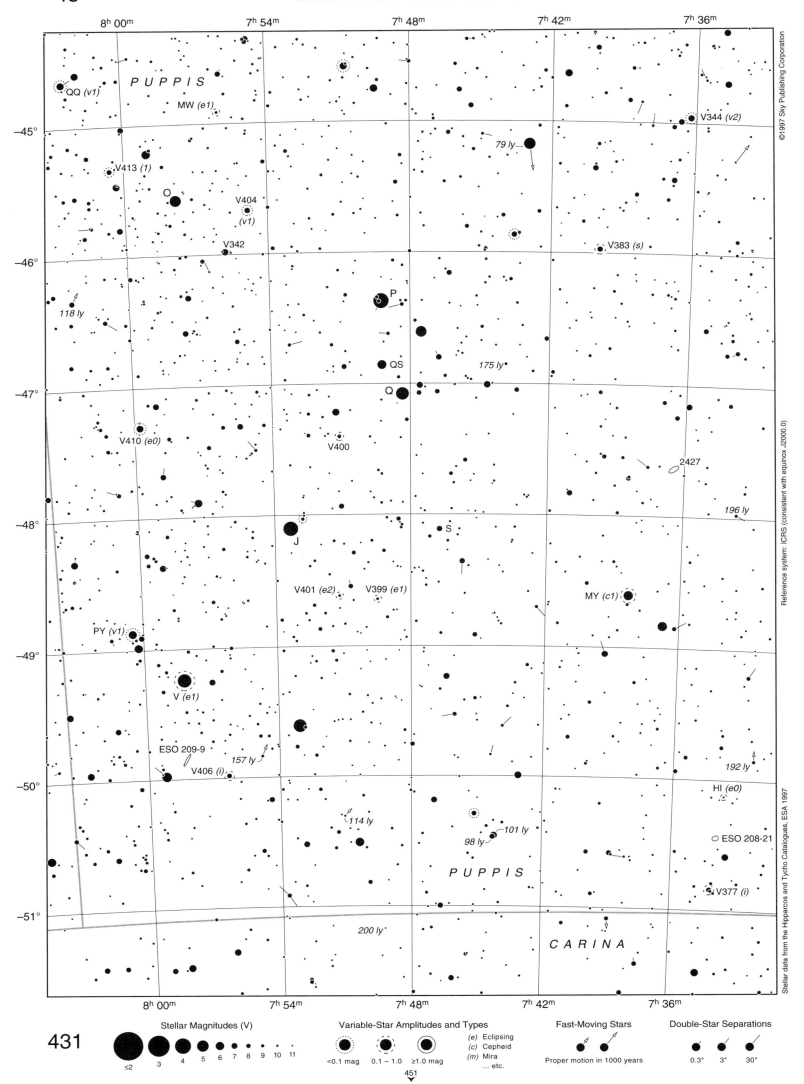

PUPPIS

QQ *(v1)*

MW *(e1)*

V413 *(1)*

O

V404
(v1)

V342

118 ly

P

V383 *(s)*

79 ly

V344 *(v2)*

QS

175 ly

Q

V410 *(e0)*

V400

2427

196 ly

J

S

V401 *(e2)*   V399 *(e1)*

MY *(c1)*

PY *(v1)*

V *(e1)*

ESO 209-9

V406 *(i)*   *157 ly*

114 ly

101 ly

98 ly

192 ly

HI *(e0)*

○ ESO 208-21

V377 *(i)*

PUPPIS

200 ly

CARINA

431

Stellar Magnitudes (V)

≤2   3   4   5   6   7   8   9   10   11

Variable-Star Amplitudes and Types

<0.1 mag   0.1 – 1.0   ≥1.0 mag

(e) Eclipsing
(c) Cepheid
(m) Mira
... etc.

Fast-Moving Stars

Proper motion in 1000 years

Double-Star Separations

0.3"   3"   30"

MILLENNIUM STAR ATLAS

−48°

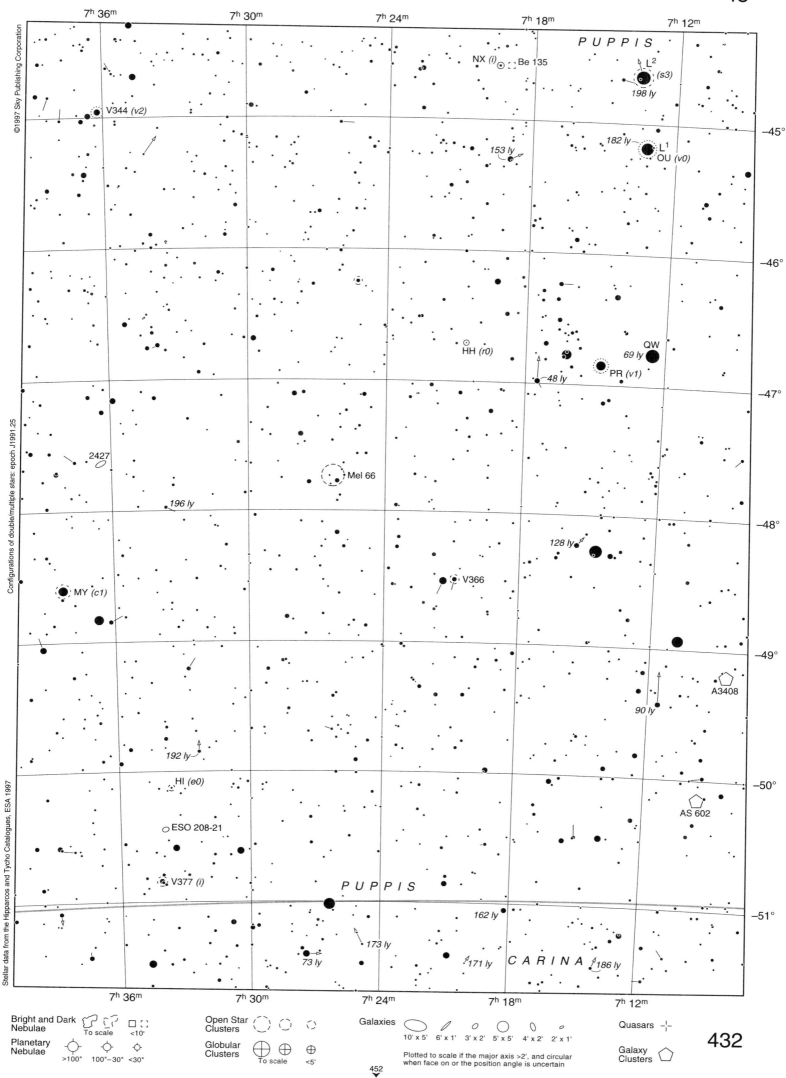

7h 36m   7h 30m   7h 24m   7h 18m   7h 12m

PUPPIS

NX *(i)* Be 135

L² *(s3)*
198 ly

−45°

182 ly L¹
OU *(v0)*

V344 *(v2)*

153 ly

−46°

HH *(r0)*

QW
69 ly

PR *(v1)*

48 ly

−47°

2427

Mel 66

196 ly

128 ly

−48°

MY *(c1)*

V366

−49°

A3408

90 ly

192 ly

−50°

HI *(e0)*

AS 602

ESO 208-21

V377 *(i)*

PUPPIS

162 ly

−51°

173 ly

73 ly

171 ly *CARINA* 186 ly

7h 36m   7h 30m   7h 24m   7h 18m   7h 12m

Bright and Dark Nebulae   To scale   <10'
Planetary Nebulae   >100" 100"−30" <30"

Open Star Clusters
Globular Clusters   To scale   <5'

Galaxies
10' x 5' 6' x 1' 3' x 2' 5' x 5' 4' x 2' 2' x 1'

Plotted to scale if the major axis >2', and circular when face on or the position angle is uncertain

Quasars

Galaxy Clusters

432

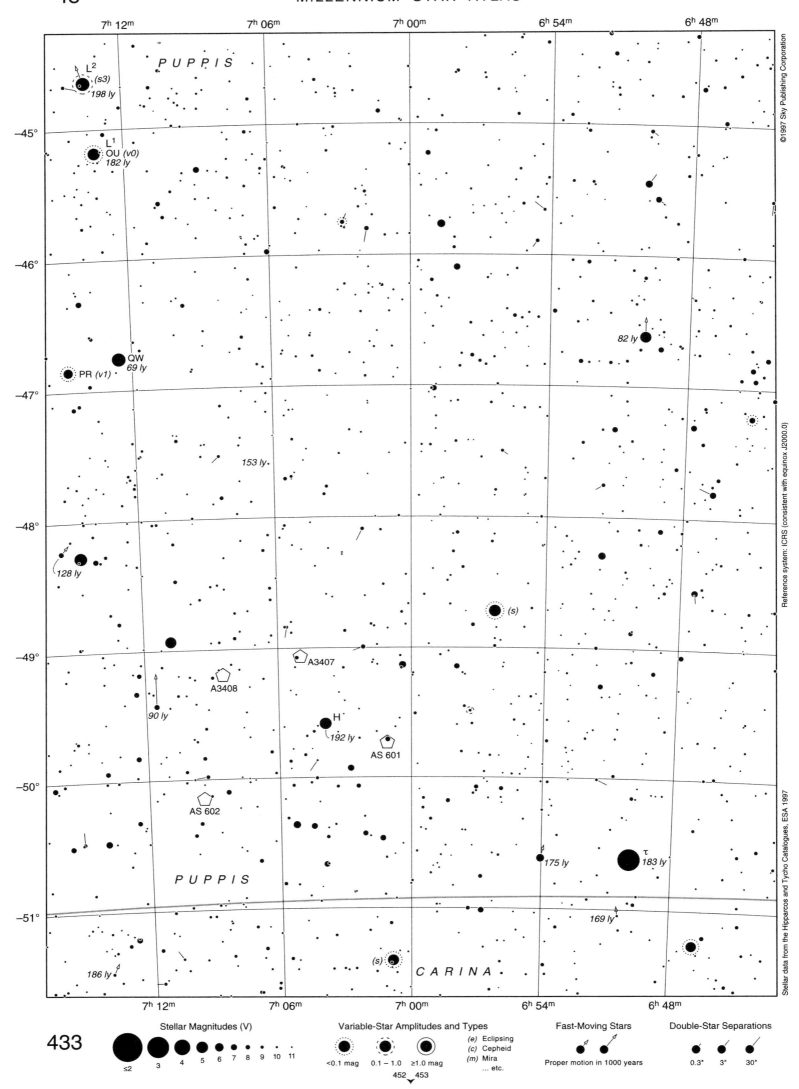

©1997 Sky Publishing Corporation

Reference system: ICRS (consistent with equinox J2000.0)

Stellar data from the Hipparcos and Tycho Catalogues, ESA 1997

PUPPIS

L²
(s3)
198 ly

L¹
OU (v0)
182 ly

QW
69 ly

PR (v1)

82 ly

153 ly

128 ly

(s)

A3407

A3408

90 ly

H
192 ly

AS 601

AS 602

τ
183 ly

175 ly

169 ly

186 ly

(s)

PUPPIS

CARINA

433

Stellar Magnitudes (V)

≤2　3　4　5　6　7　8　9　10　11

Variable-Star Amplitudes and Types

<0.1 mag　0.1 − 1.0　≥1.0 mag

(e) Eclipsing
(c) Cepheid
(m) Mira
... etc.

Fast-Moving Stars

Proper motion in 1000 years

Double-Star Separations

0.3"　3"　30"

MILLENNIUM STAR ATLAS

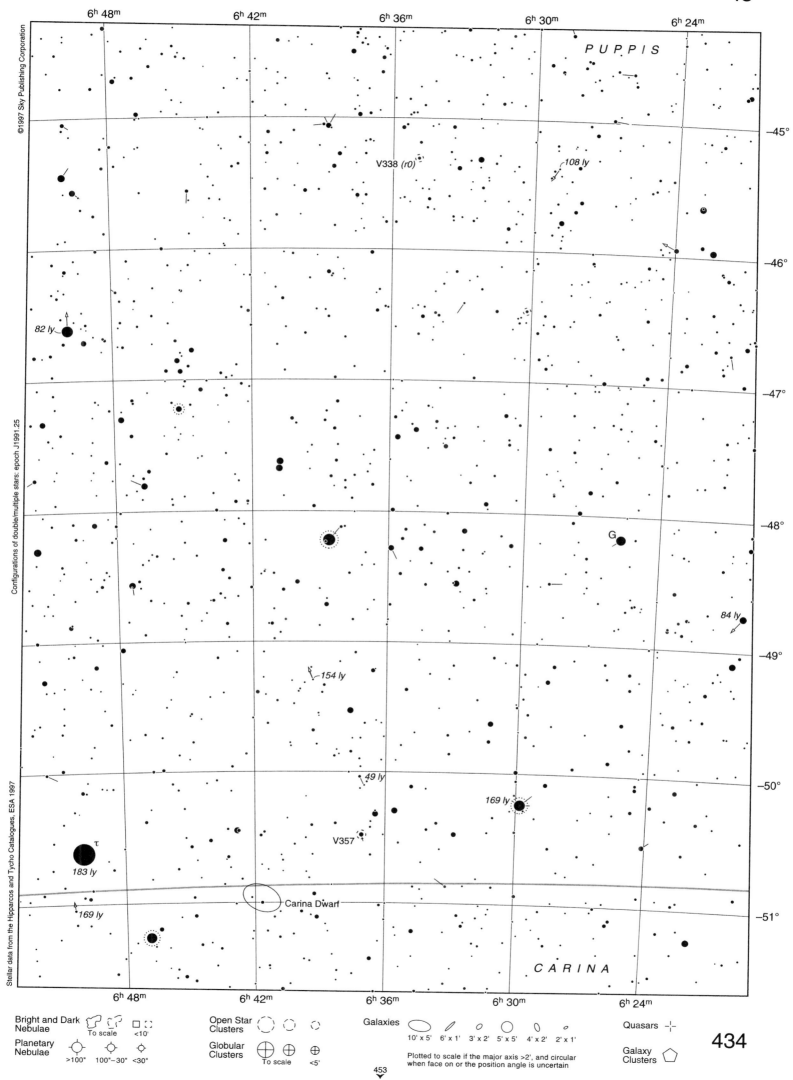

PUPPIS

6ʰ 48ᵐ   6ʰ 42ᵐ   6ʰ 36ᵐ   6ʰ 30ᵐ   6ʰ 24ᵐ

−45°

−46°

−47°

−48°

−49°

−50°

−51°

V338 *(r0)*

108 *ly*

82 *ly*

G

84 *ly*

154 *ly*

49 *ly*

169 *ly*

V357

τ

183 *ly*

169 *ly*

Carina Dwarf

CARINA

6ʰ 48ᵐ   6ʰ 42ᵐ   6ʰ 36ᵐ   6ʰ 30ᵐ   6ʰ 24ᵐ

Bright and Dark Nebulae — To scale   <10'

Planetary Nebulae   >100"   100"–30"   <30"

Open Star Clusters

Globular Clusters — To scale   <5'

Galaxies   10' x 5'   6' x 1'   3' x 2'   5' x 5'   4' x 2'   2' x 1'

Plotted to scale if the major axis >2', and circular when face on or the position angle is uncertain

Quasars

Galaxy Clusters

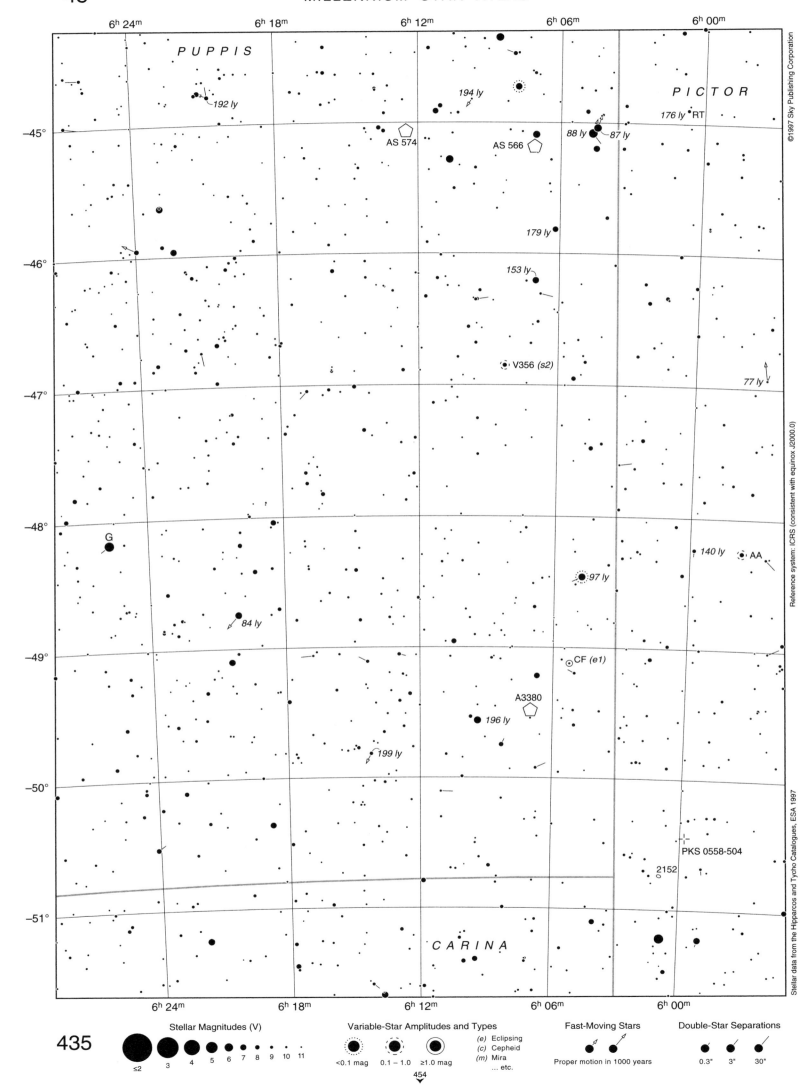

©1997 Sky Publishing Corporation

Reference system: ICRS (consistent with equinox J2000.0)

Stellar data from the Hipparcos and Tycho Catalogues, ESA 1997

PUPPIS

PICTOR

192 ly

194 ly

176 ly RT

AS 574

AS 566

88 ly   87 ly

179 ly

153 ly

V356 (s2)

77 ly

G

140 ly   AA

97 ly

84 ly

CF (e1)

A3380

196 ly

199 ly

PKS 0558-504

2152

CARINA

435

Stellar Magnitudes (V)

≤2   3   4   5   6   7   8   9   10   11

Variable-Star Amplitudes and Types

<0.1 mag   0.1 – 1.0   ≥1.0 mag

(e) Eclipsing
(c) Cepheid
(m) Mira
... etc.

Fast-Moving Stars

Proper motion in 1000 years

Double-Star Separations

0.3"   3"   30"

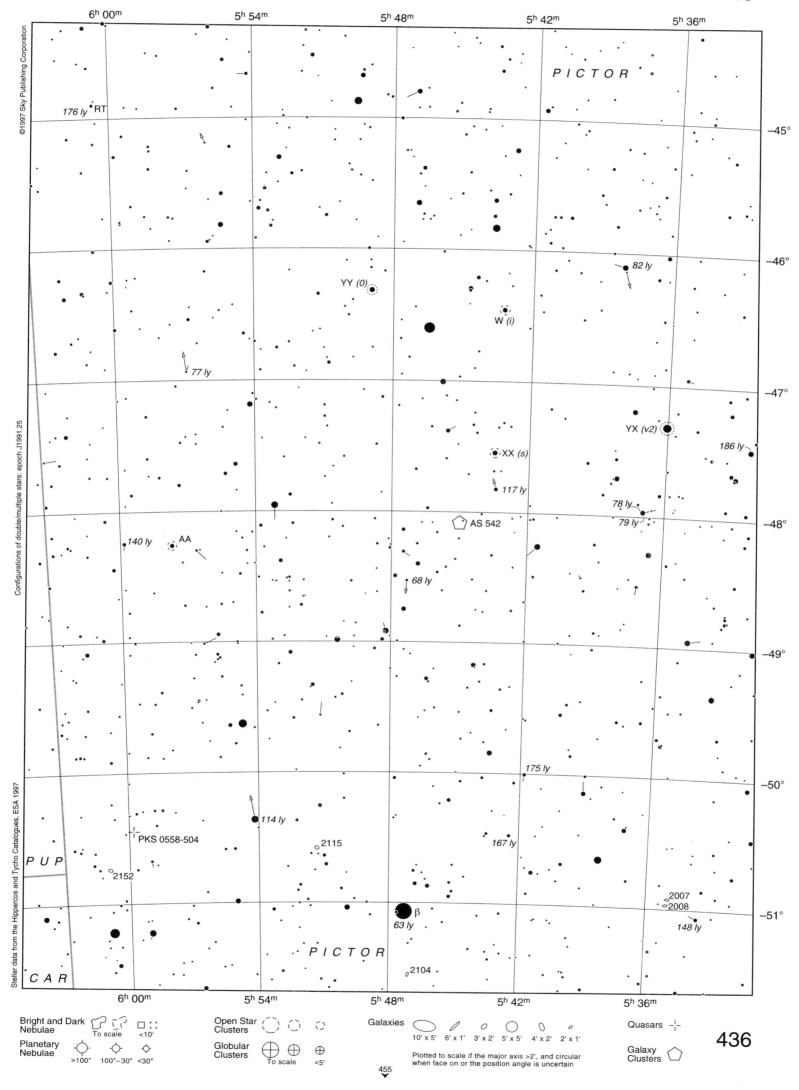

© 1997 Sky Publishing Corporation

Configurations of double/multiple stars: epoch J1991.25

Stellar data from the Hipparcos and Tycho Catalogues, ESA 1997

P I C T O R

176 ly RT

−45°

82 ly

YY *(0)*

W *(i)*

−46°

77 ly

−47°

YX *(v2)*

186 ly

XX *(s)*

117 ly

78 ly

79 ly

AS 542

−48°

140 ly AA

68 ly

−49°

175 ly

−50°

114 ly

167 ly

2115

PKS 0558-504

P U P

2152

2007
2008

148 ly

β
63 ly

−51°

C A R

P I C T O R

2104

6h 00m   5h 54m   5h 48m   5h 42m   5h 36m

Bright and Dark Nebulae — To scale — <10'

Planetary Nebulae — >100" — 100"–30" — <30"

Open Star Clusters

Globular Clusters — To scale — <5'

Galaxies — 10' x 5' — 6' x 1' — 3' x 2' — 5' x 5' — 4' x 2' — 2' x 1'

Plotted to scale if the major axis >2', and circular when face on or the position angle is uncertain

Quasars

Galaxy Clusters

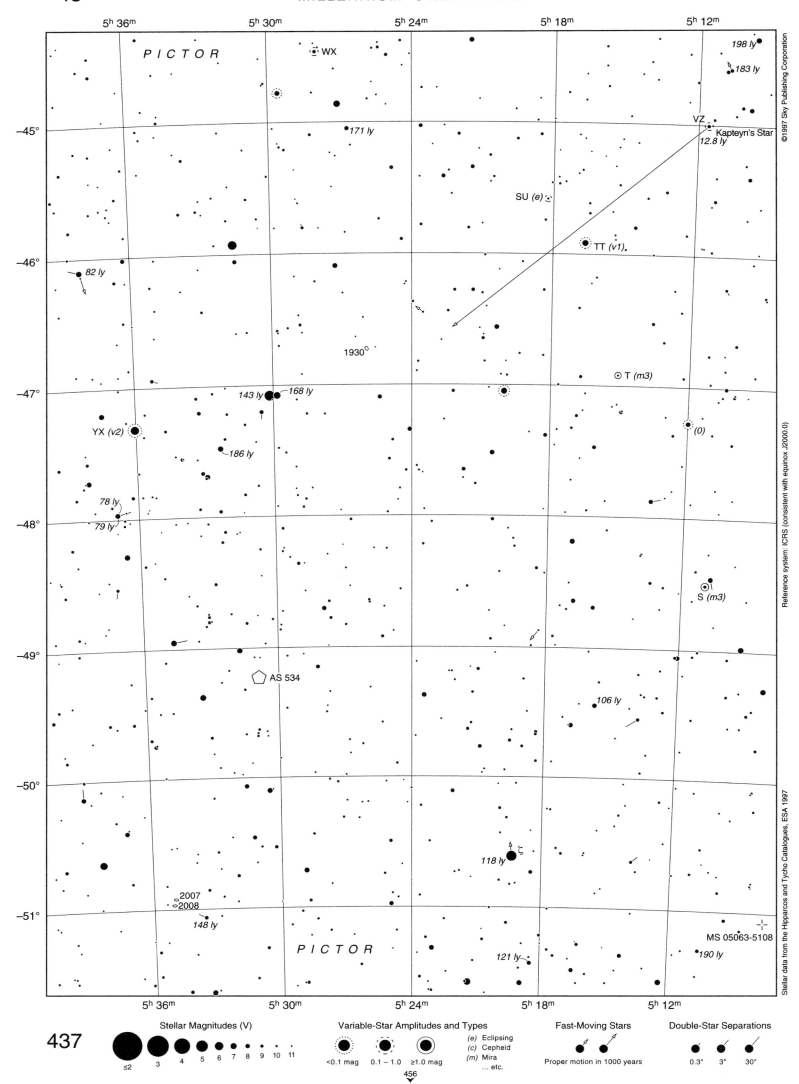

PICTOR

WX

171 ly

VZ
Kapteyn's Star
12.8 ly

SU (e)

TT (v1)

82 ly

1930°

T (m3)

143 ly 168 ly

YX (v2)

186 ly

(0)

78 ly
79 ly

S (m3)

AS 534

106 ly

118 ly ζ

2007
2008

148 ly

MS 05063-5108

PICTOR

121 ly 190 ly

©1997 Sky Publishing Corporation

Reference system: ICRS (consistent with equinox J2000.0)

Stellar data from the Hipparcos and Tycho Catalogues, ESA 1997

437

Stellar Magnitudes (V)
≤2 3 4 5 6 7 8 9 10 11

Variable-Star Amplitudes and Types

<0.1 mag   0.1 – 1.0   ≥1.0 mag

(e) Eclipsing
(c) Cepheid
(m) Mira
... etc.

Fast-Moving Stars

Proper motion in 1000 years

Double-Star Separations

0.3"   3"   30"

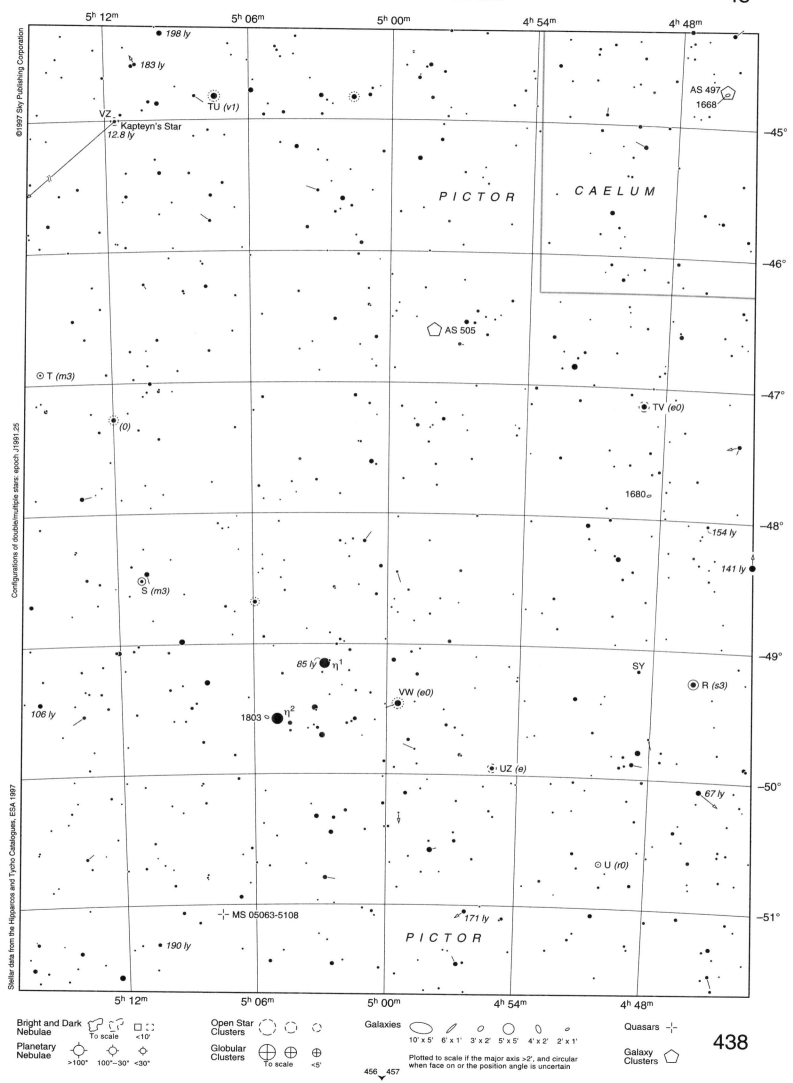

198 ly

183 ly

AS 497
1668

TU *(v1)*

VZ

Kapteyn's Star
12.8 ly

P I C T O R   *C A E L U M*

−45°

−46°

AS 505

⊙ T *(m3)*

−47°

TV *(e0)*

(0)

1680

154 ly

−48°

141 ly

⊙ S *(m3)*

85 ly   η¹

−49°

SY

R *(s3)*

VW *(e0)*

1803   η²

106 ly

UZ *(e)*

−50°

67 ly

⊙ U *(r0)*

MS 05063-5108

171 ly

−51°

190 ly

P I C T O R

5ʰ 12ᵐ   5ʰ 06ᵐ   5ʰ 00ᵐ   4ʰ 54ᵐ   4ʰ 48ᵐ

To scale   <10'

Planetary Nebulae
>100" 100"-30" <30"

Globular Clusters
To scale   <5'

10' x 5' 6' x 1' 3' x 2' 5' x 5' 4' x 2' 2' x 1'

Plotted to scale if the major axis >2', and circular when face on or the position angle is uncertain

Galaxy Clusters

438

456 457

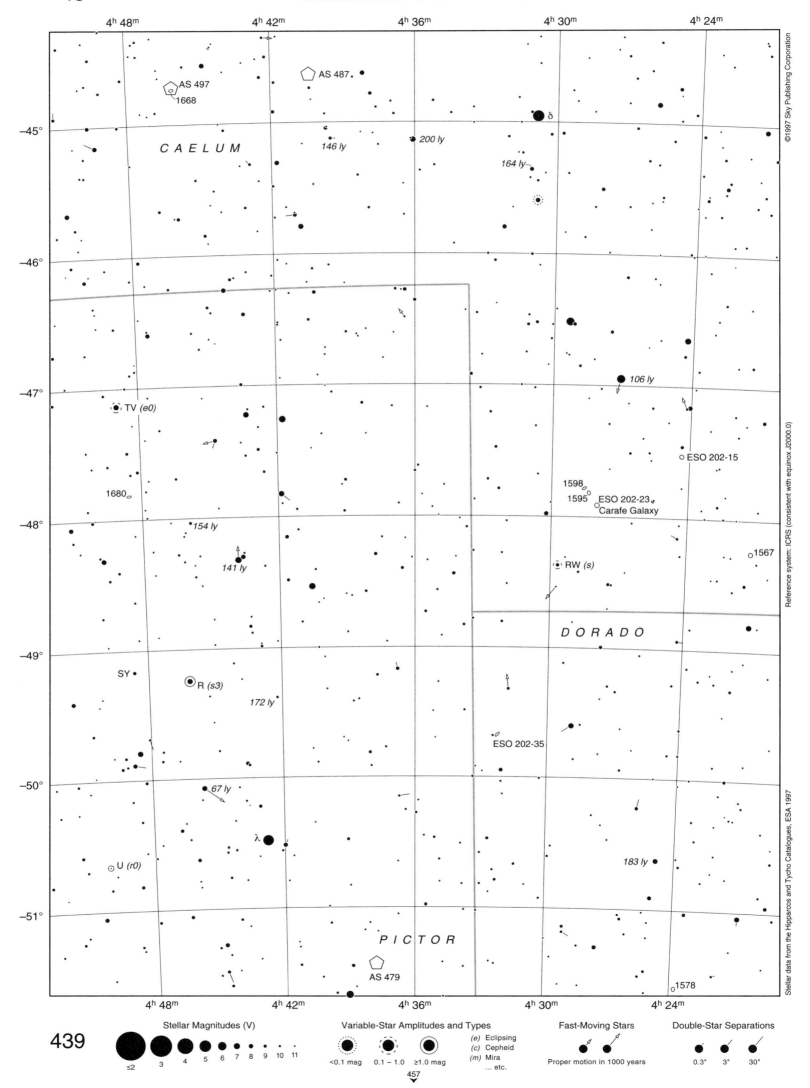

©1997 Sky Publishing Corporation

Reference system: ICRS (consistent with equinox J2000.0)

Stellar data from the Hipparcos and Tycho Catalogues, ESA 1997

CAELUM

DORADO

PICTOR

AS 497
1668
AS 487
146 ly
200 ly
δ
164 ly

TV (e0)

1680

154 ly

141 ly

106 ly
ESO 202-15

1598
1595
ESO 202-23
Carafe Galaxy

1567

RW (s)

SY
R (s3)
172 ly
ESO 202-35

67 ly
λ
183 ly
U (r0)

AS 479
1578

439

Stellar Magnitudes (V)
≤2 3 4 5 6 7 8 9 10 11

Variable-Star Amplitudes and Types
<0.1 mag   0.1 – 1.0   ≥1.0 mag

(e) Eclipsing
(c) Cepheid
(m) Mira
... etc.

Fast-Moving Stars
Proper motion in 1000 years

Double-Star Separations
0.3"   3"   30"

457

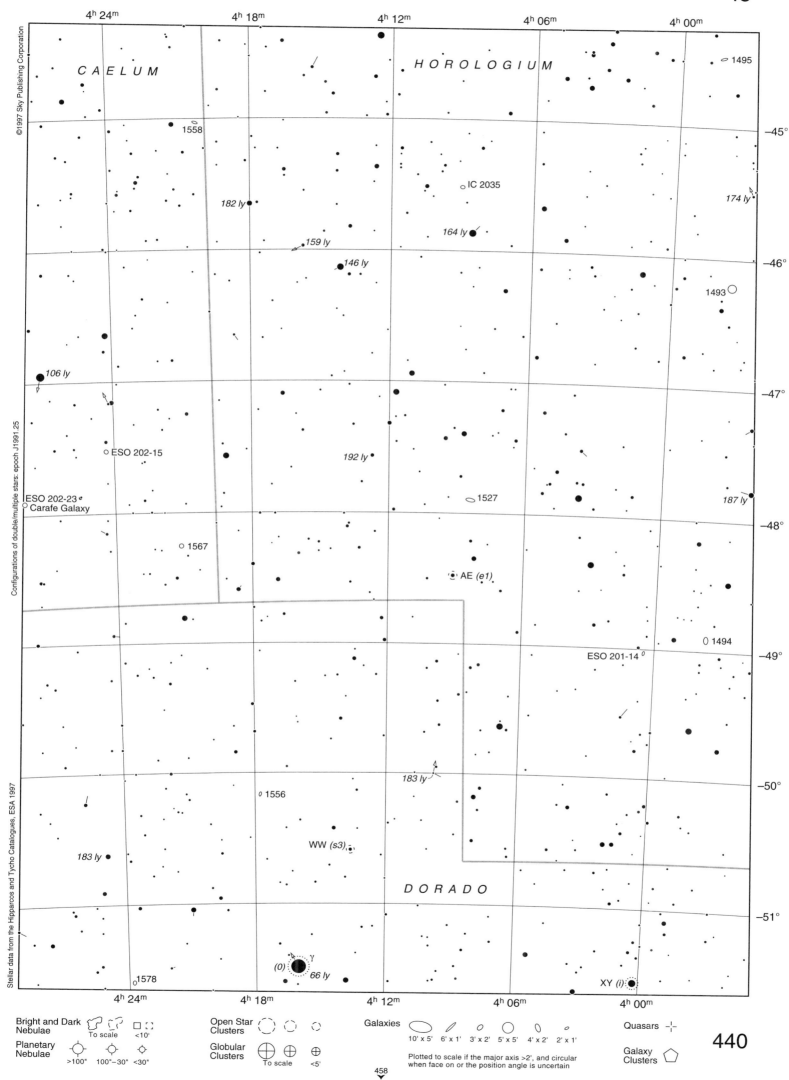

Bright and Dark Nebulae		Open Star Clusters	Galaxies

Bright and Dark Nebulae   To scale   <10'

Planetary Nebulae   >100"   100"–30"   <30'

Open Star Clusters   To scale

Globular Clusters   To scale   <5'

Galaxies   10' x 5'   6' x 1'   3' x 2'   5' x 5'   4' x 2'   2' x 1'

Plotted to scale if the major axis >2', and circular when face on or the position angle is uncertain

Quasars

Galaxy Clusters

440

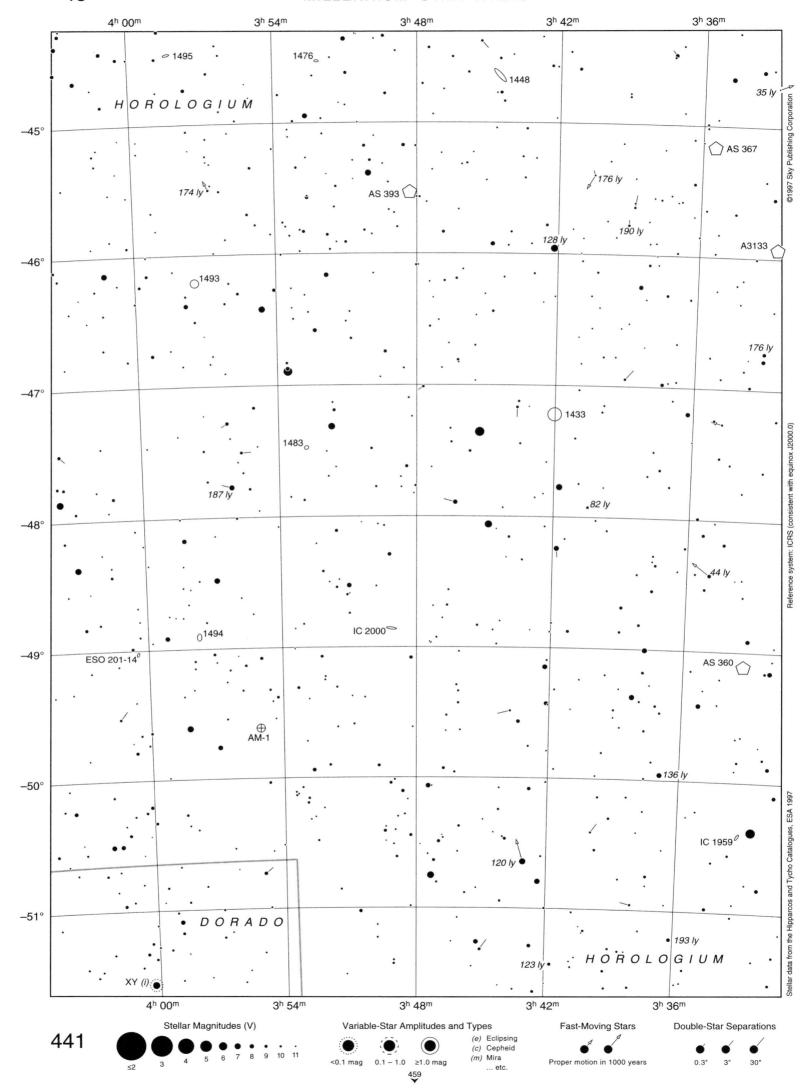

©1997 Sky Publishing Corporation

Reference system: ICRS (consistent with equinox J2000.0)

Stellar data from the Hipparcos and Tycho Catalogues, ESA 1997

441

Stellar Magnitudes (V)	Variable-Star Amplitudes and Types	Fast-Moving Stars	Double-Star Separations
≤2 3 4 5 6 7 8 9 10 11	<0.1 mag 0.1 – 1.0 ≥1.0 mag	Proper motion in 1000 years	0.3" 3" 30"

(e) Eclipsing
(c) Cepheid
(m) Mira
... etc.

459

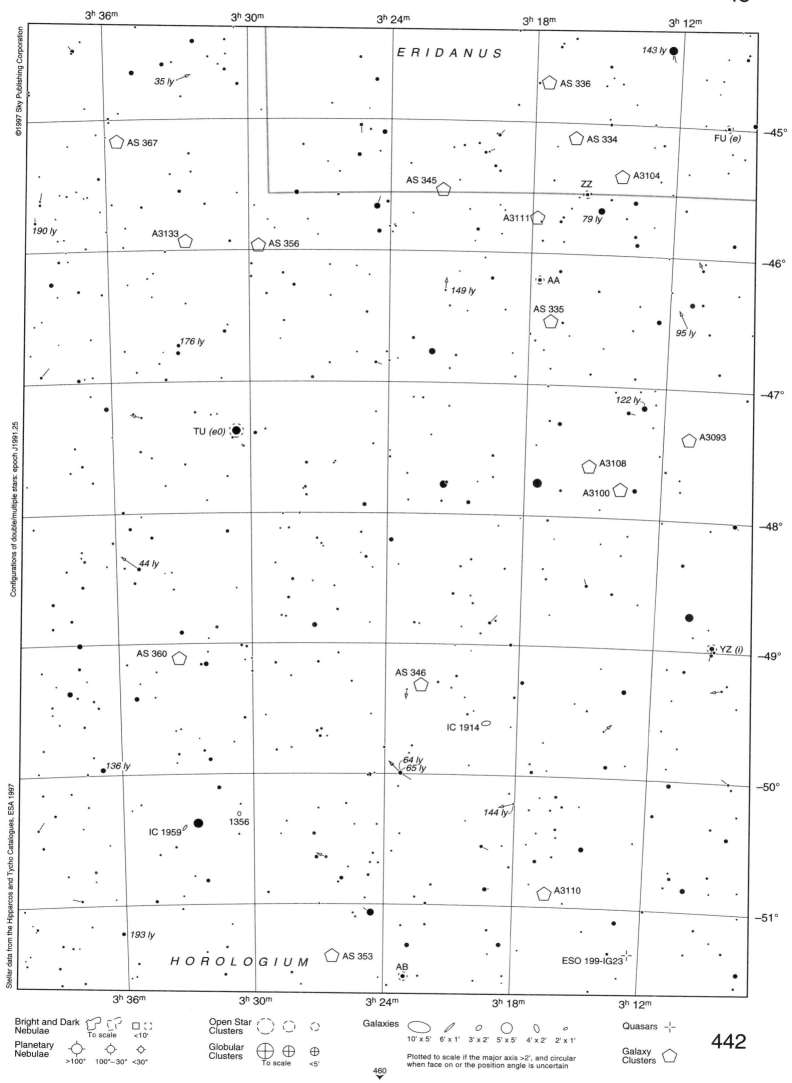

ERIDANUS

143 ly

AS 336

AS 367

AS 334

FU (e)

AS 345

A3104

ZZ

A3111

79 ly

190 ly

A3133

AS 356

149 ly

AA

176 ly

AS 335

95 ly

122 ly

TU (e0)

A3093

A3108

A3100

44 ly

AS 360

YZ (i)

AS 346

IC 1914

136 ly

64 ly
65 ly

144 ly

IC 1959

o
1356

A3110

193 ly

HOROLOGIUM

AS 353

AB

ESO 199-IG23

MILLENNIUM STAR ATLAS

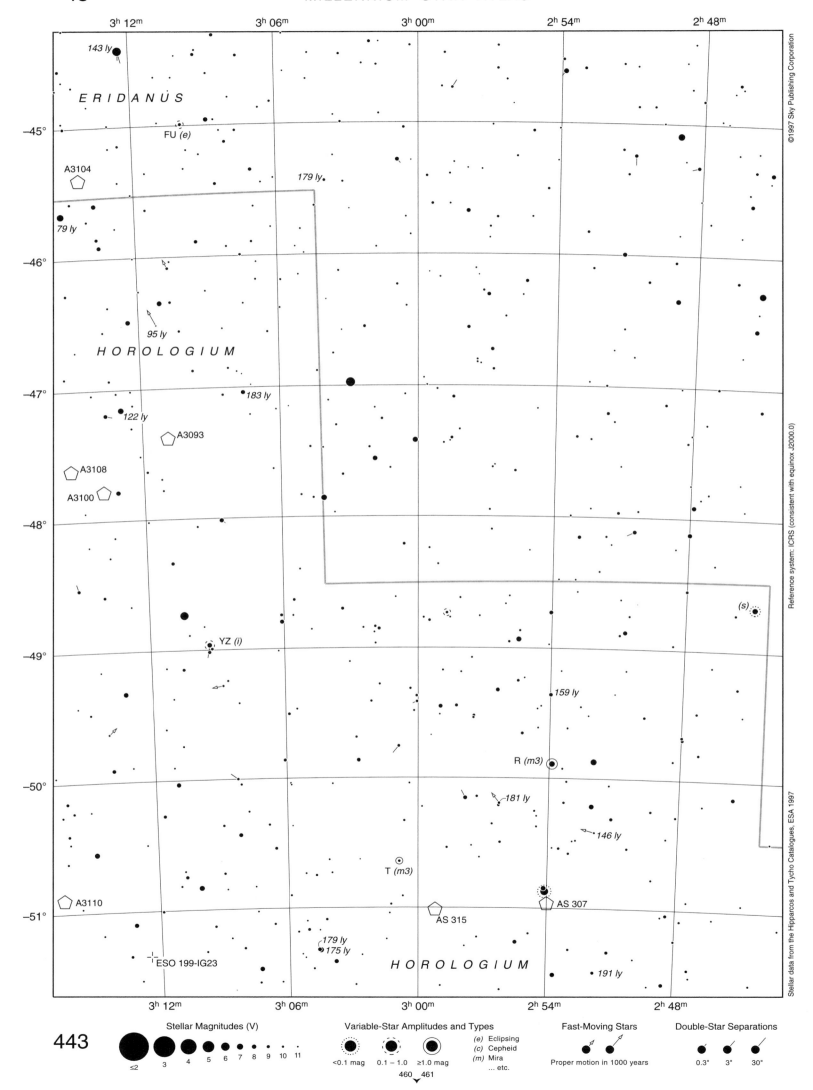

©1997 Sky Publishing Corporation

Reference system: ICRS (consistent with equinox J2000.0)

Stellar data from the Hipparcos and Tycho Catalogues, ESA 1997

443

Stellar Magnitudes (V)

≤2 3 4 5 6 7 8 9 10 11

Variable-Star Amplitudes and Types

<0.1 mag   0.1 − 1.0   ≥1.0 mag

(e) Eclipsing
(c) Cepheid
(m) Mira
... etc.

Fast-Moving Stars

Proper motion in 1000 years

Double-Star Separations

0.3" 3" 30"

460 461

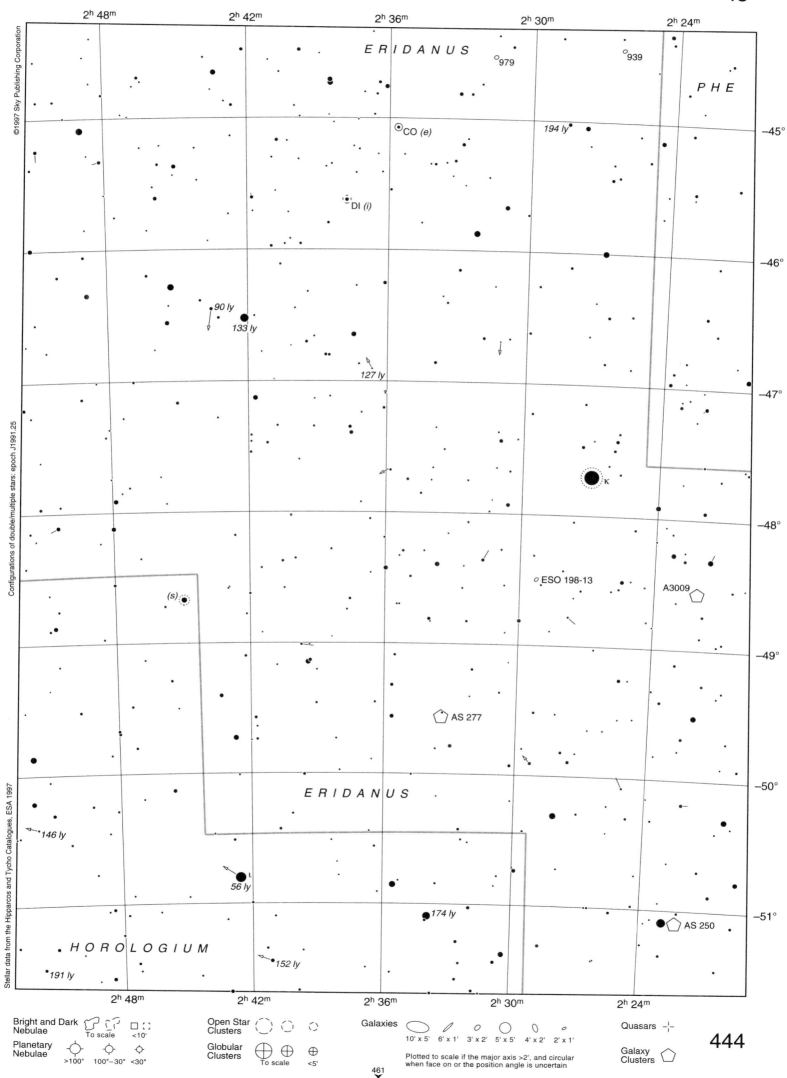

Configurations of double/multiple stars: epoch J1991.25

Stellar data from the Hipparcos and Tycho Catalogues, ESA 1997

ERIDANUS

PHE

979

939

CO (e)

194 ly

DI (i)

90 ly

133 ly

127 ly

K

(s)

ESO 198-13

A3009

AS 277

ERIDANUS

146 ly

L

56 ly

174 ly

AS 250

HOROLOGIUM

191 ly

152 ly

2ʰ 48ᵐ   2ʰ 42ᵐ   2ʰ 36ᵐ   2ʰ 30ᵐ   2ʰ 24ᵐ

| Bright and Dark Nebulae | Open Star Clusters | Galaxies | Quasars |
| Planetary Nebulae | Globular Clusters | | Galaxy Clusters |

To scale   <10'

>100°   100°−30°   <30°

To scale   <5'

10' x 5'   6' x 1'   3' x 2'   5' x 5'   4' x 2'   2' x 1'

Plotted to scale if the major axis >2', and circular
when face on or the position angle is uncertain

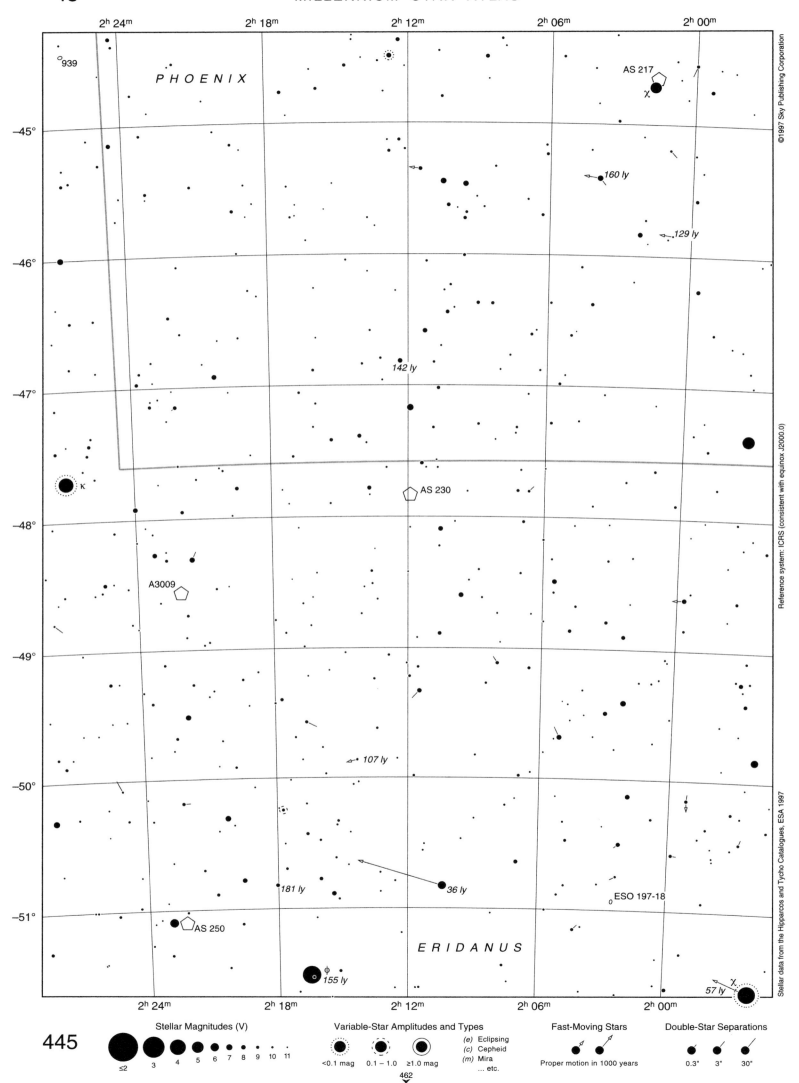

©1997 Sky Publishing Corporation

Reference system: ICRS (consistent with equinox J2000.0)

Stellar data from the Hipparcos and Tycho Catalogues, ESA 1997

PHOENIX

ERIDANUS

939

AS 217
χ

160 ly

129 ly

142 ly

κ

AS 230

A3009

107 ly

36 ly

181 ly

ESO 197-18

AS 250

φ
155 ly

χ
57 ly

Stellar Magnitudes (V)	Variable-Star Amplitudes and Types	Fast-Moving Stars	Double-Star Separations
≤2 3 4 5 6 7 8 9 10 11	<0.1 mag 0.1 – 1.0 ≥1.0 mag	Proper motion in 1000 years	0.3" 3" 30"

(e) Eclipsing
(c) Cepheid
(m) Mira
... etc.

462

MILLENNIUM STAR ATLAS

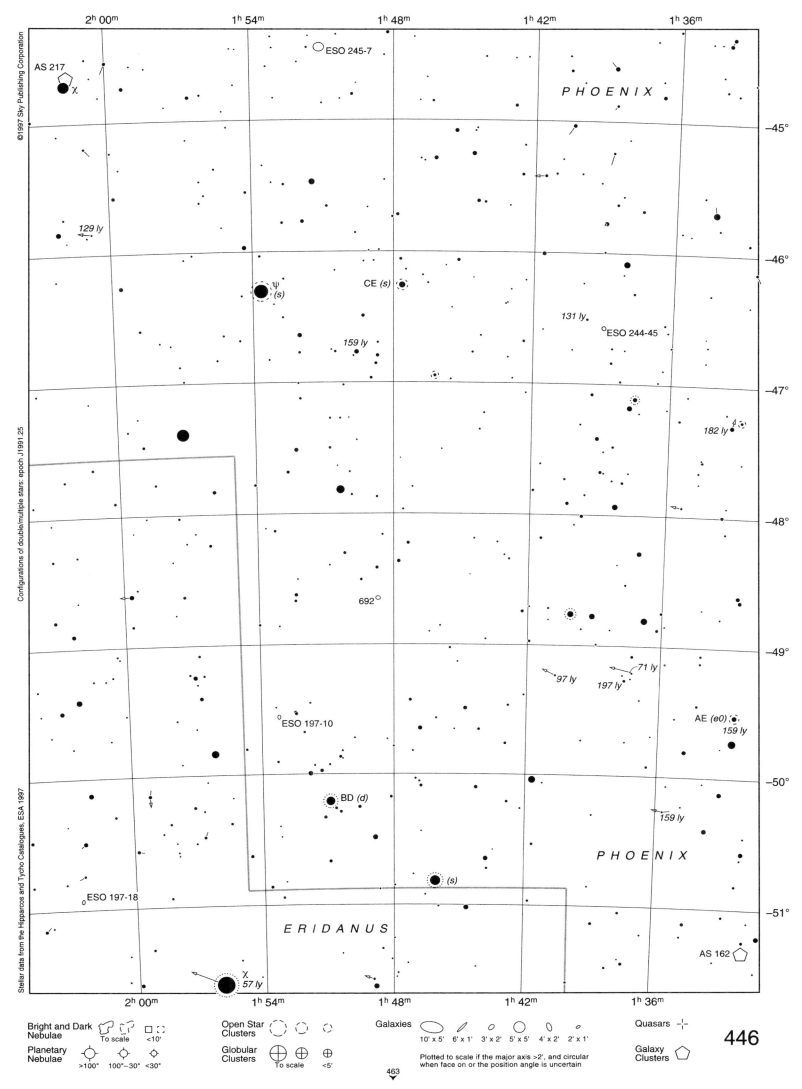

©1997 Sky Publishing Corporation

Configurations of double/multiple stars: epoch J1991.25

Stellar data from the Hipparcos and Tycho Catalogues, ESA 1997

2ʰ 00ᵐ   1ʰ 54ᵐ   1ʰ 48ᵐ   1ʰ 42ᵐ   1ʰ 36ᵐ

AS 217

χ

ESO 245-7

PHOENIX

−45°

129 ly

ψ (s)

CE (s)

131 ly

ESO 244-45

−46°

159 ly

−47°

182 ly

692

−48°

71 ly

97 ly   197 ly

AE (e0)

159 ly

ESO 197-10

−49°

BD (d)

159 ly

PHOENIX

−50°

(s)

ESO 197-18

AS 162

ERIDANUS

χ

57 ly

−51°

2ʰ 00ᵐ   1ʰ 54ᵐ   1ʰ 48ᵐ   1ʰ 42ᵐ   1ʰ 36ᵐ

Bright and Dark Nebulae	To scale <10'	
Planetary Nebulae	>100" 100"−30" <30"	
Open Star Clusters		
Globular Clusters	To scale <5'	

Galaxies   10' x 5'   6' x 1'   3' x 2'   5' x 5'   4' x 2'   2' x 1'

Plotted to scale if the major axis >2', and circular when face on or the position angle is uncertain

Quasars

Galaxy Clusters

446

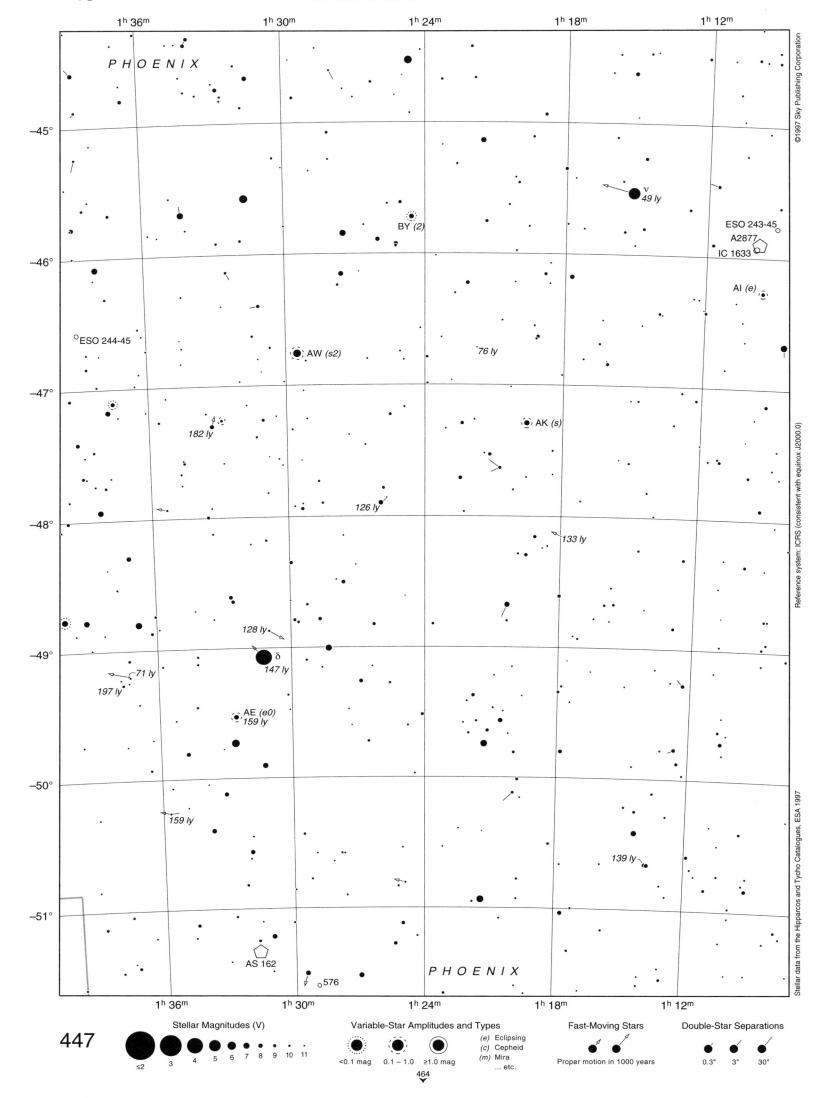

PHOENIX

ν
49 ly

ESO 243-45
A2877
IC 1633

AI (e)

ESO 244-45

AW (s2)

76 ly

182 ly

AK (s)

126 ly

133 ly

128 ly

δ
147 ly

71 ly
197 ly

AE (e0)
159 ly

159 ly

139 ly

AS 162

576

PHOENIX

©1997 Sky Publishing Corporation

Reference system: ICRS (consistent with equinox J2000.0)

Stellar data from the Hipparcos and Tycho Catalogues, ESA 1997

447

Stellar Magnitudes (V)

≤2 3 4 5 6 7 8 9 10 11

Variable-Star Amplitudes and Types

<0.1 mag   0.1 – 1.0   ≥1.0 mag

(e) Eclipsing
(c) Cepheid
(m) Mira
... etc.

Fast-Moving Stars

Proper motion in 1000 years

Double-Star Separations

0.3"   3"   30"

464

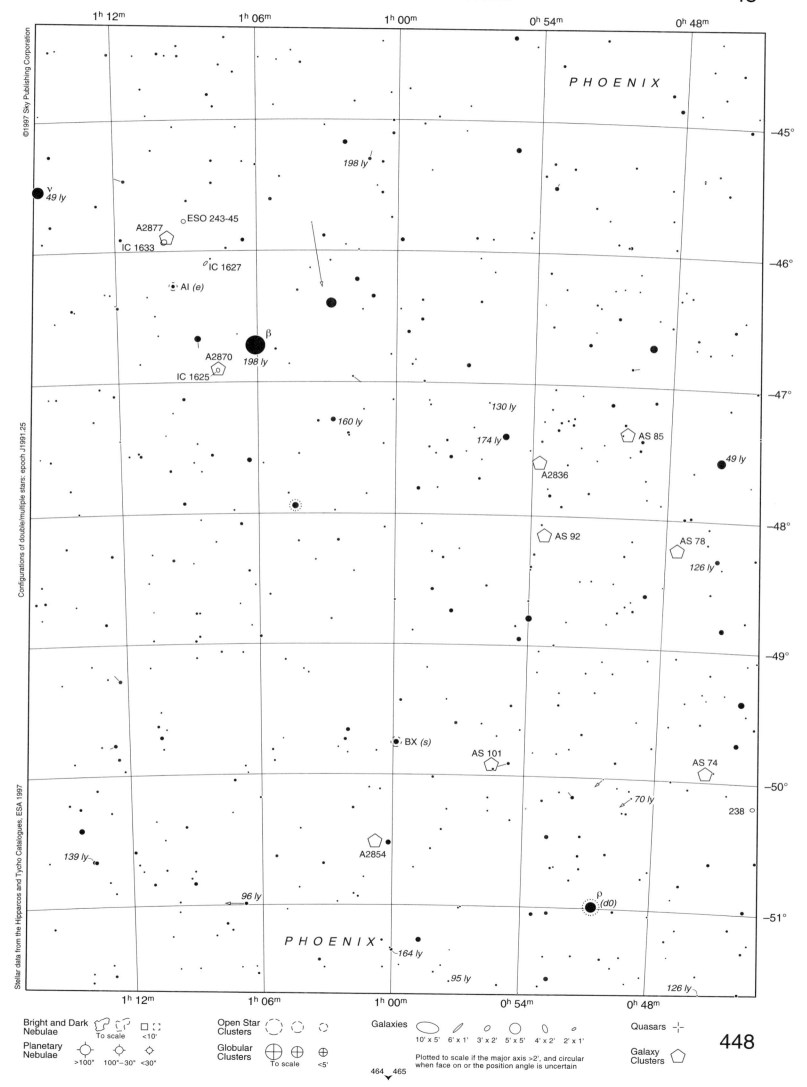

P H O E N I X

−45°

ν
49 ly

○ ESO 243-45

A2877

IC 1633

○ IC 1627

−46°

·○· AI (e)

β

A2870

198 ly

IC 1625

−47°

160 ly

130 ly

174 ly

AS 85

A2836

49 ly

−48°

AS 92

AS 78

126 ly

−49°

BX (s)

AS 101

AS 74

−50°

70 ly

238 ○

139 ly

A2854

96 ly

ρ (d0)

−51°

P H O E N I X

164 ly

95 ly

126 ly

Bright and Dark Nebulae	Open Star Clusters	Galaxies	Quasars −	−
To scale <10'	To scale <5'	10' x 5' 6' x 1' 3' x 2' 5' x 5' 4' x 2' 2' x 1'	
Planetary Nebulae	Globular Clusters		Galaxy Clusters
>100" 100"−30" <30"		Plotted to scale if the major axis >2', and circular when face on or the position angle is uncertain	

464 465

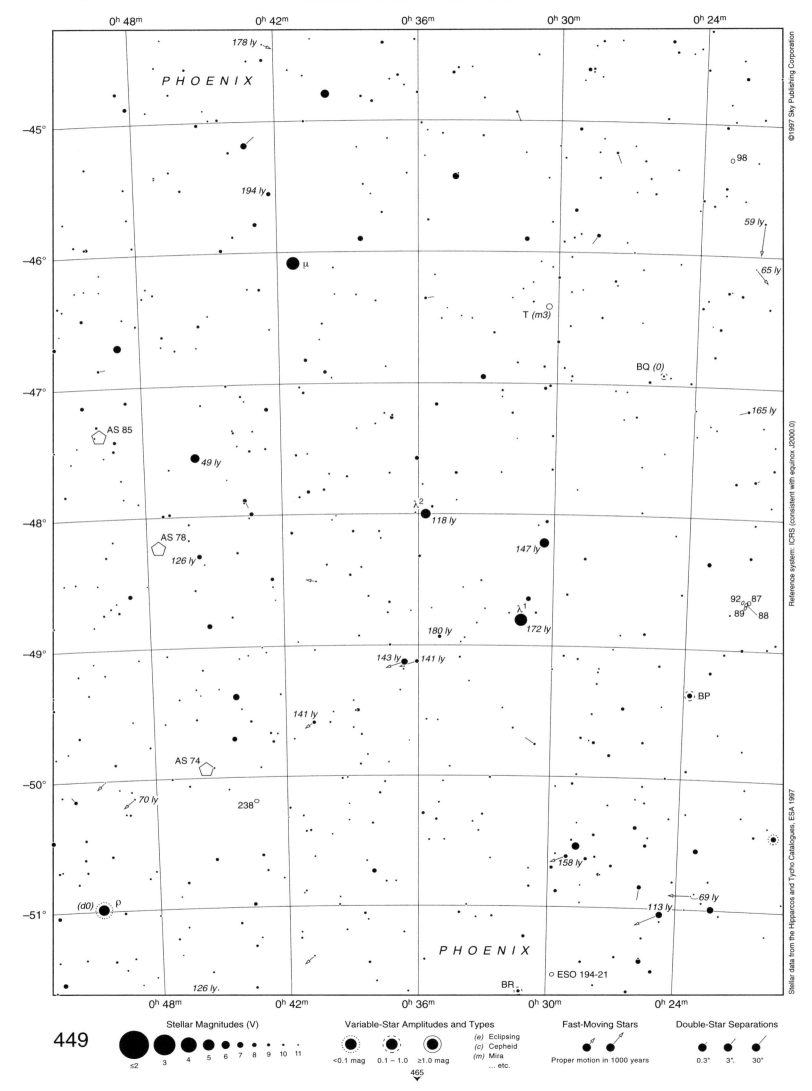

PHOENIX

PHOENIX

449

Stellar Magnitudes (V)

≤2   3   4   5   6   7   8   9   10   11

Variable-Star Amplitudes and Types

<0.1 mag   0.1 − 1.0   ≥1.0 mag

(e) Eclipsing
(c) Cepheid
(m) Mira
... etc.

Fast-Moving Stars

Proper motion in 1000 years

Double-Star Separations

0.3"   3"   30"

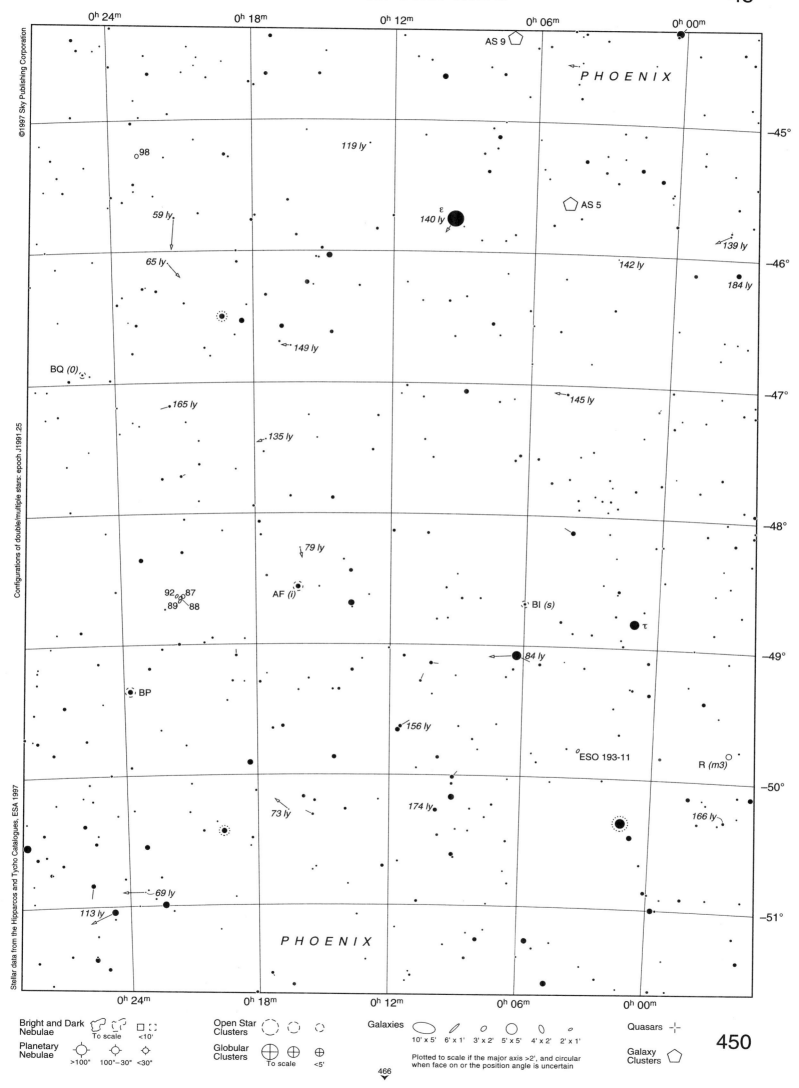

0ʰ 24ᵐ   0ʰ 18ᵐ   0ʰ 12ᵐ   0ʰ 06ᵐ   0ʰ 00ᵐ

AS 9

PHOENIX

−45°

98

119 ly

ε
140 ly

AS 5

139 ly

59 ly

142 ly

−46°

65 ly

184 ly

149 ly

BQ (0)

−47°

165 ly

145 ly

135 ly

−48°

79 ly

92 87
89 88

AF (i)

BI (s)

τ

84 ly

−49°

BP

156 ly

ESO 193-11

R (m3)

−50°

73 ly

174 ly

166 ly

69 ly

113 ly

−51°

PHOENIX

0ʰ 24ᵐ   0ʰ 18ᵐ   0ʰ 12ᵐ   0ʰ 06ᵐ   0ʰ 00ᵐ

Bright and Dark
Nebulae
To scale   <10'

Planetary
Nebulae
>100"   100"–30"   <30"

Open Star
Clusters

Globular
Clusters
To scale   <5'

Galaxies
10' x 5'   6' x 1'   3' x 2'   5' x 5'   4' x 2'   2' x 1'

Plotted to scale if the major axis >2', and circular
when face on or the position angle is uncertain

Quasars

Galaxy
Clusters

450

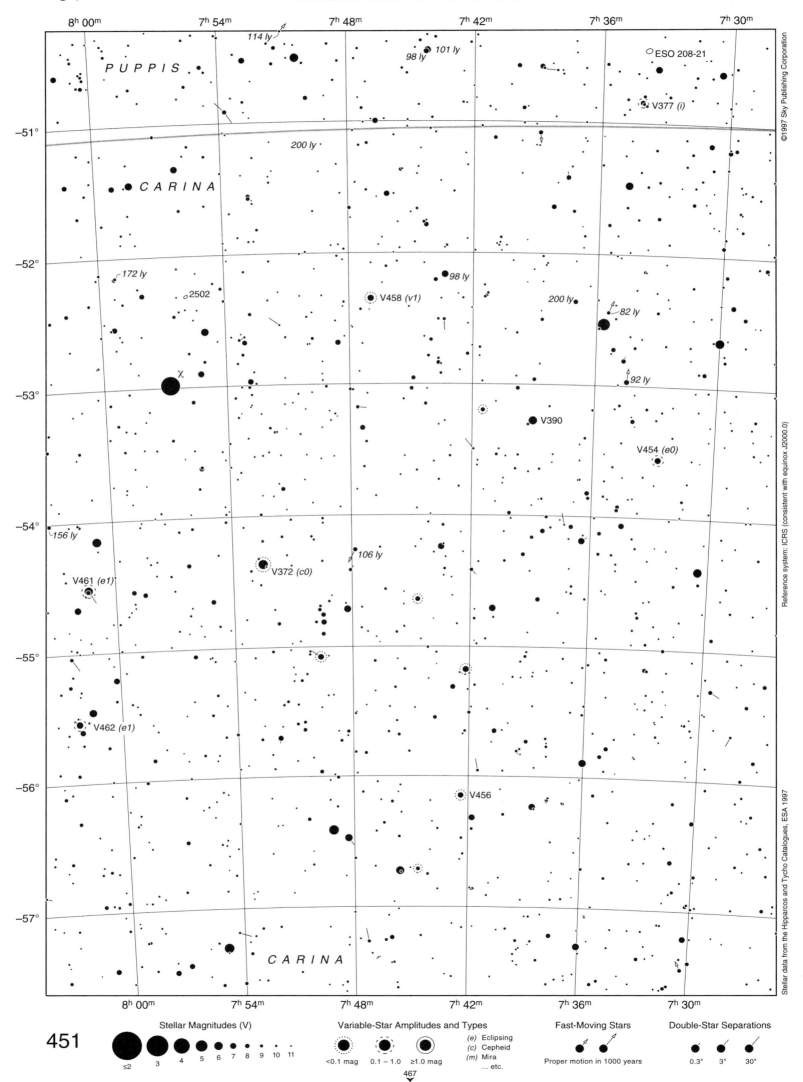

PUPPIS

CARINA

ESO 208-21

V377 (i)

200 ly

114 ly

98 ly   101 ly

172 ly

2502

98 ly

V458 (v1)

200 ly

82 ly

92 ly

V390

V454 (e0)

156 ly

106 ly

V372 (c0)

V461 (e1)

V462 (e1)

V456

CARINA

©1997 Sky Publishing Corporation

Reference system: ICRS (consistent with equinox J2000.0)

Stellar data from the Hipparcos and Tycho Catalogues, ESA 1997

Stellar Magnitudes (V)

≤2   3   4   5   6   7   8   9   10   11

Variable-Star Amplitudes and Types

<0.1 mag   0.1 – 1.0   ≥1.0 mag

(e) Eclipsing
(c) Cepheid
(m) Mira
... etc.

Fast-Moving Stars

Proper motion in 1000 years

Double-Star Separations

0.3"   3"   30"

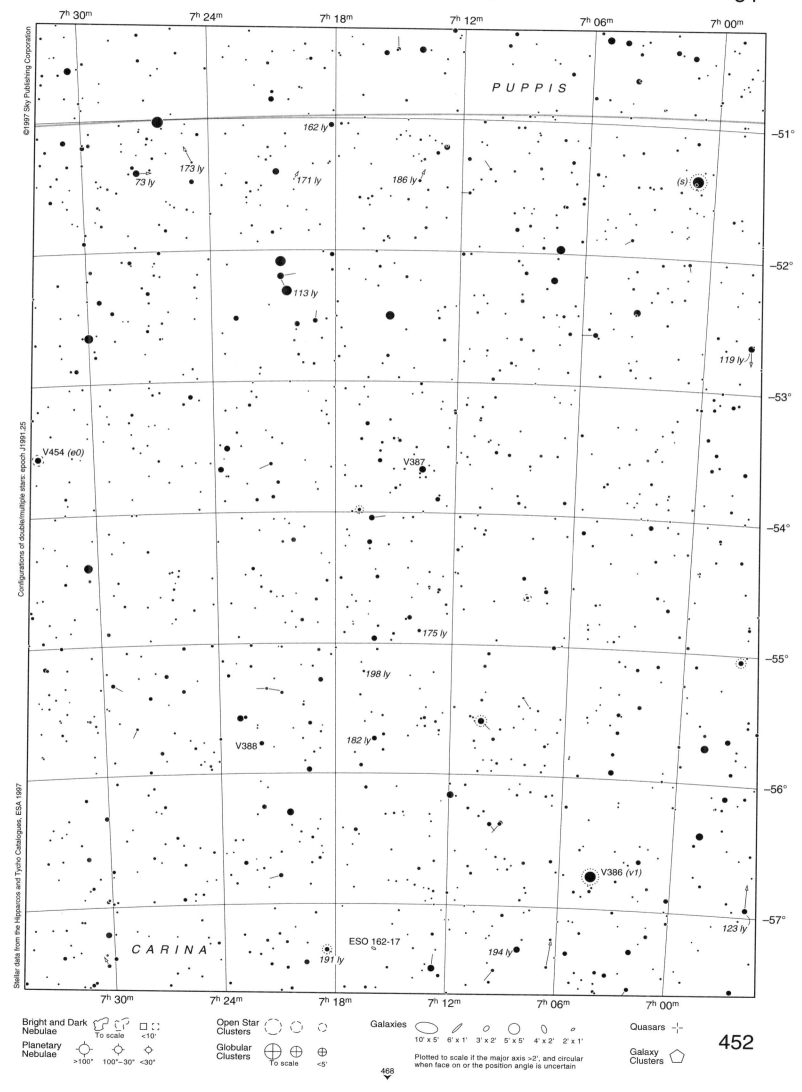

7h 30m   7h 24m   7h 18m   7h 12m   7h 06m   7h 00m

PUPPIS

−51°

162 ly

173 ly

73 ly   *171 ly*   *186 ly*

(s)

−52°

113 ly

119 ly

−53°

V454 (e0)

V387

−54°

175 ly

−55°

198 ly

V388   *182 ly*

−56°

V386 (v1)

−57°

123 ly

ESO 162-17

191 ly   *194 ly*

CARINA

7h 30m   7h 24m   7h 18m   7h 12m   7h 06m   7h 00m

Bright and Dark Nebulae   To scale   <10'

Planetary Nebulae   >100"   100"−30"   <30"

Open Star Clusters

Globular Clusters   To scale   <5'

Galaxies   10' x 5'   6' x 1'   3' x 2'   5' x 5'   4' x 2'   2' x 1'

Plotted to scale if the major axis >2', and circular when face on or the position angle is uncertain

Quasars

Galaxy Clusters

452

▼
468

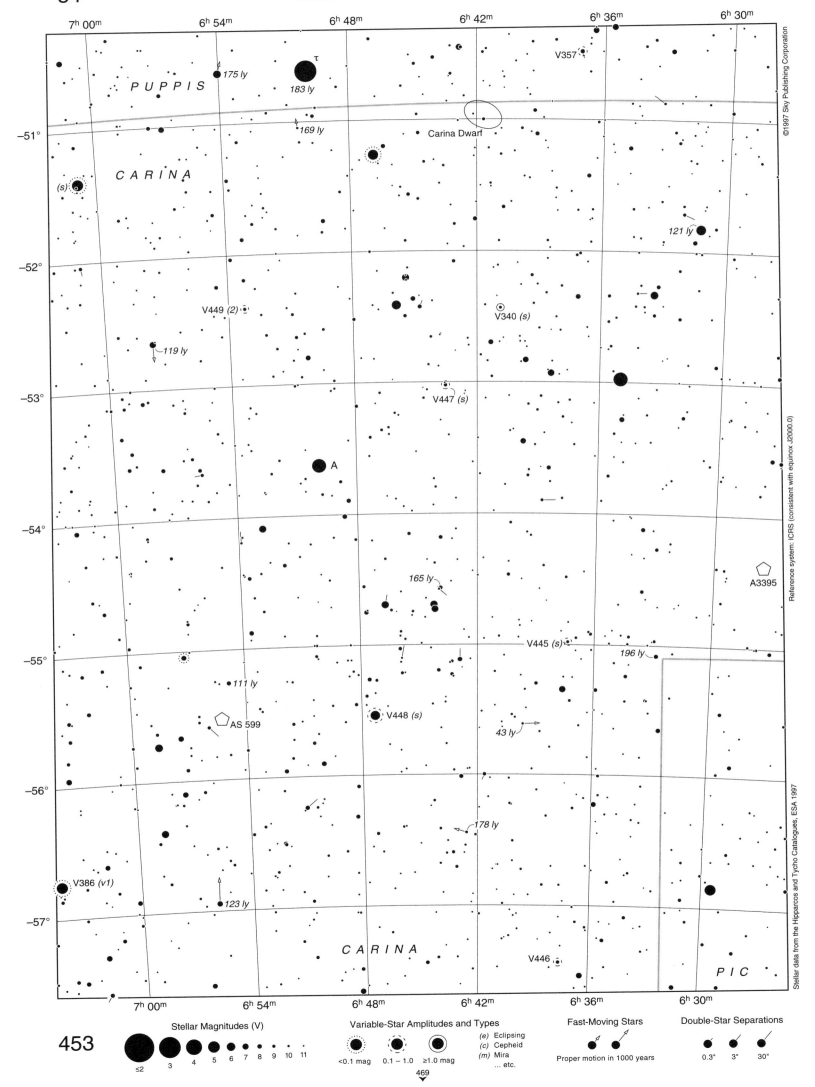

©1997 Sky Publishing Corporation

Reference system: ICRS (consistent with equinox J2000.0)

Stellar data from the Hipparcos and Tycho Catalogues, ESA 1997

PUPPIS

τ
175 ly
183 ly
169 ly

Carina Dwarf

CARINA

(s)

V357

121 ly

V449 (2)

V340 (s)

119 ly

V447 (s)

A

A3395

165 ly

V445 (s)

196 ly

111 ly

V448 (s)

AS 599

43 ly

178 ly

V386 (v1)

123 ly

CARINA

V446

PIC

453

Stellar Magnitudes (V)

≤2   3   4   5   6   7   8   9 10 11

Variable-Star Amplitudes and Types

<0.1 mag   0.1 – 1.0   ≥1.0 mag

(e) Eclipsing
(c) Cepheid
(m) Mira
... etc.

Fast-Moving Stars

Proper motion in 1000 years

Double-Star Separations

0.3"   3"   30"

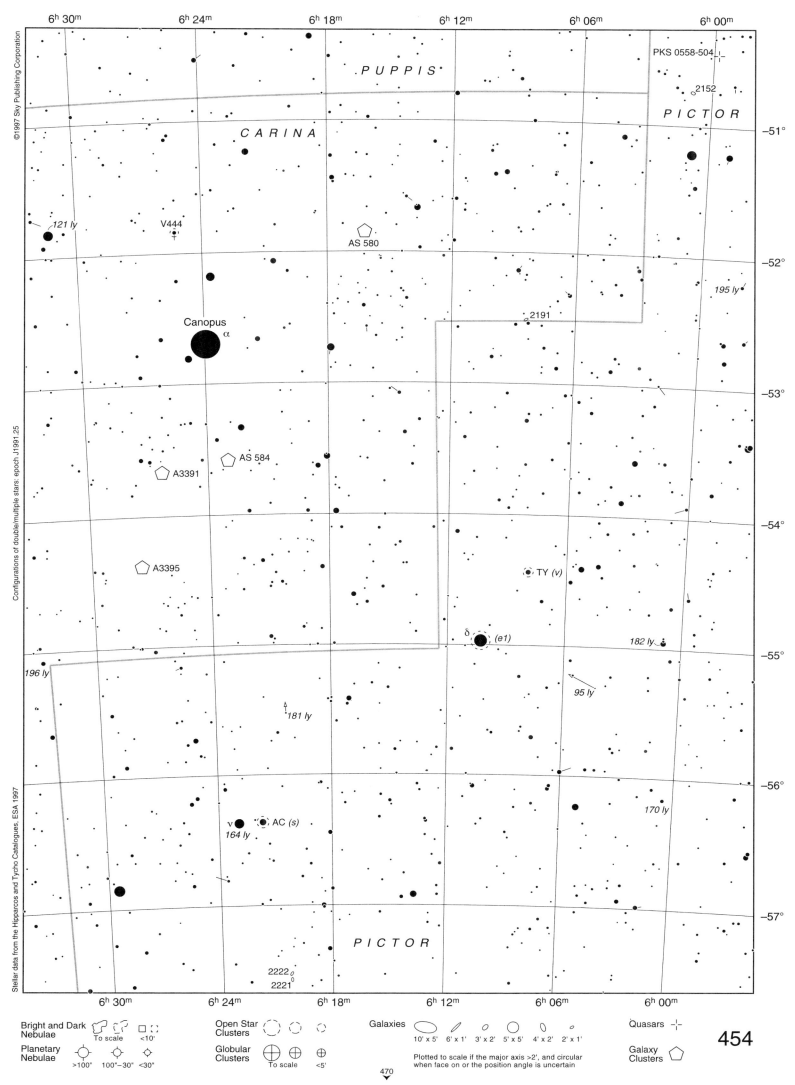

PUPPIS

CARINA

PICTOR

PKS 0558-504

2152

121 ly

V444

AS 580

195 ly

2191

Canopus
α

AS 584

A3391

182 ly

A3395

TY (v)

δ (e1)

196 ly

95 ly

181 ly

ν
164 ly

AC (s)

170 ly

PICTOR

2222
2221

Bright and Dark Nebulae
To scale   <10'

Open Star Clusters

Galaxies
10' x 5'   6' x 1'   3' x 2'   5' x 5'   4' x 2'   2' x 1'

Quasars

Planetary Nebulae
>100"   100"–30"   <30"

Globular Clusters
To scale   <5'

Plotted to scale if the major axis >2', and circular when face on or the position angle is uncertain

Galaxy Clusters

470

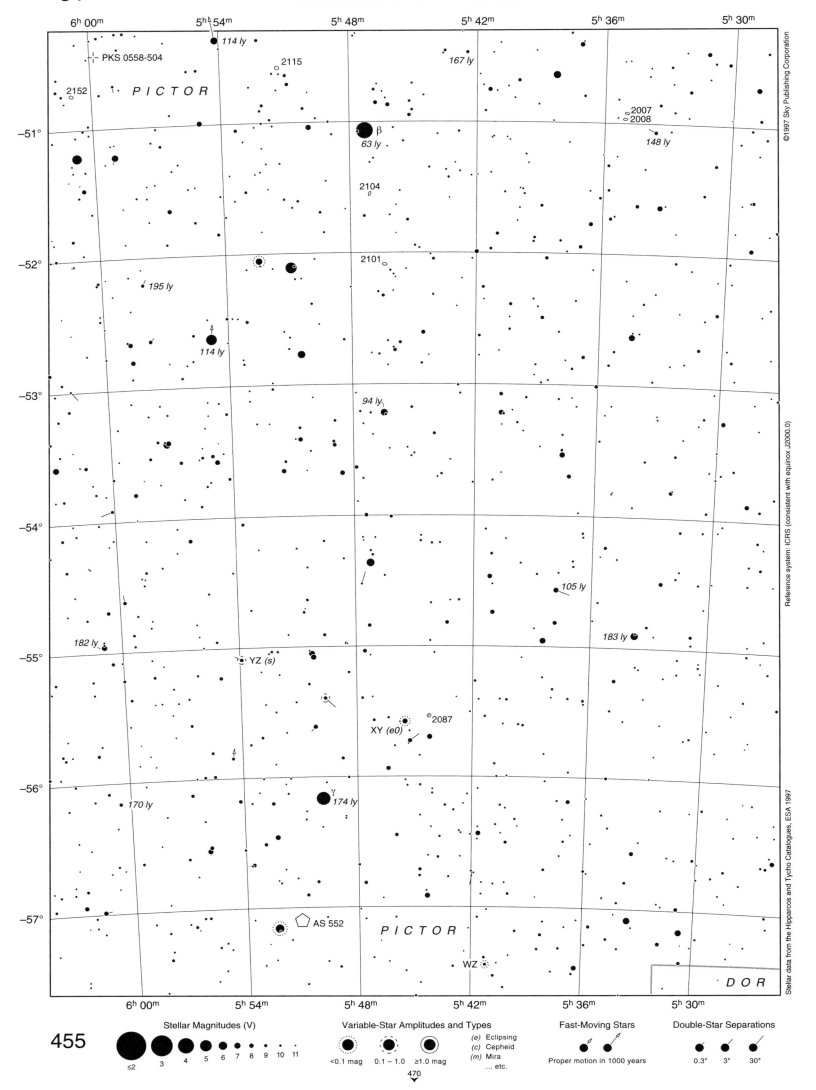

PKS 0558-504

2115

2152

P I C T O R

167 ly

2007
2008

β
63 ly

148 ly

–51°

2104

195 ly

2101

–52°

114 ly

94 ly

–53°

105 ly

183 ly

182 ly

–54°

YZ (s)

–55°

XY (e0)   2087

γ 174 ly

170 ly

–56°

AS 552   P I C T O R

–57°

WZ

D O R

©1997 Sky Publishing Corporation

Reference system: ICRS (consistent with equinox J2000.0)

Stellar data from the Hipparcos and Tycho Catalogues, ESA 1997

455

Stellar Magnitudes (V)

≤2   3   4   5   6   7   8   9   10   11

Variable-Star Amplitudes and Types

<0.1 mag   0.1 – 1.0   ≥1.0 mag

(e) Eclipsing
(c) Cepheid
(m) Mira
... etc.

Fast-Moving Stars

Proper motion in 1000 years

Double-Star Separations

0.3"   3"   30"

470

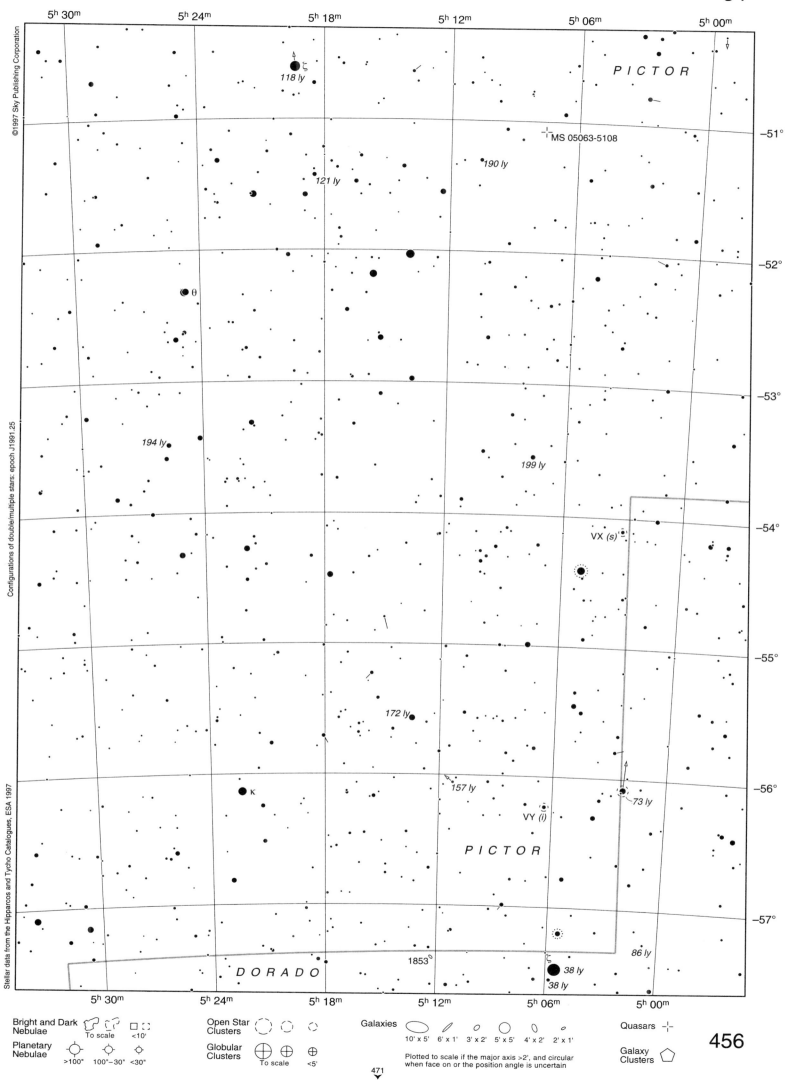

5h 30m 5h 24m 5h 18m 5h 12m 5h 06m 5h 00m

−51°
−52°
−53°
−54°
−55°
−56°
−57°

PICTOR

ζ
118 ly

MS 05063-5108
190 ly

121 ly

θ

194 ly

199 ly

VX *(s)*

172 ly

κ

157 ly

VY *(i)*

73 ly

PICTOR

1853

86 ly

DORADO

ζ
38 ly
38 ly

Bright and Dark Nebulae	Open Star Clusters	Galaxies	Quasars
To scale <10'	To scale <5'	10' x 5' 6' x 1' 3' x 2' 5' x 5' 4' x 2' 2' x 1'	
Planetary Nebulae	Globular Clusters	Galaxy Clusters	
>100" 100"–30" <30"	To scale <5'	Plotted to scale if the major axis >2', and circular when face on or the position angle is uncertain	

471

456

MILLENNIUM STAR ATLAS

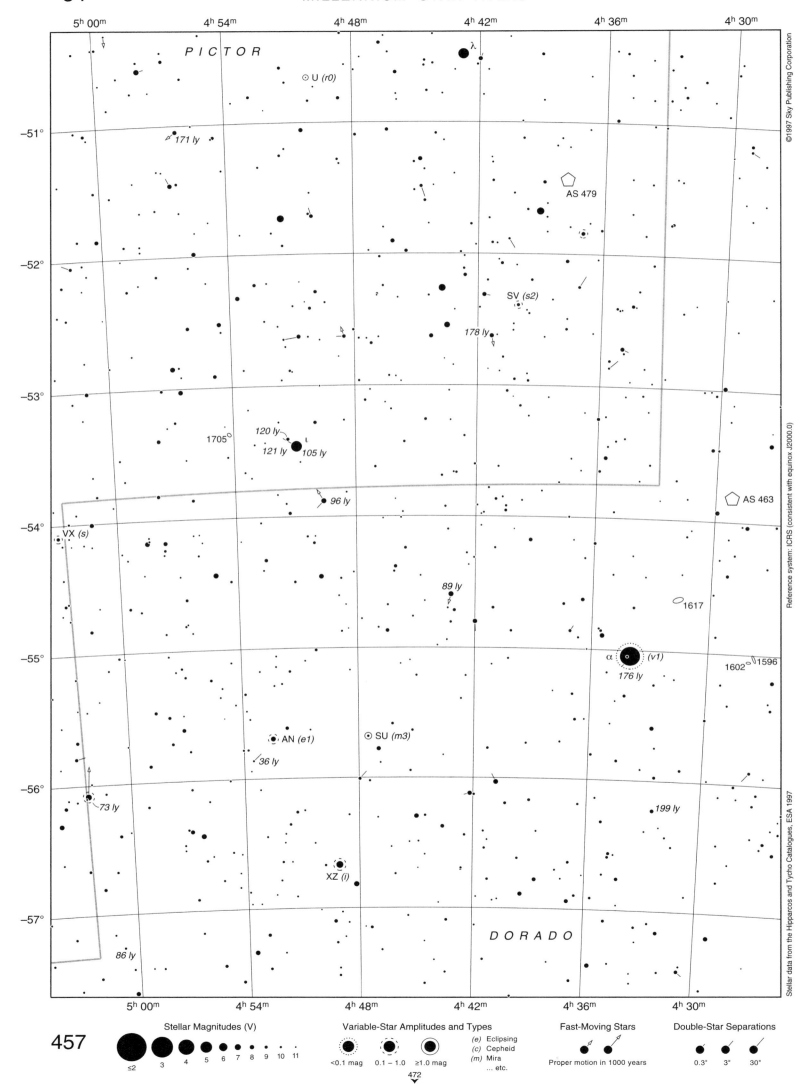

©1997 Sky Publishing Corporation

Reference system: ICRS (consistent with equinox J2000.0)

Stellar data from the Hipparcos and Tycho Catalogues, ESA 1997

P I C T O R

U (r0)

λ

171 ly

AS 479

SV (s2)

178 ly

1705

120 ly
ι
121 ly   105 ly

96 ly

AS 463

VX (s)

89 ly

1617

α   (v1)

176 ly

1602   1596

AN (e1)

SU (m3)

199 ly

36 ly

73 ly

XZ (i)

D O R A D O

86 ly

457

Stellar Magnitudes (V)

≤2   3   4   5   6   7   8   9   10   11

Variable-Star Amplitudes and Types

<0.1 mag   0.1 – 1.0   ≥1.0 mag

(e) Eclipsing
(c) Cepheid
(m) Mira
... etc.

Fast-Moving Stars

Proper motion in 1000 years

Double-Star Separations

0.3"   3"   30"

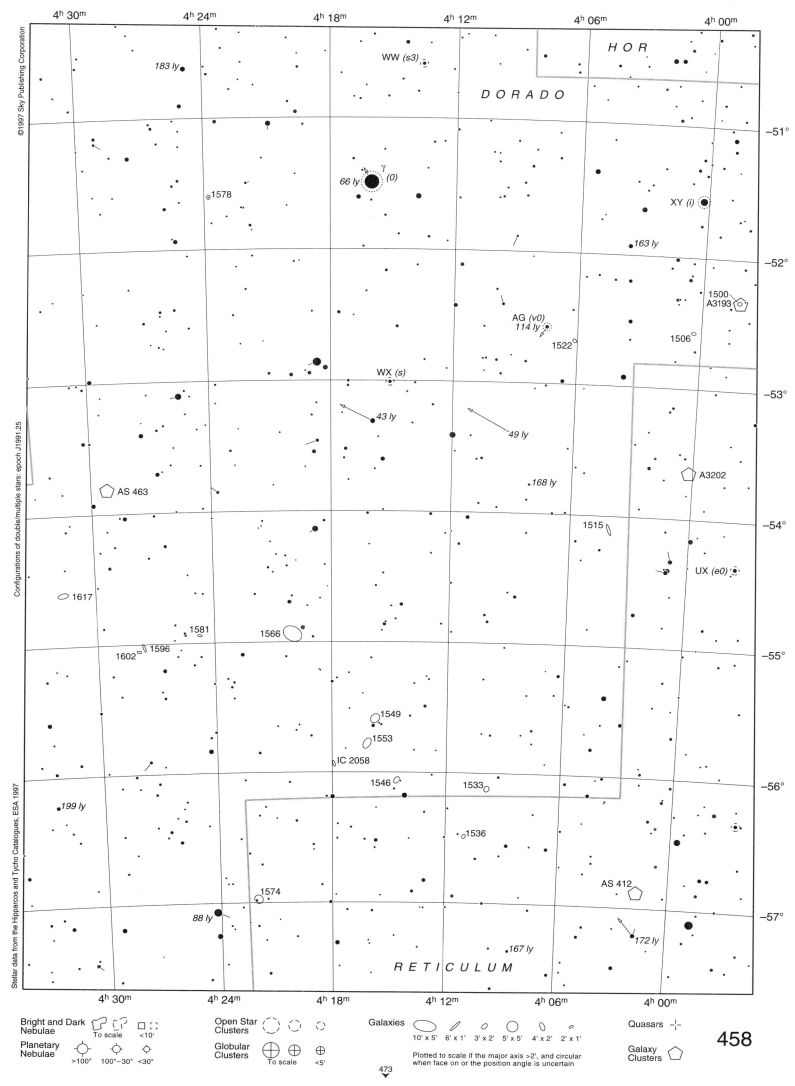

H O R

D O R A D O

WW *(s3)*

−51°

183 ly

⊙1578

γ *(0)*
66 ly

XY *(i)*

163 ly

−52°

1500
A3193

AG *(v0)*
114 ly

1522

1506

WX *(s)*

−53°

43 ly

49 ly

168 ly

A3202

AS 463

1515

−54°

UX *(e0)*

1617

1581

1566

1602 1596

−55°

1549

1553

IC 2058

1546

1533

−56°

199 ly

1536

AS 412

1574

88 ly

−57°

172 ly

167 ly

R E T I C U L U M

Bright and Dark Nebulae			Open Star Clusters			Galaxies						Quasars ┼
To scale		<10'	To scale			10' x 5'	6' x 1'	3' x 2'	5' x 5'	4' x 2'	2' x 1'	
Planetary Nebulae			Globular Clusters									Galaxy Clusters
>100"	100"−30"	<30"	To scale		<5'	Plotted to scale if the major axis >2', and circular when face on or the position angle is uncertain						

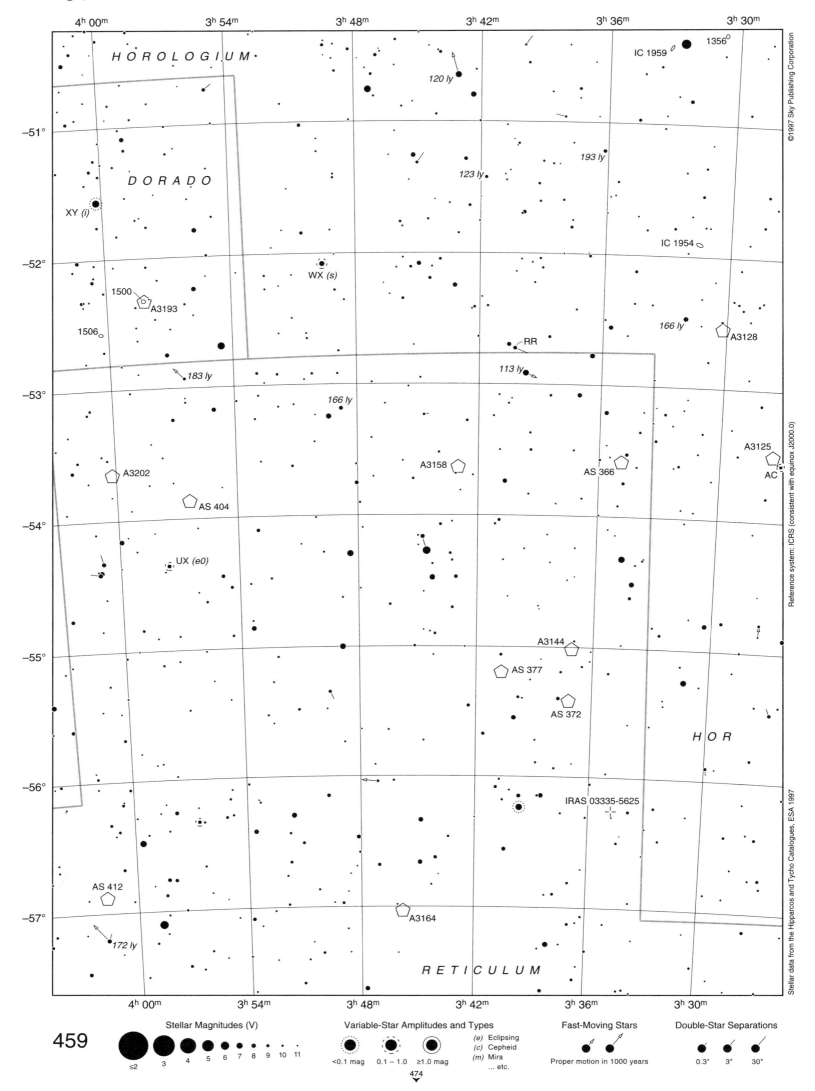

Stellar Magnitudes (V)

≤2   3   4   5   6   7   8   9   10   11

Variable-Star Amplitudes and Types

<0.1 mag   0.1 – 1.0   ≥1.0 mag

(e) Eclipsing
(c) Cepheid
(m) Mira
... etc.

Fast-Moving Stars

Proper motion in 1000 years

Double-Star Separations

0.3"   3"   30"

MILLENNIUM STAR ATLAS

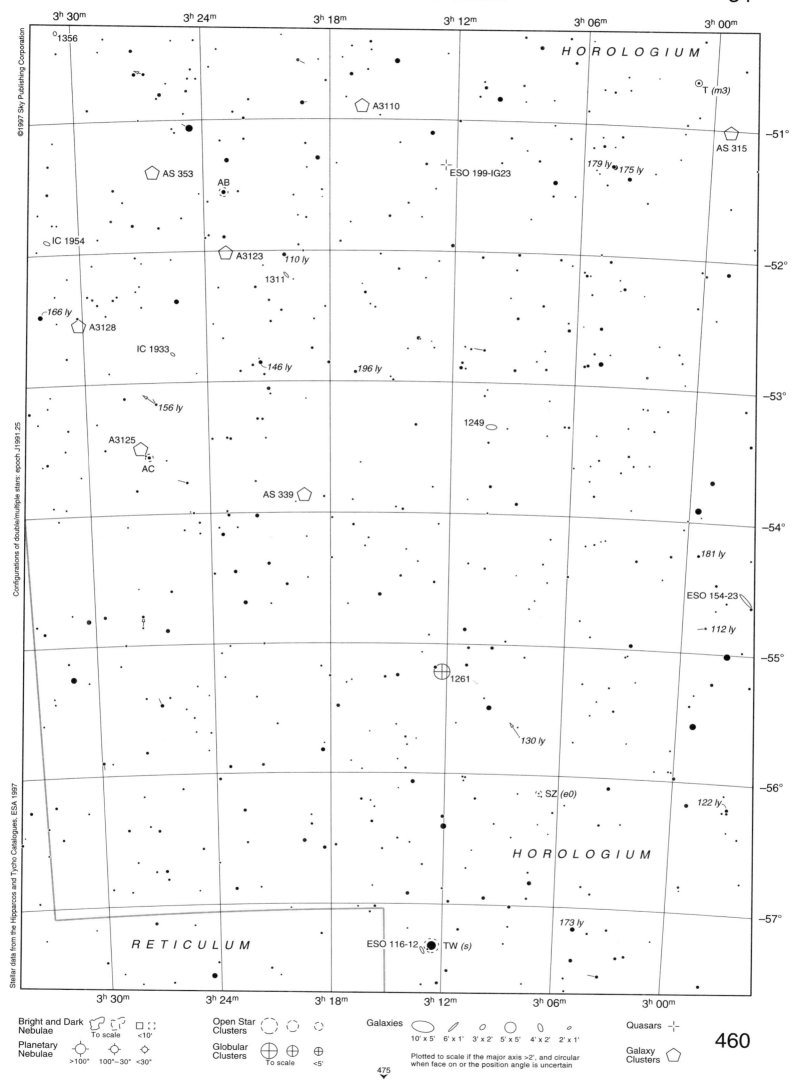

Configurations of double/multiple stars: epoch J1991.25

Stellar data from the Hipparcos and Tycho Catalogues, ESA 1997

H O R O L O G I U M

○1356

A3110

AS 353

AB

ESO 199-IG23

T *(m3)*

AS 315

179 ly ● 175 ly

○ IC 1954

A3123   *110 ly*

1311

166 ly

A3128

IC 1933 ○

146 ly   *196 ly*

156 ly

A3125

AC

AS 339

1249

181 ly

ESO 154-23

112 ly

1261

130 ly

SZ *(e0)*

122 ly

H O R O L O G I U M

173 ly

R E T I C U L U M

ESO 116-12   TW *(s)*

Bright and Dark Nebulae
To scale   <10'

Planetary Nebulae
>100"   100"−30"   <30"

Open Star Clusters

Globular Clusters
To scale   <5'

Galaxies
10' x 5'   6' x 1'   3' x 2'   5' x 5'   4' x 2'   2' x 1'

Plotted to scale if the major axis >2', and circular when face on or the position angle is uncertain

Quasars

Galaxy Clusters

460

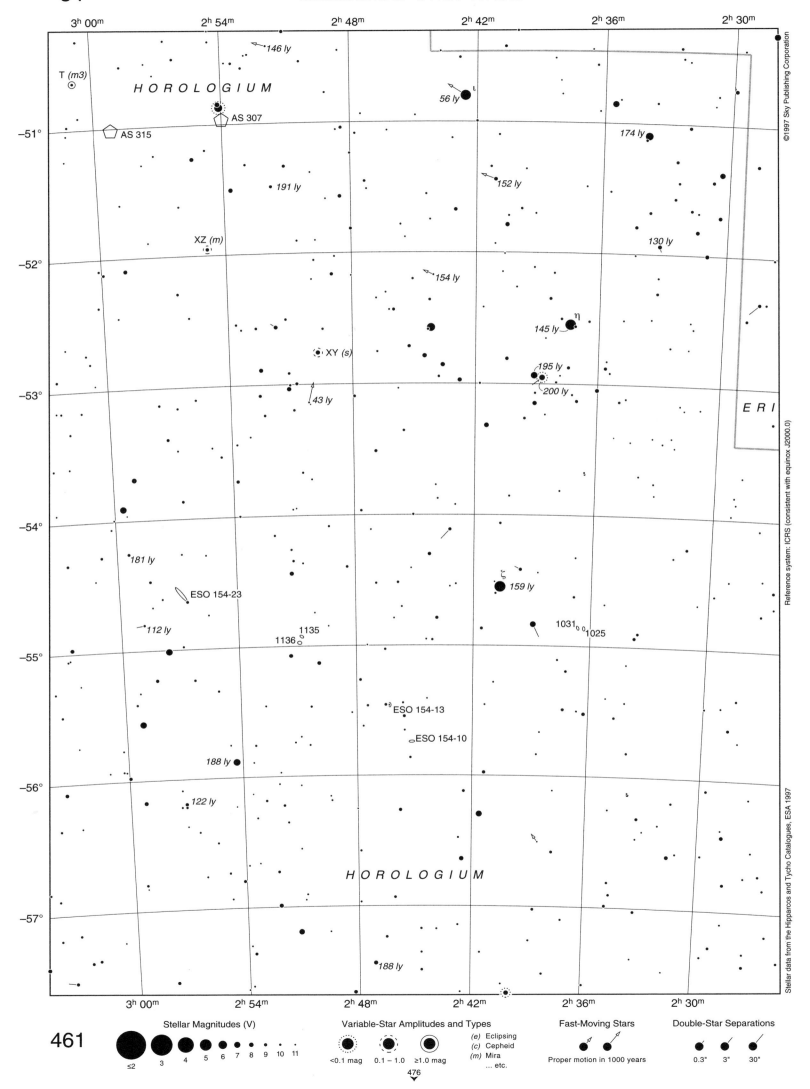

461

Stellar Magnitudes (V)

≤2 3 4 5 6 7 8 9 10 11

Variable-Star Amplitudes and Types

<0.1 mag   0.1 – 1.0   ≥1.0 mag

(e) Eclipsing
(c) Cepheid
(m) Mira
... etc.

Fast-Moving Stars

Proper motion in 1000 years

Double-Star Separations

0.3" 3" 30"

MILLENNIUM STAR ATLAS

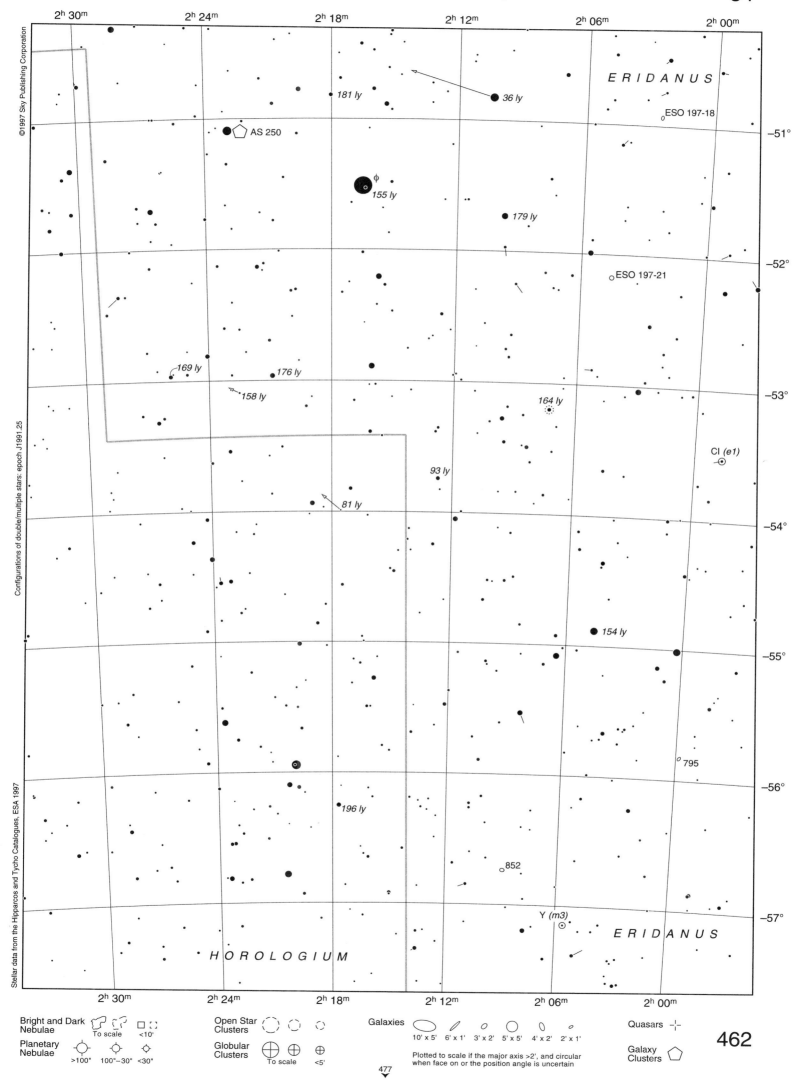

E R I D A N U S

AS 250

φ

155 ly

181 ly

36 ly

ₒESO 197-18

179 ly

ₒESO 197-21

169 ly

176 ly

158 ly

164 ly

Cl *(e1)*

93 ly

81 ly

154 ly

ₒ795

196 ly

ₒ852

Y *(m3)*

E R I D A N U S

H O R O L O G I U M

Bright and Dark Nebulae	Open Star Clusters	Galaxies	Quasars

Bright and Dark Nebulae
To scale   <10'

Planetary Nebulae
>100"   100"–30"   <30"

Open Star Clusters

Globular Clusters
To scale   <5'

Galaxies
10' x 5'   6' x 1'   3' x 2'   5' x 5'   4' x 2'   2' x 1'

Plotted to scale if the major axis >2', and circular when face on or the position angle is uncertain

Quasars

Galaxy Clusters

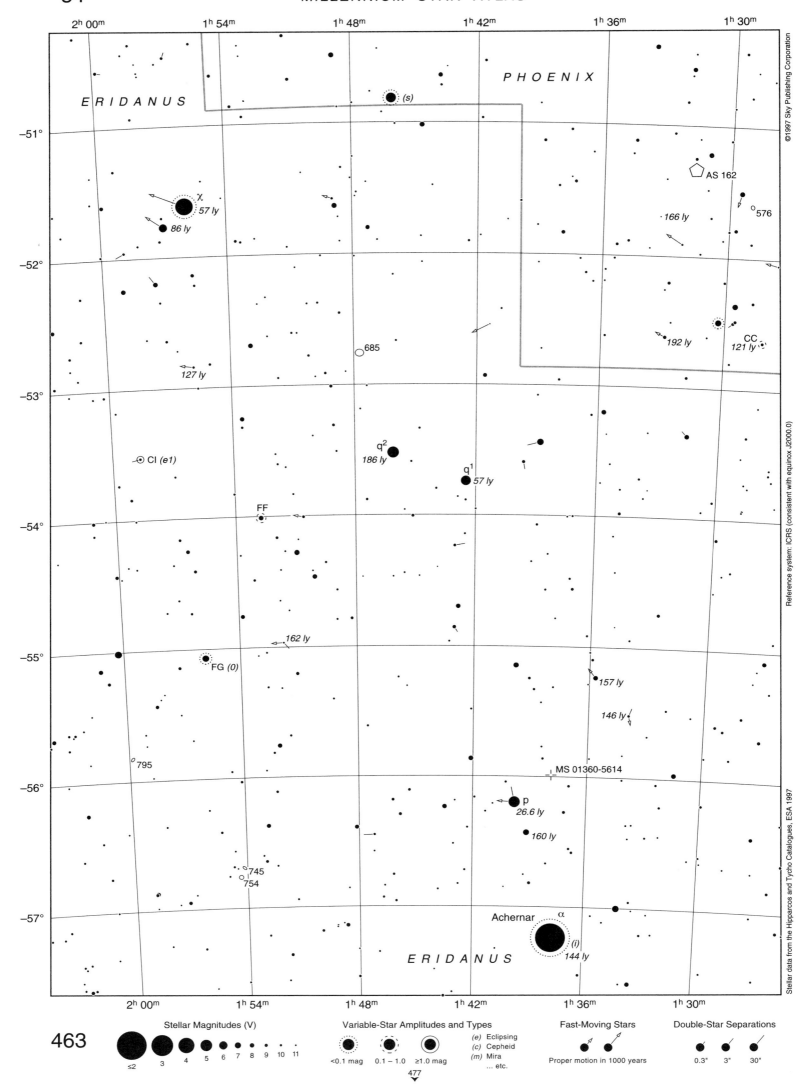

©1997 Sky Publishing Corporation

Reference system: ICRS (consistent with equinox J2000.0)

Stellar data from the Hipparcos and Tycho Catalogues, ESA 1997

P H O E N I X

E R I D A N U S

(s)

AS 162

χ
57 ly
86 ly

576

166 ly

192 ly
CC
121 ly

685

127 ly

Cl (e1)

q²
186 ly

q¹
57 ly

FF

162 ly

FG (0)

157 ly

146 ly

795

MS 01360-5614

p
26.6 ly

160 ly

745
754

Achernar   α

E R I D A N U S

(i)
144 ly

463

Stellar Magnitudes (V)

≤2   3   4   5   6   7   8   9   10   11

Variable-Star Amplitudes and Types

<0.1 mag   0.1 – 1.0   ≥1.0 mag

(e) Eclipsing
(c) Cepheid
(m) Mira
... etc.

Fast-Moving Stars

Proper motion in 1000 years

Double-Star Separations

0.3"   3"   30"

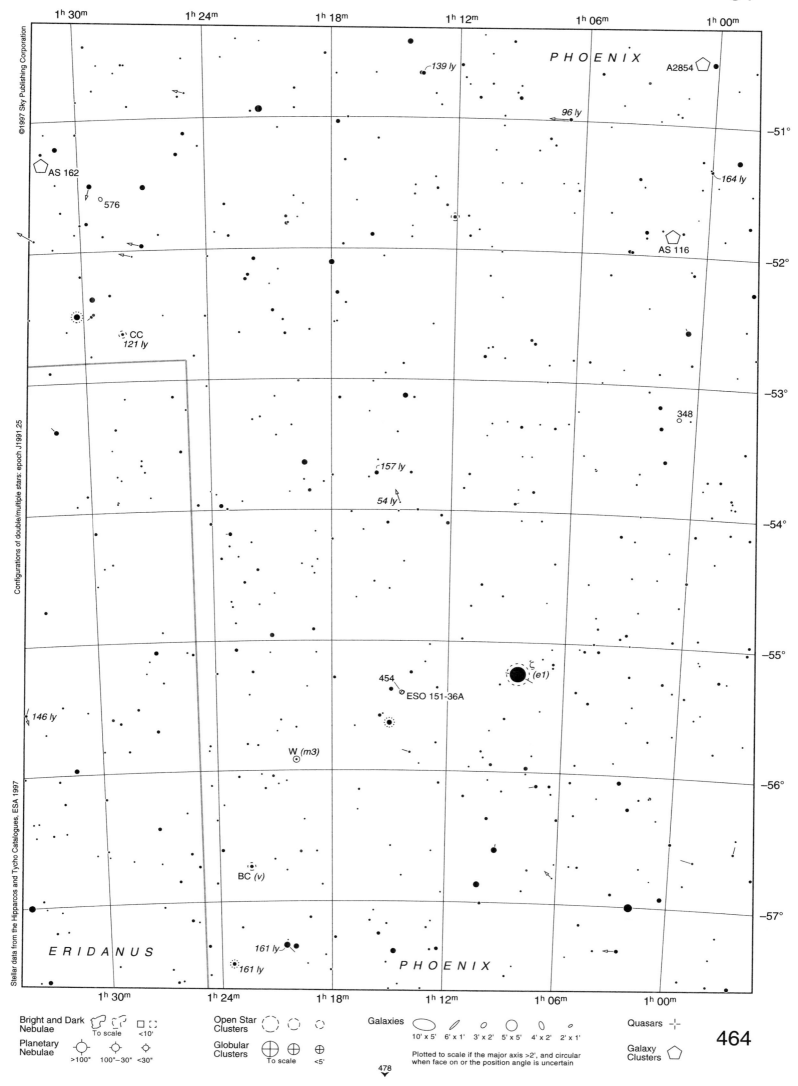

PHOENIX

A2854

139 ly

96 ly

164 ly

AS 162

576

AS 116

CC
121 ly

348

157 ly

54 ly

ζ
(e1)

454
ESO 151-36A

146 ly

W (m3)

BC (v)

146 ly

161 ly

161 ly

ERIDANUS

PHOENIX

Bright and Dark Nebulae	To scale	□ ⬚ <10'	**Quasars** −⊢−
Planetary Nebulae	>100" 100"−30" <30"		
Open Star Clusters	To scale	○ <5'	
Globular Clusters	⊕ ⊕ To scale	⊕ <5'	**Galaxy Clusters** ⬠
Galaxies	10'x5' 6'x1' 3'x2' 5'x5' 4'x2' 2'x1'		

Plotted to scale if the major axis >2', and circular when face on or the position angle is uncertain

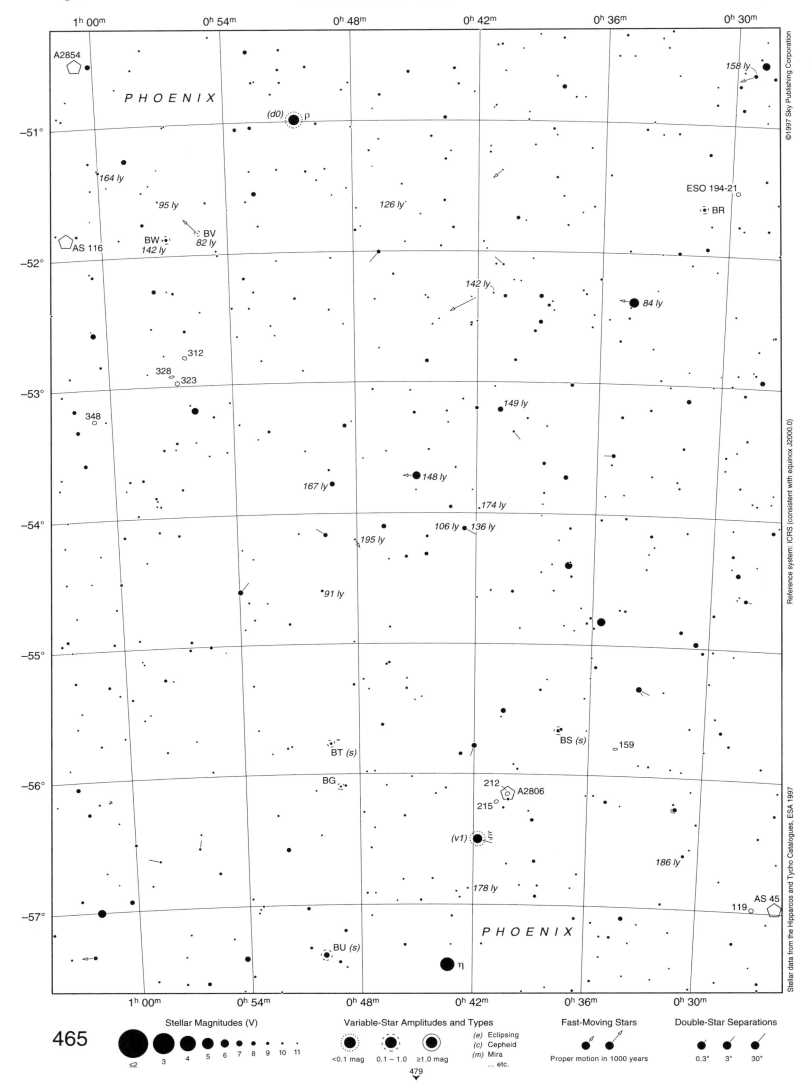

©1997 Sky Publishing Corporation

Reference system: ICRS (consistent with equinox J2000.0)

Stellar data from the Hipparcos and Tycho Catalogues, ESA 1997

Stellar Magnitudes (V)

≤2 3 4 5 6 7 8 9 10 11

Variable-Star Amplitudes and Types

<0.1 mag   0.1 − 1.0   ≥1.0 mag

(e) Eclipsing
(c) Cepheid
(m) Mira
... etc.

Fast-Moving Stars

Proper motion in 1000 years

Double-Star Separations

0.3"   3"   30"

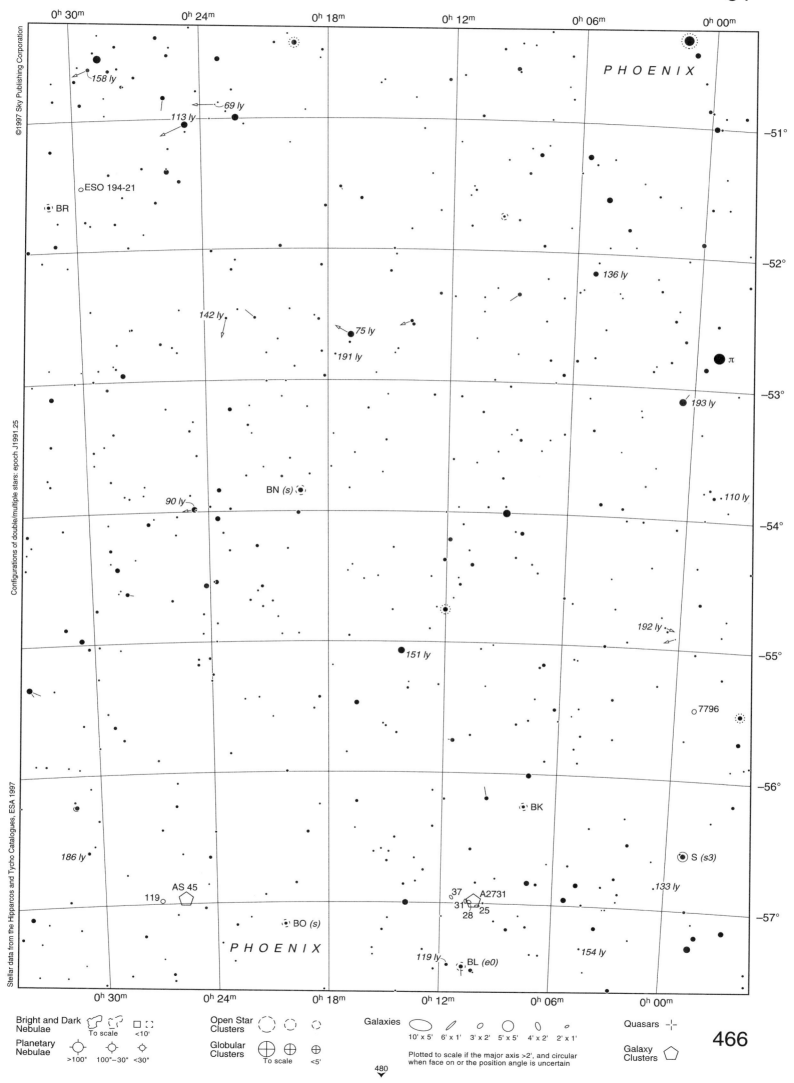

Configurations of double/multiple stars: epoch J1991.25

Stellar data from the Hipparcos and Tycho Catalogues, ESA 1997

P H O E N I X

158 ly

69 ly

113 ly

ESO 194-21

BR

136 ly

142 ly

75 ly

191 ly

π

193 ly

110 ly

BN (s)

90 ly

192 ly

151 ly

7796

186 ly

BK

S (s3)

133 ly

AS 45

119

37 A2731

31 25

28

BO (s)

P H O E N I X

119 ly

BL (e0)

154 ly

Bright and Dark Nebulae
To scale   <10'

Open Star Clusters

Galaxies
10' x 5'   6' x 1'   3' x 2'   5' x 5'   4' x 2'   2' x 1'

Quasars

Planetary Nebulae
>100"   100"−30"   <30"

Globular Clusters
To scale   <5'

Plotted to scale if the major axis >2', and circular when face on or the position angle is uncertain

Galaxy Clusters

480

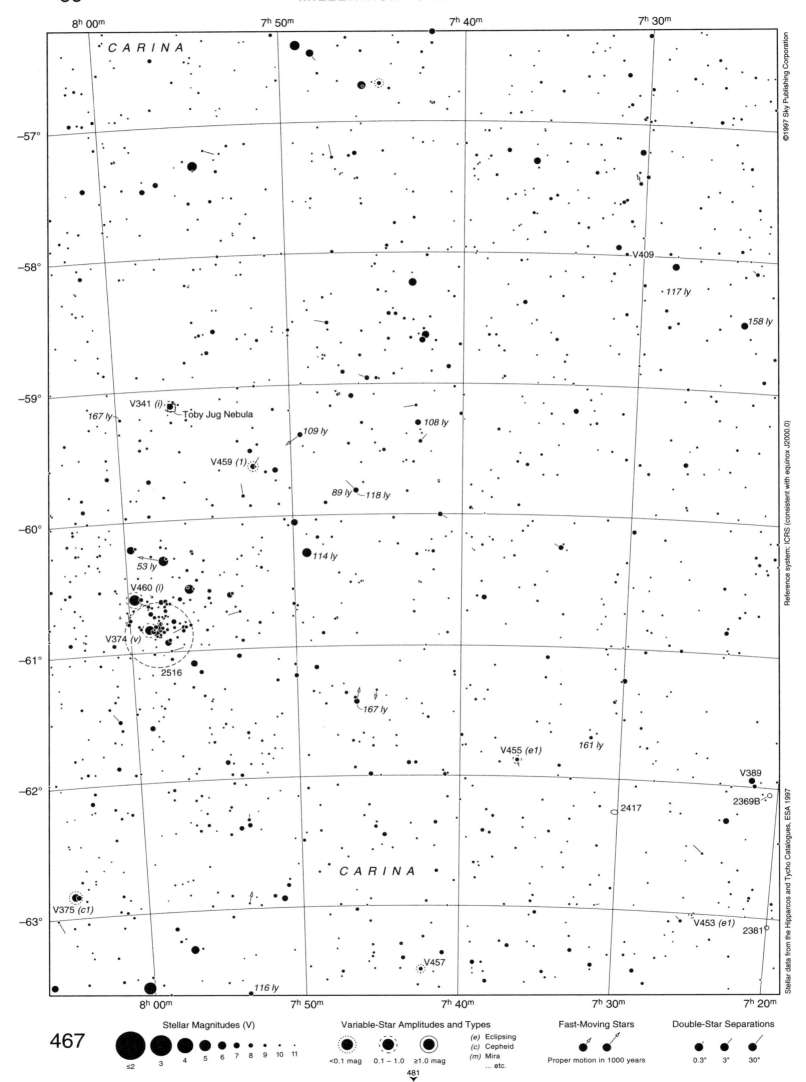

©1997 Sky Publishing Corporation

Reference system: ICRS (consistent with equinox J2000.0)

Stellar data from the Hipparcos and Tycho Catalogues, ESA 1997

CARINA

V409

117 ly

158 ly

V341 (i)

Toby Jug Nebula

167 ly

109 ly

108 ly

V459 (1)

89 ly   118 ly

114 ly

53 ly

V460 (i)

V374 (v)

2516

167 ly

V455 (e1)   161 ly

V389

2369B

2417

CARINA

V375 (c1)

V453 (e1)

2381

V457

116 ly

Stellar Magnitudes (V)

≤2   3   4   5   6   7   8   9   10   11

Variable-Star Amplitudes and Types

<0.1 mag   0.1 – 1.0   ≥1.0 mag

(e) Eclipsing
(c) Cepheid
(m) Mira
... etc.

Fast-Moving Stars

Proper motion in 1000 years

Double-Star Separations

0.3"   3"   30"

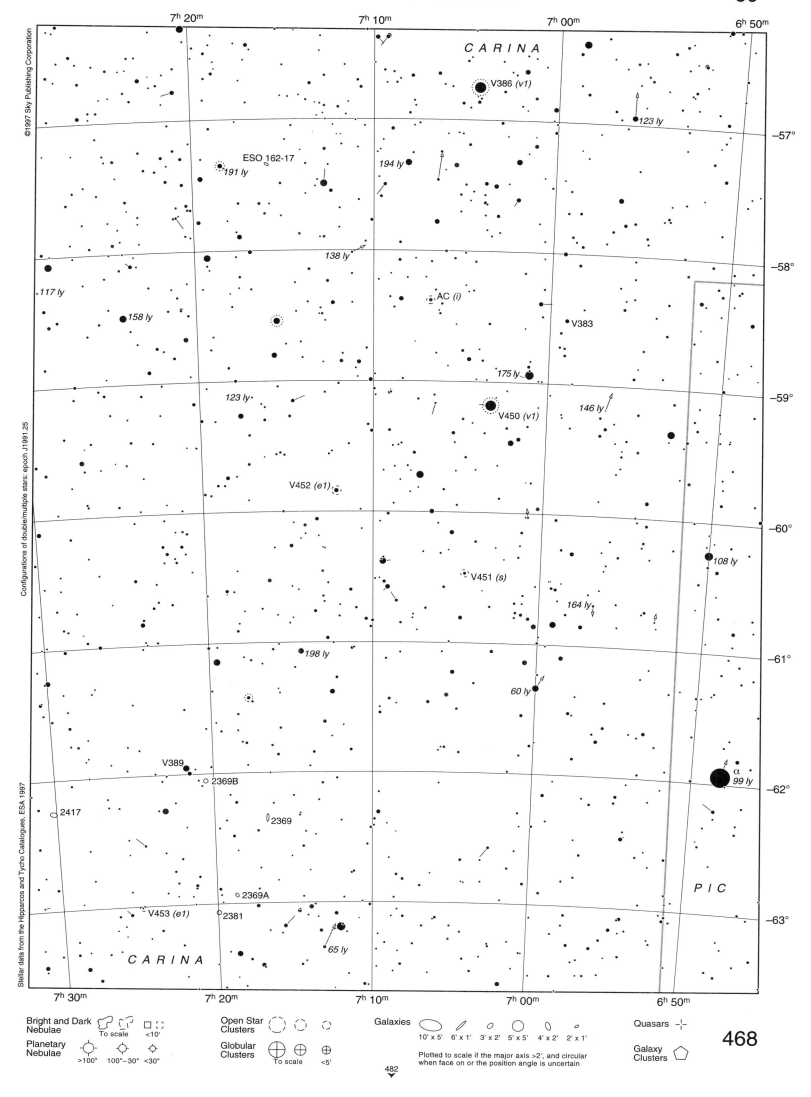

Configurations of double/multiple stars: epoch J1991.25

Stellar data from the Hipparcos and Tycho Catalogues, ESA 1997

CARINA

V386 (v1)

123 ly

−57°

ESO 162-17

191 ly

194 ly

138 ly

−58°

117 ly

AC (i)

V383

158 ly

175 ly

123 ly

V450 (v1)

146 ly

−59°

V452 (e1)

−60°

V451 (s)

108 ly

164 ly

198 ly

60 ly

−61°

α
99 ly

V389

−62°

2369B

2417

2369

PIC

2369A

V453 (e1)

2381

−63°

65 ly

CARINA

7h 30m

7h 20m

7h 10m

7h 00m

6h 50m

Bright and Dark Nebulae

To scale   <10'

Planetary Nebulae

>100"   100"–30"   <30"

Open Star Clusters

Globular Clusters

To scale   <5'

Galaxies

10' x 5'   6' x 1'   3' x 2'   5' x 5'   4' x 2'   2' x 1'

Plotted to scale if the major axis >2', and circular when face on or the position angle is uncertain

Quasars

Galaxy Clusters

482

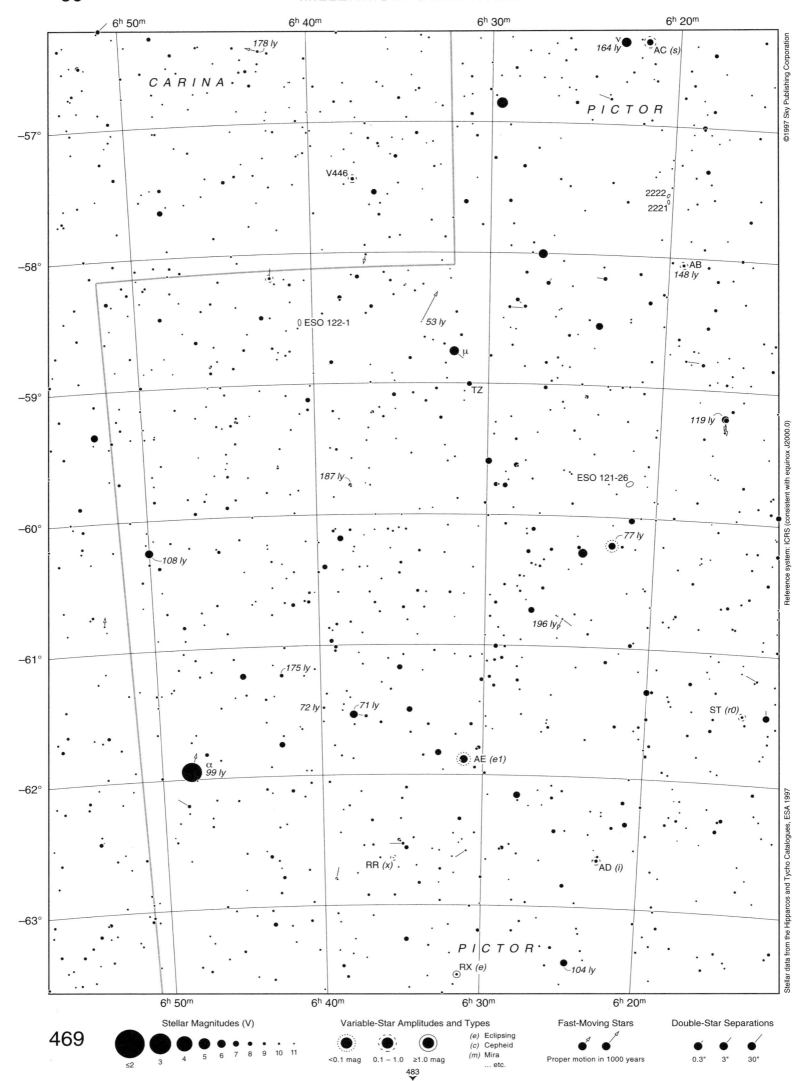

453

6h 50m
6h 40m
6h 30m
6h 20m
–57°
–58°
–59°
–60°
–61°
–62°
–63°
CARINA
PICTOR
ν 164 ly
AC (s)
178 ly
V446
2222
2221
AB 148 ly
ESO 122-1
53 ly
μ
TZ
119 ly
187 ly
ESO 121-26
77 ly
108 ly
196 ly
175 ly
72 ly
71 ly
ST (r0)
α 99 ly
AE (e1)
RR (x)
AD (i)
PICTOR
RX (e)
104 ly
©1997 Sky Publishing Corporation
Reference system: ICRS (consistent with equinox J2000.0)
Stellar data from the Hipparcos and Tycho Catalogues, ESA 1997

Stellar Magnitudes (V)
≤2
3
4
5
6
7
8
9
10
11
Variable-Star Amplitudes and Types
<0.1 mag
0.1 – 1.0
≥1.0 mag
(e) Eclipsing
(c) Cepheid
(m) Mira
... etc.
Fast-Moving Stars
Proper motion in 1000 years
Double-Star Separations
0.3"
3"
30"

483

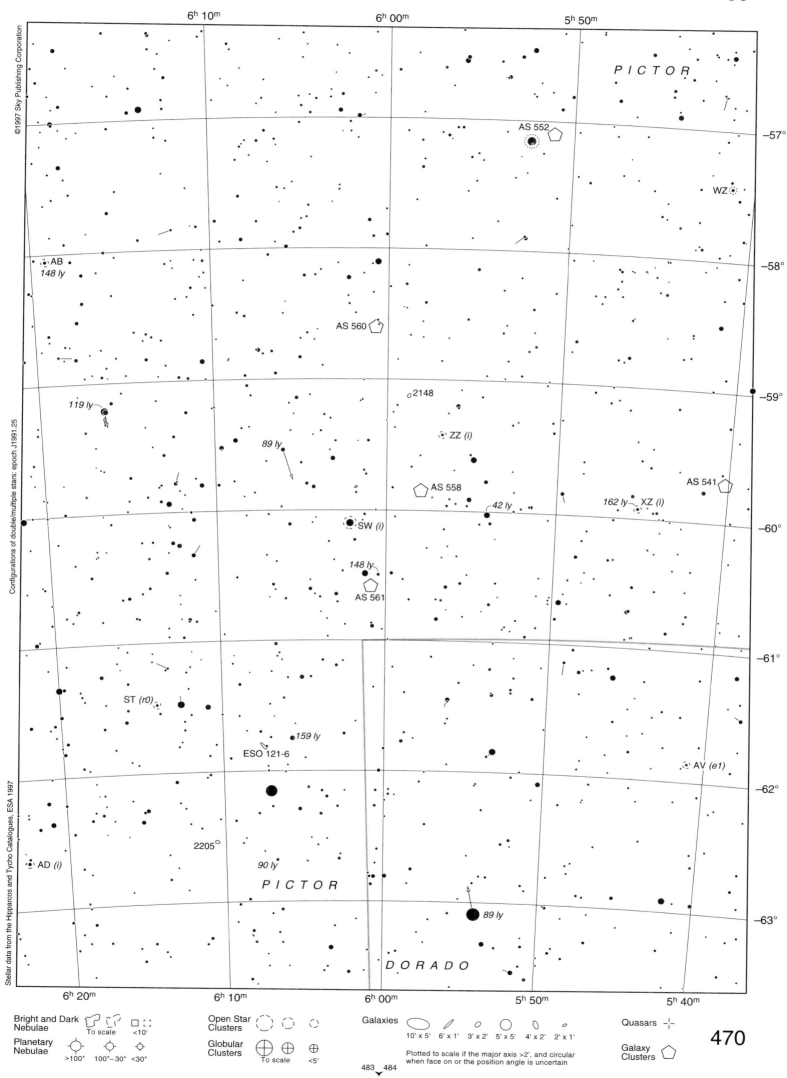

PICTOR

AS 552

WZ

AB
148 ly

AS 560

2148

119 ly

89 ly

ZZ (i)

AS 558

AS 541

162 ly   XZ (i)

42 ly

SW (i)

148 ly

AS 561

ST (r0)

159 ly

ESO 121-6

AV (e1)

2205

AD (i)

90 ly

PICTOR

89 ly

DORADO

©1997 Sky Publishing Corporation

Configurations of double/multiple stars: epoch J1991.25

Stellar data from the Hipparcos and Tycho Catalogues, ESA 1997

−57°

−58°

−59°

−60°

−61°

−62°

−63°

Bright and Dark Nebulae	Open Star Clusters	Globular Clusters	Galaxies	Quasars

Bright and Dark Nebulae — To scale — <10'

Planetary Nebulae — >100" 100"–30" <30"

Open Star Clusters

Globular Clusters — To scale — <5'

Galaxies — 10' x 5' 6' x 1' 3' x 2' 5' x 5' 4' x 2' 2' x 1'

Plotted to scale if the major axis >2', and circular when face on or the position angle is uncertain

Quasars

Galaxy Clusters

470

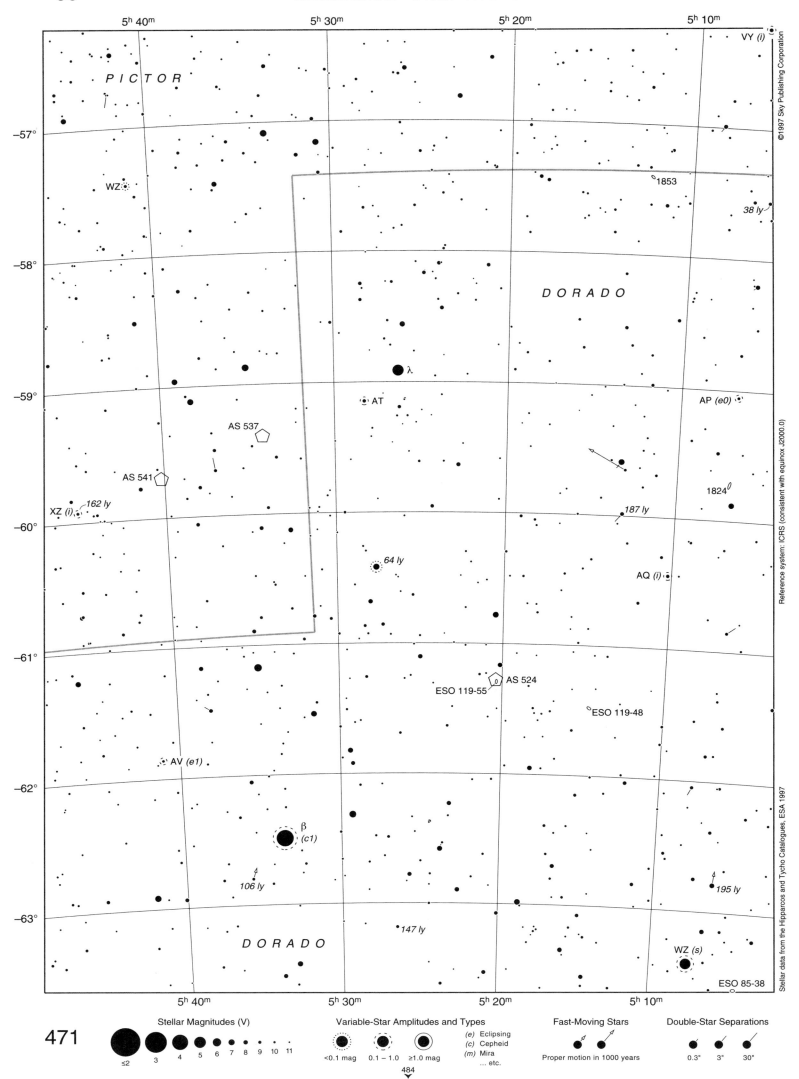

©1997 Sky Publishing Corporation

Reference system: ICRS (consistent with equinox J2000.0)

Stellar data from the Hipparcos and Tycho Catalogues, ESA 1997

PICTOR

DORADO

DORADO

WZ

1853

38 ly

λ

AT

AS 537

AP (e0)

AS 541

1824

XZ (i) 162 ly

187 ly

64 ly

AQ (i)

AS 524
ESO 119-55

ESO 119-48

AV (e1)

β
(c1)

106 ly

195 ly

147 ly

WZ (s)

ESO 85-38

471

Stellar Magnitudes (V)

≤2 3 4 5 6 7 8 9 10 11

Variable-Star Amplitudes and Types

<0.1 mag   0.1 – 1.0   ≥1.0 mag

(e) Eclipsing
(c) Cepheid
(m) Mira
... etc.

Fast-Moving Stars

Proper motion in 1000 years

Double-Star Separations

0.3"   3"   30"

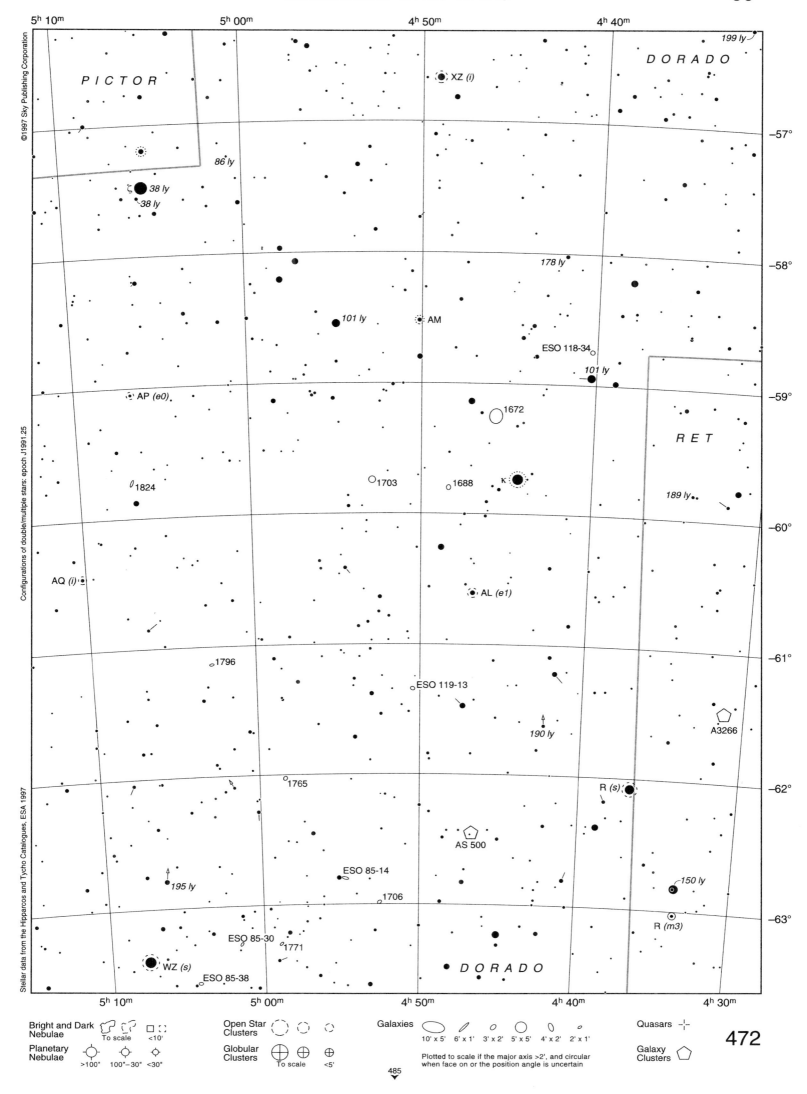

DORADO

PICTOR

199 ly

XZ (i)

86 ly

ζ 38 ly
38 ly

178 ly

101 ly   AM

ESO 118-34

101 ly

AP (e0)

1672

RET

1703   1688   κ

189 ly

θ 1824

AQ (i)

AL (e1)

1796

ESO 119-13

A3266

190 ly

1765

R (s)

AS 500

150 ly

ESO 85-14

195 ly

1706

R (m3)

ESO 85-30   1771

WZ (s)

ESO 85-38

DORADO

Bright and Dark Nebulae	Open Star Clusters	Galaxies	Quasars

Bright and Dark Nebulae — To scale — <10'

Planetary Nebulae — >100" 100"–30" <30"

Open Star Clusters

Globular Clusters — To scale — <5'

Galaxies — 10' x 5' 6' x 1' 3' x 2' 5' x 5' 4' x 2' 2' x 1'

Plotted to scale if the major axis >2', and circular when face on or the position angle is uncertain

Quasars

Galaxy Clusters

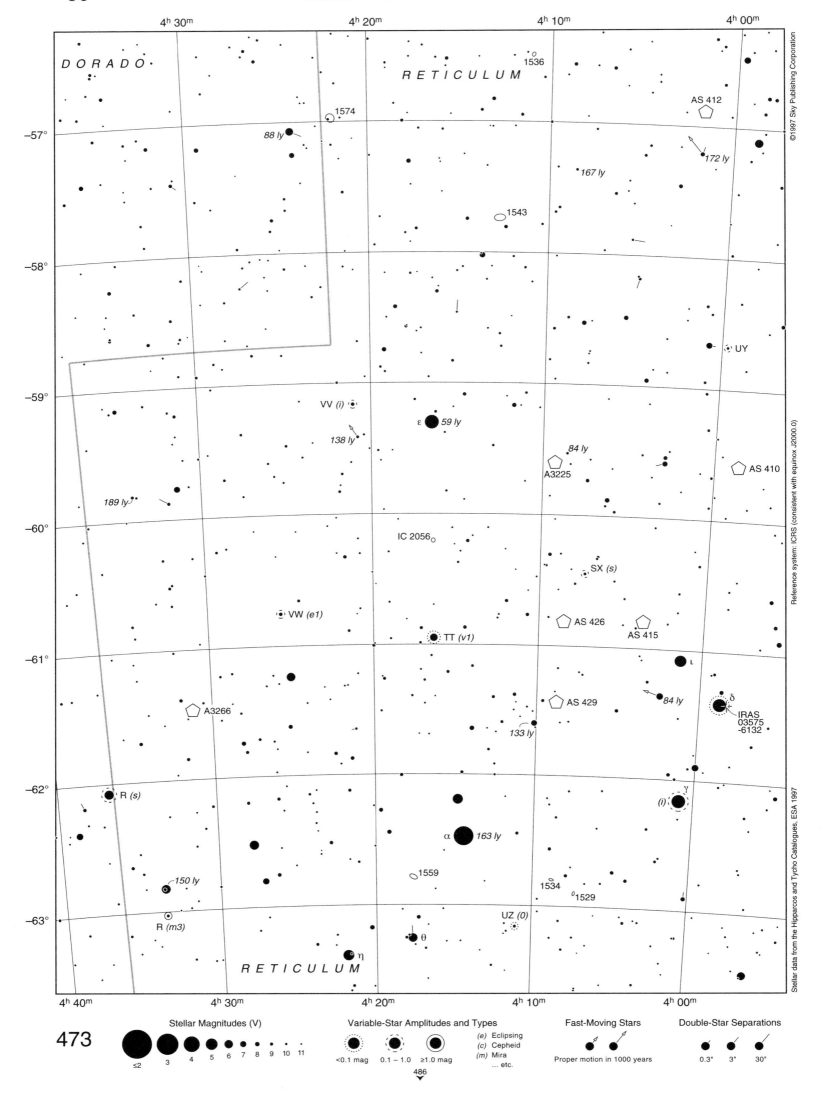

©1997 Sky Publishing Corporation

Reference system: ICRS (consistent with equinox J2000.0)

Stellar data from the Hipparcos and Tycho Catalogues, ESA 1997

DORADO

RETICULUM

1536

AS 412

1574

88 ly

172 ly

167 ly

1543

UY

VV (i)

ε   59 ly

138 ly

84 ly

A3225

AS 410

189 ly

IC 2056

SX (s)

VW (e1)

AS 426

AS 415

TT (v1)

ι

AS 429

84 ly

A3266

δ

IRAS
03575
-6132

133 ly

R (s)

γ
(i)

150 ly

α   163 ly

1559

1534

R (m3)

1529

UZ (0)

θ

η

RETICULUM

473

Stellar Magnitudes (V)

≤2   3   4   5   6   7   8   9 10 11

Variable-Star Amplitudes and Types

<0.1 mag   0.1 – 1.0   ≥1.0 mag

(e) Eclipsing
(c) Cepheid
(m) Mira
... etc.

Fast-Moving Stars

Proper motion in 1000 years

Double-Star Separations

0.3"   3"   30"

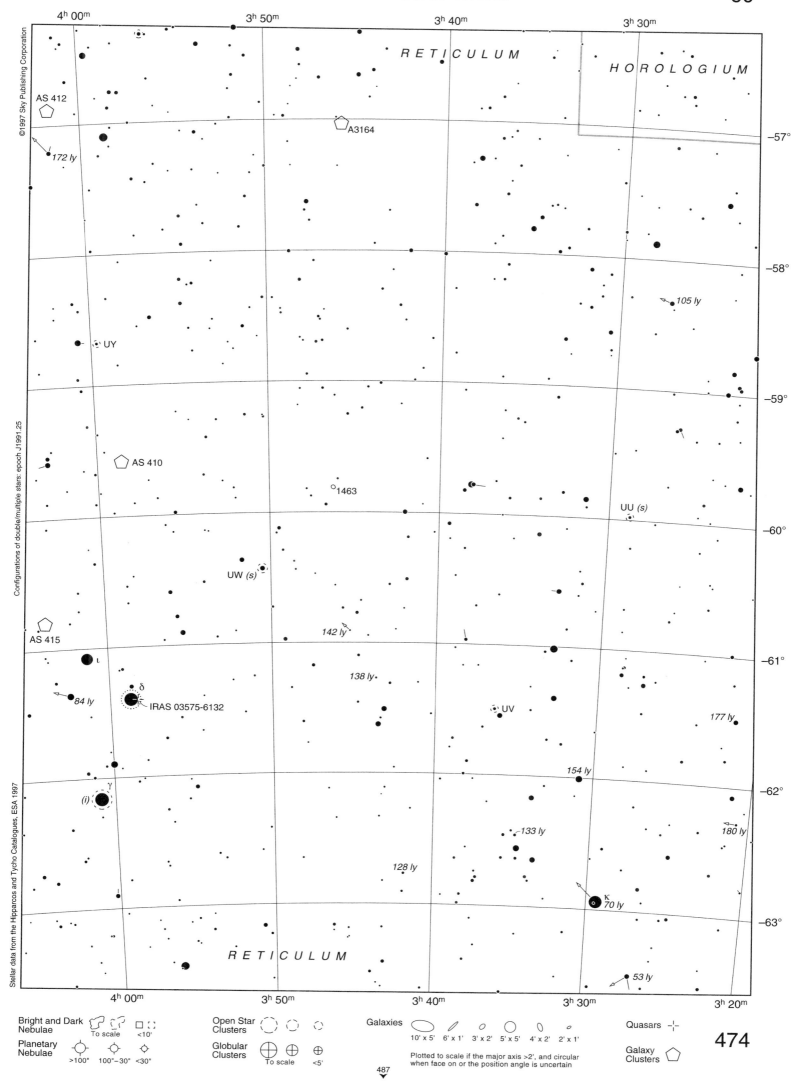

RETICULUM

HOROLOGIUM

AS 412

A3164

172 ly

105 ly

UY

AS 410

1463

UU (s)

UW (s)

AS 415

142 ly

ι

138 ly

84 ly

δ
IRAS 03575-6132

UV

177 ly

154 ly

γ
(i)

133 ly

180 ly

128 ly

κ
70 ly

RETICULUM

53 ly

−57°

−58°

−59°

−60°

−61°

−62°

−63°

4ʰ 00ᵐ 3ʰ 50ᵐ 3ʰ 40ᵐ 3ʰ 30ᵐ

4ʰ 00ᵐ 3ʰ 50ᵐ 3ʰ 40ᵐ 3ʰ 30ᵐ 3ʰ 20ᵐ

Bright and Dark Nebulae			

To scale   <10'

Planetary Nebulae
>100" 100"−30" <30"

Open Star Clusters

Globular Clusters
To scale   <5'

Galaxies
10' x 5' 6' x 1' 3' x 2' 5' x 5' 4' x 2' 2' x 1'

Plotted to scale if the major axis >2', and circular when face on or the position angle is uncertain

Quasars

Galaxy Clusters

MILLENNIUM STAR ATLAS

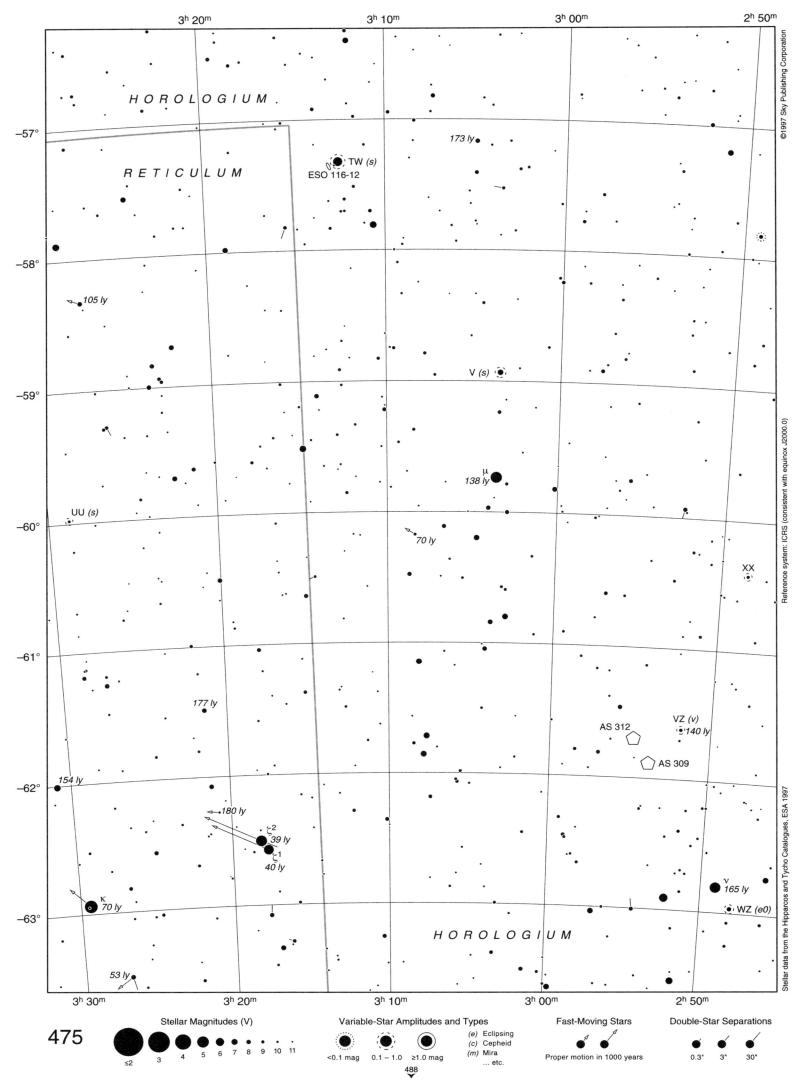

©1997 Sky Publishing Corporation

Reference system: ICRS (consistent with equinox J2000.0)

Stellar data from the Hipparcos and Tycho Catalogues, ESA 1997

HOROLOGIUM

RETICULUM

TW (s)
ESO 116-12

173 ly

105 ly

V (s)

μ
138 ly

UU (s)

70 ly

XX

177 ly

VZ (v)
AS 312   140 ly

AS 309

154 ly

180 ly

ζ²
39 ly

ζ¹
40 ly

ν
165 ly

κ
70 ly

WZ (e0)

HOROLOGIUM

53 ly

475

Stellar Magnitudes (V)										
≤2	3	4	5	6	7	8	9	10	11	

Variable-Star Amplitudes and Types		
<0.1 mag	0.1 – 1.0	≥1.0 mag

(e) Eclipsing
(c) Cepheid
(m) Mira
... etc.

Fast-Moving Stars
Proper motion in 1000 years

Double-Star Separations		
0.3"	3"	30"

MILLENNIUM STAR ATLAS

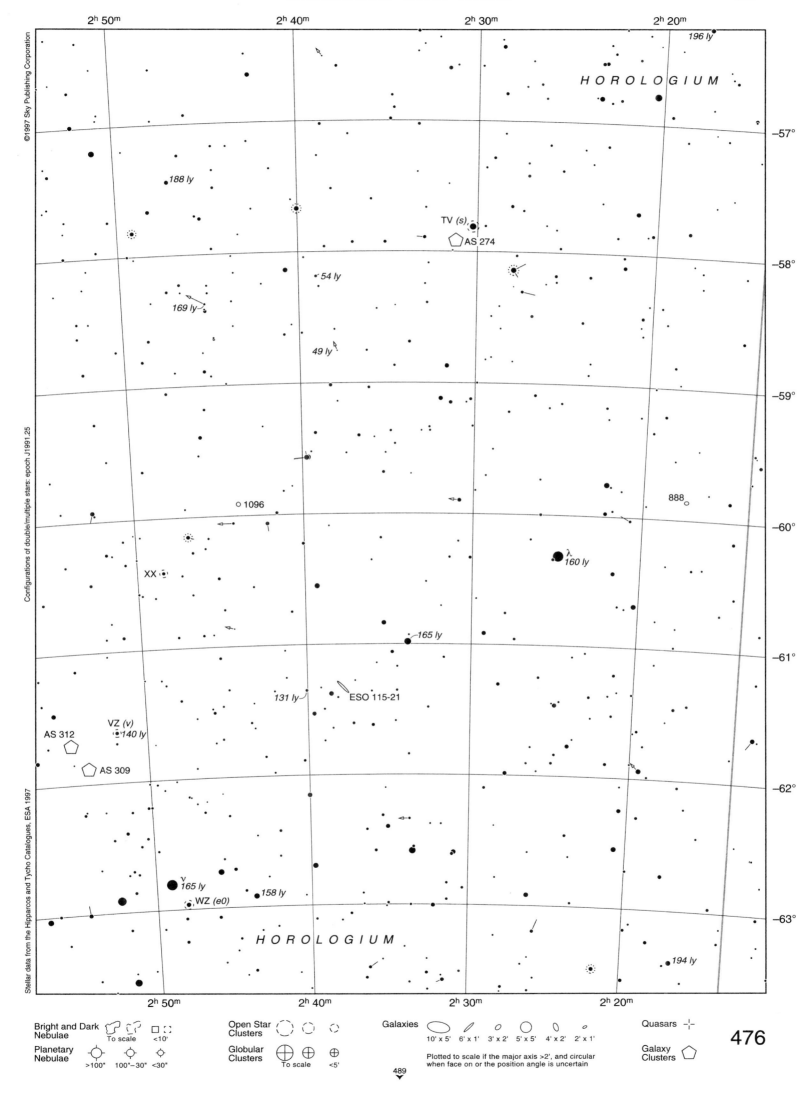

©1997 Sky Publishing Corporation

Configurations of double/multiple stars: epoch J1991.25

Stellar data from the Hipparcos and Tycho Catalogues, ESA 1997

HOROLOGIUM

HOROLOGIUM

2^h 50^m   2^h 40^m   2^h 30^m   2^h 20^m

−57°
−58°
−59°
−60°
−61°
−62°
−63°

196 ly
188 ly
54 ly
169 ly
49 ly
TV (s)
AS 274
1096
888
λ
160 ly
165 ly
XX
131 ly
ESO 115-21
VZ (v)
140 ly
AS 312
AS 309
γ
165 ly
WZ (e0)
158 ly
194 ly

Bright and Dark Nebulae	Open Star Clusters	Galaxies	Quasars

Bright and Dark Nebulae — To scale — <10'
Planetary Nebulae — >100" — 100"–30" — <30"
Open Star Clusters
Globular Clusters — To scale — <5'
Galaxies — 10' x 5' 6' x 1' 3' x 2' 5' x 5' 4' x 2' 2' x 1'
Plotted to scale if the major axis >2', and circular when face on or the position angle is uncertain
Quasars
Galaxy Clusters

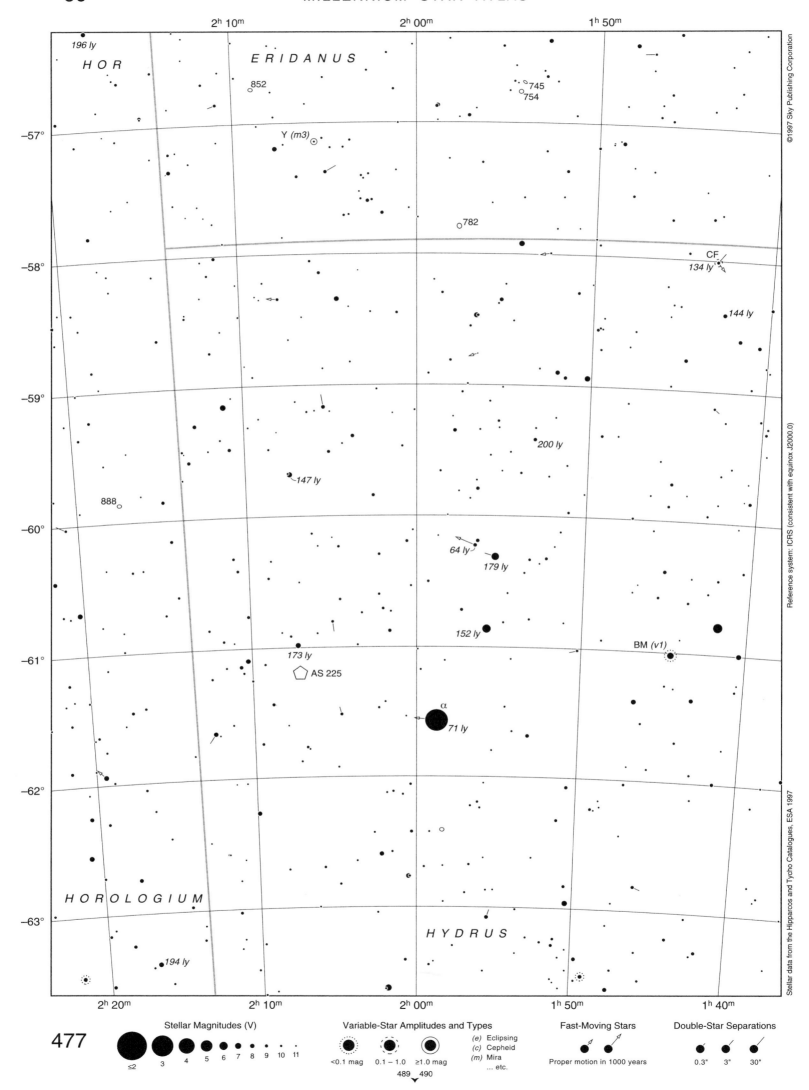

HOR

ERIDANUS

196 ly

852

745
754

Y (m3)

782

CF
134 ly

144 ly

200 ly

147 ly

888

64 ly

179 ly

152 ly

BM (v1)

173 ly

AS 225

α
71 ly

HOROLOGIUM

194 ly

HYDRUS

477

Stellar Magnitudes (V)

≤2 3 4 5 6 7 8 9 10 11

Variable-Star Amplitudes and Types

<0.1 mag   0.1 − 1.0   ≥1.0 mag

(e) Eclipsing
(c) Cepheid
(m) Mira
... etc.

489 490

Fast-Moving Stars

Proper motion in 1000 years

Double-Star Separations

0.3"   3"   30"

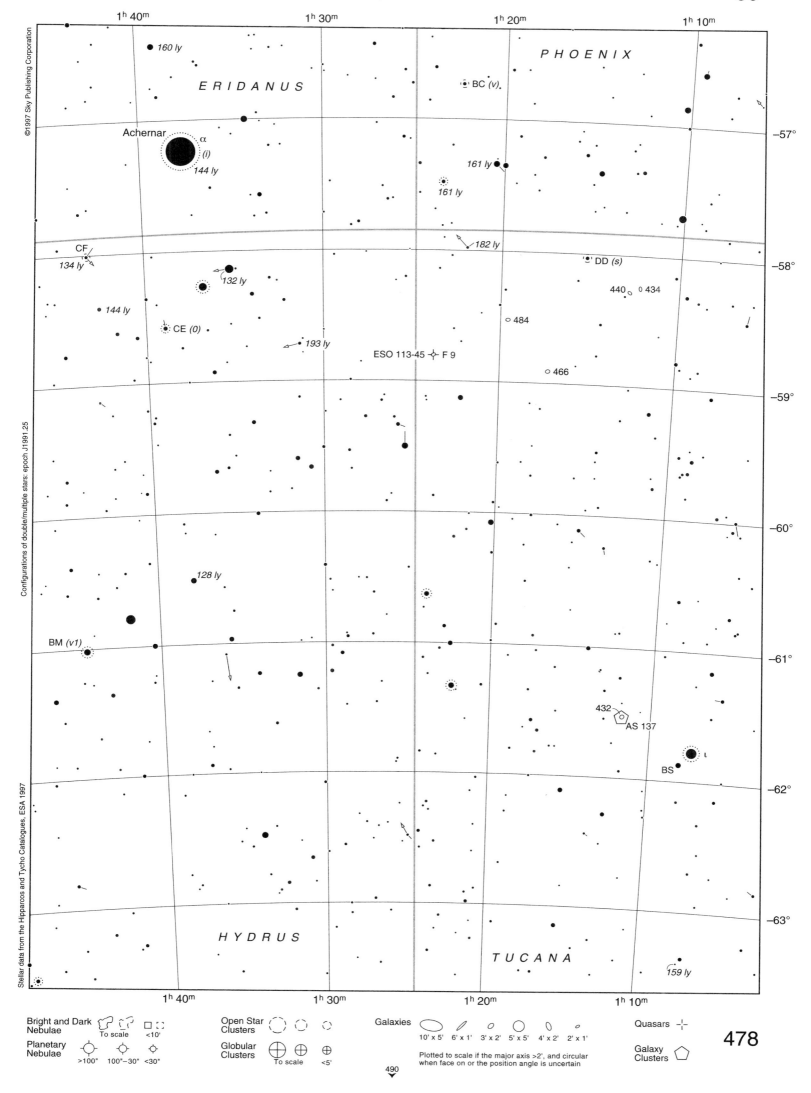

1ʰ 40ᵐ   1ʰ 30ᵐ   1ʰ 20ᵐ   1ʰ 10ᵐ

PHOENIX

ERIDANUS

160 ly

BC (v)

Achernar   α
(i)
144 ly

161 ly

161 ly

182 ly

CF
134 ly

DD (s)

132 ly

440 ○   ○ 434

144 ly

○ 484

CE (0)

193 ly

ESO 113-45 ⬩ F 9

○ 466

128 ly

BM (v1)

432
AS 137

ι
BS

HYDRUS

TUCANA

159 ly

−57°
−58°
−59°
−60°
−61°
−62°
−63°

1ʰ 40ᵐ   1ʰ 30ᵐ   1ʰ 20ᵐ   1ʰ 10ᵐ

Bright and Dark Nebulae
To scale   <10'

Open Star Clusters

Galaxies
10' x 5'   6' x 1'   3' x 2'   5' x 5'   4' x 2'   2' x 1'

Quasars

Planetary Nebulae
>100"   100"–30"   <30"

Globular Clusters
To scale   <5'

Galaxy Clusters

Plotted to scale if the major axis >2', and circular when face on or the position angle is uncertain

478

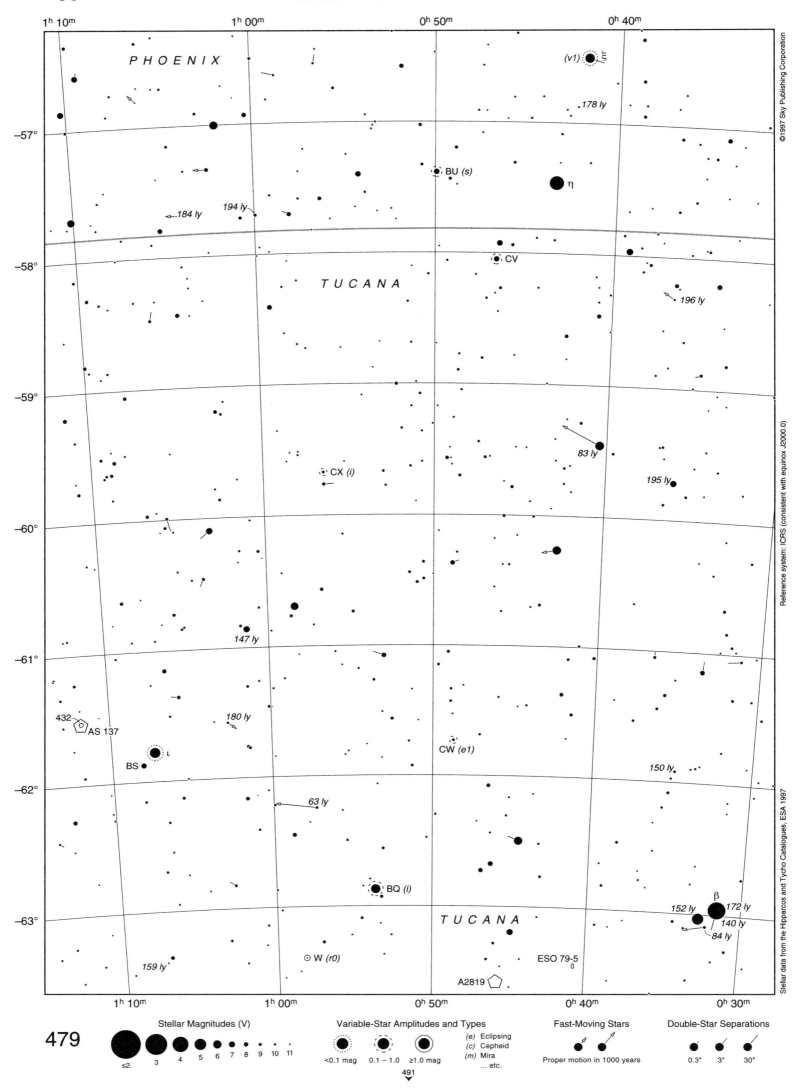

©1997 Sky Publishing Corporation

Reference system: ICRS (consistent with equinox J2000.0)

Stellar data from the Hipparcos and Tycho Catalogues, ESA 1997

P H O E N I X

T U C A N A

T U C A N A

178 ly

BU *(s)*

η

194 ly

184 ly

CV

196 ly

83 ly

195 ly

CX *(i)*

147 ly

432 AS 137

180 ly

CW *(e1)*

150 ly

ι

BS

63 ly

β

172 ly
152 ly
140 ly
84 ly

BQ *(i)*

W *(r0)*

ESO 79-5
0

A2819

159 ly

Stellar Magnitudes (V)

≤2   3   4   5   6   7   8   9 10 11

Variable-Star Amplitudes and Types

<0.1 mag   0.1 – 1.0   ≥1.0 mag

(e) Eclipsing
(c) Cepheid
(m) Mira
... etc.

Fast-Moving Stars

Proper motion in 1000 years

Double-Star Separations

0.3"   3"   30"

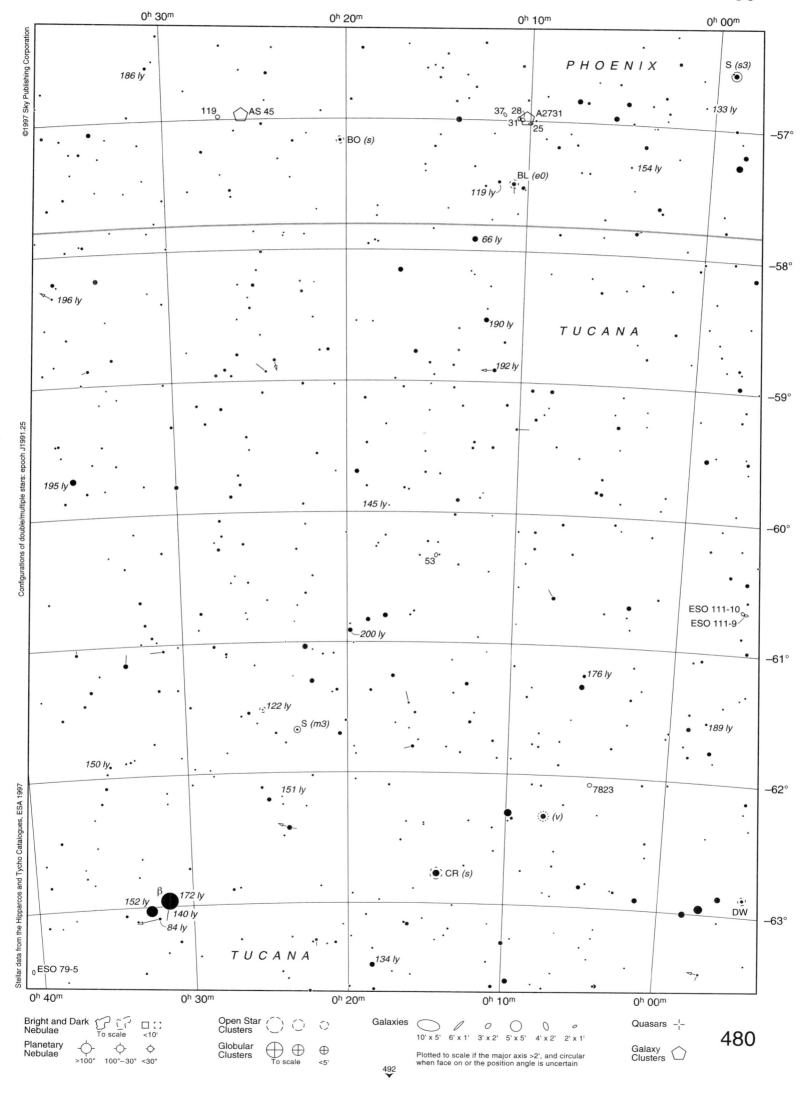

P H O E N I X

S (s3)

186 ly

119
AS 45

133 ly

37 28 A2731
31   25

BO (s)

154 ly

BL (e0)

119 ly

66 ly

T U C A N A

196 ly

190 ly

192 ly

195 ly

145 ly

53

ESO 111-10
ESO 111-9

200 ly

176 ly

122 ly

189 ly

S (m3)

150 ly

151 ly

7823

(v)

CR (s)

β
152 ly 172 ly

140 ly

84 ly

DW

T U C A N A

134 ly

ESO 79-5

Bright and Dark
Nebulae   To scale   <10'

Planetary
Nebulae   >100° 100°−30° <30°

Open Star
Clusters

Globular
Clusters   To scale <5'

Galaxies

10' x 5' 6' x 1' 3' x 2' 5' x 5' 4' x 2' 2' x 1'

Plotted to scale if the major axis >2', and circular
when face on or the position angle is uncertain

Quasars

Galaxy
Clusters

492

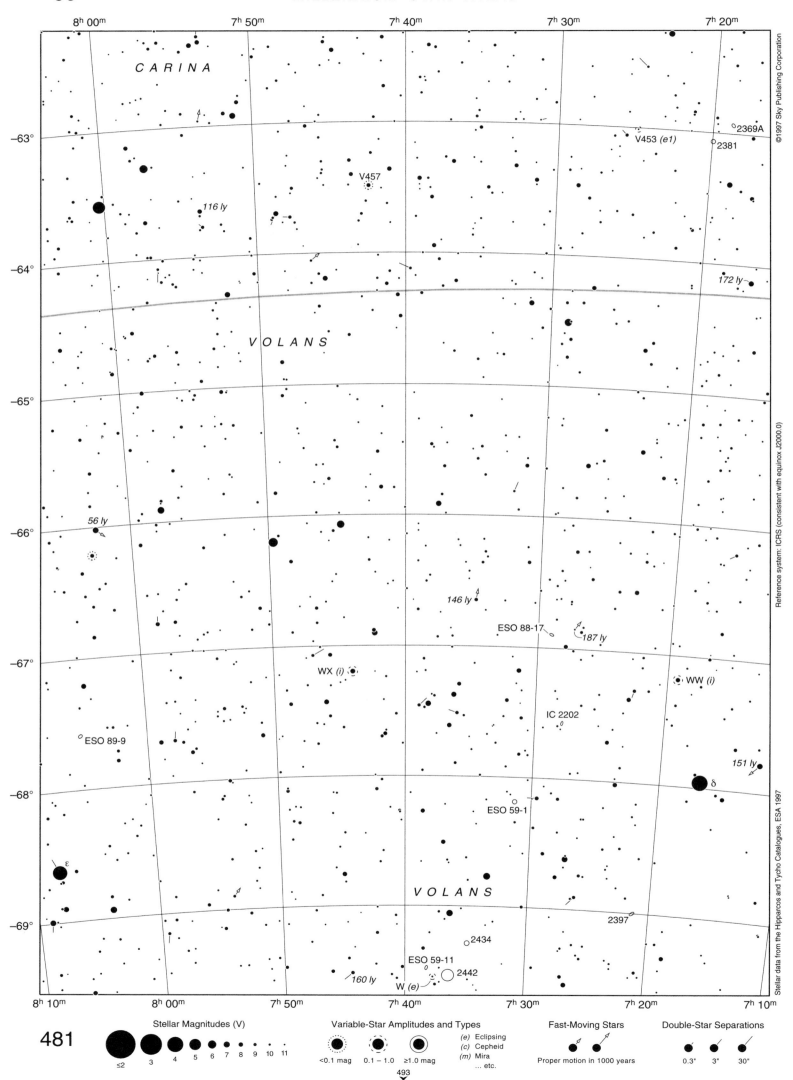

©1997 Sky Publishing Corporation

Reference system: ICRS (consistent with equinox J2000.0)

Stellar data from the Hipparcos and Tycho Catalogues, ESA 1997

CARINA

VOLANS

VOLANS

116 ly

56 ly

146 ly

172 ly

151 ly

160 ly

187 ly

V457

V453 (e1)

2369A

2381

ESO 88-17

WX (i)

WW (i)

IC 2202

ESO 89-9

ESO 59-1

δ

ε

2397

2434

ESO 59-11

2442

W (e)

481

Stellar Magnitudes (V)

≤2   3   4   5   6   7   8   9 10 11

Variable-Star Amplitudes and Types

<0.1 mag   0.1 – 1.0   ≥1.0 mag

(e) Eclipsing
(c) Cepheid
(m) Mira
... etc.

Fast-Moving Stars

Proper motion in 1000 years

Double-Star Separations

0.3"   3"   30"

MILLENNIUM STAR ATLAS

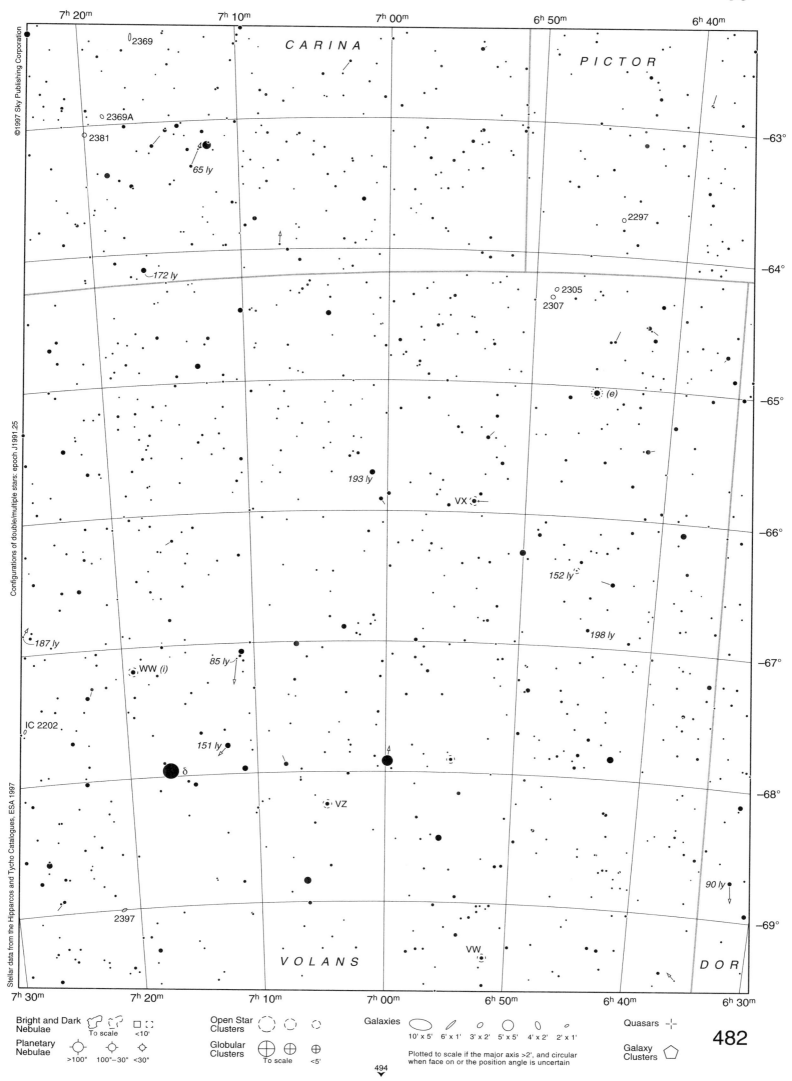

CARINA

PICTOR

VOLANS

DOR

2369
2369A
2381
65 ly
172 ly
2297
2305
2307
(e)
193 ly
VX
152 ly
198 ly
187 ly
WW (i)
85 ly
IC 2202
151 ly
δ
90 ly
VZ
2397
VW

7h 20m 7h 10m 7h 00m 6h 50m 6h 40m

−63°
−64°
−65°
−66°
−67°
−68°
−69°

7h 30m 7h 20m 7h 10m 7h 00m 6h 50m 6h 40m 6h 30m

| Bright and Dark Nebulae | | | Open Star Clusters | | | Galaxies | | | | | | Quasars |
| To scale | | <10' | To scale | | | 10' x 5' | 6' x 1' | 3' x 2' | 5' x 5' | 4' x 2' | 2' x 1' | |

Planetary Nebulae   >100"   100"–30"   <30"

Globular Clusters   To scale   <5'

Plotted to scale if the major axis >2', and circular when face on or the position angle is uncertain

Galaxy Clusters

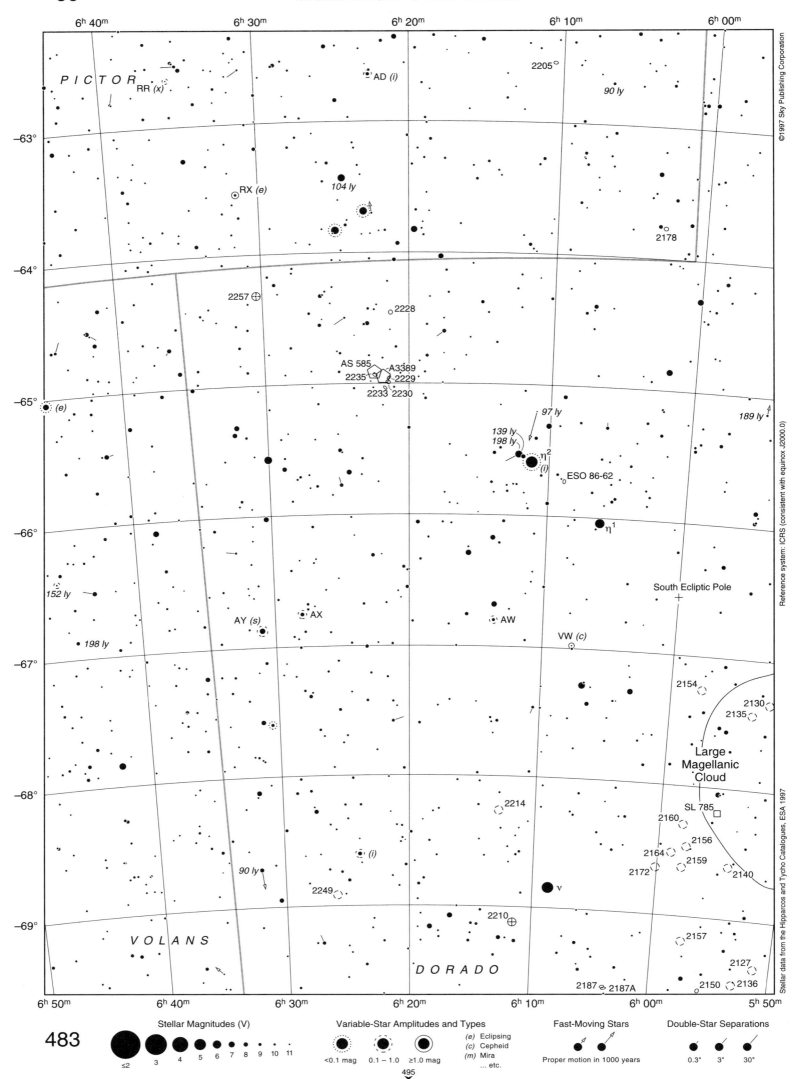

©1997 Sky Publishing Corporation

Reference system: ICRS (consistent with equinox J2000.0)

Stellar data from the Hipparcos and Tycho Catalogues, ESA 1997

PICTOR

RR (x)

AD (i)

2205

90 ly

RX (e)

104 ly

2178

2257

2228

AS 585   A3389
2235   2229
2233 2230

(e)

97 ly

139 ly
198 ly

η²
(i)

189 ly

ESO 86-62

η¹

South Ecliptic Pole

152 ly

AY (s)   AX   AW

VW (c)

198 ly

2154

2130
2135

Large
Magellanic
Cloud

2214

SL 785

2160

2156

(i)

2164   2159
2172

2140

90 ly

2249

ν

2210

2157

VOLANS   DORADO

2187 ⊘ 2187A   2150   2136

2127

483

Stellar Magnitudes (V)

≤2   3   4   5   6   7   8   9   10   11

Variable-Star Amplitudes and Types

<0.1 mag   0.1 – 1.0   ≥1.0 mag

(e) Eclipsing
(c) Cepheid
(m) Mira
... etc.

Fast-Moving Stars

Proper motion in 1000 years

Double-Star Separations

0.3"   3"   30"

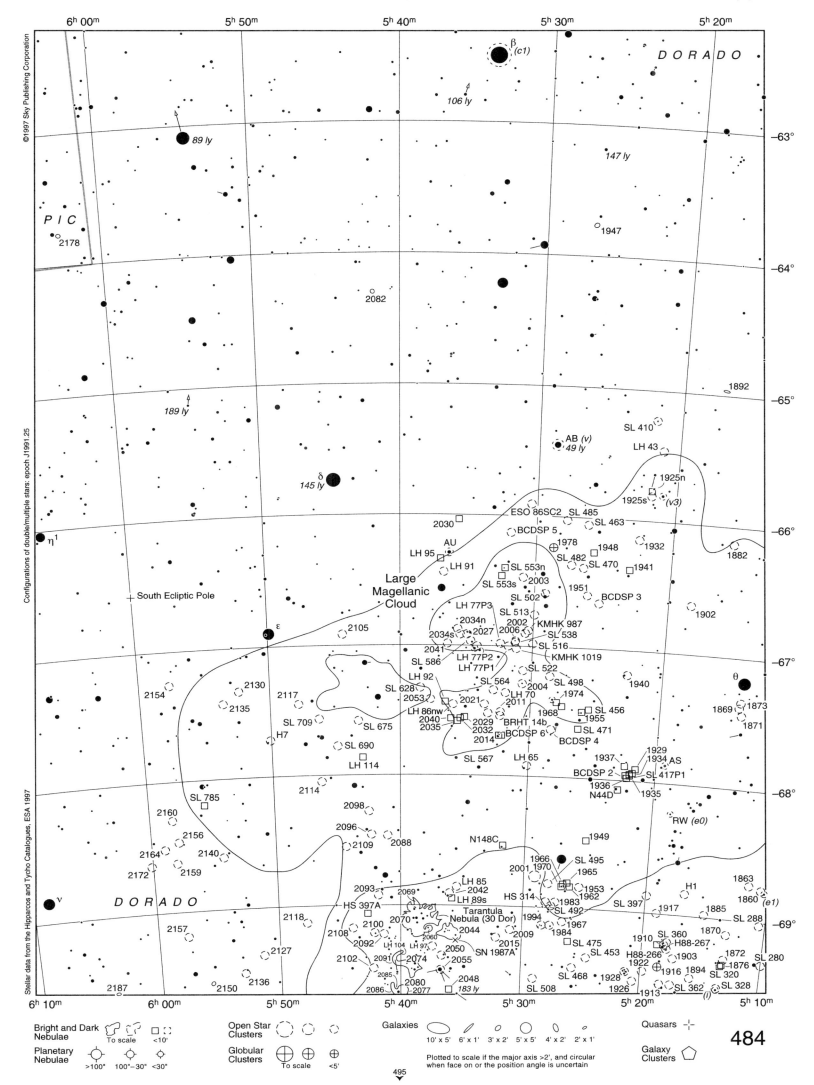

Bright and Dark Nebulae
To scale <10'

Planetary Nebulae
>100" 100"–30" <30'

Open Star Clusters

Globular Clusters
To scale <5'

Galaxies
10' x 5' 6' x 1' 3' x 2' 5' x 5' 4' x 2' 2' x 1'

Plotted to scale if the major axis >2', and circular when face on or the position angle is uncertain

Quasars

Galaxy Clusters

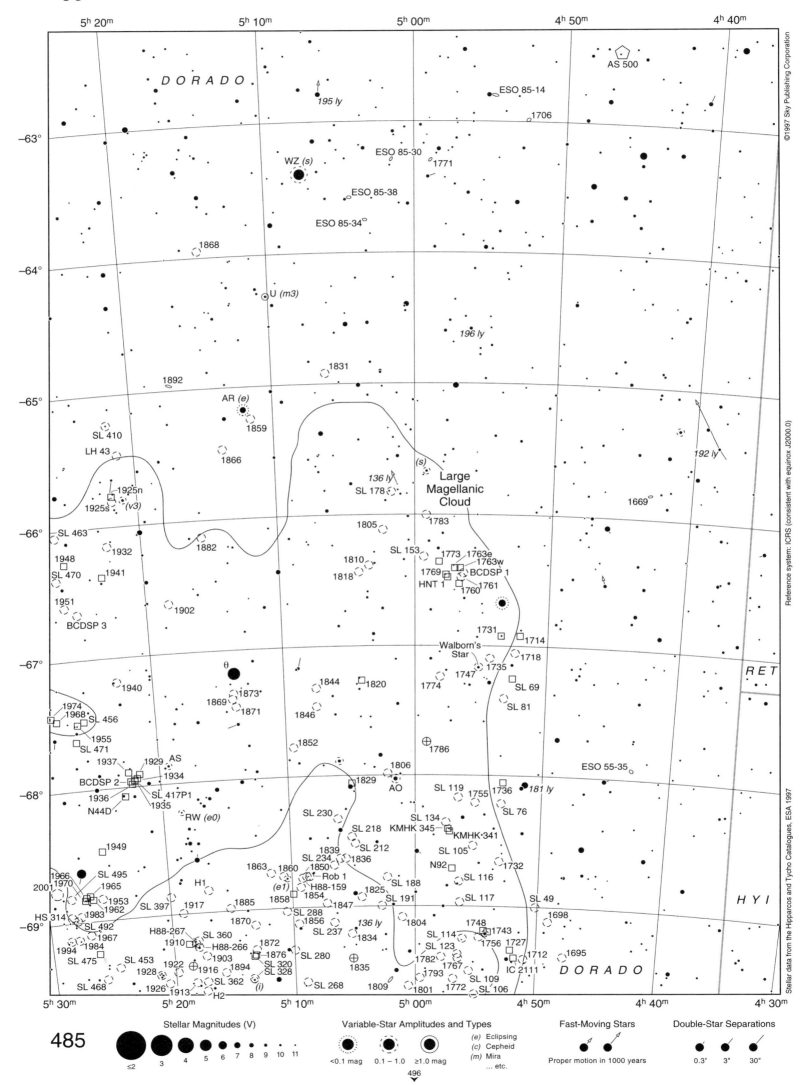

485

Stellar Magnitudes (V)

≤2 3 4 5 6 7 8 9 10 11

Variable-Star Amplitudes and Types

<0.1 mag   0.1 – 1.0   ≥1.0 mag

(e) Eclipsing
(c) Cepheid
(m) Mira
... etc.

Fast-Moving Stars

Proper motion in 1000 years

Double-Star Separations

0.3"   3"   30"

MILLENNIUM STAR ATLAS

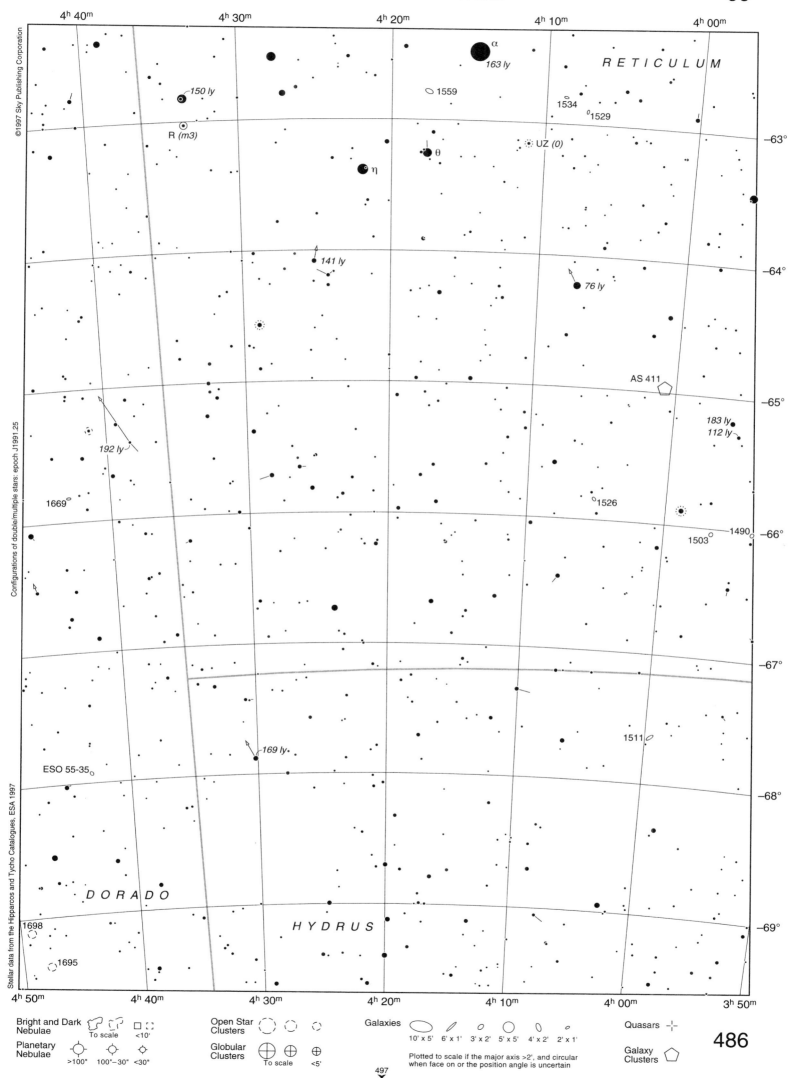

R E T I C U L U M

α
163 ly

1559

1534
1529

R *(m3)*

UZ *(0)*

θ
η

141 ly

76 ly

AS 411

183 ly
112 ly

192 ly

1669

1526

1490
1503

D O R A D O

ESO 55-35

1698

1695

169 ly

1511

H Y D R U S

−63°
−64°
−65°
−66°
−67°
−68°
−69°

4ʰ 40ᵐ   4ʰ 30ᵐ   4ʰ 20ᵐ   4ʰ 10ᵐ   4ʰ 00ᵐ

4ʰ 50ᵐ   4ʰ 40ᵐ   4ʰ 30ᵐ   4ʰ 20ᵐ   4ʰ 10ᵐ   4ʰ 00ᵐ   3ʰ 50ᵐ

Bright and Dark Nebulae	Open Star Clusters	Galaxies	Quasars

To scale   <10'

To scale   <10'

Planetary Nebulae
>100"   100"–30"   <30"

Globular Clusters
To scale   <5'

10' x 5'   6' x 1'   3' x 2'   5' x 5'   4' x 2'   2' x 1'

Plotted to scale if the major axis >2', and circular when face on or the position angle is uncertain

Galaxy Clusters

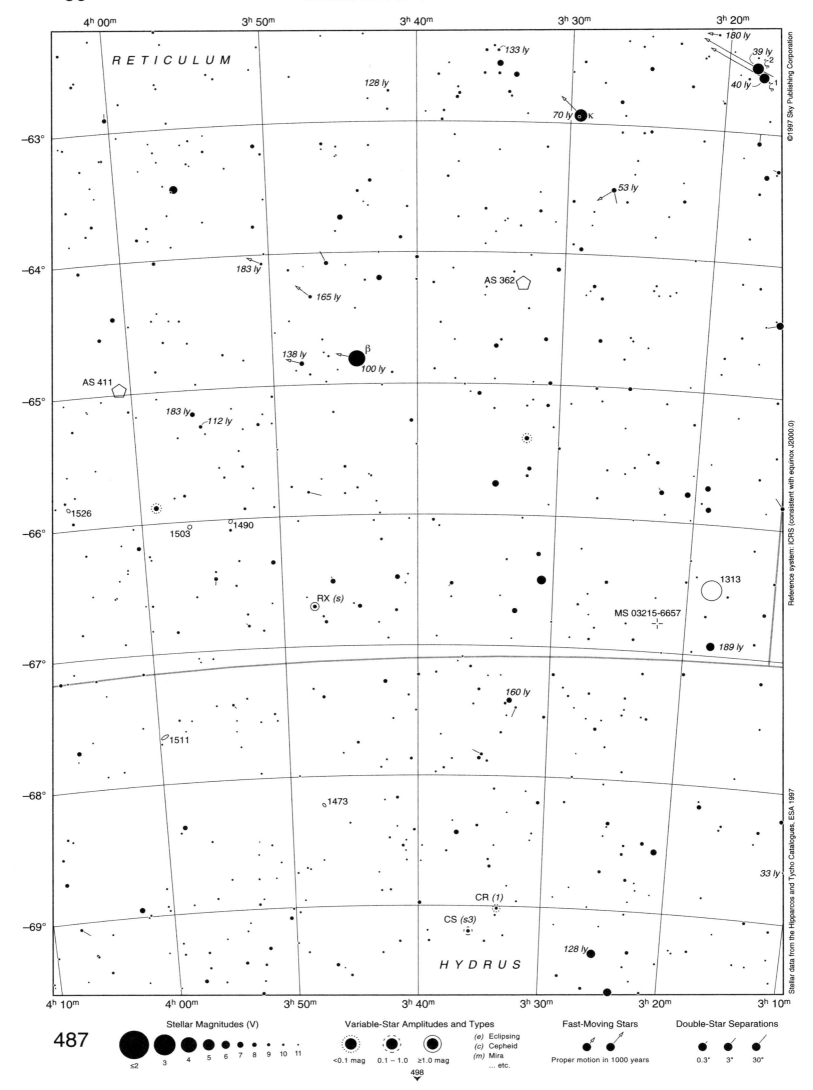

©1997 Sky Publishing Corporation

Reference system: ICRS (consistent with equinox J2000.0)

Stellar data from the Hipparcos and Tycho Catalogues, ESA 1997

R E T I C U L U M

133 ly

128 ly

70 ly ⊙ κ

180 ly

39 ly
ζ 2

40 ly
ζ 1

53 ly

183 ly

165 ly

AS 362

138 ly
β

100 ly

AS 411

183 ly
112 ly

1526

1490

1503

1313

MS 03215-6657

189 ly

RX (s)

1511

160 ly

1473

33 ly

CR (1)

CS (s3)

128 ly

H Y D R U S

487

Stellar Magnitudes (V)

≤2 3 4 5 6 7 8 9 10 11

Variable-Star Amplitudes and Types

<0.1 mag   0.1 − 1.0   ≥1.0 mag

(e) Eclipsing
(c) Cepheid
(m) Mira
... etc.

Fast-Moving Stars

Proper motion in 1000 years

Double-Star Separations

0.3"   3"   30"

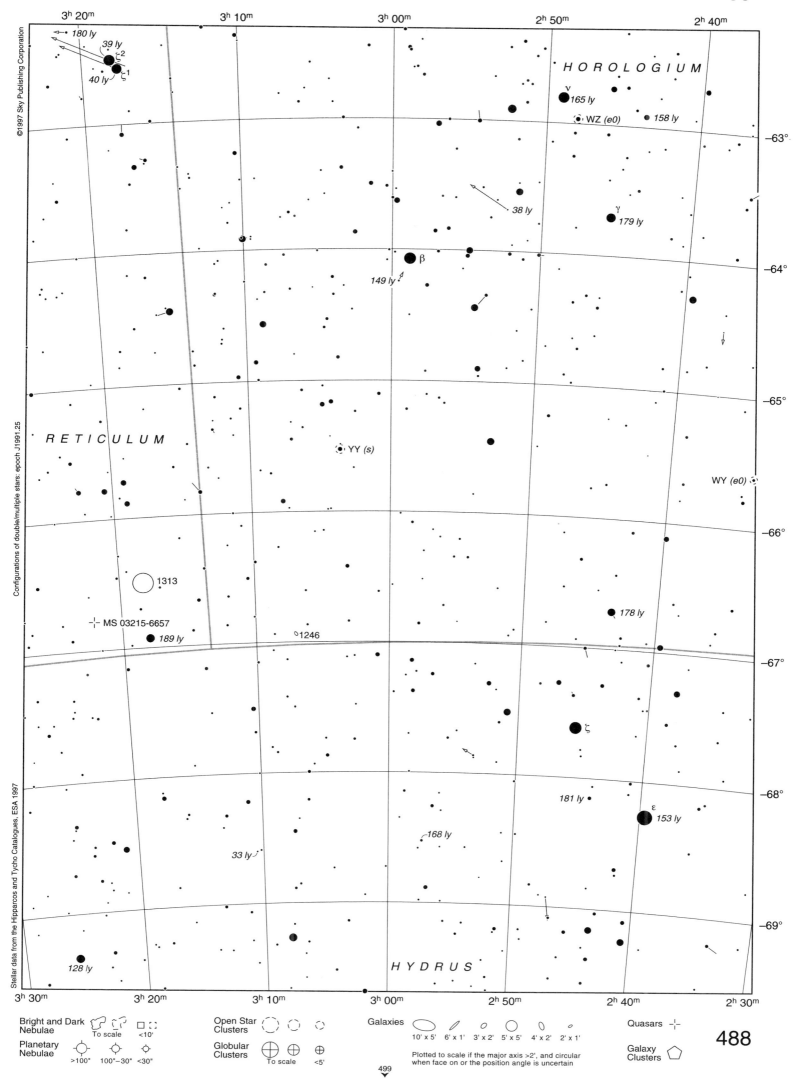

H O R O L O G I U M

ν 165 ly

WZ (e0)   158 ly

38 ly

γ 179 ly

β

149 ly

R E T I C U L U M

YY (s)

WY (e0)

1313

MS 03215-6657

189 ly

1246

178 ly

ζ

181 ly

ε 153 ly

168 ly

33 ly

128 ly

H Y D R U S

−63°
−64°
−65°
−66°
−67°
−68°
−69°

3ʰ 20ᵐ   3ʰ 10ᵐ   3ʰ 00ᵐ   2ʰ 50ᵐ   2ʰ 40ᵐ

3ʰ 30ᵐ   3ʰ 20ᵐ   3ʰ 10ᵐ   3ʰ 00ᵐ   2ʰ 50ᵐ   2ʰ 40ᵐ   2ʰ 30ᵐ

180 ly
39 ly
ζ2
40 ly   ζ1

| Bright and Dark Nebulae | Open Star Clusters | Galaxies | Quasars −┼− |
| Planetary Nebulae | Globular Clusters | | Galaxy Clusters |

To scale   <10'

>100"   100"–30"   <30"

To scale   <5'

10' x 5'   6' x 1'   3' x 2'   5' x 5'   4' x 2'   2' x 1'

Plotted to scale if the major axis >2', and circular when face on or the position angle is uncertain

488

499

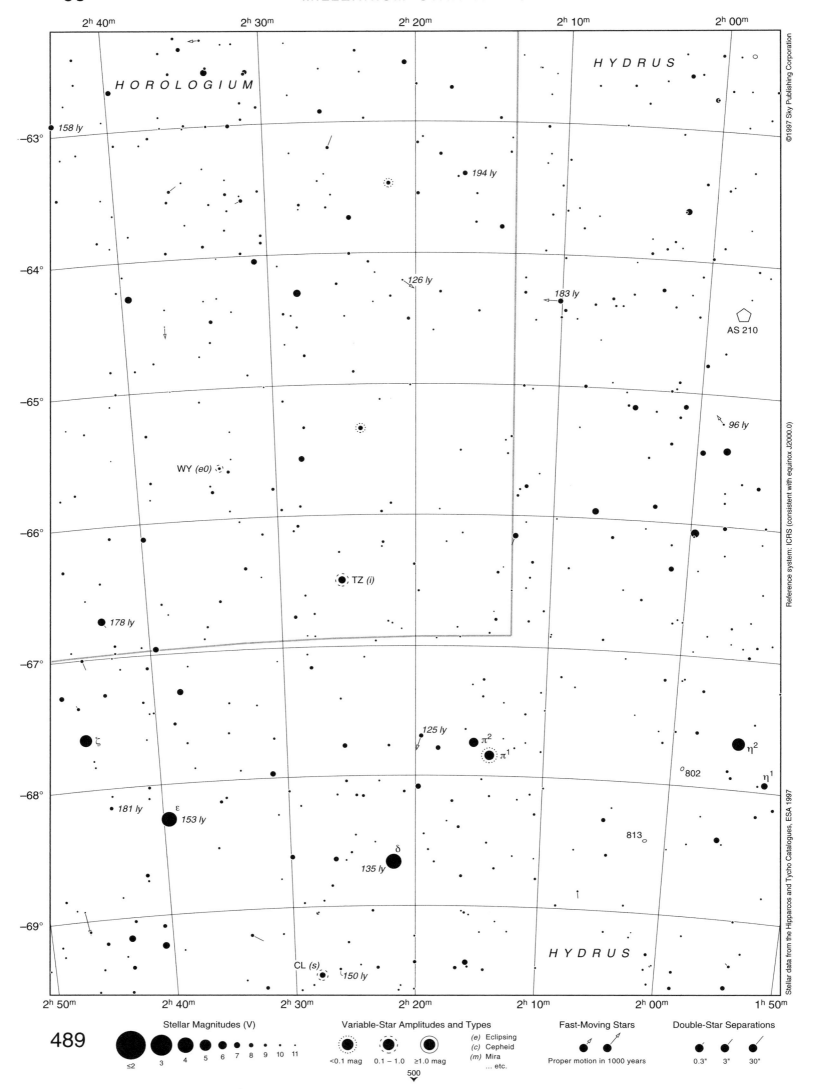

©1997 Sky Publishing Corporation

Reference system: ICRS (consistent with equinox J2000.0)

Stellar data from the Hipparcos and Tycho Catalogues, ESA 1997

489

Stellar Magnitudes (V)

≤2 3 4 5 6 7 8 9 10 11

Variable-Star Amplitudes and Types

<0.1 mag   0.1 − 1.0   ≥1.0 mag

(e) Eclipsing
(c) Cepheid
(m) Mira
... etc.

Fast-Moving Stars

Proper motion in 1000 years

Double-Star Separations

0.3"   3"   30"

500

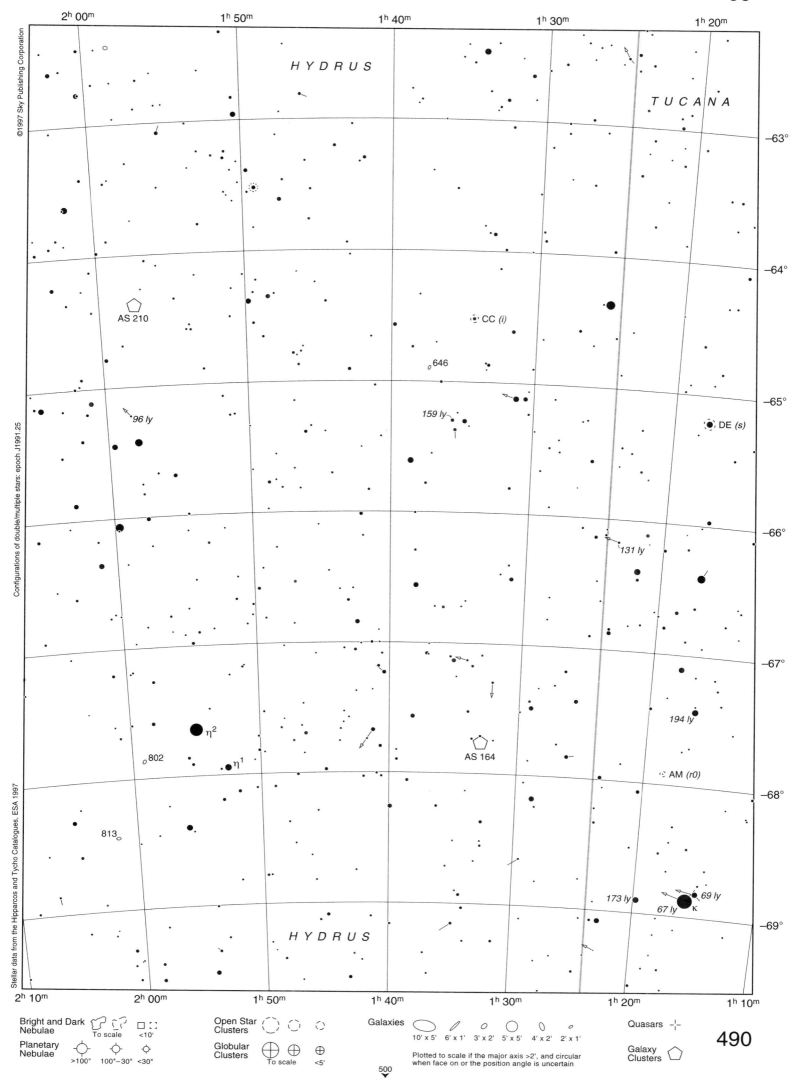

HYDRUS

TUCANA

CC *(i)*

o 646

DE *(s)*

96 ly

159 ly

AS 210

131 ly

194 ly

η²

AM *(r0)*

o 802

η¹

AS 164

813 *o*

173 ly

69 ly

67 ly κ

HYDRUS

Bright and Dark Nebulae	Open Star Clusters	Galaxies	Quasars

Bright and Dark Nebulae — To scale — <10'

Planetary Nebulae — >100" — 100"–30" — <30"

Open Star Clusters — To scale

Globular Clusters — To scale — <5'

Galaxies — 10' x 5' — 6' x 1' — 3' x 2' — 5' x 5' — 4' x 2' — 2' x 1'

Plotted to scale if the major axis >2', and circular when face on or the position angle is uncertain

Quasars

Galaxy Clusters

490

500

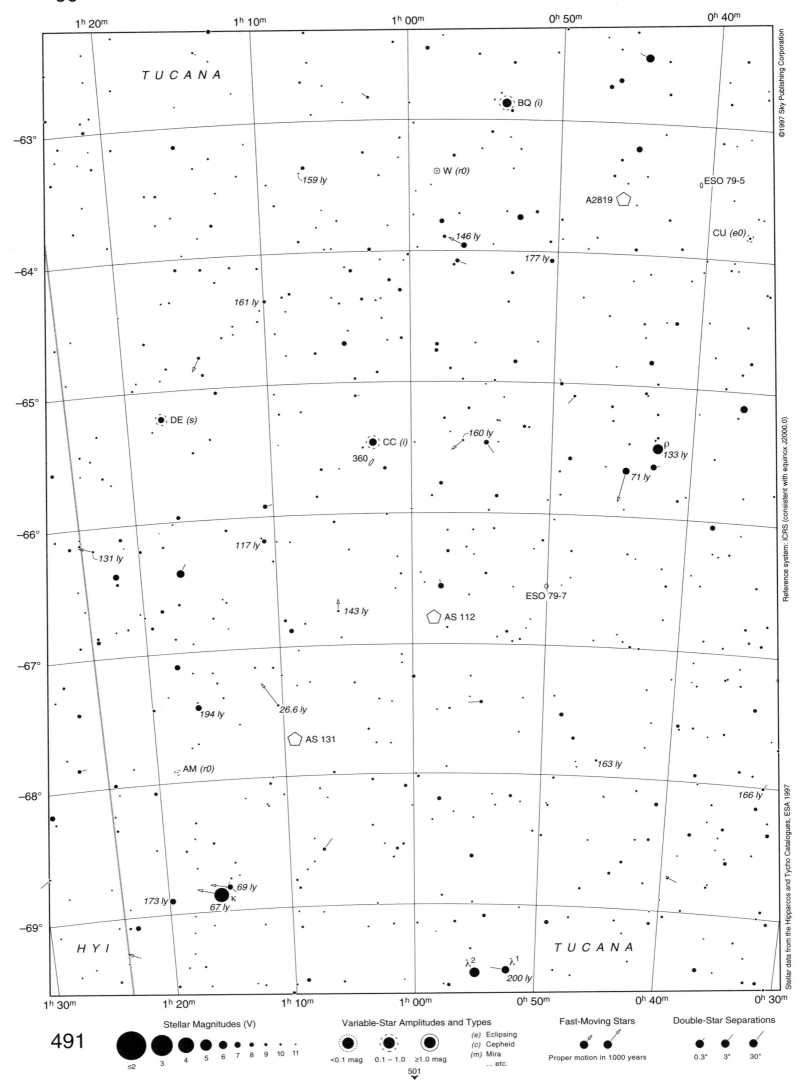

T U C A N A

159 ly

BQ (i)

⊙ W (r0)

A2819

ESO 79-5

CU (e0)

146 ly

177 ly

161 ly

DE (s)

160 ly

CC (i)

ρ
133 ly

360

71 ly

117 ly

131 ly

143 ly

ESO 79-7

AS 112

26.6 ly

194 ly

AS 131

AM (r0)

163 ly

166 ly

69 ly
K
173 ly
67 ly

H Y I

T U C A N A

λ² λ¹
200 ly

©1997 Sky Publishing Corporation

Reference system: ICRS (consistent with equinox J2000.0)

Stellar data from the Hipparcos and Tycho Catalogues, ESA 1997

Stellar Magnitudes (V)	Variable-Star Amplitudes and Types	Fast-Moving Stars	Double-Star Separations

491

≤2 3 4 5 6 7 8 9 10 11

<0.1 mag   0.1 − 1.0   ≥1.0 mag

(e) Eclipsing
(c) Cepheid
(m) Mira
... etc.

Proper motion in 1000 years

0.3" 3" 30"

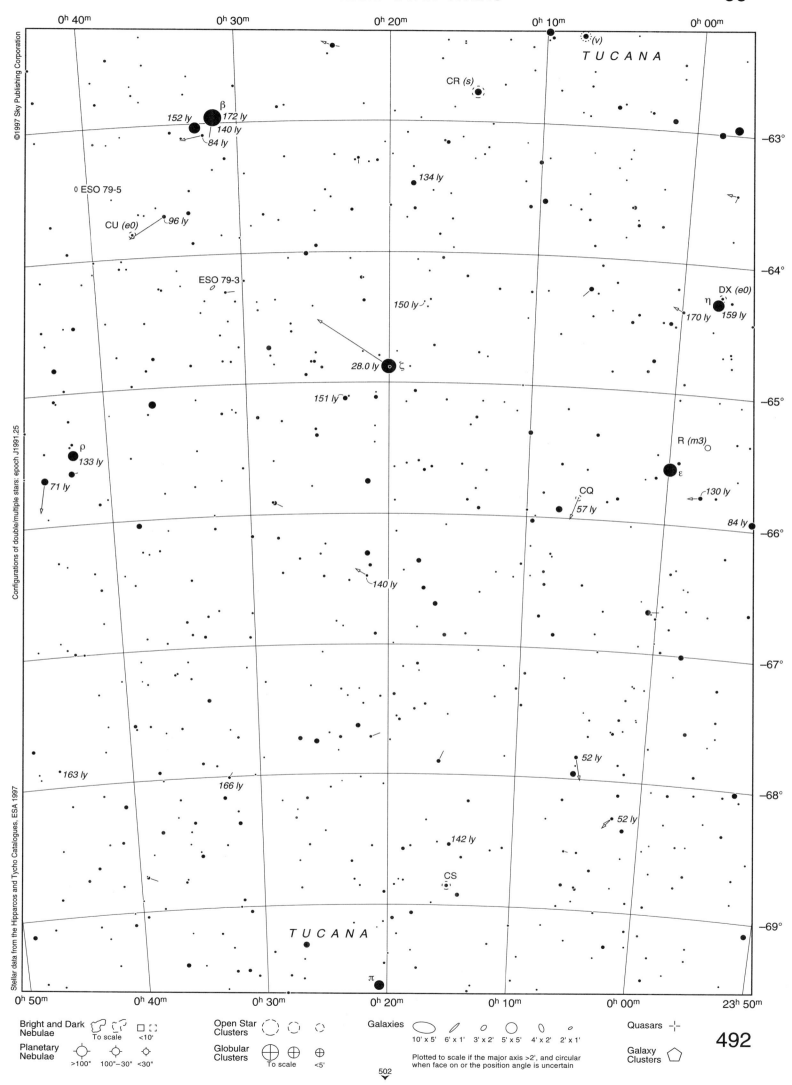

T U C A N A

CR (s)

β
152 ly 172 ly
140 ly
84 ly

0 ESO 79-5

CU (e0) 96 ly

ESO 79-3

134 ly

150 ly

28.0 ly ζ

151 ly

ρ
133 ly

71 ly

DX (e0)
η
170 ly 159 ly

R (m3)
ε

130 ly

CQ
57 ly

84 ly

140 ly

52 ly

163 ly

166 ly

52 ly

142 ly

CS

T U C A N A

π

0ʰ 50ᵐ   0ʰ 40ᵐ   0ʰ 30ᵐ   0ʰ 20ᵐ   0ʰ 10ᵐ   0ʰ 00ᵐ   23ʰ 50ᵐ

−63°
−64°
−65°
−66°
−67°
−68°
−69°

Bright and Dark Nebulae
To scale   <10'

Planetary Nebulae
>100"   100"–30"   <30"

Open Star Clusters

Globular Clusters
To scale   <5'

Galaxies
10' x 5'   6' x 1'   3' x 2'   5' x 5'   4' x 2'   2' x 1'

Plotted to scale if the major axis >2', and circular when face on or the position angle is uncertain

Quasars

Galaxy Clusters

492

502

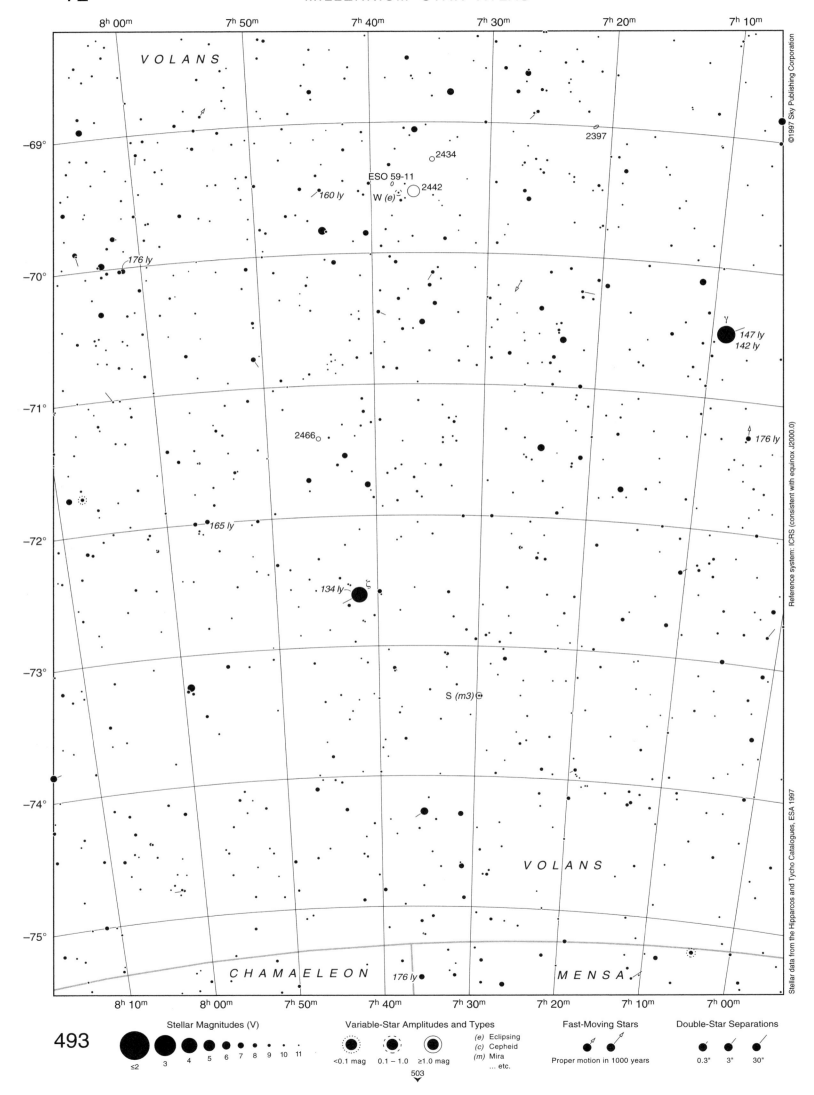

VOLANS

2397

2434

ESO 59-11

160 ly

2442

W (e)

176 ly

γ 147 ly
142 ly

2466

176 ly

165 ly

134 ly ζ

S (m3)

VOLANS

CHAMAELEON

176 ly

MENSA

493

Stellar Magnitudes (V)

≤2 3 4 5 6 7 8 9 10 11

Variable-Star Amplitudes and Types

<0.1 mag   0.1 − 1.0   ≥1.0 mag

(e) Eclipsing
(c) Cepheid
(m) Mira
... etc.

Fast-Moving Stars

Proper motion in 1000 years

Double-Star Separations

0.3"   3"   30"

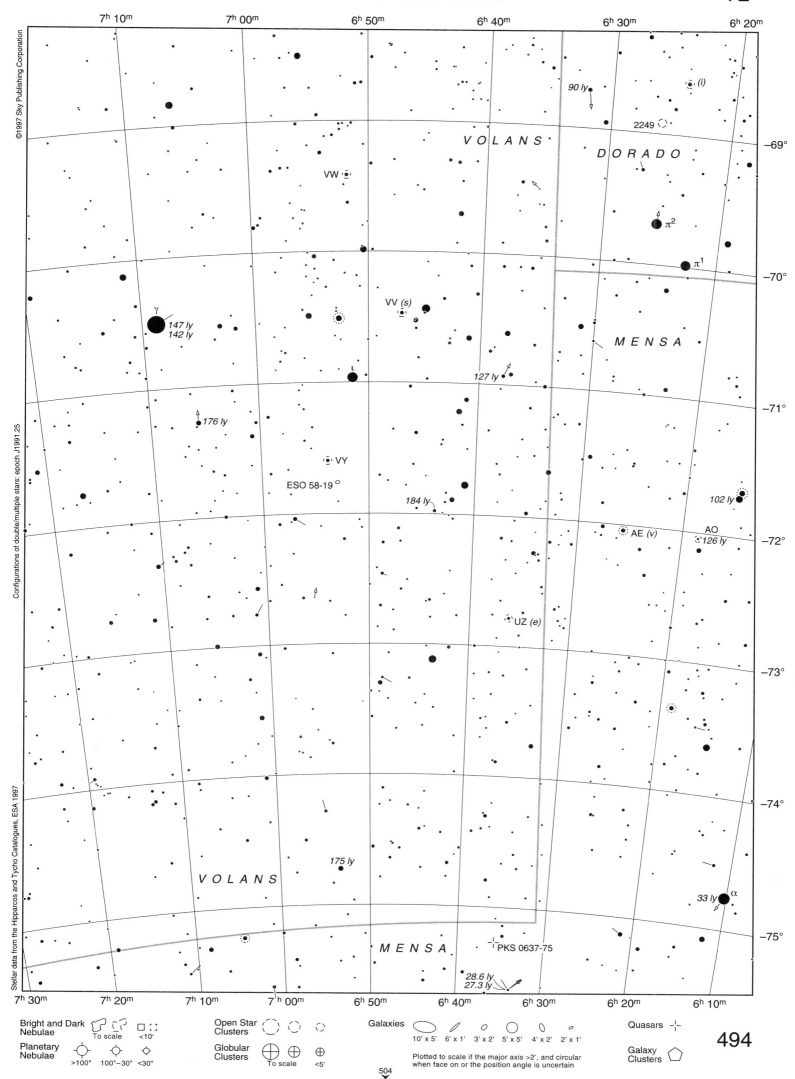

VOLANS

DORADO

MENSA

VOLANS

MENSA

90 ly

2249

VW

π²

π¹

γ
147 ly
142 ly

VV (s)

ι

127 ly

176 ly

VY

ESO 58-19

184 ly

102 ly

AE (v)

AO
126 ly

UZ (e)

175 ly

α
33 ly

PKS 0637-75

28.6 ly
27.3 ly

Bright and Dark Nebulae			Open Star Clusters			Galaxies							Quasars
To scale	<10'			To scale	<10'	10' x 5'	6' x 1'	3' x 2'	5' x 5'	4' x 2'	2' x 1'		
Planetary Nebulae			Globular Clusters										Galaxy Clusters
>100"	100"−30"	<30"	To scale	<5'									

Plotted to scale if the major axis >2', and circular when face on or the position angle is uncertain

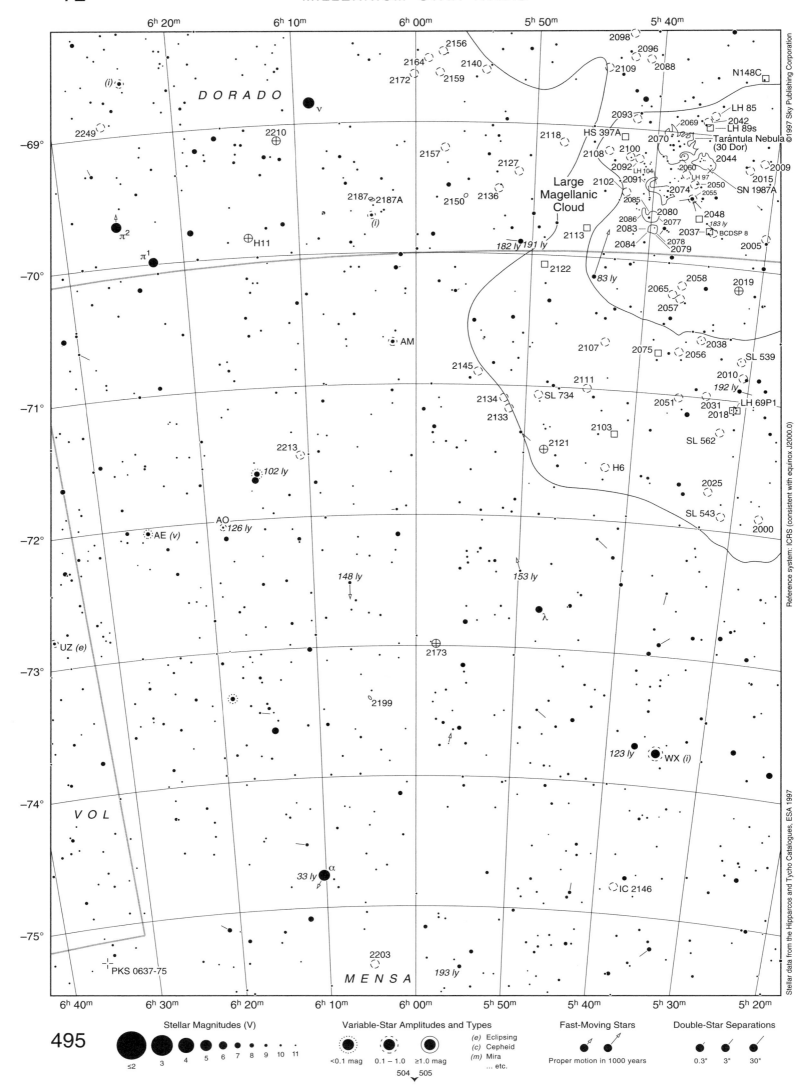

Stellar Magnitudes (V)

≤2 3 4 5 6 7 8 9 10 11

Variable-Star Amplitudes and Types

<0.1 mag   0.1 – 1.0   ≥1.0 mag

(e) Eclipsing
(c) Cepheid
(m) Mira
... etc.

Fast-Moving Stars

Proper motion in 1000 years

Double-Star Separations

0.3"   3"   30"

© 1997 Sky Publishing Corporation

Reference system: ICRS (consistent with equinox J2000.0)

Stellar data from the Hipparcos and Tycho Catalogues, ESA 1997

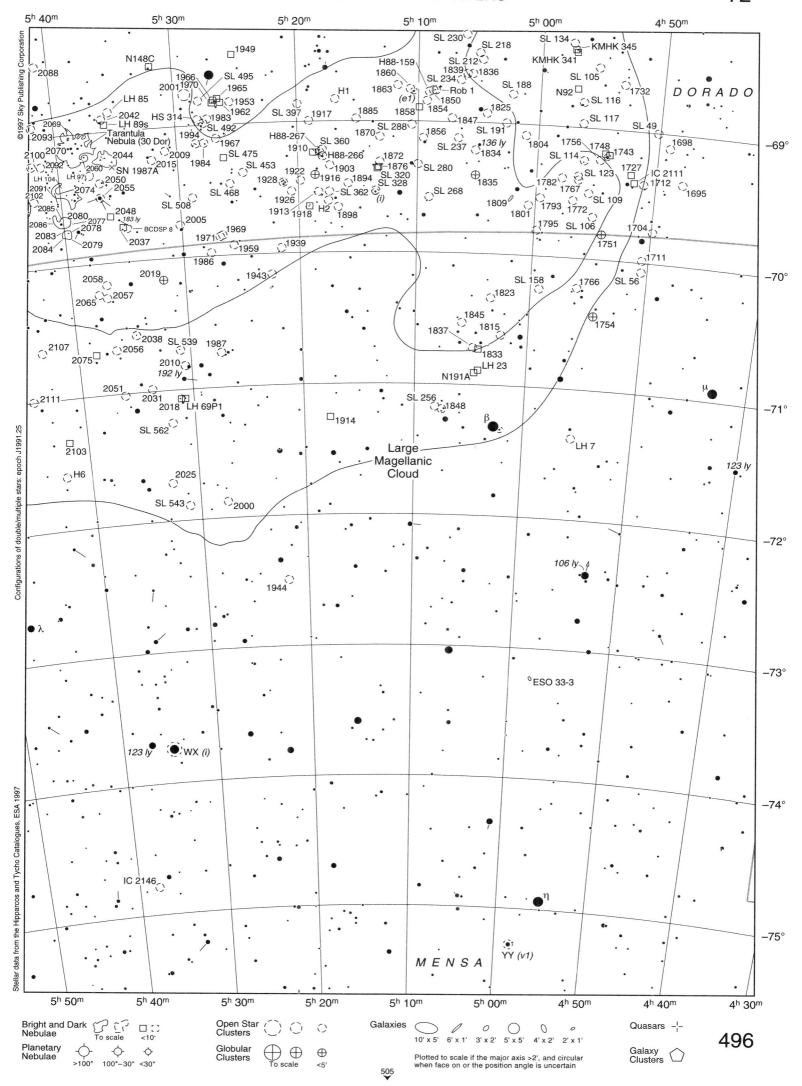

Large
Magellanic
Cloud

D O R A D O

M E N S A

Bright and Dark Nebulae		Open Star Clusters			Galaxies						Quasars
To scale	<10'				10' x 5'	6' x 1'	3' x 2'	5' x 5'	4' x 2'	2' x 1'	
Planetary Nebulae		Globular Clusters									Galaxy Clusters
>100" 100"–30" <30"		To scale	<5'		Plotted to scale if the major axis >2', and circular when face on or the position angle is uncertain						

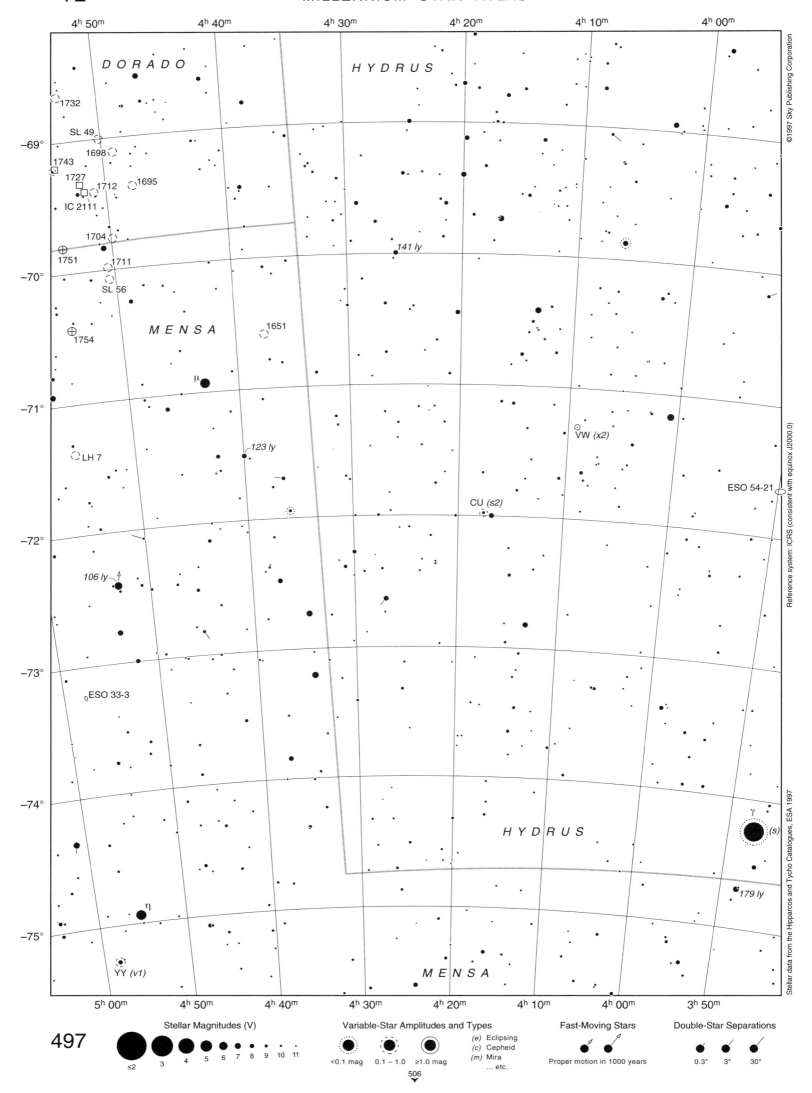

©1997 Sky Publishing Corporation

Reference system: ICRS (consistent with equinox J2000.0)

Stellar data from the Hipparcos and Tycho Catalogues, ESA 1997

497

Stellar Magnitudes (V)

≤2 3 4 5 6 7 8 9 10 11

Variable-Star Amplitudes and Types

<0.1 mag   0.1 – 1.0   ≥1.0 mag

(e) Eclipsing
(c) Cepheid
(m) Mira
... etc.

Fast-Moving Stars

Proper motion in 1000 years

Double-Star Separations

0.3"   3"   30"

MILLENNIUM STAR ATLAS

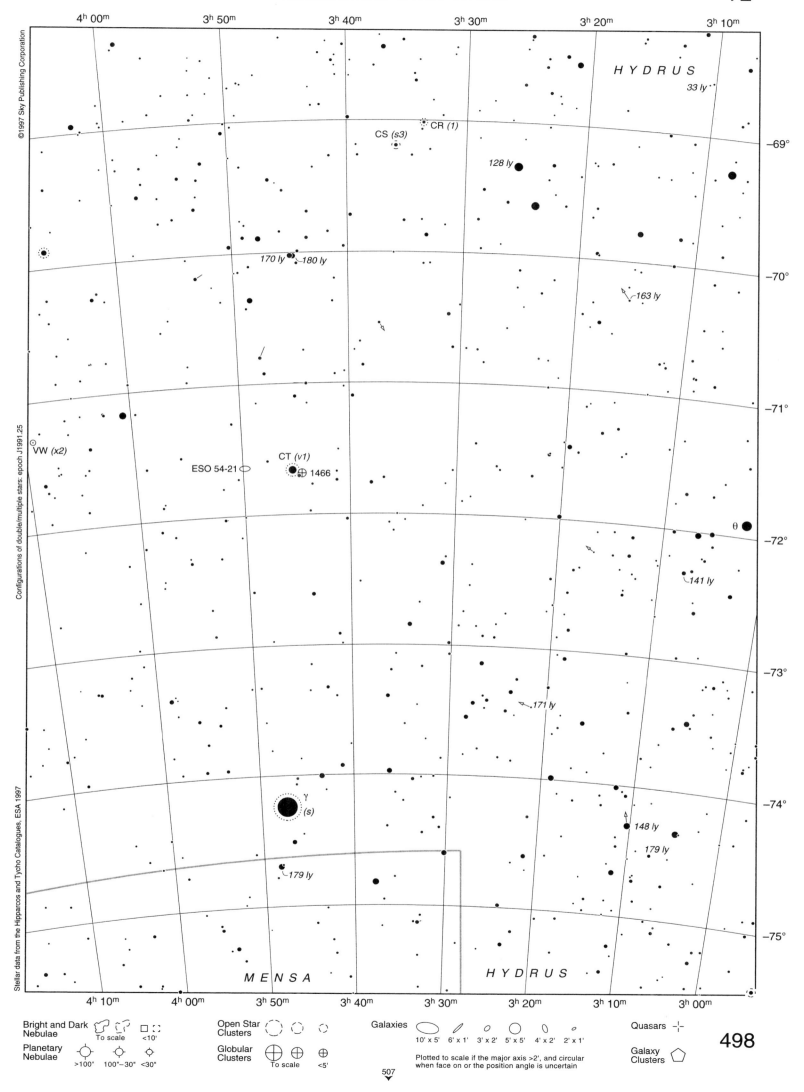

H Y D R U S

33 ly

CR (1)

CS (s3)

128 ly

170 ly 180 ly

163 ly

VW (x2)

ESO 54-21

CT (v1)

1466

θ

141 ly

171 ly

γ
(s)

148 ly

179 ly

179 ly

M E N S A   *H Y D R U S*

4ʰ 00ᵐ   3ʰ 50ᵐ   3ʰ 40ᵐ   3ʰ 30ᵐ   3ʰ 20ᵐ   3ʰ 10ᵐ

−69°
−70°
−71°
−72°
−73°
−74°
−75°

4ʰ 10ᵐ   4ʰ 00ᵐ   3ʰ 50ᵐ   3ʰ 40ᵐ   3ʰ 30ᵐ   3ʰ 20ᵐ   3ʰ 10ᵐ   3ʰ 00ᵐ

Bright and Dark Nebulae		To scale	<10'
Planetary Nebulae	>100"	100"–30"	<30"

Open Star Clusters		
Globular Clusters		To scale	<5'

Galaxies

10' x 5'   6' x 1'   3' x 2'   5' x 5'   4' x 2'   2' x 1'

Plotted to scale if the major axis >2', and circular
when face on or the position angle is uncertain

Quasars

Galaxy Clusters

498

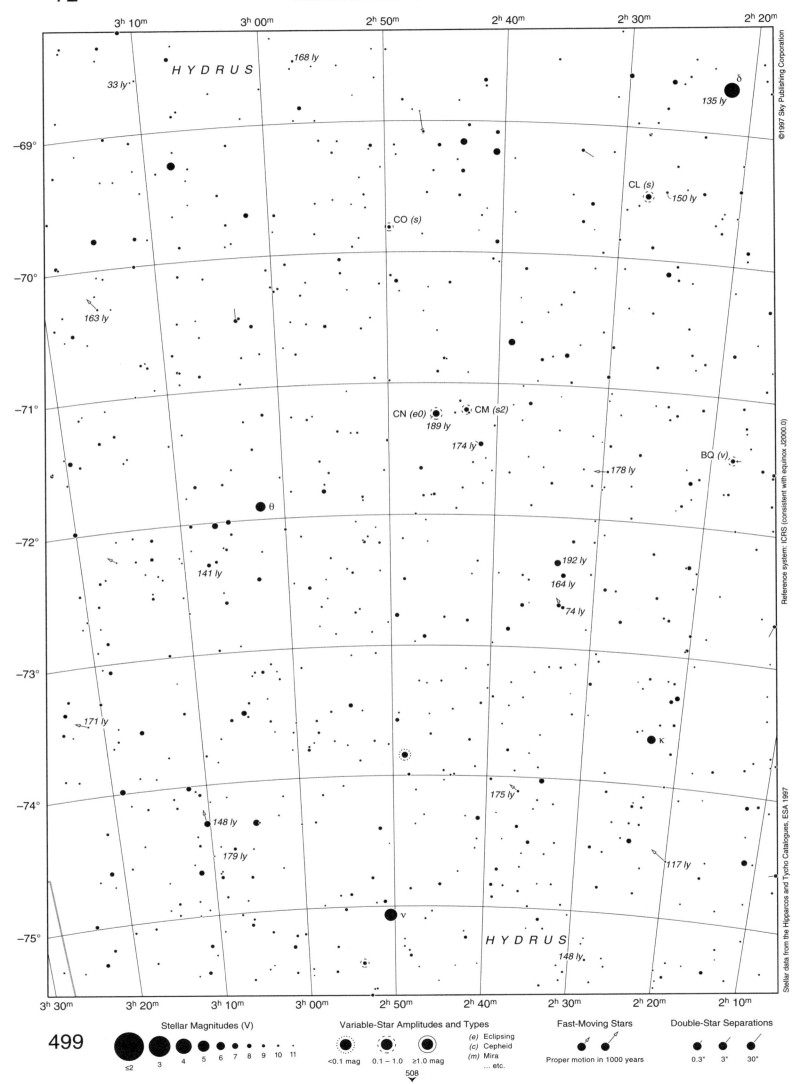

HYDRUS

168 ly

33 ly

135 ly

δ

CL (s)

150 ly

CO (s)

163 ly

CN (e0)   CM (s2)

189 ly

174 ly

BQ (v)

178 ly

θ

192 ly

141 ly

164 ly

74 ly

171 ly

κ

175 ly

148 ly

117 ly

179 ly

ν

HYDRUS

148 ly

499

Stellar Magnitudes (V)

≤2   3   4   5   6   7   8   9 10 11

Variable-Star Amplitudes and Types

<0.1 mag   0.1 – 1.0   ≥1.0 mag

(e) Eclipsing
(c) Cepheid
(m) Mira
... etc.

Fast-Moving Stars

Proper motion in 1000 years

Double-Star Separations

0.3"   3"   30"

▼
508

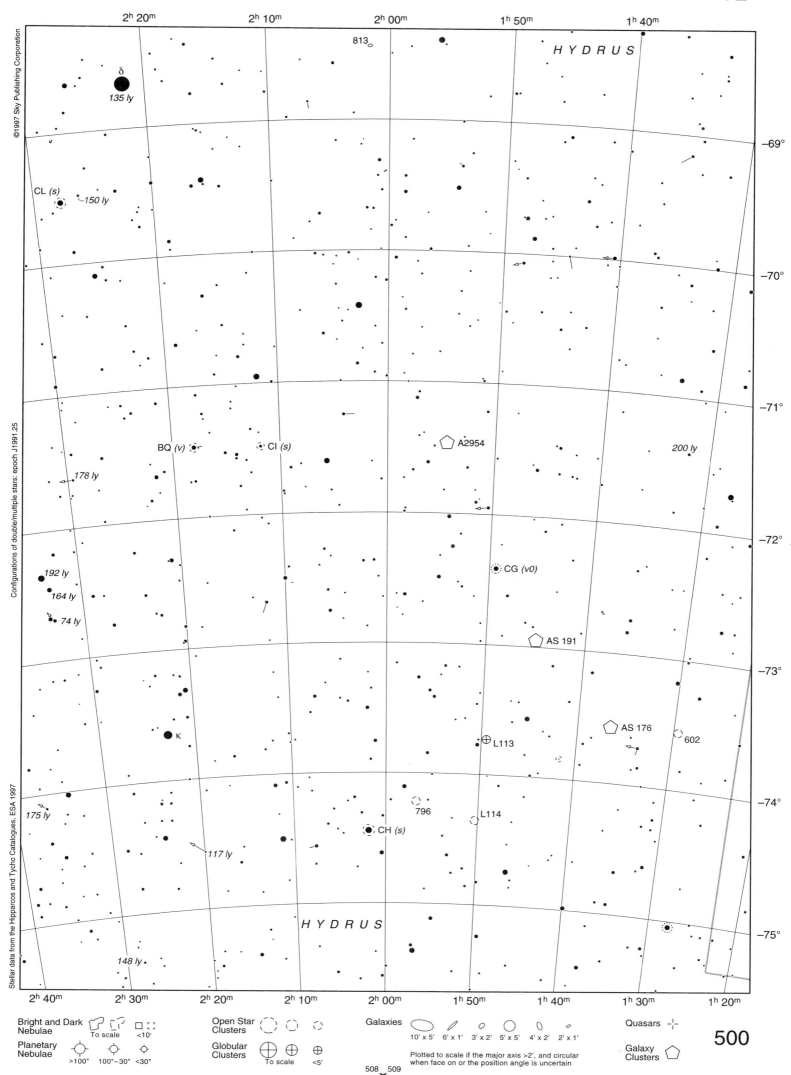

H Y D R U S

813

δ
135 ly

CL (s)
150 ly

BQ (v)
CI (s)
A2954

178 ly

200 ly

192 ly
164 ly
74 ly

CG (v0)

AS 191

κ

AS 176
L113
602

175 ly

796
L114

117 ly
CH (s)

H Y D R U S

148 ly

−69°
−70°
−71°
−72°
−73°
−74°
−75°

2ʰ 20ᵐ 2ʰ 10ᵐ 2ʰ 00ᵐ 1ʰ 50ᵐ 1ʰ 40ᵐ

2ʰ 40ᵐ 2ʰ 30ᵐ 2ʰ 20ᵐ 2ʰ 10ᵐ 2ʰ 00ᵐ 1ʰ 50ᵐ 1ʰ 40ᵐ 1ʰ 30ᵐ 1ʰ 20ᵐ

Bright and Dark Nebulae	To scale	<10'
Planetary Nebulae	>100" 100"−30" <30"	

Open Star Clusters	
Globular Clusters	To scale <5'

Galaxies
10' x 5' 6' x 1' 3' x 2' 5' x 5' 4' x 2' 2' x 1'

Plotted to scale if the major axis >2', and circular when face on or the position angle is uncertain

Quasars

Galaxy Clusters

500

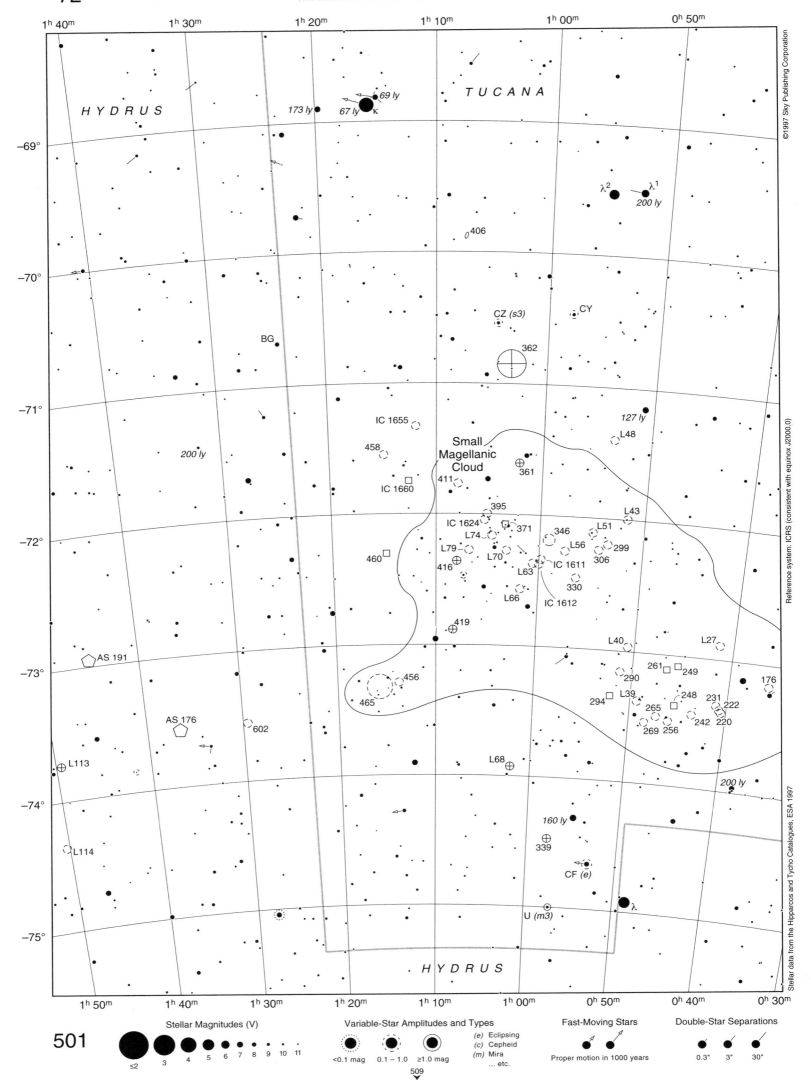

©1997 Sky Publishing Corporation

Reference system: ICRS (consistent with equinox J2000.0)

Stellar data from the Hipparcos and Tycho Catalogues, ESA 1997

H Y D R U S

T U C A N A

69 ly
173 ly   67 ly   κ

λ²   λ¹
200 ly

0 ⁴⁰⁶

CZ (s3)   CY

BG

362

127 ly

IC 1655   L48

458

Small
Magellanic
Cloud

⊕ 361

IC 1660   411

395

L43

IC 1624   371   L51

L74   346   L56   299

L79   IC 1611   306

460   416   L70   330

L63

L66   IC 1612

419

L40   L27

AS 191

456   261   249

465   290

294   L39   248   176

AS 176   265   231   222

602   269   256   242   220

⊕ L113   L68 ⊕

200 ly

160 ly

L114   339 ⊕

CF (e)

λ

U (m3)

H Y D R U S

Stellar Magnitudes (V)

≤2   3   4   5   6   7   8   9   10   11

Variable-Star Amplitudes and Types

<0.1 mag   0.1 – 1.0   ≥1.0 mag

(e) Eclipsing
(c) Cepheid
(m) Mira
... etc.

Fast-Moving Stars

Proper motion in 1000 years

Double-Star Separations

0.3"   3"   30"

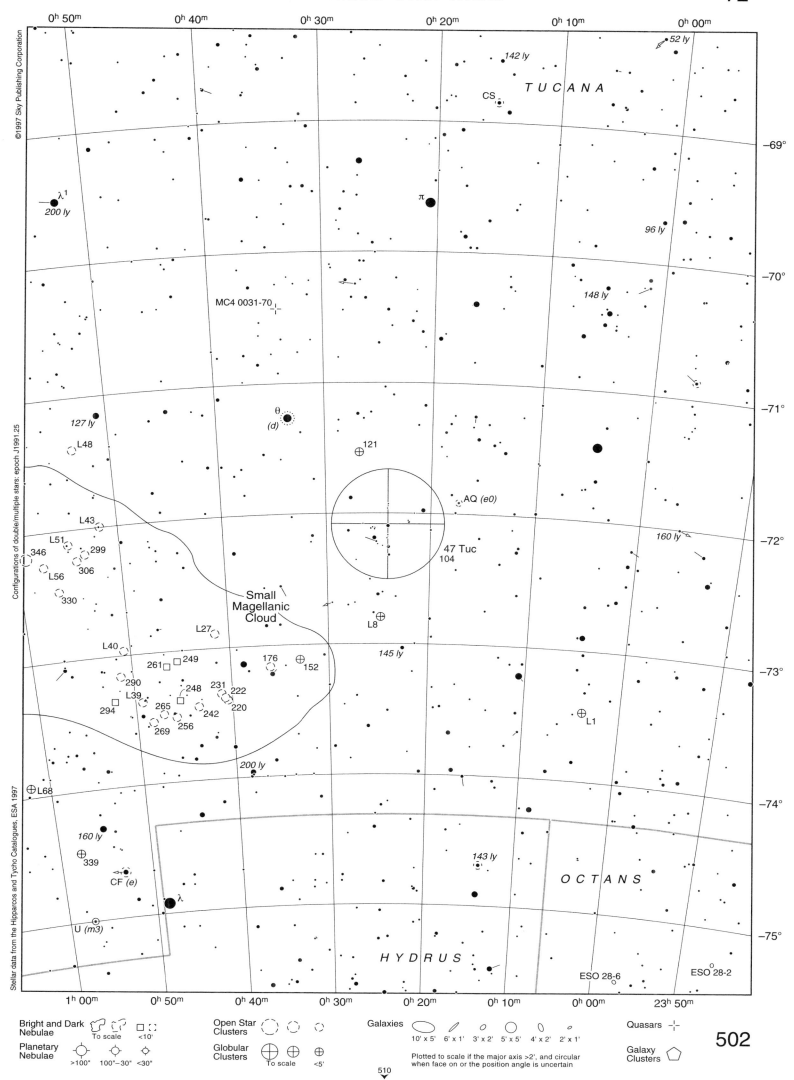

Bright and Dark Nebulae
To scale
<10'

Planetary Nebulae
>100" 100"−30" <30"

Open Star Clusters

Globular Clusters
To scale <5'

Galaxies
10' x 5' 6' x 1' 3' x 2' 5' x 5' 4' x 2' 2' x 1'

Plotted to scale if the major axis >2', and circular
when face on or the position angle is uncertain

Quasars

Galaxy Clusters

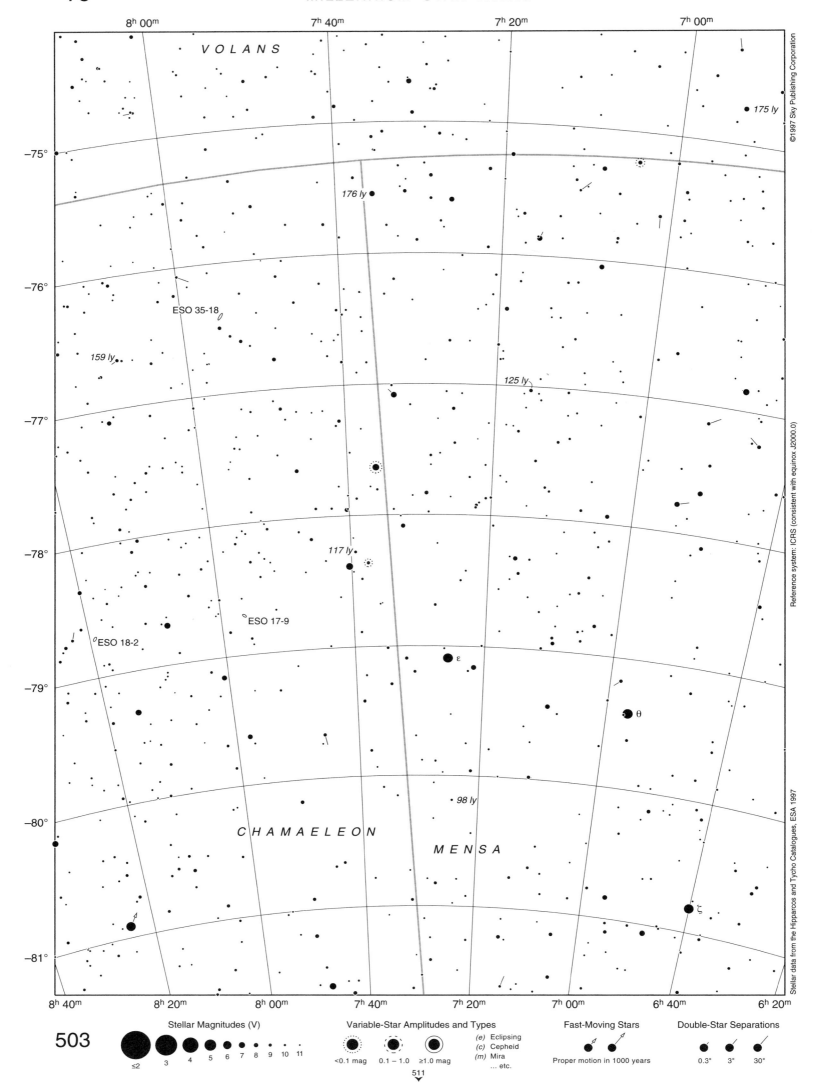

©1997 Sky Publishing Corporation

Reference system: ICRS (consistent with equinox J2000.0)

Stellar data from the Hipparcos and Tycho Catalogues, ESA 1997

VOLANS

175 ly

176 ly

ESO 35-18

159 ly

125 ly

117 ly

ESO 17-9

ESO 18-2

ε

θ

98 ly

CHAMAELEON

MENSA

ζ

503

Stellar Magnitudes (V)

≤2 3 4 5 6 7 8 9 10 11

Variable-Star Amplitudes and Types

<0.1 mag   0.1 – 1.0   ≥1.0 mag

(e) Eclipsing
(c) Cepheid
(m) Mira
... etc.

Fast-Moving Stars

Proper motion in 1000 years

Double-Star Separations

0.3"   3"   30"

MILLENNIUM STAR ATLAS

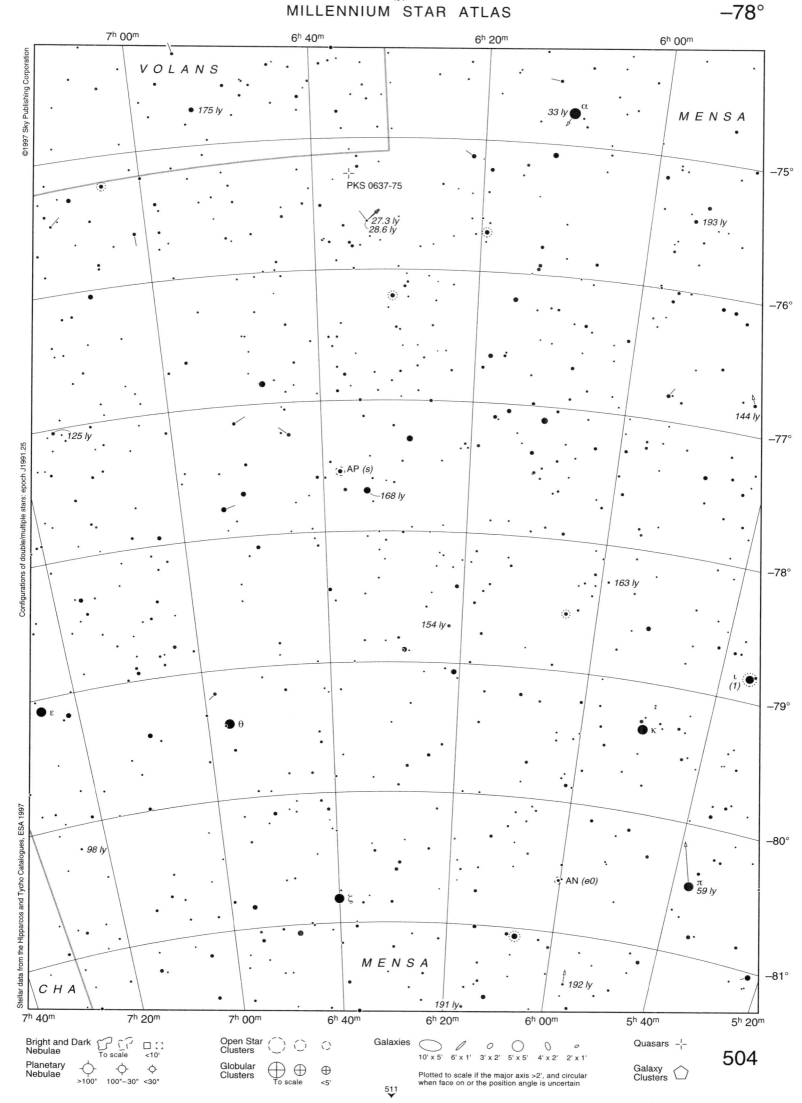

©1997 Sky Publishing Corporation

Configurations of double/multiple stars: epoch J1991.25

Stellar data from the Hipparcos and Tycho Catalogues, ESA 1997

VOLANS

MENSA

175 ly

33 ly α

193 ly

PKS 0637-75

27.3 ly
28.6 ly

144 ly

125 ly

AP (s)

168 ly

163 ly

154 ly

ι
(1)

ε

θ

κ

98 ly

AN (e0)

π
59 ly

ζ

MENSA

192 ly

CHA

191 ly

Bright and Dark Nebulae		Open Star Clusters			Galaxies						Quasars
To scale	<10'				10' x 5'	6' x 1'	3' x 2'	5' x 5'	4' x 2'	2' x 1'	
Planetary Nebulae		Globular Clusters									Galaxy Clusters
>100" 100"–30" <30"		To scale	<5'		Plotted to scale if the major axis >2', and circular when face on or the position angle is uncertain						

511

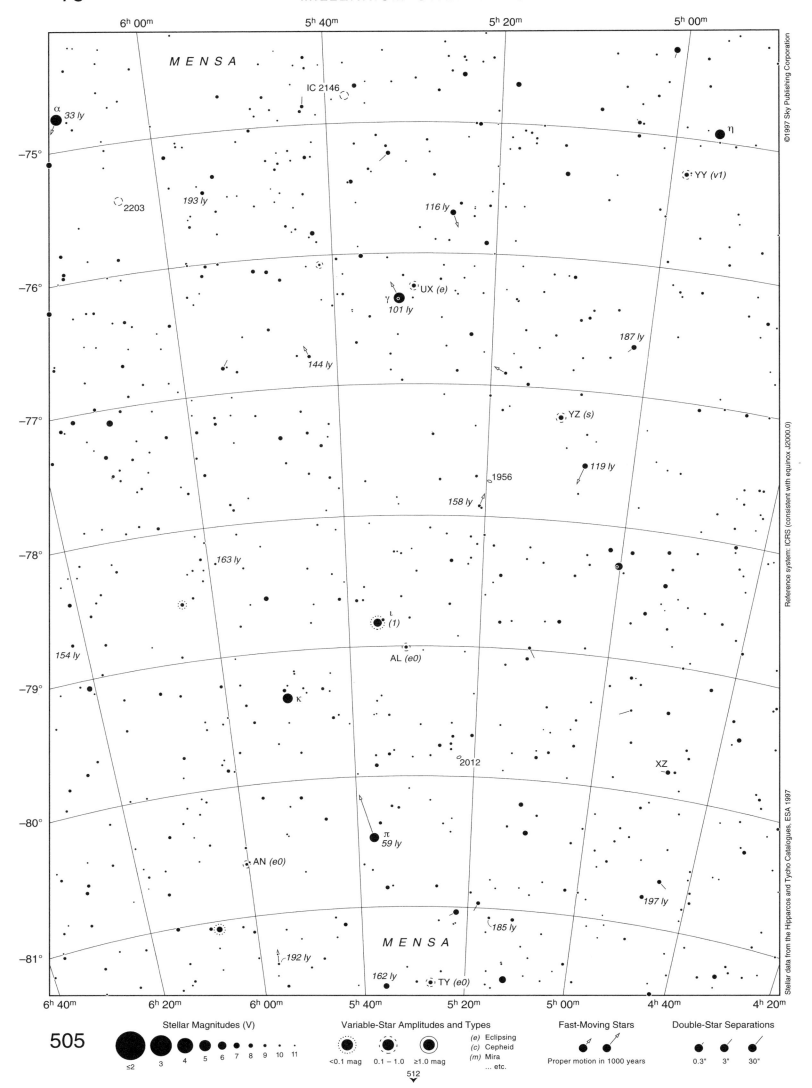

©1997 Sky Publishing Corporation

Reference system: ICRS (consistent with equinox J2000.0)

Stellar data from the Hipparcos and Tycho Catalogues, ESA 1997

M E N S A

IC 2146

2203

193 ly

α *33 ly*

η

YY *(v1)*

116 ly

UX *(e)*
γ
101 ly

187 ly

144 ly

YZ *(s)*

119 ly

1956

158 ly

163 ly

L
(1)

AL *(e0)*

154 ly

κ

2012

XZ

π
59 ly

AN *(e0)*

197 ly

185 ly

M E N S A

192 ly

162 ly

TY *(e0)*

505

Stellar Magnitudes (V)								
≤2	3	4	5	6	7	8	9	10	11

Variable-Star Amplitudes and Types

<0.1 mag   0.1 − 1.0   ≥1.0 mag

(e) Eclipsing
(c) Cepheid
(m) Mira
... etc.

Fast-Moving Stars

Proper motion in 1000 years

Double-Star Separations

0.3"   3"   30"

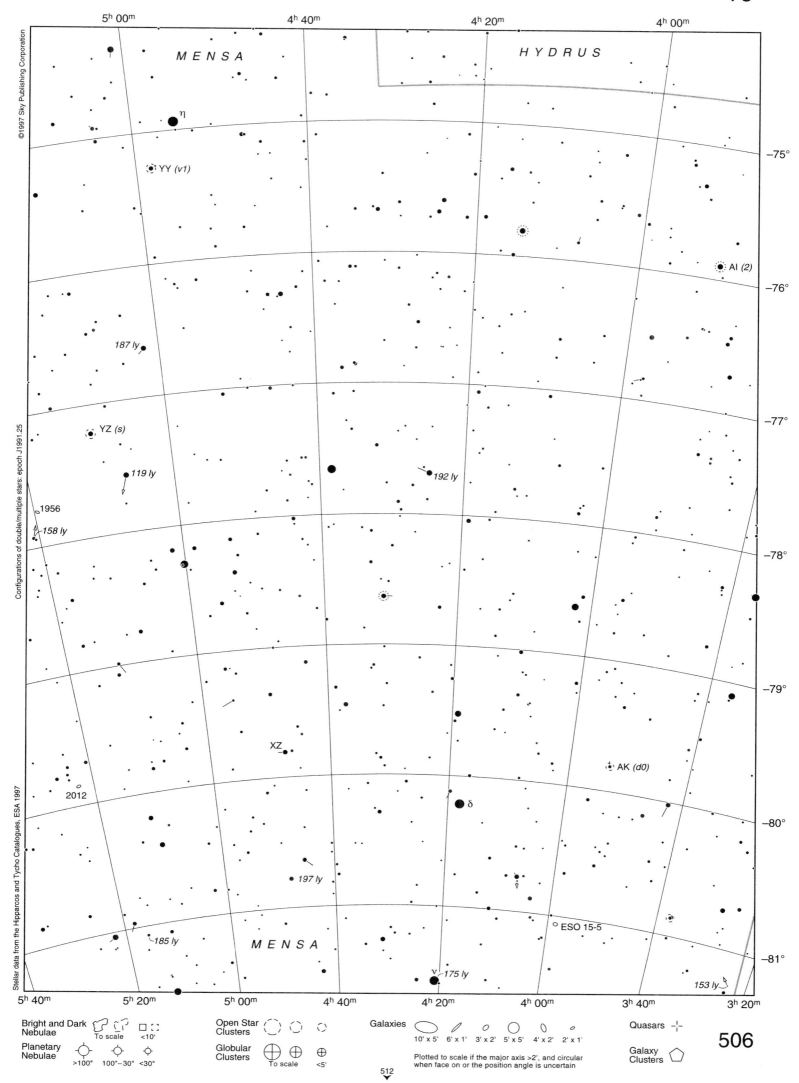

MENSA

HYDRUS

5h 00m
4h 40m
4h 20m
4h 00m

−75°
−76°
−77°
−78°
−79°
−80°
−81°

η

YY (v1)

AI (2)

187 ly

YZ (s)

119 ly

1956

158 ly

192 ly

XZ

AK (d0)

2012

δ

197 ly

ESO 15-5

185 ly

MENSA

ν 175 ly

153 ly

5h 40m
5h 20m
5h 00m
4h 40m
4h 20m
4h 00m
3h 40m
3h 20m

Bright and Dark Nebulae	To scale	<10'		
Planetary Nebulae	>100"	100"−30"	<30"	

Open Star Clusters		
Globular Clusters	To scale	<5'

Galaxies
10' x 5' 6' x 1' 3' x 2' 5' x 5' 4' x 2' 2' x 1'

Quasars

Galaxy Clusters

Plotted to scale if the major axis >2', and circular when face on or the position angle is uncertain

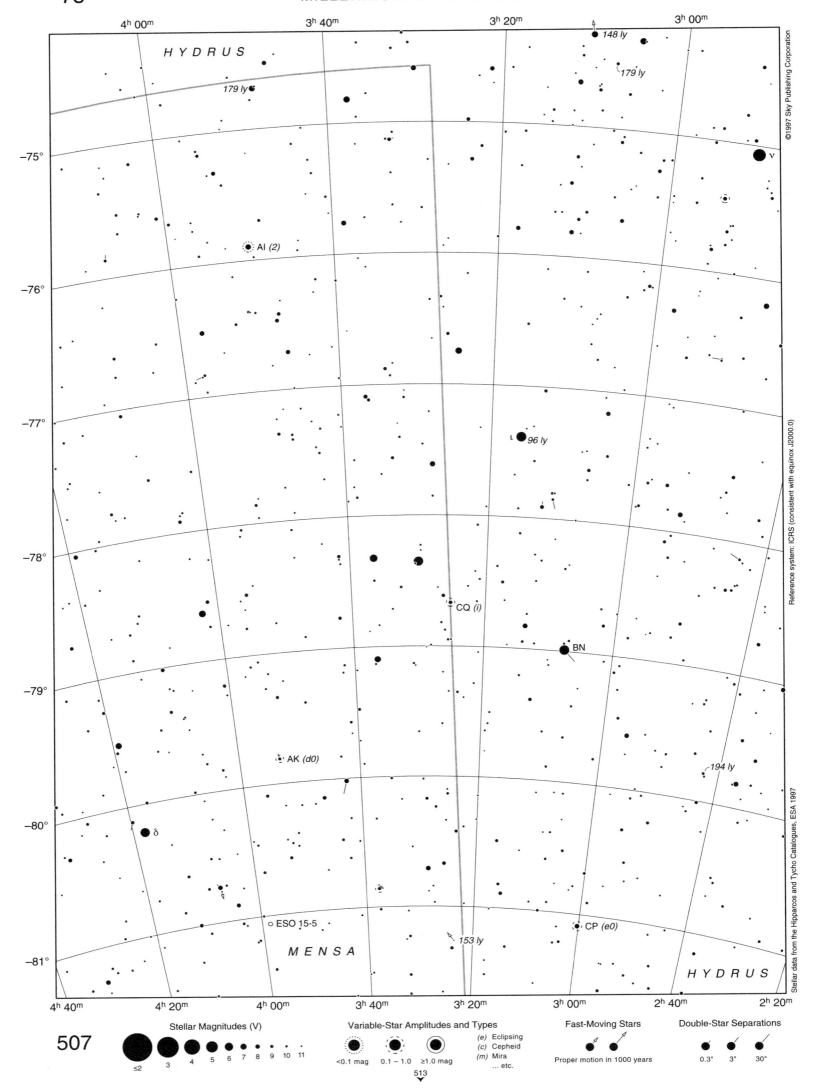

©1997 Sky Publishing Corporation

Reference system: ICRS (consistent with equinox J2000.0)

Stellar data from the Hipparcos and Tycho Catalogues, ESA 1997

HYDRUS

179 ly

AI (2)

ν

ι 96 ly

CQ (i)

BN

AK (d0)

194 ly

δ

ESO 15-5

CP (e0)

153 ly

MENSA

HYDRUS

148 ly

179 ly

507

Stellar Magnitudes (V)

≤2   3   4   5   6   7   8   9   10   11

Variable-Star Amplitudes and Types

<0.1 mag   0.1 – 1.0   ≥1.0 mag

(e) Eclipsing
(c) Cepheid
(m) Mira
... etc.

Fast-Moving Stars

Proper motion in 1000 years

Double-Star Separations

0.3"   3"   30"

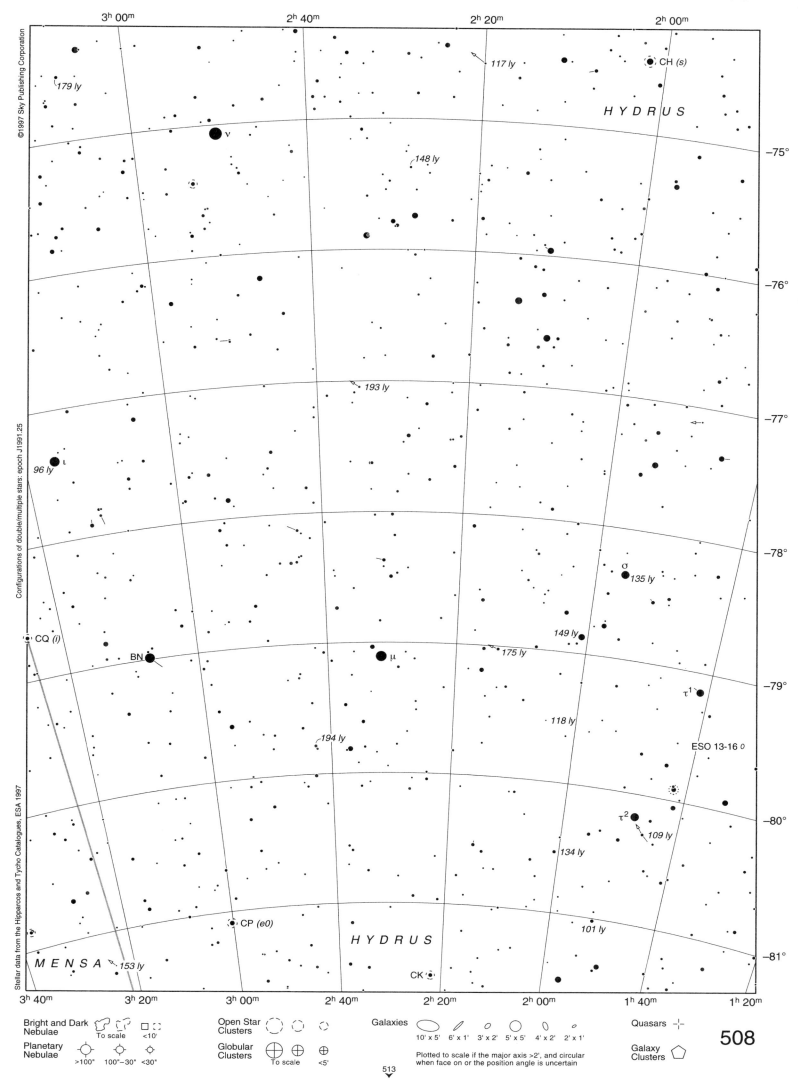

HYDRUS

HYDRUS

MENSA

508

Bright and Dark Nebulae	To scale	<10'
Planetary Nebulae	>100" 100"−30" <30'	
Open Star Clusters		
Globular Clusters	To scale <5'	

Galaxies
10' x 5' 6' x 1' 3' x 2' 5' x 5' 4' x 2' 2' x 1'

Plotted to scale if the major axis >2', and circular when face on or the position angle is uncertain

Quasars

Galaxy Clusters

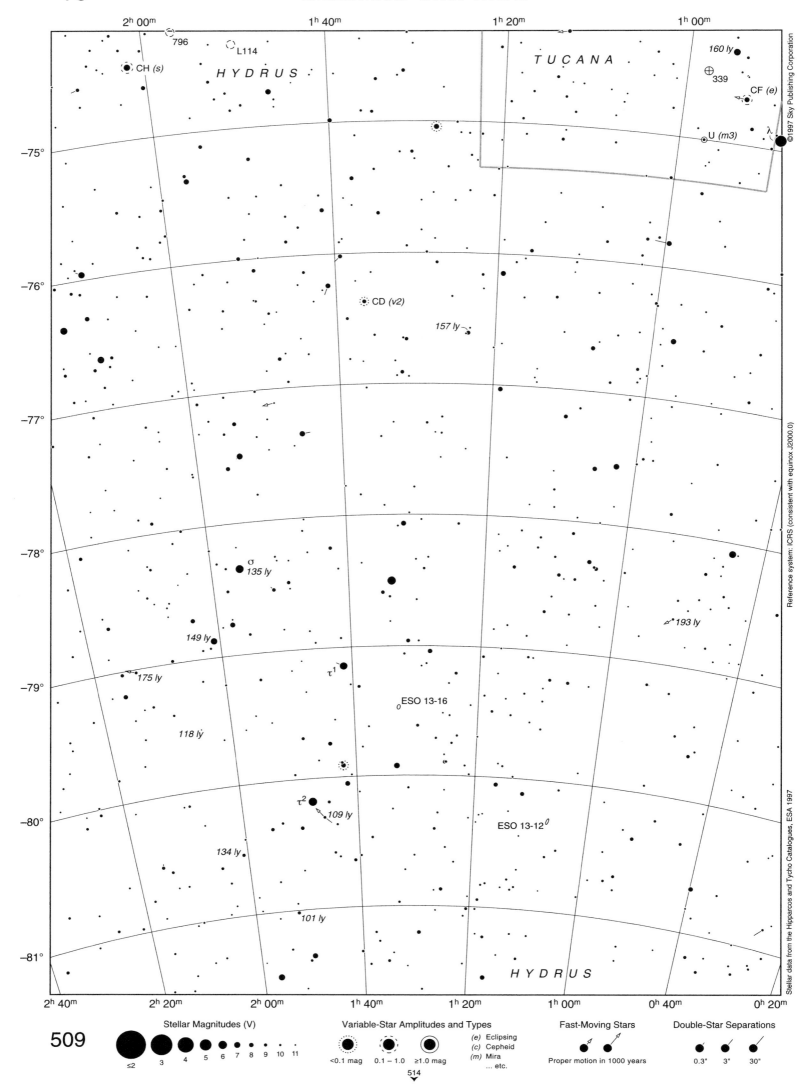

509

Stellar Magnitudes (V)

≤2　3　4　5　6　7　8　9　10　11

Variable-Star Amplitudes and Types

<0.1 mag　0.1 − 1.0　≥1.0 mag

(e) Eclipsing
(c) Cepheid
(m) Mira
... etc.

Fast-Moving Stars

Proper motion in 1000 years

Double-Star Separations

0.3"　3"　30"

514

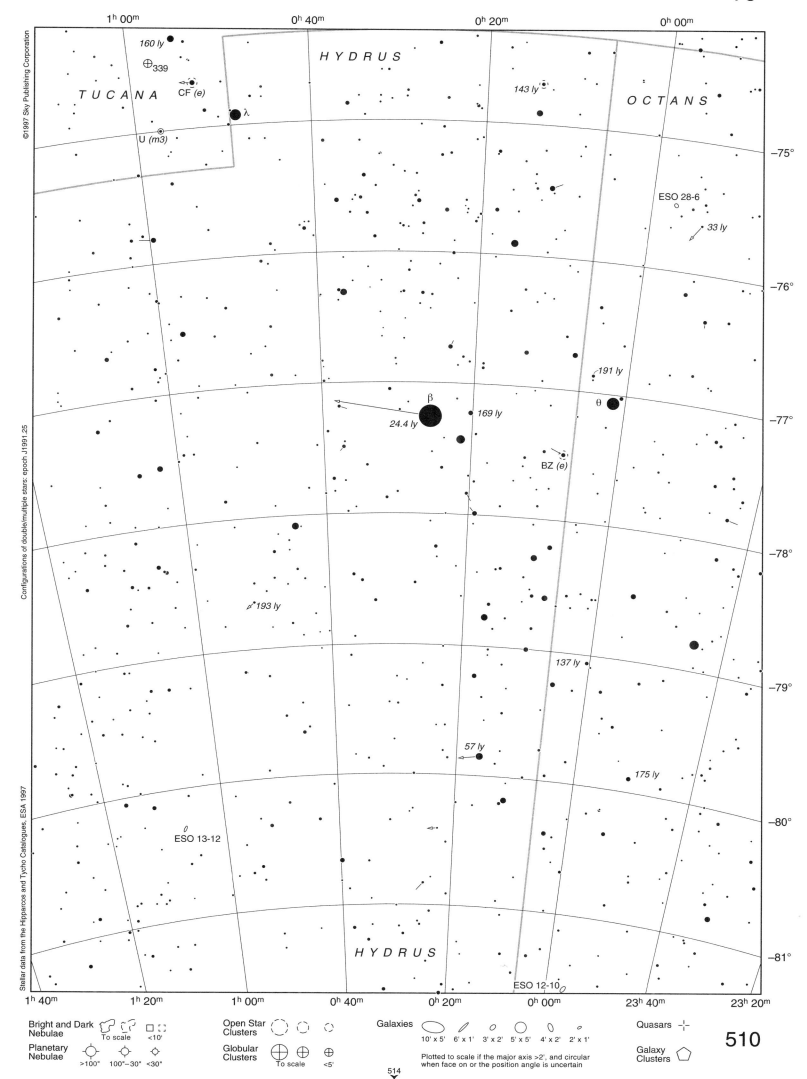

Configurations of double/multiple stars: epoch J1991.25

Stellar data from the Hipparcos and Tycho Catalogues, ESA 1997

1ʰ 00ᵐ   0ʰ 40ᵐ   0ʰ 20ᵐ   0ʰ 00ᵐ

HYDRUS

OCTANS

TUCANA

160 ly
⊕ 339
CF (e)
λ
U (m3)

143 ly
ESO 28-6
33 ly

−75°
−76°
−77°
−78°
−79°
−80°
−81°

191 ly
β
169 ly
θ
24.4 ly
BZ (e)

193 ly
137 ly
57 ly
175 ly

ESO 13-12
HYDRUS
ESO 12-10

1ʰ 40ᵐ   1ʰ 20ᵐ   1ʰ 00ᵐ   0ʰ 40ᵐ   0ʰ 20ᵐ   0ʰ 00ᵐ   23ʰ 40ᵐ   23ʰ 20ᵐ

Bright and Dark Nebulae
To scale   <10'

Planetary Nebulae
>100" 100"–30" <30'

Open Star Clusters

Globular Clusters
To scale   <5'

Galaxies
10' x 5'   6' x 1'   3' x 2'   5' x 5'   4' x 2'   2' x 1'

Plotted to scale if the major axis >2', and circular when face on or the position angle is uncertain

Quasars

Galaxy Clusters

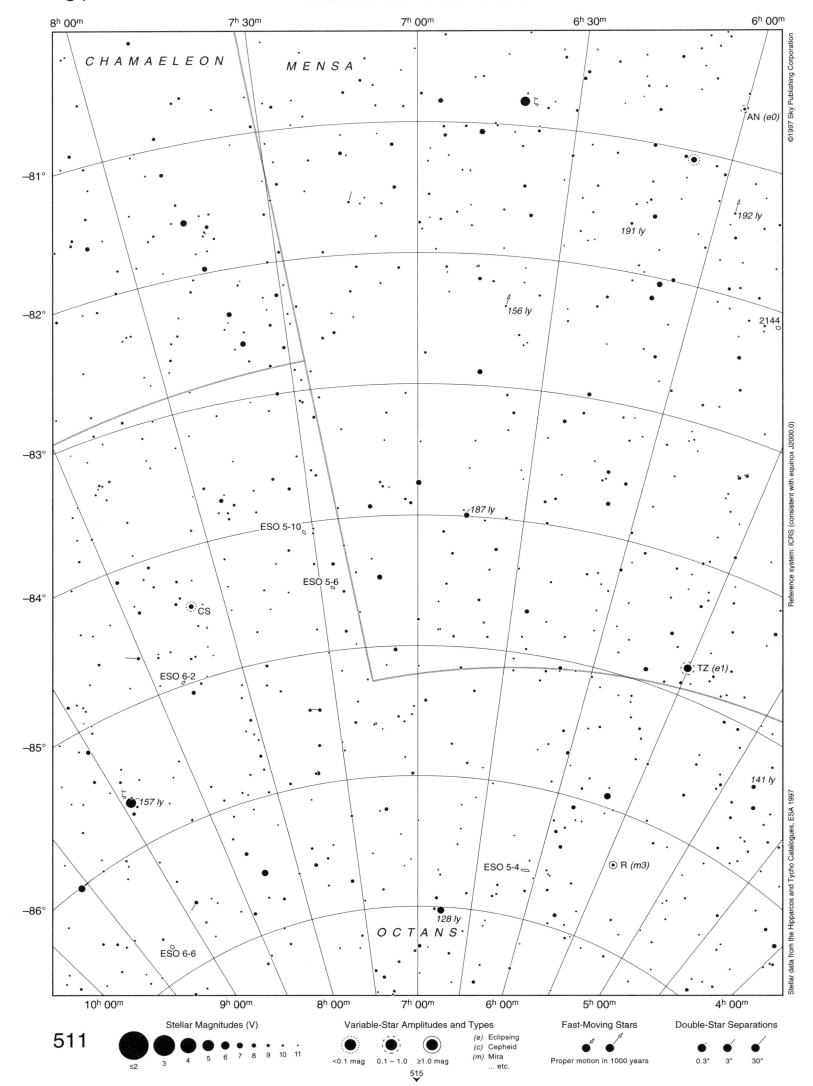

©1997 Sky Publishing Corporation

Reference system: ICRS (consistent with equinox J2000.0)

Stellar data from the Hipparcos and Tycho Catalogues, ESA 1997

CHAMAELEON

MENSA

ζ

AN (e0)

192 ly

191 ly

156 ly

2144

187 ly

ESO 5-10

ESO 5-6

CS

TZ (e1)

ESO 6-2

141 ly

ζ 157 ly

R (m3)

ESO 5-4

128 ly

OCTANS

ESO 6-6

511

Stellar Magnitudes (V)

≤2 3 4 5 6 7 8 9 10 11

Variable-Star Amplitudes and Types

<0.1 mag   0.1 − 1.0   ≥1.0 mag

(e) Eclipsing
(c) Cepheid
(m) Mira
... etc.

Fast-Moving Stars

Proper motion in 1000 years

Double-Star Separations

0.3"   3"   30"

MILLENNIUM STAR ATLAS

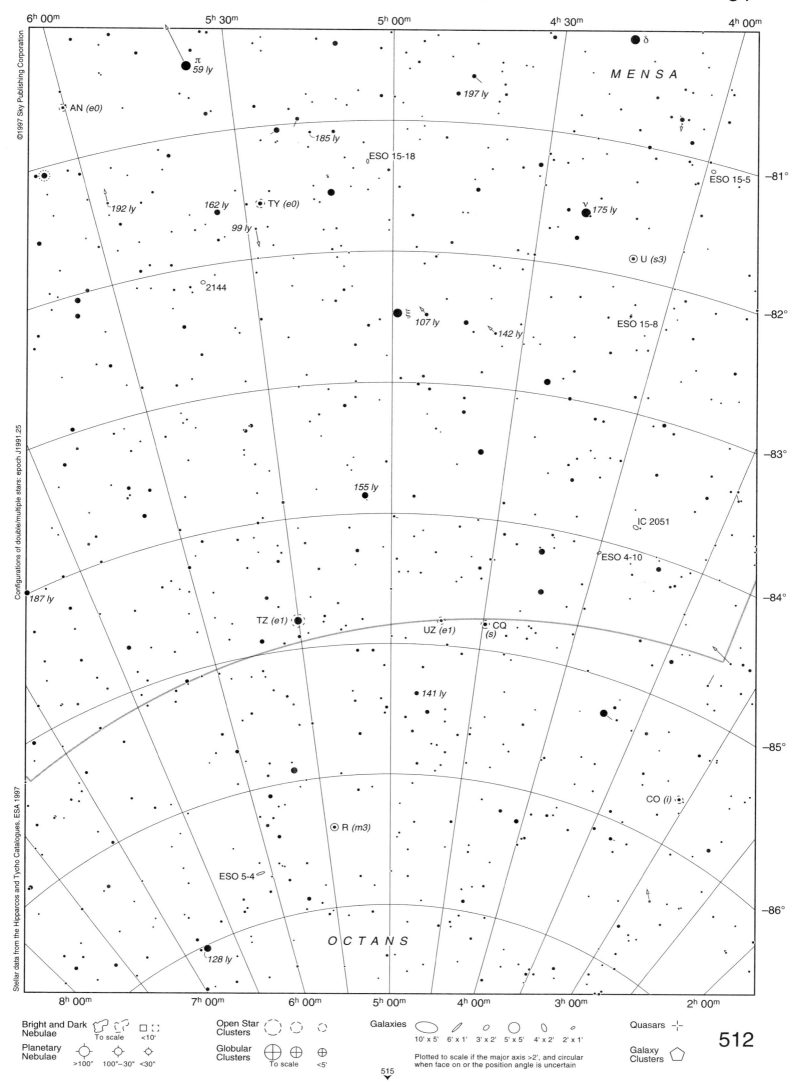

©1997 Sky Publishing Corporation

Configurations of double/multiple stars: epoch J1991.25

Stellar data from the Hipparcos and Tycho Catalogues, ESA 1997

MENSA

π
59 ly

AN *(e0)*

197 ly

185 ly

ESO 15-18

192 ly

162 ly

TY *(e0)*

99 ly

2144

ξ
107 ly

142 ly

ν 175 ly

U *(s3)*

ESO 15-5

ESO 15-8

155 ly

IC 2051

ESO 4-10

187 ly

TZ *(e1)*

UZ *(e1)*

CQ
(s)

141 ly

CO *(i)*

R *(m3)*

ESO 5-4

OCTANS

128 ly

δ

−81°

−82°

−83°

−84°

−85°

−86°

6ʰ 00ᵐ 5ʰ 30ᵐ 5ʰ 00ᵐ 4ʰ 30ᵐ 4ʰ 00ᵐ

8ʰ 00ᵐ 7ʰ 00ᵐ 6ʰ 00ᵐ 5ʰ 00ᵐ 4ʰ 00ᵐ 3ʰ 00ᵐ 2ʰ 00ᵐ

Bright and Dark Nebulae	Open Star Clusters	Galaxies	Quasars

To scale   <10'

Planetary Nebulae
>100"   100"−30"   <30"

Globular Clusters
To scale   <5'

10' x 5'   6' x 1'   3' x 2'   5' x 5'   4' x 2'   2' x 1'

Plotted to scale if the major axis >2', and circular when face on or the position angle is uncertain

Galaxy Clusters

512

515

MILLENNIUM STAR ATLAS

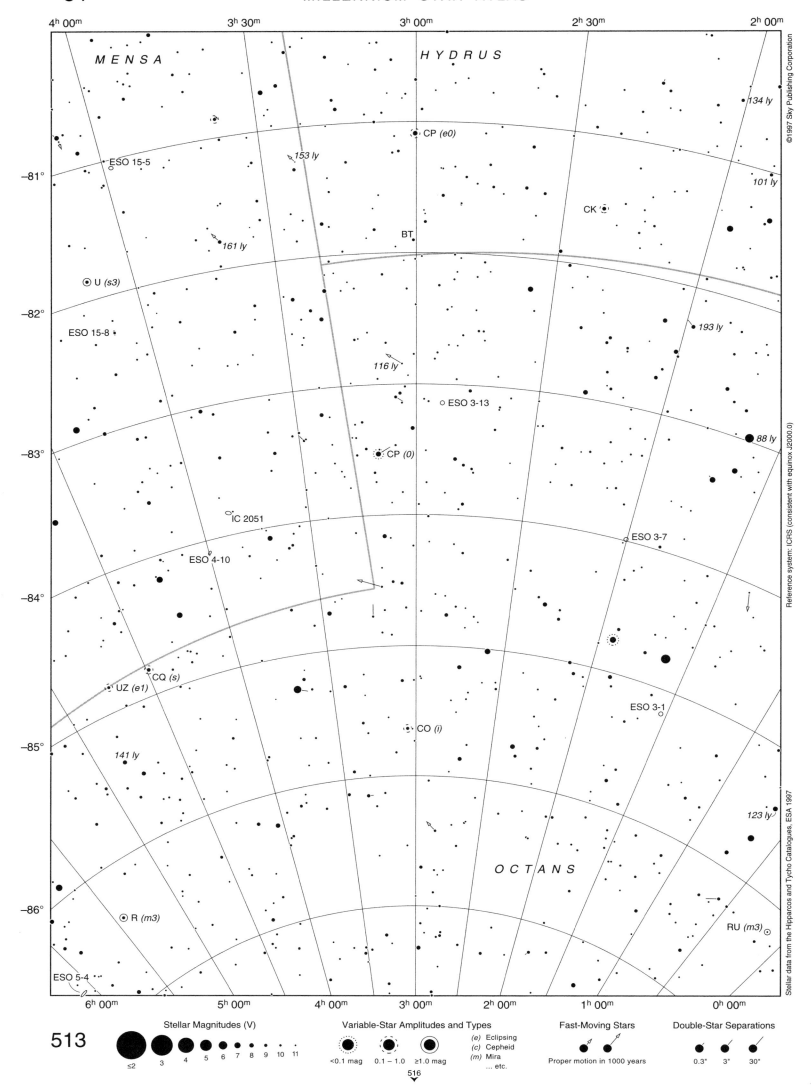

Reference system: ICRS (consistent with equinox J2000.0)

Stellar data from the Hipparcos and Tycho Catalogues, ESA 1997

513

Stellar Magnitudes (V)
≤2 3 4 5 6 7 8 9 10 11

Variable-Star Amplitudes and Types
<0.1 mag   0.1 – 1.0   ≥1.0 mag
(e) Eclipsing
(c) Cepheid
(m) Mira
... etc.

Fast-Moving Stars
Proper motion in 1000 years

Double-Star Separations
0.3"   3"   30"

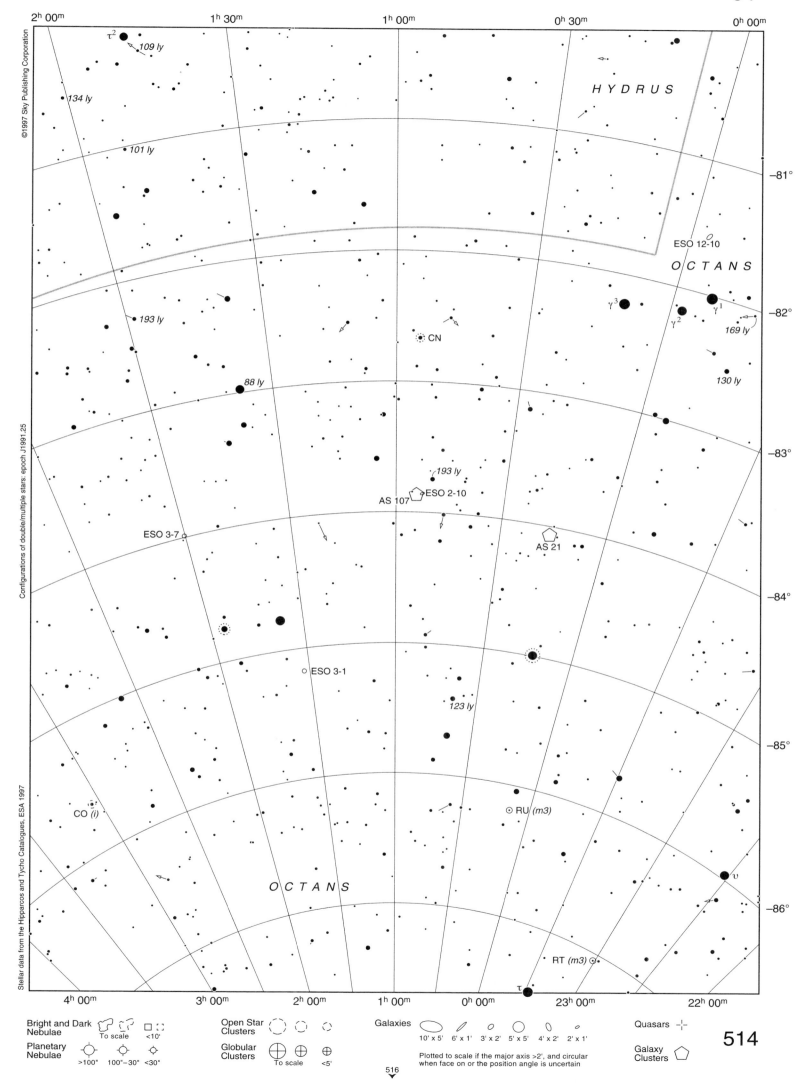

HYDRUS

OCTANS

OCTANS

τ²
109 ly
134 ly
101 ly
193 ly
88 ly
CN
ESO 12-10
γ³
γ²
γ¹
169 ly
130 ly
193 ly
AS 107 ESO 2-10
ESO 3-7
AS 21
ESO 3-1
123 ly
CO *(i)*
RU *(m3)*
υ
RT *(m3)*
τ

Bright and Dark
Nebulae
To scale   <10'

Planetary
Nebulae
>100" 100"–30" <30"

Open Star
Clusters

Globular
Clusters
To scale   <5'

Galaxies
10' x 5'   6' x 1'   3' x 2'   5' x 5'   4' x 2'   2' x 1'

Plotted to scale if the major axis >2', and circular
when face on or the position angle is uncertain

Quasars

Galaxy
Clusters

514

516

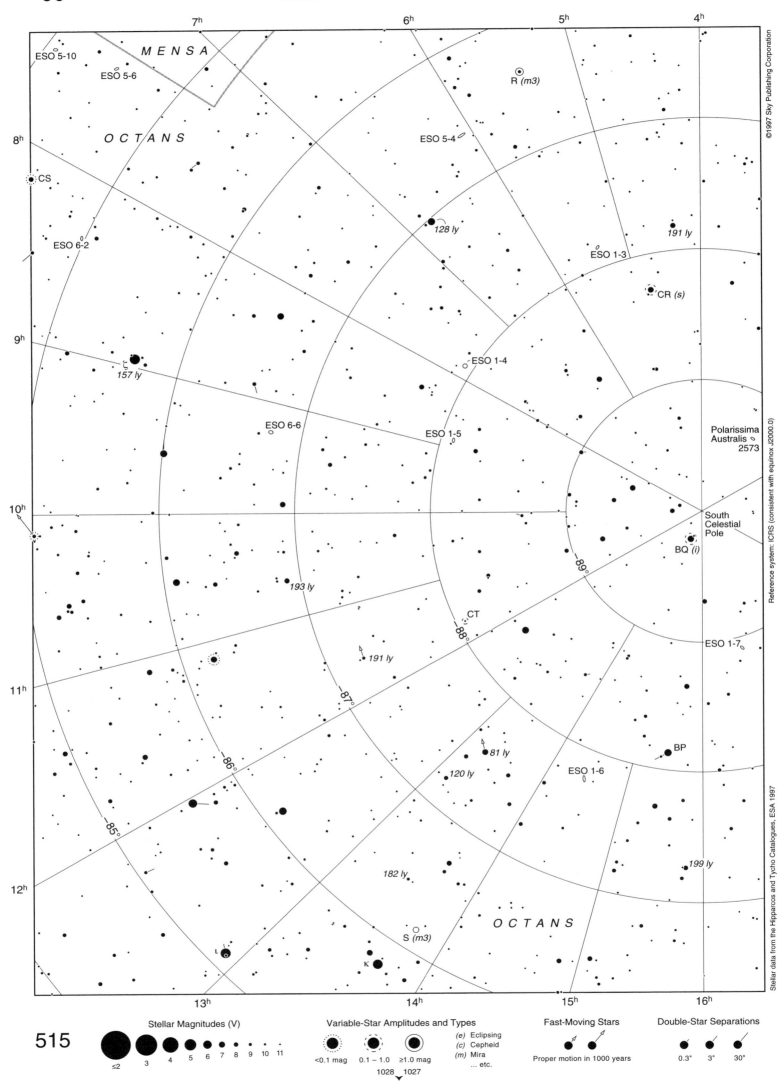

515

Stellar Magnitudes (V)									
≤2	3	4	5	6	7	8	9	10	11

Variable-Star Amplitudes and Types

<0.1 mag   0.1 − 1.0   ≥1.0 mag

(e) Eclipsing
(c) Cepheid
(m) Mira
... etc.

1028 ˄ 1027

Fast-Moving Stars

Proper motion in 1000 years

Double-Star Separations

0.3"   3"   30"

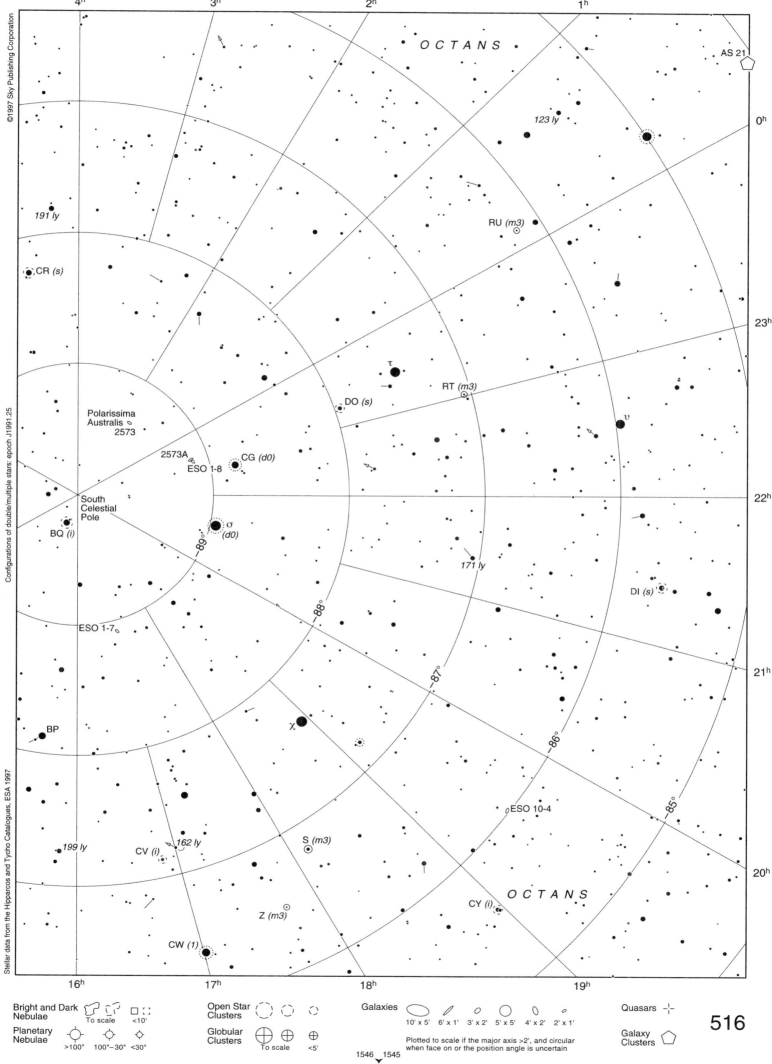

OCTANS

AS 21

123 ly

RU (m3)

191 ly

CR (s)

τ

RT (m3)

DO (s)

υ

Polarissima
Australis
2573

2573A
ESO 1-8   CG (d0)

South
Celestial
Pole

σ
(d0)

BQ (i)

89°

171 ly

DI (s)

88°

ESO 1-7

87°

χ

86°

BP

ESO 10-4

85°

199 ly

162 ly
CV (i)

S (m3)

CY (i)

OCTANS

Z (m3)

CW (1)

Bright and Dark Nebulae	Open Star Clusters	Galaxies	Quasars

Bright and Dark Nebulae — To scale — <10'

Planetary Nebulae — >100" — 100"−30" — <30"

Open Star Clusters

Globular Clusters — To scale — <5'

Galaxies — 10' x 5' 6' x 1' 3' x 2' 5' x 5' 4' x 2' 2' x 1'

Plotted to scale if the major axis >2', and circular when face on or the position angle is uncertain

Quasars

Galaxy Clusters

INDEX TO NAMED CELESTIAL OBJECTS

THESE LISTINGS PROVIDE quick pointers to those charts that contain stars and nonstellar objects with popular names and many other benchmarks in the sky. Generally just a single chart number is given, indicating the chart on which the object is most nearly centered. Any star or object near a chart's edge can be found on at least one adjacent chart as well. Multiple chart numbers are given for a few large nebulae that extend across several charts.

Charts 1–516 are found in Volume I, charts 517–1032 in Volume II, and charts 1033–1548 in Volume III.

SPECIAL ASTRONOMICAL NAMES

COMMON NAMES OF BRIGHT STARS

BRIGHT STARS BY CONSTELLATION AND BAYER LETTER

CHART KEYS

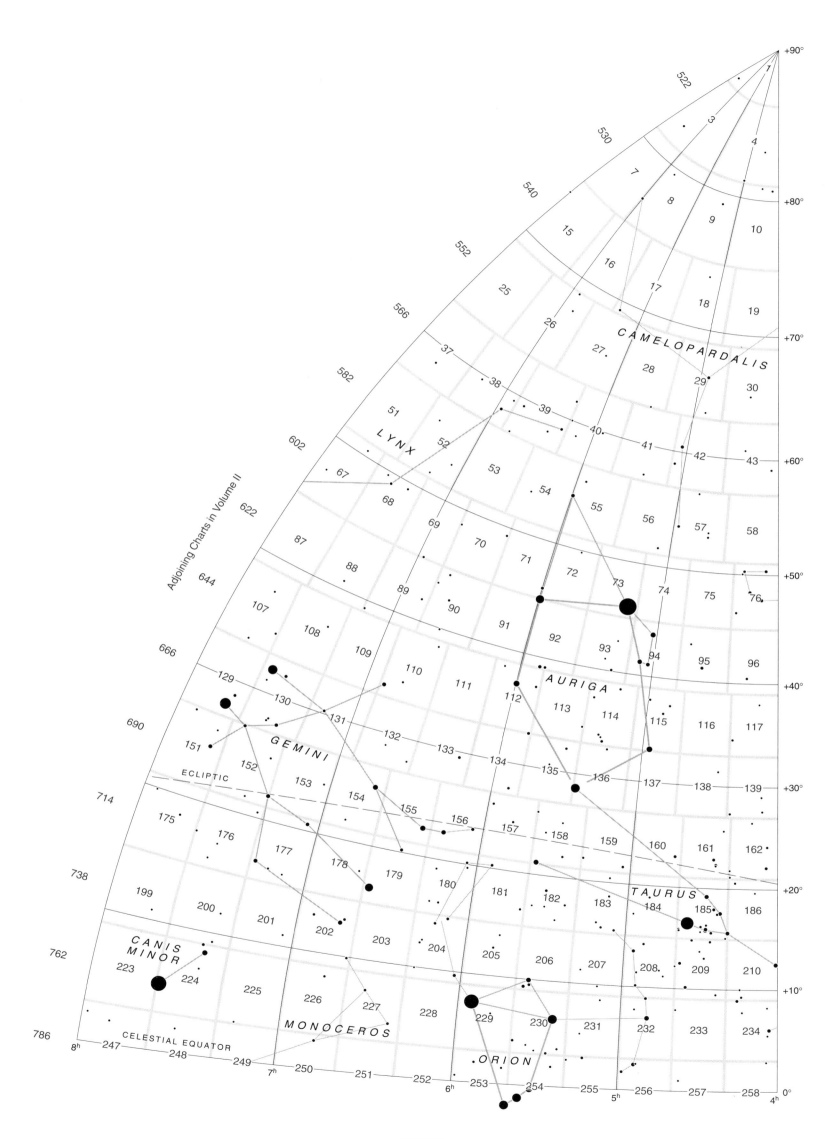

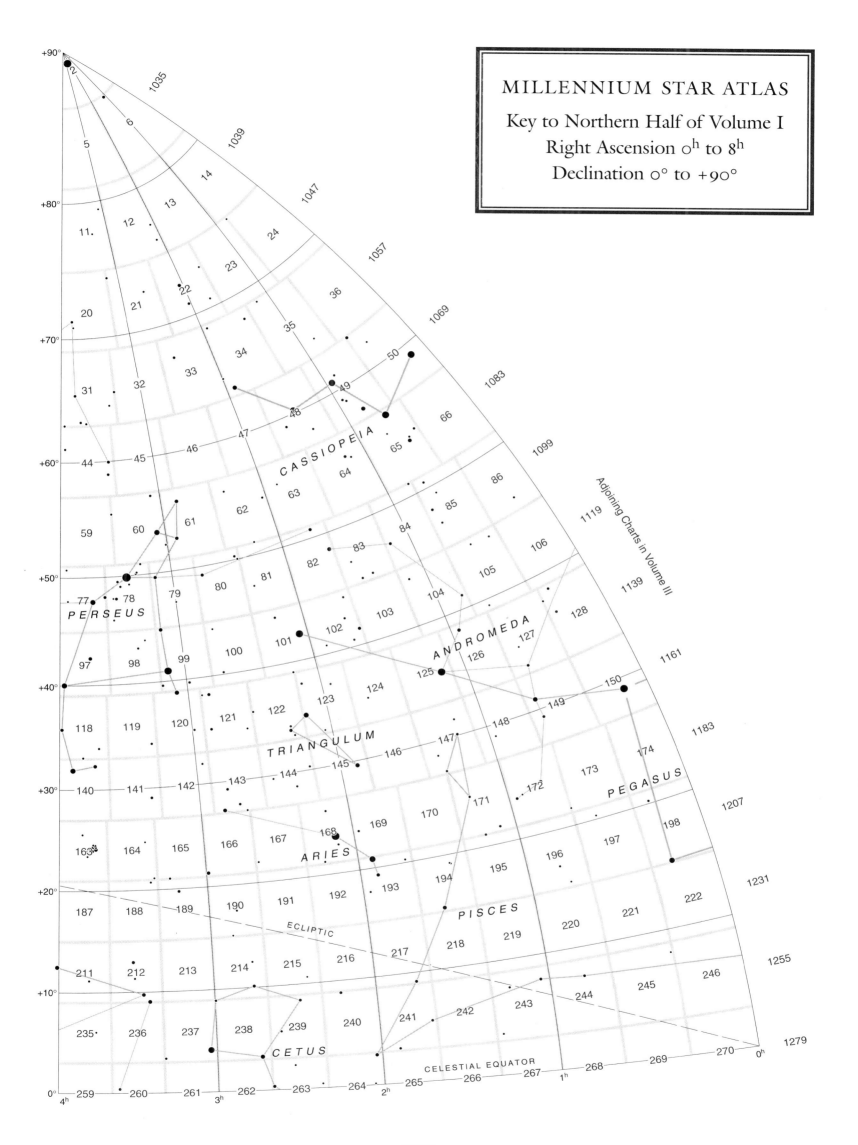

CASSIOPEIA

PERSEUS

ANDROMEDA

TRIANGULUM

PEGASUS

ARIES

PISCES

CETUS

ECLIPTIC

CELESTIAL EQUATOR

Adjoining Charts in Volume III

MILLENNIUM STAR ATLAS

Key to Southern Half of Volume I
Right Ascension 0ʰ to 8ʰ
Declination 0° to −90°

LI

CARTOGRAPHY *The charts for this atlas were prepared electronically on a Sigma Tech Pentium System using Borland Turbo Basic. Final adjustments were made in Adobe Illustrator and the book was composed in QuarkXPress on a Power Macintosh computer system.*

PREPRESS *Electronic preparation was carried out by Dartmouth Publishing, Inc., Watertown, Massachusetts, and World Color Book Services, Taunton, Massachusetts.*

PRINTING *The atlas was printed at World Color Book Services on a Cottrell web press, using direct-to-plate technology.*

PAPER *The book paper is Finch Fine 70# text stock, manufactured by Finch, Pruyn, & Co., Glens Falls, New York, and supplied by Pratt Paper Company, Boston, Massachusetts. The endleaf stock is Multicolor Slate Blue from Permalin Products, New York, New York.*

BINDING *Binding and slipcase manufacture were handled by World Color Book Services. The material is Skivertex Ubonga.*

TYPEFACES *The typefaces used are Galliard text with Mantinia display, designed by Matthew Carter. Helvetica, designed by M. Miedinger, is used in the charts, diagrams, and graphs.*

BOOK DESIGN *Typography, binding, and slipcase design are by Christopher Kuntze.*